Australia

Denis O'Byrne
Joe Bindloss
Andrew Draffen
Hugh Finlay
Paul Harding
Patrick Horton

Ly___ Gaurr
M___ ___undell
___ Murray
___ah Ross
Phillipa Saxton

LONELY PLANET PUBLICATIONS
Melbourne • Oakland • London • Paris

AUSTRALIA

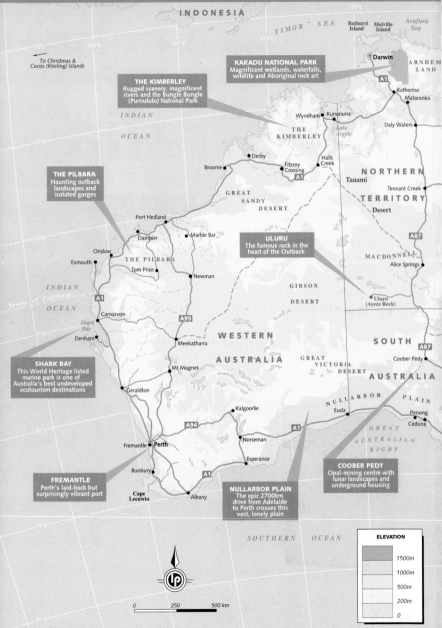

INDONESIA

TIMOR SEA

Bathurst Island   Melville Island   Arafura Sea

◉ Darwin   ARNHEM LAND

To Christmas & Cocos (Keeling) Islands

A1

Katherine
Mataranka

KAKADU NATIONAL PARK
Magnificent wetlands, waterfalls, wildlife and Aboriginal rock art

THE KIMBERLEY
Rugged scenery, magnificent rivers and the Bungle Bungle (Purnululu) National Park

Wyndham   Kununurra

Daly Waters

INDIAN

OCEAN

THE KIMBERLEY

Lake Argyle

● Derby

Fitzroy Crossing

Halls Creek

NORTHERN

Broome

A1

THE PILBARA
Haunting outback landscapes and isolated gorges

GREAT
SANDY
DESERT

Tanami   Tennant Creek

TERRITORY

Desert

Port Hedland

● Marble Bar

A87

Dampier

THE PILBARA

ULURU
The famous rock in the heart of the Outback

MACDONNELL

Onslow

Tom Price

● Newman

Alice Springs

Exmouth

INDIAN

GIBSON

DESERT

Uluru
(Ayers Rock)

Tropic of Capricorn

A1

OCEAN

Carnarvon

A95

WESTERN

SOUTH

Shark Bay

Denham

Meekatharra

A87

SHARK BAY
This World Heritage listed marine park is one of Australia's best undeveloped ecotourism destinations

AUSTRALIA

GREAT
VICTORIA
DESERT

AUSTRALIA

Coober Pedy

Mt Magnet

Geraldton

NULLARBOR   PLAIN

Kalgoorlie

Eucla

Penong
Ceduna

GREAT

A94

Norseman

A1

AUSTRALIAN

BIGHT

Fremantle ◉ Perth

Esperance

COOBER PEDY
Opal-mining centre with lunar landscapes and underground housing

Bunbury

A1

FREMANTLE
Perth's laid-back but surprisingly vibrant port

Cape Leeuwin

Albany

NULLARBOR PLAIN
The epic 2700km drive from Adelaide to Perth crosses this vast, lonely plain

SOUTHERN   OCEAN

LP

0   250   500 km

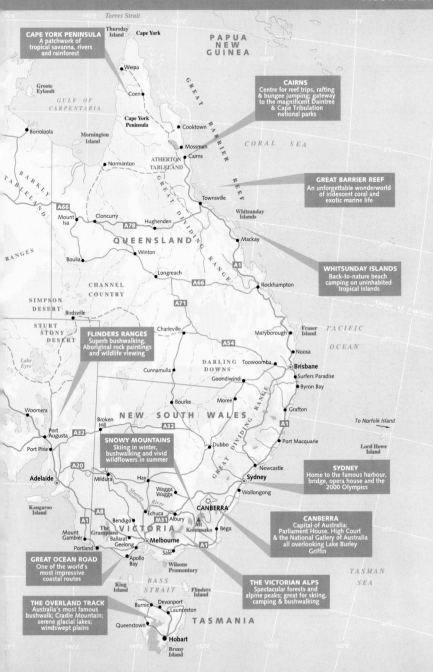

Torres Strait

PAPUA NEW GUINEA

Cape York

Thursday Island

CAPE YORK PENINSULA
A patchwork of tropical savanna, rivers and rainforest

Weipa

Coen

CAIRNS
Centre for reef trips, rafting & bungee jumping; gateway to the magnificent Daintree & Cape Tribulation national parks

Borroloola

Groote Eylandt

GULF OF CARPENTARIA

Mornington Island

Cape York Peninsula

Normanton

ATHERTON TABLELAND

Cooktown

Mossman

Cairns

CORAL SEA

GREAT BARRIER REEF
An unforgettable wonderworld of iridescent coral and exotic marine life

BARKLY TABLELAND

A66

Mount Isa

Cloncurry

Hughenden

Townsville

Whitsunday Islands

RANGES

QUEENSLAND

GREAT DIVIDING RANGE

Boulia

Winton

Mackay

A1

WHITSUNDAY ISLANDS
Back-to-nature beach camping on uninhabited tropical islands

SIMPSON DESERT

Birdsville

CHANNEL COUNTRY

Longreach

A66

Rockhampton

Tropic of Capricorn

STURT STONY DESERT

FLINDERS RANGES
Superb bushwalking, Aboriginal rock paintings and wildlife viewing

Charleville

A71

Maryborough

Fraser Island

PACIFIC OCEAN

Lake Eyre

Cunnamulla

DARLING DOWNS

Toowoomba

Noosa

Brisbane

Surfers Paradise

Byron Bay

Woomera

Bourke

Moree

Grafton

Port Augusta

A32

Broken Hill

NEW SOUTH WALES

A32

GREAT DIVIDING RANGE

A1

Port Macquarie

To Norfolk Island

Lord Howe Island

Port Pirie

A20

SNOWY MOUNTAINS
Skiing in winter, bushwalking and vivid wildflowers in summer

Dubbo

Newcastle

SYDNEY
Home to the famous harbour, bridge, opera house and the 2000 Olympics

Adelaide

Mildura

Hay

Sydney

Wollongong

Kangaroo Island

A1

A8

Wagga Wagga

Albury

CANBERRA

CANBERRA
Capital of Australia; Parliament House, High Court & the National Gallery of Australia all overlooking Lake Burley Griffin

Murray River

Echuca

M31

Bendigo

VICTORIA

Mt Kosciuszko

Bega

Mount Gambier

A1

The Grampians

Ballarat

Geelong

Melbourne

A1

Portland

GREAT OCEAN ROAD
One of the world's most impressive coastal routes

Apollo Bay

Sale

Wilsons Promontory

TASMAN SEA

King Island

BASS STRAIT

Flinders Island

THE VICTORIAN ALPS
Spectacular forests and alpine peaks; great for skiing, camping & bushwalking

THE OVERLAND TRACK
Australia's most famous bushwalk; Cradle Mountain; serene glacial lakes; windswept plains

Burnie

Devonport

Launceston

Queenstown

TASMANIA

Hobart

Bruny Island

Australia
10th edition – April 2000
First published – February 1977

6-monthly upgrades of this title available free on
www.lonelyplanet.com/upgrades

Published by
Lonely Planet Publications Pty Ltd ABN 36 005 607 983
90 Maribyrnong St, Footscray, Victoria 3011, Australia

Lonely Planet Offices
Australia Locked Bag 1, Footscray, Victoria 3011
USA 150 Linden St, Oakland, CA 94607
UK 10a Spring Place, London NW5 3BH
France 1 rue du Dahomey, 75011 Paris

Photographs
Most of the images in this guide are available for licensing from
Lonely Planet Images.
email: lpi@lonelyplanet.com.au

Front cover photograph
Manly Beach (Simon Bracken)

ISBN 1 86450 068 9

text & maps © Lonely Planet 2000
photos © photographers as indicated 2000

Printed by The Bookmaker International Ltd
Printed in China

Contents – Text

THE OLYMPIC GAMES

NEW SOUTH WALES

NORTHERN TERRITORY

QUEENSLAND

SOUTH AUSTRALIA

4 Contents – Text

TASMANIA

VICTORIA 777

WESTERN AUSTRALIA   908

GLOSSARY   1027

ACKNOWLEDGMENTS   1031

INDEX   1043

MAP LEGEND   back page

METRIC CONVERSION   inside back cover

Contents – Maps

TASMANIA

VICTORIA

WESTERN AUSTRALIA

MAP INDEX

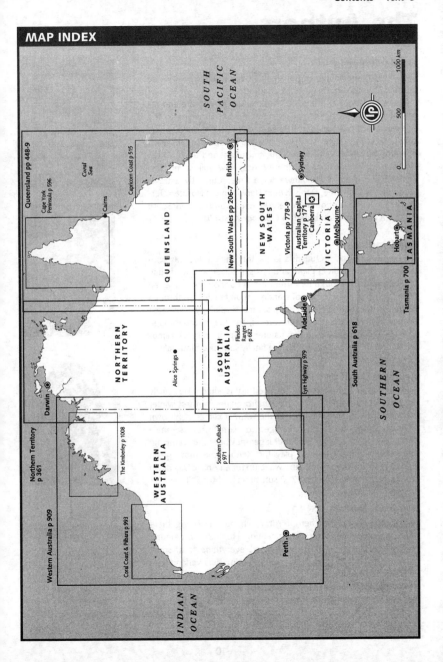

SOUTH PACIFIC OCEAN

Coral Sea

QUEENSLAND

NEW SOUTH WALES

VICTORIA

TASMANIA

NORTHERN TERRITORY

SOUTH AUSTRALIA

WESTERN AUSTRALIA

INDIAN OCEAN

SOUTHERN OCEAN

Cairns

Brisbane

Sydney

Canberra

Melbourne

Hobart

Adelaide

Alice Springs

Darwin

Perth

1000 km

500

0

The Authors

Denis O'Byrne

Denis was coordinating author of this edition and updated the introductory and South Australia chapters.

Denis was born and bred in country South Australia and received his first taste of overseas travel as a surveyor in the Australian Army. Since then he's earned a living at various pursuits, including mine surveyor, national park ranger, plant operator, builder's labourer, building consultant and travel writer. He has travelled in Europe, southern Africa, New Guinea and New Zealand and lived in Zimbabwe for a time. Currently a travel writer most of the time, Denis lives in Darwin in the Northern Territory. He is the author of Lonely Planet's *Vanuatu* and *South Australia* and has contributed to *Outback Australia*.

Joe Bindloss

Joe updated northern Queensland for this edition. He was born in Cyprus, grew up in England and has since lived and worked in several countries, though he currently calls London home. He first developed an incurable case of wanderlust on family trips through Europe in the old VW Kombi. A degree in Biology eliminated science from his future choice of careers, and Joe moved through a string of occupations – mural painter, sculptor and rock climbing tutor to name but a few – before finally settling on journalism.

Andrew Draffen

Andrew updated southern Queensland for this edition. He usually researches LP's *Brazil* and *Rio de Janeiro* guides, but last winter welcomed the opportunity to visit the warmer climes of his own country. During the trip he managed to learn to reverse-angle park, develop a taste for Eumundi lager, get back into camping, understand (almost) how to play the Keno game showing on every bar TV in Queensland, and wake up for an Anzac Day dawn service at the Agnes Water/1770 sub-branch of the RSL.

Hugh Finlay

Hugh updated the Northern Territory chapter. Deciding there must be more to life than civil engineering, Hugh took off around Australia in the mid-1970s, working at everything from spray painting to diamond prospecting before hitting the overland trail. He joined Lonely Planet in 1985 and has written *Jordan & Syria* and co-authored *Kenya*, *Morocco*, *Algeria & Tunisia* and updated *Nepal*, *Queensland* and *Australia*. He lives in central Victoria.

Paul Harding

Paul updated the Western Australia chapter and the Norfolk Island and Lord Howe Island sections of the New South .Wales chapter. Born in Melbourne, Paul grew up mostly in country Victoria and started working life as a reporter on a local newspaper. Upon throwing in that glamorous career, he spent three years travelling in Europe and South-East Asia, including a stint as editor of a minor London travel magazine. In 1996 he joined Lonely Planet as an editor but, realising he was on the wrong side of the desk, swapped his red pen for a blue one and now works as a full-time writer and 'updater'. Paul has also worked on Lonely Planet's *South-East Asia* and *India* guides.

Patrick Horton

Patrick updated the Australian Capital Territory chapter. Writer and photographer, he was born with restless feet. He travelled extensively in his native Britain before hitting the around-the-world trail as a Thatcher refugee in 1985. Since bringing his old British bikes out to Australia, he now calls Melbourne home. He prefers unusual areas of travel: he is one of the few who have visited North Korea, and has ridden a motorcycle over the Himalaya. He lives with his long-suffering partner Christine, another ardent traveller whom he met in Paris, and Mr Cat.

Lyn McGaurr

Lyn updated the Tasmania chapter. She joined the ABC in Hobart as a current affairs TV researcher and trainee reporter in her first year out of school, saving university life for her early twenties. Since then, she has worked as a sub-editor for a national magazine in Melbourne and as a graduate research assistant and information officer for the Commonwealth government in Canberra and Melbourne. After postgraduate studies, she joined Lonely Planet as an in-house editor. In 1997 she spent a fascinating six months at the Antarctic Research Centre in Hobart. Lyn has worked as a freelance editor for Lonely Planet since 1990 and lives in Hobart with her husband and three children. She updated the recent *Tasmania* guide.

Meg Mundell

Meg updated the Sydney and Blue Mountains sections of the New South Wales chapter. She is a loyal Kiwi now living in Melbourne. After studying hard for several years she realised she was too soft to be a vet, and too mad to be a psychologist. After much travel (including a nauseating but fun trans-Tasman yacht-crewing debacle) and brief stints in various ·odd occupations (zucchini sizer, ventriloquist's assistant, DJ), she now writes for and is deputy editor of *The Big Issue*, Australia.

Jon Murray

Jon updated the Victoria chapter. He spent time alternately travelling and working with various publishing houses in Melbourne, Australia, before joining Lonely Planet as an editor, then author. He co-authored Lonely Planet's *South Africa, Lesotho & Swaziland* and has written and updated books on destinations including West Africa, Papua New Guinea, Bangladesh and Hungary. He lives in country Victoria, on a bush block he shares with quite a few marsupials and a diminishing number of rabbits.

Hannah Ross

Hannah updated the northern parts of the New South Wales chapter. Among a variety of occupations, including scaffolder, she has been a journalist and freelance writer both in Australia and abroad since 1993. Born and raised in the rural outskirts of Melbourne, Hannah now resides on the heavenly far north coast of New South Wales and writes for a local daily newspaper. Hannah was ably assisted by her canine companion Josie.

Phillipa Saxton

Phillipa updated the southern parts of the New South Wales chapter. During a childhood living in several countries, and after receiving a cheque for £5 as 'Encouragement Fee' for two travel stories published at the age of 14, the seed was sown for a life of penury as a travel writer. Intervening years included studying to become the world's greatest forensic scientist (abandoned), marriage (terminated) and raising three wonderful children (completed). Despite the options her peripatetic lifestyle offered, she chose to make her home in Australia in 1968. As a 'mature-age student' Phillipa gained her motorcycle licence and has found the freedom of a bike the best way to see any country.

FROM THE AUTHORS

Denis O'Byrne Thanks to mum for allowing me to take over her dining room while I updated South Australia. As always, Phil Brennan, Peter Caust and Brett Knuckey gave enthusiastic support – fellas, next time I'll buy the beer. Special thanks also to Peter Hiscock, Bronte Leake, Jan Matthew, Tim Parnacott (STA Travel), Cheryle Pinkess and the many others who happily (or otherwise) answered my interminable questions.

Andrew Draffen Thanks to all the helpful park rangers, staff in tourist information centres, and backpackers willing to share information and experiences. Special thanks to my mate Nic Leptos for his insider insights and company on the trip, Andrea and Nic for their hospitality in Fingal, Jo Volz (Time Off), Ross MacLean (Queensland Rail), and Mr Jaffle. Love to Stella, Gabriela and Christopher, who make it all worthwhile.

Hannah Ross Thanks to Jason who has suffered many quiet nights while I struggled with information overload and to Josie for being the perfect travel companion. A big thanks to the pit stop crew from Kangaroo Campers, who drove all the way from Brisbane to ensure that my research didn't amount to a month on the side of the road in Armidale.

Lyn McGaurr Staff at visitors centres around the state and hosts at hotels, hostels and B&Bs provided invaluable information. Jayne Balmer, Nigel Ricketts, Ashley Fuller, David Machin, Kathy Van Dullemen and Geoff 'Joe' King were especially helpful. Many thanks also to Kara, Cameron, Josephine, Imogen, Tess and Erin.

Joe Bindloss Particular thanks to Kathy, Gabe, Annie, Molly and Poppy for providing a home away from home and hospitality over and above the call of duty. Thanks to all the people who helped generally, and also to the many tolerant members of the Queensland Parks and Wildlife Service who patiently answered my questions. In the UK, thanks to Piers, Nikki and Beat for providing a home to come back to and my dad and bro for providing moral support while I nursed a fever after donating blood to the mosquitoes in Cape York.

Paul Harding Thanks to all the helpful tourist office staff who pointed me in the right direction while in WA, particularly those in Kalgoorlie, Port Hedland, Mt Barker, Merredin, Northam, Carnarvon, Kalbarri, Exmouth, Broome and Derby. In Perth thanks to Marie Bowen at the Perth Tourist Lounge, Paul and Scotty at the Travellers Club, Angela at Easyrider Backpackers, Leonie at the

Arcane Bookshop, and staff at the Britannia YHA for storing my excess baggage. Special thanks to Frank Seidler in Kalbarri, Trish and Trev in Lancelin, Lesley for the ride, Barbara at Goldfields Backpackers in Kal, Pete and Paula in cyclone-battered Exmouth, Gary and Dylan at Fitzroy Crossing, Scott and Kenton in Kununurra, and Gary in Fremantle.

Patrick Horton I am indebted to Linda Roberts of the Canberra Visitors Centre who has her finger on what's happening in Canberra; to Christine Vrondou, my partner, who, despite my navigational lapses, drove me around Canberra; and to Robert Marchant, Canberra resident and old school friend whom I hadn't seen for 33 years.

Phillipa Saxton I would most like to thank my partner, Mike Ferris, who has motorcycled hundreds of kilometres to sit outside visitors centres, hotels, motels and various local attractions minding the bikes and finding space in panniers for piles of paper and brochures. I would also have been lost without the cheerful assistance of the staff at the regional visitors centres. At Lonely Planet, my thanks go to Mary Neighbour, Arabella Bamber and my friend and compatriot Claire Minty, who has raised my spirits and urged me along on numerous occasions.

This Book

From the Publisher

This 10th edition of Australia was edited in Lonely Planet's Melbourne office by Arabella Bamber, with the assistance of Joanne Newell, Kristin Odijk, Cherry Prior and Lucy Williams. Barbara Benson coordinated the design, layout and mapping, with superb back-up from Jenny Jones. Cartographers Pablo Gastar, Kusnandar, Helen Rowley and Corie Waddell assisted. Pablo produced the chapter end illustration. Simon Bracken and Indra Kilfoyle designed the cover.

Thanks to Liz Filleul for writing the Olympic Games section, Jane Bennett for the Christmas and Cocos (Keeling) Islands boxed text, Robert Allen for his contribution to the Aboriginal Art section, Bruce Cameron for the information for those travelling with a disability and to David Bamber for his contribution. Thanks also to Mark Griffiths for the 'Big Things', Jane Hart and Rowan McKinnon for updating the Travel with Children section, Angela Fiumara for information and guidance on the Snowy Mountains Hydro-Electric Authority, and to Ron Gallagher, Nancy Cowham from Ngurratjuta/Pmara Aboriginal Corporation and Will Stubbs at Buku-Larrngay Arts for their help providing artwork.

THANKS
Many thanks to the travellers who used the last edition and wrote to us with helpful hints, advice and interesting anecdotes. Your names appear in the back of this book.

Foreword

ABOUT LONELY PLANET GUIDEBOOKS

The story begins with a classic travel adventure: Tony and Maureen Wheeler's 1972 journey across Europe and Asia to Australia. Useful information about the overland trail did not exist at that time, so Tony and Maureen published the first Lonely Planet guidebook to meet a growing need.

From a kitchen table, then from a tiny office in Melbourne (Australia), Lonely Planet has become the largest independent travel publisher in the world, an international company with offices in Melbourne, Oakland (USA), London (UK) and Paris (France).

Today Lonely Planet guidebooks cover the globe. There is an ever-growing list of books and there's information in a variety of forms and media. Some things haven't changed. The main aim is still to help make it possible for adventurous travellers to get out there – to explore and better understand the world.

At Lonely Planet we believe travellers can make a positive contribution to the countries they visit – if they respect their host communities and spend their money wisely. Since 1986 a percentage of the income from each book has been donated to aid projects and human rights campaigns.

Updates Lonely Planet thoroughly updates each guidebook as often as possible. This usually means there are around two years between editions, although for more unusual or more stable destinations the gap can be longer. Check the imprint page (following the colour map at the beginning of the book) for publication dates.

Between editions up-to-date information is available in two free newsletters – the paper *Planet Talk* and email *Comet* (to subscribe, contact any Lonely Planet office) – and on our Web site at www.lonelyplanet.com. The *Upgrades* section of the Web site covers a number of important and volatile destinations and is regularly updated by Lonely Planet authors. *Scoop* covers news and current affairs relevant to travellers. And, lastly, the *Thorn Tree* bulletin board and *Postcards* section of the site carry unverified, but fascinating, reports from travellers.

Correspondence The process of creating new editions begins with the letters, postcards and emails received from travellers. This correspondence often includes suggestions, criticisms and comments about the current editions. Interesting excerpts are immediately passed on via newsletters and the Web site, and everything goes to our authors to be verified when they're researching on the road. We're keen to get more feedback from organisations or individuals who represent communities visited by travellers.

Lonely Planet gathers information for everyone who's curious about the planet – and especially for those who explore it first-hand. Through guidebooks, phrasebooks, activity guides, maps, literature, newsletters, image library, TV series and Web site we act as an information exchange for a worldwide community of travellers.

Research Authors aim to gather sufficient practical information to enable travellers to make informed choices and to make the mechanics of a journey run smoothly. They also research historical and cultural background to help enrich the travel experience and allow travellers to understand and respond appropriately to cultural and environmental issues.

Authors don't stay in every hotel because that would mean spending a couple of months in each medium-sized city and, no, they don't eat at every restaurant because that would mean stretching belts beyond capacity. They do visit hotels and restaurants to check standards and prices, but feedback based on readers' direct experiences can be very helpful.

Many of our authors work undercover, others aren't so secretive. None of them accept freebies in exchange for positive write-ups. And none of our guidebooks contain any advertising.

Production Authors submit their raw manuscripts and maps to offices in Australia, USA, UK or France. Editors and cartographers – all experienced travellers themselves – then begin the process of assembling the pieces. When the book finally hits the shops, some things are already out of date, we start getting feedback from readers and the process begins again …

WARNING & REQUEST

Things change – prices go up, schedules change, good places go bad and bad places go bankrupt – nothing stays the same. So, if you find things better or worse, recently opened or long since closed, please tell us and help make the next edition even more accurate and useful. We genuinely value all the feedback we receive. Julie Young coordinates a well travelled team that reads and acknowledges every letter, postcard and email and ensures that every morsel of information finds its way to the appropriate authors, editors and cartographers for verification.

Everyone who writes to us will find their name in the next edition of the appropriate guidebook. They will also receive the latest issue of *Planet Talk*, our quarterly printed newsletter, or *Comet*, our monthly email newsletter. Subscriptions to both newsletters are free. The very best contributions will be rewarded with a free guidebook.

Excerpts from your correspondence may appear in new editions of Lonely Planet guidebooks, the Lonely Planet Web site, *Planet Talk* or *Comet*, so please let us know if you *don't* want your letter published or your name acknowledged.

Send all correspondence to the Lonely Planet office closest to you:

Australia: Locked Bag 1, Footscray, Victoria 3011
USA: 150 Linden St, Oakland, CA 94607
UK: 10A Spring Place, London NW5 3BH
France: 1 rue du Dahomey, 75011 Paris

Or email us at: talk2us@lonelyplanet.com.au

For news, views and updates see our Web site: www.lonelyplanet.com

HOW TO USE A LONELY PLANET GUIDEBOOK

The best way to use a Lonely Planet guidebook is any way you choose. At Lonely Planet we believe the most memorable travel experiences are often those that are unexpected, and the finest discoveries are those you make yourself. Guidebooks are not intended to be used as if they provide a detailed set of infallible instructions!

Contents All Lonely Planet guidebooks follow roughly the same format. The Facts about the Destination chapters or sections give background information ranging from history to weather. Facts for the Visitor gives practical information on issues like visas and health. Getting There & Away gives a brief starting point for researching travel to and from the destination. Getting Around gives an overview of the transport options when you arrive.

The peculiar demands of each destination determine how subsequent chapters are broken up, but some things remain constant. We always start with background, then proceed to sights, places to stay, places to eat, entertainment, getting there and away, and getting around information – in that order.

Heading Hierarchy Lonely Planet headings are used in a strict hierarchical structure that can be visualised as a set of Russian dolls. Each heading (and its following text) is encompassed by any preceding heading that is higher on the hierarchical ladder.

Entry Points We do not assume guidebooks will be read from beginning to end, but that people will dip into them. The traditional entry points are the list of contents and the index. In addition, however, some books have a complete list of maps and an index map illustrating map coverage.

There may also be a colour map that shows highlights. These highlights are dealt with in greater detail in the Facts for the Visitor chapter, along with planning questions and suggested itineraries. Each chapter covering a geographical region usually begins with a locator map and another list of highlights. Once you find something of interest in a list of highlights, turn to the index.

Maps Maps play a crucial role in Lonely Planet guidebooks and include a huge amount of information. A legend is printed on the back page. We seek to have complete consistency between maps and text, and to have every important place in the text captured on a map. Map key numbers usually start in the top left corner.

Although inclusion in a guidebook usually implies a recommendation we cannot list every good place. Exclusion does not necessarily imply criticism. In fact there are a number of reasons why we might exclude a place – sometimes it is simply inappropriate to encourage an influx of travellers.

Introduction

When most people think of Australia a particular image comes to mind. It might be the Sydney Harbour Bridge, Ayers Rock, a laconic sun-burned character out of *Crocodile Dundee*, or a kangaroo hopping down a main street. Such imagery may not be particularly representative, but it does highlight the fact that in many ways Australia is different to anywhere you have been before.

The first thing you have to realise about Australia is that it's *big*, and you're not going to see very much of it on a two week holiday. Most of it is also empty – only 19 million people in an area half as big again as Europe, with most of them living in a handful of coastal cities.

If it's space you're looking for, look no further than the Outback with its vast semi-deserts, tropical wetlands and endless horizons. Here you'll find huge wilderness areas like Kakadu National Park, Cape York, the Nullarbor Plain and the Simpson Desert. It's also where Australia's Aboriginal people have best been able to preserve their ancient culture and traditions.

If you want to go where most of the people are, Aussie cities are not necessarily like every other city in the world. For example, how many can claim to be as beautiful and cosmopolitan as Sydney, as calm and dignified as Adelaide, or as remote and friendly as Perth?

Between the cities and the Outback waits another treasure trove of travel experiences, from the awe-inspiring spectacle of the Great Barrier Reef and the cathedral calm of tall native forests, to some of the world's best wineries and swimming beaches.

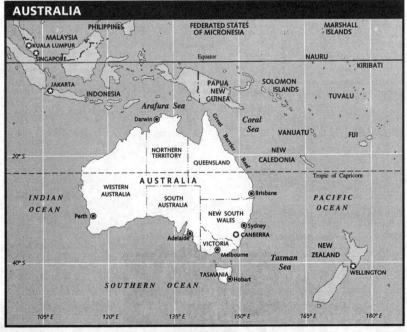

As well – even though Australia is often thought of as being rough and ready – there are many exciting events which illustrate a rich cultural diversity. These include timeless Aboriginal corroborees, the acclaimed Adelaide Festival of Arts and Sydney's outrageous Gay & Lesbian Mardi Gras. Numerous other festivals celebrate everything from wine and music to multiculturalism.

As you'll find in this book, Australia has more than enough on offer to keep you busy for months. It's a friendly, wonderfully invigorating country, and we're sure you'll enjoy it no matter how long your visit.

Facts about Australia

HISTORY

Australia was the last great landmass to be discovered by Europeans. Long before the British claimed it as their own, European explorers and traders had been dreaming of the riches to be found in the unknown – some said mythical – southern land *(terra australis)* that was supposed to form a counterbalance to the landmass north of the equator. The continent they eventually found had already been inhabited for tens of thousands of years.

Aboriginal Settlement

According to the latest archaeological findings, Australian Aboriginal (which literally means 'indigenous') society has a continuous cultural history going back at least 5000 years. Although mystery shrouds many aspects of Australian prehistory, it is almost certain that the first humans came here across the sea from South-East Asia. Just when colonisation took place is the subject of hot debate, with the favoured options being 35-45,000 and 55-60,000 years ago.

The first colonists arrived during a period when the sea level was more than 50m lower than it is today. This meant there was more land between Asia and Australia than there is now, but watercraft were still needed to cross stretches of open sea. Although much of Australia is today arid, the first migrants would have found a much wetter continent, with large forests and numerous inland lakes teeming with fish. The fauna, which was generally nonthreatening, included giant marsupials – such as 3m-tall kangaroos and cow-sized wombats – and huge, flightless birds.

Because of these favourable conditions, archaeologists suggest that Aborigines had settled much of Australia within a few thousand years. However, it's thought that the drier central areas were not occupied until about 24,000 years ago – this was at the beginning of a 12,000 year period during which these areas become larger and more arid than they are today. By 10,000 years ago the climate was improving and eventually became wetter than now. This resulted in an increase in population throughout the continent including the sandy deserts, which saw a large build up of people.

European Discovery & Exploration

It's thought that Portuguese navigators probably sighted the Australian coast in the first half of the 16th century. In 1606 the Spaniard, Luis Vaez de Torres, sailed between Cape York and New Guinea, though there's no record of his actually sighting the southern continent.

In the early 1600s Dutch sailors, in search of gold and spices, reached Cape York and several places on the west coast. They found a harsh, unpleasant country, and retreated to the kinder climes of Batavia in the Dutch East Indies (now Jakarta, Indonesia).

In 1642 the Dutch East India Company mounted an expedition to explore this southern land. Abel Tasman made two voyages from Batavia in the 1640s, during which he discovered the region he called Van Diemen's Land (renamed Tasmania some 200 years later). Although Tasman charted the coast of New Holland from Cape York to the Great Australian Bight, as well as the southern reaches of Van Diemen's Land, he did not sight the continent's east coast.

The prize for being Australia's original Pom goes to the enterprising pirate William Dampier, who made the first investigations ashore about 40 years after Tasman and nearly 100 years before Cook. His records of New Holland, from visits made to Shark Bay on the west coast in 1688 and 1698, influenced the European idea of a primitive and godless land.

Dampier's dismal continent was forgotten until 1768, when the British Admiralty instructed Captain James Cook to lead a scientific expedition to Tahiti (to observe the transit of the planet Venus), and then begin a search for the Great South Land. After

Archaeological Treasures

The early Aboriginal people left no stone buildings or statues to tickle our fancy, but archaeologists have unearthed many other treasures. The best known site by far is **Lake Mungo**, in the dry Willandra Lakes system in the south-west of New South Wales.

Mungo (the name is Scottish) is a living, evolving excavation. The true archaeologists here are time and weather. This area was once a vast system of inland lakes, dry now for some 20,000 years. The embankment of sand and mud on the eastern fringe of the ancient lake system, named the 'Walls of China' by homesick Chinese workers, has been eroded by wind in recent years, revealing human and animal skeletal remains, ancient campfires and evidence of intertribal trading.

The remains prove that ritual burial was practised here 15,000 years before the construction of the Egyptian pyramids. The fireplaces reveal that sophisticated, tertiary-chipped stone implements were fashioned by the dwellers at the edge of this now dry lake. The food they ate can be discovered in the fireplaces, and the long-extinct animals they preyed on are found in skeletal form on the dunes. This area is so important that the Willandra Lakes are now a UN World Heritage area.

Another fascinating area of study has been **Kow Swamp** in northern Victoria. This site has a rich collection of human remains that date from the late Pleistocene epoch. One body, buried 12,000 years ago, had a headband of kangaroo incisor teeth. In the lunette of **Lake Nitchie**, in western New South Wales, a man was buried 7000 to 6500 years ago with a necklace of 178 pierced Tasmanian-devil teeth.

The west and north of Australia have many significant sites. Groove-edged axes dating back 23,000 years have been found in the **Malangangerr** rock-shelter in Arnhem Land. Other rich sources of artefacts are the **Miriwun** rock-shelter on the Ord River in the Kimberley; the **Mt Newman** rock-shelter in the Pilbara; and the **Devil's Lair** near Cape Leeuwin in the far south-west of the continent. Fragments and stone tools dating back 38,000 years were found in the nearby **Swan Valley**.

Ice-age rock engravings (petroglyphs) have been found throughout the continent. Those in **Koonalda Cave**, on the Nullarbor in South Australia, are perhaps the oldest. Flint miners often visited the cave 24,000 to 14,000 years ago, and unexplained patterns were left on the wall – perhaps it's art, perhaps not. Other places where petroglyphs are easily seen are on the **Burrup Peninsula** near Dampier, Western Australia; **Mootwingee National Park**, between Tibooburra and Broken Hill in far western New South Wales; the **Lightning Brothers** site, Flora River, Northern Territory; and at the **Early Man shelter** near Laura in Queensland.

Josephine Flood's *Archaeology of the Dreamtime* (Collins, Sydney, 1983) provides a fascinating account of archaeological research into Australia's first inhabitants.

Warning

In Australia it is illegal to remove archaeological objects or to disturb human remains. Look but don't touch.

---

circumnavigating both islands of New Zealand, Cook set sail for the unexplored eastern coast of New Holland.

On 19 April 1770 the extreme south-eastern tip of the continent was sighted and named Point Hicks. When the *Endeavour* was a navigable distance from shore Cook turned north to follow the coast and search for a suitable landfall. It was nine days before an opening in the cliffs was sighted and the ship and crew found sheltered anchorage in a harbour they named Botany Bay.

During their forays ashore the expedition's scientists, under the botanist Joseph Banks, recorded descriptions of plants, animals and birds, the likes of which they had never seen. They saw Aboriginal people and attempted to communicate with them, but found themselves all but ignored. Cook wrote of the blacks: 'All they seemed to want was for us to be gone'.

After leaving Botany Bay, Cook continued north, charting the coastline and noting that the east coast was a different story from the inhospitable land earlier explorers had reported to the north, south and west. When the *Endeavour* was badly damaged on a reef off north Queensland, Cook was forced to make a temporary settlement. It took six weeks to repair the ship, during which time Cook and the scientists investigated their surroundings further, this time making contact with the local Aboriginal people.

After repairing the *Endeavour*, navigating the Great Barrier Reef and rounding Cape York, Cook again put ashore to raise the Union Jack, rename the continent New South Wales (NSW) and claim it for the British in the name of King George III.

James Cook was resourceful, intelligent, and popularly regarded as one of the greatest and most humane explorers of all time. His incisive reports of his voyages make fascinating reading even today. By the time he was killed, in the Sandwich Islands (now Hawaii) in 1779, he had led two further expeditions to the South Pacific.

Convicts & Settlement

Following the American Revolution, Britain was no longer able to transport convicts to North America. With jails and prison hulks already overcrowded, it was essential that an alternative be found. In 1779 Joseph Banks suggested NSW as a fine site for a colony of thieves, and in 1786 Lord Sydney announced that the king had decided upon Botany Bay as a place for convicts under sentence of transportation. That the continent was already inhabited was not considered significant.

MICK WELDON **Captain James Cook**

Less than two years later, in January 1788, the First Fleet sailed into Botany Bay under the command of Captain Arthur Phillip, who was to be the colony's first governor. Phillip was immediately disappointed with the landscape and sent a small boat north to find a more suitable landfall. The crew soon returned with the news that in Port Jackson they had found the finest harbour in the world and a good sheltered cove.

The fleet comprised 11 ships carrying 1030 people, including 548 male and 188 female convicts, four companies of marines and enough livestock and supplies for two years. It weighed anchor again and headed for Sydney Cove to begin settlement.

For the new arrivals, NSW was a harsh and horrible place. The crimes punished by transportation were often minor and the sentences, of no less than seven years with hard labour, were tantamount to life sentences as there was little hope of returning home.

Although the colony of soldiers, sailors, pickpockets, prostitutes, sheep stealers and petty thieves managed to survive the first difficult years, the cruel power of the military guards made the settlement a prison hell.

At first, until farming could be developed, the settlers were dependent upon supplies from Europe and a late or, even worse, a wrecked supply ship would have been disastrous. The threat of starvation hung over the colony for at least 16 years.

The Second Fleet arrived in 1790 with more convicts and some supplies, and a year later, following the landing of the Third Fleet, the population increased to around 4000.

As crops began to yield, NSW became less dependent on Britain for food. There were still, however, huge social gulfs in the fledgling colony: officers and their families were in control and clinging desperately to a modicum of civilised British living; soldiers, free settlers and even emancipated convicts were beginning to eke out a living; yet the majority of the population was still in chains, regarded as the dregs of humanity and living in squalid conditions.

Little of the country was explored during those first years; few people ventured further than Sydney Cove, and though Governor Phillip had instructed that every attempt should be made to befriend the blacks, this was not to be.

Phillip believed NSW would not progress if the colony continued to rely solely on the labour of convicts, who were already busy constructing government roads and buildings. He believed prosperity depended on attracting free settlers, to whom convicts could be assigned as labourers, and in the granting of land to officers, soldiers and worthy emancipists (convicts who had served their time).

This had begun by the time Phillip returned to England and his second in command, Grose, took over. In a classic case of 'jobs for the boys', Grose tipped the balance of power further in favour of the military by granting land to officers of the NSW Corps.

With money, land and cheap labour suddenly at their disposal, the officers became exploitative, making huge profits at the expense of the small farmers. To encourage convicts to work, the officers paid them in rum. The officers quickly prospered and were soon able to buy whole shiploads of goods and resell them for many times their original value. NSW was becoming an important port on trade routes, and whaling and sealing were increasing.

Meeting little resistance, the officers did virtually as they pleased. In particular, one John Macarthur managed to upset, defy, out-manoeuvre and outlast three governors, including William Bligh of the *Bounty* mutiny fame.

As governor, Bligh faced a second mutiny in 1808 when the officers rebelled and ordered his arrest. The Rum Rebellion, as it became known, was the final straw for the British government, which dispatched Lieutenant-Colonel Lachlan Macquarie with his own regiment and orders for the return to London of the NSW Corps.

John Macarthur, incidentally, was to have far-reaching effects on the colony's first staple industry, wool. His understanding of the country's grazing potential fostered his own profitable sheep-breeding concerns and prompted his introduction of the merino, in the belief that careful breeding could produce wool of exceptional quality. Although it was his vision, his wife, Elizabeth, did most of the hard work – Macarthur himself remained in England for nearly a decade for his part in the Rum Rebellion.

Governor Macquarie, having broken the stranglehold of the Corps, set about laying the groundwork for significant social reforms. He felt that convicts who had served their time should be allowed rights as citizens, and began appointing emancipists to public positions.

While this meant the long-term future for convicts didn't appear quite so grim, by the end of Macquarie's term in 1821 NSW was still basically a convict society and there were often clashes between those who had never been imprisoned and those who had been freed.

During the 1830s and 1840s the number of free settlers to the colonies of NSW, Western Australia (WA), Van Diemen's Land (present-day Tasmania) and Port Phillip (Victoria) was increasing, although it was the discovery of gold in the 1850s that was truly to change the face of the young country.

By the time transportation was abolished (1852 in the eastern colonies and 1868 in the west) more than 168,000 convicts had been shipped to Australia.

Colonial Exploration & Expansion

Australia never experienced the systematic push westward that characterised the European settlement of America. Exploration and expansion basically took place for one of three reasons: to find suitable places of secondary punishment, like the barbaric penal settlement at Port Arthur in Van Diemen's Land; to occupy land before anyone else arrived; or in later years, because of the quest for gold.

By 1800 there were only two small settlements in Australia – at Sydney Cove and Norfolk Island. While unknown areas on world maps were becoming few and far between, most of Australia was still one big blank. It was even suspected that it might be two large, separate islands and it was hoped there might be a vast sea in the centre.

The ensuing 40 years was a great period of discovery, as the vast land was explored and settlements were established at Hobart, Brisbane, Perth, Adelaide and Melbourne. Some of the early explorers, particularly those who braved the hostile centre, suffered great hardship.

George Bass charted the coast south of Sydney almost down to the present location of Melbourne during 1797 and 1798. Also in 1798, he sailed around Van Diemen's Land with Matthew Flinders, establishing that it was an island. Flinders went on in 1802 to sail right round Australia.

The first settlement in Van Diemen's Land, in 1803, was close to the present site of Hobart; by the 1820s Hobart Town rivalled Sydney in importance. The island was not named Tasmania, after its original European discoverer, until 1856 when, after the end of transportation, the inhabitants requested the name be changed to remove the stigma of what had been a vicious penal colony.

On the mainland, the Blue Mountains at first proved an impenetrable barrier, fencing in Sydney to the sea, but in 1813 a track was finally forced through and the western plains were reached by the explorers Blaxland, Wentworth and Lawson.

Port Phillip Bay in Victoria was originally considered as the site for a second settlement in Australia but was rejected in favour of Hobart. It was not looked at again until 1835 when settlers from Tasmania, in search of more land, selected the present site of Melbourne. Perth was first settled in 1829, but as it was isolated from the rest of the country, growth there was very slow.

The first settlement in the Brisbane area was made by a party of convicts sent north from Sydney because the (by then) good citizens of that fair city were getting fed up with having all those crims about the place. By the time the Brisbane penal colony was abandoned in 1839, free settlers had arrived in force.

Adelaide, established in 1837, was initially an experiment in free-enterprise colonisation. It failed due to bad management and the British government had to take over from the bankrupt organisers and bail the settlement out of trouble.

In 1824 the explorers Hume and Hovell, starting from near present-day Canberra, made the first overland journey southwards, reaching the western shores of Port Phillip Bay. On the way they discovered a large river and named it after Hume, although it was later renamed the Murray by another great explorer, Charles Sturt. In 1829, Sturt established how the Murrumbidgee and Darling river systems tied in with the Murray, and where the Murray met the sea. Until that time there had been much speculation that many of the inland rivers might in fact drain into the anticipated inland sea.

Twelve years later the colony's surveyor-general, Major Mitchell, wrote glowing reports of the beautiful and fertile country he had crossed in his expedition across the Murray River and as far south as Portland Bay. He dubbed the region (now Victoria) Australia Felix, or 'Australia Fair'.

In 1840 Edward Eyre left Adelaide to try to reach the centre of Australia. He gave up at Mt Hopeless and then attempted a crossing to Albany in WA. This formidable task nearly proved too much as both food and water were virtually unobtainable and Eyre's companion, Baxter, was killed by two Aboriginal guides. Eyre struggled on, encountering a French whaling ship in Rossiter Bay;

reprovisioned, he managed to reach Albany. The road across the Nullarbor Plain from South Australia (SA) to WA is named the Eyre Highway.

From 1844 to 1845 a German scientist, by the name of Ludwig Leichhardt, travelled through northern Queensland, skirting the Gulf of Carpentaria, to Port Essington, near modern-day Darwin. He failed in 1846 and 1847 to cross Australia from east to west, and disappeared on his second attempt; he was never seen again.

In 1848 Edmund Kennedy set out to travel up Cape York Peninsula by land while a ship, HMS *Rattlesnake*, explored the coast and islands. Starting from Rockingham Bay, south of Cairns, the expedition almost immediately struck trouble when its heavy supply carts could not be dragged through the swampy ground around Tully. The rugged land, harsh climate, lack of supplies, hostile Aboriginal people and missed supply drops all took their toll and nine of the party of 13 died. Kennedy himself was speared to death by Aborigines when he was only 30km from the end of the fearsome trek. His Aboriginal servant, Jacky Jacky, was the only expedition member to finally reach the supply ship.

Beginning in Melbourne in 1860, the legendary attempt by Robert Burke and William Wills to cross the continent from south to north was destined to be one of the most tragic. Unlike earlier explorers, they tried to manage without Aboriginal guides. After reaching a depot at Cooper Creek in Queensland they intended to make a dash north to the Gulf of Carpentaria with a party of four. Their camels proved far slower than anticipated in the swampy land close to the gulf and on their way back one of the party died of exhaustion.

Burke, Wills and the third member, John King, eventually struggled back to Cooper Creek, at the end of their strength and nearly two months behind schedule, only to find the depot group had given up hope and left for Melbourne just hours earlier. They remained at Cooper Creek, but missed a returning search party and never found the supplies that had been left for them. Burke

and Wills finally starved to death, literally in the midst of plenty; King was able to survive on food provided by local Aboriginal people until a rescue party arrived.

Departing from Adelaide in 1860, and chasing a £2000 reward for the first south-north crossing, John McDouall Stuart reached the geographical centre of Australia, Central Mt Stuart, but shortly after was forced to turn back. In 1861 he got much closer to the Top End before he again had to return. Finally, in 1862, Stuart reached the north coast near Darwin. The overland telegraph line, completed in 1872, and the modern Stuart Highway follow a similar route.

Devastation of the Aborigines

When Sydney Cove was first settled by the British, it is believed there were about 300,000 Aboriginal people in Australia and around 250 different languages, many as distinct from each other as English is from Chinese. Tasmania alone had eight languages, and tribes living on opposite sides of present-day Sydney Harbour spoke mutually unintelligible languages.

In such a society, based on family groups with an egalitarian political structure, a co-ordinated response to the European colonisers was not possible. Despite the presence of Aboriginal people, the newly arrived Europeans considered the new continent to be *terra nullius* – a land belonging to no-one. Conveniently, they saw no recognisable system of government, no commerce or permanent settlements and no evidence of landownership. (Had there been such systems, and had the Aboriginal people offered coordinated resistance, the British might have been forced to legitimise their colonisation by entering into a treaty with the Aboriginal landowners, as happened in New Zealand with the Treaty of Waitangi.)

Many Aborigines were driven from their land by force, and many more succumbed to exotic diseases such as smallpox, measles, venereal disease, influenza, whooping cough, pneumonia and tuberculosis.

The delicate balance between Aboriginal people and nature was broken, as the European invaders cut down the forests and

PHOTO COURTESY OF THE NATIONAL LIBRARY OF AUSTRALIA

Taking control of Aboriginal land meant the systematic slaughter and repression of its traditional owners. Aboriginal people suffered inhuman treatment with dignity, and often fought back.

introduced numerous feral and domestic animals – by 1860 there were 20 million sheep in Australia. Sheep and cattle destroyed water holes and ruined the habitats that had sustained mammals, reptiles and vegetable foods for tens of thousands of years. Starving Aborigines speared sheep and cattle and then suffered reprisal raids which often left many dead. For the first 100 years of 'settlement' very few Europeans were prosecuted for killing Aboriginal people, although the practice was widespread.

In many parts of Australia, Aboriginal people defended their lands with desperate guerrilla tactics. Warriors such as Pemulwy, Yagan, Dundalli, Jandamarra (known to the whites as 'Pigeon') and Nemarluk were feared by the colonists for a time, and some settlements had to be abandoned. Until the 1850s, when Europeans had to rely on inaccurate and unreliable flintlock rifles, Aboriginal people sometimes had the benefit of superior numbers, weapons and tactics. However, with the introduction of breach-loading repeater rifles in the 1870s, armed resistance was quickly crushed (although whites were still being speared in central and northern Australia as late as the 1920s). Full-blood Aboriginal people in Tasmania were wiped out, and Aboriginal society elsewhere in Australia suffered terribly. By the 1880s only relatively small groups in the far Outback were still unscathed by the European invasion.

Gold, Stability & Growth

The discovery of gold in the 1850s brought about the most significant changes in the social and economic structure of Australia, particularly in Victoria where most of the gold was found.

Earlier gold discoveries had been all but ignored, partly because they were only small finds and mining skills were still undeveloped, but mostly because the law stated that all gold discovered belonged to the government.

The discovery of large quantities near Bathurst in 1851, however, caused a rush of hopeful miners from Sydney and forced the government to abandon the law of ownership. Instead, it introduced a compulsory diggers' licence fee of 30 shillings a month, whether the miners found gold or not, to ensure the country earned some revenue from the incredible wealth that was being unearthed. Victorian businesspeople at the time, fearing their towns would soon be devoid of able-bodied men, offered a reward for the discovery of gold in their colony.

In 1851 one of the largest gold discoveries in history was made at Ballarat, followed by others at Bendigo and Mt Alexander (near Castlemaine), starting a rush of unprecedented magnitude.

While the first diggers at the goldfields that soon sprang up all over Victoria came from the other Australian colonies, it wasn't long before they were joined by thousands of migrants. The Irish, Scots and English, as well as other Europeans and Americans, began arriving in droves, and within 12 months there were about 1800 hopeful diggers disembarking at Melbourne every week.

Similar discoveries in other colonies, particularly in WA in the 1890s, further boosted populations and levels of economic activity.

The gold rushes also brought floods of diligent Chinese miners and market gardeners onto the Australian diggings, where violent white opposition led to race riots and a morbid fear of Asian immigration which persists, to some extent, to this day. Although few people actually made their fortunes on the goldfields, many stayed to settle, as farmers, workers and shopkeepers. At the same time the Industrial Revolution in England started to produce a strong demand for raw materials. With its vast agricultural and mineral resources, Australia's economic base became secure.

Besides the population and economic growth that followed the discovery of gold, the rush contributed greatly to the development of a distinctive Australian folklore. The music brought by the Scots, English and Irish, for instance, was tuned to life on the diggings, while poets, singers and writers told stories of the people, the roaring gold towns and the boisterous hotels, the squatters and their sheep and cattle stations, the swagmen, and the derring-do of the notorious bushrangers, many of whom became folk heroes.

Federation & WWI

During the 1890s calls for the separate colonies to federate became increasingly strident. Supporters argued that it would improve the economy and the position of workers by enabling the abolition of intercolonial tariffs and protection against competition from foreign labour.

Each colony was determined, however, that its interests should not be overshadowed by those of the other colonies. For this reason, the constitution that was finally adopted gave only very specific powers to the Commonwealth, leaving all residual powers with the states. It also gave each state equal representation in the upper house of parliament (the Senate) regardless of size or population. Today Tasmania, with a population of less than half a million, has as many senators in Federal parliament as NSW, with a population of around six million. As the Senate is able to reject legislation passed by the lower house, this legacy of Australia's colonial past has had a profound effect on its politics, entrenching state divisions and ensuring that the smaller states have remained powerful forces in the government of the nation.

With federation, which came on 1 January 1901, Australia became a nation, but its loyalty and many of its legal and cultural ties to Britain remained. The mother country still expected military support from its Commonwealth allies in any conflict, and Australia fought beside Britain in battles as far from Australia's shores as the Boer War in South Africa. This willingness to follow western powers to war would be demonstrated time and again during the 20th century. Seemingly unquestioning loyalty to Britain and later the USA was only part of the reason. Xenophobia – born of isolation, an Asian location and a vulnerable economy – was also to blame.

The extent to which Australia regarded itself as a European outpost became evident with the passage of the Immigration Restriction Bill of 1901. The bill, known as the

White Australia policy, was designed to prevent the immigration of Asians and Pacific Islanders. Prospective immigrants were required to pass a dictation test in a European language. This language could be as obscure a tongue as the authorities wished. The dictation test was not abolished until 1958.

The desire to protect the jobs and conditions of white Australian workers that had helped bring about the White Australia policy did, however, have some positive results.

The labour movement had been a strong political force for many years, and by 1908 the principle of a basic wage sufficient to enable a male worker to support himself, a wife and three children had been established. By that time also, old age and invalid pensions were being paid.

When war broke out in Europe in 1914, Australian troops were again sent to fight thousands of kilometres from home. From Australia's perspective, the most infamous

The Flying Doctor

Before the late 1920s the outback's far-flung residents had little or no access to medical facilities. The nearest doctor was often weeks away over rough tracks, so if you fell seriously ill or met with a bad accident, your chances of recovery were slim. Difficult pregnancies and illnesses such as rheumatic fever and acute appendicitis were almost a death sentence. If you were lucky, you fell ill near a telegraph line, where your mates could treat you – or even operate – under instructions received in Morse code.

In 1912 the Reverend John Flynn of the Presbyterian Church helped establish the outback's first hospital at Oodnadatta. Flynn was appalled by the tragedies resulting from the lack of medical facilities and was quick to realise the answer lay in radios and aircraft. However, these technologies – particularly radio – were still very much in their infancy.

Flynn knew nothing of either radios or aviation but his sense of mission inspired others who did, such as radio engineer Alfred Traeger. In 1928, after years of trial and error, Traeger developed a small, pedal-powered radio transceiver that was simple to use, inexpensive and could send and receive messages over 500km. The outback's great silence was broken at last.

Aircraft suitable for medical evacuations had become available in 1920 but it was the lack of a radio communication network that delayed their general use for this purpose. Traeger's invention was the key to the establishment of Australia's first Flying Doctor base in Cloncurry, Queensland, in 1928. Cloncurry was then the base for the Queensland & Northern Territory Aerial Services (Qantas), which provided the pilot and an aircraft under lease.

The new service proved an outstanding success and areas beyond the reach of Cloncurry soon began to clamour for their own Flying Doctor. However, the Presbyterian Church had insufficient resources to allow a rapid expansion. In 1933 it handed the aerial medical service over to 'an organisation of national character' and so the Royal Flying Doctor Service (RFDS) was born. Flynn's vision of a 'mantle of safety' over the outback had become a reality.

Today, twelve RFDS base stations provide a sophisticated network of radio communications and medical services to an area as large as Western Europe and about two-thirds the size of the USA. Emergency evacuations of sick or injured people are still an important function, but these days the RFDS provides a comprehensive range of medical services, including routine clinics at communities that are unable to attract full-time medical staff. It also supervises numerous small hospitals that normally operate without a doctor; such hospitals are staffed by registered nurses who communicate by telephone or radio with their RFDS doctor.

The administration of RFDS bases is divided between seven nonprofit organisations funded by government grants and private donations.

of the WWI battles in which Diggers took part was that intended to force a passage through the Dardanelles to Constantinople. Australian and New Zealand troops landed at Gallipoli only to be slaughtered by well-equipped and strategically positioned Turkish soldiers. The sacrifices made by Australian soldiers are commemorated annually on Anzac Day, 25 April, the anniversary of the Gallipoli landing.

Interestingly, while Australians rallied to the aid of Britain during WWI, the majority of voters were prepared to support voluntary military service only. Efforts to introduce conscription during the war led to bitter debate, both in parliament and in the streets, and in referenda compulsory national service was rejected by a small margin.

Australia was hard hit by the Depression; prices for wool and wheat – two mainstays of the economy – plunged. In 1931 almost a third of breadwinners were unemployed and poverty was widespread. Swagmen became a familiar sight, as they had been in the 1890s depression, as thousands of men took to the 'wallaby track' in search of work in the countryside. By 1933, however, Australia's economy was starting to recover, a result of rises in wool prices and a rapid revival of manufacturing.

Also on the rise was the career of Joseph Lyons, who had become prime minister after defeating the Labor government, headed by James Scullin, at election in 1932. Lyons, a former Labor minister, had defected and formed the conservative United Australia Party, which stayed in power through the 1930s. The death of Lyons in 1939 saw the emergence of a figure who was set to dominate the Australian political scene for the next 25 years – Robert Gordon Menzies. He was prime minister from 1939 until forced by his own party to resign in 1941, after which time he formed a new conservative party, the Liberal Party, before regaining office in 1949, a post he held for a record 16 years.

'Protection' of Aboriginal People

By the early 1900s, legislation designed to segregate and 'protect' Aboriginal people was passed in all states. The legislation imposed restrictions on their rights to own property and seek employment. As well, the Aboriginals Ordinance of 1918 allowed the state to remove children from their Aboriginal mothers if it was suspected that the father was not an Aborigine – the parents were considered to have no rights over their children, who were placed in foster homes or childcare institutions. This practice continued up until the 1960s.

Many Aboriginal people are still angry about having been separated from their families and forced to grow up apart from their people, not to mention their mistreatment at the hands of some of the institutions to which they were sent. These people have become known as the 'Stolen Generation'. In a landmark test case now before the Federal Court of Australia, two members of the Stolen Generation are alleging that their treatment was illegal under the laws of the day, and are seeking compensation for pain and suffering.

WWII & Postwar Australia

In the years before WWII Australia became increasingly fearful of Japan. When war did break out, Australian troops fought alongside the British in Europe but after the Japanese bombed Pearl Harbor, Australia's own national security finally began to take priority.

Singapore fell, the northern Australian towns of Darwin and Broome and the New Guinean town of Port Moresby were bombed, the Japanese advanced southward, and still Britain called for more Australian troops. This time the Australian prime minister, John Curtin, refused. Australian soldiers were needed to fight the Japanese advancing over the mountainous Kokoda Trail towards Port Moresby. In appalling conditions, Australian soldiers confronted and defeated the Japanese at Milne Bay, east of Port Moresby, and began the long struggle to push them from the Pacific.

Ultimately it was the USA, not Britain, that helped protect Australia from the Japanese, defeating them in the Battle of the Coral Sea. This event was to mark the beginning of a profound shift in Australia's

20th Century Exploration

Around the turn of the century, Baldwin Spencer, a biologist, and Francis Gillen, an anthropologist, teamed up to study the Aboriginal people of central Australia and Arnhem Land. Other expeditions to northern Australia and Arnhem Land were led by the British polar explorer GH Wilkins (in 1923) and Donald Mackay (in 1928). Donald Thomson led his first expedition to Arnhem Land in 1935 and his work in northern Australia still receives accolades from anthropologists and naturalists.

In the 1930s aerial mapping of the Centre began in earnest, financed by Mackay. Surveys were carried out over the Simpson Desert, the only large stretch of the country still to be explored on foot by Europeans. In 1939 CT Madigan led an expedition that crossed this forbidding landscape from Old Andado to Birdsville.

In 1948 the largest scientific expedition ever undertaken in Australia was led into Arnhem Land by Charles Mountford. Financed by the National Geographic Society and the Australian government, it collected over 13,000 fish, 13,500 plant specimens, 850 birds and over 450 animal skins, along with thousands of Aboriginal implements and weapons.

During the 1950s the Woomera Rocket Range and the atomic-bomb test sites of Emu Junction and Maralinga were set up. The vast central-western desert region was opened up by the surveyor Len Beadell, who pushed a number of 'bomb roads' throught the previously trackless wilderness. He is widely regarded as the last Australian explorer.

allegiance away from Britain and towards the USA. Although Australia continued to support Britain in the war in Europe, its appreciation of its own vulnerability had been sharpened immeasurably by the Japanese advance.

One result of this was the postwar immigration program, which offered assisted passage not only to the British but also to refugees from eastern Europe, in the hope that the increase in population would strengthen Australia's economy and its ability to defend itself. 'Populate or Perish' became the catch phrase. Between 1947 and 1968 more than 800,000 non-British European migrants came to live in Australia. They have since made an enormous contribution to the country, enlivening its culture and broadening its vision.

The standard of living improved rapidly after the war (due largely to a rapid increase in the demand for Australian raw materials), and the Labor government of Ben Chifley put in place a reconstruction program, which saw, among other things, the establishment of the massive Snowy Mountains Hydroelectric Scheme.

Postwar Australia came to accept the American view that it was not so much Asia but communism in Asia that threatened the increasingly Americanised Australian way of life. Accordingly Australia, again under Menzies by this stage, followed the USA into the Korean War and joined it as a signatory to the treaties of ANZUS and the anti-communist Southeast Asia Treaty Organization (SEATO). During the 1950s Australia also provided aid to South-East Asian nations under the Colombo Plan of 1950, a scheme initiated by Australia but subscribed to by many other countries (including the USA, Britain, Canada and Japan) as a means to prevent the spread of communism throughout the region.

In the light of Australia's willingness to join SEATO, it is not surprising that the Menzies government applauded the USA's entry into the Vietnam War and, in 1965, committed troops to the struggle. Support for involvement was far from absolute, however. Arthur Calwell, the leader of the Australian Labor Party, believed the Vietnam conflict to be a civil war in which Australia had no part. Still more troubling for many young

Australian men was the fact that conscription was introduced in 1964 and those undertaking national service could now be sent overseas. By 1967 as many as 40% of Australians serving in Vietnam were conscripts.

'Assimilation' of Aboriginal People

The process of social change for Aboriginal people was accelerated by WWII. After the war 'assimilation' of Aboriginal people into white society became the stated aim of the government. To this end, the rights of Aboriginal people were subjugated even further – the government had control over everything, from where they could live to whom they could marry. Many people were forcibly moved from their homes to townships, the idea being that they would adapt to European culture, which would in turn aid their economic development. This policy was a dismal failure.

In the 1960s the assimilation policy came under a great deal of scrutiny, and white Australians became increasingly aware of the inequity of their treatment of Aboriginal people. In 1967 non-Aboriginal Australians voted to give Aborigines and Torres Strait Islanders the status of citizens, and gave the Federal government power to legislate for them in all states. The states had to provide them with the same services as were available to other citizens, and the Federal government set up the Department of Aboriginal Affairs to identify and legislate for the special needs of Aboriginal people.

The assimilation policy was finally dumped in 1972, to be replaced by the government's policy of 'self-determination', which for the first time enabled Aboriginal people to participate in decision-making processes by granting them rights to their land. (See the Government & Politics section later in this chapter for more on Aboriginal land rights.)

Although the outcome of the Mabo case (see Aboriginal Land Rights under Government & Politics later in this chapter) gives rise to cautious optimism, many Aboriginal people still live in appalling conditions, and alcohol and substance abuse remain widespread problems, particularly among young and middle-aged men. Aboriginal communities have taken up the challenge to try to eradicate these problems – many communities are now 'dry', and there are a number of rehabilitation programs for alcoholics, petrol-sniffers and others with drug problems. Thanks for much of this work goes to Aboriginal women, many of whom have found themselves on the receiving end of domestic violence.

The 1970s & Beyond

The civil unrest aroused by conscription was one factor that contributed to the rise to power, in 1972, of the Australian Labor Party, under the leadership of Gough Whitlam, for the first time in more than 25 years. The Whitlam government withdrew Australian troops from Vietnam, abolished national service and higher-education fees, instituted a system of free and universally available health care, and supported land rights for Aboriginal people.

The government, however, was hampered by both a hostile Senate and much talk of mismanagement. On 11 November 1975, the governor-general (the British monarch's representative in Australia) dismissed the parliament and installed a caretaker government led by the leader of the opposition Liberal Party, Malcolm Fraser. Labor supporters were appalled. Such action was unprecedented in the history of the Commonwealth of Australia and the powers that the governor-general had been able to invoke had long been regarded by many as an anachronistic vestige of Australia's now remote British past.

Nevertheless, it was a conservative Liberal and National Country Party coalition that won the ensuing election. A Labor government was not returned until 1983, when a former trade union leader, Bob Hawke, led the party to victory. In 1990 Hawke won a third consecutive term in office (a record for a Labor prime minister), thanks in no small part to the lack of better alternatives offered by the Liberals. He was replaced as prime minister by Paul Keating, his long-time treasurer, in late 1991.

Mt Feathertop, Victorian Alps, Victoria (Vic)

RICHARD I'ANSON

Kata Tjuta (The Olgas), Uluru-Kata Tjuta National Park, Northern Territory (NT)

RICHARD I'ANSON

War Memorial and Parliament House, Canberra, ACT

Captain Cook Memorial Water Jet, Canberra, ACT

Rats of Tobruk War Memorial, Canberra, ACT

Consequences of Dispossession

Aboriginal Australians are the most disadvantaged socio-economic group in Australia. They continue to suffer the effects of British colonisation under the doctrine of *terra nullius*, whereby the land was deemed unoccupied at the time of settlement. As a result, their spiritual and economic attachments to the land were ignored. They were dispossessed of their land and killed in large numbers by hunting parties and introduced diseases as pastoralists took up their lands. Aborigines on more viable agricultural land were almost wiped out.

Aborigines in remote regions survived in greater numbers, but they too were forced off their traditional lands and into missions as cattle grazing spread to arid regions. Their culture was attacked, both by separation from their sacred sites and by direct assault on their values by the missionaries, and, in more recent times, by the media of white culture. Many were forced on to missions because of hunger as cattle grazing destroyed their hunting lands.

The last 200 years of mistreatment and the continuing reluctance of governments to deal with Aboriginal disadvantage on the scale necessary to make serious inroads into their problems has left Aboriginal welfare in an appalling state. The Human Rights and Equal Opportunity Commission's Social Justice Statistics report of 1996 shows that, compared with non-Aboriginal Australians, Aborigines die on average 20 years younger and are 20 times more likely to be homeless. Indigenous children are placed on guardianship orders at almost 16 times the rate of non-indigenous children. While the total unemployment rate of the general Australian labour force was 10.5% in 1994, that of Aboriginal and Torres Strait Islanders was 38%. Only 11% of indigenous Australians have an income of $25,000 or more.

Given the scale of their displacement and these appalling social circumstances, it is not surprising that alcohol and other substance abuse, including petrol sniffing, is a major problem.

In an effort to address the problem, many Aboriginal communities have chosen to be 'dry' communities and on such lands it is an offence to possess or consume liquor. Many Aborigines do not drink liquor at all or only drink it occasionally or in moderation. For example, the Commonwealth Department of Human Services and Health's 1993 National Drug Strategy survey showed that only 33% of urban Aboriginal and Torres Strait Islanders were regular drinkers.

However, many problem drinkers from 'dry' communities tend to drift into population centres, such as Alice Springs, where they can obtain liquor. Often they are homeless, unemployed and away from the moderating influence of their communities. They tend to obtain liquor in its cheapest form from takeaway outlets and drink in open spaces. This means they become highly visible both to the police and the community generally.

The high visibility of Aboriginal problem-drinkers can lead to stereotyping, which is unfair to the majority of Aborigines who are sober and hard working. Even the problem-drinkers deserve compassion and understanding, given the appalling social conditions out of which the problems have arisen.

By 1991 Australia was in recession, mainly as a result of domestic economic policy but also because Australia is particularly hard hit when demand (and prices) for primary produce and minerals falls on world markets. Unemployment was the highest it had been since the early 1930s, hundreds of farmers were forced off the land because they couldn't keep afloat financially, there was a four-million-bale wool stockpile that no-one seemed to know how to shift, and the building and manufacturing industries faced a huge slump amid a general air of doom and gloom. The Federal election in 1993 was won by Paul Keating, against all expectations. The economy took a slight turn for the better, but not enough for the electorate to maintain its faith in the Labor government.

Cutting Ties with Britain

With the turn of the millennium, and with it the 2000 Olympic Games in Sydney followed closely by the centenary of Australian federation, the debate about Australia's national identity has become a major issue. At the core of the debate is the current constitution, in which Britain's monarch is the Australian head of state. On one side are the republicans, who want an Australian as head of state, on the other the monarchists, who favour the status quo.

In a nutshell, the republican argument is that Australia over the past 40 years has become a multicultural society, with immigrants from at least 100 countries, a far cry from the Anglo-Celtic-dominated population of a century ago. Therefore, the current constitutional set up is an anachronism. The monarchists believe that the system has served Australia well, and if it ain't broke why fix it?

The republic issue has been simmering since the early 90s when it became a hobby horse of the then prime minister, Paul Keating. It seemed back then that a republic was a sure bet, and that it would happen probably sooner rather than later. However, the process slowed with the 1996 election victory of John Howard, an avowed monarchist.

Still, Howard did – if grudgingly – set up a constitutional convention in early 1998, but put the onus on the 152 delegates to come up with a 'workable' republic model. If they were able to do this, and the model was passed by a referendum to be held in 1999, Australia would become a republic on 1 January 2001. This would be exactly 100 years after the current constitution, which saw the federation of the six colonies, came into being.

The convention led to the adoption of a republic model. It allowed for an Australian president chosen by the prime minister from a list prepared by a 15-member committee from public nominations, and the choice agreed to by the Opposition leader and a two-thirds majority of parliament. While this model was not the one favoured by the majority of the roughly 60% of Australians who want a republic (they would prefer to see a president directly elected by popular vote), it was the one put to the referendum vote on 6 November 1999.

Change doesn't come easily. Of the entire nation, only the ACT voted for a republic. Although the republican movement maintains the issue is not dead, another chance to achieve constitutional change is probably a decade away.

With unemployment remaining high at around 9%, in early 1996 Keating was defeated in a landslide victory to the Coalition, led by John Howard.

The Coalition was re-elected in late 1998, but with a much-reduced majority due largely to voter concerns about broken promises and proposed tax reforms – the government had stated its intention to introduce a goods and services tax, and this legislation was introduced to the Senate for debate early in 1999. By now commodity prices had slumped even further with the economic turmoil in Asia, which has the largest markets for Australian primary producers. However, the unemployment rate had marginally improved (to 7.5%) and the national economy was growing strongly – ironically due to increased consumer spending.

Despite the economic uncertainty of recent times, most non-Aboriginal Australians have an extremely high standard of living; it's a disgrace that the same can't be said for most of their Aboriginal counterparts. Many Aboriginal people still live in deplorable conditions, with outbreaks of preventable diseases and infant mortality running at a rate higher even than in many Third World countries. While some progress has been made with the Federal government's Native Title legislation (see the Government & Politics section in this chapter for details), there's still a long way to go before Aboriginal people can enjoy an improved standard of living.

Socially and economically, Australia is still coming to terms with its strategic location in Asia. While it has accepted large numbers of Vietnamese and other Asian migrants during the past two decades, it has never really considered itself a part of Asia, nor has it exploited the area's economic potential. One of the key aims of the former Labor government was to make Australia a more important player in the Asia-Pacific arena, shifting the focus away from traditional ties with Britain, the USA and Europe. However, the Coalition government places far less importance on this.

Another issue dominating Australian thinking in the late 1990s is republicanism, as increasing numbers of people feel constitutional ties with Britain are no longer relevant. (See Cutting Ties with Britain boxed text.) This is especially true with Sydney hosting the Olympic Games in the year 2000 – many feel it would be fitting that the games be opened by the constitutional head of a new Republic of Australia. However, it seems that Prime Minister John Howard has strong traditional ties to the monarchy and it may be a long time yet before the governor-general is replaced.

GEOGRAPHY

Australia is an island continent whose landscape – much of it inhospitable – is the result of gradual changes wrought over millions of years. Although there is still seismic activity in the eastern and western highland areas, Australia is one of the most stable land masses. For about 100 million years it has been free of the forces that have given rise to huge mountain ranges elsewhere.

From the east coast a narrow, fertile strip merges into the greatly eroded Great Dividing Range, that is almost continent-long. The mountains are mere reminders of the mighty range that once stood here. Only in the section straddling the NSW border with Victoria, and in Tasmania, are they high enough to have winter snow.

West of the range the country becomes increasingly flat and dry. The endless flatness is broken only by salt lakes, occasional mysterious protuberances like Uluru (Ayers Rock) and Kata Tjuta (the Olgas), and some starkly beautiful mountains like the MacDonnell Ranges near Alice Springs. In places, the scant vegetation is sufficient to allow some grazing. However, much of the Australian Outback is a barren land of harsh semideserts and dry salt pans.

The extreme north of Australia, the Top End, is a tropical area within the monsoon belt. Although its annual rainfall looks adequate on paper, it comes in more or less one short, sharp burst. This has prevented the Top End from becoming seriously productive agriculturally.

The west of Australia consists mainly of a broad plateau. In the far west a mountain range and fertile coastal strip heralds the Indian Ocean, but this is only to the south. In the north-central part of WA, the dry country runs right to the sea. The rugged Kimberley region in the state's far north is spectacular.

Australia is the world's sixth largest country. Its area is 7,682,300 sq km, about the same size as the 48 mainland states of the USA and half as large again as Europe, excluding the former USSR. It constitutes approximately 5% of the world's land surface. Lying between the Indian and Pacific oceans, Australia is about 4000km from east to west and 3200km from north to south, with a coastline 36,735km long.

GEOLOGY

Along with Africa, South America, Antarctica and India, Australia once formed part of the supercontinent Gondwana, which was formed about 600 million years ago when its various components bumped into each other and bonded together. Australia only became separate a continent about 100 million years ago when it broke away from Antarctica. Since then it has been drifting north – its current rate of drift is about 55mm per year.

Australia can be divided into two broad geological zones: the Tasman Fold Belt and the Australian Craton. These are situated east and west, respectively, of a line drawn roughly between Kangaroo Island in SA and Princess Charlotte Bay, near Cooktown in far north Queensland.

The Remarkable Rocks, Flinders Chase National Park, Kangaroo Island

The Australian Craton is geologically ancient, its basement metamorphic and igneous rocks ranging in age from 570 million to 3.7 billion years. Its oldest rock formations – in WA's Pilbara region – contain crystals that formed 4.3 billion years ago, making them part of the earth's original crust. At North Pole, also in the Pilbara, are the fossil remains of stromatolites that lived 3.5 billion years ago.

The Australian Craton is actually made up of several small crustal blocks of igneous material such as granite that became welded together about a billion years ago. Today these blocks are mostly buried by sedimentary material, although they emerge at places like Mt Isa, Broken Hill and in the Tanami Desert. All these areas contain rich mineral deposits that today sustain major mining developments. The eroded remnants of the original sandstone blanket form the rugged landscapes we now admire in the north-west Kimberley region and Kakadu, in the Top End.

About 500 million years ago, the first of a series of mountain-building episodes threw up an Andes-like mountain range along the Australian Craton's eastern side. Over a period of 110 million years these events gradually pushed the coastline 1000km eastwards.

Most of the Australian Craton was dry land between 250 and 140 million years ago, after which a major rise in sea level created an inland sea covering a third of the continent. Marine siltstones from this period contain precious opal, now mined at a number of places including Coober Pedy in SA and White Cliffs in NSW. Another inundation occurred 10 to 15 million years ago, creating the limestone deposits that today make up the Nullarbor Plain.

The Great Artesian Basin, one of the world's largest groundwater resources, underlies about 20% of the continent. Much of eastern inland Australia is almost totally reliant on it for its water needs.

CLIMATE

Australian seasons are the antithesis of those in Europe and North America. It's hot in December and many Australians spend Christmas at the beach, while in July and

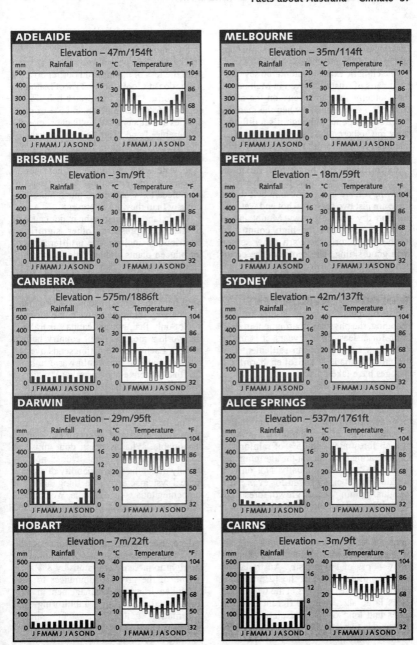

August it's midwinter. Summer starts in December, autumn in March, winter in June and spring in September.

The climatic extremes aren't too severe in most parts of Australia. Even in Melbourne, the southernmost capital city on the mainland, it's a rare occasion when the mercury hits freezing point, although it's a different story in Canberra, the national capital. Tasmanians, further to the south, have a good idea of what cold is.

As you head north the seasonal variations become fewer until, in the far north around Darwin, you are in the monsoon belt where there are just two seasons – hot and wet, and hot and dry. In the Snowy Mountains of southern NSW and the high country of north-east Victoria there's a snow season with good skiing. The centre of the continent is arid – hot and dry during the day, but often bitterly cold at night.

ECOLOGY & ENVIRONMENT

While humans have been living in, and changing, the physical environment in Australia for at least 50,000 years, it is in the 200 years since European settlement that the most dramatic – and often harmful – changes have taken place.

With the spread of settlement and the increase in pastoral use came clearing of native bush. The last 200 years have seen the loss or severe altering of 70% of all native vegetation, including the total loss of 40% of total forest area and 75% of rainforests. Land clearing continues at the alarming rate of 600,000 hectares annually. Not only is marginal land being cleared for even more marginal farming but old growth forests are logged for timber products – notably wood chips.

This drastic modification of the environment has led to probably the most significant environmental problem in Australia today – loss of biodiversity. Australia has been identified as one of the 12 most biologically diverse countries in the world, due to its large size, many different climatic zones and long period of isolation. It has thousands of unique plants and animals, especially marsupials (with 144 species),

which have evolved and adapted to survive in the unique environment.

The loss of species goes hand in hand with the loss of habitat, and our report card so far doesn't look good – 23% of mammal, 9% of bird, 9% of freshwater fish, 7% of reptile, 16% of amphibian and 5% of plant species are either already extinct or severely vulnerable. Land clearing also contributes significantly to other environmental problems such as soil salinity, degradation of inland waterways, erosion and increases in greenhouse-gas emissions. All these problems need to be addressed much more vigorously than they are at present.

While land clearing is the major cause of biodiversity pressure, other significant contributors include the proliferation of introduced plants and animals and the diseases that they can carry. Tourism plays its part too, with large numbers of visitors putting pressure on fragile natural and cultural heritage areas, in some cases damaging the very thing they have come to see.

Not only that, but per capita Australia is the world's most wasteful country behind the US. Each year the nation sends over 18 million tonnes of household waste to landfill (that's a tonne per Australian), which is enough to cover the state of Victoria to a depth of 100mm. Australians use six billion plastic shopping bags annually.

The key word when judging environmental practices and effects these days is sustainable. What is being done must be done in such a way that it does not adversely affect the future viability of an ecological system, clearly something that is not happening today – in Australia, World Heritage areas are mined, groundwater is used faster than it is being replenished, and there is an unwillingness by the government to reduce greenhouse-gas emissions (at the 1997 Kyoto Climate Summit, Australia won the right to increase emissions by 8%).

One of the greatest hindrances to successful environmental management in Australia is the fact that monitoring and information gathering systems simply aren't in place. This makes it almost impossible to accurately gauge the true impact of human activity and the effectiveness of management programs.

The news is not all bad, however, especially when compared with many other industrialised countries. As Australia is a huge, sparsely populated country with a highly urbanised population (88%), large areas are still in good condition, pollution of all kinds is relatively low, recycling is becoming much more widespread and general environmental awareness has risen dramatically.

While Australia lacks a coordinated approach to environmental management and sustainable development, there are many bodies – from Federal government right through to local community level – working towards that goal. Organisations such as Greening Australia and the very successful Landcare movement do great things locally, while Federal programs such as the One Billion Trees initiative and the listing and protection of areas under the World Heritage convention are all steps in the right direction.

See the Useful Organisations section in the Facts for the Visitor chapter for details of environmental groups.

NATIONAL PARKS & RESERVES

Australia has more than 500 national parks – non-urban protected wilderness areas of environmental or natural importance. Each state defines and runs its own national parks, but the principle is the same throughout Australia. National parks include rainforests, vast tracts of empty Outback, strips of coastal dune land and rugged mountain ranges.

Public access is encouraged if safety and conservation regulations are observed. In all parks you're asked to do nothing to damage or alter the natural environment. Approach roads, camping grounds (often with toilets and showers), walking tracks and information centres are often provided for visitors. In most national parks there are restrictions on bringing in pets.

Some national parks are so isolated, rugged or uninviting that you wouldn't want to go there unless you were an experienced bushwalker or 4WD traveller. Other parks, however, are among Australia's major attractions. Some of the most beautiful are included on the World Heritage List (a United Nations list of natural or cultural places of world significance that would be an irreplacable loss to the planet if they were altered).

Internationally, the World Heritage List includes more than 400 sites such as the Taj Mahal and the Grand Canyon. Australia has 13 areas: the Great Barrier Reef; Kakadu and Uluru-Kata Tjuta national parks in the Northern Territory (NT); the Willandra Lakes region of far western NSW; the Lord

The Environment: What You Can Do

Tourism places strains on the environment, although often inadvertently and often despite the best of intentions. Whether you're an international tourist or a local visitor, there are certain things you can do to minimise your impact on Australia's fragile and unique environment:

- When travelling by 4WD, never venture off established tracks, especially in sensitive areas such as Fraser Island, Uluru-Kata Tjuta and other national parks.
- Bushwalkers will find that there are fewer and fewer places where they can light a camp or cooking fire, so be prepared and carry a fuel stove. All rubbish should be carried out and disposed of properly.
- It seems obvious, but don't light fires on days of Total Fire Ban. Ignorance of a ban is no excuse – keep yourself informed and be aware of the dangers (and the penalties!).
- The Great Barrier Reef is a national park, so the usual rules apply – don't damage or remove anything, and definitely do not walk on or otherwise touch the coral.
- When taking organised adventure tours through remote and fragile areas, if possible, try to choose operators who are aware of environmentally sound practices and stick to them. Unfortunately, there are plenty of cowboys out there whose bank balance means much more than any eco-balance.

Crater Lake in the World-Heritage-listed Cradle Mountain-Lake St Clair National Park, Tasmania

Howe Island group off NSW; the Tasmanian Wilderness (the Franklin-Gordon Wild Rivers and Cradle Mountain-Lake St Clair national parks); the Central Eastern Rainforest Reserves (15 reserves covering 1000 sq km in the eastern highlands of NSW); the Wet Tropics of far north Queensland; Shark Bay in WA; Fraser Island off the Queensland coast; the fossil-mammal sites of Riversleigh (north-western Queensland) and Naracoorte (coastal SA); Macquarie Island (Australian external territory near Antarctica); and Heard Island and the McDonald Islands group (also external territories off Antarctica).

The Great Barrier Reef, the Tasmanian Wilderness, the Wet Tropics of Queensland and Shark Bay meet all four World Heritage criteria for natural heritage, with Kakadu National Park, Uluru-Kata Tjuta National Park, Willandra Lakes and the Tasmanian Wilderness being listed for both natural and cultural criteria. These sites are among the very few on the World Heritage List selected for both natural and cultural heritage reasons, or because they meet all four natural criteria.

Before a site or area is accepted for the World Heritage List it has first to be proposed by its country and then must pass a series of tests at the UN, culminating, if it is successful, in acceptance by the UN World Heritage Committee, which meets at the end of each year. Any country proposing one of its sites or areas for the list must agree to protect the selected area, keeping it for the enjoyment of future generations even if to do so requires help from other countries.

While state governments have authority over their own national parks, the Federal government is responsible for ensuring that Australia meets its international treaty obligations, and in any dispute arising from a related conflict between a state and the Federal government, the latter can override the former. In this way the Federal government can force a state to protect an area with World Heritage listing, as it did in the early 1980s when the Tasmanian government wanted to dam the Gordon River in the south-west of the state and thereby flood much of the wild Franklin River.

Unfortunately, however, there appear to be no such constraints on the Federal government which, in 1998, approved the development of a major new uranium mine in Kakadu National Park. As a result, the UN considered down-grading the park's World Heritage listing, but decided against it. Mining can continue at Ranger until 2009 and can start at Jabiluka in 2001.

For national park authority addresses see Useful Organisations in the Facts for the Visitor chapter.

State Forests

Another form of nature reserve is the state forest. These are owned by state governments and have fewer regulations than national parks. In theory, state forests can be logged, but often they are primarily recreational areas with camping grounds, walking trails and signposted forest drives. Some permit horses and dogs.

The logging of state forests for woodchips has long been a contentious issue in Australia, and in recent times has once again come to the fore. The Federal government issues the woodchip licences and decides which forests will go and which will stay. Its current policy sets aside a number of areas for woodchipping, while protecting others. The loggers say more should be logged, the conservationists naturally enough say it should be less, and the confrontation often gets quite ugly. One of the more high-profile campaigns by the pro-logging lobby in recent years saw hundreds of logging trucks descend on Canberra, blockading Parliament House and forcing the politicians to walk the last bit to work.

GOVERNMENT & POLITICS

Australia is a federation of six states and two territories. Under the written Constitution, which came into force on 1 January 1901 when the colonies joined to form the Commonwealth of Australia, the Federal government is mainly responsible for the national economy and Reserve Bank, customs and excise, immigration, defence, foreign policy and the postal system. The state governments are chiefly responsible for health, education, housing, transport and justice. There are both Federal and State police forces.

Australia has a parliamentary system of government based on that of the UK, and the state and Federal structures are broadly similar. In Federal parliament, the lower house is the House of Representatives, the upper house the Senate. The House of Representatives has 148 members, divided among the states on a population basis (NSW 50, Victoria 37, Queensland 27, SA 12, WA 14, Tasmania five, Australian Capital Territory (ACT) two and NT one). Elections for the House of Representatives are held at least every three years. The Senate has 12 senators from each state, and two each from the ACT and the NT. State senators serve six-year terms, with elections for half of them every three years; territory senators serve only three years, their terms coinciding with elections for the House of Representatives. Queensland's upper house was abolished in 1922. The Federal government is run by a prime minister, while the state governments are led by a premier and the NT by a chief minister. The party holding the greatest number of lower-house seats forms the government.

Australia is a monarchy, but although Britain's king or queen is also Australia's, Australia is fully autonomous. The British sovereign is represented by the governor-general as well as state governors, whose nominations for their posts by the respective governments are ratified by the monarch of the day.

Federal parliament is based in Canberra, the capital of the nation. Like Washington DC in the USA, Canberra is in its own separate area of land, the ACT, and is not under the rule of one of the states. Geographically, however, the ACT is completely surrounded by NSW. The state parliaments are in each state capital.

The Federal government is elected for a maximum of three years but elections can be (and often are) called earlier. Voting is by secret ballot and is compulsory for people 18 years of age and over. Voting can be somewhat complicated as a preferential system is used whereby each candidate has to be listed in order of preference. This can result, for example in Senate elections with 50 or more candidates to be ranked.

The Constitution can only be changed by referendum, and only if a majority of voters in at least four states favour it. Since federation in 1901, of the 43 proposals that have been put to referendum, only eight have been approved.

In Federal parliament, the two main political groups are the Australian Labor Party (ALP) and the coalition between the Liberal Party and the National Party. These parties also dominate state politics but sometimes the Liberal and National parties are not in coalition. The latter was once known as the National Country Party since it mainly represents country seats.

The only other political party of any real substance is the Australian Democrats, which has largely carried the flag for the ever-growing 'green' movement. The Democrats have been successful in recent times. Although the 1998 election gave a majority to the Coalition in the House of Representatives, the balance of power is held in the Senate by the Democrats. (The new and controversial One Nation Party won over 10% of the primary vote for the House of Representatives in the 1998 Federal election, and has won significant support in recent state elections in Queensland and NSW. The party is reviled by many Australians for its allegedly racist policies.)

The Cabinet, presided over by the prime minister, is the government's major policy-making body, and it comprises about half of the full ministry. It's a somewhat secretive body which meets in private (usually in Canberra) and its decisions are ratified by the Executive Council, a formal body presided over by the governor-general.

Aboriginal Land Rights

Britain founded the colony of NSW on the legal principle of *terra nullius*, a land belonging to no-one, which meant that Australia was legally unoccupied. The settlers could take land from Aboriginal people without signing treaties or providing compensation. The European concept of land

ownership was completely foreign to Aboriginal people and their view of the world in which land did not belong to individuals: people belonged to the land, were formed by it and were a part of it like everything else.

After WWII, Australian Aboriginal people became more organised and better educated, and a political movement for land rights developed. In 1962 a bark petition was presented to the Federal government by the Yolngu people of Yirrkala, in north-east Arnhem Land, demanding that the government recognise Aboriginal peoples' occupation and ownership of Australia since time immemorial. The petition was ignored, and the Yolngu people took the matter to court – and lost. In the famous Yirrkala Land Case 1971, Australian courts accepted the government's claim that Aboriginal people had no meaningful economic, legal or political relationship to land. The case upheld the principle of *terra nullius*, and the common-law position that Australia was unoccupied in 1788.

Because the Yirrkala Land Case was based on an inaccurate (if not outright racist) assessment of Aboriginal society, the Federal government came under increasing pressure to legislate for Aboriginal land rights. In 1976 it eventually passed the Aboriginal Land Rights (NT) Act – often referred to as the Land Rights Act.

Land Rights Acts The Aboriginal Land Rights (NT) Act of 1976, which operates in the NT, remains Australia's most powerful and comprehensive land rights legislation. Promises were made to legislate for national land rights, but these were abandoned after opposition from mining companies and state governments. The act established three Aboriginal Land Councils that are empowered to claim land on behalf of traditional Aboriginal owners.

However, under the act the only land claimable is unalienated NT land outside town boundaries – land that no-one else owns or leases, usually semidesert or desert. Thus, when the Anangu traditional owners of Uluru (Ayers Rock) claimed ownership of Uluru and Kata Tjuta (the Olgas), their claim was disallowed because the land was within a national park and thus alienated. It was only by amending two acts of parliament that Uluru-Kata Tjuta National Park was handed back to traditional Anangu owners on the condition that it be immediately leased back to the Federal government as a national park. At present, about half of the NT has either been claimed, or is under claim, by its traditional Aboriginal owners. The claim process is extremely tedious and can take many years to complete, largely because almost all claims have been opposed by the NT government. Claimants must prove that under Aboriginal law they are responsible for the sacred sites on the land being claimed. A great many elderly claimants die before the matter is resolved.

Once a claim is successful, Aboriginal people have the right to negotiate with mining companies and ultimately to accept or reject exploration and mining proposals. This right is strongly opposed by the mining lobby, despite the fact that traditional Aboriginal owners in the NT only reject about a third of these proposals outright.

The Pitjantjatjara Land Rights Act 1981 (SA) is Australia's second-most powerful and comprehensive land rights law. This gives Anangu Pitjantjatjara and Yankunytjatjara people freehold title to 10% of SA. The land, known as the Anangu Pitjantjatjara Lands, is in the far north of the state.

Just south of the Anangu Pitjantjatjara Lands lie the Maralinga Lands, which comprise 8% of SA. The area, much of which was contaminated by British nuclear tests in the 1950s, was returned to its Anangu traditional owners by virtue of the Maralinga Tjarutja Land Rights Act 1984 (SA).

Under these two South Australian acts, Anangu can control access to land and liquor consumption. However, if Anangu traditional owners cannot reach agreement with mining companies seeking to explore or mine on their land, they cannot veto mining activity; an arbitrator decides if mining will go ahead. If mining is given the green light, the arbitrator will bind the mining company with terms and conditions and ensure that reasonable monetary payments are made to Anangu.

In SA, other Aboriginal reserves exist by virtue of the Aboriginal Land Trust Act 1966 (SA). However, this act gives Aboriginal people little control over their land.

Outside the NT and SA, Aboriginal land rights are extremely limited. In Queensland, less than 2% of the state is Aboriginal land and, what's more, the only land that can be claimed under the Aboriginal Land Act 1991 (Queensland) is land that has been gazetted by the government as land available for claim. Under existing Queensland legislation, 95% of the state's Aboriginal people can't claim their traditional country.

Since the passing of the Nature Conservation Act 1992 (Queensland), Aboriginal people in the state also have very limited claim to national parks. If Aboriginal people successfully claim a Queensland park, they must permanently lease it back to the government without a guarantee of a review of the lease arrangement or a majority on the board of management. This is quite different to the arrangements at Uluru-Kata Tjuta National Park, where the traditional owners have a majority on the board, with a 99-year lease-back that is renegotiated every five years.

In WA, Aboriginal reserves comprise about 13% of the state. Of this land about one-third is granted to Aboriginal people under 99-year leases; the other two-thirds is controlled by the government's Aboriginal Affairs Planning Authority. Control of mining and payments to communities are a matter of ministerial discretion.

In NSW, the Aboriginal Land Rights Act 1983 (NSW) transferred freehold title of existing Aboriginal reserves to Aboriginal people and gave them the right to claim a minuscule amount of other land. Aboriginal people also have limited rights to the state's national parks, but these rights fall short of genuine control and don't permit Aboriginal people to live inside parks. In Victoria and Tasmania, land rights are extremely limited.

Mabo & the Native Title Act It was only very recently that the non-Aboriginal community, including the Federal government, came to grips with the fact that a meaningful reconciliation between white Australia and its indigenous population was vital to the psychological well-being of all Australians.

In May 1982, five Torres Strait Islanders, led by Eddie Mabo, began an action for a declaration of native title over Murray Island, off the tip of Cape York. They argued that the legal principle of *terra nullius* had wrongfully usurped their title to land, as for thousands of years Murray Islanders had enjoyed a relationship with the land that included a notion of ownership. In June 1992 the High Court of Australia rejected *terra nullius* and the myth that Australia had been unoccupied. In doing this, it recognised that a principle of native title existed before the arrival of the British.

The High Court's judgment became known as the Mabo decision, one of the most controversial decisions ever handed down by an Australian court. It was ambiguous, as it didn't outline the extent to which native title existed in mainland Australia. It received a hostile reaction from mining and other industry groups, but was hailed by Aboriginal people and the prime minister of the time, Paul Keating, as an opportunity to create a basis of reconciliation between Aboriginal and non-Aboriginal Australians.

To define the principle of native title, the Federal parliament passed the Native Title Act in December 1993. Despite protest from the mining industry, the act gives Aboriginal people very few new rights. It limits the application of native title to land which no-one else owns or leases, and also to land with which Aboriginal people have continued to have a physical association. The act states that existing ownership or leases extinguish native title, although native title may be revived after mining leases have expired. If land is successfully claimed by Aboriginal people under the act, they will have no veto over developments, including mining.

The Wik Decision Several months before the Native Title Act become law, the Wik and Thayorre peoples had made a claim in the Federal Court for native title to land on Cape York Peninsula. The area claimed included two pastoral leases, neither of which had ever been permanently occupied for that purpose. The Wik and Thayorre peoples, however, had been in continuous occupation of them. They argued that native title coexisted with the pastoral leases.

In January 1996 the Federal Court decided that the claim could not succeed as the granting of pastoral leases under Queensland law extinguished any native title rights. The Wik people appealed that decision in the High Court, which subsequently overturned it.

The High Court determined that, under the law that created pastoral leases in Queensland, native title to the leases in question had not been extinguished. Further, it said that native title rights could continue at the same time that land was under lease, and that pastoralists did not have exclusive right of possession to their leases. Importantly, it also ruled that where the two were in conflict, the rights of the pastoralists would prevail.

Despite the fact that lease tenure was not threatened, the Wik decision brought a hue and cry from pastoral lessees across Australia. They demanded that the Federal government step in to protect them by legislating to limit native title rights, as was intended in the original act. Aboriginal leaders were equally adamant that native title must be preserved.

In late 1997 the government responded with its so-called 10 Point Plan, a raft of proposed legislative amendments to the Native Title Act which further entrenched the pastoralists' position. Thanks largely to the independent senator Brian Harradine, the Native Title Amendment Act 1998 is an improvement on the government's intended bill, but it still contains serious negatives for Aboriginal people. These include the removal of the 'right to negotiate' on the way that pastoral leases and reserved lands are used, and the degree to which native title has been extinguished.

ECONOMY

Australia is a relatively affluent and industrialised nation but much of its wealth still comes from agriculture and mining. It has a small domestic market and its manufacturing sector is comparatively weak. Nevertheless, a substantial proportion of the population is employed in manufacturing, and for much of Australia's history it has been argued that these industries need tariff protection from imports to ensure their survival.

Today, however, tariff protection is on the way out and efforts are being made to increase Australia's international competitiveness. This has become more important as prices of traditional primary exports have become more volatile. During the 1980s and early 90s, Labor sought to restrain the growth of real wages with the assistance of the Australian Council of Trade Unions (ACTU), to make Australian products more competitive overseas. This Accord, as it was known, ended with the 1996 election of the conservative Howard government.

An increasingly important source of income is the tourism industry, with the numbers of visitors rising each year and projections for even greater numbers in the future. That vision has been dampened somewhat by the downturn that hit the once booming economies of South-East Asia in late 1997. However Australia remains well positioned to enter these markets – more than half of Australia's exports go to the Asian region.

Agriculture, formerly the cornerstone of the Australian economy, today accounts for about 4% of production, while mining contributes about 8% and manufacturing about 16%. Major commodity exports include wool (Australia is the world's largest supplier), wheat, barley, sugar, coal and iron ore.

Japan is Australia's biggest trading partner, but the economies of China, Korea and Vietnam are becoming increasingly important. Regionally, Australia has initiated the establishment of the Asia-Pacific Economic Cooperation (APEC) group, a body aimed at furthering the economic interests of the Pacific nations.

The Australian economy is growing at the rate of around 4% per year and inflation is low, at around 2%.

POPULATION & PEOPLE

Australia's population is about 18.8 million. The most populous states are NSW (6.4 million) and Victoria (4.7 million), which also have the two largest cities respectively – Sydney (four million) and Melbourne (3.3 million). The population is concentrated along the east coast from Adelaide to Cairns and in a similar, but much smaller, coastal region in the south-western corner of WA. The centre of the country is very sparsely populated.

Until WWII Australians were mostly of British and Irish descent but that has changed dramatically. Since the war, heavy migration from Europe has created major Greek and Italian populations, also adding Germans, Dutch, Maltese, Yugoslavs, Lebanese, Turks and other groups.

More recently Australia has had large influxes of Asians, particularly Vietnamese after the Vietnam War. In proportion to its population, Australia has probably taken more Vietnamese refugees than any other western nation. On the whole they have been well accepted and 'multiculturalism' is a popular concept in Australia.

According to the 1996 census there are around 350,000 people who identified themselves as Aboriginal or being of indigenous origin. This is a large increase on previous census figures, a reflection of the fact that these days people are far more willing to declare their indigenous origins. They are concentrated in northern and central Australia. Most of the 28,000 Torres Strait Islanders, primarily a Melanesian people, live in north Queensland and on the islands of Torres Strait between Cape York and Papua New Guinea.

ARTS
Ballet

Australia's national ballet company, the Australian Ballet founded in 1962, is considered one of the world's finest. It tours extensively both locally and internationally, and has a large and diverse repertoire bolstered by the inclusion of guest choreographers of renown. Queensland and WA each has a classical ballet company.

Music

Classical Music Australia's large urban population supports a vibrant classical music culture. Every state and territory has its own symphony orchestra as well as youth and chamber orchestras in some states. Musica Viva Australia, sponsored by such companies as Qantas, the Australia Council for the Arts and the British Council, is the world's largest entrepreneur of fine music, presenting around 2,500 concerts each year across Australia. While Sydney and Melbourne are the main centres, classical music goes to the bush too; the Darwin Symphony Orchestra has held concerts in Katherine Gorge and at Nourlangie Rock, Kakadu, and most of the state orchestras also tour the country.

Popular Music Australia's participation in the flurry of popular music since the 1950s has been a frustrating mix of good, indifferent, lousy, parochial and excellent. In the early days the local industry suffered from severe cultural cringe, the highest praise being that it was 'good enough to have come from the UK/USA'.

Fortunately that has all changed. The 1970s saw music with a distinctly Australian flavour start to emerge, with bands such as Skyhooks leading the way. The music has since evolved to the stage where the local scene is flooded with great talent playing Australian rock. Popular bands and performers to look out for include: Midnight Oil, Cruel Sea, You Am I, The Black Sorrows, Spiderbait, silverchair, Magic Dirt, Custard, Regurgitator, Stephen Cummings, Mark Seymour, Deborah Conway, Screamfeeder, Paul Kelly, Deadstar, Dave Graney and Nick Cave.

The last decade or so has also seen huge success for Aboriginal music and performers. The most obvious name that springs to mind is Yothu Yindi. Their song about the dishonoured white-man's agreement, 'Treaty', perhaps did more than anything else to popularise Aboriginal land-rights claims. The band's lead singer, Mandawuy Yunupingu, was named Australian of the Year in 1993.

Other Aboriginal musicians include Blekbala Mujik, Coloured Stone, Kev Carmody, Archie Roach, Ruby Hunter, Bart Willoughby, the Sunrise Band, Christine Anu (from the Torres Strait Islands), and the bands that started it all but no longer exist, No Fixed Address and Warumpi Band.

White country music owes much to Irish heritage and American country influences, often with a liberal sprinkling of dry Outback humour. Names to watch out for include Slim Dusty, Ted Egan, John Williamson, Lee Kernaghan, Neil Murray, Gondwanaland and Smokey Dawson.

Folk Music Australian folk music is derived from English, Irish and Scottish roots. Fiddles, banjos and tin whistles feature prominently in bush bands, plus there's the indigenous 'lagerphone', a percussion instrument made from a great many beer bottle caps nailed to a stick. If you have a chance to go to a bush dance or folk festival, don't pass it up.

Opera

Australians are among the world's most dedicated opera-goers, and in fact Australia has produced several great opera singers (eg June Bronhill and Dame Joan Sutherland). There are around 300 operatic performances each year across the country – the busy national company Opera Australia performs in Melbourne and Sydney, and will be taking part in major arts festivals leading up to and during the Olympic Games. The other states have their own opera companies.

Literature

Bush Ballads & Yarns 'The bush' was a great source of inspiration for many popular ballads and stories. These were particularly in vogue at the turn of the century but they have an enduring quality.

Adam Lindsay Gordon was the forerunner of this type of literature, having published *Bush Ballads and Galloping Rhymes* in 1870. The two most famous exponents of the ballad style were AB 'Banjo' Paterson and Henry Lawson. Paterson grew up in the bush in the second half of the 19th century and became one of Australia's most important bush poets. He was familiar with all aspects of station life and wrote with great optimism. *Clancy of the Overflow* and *The Man From Snowy River* are both well known, but Paterson is probably best remembered as the author of Australia's alternative national anthem, *Waltzing Matilda*, in which he celebrates an anonymous wanderer of the bush.

Henry Lawson was a contemporary of Paterson, but was much more of a social commentator and political thinker and less of a humorist. Although he wrote a good many poems about the bush – pieces such as *Andy's Gone with Cattle* and *The Roaring Days* are among his best – his greatest legacy is his short stories of life in the bush. Good examples are *A Day on a Selection* (a selection was a tract of crown land for which annual fees were paid) and *The Drover's Wife*; the latter epitomises one of Lawson's 'battlers' who dreams of much

better things as an escape from the ennui of her isolated circumstances.

There were many other balladeers. George Essex Evans is the author of a tribute to Queensland's women pioneers, *The Women of the West*; Will Ogilvie wrote of the great cattle drives; and Barcroft Boake's *Where the Dead Men Lie* celebrates the people who opened up never-never country where 'heat-waves dance forever'. Conversely, Barbara Baynton depicts the Outback as a cruel, brutal environment, and romantic imagery is absent in the ferocious depiction of the lot of *Squeaker's Mate* in *Bush Studies* (1902).

Outback Novelists The author's name if not the content would have encouraged many overseas visitors to read DH Lawrence's *Kangaroo* (1923), which, in places, presents his frightened interpretations of the bush. Later, Nevil Shute's *A Town Like Alice* (1950) would have been the first Outback-based novel that many

Australia's Literary Hoaxes

Australia's rich tradition of literary hoaxes began in the 1940s with the Ern Malley Hoax. An edition of the literary magazine, *Angry Penguins*, edited by Adelaide poet Max Harris, featured 16 poems grouped under the title *The Darkening Ecliptic* – the entire works of the newly discovered (but supposedly deceased) Australian poet, Ern Malley. It was soon revealed that Malley was a hoax, created by two young poets James McAuley and Harold Stewart, who had concocted the poems in a single afternoon. It seems their aim was to expose Harris and others who they blamed for 'the gradual decay of meaning and craftsmanship in poetry'.

In 1995 the winner of the prestigious Miles Franklin Award was the author Helen Demidenko. Her winning work, *The Hand that Signed the Paper*, supposedly related events experienced by her family during famine in the Ukraine in the 1930s. Initially the quality of the work was the subject of debate, but this became a furore when it was discovered that Demidenko was in fact the very un-Ukrainian Helen Darville, who not only had no experience of the subject matter but had plagiarised much of her material. Amazingly, the judges stood by their decision and the award stood; the book was initially withdrawn, then republished with the author's correct name.

More recently the Wanda Koolmatrie deception has been the one to capture the spotlight. Wanda Koolmatrie was supposedly a Kimberley Aboriginal woman and author of the book *In My Own Sweet Time*. The book had won an award for the best first publication by a female writer and was set to become part of the NSW secondary school syllabus. It was only when the book's publisher insisted on actually meeting the author that 'she' confessed to being Leon Carmen, a non-Aboriginal man from Sydney!

people read. Other Shute titles with outback themes are *In the Wet* (1953) and *Beyond the Black Stump* (1956).

Perhaps the best local depicter of the Outback was Katharine Susannah Prichard. She produced a string of novels with outback themes into which she wove her political thoughts. *Black Opal* (1921) was the study of the fictional opal mining community of Fallen Star Ridge; *Working Bullocks* (1926) examined the political nature of work in the karri forests of WA; and *Moon of Desire* (1941) follows its characters in search of a fabulous pearl from Broome to Singapore. Her trilogy of the Western Australian goldfields was published separately as *The Roaring Nineties* (1946), *Golden Miles* (1948) and *Winged Seeds* (1950).

Xavier Herbert's *Capricornia* (1938), with its sweeping descriptions of the northern country, stands as one of the great epics of outback Australia. His second epic, *Poor Fellow My Country* (1975), is an over-long documentary of the fortunes of a northern station owner.

One of the great nonfiction pieces is Mary Durack's family chronicle, *Kings in Grass Castles* (1959), which relates the white settlement of the Kimberley ranges. Her sequel was *Sons in the Saddle* (1983).

Australia's Nobel prize-winner, Patrick White, used the Outback as the backdrop for a number of his monumental works. The most prominent character in *Voss* (1957) is an explorer, perhaps loosely based on Ludwig Leichhardt; *The Tree of Man* (1955) has all the Outback happenings of flood, fire and drought; and the journey of *The Aunt's Story* (1948) begins on an Australian sheep station.

Kenneth Cook's nightmarish novel set in outback NSW, *Wake in Fright* (1961), has been made into a film.

Miles Franklin was one of Australia's early feminists and decided early in life to become a writer rather than the traditional wife and mother. Her best-known book, *My Brilliant Career*, was also her first. It was published in 1901 when the author was only 20, and brought her both widespread fame and criticism. On her death she endowed an annual award for an Australian novel; today the Miles Franklin Award is the most prestigious in the country.

Late 20th Century Writers Peter Carey is one of Australia's most successful contemporary writers and all his books are worth reading. His first novel, *Bliss* (1981), won the Miles Franklin Award and was made into a film. *Illywhacker* (1985) is set mostly in Melbourne, while *The Tax Inspector* (1991) in outer-suburban Sydney. In 1988 *Oscar and Lucinda* won the Miles Franklin Award and the Booker Prize; his most recent novel, *Jack Maggs* (1997), is his third to win the Miles Franklin Award.

Other writers with a strong sense of place include Helen Garner (*Monkey Grip*, 1987) – Melbourne, Peter Corris (the Cliff Hardy stories, including *Matrimonial Causes*, 1994, *Beware of the Dog*, 1992, and *Wet Graves*, 1990) – Sydney, and David Ireland (*The Glass Canoe*, 1993) – Sydney.

Set in Tasmania, Richard Flanagan's *The Sound of One Hand Clapping* (1997) is the compelling story of a dysfunctional family that emigrated from Europe in the 1950s. It promises to become an Australian classic.

Thomas Keneally is well known for his novels which deal with the suffering of oppressed peoples, for example *The Chant of Jimmy Blacksmith* (1972) and the Booker Prize-winning *Schindler's Ark* (1982), upon which the Spielberg film *Schindler's List* was based.

Thea Astley is not a household name, yet she is one of the finest writers in the country. Her books include *Vanishing Points* (1992), *The Slow Natives* (1965), *An Item from the Late News* (1982) and *It's Raining in Mango* (1987), the last of which is probably her finest work and expresses her outrage at the treatment of Aboriginal people.

A sense of outrage is also apparent in *Snake Dreaming*, the powerful autobiography of Roberta Sykes, one of Australia's most well known activists for Aboriginal rights. Her story is to be in three volumes – *Snake Cradle* (1997) and *Snake Dancing* (1998) have been published to date. *Snake Cradle* won the 1997 *Age* Book of the Year Award.

Two-tonne trout, Adaminaby, NSW

Looming lobster, Kingston SE, SA

Big bovine, Nambour, Qld

Over-sized orange, Berri, South Australia (SA)

'Normous 'nana, Coffs Harbour, NSW

Prominent pineapple, Nambour, Qld

PATRICK HORTON

Gargantuan guitar, Tamworth, NSW

PATRICK HORTON

Colossal crustacean, Ballina, NSW

PHILIP CAME

Killer koala, Dadswells Bridge, Vic

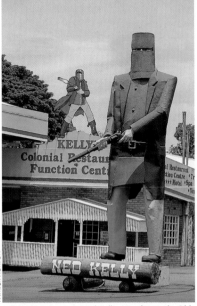

PATRICK HORTON

Big bad bushranger Ned Kelly, Maryborough, Qld

Elizabeth Jolley is well known as a short-story writer and novelist with a keen eye for the eccentric. Her works include *Mr Scobie's Riddle* (1983), *My Father's Moon* (1989), *Cabin Fever* (1990) and *The Georges' Wife* (1993). *Fellow Passengers* (1997) is a collection of her best short fiction.

David Malouf has won just about every award there is to be won in Australian literature, including the NSW Premier's Literary Award for *An Imaginary Life* (1978) in 1979, the *Age* Book of the Year Award in 1982 for *Fly Away Peter* (1981), the Miles Franklin Award in 1991 and the 1991 Commonwealth Prize for fiction for *The Great World* (1991). In 1996 he won the first International IMPAC Dublin Literary Award for *Remembering Babylon*.

David Foster, until recently a largely overlooked writer, won the 1997 Miles Franklin Award for his impenetrable, rambling and complex novel *The Glade Within the Grove* (1996), his ninth book. Other works by him include *Dog Rock* (1989) and *The Pale Blue Crochet Coathanger Cover* (1998).

Christopher Koch is a writer who, for many years, has been exploring Australia's relationship with Asia. Although *The Year of Living Dangerously* (1978) is probably his best known work, *The Doubleman* (1985) won him the Miles Franklin Award in 1985, and *Highways to a War* (1996), which looks at Australia's role in Vietnam, was the 1996 winner.

Tim Winton is widely regarded as one of the best writers in Australia today. Winton's evocation of coastal WA is superb, particularly in his best-selling *Cloudstreet* (1991). Other works worth reading include *The Riders* (1994), *Shallows* (1982) and *An Open Swimmer* (1984).

Architecture

Australia's first European settlers arrived in the country with memories of Georgian grandeur, but the lack of materials and tools meant that most of the early houses were almost caricatures of the real thing. One of the first concessions to the climate, and one which was to become a feature of Australian houses, was the addition of a wide verandah which kept the inner rooms of the house dark and cool.

The prosperity of the gold rush era in the second half of the 19th century saw a spate of grand buildings in the Victorian style in most major towns. Many of these buildings survive, and are a fine reminder of a period of great wealth, confidence and progress. The houses of the time became much more elaborate, with ornamentation of all sorts gracing the facades.

Increasing population in the major towns saw the rise of the terrace house, simple single and later double-storey houses which, although cramped at the time, today provide comfortable dwellings for thousands of inner-city residents.

By the turn of the century, at a time when the separate colonies were now combining to form a new nation, a simpler, more 'Australian' architectural style evolved, and this came to be known as Federation style. Built between about 1890 and 1920, Federation houses typically feature red-brick walls and an orange-tiled roof decorated with terracotta ridging and chimney pots. Another feature was the rising-sun motif on the gable ends, symbolic of the dawn of a new age for Australia.

The Californian bungalow, a solid house style which developed in colonial British India, became the rage in the 1920s and 30s, and its simple and honest style fitted well with the emerging Australian tendency towards a casual lifestyle.

Differing climates led to some interesting regional variations. In the tropical north the style known as the Queenslander evolved – elevated houses with plenty of ventilation to make the most of cooling breezes. In the 1930s the first buildings in Darwin appeared with the same features, and have developed into the modern 'Troppo' (tropical) style of architecture.

The immigration boom that followed WWII led to urban sprawl – cities and towns expanded rapidly, 'brick veneer' became the dominant housing medium, and it remains so today. On the fringe of any Australian city you'll find acres of low-cost, brick-veneer suburbs – as far as the

GLENN BEANLAND

Victorian, Gothic and Federation architecture lined up in George St, with the modern Sydney behind

eye can see it's a bleak expanse of terracotta roofs and bricks in various shades.

Modern Australian architecture struggles to maintain a distinctive style, with overseas trends dominating large projects. Often the most interesting 'modern' buildings are in fact recycled Victorian or other era buildings. There are some exceptions, notable ones being the Convention Centre at Sydney's Darling Harbour, designed by Phillip Cox, Melbourne Museum, designed by Denton Corker Marshall and the Cultural Centre at Uluru-Kata Tjuta National Park in central Australia, designed in consultation with the park's traditional owners.

Painting

In the 1880s a group of young artists developed the first distinctively Australian style of watercolour painting. Working from a permanent bush camp in Melbourne's (then) outer suburb of Box Hill, the painters captured the unique qualities of Australian life and the bush. The work of this group is generally referred to as the Heidelberg School, although the majority of the work was done at Box Hill.

In Sydney a contemporary movement worked at Sirius Cove on Sydney Harbour. Both groups were influenced by the French plein-air painters, whose practice of working outdoors to capture the effects of natural light led directly to impressionism. The main artists were Tom Roberts, Arthur Streeton, Frederick McCubbin, Louis Abrahams, Charles Conder, Julian Ashton and, later, Walter Withers. Their works can be found in most of the major galleries and are well worth seeking out.

In the 1940s, under the patronage of John and Sunday Reed at their home in suburban Melbourne, a new generation of artists redefined the direction of Australian art. This group included some of Australia's most famous contemporary artists, such as Sir Sidney Nolan and Arthur Boyd.

More recently the work of painters such as Fred Williams, John Olsen and Brett Whiteley has made an impression on the international art world. Whiteley, probably Australia's most well known modern artist, died in 1992.

See also the Aboriginal Art special section following the Facts for the Visitor chapter.

Film

The Australian film industry began as early as 1896, a year after the Lumiere brothers opened the world's first cinema in Paris. Maurice Sestier, one of the Lumieres' photographers, came to Australia and made the first films in the streets of Sydney and at Flemington Racecourse during the Melbourne Cup.

Cinema historians regard an Australian film, *Soldiers of the Cross*, as the world's first 'real' movie. It was originally screened at the Melbourne Town Hall in 1901, cost £600 to make and was shown throughout the USA in 1902.

The next significant Australian film, *The Story of the Kelly Gang*, was screened in 1907, and by 1911 the industry was flourishing. Low-budget films were being made in such quantities that they could be hired out or sold cheaply. Over 250 silent feature films were made before the 1930s when the talkies and Hollywood took over.

In the 1930s, film companies such as Cinesound sprang up. Cinesound made 17 feature films between 1931 and 1940, many based on Australian history or literature. *Forty Thousand Horsemen*, directed by Cinesound's great film maker Charles Chauvel, was a highlight of this era of locally made and financed films which ended in 1959, the year of Chauvel's death. Early Australian actors who became famous both at home and overseas include Errol Flynn and Chips Rafferty (born John Goffage).

Before the introduction of government subsidies during 1969 and 1970, the Australian film industry found it difficult to compete with US and British interests. The New Wave era of the 1970s, a renaissance of Australian cinema, produced films such as *Picnic at Hanging Rock*, *Sunday Too Far Away*, *Caddie* and *The Devil's Playground*, which appealed to large local and international audiences.

Since the 70s, Australian actors and directors such as Mel Gibson, Nicole Kidman, Judy Davis, Toni Collette, Hugo Weaving, Cate Blanchett, Paul Hogan, Geoffrey Rush, Bruce Beresford, Peter Weir, Gillian Armstrong and Fred Schepisi have gained international recognition. Films such as *Gallipoli*, *The Year of Living Dangerously*, *Mad Max*, *Malcolm*, *Crocodile Dundee*, *Proof*, *The Year My Voice Broke*, *Strictly Ballroom*, *The Adventures of Priscilla – Queen of the Desert*, *Death in Brunswick*, *Muriel's Wedding*, *Babe* and more recently *Shine* have entertained and impressed audiences worldwide.

Love and Other Catastrophes and *Strange Planet* by Emma-Kate Croghan and *Two Hands* by Gregor Jordan are examples of recent innovative work by Australian writer-directors.

RELIGION

A shrinking majority of people in Australia (around 58%) are at least nominally Christian. Most Protestant churches have merged to become the Uniting Church, although the Church of England has remained separate. The Catholic Church is popular (almost half of Australia's Christians are Catholics), with the original Irish adherents now joined by large numbers of Mediterranean immigrants.

Non-Christian minorities abound, the main ones being Buddhist (1.13% of the total population), Jewish (0.45%) and Muslim (1.13%). Almost twenty per cent of the population describe themselves as having no religion.

LANGUAGE

While English is the main language of Australia, languages other than English are in common use as you'd expect in a country with such a diverse ethnic mix. The 1996 census found that 240 languages other than English were being spoken at home, and almost 50 of these were indigenous languages. This amounts to a language other than English being used in 15% of Australian households.

The most commonly used non-English languages are, in order, Italian, Greek, Cantonese, Arabic and Vietnamese. Languages rapidly growing in use are Mandarin, Vietnamese and Cantonese, while those most in decline include Dutch, German, Italian and Greek. See the Glossary at the end of the book for more on Australian English.

Aboriginal Culture

TRADITIONAL SOCIETY

Australia's Aboriginal people were (and still are in many places) tribal, living in extended family groups or clans, with clan members descending from a common ancestral being. Tradition, rituals and laws linked the people of each clan to the land they occupied – each clan had various sites of spiritual significance, places to which their spirits would return when they died. Clan members came together to perform rituals to honour their ancestral spirits and the creators of the Dreaming. These beliefs were the basis of the Aboriginal peoples' ties to the land they lived on.

In traditionally-oriented areas it is the responsibility of the clan, or particular members of it, to maintain and protect the sites so that the ancestral beings are not offended and continue to protect the clan. Traditional punishments for those who neglect these responsibilities can still be severe, as their actions can easily affect the well-being of the whole clan – food and water shortages, natural disasters or mysterious illnesses can all be attributed to disgruntled or offended ancestral beings.

Many Aboriginal communities were seminomadic, others sedentary, one of the deciding factors being the availability of food. Where food and water were readily available, the people tended to remain in a limited area. When they did wander, however, it was to visit sacred places to carry out rituals, or to take advantage of the availability of seasonal foods. They did not, as is still often believed, roam aimlessly and desperately over the landscape in search of food and water.

The traditional role of the men was that of hunter, tool-maker and custodian of male law; the women reared the children, and gathered and prepared food. There was also female law and ritual for which the women were responsible. Ultimately, the shared efforts of men and women ensured the continuation of their social system.

Wisdom and skills obtained over millennia enabled Aboriginal people to use their environment to the maximum. An intimate knowledge of the behaviour of animals and the correct time to harvest the many plants they utilised ensured that food shortages were rare. As is the case with other hunter-gatherer peoples, Aboriginal people were true ecologists.

Aboriginal people neither cultivated crops (in the sense that Europeans and Asians do) nor domesticated livestock. Thus their only major modification of the landscape was the selective burning of undergrowth in forests and dead grass on the plains. This encouraged new growth, which in turn attracted game animals to the area. It also prevented the build-up of combustible material in the forests, making hunting easier and reducing the possibility of major bushfires. Dingoes were domesticated to assist in the hunt and to guard the camp from intruders.

Similar technology – for example the woomera and spear – was used throughout the continent, but techniques were also adapted to the environment and the species being hunted. In the wetlands of northern Australia, fish traps hundreds of metres long made of bamboo and cord were built to catch fish at the end of the wet season. In the area now known as Victoria, stone weirs many kilometres long were used to trap migrating eels, while in the tablelands of Queensland finely woven nets were used to snare herds of wallabies and kangaroos.

Dwellings varied from simple windbreaks to more permanent structures. Stone was used in western Victoria, while in Tasmania conical thatch shelters which could house up to 30 people were constructed. Such dwellings were used mainly for sleeping.

Aboriginal people were also traders. Trade routes crisscrossed the country, dispersing a variety of raw materials (ochre and hardwood, for example) and manufactured goods. Many items traded, such as certain types of stone or shell, were rare and had great ritual significance. Along the networks which developed, large numbers of people would meet for 'exchange ceremonies', where not only goods but also songs and dances were passed on.

Injinoo Aborigines in traditional dress, Somerset, Cape York Peninsula

MITCH REARDON

BELIEFS & CEREMONIES

Early European settlers and explorers usually dismissed the entire Aboriginal population as 'savages' and 'barbarians'. It was some time before the Aboriginal peoples' deep, spiritual bond with the land, and their relationship to it, began to be understood by white Australians.

The perceived simplicity of the Aboriginal peoples' technology contrasts with the sophistication of their cultural life. Religion, history, law and art are integrated in complex ceremonies which depict the activities of their spirit ancestors, and also prescribe codes of behaviour and responsibilities for looking after the land.

The link between the people and their spirit ancestors are totems, each person having their own totem, or Dreaming. These totems take many forms, such as trees, caterpillars, snakes, fish and magpies. Songs explain how the landscape contains these powerful creator ancestors, who can exert either a benign or a malevolent influence. They tell of the best places and the best times to hunt, and where to find water in drought years. They can also specify kinship relations and identify correct marriage partners.

Traditional ceremonies are still performed in many parts of Australia; many sacred sites are believed to be dangerous and entry is prohibited under traditional Aboriginal law. These restrictions may seem merely the result of superstition, but in many cases they have a pragmatic origin. For example one site in northern Australia was believed to cause sores to break out all over the body of anyone visiting the area. Subsequently, the area was found to have a dangerously high level of radiation from naturally occurring radon gas.

Many Aboriginal people – particularly those living in more remote areas – still speak their indigenous language (or a creolised mix) on a daily basis, and mix largely with other Aboriginal people. Much of their knowledge of the environment, bush medicine and food ('bush tucker'), such as the favourite delicacy, the honey-ant, has been retained, and many traditional rites and ceremonies are still practiced.

For more on Aboriginal beliefs, ceremonies and sacred sites see the Religion section later in this chapter. Also see the Aboriginal Art special section after the Facts for the Visitor chapter.

KATE NOLAN

Honey-ants make a great appetiser!

SONG & NARRATIVE

Aboriginal oral traditions are loosely and misleadingly described as 'myths and legends'. Their single uniting factor is the Dreamtime, or creation time, when the totemic ancestors formed the landscape, fashioned the laws and created the people who would inherit the land. Translated and printed in English, these renderings of the Dreamtime often lose much of their intended impact. Gone are the sounds of clap sticks and the rhythm of dance that accompany each poetic line; alone, the words fail to fuse past and present, and the spirits and forces to which the lines refer lose much of their animation.

In the early 19th century, Catherine Langloh Parker collected Aboriginal legends and used her outback experience to interpret them sincerely but synthetically. She compiled *Australian Legendary Tales: Folklore of the Noongah-burrahs* (1902).

Professor Ted Strehlow was one of the first methodical translators, and his *Aranda Traditions* (1947) and *Songs of Central Australia* (1971) are important works. Equally important is the combined effort of Catherine and Ronald Berndt. There are 188 songs in the Berndt collection *Djanggawul* (1952), and 129 sacred and 47 secular songs in the collection *Kunapipi* (1951). *The Land of the Rainbow Snake* (1979) focuses on children's stories from western Arnhem Land.

More recently, many Dreamtime stories have appeared in translation, illustrated and published by Aboriginal artists. Some representative collections are *Joe Nangan's Dreaming: Aboriginal Legends of the North-West* (Joe Nangan & Hugh Edwards,

1976); *Milbi: Aboriginal Tales from Queensland's Endeavour River* (Tulo Gordon & J B Haviland, 1980); *Visions of Mowanjum: Aboriginal Writings from the Kimberley* (Kormilda Community College, Darwin, 1980); and *Gularabulu* (Paddy Roe & Stephen Muecke, 1983).

Modern Aboriginal Literature

Modern Aboriginal writers have fused the English language with aspects of their traditional culture. The result is often carefully fashioned to expose the injustices they have been subjected to, especially as urban dwellers. The first Aboriginal writer to be published was David Unaipon in 1929 *(Native Legends)*.

Aboriginal literature now includes drama, fiction and poetry. The poet Oodgeroo Noonuccal (Kath Walker), one of the most well known of modern Aboriginal writers, was the first Aboriginal woman to have work published (*We Are Going*, 1964). *Paperbark: A collection of Black Australian writings* (1990) presents a great cross-section of modern Aboriginal writers, including dramatist Jack Davis and novelist Mudrooroo (Colin Johnson). The book has an excellent bibliography of black Australian writing.

There are a number of modern accounts of Aboriginal life in remote parts of Australia. *Raparapa Kularr Martuwarra: Stories from the Fitzroy River Drovers* (1988) is a Magabala Books production. This company, based in Broome, energetically promotes Aboriginal literature.

In *Grog War* (1997), Aboriginal writer Alexis Wright tells of the huge grog problems being experienced in Tennant Creek, an outback town in the NT. She describes how the town tackled these problems and how its residents (both black and white) eventually develop a collective sense of community responsibility.

Autobiography and biography have become an important branch of Aboriginal literature – look for *Moon and Rainbow* (Dick Roughsey, 1971), *My Country of the Pelican Dreaming* (Grant Ngabidj, 1981) and *My Place* (Sally Morgan, 1987).

Aborigines in White Literature

Aboriginal people have often been used as characters in white outback literature. Usually the treatment was patronising and somewhat short-sighted. There were exceptions, especially in the subject of interracial sexuality between white men and Aboriginal women.

Rosa Praed, in her short piece *My Australian Girlhood* (1902), drew heavily on her outback experience and her affectionate childhood relationship with Aboriginal people. Jeannie Gunn's *Little Black Princess* was published in 1904, but it was *We of the Never Never* (1908) which brought her renown. Her story of the life and trials on Elsey Station includes an unflattering, patronising depiction of the Aboriginal people on and around the station.

Catherine Martin, in 1923, wrote *The Incredible Journey*. It follows the trail of two black women, Iliapo and Polde, in search of a little boy who had been kidnapped by a white man. The book describes in careful detail the harsh desert environment they traverse.

Katharine Susannah Prichard contributed a great deal to outback literature in the 1920s. A journey to Turee Station in the cattle country of the Ashburton and Fortescue rivers in 1926 inspired her lyric tribute to the Aborigine, *Coonardoo* (1929). It delved into the then almost taboo love between an Aboriginal woman and a white station boss. Later, Mary Durack's *Keep Him My Country* (1955) explored the theme of a white station manager's love for an Aboriginal girl, Dalgerie.

More recent works incorporating Aboriginal themes include Rodney Hall's *The Second Bridegroom* (1991), Thomas Keneally's *Flying Hero Class* (1991) and David Malouf's *Remembering Babylon* (1993).

RELIGION

Aboriginal religious beliefs centre on the continuing existence of spirit beings that lived on earth during the creation time (or Dreamtime), which occurred before the arrival of humans. These beings created all the features of the natural world and were the ancestors of all living things. They took different forms but behaved as people do, and as they travelled about they left signs to show where they had passed.

Despite being supernatural, the ancestors were subject to ageing and eventually they returned to the sleep from which they'd awoken at the dawn of time. Here their spirits remain as eternal forces that breathe life into the newborn and influence natural events. Each ancestor's spiritual energy flows along the path it travelled during the Dreamtime and is strongest at the points where it left physical evidence of its activities, such as a tree, hill or claypan. These features are called 'sacred sites'.

Every person, animal and plant is believed to have two souls – one mortal and one immortal. The latter is part of a particular ancestral spirit and returns to the sacred sites of that ancestor after death, while the mortal soul simply fades into oblivion. Each person is spiritually bound to the sacred sites that mark the land associated with his or her spirit ancestor. It is the individual's obligation to help care for these sites by performing the necessary rituals and singing the songs that tell of the ancestor's deeds. By doing this, the order created by that ancestor is maintained.

Aboriginal people believe that to destroy or damage a sacred site threatens not only the living but also the spirit inhabitants of the land. It is a distressing and dangerous act, and one that no responsible person would condone. These days the importance of sacred sites is more widely recognised among the non-Aboriginal community, and most state governments have legislated to give these sites a measure of protection. However, their presence can still lead to headline-grabbing controversy when they stand in the way of developments such as roads, mines and dams.

See Beliefs & Ceremonies earlier in this section for more on sacred sites.

LANGUAGE

At the time of European settlement it is thought that Australia had around 250 separate languages comprising about 700 dialects. It is believed that all these languages evolved from a single language family as the Aboriginal people gradually moved out over the entire continent and split into new groups. There are a number of words that occur right across the continent, such as *jina* (foot) and *mala* (hand), and similarities also exist in the often complex grammatical structures.

Following European settlement the number of Aboriginal languages was drastically reduced. Today, only around 30 are regularly spoken and being taught to children.

Aboriginal Kriol is a new language that has developed since European arrival in Australia. It is spoken across northern Australia and has become the 'native' language of many young Aboriginal people. It con-

tains many English words, but the pronunciation and grammatical usage are along Aboriginal lines, the meaning is often different, and the spelling is phonetic. For example, the English sentence 'He was amazed' becomes 'I bin luk kwesjinmak' in Kriol.

There are a number of generic terms which Aboriginal people use to describe themselves, and these vary according to the region. The most common of these is Koori, used for the people of south-east Australia. Nunga is used to refer to the people of coastal SA, Murri for those from the north-east, and Nyoongah is used in the country's south-west.

Lonely Planet's excellent *Australian Phrasebook* gives a detailed account of Aboriginal languages.

FAUNA & FLORA

FAUNA & FLORA

The Australian landmass is one of the most ancient on earth. The sea has kept it cut off from other continents for more than 50 million years, and its various indigenous plants and animals have experienced an unusually long, uninterrupted period of evolution in isolation.

Australia's characteristic vegetation began to take shape about 55 million years ago when Australia broke from the supercontinent of Gondwanaland. At this time, Australia was completely covered by cool-climate rainforest, but as the continent drifted towards warmer climes, it gradually dried out, the rainforests retreated, plants like eucalypts and wattles *(acacias)* took over and grasslands expanded, resulting in the distinctive habitats found today.

Kookaburra sits in the old gum tree.

FAUNA

Australia has a fascinating mix of native fauna, which ranges from the primitive to the highly evolved – some creatures are unique survivors from a previous age, while others have adapted so acutely to the natural environment that they can survive in areas other animals would find uninhabitable.

Since the European colonisation of Australia, 17 species of mammal have become extinct and at least 30 more are endangered. Many introduced non-native animals have been allowed to run wild. Introduced animals include the fox, cat, pig, goat, camel, donkey, water buffalo, horse, starling, blackbird, cane toad and the notorious rabbit. Foxes and cats kill small native mammals and birds, rabbits denude vast areas of land, pigs carry disease and introduced birds take over the habitat of the local species.

Cane toad

Monotremes

The monotremes are often regarded as living fossils and, although they display some intriguing features from their reptile ancestors, such as laying eggs, they are now recognised as a distinct mammalian lineage rather than a primitive stage in mammalian evolution. It's an exclusive club with two members – the platypus, found solely in Australia, and the echidna, which is also found in Papua New Guinea. The newly hatched young are suckled on milk. They are both superbly adapted and consequently fairly common within their distributions.

Title Page: Yellow-footed rock wallaby and joey. Photograph by Mitch Reardon

JASON EDWARDS

Platypus

CHRIS MELLOR

An echidna searching for ants

TOM BOYDEN

Western grey kangaroo

Platypus

The platypus (*Ornithorhynchus anatinus*) is well equipped for its semi-aquatic lifestyle. It has a duck-like bill, which is actually quite soft, short legs, webbed feet and a short, thick, beaver-like tail. Adult males are about 50cm long, with 10 to 13cm tails, and weigh about 2kg; females are slightly smaller.

A platypus lives in the extensive burrows that it digs along river banks; it spends the rest of its time in the water foraging for food with its electrosensitive bill or sunning itself in the open. Its diet is mainly small crustaceans, worms and tadpoles.

The platypus is confined to eastern Australia and Tasmania.

Echidna

The short-beaked echidna (or spiny anteater; *Tachyglossus aculeatus*) is a small monotreme which is covered on the back with long, sharp spines and on the underside with fur. When fully grown it weighs around 4.5kg and measures around 45cm long. The elongated, beak-like snout is around 7.5cm long and it has a long, sticky tongue that it can whip out some 15cm beyond the snout – perfect for catching ants and termites, which comprise the major portion of its diet. At the first sign of danger, the echidna rapidly buries its body in the dirt, leaving only its formidable spines exposed.

Short-beaked echidnas are found in a great range of habitats, from hot, dry deserts to altitudes of 1800m in the Alps.

Marsupials

Marsupials are mammals that raise their young in a pouch, or *marsupium*. They are largely confined to Australia, and included in this group of around 120 species are some of the country's most distinctive – kangaroos, wallabies, koalas, wombats and possums – as well as others less well known, such as bandicoots and quolls.

The young are usually minute at birth and spend a long time in the pouch before being sufficiently developed to live independent of their mothers.

Kangaroos & Wallabies

Kangaroos are probably the most recognisable Australian mammal and hardly need a description, although the name is applied to many species.

There are now more kangaroos in Australia than there were when Europeans arrived, a result of the better availability of water and the creation of grasslands for sheep and cattle. Certain species, however, are threatened with extinction through habitat destruction and predation from feral cats and foxes. About three million kangaroos are culled legally each year. Many more are killed for sport or by farmers who believe the cull is insufficient to protect their paddocks. Kangaroo meat has been exported for some time but has only started to appear on Australian menus in recent years.

Red kangaroos

Red Kangaroo The distinctive red kangaroo *(Macropus rufus)* is the largest and most widespread of the kangaroos. A fully grown male can be 2.4m long and up to 2m high. It's usually only the males that are brick-red; females are often a blue-grey colour. They range over most of arid Australia.

Grey Kangaroo The eastern grey kangaroo *(M. giganteus)* is about the same size as the red, and is found throughout the dry sclerophyll forests of south-eastern Australia, from Queensland to Tasmania. The western grey *(M. fuliginosus)* is very similar, although slightly darker in colour, and is common in the southern regions of Western Australia (WA) and South Australia (SA), central and western New South Wales (NSW) and western Victoria. Mixed populations of eastern and western greys occur in Victoria and NSW but there have been no recordings of natural hybrids.

Red-necked wallaby

Wallaby Wallabies come in a variety of shapes and sizes. The most commonly seen are the red-necked *(M. rufogriseus)*, agile *(M. agilis)* and the swamp wallaby *(Wallabia bicolor)*, all of which are about 1.7m long when fully grown.

The various rock-wallabies are small (around 1m long) and are confined to cliffs and rocky habitats. One of the most widespread is the brush-tailed rock-wallaby *(Petrogale penicillata)*, which is found along the Great Dividing Range in eastern Australia.

Quokka The quokka *(Setonix brachyurus)* is a small, nocturnal mammal found only in south-western WA, including Rottnest Island, where it very common. They are gregarious creatures and can move in groups of more than 100.

Quokka

Western barred bandicoot

Bilby

Common ringtail possum

Tree Kangaroo The two Australian species of tree kangaroo, Bennett's *(Dendrolagus bennettianus)* and Lumholtz's *(D. lumholtzi)*, are about the size of a cat and, as the name suggests, live in the trees. Unlike other kangaroos they have strong forelimbs, but are rather ungainly climbers.

Both species are restricted to the north Queensland rainforest, and their habitat has come under extreme pressure from logging activities.

Bandicoots & Bilbies

The small, rat-like bandicoots and bilbies have been among the principal victims of domestic and feral cats.

Although largely nocturnal, bandicoots can occasionally be seen scampering through the bush. They mainly eat insects and some plant material.

One of the most common varieties is the southern brown bandicoot *(Isoodon obesulus)*, found in eastern and western Australia. Others, such as the eastern barred bandicoot *(Perameles gunnii)*, are now in very limited areas. The rare bilby *(Macrotis lagotis)* lives mainly in the Northern Territory (NT). Major efforts have been made to ensure its survival. Its rabbit-like ears have caused it to be promoted as Australia's own Easter bilby, versus the Easter bunny!

Possums

There is an enormous range of possums (or phalangers) in Australia. They have adapted to a variety of habitats, including the city, where they're often seen in parks. Some large species live in suburban roofs and eat garden plants and food scraps. Possums are common visitors at camp sites in treed country, and will help themselves to food left out.

Probably the most familiar of all possums is the common brushtail (or grey) possum *(Trichosurus vulpecula)*, which occurs widely throughout the mainland and Tasmania.

The sugar glider *(Petaurus breviceps)* has membranes between its front and rear legs, which when spread enable it to glide from one tree to the next, covering up to 100m in one swoop – a remarkable sight.

Koala

Another instantly recognisable mammal is the koala *(Phascolarctos cinereus)*. The name is an Aboriginal word meaning 'no water', which refers to the koala's alleged ability to get all the moisture it needs from gum leaves, although it does drink water from pools.

Koalas are protected and their survival is assured, but large numbers of females are infertile due to chlamydia, a sexually transmitted disease.

When fully grown a koala measures about 70cm and weighs around 10kg. Their most distinctive features are their tufted ears and hard, black nose.

Koalas feed only on the leaves of certain types of eucalypt and are particularly sensitive to changes to their habitat. They are found along the east coast from around Townsville down to Melbourne, and have been reintroduced in SA, where they had previously been driven to extinction.

Wombats

Wombats are slow, solid, powerfully built marsupials with broad heads and short, stumpy legs.

Adult wombats are about one metre long and weigh up to 35kg. Their strong front legs are excellent burrowing tools, and the rear legs are used for pushing the earth away. Their diet consists of grasses, roots and tree barks.

There are three species of wombat, the most prevalent being the common wombat *(Vombatus ursinus)*, in the forested areas of south-eastern Australia. The other species are the rare and endangered northern hairy-nosed *(Lasiorhinus krefftii)*, and the southern hairy-nosed *(Lasiorhinus latifrons)*, which is also vulnerable and lives inland of the Great Australian Bight.

Dasyuroids

Dasyuroids are predatory marsupials, such as quolls, numbats and the Tasmanian devil. Their main distinguishing feature is a pointy, elongated snout.

Quoll Australia's spotted quolls, or native cats, are about the size of domestic cats and may be even more efficient killers. Nocturnal creatures, spending most of their time in trees, they are not often seen.

Species include the eastern*(Dasyurus viverrinus)*, the western *(D. geoffroii)* and the northern quoll *(D. hallucatus)*. The eastern is now rare on the mainland but is still found widely in Tasmania. The spotted-tailed quoll *(D. maculatus)*, also known as the tiger cat, is one of the most ferocious hunters in the bush.

Tasmanian Devil The carnivorous Tasmanian devil *(Sarcophilus harrisii)*, the largest of the dasyuroids, is as fierce as it looks. It's solitary and nocturnal and has

A snoozing koala

Common wombat

An inquisitive northern quoll

MITCH REARDON

Tasmanian devil

JASON EDWARDS

A nosey numbat

JOHN HAY

Dingo

a fierce whining growl. The body is black with a white stripe across the chest, and measures around 60cm long, with a tail about 25cm long. Its diet consists of small birds and mammals, insects and carrion.

Numbat The attractive numbat *(Myrmecobius fasciatus)* is a pouchless marsupial and is unusual in that it is most active during the day. It has striking rust-red fur with seven white stripes across the rump. Adult numbats are about rat-sized and weigh around 500g.

Numbats live in hollow, fallen wandoo trees *(Eucalyptus redunca)* in the forests of south-western Australia; their numbers are dwindling.

Eutherians

Australia's native eutherians, or placental mammals, include the marine mammals and the 'recent' invaders, who arrived no more than 15 million years ago, which include the native dog or dingo and numerous species of bat and rodent.

Dingo

The dingo *(Canis familiaris dingo)* is thought to have arrived in Australia around 6000 years ago, and was domesticated by Aborigines. It differs from the domestic dog in that it howls rather than barks and breeds once a year (rather than twice), although the two can interbreed.

Dingoes prey on rabbits, rats and mice. When food is scarce they sometimes attack livestock (usually sheep or calves), and for this reason are considered vermin by many farmers. Efforts to control dingo numbers have been largely unsuccessful.

Marine Mammals

Humpback Whale This massive marine mammal *(Megaptera novaeangliae)* migrates northwards from feeding grounds in the polar seas to breed in subtropical waters in winter. Adult humpbacks range from 14 to 19m in length and can live for over 30 years. They are a regular sight along the east and west coasts of Australia.

Southern Right Whale The southern right whale *(Eubalaena australis)*, so-called because it was the 'right' whale to kill, was hunted almost to the point of extinction but, since the cessation of whaling, has returned to Australian waters. It can be seen in the

FAUNA & FLORA

Great Australian Bight, and is easily recognised by its strongly down-turned mouth with long baleen plates (these filter water for planktonic krill).

Dugong This is a herbivorous aquatic mammal (*Dugong dugon*), or 'sea cow', found along the northern coast, from Shark Bay in WA to the Great Barrier Reef in Queensland. The Shark Bay population is estimated to be over 10,000, about 10% of the world's dugong population. They live in shallow tropical waters where they feed on seagrasses and algae.

The massive tail of a humpback whale

Birds

Australian birdlife is beautiful and varied, with over 750 recorded species, many of them endemic. Birds Australia (☎ 03-9882 2622) runs bird observatories in NSW, Victoria, SA and WA, providing accommodation and guides.

Emu

The emu (*Dromaius novaehollandiae*) is a shaggy feathered bird that stands 2m high. The only bird larger than the emu is the African ostrich, also flightless. Emus are found across the country, in areas away from human habitation. After the female lays her six to 12 large, dark green eggs the male hatches them and raises the young.

Kookaburra

The laughing kookaburra (*Dacelo novaeguinae*) is common throughout coastal Australia, particularly in the east and south-west of the country. The blue-winged kookaburra (*D. leachii*) is found in northern coastal woodlands. Kookaburras are the largest members of the kingfisher family. They are heard as much as they are seen – you can't miss the loud, cackling laugh. Kookaburras can become quite tame.

Emu

Bowerbird

The stocky, stout-billed bowerbird, of which there are at least half a dozen species, is best known for its unique mating practice. The brightly coloured male builds a bower that he decorates with various coloured objects to attract the less showy female. The female is impressed by the male's bower and attractively displayed treasures, but once they've mated all the hard work is left to her. The three most common species are the great (*Chlamydera nuchalis*),

Male regent bowerbird

Magpie

DAVID CURL

A pair of wedge-tailed eagles

JASON EDWARDS

Rainbow lorikeet

JASON EDWARDS

the spotted *(C. maculata)* and the satin *(Ptilonorhynchus violaceus)*.

Magpie

The magpie *(Gymnorhina* spp) is widespread throughout Australia. One of the most distinctive sounds of the bush is the melodious song of the magpie, heard especially at dawn. The way they swoop on people who approach their nests in spring is less endearing. The several species of magpie look much alike to the untrained eye, but differ in the arrangement of their black and white markings.

Wedge-Tailed Eagle

With a wing span of up to 2m, the wedge-tailed eagle *(Aquila audax)* is Australia's largest bird of prey. It is easily identified in flight by its distinctive wedge-shaped tail. 'Wedgies' are often seen in outback Australia, soaring to great heights, or feeding on road-kill.

Parrots, Rosellas, Lorikeets & Cockatoos

There is an amazing variety of these birds throughout Australia.

Rosella Most of the number of species of rosella *(Platycercus* spp) are brilliantly coloured. The red, yellow and blue eastern rosella *(P. eximius)* is the most widespread and is found throughout south-eastern Australia. They are not shy and will take a free feed from humans.

Galah The pink and grey galah *(Cacatua roseicapilla)* is among the most common, and is often sighted scratching for seeds on the roadside.

Rainbow Lorikeet The rainbow lorikeet *(Trichoglossus haematodus)* is extravagantly colourful with its blue head, orange breast and green body. Lorikeets have a brush-like tongue for extracting nectar from flowers.

Budgerigar Budgies *(Melopsittacus undulatus)* are widespread over inland Australia where they can be seen in flocks of thousands flying in tight formation.

Black Cockatoo There are six species of black cockatoo. The most widespread are the large red-tailed black cockatoo *(Calyptorhynchus magnificus)* and the yellow-tailed black cockatoo *(C. funereus)*.

FAUNA & FLORA

Sulphur-Crested Cockatoo Often seen in raucous flocks, this noisy cocky *(Cacatua galerita)* is found throughout eastern and northern Australia. When the flock is feeding on the ground, several individuals will fly to vantage points to watch for and signal danger.

Lyrebird

The shy, superb lyrebird *(Menura novaehollandiae)* is a ground-dwelling rainforest bird found in south-eastern Australia. The male has tail feathers that form a lyre shape when displayed to attract a mate. The similar Albert lyrebird *(M. alberti)* is found in the rainforests of southern Queensland and northern NSW. Lyrebirds have a beautiful song and are also clever mimics.

Jabiru

The jabiru (or black-necked stork, *Xenorhynchus asiaticus*) is found throughout northern and eastern Australia, although it is rarely seen. It stands over 1m high, and has an iridescent green-black neck, black and white body, and orange legs.

Magpie Goose

The magpie (or pied) goose *(Anseranas semipalmata)* is commonly seen in the tropical wetlands of northern Australia. When water becomes scarce towards the end of the Dry (October) they gather in huge numbers on the retreating wetlands.

Brolga

This crane known as the brolga *(Grus rubicundus)* is commonly seen in wetland areas of northern and, to a lesser extent, eastern Australia. It stands over 1m high, is grey in colour and has a distinctive red head.

Black Swan

Commonly seen in large flocks near fresh or brackish water from the Top End to Tasmania are black swans *(Cygnus atratus)*. They nest among reeds or on islands in lakes and both parents take on nesting duties.

Reptiles
Snakes

There are seven different families of snakes in Australia; the most common is the *Elapidae* group. Most snakes are shy and avoid humans. A few, however, are deadly. The most dangerous are the taipan and tiger snake, although death adders, copperheads,

Sulphur-crested cockatoo

A brilliant jabiru

DAVID CURL

Saltwater crocodile

MITCH REARDON

Yellow-spotted goanna

ROHAN CLARKE

Frilled lizard

brown snakes and red-bellied black snakes should also be avoided. Tiger snakes actually attack.

Crocodiles

There are two types of crocodile in Australia: the extremely dangerous saltwater crocodile *(Crocodylus porosus)*, or 'saltie', and the less aggressive freshwater crocodile *(C. johnstoni)*, or 'freshie'. Both are prolific in northern Australia. It is important to be able to distinguish between them.

Saltwater Crocodile Salties are not confined to salt water. They inhabit estuaries, and after floods may be found many kilometres from the coast. They are even found in permanent fresh water more than 100km inland. Salties, which can grow to 7m, will attack and kill humans.

Freshwater Crocodile Freshies are smaller, under 4m, and more finely built than salties. They have much narrower snouts and smaller teeth and, though unlikely to seek human prey, have been known to bite.

Lizards

Goanna Goannas are large and sometimes aggressive lizards, up to 2m long. With their forked tongues and loud hiss they can be quite formidable, and are best left undisturbed as they will stand their ground. The largest goanna is the carnivorous perentie *(Varanus giganteus)*, in central Australia.

Frilled Lizard The frilled lizard *(Chlamydosaurus kingii)* is commonly seen in bushland in eastern and northern Australia. The frill is a loose flap of skin, which normally hangs flat around the neck. When alarmed or threatened, the lizard raises its frill and opens its mouth to give a more ferocious appearance.

Spiders

The notorious redback *(Latrodectus hasselti)* is generally glossy black with a red streak down its back. Woodheaps and garden sheds are favourite hang-outs, and its bite can be lethal. The funnel-web *(Dipluridae* family) is a large, aggressive ground-dwelling spider found mainly in NSW. Sydney's funnel-web is particularly venomous; its bite can be fatal.

FLORA

Despite vast tracts of dry and barren land, much of Australia is well vegetated. Forests cover 5%, or 410,000 sq km. Plants are found in the arid centre, though many of them grow and flower erratically.

The arrival of Europeans just over 200 years ago saw the introduction of new flora, fauna and tools. Rainforests were logged, new crops and pasture grasses spread, hoofed animals such as cows, sheep and goats damaged the soil, and watercourses were altered. Irrigation, combined with excessive tree clearing, gradually resulted in salination of the soil. Despite all this, most species of Australian flora have survived.

Spinifex and snappy gums

Native Grasses

There are more than 700 native Australian grasses found in a variety of habitats across the country.

Spinifex

The hardiest and most common desert plant is the desert grass, spinifex. It forms a dense, dome-shaped mass of long, needle-like leaves on sandy soils and rocky areas. It covers vast areas of central Australia and supports large populations of reptiles.

Mitchell Grass

Mitchell grass covers huge areas of arid land in northern Australia, and is the saviour of the cattle industry in the Top End. It has a well-developed root system and is therefore very drought resistant. The grass usually grows in tussocks on clay soils.

Callistemon (bottlebrush)

Shrubs & Flowers

Callistemons

Callistemons, or bottlebrushes (after the brush-like flowers), are found across the country, but especially in NSW. They are attractive, hardy and draw many native birds. There are some 25 different species, from one to 10m high. Some of the most common are the crimson *(C. citrinus)*, the weeping *(C. viminalis)* and the prickly bottlebrush *(C. brachycandrus)*.

Grevilleas

Grevilleas are another major family of shrub. Of the 250 or so varieties, all but 20 are native to Australia. There are a variety of sizes and flower colours. Most grevilleas are small to medium shrubs, such as Banks

Magnificent grevillea in flower

MITCH REARDON

Sturt's desert pea

ROB BLAKERS

Soft tree fern

TREVOR CREICHTON

Cabbage palms

grevillea *(G. banksii)*, which has beautiful red flower spikes. A flowering silky oak *(G. robusta)*, which can grow to a height of 30m, is truly spectacular.

Kangaroo Paw
Kangaroo paw (*Anigozanthos* spp) grows wild only in south-western WA; Mangle's kangaroo paw *(A. manglesii)* is the state's floral emblem. They are commonly grown in gardens in the eastern states. The plant takes its name from the distinctive, tubular flowers that are covered in velvet-like hair and are a variety of colours – from black to red, green and yellow. The plants were used for medicinal purposes by Aborigines.

Sturt's Desert Pea
A small, annual flower, Sturt's desert pea *(Clianthus formosus)* flourishes in the drier areas of inland Australia, particularly after heavy rain. The plant is the floral emblem of SA, and has distinctive red flowers with black centres.

Saltbush
Millions of sheep and cattle owe their survival in the arid zone to dry, shrubby saltbush, named for its tolerance to saline conditions. There are 30 species of saltbush which is extremely widespread.

Cycads & Ferns
MacDonnell Ranges Cycad
The MacDonnell Ranges cycad *(Macrozamia macdonnelli)* is one of 18 species in Australia belonging to the ancient cycad family. It is a very slow-growing plant, often seen high up on rocky hillsides and gorges. Seed cones grow at the tip of the short trunk on female plants, while male cones carry the pollen.

Tree Ferns
The beautifully ornate rough tree fern (*Cyathea* spp) and the soft tree fern *(Dicksonia antarctica)* are found in the temperate rainforests of eastern Australia. Some varieties can be up to 20m high, and all are topped by a crown of green fronds.

Trees
Cabbage Palms
There are 40 palm species in Australia. One of the more notable is the cabbage palm *(Livistona mariae)* of Palm Valley in the Finke Gorge National Park near

Alice Springs. The tree grows up to 30m high, and is unique to this area. The growing tip of the tree consists of tender green leaves, which were a source of bush tucker to Aborigines. The mature leaves were woven into hats by early European inhabitants of the Centre.

Acacias

There are over 660 species of the genus *Acacia*, or 'wattle', in Australia. They vary from small shrubs to towering blackwoods. Most species flower during late winter and spring, when the countryside is ablaze with yellow flowers.

Cootamundra wattle

Blackwood The largest of the acacias, the blackwood (*A. melanoxylon*) can grow more than 30m high in good soil and is generally found on the eastern and southern ranges.

Mulga The mulga (*A. aneura*) is the dominant species in huge areas of inland Australia. It is very drought tolerant, and the hard wood was preferred by Aborigines for making spears and other implements.

Golden Wattle The golden wattle (*A. pycnantha*), Australia's floral emblem, is one of the most widespread acacias. It grows best in hot and arid areas, but is common throughout south-eastern Australia.

Banksias

There are about 60 species of Banksias (*Banksia* spp), named after Sir Joseph Banks, the botanist who accompanied Captain James Cook on his exploratory voyage of eastern Australia. They are often found in poor soils unsuitable for most other plants. The majority have upright spikes covered with brilliant orange, red or yellow flowers, one of the most spectacular being the scarlet banksia (*B. coccinea*). The nectar of these flowers was popular with Aborigines, who would dip the spikes in water to make a sweet drink.

Casuarinas

Also known as sheoaks, these hardy trees are almost as much a part of the Australian landscape as eucalypts. They grow in a variety of habitats, and are characterised by feather-like 'leaves', which are actually branchlets; the true leaves are small scales at the joints of the branchlets.

Banksia serrata

RICHARD I'ANSON

Desert oaks

PAUL SINCLAIR

Ghost gum

Desert Oak Its height, broad shady crown, dark weeping foliage and the sighing music of the wind in its leaves make the desert oak *(Allocasuarina decaisneana)* an inspiring feature of its sand-plain habitat. These magnificent trees are confined to the western arid zone of central Australia and are common around Uluru and Kings Canyon, near Alice Springs. Young desert oaks resemble tall hairy broomsticks, quite unlike the adult trees, and many people think that they're a different species altogether.

River Sheoak The river sheoak *(Casuarina cunninghamania)* is a tall tree, highly valued for its ability to bind river banks, which greatly reduces erosion.

Eucalypts

The eucalypt *(Eucalyptus* spp), or gum tree, is ubiquitous in Australia except in the rainforests and the most arid regions. Of the 700 species of the genus eucalyptus, 95% occur naturally in Australia.

Gum trees vary in form and height from the tall, straight hardwoods such as jarrah, karri and mountain ash to the stunted, twisted, shrub-like Mallee gum.

River Red Gum River red gums *(E. camaldulensis)* are generally confined to watercourses where their roots have access to a reliable water source. They are massive trees which can grow up to 40m high and live for up to 1000 years.

Coolabah Coolabah trees *(E. Microtheca)* are widespread throughout inland and northern Australia. They grow to about 20m high, and are not the prettiest of trees, with an uneven, spreading form and a twisted trunk. The coolabah was immortalised in Banjo Paterson's poem, *Waltzing Matilda.*

Ghost Gum The ghost gum *(E. papuana)* is one of the most attractive eucalypts and is found throughout central and northern Australia. Its bright green leaves and smooth white bark contrast with the red rocks and soil of the Centre; and, not surprisingly, it is a common subject for artists.

Melaleucas

The loose, papery bark hanging in thin sheets around the trunk characterises paperbarks, or *Melaleucas.* This is actually dead bark that stays on the tree, insulating the trunk from extreme temperature and moisture loss. The trees have been put to many uses by Aborigines for centuries – drinkable water is obtainable from the trunk, and the bark has been used for water carriers, rafts, shelters and food coverings.

Some of the most common varieties are the swamp (*M. ericifolia*), the bracelet honey-myrtle (*M. armillaris*) and the long-leaved paperbark (*M. leucadendron*).

Waratah

The waratah *(Telopea Speciosissima)* has a spectacular red flower. The scientific name, *Telopea*, means 'seen from afar', which gives some idea of its impact in the bush. The small tree is limited to NSW, of which it is the floral emblem, and Victoria. Genera other than *Telopea* are also given the name waratah, such as the waratah tree *(Oreocallis pinnata)* of Queensland and NSW.

Boab

The boab *(Adansonia gregorii)* is found only from the south-western Kimberley to the NT's Victoria River, where it grows on flood plains and rocky areas. Its huge, grey, swollen trunk topped by a mass of contorted branches makes it a fascinating sight, particularly during the Dry when it loses its leaves and becomes 'the tree that God planted upside-down'. Although boabs rarely grow higher than 20m, their moisture-storing trunks can be over 23m in girth.

Conifers

There are several families of native Australian conifers.

Bunya Pine One of the most unusual pines is the bunya pine *(Araucaria bidwillii)*, which is found in rainforest in southern Queensland. The huge cones can weigh up to 7kg. The seeds inside these cones were once a favourite food of Aborigines.

Norfolk Island Pine The Norfolk Island pine *(A. heterophylla)* is native to Norfolk Island. Their tall straight form prompted Captain Cook to suggest they would make excellent masts. Their symmetry has made them a popular tree for streets and parks.

Pencil Pine Endemic to Tasmania, the pencil pine *(Athrotaxis cupressoides)* is found in high-altitude rainforests.

Boab tree

Pencil pine

Facts for the Visitor

HIGHLIGHTS

In a country as large and geographically diverse as Australia the list of highlights is virtually endless, although one person's highlight·can easily be another's disappointment. However, each state has features that shouldn't be missed:

Australian Capital Territory (ACT)
The national capital is a picturesque, planned city, the focal points being Lake Burley Griffin and impressive, modern buildings such as Parliament House and the High Court. The fine National Gallery should not be missed, while Namadgi National Park is wonderful for walks and wildlife.

New South Wales (NSW)
Sydney, the capital of NSW and host for the year 2000 Olympic Games, has simply one of the most stunning locations you're likely to come across, as well as the beautiful Blue Mountains nearby. The coastal beaches, northern rainforests, Snowy Mountains National Park and wide expanse of the interior also have plenty to offer.

Northern Territory (NT)
The obvious attraction is Uluru (Ayers Rock), probably Australia's most readily identifiable symbol after the Sydney Opera House. There's also the World Heritage listed Kakadu National Park with its abundant flora and fauna and superb wetlands. The Territory is where Australia's Aboriginal cultural heritage is at its most accessible – the rock-art sites of Kakadu, and Aboriginal-owned and run tours of Arnhem Land, Manyallaluk (near Katherine) and Uluru are just a few of the possibilities.

Queensland
The Great Barrier Reef, and its many water-based activities, is outstanding. The state's varied terrain offers visitors secluded beach and island resorts, the rainforested Daintree, inland deserts and 'one-horse towns', cattle country and the remote Cape York Peninsula.

South Australia (SA)
The big drawcards here are the Barossa Valley, with its excellent wineries, and the Flinders Ranges, which offer superb bushwalking and stunning scenery. In the northern areas of South Australia you can get a real taste of the Outback along famous tracks such as the Strzelecki, Oodnadatta and Birdsville. The opal-

mining town of Coober Pedy, where many people live in underground houses, is unique.

Tasmania
There's the rich heritage of the convict era at places such as Port Arthur, as well as some of the most beautiful wilderness areas in the country. The Cradle Mountain-Lake St Clair World Heritage area is popular with bushwalkers, as is the rugged south-west corner of the state.

Victoria
No visit to Victoria would be complete without an exploration of the enchanting Grampians range, famous for its natural beauty and great bushwalks. Other highlights include the fairy penguins at Phillip Island, the re-created gold-mining township of Sovereign Hill at Ballarat, the snowfields and forests of the Victorian Alps, and the Great Ocean Road, one of the world's most spectacular coastal routes. Melbourne too has a charm that's well worth discovering.

Western Australia (WA)
Vast distances and wide open spaces are the big attractions here. In the south is Fremantle, an eclectic port not far from the state capital, Perth. Spectacular sights include the tall eucalypt forests of the south-west, Karijini National Park in the Pilbara, and the Bungle Bungle (Purnululu) National Park in the rugged Kimberley.

SUGGESTED ITINERARIES

The toughest part about visiting Australia is deciding what to see now and what to leave for next time. The biggest influence on any decisions you make will be whether you are travelling by land or air. In a country where it takes a week or more to drive from coast to coast, clearly a driving or bus holiday of a couple of weeks is going to limit you to a relatively small area (Tasmania, for instance), whereas by air you could hop between a number of widely spaced points.

The main thing to bear in mind when trying to plan ahead is that Australia is *big* – that line on the map between two cities may look like an easy day's drive, but it may be 1000km or more! A leisurely trip through a small area is going to be much more enjoyable (and safer) than a mad, 500km-a-day dash around the place. In the Outback and in sparsely populated country areas, 500km is not an unrealistic day's driving if you don't plan to stop much along the way; on the east coast you can only expect to cover half the distance.

While everybody travels at a different pace, the following suggestions assume that you want to see things along the way, don't want to spend 12 hours a day behind the wheel and would like to finish your trip feeling more relaxed than when you started.

One Month
One of the most popular routes is the run along the east coast between Sydney and Cairns. To drive (or bus) this comfortably would take about a month, although you could easily spend three months doing it. Another four week drive could be from Cairns across Queensland to Darwin and Kakadu, and even down to the Centre to Alice Springs, with a side trip to Uluru. You could also attack the Centre from the other direction, starting in Sydney or Melbourne and heading north via Adelaide and the Flinders Ranges. The trek between Perth and the east coast would take a comfortable four weeks, but that wouldn't allow for much time at either end.

Three Months
With three months at your disposal you can start getting serious: Sydney to Cairns via the Centre and Darwin; Sydney to Adelaide via Cairns, Darwin and the Centre; Perth to Cairns via the Kimberley and Darwin; or Melbourne to Cairns via the coast.

Six Months
Six months gives you enough time to do the big loop that takes in the east coast, Darwin, central Australia, Adelaide and Melbourne, with perhaps a stop for a month to work or hang out somewhere along the way. Cairns to Perth via the eastern and southern coasts would also be a viable proposition.

PLANNING
When To Go

Any time is a good time to be in Australia, but as you'd expect in a country this large, different parts are at their best at different times.

The southern states are most popular during summer (December through February), as there's often good weather for swimming and being outdoors. In the centre of the country, summer is just too damn hot to do

anything much, while in the far north it's the Wet season, when the heat and humidity can make life pretty uncomfortable. To make matters worse, swimming in the sea up north in summer is considered dangerous because of the 'stingers' (box jellyfish) that frequent the waters at this time. On the other hand, if you want to see the Top End green and free of dust, be treated to some spectacular electrical storms and have the best of the barramundi fishing while all the other tourists are down south, this is the time to do it.

In winter (June through August) the focus swings to the north, when the humidity has faded and the temperature is perfect. This is the most popular time for visits to far north Queensland and the Top End. Central and outback Australia are also popular at this time, as the extreme heat of summer has been replaced by warm sunny days and surprisingly cool – even cold – nights. The cooler weather also deters the bush flies, which in the warmer months can be an absolute nightmare. The southern states, however, are not without their own attractions in winter. Snow skiers can head for the Victorian Alps or the Snowy Mountains in NSW for good cross-country or downhill skiing – although snow cover ranges from excellent one year to virtually nonexistent the next.

Spring and autumn give the greatest flexibility for a short visit as you can combine highlights of the whole country while avoiding the extremes of the weather. Late winter and early spring are the times for wildflowers in the Outback (particularly in central and Western Australia) – these can be absolutely stunning, but like the rainfall the displays vary in intensity from year to year.

The other major consideration when travelling in Australia is school holidays. Australian families take to the road (and air) en masse at these times and many places are booked out, prices rise and things generally get a bit crazy. (See the Public Holidays & Special Events section later in this chapter for details.)

Maps
There's no shortage of maps available, although many of them are of pretty average

quality. Road maps published by the various oil companies – Shell, BP, Mobil etc – are available from service stations. The various state motoring organisations are another good source of maps, and theirs are often a lot cheaper (and better) than the oil company maps (see the Car section of the Getting Around chapter for addresses). Lonely Planet produces convenient city maps of Melbourne and Sydney. Commercially available city street guides, such as those produced by Ausway (publishers of *Melway* and *Sydway*), Gregorys and UBD, are also useful.

For bushwalking, ski-touring and other activities that require large-scale maps, the topographic sheets put out by the Australian Surveying & Land Information Group (AUSLIG) are the ones to get. Many of the more popular sheets are usually available over the counter at shops that sell specialist bushwalking gear and outdoor equipment. AUSLIG also has special-interest maps showing various types of land use, population densities or Aboriginal land. For more information, or a catalogue, you can contact AUSLIG at the Department of Industry, Science and Resources, PO Box 2, Belconnen, ACT 2616 (☎ 02-6201 4201). Its Web site is www.auslig.gov.au.

TOURIST OFFICES

There are a number of information sources for visitors to Australia and, like many other tourist-conscious western countries, you can easily bury yourself in brochures and booklets, maps and leaflets.

Local Tourist Offices

Within Australia, tourist information is handled by various state and local offices. Each state and territory has a tourist office of some kind and you will find information about them in later chapters. Apart from main offices in the capital cities, they often have regional offices in major tourist centres and also in other states.

As well as supplying brochures, price lists, maps and other information, the state offices will often book transport, tours and accommodation for you. Unfortunately, very few of the state tourist offices maintain information

desks at airports and, furthermore, the opening hours of the city offices are too often the 9-to-5-weekdays and Saturday-morning-only variety.

The main sources of information are:

Australian Capital Territory
    Canberra Visitors Centre (☎ 02-6205 0044, 1800 026 166, fax 6205 0776)
    330 Northbourne Ave (PO Box 673), Dickson, ACT 2602, Web site www.canberratourism .com.au
New South Wales
    Sydney Visitor Centre (☎ 13 2077)
    106 George St, The Rocks, NSW 2000, Web site www.tourism.nsw.gov.au
Northern Territory
    Northern Territory Holiday Centre (☎ 1800 621 336)
    PO Box 2532, Alice Springs, NT 0871, Web site www.nttc.com.au
Queensland
    Queensland Government Travel Centre (☎ 13 1801, 07-3874 2800, fax 3221 5320)
    243 Edward St (GPO Box 9958), Brisbane, Queensland 4001, Web site www.queensland -travel-centre.com.au
South Australia
    South Australian Travel Centre (☎ 08-8303 2033, 1300 366 770, fax 8303 2231)
    1 King William St, (PO Box 1972) Adelaide, SA 5000, Web site www.tourism.sa.gov.au
Tasmania
    Tasmanian Travel & Information Centre (☎ 03-6230 8233, fax 6224 0289)
    Corner of Davey and Elizabeth Sts, Hobart, Tasmania 7000
    Tourism Tasmania (☎ 03-6230 8235, 1800 806 846, fax 6230 8353)
    GPO Box 399, Hobart, Tasmania 7001, Web site www.tourism.tas.gov.au
Victoria
    RACV Travel Centre (☎ 1800 337 743)
    360 Bourke St, Melbourne, Victoria 3000
    Victorian Tourism Information Service (☎ 13 2842, fax 03-9653 9744)
    GPO Box 2219T, Melbourne, Victoria 3001, Web site www.tourism.vic.gov.au
Western Australia
    Western Australian Tourist Centre (☎ 1800 812 808, fax 08-9481 0190)
    Forrest Place, Perth, WA 6000, Web site www .westernaustralia.net

A step down from the state tourist offices are the local or regional offices. Almost every major town in Australia seems to maintain a tourist office of some type and in many cases they are excellent, with much local information not readily available from the state offices. This particularly applies where there is a strong local tourist trade.

Tourist Offices Abroad

The Australian Tourist Commission (ATC) is the government body intended to inform potential visitors about the country. There's a very definite split between promotion outside and inside Australia. The ATC is strictly an external operator; it does minimal promotion within the country and has little contact with visitors once they have arrived in Australia. Within the country, tourist promotion is handled by state and regional tourist offices.

ATC offices overseas have a useful, free, magazine-style periodical booklet called *Australia Travellers Guide*, which has some handy info for potential visitors. Its *Australia Unplugged* is a good introduction to Australia for young people, giving some information about the country in general and snapshots of major cities – it is not available in some regions of the world.

The ATC publishes 'Fact Sheets' on various topics such as camping, fishing, skiing, disabled travel and national parks, and these can be a useful introduction to the subject. It has a handy map of the country, which is available for a small fee. This literature is intended for distribution overseas only; if you want copies, find them on the ATC Web site at www.australia.com or contact an 'Aussie Specialist' – travel agents who specialise in marketing Australia to international visitors.

VISAS & DOCUMENTS

All important documents (passport, credit cards, travel insurance, air/bus/train tickets, driving licence etc) should be photocopied before you leave home. Leave a copy with someone at home and keep another with you, separate from the originals.

Visas

All visitors to Australia need a visa – only New Zealand nationals are exempt, and even they receive a 'special category' visa on arrival. Check the Department of Immigration & Multicultural Affairs' Web site at www.immi.gov.au for lots of useful pre-departure information on visas, as well as on customs and health issues. It includes *An Australian Government Guide to Visiting Australia*. Visa application forms are available from either Australian diplomatic missions overseas or travel agents, and you can apply by mail or in person. There are several different types of visa, depending on the reason for your visit.

Tourist Visas Tourist visas are issued by Australian diplomatic missions abroad; they are valid for a stay of up to six months and there is a $50 application fee. The visa is valid for use within 12 months of the date of issue and can be used to enter and leave Australia several times within that 12 months.

When you apply for a visa, you need to present your passport and a passport photo, as well as sign an undertaking that you have an onward or return ticket and 'sufficient funds' to support yourself during your stay – the latter is obviously open to interpretation.

You can also apply for a long-stay visa, which is a multiple-entry, four year visa allowing stays of up to six months on each visit. These also cost $50.

Electronic Travel Authority (ETA) Visitors who require a tourist visa of up to three months can get a free ETA through an International Air Transport Association (IATA)-registered travel agent abroad – the agent makes the application direct and issues the traveller with an ETA, which replaces the usual visa stamped in your passport. This system, which was introduced in 1997, is so far only available to passport holders of the UK, the USA, most European and Scandinavian countries, Malaysia, Singapore, Japan and Korea. The list is likely to grow significantly. To avoid later complications, make sure the details shown on your ETA slip are correct.

Working Holiday Visas Young, single visitors from the UK, Canada, Korea, the

Netherlands, Malta, Ireland and Japan may be eligible for a 'working holiday' visa. 'Young' is fairly loosely interpreted as between 18 and 25, although people from countries with which Australia has working holiday agreements, such as Britain, can obtain work visas up to the age of 30. At the time of writing, similar agreements were being negotiated with other countries such as USA, France, Italy, Greece and Singapore.

A working holiday visa allows for a stay of up to 12 months. As the emphasis is on casual rather than full-time employment, you are only supposed to work for any one employer for three months at a time – there's nothing to stop you from working for more than one employer in the 12 months. This visa can only be applied for at Australian diplomatic missions abroad (citizens of the UK, Ireland, Canada and the Netherlands can apply at any Australian diplomatic mission, while all others must apply in their home country). You can't change from a tourist visa to a working holiday visa.

You can apply for a working holiday visa up to 12 months in advance – it's a good idea to apply as early as possible as there is a limit on the number of visas issued each year. Conditions attached to a working holiday visa include having sufficient funds for a ticket out, and having private health insurance unless there is a reciprocal arrangement between Australia and your country of citizenship (see the Medicare Card entry later in this section). There is an application fee of $145.

See the section on Work later in this chapter for details of what sort of work is available and where.

Visa Extensions Visitors are allowed a maximum stay of one year, including extensions. Visa extensions are made through Department of Immigration & Multicultural Affairs offices in Australia (☎ 13 1881) and it's best to apply two or three weeks before your visa expires. There is an application fee of $145, but beware – even if they turn down your application they still keep your money.

If you'd like to stay for longer in Australia the books *Temporary to Permanent Residence in Australia* and *A Practical Guide to Obtaining Permanent Residence in Australia*, both by Adrian Joel, might be useful.

Driving Licence

You can generally use your own foreign driving licence in Australia, as long as it is in English (if it's not, a certified translation must be carried). Confusingly, some states prefer that you have an International Licence, which must be supported by your

---

Travel Insurance

A travel insurance policy to cover theft, loss and medical problems is a good idea. The policies handled by STA Travel and other student travel organisations are usually good value. Some policies offer lower and higher medical-expense options; the higher ones are chiefly for countries that have extremely high medical costs, such as the USA. There is a wide variety of policies available: compare the small print.

Some policies specifically exclude 'dangerous activities' such as scuba diving, parasailing, bungee jumping, motorcycling and even trekking. A locally acquired motorcycle licence is not valid under some policies.

You may prefer a policy that pays doctors or hospitals direct rather than you having to pay on the spot and claim later. If you have to claim later make sure you keep all documentation. Some policies ask you to call back (reverse charges) to a centre in your home country where an immediate assessment of your problem is made.

Check that the policy covers ambulances and emergency medical evacuations by air.

home licence. To avoid potential hassles we suggest you carry both.

Medicare Card

Under reciprocal arrangements, residents of the UK, New Zealand, the Netherlands, Sweden, Finland, Malta and Italy are entitled to free or subsidised medical treatment under Medicare, Australia's compulsory national health insurance scheme. To enrol you need to show your passport and health-care card or certificate from your own country, after which you are given a Medicare card.

A Medicare card entitles you to free, necessary public-hospital treatment. While residents of southern Ireland cannot get a Medicare card, they can present their passport at a public hospital and be given free necessary treatment.

Visits to a private doctor are also claimable under Medicare, although depending on the claim method used by the doctor you may have to pay the bill first and then make a claim yourself from Medicare. You also need to find out how much the doctor's consultation fee is, as Medicare only covers you for a certain amount and you will need to pay the balance. Clinics that advertise 'bulk billing' are the easiest to use as they charge Medicare direct.

For more information phone Medicare on ☎ 13 2011.

EMBASSIES
Australian Embassies Abroad

The Department of Foreign Affairs & Trade's Web site at www.dfat.gov.au has a full listing of Australian diplomatic missions overseas. They include:

Canada
(☎ 613-236 0841, fax 236 4376)
Suite 710, 50 O'Connor St, Ottawa, Ontario K1P 6L2
Also in Vancouver

France
(☎ 01-4059 3300, fax 4059 3310)
4 Rue Jean Rey, 75724 Cedex 15, Paris

Germany
(☎ 30-880 0880, fax 880 08899)
Friedrich St 200, 10117 Berlin

Indonesia
(☎ 021-522 7111, fax 526 1690)
Jalan HR Rasuna Said Kav C15-16, Kuningan,
Jakarta Selatan 12940
(☎ 0361-23 5092, fax 23 1990)
Jalan Prof Moh Yamin 4, Renon, Denpasar, Bali

Ireland
(☎ 01-676 1517, fax 678 5185)
Fitzwilton House, Wilton Terrace, Dublin 2

Malaysia
(☎ 03-246 5555, fax 241 5773)
6 Jalan Yap Kwan Seng, Kuala Lumpur 50450

Netherlands
(☎ 070-310 8200, fax 310 7863) Carnegielaan 4, The Hague 2517 KH

New Zealand
(☎ 04-473 6411, fax 498 7135)
72-78 Hobson St, Thorndon, Wellington
(☎ 09-303 2429, fax 377 0798)
Union House, 132-38 Quay St, Auckland

Papua New Guinea
(☎ 325 9333, fax 325 9183)
Godwit Rd, Waigani NCD, Port Moresby

Philippines
(☎ 02-750 2850, fax 754 6268)
Dona Salustiana Ty Tower, 104 Paseo de Roxas Ave, Makati, Metro Manila

Singapore
(☎ 863 4100, fax 737 5481)
25 Napier Rd, Singapore 258507

Thailand
(☎ 02-287 2680, fax 287 2029)
37 South Sathorn Rd, Bangkok 10120

UK
(☎ 020-7379 4334, fax 7465 8217)
Australia House, The Strand, London WC2B 4LA
Also in Manchester

USA
(☎ 202-797 3000, fax 797 3168)
1601 Massachusetts Ave NW, Washington DC 20036
Also in Los Angeles and New York

Vietnam
(☎ 04-831 7755, fax 831 7711)
Van Phuc Compound, Ba Dinh District, Hanoi
Also in Ho Chi Minh City

Foreign Embassies in Australia

The principal diplomatic representations to Australia are in Canberra. There are also representatives in other major cities, particularly from countries with a strong connection with Australia like the USA, UK or New Zealand; or in cities with important connections, like Darwin, which has an Indonesian consulate.

Big cities like Sydney and Melbourne have nearly as many consular offices as Canberra, although visa applications are usually handled in Canberra. Addresses of important offices follow (look under Consulates & Legations in the *Yellow Pages* telephone book for more):

Canada
   (☎ 02-6270 4000)
   Commonwealth Ave, Yarralumla, ACT 2600
   (☎ 02-9364 3050)
   Level 5/111 Harrington St, Sydney, NSW 2000
France
   (☎ 02-6216 0100)
   6 Perth Ave, Yarralumla, ACT 2600
   (☎ 02-9261 5779)
   31 Market St, Sydney, NSW 2000
   (☎ 03-9820 0921)
   492 St Kilda Rd, Melbourne, Victoria 3004
Germany
   (☎ 02-6270 1911)
   119 Empire Circuit, Yarralumla, ACT 2600
   (☎ 02-9328 7733)
   13 Trelawney St, Woollahra, NSW 2025
   (☎ 03-9828 6888)
   480 Punt Rd, South Yarra, Victoria 3141
Indonesia
   (☎ 02-6250 8600)
   8 Darwin Ave, Yarralumla, ACT 2600
   (☎ 02-9344 9933)
   236 Maroubra Rd, Maroubra, NSW 2035
   (☎ 08-8941 0048)
   20 Harry Chan Ave (PO Box 1953), Darwin, NT 0801
   (☎ 03-9525 2755)
   72 Queens Rd, Melbourne, Victoria 3004
Ireland
   (☎ 02-6273 3022)
   20 Arkana St, Yarralumla, ACT 2600
Malaysia
   (☎ 02-6273 1543)
   7 Perth Ave, Yarralumla, ACT 2600
   (☎ 02-9327 7565)
   67 Victoria Rd, Bellevue Hill, NSW 2023
Netherlands
   (☎ 02-6273 3111)
   120 Empire Circuit, Yarralumla, ACT 2600
   (☎ 02-9387 6644)
   500 Oxford St, Bondi Junction, Sydney, NSW 2022
   (☎ 03-9867 7933)
   499 St Kilda Rd, Melbourne, Victoria 3004
New Zealand
   (☎ 02-9247 1344)
   Level 14/1 Alfred St, Circular Quay, Sydney, NSW 2000

Papua New Guinea
   (☎ 02-6273 3322)
   39-41 Forster Crescent, Yarralumla, ACT 2600
   (☎ 02-9299 5151)
   100 Clarence St, Sydney, NSW 2000
   (☎ 07-4052 1033)
   Level 15/15 Lake St, Cairns, Queensland 4870
Singapore
   (☎ 02-6273 3944)
   17 Forster Crescent, Yarralumla, ACT 2600
Thailand
   (☎ 02-6273 1149)
   111 Empire Circuit, Yarralumla, ACT 2600
   (☎ 02-9241 2542)
   131 Macquarie St, Sydney, NSW 2000
   (☎ 07-3846 7771)
   87 Annerley Rd, South Brisbane, Queensland 4102
   (☎ 03-9650 1714)
   277 Flinders Lane, Melbourne, Victoria 3000
UK
   (☎ 02-6270 6666)
   Commonwealth Ave, Yarralumla, ACT 2600
   (☎ 03-9650 3699)
   17/90 Collins St, Melbourne, Victoria 3000
   (☎ 02-9247 7521)
   16/1 Macquarie Place, Sydney Cove, Sydney, NSW 2000
USA
   (☎ 02-6214 5600)
   21 Moonah Place, Yarralumla, ACT 2600
   (☎ 02-9373 9200)
   19 Martin Place, Sydney, NSW 2000
   (☎ 03-9526 5900)
   553 St Kilda Rd, Melbourne, Victoria 3004

It's important to realise what your own embassy – the embassy of the country of which you are a citizen – can and can't do to help you if you get into trouble.

Generally speaking, it won't be much help in emergencies if the trouble you're in is remotely your own fault. Remember that while in Australia you are bound by Australian laws. Your embassy will not be sympathetic if you end up in jail after committing a crime locally, even if such actions are legal in your own country.

In genuine emergencies you might get some assistance, but only if other channels have been exhausted. For example, if you need to get home urgently, a free ticket home is exceedingly unlikely – the embassy would expect you to have insurance. If you have all your money and documents stolen, it might assist with getting a new passport, but a loan for onward travel is out of the question.

CUSTOMS

When entering Australia you can bring most articles in free of duty provided that customs is satisfied they are for personal use and that you'll be taking them with you when you leave. There's also a duty-free, per-person quota of 1125mL of alcohol, 250 cigarettes and dutiable goods up to the value of A\$400.

With regard to prohibited goods, two areas need particular attention. Number one is, of course, drugs – Australian customs can be extremely efficient when it comes to finding them. Unless you want to make first-hand investigations of conditions in Australian jails, don't bring illegal drugs with you.

Problem two is animal and plant quarantine. You will be asked to declare all goods of animal or vegetable origin – wooden spoons, straw hats, the lot – and show them to an official. The authorities are naturally keen to prevent weeds, pests or diseases getting into the country – Australia has so far managed to escape many of the agricultural pests and diseases prevalent in other parts of the world. Fresh food is also unpopular, particularly meat, cheese, fruit, vegetables and flowers, and there are restrictions on taking fruit and vegetables between states (see the boxed text on Interstate Quarantine in the Getting Around chapter).

Weapons and firearms are either prohibited or require a permit and safety testing. Other restricted goods include products (such as ivory) made from protected wildlife species, unapproved telecommunications devices and live animals.

There are duty-free stores at the international airports and their associated cities. Treat them with healthy suspicion: 'duty-free' is one of the world's most overworked catch phrases, and it is often just an excuse to sell things at prices you can easily beat by a little shopping around.

MONEY
Currency

Australia's currency is the Australian dollar, which comprises 100 cents. There are 5c,

10c, 20c, 50c, \$1 and \$2 coins, and \$5, \$10, \$20, \$50 and \$100 notes.

Although the smallest coin in circulation is 5c, prices are still marked in single cents, and then rounded to the nearest 5c when you come to pay.

There are no notable restrictions on importing or exporting travellers cheques. Cash amounts in excess of the equivalent of A\$5000 (any currency) must be declared on arrival or departure.

In this book, unless otherwise stated, all prices given in dollars refer to Australian dollars.

Exchange Rates

The Australian dollar fluctuates quite markedly against the US dollar, but it seems to stay pretty much around US\$0.65.

country	unit		A\$
Canada	C\$1	=	\$1.06
euro	€1	=	\$1.63
France	10FF	=	\$2.49
Germany	DM1	=	\$0.83
Hong Kong	HK\$10	=	\$2.00
Ireland	IR£1	=	\$2.07
Japan	¥100	=	\$1.48
New Zealand	NZ\$1	=	\$0.80
UK	UK£1	=	\$2.55
USA	US\$1	=	\$1.55

Exchanging Money

Changing foreign currency or travellers cheques is usually no problem at banks or licensed moneychangers such as Thomas Cook or American Express.

Travellers Cheques There is a variety of ways to carry your money. If your stay is limited, then travellers cheques are the most straightforward and generally enjoy a better exchange rate than foreign cash in Australia.

American Express, Thomas Cook and other well known international brands of travellers cheques are widely used. While a passport will usually be adequate for identification, it would be sensible to also carry a driver's licence or other form of identification.

Fees for changing foreign currency travellers cheques vary from bank to bank and from year to year. Currently, the 'big four' banks are ANZ, Commonwealth, National and Westpac (which is 'Bank of Melbourne' in Victoria and 'Challenge Bank' in WA). ANZ charges $6.50 for up to the equivalent of A$3000 (free for Visa travellers cheques or for more than A$3000), Westpac charges $7 for up to A$500 (free above that amount), and at the National and Commonwealth it's $5 and $7 respectively, regardless of the amount or number of cheques.

Buying Australian dollar travellers cheques is an option worth looking at. These can be exchanged immediately with the bank teller without being converted from a foreign currency and incurring commissions, fees and exchange rate fluctuations.

Credit Cards Credit cards are an alternative to carrying large numbers of travellers cheques. Visa, MasterCard, Diners Club and American Express (AMEX) are all widely accepted in Australia.

Cash advances from credit cards are available over the counter and from many automatic teller machines (ATMs), depending on the card.

If you're planning to rent cars, a credit card makes life much simpler; they're looked upon with much greater favour by rent-a-car agencies than nasty old cash; many agencies simply won't rent you a vehicle if you don't have a card.

Bank Accounts & ATMs

If you're planning to stay longer than just a month or so, it's worth considering other ways of handling money that give you more flexibility and are more economical.

Most travellers these days opt for an account that includes a cash card, which you can use to access your cash from ATMs all over Australia. Westpac, ANZ, National and Commonwealth bank branches are found nationwide. However, many smaller country towns don't have ATMs, so don't count on being able to find one everywhere.

ATMs can be used day or night, and most will accept cards from other banks. There is a limit on how much you can withdraw (usually around $1000 per day).

A great many businesses, including service stations, camping gear shops, restaurants and convenience stores, are linked into the EFTPOS (Electronic Funds Transfer at Point Of Sale) system. Here you can use your bank cash card to pay for services or purchases direct, and often withdraw cash as well. Credit cards can also be used to make local, Subscriber Trunk Dialling (STD) and international phone calls in special public telephones, found in most towns throughout the country.

Opening an account at an Australian bank is easy for overseas visitors provided they do it within six weeks of arrival. You simply present your passport and away you go. After six weeks it's much more complicated. A points system operates and you need to score a minimum of 100 points before you can have the privilege of letting the bank take your money. Passports and birth certificates are worth 70 points; an international driver's licence with photo earns you 40 points; and minor IDs such as credit cards get you 20 points. Just like a game show really! You must have at least one ID with a photograph.

If you don't have an Australian Tax File Number (TFN), interest earned from your funds will be taxed at the rate of 47% (see Work later in this chapter).

Costs

Compared with the USA, Canada and European countries, Australia is cheaper in some ways and more expensive in others. Manufactured goods tend to be more expensive: if they are imported they have the additional costs of transport and duties, and if they're locally manufactured they suffer from the extra costs entailed in making things in comparatively small quantities. Thus you pay more for clothes, cars and other manufactured items. On the other hand, food is normally both high in quality and low in cost.

Accommodation is also very reasonably priced. In virtually every town where backpackers are likely to stay there'll be a backpackers' hostel with dorm beds from $12 to $17, or a caravan park with camp sites for around $14 for two people and on-site vans from around $30, also for two.

The biggest cost in any trip to Australia will be transport, simply because it's such a vast country. If there's a group of you, buying a second-hand car is probably the most economical way to go – see Car in the Getting Around chapter.

How much to allow for your budget is obviously going to depend on what you'll be doing. We had a detailed letter from one reader who, in 96 days, averaged around $35 a day on accommodation (she mainly stayed in hostels), transport (she bought a 10,000km ticket with one of the major bus companies) and food (she mostly prepared her own meals).

The GST The Goods and Services Tax, to be introduced on 1 July 2000, will replace several other taxes (most notably the Wholesale Sales Tax). As a result, many services may increase in price, but the cost of a wide range of goods may fall. Shelf prices will include the GST – there will be no add-on such as occurs in the USA.

International air and sea travel to/from Australia will be GST-free, as will domestic air travel when purchased outside Australia by nonresidents. As well, if you purchase new or second-hand goods with a total minimum value of $300 from any one supplier within 28 days of departure from Australia, you will be entitled to a refund of any GST paid – ring the Australian Tax Office general inquiry line on ☎ 132861 for details.

Tipping

In Australia tipping isn't entrenched. It's only customary to tip in more expensive restaurants and only then if you feel it's necessary. If the service has been especially good and you decide to leave a tip, 10% of the bill is the usual amount. Taxi drivers don't expect tips (of course, they don't hurl it back at you if you decide to leave the change).

POST & COMMUNICATIONS
Postal Rates
Letters Australia's postal services are relatively efficient and reasonably cheap. It costs 45c to send a standard letter or postcard within Australia.

Australia Post has divided international destinations into two: Asia Pacific and Rest of the World and airmail letters cost $1.00/1.50 respectively. The cost of a postcard or aerogram is the same to any country: $1.00/80c respectively.

Parcels Only available to Europe and the USA, a seamail 1/1.5/2kg parcel costs $14/20/26. Each 500g over 2kg costs $3 with a maximum of 20kg. Airmail rates are considerably more expensive.

To all other destinations, including New Zealand, airmail is the only option. A 1/1.5/2kg parcel sent by 'economy air' to New Zealand and other Asia Pacific destinations costs $12/17/22 and $14/20/26 respectively, with a maximum of 20kg.

Sending Mail
Post offices are open Monday to Friday from 9 am to 5 pm. You can buy stamps on Saturday morning at post office agencies (operated from newsagencies) and from Australia Post shops in the major cities.

Receiving Mail
All post offices will hold mail for visitors, and some city GPOs (main post offices) have very busy poste restante sections. You can also have mail sent to you at American Express offices in big cities if you have an Amex card or carry Amex travellers cheques.

There are also a number of companies that, for a fee, will hold and forward mail to you.

Telephone
The Australian telecommunications industry is deregulated and there are a number of providers offering various services. Private phones are serviced by the two main players, Telstra and Optus, but it's in the mobile phone and payphone markets that other companies such as Vodafone, One.Tel, Unidial, Global One and AAPT are also operating, and it's where you'll find the most competition.

Payphones & Phonecards There's a wide range of local and international phonecards. Lonely Planet's eKno Communication Card is aimed specifically at independent travellers and provides budget international calls, a wide range of messaging services and free email. For local calls, you're usually better off with a local card.

You can join by phone from anywhere in Australia by dialling ☎ 1800 674 100 or online at www.ekno.lonelyplanet.com. Once you have joined, you can access the really cheap eKno local access rates from Sydney by dialling ☎ 02-8208 3000 and from Melbourne by dialling ☎ 03-9909 0888. If you are elsewhere in Australia, you can use eKno by dialling ☎ 1800 114 478.

Phonecards can be used in any Telstra public phone that accepts cards (virtually all do these days), or from a private phone by dialling a toll-free access number.

Long-distance calls made from payphones are considerably more expensive than calls made from private phones. If you will be using payphones to make a large number of calls it pays to look into the various cards available from providers other than Telstra.

The important thing is to know exactly how your calls are being charged, as the charges for calls vary from company to company. An explanatory booklet should be available from the card outlet – usually a newsagent or other shop.

Some public phones are set up to take only credit cards, and these too are convenient, although you need to keep an eye on how much the call is costing as it can quickly mount up. The minimum charge for a call on one of these phones is $1.20.

Local Calls Local calls from public phones cost 40c for an unlimited amount of time, while local calls from private phones cost 25c. Calls to mobile phones attract higher rates.

Long-Distance Calls & Area Codes It's also possible to make long-distance (sometimes known as STD) calls from virtually any public phone. Long-distance calls are cheaper in off-peak hours (basically outside normal business hours), and different service providers have different charges.

For the purpose of area (or STD) codes, Australia is divided into just four areas. All regular numbers (ie numbers other than mobiles or information services) have one of four area codes followed by an eight digit number. Long-distance calls (ie to more than about 50km away) within these areas are charged at long-distance rates, even though they have the same area code. Broadly, the 02 code covers NSW, 03 Victoria and Tasmania, 07 Queensland and 08 SA, WA and the NT. Keep in mind that area code boundaries do not necessarily coincide with state borders – for example, NSW has all four codes.

Generally, you don't have to dial the area code if you're making a call to someone with the same code as yours.

International Calls From most payphones you can also make ISD (International Subscriber Dialling) calls, although calls are often cheaper if using a provider other than Telstra, particularly at off-peak times.

When making overseas calls, the international dialling code will vary depending on which provider you are using.

International calls from Australia are among the cheapest you'll find anywhere, and there are often specials that bring the rates down even further. Off-peak times, if available, vary depending on the destination – call ☎ 12 552 for more details.

Country Direct is a service that gives callers in Australia direct access to operators in nearly 60 countries, to make reverse-charge (collect) or credit-card calls. For a full list of the countries hooked into this system, check any local White Pages telephone book.

Toll-Free Calls Many businesses and some government departments operate a toll-free service (prefix 1800), so no matter where you are ringing from around the country, it's a free call. Having said that, these numbers may not be accessible from certain areas, or from mobile phones, in which case you'll have to dial the normal number.

Many companies, such as the airlines, have numbers beginning with 13 or 1300, and these are charged at the rate of a local call. Often these numbers are Australia-wide, or may be applicable to a specific state or STD district only. Unfortunately, as with 1800 numbers, there's no way of telling without actually ringing the number.

Calls to these services still attract charges if you are calling from a mobile phone.

Information Calls Other odd numbers you may come across are those starting with 190. These numbers, usually recorded information services and the like, are provided by private companies, and your call is charged at anything from 35c to $5 or more per minute (more from mobile and payphones).

Mobile Phones Australia has two separate mobile networks: digital and the digitally-based CDMA. The latter has replaced the analogue network, which will be completely phased out during 2000. Ask the carrier you use in your home country whether your mobile phone will work in Australia.

While these two networks service more than 90% of the population, vast tracts of the country are not covered at all – the various service providers have coverage maps and you should check these before signing up. Basically the east coast and south-east of the continent are covered; it's when you move inland that it begins to thin out.

Phone numbers with the prefixes 014, 015, 017, 018, 019 (analogue) or 04xx or 04xxx (digital) are mobile phones – analogue numbers will cease operating with the phasing out of that network. The main mobile operators are the mostly government-owned Telstra, and two private companies Optus and Vodafone.

The caller is charged mobile rates on calls both to and from mobiles.

Email & Internet Access
If you've brought your computer and want to surf the Net, even just to access your email, there are service providers in all the capital cities and in many regional areas. The current major players include:

Australia On Line
☎ 1800 621 258, Web site www.ozonline .com.au (services Melbourne and Sydney only)
Oz Email
☎ 1800 805 874, Web site www.ozemail .com.au
Telstra Big Pond
☎ 1800 804 282, Web site www.bigpond.com

CompuServe users who want to access the service locally should phone CompuServe (☎ 1300 307 072) to get the local log-in numbers. There's a US$4 surcharge for non-Pacific customers.

Australia uses RJ-45 telephone plugs and Telstra EXI-160 four-pin plugs. Neither are universal – electronics shops such as Tandy and Dick Smith should be able to help if your plug doesn't suit. Check the Electricity section later in this chapter to see if your laptop will plug into the local power supply.

Keep in mind too that your PC-card modem may not work in Australia. The safest option is to buy a reputable 'global' modem before you leave home or buy a local PC-card modem once you get to Australia.

If you're not carrying a computer with you, cybercafes are popping up all over the place and many hostels have coin-operated Internet machines. These days most public libraries also have Internet access – it's normally free but you have to book. While all the larger libraries have terminals, not all will allow you to access your email.

The most convenient (and often the only) way to send and receive email from these places is to open an account with one of the free Web-based email services, such as Hot-Mail or Rocket Mail. This will allow you to access your mail from any Internet-connected machine running a standard Web browser.

Telecentres
In rural WA a government initiative has set up these community facilities. Telecentres provide Internet and email, fax and photocopying facilities and are mostly in the smaller towns.

INTERNET RESOURCES

The World Wide Web is a rich resource for travellers. You can research your trip, hunt down bargain air fares, book hotels, check on weather conditions or chat with locals and other travellers about the best places to visit (or avoid!).

At the Lonely Planet Web site (www.lonelyplanet.com) you'll find succinct summaries on travelling to Australia, postcards from other travellers and the Thorn Tree bulletin board, where you can ask questions before you go or dispense advice when you get back. You can also find travel news and updates to many of our most popular guidebooks, and the sub-WWWay section links you to the most useful travel resources elsewhere on the Web.

In addition to other sites listed throughout this chapter, try these useful Australian sites:

Guide to Australia
  www.csu.edu.au/education/australia.html
  (maintained by the Charles Sturt University in NSW, a mine of information, with links to Australian government departments, weather information, books, maps etc)
The Aussie Index
  www.aussie.com.au
  (fairly comprehensive list of Australian companies, educational institutions and government departments that maintain Web sites)

BOOKS

All good bookshops in the country have a section devoted to Australiana, with books on every Australian subject you care to mention. Some of the better-known bookshops are mentioned in the various city sections of later state chapters. If you find that any of the books listed in the following entries are out of print or are not available in bookstores, try a public library.

Lonely Planet

For more detail than is provided in this guide, Lonely Planet has *New South Wales*, *Northern Territory*, *Queensland*, *South Australia*, *Tasmania*, *Victoria* and *Western Australia* state guides, *Melbourne* and *Sydney* city guides and *Out to Eat* restaurant guides to Melbourne and Sydney.

Lonely Planet's *Bushwalking in Australia* describes 35 walks of different lengths and difficulty in various parts of the country. For trips into the Outback in your own vehicle *Outback Australia*, is the book to get.

Sean & David's Long Drive, a hilarious, offbeat road book by young Australian author Sean Condon, is one of the titles in Lonely Planet's 'Journeys' travel literature series.

Included in the Lonely Planet stable are the *Islands of Australia's Great Barrier Reef* and also the 'Pisces' diving guides. The Australian titles are *Coral Sea & Great Barrier Reef* and *Southeast Coast & Tasmania*.

Other Guidebooks

Burnum Burnum's Aboriginal Australia is subtitled 'a traveller's guide'. If you want to explore Australia from the Aboriginal point of view, this large and lavish hardback is the book for you.

There are a number of books about vehicle preparation and driving in the Outback, including *Explore Australia by Four-Wheel Drive* by Peter & Kim Wherrett.

Surfing Australia's East Coast by Aussie surf star Nat Young is a slim, cheap, comprehensive guide to the best breaks from Victoria to Fraser Island. He's also written the *Surfing & Sailboard Guide to Australia*, which covers the whole country.

For the complete story on the Great Barrier Reef, the *Reader's Digest Book of the Great Barrier Reef* is the one to go for. It's a hefty but comprehensive volume. There's also a cheaper abbreviated paperback version. *Australia's Wonderful Wildlife* is the shoestringer's equivalent of a coffee-table book – a cheap paperback published by the Womens Weekly with lots of great photos of the animals you didn't see, or those that didn't stay still when you pointed your camera at them.

There are state-by-state Reader's Digest guides to coasts and national parks, such as the *Coast of New South Wales*, and Gregory's guides to national parks, such as *National Parks of New South Wales* (a handy reference listing access, facilities, activities and so on for all parks).

Travel

Other accounts of travels in Australia include the marvellous *Tracks*, by Robyn Davidson. It's the amazing story of a young woman who set out alone to walk from Alice Springs to the Western Australia coast with her camels – proof that you can do anything if you try hard enough. It almost single-handedly inspired the current Australian interest in camel safaris!

Quite another sort of travel tale is Tony Horwitz's *One for the Road*, an entertaining account of a high-speed hitchhiking trip around Australia (Oz through a windscreen). In contrast, *The Ribbon and the Ragged Square*, by Linda Christmas, is an intelligent, sober account of a nine month investigatory trip around Oz by a *Guardian* journalist from England. There's lots of background, history, first-hand reporting and interviews.

Howard Jacobson's *In the Land of Oz* recounts his circuit of the country. It's quite amusing, but through most of the book you're left wondering when the long-suffering Ros is finally going to thump the twerp!

The late Bruce Chatwin's *The Songlines* tells of his experiences among central Australian Aborigines. It probably reveals more about the author than Aboriginal people, its best feature perhaps being some excellent, pithy anecdotes about modern Australia.

The journals of the early European explorers can be fairly hard going but make fascinating reading. The hardships that many of them endured is nothing short of incredible; you'll find their accounts in bookshops and public libraries.

History & Politics

For a good introduction to Australian history, read *A Short History of Australia*, a most accessible and informative general history by the late Manning Clark, the respected Aussie historian, or *The Fatal Shore*, Robert Hughes' bestselling account of the convict era.

Geoffrey Blainey's *The Tyranny of Distance* is an engrossing study of the problems of transport in this harsh continent and how it shaped the pattern of white settlement.

Finding Australia, by Russel Ward, traces the period from the first Aboriginal arrivals up to 1821. It's strong on Aborigines, women and the full story of foreign exploration, not just Cook's role. There's lots of fascinating detail, including information about the appalling crooks who ran the early colony. It's intended to be the first of a series.

The Exploration of Australia, by Michael Cannon, is a coffee-table book in size, presentation and price, but it's a fascinating reference book about the gradual European uncovering of the continent.

The Fatal Impact, by Alan Moorehead, begins with the voyages of Cook, regarded as one of the greatest and most humane explorers, and tells the tragic story of the European impact on Australia, Tahiti and Antarctica in the years that followed. It details how good intentions and the economic imperatives of the time led to disaster, corruption and annihilation. *Cooper's Creek*, also by Moorehead, is a classic account of the ill-fated Burke and Wills expedition; it dramatises the horrors and hardships faced by the early explorers.

John Pilger's *A Secret Country* is a vividly written book that deals with Australia's historical roots and its shabby treatment of Aboriginal people. It also posits an interesting theory on the dismissal of the Whitlam government in 1975.

To get an idea of life on a Kimberley cattle station last century, *Kings in Grass Castles* and *Sons in the Saddle*, both by Dame Mary Durack, are well worth getting hold of. Other books giving an insight into the pioneering days in the Outback include *Packhorse & Waterhole* by Gordon Buchanan, son of legendary drover Nat Buchanan who opened up large areas of the Northern Territory; *The Big Run*, by Jock Makin, a history of the Victoria River Downs cattle station in the Northern Territory; and *The Cattle King* by Ion Idriess, which details the life of the remarkable Sir Sidney Kidman, who set up a chain of stations in the Outback early this century.

Aboriginal People

The Australian Aborigines by Kenneth Maddock is a good cultural summary. The award-winning *Triumph of the Nomads*, by Geoffrey Blainey, chronicles the life of Australia's original inhabitants, and it convincingly demolishes the myth that Aborigines were 'primitive' people trapped on a hostile continent. They were in fact extremely successful in adapting to and overcoming the difficulties presented by the climate and seeming lack of resources – it's an excellent read.

For a sympathetic historical account of what's happened to the original Australians since Europeans arrived, read *Aboriginal Australians* by Richard Broome. *A Change of Ownership*, by Mildred Kirk, covers similar ground to Broome's book, but does so more concisely, focusing on the land rights movement and its historical background.

The Other Side of the Frontier, by Henry Reynolds, uses historical records to give a vivid account of an Aboriginal view of the arrival and takeover of Australia by Europeans. His *With the White People* identifies the essential Aboriginal contributions to the survival of the early white settlers. *My Place*, Sally Morgan's prize-winning autobiography, traces her discovery of her Aboriginal heritage. *The Fringe Dwellers*, by Nene Gare, describes just what it's like to be an Aborigine growing up in a white-dominated society.

Don't Take Your Love to Town by Ruby Langford and *My People* by Oodgeroo Noonuccal (Kath Walker) are also recommended reading for people interested in the experiences of Aboriginal people.

Songman, by Allan Baillie, is a fictional account of the life of an adolescent Aboriginal boy growing up in Arnhem Land in the days before white settlement.

General

If you want a souvenir of Australia, such as a photographic record, try one of the numerous coffee-table books like *A Day in the Life of Australia*. *Local Color – Travels in the Other Australia*, by Bill Bachman, is a photographic essay that includes fine prose by Tim Winton.

There are many other Australian books that make good gifts: books for children, with Australian illustrations, like Julie Vivar and Mem Fox's *Possum Magic*, Norman Lindsay's *The Magic Pudding*, Dorothy Wall's *Blinky Bill*, and *Snugglepot & Cuddlepie* by May Gibbs (one of the first bestselling Australian children's books), or cartoon books by excellent Australian cartoonists such as Michael Leunig and Kaz Cooke.

NEWSPAPERS & MAGAZINES

Australia's print media is dominated by a few big companies (Rupert Murdoch's News Corporation and Kerry Packer's Publishing & Broadcasting Ltd being the best known).

Each major city has at least one important daily, often backed up by a tabloid. The Fairfax group's *Sydney Morning Herald* and Melbourne *Age* are two of the most important dailies. There's also the *Australian*, a Murdoch-owned paper and the country's only national daily. The *Australian Financial Review* is the country's business daily.

Weekly newspapers and magazines include an Australian edition of *Time* and a combined edition of the Australian news magazine the *Bulletin* and *Newsweek*. The *Guardian Weekly* is widely available and good for international news, while the *Business Review Weekly* explores business matters in depth on a weekly basis.

Good outdoor and adventure magazines include *Wild* and *Outdoor Australia*, published quarterly, and *Rock*, published monthly.

Magazines from the UK and USA are also available, but usually with a delay of a month or so.

RADIO & TV

The national advertising-free TV and radio network is the Australian Broadcasting Corporation (ABC). In most places there are a couple of ABC radio stations and a host of commercial stations, both AM and FM, featuring the whole gamut of radio possibilities. Triple J is the ABC's youth FM radio station; it broadcasts nationally and is an excellent place to hear music (Australian and overseas) that's outside the pop mainstream, and to plug in to Australia's youth culture.

In Sydney and Melbourne there are the ABC, three commercial TV stations (Seven, Nine and Ten networks) and SBS, a government-sponsored multicultural TV station beamed to the capital cities and main regional centres. Around the country the number of TV stations varies from place to place; there are regional TV stations but in some remote areas the ABC may be all you can receive.

Imparja is an Aboriginal-owned and run commercial TV station that operates out of Alice Springs and has a 'footprint' that covers one-third of the country (mainly the NT, SA and western NSW). It broadcasts a variety of programs, ranging from 'soaps' to pieces made by and for Aboriginal people.

Pay TV is still in its infancy in Australia, with the major players (Optus Vision and Murdoch's Foxtel) jockeying for position and market share. Austar is the only provider outside the metropolitan areas.

VIDEO SYSTEMS
Australia uses the PAL system, and so prerecorded videos purchased in Australia may be incompatible with overseas systems. Check this before you buy.

PHOTOGRAPHY & VIDEO
Film & Equipment
Australian film prices are not too far out of line with those of the rest of the western world. A roll of 36-exposure Kodachrome 64 or Fujichrome 100 slide film costs around $26, including developing – less if you buy it in quantity.

There are plenty of camera shops in all the big cities and the standard of camera service is usually good. Many places offer one hour developing of print film. Melbourne is the main centre for developing Kodachrome slide film in the South-East Asian region.

Technical Tips
In the Outback you have to allow for the exceptional intensity of the light. Best results are obtained early in the morning and late in the afternoon. As the sun gets higher, colours appear washed out. You must also allow for the intensity of reflected light when taking

shots on the Barrier Reef or at other coastal locations. Especially in the summer, allow for temperature extremes and do your best to keep film as cool as possible, particularly after exposure. Other film and camera hazards are dust in the Outback and humidity in the far north tropical regions.

Photographing People
As in any country, politeness goes a long way when taking photographs; ask before taking pictures of people. Note that many Aboriginal people don't like having their photo taken, even from a distance.

TIME
Australia is divided into three time zones: the Western Standard Time zone (GMT/UTC plus eight hours) covers WA; Central Standard Time (plus 9½ hours) covers the NT and SA; and Eastern Standard Time (plus 10 hours) covers Tasmania, Victoria, NSW and Queensland. When it's noon in WA it's 1.30 pm in the NT and SA and 2 pm in the rest of the country.

'Daylight saving' – for which clocks are put forward an hour – operates in most states during summer and a month or so either side. However, things can get pretty confusing, what with WA, the NT and Queensland staying on standard time, while in Tasmania daylight saving starts a month earlier and finishes up to a month later than SA, Victoria and NSW.

ELECTRICITY
Voltage is 220-240V and the plugs are three-pin, but not the same as British three-pin plugs. Users of electric shavers or hairdryers should note that, apart from in fancy hotels, it's difficult to find converters to take either US flat two-pin plugs or the European round two-pin plugs. Adaptors for British plugs can be found in good hardware shops, chemists and travel agents. You can easily bend the US plugs to a slight angle to make them fit.

WEIGHTS & MEASURES
Australia uses the metric system. Petrol and milk are sold by the litre, apples and potatoes

by the kilogram, distance is measured by the metre or kilometre, and speed limits are in kilometres per hour (km/h). Colloquially, distance is often measured in the time it takes to get there, rather than in kilometres, eg Geelong is two hours drive away.

For those who need help with metric there's a conversion table at the back of this book.

HEALTH

Australia is a remarkably healthy country in which to travel, considering that such a large portion of it lies in the tropics. Tropical diseases such as malaria and yellow fever are unknown, diseases of insanitation such as cholera and typhoid are unheard of, and even some animal diseases such as rabies and foot-and-mouth disease have yet to be recorded.

Travel health depends on your predeparture preparations, your daily health care while travelling and how you handle any medical problem that does develop. While the potential dangers can seem quite frightening, in reality few travellers experience anything more than an upset stomach.

Lonely Planet's *Healthy Travel: Australia, New Zealand & the Pacific* is a handy pocket size and packed with useful information including pretrip planning, emergency first aid, immunisation and disease information and what to do if you get sick on the road. *Travel with Children* from Lonely Planet also includes advice on travel health for younger children.

There are also a number of excellent travel health sites on the Internet. From the Lonely Planet home page there are links at www.lonelyplanet.com/weblinks/wlprep.htm #heal to the World Health Organization and the US Centers for Disease Control & Prevention.

Predeparture planning

Immunisations There are no vaccination requirements for travel to Australia. If you are coming to Australia from a yellow-fever-infected country you will need proof of vaccination. It's always a good idea to keep childhood vaccinations, such as polio, tetanus and diphtheria, up to date.

Other Preparations Make sure you're healthy before you start travelling. If you are going on a long trip make sure your teeth are OK. If you wear glasses take a spare pair and your prescription.

If you require a particular medication take an adequate supply, as it may not be available. Take part of the packaging showing the generic name rather than the brand, which will make getting replacements easier. It's a good idea to have a legible prescription or letter from your doctor to show that you legally use the medication to avoid any problems.

Basic Rules

Water While town water supplies are generally safe to drink, many outback towns rely on bore water that may be unsuitable for human consumption – in these places, such as Marree in SA, the locals drink rainwater. Be wary of water from rivers, creeks and lakes as it may be polluted. If you aren't sure of the water quality, the best way to purify water is to boil it for at least 10 minutes.

Environmental Hazards

Asthma Australia poses a significant risk for visiting asthmatics, with air-borne allergens such as dust and pollen being the main culprits – in fact, Australia has one of the world's highest incidences of asthma. The main danger periods are winter in the south and April/May and October in the north.

Inhalers (or puffers) are available without prescription at pharmacies.

Heat Exhaustion Dehydration and salt deficiency can cause heat exhaustion. Take time to acclimatise to high temperatures, drink sufficient liquids and do not do anything too physically demanding.

Salt deficiency is characterised by fatigue, lethargy, headaches, giddiness and muscle cramps; salt tablets may help, but adding extra salt to your food is better.

Heatstroke This serious, occasionally fatal, condition can occur if the body's heat-regulating mechanism breaks down and the body temperature rises to dangerous levels.

Long, continuous periods of exposure to high temperatures and insufficient fluids can leave you vulnerable to heatstroke.

The symptoms are feeling unwell, not sweating very much (or at all) and a high body temperature (39 to 41°C or 102 to 106°F). Where sweating has ceased, the skin becomes flushed and red. Severe, throbbing headaches and lack of coordination will also occur, and the sufferer may be confused or aggressive. Eventually the victim will become delirious or convulse. Hospitalisation is essential, but in the interim get victims out of the sun, remove their clothing, cover them with a wet sheet or towel and then fan continually. Give fluids if they are conscious.

Prickly Heat Prickly heat is an itchy rash caused by excessive perspiration trapped under the skin. It usually strikes people who have just arrived in a hot climate. Keeping cool, bathing often, drying the skin and using a mild talcum or prickly heat powder or resorting to air-conditioning may help.

Sunburn In the tropics, the desert or at high altitude, you can get sunburnt surprisingly quickly, even through cloud. Use a sunscreen, a hat, and a barrier cream for your nose and lips. Calamine lotion or a commercial after-sun preparation are good for mild sunburn. Protect your eyes with good quality sunglasses, particularly if you will be near water, sand or snow.

Hypothermia Too much cold can be just as dangerous as too much heat. If you are hiking in cold climates, such as in the alpine areas of NSW, Victoria and Tasmania, you should always be prepared for cold, wet or windy conditions.

Hypothermia occurs when the body loses heat faster than it can produce it and the core temperature of the body falls. It is surprisingly easy to progress from very cold to dangerously cold due to a combination of wind, wet clothing, fatigue and hunger, even if the air temperature is above freezing. It is best to dress in layers; silk, wool and some of the new artificial fibres are all good insulating materials. A hat is important, as a lot of heat is lost through the head. A strong, waterproof outer layer (and a 'space' blanket for emergencies) is essential. Carry basic supplies, including food containing simple sugars to generate heat quickly, and fluid to drink.

Symptoms of hypothermia are exhaustion, numb skin (particularly of the toes and fingers), shivering, slurred speech, irrational or violent behaviour, lethargy, stumbling, dizzy spells, muscle cramps and violent bursts of energy. Irrationality may take the form of sufferers claiming they are warm and trying to take off their clothes.

To treat mild hypothermia, first get the person out of the wind and/or rain, remove their clothing if it's wet and replace it with dry, warm clothing. Give them hot liquids – not alcohol – and some high-kilojoule, easily digestible food. Do not rub victims: instead, allow them to slowly warm themselves. This should be enough to treat the early stages of hypothermia. The early recognition and treatment of mild hypothermia is the only way to prevent severe hypothermia, which is a critical condition.

Motion Sickness Eating lightly before and during a trip will reduce the chances of motion sickness. If you are prone to motion sickness try to find a place that minimises movement – near the wing on aircraft, close to midships on boats, near the centre on buses. Fresh air usually helps; reading and cigarette smoke don't. Commercial motion-sickness preparations, which can cause drowsiness, have to be taken before the trip commences. Ginger (available in capsule form) and peppermint (including mint-flavoured sweets) are natural preventatives.

Infectious Diseases

Diarrhoea Simple things like a change of water, food or climate can all cause a mild bout of diarrhoea, but a few rushed toilet trips with no other symptoms is not indicative of a major problem.

Dehydration is the main danger with any diarrhoea, particularly in children or the elderly as it can occur quite quickly. Under all circumstances *fluid replacement* (at least equal to the volume being lost) is the most important thing to remember. Weak black tea with a little sugar, soda water, or soft drinks allowed to go flat and diluted 50% with clean water are all good. With severe diarrhoea a rehydrating solution is preferable to replace minerals and salts lost. Commercially available oral rehydration salts (ORS) are very useful; add them to boiled or bottled water. In an emergency you can make up a solution of six teaspoons of sugar and a half teaspoon of salt to a litre of boiled or bottled water. You need to drink at least the same volume of fluid that you are losing in bowel movements and vomiting. Urine is the best guide to the adequacy of replacement – if you have small amounts of concentrated urine, you need to drink more. Keep drinking small amounts often. Stick to a bland diet as you recover.

Gut-paralysing drugs such as loperamide or diphenoxylate can be used to bring relief from the symptoms, although they do not actually cure the problem. Only use these drugs if you do not have access to toilets, eg if you *must* travel. Note that these drugs are not recommended for children under 12 years.

Fungal Infections Fungal infections occur more commonly in hot weather and are usually found on the scalp, between the toes (athlete's foot) or fingers, in the groin and on the body (ringworm). You get ringworm (which is a fungal infection, not a worm) from infected animals or other people. Moisture encourages these infections.

To prevent fungal infections wear loose, comfortable clothes, avoid artificial fibres, wash frequently and dry yourself carefully. If you do get an infection, wash the infected area at least daily with a disinfectant or medicated soap and water, and rinse and dry well. Apply an antifungal cream or powder like tolnaftate. Try to expose the infected area to air or sunlight as much as possible and wash all towels and underwear in hot water, change them often and let them dry in the sun.

HIV/AIDS Infection with the human immunodeficiency virus (HIV) may lead to acquired immune deficiency syndrome (AIDS), which is a fatal disease. Any exposure to blood, blood products or body fluids may put the individual at risk. The disease is often transmitted through sexual contact or dirty needles.

Sexually Transmitted Diseases (STDs)
STDs include gonorrhoea, herpes and syphilis; sores, blisters or rashes around the genitals and discharges or pain when urinating are common symptoms. With some STDs, such as wart virus or chlamydia, symptoms may be less marked or not observed at all, especially in women. Chlamydia infection can cause infertility in men and women before any symptoms have been noticed. Syphilis symptoms eventually disappear completely but the disease continues and can cause severe problems in later years. While abstinence from sexual contact is the only 100% effective prevention, using condoms is also effective. The treatment of gonorrhoea and syphilis is with antibiotics. The different sexually transmitted diseases each require specific antibiotics.

Insect-Borne Diseases

Dengue Fever Small outbreaks of this viral disease have been reported from Far North Queensland. Unlike the malaria mosquito, the *Aedes aegypti* mosquito, which transmits the dengue virus, is most active during the day, and is found mainly in urban areas, in and around human dwellings.

Signs and symptoms of dengue fever include a sudden onset of high fever, headache, joint and muscle pains (hence its old name, 'breakbone fever'), nausea and vomiting. A rash of small red spots sometimes appears three to four days after the onset of fever. In the early phase of illness, dengue may be mistaken for other infectious diseases, including malaria and influenza. Minor bleeding such as nose bleeds may occur in the course of the illness. Severe complications of the disease are unknown in Australia. Recovery even from simple dengue fever may be prolonged, with tiredness lasting for several weeks.

You should seek medical attention as soon as possible if you think you may be infected. A blood test can exclude malaria and indicate the possibility of dengue fever. There is no specific treatment for dengue. Aspirin should be avoided, as it increases the risk of haemorrhaging. There is no vaccine against dengue fever. The best prevention is to avoid mosquito bites at all times by covering up, using insect repellents containing the compound DEET, and mosquito nets.

Ross River Fever This viral disease, properly known as epidemic polyarthritis, is transmitted by some species of mosquito. The disease is mostly found in eastern Australia where outbreaks are most likely to occur in January and February. Epidemics have also occurred in the NT. Flu-like symptoms (muscle and joint pain, rashes, fever, headache and tiredness) are possible indicators, but blood tests are necessary for a positive diagnosis. Risk of infection for travellers is usually very low.

Unfortunately, there is no treatment for Ross River Fever, although the symptoms can be relieved. Conventional wisdom has it that the symptoms do not last for more than a few months, but there are now some serious doubts about this as some people still feel the effects, mainly chronic fatigue, some years after contracting the disease. Avoiding mosquito bite is the best preventative against the disease.

Cuts, Bites & Stings

Cuts & Scratches Wash well and treat any cut with an antiseptic such as povidone-iodine. Where possible avoid bandages and Band-Aids, which can keep wounds wet. Coral cuts are notoriously slow to heal and if they are not adequately cleaned, small pieces of coral can become embedded in the wound.

Bites & Stings Bee and wasp stings are usually painful rather than dangerous. However, people who are allergic to them may have severe breathing difficulties and require urgent medical care. Calamine lotion or a sting relief spray will give relief and ice packs will reduce the pain and swelling. There are some spiders with dangerous bites but antivenins are usually available.

Scorpions, which often shelter in shoes or clothing, can give you a very painful sting. Certain cone shells found in Australia can sting dangerously or even fatally and there are various fish, such as stone fish, and other sea creatures that can sting or bite dangerously or are dangerous to eat – seek local advice.

Jellyfish Avoid contact with these sea creatures, which have stinging tentacles – seek local advice before swimming. The sting from the box jellyfish found in coastal waters around northern Australia is potentially fatal, but stings from most jellyfish are simply rather painful. Dousing in vinegar will deactivate any stingers that have not 'fired'. For minor stings, calamine lotion, antihistamines and analgesics may reduce the reaction and relieve the pain.

See Dangers & Annoyances later in this chapter for more information.

Leeches & Ticks Leeches may be present in damp rainforest conditions; they attach themselves to your skin to suck your blood. Trekkers often get them on their legs or in their boots. Salt or a lighted cigarette end will make them fall off. Do not pull them off, as the bite is then more likely to become infected. Clean and apply pressure if the point of attachment is bleeding. An insect repellent may keep them away.

You should always check all over your body if you have been walking through a potentially tick-infested area as ticks can cause skin infections and other more serious diseases. If a tick is found attached, press down around the tick's head with tweezers, grab the head and gently pull upwards. Avoid pulling the rear of the body as this may squeeze the tick's gut contents through the attached mouth parts into the skin, increasing the risk of infection and disease. Smearing chemicals on the tick will not make it let go and is not recommended.

Snakes To minimise your chances of being bitten, always wear boots, socks and long trousers when walking through undergrowth where snakes may be present. Don't put your hands into holes and crevices, and be careful when collecting firewood.

Snake bites do not cause instantaneous death and antivenins are usually available. Immediately wrap the bitten limb tightly, as you would for a sprained ankle, and then attach a splint to immobilise it. Keep the victim still and seek medical help. Having as complete a description as possible of the snake will help ensure the right treatment is given. Don't attempt to catch the snake if there is a possibility of being bitten again. Tourniquets and sucking out the poison are now comprehensively discredited.

Women's Health
Gynaecological Problems Antibiotic use, synthetic underwear, sweating and contraceptive pills can lead to fungal vaginal infections, especially when travelling in hot climates. Fungal infections are characterised by a rash, itch and discharge and can be treated with a vinegar or lemon-juice douche, or with yogurt. Nystatin, miconazole or clotrimazole pessaries or vaginal cream are the usual treatment. Maintaining good personal hygiene and wearing loose-fitting clothes and cotton underwear may help prevent these infections.

Sexually transmitted diseases are a major cause of vaginal problems. Symptoms include a smelly discharge, painful intercourse and sometimes a burning sensation when urinating. Medical attention should be sought and male sexual partners must also be treated. For more details see the section on sexually transmitted diseases earlier in this chapter. Besides abstinence, the best thing is to practise safer sex using condoms.

WOMEN TRAVELLERS
Australia is generally a safe place for women travellers, although it's probably best to avoid walking alone late at night in any of the major cities and towns. Sexual harassment is unfortunately still second nature to many Aussie males and it's hard to say when you might be confronted by these individuals. It's mostly true to say that the further you get from 'civilisation' (ie the big cities), the less enlightened your average

Aussie male is going to be about women's issues; you're far more likely to meet an 'ocker' than a 'snag' (sensitive new-age guy)!

Female hitchers should exercise care at all times (see the section on hitching in the Getting Around chapter).

GAY & LESBIAN TRAVELLERS
Australia is a popular destination for gay and lesbian travellers. Certainly the profile of gay and lesbian travel has risen significantly in the last few years, partly as a result of the publicity surrounding the Gay & Lesbian Mardi Gras in Sydney. Throughout the country, but especially on the east coast, there are tour operators, travel agents, resorts and accommodation places that are exclusively gay and lesbian, or gay friendly.

Certain areas are the focus of the gay and lesbian communities: Cairns and Noosa in Queensland, Sydney, the Blue Mountains and the south coast in NSW, and Melbourne, Daylesford and Hepburn Springs in Victoria, are all popular areas.

As is the case with the attitude to women, the further into the country you get, the more likely you are to run into fairly rampant homophobia. Homosexual acts are legal in all states.

The gay telephone counselling services (you'll find them in most capital cities) are often a useful source of general information.

Publications
Australia's gay community produces a wide range of publications. All major cities have gay newspapers, which are available from major gay and lesbian venues and from newsagents in popular gay and lesbian residential areas. You'll also find gay business directories that list, among other things, travel agents, tour operators and accommodation.

National gay lifestyle magazines include *OutRage*, *Campaign*, *Lesbians on the Loose* and the art magazine, *Blue*.

Tour Operators
Tour operators that cater exclusively or partly for gay and lesbian travellers include:

BreakOut Travel & Tours
   (☎ 02-9558 8229, fax 9332 3326)
   77 Oxford St, Darlinghurst, Sydney, NSW
   2010, Web site www.fod.com.au
Friends of Dorothy
   (☎ 02-9360 3616, fax 9332 3326)
   77 Oxford St, Darlinghurst, Sydney, NSW
   2010, Web site www.fod.com.au
Beyond the Blue
   (☎ 02-9221 6377, fax 9557 4332)
   300 George St, Sydney NSW 2000, Web site
   www.beyondblue.com.au

Organisations

The Australian Gay & Lesbian Tourism Association, PO Box 208, Darlinghurst, NSW 2010, promotes gay and lesbian travel – it's not a booking office but has a lot of useful information on gay-friendly operators in all states. Its Web site is www.aglta.asn.au.

TRAVEL WITH CHILDREN

There are no special considerations when travelling with children in Australia. Relatively few places are reluctant to accept kids, and in fact children are fairly well catered for.

All cities and most major towns have centrally located public rooms where mothers (and sometimes fathers) can go to nurse their baby or change its nappy – check with the local tourist office or city council for details. While many Australians have a relaxed attitude about breast-feeding in public, others frown on it.

Most motels and the better-equipped caravan parks supply cots and baby's baths, and many have playgrounds and swimming pools – many motels also have in-house children's videos and child-minding services. While a lot of cafes and restaurants don't exactly welcome small children with open arms, others have high chairs and kids' menus – or will happily provide small serves from the main menu. The larger car-rental companies will provide baby seats, but parents are expected to secure the seat in the car.

If you want to leave junior behind for a few hours, some of Australia's numerous licensed child-care agencies have places set aside for casual care. To find them, check under 'Child

Care Centres' in the *Yellow Pages* telephone book, or phone the local council for a list of local centres. Typically they look after children aged from one to five years; many do not accept very young infants. Licensed centres are subject to government regulation and usually have a high standard – to be on the safe side avoid unlicensed ones.

Child concessions often apply for such things as accommodation, tours, entry fees and air, bus and train transport. Discounts can be as high as 50% of the adult rate. However, the definition of 'child' varies from under 12 to under 18 years.

For accommodation, concessions generally apply to children under 12 years sharing the same room as adults. With the major airlines, infants travel free provided they don't occupy a seat – child fares apply between the ages of three and 15 years, but student and normal adult discount fares are usually more attractive. Bus companies have various discounting arrangements for children. Greyhound, for example, give a 20% discount to children over three years and all students. Children under three can travel free if they are nursed, or can have a seat for half the adult fare.

Lonely Planet's *Travel with Children* contains plenty of useful information. As well, the various Travellers Medical & Vaccination Centres around Australia (there's at least one in every capital city) have a leaflet on the subject.

USEFUL ORGANISATIONS
National Parks Organisations

The Biodiversity Group of Environment Australia (EABG) is a Commonwealth body responsible for Kakadu and Uluru national parks in the Northern Territory, national parks in the ACT, some offshore areas such as the Cocos (Keeling) Islands and Norfolk Island, and also international conservation issues such as whaling and migratory bird conventions. It's based at John Gorton Building, King Edward Terrace, Parkes, ACT 2600 (GPO Box 787, Canberra 2601, ☎ 02-6274 1111, fax 6274 1123). Look under 'biodiversity' on Environment Australia Online's Web site at www.ea.gov.au.

Otherwise, Australia's conservation areas are managed by the various states. The main addresses for information are:

New South Wales
National Parks & Wildlife Service (☎ 02-9585 6333, fax 9585 6527),
Level 1, 43 Bridge St, PO Box 1967, Hurstville, NSW 2220, Web site www.npws.nsw.gov.au

Northern Territory
Parks & Wildlife Commission of the NT (☎ 08-8999 5511, fax 8999 4558),
25 Chung Wah Terrace, Palmerston, NT 0830, (PO Box 496, Palmerston, NT 0831), Web site www.nt.gov.au/paw
Parks Australia North (an arm of Environment Australia; ☎ 08-8946 4300, fax 8981 3497), 80 Mitchell St, Darwin, NT 0800 (PO Box 1260, Darwin NT 0801)

Queensland
Environmental Protection Agency (☎ 07-3227 8186, fax 3227 8749)
160 Ann St, Brisbane, Queensland 4000 (PO Box 155, Brisbane Albert St 4002), Web site www.env.qld.gov.au

South Australia
National Parks & Wildlife SA (☎ 08-8204 1910, fax 8204 1919)
The Environment Shop, 77 Grenfell St, Adelaide, SA 5000 (GPO Box 1047, Adelaide 5001)

Tasmania
Tasmania Parks & Wildlife Service (☎ 03-6233 6191, fax 6233 2158)
134 Macquarie St, Hobart, Tasmania 7000 (PO Box 44A, Hobart, Tasmania 7001), Web site www.parks.tas.gov.au

Victoria
Department of Natural Resources & Environment (☎ 03-9637 8000, fax 9637 8150)
8 Nicholson St, PO Box 500, East Melbourne, Victoria 3002, Web site www.nre.vic.gov.au

Western Australia
Department of Conservation & Land Management (☎ 08-9334 0333, fax 9334 0498)
50 Hayman Rd, Como, Perth, WA 6152 (Locked Bag 104, Bentley DC, WA 6983), Web site www.calm.wa.gov.au

Australian Conservation Foundation

The Australian Conservation Foundation (ACF) is the largest nongovernment organisation involved in conservation. It covers a wide range of issues, including the greenhouse effect and depletion of the ozone layer, the negative effects of logging, the preservation of rainforests and the problems of land degradation. With the growing focus on conservation issues and the increasing concern of the Australian public in regard to their environment, the conservation vote is becoming more and more important to all political parties.

ACF's contact details are (☎ 03-9416 1166, fax 9416 0767) 340 Gore St, Fitzroy, Victoria 3065, Web site www.acfonline.org.au.

Wilderness Society

The Wilderness Society was formed by conservationists who had been unsuccessful in preventing the damming of Lake Pedder in south-western Tasmania, but were determined to prevent a hydroelectricity project being built on the wild Franklin River, also in Tasmania's south-west. This was one of Australia's first major conservation confrontations. It ended in success in 1983 when the Australian High Court ruled against damming the Franklin.

The Wilderness Society is involved in issues such as forest management and logging throughout Australia. All its income is derived from memberships, donations and merchandising – there are Wilderness Society shops in most states where you can buy books, T-shirts, posters, badges etc.

Its head office is at 130 Davey St, Hobart, Tasmania 7000 (☎ 03-6234 9799, fax 6224 1497) and its Web site is www.wilderness.org.au.

Australian Trust for Conservation Volunteers

This nonprofit group, known as ATCV, organises practical conservation projects (such as tree planting, walking track construction and flora and fauna surveys) for volunteers – overseas visitors are welcome. It's an excellent way to get involved with the conservation movement and visit some interesting areas of the country. Past volunteers have found themselves working in places such as Tasmania, Kakadu and Fraser Island.

Australia for the Traveller with a Disability

Disability awareness in Australia is reasonably high, especially in the lead-up to the 2000 Paralympics in New South Wales. Most tourist commissions are gathering information in their state about accessible tourist attractions and accommodation. Legislation requires that new accommodation must meet accessibility standards and tourist operators must not discriminate.

Many of Australia's key tourist attractions provide access so call ahead to confirm your needs. Tour operators with accessible vehicles operate from most capital cities. Contact the local disability organisation or even the tourist office for a referral.

Information

Reliable information is the key ingredient for travellers with a disability and the best source is the National Information Communication and Recreation Network or NICAN (☎/TTY 02-6285 3713, TTY 1800 806 769, fax 02-6285 3714, nican@spirit.com.au), PO Box 407, Curtin, ACT 2605. It's an Australia-wide directory providing information on access issues, accessible accommodation, sporting and recreational activities, transport and specialist tour operators.

The Australian Tourist Commission (see the Tourist Offices section earlier in this chapter for contact details) publishes *Travel in Australia for People with Disabilities*, which contains travel tips and transport and contact addresses of organisations on a state-by-state basis.

Other sources of quality information are the Disability Information Resource Centre (DIRC) in SA (☎ 08-8223 7522, dirc@dircsa.org.au) and the Independent Living Centre in WA (☎ 08-9382 2011, ilcwa@iinet.com.au), and Vicnet's Web site Disability page, www.vicnet.net.au/disability.

Easy Access Australia can be ordered from easyaccessaustralia.com.au. *Accessing Sydney* was being updated at the time of writing, while *Accessing Melbourne is* available from RACV outlets and the Melbourne Information Centre. Brisbane City Council's *Access Brisbane* is available from council offices. *Accessible Queensland* is a schedule of service providers, published by Tourism Queensland. *Darwin Without Steps* is available from local councils.

Places to Stay

Accessible accommodation in Australia is generally good – check with NICAN, state-based disability organisations and easyaccessaustralia.com.au. The state motoring organisations publish comprehensive accommodation guides and give some wheelchair-access information. However, it is best to confirm that facilities suit your needs. Ask at information centres for lists of accessible accommodation and tourist attractions, a good example is Toowomba's 'Access the Best'. Beware that some information may not have been independently assessed.

Hotels in the capital cities such as Hyatt, Hilton, Sheraton, Accor and All Seasons have accessible rooms. More affordable are Novotel and Ibis Hotels, while motel chains such as Flag, Best Western and Budget have properties with accessible rooms (but of varying quality – check first).

Youth Hostel Association (YHA) hostels have limited accessible accommodation (see the Accommodation section later in this chapter for YHA membership and travel centres). *YHA Central (☎ 02-9281 9111)*, opposite Sydney's Central station, has seven excellent accessible rooms.

Two wheelchair-accessible resorts in NSW are *Clark Bay Farm (☎/fax 02-4476 1640)* at Narooma and *Byron Bay Rainforest Resort (☎ 02-6685 6139, fax 6685 8754, 39-75 Broken Head Rd, Byron Bay)*.

Getting Around

Air The Carers Concession Card, which is accepted by Qantas (☎ 13 1313, TTY 1800 652 660) and Ansett (☎ 13 1300, TTY 1800 623 195), entitles a disabled person and the carer travelling

Australia for the Traveller with a Disability

with them to a 50% discount on the full economy fare; call NICAN for eligibility and an application form. Ansett also has its ANSACARE system to record your details and needs – done once only, eliminating repetition. Some of their aircraft have a larger 'accessible' toilet. All of Australia's major airports have dedicated parking spaces, wheelchair access to terminals, accessible toilets and skychairs to convey passengers onto planes via airbridges. At some regional airports a fork-lift arrangement is used to lift wheelchair passengers to the plane.

Bus This form of travel is not generally an option for wheelchair users. However, there can be good facilities on other forms of transport.

Train NSW Countrylink (☎ 02-9379 4850, reservations ☎ 13 2232) operates the XPT from Sydney to Melbourne, Brisbane (via Murwillumbah), Coffs Harbour, Dubbo and Wagga Wagga, while the Xplorer travels to Moree, Tamworth and Canberra. Each train has at least one carriage (usually the buffet car) with an accessible toilet and a seat removed for a wheelchair. Countrylink's *Guide for People with Special Requirements* details this and other services. Accessible public transport in Sydney is limited but the monorail from Darling Harbour and Sydney light rail from Central station cover parts of the city.

The *Indian Pacific* (see Train in the Getting Around chapter) provides wheelchair access with an en suite bathroom with grab rails – but it will not suit all.

Queensland Rails' *Tilt Train* from Brisbane to Rockhampton has a wheelchair accessible carriage giving access to Maryborough (Hervey Bay via accessible coach).

Melbourne's suburban rail network is accessible and V/Line's country trains and stations are equipped with ramps. Some rural services employ hoist-equipped accessible coaches. Twenty-four hours advance booking is required; V/Line Customer Service (☎ 9619 2578; ask for wheelchair reservations) is at Spencer St station. Ring ☎ 13 1638 for metropolitan, ☎ 13 1196 for country and ☎ 13 2147 for interstate services information. The Travellers' Aid Society (☎ 03-9670 2873), also at Spencer St station, provides a meet-and-greet service (arrange in advance). It is also at 169 Swanston St (☎ 9654 7690), where there are carers, a cafe and accessible showers and toilets.

Car Avis (☎ 1800 225 533) and Hertz (☎ 13 3039) offer hire cars with hand controls at no extra charge for pick-up at capital cities and the major airports, but advance notice is required. Several hire vehicle companies offering a range of vehicles are available in NSW – check with Paraquad Assn NSW or AQA NSW.

Parking The international wheelchair symbol (blue on a white background) for parking in allocated bays is recognised. Maps of central business districts showing accessible routes, toilets etc are available from major city councils, some regional councils and at information centres.

Taxi Most taxi companies in major cities and towns have modified vehicles to take wheelchairs.

Ferry TT Line's *Spirit of Tasmania* (reservations ☎ 13 2010) operates between Melbourne and Devonport in Tasmania. It has four accessible cabins and wheelchair access to the public areas on the ship.

Bruce Cameron

Most projects are either for a weekend or a week and all food, transport and accommodation is supplied in return for a small contribution to help cover costs. Most travellers who take part in ATCV join a Conservation Experience package that lasts six weeks and includes up to six different projects. The cost is $840, and further days/weeks can be added for $20/140. Check out its Web site at www.atcv.com.au.

Contact the head office (☎ 03-5333 1483, fax 5333 2166) at PO Box 423, Ballarat, Vic 3350, or the state offices listed below.

New South Wales
  (☎ 02-9564 1244, fax 9564 1474)
  18/42 Addison Rd, Marrickville, NSW 2048
Northern Territory
  (☎ 08-8981 3206, fax 8981 9052)
  PO Box 2358, Darwin, NT 0801
Queensland
  (☎ 07-3846 0893, fax 3846 0894)
  GPO Box 2673, Brisbane, Queensland 4101
South Australia
  (☎ 08-8207 8747, 8207 8755)
  PO Box 419, Campbelltown, Adelaide, SA 5074
Tasmania
  (☎ 03-6224 4911, fax 6224 4913)
  PO Box 940, Hobart, Tasmania 7001
Victoria
  (☎ 03-9686 5554, fax 9686 5557)
  534 City Rd, South Melbourne, Victoria 3205
Western Australia
  (☎ 08-9336 6911, fax 9336 6811)
  PO Box 188, North Fremantle, WA 6159

National Trust

The National Trust is dedicated to preserving historic buildings and artefacts, as well as important natural features, in all parts of Australia. It owns and manages a large number of properties, most of which are open to the public. Many other heritage sites are 'classified' by the National Trust to ensure their preservation.

The National Trust produces some excellent literature, including a fine series of walking-tour guides to many cities, large and small. These guides are often available from local tourist offices or from National Trust offices and are usually free whether you're a member of the National Trust or

not. Membership is well worth considering, however, because it entitles you to free entry to most of its properties.

Annual membership costs $49 for individuals ($35 concession) and $68 for families ($49 concession), and there is a $30 joining fee. This includes the monthly or quarterly magazine put out by the state organisation that you join. Addresses of the National Trust state offices are:

Australian Capital Territory
  (☎ 02-6239 5222, fax 6239 5333)
  2 Light St, Griffith, ACT 2603
New South Wales
  (☎ 02-9258 0123, fax 9251 1110)
  Observatory Hill, via Watson Rd, The Rocks, NSW 2000
Northern Territory
  (☎ 08-8981 2848, fax 8981 2379)
  4 Burnett Place, Myilly Point, Darwin, NT 0800
Queensland
  (☎ 07-3229 1788, fax 3229 0146)
  Old Government House, QUT Campus, 2 George St, Brisbane, Queensland 4000
South Australia
  (☎ 08-8223 1655, fax 8232 2856)
  452 Pulteney St, Adelaide, SA 5000
Tasmania
  (☎ 03-6344 6233, fax 6344 4033)
  Franklin House, 413 Hobart Rd, Launceston, Tasmania 7250
Victoria
  (☎ 03-9654 4711, fax 9650 5397)
  Tasma Terrace, 4 Parliament Place, Melbourne, Victoria 3002
Western Australia
  (☎ 08-9321 6088, fax 9324 1571)
  Old Observatory, 4 Havelock St, West Perth, WA 6005

WWOOF

WWOOF (Willing Workers on Organic Farms) is well established in Australia. The idea is that you do a few hours work each day on a farm in return for bed and board. Some places have a minimum stay of a couple of days but many will take you for just a night.

There are about 1300 WWOOF associates in Australia, mostly in Victoria, New South Wales and Queensland. As the name says, the farms are supposed to be organic but that isn't always so. Some places aren't even farms – you might help out at a pottery or do the books at a seed wholesaler. Whether they have a farm or just a vegie patch, most participants in the scheme are concerned to some extent with alternative lifestyles.

To join WWOOF send $35/40 for singles/couples to WWOOF, Mt Murrindal Coop, Buchan, Victoria 3885 (☎ 03-5155 0218, fax 5155 0342). It has a Web site at www.wwoof.com.au. WWOOF will send you a membership number and a booklet that lists participating places all over Australia.

DANGERS & ANNOYANCES
Animal Hazards
There are a few unique and sometimes dangerous creatures, although it's unlikely that you'll come across any of them, particularly if you stick to the cities. Here's a rundown just in case.

Snakes The best-known danger in the Australian bush, and the one that captures the imagination of most visitors, is snakes. There are many venomous snakes but few are aggressive – unless you're interfering with one, or have the bad fortune to stand on one, it's extremely unlikely that you'll be bitten. The golden rule is 'if you see a snake leave it alone.' *Don't* try to catch or kill it.

See the Health section earlier in this chapter for treating snake bites.

Spiders Nasty spiders include the funnel-web, the redback and the white-tail. The funnel-web spider is found in NSW (and some parts of southern Queensland and eastern Victoria) and its bite is treated in the same way as snake bite. For redback bites, apply ice and seek medical attention.

Insects For four to six months of the year you'll have to cope with those two banes of the Australian outdoors – the fly and the mosquito (mozzie).

In the cities the flies are not too bad; it's in the country that they start getting out of hand, and the further 'out' you get the worse the flies seem to be. In central Australia the flies come out with the warmer spring weather (late August), particularly if there has been good winter rain, and last until the next frosts kill them off. The humble fly net – which fits on a hat and is rather like a string onion bag – is very effective. Repellents such as Aerogard and Rid may also help to deter the little bastards.

Mozzies can be a problem, especially near wetlands in tropical areas – some species are carriers of Ross River Fever (see the Health section earlier in this chapter).

Also see the Health section for information on leeches and ticks.

Crocodiles Up north, saltwater crocodiles ('salties') are a real danger – they are known to sample human. As well as living around the coast they are found in estuaries, creeks and rivers, sometimes a long way inland. Observe safety signs or ask locals whether waterholes are croc-free before plunging in.

Box Jellyfish Also known as the sea wasp or 'stinger', this is another dangerous creature of the northern coast. There have been numerous fatal encounters between swimmers and these large jellyfish, whose venomous tentacles are up to 3m long – you can be stung in any month, but the worst time is October through to the end of April. Stay out of the water during this period unless you're wearing protective clothing such as a 'stinger suit' – available from swimwear and sporting shops in the stinger zone.

If someone is stung, they are likely to run screaming from the sea and collapse on the beach, with weals on their body as though they've been whipped. Douse the stings with vinegar (you should have some with you if you're going for a swim in stinger country), and don't try to remove the tentacles from the victim's skin. Be prepared to resuscitate the victim, who may stop breathing.

See the earlier Health section in this chapter for treatment of stings.

On the Road
See under Car in the Getting Around chapter for road hazards.

Bushfires & Blizzards
Bushfires happen every year in Australia. Don't be the mug who starts one. In hot,

dry, windy weather, be extremely careful with any naked flame – cigarette butts thrown out of car windows have started many a fire. On a total fire ban day (listen to the radio or watch the billboards on country roads), it is forbidden even to use a camping stove in the open. The locals will not be amused if they catch you breaking this particular law; they'll happily dob you in, and the penalties are severe.

If you're unfortunate enough to find yourself driving through a bushfire, stay inside your car and try to park off the road in an open space, away from trees, until the danger has passed. Lie on the floor under the dashboard and cover up with a wool blanket or protective clothing – heat radiation is the big killer in bushfire situations. The front of the fire should pass quickly, and you will be much safer than if you were out in the open.

Bushwalkers should take local advice before setting out. On a day of total fire ban, don't go – delay your trip until the weather has changed. Chances are that it will be so unpleasantly hot and windy you'll be better off anyway in an air-conditioned pub sipping a cool beer.

If you're out in the bush and you see smoke, even at a great distance, you should

take it seriously. Go to the nearest open space, downhill if possible. A forested ridge is the most dangerous place to be. Bushfires move very quickly and change direction with the wind.

Having said all that, more bushwalkers die of cold than in bushfires! Even in summer, temperatures can drop below freezing at night in the mountains (see the Health section earlier in this chapter for treatment of hypothermia). Blizzards in Tasmanian, Victorian and NSW mountains can occur at almost any time of the year, even January!

Swimming

Ocean Beaches Be aware that many surf beaches can be dangerous places to swim if you are not used to the conditions. Undertows (or 'rips') are the main problem, but a number of people are paralysed each year by diving into waves in shallow water and hitting a sand bar – check first.

Many popular beaches are patrolled by surf lifesavers, and patrolled areas are marked off by flags. If you swim between the flags help should arrive quickly if you get into trouble; raise your arm if you need help. Outside the flags and on unpatrolled beaches you are on your own.

If you find yourself being carried out by a rip, the main thing to do is just keep afloat; don't panic or try to swim against the rip. In most cases the current stops within a couple of hundred metres of the shore, and you can then swim parallel to the shore for a short way to get out of the rip and then make your way back to the shore.

BUSINESS HOURS

Most shops close weekdays at 5 or 5.30 pm, and on Saturday at either noon or 5 pm. Sunday trading is becoming increasingly common, but it's currently limited to the major cities and, to a lesser extent, regional Victoria. In most towns there are usually one or two late shopping nights each week, when the doors stay open until 9 or 9.30 pm. Usually it's Thursday and/or Friday night.

Banks are open from 9.30 am to 4 pm Monday to Thursday, and until 5 pm on Friday. Some large city branches are open

Not all the nasties in Australia will appear on your doorstep at once!

Monday to Friday from 8 am to 6 pm. Some are also open Friday to 9 pm. Of course there are some exceptions to Australia's unremarkable opening hours and all sorts of places stay open late and all weekend – particularly milk bars, convenience stores, supermarkets, delis and city bookshops. The big chain supermarkets in large city shopping centres are also often open 24 hours a day.

PUBLIC HOLIDAYS & SPECIAL EVENTS
School Holidays
The Christmas holiday season, from mid-December to late January, is part of the summer school vacation – it's the time you are most likely to find accommodation booked out and long queues. There are three other shorter school holiday periods during the year, but they vary by a week or two from state to state. They fall from early to mid-April, late June to mid-July, and late September to early October.

Public Holidays
Public holidays also vary quite a bit from state to state. The following is a list of the main national and state public holidays; for precise dates (which vary from year to year), check locally (* indicates holidays are only observed locally):

National

New Year's Day	1 January
Australia Day	26 January
Easter (Good Friday to Easter Monday inclusive)	March/April
Anzac Day	25 April
Queen's Birthday (except WA)	2nd Monday in June
Queen's Birthday (WA)	Last Monday in September
Christmas Day	25 December
Boxing Day	26 December

Australian Capital Territory

Canberra Day	March
Bank Holiday	1st Monday in August
Labour Day	1st Monday in October

New South Wales

Bank Holiday	1st Monday in August
Labour Day	1st Monday in October

Northern Territory

May Day	1st Monday in May
Show Day	
Alice Springs	1st Friday in July *
Tennant Creek	2nd Friday in July *
Katherine	3rd Friday in July *
Darwin	4th Friday in July *
Picnic Day	1st Monday in August

Queensland

Labour Day	1st Monday in May
RNA Show Day (Brisbane)	August *

South Australia

Adelaide Cup Day	3rd Monday in May *
Labour Day	1st Monday in October
Proclamation Day	Last Tuesday in December

Tasmania

Regatta Day	14 February
Launceston Cup Day	February *
Eight Hours Day	1st Monday in March
Bank Holiday	Tuesday following Easter Monday
King Island Show	March
Launceston Show Day	October *
Hobart Show Day	October *
Recreation Day (northern Tasmania only)	1st Monday in November *

Victoria

Labour Day	2nd Monday in March
Melbourne Cup Day	1st Tuesday in November *

Western Australia

Labour Day	1st Monday in March
Foundation Day	1st Monday in June

Special Events
Some of the most enjoyable Australian festivals are, naturally, the most typically Australian – like the surf life-saving competitions on beaches all around the country during summer; or outback race meetings, which draw together isolated communities and more than a few eccentric bush characters.

There are happenings and holidays in Australia year-round – the following is just a brief overview (inquire at relevant state tourist authorities for precise dates and more details):

January

Sydney to Hobart Yacht Race – Tasmania
Yachts competing in this world-class event arrive in Hobart from 29 December to 2 January. Competitors in the Melbourne to Hobart Yacht Race arrive soon after.

Hobart Summer Festival – Tasmania
Month-long festival beginning at the completion of the Sydney to Hobart Yacht Race, and incorporating the Taste of Tasmania food festival at the docks.

Sardine Festival – WA
Great music festival held at historic Fremantle, south of Perth, also features distinctively Australian food and street theatre.

Sydney Fringe Festival – NSW
Multi-arts festival based around the pavilion at Bondi Beach.

Tunarama Festival – SA
Held at Port Lincoln, this festival features, among other things, a tuna tossing competition.

Australia Day
This national holiday, commemorating the arrival of the First Fleet in 1788, is observed on 26 January.

Sydney Festival & Carnivale – NSW
A three week arts, music, food and dance festival.

Australasian Country Music Festival – NSW
Tamworth *is* country music in Australia, and this festival held on the Australia Day long weekend is the showcase for the country's top Country and Western artists.

International Jazz Festival – Victoria
Australia's biggest jazz festival is held in Melbourne.

Midsumma Festival – Victoria
Melbourne's gay festival runs through January and February, starts with a street party in Brunswick St, includes the famous Red Raw dance party and ends with Midsumma Carnival in early February.

Hunter Vintage Festival – NSW
Wine enthusiasts flock to the Hunter Valley (north of Sydney) for wine tasting, and grape-picking and treading contests. Runs throughout January to March.

February

Royal Hobart Regatta – Tasmania
This is the largest aquatic carnival in the southern hemisphere, with boat races and other activities.

Sydney Gay & Lesbian Mardi Gras – NSW
It's fun – there's a huge procession with extravagant costumes, and an incredible party along Oxford St.

Festival of Perth – WA
This huge cultural festival features three weeks of performances by local and international artists.

Melbourne Music Festival – Victoria
The main contemporary music festival in the country.

Antipodes International Festival – Victoria
Melbourne's Greek community celebrates its culture and achievements.

March

Adelaide Festival of Arts – SA
Held on even-dated years, this is three weeks of music, theatre, opera, ballet, art exhibitions, light relief and plenty of parties. The Adelaide Fringe Festival accompanies the main festival.

Moomba – Victoria
This week-long festival in Melbourne features cultural and sporting events and culminates in a huge evening street procession.

Port Fairy Folk Festival – Victoria
Every Labour Day weekend the small coastal town of Port Fairy comes to life with music, dancing, workshops, storytelling, spontaneous entertainment and stalls. Australia's biggest folk music festival attracts all sorts of people and for three days the population swells from 2500 to over 10,000.

Australian Formula One Grand Prix – Victoria
This premier motor race takes place on a circuit around Albert Park Lake in inner suburban Melbourne.

Canberra Festival – ACT
A ten day festival to mark the founding of Canberra.

March to April

Melbourne International Comedy Festival – Victoria
No joke, one of the largest comedy festivals in the world.

Royal Easter Show – NSW
Livestock contests and exhibits, ring events, sideshows and rodeos are features of the Sydney show, held at Easter.

Byron Bay Blues & Roots Festival – NSW
Also held over Easter, a four day explosion of blues music with artists from all over the world.

Bell's Beach Surf Classic – Victoria
The longest-running professional surfing event in the world is held over the Easter weekend at Bell's Beach, south-west of Melbourne.

National Folk Festival – ACT
Large music festival held at Easter in Canberra.

Port Fairy Folk Festival – Victoria
Another major folk festival.

Queer Film & Video Festival – Victoria
Showcase festival for film and video work by gay artists.

April

Anzac Day
This national public holiday on 25 April commemorates the landing of Anzac troops at Gallipoli in 1915. Memorial marches by the returned soldiers of both world wars and the veterans of Korea and Vietnam are held all over the country.

Bright Autumn Festival – Victoria
Two week festival in country Victoria; the main feature being a prestigious art exhibition.

May

Outback Muster – Queensland
Held at the famed Stockman's Hall of Fame in Longreach, this unusual three day festival features a variety of events related to droving.

June

Barunga Wugularr Sports & Cultural Festival – NT
Held on the four days over the Queen's Birthday long weekend in June, Barunga, 80km southeast of Katherine, becomes a gathering place for Aboriginal people from all over the Territory. There are traditional arts and crafts on display, as well as dancing and athletics competitions.

Merrepen Arts Festival – NT
In June or July, Nauiyu Nambiyu on the banks of the Daly River is the venue for this festival where several Aboriginal communities from around the district, such as Wadeye, Nauiyu and Peppimenarti, display their arts and crafts.

Blackrock Stakes – WA
Held in the iron-ore mining Pilbara region, the Blackrock Stakes is a 122km race from Whim Creek to Port Hedland. Contestants (teams or solo) push wheelbarrows weighed down with iron ore.

July

Melbourne International Film Festival – Victoria
This is Australia's longest-running international film event, presenting the best in contemporary world cinema.

Alice Springs Camel Cup – NT
Camel races and charity fundraising day.

Great Goat Race – NSW
Annual wild goat race through the main street of Lightning Ridge in outback NSW!

August

Darwin Beer Can Regatta – NT
Races for boats constructed entirely out of beer cans, of which there are plenty in this heavy drinking city.

Yuendumu Festival – NT
Aboriginal people from the central and western desert region meet in Yuendumu, northwest of Alice Springs, over a long weekend in early August. There's a mix of traditional and modern sporting and cultural events.

Sydney City to Surf – NSW
Australia's biggest foot race takes place with up to 25,000 competitors running the 14km from Hyde Park to Bondi Beach.

Melbourne Writers Festival – Victoria
Readings and discussions of works by Australian and international authors, held during the last week of August.

Mt Isa Rodeo – Queensland
Three days of rodeo events and street parties.

August to September

Shinju Matsuri (Festival of the Pearl) – WA
Held in the old pearling port of Broome during the week of the full moon, this festival highlights and celebrates the town's Asian cultural heritage.

September

AFL Grand Final – Victoria
Sporting attention turns to Melbourne with the Grand Final of Aussie rules football, when a crowd close to 100,000 assembles at the MCG (Melbourne Cricket Ground). It's the biggest sporting event in Australia.

Royal Melbourne Show – Victoria
This attracts agricultural folk for the judging of livestock and produce, and lots of families for the sideshows and showbags.

Royal Perth Show – WA
Has agricultural displays and demonstrations, with sideshows, novelty rides etc.

Royal Adelaide Show – SA
One of the oldest royal shows in the country, with major agricultural and horticultural exhibits and entertainment.

Birdsville Races – Queensland
The famous outback race meeting where visitors flock in their droves from around the country for a weekend of horse races and heavy drinking. Proceeds go to the Royal Flying Doctor Service.

Floriade – ACT
Month-long spring festival in Canberra with thousands of bulbs and annuals in bloom, and activities.

October

Henley-on-Todd Regatta – NT
A series of races for leg-powered bottomless boats on the (usually) dry Todd River, Alice Springs.

World Solar Car Challenge – NT
Numerous weird and wonderful solar-powered vehicles compete in a race down the Stuart Hwy from Darwin to Adelaide. The event attracts contestants from around the world.

Royal Shows – Tasmania
The royal agricultural and horticultural shows of Hobart and Launceston are held this month.

Tasmanian Craft Fare
Held in Deloraine over four days, this is claimed to be Australia's largest working craft fair.

Melbourne Festival – Victoria
An annual festival offering some of the best of opera, theatre, dance and the visual arts from around Australia and the world.

Melbourne Fringe Festival – Victoria
Three weeks of theatre, dance, comedy, cabaret, readings, exhibitions and other events help Melbourne celebrate the 'alternative' arts.

Australian Motorcycle Grand Prix – Victoria
The last round of the 500cc world championships is held at the Phillip Island circuit.

Stompen Festival – WA
Month-long festival of Aboriginal culture and arts from the Kimberley, held in Broome.

November

Melbourne Cup – Victoria
On the first Tuesday in November, Australia's premier horse race is run at Flemington. It's a public holiday in Melbourne, but the whole country comes to a virtual standstill for the race.

Bathurst 1000 Touring Car Race – NSW
Motor racing enthusiasts flock to Bathurst for the annual 1000km, touring car race on the superb Mt Panorama circuit.

Land of the Beardies Bush Festival – NSW
Country festival with performances by Aboriginal and non-Aboriginal singers, dancers and musicians at Glen Innes; long beard competition.

Ngangirra Festival – NSW
Held at Mungabareena on the Murray River, this three day Aboriginal festival features the art, music, dance and language of seven regional Aboriginal groups.

December to January
These are the busiest summer months with Christmas, school holidays and lots of beach activities, rock and jazz festivals, international sporting events, including tennis and cricket, a whole host of outdoor activities and lots of parties.

Sydney to Hobart Yacht Race – NSW
Sydney Harbour is a sight to behold on Boxing Day (26 December) when boats of all shapes and sizes crowd its waters to farewell the yachts competing in this gruelling race. It's a fantastic sight as the yachts stream out of the harbour and head south. In Hobart there's a mardi gras to celebrate the finish of the race.

Woodford Folk Festival – Queensland
Held between Christmas and New Year, this five day festival is the largest folk festival in the country, attracting up to 70,000 people.

ACTIVITIES

There are plenty of activities that you can take part in while travelling around the country. Here we've just given an idea of what's available; for specifics, check the Activities section at the start of each state chapter.

Cycling

You can cycle all around Australia; for the athletic there are long, challenging routes and for the not so masochistic there are plenty of great day trips. In most states there are excellent cycling routes and helpful bicycle societies that have lots of maps and useful tips and advice. Around the country there are a number of specialist bicycle tour companies.

See the Getting Around and individual state chapters for more on cycling.

Skiing

Australia has a flourishing skiing industry – a fact that takes a number of travellers by surprise – with snowfields straddling the NSW-Victoria border. There's skiing information in the Victorian Alps section of the Victoria chapter, and in the Snowy Mountains section of the NSW chapter. Tasmania's snowfields aren't as developed as those of Victoria and NSW – if you want to ski in Tassie, see the Activities section of the Tasmania chapter.

Bushwalking

One of the best ways of really getting away from it all in Australia is to go bushwalking. There are many fantastic walks in the various national parks around the country and information on how to get there is in Lonely Planet's *Bushwalking in Australia*.

Some walks include the Overland and South-West Tracks in Tasmania; the Bogong High Plains Circuit in Victoria's High Country; Fraser Island and Bellenden Ker in Queensland; the Flinders Ranges in SA; and the Larapinta Trail west of Alice Springs in the Centre.

Surfing

If you're interested in surfing you'll find great beaches and surf in various states (see the boxed text 'Where to Surf in Australia').

Scuba Diving

There's great scuba diving at a number of places around the coast, particularly along the Great Barrier Reef where there are also many dive schools. Open-water Professional Association of Diving Instructors' (PADI) courses typically cost $300 to $550 for five days, depending on how much time you actually spend on the reef. See the Queensland chapter for more information.

Diving courses are available in all other states as well – in WA the Ningaloo Reef is becoming a popular dive site, with courses available at Coral Bay and Exmouth.

Horse Riding

Horseback is a great way to get out into the bush and experience the silence and space in a way not possible by vehicle. You can find horses to hire at any number of places around the country, and you can opt for anything from a half-hour stroll to extended trail rides.

In Victoria you can go horse riding in the High Country and follow the spectacular routes of the Snowy Mountains cattle people, whose lives were the subject of the film *The Man from Snowy River*, which in turn was based on the poem by Banjo Paterson. Rides in the Alps in NSW are also popular.

In northern Queensland you can ride horses through rainforests and along sand dunes, and swim with them in the sea.

There are plenty of places to ride in the NT, particularly in the Centre. Ossie's Outback Trail Rides in Alice Springs offers extended

trail rides and Juno Horse Centre near Tennant Creek also has cattle mustering rides.

In WA, Kimberley Pursuits (near Wyndham in the Kimberley) has riding tours lasting from two to seven days, exploring remote country with 4WD back-up. The South West Timber Trekking Company does similar things in the south-west corner of the state, except its tours are for two or three days.

Camel Riding

Camel riding has taken off around the country, especially in central Australia and outback SA. If you've done it in India or Egypt or you just fancy yourself as the explorer/outdoors type, then here's your chance. You can take anything from a five minute stroll to a 14 day expedition.

Bird-Watching

Birds Australia (formerly the Royal Australasian Ornithologists Union) runs bird observatories in NSW, Victoria, SA and WA. Its headquarters are at 415 Riversdale Rd, Hawthorn East, Victoria 3123 (☎ 03-9882 2622, fax 9882 2677). Its Web site is: avoca.vicnet.net.au/~birdsaus/.

Other Activities

Windsurfing, paragliding, rafting, hot-air ballooning, bungee-jumping and hang-gliding are among the many other outdoor activities available. The places with the most activities on offer are usually also those with the most backpackers; places like Airlie Beach and Cairns in Queensland have a huge range.

WORK

If you come to Australia on a tourist visa then you're not allowed to work. Many travellers on tourist visas do find casual work, usually in the tourism and fruit industries, but the work is not well paid and as you are not working legally you are open to being exploited. Not only that, if you're caught breaching your visa conditions you can be expelled from the country and placed on a banned list for up to three years.

With a working holiday visa (see the Visas & Documents section earlier in this chapter),

Considerations for Responsible Bushwalking

The popularity of bushwalking is placing great pressure on wilderness areas. Please consider the following tips when trekking and help preserve the ecology and beauty of the Australian bush.

Wildlife Conservation

- Do not engage in or encourage hunting. It's illegal in all parks and reserves.
- Don't assume animals in huts are nonindigenous vermin and attempt to exterminate them. In wild places they are likely to be protected native animals.
- Discourage the presence of wildlife at your camp site by not leaving food scraps behind you. Place gear out of reach and tie packs to rafters or trees.
- Do not feed the wildlife as this can lead to animals becoming dependent on trekker handouts, to unbalanced populations and to diseases such as 'lumpy jaw'.

Rubbish

- Carry out all your rubbish. If you've carried it in you can carry it out. Don't overlook those easily forgotten items, such as silver paper, orange peel, cigarette butts and plastic wrappers. Empty packaging weighs very little anyway and should be stored in a dedicated rubbish bag. Make an effort to carry out rubbish left by others.
- Never bury your rubbish: digging disturbs soil and ground-cover and encourages erosion. Buried rubbish will more than likely be dug up by animals such as goannas and dingoes, which may be injured or poisoned by it. What's more, it may take years to decompose.
- Minimise waste by taking minimal packaging. If you can't buy in bulk, unpack small-portion packages and combine their contents in one container before your trek. Take re-useable containers or stuff sacks.
- Sanitary napkins, tampons and condoms should also be carried out despite the inconvenience. They burn and decompose poorly.

Human Waste Disposal

- Contamination of water sources by human faeces can lead to the transmission of hepatitis, typhoid and intestinal parasites, such as giardiasis, amoebas and round worms. It can cause severe health risks not only to members of your party, but also to local residents and wildlife.
- Where there is a toilet, please use it. Where there is none, bury your waste. Dig a hole 20cm deep and at least 100m from any watercourse – consider carrying a lightweight trowel for this purpose. Cover the waste with soil and a rock. Use toilet paper sparingly and bury it with the waste. In snow, dig down to the soil otherwise your waste will be exposed when the snow melts. If the area is inhabited, ask local people if they have any concerns about your chosen toilet site.
- Ensure that these guidelines are applied to a portable toilet tent if one is being used by a large trekking party. Encourage all party members to use the site.

---

the possibilities for finding temporary employment are many. With the current boom in tourism, work is often easy to find in the peak season at the major tourist centres. Places like Alice Springs, Cairns and various other places along the Queensland coast, and the ski fields of Victoria and NSW, are all good prospects, but opportunities are usually limited to the peak holiday seasons.

Other good prospects for casual work include factory work, bar work, waiting on tables, other domestic chores at outback roadhouses, nanny work, fruit picking, working as a station hand (jackaroo/jillaroo) and collecting for charities. People with computer or secretarial skills should have little difficulty finding work in the major cities, and for qualified nurses agency work is often avail-

Considerations for Responsible Bushwalking

Fires & Low Impact Cooking

- Don't depend on open fires for cooking. Cutting wood for fires in popular trekking areas can cause rapid deforestation. Cook on a lightweight kerosene, alcohol or Shellite (white gas) stove and avoid those powered by disposable butane gas canisters. Open fires are banned in many Australian national parks, and even stoves may be banned on days of total fire ban.
- Fires may be acceptable in areas that get very few visitors. If you light a fire, use an existing fireplace rather than creating a new one – don't surround fires with rocks as this creates a visual scar. Use only dead, fallen wood. Remember the adage 'the bigger the fool, the bigger the fire'. Use minimal wood, just what you need for cooking. In huts leave wood for the next person.
- Ensure that you fully extinguish a fire after use. Spread the embers and douse them with water. A fire is only truly safe to leave when you can comfortably place your hand in it.

Washing

- Don't use detergents or toothpaste in or near watercourses, even if they are biodegradable. For personal washing, use biodegradable soap and a water container (or even a lightweight, portable basin) at least 50m away from the watercourse. Widely disperse the waste water to allow the soil to filter it fully before it finally makes it back to the watercourse.
- Wash cooking utensils 50m from watercourses using a scourer, sand or snow instead of detergent.

Erosion

- Hillsides and mountain slopes are prone to erosion. It is important to stick to existing tracks and avoid short cuts that bypass a switchback. If you blaze a new trail straight down a slope it may turn into a gutter with the next heavy rainfall and eventually cause deep scarring. If a well-used track passes through a mud patch, walk through the mud: walking around the edge will increase the size of the patch.
- Avoid removing the plant life that keeps topsoils in place.

Camping & Walking on Private Property

- Seek permission to camp from landowners.

Park Regulations

- Take note of and observe any rules and regulations particular to the national park or reserve that you are visiting.

Environmental Organisations

- See Useful Organisations later in this chapter for the contact addresses of active environmental groups in Australia.

---

able. We even got one letter from a traveller who was employed as an ostrich babysitter!

The various backpacker magazines, newspapers and hostels are good information sources – some local employers even advertise on their notice boards. As well, ask at country hotels about local work opportunities and check the classified section of the daily papers under Situations Vacant.

Workabout Australia, by Barry Brebner, gives a comprehensive state by state breakdown of seasonal work opportunities.

Tax File Number

If you have a working holiday visa, it's important to apply for a Tax File Number (TFN). This is not because it's a condition of employment, but because without it tax

Where to Surf in Australia

In the summer of 1915, Hawaiian surfer Duke Kahanamoku came to Australia and introduced the art of surfboard riding. He fashioned a board from local timbers and gave a demonstration at Freshwater, on Sydney's north shore. From that point on the sport grew steadily and today Australia boasts several world champions and many world class breaks.

Queensland Surfers Paradise, south of Brisbane, is not what the name suggests. The Gold Coast, however, is generally a good place to surf – Burleigh Heads and Kirra are the more well known breaks with good rights on a solid ground swell. Also check Coolangatta's Greenmount Point and Duranbah on the other side of the Point Danger headland.

Just north of Surfers Paradise, South Stradbroke Island has some big and powerful beach breaks.

North of Brisbane is the Sunshine Coast, which has a variety of breaks at Caloundra and Maroochydore.

When it works, Noosa Heads National Park has a good right but does draw large crowds. Double Island Point, north of Noosa, is worth getting to but you'll need a 4WD.

New South Wales Name practically any coastal town in NSW and there will be good surf nearby.

Sydney's northern beaches are well known for their good surf, with Manly, Dee Why, Narrabeen and Avalon the more popular. To the east of Sydney check out the areas around Bondi and to the south there's good surf around Cronulla.

On the far north coast are Byron Bay, Lennox Head and Angourie, Coffs Harbour and Nambucca Heads on the mid-north coast and the beaches off Newcastle on the lower north coast. Down on the south coast try the beaches off Wollongong, Jervis Bay, Ulladulla, Merimbula and Pambula.

Victoria Bells Beach has become synonymous with surfing in Australia and does have a classic right-hander if the swell is up. There are many other excellent breaks throughout the state.

---

will be deducted from any wages you receive at the maximum rate (currently 47%!). To get a TFN, contact the local office of the Australian Taxation Office (ATO, ☎ 13 2861) for a form. It's a straightforward procedure, but you will have to supply adequate identification (your passport plus driver's licence, or similar ID) and show that you have a working holiday visa. The issuing of a TFN takes about four weeks.

Paying Tax

If you have supplied your employer with a TFN, tax will be deducted from your wages at the rate of 29% if your weekly income is below $397. As your income increases, so does the tax rate – the maximum rate of 47% is deducted from weekly incomes above $961 (this rate only applies to the amount by which $961 is exceeded).

If you have had tax deducted at the correct rate as you earn, it is unlikely you'll be entitled to a tax refund when you leave Australia. However, if you have had tax deducted at 47% because you did not submit a TFN, you will be entitled to a partial refund of the tax paid. To get the refund you must lodge a tax return with the ATO.

Before you can lodge a tax return, however, you must have a TFN. As well, the tax return must include a Group Certificate (an official summary of your earnings and tax payments) provided by your employer, who must be given written advice at least 14

Where to Surf in Australia

Phillip Island, the Mornington Peninsula and the west coast are all within a two hour drive from Melbourne. On Phillip Island check Woolamai, Surfies Point, Smiths Beach and Cat Bay. The best places on the Mornington Peninsula are Point Leo, Flinders, Gunamatta, Rye and Portsea. On the west coast you can try Barwon Heads, Torquay, Bells Beach and other spots along the Great Ocean Road.

In Gippsland try Lakes Entrance and Wilsons Promontory.

There is also the big and powerful shipwreck coast near Port Campbell, which only experienced surfers should attempt.

Tasmania Despite the cold water, Tasmania has some fine surfing. The best places on the exposed west coast are around Marrawah and there are many quality spots along the east coast. Check north and south of St Helens, around Eaglehawk Neck on the Tasman Peninsula and Shelly Beach near Orford. Bruny Island also has some surfable waves and closer to Hobart try Cremorne Point and Clifton Beach.

South Australia Cactus Beach, west of Ceduna on remote Point Sinclair, is SA's best known surf spot, and is also renowned worldwide as one of Australia's best remote waves. Other places to check are the Eyre and southern York peninsulas, while closer to Adelaide and near Victor Harbor there are good waves on the west and south side of the Fleurieu Peninsula.

Western Australia WA's best known surfing spot is probably Margaret River and the surf here can be huge. The beaches and points north and south of Margaret River also offer some excellent surf.

Trig and Scarborough beaches north of Perth have beginners' surf and Rottnest Island has some good breaks, too.

Further north, Geraldton, Kalbarri and Carnarvon are also well worth checking out. However, you may need a 4WD on the coast road north of Carnarvon, and only experienced surfers should attempt these waves.

Andrew Tudor

---

days in advance that you want the certificate on your last day at work – otherwise you may have to wait until the end of the financial year (30 June).

Australia's tax system will change in July 2000 with the introduction of a 10% GST. Income tax rates will alter as a result, for example, no tax will be paid on annual income under $6000, from $6001 to $20,000 the rate is 17% and the maximum rate remains 47%. For more information ring the ATO GST information line on ☎ 13 6140.

Superannuation

As part of the government's compulsory superannuation scheme, if you're earning more than $450 per calendar month your employer must make contributions on your behalf to a retirement or superannuation (super) fund. These contributions are at the rate of 7% of your wage, and the money must remain in the fund until you reach 'preservation age' (sounds nasty!), which is currently 55.

Current legislation does not allow for the early release of superannuation funds. You can find out the latest on this from the ATO on ☎ 13 1020; also check with the super fund with which your contributions have been lodged.

Casual Employment Seasons

The table below lists the main times and regions where casual employment, mainly fruit-picking, is a possibility:

New South Wales

job	time	region/s
Apples	Feb-Apr	Orange
	Dec-Jan	Forbes
Bananas	Nov-Jan	North Coast
Cherries	Nov-Jan	Orange
Citrus	Dec-Mar	Griffith
Grapes	Feb-Mar	Griffith, Hunter Valley
Tomatoes	Jan-Mar	Forbes

Northern Territory

job	time	region/s
Mangoes	Oct-Nov	Darwin
Tourism	May-Sep	Darwin, Alice Springs, Katherine

Queensland

job	time	region/s
Apples	Feb-Mar	Warwick
Asparagus	Aug-Dec	Warwick
Bananas	year-round	Tully
Fishing trawlers	May-Aug	Cairns
Grapes	Jan-Apr	Stanthorpe
Mangoes	Dec-Jan	Atherton
Tomatoes	Oct-Dec	Bundaberg
Tourism	Apr-Oct	Cairns
Vegies	May-Nov	Bowen

South Australia

job	time	region/s
Apples/ pears	Feb-July	Adelaide Hills
Apricots	Dec	Riverland
Grapes	Feb-Apr	Riverland, Barossa, Clare
Peaches	Feb-June	Riverland
Pruning	Aug-Dec	Adelaide Hills
Tomatoes	Jan-Feb	Riverland

Tasmania

job	time	region/s
Apples/ pears	Mar-Apr	Huon/Tamar Valleys
Cherries	Dec-Jan	Huonsville
Grapes	Mar-Apr	Tamar Valley
Strawberries/ raspberries	Jan-Apr	Huonville

Victoria

job	time	region/s
Apples	Mar-May	Bendigo
Cherries	Nov-Dec	Dandenongs
Grapes	Feb-Mar	Mildura
Peaches/ pears	Feb-Mar	Shepparton
Strawberries	Oct-Dec	Echuca, Dandenongs
Tomatoes	Jan-Mar	Shepparton, Echuca
Ski fields	June-Oct	Wangaratta/Alps

Western Australia

job	time	region/s
Apples/ pears	Feb-Apr	Donnybrook, Manjimup
Bananas	Apr-Dec year-round	Kununurra Carnarvon
Flowers	Sep-Nov	Midlands
Grapes	Feb-Mar	Albany, Margaret River, Mt Barker, Manjimup
Lobsters	Nov-May	Esperance
Prawn trawlers	Mar-June	Carnarvon
Tourism	May-Dec	Kununurra
Vegies	May-Nov	Kununurra, Carnarvon

ACCOMMODATION

Australia is very well provided with youth hostels, backpacker hostels and caravan parks with camp sites – the cheapest shelter you can find. Furthermore, there are plenty of hotels, motels, guesthouses and B&Bs, particularly in places where tourists congregate.

A typical town of a thousand people will have a basic motel, an old pub or two with twin or double rooms (shared bathrooms), and a caravan park with camp sites, on-site vans and cabins. If the town is on a main road it may have several of each. You'll rarely have much trouble finding *somewhere* to lay your head, unless it's a peak time and you've forgotten to book. If there's a group of you, the rates for three or four people in a room are always worth checking – many hotels have 'family' rooms, and caravan park cabins sleep at least three people.

There are a couple of free backpacker newspapers and booklets available at hostels around the country, and these have fairly up-to-date listings of hostels, although they give neither prices nor details of each hostel.

For more comprehensive accommodation listings, the state automobile clubs produce directories listing caravan parks, hotels, motels, holiday flats and hostels in practically every town in the country. They're updated every year so the prices are fairly current. They're available from the clubs for a nominal charge if you're a member.

There's a wide variation in seasonal prices for accommodation. At peak times – school holidays in particular – prices are at their highest, whereas at other times useful discounts can be found. This particularly applies to the Top End, where the Wet season (summer) is the low season and prices can drop by as much as 30%. In this book high-season prices are used unless indicated otherwise.

Camping & Caravanning

The camping story in Australia is partly excellent and partly rather annoying! The excellent side is that there is a large number of caravan parks and except at peak times you'll generally find space available. If you want to get around Australia on the cheap then camping is the cheapest way of all, with nightly costs for two of around $10 to $15, slightly more if you want power.

On the downside, camp sites are often intended more for caravanners (house trailers for any North Americans out there) than for campers. The fact that most of the sites are called 'caravan parks' indicates who gets most attention. In many Australian caravan parks gravel is laid down to make the ground more suitable for cars and caravans, so pitching a tent becomes very hard work.

Equally bad, although probably true the world over, is that in most big cities camp sites are well away from the centre of town, although public transport is invariably close by.

Most Australian caravan parks are well kept and excellent value – almost all will have hot showers, flush toilets and laundry facilities. Many have on-site vans that you can rent for the night. These give you the comfort of a caravan without the inconvenience of actually towing one of the damned things. On-site cabins are also widely available. They usually have separate bedrooms, or at least an area that can be screened off from the rest of the unit – and many have their own bathroom and toilet. They are much less cramped than a caravan, and the price difference is not always that great – say $30 to $35 for an on-site van for two people, $35 to $45 for a cabin with kitchenette. In winter, if you're going to be using this sort of accommodation on a regular basis, it's worth investing in a small heater of some sort as many vans and cabins are unheated.

Camping in the bush, either in national parks and reserves or in the open, is for many people one of the highlights of a visit to Oz. In the Outback you won't even need a tent – swags are the way to go, and nights spent around a campfire under the stars are unforgettable.

Hostels

Youth Hostels YHA hostels provide basic accommodation, usually in small dormitories or bunk rooms, although more and more are providing twin rooms. The nightly charges are usually between $9 and $18 a night for members – most hostels also take non-YHA members, who are charged an extra $3. Accommodation can usually be booked directly with the manager or through a Membership & Travel Centre – see the YHA handbook for details.

Australia has a very active Youth Hostel Association (YHA) and you'll find its places all over the country – there are over 130 YHA hostels, including associates. YHA is part of the International Youth Hostel Federation (IYHF, also known as HI, Hostelling International), so if you're already a member of the YHA in your own country, your membership entitles you to use Australian hostels.

A Hostelling International Card (for visitors to Australia) costs $30. For an Australian resident to become a full YHA member costs $47 a year. You can join at a state office or at any youth hostel.

There's also an introductory membership, where you pay no initial membership, but instead pay an additional $3 per night at any hostel. Once you have stayed for 10 nights, you get a full membership. Alternatively, the YHA's Accommodation Packs allow you to prepay accommodation and get healthy discounts. These cost $150/280 for 10/20 nights at any Australian YHA hostel.

To stay in a hostel you must have bed linen. If you haven't got sheets they can be hired at many hostels (usually for $3), but it's cheaper after a few nights' stay to have your own. YHA offices and some larger hostels sell the official YHA sheet bag.

Most hostels have 24-hour access, cooking facilities and a communal area where you can sit and talk. There are usually laundry facilities and, in the larger hostels, excellent notice boards and travel offices. Many have a maximum-stay period (usually five to seven days).

The YHA classes its main hostels as simple, standard or superior. Rural hostels get a gum-leaf rating – from one to three gum leaves depending on how much of a wilderness experience the visitor can expect.

The annual *YHA Accommodation & Discounts Guide* booklet, which is available from all local YHA offices and from some YHA offices overseas, lists all YHA hostels in Australia, with maps showing how to find them. It also lists the discounts (eg bus transport, car hire, activities, accommodation) that members are entitled to.

The Australian head office is in Sydney, at the Australian Youth Hostels Association, 10 Mallett St, Camperdown, NSW 2050 (☎ 02-9565 1699, fax 9565 1325) and its Web site is www.yha.com.au. If you can't get a YHA hostel booklet in your own country, write to the above address, but otherwise deal with the Membership & Travel centres:

New South Wales
  (☎ 02-9261 1111, fax 9261 1969)
  422 Kent St, Sydney, NSW 2001
Northern Territory
  (☎ 08-8981 6344, fax 8981 6674)
  Darwin City Hostel, 69A Mitchell St, Darwin, NT 0800

Queensland
  (☎ 07-3236 1680, fax 3236 0647)
  154 Roma St, Brisbane, Queensland 4000
South Australia
  (☎ 08-8231 5583, 8231 4219)
  38 Sturt St, Adelaide, SA 5000
Tasmania
  (☎ 03-6234 9617, fax 6234 7422)
  1st floor, 28 Criterion St, Hobart, Tasmania 7000
Victoria
  (☎ 03-9670 3802, fax 9670 9840)
  Level 1, 377 Little Lonsdale St, Melbourne, Victoria 3000
Western Australia
  (☎ 08-9227 5122, 1800 811 420, fax 9227 5123)
  236 William St, Northbridge, Perth, WA 6003

Backpacker Hostels Australia has many backpacker hostels and standards vary enormously. Some are run-down, inner-city hotels where the owners have tried to fill empty rooms; unless renovations have been done, these places are generally pretty gloomy and depressing. Occasionally you'll come across those that are former motels, so each unit, typically with four to six beds, will have a fridge, TV and bathroom. The drawback with these places is that the communal areas and cooking facilities are often lacking. You may also find yourself sharing a room with someone who wants to watch TV all night.

Still others are purpose-built as backpacker hostels, and these are usually the best places in terms of facilities. However, sometimes they are simply too big and therefore lack any personalised service.

As often as not, hostel owners have backpackers running their places, in which case it's usually not too long before standards start to slip. Some actively promote themselves as 'party' hostels, so avoid them if you want a quiet time. The best places tend to be the smaller, more intimate hostels where the owner is also the manager.

With the proliferation of hostels has come intense competition. Hop off a bus in any town where there are more than two or three hostels and chances are there'll be touts waiting to lure you in. To this end many have introduced inducements such as the first night free, or free breakfasts. The busier hostels often have courtesy buses.

Some places will only admit overseas backpackers. This happens mostly in cities when the hostel in question has had problems with locals misbehaving. Hostels that discourage or ban Aussies say it's only a rowdy minority that makes trouble, but they can't take the risk. If you're an Aussie and encounter this kind of reception, the best you can do is persuade the desk people that you're genuinely travelling the country, and aren't just looking for a cheap place to crash.

Prices at backpacker hostels are typically $12 to $18, although discounts can reduce this.

Hostel Organisations There are a couple of backpacker hostel organisations and these might be worth joining.

VIP Backpacker Resorts has 134 hostel franchisees in Australia and many more overseas. For $25 you'll receive 12 month's membership, which entitles you to a $1 discount on accommodation and a 5-15% discount on other products such as air and bus transport, tours and activities. You can join at VIP hostels, Greyhound Pioneer terminals, or the larger agencies dealing in backpacker travel. Alternatively, contact the VIP office at PO Box 600, Cannon Hill, Queensland 4170 (☎ 07-3395 6111, fax 3395 6222). Its Web site is www.backpackers.com.au.

Nomads Backpackers has around 40 franchisees in Australia and more in New Zealand. Membership ($25 for 12 months) likewise entitles you to a range of discounts. You can join at any participating hostel or backpacker travel agency, or by writing to the Nomads office at 288 North Terrace, Adelaide SA 5000 (☎ 1800 819 883, fax 08-8224 0972). You can have a look at its Web site at www.nomads-backpackers.com.

Guesthouses & B&Bs

This is the fastest-growing segment of the accommodation market. New places are opening all the time, and the options include everything from restored miners' cottages, converted barns, rambling old guesthouses, upmarket country homes and romantic escapes to a simple bedroom in a family home. Many of these places are listed throughout the book. Tariffs cover a wide range, but are typically in the $50 to $100 (per double) bracket.

Hotels

For the budget traveller, hotels in Australia are usually older places – almost all the new ones are of the Hilton variety. Relatively few old hotels in the city still have rooms to rent, but most in the country do. In Australia, these old-style hotels are known as 'pubs'.

In country towns, hotels are invariably found in the town centre. Many were built during 'boom' economic times, so they're often among the largest and most extravagant buildings in town – they're typically double storey, with huge balconies and lots of iron lacework. However, the rooms themselves can be pretty old-fashioned and unexciting, while heating and cooling may be inadequate or nonexistent. Never book a room above the bar if you're a light sleeper. On the plus side, country hotels are often the town's social focus so staying there is a good way to find out what makes the place tick. You can also usually get substantial meals for very reasonable prices.

Generally, hotels will have twin rooms with shared facilities for around $25 to $35 (more with private bathroom). Few have a separate reception area – you have to ask in the bar if there are rooms available.

Motels, Serviced Apartments & Holiday Flats

If you've got transport and want a more modern place with your own bathroom and other facilities, then you're moving into the motel bracket. Motels are usually located away from the city centres. Prices vary and at motels, unlike hotels, singles are rarely much cheaper than doubles. You'll sometimes find motel rooms for less than $40, but in most places they'll be at least $50. Most motels provide at least tea and coffee-making facilities and a small fridge.

Holiday flats are found in holiday areas, and serviced apartments in cities. A holiday flat is much like a motel unit but has a kitchen or cooking facilities. Usually holiday flats are not serviced like motels – you don't get your bed made up every morning or the cups washed up. In some holiday flats you have to provide your own sheets and bedding.

Holiday flats are often rented on a weekly basis but it's still worth asking if daily rates are available. Paying for a week, even if you're only staying for a few days, can still be cheaper than paying the higher daily rate. If there are more than two of you, another advantage of holiday flats is that you can often find them with two or more bedrooms. A two-bedroom holiday flat is typically priced at about 1½ times the cost of a comparable single-bedroom flat.

In holiday areas like the Queensland coast, there's nothing really to distinguish motels from holiday flats.

Other Possibilities

There are lots of less conventional accommodation possibilities. You don't have to camp in caravan parks, for example, as there are plenty of roadside rest areas where short-term camping is permitted. Australia has lots of bush where nobody is going to complain about you sleeping in the back of your car or rolling out a swag for a night.

Australia is a land of farms and many offer accommodation – some let you sit back and watch how it's done, while others like to get you involved in day-to-day activities. With commodity prices falling daily, mountainous wool stockpiles and a general rural crisis, tourism offers the hope of at least some income for farmers. The state tourist offices can advise you on what's available.

Finally, how about life on a houseboat? See the Murray River sections in the Victoria and South Australia chapters.

Long-Term Accommodation

If you want to stay longer, the first place to look for a shared flat or a room in the cities is the classified ad section of the daily newspaper. Wednesday and Saturday are the best days for these ads. Notice boards in universities, hostels, certain popular bookshops and cafes are good places to look for flats/houses to share or rooms to rent.

FOOD

The culinary delights can be one of the real highlights of Australia. There was a time – like 25 years ago – when Australia's food (mighty steaks apart) had a reputation for being like England's, only worse. But miracles happen and Australia's miracle was immigration. The Greeks, Yugoslavs, Italians, Lebanese and many others who flooded into Australia in the 50s and 60s brought their food with them. More recent arrivals include the Vietnamese, whose communities are thriving in several cities.

In Australia today you can have excellent Greek moussaka (and a bottle of retsina to wash it down), delicious Italian saltimbocca and pasta, or good, heavy German dumplings; you can perfume the air with garlic after stumbling out of a French bistro, or try all sorts of Middle Eastern treats. The Chinese have been sweet-and-souring since the gold-rush days, while more recently, Indian, Thai and Malaysian restaurants have been all the rage. And for cheap eats, you can't beat some of the Vietnamese places.

Australian

Although there is no real Australian cuisine there is certainly some excellent Australian food to try. There's been a great rise in popularity of exotic local and 'bush' foods, and for the adventurous these dishes offer something completely different. So in a swish Melbourne restaurant or Sydney bistro you might find braised kangaroo tail samosas, emu pate, gum-leaf smoked venison, saltbush lamb, native aniseed frittata, Warrigalgreens salad or wattle-seed ice cream.

There are also cafes and restaurants in all the major cities serving food that can be termed 'modern Australian'. These dishes borrow heavily from a wide range of foreign cuisines, but have a definite local flavour. At these places seemingly anything goes, so you might find Asian-inspired curry-type dishes sharing a menu with European or Mediterranean-inspired dishes. It all adds up to exciting dining.

The Kangaroo-Meat Debate

Kangaroos – should we eat them? On one hand, the animal rights lobby claims that killing kangaroos is cruel and that the meat itself may not be disease-free. On the other, farmers and ecologists say the culling of kangaroos is a humane way to bring population numbers down to levels the environment can tolerate. Meat-industry representatives say that meat harvested by licensed shooters is properly inspected and safe to eat; it's generally accepted that kangaroo meat is a healthy low-cholesterol alternative to beef and mutton.

A lot is at stake. The kangaroo meat and hide industry employs about 4000 people in Australia and generates more than A$200 million a year. In Britain, kangaroo meat sales have been booming, helped along by fears of mad-cow disease, which have put people off beef. However, in September 1997 giant British supermarket chain Tesco banned kangaroo meat from 350 stores after a Sunday newspaper ran a disturbing feature, with pictures, on a kangaroo hunt in the Australian Outback. The farmer involved was not a licensed hunter and was not working in the meat industry. Nevertheless, kangaroo meat was taken off the shelves. This left Australian meat-industry representatives fuming, as kangaroo meat sold for human consumption in supermarkets and restaurants comes from licensed hunters governed by a code of practice, and is subject to strict hygiene standards.

Kangaroos are indigenous to Australia and the species hunted for human consumption are not endangered. Government estimates put the total population at between 15 million and 25 million (depending on the availability of food and water from one season to another). Each year the government earmarks a certain number (about 10% to 15% of the total) for harvesting. State and territory governments issue permits to shooters who may then, with landholders' consent, hunt on private property (national parks and reserves are off-limits).

While emus and crocodiles are farmed for their meat, the kangaroo is shot in the field at night, using spotlights, high calibre rifles and telescopic sights. Hunters and wildlife authorities claim that a bullet shot straight into the head is quick and humane; certainly better than steel traps or poison. However, animal rights advocates claim otherwise. They claim the hunt itself (with its lights and noise), let alone the killing, is highly stressful. Others would say this is a lot less stressful than death by starvation.

Unfortunately, a fair amount of killing goes on by unlicensed hunters who aren't working for the meat industry, and distressing tales of cruelty surface from time to time. The RSPCA and conservation agencies prosecute occasionally, but it's difficult to positively identify the perpetrators.

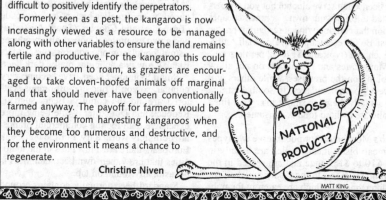

Formerly seen as a pest, the kangaroo is now increasingly viewed as a resource to be managed along with other variables to ensure the land remains fertile and productive. For the kangaroo this could mean more room to roam, as graziers are encouraged to take cloven-hoofed animals off marginal land that should never have been conventionally farmed anyway. The payoff for farmers would be money earned from harvesting kangaroos when they become too numerous and destructive, and for the environment it means a chance to regenerate.

Christine Niven

MATT KING

For something less exotic you can try a meat pie. These vary from approaching gourmet standard to an awful concoction of anonymous meat and dark gravy in a soggy pastry case. You'll have to try one as it's a real part of Australian culture. A pie'n'sauce at the 'footy' on a Saturday afternoon in winter is something plenty of Aussies can relate to.

Even more a part of Australian food culture is Vegemite. This dark yeast extract, similar to British Marmite, looks and spreads like thick tar and smells like, well, Vegemite. Australians spread Vegemite on bread and become positively addicted to the stuff.

Vegetarian

Vegetarians are catered for in most major centres. While there are few dedicated vegetarian restaurants, most modern cafes and restaurants have a few vegetarian dishes on the menu.

Where to Eat

Restaurants & Cafes The best Australian eateries serve food as exciting and as innovative as you'll find anywhere, and it doesn't need to cost a fortune. Best value are the modern and casual cafes, where you can get an excellent feed for less than $20. Otherwise most pubs have substantial if basic meals for under $10.

All over Australia you'll find restaurants advertising that they're BYO, which stands for 'Bring Your Own'. This means they're not licensed to serve alcohol but you are permitted to bring your own – a much cheaper option than buying wine at restaurant prices. Most BYO restaurants have a small 'corkage' charge (typically $1 to $2 per person).

Many cafes and restaurants do not allow smoking on the premises, while others will have a 'no smoking' area. In South Australia it's actually illegal to smoke in any confined public area where food is consumed.

Pubs Most hotels (or pubs) serve two types of meal: bistro meals, which are usually in the $10 to $15 range and are served in the dining room or lounge bar; and bar (or counter) meals, which are eaten in the public bar and usually cost between $5 and $10.

While pub food is often fairly basic, it's also generally pretty good value. The usual meal times are from noon to 2 pm and 6 to 8 pm.

Markets Where the climate allows there are often outdoor food stalls and markets. These can be an excellent place to sample a variety of cuisines, with Asian being the most popular. Darwin's Thursday evening (during the Dry) Mindil Beach market is probably the largest of its type in the country, and has an impressive range of cuisines.

DRINKS
Beer

The consistency of Australian beer will be fairly familiar to North Americans; it's also similar to what's known as lager in the UK. It may taste like lemonade to the European real-ale addict, but it packs quite a punch. It is invariably chilled before drinking.

Fosters is the best known international brand with a worldwide reputation, but there's a bewildering array of Australian beers. Among the most well known are XXXX (pronounced 'four-ex'), Tooheys Red, Fosters, Carlton Draught and VB (Victoria Bitter). Recent additions to the stable of old favourites include lower alcohol beers such as Fosters Light Ice, and styles other than your average Aussie lager, such as Blue Bock and Old Black Ale, both made by Tooheys.

However, the best beer is usually produced by the smaller breweries – Cascade (Tasmania) and Coopers (South Australia) being two examples. Coopers also produces a stout, popular among connoisseurs, and its Black Crow is a delicious malty, dark beer.

Small 'boutique' beers have become very popular, so you'll find one-off brands scattered around the country. Beers such as Redback and Dogbolter, while being more expensive than the big commercial brands, are definitely worth a try. For the homesick European, there are a few pubs in the major cities that brew their own beer. Guinness is occasionally found on tap.

Standard beer normally contains around 5% alcohol, although the trend in recent

A Beer, By Any Other Name ...

Around Australia, beer, the containers it comes in, and the receptacles you drink it from are all called by different names. The standard bottle is 750mL, and costs around $3 for full-strength beer and $2.50 for light. Cans (or tinnies) hold 375mL and come in cartons of 24, known as slabs, and these cost around $30/25 for full-strength/light, although you can of course buy them as individual cans.

Half-size bottles with twist-top caps are known as stubbies (echoes in SA), except in the NT where a stubby is also a 1.25 litre bottle, although these are not in everyday use and are really only a novelty souvenir. Low-alcohol beer is marginally cheaper than full-strength beer. Boutique beers generally only come in stubbies, and are significantly more expensive than your common or garden variety.

Ordering at the bar can be an intimidating business for the uninitiated. Beer by the glass basically comes in three sizes – 200, 285 and 425mL – but knowing what to ask for when the barman/maid queries you with an eloquent 'Yeah, mate?' is not quite so simple. A 200mL (7oz) beer is a 'glass' (Victoria and Queensland), a 'butcher' (SA) or a 'beer' (WA or NSW). Tasmanians like to be different, and so there they have a 6oz glass. A 285mL (10oz) beer is a 'pot' (Victoria and Queensland), a 'schooner' (SA), a 'handle' (NT), a 'middie' (NSW and WA) or a '10 ounce' (Tasmania). Lastly, there's the 425mL (15oz) glass, which is a 'schooner' (NSW and NT) or a 'pint' (SA).

years has been towards low-alcohol beers (between 2% and 3.5%). Tooheys Blue is a particularly popular light beer. While Australians are generally considered to be heavy beer drinkers, per capita beer consumption has fallen by 20% in the past decade.

And a warning: people who drive under the influence of alcohol risk a heavy fine and the loss of their licence (see Car in the Getting Around chapter).

Wine

If you don't fancy beer, then try the wines. Australia has a great climate for wine producing and Australian wine is rapidly gaining international recognition – it's also one of our fastest-growing exports.

The best known wine-growing regions are the Hunter Valley of NSW and the Barossa Valley of SA, but there are plenty of other fine areas too. In Victoria the main region is the Rutherglen/Milawa area of the north-east, and there's also the Yarra Valley (where the French company, Moët et Chandon, makes top quality sparkling wines), the Mornington Peninsula and the Geelong areas, all within easy reach of Melbourne.

SA also has the Coonawarra, McLaren Vale and the picturesque Clare Valley districts. In WA, increasingly sophisticated wines are being produced in the Margaret River area. There's even a winery (albeit a modest one) in Alice Springs.

Australia's wines are reasonably cheap and readily available. For $10 or so you can get a bottle of wine that you could take to someone's place without having to hide the label; $20 gets you something very good indeed.

It takes a little while to become familiar with Australian wineries and their styles but it's an effort worth making. The best – and most enjoyable – way to do this is to get out to the wineries and sample the wine at the cellar door. Most wineries have tastings: you just walk in and say what you'd like to try. However, free wine tastings do not mean open slather drinking – the glasses are often thimble-sized and it's expected that you will buy something if, for example, you taste every Chardonnay that vineyard has ever produced. Many wineries have decided that enough is enough and now have a small 'tasting fee' of a couple of dollars; refundable if you buy.

Each wine-growing area is generally renowned for a particular style of wine, although there's much more experimentation and blending of grapes these days. The Hunter Valley is famous for its whites (especially Chardonnay), the Barossa is even more famous for its Shiraz, the Coonawarra produces excellent heavy reds and the Rutherglen region of Victoria is great for port and Muscat.

Other Alcoholic Drinks

So-called 'designer drinks' are all the rage in hip cafes and bars. Two Dogs Lemonade, an alcoholic lemonade, was the first in what was thought to be a novelty part of the market. This was followed by the phenomenally popular Sub Zero, a basically tasteless alcoholic soda which, when mixed with the obligatory dash of raspberry cordial, is *de rigueur*.

Other alcoholic oddities available in Australia are Strongbow White, a cider with a real kick; Stolichnaya Lemon Ruski (vodka and lemon soda); a shandy (half beer, half lemonade) called Razorback Draught; XLR8, an alcoholic cola; and Finlandia Vodka Pulp Finlandia Cranberry.

ENTERTAINMENT
Discos & Nightclubs

Yep, no shortage of these either, but they are confined to the larger cities and towns. Clubs range from the exclusive 'members only' variety to barn-sized discos where anyone who wants to spend the money is welcomed with open arms. Admission charges range from around $6 to $12.

Some places have certain dress standards, but it is usually left to the discretion of the people at the door – if they don't like the look of you, bad luck. The more 'upmarket' nightclubs attract an older, more sophisticated and affluent crowd, and often have stricter dress codes, smarter decor – and higher prices.

Live Music

Many suburban pubs have live music, and these are often great places for catching bands, either nationally well known names or up-and-coming performers trying to make a name for themselves – most of Australia's popular bands started out on the pub circuit.

The best way to find out about the local scene is to get to know some locals, or travellers who have spent some time in the place. Otherwise, there are often comprehensive listings in newspapers, particularly on Friday. Free street papers are also good places to look – check out *Drum Media*, *Beat* and *3D World* in Sydney; *Son of Barfly* in Cairns; *Beat* and *Inpress* in Melbourne; *Xpress* in Perth; *Time Off*, *Rave* and *The Scene* in Brisbane and *Pulse* in Darwin.

Cinema

In main cities there are commercial cinema chains, such as Village, Hoyts and Greater Union, usually in two to 10-screen complexes. Smaller towns have just the one cinema (if they're lucky), and many of these are almost museum pieces in themselves. Seeing a new-release mainstream film costs around $11 ($8 for children under 15) in the big cities, less in country areas and less on certain nights at the bigger cinema chains.

Also in the cities you'll find art-house and independent cinemas – these places generally screen either films that aren't made for mass consumption or specialise purely in re-runs of classics and cult movies. Cinemas such as the Westgarth and Astor in Melbourne, the Valhalla (closed for renovations at the time of writing) and Paddington Academy Twin in Sydney, the Palace East End in Adelaide and the Astor in Perth all fall into this category.

SPECTATOR SPORTS

If you're an armchair – or wooden bench – sports fan, Australia has plenty to offer. Australians play at least four types of football, each type being called 'football' by its aficionados. The seasons run from about March to September.

Australian Rules (Footy)

Australian (Aussie) Rules is unique – only Gaelic football is anything like it. It's played by teams of 18 on an oval field with an oval ball that can be kicked, caught, hit with the hand or carried and bounced. You get six points for kicking the ball between two central posts (a goal) and one point for kicking it through side posts (a behind). A game lasts for four quarters of 25 minutes each. To take a 'mark' players must catch a ball on the volley from a kick – in which case they then receive a free kick. A typical final score for one team is between 70 and 110 points.

Players cannot be sent off in the course of a game; disciplinary tribunals are usually held the following week. Consequently there can be spectacular brawls on field – while the crowds, in contrast, are noisy but remarkably peaceful (a pleasant surprise for visiting soccer fans).

Melbourne is the national (and world) centre for Australian Rules, and the Australian Football League (AFL) is the national competition. Nine of its 16 teams are from Melbourne; the others are from Geelong, Perth, Fremantle, Sydney, Brisbane and Adelaide (two teams). Crowds in Melbourne regularly exceed 30,000 at top regular games and 80,000 at finals.

The top eight sides compete in the finals in September, and the season culminates with the AFL Grand Final on the last Saturday in September – it's being brought forward in 2000 so as not to coincide with the Olympics.

Aussie Rules is a great game to get to know. Fast, tactical, skilful, rough and athletic, it can produce gripping finishes when even after 80 minutes of play the outcome hangs on the very last kick. It also inspires fierce spectator loyalties and has made otherwise obscure Melbourne suburbs (eg Hawthorn, Essendon, Collingwood, St Kilda) national names.

Soccer
Soccer is a bit of a poor cousin: it's widely played on an amateur basis but the national league is only semiprofessional and attracts a pathetically small following. It's slowly gaining popularity thanks in part to the success of the national team. At the local level, there are ethnically based teams representing a wide range of origins.

Rugby
Rugby is the main game in NSW and Queensland, and it's rugby league, the 13-a-side version, that attracts the crowds. The national competition – the National Rugby League (NRL) – has 17 teams consisting of one each from Melbourne, Canberra and New Zealand, two from Queensland and the rest from Sydney. The grand final takes place on the last Saturday in September.

Rugby union, the 15-a-side game originally for amateurs but now professional, has a large following. Union is a much more global game than league, which is mainly played in Australia, England and New Zealand.

Cricket
During the other (nonfootball) half of the year, there's cricket. The Melbourne Cricket Ground (MCG) is the world's biggest, and international Test and one-day matches are played every summer there and in Sydney, Adelaide, Perth, Brisbane and Hobart. There is also an interstate competition (the Sheffield Shield) and state-based district cricket.

Basketball & Hockey
Basketball too is growing in popularity and there is a National Basketball League, the NBL. Australia's women's netball team won the world cup in 1995 and Australia also has world-class hockey teams (both men and women).

Horse Racing
Australians love a gamble, and hardly any town of even minor import is without a horse-racing track or a Totalisator Agency Board (TAB) betting office or pub. Melbourne and Adelaide must be among the only cities in the world to give a public holiday for horse races. The prestigious Melbourne Cup is held on the first Tuesday in November.

Motor Sports
Each year Victoria hosts the Australian Formula One Grand Prix (held in Melbourne in March), and the Australian round of the World 500cc Motorcycle Grand Prix (held at Phillip Island in October).

Other major events are the Bathurst 1000 held at the Mt Panorama circuit in NSW every October, the Targa Tasmania race in April, and the Finke Desert Race in central Australia in June.

Other Sports

The grand slam tennis event, the Australian Open, is played in Melbourne in January.

Surfing competitions, such as that held each year at Bell's Beach, Victoria, are world-class.

Bookings & Tickets

Tickets for most major events in each state, including concerts, are handled by one or two central booking agencies in that state.

ACT Ticketek	☎ 02-6248 7666
NSW Ticketek	☎ 02-9266 4800
Ticketmaster (NSW)	☎ 02-9320 9000
Queensland Ticketek	☎ 07-3404 6644
Bass Adelaide (SA)	☎ 08-8400 2205
Centertainment (Tasmania)	☎ 03-6234 5998
Ticketmaster (Victoria)	☎ 13 6100
Ticketek (Victoria)	☎ 13 2849
BOCS Ticketing (WA)	☎ 08-9484 1133
Red Ticket (WA)	☎ 1800 199 991

SHOPPING

There are lots of things definitely not to buy – like plastic boomerangs, fake Aboriginal ashtrays and T-shirts and all the other terrible souvenirs you find seemingly everywhere. Most of them come from Taiwan or Korea anyway. Before buying an Australian souvenir, turn it over to check that it was actually made here.

Australiana

The term 'Australiana' is a euphemism for all those things you buy as gifts for friends, aunts and uncles, nieces and nephews, and other sundry bods back home. They are supposedly representative of Australia and its culture, although many are extremely dubious as such.

The seeds of many native plants are on sale all over the place. Try growing kangaroo paws back home (if your own country will allow them in).

For those last-minute gifts, drop into a deli. Australian wines are well known overseas, but why not try honey (leatherwood honey is one of a number of powerful local varieties), macadamia nuts (native to Queensland) or Bundaberg Rum with its unusual sweet flavour.

Also gaining popularity are 'bush tucker' items such as tinned witchetty grubs, or honey ants.

Opals

The opal is Australia's national gemstone, and opals and jewellery made with it are popular souvenirs. It's a beautiful stone, but buy wisely and shop around – quality and prices can vary widely from place to place.

Aboriginal Art

Aboriginal art has been 'discovered' by the international community, and prices are correspondingly high. There's also a growing problem with fakes.

For most people the only readily affordable things are small carvings and some very beautiful screen-printed T-shirts produced by Aboriginal craft cooperatives. Didgeridoos and boomerangs are also popular purchases, but just be aware that unless you pay top dollar, what you are getting is something made purely for the tourist trade – certainly not the real thing.

See the following Aboriginal Art section for more information on buying Aboriginal art and artefacts.

ABORIGINAL
ART

Visual imagery is a fundamental part of Aboriginal life, a connection between past and present, between the supernatural and the earthly, between people and the land. The early forms of Aboriginal artistic expression were rock carvings (petroglyphs), body painting and ground designs, and the earliest engraved designs known to exist date back at least 30,000 years.

While it has always been an integral part of Aboriginal culture, Aboriginal art, with some notable exceptions, was either largely ignored by non-Aboriginals or simply seen as a anthropological curiosity. Then, in 1971 an event took place that changed non-Aboriginal perceptions of Aboriginal art. At **Papunya**, north-west of Alice Springs, Long Jack Phillipus Tjakamarra and Billy Stockman Tjapaltjarri, both elders of the community and employed as groundsmen at the Papunya school, were encouraged to paint a mural on one of the school's external walls. Shortly after work commenced other members of the community became enthused by the project and joined in creating the mural named *Honey Ant Dreaming*. Government regulations later saw the mural destroyed, but its effect on the community was still profound. Images of spiritual significance had taken on a permanent and very public form. Notwithstanding the debate the mural caused in the community, other members of the community expressed a desire to paint. Initially the paintings were executed on smallish boards, but within a short time canvases were used.

From this quiet beginning in a remote Aboriginal community one of the most important arts movements of the late 20th century grew and spread. That it developed in Papunya is not without irony. Papunya was established in 1960 under the auspices of the Australian government's cultural assimilation policy – a policy designed in combination

Title Page: *Walka* by Tjangali George; acrylic on canvas; 51 x 90 cm; 1999. Kaltjiti Arts and Crafts, Fregon, SA

Below: Ewaninga rock engravings, south of Alice Springs; courtesy of the NT Tourist Commission

with others, such as the forced removal of Aboriginal children from their families, to undermine Aboriginal culture. *Honey Ant Dreaming* and the creative and cultural energy it unleashed helped to strengthen Aboriginal culture and led to the abandonment of assimilation as the foundation stone of non-Aboriginal social policy.

While paintings from the central Australian Aboriginal communities are among the more readily identifiable and probably most popular form of contemporary Aboriginal art, there's a huge range of material being produced across Australia including bark paintings from Arnhem Land, ironwood carving and silk-screen printing from the Tiwi Islands north of Darwin, batik and wood carving from central Australia, didgeridoos and more.

Of particular importance is the strength of artistic expression emanating from Aboriginal artists living in the cities and rural townships of

Right: *Possum Snake, Potato Dreaming* by Paddy Japaljarri Sims and Bessie Nakamarra Sims; acrylic on linen; 91 x 153cm; 1992; Warlukurlangu Artists Association, Yuendumu, NT; courtesy of DESART

Art & the Dreaming

All early Aboriginal art was based on the various peoples' ancestral Dreaming – the 'Creation', when the earth's physical features were formed by the struggles between powerful supernatural ancestors such as the Rainbow Serpent, the Lightning Men and the Wandjina. Codes of behaviour were also laid down in the Dreaming, and although these laws have been diluted and adapted in the last 200 years, they still provide the basis for today's Aborigines. Ceremonies, rituals and sacred paintings are all based on the Dreaming.

A Dreaming can relate to a person, an animal or a physical feature, while others are more general, relating to a region, a group of people, or natural forces such as floods and wind. Australia is covered by a vast network of Dreamings, and any one person may have connections to several.

south-eastern Australia whose ancestors felt the full brunt of colonial occupation. The level of brutality the Aboriginal peoples of south-east Australia endured through the 19th and well into the 20th century is difficult for non-Aboriginal Australians to imagine, in fact, to the point that some in government refuse to utter the word sorry.

While the art of the more traditional communities differs in style from urban works, a common theme that appears to run through all the works, be it a painting by Rover Thomas or Trevor Nicholls, is the strong and ancient connection Aboriginal people have with the land, mixed with a deep sense of loss occasioned by the horror of the last 200 years. Ultimately, however, the viewer is left with a sense of Aboriginal cultural strength and renewal.

Below: Rock paintings, Nourlangie Rock, Kakadu National Park; courtesy of the NT Tourist Commission

ROCK ART
Arnhem Land

Arnhem Land, in Australia's tropical Top End, is an area of rich artistic heritage. Recent finds suggest that rock paintings were being produced as early as 60,000 years ago, and some of the rock art galleries in the huge sandstone Arnhem Land plateau are at least 18,000 years old.

The rock art of Arnhem Land depicts Dreaming stories literally, with easily recognisable (though often stylised) images of ancestors, animals, and Macassans – Indonesian mariners from Sulawesi who regularly visited the north coast until banned by government regulations in 1906.

The paintings contained in the Arnhem Land rock art sites range from hand prints to paintings of animals, people, mythological beings and European ships, constituting one of the world's most important and fascinating rock art collections. They provide a record of changing environments and lifestyles over the millennia.

In some places they are concentrated in large 'galleries', with paintings from more recent eras sometimes superimposed over older paintings. Some sites are kept secret – not only to protect them from

Right: Lightning Brothers rock art site at Katherine River; courtesy of the NT Tourist Commission

Hollow-Log Coffins

Hollowed-out logs were often used for reburial ceremonies in Arnhem Land, and were also a major form of artistic expression. They were highly decorated, often with many of the Dreaming themes, and were known as *dupun* in eastern Arnhem Land and *lorrkon* in western Arnhem Land.

In 1988 a group of Arnhem Land artists made a memorial as their contribution to the movement highlighting injustices against Aborigines – this was, of course, the year when non-Aboriginal Australians were celebrating 200 years of European settlement. The artists painted 200 log coffins – one for each year of settlement – with traditional clan and Dreaming designs, and these now form a permanent display in the National Gallery in the ACT.

damage, but also because they are private or sacred to the Aboriginal owners. Some are believed to be inhabited by dangerous beings, who must not be approached by the ignorant. However, two of the finest sites have been opened up to visitors, with access roads, walkways and explanatory signs. These are **Ubirr** and **Nourlangie** in Kakadu National Park.

The rock paintings show how the main styles succeeded each other over time. The earliest hand or grass prints were followed by a 'naturalistic' style, with large outlines of people or animals filled in with colour. Some of the animals depicted, such as the thylacine (Tasmanian tiger), have long been extinct on mainland Australia.

After the naturalistic style came the 'dynamic', in which motion was often depicted (a dotted line, for example, to show a spear's path through the air). In this era the first mythological beings appeared, with human bodies and animal heads.

The next style mainly showed simple human silhouettes, and was followed by the curious 'yam figures', in which people and animals were drawn in the shape of yams (or yams in the shape of people and animals!). The painting known as the 'x-ray' style, displaying the internal organs and bone structure of animals, appeared around this time.

By about 1000 years ago many of the salt marshes had turned into freshwater swamps and billabongs. The birds and plants that provided new food sources in this landscape appeared in the art of this time.

From around 400 years ago, Aboriginal artists also depicted the human newcomers to the region – Macassan traders and, more recently, Europeans – and the things they brought, or their modes of transport such as ships and horses.

The Kimberley

The art of the Kimberley is best known for its images of the **Wandjina**, a group of ancestor beings who came from the sky and sea and were associated with fertility. They controlled the elements and were responsible for the formation of the country's natural features.

Wandjina images are found painted on rock as well as on more recent portable art media, with some of the rock images being more than 7m long. They generally appear in human form, with large black eyes, a nose but no mouth, a halo around the head (representative of both hair and clouds), and a black oval shape on the chest.

The other significant style of painting found in the Kimberley is that of the so-called **Bradshaw figures** (named after the first European who saw them). The Bradshaw figures are generally small and seem to be of ethereal beings depicted engaged in ceremony or dance. It is believed that they predate the Wandjina paintings though little is known of what significance or meaning they have.

North Queensland

In North Queensland rock art again predominates. The superb Quinkan galleries at Laura on the Cape York Peninsula, north-west of Cairns, are among the best known in the country. Among the many creatures depicted on the walls, the main ones are the Quinkan spirits, which are shown in two forms – the long and stick-like Timara, and the crocodile-like Imjim with their knobbed, club-like tails.

Right: Quinkan rock art, Laura, far north Queensland; photograph reproduced with the permission of the Aboriginal community of the Quinkan district, Cape York Peninsula

Left: *Kadaitja Man* by Ronnie Tjampitjinpa; acrylic on linen; 122 x 61cm; 1993; Papunya Tula Artists Pty Ltd, Alice Springs, NT; courtesy of DESART

PAINTING
Western Desert Painting

Following the developments at Papunya (see introduction) and with the growing importance of art, both as an economic and a cultural activity, an association was formed to help the artists sell their work. The **Papunya Tula** company in Alice Springs is still one of the relatively few galleries in central Australia to be owned and run by Aboriginal people.

Painting in central Australia has flourished to such a degree that it is now an important educational activity for children, through which they can learn different aspects of religious and ceremonial knowledge. This is especially true now that women are so much a part of the painting movement.

Dot painting partly evolved from 'ground paintings', which formed the centrepiece of dances and songs. These were made from pulped plant material, and the designs were made on the ground using dots of this mush. Dots were also used to outline objects in rock paintings, and to highlight geographical features or vegetation.

While dot paintings may look random and abstract, they usually depict a Dreaming journey, and so can be seen almost as aerial landscape maps. Many paintings feature the tracks of birds, animals and humans, often identifying the ancestor. Subjects may be depicted by the imprint they leave in the sand – a simple arc depicts a person (as that is the print left by someone sitting), a coolamon (wooden carrying dish) is shown by an oval shape, a digging stick by a single line, a camp fire by a circle. Males or females are identified by the objects associated with them – digging sticks and coolamons for women, spears and boomerangs for men. Concentric circles usually depict Dreaming sites, or places where ancestors paused in their journeys.

While these symbols are widely used, their meaning within each individual painting is known only by the artist and the people closely associated with him or her – either by group or by the Dreaming – and different groups apply different interpretations to each painting. In this way sacred stories can be publicly portrayed, as the deeper meaning is not evident to most viewers.

Bark Painting

Bark painting is an important part of the cultural heritage of Arnhem Land Aboriginal people. It's difficult to establish when bark was first used, partly because it is perishable, so very old pieces don't exist. The paintings were never intended to be permanent records. European visitors in the early 19th century noted the practice of painting the inside walls of bark shelters.

The bark used is from the stringy-bark tree (Eucalyptus tetradonta), and it is taken off the tree in the Wet season when it is moist and supple. The rough outer layers are removed and the bark is dried by

Albert Namatjira

Australia's most well-known Aboriginal artist was probably Albert Namatjira (1902-59). He lived at the Hermannsburg Lutheran Mission, about 130km west of Alice Springs, and was introduced to European-style watercolour painting by a non-Aboriginal artist, Rex Batterbee, in the 1930s.

Namatjira successfully captured the essence of the Centre using a heavily European-influenced style. At the time his paintings were seen purely as picturesque landscapes. These days, however, it is thought he chose his subjects carefully, as they were Dreaming landscapes to which he had a great bond.

Namatjira supported many of his people on the income from his work, as was his obligation under tribal law. Because of his fame he was allowed to buy alcohol at a time when this was otherwise illegal for Aborigines. In 1957 he became the first Aboriginal person to be granted Australian citizenship, but in 1958 he was jailed for six months for supplying alcohol to Aborigines. He died the following year aged only 57.

Although Namatjira died very disenchanted with white society, he did much to change the extremely negative views of Aborigines that prevailed at the time. At the same time he paved the way for the Papunya painting movement that emerged just over a decade after his death.

WENDY HART

Albert Namatjira with some of his paintings at Areyonga, south-west of Alice Springs (1952)

placing it over a fire and then under weights on the ground to keep it flat. In a couple of weeks the bark is dry and ready for use. A typical bark painting made today has sticks across the top and bottom of the sheet to keep it flat.

The pigments used in bark paintings are mainly red and yellow (ochres), white (kaolin) and black (charcoal). The colours were gathered

Right: *Wuyal* (detail) by Wolpa Wanambi; earth pigments on bark; Buku Larrngay Arts, Yirrkala, eastern Arnhem Land, NT

from special sites by the traditional owners, and they were then traded. Even today these natural pigments are used, giving the paintings their superb soft and earthy finish. Binding agents such as egg yolks, wax and plant resins were added to the pigments. Recently these have been replaced by synthetic agents such as wood glue. Similarly, the brushes used in the past were obtained from the bush materials at hand – twigs, leaf fibres, feathers, human hair and the like – but these too have largely been replaced by modern brushes.

One of the main features of Arnhem Land bark paintings is the use of cross-hatching designs. These designs identify the particular clans, and are based on body paintings of the past. The paintings can also be

broadly categorised by their regional styles. In the west the tendency is towards naturalistic images and plain backgrounds, while to the east the use of geometric designs is more common.

The art reflects Dreaming themes that vary by region. In eastern Arnhem Land the prominent ancestor beings are the Djangkawu, who travelled the land with elaborate dilly bags (carry bags) and digging sticks (for making waterholes), and the Wagilag Sisters, who are associated with snakes and waterholes. In western Arnhem Land the Rainbow Serpent, Yingarna, is the significant being (according to some clans), as is one of her offspring, Ngalyod. Other groups paint

Left: *Minhala at Gangan* by Nawurapu Wunung-murra; earth pigments on bark; Buku Larrngay Arts, Yirrkala, eastern Arnhem Land, NT

Nawura as the principal ancestral being – he travelled through the rocky landscape creating sacred sites and giving people the attributes of culture.

The mimi spirits are another feature of western Arnhem Land art, both on bark and rock. These mischievous spirits are attributed with having taught the Aborigines of the region many things, including hunting, food gathering and painting skills.

It's worth visiting the Buku Larrnggay Arts Centre (☎ 8987 1701) and you can also buy locally made crafts at the Nambara Arts & Crafts Aboriginal gallery (☎ 8987 2811).

Contemporary Painting

Ngukurr

Since the late 1980s the artists of Ngukurr ('nook-or'), a settlement near Roper Bar in south-eastern Arnhem Land, have been producing works using acrylic paints on canvas. People from a number of language groups live at Ngukurr. This is reflected stylistically in the art created, as can be seen in paintings by Ginger Munduwalawala Riley, Amy Johnson and Willie Gububi. Although ancestral beings still feature prominently, the works are generally much more modern, with free-flowing forms and often have little in common with traditional formal structure.

The Kimberley

Contemporary art in the eastern Kimberley also features elements of the works of the desert peoples of central Australia, a legacy of the

Right: *Pelican Story* by Amy Jirwulurr Johnson; acrylic on canvas; 185 x 175cm; 1994; Ngukurr, NT; represented by Alcaston Gallery, Melbourne

forced relocation of people during the 1970s. The community of Warmun, at Turkey Creek on the Great Northern Hwy, has been particularly active in ensuring that Aboriginal culture through painting and dance remains strong.

Left: *Devil Devil Man* by Djambu Barra Barra; acrylic on canvas; 1997; Ngukurr, NT; represented by Alcaston Gallery, Melbourne

Right: Untitled, Douglas Abbott; watercolour on board; 35 x 22cm; 1998; Ngurratjuta/Pmara Ntjarra Aboriginal Corporation, Alice Springs, NT

Western Aranda artist Douglas Abbott is a contemporary of the late Albert Namatjira (see the boxed text). Started in the 1930s, painting in watercolour continues to be a vibrant art form, particularly in central Australia.

Balgo

On the edge of the Great Sandy Desert, Balgo was established as a Catholic mission in 1939. While the community is a fair distance from the communities of Papunya and Yuendumu, there are strong cultural connections with the two communities, as there are with the Kimberleys to the north. It was not until the mid-1980s that Balgo artists embraced painting for people outside the community with gusto. Like artists from the other Central Desert communities, the geometric form is favoured, though in what seems a more free flowing or adventurous manner. The art from Balgo is also characterised by the vivid use of colour, as best seen in works by Peter Sunfly (Sandfly) Tjampitjin, Susie Bootja Bootja Napangarti and Donkeyman Lee Tjupurrula.

Utopia

This community north-east of Alice Springs came into existence in 1977 when the Anmatyerre and Alyawerre people re-established their community on traditional land taken from them to create what had been Utopia Station for 50 years. Initially, batik was produced following, like other communities, the influence of the women batik artists of Ernabella. In the 1980s members of the community started to paint on canvases with acrylics, largely abandoning batik. While some men in the community paint, Utopia is known for the work produced by its women artists, in particular Emily Kame Kngwarreye (1910-96), Ada Bird Petyarre, Kathleen Petyarre and Gloria Petyarre. Of this group of extremely talented artists the late **Emily Kame Kngwarreye** holds a special place. Her life as an artist only commenced when she was in her late 70s, first with batik and then in the late 1980s with acrylic paints. Thematically, Kngwarreye's paintings are closely connected to her people's relationship with the land. This is evident throughout, though simultaneously her paintings, with their beautiful use of textured colour, are reminiscent of expressionist paintings. Another startling feature of her work is the number of stylistic changes made over her painting life of a mere eight years. The Australian National Gallery in Canberra, the New South Wales Art Gallery in Sydney and the National Gallery of Victoria hold particularly fine examples of Kngwarreye's paintings.

Tiwi Island Art

Due to their isolation, the Aborigines of the Tiwi Islands (Bathurst and Melville islands, off the coast of Darwin) have developed art forms – mainly sculpture – not found anywhere else, although there are some similarities with the art of Arnhem Land.

The *pukumani* burial rites are one of the main rituals of Tiwi religious life, and it is for these ceremonies that many of the art works are created – *yimwalini* (bark baskets), spears and *tutini* (burial poles). These carved and painted ironwood poles, up to 2.5m long, are placed around the grave, and represent features of the deceased person's life.

In the last 50 or so years the Tiwi islanders have been producing sculptured animals and birds, many of these being Creation ancestors (the Darwin Museum of Arts & Sciences has an excellent display). More recently, bark painting and silk-screen printing have become popular, and there are workshops on both islands where these items are produced.

Right: Pukamani funerary poles and bark baskets installation; Milikapiti, Melville Island, NT; represented by Alcaston Gallery, Melbourne

Artists Working Outside Traditional Communities

While the quantity of work being produced in the desert and Arnhem Land communities has resulted in the work of Aboriginal artists based in the city being somewhat overshadowed, the work produced by artists such as Fiona Foley, Harry Wedge, Trevor Nicholls and Gordon Bennett, to name but a few, is both thought-provoking and at times deeply confronting The works often illustrate the terrible injustices of the past 200 years while raising issues of the place of Aboriginal culture and the artist in the modern post-colonial world. By their very creation, the paintings speak of the strength and unity of Aboriginal culture.

ARTEFACTS & CRAFTS

Objects traditionally made for practical or ceremonial uses, such as weapons and musical instruments, often featured intricate and symbolic decoration. In recent years many communities have also developed non-traditional craft forms that have created employment and income, and the growing tourist trade has seen demand and production increase steadily.

Didgeridoos

The most widespread craft items seen for sale these days are didgeridoos. There has been a phenomenal boom in their popularity and they can be found in shops around the country.

Originally they were used as ceremonial musical instruments by Aboriginal people in Arnhem Land (where they are known as *yidaki*). The traditional instrument was made from particular eucalypt branches that had been hollowed out by termites. The tubes were often fitted with a wax mouthpiece made from sugarbag (native honeybee wax) and decorated with traditional designs.

Although they may look pretty, most didgeridoos made these days

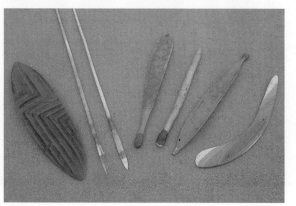

Above: Didgeridoo by Djambu Barra Barra; private collection; Ngukurr, NT; represented by Alcaston Gallery, Melbourne

Left: Traditional weapons and tools from the western desert region of central Australia; Maruku Arts & Crafts, Uluru, NT; courtesy of DESART

bear little relation to traditional ones: they may be made from the wrong or inferior wood, have been hollowed out using mechanical or other means, have poor sound quality, and most have never had an Aboriginal person anywhere near them! (See Buying Aboriginal Art & Artefacts.)

Boomerangs

Boomerangs are curved wooden throwing sticks used for hunting and also as ceremonial clapping sticks. Contrary to popular belief, not all boomerangs are designed to return when thrown – the idea is to hit the animal being hunted! Returning boomerangs were mostly used in south-eastern and western Australia. Although they all follow the same fundamental design, boomerangs come in a huge range of shapes, sizes and decorative styles, and are made from a number of different wood types.

Wooden Sculptures

Traditionally, most wooden sculptures were made to be used for particular ceremonies. Arnhem Land artists still produce soft-wood carvings of birds, fish, animals and ancestral beings. The lightweight figures are engraved and painted with intricate symbolic designs.

Early in the 20th century, missionaries encouraged some communities and groups to produce wooden sculptures for sale.

Below: Decorative central Australian scorched carvings made from river red gum root; Maraku Arts & Crafts; Uluru (Ayers Rock), NT; courtesy of DESART

Scorched Carvings

Also very popular are the wooden carvings that have designs scorched into them with hot fencing wire. These range from small figures, such as possums, up to quite large snakes and lizards. Many are connected with Dreaming stories from the artists' country. In central Australia one of the main outlets for these is the Maruku Arts & Crafts centre at the

ABORIGINAL ART

Uluru-Kata Tjuta National Park Cultural Centre, where it's possible to see the crafts being made. Although much of the artwork is usually done by women, men are also involved at the Maruku centre. The Mt Ebenezer Roadhouse, on the Lasseter Hwy (the main route to Uluru), is another Aboriginal-owned enterprise and one of the cheapest places for buying sculpted figures.

Ceremonial Shields

Around the country many types of weapons were traditionally produced, including spears, spear-throwers (woomeras), clubs (nulla nullas) and shields. The shields were made from timber or bark in different shapes and sizes, and were often richly decorated with carved and painted surfaces showing the owner's ancestry or Dreaming. They were mainly used for ceremonial purposes, but they were also put to practical use when fighting between clans occurred.

Fibre Craft

Articles made from fibres are a major art form among women. String or twine was traditionally made from bark, grass, leaves, roots and

Left: *Bush Tucker and Flowers*, silk scarf by Rosemary Petyarre; courtesy Utopia Batik Pty Ltd

other materials, hand-spun and dyed with natural pigments, then woven to make dilly bags, baskets, garments, fishing nets and other items. Strands or fibres from the leaves of the pandanus palm (and other palms or grasses) were also woven to make dilly bags and mats. While all these objects have utilitarian purposes, many also have ritual uses.

Other Crafts

The **Ernabella** Presbyterian Mission, in northern SA, was another place where craftwork was encouraged. A 1950 mission report stated that: 'A mission station must have an industry to provide work for and help finance the cost of caring for the natives'. As the mission had been founded on a sheep station, wool craft techniques of spinning, dyeing and weaving were introduced. The Pitjantjatjara ('pigeon-jara') women made woollen articles such as rugs, belts, traditional dilly bags and scarves, using designs incorporating aspects of women's law *(yawilyu)*. With the introduction of batik fabric dyeing in the 1970s, weaving at Ernabella virtually ceased.

While probably better-known for their traditional watercolour artists, in particular Albert Namatjira, the Arrernte community of **Hermannsburg** has recently begun to work with **pottery**, a craft that is not traditionally Aboriginal. They have incorporated moulded figures and surface treatments adapted from Dreaming stories.

Another art form, from the western Kimberley, is the engraved **pearl-shell pendants** that come from the Broome area. It is believed that the Aboriginal people of the area were using pearl shell for decoration before the arrival of Europeans, but with the establishment of the pearling industry in Broome in the late 19th century the use of pearl

Right: *My Country* by Elaine Namatjira; terracotta with underglazes; Hermannsburg, NT; represented by Alcaston Gallery, Melbourne

shell increased markedly. The highly prized shells were engraved and used for ceremonial purposes, as well as for personal decoration and trade – examples of this art have been found as far away as Queensland and SA.

The designs engraved into the shells were usually fairly simple geometric patterns that had little symbolic importance. The practice of pearl-shell engraving has largely died out, although the decorated shells are still highly valued.

BUYING ABORIGINAL ART & ARTEFACTS

One of the best and most evocative reminders of your trip is an Aboriginal work of art or artefact. By buying authentic items you are supporting Aboriginal culture and helping to ensure that traditional skills and designs endure. Unfortunately, much of the so-called Aboriginal art sold as souvenirs is either ripped-off from Aboriginal people or is just plain fake. Admittedly it is often difficult to tell whether an item is genuine, or whether a design is being used legitimately, but it is worth trying to find out.

The best place to buy artefacts is either directly from the communities that have craft outlets or from galleries and shops that are owned and operated by Aboriginal communities (see the following list for some suggestions). This way you can be sure that the items are genuine and that the money you spend goes to the right people. There are many Aboriginal artists who get paid very small sums for their work, only to find it being sold for thousands in big city galleries.

Didgeridoos are the hot item these days, and you need to decide whether you want a decorative piece or an authentic and functional musical instrument. Many of the didgeridoos sold are not made by Aboriginal people, and there are even stories of backpackers in Darwin earning good money by making or decorating didgeridoos. From a community outlet such as Injalak or Manyallaluk in NT you could expect to pay $100 to $200 for a functional didgeridoo that has been painted with ochre paints, and you may even get to meet the maker. On the other hand, from a souvenir shop in Darwin or Cairns you could

Top: A collection of handpainted gumnut necklaces; 1993; Keringke Arts; Santa Teresa, NT; courtesy of DESART

pay anything from $200 to $400 or more for something that looks pretty but is really little more than a painted bit of wood.

If you're interested in buying a painting, possibly in part for its investment potential, then it's best to purchase the work from a community art centre, Aboriginal-owned gallery or reputable non-Aboriginal-owned gallery. Regardless of its individual aesthetic worth, a painting purchased without a certificate of authenticity from either a reputable gallery or community art centre, in most cases, will not be easy to resell at a later time – even if the painting is attributed to a well known artist.

For general shops and galleries, see the Shopping sections of the major cities in the main text.

Major Aboriginal Craft Outlets

The following are some Aboriginal owned and operated places where you can buy artefacts and crafts:

Alice Springs
Aboriginal Arts & Culture Centre
　　(☎ 08-8952 3408, aborart@ozemail.com.au)
　　86 Todd St. Gallery and craft outlet with a good variety of dot paintings and other desert crafts.
DESART
　　(☎ 08-8953 4736, fax 8953 4517)
　　Suite 1, Heenan Bldg, Gregory Terrace. A resource and advocacy organisation representing 22 owner-operated Aboriginal art centres in central Australia.
Papunya Tula Artists
　　(☎ 08-8952 4731, fax 8953 2509)
　　78 Todd St. Specialising in western desert dot paintings; high prices but good quality.

Darwin
Raintree Aboriginal Fine Arts
　　(☎ 08-8941 9933)
　　20 Knuckey St. One of the major commercial outlets in Darwin, with medium to high prices but top quality paintings and artefacts.

Kakadu National Park
Injalak Arts & Crafts
　　(☎ 08-8979 0190, fax 8979 0119)
　　Oenpelli. Just over the East Alligator River from Ubirr in Kakadu National Park, Injalak has probably the best selection of Top End arts and crafts anywhere; prices are very reasonable and the staff can pack and ship orders (permits required to visit, but easily available on the spot).
Warradjan Aboriginal Cultural Centre
　　(☎ 08-8979 0051)
　　Cooinda, Kakadu National Park. High exposure and consequently high prices, but good fabrics, T-shirts and didgeridoos.

Katherine Region

Manyallaluk Community
(☎ 08-8975 4727, fax 8975 4724)
PMB 134, Katherine. This small community of Top End Aboriginal people, 100km from Katherine, has a small but impressive array of artefacts including didgeridoos and bark paintings, and some of the best prices you'll come across anywhere.

Uluru-Kata Tjuta National Park

Maruku Arts & Crafts
(☎ 08-8956 2153, fax 8956 2410)
Uluru-Kata Tjuta Cultural Centre. Good for artefacts, especially scorched wood carvings; craftspeople usually work on the site.

Yirrkala – Arnhem Land

Buku Larrnggay Arts
(☎ 08-8987 1701, fax 8987 2701, yirrkala-arts@octa4.net.au)
Museum and award-winning gallery selling art exclusively from north-eastern Arnhem land.

Cairns

Tjapukai Aboriginal Cultural Park
(☎ 07-4042 9999, fax 4042 9900)
Kamerunga Rd, Smithfield. Located at the Skyrail terminus in Cairns with a good range of art, craft and fabrics from a variety of sources.

Below: Detail of hand-painted silk fabric, Kathleen Wallace; 1997; Keringke Arts; Santa Teresa, NT; courtesy of DESART

Getting There & Away

AIR

Australia is a long way from just about everywhere, and getting there basically means flying. Coming from Asia, Europe or North America there are lots of competing airlines and a wide variety of air fares, but there's no way you can avoid those great distances. Australia's current international popularity means that flights are often heavily booked – inbound traffic will almost certainly be chock-a-block leading up to the Olympic Games. If you want to fly to Australia at a particularly popular time of year (the middle of summer – ie Christmas – is notoriously difficult) or on a particularly popular route (eg Hong Kong or Singapore to Sydney or Melbourne) then you need to plan well ahead.

Australia has a number of international gateways. Sydney and Melbourne are the two busiest. Perth gets many flights from Asia and Europe and has direct flights to New Zealand and Africa. Other international airports are Hobart (New Zealand only), Adelaide, Port Hedland (Bali only), Darwin, Cairns and Brisbane. One place you can't fly to direct from overseas is Canberra, the national capital.

Sydney airport is a good place to avoid – it's stretched way beyond its capacity and flights are frequently delayed on arrival and departure. If you're planning to explore Australia fairly seriously then think about starting at a quieter entry port like Cairns or Darwin.

Buying Tickets

The plane ticket will probably be the single most expensive item in your budget, and buying it can be an intimidating business. There is likely to be a multitude of airlines and travel agents hoping to separate you from your money, and it is always worth putting aside a few hours to research the current state of the market. Start early: some of the cheapest tickets have to be bought months in advance, and some popular flights sell out early. Talk to other recent travellers – they may be able to stop you

making some of the same old mistakes. Look at ads in newspapers and magazines, consult reference books and watch for special offers. Then phone around travel agents for bargains. (Airlines can supply information on routes and timetables; however, except at times of inter-airline warfare, they do not supply the cheapest tickets.) Find out the fare, the route, the duration of the journey and any restrictions on the ticket. Then sit back and decide which is best for you.

You may discover that those impossibly cheap flights are 'fully booked, but we have another one that costs a bit more ...' Or the flight is on an airline notorious for its poor safety standards and leaves you in the world's least favourite airport mid-journey for 14 hours. Or the agents claim to have the last two seats available for that country for the whole of July, which they will hold for you for a maximum of two hours. Don't panic – keep ringing around.

Use the fares quoted in this book as a guide only. They are approximate and based on the rates advertised by travel agents at the time of going to press. Quoted air fares do not necessarily constitute a recommendation for the carrier. If you are travelling from the UK or the USA, you will probably find that the cheapest flights are being advertised by obscure bucket shops whose names haven't yet reached the telephone directory. Many such firms are honest and solvent, but there are a few rogues who will take your money and disappear, to reopen elsewhere a month or two later under a new name. If you feel suspicious about a firm, don't give them all the money at once – leave a deposit of 20% or so and pay the balance when you get the ticket. If they insist on cash in advance, go somewhere else. And once you have the ticket, ring the airline to confirm that you are actually booked on the flight.

You may decide to pay more than the rock-bottom fare by opting for the safety of a better-known travel agent. Firms such as STA Travel, which has offices worldwide,

Air Travel Glossary

Baggage Allowance This will be written on your ticket and usually includes one 20kg item to go in the hold, plus one item of hand luggage.

Bucket Shops These are unbonded travel agencies specialising in discounted airline tickets.

Bumped Just because you have a confirmed seat doesn't mean you're going to get on the plane (see Overbooking).

Cancellation Penalties If you have to cancel or change a discounted ticket, there are often heavy penalties involved; insurance can sometimes be taken out against these penalties. Some airlines impose penalties on regular tickets as well, particularly against 'no-show' passengers.

Check-in Airlines ask you to check in a certain time ahead of the flight departure (usually one to two hours on international flights). If you fail to check in on time and the flight is overbooked, the airline can cancel your booking and give your seat to somebody else.

Confirmation Having a ticket written out with the flight and date you want doesn't mean you have a seat until the agent has checked with the airline that your status is 'OK' or confirmed. Meanwhile you could just be 'on request'.

Courier Fares Businesses often need to send urgent documents or freight securely and quickly. Courier companies hire people to accompany the package through customs and, in return, offer a discount ticket which is sometimes a phenomenal bargain. In effect, what the companies do is ship their freight as your luggage on regular commercial flights. This is a legitimate operation, but there are two shortcomings – the short turnaround time of the ticket (usually not longer than a month) and the limitation on your luggage allowance. You may have to surrender all your allowance and take only hand luggage.

Full Fares Airlines traditionally offer 1st class (coded F), business class (coded J) and economy class (coded Y) tickets. These days there are so many promotional and discounted fares available that few passengers pay full economy fare.

ITX An ITX, or 'independent inclusive tour excursion', is often available on tickets to popular holiday destinations. Officially it's a package deal combined with hotel accommodation, but many agents will sell you one of these for the flight only and give you phoney hotel vouchers in the unlikely event that you're challenged at the airport.

Lost Tickets If you lose your airline ticket an airline will usually treat it like a travellers cheque and, after inquiries, issue you with another one. Legally, however, an airline is entitled to treat it like cash and if you lose it then it's gone forever. Take good care of your tickets.

MCO An MCO, or 'miscellaneous charge order', is a voucher that looks like an airline ticket but carries no destination or date. It can be exchanged through any International Association of Travel Agents (IATA) airline for a ticket on a specific flight. It's a useful alternative to an onward ticket in those countries that demand one, and is more flexible than an ordinary ticket if you're unsure of your route.

No-Shows No-shows are passengers who fail to show up for their flight. Full-fare passengers who fail to turn up are sometimes entitled to travel on a later flight. The rest are penalised (see Cancellation Penalties).

Air Travel Glossary

On Request This is an unconfirmed booking for a flight.

Onward Tickets An entry requirement for many countries is that you have a ticket out of the country. If you're unsure of your next move, the easiest solution is to buy the cheapest onward ticket to a neighbouring country or a ticket from a reliable airline which can later be refunded if you do not use it.

Open Jaw Tickets These are return tickets where you fly out to one place but return from another. If available, this can save you backtracking to your arrival point.

Overbooking Airlines hate to fly empty seats and since every flight has some passengers who fail to show up, airlines often book more passengers than they have seats. Usually excess passengers make up for the no-shows, but occasionally somebody gets 'bumped' onto the next available flight. Guess who it is most likely to be? The passengers who check in late.

Point-to-Point Tickets These are discount tickets that can be bought on some routes in return for passengers waiving their rights to a stopover.

Promotional Fares These are officially discounted fares, available from travel agencies or direct from the airline.

Reconfirmation If you don't reconfirm your flight at least 72 hours prior to departure, the airline may delete your name from the passenger list. Ring to find out if your airline requires reconfirmation.

Restrictions Discounted tickets often have various restrictions on them – such as needing to be paid for in advance and incurring a penalty to be altered. Others are restrictions on the minimum and maximum period you must be away, such as a minimum of 14 days or a maximum of one year.

Round-the-World Tickets RTW tickets give you a limited period (usually a year) in which to circumnavigate the globe. You can go anywhere the carrying airlines go, as long as you don't backtrack. The number of stopovers or total number of separate flights is decided before you set off and they usually cost a bit more than a basic return flight.

Stand-by This is a discounted ticket where you only fly if there is a seat free at the last moment. Stand-by fares are usually available only on domestic routes.

Transferred Tickets Airline tickets cannot be transferred from one person to another. Travellers sometimes try to sell the return half of their ticket, but officials can ask you to prove that you are the person named on the ticket. This is less likely to happen on domestic flights, but on an international flight tickets are compared with passports.

Travel Agencies Travel agencies vary widely and you should choose one that suits your needs. Some simply handle tours, while full-service agencies handle everything from tours and tickets to car rental and hotel bookings. If all you want is a ticket at the lowest possible price, then go to an agency specialising in discounted fares.

Travel Periods Ticket prices vary with the time of year. There is a low (off-peak) season and a high (peak) season, and often a low-shoulder season and a high-shoulder season as well. Usually the fare depends on your outward flight – if you depart in the high season and return in the low season, you pay the high-season fare.

Council Travel in the USA, or Travel CUTS in Canada are not going to disappear overnight, leaving you clutching a receipt for a nonexistent ticket, and they do offer good prices to most destinations.

Once you have your ticket, write down its number, together with the flight number and other details, and keep the information somewhere separate. If the ticket is lost or stolen, this will help you get a replacement. It's sensible to buy travel insurance as early as possible. If you buy it the week before you fly, you may find, for example, that you're not covered for delays to your flight caused by industrial action.

Round-the-World Tickets Round-the-world (RTW) tickets are often real bargains. They are usually put together by a combination of two airlines and permit you to fly anywhere you want on their route systems so long as you do not backtrack. There may be restrictions on how many stops you are permitted and usually the tickets are valid for 90 days up to a year. The cost of a South Pacific RTW ticket including Australia is typically in the US$2100 to US$4400 range.

An alternative type of RTW ticket is one put together by a travel agent using a combination of discounted tickets. A good UK agent like Trailfinders can put together interesting London-to-London RTW combinations that include Australia for £800 to £1200.

Also worth investigating is the Global Explorer – a RTW ticket put together by Qantas, British Airways, American Airlines and several others. The number of stops on this one is normally limited to 15.

Circle Pacific Tickets Circle Pacific tickets use a combination of airlines to circle the Pacific – combining Australia, New Zealand, North America and Asia. As with RTW tickets, there are advance purchase restrictions and limits to how many stopovers you can take. However, these fares are likely to be around 15% cheaper than RTW tickets.

Travellers with Special Needs
If you have special needs of any sort – you've broken a leg or you're vegetarian,

travelling in a wheelchair, taking the baby, terrified of flying – you should let the airline know as soon as possible so that they can make arrangements accordingly. You should remind them when you reconfirm your booking (at least 72 hours before departure) and again when you check in at the airport. It may also be worth ringing round the airlines before you make your booking to find out how they can handle your particular needs.

Airports and airlines can be surprisingly helpful, but they do need advance warning. Most international airports will provide escorts from check-in desk to plane where needed, and there should be ramps, lifts, accessible toilets and reachable phones. Aircraft toilets, on the other hand, are likely to present a problem; travellers should discuss this with the airline at an early stage and, if necessary, with their doctor.

Guide dogs for the blind will often have to travel in a specially pressurised baggage compartment with other animals, away from their owners; smaller guide dogs may be admitted to the cabin. All guide dogs will be subject to the same quarantine laws (six months in isolation etc) as other animals when entering or returning to countries currently free of rabies such as Australia.

Deaf travellers can ask for airport and in-flight announcements to be written down for them.

Children under two travel for 10% of the standard fare (or free, on some airlines), as long as they don't occupy a seat. They don't get a baggage allowance either. 'Skycots' should be provided by the airline if requested in advance; these will take a child weighing up to about 10kg. Children between two and 12 can usually occupy a seat for half to two-thirds of the full fare and do get a baggage allowance. Push chairs can often be taken as hand luggage.

The UK
Trailfinders in west London produces a lavishly illustrated brochure which includes air fare details. Look in the Sunday papers and *Exchange & Mart* for ads. Also look out for the free magazines widely available in London – start by looking outside the main train

and underground stations. STA Travel also has branches in the UK.

Most British travel agents are registered with the Association of British Travel Agents (ABTA). If you bought your ticket from an ABTA-registered agent which then goes out of business, ABTA will guarantee a refund or an alternative. Unregistered 'bucket shops' are riskier but also sometimes cheaper.

Trailfinders (☎ 020-7938 3366) at 194 Kensington High St, London W8 7RC, and STA Travel (☎ 020-7581 4132) at 86 Old Brompton Rd, London SW7 3LQ, and 117 Euston Rd, London NW1 2SX (☎ 020-7465 0484), are good, reliable agents for cheap tickets.

The cheapest flights from London to Sydney, Melbourne or Adelaide are Britannia Airways charter flights for an amazing £399 return. This price is valid for one departure in November involving a stay of 10 weeks.

Typical direct fares from London to Sydney and Perth are £335/490 one way/return during the low season (March to June), including tax. In September and mid-December fares go up by as much as 30% while the rest of the year they're somewhere in between. Typical high-season fares are £390/560 one way/return including tax.

From Australia you can expect to pay around A$705/1435 one way/return to London and other European capitals (with stops in Asia on the way) in the low season and A$1020/2000 in the high season.

The USA

There are a variety of connections across the Pacific from Los Angeles and San Francisco to Australia, including direct flights, flights via New Zealand, island-hopping routes and more circuitous Pacific rim routes via nations in Asia. Qantas, Air New Zealand and United Airlines fly USA-Australia. An interesting option from the east coast is Japan Airlines' flight via Japan.

The *New York Times*, the *LA Times*, the *Chicago Tribune* and the *San Francisco Examiner* all produce weekly travel sections in which you'll find any number of travel agents' ads. The magazine *Travel Unlimited*

publishes details of the cheapest air fares and courier possibilities for destinations all over the world from the USA. Council Travel and STA Travel have offices in major cities nationwide.

You can typically get a one way/return ticket from the west coast for US$535/845 in the low season, US$1080/1265 in the high season (Australian summer/Christmas period) or from the east coast for US$680/1180 one way/return in the low season and US$1375/1600 in the high season.

Return fares from Australia include: San Francisco A$1535 low season, A$1640 high season and New York A$1795 low season, A$1895 high season.

If Pacific island-hopping is your aim, check out the airlines of Pacific island nations, some of which have good deals on indirect routings. Qantas can give you Fiji or Tahiti along the way, while Air New Zealand can offer both and the Cook Islands as well.

Canada

To find good fares from Canada to Australia check the travel sections of papers like the Toronto *Globe & Mail* and the *Vancouver Sun*. Travel CUTS has offices in all major cities. Qantas, Air New Zealand, Japan Airlines and Canadian Airlines International all fly Canada-Australia.

Fares out of Vancouver will be similar to those from the US west coast. From Toronto, fares go from around C$1884 return during the low season and C$2307 in the high season.

In the low season, expect to pay around A$1199 for a return fare from Sydney to Vancouver. In the high season, fares start at around A$1870.

See the USA section earlier for other options from North America.

New Zealand

Air New Zealand, Ansett and Qantas operate a network of trans-Tasman flights linking Auckland, Wellington and Christchurch in New Zealand with most major Australian gateway cities. STA Travel and Flight Centres International are popular travel agents in New Zealand.

From New Zealand to Sydney you're looking at around NZ$450/900 one way/return full economy in the low season and NZ$450/1000 in the high season – it costs a little more to Melbourne. There is a lot of competition on these routes, so there is bound to be some good discounting going on.

Cheap fares to New Zealand from Europe will usually be for flights via the USA. A straightforward London-Auckland return bucket-shop ticket costs around £572 in the low season, £739 high season. Coming via Australia you can continue right around with a comprehensive choice of stopovers on a RTW ticket which will cost from around £818.

Asia

Ticket discounting is widespread in Asia, particularly in Singapore, Hong Kong, Bangkok and Penang. There are a lot of fly-by-nights in the Asian ticketing scene so a little care is required. STA Travel, which is reliable, has branches in Hong Kong, Tokyo, Singapore, Bangkok and Kuala Lumpur.

Also, the Asian routes have been particularly caught up in the capacity shortages on flights to Australia. Flights between Hong Kong and Australia are notoriously heavily booked while flights to or from Bangkok and Singapore are often part of the longer Europe-Australia route so they are also sometimes full. Plan ahead. For more information on South-East Asian travel, and travel on to Australia, see Lonely Planet's *South-East Asia on a shoestring*.

Typical one-way fares to Australia from Singapore are S$450 to Darwin or Perth, S$510 to Sydney or Melbourne.

From east-coast Australia, return fares to Singapore, Kuala Lumpur and Bangkok range from A$710 to A$1050, and to Hong Kong from A$950 to A$1350.

The cheapest way out of Australia is to take one of the flights operating between Darwin and Kupang (Timor, Indonesia). See Darwin's Getting There & Away section in the Northern Territory chapter.

Africa

There are a number of direct flights each week between Africa and Australia, but only between Perth and Harare or Johannesburg. Fares vary but from Perth to Johannesburg you can expect to pay A$1045/1590 one way/return in the low season, A$1240/2050 in the high season – a little more to Harare. Qantas, South African Airways and Air Zimbabwe fly these routes.

Other airlines which connect southern Africa and Australia include Malaysia Airlines (via Kuala Lumpur), Singapore Airlines (via Singapore) and Air Mauritius (via Mauritius).

From East Africa the options are to fly via Mauritius or Zimbabwe, or via the Indian subcontinent and on to South-East Asia, then connect from there to Australia.

South America

Two routes operate between South America and Australia. The Chile connection involves Lan Chile's Santiago-Easter Island-Tahiti twice-weekly flight, from where you fly Qantas or another airline to Australia. One way fares cost from around US$1600 to Sydney, Melbourne and Brisbane, plus a raft of taxes. Alternatively, Aerolineas Argentinas flies twice weekly from Buenos Aires to Auckland and Sydney.

SEA

Yacht

It is possible to make your way to other countries such as New Zealand, Papua New Guinea or Indonesia by hitching rides or crewing on yachts. Ask around at harbours, marinas, yacht or sailing clubs. Good places on the east coast include Coffs Harbour, Great Keppel Island, Airlie Beach/the Whitsundays, Cairns – anywhere where boats call. Usually you have to contribute something towards food. A lot of boats move north to escape the winter, so April is a good time to look for a berth in the Sydney area.

Ship

There are no passenger liners operating to/from Australia any more, and finding a berth on a cargo ship isn't particularly easy – travel agencies that know about passenger-carrying cargo services seem to be few and far between (in London try Strand Cruises and Travel Centre, in New York try Trav'l Tips). Probably the quickest way to find a ship is to get hold of a telephone book and start ringing the shipping companies.

DEPARTURE TAXES

There is a $30 departure tax when leaving Australia, but this is incorporated into the price of your air ticket so is not paid separately.

WARNING

The information in this chapter is particularly vulnerable to change – prices for international travel are volatile, schedules change, rules are amended, special deals come and go and routes are introduced and cancelled. Airlines and governments seem to take a perverse pleasure in making price structures and regulations as complicated as possible: you should check directly with the airline or travel agent to make sure you understand how a fare (and any ticket you may buy) works. In addition, the travel industry is highly competitive and there are many lurks and perks.

The upshot of this is that you should get quotes and advice from as many airlines and travel agents as possible before you part with your hard-earned cash. The details given in this chapter should be regarded only as pointers and cannot be any substitute for your own careful, up-to-date research.

Getting Around

AIR

Australia is so vast (and often so empty) that unless your time is unlimited you will probably have to take to the air at some stage.

The two main domestic carriers are Qantas Airways and Ansett Australia. At the time of going to press, Virgin and some other smaller companies were attempting to enter the market, offering discount fares between major cities, thus introducing some welcome competition.

Note that all domestic flights in Australia are nonsmoking. Qantas flights with numbers from QF001 to QF399 operate from international terminals; flight numbers QF400 and above operate from domestic terminals.

For inquiries and reservations contact Ansett on ☎ 13 1300 and Qantas on ☎ 13 1313. Their respective Web sites are www .ansett.com.au and www.qantas.com.au.

Cheap Fares

Random Discounting A major feature of the deregulated air-travel industry is random discounting. As the airlines compete to fill planes, they often offer substantial discounts on selected routes. There are usually conditions attached to the discounted fares, such as booking 14 or so days in advance, or only flying on weekends or between certain dates. Also the number of seats available per flight for these deals is usually fairly limited. The further ahead you can plan the better.

On virtually any route in the country covered by Qantas or Ansett the full economy fare will not be the cheapest way to go. However, because the situation is so fluid, full economy fares are the ones we list throughout the book. Many airports charge a landing tax. This is usually incorporated into the price of the ticket, but may not be included in the price quoted to you by the airlines.

Discounts are generally greater for return than for one-way travel.

If you're planning a return trip and you have 21 days up your sleeve then you can save around 55% by travelling Apex. You have to book and pay for your tickets 21 days in advance and you must stay away at least one Saturday night. Flight details can be changed at any time (with 21 days notice), but the tickets are nonrefundable. If you book 14 days in advance the saving is 50% of the full fare. With five days advance notice you can save 10% of the full one-way or return fares.

University or other higher education students under the age of 26 can get a 25% discount on the regular economy fare. An airline tertiary concession card (available from the airlines) is required for Australian students. Overseas students can use their International Student Identity Card.

All nonresident international travellers can get up to a 30% discount on internal Qantas flights and 25% on Ansett flights, simply by presenting their international ticket when booking. It seems there is no limit to the number of domestic flights you can take, it doesn't matter which airline you fly into Australia with, and it doesn't have to be on a return ticket. Note that the discount applies only to the full economy fare, and so in many cases it will be cheaper to take advantage of other discounts offered. The best advice is to ring around and explore the options before you buy.

Air Passes

With discounting being the norm these days, air passes do not represent the value they did in pre-deregulation days. However, there are a few worth checking out.

Qantas Qantas offers two passes. The **Boomerang Pass** can only be purchased overseas and involves purchasing coupons for either short-haul flights (eg Hobart to Melbourne) at $250 one way, or for long-haul sectors (eg from just about anywhere to Yulara, near Uluru) for $365. You must purchase a minimum of two coupons before you arrive in Australia, and once here you can buy up to eight more.

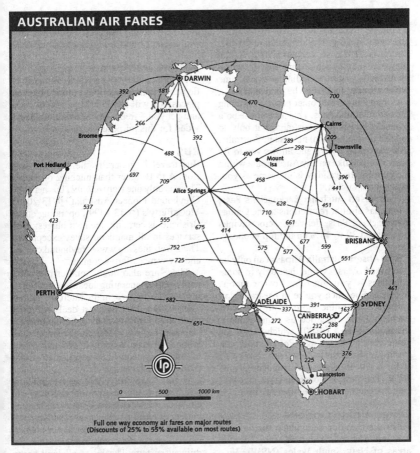

AUSTRALIAN AIR FARES

Full one way economy air fares on major routes
(Discounts of 25% to 55% available on most routes)

There is also the **Qantas Backpackers Pass**, which can only be bought in Australia with proof of membership of the YHA, VIP, Independent Backpackers, Nomads Australia or other acceptable organisation. You must purchase a minimum of three sectors in the first transaction – this journey must take at least seven days – and you can buy two to six coupons afterwards, staying a minimum of two nights at each stop. The discount is quite substantial; a sample fare using this pass is Sydney to Adelaide for $240 one way, as against the full economy fare of $391.

Ansett The **Kangaroo Airpass**, which is available only in Australia, gives you two options: 6000km with two to three stopovers for $949; and 10,000km with three to seven stopovers for $1499.

A number of restrictions apply. Minimum/maximum travel times are 10/45 nights, and travel must be in a continuous direction. One stop must be at a non-capital-city destination and be for at least four nights, and you can only stay overnight at each destination once. All sectors must be booked when you purchase the ticket, although these can be changed without penalty.

On a 6000km air pass you could, for example, fly Sydney-Alice Springs-Cairns-Brisbane-Sydney. The regular fare for that circuit is $1825, so you save $876. While there are better deals, this pass is worth checking if you're travelling at a peak time when cheaper fares may be unavailable.

Ansett has several other passes, including the **See Australia Pass**. This is available both overseas and within Australia, but only to holders of international tickets into Australia. The pass costs $1278 and allows you to fly wherever you like on any Ansett route within the country. Its validity is the same as your international ticket.

The **Ansett Australia Backpackers Pass**, which has similar restrictions to the Qantas Backpackers Pass, delivers sector savings of between 30 to 40% on the full economy fare.

The **Ansett Australia Airpass** can only be purchased overseas, and then only in some countries – you must buy two coupons overseas, and once you're in Australia you can buy up to nine more. With this pass, each sector is classified as either Zone 1 ($240) or Zone 2 ($300), which makes for some very good savings. For example, the Perth-Cairns sector is Zone 2, so you can do it for $300 as against the regular fare of $709. The pass is nonrefundable, but you can change the dates and upgrade it.

Other Airline Options

Australia's major secondary operator is Kendell Airlines, which services country areas of New South Wales (NSW), Victoria, South Australia (SA) and Tasmania. There are numerous other smaller operators. Sunstate operates services in Queensland including some to a number of islands. They also have a couple of routes in the south to Mildura and Broken Hill. Skywest flies a number of routes within Western Australia (WA).

Eastern Australia Airlines operates up and down the NSW coast and also inland from Sydney as far as Bourke and Cobar. Airnorth connects Darwin and Alice Springs with many small towns in the Northern Territory (NT).

These smaller airlines are usually affiliated with either Qantas or Ansett, and their flights can be booked through that affiliate.

Airport Transport

All major country airports have either shuttle bus or taxi connections to town. In some places you will have to ring a taxi to come and get you – free telephones are often provided for this purpose.

BUS

Bus travel is generally the cheapest way from A to B, other than hitching of course. There is only one truly *national* bus network, Greyhound Pioneer Australia (☎ 13 2030). McCafferty's (☎ 13 1499), operating out of Brisbane, is certainly the next biggest, with services in all mainland states except WA. Their Web sites are www.greyhound.com.au and www.mccaffertys.com.au.

There are also many smaller bus companies either operating locally or specialising in one or two main intercity routes. These often offer the best deals – Firefly charges $50 from Sydney to Melbourne, for example. In SA, Premier Stateliner operates around the state. Westrail in WA and V/Line in Victoria operate bus services to places trains no longer go.

A great many travellers see Australia by bus because it's one of the best ways to come to grips with the country's size and variety of terrain, and because the bus companies have such comprehensive route networks – far more comprehensive than the railway system. The buses all look pretty similar and are equipped with air-con, toilets and videos. Smoking is not permitted on any bus.

In most places there is just one bus terminal. Big city terminals are usually well equipped with toilets, showers and other facilities.

Greyhound Pioneer and McCafferty's have a variety of passes, so you should be able to find one that suits your needs. One possible problem with the longer passes is that you are locked into one mode of travel, which may not be convenient if there are more interesting alternatives to straight A to

Interstate Quarantine

When travelling in Australia, whether by land or air, you'll come across signs (mainly in airports, interstate railway stations and at state borders) warning of the possible dangers of carrying fruit, plants and vegetables (which may be infected with a disease or pest) from one area to another. Certain pests and diseases – such as fruit fly, cucurbit thrips, grape phylloxera and potato cyst nematodes, to name a few – are prevalent in some areas but not in others, and so for obvious reasons authorities would like to limit their spread.

There are quarantine inspection posts on some state borders and occasionally elsewhere. While quarantine control often relies on honesty, many posts are staffed and the officers are entitled to search your car for undeclared items. Generally they'll confiscate all fresh fruit and vegetables, so it's best to leave shopping for these items until the first town past the inspection point.

B travel (eg see Other Bus Options later in this section). Both companies give a 10% discount for members of YHA, VIP, Nomads and other approved organisations.

Greyhound Pioneer Passes

Aussie Kilometre Pass This gives you a specified amount of travel to be completed within 12 months, the shortest being 2000km ($185), going up in increments of 1000km to a maximum of 20,000km ($1400). This pass is valid for 12 months; you can travel where and in what direction you like, and stop as many times as you like. For example, a 2000km pass will get you from Cairns to Brisbane, 4000km ($325) from Cairns to Melbourne, and 12,000km ($865) will cover a loop from Sydney to Melbourne, Adelaide, central Australia, Darwin, Cairns and back to Sydney.

Aussie Day Pass This is like the Kilometre pass, except that you are limited by days of travel rather than by distance. Passes for seven ($499), 10 ($640) and 15 ($745) days

of travel are valid for 30 days; a 21 day pass ($982) is valid for 60 days.

Aussie Explorer Pass This set-route pass is more popular, giving you from two to 12 months to cover a set route – the validity period depends on distance. You haven't got the go-anywhere flexibility of the Kilometre Pass, but if you can find a set route which suits you – and there are 24 to choose from – it generally works out cheaper.

The main limitation with this pass is that you can't backtrack, except on 'dead-end' short sectors such as Darwin to Kakadu, Townsville to Cairns or the Stuart Hwy to Uluru. When a pass follows a circular route, you can start anywhere along the loop, and finish at the same spot.

The Aussie Highlights Pass allows you to loop around the eastern half of Australia from Sydney, taking in Melbourne, Adelaide, Coober Pedy, Alice Springs, Darwin, Cairns, Townsville, the Whitsundays, Brisbane and Surfers Paradise for $920, including tours of Uluru-Kata Tjuta and Kakadu national parks.

Or there are one-way passes, such as the Reef & Rock, which goes from Sydney to Alice Springs (and Uluru) via Cairns and Darwin (and Kakadu) for $710; or Top End Explorer which takes in the Cairns to Darwin (and Kakadu) section only, for $290.

There's even an All Australia Pass which takes you right around the country, including up or down through the Centre, for $1555.

McCafferty's Passes

The **Australian Roamer Pass** is similar to Greyhound Pioneer's Aussie Kilometre Pass. You can travel in 1000km increments from between 2000km ($190) to 15,000km ($1050).

McCafferty's also has the **Travel Australia Pass**. There are seven set-route passes to choose from and these are valid for between three and 12 months. The Best of the East & Centre, which is the equivalent of Greyhound Pioneer's Aussie Highlights, costs $845 ($975 including Uluru and Kakadu tours). The Outback Wanderer goes from Cairns to Sydney via the centre for

$485 ($550 including tours), or there's the Sun & Centre, from Sydney to Alice Springs via Cairns and Darwin, for $670 ($750 including tours).

Other Bus Options

Other companies offer transport options for budget travellers in various parts of the country. While most of these are really organised tours, they do also get you from A to B, so are a good alternative to the big bus companies – it's definitely a much more interesting way to travel. Readers recommend the following:

The Wayward Bus

(☎ 1800 882 823) This company has a excellent reputation. It offers six trips, most of which allow you to get on or off where you like. Face the Outback is an eight day run from Adelaide to Alice Springs via Wilpena Pound, the Oodnadatta Track, Coober Pedy and Uluru for $670 including all meals, camping and hostel charges, and national park entry fees. The return trip (Mad Cow) is a simple two day dash down the Stuart Hwy for $75, a good deal if you're in a hurry. You can check out its Web site at www.waywardbus.com.au.

The Classic Coast is a three day trip along the spectacular Great Ocean Road between Adelaide and Melbourne, running twice a

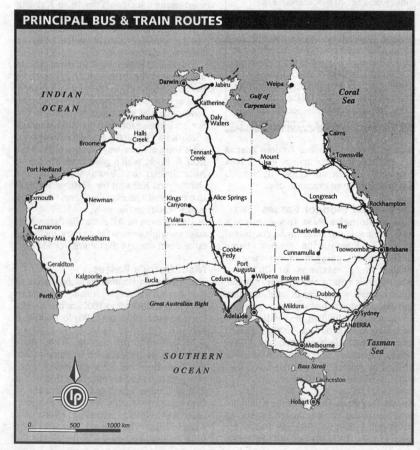

PRINCIPAL BUS & TRAIN ROUTES

week in each direction ($180 including lunches). Another one is Over the Top, a weekly five day run between Sydney and Melbourne via Canberra, Kosciusko National Park and the Alpine Way ($190 travel only).

Nullarbor Traveller

(☎ 1800 816 858) This is a small company running relaxed minibus tours around the coast between Adelaide and Perth. They have two trips – seven days ($529) and nine days ($699) – and these can include activities such as surfing, bushwalking, whale watching and swimming with sea lions and dolphins. The prices include accommodation (camping and hostels), entry fees, and most meals. Its Web site is www.southaustralia.com/nullarbor.

Heading Bush 4WD Adventures

(☎ 1800 639 933, headbush@dove.net.au) This company also does the route from Adelaide to Alice Springs, taking 10 days and going via Dalhousie Springs (except summer) and the Painted Desert. The small group size (10 maximum) makes this a good personal tour – it emphasises that it's an expedition, not a tour, so it's best if you don't mind roughing it. The all-inclusive cost is $750; you can do its express two day return run for $79.

Groovy Grape

(☎ 08-8395 4422, 1800 661 177) Offering yet another option for the Adelaide-Alice run, this company follows much the same route as Wayward, but the groups are smaller (maximum 18). Its seven day camping trips, which depart on Friday, cost $590 including all meals, camping ground charges and national park entry fees. The two day express return costs $85. Its Web site is www.groovygrape.com.au.

TRAIN

Rail travel in Australia today is basically something you do because you really want to – not because it's cheaper, and certainly not because it's fast. It's generally the slowest way to get around. On the other hand the trains are comfortable and you certainly see Australia at ground level in a way no other means of travel permits.

Discounts of up to 40% are possible, subject to availability, making prices comparable to the private bus lines; Australian students get a 50% discount on economy fares. Discount tickets work on a first-come/first-served quota basis. Unless it's a public or school holiday, you stand a pretty good chance of getting one, even if you purchase your ticket on the day of departure; book in advance to be sure.

On interstate journeys you can arrange free stopovers on economy and student tickets, but not on discounted tickets.

Rail services within each state are run by that state's rail body, either government or private. The three major interstate services in Australia (*The Ghan* from Melbourne to Alice Springs via Adelaide, the *Indian Pacific* between Sydney and Perth, and the *Overland* between Melbourne and Adelaide) are operated by Great Southern Railway (☎ 13 2147). Queensland Rail (☎ 13 2232) operates services between Brisbane and Cairns.

The corridor for a train link between Alice Springs and Darwin has been acquired and permission obtained from local Aboriginal people to build the line. At the time of this update, negotiations on a proposal to construct and operate the line were under way between a private developer and the NT and SA governments.

Rail Passes

With the **Austrail Pass** you can travel in economy class anywhere on the Australian rail network during a set period. The cost is $575 for a 14 day pass, $750 for 21 days and $900 for 30 days. A seven day extension to any of these passes costs $300.

Alternatively, the **Austrail Flexipass** allows a set number of economy-class travelling days within a six month period. The cost is $475 for eight days of travel, $685 for 15 days, $965 for 22 days and $1250 for 29 days. The eight day pass cannot be used for travel between Adelaide and Perth or on any of the Ghan trains.

These two passes are only available to holders of non-Australian passports and must be purchased prior to arrival in Australia.

The **East Coast Discovery Pass** covers sections between Melbourne and Cairns, with several options available – eg you can go from Sydney to Cairns via Murwillumbah or direct (both $199). The full pass is restricted to overseas visitors, but an abbreviated version, just covering the most direct route, is available to domestic travellers.

Passes which cover travel in one state are available for NSW and Queensland (see the Getting Around sections in the chapters covering those states for details).

As the railway booking system is computerised, any station (other than those on metropolitan lines) can make a booking for any journey throughout the country. For reservations telephone ☎ 13 2232 during office hours; this will connect you to the nearest mainline station.

CAR

Australia is a vast, generally sparsely populated country where public transport is more often than not neither comprehensive nor convenient. Many travellers find that the best way to see the place is to buy a car. With three or four of you the costs are reasonable and the benefits many, provided you don't have a major mechanical problem.

Road Rules

Driving in Australia holds few real surprises. Australians drive on the left-hand side of the road just like in the UK, Japan and most countries in South-East Asia and the Pacific.

An important road rule is 'give way to the right' – if an intersection is unmarked (unusual), you must give way to vehicles entering the intersection from your right.

The general speed limit in built-up areas in Australia is 60km/h and on the open highway it's usually 100 or 110km/h, although in the NT there is no speed limit outside built-up areas. The police have speed radar guns and cameras and are very fond of using them in carefully hidden locations. However, far from the cities where traffic is light, you'll see a lot of vehicles moving a lot faster than the speed limit. Oncoming drivers who flash their lights at you may be giving you a friendly warning of a speed camera ahead – or they may be telling you that your headlights are on. Whatever, it's polite to wave back if someone does this.

All new cars in Australia have seat belts back and front and if your seat has a belt you're required to wear it – you're likely to get a fine if you don't. Small children must be belted into an approved safety seat.

On the Road

Road Conditions Australia has few multi-lane highways, although there are stretches

DISTANCES BY ROAD

	Adelaide	Alice Springs	Brisbane	Broome	Cairns	Canberra	Darwin	Melbourne	Perth
Alice Springs	1690								
Brisbane	2130	3060							
Broome	4035	2770	4320						
Cairns	2865	2418	1840	4126					
Canberra	1210	2755	1295	5100	3140				
Darwin	3215	1525	3495	1965	2795	4230			
Melbourne	755	2435	1735	4780	3235	655	3960		
Perth	2750	3770	4390	2415	6015	3815	4345	3495	
Sydney	1430	2930	1030	4885	2870	305	4060	895	3990

These are the shortest distances by road; other routes may be considerably longer. For distances by coach, check the companies' leaflets.

of divided road in some particularly busy areas – eg the Princes Hwy from Murray Bridge to Adelaide, the Pacific Hwy from Sydney to Newcastle and the Surfers Paradise-Brisbane road. Elsewhere the major routes are sealed and have two lanes.

You don't have to get far off the beaten track to find yourself on dirt roads. In fact, anybody who sets out to see the country in reasonable detail will have to expect some dirt-road travelling. If you seriously want to explore, you'd better plan on having four-wheel drive (4WD) and a winch. A few useful spare parts, such as fan belts and radiator hoses, are worth carrying if you're travelling in remote areas where traffic is light and garages are few and far between.

Drink-Driving Drink-driving is a real problem, especially in country areas. Serious attempts are being made to reduce the resulting road toll – random breath tests are not uncommon in built-up areas. If you're caught with a blood-alcohol level of more than 0.05% be prepared for a hefty fine and the loss of your licence.

Fuel Fuel (super, diesel and unleaded) is available from stations sporting the well known international brand names. Prices vary from place to place and from price war to price war but generally they're in the range of 65c to 80c. Once away from the major cities, however, prices soar towards (or over) $1 a litre. Distances between fill-ups can be long in the Outback.

Hazards Kangaroos are common hazards on country roads, and cows too in the Outback. Kangaroos are most active around dawn and dusk, and they often travel in groups. If you see one hopping across the road in front of you, slow right down – its friends may be just behind it. Many Australians avoid travelling altogether after dark because of the hazards posed by animals.

If you are travelling at night and a large animal appears in front of you, hit the brakes, dip your lights (so you don't continue to dazzle and confuse it) and only swerve if it's safe to do so. Numerous travellers have been killed in accidents caused by swerving to miss even rabbits and lizards, as well as larger creatures. It's better to damage your car and perhaps kill the animal than cause the death of yourself and your passengers.

In many outback areas you'll also meet road trains – huge trucks (a prime mover plus two or three trailers) up to 50m long. When trying to overtake one make sure you have plenty of room to complete the manoeuvre – allow about a kilometre. When you see a road train approaching on a narrow bitumen road, slow down and pull over – if it has to put its wheels off the road to pass you, the shower of stones that results will almost certainly smash your windscreen. Road trains throw up a lot of dust on dirt roads, so if you see one coming it's best to pull over and stop until it's gone past.

Outback Travel

You can drive all the way round Australia on Hwy 1 and through the centre from Adelaide to Darwin without ever leaving sealed roads. However, if you really want to see outback Australia, there are plenty of routes that put new meaning into 'off the beaten track'. Some of these can be pretty rugged, particularly if it's been a while since a grader went through – if it ever has!

While you may not need 4WD or fancy expedition equipment to tackle most of these roads, you do need to be carefully prepared for the loneliness and lack of facilities. Vehicles should be in good condition and have reasonable ground clearance. Always carry a tow rope so that some passing Good Samaritan can pull your broken-down car to the next garage. The state automobile associations, which can advise on preparation, supply good-quality touring maps.

When travelling to really remote areas, such as the central desert areas, it's advisable to carry a HF radio transceiver equipped to pick up the relevant Royal Flying Doctor Service bases. A satellite phone and GPS position finder can also be handy.

You will of course need to carry plenty of water. In warm weather allow five litres per person per day and an extra amount for the radiator. Carry it in several containers, so that if one breaks you won't necessarily have to make a dash for the nearest tap. Food is less important – if space is tight it might be better allocated to an extra spare tyre.

In arid areas it's not wise to attempt the tougher routes during the hottest part of the year (October to April inclusive) – apart from the risk of heat exhaustion, simple mishaps can easily lead to tragedy at this time. Conversely, there's no point going anywhere on dirt roads in the Outback if there has been recent flooding.

If you do run into trouble in the back of beyond, stay with your car. It's easier to spot a car than a human being from the air, and you wouldn't be able to carry a heavy load of water very far anyway. For the full story on safe outback travel, get hold of Lonely Planet's *Outback Australia*.

Some worthwhile outback tracks are:

Birdsville Track
Running 499km from Marree in SA to Birdsville just across the border in Queensland, this old droving trail is one of the best-known outback routes in Australia. These days it is generally quite feasible in any well-prepared, conventional vehicle.

Strzelecki Track
This track covers much the same territory, starting south of Marree at Lyndhurst and going to Innamincka, 473km north-east and close to the Queensland border. This route has been much improved due to work on the Moomba gas fields. It was at Innamincka that the hapless explorers Burke and Wills died.

Oodnadatta Track
Running mainly parallel to the old Ghan railway line to Alice Springs, this track is comprehensively bypassed by the sealed Stuart Hwy to the west. It's 465km from Marree to Oodnadatta then another 202km from there to the Stuart Hwy at Marla. Any well-prepared conventional vehicle should be able to manage this fascinating route.

Simpson Desert
Crossing the Simpson Desert from Mt Dare Homestead to Birdsville is becoming increasingly popular, but this route is still a real test. Four-wheel drive is definitely required and you should be in a party of at least three vehicles equipped with HF radio communications.

Warburton Road/Gunbarrel Hwy
This route runs west from Uluru to Laverton in WA, from where you can drive down to Kalgoorlie and on to Perth. The route, which is normally OK for conventional vehicles, passes through Aboriginal land for which travel permits must be obtained in advance. From the Yulara resort at Uluru to Warburton is 567km, and it's another 568km from there to Laverton. It's then 361km on a sealed road to Kalgoorlie. For 300km near the Giles Meteorological Station the Warburton Road and the Gunbarrel Hwy run on the same route. Taking the old Gunbarrel (to the north of Warburton) to Wiluna in WA is a much rougher trip requiring 4WD. The Warburton Road is often (and inaccurately) referred to as the Gunbarrel.

Tanami Track
Turning off the Stuart Hwy just north of Alice Springs this route goes north-west across the Tanami Desert to Halls Creek in WA. It's a popular short cut for people travelling between the centre and the Kimberley. The road has been extensively improved in recent years and conventional vehicles are normally quite OK, although there are sandy stretches on the WA side. Be warned that the Rabbit Flat roadhouse in the middle of the desert is only open from Friday to Monday.

Canning Stock Route
This old 1700km cattle droving trail runs south-west from Halls Creek to Wiluna in WA. It crosses the Great Sandy Desert and Gibson Desert and, since the track is entirely unmaintained, it's a route to be taken very seriously. Like the Simpson Desert crossing, you should only travel in a well-equipped 4WD party.

Plenty & Sandover Hwys
These two routes run east from the Stuart Hwy, to the north of Alice Springs, into Queensland. They're normally suitable for conventional vehicles.

Cape York
The Peninsula Developmental Road up to the top of Cape York has a number of river crossings, so can only be attempted in the dry season. The original road along the old telegraph line definitely requires 4WD. Conventional vehicles can take the new 'Heathlands' road to the east beyond the Wenlock River, bypassing the difficult sections, but the Wenlock River itself can be a formidable obstacle.

Gibb River Road
This 'short cut' between Derby and Kununurra runs through the heart of the spectacular Kimberley in northern WA – it's 720km, compared with about 920km via Hwy 1. Although badly corrugated in places, it can be easily negotiated by conventional vehicles in the dry season.

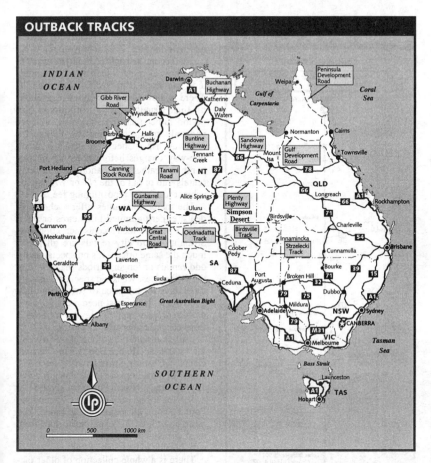

OUTBACK TRACKS

INDIAN OCEAN

Darwin · A1

Buchanan Highway

Gulf of Carpentaria

Weipa

Peninsula Development Road

Coral Sea

Gibb River Road

Katherine

Wyndham

Daly Waters

Derby · A1 · Halls Creek
Broome

Buntine Highway

Sandover Highway

Normanton · Cairns

Port Hedland

Tennant Creek

Mount Isa

Gulf Development Road · 78

Townsville

Canning Stock Route

Tanami Road

NT

87

66

Gunbarrel Highway

Alice Springs

Plenty Highway

QLD

Longreach

66

A1

Rockhampton

WA

Uluru

Simpson Desert

66

95

Warburton

Great Central Road

Oodnadatta Track

Birdsville Track

Birdsville

71

Charleville

54

Carnarvon
Meekatharra

Innamincka
Strzelecki Track

Cunnamulla

Brisbane

Geraldton

Laverton

Coober Pedy

15

91

Kalgoorlie

SA

87

Bourke

39

Perth · A1

94

Eucla

Esperance

Great Australian Bight

Ceduna

Port Augusta

Broken Hill

32

71

Dubbo

A1

Sydney

Albany

79

75

Mildura

79

M31

CANBERRA

NSW

Adelaide

VIC

A1

Melbourne

Tasman Sea

Bass Strait

SOUTHERN OCEAN

Launceston

A1 · **TAS**

Hobart

0   500   1000 km

Rental

If you've got the cash there are plenty of car rental companies ready and willing to put you behind the wheel. Competition is pretty fierce so rates tend to be variable and lots of special deals pop up and disappear again. Whatever your mode of travel on the long stretches, it can be very useful to have a car for some local travel. Between a group it can even be reasonably economical. There are many places – like around Alice Springs – where if you haven't got your own transport you have little choice but to choose between a tour and a rented vehicle.

The three major companies are Budget, Hertz and Avis, with offices in most major towns. A second-string company which is also represented almost everywhere in the country is Thrifty. Then there is a vast number of local firms, or firms with outlets in a limited number of locations. The big operators generally have higher rates than the local firms.

The big firms have a number of advantages, however. First, Avis, Budget, Hertz and Thrifty are represented at all the country's entry airports. If you want to pick up or leave a car at the airport then they're the

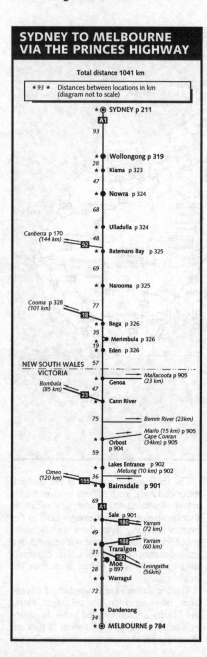

SYDNEY TO MELBOURNE VIA THE PRINCES HIGHWAY

Total distance 1041 km

★ 93 ★   Distances between locations in km (diagram not to scale)

★ ◉ **SYDNEY** p 211
A1

93

★ ● **Wollongong** p 319
28
★ ● **Kiama** p 323

47

★ ● **Nowra** p 324

68

★ ● **Ulladulla** p 324
Canberra p 170   48
(144 km)   **52**
★ ● **Batemans Bay** p 325

69

★ ● **Narooma** p 325

Cooma p 328   77
(101 km)
18
★ ● **Bega** p 326
35
★ ● **Merimbula** p 326
19
★ ● **Eden** p 326
★

NEW SOUTH WALES   57
VICTORIA
★ ━━━━ *Mallacoota* p 905
Bombala   **Genoa**   (23 km)
(85 km)   47
23
★ **Cann River**

75 ━━━━ *Bemm River (23km)*

Marlo (15 km) p 905
Cape Conran
★ **Orbost**   (34km) p 905
p 904
59

★ **Lakes Entrance**   p 902
Metung (10 km) p 902
Omeo   36
(120 km)   **195**
★ ● **Bairnsdale** p 901

69
A1
★ ● **Sale** p 901
180 ━━━━ *Yarram*
49   (72 km)

★ ● **188** ━━━━ *Yarram*
Traralgon   (60 km)
31
★ ● **182**
● **Moe** ━━━━ *Leongatha*
28   p 897   (56km)
★ ● **Warragul**

72

★ ● **Dandenong**
34
★ ◉ **MELBOURNE** p 784

best ones to deal with. Some other companies will also arrange to pick up or leave a car there for you.

The second advantage is if you want to do a one-way rental – pick up a car in Adelaide and leave it in Sydney, for example. There is, however, a variety of restrictions on this. Usually there's a minimum hire period rather than 'repositioning' charges and only certain cars may be eligible for one-way trips. Check the small print on one-way charges before deciding on one company rather than another. One way rentals into or out of the NT or WA may be subject to a hefty repositioning fee.

The major companies offer a choice of deals, either unlimited kilometres or a flat charge plus so many cents per kilometre. Straightforward city rentals are all pretty much the same price – it's on special deals, odd rentals or longer periods that you find the differences. Weekend specials – usually three days for the price of two – are often good value. If you just need a car for three days to drive around Sydney try to make it the weekend rather than midweek.

Daily rates are typically about $50 a day for a small car (Holden Barina, Ford Festiva, Daihatsu Charade, Suzuki Swift), about $75 a day for a medium car (Mitsubishi Magna, Toyota Camry, Nissan Pulsar) or about $100 a day for a big car (Holden Commodore, Ford Falcon), all including insurance. You must be at least 21 years old to hire from most firms – if you're under 25 you may only be able to hire a small car.

There is a whole collection of other factors to bear in mind about this rent-a-car business. For a start, if you're going to want it for a week, a month or longer then they all have significantly lower rates. If you're in Tasmania there are often lower rates, especially in the low season.

OK, that's the big hire companies, what about all the rest of them? Well, some of them are still pretty big in terms of numbers of shiny new cars. In Tasmania, for example, the car-hire business is huge since many people don't bring their cars with them. There's a plethora of hire companies and lots of competition. In many cases local companies are markedly cheaper than the big boys, but in others what looks like a cheaper rate can end up quite the opposite if you're not careful. In the NT, Territory Thrifty Car Rental is at least as big as the others and its rates are very competitive. It also hires camping gear for $25 a day for up to four people.

And don't forget the 'rent-a-wreck' companies. They specialise in renting older cars and have a variety of rates, typically around $30 a day. If you just want to travel around the city, or not too far out, they can be worth considering.

Be aware that if you are travelling on dirt roads you will probably not be covered by insurance – in other words, if you have an accident you'll be liable for all the costs involved. We can't emphasise enough that you should know exactly what your liability is in the event of an accident. Rather than risk paying out thousands of dollars if you do have an accident, you can take out your own comprehensive insurance on the car, or pay an additional daily amount to the renter for an 'insurance excess reduction' policy (see the following 4WD Rental section).

4WD Rental Having 4WD enables you to get right off the beaten track and out to some of the Australian natural wonders that most travellers miss.

Renting a 4WD is within a reasonable budget range if a few people get together. Something small like a Suzuki Vitara or Toyota Rav4 costs around $100 per day; for a basic Toyota Landcruiser you're looking at around $140, which should include insurance and some free kilometres (typically 100 to 200km per day).

Check the insurance conditions, especially the excess, as they can be onerous – in the NT $4000 is typical, although this can often be reduced to around $1000 on payment of an additional daily charge (around $20). Even for a 4WD the insurance of most companies does not cover damage caused when travelling 'off-road', which basically means anything that is not a maintained bitumen or dirt road. Read the fine print.

Hertz, Budget and Avis have 4WD rentals, with one way rentals possible between the

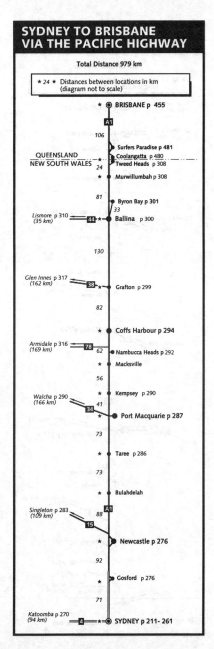

SYDNEY TO BRISBANE VIA THE PACIFIC HIGHWAY

Total Distance 979 km

★ 24 ★ Distances between locations in km
(diagram not to scale)

★ ◉ BRISBANE p 455

A1

106

Surfers Paradise p 481
Coolangatta p 480
QUEENSLAND
NEW SOUTH WALES   24   Tweed Heads p 308
★   Murwillumbah p 308

81
Byron Bay p 301
33
Lismore p 310   44 ★   Ballina p 300
(35 km)

130

Glen Innes p 317   38 ★   Grafton p 299
(162 km)

82

★ Coffs Harbour p 294

Armidale p 316   78
(169 km)   62   Nambucca Heads p 292

★   Macksville

56

Walcha p 290   ★   Kempsey p 290
(166 km)   41
34
★ Port Macquarie p 287

73

★   Taree p 286

73

★   Bulahdelah

A1
Singleton p 283   88
(109 km)
15
★   Newcastle p 276

92

★ Gosford p 276

71

Katoomba p 270
(94 km)   4 ★ ◉ SYDNEY p 211- 261

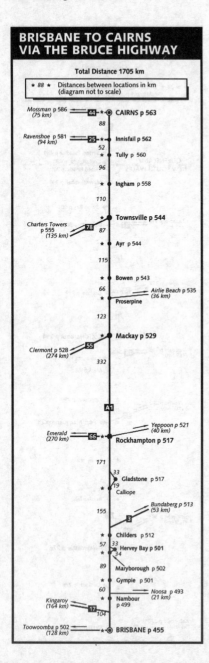

BRISBANE TO CAIRNS VIA THE BRUCE HIGHWAY

Total Distance 1705 km

★ *88* ★ Distances between locations in km (diagram not to scale)

Mossman p 586 (75 km) — **44** ★–◉ **CAIRNS p 563**

88

Ravenshoe p 581 (94 km) — **25** ★–★ **Innisfail p 562**

52

★ **Tully** p 560

96

★ **Ingham** p 558

110

★ **Townsville p 544**

Charters Towers p 555 (135 km) — **78** 87

★ **Ayr** p 544

115

★ **Bowen** p 543

66 — **Airlie Beach** p 535 (36 km)
★ **Proserpine**

123

★ **Mackay p 529**

Clermont p 528 (274 km) — **55**

332

A1

Emerald (270 km) — **66** ★ — *Yeppoon* p 521 (40 km)
Rockhampton p 517

171

33
★ **Gladstone** p 517
19
★ **Calliope**

155 — *Bundaberg* p 513 (53 km)

3

★ **Childers** p 512

57 *33*
★ **Hervey Bay** p 501
34
★ **Maryborough** p 502

89

★ **Gympie** p 501

60 — *Noosa* p 493 (21 km)
★ **Nambour** p 499

Kingaroy (164 km) — **17**
104

Toowoomba p 502 (128 km) — ★–◉ **BRISBANE p 455**

eastern states and the NT. Territory Thrifty Car Rental rents 4WDs from Darwin and Alice Springs.

Britz:Australia (☎ 1800 331 454) hires fully equipped 4WDs fitted out as campervans. These are extremely popular and cost around $130 per day for unlimited km, plus insurance ($20 per day, or $40 to cover everything, including windscreen and tyres). Britz:Australia has offices in all the mainland capitals except Canberra, as well as in Alice Springs, Broome and Cairns, so one-way rentals are also possible. Its Web site is www.britz.com.

Renting Other Vehicles There are lots of vehicles you can rent apart from cars and motorcycles. In many places you can rent campervans – they're particularly popular in Tasmania. Motorscooters are also available in a number of locations – they are popular on Magnetic Island and in Cairns for example – and you only need a car licence to ride one. Best of all, in many places you can rent bicycles.

Buying & Selling

Second-hand cars in Australia can be reasonably cheap. You should be able to pick up a 1982 to 1984 XE Ford Falcon station wagon (a very popular model with backpackers) in good condition for around $2500. The XF Falcon (1985 to 1986) is also popular and costs around $3500. Japanese cars of a similar size and age are considerably more expensive.

Shopping around for a used car involves much the same rules as anywhere in the Western world but with a few local variations. Used-car dealers in Australia are just like used-car dealers from Los Angeles to London – they'll do nearly anything if it turns a dollar. You'll probably get any car cheaper by buying privately through the newspaper than through a car dealer. Buying through a dealer does have the advantage of some sort of guarantee, but this is not much use if you're buying a car in Sydney for a trip to Perth. Used-car guarantee requirements vary from state to state – check with the local automobile organisations.

There's a great deal of discussion among travellers about where the best place is to buy used cars. It's quite possible that prices do vary but don't count on turning it to your advantage. See the section on buying cars in Sydney for the situation at that popular starting/finishing point.

What is rather more certain is that the further you get from civilisation, the better it is to be in a Holden or a Ford. New cars are a different ball game of course, but if you're in an older vehicle that's likely to have the odd hiccup, life is much simpler if it's a make for which spare parts are more readily available.

In Australia third-party personal injury insurance is always included in the vehicle registration cost. This ensures that every vehicle (as long as it's currently registered) carries at least minimum insurance. You'd be wise to extend that minimum to at least third-party property insurance as well – minor collisions with other vehicles can be amazingly expensive.

When you come to buy or sell a car every state has its own regulations, particularly with registration (rego). In Victoria, for example, a car has to have a compulsory safety check (Road Worthy Certificate – RWC) before it can be registered in the new owner's name – the seller will indicate whether the car already has a RWC. In NSW and the NT, on the other hand, safety checks are compulsory every year when you come to renew the registration. Stamp duty has to be paid when you buy a car and, as this is based on the purchase price, it's not unknown for buyer and seller to agree privately to understate the price.

Note that it's much easier to sell a car in the same state that it's registered in, otherwise you (or the buyer) must re-register it in the new state, and that's a hassle. Vehicles with interstate plates are particularly hard to get rid of in WA.

One way of getting around the hassles of buying and selling a vehicle privately is to enter into a buy-back arrangement with a car or motorcycle dealer. However, dealers will often find ways of knocking down the price when you return the vehicle, even if it

was agreed to in writing – often by pointing out expensive repairs that allegedly will be required to gain the dreaded RWC needed to transfer the registration. The cars on offer have often been driven around Australia a number of times, often with haphazard or minimal servicing, and are generally pretty tired. The main advantage of these schemes is that you don't have to worry about being able to sell the vehicle quickly at the end of your trip, and can usually arrange insurance, which short-term visitors may find hard to get. See the Sydney Getting There & Away section in the NSW chapter for more details.

A company that specialises in buy-back arrangements on cars and motorcycles, with fixed rates and no hidden extras, is Car Connection Australia (☎ 03-5473 4469, fax 5473 4520). Here a used Ford Falcon station wagon or Yamaha XT600 trail bike will set you back a fixed sum of $1950 for any period up to six months; a diesel Toyota Landcruiser, suitable for serious outback exploration, is $4500, also for up to six months. Its Web site is www.carconnection.com.au; information and bookings are handled by its European agent: Travel Action GmbH (☎ 0276-47824; fax 7938), Einsiedeleiweg 16, 57399 Kirchhundem, Germany.

Finally, make use of the automobile associations. They can advise you on any local regulations to be aware of, give general guidelines about buying and selling and, for a fee (around $100 for members) will check over a used car and report on its condition before you agree to purchase it. They also offer car insurance to their members. Note that membership is on a personal basis – it does not transfer with the sale of a vehicle.

Automobile Associations

The national Australian Automobile Association (www.aaa.asn.au) is an umbrella organisation for the various state associations and maintains links with similar bodies throughout the world. Day-to-day operations are handled by the state organisations, which provide emergency breakdown services, literature, excellent touring maps and detailed guides to accommodation and camp sites.

The state organisations have reciprocal arrangements with other states in Australia and with similar organisations overseas. So, if you're a member of the National Roads and Motorists Association (NRMA) in NSW, for example, you can use the Royal Automobile Club of Victoria's (RACV) facilities in Victoria. Similarly, if you're a member of the AAA in the USA, or the RAC or AA in the UK, you can use any of the state organisations' facilities. Bring proof of membership with you.

The main state offices are:

New South Wales
(☎ 13 2132, fax 02-9292 9049)
NRMA, 388 George St, Sydney, NSW 2000,
www.nrma.com.au

Northern Territory
(☎ 08-8981 3837, fax 8941 2965)
Automobile Association of the Northern Territory (AANT), 79-81 Smith St, Darwin, NT 0800

Queensland
(☎ 07-3361 2444, fax 3849 0610)
Royal Automobile Club of Queensland (RACQ), 300 St Pauls Terrace, Fortitude Valley, Queensland 4006, www.racq.com.au

South Australia
(☎ 08-8202 4500, fax 8202 4520)
Royal Automobile Association of South Australia (RAA), 41 Hindmarsh Square, Adelaide, SA 5000, www.raa.net

Tasmania
(☎ 03-6232 6300, fax 6234 8784, travel@ract .com.au)
Royal Automobile Club of Tasmania (RACT), Cnr Patrick and Murray Sts, Hobart, Tasmania 7000

Victoria
(☎ 13 1955, fax 03-9790 2844)
Royal Automobile Club of Victoria (RACV), 360 Bourke St, Melbourne, Victoria 3000, www.racv.com.au

Western Australia
(☎ 08-9421 4444, fax 9221 2708)
Royal Automobile Club of Western Australia (RACWA), 228 Adelaide Terrace, Perth, WA 6000, www.rac.com.au

MOTORCYCLE

Motorcycles are a very popular way of getting around. The climate is just about ideal for bikes for much of the year, and the many small trails from the road into the bush often lead to perfect spots to spend the night.

The long, open roads are really made for large-capacity machines above 750cc, which Australians prefer once they outgrow their 250cc learner restrictions. But that doesn't stop enterprising individuals from tackling the length and breadth of the continent on 250cc trail bikes. Doing it on a small bike is not impossible, just tedious at times.

If you want to bring your own motorcycle into Australia you'll need a customs licence; if and when you try to sell it you'll get less than the market price because of restrictive registration requirements. Shipping from just about anywhere is expensive.

However, with a little bit of time up your sleeve, getting mobile on two wheels in Australia is quite feasible, thanks largely to the chronically depressed motorcycle market. The beginning of the southern winter is a good time to strike out. Australian newspapers and the local bike press have classified advertisement sections where $4000 should get you something that will take you around the country – provided you know a bit about bikes. The main drawback is that you'll have to try to sell it again afterwards.

An easier option is a buy-back arrangement from a large motorcycle dealer in a major city. They're usually keen to do business, and basic negotiating skills allied with a wad of cash (say, $8000) should secure an excellent second-hand road bike with a written guarantee that they'll buy it back in good condition minus around $2000. Very few dealers are interested in buy-back schemes on trail bikes.

You'll need a rider's licence and a helmet. A fuel range of 350km will cover fuel stops up the centre and on Hwy 1 around the continent. Beware of dehydration in the dry, hot air – force yourself to drink *plenty* of water, even if you don't feel thirsty. Carry at least two litres on major roads in central Australia, more off the beaten track.

If riding in Tasmania (a top motorcycling destination) or southern and eastern Victoria you should be prepared for rotten weather in winter, and rain any time of year.

It's worth carrying some spares and tools even if you don't know how to use them, because someone else often does. If you do know, you'll probably have a fair idea of what to take. If not, the major motoring organisations (see the earlier Car section) can give members advice on preparation. Carry a workshop manual for your bike and spare elastic (octopus) straps for securing your gear.

And finally, if something does go hopelessly wrong in the back of beyond, park your bike where it's clearly visible and observe the cardinal rule: *don't leave your vehicle.*

For general tips on road safety see the earlier Car section.

BICYCLE

Whether you're hiring a bike to ride around a city or wearing out your Bio-Ace chainwheels on a Melbourne-Darwin marathon, you'll find that Australia is a great place for cycling. There are bike tracks in most cities, and in the country you'll find thousands of kilometres of good roads which carry so little traffic that the biggest hassle is waving back to the drivers. Especially appealing is that in many areas you'll ride a very long way without encountering a hill.

Bicycle helmets are compulsory in all states and territories.

There are countless touring options. A day or two cycling around SA's wineries is popular, or you could meander along beside the Murray or Murrumbidgee rivers for weeks. Tasmania is very popular for touring, and mountain bikers love Australia's deserts – and its so-called mountains too, for that matter. Try the Australian Alps between Canberra and Melbourne, and the Flinders Ranges in SA.

If you're coming specifically to cycle, it makes sense to bring your own bike – check your airline for costs and the degree of dismantling/packing required. Within Australia you can load your bike onto a bus or train to skip the boring bits. Note that bus companies require you to dismantle your bike, and some don't guarantee that it will travel on the same bus as you. Trains are easier, but supervise the loading and if possible tie your bike upright, otherwise you may find that

the guard has stacked crates of Holden spares on your fragile alloy wheels.

If you haven't brought a bike and don't want to buy one, many places have a commercial operator or two who rent out touring bikes and equipment. It's rare to find a good sized town that doesn't have a shop stocking at least basic bike parts.

Much of eastern Australia was settled on the principle of not having more than a day's horse ride between pubs, so here it's possible to plan even ultra-long routes and still get a shower at the end of each day. Most people do carry camping equipment, but, on the east coast at least, it's feasible to travel from town to town staying in hostels, hotels or on-site vans.

You can get by with standard road maps, but as you'll probably want to avoid both the highways and the low-grade unsealed roads, the Government series is best. The 1:250,000 scale is the most suitable, though you'll need a lot of maps if you're going far. The next scale up, 1:1,000,000, is adequate. They are widely available in specialty map shops.

No matter how fit you are, water is vital. Dehydration is no joke and can be life threatening. See the Health section in the Facts for the Visitor chapter. One Lonely Planet author rode his first 200km day on a bowl of cornflakes and a round of sandwiches, but the Queensland sun forced him to drink nearly five litres of water.

It can get very hot in summer, and you should take things slowly until you're used to the heat. Cycling in 35°C-plus temperatures isn't too bad if you wear a hat and plenty of sunscreen, and drink *lots* of water (not soft drinks). In the south, be aware of the blistering hot 'northerlies' that can make a north-bound cyclist's life hell in summer. The South-East Trades begin to blow in April, when you can have (theoretically at least) tailwinds all the way to Darwin.

Of course, you don't have to follow the larger roads and visit towns. It's possible to fill your bike's panniers with muesli, head out into the mulga, and not see anyone for days – or ever again, for that matter, as outback travel is very risky if not properly planned. Drinking water is the main problem in the 'dead heart'. Those isolated water sources (bores, tanks, creeks and the like) shown on your map may be dry or the water undrinkable, so you can't depend on them.

Check with locals if you're heading into remote areas, and notify someone who cares about you if you're about to do something particularly adventurous (or foolhardy).

Useful Organisations

In each state there are touring organisations that can help with information, tell you about tour operators and bike hirers, and put you in touch with touring clubs:

Australian Capital Territory
　(☎ 02-6248 7995, fax 6248 7774)
　Pedal Power ACT, PO Box 581, Canberra, ACT 2601, www.sunsite.anu.edu.au/community/pedalpower

New South Wales
　(☎ 02-9283 5200, fax 9283 5246)
　Bicycle New South Wales, 209 Castlereagh St, Sydney, NSW 2000, www.ozemail.com.au/bikensw

Queensland
　(☎/fax 07-3844 1144) Bicycle Queensland, PO Box 8321, Woolloongabba, Brisbane, Qld 4102; www.uq.net.au/~zzdmcdon/

South Australia
　(☎ 08-8410 1046, fax 8410 1455
　Bicycle SA, 1 Sturt St, Adelaide 5000, www.bikesa.asn.au

Tasmania
　(☎ 03-6233 6619) Bicycle Tasmania, c/o Environment Centre, 102 Bathurst St, Hobart, Tasmania 7000, www.netspace.net.au/spoke/biketas.html

Victoria
　(☎ 03-9328 3000, fax 9328 2288)
　Bicycle Victoria, 19 O'Connell St, North Melbourne, Victoria 3051, www.bv.com.au

Western Australia
　Bicycle Transportation Alliance, www.sunsite.anu.edu.au/wa/bta

Organised Bicycle Tours

There are many organised tours of varying lengths. Apart from being a great way to meet other cycling enthusiasts, most provide a support vehicle and take care of accommodation and cooking.

Remote Outback Cycle Tours (☎ 08-9244 4614, 1800 244 614, fax 9244 4615) based in Perth does fully supported tours from Perth to Broome in four stages via Uluru, Alice Springs and Darwin. The routes covered include the Warburton Road between Kalgoorlie and Uluru, and the Gibb River Road between Kununurra and Broome, in the Kimberley. The cost works out at about $130 per day all inclusive. Its comprehensive Web site is at www.cycletours.com.au.

HITCHING

Hitching is not a particularly safe practice in Australia and we don't recommend it. Travellers who decide to hitch should understand that they are taking a potentially serious risk – Queensland in particular is notorious for attacks on women hitchhikers, and there have been plenty in other states (those dubbed the 'backpacker murders' of the early 1990s in NSW, for example). Even people hitching in pairs are not entirely safe.

Before deciding to hitch, talk to local people about the dangers. If you do decide to go ahead, the advice that follows should help to make your journey reasonably safe.

Factor one is numbers – solo hitching is unwise for men as well as women. Two women hitching together may be vulnerable, while two men can expect long waits. The best option is for a woman and a man to hitch together.

Factor two is knowing when to say no. While refusing a ride with a car-load of drunks is pretty obvious, many violent types are often not so easy to identify at face value. Always be prepared to abandon a ride if you begin to feel uneasy for any reason. Don't sit there hoping for the best; make an excuse and get out at the first opportunity.

Also don't accept rides that are going to drop you at some lonely intersection in the middle of nowhere. Travel from town to town, or roadhouse to roadhouse.

Just as hitchers should be wary when accepting lifts, drivers who pick up fellow travellers to share the costs should also be aware of the risks involved.

BOAT

Not really. The only regular passenger service of note is the vehicle ferry *Spirit of Tasmania* that operates between Melbourne and Devonport. A second ferry, the *Devil Cat,* has operated on that route in recent years, but only in the summer and its future is uncertain.

ORGANISED TOURS

There are all sorts of tours around Australia available including some interesting camping tours. Adventure tours include 4WD safaris in the central deserts, the NT and up into far north Queensland. Some of these go to places you simply couldn't get to on your own without large amounts of expensive equipment. You can also walk, ski, boat, raft, canoe, ride a horse or camel or even fly.

YHA tours are good value – find out about them at YHA Travel offices in capital cities (see Accommodation in the Facts for the Visitor chapter for addresses). In major tourist centres like Sydney, Darwin and Cairns there are many tours aimed at backpackers – good prices, good destinations and usually good fun.

Several operators offer organised motorcycling tours in Australia. One of these is Bike Tours Australia, which also operates under the name Car Connection Australia (see the earlier Car section for details).

STUDENT TRAVEL

STA Travel is the main agent for student travellers in Australia. They have a network of travel offices around the country and apart from selling normal tickets also have special student discounts and tours. STA Travel doesn't only cater to students – they also act as travel agents to the public in general. The STA Travel head office is in Melbourne, but there are a number of other offices around the various cities and at the universities. Its Web site is www.statravel.com.au and the national telephone sales number is ☎ 1300 360 960. The main offices are:

Australian Capital Territory
  (☎ 02-6247 8633)
  13-15 Garema Place, Canberra, ACT 2601
New South Wales
  (☎ 02-9212 1255)
  855 George St, Sydney, NSW 2000
Northern Territory
  (☎ 08-8941 2955)
  Shop T17, Smith St Mall, Darwin, NT 0800
Queensland
  (☎ 07-3221 3722)
  Shop 25-26, Brisbane Arcade, 111 Adelaide St, Brisbane, Queensland 4000
South Australia
  (☎ 08-8223 2426)
  235 Rundle St, Adelaide, SA 5000
Victoria
  (☎ 03-9347 6911)
  224 Faraday St, Carlton, Melbourne, Victoria 3053
Western Australia
  (☎ 08-9227 7569)
  100 James St, Northbridge, Perth, WA 6003

Australian Capital Territory

When the separate colonies of Australia were federated in 1901 and became states, a decision to build a national capital was included in the constitution. American architect Walter Burley Griffin won an international competition to design the city and the site was selected in 1908, diplomatically situated between arch rivals Sydney and Melbourne. In 1911 the Commonwealth government bought land for the Australian Capital Territory (ACT) and in 1913 decided to call the capital Canberra, believed to be an Aboriginal term for 'meeting place'.

Development of the site was slow and was virtually halted during the Depression. Melbourne was the seat of the national government until 1927, when parliament first convened in Canberra. Real expansion of the city only got under way after WWII. In 1960 the ACT's population was 50,000; by 1967 it had topped 100,000. Today, it has reached around 309,000.

HIGHLIGHTS

Telephone code: ☎ 02
Population: 308,411
Area: 2366 sq km

- Taking a tour of the architecturally fascinating, grass-topped Parliament House
- Following the Aboriginal plant trail through the Australian National Botanic Gardens
- Appreciating the Australian art collection at the National Gallery of Australia
- Admiring the display of Canberra's spring flowers at the Floriade Festival in October and November
- Cycling on the path around beautiful Lake Burley Griffin
- Bushwalking in Tidbinbilla Nature Reserve or Namadgi National Park, both home to a variety of Australian fauna and flora

Canberra

☎ 02   • postcode 2601   • pop 308,086

Canberra is well worth visiting. The first things you'll notice about the city are the space and how green it is – some 12 million trees have been planted so far. Examples of the best modern architecture in Australia are to be found here, and the design of the city is fascinating because, unlike so much of Australia, it was totally planned and therefore seems very orderly. Canberra is a place of government with few industries so it has a unique atmosphere that is found only in dedicated national capitals. Surrounded by hills, it has a beautiful setting and is close to good bushwalking and skiing areas.

Canberra has all the furnishings of a national centre – the exciting National Gallery of Australia, the splendid Parliament House and the excellent Australian National Botanic Gardens. Canberra also has quite a young population, including a lot of stu-

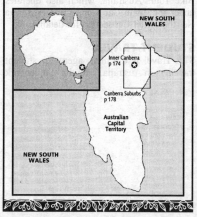

dents, and its entertainment scene is livelier than one would imagine. Finally, this is the only city in Australia where it's possible to bump into kangaroos – they've been spotted swimming across Lake Burley Griffin and grazing in the grounds of Parliament House.

AUSTRALIAN CAPITAL TERRITORY

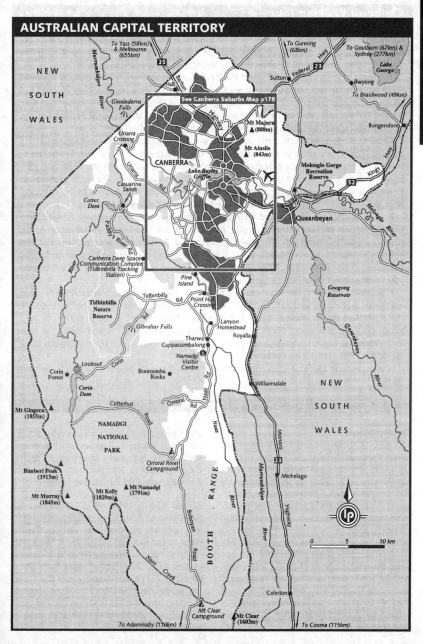

See Canberra Suburbs Map p178

To Yass (58km) & Melbourne (655km)

To Gunning (68km)

To Goulburn (67km) & Sydney (277km)

NEW SOUTH WALES

Ginninderra Falls

Uriarra Crossing

Sutton

Federal Hwy

Lake George

Bwyong

To Braidwood (49km)

Mt Majura (888m)

CANBERRA

Mt Ainslie (843m)

Bungendore

Casuarina Sands

Lake Burley Griffin

Molonglo Gorge Recreation Reserve

Kings Hwy

Cotter Dam

Queanbeyan

Canberra Deep Space Communication Complex (Tidbinbilla Tracking Station)

Pine Island

Googong Reservoir

Tidbinbilla Rd

Point Hut Crossing

Tidbinbilla Nature Reserve

Gibraltar Falls

Lanyon Homestead

Royalla

Tharwa

Cuppacumbalong

Corin Forest

Lookout

Corin

Namadgi Visitor Centre

Booroomba Rocks

Williamsdale

NEW SOUTH WALES

Corin Dam

Cotterhut

Orroral Rd

Mt Gingera (1855m)

NAMADGI NATIONAL PARK

Monaro Hwy

Bimberi Peak (1913m)

Orroral River Campground

Michelago

Mt Murray (1845m)

Mt Kelly (1829m)

Mt Namadgi (1791m)

BOOTH RANGE

0 5 10 km

To Adaminaby (110km)

Mt Clear Campground

Mt Clear (1603m)

Colinton

To Cooma (115km)

AUSTRALIAN CAPITAL TERRITORY

Canberra Walking Tour

Canberra is widely spread out, but many of the major attractions are near or around Lake Burley Griffin, within the 'parliamentary triangle' bounded by the lake, Commonwealth Ave and Kings Ave. You'll need to allow three to four hours for the following walk.

The focus of the triangle is **Parliament House** on Capital Hill. Starting from there, if you head north towards the lake along Commonwealth Ave you'll pass the Canadian, New Zealand and UK **high commissions** on your left. Turning right (east) at Coronation Drive brings you to King George Terrace and **Old Parliament House**, which also houses the **National Portrait Gallery**, and the **Aboriginal Tent Embassy** on the lawns in front of Old Parliament House.

Crossing diagonally (north-west) across the lawn in front of Old Parliament House to King Edward Terrace you arrive at the **National Library of Australia** near the lake. Beside the library is the **National Science & Technology Centre** (aka Questacon), the city's interesting interactive science museum. Along King Edward Terrace towards Kings Ave is the grand **High Court** with its ornamental watercourse burbling alongside the path leading to the entrance. Next door, across Parkes Place, is the wonderful **National Gallery of Australia**.

From there, follow King Edward Terrace onto Kings Ave, turn left (north-east) and follow the avenue over the lake to the other side. As you cross over you'll see the **Carillon** on Aspen Island on your left-hand side. The avenue ends at the **Australian-American Memorial**, but before you reach it, turn left (north-west) at the roundabout onto Parkes Way, which follows the northern side of the lake. After about a kilometre and off Parkes Way to the left (south) you'll come across the modest **Blundells' Cottage**.

Continuing along Parkes Way you'll come to another roundabout. **Anzac Parade** leads north-east from there and has a number of memorials, ending with the largest of them all, the **Australian War Memorial**. Back on Parkes Way, follow it to Commonwealth Ave. Turn left (south) and after about 500m, turn left (east) again onto Albert St and follow the path to the **National Capital Exhibition** at Regatta Point. From there you can see the **Captain Cook Memorial Water Jet** out on the lake.

If you continue south on Commonwealth Ave you will eventually come back to Parliament House.

Orientation

The city is arranged around the natural-looking (but artificial) Lake Burley Griffin. On the north side the main arterial road, Northbourne Ave, runs through Canberra's city centre, Civic. The post office, banks and bus terminals are nearby, and the pedestrian malls to the east are Canberra's main shopping areas.

South of Civic, Northbourne Ave becomes Commonwealth Ave and crosses Lake Burley Griffin to Capital Circle. This circular road surrounds the new Parliament House on Capital Hill and is the apex of Burley Griffin's parliamentary triangle, formed by Commonwealth Ave, Kings Ave (crossing the lake on the north-eastern side) and Constitution Ave. This triangle encompasses a number of important buildings, such as the National Library of Australia, the High Court, the National Gallery of Australia and Old Parliament House.

Maps The NRMA (☎ 13 2132) at 92 Northbourne Ave has an excellent map ($5) of Canberra; the Canberra Visitors Centre (see the Information entry) has a black and white version as well as topographic maps of the ACT. The Government Info Shop (☎ 6247 7211), 10 Mort St, near the Civic bus interchange, and the Travellers Maps & Guides shop (☎ 6249 6006) in the Jolimont Centre on Northbourne Ave also have a wide range of maps.

Information

Tourist Offices The Canberra Visitors Centre (☎ 6205 0044, 1800 026 166), 330 Northbourne Ave, about 2km north of Vernon Circle, is open daily from 9 am to 5.30 pm and weekends until 4 pm. Its Web site is at www.canberratourism.com.au. The friendly Travellers Maps & Guides (☎ 6249 6006) in the Jolimont Centre on Northbourne Ave is also an excellent source of information on Canberra.

There's also a Women's Information & Referral Centre (☎ 6205 1075), Level 1, Block A, Callam Offices, Easty St, Woden, which is open Monday to Friday from 9 am to 5 pm.

Money Apart from the banks scattered around Civic, you'll find American Express in the Centrepoint Building, on the corner of Petrie St and City Walk, and Thomas Cook, in the Canberra Centre on Bunda St. The Casino Canberra is good for after-hours money changing.

Post & Communications Poste restante mail can be addressed to Canberra City Post Office, 53-73 Alinga St, Civic, ACT 2601. It's open Monday to Friday from 8.30 am to 5.30 pm. There are payphones and credit-card phones outside the post office, as well as in the nearby Jolimont Centre and elsewhere.

The National Library, the Civic Library and many of the suburban libraries have Internet facilities. Both the YHA and Victor Lodge have terminals, as does the ground floor of the Jolimont Centre. Cyberchino in Kingston (see the Places to Eat section later in the chapter) is an Internet cafe.

Bookshops Canberra has many good bookshops. The Co-op Bookshop in the ANU Concessions area at the southern end of North Rd, Acton, has an extensive selection of books. The Government Info Shop, 10 Mort St, has Australiana publications that make good souvenirs or presents. Smiths Alternative Bookshop, 76 Alinga St, stocks a range of alternative titles, while Paperchain Bookstore on Furneaux St in Manuka stocks more general books.

Electric Shadows on City Walk, near the cinema of the same name, has books on theatre, film and the arts, and the more eclectic videos for rent. It's open daily.

Book Lore, 94 Wattle St, next to Tilley's in Lyneham, is an excellent second-hand bookshop.

Cultural Centres Canberra is well stocked with overseas information centres and clubs, including Alliance Française (☎ 6247 5027) on McCaughey St, Turner; Das Zentrum (☎ 6230 0441), a German-Australian Cultural Centre in the Community Centre, 19 Bunda St; and the Spanish-Australia Club (☎ 6295 6506) on Jerrabomberra Ave, Narrabundah.

Laundry Many of the major shopping areas have laundrettes. In Dickson there's a coin laundrette on Cope Street; there's one also masquerading as a post office in the same block as Tilley's on Wattle St, Lyneham, and the Kingston Coin-Op Laundry is in the Cusak Centre on Eyre St in the Kingston shopping centre.

Medical Services The Travellers' Medical & Vaccination Centre (☎ 6257 7154), upstairs in the City Walk Arcade near the Civic bus interchange, is open weekdays from 8.30 am to 4.30 pm. Treatment is by appointment only. Several other clinics are nearby.

Emergency Emergency phone numbers include ☎ 000 for ambulance, fire and police; ☎ 13 1114 for Lifeline (emergency counselling); and ☎ 6247 2525 for the Rape Crisis Centre.

Lookouts

There are fine views of Canberra from the surrounding hills. West of Civic, **Black Mountain** rises to 812m and is topped by the 195m **Telstra Tower**, complete with revolving restaurant. The tower also houses a display on the history of telecommunications. The tower is open daily from 9 am to 10 pm ($3/1 for adults/children). There are also splendid vistas from the approach road.

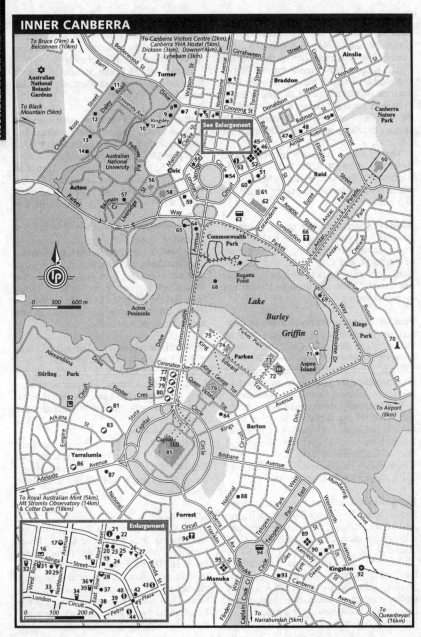

AUSTRALIAN CAPITAL TERRITORY

INNER CANBERRA

INNER CANBERRA

PLACES TO STAY
2   Quality Inn Downtown
3   Holiday Inn
4   Canberra Central
    Apartments
8   Toad Hall
11 Bruce Hall
12 Burton & Garran Hall
13 Ursula College
14 Burgmann College
19 City Walk Hotel
48 Acacia Motor Lodge
49 Olim's Canberra Hotel
59 Capital Towers Apartments
88 Macquarie Private Hotel
90 Motel Monaro
91 Victor Lodge
93 Kingston Hotel

PLACES TO EAT
5   Psychedeli
6   Fringe Benefits
10 University Union
25 Mama's Café & Bar; Happy's
26 Sammy's Kitchen; Gus'Café;
    Café Essen
27 Ali Baba; Heaven Nite Club
29 Little Saigon
33 Lemon Grass
36 Canberra Vietnamese
    Restaurant
38 Bailey's Corner; Tosolini's
39 Antigo Café
45 Sizzle City

OTHER
1   NRMA
7   Environment Centre
9   Drill Hall Gallery
15 Canberra Workers' Club
16 Main Post Office

17 Jolimont Centre
    (Countrylink Travel Centre,
    Airlines, Bus Station, Trav-
    ellers Maps & Guides)
18 Pandora's
20 Greater Union cinemas
21 Government Info Shop
22 Das Zentrum
23 Cinema Centre
24 Travellers' Medical &
    Vaccination Centre
28 Civic Bus Interchange
30 Smiths Bookshop
31 PJ O'Reilly's
32 Wig & Pen
34 Moosehead's Pub
35 Phoenix
37 Civic Library
40 ANZ Bank
41 Merry-go-round
42 American Express
43 Commonwealth Bank
44 Westpac Bank
46 City Market
47 Gorman House Community
    Arts Centre & Café Luna
50 Australian War Memorial
51 Canberra Blade Centre
52 Canberra Centre;
    Thomas Cook
53 National Australia Bank
54 Canberra Theatre Centre
55 Canberra City Police Station
56 SoundScreen Australia
57 University House
58 Australian Academy of
    Science
60 Electric Shadows Cinema
    & Bookshop
61 Casino Canberra
62 National Convention Centre

63 Olympic Swimming Pool
64 Mr Spokes Bike Hire
65 Acton Park Ferry Terminal &
    Boat Hire
66 Church of St John the
    Baptist; St John's School-
    house Museum
67 National Capital Exhibition
68 Captain Cook Memorial
    Water Jet
69 Blundells' Cottage
70 Australian-American
    Memorial
71 Carillon
72 National Gallery of Australia
73 High Court
74 National Science &Tech-
    nology Centre (Questacon)
75 National Library of Australia
76 Old Parliament House
77 UK High Commission
78 NZ High Commission
79 Canadian High Commission
80 PNG High Commission
81 Indonesian Embassy
82 Canberra Mosque
83 US Embassy
84 National Archives
85 Parliament House
86 Thai Embassy
87 The Lodge
89 Kingston Shopping Centre;
    Cyberchino; Café Keru; Filthy
    McFadden's; Durham Castle
    Arms
92 Kingston Train Station
94 Manuka Swimming Pool
95 Manuka Shopping Centre;
    My Café; Alanya; Daniel's;
    Timmy's Kitchen
96 Serbian Orthodox Church

Murray's Canberra Explorer (see the Getting Around section later in this chapter) runs to the tower, or you can walk up a 2km trail through bush, starting on Frith Rd. Additional bushwalks, accessible from Belconnen Way and Caswell Drive, wander to the north-west around the back of the mountain.

Other lookouts, all with road access, are **Mt Ainslie** (843m), **Red Hill** (720m) and **Mt Pleasant** (663m). Mt Ainslie is close to and north-east of the city and has particularly fine views, day or night. Foot trails lead up to Mt Ainslie from behind the Australian War Memorial, and then go north-west to **Mt Majura** (888m), 4km away. You may see kangaroos on the hike up. The Canberra Visitors Centre has basic maps for these and other local bushwalks.

Lake Burley Griffin

The lake was named after Canberra's designer, but wasn't created until the Molonglo River was dammed in 1963. Swimming in the lake is not recommended, but it is suitable for boating (beware of sudden strong winds) and is great to cycle around. Boats, bikes and in-line skates are available for hire at the Acton Park ferry terminal on the northern side of the lake.

There are many places of interest around the lake's 35km shore. The most visible is the **Captain Cook Memorial Water Jet**, which flings a six tonne column of water 147m into the air and gives you a free shower if the wind is blowing from the right direction (despite an automatic switch-off if wind speeds get too high). The jet, built in 1970 to commemorate the bicentenary of Captain Cook's visit to Australia, operates daily from 10 am to noon and 2 to 4 pm (plus 7 to 9 pm during daylight-saving time). At **Regatta Point**, nearby on the north shore, is a skeleton globe with Cook's three great voyages traced onto it.

The **National Capital Exhibition**, also at Regatta Point, is open daily from 9 am to 5 pm (winter) or 6 pm (summer) and has interesting displays on the growth of Canberra (entry is free). Further east around the lake is **Blundells' Cottage** (circa 1860). This simple stone-and-slab cottage, a reminder of the area's early farming history, is open Tuesday to Sunday from 10 am to 4 pm (entry $2).

A little further around the lake, at the far end of Commonwealth Park, is the **Carillon** on Aspen Island. The 53-bell tower was a gift from Britain in 1963 for Canberra's 50th anniversary. The bells weigh from 7kg to six tonnes. There are recitals on weekdays from 12.45 to 1.30 pm, and weekends and public holidays from 2.45 to 3.30 pm.

Parliament House

South of the lake, a four-legged flag mast on top of Capital Hill marks the location of Parliament House. This is the most recent aspect of Burley Griffin's vision to become a reality. Opened in 1988, it cost $1.1 billion, took eight years to build and replaced the 'temporary' parliament house down the hill on King George Terrace, which served for 11 years longer than its intended 50 year life. The new parliament was designed by the US-based Italian Romaldo Giurgola, who won a competition entered by more than 300 architects.

The structure was built into the top of the hill and the roof grassed over to preserve

RICHARD I'ANSON

Parliament House

the shape of the original hill top. The interior design and decoration is splendid – a different combination of Australian timbers is used in each of the main sections. Seventy Australian art and craft works were commissioned and a further 3000 were bought for the building.

Its main axis runs from north-east to south-west and in a direct line from Old Parliament House, the Australian War Memorial across the lake and Mt Ainslie. On either side of this axis, two high, granite-faced walls curve out from the centre to the corners of the site. The House of Representatives is to the east of these walls and the Senate to the west. They're linked to the centre by covered walkways.

Extensive areas of Parliament House are open daily to the public from 9 am to 5 pm. Entry is through the white marble **Great Verandah** at the north-eastern end of the main axis, where Michael Tjakamarra Nelson's *Meeting Place* mosaic represents a gathering of Aboriginal tribes.

Inside, the grey-green marble columns of the foyer symbolise a forest, and marquetry panels on the walls depict Australian flora. The 1st floor looks down on the **Great Hall**, with its 20m long Arthur Boyd tapestry. A public gallery above the Great Hall has a 16m embroidery, created by over 500 people.

Beyond the Great Hall is the gallery, which is above the Members' Hall. The gallery is the central 'crossroads' of the building, with the flag mast above it and passages to the debating chambers on each side. One of only four known originals of **Magna Carta** is on display here. Committee rooms and ministers' offices are south of the Members' Hall. The public can view the committee rooms and attend some of the proceedings. It is also possible to wander over the grassy top of the building. If you want to ensure a place in the **House of Representatives** gallery, book by phone (☎ 6277 4889) or write to the Sergeant at Arms Office, House of Representatives, Parliament House, Canberra, ACT 2000. Some seats are left unbooked, but on days when parliament is sitting you have to queue early to get a place. Seats in the **Senate** gallery are usually available.

On nonsitting days there are free **guided tours** every half hour from 9 am; on sitting days there's a shorter tour.

Murray's Canberra Explorer (see Getting Around later in this chapter) and bus Nos 34 and 39 run to Parliament House.

Old Parliament House

On King George Terrace, halfway between the new Parliament House and the lake, this building was the seat of government from 1927 to 1988. Its parliamentary days ended in style: as the corridors of power echoed to the defence minister's favourite Rolling Stones records, the prime minister and leader of the opposition sang together arm in arm, and bodies were seen dragging themselves away well after dawn the next morning – and that's just what got into print!

There are 40-minute guided tours of the building but if you want to take yourself around there's a set of notes available that describe life in the legislative chambers, parliamentarians' offices and prime minister's office. The building is also home to the **National Portrait Gallery** (☎ 6273 4723) and there are often special exhibitions. Old Parliament House is open daily from 9 am to 4 pm ($2/1).

On the lawn in front of Old Parliament House is the **Aboriginal Tent Embassy**. Established in 1972 to persuade the Federal Government to recognise the legitimacy of Australian and Torres Strait Islander land claims, it's now recognised by the Australian Heritage Commission as a site of special cultural significance. It was here that the Aboriginal flag first gained prominence.

National Gallery of Australia

This excellent art gallery (☎ 6240 6411/6502) is on Parkes Place beside the High Court on the south of Lake Burley Griffin. The Australian collection ranges from traditional Aboriginal art to 20th century works by Arthur Boyd, Sidney Nolan and Albert Tucker. Aboriginal works include bark paintings from Arnhem Land, *pukumani* burial poles from the Tiwi people of

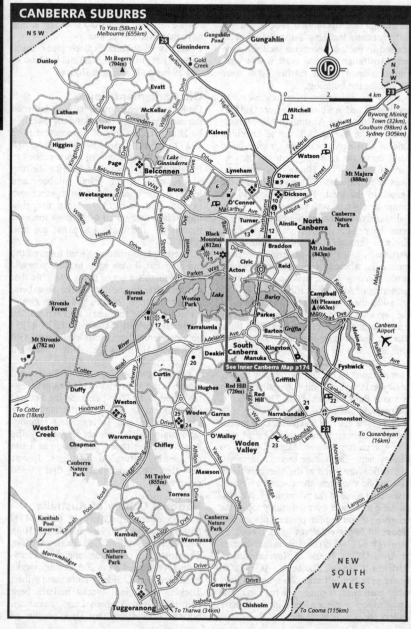

CANBERRA SUBURBS

AUSTRALIAN CAPITAL TERRITORY

CANBERRA SUBURBS

PLACES TO STAY
3   Canberra Lakes Carotel
5   Canberra Motor Village
7   Canberra YHA Hostel
9   Blue & White Lodge; Blue Sky;
    Parkview; Miranda; Northbourne Lodge
12 Fenner Hall
22 Canberra South Motor Park

OTHER
1   Gold Creek attractions
    (Australian Reptile Centre;
    National Dinosaur Museum;
    Ginnidera Village; Cockington Green)
2   National Motorcycle Museum
4   Belconnen Shopping Centre
6   Australian Institute of Sport
8   Lyneham Shopping Centre; Tilley's
10 Dickson Shopping Centre;
    Canberra Tradesmen's Union Club;
    Downer Club
11 Canberra Visitors Centre
13 Alliance Française
14 Australian National Botanic Gardens
15 Black Mountain Lookout; Telstra Tower
16 Government House
17 Scrivener Dam Lookout
18 National Aquarium & Wildlife Sanctuary
19 Mt Stromlo Observatory; Red Belly Black Café
20 Royal Australian Mint
21 Spanish-Australia Club
23 Mugga Lane Zoo
24 Women's Information & Referral Centre
25 Woden Plaza
26 Weston Shopping Centre
27 Tuggeranon Hyperdome

Melville and Bathurst islands off Darwin, printed fabrics by the women of Utopia and Ernabella in central Australia, and paintings from Yuendumu, also in central Australia. There are often temporary exhibitions from the Kimberley and other areas where Aboriginal art is flourishing.

In addition to works from the early decades of European settlement and the 19th century romantics, there are examples of the early nationalistic statements of Charles Conder, Arthur Streeton and Tom Roberts. The collection is not confined to paintings: sculptures, prints, drawings, photographs, furniture, ceramics, fashion, textiles and silverware are all on display. The Sculpture Garden (always open) has a variety of striking sculptures. The garden is a great place to listen to carillon recitals.

The gallery is open daily from 10 am to 5 pm, and entry is free except for special exhibitions. There are tours at 11 am and 2 pm, and a tour focuses on Aboriginal art every Thursday and Sunday at 11 am. The gallery often provides free lectures relating to its exhibitions and presents films on Friday at 12.45 pm. Phone the gallery for details or check Saturday's *Canberra Times*.

Foreign Consulates
There are about 60 embassies and high commissions in Canberra. A few are worth looking at, although many operate from nondescript suburban houses. Most are in Yarralumla, west and north of Parliament House. Periodically, a number of them are open to the public; ask at the Canberra Visitors Centre for details.

The US embassy is a facsimile of a southern mansion, in the style of those in Williamsburg, Virginia. Opposite is the Mughal-inspired Indian high commission. The Thai embassy, with its pointed, orange-tiled roof, is in a style similar to that of Bangkok temples. Beside the dull Indonesian embassy building is a small centre exhibiting Indonesia's colourful culture. It's open Monday to Wednesday from 9.30 am to 12.30 pm and 2 to 5 pm. Papua New Guinea's high commission looks like a *haus tambaran* (spirit house) from the Sepik region. A display room containing colour photographs and artefacts is open weekdays from 10.30 am to 1 pm and 2.30 to 4.30 pm.

See the Embassies section in the Facts for the Visitor chapter for the addresses of embassies and high commissions.

High Court
The High Court building (☎ 6270 6811) on Parkes Place, by the lake and next to the National Gallery of Australia, is open Monday to Friday from 9.45 am to 4.30 pm (entry free). Opened in 1980, its grandiose magnificence caused it to be dubbed 'Gar's Mahal', a reference to Sir Garfield Barwick, chief justice during the building's construction.

High Court sittings are open to the public (call for times).

National Archives

On Queen Victoria Terrace is the former Old Parliament post office that now houses the National Archives of Australia. Comprising photographs, files, posters, films, maps and audio tapes, these are the records of the Commonwealth government since Federation. In addition to regular exhibitions there are facilities for research. The archives are open Monday to Saturday from 9 am to 5 pm and from noon to 5 pm Sunday (entry is free).

National Science & Technology Centre (Questacon)

This 'hands-on' science museum is in the building between the High Court and the National Library of Australia. There are 200 'devices' in the centre's five galleries and outdoor areas. Using 'props', you can get a feeling for a scientific concept and then see it applied to an everyday situation. It might be educational, but it's also great fun.

It's open daily from 10 am to 5 pm ($8/5/4 for adults/concessions/children).

National Library of Australia

Also on Parkes Place beside the lake is the National Library of Australia (☎ 6262 1111), one of the most elegant buildings in Canberra. The visitor information desk is staffed weekdays from 9 am to 5 pm.

The library has more than five million books. Among its displays are rare books, paintings, early manuscripts, photographs, oral histories and maps. There are guided tours at 12.30 pm on Tuesday. You can use the Internet terminal in the foyer.

The library is open Monday to Thursday from 9 am to 9 pm, Friday and Saturday until 5 pm and Sunday from 1.30 to 5 pm.

Royal Australian Mint

The mint (☎ 6202 6999), south of the lake on Denison St, Deakin, produces Australia's coins. There's a gallery with displays showing the history of Australian coins, and through plate-glass windows (keeping you at arm's length) you can see the production

process from raw materials to finished coins. The nearest you get to new coins is being able to mint your own $1 coin, but the pleasure costs you $2. The mint is open weekdays from 9 am to 4 pm and weekends from 10 am to 3 pm (entry is free). Murray's Canberra Explorer and bus Nos 30, 31, 32 and 82 run past.

Australian War Memorial

The massive war memorial, north of the lake and at the foot of Mt Ainslie, looks along Anzac Parade to Old Parliament House across the lake. It was conceived in 1925 and finally opened in 1941. The memorial houses an amazing collection of pictures, dioramas, relics and exhibitions detailing the horrors and stupidity of war, the suffering and the individual acts of bravery. Allow at least a couple of hours for this exhibition. Entombed here is the Unknown Australian Soldier, whose remains were returned from a WWI battlefield in 1993.

The memorial is open daily from 10 am to 5 pm (when the 'Last Post' is played) and entry is free. Several free tours are held each day, some focusing on the artworks. Phone (☎ 6243 4211) for times. Murray's Canberra Explorer and bus No 33 stop here.

Along Anzac Parade there are memorials to several conflicts and campaigns.

Larger war relics, such as tanks and aircraft, are housed at the **Treloar Technology Centre** on the corner of Vickers and Callan Sts in Mitchell. The centre is open on Wednesday and Sunday from 11 am to 4 pm; entry is $3/2 for an adult/child.

Australian National University (ANU)

The ANU's attractive grounds take up most of the area between Civic and Black Mountain and are pleasant to wander through. The University Union on University Ave offers a variety of cheap eats and entertainment. On Kingsley St near the junction with Hutton St is the **Drill Hall Gallery** (☎ 6249 5832), an offshoot of the National Gallery of Australia, with changing exhibitions of contemporary art. It's open Wednesday to Sunday from noon to 5 pm (entry is free).

SoundScreen Australia

The former National Film & Sound Archive (☎ 6248 2000) is in an Art Deco building on McCoy Circuit at the south-eastern edge of the university area. There are interesting exhibitions and frequent film festivals. It is open daily from 9 am to 5 pm (entry is $2).

Australian National Botanic Gardens

On the lower slopes of Black Mountain, behind the ANU, the beautiful 50 hectare botanic gardens are devoted to Australian flora. There are educational walks, including one among plants used by Aborigines. A highlight is the **rainforest area**, achieved in this dry climate by a 'misting' system, while the **eucalypt lawn** has 600 species of this ubiquitous Australian tree.

There are guided walks Monday to Friday at 11 am and on weekends at 11 am and 2 pm. The information centre (☎ 6250 9540), open daily from 9.30 am to 4.30 pm, shows an introductory video about the gardens. Near where the walks start and finish is the *Kookaburra Café*, which has a pleasant outdoor area.

The gardens are open daily from 9 am to 5 pm and are reached from Clunies Ross St (take Murray's Canberra Explorer).

Australian Institute of Sport (AIS)

The AIS (☎ 6214 1444) is on Leverrier Crescent in the northern suburb of Bruce. It provides training facilities for the country's top athletes, who lead 90-minute tours of the institute daily at 11.30 am and 2.30 pm (adults/children $8/4). The tour covers sporting history, training routines and diets, and there's a chance to try out your own skills. Murray's Canberra Explorer gets there at 2.17 pm, in time for the 2.30 pm tour, or catch bus No 80 from Civic.

National Aquarium & Wildlife Sanctuary

The impressive aquarium is about 6km south-west of the city centre on Lady Denman Drive near Scrivener Dam at the western end of Lake Burley Griffin. It also has a sanctuary for native fauna. It's open daily from 9 am to 5.30 pm ($10/6). Take Murray's Canberra Explorer bus.

National Museum of Australia

This long-awaited museum will be built on Acton Peninsula, west of the Commonwealth Ave Bridge. It is due to open in 2001 to coincide with the centenary of Federation.

Other Attractions

You can do no more than drive by and peek through the gates of the prime minister's official Canberra residence, **The Lodge**, on Adelaide Ave, Deakin. The same is true of **Government House**, the residence of the Governor-General, which is on the south-western corner of Lake Burley Griffin. However, there's a lookout beside Scrivener Dam at the end of the lake, giving a good view of the building.

The **Australian-American Memorial** at the eastern end of Kings Ave is a 79m high pillar topped by an eagle, although from a distance it looks more like the ears of Bugs Bunny. The memorial recognises US support for Australia during WWII.

The **Church of St John the Baptist** in Reid, just east of Civic, was built between 1841 and 1845. The stained glass windows were donated by pioneering families of the region. The adjoining **St John's Schoolhouse Museum** has memorabilia of Canberra's first school and is open on Wednesday from 10 am to noon and weekends from 2 to 4 pm (entry $1.50).

The enterprising **Canberra Tradesmen's Union Club**, 2 Badham St, Dickson, is an amazing social club that has a large collection of old and unusual bicycles and 10 restored trams. The club/museum is well worth visiting.

The club also runs the **Downer Club**, nearby on Hawdon St, and has an Antarctic igloo on display. If that doesn't interest you, the observatory there has an astronomer on duty at 7.30, 8.30 and 9.30 pm (Tuesday to Saturday) for sessions with a telescope. Entry is $8/5.50. There is also a planetarium with sessions on Tuesday to Saturday at 7 and 8.30 pm. Entry is also $8/5.50.

The **National Motorcycle Museum** (☎ 6241 8131) at 25 Kemble Court, Mitchell, is well worth a look. The museum has over 250 motorcycles dating from the 1930s, including two examples of very rare Australian models. The display could do with more room and there are vague plans to move the museum sometime to Nabiac in New South Wales (NSW), so check before you go. The museum is open daily from 9 am to 4.30 pm, and entry is $10/3. Bus Nos 48 and 50 take you near the museum.

Activities

Bushwalking Tidbinbilla Nature Reserve, south-west of the city centre, has marked trails; see the Around Canberra section later in the chapter for details. Contact the Canberra Bushwalking Club through the Environment Centre (☎ 6247 3064) on Kingsley St on the ANU campus. Here you can buy *Above the Cotter*, which details walks and drives in the area, Graeme Barrow's *Exploring Namadgi National Park and Tidbinbilla Nature Reserve*, and other useful books. There are also some good rock climbing areas in Namadgi National Park.

Bushwalking information is also available from the Government Info Shop at 10 Mort St.

Water Sports Dobel Boat Hire (☎ 6249 6861), at the Acton Park ferry terminal on the northern shore of Lake Burley Griffin, rents canoes for $16 an hour, as well as paddle boats and surf skis. Canoeing on the Murrumbidgee River, about 20km west of Canberra at its closest point, is also popular.

Swimming pools around the city include the Olympic Swimming Pool on Allara St, Civic, and the pool in Manuka. Swimming in Lake Burley Griffin is not recommended.

Paddle Power (☎ 6287 3973) offers one-day rafting trips on the upper Murray river for $140 and canoeing on the Murrumbidgee for $95.

Cycling Canberra has a great network of bicycle tracks – probably the best in Australia. See the Getting Around section later in this chapter for more information.

In-Line Skating Several places hire skates. Mr Spokes Bike Hire (☎ 6257 1188), near the Acton Park ferry terminal, charges $10 for the first hour and $5 for subsequent hours. Canberra Blade Centre (☎ 6257 7233), 38 Akuna St, Civic, charges $15 for the first two hours and $5 for subsequent hours. Both fees include all safety wear.

Organised Tours

The Canberra Visitors Centre (☎ 6205 0044, 1800 026 166) has details of the many tours of the city and the ACT. Half-day city tours start at around $30. Australian Capital Cruises offers a 1½ hour cruise on Lake Burley Griffin for $15; for a different experience, Canberra Steam Boats (☎ 014 685 684) runs a one hour trip in a 19th century steamboat for $8.

Umbrella Tours (☎ 6285 2605) offers daily 1½-hour walking tours ($15) covering Canberra's history, and also runs market and restaurant tours for $15.

Round About Tours (☎ 6259 5999) runs a 'roos and views' tour in Canberra to spot kangaroos and then watch the sunset from a lookout. The tours run on on Thursday and Sunday and cost $20.

Taking a flight is a good way of seeing the grand scale of the city's plan, and several outfits offer aeroplane flights. The Canberra Flight Training Centre (☎ 6257 6331), based at the airport, has 30-minute scenic flights for $80 (minimum of two people). For a more leisurely pace try Dawn Drifters (☎ 6285 4450), which offers an hour long balloon ride for $155/$195 per person for weekday/weekend flights. The tours are at dawn and a champagne breakfast is included. Balloon Aloft (☎ 6285 1540) offers the same experience at a similar price.

Special Events

An event that may appeal to petrolheads is the Summernats festival of hot rods and custom cars that revs up every January. For a very different feel, the Canberra Festival takes place over 10 days in March and celebrates the city's birthday with fun events, many of which are held in Commonwealth Park. The National Folk Festival, one of the country's largest, is held every April. In September and October, the Floriade Festival is dedicated to Canberra's spectacular spring flowers but has many other events, including music, dance and circus-style entertainment.

Places to Stay – Budget

Camping *Canberra Motor Village* (☎ 6247 5466), 6km north-west of the city centre on Kunzea St, O'Connor, has a peaceful bush setting. Charges are from $10/22 for unpowered/powered camp sites; on site vans and cabins cost $66 a double (supply your own linen) and a motel room is $76. There's a restaurant, kitchen, tennis court and swimming pool.

Canberra South Motor Park (☎ 6280 6176) is 8km south-east of the city in Fyshwick, on Canberra Ave, which is the main road to Queanbeyan. A camp site costs $12, or $17 with power; cabins are $45 to $70 a double.

Hostels In the centre of Canberra, the *City Walk Hotel* (☎ 6257 0124, 2 Mort St) on the corner of City Walk has dorm beds for $18 to $20 and singles/doubles for $40/50; most rooms share bathrooms. This place is a reasonable option – it has a spacious TV lounge and kitchen facilities.

The *Canberra YHA Hostel* (☎ 6248 9155, 191 Dryandra St, O'Connor), about 6km north-west of Civic, has deservedly been named the second most popular YHA hostel worldwide. It's purpose built, and well designed and equipped. There is a travel desk which handles domestic and international travel, an Internet terminal and bicycles for hire. Dorm beds cost $16 to $18 and twin rooms are $44/48 with a shared/private bathroom. Add $3 if you're not a YHA member. The office is open from 7 am to 10.30 pm with check-in until midnight if you give advance warning. Bus No 35 runs to the YHA from Civic.

Guesthouses *Victor Lodge* (☎ 6295 7777, 29 Dawes St, Kingston) is a clean and friendly place about 500m from the Kingston train station and 2km south-east

of Parliament House. Rooms with shared bathrooms are $39/49 for a single/double; beds in a four or five bunk room cost $19, which includes a light breakfast. It has basic outdoor cooking facilities, an Internet terminal and bike rental for $12 a day. Bus Nos 38, 39 and 50 go to the nearby Kingston shops, or phone for a pick up from the Jolimont Centre bus terminal.

Hotels The *Kingston Hotel* (☎ 6295 0123) is a large, popular pub on the corner of Canberra Ave and Giles St in Manuka, about 2km south-east of Parliament House. It offers shared accommodation for $12 with optional linen hire ($4). There are cooking facilities, although counter meals are available. Catch bus No 38 from the city interchange.

Colleges The ANU in Acton is a pleasant place to stay. A selection of residential colleges rent out rooms during university holidays in Easter (one week), June/July (three weeks), September (two weeks) and late-November to late-February.

Toad Hall (☎ 6267 4999) on Kingsley St near the corner of Barry Drive is the closest college to the city centre and has basic rooms for $21/35 a day for students/non-students.

Most other colleges are along Daley Rd at the western end of the campus near Clunies Ross St. At *Burgmann College* (☎ 6267 5222) daily rates for students/non students are $32/44 with breakfast or $40/52 for full board. *Bruce Hall* (☎ 6267 4050) and *Burton & Garran Hall* (☎ 6267 4333) have rooms for $16/31 a night. *Ursula College* (☎ 6279 4300) has rooms for $20/25. *Fenner Hall* (☎ 6279 9000, 210 Northbourne Ave) has basic rooms for $25/120 a day/week.

Places to Stay – Mid-Range

The Canberra Visitors Centre accommodation booking service (☎ 13 1251) often has special deals for the more expensive hotels so it's always worthwhile checking with them before making a final choice.

South of the lake, the modern *Macquarie Private Hotel* (☎ 6273 2325, 18 National Circuit) on the corner of Bourke St has over

500 rooms, all with shared bathrooms. Singles cost $35 to $50 and doubles are $65. Breakfast is included in the price. Bus No 35 from the city stops at the front door.

Entering Canberra from the north, there's a cluster of guesthouses on the east side of Northbourne Ave in Downer, south of the junction with the Barton Hwy from Yass. All are clean, straightforward and comfortable. It's 4km or so into town, but buses run past and Dickson shopping centre isn't far away.

At No 524 the *Blue & White Lodge* (☎ 6248 0498), which also runs the similarly priced *Blue Sky* at No 528, has singles for $70 to $90 and doubles from $80. Prices include a cooked breakfast and rooms have a TV and fridge, but most bathrooms are shared. The staff can collect guests from the bus station. *Parkview* (☎ 6248 0655) at No 526 also does pick-ups and charges $60/75 for singles/doubles with private bathroom; rates include a cooked breakfast. *Miranda* (☎ 6249 8038) at No 534 has rooms for $68/80, including breakfast. *Northbourne Lodge* (☎ 6257 2599) at No 522 is a pleasant place with rooms for $55/68 or $65/80 with bathroom (both include breakfast).

Canberra Central Apartments (☎ 6230 4781, 1800 629 700, 79 Northbourne Ave) has one-bedroom apartments with cooking facilities for $65 a night or $350 a week. It also has single rooms without cooking facilities for $55 a night.

The *Acacia Motor Lodge* (☎ 6249 6955, 65 Ainslie Ave, Braddon) is near the city centre but the rooms are small. It charges from $69/75 for its rooms, including a light breakfast. South of the city centre, next to and owned by Victor Lodge, is *Motel Monaro* (☎ 6295 2111, 27 Dawes St, Kingston), which has rooms for $76/79.

Places to Stay – Top End

More expensive places include the old but pleasant *Olim's Canberra Hotel* (☎ 6248 5511) on the corner of Ainslie and Limestone Aves, Braddon. Rooms cost from $95 a single or double. The *Holiday Inn* (☎ 6243 2500, 84 Northbourne Ave) has rooms for $99, including breakfast, subject to availability. Otherwise, rooms are $230 a night.

There are a number of hotels providing apartment accommodation with an equipped kitchen. *Capital Tower Apartments* (☎ 6276 3444, 2-6 Marcus Clarke St) has apartments for $195. As these can take up to five people they are an attractive proposition – especially with access to the pool, sauna, gym and tennis court.

Places to Eat

Canberra has a fine eating scene. Most places are around Civic, with an upmarket selection in Manuka, a mid-range variety in Kingston, an Asian strip in Dickson and other possibilities scattered around the suburbs. Smoking isn't allowed in Canberra's eateries.

City Centre There's a food hall in the lower section of the *Canberra Centre* on City Walk where you can fill up on burgers, pasta, croissants and more for $4 to $7. There's a more intimate food hall in *City Market* on Bunda St, where the excellent *Sizzle City* has cheap Japanese lunch packs.

Upstairs in the Sydney Building at 21 East Row, the *Canberra Vietnamese Restaurant* has main courses for less than $10. *Bailey's Corner*, on the corner of East Row and London Circuit, has a couple of places with outdoor tables. *Tosolini's* is an Italian bistro, good for a drink or a meal. It has breakfast available; lunchtime specials start at $12; and in the evening, pasta dishes are $9 and mains $17. Its cakes are to die for.

On the southern end of the Melbourne Building, *Lemon Grass* is an award-winning Thai restaurant with seafood mains for $14 and a good selection of vegetarian dishes for $11. *Little Saigon*, on the corner of Alinga St and Northbourne Ave, gives quick service even when it's very crowded. Main courses are $8, seafood meals are $12 and the restaurant does a $5 lunchbox.

Garema Place, just north-east of London Circuit, is a rather ugly concrete plaza but it is full of restaurants and cafes. *Happy's* is a popular, reasonably priced Chinese restaurant with dishes from $7 to $11.50. Nearby, *Mama's Cafe & Bar* serves homemade pasta for $9.50 and other meals for around $13, in a good atmosphere.

For the caffeine enthusiast, *Café Essen* in Garema Arcade has 30 varieties of coffee that can be served in 18 different ways. For the tea sipper there are 22 varieties to choose from. Breakfast is offered all day for $2 to $8 and snacks are $3.50 to $8. The cakes are scrumptious.

Around the corner on Bunda St, *Gus' Café* has outdoor tables and serves inventive food (only semi-dried rather than sun-dried tomatoes cross this doorway). Soup is $6 and pasta is $8.50. Not far away, the Chinese/Malaysian *Sammy's Kitchen* has a good reputation and a variety of dishes from $7.50 to $14. *Ali Baba*, on the corner of Bunda St and Garema Place, does Lebanese takeaways, including shawerma and felafel for around $4 and meals for $9 to $10.50.

There are a couple of good eating options on Marcus Clarke St, north-west of Civic. The excellent *Fringe Benefits (54 Marcus Clarke St)* is a brasserie that has regularly won national wine and food awards, and has main courses for around $20. Nearby at No 60, *Psychedeli* has good coffee, foccacia and pizza.

Manuka South of Capital Hill is the Manuka shopping centre, which services the diplomatic corps and well-heeled bureaucrats from surrounding neighbourhoods. There are plenty of cafes and restaurants on Franklin, Fourneaux and Bougainville Sts, and on Flinders Way.

My Café on Franklin St has bagels and foccacia for $4.50, and main courses for $10 to $12. Upstairs in the nearby Style Arcade, *Alanya* is a good Turkish restaurant offering lunch for two for $30, with entrees for $8 to $10 and mains (including vegetarian) for $10 to $15. Also here is *Daniel's*, one of Canberra's better restaurants, which serves French and Moroccan food. Its creative main courses usually cost around $20, but it has a lunchtime two course special for $15.

Booking is essential for *Timmy's Kitchen (☎ 6295 6537)* on Fourneaux St. This is a very popular, friendly and unpretentious Malaysian/Chinese restaurant with main courses for $8.80 to $13.70; it also has a good vegetarian selection.

Kingston Kingston has plenty of restaurants and cafes. *Cyberchino (33 Kennedy St)* is an Internet cafe with seven terminals and a computer-infected menu – dishes include Yahoo chicken, Netscape fettuccine and Dot.com, which proves the power of its Internet connections as it has been able to download Nile perch for this dish. *Cafe Keru (38 Giles St)* serves Turkish *pides* (similar to pizza) for $12 and has a pleasant courtyard.

Dickson The Dickson shopping area, a few kilometres north of Civic, is a thriving restaurant district sometimes called Little China because of its many Asian restaurants.

Dickson Asian Noodle House (29 Woolley St) is a popular Lao and Thai café, with dishes for around $9. The Japanese *Sakura*, at No 51, opposite the BP service station, has mains from $16. The Malaysian *Rasa Sayang*, at No 43, charges reasonable prices, with noodles for $8.80 and a good vegetarian selection.

Elsewhere There's cheap food at the student union *Refectory* on University Ave at the ANU. The *Red Belly Black Cafe* at the Mt Stromlo Observatory (see the Observatories & Tracking Stations section) has mountain and forest views, and is *the* place to be seen for Sunday lunch.

In Lyneham, *Tilley's (96 Wattle St)*, on the corner of Brigelow St, is a well known cafe and bar. The food is healthy (if you don't count the great cakes), with an emphasis on vegetarian dishes, the clientele is diverse and there is often entertainment. Meals are from $10 and breakfast starts at $5.50.

Entertainment

Canberra is livelier than its reputation suggests. Liberal licensing laws allow hotels unlimited opening hours and there are some 24-hour bars. Underage drinking is strictly policed; if you don't have ID proving you're over 18, forget it. The 'Good Times' section in the Thursday *Canberra Times* has entertainment listings, and the free monthly *BMA* magazine lists bands and other events.

Pubs, Bars & Nightclubs Friday night is the big drinking night in Canberra, when everyone winds down after a hard week.

There's live music two or three nights a week during term time at the *ANU union bar*, which is a good place for a drink even when there's no entertainment. Big touring acts often play at the *Refectory* here.

In Civic, the Sydney Building has a number of venues, including the popular *Moosehead's Pub (105 London Circuit)* on the south side. The *Phoenix (21 East Row)* has poetry and quiz nights. Not far away is *Pandora's*, on the corner of Alinga and Mort Sts, which caters for all ages, and has a bar downstairs and a dance club upstairs.

For the gay scene, try the popular *Heaven Nite Club* on Garema Place or the *Meridian Club (34 Mort St, Braddon)*.

The *Wig & Pen*, on the corner of West Row and Alinga St, is a British-style pub. For those jaded by the uniform blandness of many Australian beers, here's a chance to try real English ale, served without gas and at the right temperature. There are bands most nights and a quiz night on Monday; the pub is closed on Sunday.

Just down Alinga St on the corner with West Row is *P.J. O'Reilly's*, a large Irish theme pub with cosy corners. Bands play here most nights.

In the Green Square shopping area in Kingston, *Filthy McFadden's (62 Jardine St)* is an Irish pub with character that has music on most nights. Nearby, the *Durham Castle Arms* occasionally has live bands performing jazz and blues.

In Lyneham, *Tilley's (96 Wattle St)* has live music – often international and Australian touring acts – on weekends. It also has poetry nights and sessions by guest writers.

Other places that occasionally have bands include the *Canberra Workers' Club* on Childers St in Civic and the *Tradesmen's Union Club (2 Badham St, Dickson)*. Twenty-four hour venues like this one are the best places to watch major overseas sporting events broadcast at odd times in the night.

Cinemas There are several cinemas in the Civic Square and London Circuit area.

Electric Shadows is an art house cinema on City Walk near Akuna St. The *National Gallery of Australia* has screenings on art-related topics on Friday at 12.45 pm and *SoundScreen Australia (☎ 6209 3111)*, on McCoy Circuit, occasionally shows films.

Performing Arts The *Canberra Theatre Centre (☎ 6257 1077)* on Civic Square has several theatres that showcase a varied range of events. *Gorman House Community Arts Centre (☎ 6249 7377, Ainslie Ave, Braddon)* is home to several theatre and dance companies that put on occasional performances and exhibitions.

Casino The *Casino Canberra (21 Binara St)*, near the National Convention Centre, is open daily from noon to 6 am. It's a fairly casual place: before 7 pm T-shirts, jeans and runners are OK, but after 7 pm men have to wear a shirt with a collar and 'proper' shoes. The casino has a nightclub, *Deja Vu*, open from 7 pm until you drop.

Shopping

Artwares Gift Gallery, at Gorman House Community Arts Centre on Ainslie Ave, sells craftwork by local and international artisans. There's also an interesting craft market at the centre on Saturday.

The Old Bus Depot Market, on Wentworth Ave in Kingston, is held every Sunday, with stalls selling art and craft with a New Age slant, as well as international food.

The Community Aid Abroad shop at 112 Alinga St sells artefacts from around the world, and the Bogong Environment Shop, in the Environment Centre on Kingsley St, sells books, gifts and other products with an ecological theme.

Getting There & Away

Air Canberra doesn't have an international airport. Sydney is about half an hour away and a standard one way fare with the two major airlines is $163; Melbourne is about an hour's flight away ($232), while direct flights to Adelaide and Brisbane cost $337 and $341 respectively.

Qantas (☎ 13 1313) and Ansett (☎ 13 1300) are both in the Jolimont Centre.

Other smaller airlines fly to NSW country destinations. Air Facilities (☎ 6041 1210) flies daily to Albury.

Bus Several bus lines have their booking offices and their main terminus at the Jolimont Centre. Greyhound (☎ 13 2030) has the most frequent Sydney service ($28, or $33 for express). It also runs to Adelaide ($96) and Melbourne ($45, or $54 express). Services to Cooma ($25) and to Thredbo in the NSW snowfields ($44, or $54 express) are frequent in winter, less so at other times.

Murrays (☎ 13 2251) has daily express buses to Sydney ($28) and to the NSW coast at Batemans Bay ($22), and connects with buses running up to Nowra ($39).

McCafferty's (☎ 13 1499) has buses to Sydney ($28), Melbourne ($45) and Adelaide ($96); bookings can be made at the Travellers Maps & Guides shop in the Jolimont Centre.

Transborder Express (☎ 6241 0033) runs to Yass for $10 one way; a same-day return is $12. Sid Fogg's (☎ 4928 1088) runs between Newcastle and Canberra on Monday, Wednesday and Friday for $45 one way.

The Jolimont Centre is a useful place for travellers: it has left luggage lockers, showers, an Internet terminal and free phone lines to the Canberra Visitors Centre as well as some of the budget accommodation places.

Train The Kingston train station (☎13 2232) is on Wentworth Ave in Kingston. You can make bookings for trains and connecting buses at the Countrylink Travel Centre (☎ 6257 1576) in the Jolimont Centre. Three trains a day make the four hour trip to Sydney ($42 one way).

There's no direct train to Melbourne. The daily V/Line Canberra Link service involves taking a train between Melbourne and Wodonga and a connecting bus to Canberra ($49, about nine hours). A longer but more interesting bus/train service to Melbourne is the V/Line Capital Link that runs via Cooma and the forests of Victoria's East Gippsland, then down the Princes Hwy to

Sale, where you catch a train. This trip takes over 11 hours and costs $49.

The Wayward Bus (☎ 1800 882 823) goes from Canberra on a three day journey to Melbourne for $140 via the Alps or the coastal route. A two day trip to Sydney costs $110.

Car & Motorcycle The Hume Hwy connects Sydney and Melbourne and passes about 50km north of Canberra. The Federal Hwy runs north of the Hume near Goulburn, while the Barton Hwy meets the Hume near Yass. To the south, the Monaro Hwy connects Canberra with Cooma.

Major car-rental companies with offices in the city, as well as desks at the airport, are:

Avis
  (☎ 6249 6088) 17 Lonsdale St, Braddon
Budget
  (☎ 6257 1305) Corner of Mort and Girrahween Sts, Braddon
Hertz
  (☎ 6257 4877) 32 Mort St, Braddon
Thrifty
  (☎ 6247 7422) 29 Lonsdale St, Braddon

Cheaper outfits include Rumbles (☎ 6280 7444), 11 Paragon Mall, Gladstone St, Fyshwick, and Noss Car Rentals (☎ 6280 0320), 41 Whyalla St, Fyshwick. Rentals start from $25 a day.

Getting Around
To/From the Airport The airport is 7km south-east of the city centre. You will notice all the government cars lined up outside, waiting to pick up 'pollies' and public servants. Bus No 80 serves the airport from the city interchange on weekdays only. The taxi fare from the airport to Civic is around $12.

Bus Buses operated by the Australian Capital Territory Internal Omnibus Network (ACTION; ☎ 6207 7611) run reasonably frequently.

The main city interchange is in the area of Alinga St, East Row and Mort St in Civic. The information kiosk on the corner of Alinga St and East Row is open daily until about 11.30 pm, though it only sells tickets until 6 pm. If you'll be using buses a lot it's worth buying the *ACTION Bus Pack* ($2) here or from the Canberra Visitors Centre. The pack has an invaluable route map.

Canberra is divided into three fare zones: north, central and south. A one zone ticket costs $2 for a single ride with a transfer ticket available for another ride in the same zone within one hour. An all-zones ticket costs $4, but the best deal is an all-day, all-zones ticket for $7. Tickets can be bought from the driver.

Special Services Murray's Canberra Explorer (☎ 13 2251) runs a 25km route around 18 points of interest; you can get on and off at any stop. This daily service leaves the Jolimont Centre at 8.40 and 10.40 am and 12.40 and 2.40 pm; tickets ($18/15 for adults/children) are sold on the bus or at the Murray's counter in the Jolimont Centre. A half-day pass for $129 allows for a complete circuit and one two-hour stop.

Car & Motorcycle Canberra's road system is as circuitous as a politician's answer to a straight question, but the wide and relatively uncluttered main roads make driving easy. A map is essential.

Taxi Call Canberra Cabs (☎ 6285 9222).

Bicycle Canberra is a cyclist's paradise, with bike paths making it possible to ride around the city hardly touching a road. One popular track circles the lake; there are also peaceful stretches of bushland along some suburban routes. Get a copy of the *Canberra Cycleways* map ($5.95) from bookshops or the Canberra Visitors Centre.

Mr Spokes Bike Hire (☎ 6257 1188), near the Acton Park ferry terminal, charges $8 an hour and $7 for subsequent hours. Both the YHA and Victor Lodge rent out bicycles.

Around Canberra

The ACT is about 88km from north to south and about 30km from east to west. There's plenty of unspoiled bush just outside the urban area and a network of roads into it. The NRMA's *Canberra & District* map and the Canberra Visitors Centre's *Canberra Sightseeing Guide with Tourist Drives* are helpful.

The plains and isolated hills around Canberra rise to rugged ranges in the south and west of the ACT. The Murrumbidgee River flows across the ACT from south-east to north-west. Namadgi National Park in the south covers 40% of the ACT and adjoins Kosciuszko National Park. The Canberra Visitors Centre has leaflets on walking trails, swimming spots and camp sites.

Picnic, Swimming & Walking Areas

Picnic and barbecue spots, many with gas facilities, are scattered throughout and around Canberra. There's no public transport to most of them. **Black Mountain**, west of the city, is convenient for picnics, and there are swimming spots along the Murrumbidgee and Cotter rivers. Other riverside areas include **Uriarra Crossing**, 24km north-west of the city, on the Murrumbidgee near its meeting with the Molonglo River; **Casuarina Sands**, 19km west of the city at the meeting of the Cotter and Murrumbidgee rivers; **Kambah Pool Reserve**, about 14km further south upstream on the Murrumbidgee; **Cotter Dam**, 23km west of the city on the Cotter River, which also has a camping ground; **Pine Island** and **Point Hut Crossing**, on the Murrumbidgee upstream of Kambah Pool Reserve; and **Gibraltar Falls**, roughly 45km south-west of the city. There's camping also at **Woods Reserve**, on the Corin Rd south of Tidbinbilla Nature Reserve.

There are good walking tracks along the Murrumbidgee from Kambah Pool Reserve to Pine Island (7km) or Casuarina Sands (about 14km).

The spectacular **Ginninderra Falls** (☎ 6278 4222) at Parkwood, north-west of Canberra and across the NSW border, is open daily (adults $4, concession $2); there are gorges and a nature trail, and canoes available for hire.

Tidbinbilla Nature Reserve, in hills 45km south-west of the city, has bushwalking tracks, some leading to interesting rock formations. There is plenty of wildlife here, with the opportunity to see emus, kangaroos, wallabies, koalas and maybe a platypus. The reserve is open daily from 9 am to 6 pm (later during daylight-saving time); the visitors centre is open weekdays from 9 am to 4.30 pm and weekends until 5.30 pm. Round About Tours (☎ 6259 5999) has a Wednesday tour for $55 ($10 reduction for YHA and VIP cardholders), which includes food and a pickup/drop-off service.

South-west of the reserve in **Corin Forest**, there's a 1.2km 'bobsled' run on weekends, public holidays and during school holidays; six rides cost $18. There's also a flying fox.

Other good walking areas include **Mt Ainslie**, to the north-east of the city; **Mt Majura** behind it (the combined area forms part of Canberra Nature Park); and **Molonglo Gorge** near Queanbeyan.

Namadgi National Park, occupying the south-west of the ACT, has eight peaks higher than 1700m and offers challenging bushwalking. Two kilometres south of **Tharwa** is the Namadgi Visitors Centre (☎ 6237 5222) on Naas Rd. Wild Thing Tours (☎ 6254 6303) has half-day bushwalking tours of Namadgi ($40) which give you the opportunity to see animals in their natural habitat. Many overseas visitors report seeing their first kangaroos on this tour and the operator promises your money back if you don't see at least 500.

Round About Tours (☎ 6259 5999) also has a bushwalking tour of the park on Saturday for $55 ($10 less for YHA and VIP cardholders), which includes food and a pickup/drop-off service.

There are picnic and camping facilities at the Orroral River crossing, Honeysuckle Creek and Mt Clear. Contact the Namadgi Visitor Centre for details.

Observatories & Tracking Stations

The ANU's **Mt Stromlo Observatory**, 16km south-west of Canberra, has a 188cm telescope plus a visitors' annexe, open daily from 9.30 am to 4.30 pm. Guided telescope tours are daily at 11 am and 2 pm.

The **Canberra Space Centre**, in the grounds of the Canberra Deep Space Communication Complex, is 40km south-west of Canberra. There are spacecraft displays and deep-space tracking technology, plus a piece of moon rock securely tucked away behind thick glass. It's open daily from 9 am to 5 pm (to 8 pm during daylight-saving time); entry is free. The area is popular for bushwalks and barbecues.

Gold Creek

Near the Barton Hwy, about 11km northwest of the city, Gold Creek has a number of attractions. Hard to resist is the **National Dinosaur Museum**, which is a private collection with replica skeletons of 10 dinosaurs and many bones and fossils. It's open daily from 10 am to 5 pm (from 9 am during school holidays); entry is $8/5 for adults/children.

You can get up close to some deadly Australians and also cuddle a friendly python at the **Australian Reptile Centre**. The centre has a selection of some of the most venomous snakes in the world, which just happen to live in Australia, but they're safely behind glass. Entry is $6/3. It's open daily from 10 am to 5 pm.

Ginninderra Village is a collection of craft workshops and galleries open daily from 10 am to 5 pm (entry is free). Next door, **Cockington Green** is a miniature replica of an English village and is open daily from 9.30 am to 4 pm. Entry is $8.50/4.30.

Other Attractions

Bywong Mining Town, about 30km northeast of Canberra on Millyn Rd off the Federal Hwy in NSW, is a re-creation of a mining settlement. It's open daily from 10 am to 4 pm, with tours at 10.30 am, and 12.30 and 2 pm. Entry is $7/4.50.

The beautifully restored, National Trust **Lanyon Homestead**, on Tharwa Drive off the Monaro Hwy beside the Murrumbidgee River, is about 30km south of Canberra. The early stone cottage on the site was built by convicts and the grand homestead was completed in 1859. A major attraction that documents the life of the region before Canberra existed is the **Nolan Gallery**, containing a collection of Sidney Nolan's paintings. The homestead and gallery are open Tuesday to

Sunday from 10 am to 4 pm. Combined entry is $6/3.

Cuppacumbalong, on Naas Rd near Tharwa, is another old homestead, now a craft studio and gallery, and is open Wednesday to Sunday from 11 am to 5 pm.

Day Trips

A popular drive is the journey on the Kings Hwy east into NSW through **Bungendore**, which has craft galleries and some old buildings, to pretty **Braidwood** (an hour from Canberra) with its many antique and craft shops and restaurants. Another good route takes in **Tharwa** in hilly grazing lands.

QUEANBEYAN

☎ 02 • postcode 2620 • pop 29,000

Across the NSW border, about 12km south-east of Canberra, is Queanbeyan, now virtually a suburb of the capital it predates. It was known as 'Queen Bean' until 1838, when it was proclaimed a township. The Queanbeyan Information & Tourist Centre (☎ 1800 026 192) is at 1 Farrer Place.

There's a **museum**, which displays the town's history, and good lookouts on **Jerrabomberra Hill** (5km west) and **Bungendore Hill** (4km east).

Motel accommodation here is cheaper than in Canberra.

THE OLYMPIC GAMES

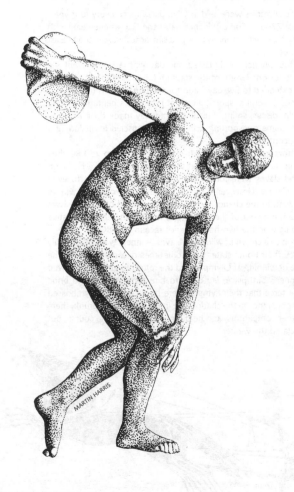

MARTIN HARRIS

In September 2000, sportspeople from all over the globe will converge on Sydney to take part in the world's greatest sporting event – the Olympic Games. For two weeks, the eyes of the world will be on these athletes as they strive to become the first Olympic gold medallists of the new millennium.

ANCIENT OLYMPICS

The Ancient Olympics were held in Olympia, Greece every four years from at least 776 BC. Some evidence dates the Games even earlier, to around 900 BC; other historians believe a similar festival existed at least four centuries previously.

Initially the Olympics only lasted one day with a single event – a running race for one length of the stadium (about 190m). In time the event was extended to five days, and four running events (including a race in armour), combat sports, a chariot race and a pentathlon (long jump, javelin, discus, sprint, wrestling) gradually made their way into the Games. Some nonsporting activities also muscled in, including a trumpeting contest.

Competitors had to be free-born male Greeks. From 750 BC they competed in the nude; prior to that they wore a shorts-like garment. Women and slaves were forbidden, under threat of death, to even attend the Games. However, it was possible for a woman to win an Olympic event. In the chariot race the crown of wild olive leaves was awarded to the owner of the horses and not the drivers. So Belistike of Macedonia won the two-horse chariot race in 268 BC.

In addition to a crown of wild olive leaves, winners were often richly rewarded by their home states and sometimes became wealthy. The importance of winning at Olympia, and the reflected glory it bestowed on the winner's birthplace, led cities to hire professionals and bribe judges. The farce that the Olympics were to become was symbolised by Nero's appearance in the chariot race in 66 AD: he was drunk, there were no other competitors, and he did not even finish the course, but he was declared the winner.

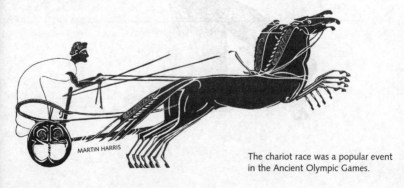

MARTIN HARRIS

The chariot race was a popular event in the Ancient Olympic Games.

Dead Good

In the Ancient Olympics, the *pankration* event was a brutal combination of boxing and wrestling in which virtually anything was permitted. Arrachion of Phigalia was awarded the title in 564 BC because his opponent 'gave up' – though Arrachion himself was by then lying dead in the arena. He remains the only dead person to become an Olympic champion.

The Myth of the Marathon

Everyone thinks they know the story of the marathon – even if you don't, the story gets another run (so to speak) every Olympic Games. In 490 BC, the small army of the Athenians, having defeated the much larger Persian forces at the battle of Marathon, sent a famed runner, Pheidippides, to Athens, a distance of 26 miles and 385 yards (about 42km), to deliver the good news. He had just completed a 300 mile (480km) round trip to Sparta in a vain attempt to enlist their support; nevertheless, he ran to Athens, gasped out his message and, in extreme exhaustion, collapsed and died.

So, is it true? Well, partly, but not the most famous bit that everyone believes. Pheidippides certainly did exist: Herodotus, the earliest and most reliable historian of this era, mentions him in two paragraphs (Book VI, 105-6), written about 40 years later. These clearly state that Pheidippides ran to Sparta and back in about three days – and that's it. There's no mention of him at Marathon.

Subsequently, though, Pheidippides ran out of the pages of history and into the realm of mythology. The modern marathon was supposed to be the exact distance he ran from Marathon to Athens. But there is no record of this in Herodotus; later Greek and Roman historians invented the more romantic 'Marathon' story.

Pheidippides was a professional messenger; even so, his run to Sparta is one of the great feats of endurance in history, especially as much of it was through very rugged terrain. Thus, Pheidippides' actual deeds far surpass any mere marathon. So the modern marathon rightly celebrates Pheidippides' prowess – only in not quite the way most people think. So when you're lining the marathon route among the wildly cheering crowds at Sydney 2000, spare a thought for Pheidippides and the real story of his remarkable run.

Greg Alford

In 393 AD the Olympics were abolished by the Christian emperor Theodosius, and Olympia was buried under earthquakes until excavated between 1875 and 1881: it was these excavations that turned Baron Pierre de Coubertin's mind towards resurrecting the Games.

MODERN OLYMPIC HISTORY

The history of the modern Olympic Games has been a turbulent one. Almost from their inception, the Games have faced disruption courtesy of political crises – including two world wars, boycotts and terrorist attacks – and their demise has frequently been predicted. Despite this, the Games have always gone on and, 104 years after the first Olympics of the modern era took place in Athens, winning an Olympic gold medal remains the ultimate ambition of sportspeople throughout the world.

The modern Olympic Games was the brainchild of the Frenchman Baron de Coubertin. In 1892, inspired by epic tales of the Ancient Olympics and by the public school games of 19th century Britain, de Coubertin proposed the idea of reviving the Olympic Games. He invited interested parties to participate in a world sports congress in Paris in 1894. This congress spawned the International Olympic Committee (IOC) and, consequently, the decision to revive the Olympics in 1896.

The man who started it all: Pierre de Coubertin.

De Coubertin intended the Games to be for amateurs only (with the exception of professional fencing masters), that competitors should be adult males, and that the Olympics should be held every four years in different venues. At the turn of the 21st century the only stipulation that has stood the test of time is that the Games are staged in different cities.

The 1896 Games, which were jointly funded by wealthy Greek architect Georgios Averoff, a lottery, and the world's first collection of sporting postage stamps, were well attended and successful. However, the following two Games, held in Paris and St Louis, were appalling: they were staged as an appendage to the World Exhibition, and the sporting events were held over a periods of five and 4½ months respectively. Additionally, the organisation was so bad that in Paris many competitors had no idea they were taking part in the Olympics, and in St Louis many of the events were open only to Missouri residents.

The Olympic movement might have died then, had it not been for the successful 'Intercalated' Games held in Athens in 1906 to mark the ten-year anniversary of the Games. The London Games of 1908 were marked by controversy, with the USA in particular accusing the British officials of favouring British athletes. However, the well organised Games of Stockholm in 1912 attracted athletes from five continents, and the future of the Olympics at last looked promising. WWI prevented the 1916 Games from going ahead, and the fact that athletes gathered for the Games in war-torn Antwerp in 1920 was a major achievement for the IOC.

Famous Five

Only five sports have been on the program of every modern Olympic Games since 1896 – cycling, fencing, gymnastics, swimming and track and field athletics. Rowing should have been included with them, but rough seas caused its cancellation in 1896.

The post-WWI years saw increased public interest in the Games, with distance runner Paavo Nurmi and swimmer Johnny Weissmuller (who later played Tarzan in the films of the 1930s and 40s) becoming the first 'household names' of Olympic sport. The 1920s and 30s also witnessed the gradual admission of more female competitors in the Games, with track and field and gymnastics being added to the women's program in Amsterdam in 1928. The final Games before the outbreak of WWII were held in Berlin in 1936.

Nova Peris-Kneebone will be the first torchbearer in Australia.

D BRAYBROOK / SPORT • THE LIBRARY •

The Journey of the Olympic Torch

The world has the Nazis to thank for the concept of the Olympic flame and torch relay. The brainchild of Carl Diem, head of the organising committee for the Berlin Olympics, the Olympic flame was ignited in Olympia, Greece for the first time in 1936, and was carried from there to Berlin by 3075 torchbearers, all running just slightly over one mile of the journey.

The Sydney 2000 Olympic torch relay will travel over 27,000km and be carried by 10,000 torchbearers in what is to be the longest torch relay in Olympic history.

Apart from being carried by torchbearers, the Olympic flame will travel on a surf boat at Bondi Beach, on the *Indian Pacific* train across the Nullarbor Plain, on a Royal Flying Doctor Service aircraft in the remote outback, and by camel on Cable Beach at Broome. Before reaching Australia, the torch will be taken by plane to Guam, where it will begin a 20 day journey visiting the 12 Pacific Island countries that make up the Oceania ring of the Olympic nations. It will then visit every state and territory in Australia over 100 days. The first person to carry the torch in Australia will be Australian Olympic hockey gold medallist-turned-sprinter Nova Peris-Kneebone.

History at a Glance

Olympic Games	Highlights	Leading Nations
1896 – Athens, Greece Male (M): c. 200, Female (F): 0	Greek peasant Spiridon Louis wins the marathon.	USA (11 gold), Greece (10), Germany (7)
1900 – Paris, France M: 1206, F: 19	Australian Frederick Lane wins swimming's obstacle race – climbing over and diving under boats.	France (29), USA (20), GB (17)
1904 – St Louis, USA M: 681, F: 6	'Winner' Fred Lotz, an American, is disqualified from the marathon for taking a lift.	USA (80), Germany (5), Cuba (5)
1908 – London, GB M: 1999, F: 36	First gold medals awarded. Briton Wyndham Halswelle wins a 'walkover' 400m courtesy of partisan judging.	GB (56), USA (23), Sweden (7)
1912 – Stockholm, Sweden M: 2490, F: 57	The photo finish and electronic timer are introduced. American Jim Thorpe wins the pentathlon and decathlon, but is later stripped of his medal due to his professional status.	Sweden (24), USA (23), GB (10)
1920 – Antwerp, Belgium M: 2591, F: 77	French Wimbledon champion Suzanne Lenglen takes tennis gold.	USA (41), Sweden (17), GB (15)
1924 – Paris, France M: 2956, F: 136	Finnish athlete Paavo Nurmi takes his total of gold medals to five.	USA (45), Finland (14), France (13)
1928 – Amsterdam, Netherlands M: 2724, F: 290	American Johnny Weissmuller takes his gold medal tally to five.	USA (22), Germany (10) Finland (8)
1932 – Los Angeles, USA M: 1281, F: 127	American Babe Didrikson wins two athletics golds.	USA (41), Italy (12), France (10)
1936 – Berlin, Germany M: 3738, F: 328	American Jesse Owens wins four athletics golds to dominate the 'Aryan Games'.	Germany (33), USA (24), Hungary (10)
1948 – London, UK M: 3714, F: 385	Fanny Blankers-Koen of the Netherlands wins four athletics golds.	USA (38), Sweden (16), France (10)
1952 – Helsinki, Finland M: 4407, F: 518	Czech Emil Zatopek wins the 5000m, 10,000m and the marathon and his wife, Dana, wins gold in the javelin.	USA (40), USSR (22), Hungary (16)
1956 – Melbourne, Australia M: 2813, F: 371	Australian Dawn Fraser wins the first of three consecutive 100m freestyle golds.	USSR (37), USA (32), Australia (13)

BERGMAN / SPORT • THE LIBRARY •

History at a Glance

Olympic Games	Highlights	Leading Nations
1960 – Rome, Italy M: 4736, F: 610	Ethiopian Abebe Bikila wins the marathon barefoot.	USSR (42), USA (34), Italy (13)
1964 – Tokyo, Japan M: 4457, F: 683	The first Games televised internationally. Soviet sisters Irina and Tamara Press take three gold medals between them.	USA (36), USSR (30), Japan (16)
1968 – Mexico City, Mexico M: 4749, F: 781	American Bob Beamon sets long jump world record. American sprinters Tommie Smith and John Carlos give 'black power' salute on victory podium and are sent home.	USA (45), USSR (29), Japan (11)
1972 – Munich, FRG M: 6065, F: 1058	American Mark Spitz wins seven golds in swimming.	USSR (50), USA (33), GDR (20)
1976 – Montreal, Canada M: 4781, F: 1247	Romanian gymnast Nadia Comaneci scores seven perfect tens.	USSR (49), GDR (40), USA (34)
1980 – Moscow, USSR M: 4043, F: 1124	British arch rivals Steve Ovett and Seb Coe win a gold each in middle distance running.	USSR (80), GDR (47), Bulgaria (8)
1984 – Los Angeles, USA M: 5230, F: 1567	American Carl Lewis wins four athletics golds.	USA (83), Romania (20), FRG (17)
1988 – Seoul, South Korea M: 6279, F: 2186	East Germany's Kristin Otto wins six gold medals. American Ben Johnson is stripped of his 100m gold after testing positive to anabolic steroids.	USSR (55), GDR (37), USA (36)
1992 – Barcelona, Spain M: 6657, F: 2707	South Africa competes in Games for the first time since 1960 and Germany competes as one nation for the first time since 1964. The USA's 'Dream Team' dominates the men's basketball.	Unified Team* (45), USA (37), Germany (33)
1996 – Atlanta, USA M: 6797, F: 3513	Ireland's Michelle Smith wins more golds individually (three) than any Irish team in the history of the Games. American Michael Johnson takes the 200m and 400m double.	USA (44), Russia (26), Germany (20)

The Unified Team was made up of representatives of the Commonwealth of Independent States, the former USSR.

DAVID CALLOW / SPORT • THE LIBRARY •

The Nazis turned them into a propaganda event, presenting the image of a democratic, peace-loving Third Reich. However, Hitler's hope that the Games would prove the superiority of the Aryan athletes was undermined by the performances of USA's black athletes, in particular the incredible Jesse Owens, winner of four gold medals for track and field.

The post-war era saw the Olympics used as a battleground between the capitalist countries of the western world and the communist countries of Eastern Europe to 'prove' which ideology was best. The Eastern European practice of mass-producing athletes in elitist sports schools led to accusations of 'shamateurism' by western nations who found they could not effectively compete against the USSR and East Germany. There were boycotts of Olympic Games held between 1954 and the end of the Cold War era. Some of the world events that influenced the boycotts were: the Soviet invasions of Hungary (1956), Czechoslovakia (1968) and Afghanistan (1979); the apartheid regimes of South Africa and Rhodesia; and the British intervention in the Suez crisis (1956). The boycotts hit their peak in 1980 when the USA, Canada and Germany refused to attend the Moscow Olympics because of the Soviet invasion of Afghanistan. Four years later the Soviets and most of their East European satellites carried out a tit-for-tat boycott of the Los Angeles Olympics.

PRESSE SPORTS / SPORT • THE LIBRARY •

Carl Lewis wins one of four golds in the 100m at the LA Games in 1984.

The use of the Olympics for political ends turned to tragedy in 1972 when 11 Israeli athletes were killed by Palestinian terrorists during the Munich Games. It is to the credit of the athletes that the Games continued to increase in prestige and public popularity during the 1960s and 1970s – Bob Beamon's world record long jump in Mexico, swimmer Mark Spitz's seven gold medals in Munich, and Nadia Comaneci's perfect ten scores in Montreal remained in the memories of sports fans long after boycotts and terrorism had almost been forgotten.

The LA Games marked a turning point in Olympic history. Up till that point, Olympic Games had proved far from lucrative and countries showed little interest in staging an event that had become a security nightmare as well as a financial one. Montreal was still paying off debts accrued from its Olympics way into the 1990s.

But LA turned the Games into a commercial success thanks to marketing, sponsorship and revenue from TV rights. Since then, cities have clamoured for the right to stage the Games, now regarded as a huge money-spinner. With the dismantling of the Eastern Bloc in 1989-90, the days of tit-for-tat boycotts were over, so all the top sportspeople started turning up for the Games. Additionally, professionals were allowed to take part in the Games from 1988 onwards, and 'shamateurism' became a term of the past.

Today some aspects of this commercialisation of the Olympics undermine their integrity and public image. Pressure on athletes to perform is immense. The issue of drugs also refuses to go away. Ben Johnson's positive test of 1988 led many sports bodies and fans to believe that plenty of other athletes remained uncaught. There have been allegations – most notably by Andrew Jennings, author of .*The Lords of the Rings* (1992) and *The New Lords of the Rings* (1996) – that positive tests have been covered up in recent Olympics.

Jennings' books also revealed another 'dark side' to the Olympics: corruption and bribery, he claimed, was rife in the bidding process for Olympic Games, with organising committees showering IOC officials and their families with gifts to encourage them to vote for their city. In 1998-99 these allegations were taken more seriously when the IOC admitted that some of its officials had accepted bribes from the organising committee of the Salt Lake City Winter Games of 2002. In 1999 Australian Olympic Committee president John Coates admitted that inducement payments were made to Kenyan and Ugandan officials to encourage them to vote for the Sydney bid.

The anger these revelations provoked among athletes, sports fans and the organisers of failed Olympic bids resulted in IOC president Juan Antonio Samaranch ordering an inquiry into the bribery scandal. But the news that he had received gifts from Nagano and Salt Lake City prior to their cities being granted the Winter Olympics of 1998 and 2002 respectively did not instil critics with confidence in his ability to weed out corruption. (Incidentally, as IOC president, Samaranch is not entitled to a vote during the bidding process ...)

At present corruption and drugs seem to pose the greatest threat to the future of the Greatest Show on Earth. However, the Games have survived plenty of turmoil over the past 104 years and it has always been the marvellous performances of the athletes that has helped to sustain them. Whatever else happens in Sydney, it will be the performances of the next Carl Lewis or Nadia Comaneci that will be remembered after external politics have been forgotten.

Identity Crisis

In the early Olympic years, competitors were regarded as individuals and so could represent any country. For example, Stanley Rowley (Australia) won bronze medals in the 60m, 100m and 200m in 1900 representing Australasia. He was then drafted into the British team for the 5000m team race and won a gold medal, although he didn't finish the race.

Women at the Olympics

Like the ancient Greeks before him, de Coubertin believed that 'Women have but one task, that of crowning the winner with garlands'. So the first Olympics was for men only. Ironically, women made their Olympic debut in de Coubertin's home city – but they were permitted to compete only in 'genteel' sports like tennis and golf. The first female Olympic champion was Charlotte Cooper of Great Britain, who won the tennis singles and went on to win the mixed doubles.

After 1900, women's participation in Olympic sport evolved torturously slowly. Women's swimming (the 100m freestyle and a relay) and highboard diving were added to the program in 1912. It was not until 1928 that women were allowed to compete in track and field events. Unfortunately, so many competitors collapsed after the 800m that the distance was declared unsafe for women, and women weren't permitted to run farther than 200m in Olympic Games until 1960. Since the late 1970s, the IOC has made a concerted effort to increase women's Olympic participation and in Sydney women will compete in some 24 sports including, for the first time, weightlifting.

Paralympic Games

The Paralympics began when the British government set up a spinal injuries centre for ex-servicemen at Stoke Mandeville hospital in 1944. As part of their therapy, patients were introduced to a number of sports and in 1948 a sports competition involving patients from various rehabilitation centres took place. Three years later, competitors from Holland took part in these games and the international Paralympic movement was born. Now, the Paralympics – the name is derived from 'parallel to the Olympics' – take place every four years, in the wake of the Olympics. Since 1976 the Winter Paralympics have followed the Winter Games.

No Handicap

Perhaps the most amazing Olympic competitor of all time was American gymnast George Eyser. In 1904 he won three gymnastics events, despite the fact that he was well over 30 and had a wooden leg! Incredibly, he also competed in the all-around track and field contest (forerunner of the decathlon).

THE SYDNEY GAMES

The 2000 Olympic Games will take place in Sydney from 15 September to 1 October, bringing together more than 10,000 competitors from 198 countries.

Sydney 2000 will feature 28 sports (seven of which include multiple disciplines – eg swimming, diving, synchronised swimming and water polo are disciplines in the sport of aquatics) including, for the first time, the triathlon and taekwondo.

Shortly after the Olympic Games have finished, disabled sportspeople from some 198 countries will converge on Sydney for the 2000 Paralympic Games, held from 18 to 29 October.

Harbour of Life Arts Festival

If you're in Sydney during the 2000 Games you'll find a variety of things to do. In addition to the Games, there'll be the Harbour of Life Arts Festival, which will begin in August 2000 and continue until the conclusion of the Paralympic Games on 24 October. There'll be plenty of street entertainment including outdoor concerts, performing arts, visual arts, film, literature and music activities. Tickets for the festival went on sale in October 1999.

For up-to-the-minute information on all the events taking place, check the daily papers and the official Web site for the Games (www.Sydney.Olympic.org) or call the info service on ☎ 13 63 63.

Venues

Most of the Olympic events will take place at Sydney Olympic Park in Homebush Bay, with some sports being held in western Sydney, eastern Sydney and Darling Harbour.

The centrepiece of Sydney Olympic Park is the 110,000-capacity Stadium Australia. The stadium will stage the opening and closing ceremonies as well as the athletics events and the soccer (football) final.

Also in the Olympic Park is the Sydney International Aquatic Centre, which holds 17,500 people. The gymnastics events and the basketball finals will be held in the 18,000-seat Sydney Superdome. The Baseball Stadium, Hockey Centre, Tennis Centre and Bicentennial Park (where the modern pentathlon will take place) are also in Olympic Park.

Western Sydney will stage the water polo at Ryde Water Polo Pool, rowing and canoeing at the Regatta Centre in Penrith, the cycling at Dunc Gray Velodrome, Bankstown and the three day eventing at the appropriately named Horsley Park.

In eastern Sydney, spectators can watch sailing at Rushcutters Bay, beach volleyball at Bondi Beach, and football at Sydney Football Stadium.

Boxing, weightlifting, judo and fencing will take place at the Sydney Exhibition Centre and Convention Centre in Darling Harbour. Finally, preliminary soccer matches will take place at various venues in Australia: Brisbane's Gabba, Adelaide's Hindmarsh Stadium, Canberra's Bruce Stadium and Melbourne's MCG.

Tickets

Olympic tickets range from A$105 to A$1382 for the opening and closing ceremonies, through A$65 to $455 for athletics events, down to A$30 to $80 for rowing. For Australians, ticket applications closed in July 1999. However, tickets for less popular sports will possibly remain on sale right up to and during the Games themselves. Keep an

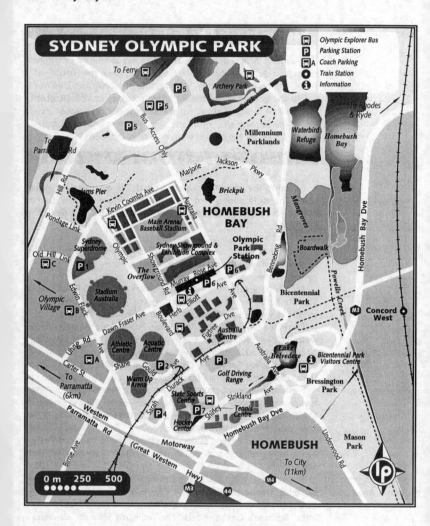

SYDNEY OLYMPIC PARK

Legend:
- Olympic Explorer Bus
- Parking Station
- Coach Parking
- Train Station
- Information

To Ferry
Archery Park
To Rhodes & Ryde
P5
P5
P5
Millennium Parklands
Waterbird Refuge
Homebush Bay
Bus Access Only
To Parramatta Rd
Jackson Pkwy
Marjorie
Jams Pier
Hill Rd
Kevin Coombs Ave
Brickpit
HOMEBUSH BAY
Mangroves
Pondage Link
Main Arena/ Baseball Stadium
Australia
Olympic Park Station
Boardwalk
Sydney Superdrome
Sydney Showground & Exhibition Complex
Homebush Bay Dve
Old Hill Link
P1
Showground Rd
The Overflow
Murray
Rose Ave
P6
P6
Bennelong Rd
Bicentennial Park
Powells Creek
M3 Concord West
Olympic Village
Stadium Australia
Edwin Flack
Herb
Elliott
Ave
Dawn Fraser Ave
Boulevard
Figtree
Dve
Australia Ave
Uhrig Rd
Athletic Centre
Aquatic Centre
Shane
Gould
Lake Belvedere
Bicentennial Park Visitors Centre
Carter St
To Parramatta (6km)
Warm Up Arena
P2
Ave
P3
Golf Driving Range
Bressington Park
Durack
Western Parramatta Rd
Sarah
P4
State Sports Centre
P7
Strikland
Shirley
Tennis Centre
Homebush Bay Dve
Mason Park
Birnie Ave
Hockey Centre
Motorway
(Great Western Hwy)
HOMEBUSH
Underwood Rd
To City (11km)
M3
44
M4

0 m 250 500

Overseas visitors can purchase tickets for the Olympics through agents appointed by their National Olympic Committee. See the Web site www.olympic.org/ioc/e/org/noc/noc_list_e.html for a list of all the

Marvellous Melbourne

This will be the second time the Olympics have been staged in Australia – Melbourne hosted the Games in 1956. The Melbourne Games were memorable for the gold-medal-winning performances of the host nation, especially in the pool, and for Soviet runner Vladimir Kuts' victories in the 5000m and 10,000m. Melbourne also marked the first and only time that the complete Olympic program could not take place within the host country – Australia's quarantine laws meant that the equestrian events had to be staged in Sweden.

committees around the world. Some National Olympic Committees are listed below.

Australia
   (☎ 02-9245 2000, fax 9245 2098)
   Level 13, The Maritime Centre, 207 Kent St, Sydney NSW 2000
Canada
   (☎ 514-861 3371, fax 861 2896)
   Olympic House, Ave Pierre Dupuy 2380, Montreal, Quebec H3C 3R4
France
   (☎ 01-40 78 28 00, fax 40 78 29 51)
   Maison du Sport Français, 1 Ave Pierre de Coubertin, 75640 Paris, Cedex 13
Great Britain
   (☎ 020-8871 2677, fax 8871 9104)
   1 Wandsworth Plain, London SW18 1EH
Germany
   (☎ 69-670 02 02, fax 677 12 29)
   Postfach 71 02 63, 60492 Frankfurt-am-Main
Ireland
   (☎ 01-668 04 44, fax 668 06 50)
   27 Mespil Rd, Dublin 4
Japan
   (☎ 03-3481 2286, fax 3481 0977)
   1-1-1 Jinnan, Tokyo 150-8050
Netherlands
   (☎ 26-483 44 00, fax 483 44 44)
   PO Box 302, Papendallaan 60, 6800 AH Arnhem
New Zealand
   (☎ 04-385 0070, fax 385 0090)
   Olympic House, 3rd Floor, 97-99 Courtenay Place, Wellington
USA
   (☎ 719-632 5551, fax 632 4180)
   Olympic House, 1750 East Boulder St,
   Colorado Springs, CO 80909-5764

Freebies

You won't have to be wealthy to watch Olympic sport live. In fact, some of the Sydney events can be seen free of charge. These are:

Marathons The women's marathon will take place from 9 am on 24 September, and the men's will be on 1 October from 4 pm (followed by the closing ceremony). The 42km course runs from North Sydney Oval through the city centre and out to Stadium Australia in Homebush, and thousands are expected to watch from the roadside.

Racewalking The men's 20km and 50km walks and the women's 20km walk will also take place in Sydney's streets, on 22, 28 and 29 September.

Cycling The road race route will go through Sydney's eastern suburbs, starting and finishing at Moore Park. Road racing can be seen on 25 (training only), 26 and 27 September.

Triathlon Spectators will be able to watch the swimming stage of this event free from the harbourside. The event will take place from 10 am to 1 pm on 16 and 17 September.

Sailing Sydney's famous harbour will play host to the sailing events. Yachts will carry special symbols, probably their national flag, to help spectators identify them. The sailing events will take place every day from 16 to 30 September, from noon.

In addition to the sporting events, free concerts and street entertainment will be provided for the duration of the Games. These events will be centred on the Olympic Boulevard and Millennium Park at Homebush Bay, and around the waterfront at Circular Quay and Darling Harbour.

Transport

Games ticket holders can travel free on the Sydney Olympic transport system on the day of the event until 4 am the following day. Transport will run 24 hours a day. The system covers all CityRail trains and the bus network covering the venues. Olympic Park train station will run up to 30 trains an hour and there will be frequent buses to Olympic Park and the other venues. The free transport zone includes central Sydney and extends to Newcastle, Dungog and Scone in the north of NSW, to Port Kembla and Nowra in the south, Goulburn in the southwest and Bathurst in the west.

Further Reading

Chronicle of the Olympics, pub. Dorling Kindersley
The Complete Book of the Olympics, David Wallechinsky
The History of the Olympics, ed. Martin Tyler & Phil Soar
The Lords of the Rings, Andrew Jennings
The New Lords of the Rings, Andrew Jennings
The Olympics at 100, Associated Press

Liz Filleul

MARTIN HARRIS

New South Wales

Captain Cook first landed in Australia in what is now New South Wales (NSW), and it is where the first permanent European settlement was established. Today it's Australia's most populous state and it has the country's largest city, Sydney. Those expecting NSW to be little more than Sydney's hinterland are in for a real surprise. The state is rich in history, some of it tainted with the brutality of the early penal settlement, but much of it bound up with the gold rush and expansion westward. The state has fabulous coastal and mountain scenery and dry western plains stretching all the way to the 'back of Bourke'.

The state capital, with its opera house, harbour and bridge, is a good place to start your exploration of NSW. It was at Sydney Cove, where the ferries run from Circular Quay today, that the first European settlement was established in 1788, so it's not surprising that Sydney has an air of history which is missing from many Australian cities. That doesn't stop the city being far brasher and more lively than many of its younger Australian counterparts though.

The Pacific Hwy runs north from Sydney and leads to the great beaches, surf and scenery of NSW's northern coastal strip. The Princes Hwy heads south from the capital along the state's less-developed southern coast.

ABORIGINAL PEOPLE

When the British arrived at Sydney Cove, over 200 years ago, there were somewhere between 500,000 and one million Aborigines in Australia, and more than 250 regional languages – many as distinct from each other as English is from Chinese.

Around what is now Sydney, there were approximately 3000 Aborigines using three main languages to communicate, encompassing several dialects and subgroups. Although there was considerable overlap, Ku-ring-gai was generally spoken on the northern shore, Dharawal along the coast

HIGHLIGHTS

Telephone code: ☎ 02 (also 03, 07 and 08)
Population: 6.34 million
Area: 802,000 sq km

- Cruising on Sydney Harbour, the best way to view the harbour city
- Sampling the wineries of the Hunter Valley region
- Bushwalking in the Blue Mountains
- Skiing in the Snowy Mountains beneath Mt Kosciuszko, Australia's highest mainland peak
- Catching a wave at Byron Bay, Australia's surfing mecca
- Exploring the extraordinary archaeological record of Lake Mungo
- Watching the flamboyant Mardi Gras parade – or joining in!
- Venturing into the remote outback, 'back of Bourke'

QUEENSLAND
Byron Bay p 304
Far North Coast p 300
Mid North Coast p 291
Coffs Harbour p 296
Broken Hill p 354
Dubbo p 346
Port Macquarie p 288
Lower North Coast p 285
Newcastle p 278
Around Sydney p 263
Katoomba p 272
Central Sydney pp 212-13
Wollongong p 321
Kosciuszko National Park p 332
Darling Harbour & Chinatown p 223
CANBERRA
Kings Cross p 228
ACT
Manly p 233
Sydney Harbour & Inner Suburbs p 231
VICTORIA
South Coast p 319

south of Botany Bay; Dharug and its dialects were spoken on the plains at the foot of the Blue Mountains.

Today, more Aboriginal people live in Sydney than in any other Australian city. The

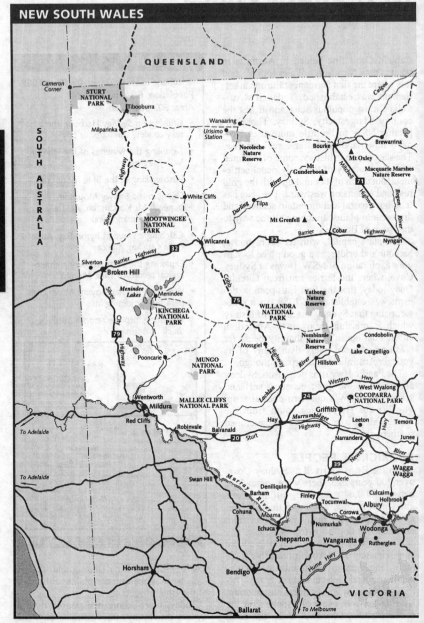

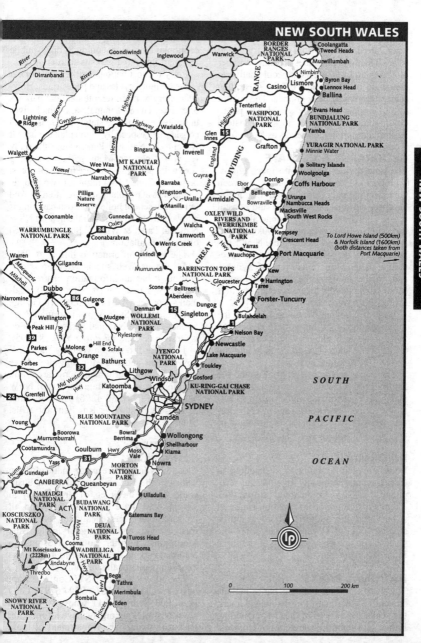

Sydney region is estimated to have around 30,800 indigenous inhabitants, most of whom are descended from migratory inland tribes. This figure includes a smaller number of Torres Strait Islanders, a people native to the group of islands just off the Australian coast, near Papua New Guinea. The suburb of Redfern has a large and vital Koori population (many Aborigines in south-eastern Australia describe themselves as Kooris).

GEOGRAPHY & CLIMATE

The state divides neatly into four regions. The narrow coastal strip runs between Queensland and Victoria and has many beaches, national parks, inlets and coastal lakes. The Great Dividing Range also runs the length of the state, about 100km inland from the coast, and includes the New England tablelands north of Sydney, the spectacular Blue Mountains west of Sydney, and, in the south of the state, the Snowy Mountains, which offer excellent winter skiing and summer bushwalking.

West of the Great Dividing Range is the farming country of the western slopes and the dry western plains, which cover two-thirds of the state. The plains fade into the barren Outback in the far west.

The major rivers are the Murray and the Darling, which meander westward across the plains. As a general rule of thumb, it gets hotter the further north you go and drier the further west. In winter, the Snowy Mountains are, not surprisingly, covered with snow.

INFORMATION

NSW travel information is distributed to travel agents nationally or you can telephone ☎ 13 2077 for recorded information. There's also a major information centre at Albury, on the Victorian border, and a smaller one at Tweed Heads, on the Queensland border. Most towns have tourist information centres.

NATIONAL PARKS

The state's 70-odd national parks include stretches of coast, vast forested inland tracts, the peaks and valleys of the Great Dividing Range, and some epic stretches of Outback.

Most parks can be reached by conventional vehicles in reasonable weather. With the exception of those surrounding Sydney, public transport into most parks is scarce.

Entry to most national parks is $9 per car – less for motorcycles and pedestrians. However, entry to more remote national parks is often free. The $60 annual pass, which gives unlimited entry to the state's parks, is worth considering, especially if you plan to visit Mt Kosciuszko National Park, where the daily fee is $14 per car. Many parks have camp sites with facilities; some are free, others cost between $5 and $15 a night for two people. Camp sites at popular parks are often booked out during school holidays. Bush camping is allowed in some parks; call the nearest NSW National Parks & Wildlife Service (NPWS) office for regulations.

The NPWS information line is ☎ 9585 6444 and its Web site is www.npws.nsw .gov.au. It has an information centre at 43 Bridge St, Hurstville (☎ 9585 6333). Cadman's Cottage (☎ 9247 5033), 110 George St, The Rocks, Sydney has information on Sydney Harbour National Parks. Also handy is Gregory's *National Parks NSW* ($18.95).

The state forests – owned by the NSW government and used for logging – have drives, camping grounds, picnic areas and walking tracks. The State Forests of NSW head office (☎ 9980 4296) is at Building 2, 423 Pennant Hills Rd, Pennant Hills, Sydney.

ACTIVITIES
Bushwalking

Close to Sydney, there are dramatic cliff-top walks in the Royal National Park, bushwalks around the inlets of Broken Bay in Ku-ring-gai Chase National Park, and all the sandstone bluffs, eucalyptus forests and fresh air you could wish for in the Blue Mountains. Further south, Kosciuszko National Park, in the Snowy Mountains, has excellent alpine walks in summer.

The NPWS and the NSW Confederation of Bushwalking Clubs (☎ 9294 6797), GPO Box 2090, Sydney 1043, whose Web site is www.bushwalking.org.au, have information on bushwalking. The Department of Land

& Water Conservation (DLWC; ☎ 9228 6111), 23-33 Bridge St, Sydney, has free brochures and discovery kits ($10) on the 250km Great North Walk, linking Sydney with the Hunter Valley, and the Hume & Hovell Track running through the High Country between Yass and Albury.

Lonely Planet's *Bushwalking in Australia* details some walks in NSW. Other useful books are *100 Walks in New South Wales* by Tyrone Thomas and *Sydney and Beyond* by Andrew Mevissen.

Water Sports

Swimming & Surfing The state's 1900km coastline is liberally sprinkled with beaches offering excellent swimming (see the Sydney section for surf beaches within the metropolitan area). North of Sydney, surfing spots include Newcastle, Port Macquarie, Seal Rocks, Crescent Head, Nambucca Heads, Coffs Harbour, Angourie, Lennox Head and Byron Bay. South of Sydney, you could try Wollongong, Jervis Bay, Ulladulla, Merimbula or Eden. Contact Surfing NSW (☎ 9518 9410), PO Box 330, Manly, NSW 2095, for detailed information.

Surf carnivals start in December and run until April. Contact Surf Life Saving NSW (☎ 9984 7188) for dates and venues.

Diving & Snorkelling North of Sydney, try Terrigal, Port Stephens, Seal Rocks, Coffs Harbour or Byron Bay. On the south coast, head to Jervis Bay, Merimbula or Eden.

Sailing Sydney Harbour and Pittwater both offer exceptional sailing (see the Sydney section for details). Lake Macquarie, south of Newcastle, and Myall Lakes, just to the north, are also good. Contact the Yachting Association of NSW (☎ 9660 1266) for information on sailing clubs and courses.

White-Water Rafting & Canoeing Good rafting spots include the upper Murray and Snowy rivers in the Snowy Mountains, and the Shoalhaven River, 220km south of Sydney. In the north, there's rafting on the Nymboida and Gwydir rivers. Albury, Jindabyne and Nowra are the centres for the southern rivers; Coffs Harbour and Nambucca Heads for the northern. A day trip costs around $100.

JIM SWANSON

White water rafting

NEW SOUTH WALES

There's an abundance of canoeing spots in NSW, but in particular you might like to try Port Macquarie, Barrington Tops (for white-water canoeing), Myall Lakes, Jervis Bay and the Murrumbidgee River near Canberra. The NSW Canoe Association (☎ 9660 4597) can provide information, and publishes *The Canoeing Guide to NSW* ($24.95).

Cycling
Bicycle NSW (☎ 9283 5200), 209 Castlereagh St, Sydney 2000, can provide information on cycling routes throughout the state.

Skiing
See the Snowy Mountains section for skiing information.

GETTING THERE & AWAY
See Getting There & Away in the Sydney section for information on international and interstate air, rail and bus links.

GETTING AROUND
Air
Smaller airlines like Hazelton (☎ 13 1713) and Eastern Australia Airlines (a Qantas subsidiary, ☎ 13 1313) operate comprehensive networks within the state, and other airlines serve particular regions. The chart shows some routes and standard economy one-way fares. In many instances, discount return tickets are as cheap as economy one-way fares. Discounted tickets generally require purchase 21 days in advance and carry restrictions.

Bus
Buses are often quicker and cheaper than trains, but not always. If you want to make stops on the way to your ultimate destination, look for cheap stopover deals rather than buying separate tickets. Once you have reached your destination, there are usually local bus lines, although services may not be frequent. In remote areas, school buses may be the only option. The drivers will usually pick you up, but they are not obliged to do so.

NSW AIR FARES

Train
Countrylink has the most comprehensive state rail service in Australia and will, in conjunction with connecting buses, take you to most sizeable towns in NSW. All Countrylink services must be booked in advance (☎ 13 2242 daily between 6.30 am and 10 pm). You can do this in person at Central station or the Countrylink Travel Centre, corner York and Margaret Sts (both in Sydney). Passage for bicycles and surfboards ($10 one way) must also be reserved in advance.

The frequency of services and their value for money is variable so compare options with private bus services. Countrylink offers first and economy-class tickets and a quota of discount tickets; return fares are double the single fare. Australian students travel for half the economy fare.

Intrastate services and one-way economy fares from Sydney include Albury, 643km, $75; Armidale, 569km, $69; Bathurst, 223km, $32; Bourke, 835km, $85; Broken Hill, 1125km, $102; Byron Bay, 883km, $85; Canberra, 326km, $42; Coffs Harbour, 608km, $69; Cooma, 441km, $57; Dubbo, 462km, $57; Port Macquarie, 474km, $62; and Tamworth, 455km, $62.

Frequent commuter-type trains run between Sydney and Wollongong ($7.20), Katoomba ($9.40), Lithgow ($14.60), Newcastle ($14.60) and, less frequently, Goulburn ($29).

A one month NSW Discovery Pass offers economy-class travel and unlimited stopovers on the state network for $249.

Sydney

☎ 02   • postcode 2000 (city central)
• pop 3,986,700

Australia's oldest and largest settlement is a vibrant city built around one of the most spectacular harbours in the world. Instantly recognisable thanks to its opera house, harbour and bridge, Sydney also boasts lesser-known attractions like the historic Rocks, Victorian-era Paddington, heavenly beaches such as Bondi and Manly, and two superb coastal national parks on the city fringe.

The city is built on land once occupied by the Eora tribe, whose presence lingers in the place names of many suburbs and whose artistic legacy can be seen at many Aboriginal engraving sites around the city. After its brutal beginnings, and a long period when it seemed content to be a second-rate facsimile of a British city, Sydney has finally come of age. After being selected to host the 2000 Olympic Games, it has undergone a period of rejuvenation aimed at putting its cityscape on a level with its natural charms.

An array of ethnic groups contribute to the city's social life – the dynamism of the Chinese community in particular has played an important role in altering the city's Anglo-Mediterranean fabric, and preparing it to become a key player in Asia.

ORIENTATION

The harbour divides Sydney into northern and southern halves, with the Sydney Harbour Bridge and the Harbour Tunnel joining the two shores. The city centre and most places of interest are south of the harbour. The central area is long and narrow, stretching from the Rocks and Circular Quay in the north to Central station in the south. It is bounded by Darling Harbour to the west and a string of pleasant parks to the east.

East of the city centre are the innercity suburbs of Darlinghurst, Kings Cross and Paddington. Further east again are exclusive suburbs like Double Bay and Vaucluse. To the south-east of these are the ocean-beach suburbs of Bondi and Coogee. Sydney's Kingsford-Smith airport is in Mascot,

10km south of the city centre, jutting into Botany Bay.

West of the centre is the radically changing suburb of Pyrmont, and the peninsula suburbs of Glebe and Balmain. The inner west includes Newtown and Leichhardt.

Suburbs stretch a good 20km north and south of the centre, their extent limited by national parks. The suburbs north of the bridge are known collectively as the North Shore. The western suburbs sprawl for 50km to reach the foothills of the Blue Mountains, encompassing the once separate settlements of Parramatta and Penrith.

Maps

Just about every brochure you pick up includes a map of the city centre, but the Lonely Planet's *Sydney City Map* ($7.95) has good coverage of the city centre and also covers the Blue Mountains and Homebush Bay. If you're intending to drive around the city, the *Sydney UBD* street directory ($33.95) is invaluable. For topographic maps, visit the DLWC (☎ 9228 6111), 23-33 Bridge St.

INFORMATION
Tourist Offices

The NSW Travel Centre, in the international terminal at the airport (☎ 9667 6050), is open daily from 6 am to midnight. It can book discounted hotel rooms, and has a notice board listing hostel accommodation, with free telephone links to hostels.

The useful Travellers Information Service (☎ 9281 9366), in the coach terminal outside Central station, is open daily from 6 am until 10.30 pm for bus and hotel accommodation bookings; there's also a hostel notice board. Inside the station, the Travellers Aid Society (☎ 9211 2469) provides general information, travel assistance, and hot showers ($3). It's open weekdays from 6.45 am to 5 pm, weekends 7 am to midday.

Citi Host tourist information kiosks are located at Circular Quay, Town Hall and Martin Place. They're open from 9 am to 5 pm in winter, 10 am to 6 pm in summer.

The excellent Sydney Visitors Centre (☎ 9255 1788, or 1800 067 676), at 106

NEW SOUTH WALES

CENTRAL SYDNEY

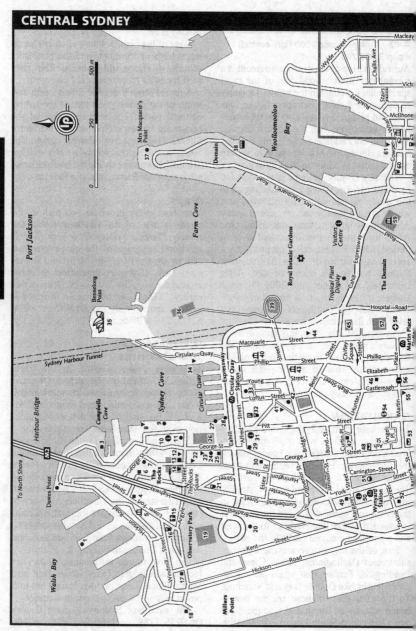

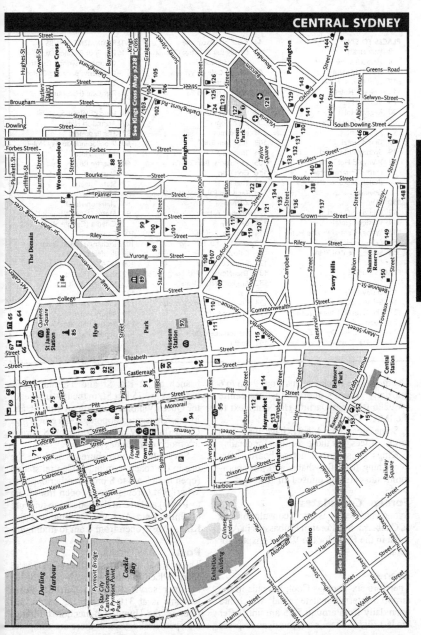

CENTRAL SYDNEY

NEW SOUTH WALES

CENTRAL SYDNEY

PLACES TO STAY

3 Park Hyatt
4 Harbour View Hotel
6 Mercantile Hotel
17 Lord Nelson Hotel
18 Palisade Hotel
25 Russell Hotel
30 Regent Hotel
46 Sydney City Centre
Apartments
47 Grand Hotel
49 Sydney Vista Hotel
52 Wynyard Hotel
88 Forbes Terrace Hotel
106 L'Otel; Backdoor Café;
Govinda's
110 YWCA
112 CB Private Hotel
114 Westend Hotel
115 Sydney Central Private Hotel
150 Excelsior Hotel
153 Sydney Central YHA

PLACES TO EAT

8 Quay
12 G'Day Cafe
14 Bel Mondo; anti bar
22 The Gum Nut Tea Garden
23 Rockpool
34 Sydney Cove Oyster Bar
41 Obelisk; Customs House Bar

44 Kiosk on Macquarie
55 Dendy Bar & Bistro; Cinema
(Martin Place)
61 Harry's Cafe de Wheels
67 Carruthers
91 Parma Espresso Bar
98 Pacifico
99 Hard Rock Cafe
100 Bill & Toni's
101 No Names
103 Tum Tum Thai
104 Tropicana
105 La Bussola; Bar Coluzzi
116 Don Don
117 Thai Panic
118 Tandoori Palace; Betty's Soup
Kitchen
120 Roobar; Fatz
121 Bach Hy
124 Fishface; Eca Bar
125 Fu-Manchu; Fez; Oh
Calcutta!
127 Bandstand Cafe
131 Thai-Nesia; Vin Ha Long
132 Angkor Wat; Balkan
133 Cafe 191
134 Courthouse Hotel; Kinselas
135 Maltese Cafe
137 Mali
138 Metronome Café
151 Bodhi

ENTERTAINMENT & PUBS

1 Pier Four (Sydney Dance
Company; Sydney Theatre
Company; Bangarra Dance
Theatre)
2 Pier One (Harbourside
Brasserie)
16 Hero of Waterloo Hotel
21 Australian Hotel
32 The Basement
60 Woolloomooloo Bay Hotel
63 Tilbury Hotel
68 Theatre Royal
71 Soup Plus
77 State Theatre
80 Marble Bar
84 Sheraton Hotel
94 Metro (Music Venue); Dendy
Cinema (George St)
102 Cauldron
107 Exchange Hotel; Q Bar
108 Burdekin Hotel
109 DCM
113 Capitol Theatre
119 Midnight Shift
122 Oxford Hotel
126 Green Park Hotel
129 Albury Hotel
130 Beauchamp Hotel
136 Bentley Bar
139 Beresford Hotel; Barracks Bar

George St, the Rocks, opens from 9 am to 6 pm daily. There's another visitors centre (☎ 9286 0111) at Darling Harbour, next to the IMAX Cinema.

Some areas, like Manly, have their own tourist offices (see those sections for details).

Kings Cross hostel notice boards offer everything from flat-shares and job opportunities to cars and unused air tickets.

Foreign Consulates

Sydney has nearly as many consular offices as Canberra. See Foreign Embassies in Australia in the Facts for the Visitor chapter for details.

Money

There are six Thomas Cook bureaus in the airport's international terminal, which are open daily from around 5.15 am until after the last flight. There's an American Express branch at 92 Pitt St and Thomas Cook branches at 175 Pitt St, in the lower level of the Queen Victoria Building on York St, and in the Kingsgate shopping centre in Kings Cross (but they're all closed on Saturday afternoon and Sunday).

Seven-day change bureaus include the one in the coach terminal at Central station (open from 8 am to 8 pm), another opposite Wharf 6 at Circular Quay (open from 8 am to 10 pm) and one at the pedestrian juncture of Springfield Ave and Darlinghurst Rd, Kings Cross (open from 8 am to midnight).

Post

The original main post office (GPO) is in Martin Place, but there's another post office (counter service) at 130 Pitt St. Poste Restante is at 310 George St, on the 3rd floor of the Hunter Connection building; it's open weekdays, and there are computer

CENTRAL SYNDEY

140 Flinders Hotel
141 Palace Academy Twin; Mister Goodbar
142 Verona Cinema
146 Palace Hotel
147 Cricketers Arms
148 Hopetoun Hotel
149 Forresters Hotel

ATTRACTIONS
5 Colonial House Museum
15 Garrison Church
19 Sydney Observatory
20 National Trust Centre
26 Museum of Contemporary Art
33 Customs House
35 Sydney Opera House
36 Government House
37 Mrs Macquarie's Chair
39 Sydney Conservatorium of Music
40 Justice & Police Museum
42 Macquarie Place
43 Museum of Sydney
45 State Library of NSW
57 Parliament House
59 Art Gallery of NSW
62 Artspace
64 Hyde Park Barracks
65 Mint Building

66 St James Church
75 Sydney Tower & Centrepoint
82 Great Synagogue
85 Archibald Fountain
86 St Mary's Cathedral
89 Australian Museum
93 St Andrew's Cathedral
97 Anzac Memorial
123 Jewish Museum
145 Victoria Barracks

OTHER
7 Australian Conservation Foundation Shop
9 Overseas Passenger Terminal
10 Sydney Visitors Centre
11 Cadman's Cottage
13 Rocks Centre
24 Aboriginal & Tribal Art Centre
27 Commissioners & Harbour-master's Steps
28 Australian Travel Specialists
29 Australian Wine Centre
31 Citi Host Information Kiosk
38 Boy Charlton Pool
48 Post Restante (Hunter Connection)
50 Tourism NSW
51 Wynyard Park Bus Terminal
53 GPO

54 American Express
56 Sydney City Host Information Kiosk
58 Sydney Hospital
69 GPO (Counter Service)
70 NRMA
72 Strand Arcade
73 Travellers Medical & Vaccination Centre; Travellers Contact Point; Dymocks Books
74 Skygarden Arcade
76 City Centre Monorail Station
78 Queen Victoria Building (QVB)
79 Darling Park Monorail Station
81 Park Plaza Monorail Station
83 Ticketek
87 Eastern Distributor Road Exit
90 Telstra Payphone Centre
92 Citi Host Information Kiosk
95 World Square Monorail Station
96 Whilton Camera Service
111 Kinko's; Travel Bookshop
128 St Vincent's Hospital
143 Ariel Bookshop
144 Wooly's Wheels
152 Sydney Coach Terminal & Travellers Information Service
154 Thomas Cook Bush Gear

terminals that indicate whether mail is being held for you. You can have your mail redirected to any suburban post office for $5 a month.

There are several travel agencies offering mail-holding and forwarding services, including Travellers Contact Point (☎ 9221 8744), 7th floor, 428 George St and Backpackers World (☎ 9380 2700), 212 Victoria St, Kings Cross.

Telephone & Fax
There are phone booths at the Telstra Payphone Centre, 231 Elizabeth St. You can make discounted calls and send faxes from Global Gossip (☎ 9326 9777), 111 Darlinghurst Rd, Kings Cross.

Email & Internet Access
Internet cafes have been popping up all over Sydney recently, especially around Kings

Cross and Oxford St. Some stay open 24 hours. Rates vary, so shop around.

You can check email at Travellers Contact Point (☎ 9221 8744), 7th floor, 428 George St, Backpackers World (☎ 9380 2700), 212 Victoria St, Kings Cross and Global Gossip (☎ 9326 977), 111 Darlinghurst Rd, Kings Cross (also in Oxford and George Sts). There's a pricier net cafe (closed on Sunday) upstairs at the Hotel Sweeney (☎ 9267 1116), 236 Clarence St in the city. The Idle Tank book and CD shop at 84 Campbell St, Bondi Beach, has Internet access. Well Connected, 35 Glebe Point Rd, Glebe, is a surf-and-snack cafe. Many hostels have coin-operated Internet machines; most libraries offer free Net access, but you'll need to book ahead.

Travel Agencies
The YHA Membership & Travel Centre (☎ 9261 1111), 422 Kent St, between Market

and Druitt Sts, offers normal travel agency services and enables travellers to make national and international hostel bookings. There's another travel centre in the Sydney Central YHA (☎ 9281 9444) on the corner of Pitt St and Rawson Place; Backpackers World (☎ 9380 2700), 212 Victoria St, Kings Cross, is also a backpacker-friendly travel agent.

Bookshops

The Travel Bookshop (☎ 9261 8200), 175 Liverpool St, has a comprehensive range of guidebooks and travel literature. Dymocks Booksellers (☎ 9224 0411), 424-428 George St, claims to be the largest bookshop in the southern hemisphere. Other good bookshops are Gleebooks, 49 Glebe Point Rd, Glebe, and Ariel, 42 Oxford St, Paddington. Gould's, 33 King St, Newtown, is an amazing muddle of second-hand tomes; it's open daily till midnight.

Publications

TNT is a free monthly magazine aimed at backpackers. It's full of stuff to know, budget accommodation and activities and is available from hostels and tourist offices. OVG ('overseas visitors guide') is a free monthly available from the airport that combines maps and places of interest with what's-on listings. This Month in Sydney is similar, if a bit twee.

The Metro lift-out in Friday's Sydney Morning Herald provides a comprehensive listing of what's on in the city over the coming week. The free music and entertainment newspapers delivered to pubs, cafes and record shops list those clubs that open and close so fast that you hardly have time to find out where they are. They include Drum Media, Revolver, 3D World, Capital Q Weekly and Sydney Star Observer (both gay). The excellent Sydney City Hub is full of culturally savvy listings for the innercity groover.

There are plenty of guidebooks to Sydney. Lonely Planet's Sydney guide and New South Wales are general guides and there is also their new, briefer Sydney Condensed. Untourist Sydney by Jacqueline Huié is a difficult to navigate 'insider's guide' to the city.

A great piece of travel literature is Sydney by Jan Morris. For a literary journey through the mean streets of Sydney, try one of Peter Corris' Cliff Hardy thrillers.

Gay & Lesbian Travellers

Gay and lesbian culture forms a vital and colourful part of Sydney's social fabric.

The Gay & Lesbian Mardi Gras in February/March is Australia's biggest annual tourist event, and the hedonistic Oxford St parade is watched by over half a million people. (See the boxed text 'Out & About in Gay Sydney' in the Entertainment section.) The Taylor Square region of Oxford St is the hub of the second-largest gay community in the world.

However, there's still a homophobic side to some 'true blue' Aussies, and violence against homosexuals isn't unheard-of. For the record, in NSW the age of consent for homosexual sex is 18 for men, and 16 for women.

The Sydney Gay & Lesbian Mardi Gras has established an on-line travel service, Mardi Gras Travel, at www.mardigras.com.au to assist gay and lesbian travellers coming to Australia.

For counselling and referral call the Gay & Lesbian Line (☎ 9207 2800 or 1800 805 379), from 4 pm to midnight daily.

Laundry

Most hostels and hotels provide laundry facilities or services. My Favourite Laundrette (☎ 9332 1843), 249 Darlinghurst Rd, Darlinghurst, will wash your grubby gear for you. Self-service laundrettes include Associated Laundries in Llankelly Place, Kings Cross, and Pacific Laundry (☎ 9130 3987), 10-12 Campbell Parade, Bondi Beach, near Nomad's backpackers.

Left Luggage

There is a cloakroom at Central train station, which charges $1.50 per item per day (as long as you pay the fee daily – otherwise you're charged $4.50 per day). Luggage lockers at the airport's international terminal and the Sydney coach terminal, on the corner of Pitt St and Eddy Ave, cost $4 to

$8 a day, depending on the size of your swag. Travellers Contact Point (☎ 9221 8744), 7th floor, 428 George St, stores luggage for $10 to $15 per piece per month.

Medical Services

The Travellers Medical & Vaccination Centre (☎ 9221 7133), Level 7, 428 George St, and the Kings Cross Travellers' Clinic (☎ 9358 3376), Suite 1, 13 Springfield Ave, Kings Cross, are both open weekdays and Saturday mornings. It's best to book. If you break a leg in central Sydney, hobble up to Sydney Hospital (☎ 9382 7111), on Macquarie St.

Other Services

The NRMA head office is on the corner of King and George Sts in the city (☎ 13 2132).

If your backpack is busted, try Custom Luggage (☎ 9261 1109), 317 Sussex St. Cameras can be repaired at Whilton Camera Service (☎ 9267 8429), 251 Elizabeth St, opposite Hyde Park.

If you just need a damn good wash, grab a shower at Travellers Aid in Central station (☎ 9211 2469) for $3 on weekdays between 7 am and 4.30 pm, or on weekends before 11.30 am.

Emergency

The Wayside Chapel (☎ 9358 6577), 29 Hughes St, Kings Cross, is a crisis centre which can handle personal problems.

Other emergency support services include Lifeline (☎ 13 1114) and the Rape Crisis Centre (☎ 9819 6565).

Dangers & Annoyances

Sydney isn't an especially dangerous city but you should remain alert. The usual big-city rules apply: never leave luggage unattended, never flaunt money and never get drunk in the company of strangers. Harassment of gays, lesbians, women in general and non-Anglo-Saxons is not rife but it does happen. Use extra caution in Kings Cross, which attracts dodgy characters.

SYDNEY HARBOUR

The harbour has melded and shaped the Sydney psyche since the first days of settlement, and today it's both a major port and the city's playground. Its waters, beaches, islands and waterside parks offer all the swimming, sailing, picnicking and strolling you could wish for.

Officially called **Port Jackson**, the harbour stretches some 20km inland to join the

---

Harbour Walks

The 10km **Manly Scenic Walkway** from Manly Cove to Spit Bridge is one of the best ways for landlubbers to experience the harbour. It passes through native bushland at Dobroyd Head, runs close to several hideaway beaches, passes Aboriginal engravings and a charming lighthouse at Grotto Point, and has panoramic views of Sydney Harbour and Middle Harbour. It can be a complicated walk to follow, so pick up a leaflet at Cadman's Cottage in the Rocks or at the Manly Visitors Information Bureau on South Steyne, Manly. Bus Nos 169, 175, 185 and 248 run from Spit Bridge back to the city centre. The best way to get to Manly Cove is by ferry from Circular Quay.

There's a 4km walking track in **Ashton Park**, south of Taronga Zoo, which passes Bradleys Head and Taylor Bay. At Bradleys Head there are military fortifications and memorabilia. Take the Taronga Zoo ferry from Circular Quay to get to Ashton Park.

The walking track along the **Hermitage Foreshore**, in Nielsen Park, has spectacular views back to the city, and you can cool off at netted Shark Beach (known locally by the less scary name of Nielsen Park Beach). Bus No 325 from the city passes Nielsen Park via Kings Cross and terminates at Watsons Bay. **South Head**, near Watsons Bay, is a good spot for a cliff-top stroll.

Sydney Harbour Ferries publishes a useful pamphlet detailing some picturesque harbourside strolls.

NEW SOUTH WALES

NEW SOUTH WALES

mouth of the Parramatta River. The headlands at the entrance are known as North Head and South Head. The city centre is about 8km inland and the most scenic part of the harbour is between the Heads and the Harbour Bridge. **Middle Harbour** is a large inlet that heads north-west a couple of kilometres inside the Heads.

The best way to view the harbour is to persuade someone to take you sailing, to join a cruise or to catch one of the numerous ferries plying its waters. The Manly ferry offers vistas of the harbour east of the bridge, while the Parramatta RiverCats cover the west.

Sydney's **harbour beaches** are generally sheltered, calm coves with little of the frenetic activity of the ocean beaches. On the south shore, they include Lady Bay (nude), Camp Cove and Nielsen Park; all accessible by bus No 325 from Watsons Bay.

On the North Shore there are harbour beaches at Manly Cove, Reef Beach (nude but not very secluded), Clontarf, Chinaman's Beach and Balmoral. The Manly ferry docks at Manly Cove, and Reef Beach is a couple of kilometres walk along the Manly Scenic Walkway.

To get to Balmoral, take the No 247 from Wynyard to Mosman Junction, then change to the No 257. For Clontarf, catch the No 131 or 132 from Wynyard. The other beaches are accessible, with a bit of walking, by catching bus No 175 or 178, which depart from Wynyard, travel along Military Rd and cross Spit Bridge.

Sydney Harbour National Park

This park protects the scattered pockets of bushland around the harbour and includes several small islands. It offers some great walking tracks, scenic lookouts, Aboriginal carvings and a handful of historic sites. On the south shore it incorporates South Head and Nielsen Park; on the North Shore it includes North Head, Dobroyd Head, Middle Head and Ashton Park. Fort Denison, Goat, Clarke, Rodd and Shark islands are also part of the park. Pick up information at Cadman's Cottage (☎ 9247 5033), in the Rocks.

Previously known as Pinchgut, **Fort Denison** is a small fortified island off Mrs

Macquarie's Point, originally used to isolate troublesome convicts. The fort was built during the Crimea War amid fears of a Russian invasion. At the time of writing, Fort Denison was closed for conservation work, but tours will resume.

There are tours of **Goat Island**, just west of the Harbour Bridge, which has been a shipyard, quarantine station, gunpowder depot and, more recently, part of the set for the popular Water Rats television show. Depending on your obsessions, you can take a Water Rats tour ($13), a heritage tour ($12) or a Gruesome Tales tour ($18). Ask at Cadman's Cottage for details.

Clarke Island, off Darling Point, and **Shark Island**, off Rose Bay, are great picnic spots, but you'll need a permit ($3 per person, ☎ 9247 5033).

THE ROCKS

Sydney's first European settlement was on the rocky spur of land on the western side of Sydney Cove, from which the Harbour Bridge now crosses to North Shore. It was a squalid, raucous place full of convicts, whalers, prostitutes and street gangs, though in the 1820s the nouveaux riches inexplicably built three-storey houses on the ridges overlooking the slums.

It later became an area of warehouses and maritime commerce and then slumped into decline as modern shipping and storage facilities moved away from Circular Quay. An outbreak of bubonic plague in the early 20th century led to whole streets being razed and the construction of the Harbour Bridge resulted in further demolition.

Since the 1970s, redevelopment has turned the Rocks into a sanitised, historical tourist precinct, full of narrow cobbled streets, fine colonial buildings, converted warehouses, tea rooms and stuffed koalas. If you ignore the kitsch, it's a delightful place to stroll around, especially in the poky backstreets and in the less developed, tight-knit, contiguous community of Millers Point.

Pick up a self-guided tour map ($1) of the area from the Sydney Visitors Centre (☎ 9255 1788, 1800 067 676), in the old Sailors Home at 106 George St. The best guided tour of the

Rocks is Master Christopher's atmospheric night tour (☎ 9555 2700 or ask at the Visitors Centre). Tours start at 6 pm and cost $17 ($13 concession). If you'd rather soak it up at your own pace, hire a Rocks Walking Adventure cassette for $8 (☎ 018 111 011).

Next door to the Heritage Centre, at 110 George St, is **Cadman's Cottage** (1816), the oldest house in Sydney. It once housed longboats and was home to the last Government Coxswain, John Cadman; it's now home to the Sydney Harbour National Parks Information Centre (☎ 9247 5033).

Despite all the helpful tourist infrastructure, the beauty of the Rocks is that it's as much fun to wander around aimlessly as it is to visit particular attractions. Soak up the atmosphere, sample the frequent entertainment in The Rocks Square on Playfair St, browse around the vibrant **Rocks Centre** for that Aussie present, dine at an outdoor cafe, admire the views of Circular Quay and **Campbell Cove**, and join the melee at the weekend **Rocks Market**.

A short walk west along Argyle Street, through the convict-excavated **Argyle Cut**, takes you to the other side of the peninsula and **Millers Point**, a delightful district of early colonial homes with a quintessential English village green. Nearby are the **Garrison Church** and the more secular delights of the Lord Nelson Hotel and the Hero of Waterloo Hotel, which tussle over the title of Sydney's oldest pub. The **Colonial House Museum** (☎ 9247 6008), on Lower Fort St, is crammed with period bric-a-brac, reminiscent of a rampant great aunt's attic. It's open daily from 10 am to 4.30 pm ($1).

Sydney Observatory (☎ 9217 0485) has a commanding position atop Observatory Park overlooking Millers Point and the harbour. The observatory is open from 10 am to 5 pm. Day admission is free, but night visits ($8, $3 concession) must be booked in advance.

In the old military hospital building close by, the **National Trust Centre** houses an art gallery, bookshop and cafe. It's open Tuesday to Friday from 11 am to 5 pm, and weekends from 12 to 5 pm. Admission to the gallery is $6.

At Dawes Point, on Walsh Bay, just west of the Harbour Bridge, are several renovated wharves. **Pier One** is being developed into a shopping and leisure complex; **Pier Four** is beautifully utilised as the home of the prestigious Sydney Theatre, Bangarra Dance Theatre and Sydney Dance companies.

SYDNEY HARBOUR BRIDGE

The much-loved, imposing 'old coat hanger' crosses the harbour at one of its narrowest points, linking the southern and northern shores and joining central Sydney with the satellite business district in North Sydney. The bridge was completed in 1932 at a cost of $20 million and has always been a favourite icon, partly because of its sheer size, partly because of its function in uniting the city and partly because it boosted employment during the Depression.

You can climb inside the south-eastern stone pylon, which houses the Harbour Bridge Museum, or you can join a climbing group and scale the bridge itself (see the earlier 'Harbour Walks' boxed text).

Cars, trains, cyclists, joggers and pedestrians use the bridge. The cycleway is on the western side and the pedestrian walkway on the eastern; stair access is from Cumberland St in the Rocks and near Milsons Point station on the North Shore.

The best way to experience the bridge is undoubtedly on foot; don't expect much of a view crossing by car or train. Driving south (only) there's a $2 toll.

The **Harbour Tunnel** shoulders some of the bridge's workload. It begins about half a kilometre south of the opera house, crosses under the harbour just to the east of the bridge, and rejoins the highway on the northern side. There's a southbound (only) toll of $2. If you're heading from the North Shore to the eastern suburbs, it's much easier to use the tunnel.

SYDNEY OPERA HOUSE

The world famous Sydney Opera House is dramatically situated on the eastern headland of Circular Quay. Its soaring sail-like, shell-like roofs were actually inspired by palm fronds.

It's a memorable experience to attend a performance here, or to just loiter at an outdoor cafe and watch harbour life go by.

The opera house has four main auditoriums and hosts classical music, ballet, theatre and film, as well as opera. There is also a new venue, The Studio, staging contemporary arts events. On Sunday there is a bustling craft market in the forecourt.

Popular operas sell out quickly (despite the three-figure sums for the best seats) but there are often 'restricted view' tickets available for $35 for those with a long neck or a good imagination. Decent seats to see a play or hear the Sydney Symphony Orchestra are more affordable from around $28. The varied 'Sundays around the house' program offers some of the best deals, with most tickets around $20.

The box office (☎ 9250 7777) is open Monday to Saturday between 9 am and 8.30 pm and 2½ hours prior to a Sunday performance.

Worthwhile one-hour tours of the Opera House buildings are run daily between 9 am and 4 pm (☎ 9250 7250). They depart from the concourse and cost $12.90 ($8.90 concession). Not all tours can visit all theatres because of rehearsals, but you're more likely to see everything if you take an early tour. There are also backstage tours ($20.90).

CIRCULAR QUAY

Circular Quay, built around Sydney Cove, is one of the city's major focal points. The first European settlement grew around the Tank Stream, which now runs underground into the harbour near Wharf 6. For many years this was the shipping centre of Sydney, but it's now both a commuting hub and a recreational space, combining ferry quays, a train station and the Overseas Passenger Terminal, with harbour walkways, parks, restaurants, buskers and fisherfolk.

The **Museum of Contemporary Art** (MCA) (☎ 9241 5892 or 9252 4033) is in the stately Art Deco building dominating Circular Quay West. It shows eclectic modern art and is open Wednesday to Monday from 10 am to 6 pm (till 4 pm in winter); entry is $6 ($4 concession). The grand old **Customs House** (☎ 9247 2285) fronting Circular Quay now houses an excellent arts and cultural centre; exhibits include modern visual and Aboriginal art, and a scale model of Sydney. Entry to most sections is free.

MACQUARIE PLACE & SURROUNDS

Narrow lanes lead south from Circular Quay towards the centre of the city. At the corner of Loftus and Bridge Sts, under the shady Moreton Bay figs in Macquarie Place, are a cannon and anchor from the

The Soap Opera House

The hullabaloo surrounding the construction of the Sydney Opera House was an operatic blend of personal vision, long delays, bitter feuding, cost blowouts and narrow-minded politicking. Construction began in 1959 after Danish architect Joern Utzon won an international design competition with his plans for a $7 million building.

After political interference, Utzon quit in disgust in 1966, leaving a consortium of Australian architects to design a compromised interior. The parsimonious state government financed the eventual $102 million bill through a series of lotteries. The building was finally completed in 1973, but it was lumbered with an internal design that was impractical (too small, for one thing) for staging operas.

After all the brawling, the first public performance at the Opera House was, appropriately, Prokofiev's War & Peace. The preparations were reported to be a debacle and a possum appeared on stage during one of the dress rehearsals. An opera, The Eighth Wonder, has even been written about the building of the Opera House – it was performed there by the Australian Opera in 1995.

First Fleet flagship, HMS *Sirius*, and an **obelisk**, erected in 1818, indicating road distances to various points in the nascent colony. The square has a couple of pleasant outdoor cafes and is overlooked by the rear facade of the imposing 19th century **Lands Department building** on Bridge St.

The excellent **Museum of Sydney** (☎ 9251 5988) is east of here, on the corner of Bridge and Phillip Sts, on the site of the first and infamously fetid Government House built in 1788. Sydney's early history comes to life here in whisper, argument, gossip and artefacts. It's open daily ($6, $3 concession).

The **Justice & Police Museum** (☎ 9252 1144) is in the old Water Police Station, on the corner of Phillip and Albert Sts. It's set up as a turn-of-the-century police station, and is open weekends from 10 am to 5 pm ($6, $3 concession).

CITY CENTRE

Central Sydney stretches from Circular Quay in the north to Central station in the south. The business hub is towards the northern end, but most redevelopment is occurring at the southern end and this is gradually shifting the focus of the city.

Sydney lacks a true civic centre, but **Martin Place** lays claim to the honour, if only by default. This grand, revamped pedestrian mall extends from Macquarie St to George St and is impressively lined by the monumental buildings of financial institutions and the colonnaded Victorian post office. There's plenty of public seating, a Cenotaph commemorating Australia's war dead and an amphitheatre for lunchtime entertainment.

The **Town Hall**, a few blocks south of here, on the corner of George and Druitt Sts, was built in 1874. Its outrageously ornate exterior is matched by the elaborate chamber

NEW SOUTH WALES

A Sydney Walking Tour

Setting out on foot is a good way to explore Australia's largest city. This walk covers about 7km and takes about 2½ to three hours.

Start in **Hyde Park** at Museum Station's Liverpool St exit. Walk north-east through the park past the **Anzac Memorial**. On the right, on College St, is the **Australian Museum**. From here William St (the eastward extension of Park St) heads east to **Kings Cross**. Across Park St, at the end of the avenue of trees is the wonderful **Archibald Fountain**. To the east, on College St, is the impressive **St Mary's Cathedral**.

Keep going north to reach **Macquarie St** with its collection of early colonial buildings and, after a few blocks, **Circular Quay** and the spectacular **Sydney Opera House**. On the west side of Circular Quay, behind the **Museum of Contemporary Art**, George St runs through **the Rocks**.

Walk north on George St, which curves around under the **Harbour Bridge** into Lower Fort St. Turn right (north) for the waterfront or left to climb **Observatory Park**. From here Argyle St heads east, through the **Argyle Cut** and back to the Rocks.

Nearby, on Cumberland St, you can climb stairs to the Harbour Bridge and walk across to **Milsons Point** on the North Shore; from here you can take a train back to the city.

It's also worth strolling along Oxford St from Hyde Park's south-eastern corner to **Paddington**. You can catch a bus back to the city from Paddington, or, if you keep going to **Bondi Junction**, catch a train.

West of Hyde Park you can walk along Market St, which leads to Pyrmont Bridge (for pedestrians and the monorail only) and **Darling Harbour**. Pyrmont Bridge Rd crosses Darling Harbour and leads to **Glebe Island Bridge**, the **Pyrmont Fish Markets** and eventually to **Glebe** itself.

See The Rocks, earlier, and Organised Tours later in this chapter for guided walks.

room and concert hall inside. The Anglican **St Andrew's Cathedral**, built around the same time, is the oldest cathedral in Australia. At the time of writing it was being renovated, but free lunchtime organ recitals (Thursday) will recommence on completion.

The city's most sumptuous shopping complex, the Byzantine **Queen Victoria Building** (QVB), is next to the Town Hall and takes up an entire city block bordered by George, Druitt, York and Market Sts. Other interesting shopping centres include the lovingly restored Strand Arcade and the modern Skygarden arcade nearby.

Opposite the QVB, underneath the Royal Arcade linking George and Pitt Sts, is a bar and extravagant piece of Victoriana called the **Marble Bar**. The splendidly gothic **State Theatre**, just to the north at 49 Market St, is just as ostentatious; tours (☎ 9373 6660) operate Tuesday to Saturday ($12, $8 for children).

To the south-west are **Spanish Town** and **Chinatown**, two lively areas in a part of the city that includes a number of unsightly holes in the ground where development projects in the 1980s fell foul of economic downturn. Chinatown is still bustling though (despite the Asian economic crisis) and this dynamic area is spreading to breathe life into the city's dead · southeastern zone, where Central station lies isolated on the southern periphery.

DARLING HARBOUR

This huge, purpose-built waterfront leisure park on the city centre's western edge was once a thriving dockland area (see the Darling Harbour & Chinatown map). After sinking to the level of an urban eyesore, it was reinvented in the 1980s by a combination of vision, politicking, forbearance and huge amounts of cash. The supposed centrepiece is the graceful **Harbourside** centre – crammed with shops and tacky food outlets – but the real attractions are the stunning aquarium, excellent museums, the Chinese Garden and nifty water sculptures.

Until recently, the emphasis was on casual fun of the kind appreciated by families and coach tourists, but the snazzy new wining and dining precinct of **Cockle Bay**

Wharf, built opposite Harbourside, has lent the area a bit more kudos in the food and nightlife departments.

The **monorail** and **light rail** link Darling Harbour to the city centre.

Ferries leave from Circular Quay and stop at Darling Harbour's Aquarium and Pyrmont Bay Wharves every 30 minutes ($3.20). The Rocket Express ferry departs every 20 minutes from the Harbourmaster's Steps at Circular Quay West ($3.25). The Sydney Explorer bus (see the Sydney Getting Around section) stops at four points around Darling Harbour every 20 minutes. A dinky People Mover snakes around Darling Harbour's attractions – a ride costs $2.50.

The main pedestrian approaches are across footbridges from Market and Liverpool Sts. The one from Market St leads to **Pyrmont Bridge**, now a pedestrian-and-monorail-only route, but once famous as the world's first electrically operated swing-span bridge.

The Darling Harbour Visitors Centre (☎ 9286 0111) is under the highway and is open daily.

Sydney Aquarium

This aquarium, displaying the richness of Australian marine life, should not be missed. Three 'oceanariums' are moored in the harbour with sharks, rays and big fish in one, and Sydney Harbour marine life and seals in the others. There are also informative and well-presented exhibits of freshwater fish and coral gardens. The transparent underwater tunnels are eerily spectacular.

The Aquarium (☎ 9262 2300) is near the eastern end of Pyrmont Bridge and is open daily from 9.30 am to 9 pm ($15.90, students $10).

National Maritime Museum

This thematic museum (☎ 9552 7777) tells the story of Australia's relationship with the sea, from Aboriginal canoes and the First Fleet to surf culture and the America's Cup. A naval destroyer, a racing yacht and a Vietnamese refugee boat are moored outside awaiting exploration. Free guided tours occur on the hour between 10 am and 3 pm.

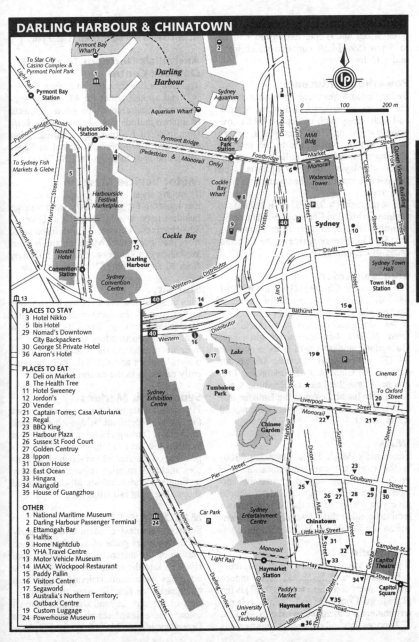

DARLING HARBOUR & CHINATOWN

0   100   200 m

PLACES TO STAY
3   Hotel Nikko
5   Ibis Hotel
29 Nomad's Downtown
    City Backpackers
30 George St Private Hotel
36 Aaron's Hotel

PLACES TO EAT
7   Deli on Market
8   The Health Tree
11 Hotel Sweeney
12 Jordon's
20 Vender
21 Captain Torres; Casa Asturiana
22 Regal
23 BBQ King
25 Harbour Plaza
26 Sussex St Food Court
27 Golden Centruy
28 Ippon
31 Dixon House
32 East Ocean
33 Hingara
34 Marigold
35 House of Guangzhou

OTHER
1   National Maritime Museum
2   Darling Harbour Passenger Terminal
4   Ettamogah Bar
6   Halftix
9   Home Nightclub
10 YHA Travel Centre
13 Motor Vehicle Museum
14 IMAX; Wockpool Restaurant
16 Visitors Centre
17 Paddy Pallin
18 Australia's Northern Territory;
    Outback Centre
19 Custom Luggage
24 Powerhouse Museum
15 Segaworld

The museum is near the western end of Pyrmont Bridge and is open daily from 9.30 am to 5 pm ($9, $4.50 concession, children under 15 free).

Powerhouse Museum

Sydney's most spectacular museum covers the decorative arts, social history, science and technology with eclectic exhibits covering everything from costume jewellery and Australian rock music to locomotives and space capsules. The collections are superbly displayed and the emphasis is on hands-on interaction and education through enjoyment.

The museum (☎ 9217 0111) is behind the Sydney Exhibition Centre, at 500 Harris St, Ultimo, and is open daily from 10 am to 5 pm ($8, $3 concession, free on the first Saturday of each month).

Chinese Garden

The exquisite Chinese Garden (☎ 9281 6863/0111), in the south-eastern corner of Darling Harbour, is an oasis of tranquillity. It was designed by landscape architects from NSW's Chinese sister province, Guangdong, and it's worth every cent of the $4 ($2 concession) entrance fee. Enter through the Courtyard of Welcoming Fragrance, circle the Lake of Brightness and finish with tea and cake in the Chinese teahouse. The garden is open daily from 9.30 am to sunset.

IMAX

Panasonic's IMAX Theatre (☎ 9281 3300) is the world's biggest movie screen. If you're into being wowed by massive images, some in 3D, then the IMAX should give you plenty of thrills. Movies shown tend to be either thrill-fests or nature docos; tickets are $13.95 ($10.95 concession).

Segaworld

If you like your fun other-worldly, or likely to bring on an acid flashback, Sega's indoor entertainment complex (☎ 9273 9273) is the place to go. Cool rides and cinema-style entertainment are included in a day pass ($28, $22 concession and children). Segaworld is open weekdays from 11 am and weekends from 10 am (last admission is at 9 pm).

Australia's Northern Territory & Outback Centre

This centre is both a tourist agency for the NT, and a retail outlet for Aboriginal artefacts and Australiana-type goods. Objects of interest include *woomeras* (spears), *kalis* (jumbo-sized boomerangs), musical clap sticks and bull-roarers. It's next to Segaworld and is open daily (☎ 9283 7477).

Motor Vehicle Museum

There are over 175 vehicles on display at this museum (☎ 9552 1210), from vintage beauties to Morris Minors. It's at Level 1, 320 Harris St, Ultimo, a fume-filled walk from the Powerhouse Museum, and is open Wednesday to Sunday and school holidays, from 10 am to 5 pm ($10, $5 concession).

Star City

This massive new complex has taken shape in Pyrmont on the north-western headland of Darling Harbour. Star City includes a **casino** and two **theatres** as well as the inevitable nightclub, flash hotel and retail outlets. Ferries and the light rail conveniently run right to the casino.

Sydney Fish Markets

Fish auctions are held here on weekdays, on the corner of Pyrmont Bridge Rd and Bank St, west of Darling Harbour. They begin at 5.30 am and last from three to six hours, depending on the size of the catch. The complex includes eateries (dinner Wednesday to Sunday) and fabulous all-day seafood shops. The light rail stops here.

MACQUARIE ST

Sydney's greatest concentration of early public buildings grace Macquarie St, which runs along the eastern edge of the city from Hyde Park to the opera house. Many of the buildings were commissioned by Lachlan Macquarie, the first governor to have a vision of the city beyond that of a convict colony. He enlisted convict forger Francis Greenway as an architect to realise his plans.

Two Greenway gems on Queens Square, at the northern end of Hyde Park, are **St James Church** (1819-24) and the Georgian-style **Hyde Park Barracks** (1819). The barracks were built originally as convict quarters, then became an immigration depot, and later a court. They now house a museum which details the history of the building and provides an interesting perspective on Sydney's social history. The museum (☎ 9223 8922) is open daily from 9.30 am to 5 pm ($6, $3 concession).

Next to the barracks is the lovely **Mint Building** (1814), which was originally the southern wing of the infamous Rum Hospital built by two Sydney merchants in return for a monopoly on the rum trade. It became a branch of the Royal Mint in 1854.

The Mint's twin is **Parliament House**, which was originally the northern wing of the Rum Hospital. This simple, proud building is now home to the Parliament of NSW. It's open to the public on weekdays between 9 am and 4 pm (admission is free). There are free tours of the chambers at 10 and 11 am and 2 pm on non-sitting weekdays. The public gallery is open on sitting days.

Next to Parliament House is the **State Library of NSW** (☎ 9273 1414), which is more of a cultural centre than a traditional library. It houses the Australian Research Collections, which document early life in Australia, and hosts innovative temporary exhibitions in its galleries. The library is open daily, except the Australian Research Collection, which is closed on Sunday. There are free guided tours at 11 am Tuesday and 2 pm Thursday.

The **Sydney Conservatorium of Music** was built by Greenway as the stables and servants' quarters of Macquarie's planned new government house. Macquarie was replaced as governor before the house could be finished, partly because of the project's extravagance. The conservatorium was being renovated at the time of writing, but its students continue to pursue their studies in temporary premises, and host performances around the city, including free lunchtime concerts – phone ☎ 9351 1222 to see what's cooking.

Art Gallery of NSW

This gallery (☎ 9225 1744) has an excellent permanent display of Australian, Aboriginal, European and Asian art, and some inspired temporary exhibits. It's in the Domain, east of Macquarie St, and is open daily from 10 am to 5 pm. Admission is free but fees may apply to special exhibitions. There are free guided tours at noon, and at 1 and 2 pm most days, and a free Aboriginal dance performance at noon Tuesday to Saturday.

Australian Museum

This natural history museum has an excellent Australian wildlife collection and a gallery tracing Aboriginal history and the Dreamtime. It's on the eastern flank of Hyde Park, on the corner of College and William Sts and is open daily from 9.30 am to 5 pm ($5, $3 concession). There are free tours on the hour between 10 am and 4 pm.

PARKS

The city's favourite picnic spot, jogging route and place to stroll is the enchanting **Royal Botanic Gardens** (☎ 9231 8111), which border Farm Cove, east of the opera house. The gardens were established in 1816 and feature plant life from the South Pacific. They include the site of the colony's first paltry vegetable patch, which has been preserved as the First Farm exhibit.

The tropical plant display in the Arc and Pyramid glasshouses is worth seeing, although at the time of writing the pyramid glasshouse was closed for repairs (the $2 entry fee will rise when it reopens). The visitors centre (☎ 9231 8125) is open daily from 9.30 am to 4.30 pm. Free guided walks begin at the centre daily at 10.30 am.

Government House (☎ 9931 5255) dominates the western headland of Farm Cove and, until early 1996, was the official residence of the Governor of NSW. The grounds are open to the public from 10 am to 4 pm daily. The house is open from 10 am to 3 pm Friday to Sunday; admission is free.

The **Domain** is a pleasant grassy area east of Macquarie St which was set aside by Governor Phillip for public recreation. Today it's used by city workers as a place to escape the city hubbub, and on Sunday afternoon it's the gathering place for soapbox speakers who do their best to entertain or enrage their listeners.

On the eastern edge of the city centre is the formal **Hyde Park**, which was once the colony's first racetrack and cricket pitch. It has a grand avenue of trees, delightful fountains, and a giant public chess board. It contains the dignified **Anzac Memorial**, which has a free exhibition on the ground floor covering the nine overseas conflicts in which Australians fought. **St Mary's Cathedral** overlooks the park from the east and the **Great Synagogue** from the west. There are free tours of the synagogue on Tuesday and Thursday at noon (enter from 166 Castlereagh St).

Sydney's biggest park is **Centennial Park**, which has running, cycling, skating and horse riding tracks, duck ponds, barbecue sites and sports pitches. It's 5km from the centre, just east of Paddington. You can hire bikes on Clovelly Rd, near the south-eastern edge of the park, inline skates in Oxford St (see Activities), or horses ($35) from one of five stables situated around the park – contact the stable manager (☎ 9332 2809).

Moore Park abuts the western flank of Centennial Park and contains sports pitches, a golf course, an equestrian centre, the Fox film studio and entertainment complex, the Sydney Football Stadium (SFS) and the Sydney Cricket Ground (SCG). Sportspace (☎ 9380 0383) offers behind-the-scenes guided tours (1¾ hours) of the SCG and SFS. Tours are held daily at 10 am and 1 and 3 pm (unless they clash with a sporting event) and cost $18 ($12 concession).

Pyrmont Point Park is a bit sterile, but it's not a bad place to fish, picnic and contemplate the changing face of Sydney. Take the

City Views

Sydney is an ostentatious city that offers visitors a dramatic spectacle. You can see the complete panorama by whooshing to the top of **Sydney Tower**, a needle-like column with an observation deck and revolving restaurants set 305m above the ground. The view, extending as far as the Blue Mountains to the west, gives you an idea of the city's geography. The tower is on top of the Centrepoint complex on Market St, between Pitt and Castlereagh Sts. It's open daily from 9 am to 10.30 pm (11.30 pm on Saturday); entry costs $10 ($8 concession).

The Harbour Bridge is another obvious vantage point, but even many locals have never visited the small **Harbour Bridge Museum** and climbed the 200 stairs inside the southeastern pylon to enjoy the dazzling view. The pylon and museum are open daily between 10 am and 5 pm; admission is $2. Enter from the bridge's pedestrian walkway, accessible from Cumberland St in the Rocks, or from near Milsons Point station on the North Shore. For the intrepid view-seeker, Bridgeclimb (☎ 9252 0077) offers a breathtaking 1500m climb to the top of the bridge for $98 during the week, $120 on the weekend. Wear rubber-soled shoes, and don't drink alcohol beforehand – you may be breath-tested!

There are impressive ground-level views of the city and harbour from **Mrs Macquarie's Point**, and from **Observatory Hill** in Millers Point. **Blues Point Reserve** and **Bradleys Head** are the best vantage points on the North Shore.

The most enjoyable and atmospheric way to view Sydney is by boat. If you can't persuade someone to take you sailing, jump aboard a ferry at Circular Quay. The Manly ferry offers an unforgettable cruise down the length of the harbour east of the bridge for a mere $4. If you're looking for a bird's-eye view, Heli-Aust (☎ 9317 3402) offers 15-minute helicopter flights over the harbour daily for a cool $99.

If you're in the vicinity of Kings Cross, the northern end of Victoria St in Potts Point is an excellent vantage point to take in the cityscape and its best-known icons, especially at night.

light rail to John St Square and walk downhill along Harris St towards the water.

On the North Shore, **Davidson Park** is an 8km corridor of bushland stretching northwest from Middle Harbour to Ku-ring-gai Chase National Park.

The **Lane Cove National Park** runs between the suburbs of Ryde and Chatswood, and has extensive walking tracks along the picturesque (but polluted) Lane Cove River. Vehicle entry to the park is free on weekdays; on weekends and public holidays it's $5 per car.

See the Sydney Harbour section for information on the parks and bushland that comprise the Sydney Harbour National Park.

KINGS CROSS

The Cross is a cocktail of strip joints, prostitution, crime and drugs shaken and stirred with a handful of classy restaurants, designer cafes, upmarket hotels and backpacker hostels. It attracts an odd mix of low-life, sailors, travellers, innercity trendies, tourists by the busload and suburbanites looking for a big night out.

The Cross has always been a bit raffish, from its early days as a centre of bohemianism to the Vietnam War era, when it became the vice centre of Australia. While the vice is real and nasty enough, Sydneysiders are quite fond of the Cross. It appeals to the larrikin spirit, which always enjoys a bit of devil-may-care and 24-hour drinking. Many travellers begin and end their Australian adventures in the Cross, and it's a good place to swap information, meet up with friends, pick up work, browse the hostel notice boards and buy or sell a car.

Darlinghurst Rd is the trashy main drag. This doglegs into Macleay St which continues into the more salubrious suburb of Potts Point. Most of the hostels are on Victoria St, which diverges from Darlinghurst Rd just north of William St, near the iconic Coca-Cola sign. The thistle-like **El Alamein Fountain**, in the Fitzroy Gardens, is the psychological centre of the area, and there's a market here every Sunday.

In the dip between the Cross and the city is **Woolloomooloo**, one of Sydney's oldest areas. Sensitive urban restoration has made it a lovely place to stroll around. Its huge disused wharf is being redeveloped. Harry's Cafe de Wheels, next to the wharf, must be one of the few pie carts in the world to be a tourist attraction. It opened in 1945, stays open 18 hours a day and is *the* place to go for a late-night chicken and mushroom fill-up. The innovative Artspace gallery is opposite.

The easiest way to get to the Cross from the city is by train ($1.60 one way offpeak). It's the first stop outside the city loop on the line to Bondi Junction. Bus Nos 324, 325 and 327 from Circular Quay pass through the Cross. You can stroll from Hyde Park along William St in 15 minutes. A longer, more interesting route involves crossing the Domain, traversing the pedestrian bridge behind the Art Gallery of NSW, walking past Woolloomooloo's wharf and climbing McElhone Stairs to the northern end of Victoria St.

INNER EAST

The lifeblood of Darlinghurst, Surry Hills and Paddington, **Oxford St** is one of the more happening places for late-night action. It's a strip of shops, cafes, bars and nightclubs whose flamboyance and spirit can be largely attributed to the vibrant and vocal gay community. The route of the Sydney Gay & Lesbian Mardi Gras parade passes this way.

The main drag of Oxford St runs from the south-eastern corner of Hyde Park to the north-western corner of Centennial Park, though it continues in name up to Bondi Junction. Taylor Square is the social hub. (An orientation warning: Oxford St's street numbers restart on the Darlinghurst-Paddington border, west of the junction with South Dowling and Victoria Sts.) Bus Nos 380 and 382 from Circular Quay, and No 378 from Railway Square, run the length of the street.

The innercity mecca for bright young things wanting to be close to the action and the ubiquitous cafe lattes is **Darlinghurst**. It's a vital area of urban cool that's fast developing a cafe monoculture, and there's no better way to soak up its studied ambience than to loiter in a few outdoor cafes and do as the others do. Darlinghurst is wedged between

NEW SOUTH WALES

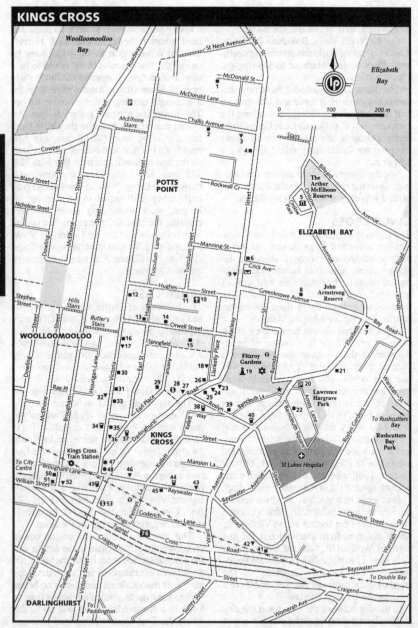

KINGS CROSS

Woolloomooloo Bay

Elizabeth Bay

St Neot Avenue

McDonald St

McDonald Lane

Challis Avenue

McElhone Stairs

POTTS POINT

Rockwall Cr

The Arthur McElhono Reserve

ELIZABETH BAY

Bland Street

Nicholson Street

Manning St

Crick Ave

Hughes Street

Tusculum Lane

Tusculum Street

Greenknowe Avenue

John Armstrong Reserve

Stephen Street

Hills Stairs

Butler's Stairs

Hughes La

Orwell Street

Springfield

Bay Road

WOOLLOOMOOLOO

Earl St

Llankelly Place

Fitzroy Gardens

Baroda

Elizabeth Bay

Hourigan Lane

Victoria Street

Earl Place

Roslyn

Barncleuth La

Lawrence Hargrave Park

Amos Lane

Rushcutters Bay Park

Roslyn Gardens

To Rushcutters Bay

Brougham Street

McElhone

Rae Pl

Darlinghurst Road

KINGS CROSS

Kellett Street

Barncleuth Square

St Lukes Hospital

To City Centre

Kings Cross Train Station

Brougham Lane

Kellett Way

Mansion La

Bayswater Avenue

Waratah St

William Street

Pennys La

Bayswater

Goderich Lane

Clement Street

Kings Cross Tunnel

Craigend

To Double Bay

DARLINGHURST

Kirketon Road

Darlinghurst Road

Victoria Street

Surrey Street

Womerah Ave

Craigend

Bayswater

To Paddington

Cowper

Dowling Street

Wharf Road

Wylde St

Onslow Place

Onslow Avenue

Billyard Avenue

Ithaca Road

Oxford and William Sts, and encompasses the vibrant 'Little Italy' of Stanley St in East Sydney. Sydney's **Jewish Museum**, on the corner of Darlinghurst Rd and Burton St, has evocative exhibits on Australian Jewish history and the Holocaust. It's open daily except Saturday and closes at 2 pm on Friday ($6, $4 concession).

South of Darlinghurst is **Surry Hills**, home to a mishmash of innercity residents and a swag of good pubs. Once the undisputed centre of Sydney's rag trade and print media, many of its warehouses have been converted, or razed to make way for expensive yuppie dogboxes. The Surry Hills Market is held on the first Saturday of the month in Shannon Reserve, on the corner of Crown and Foveaux Sts. The Brett Whiteley Studio, 2 Raper St, is in the artist's old home and studio, and is open on weekends between 10 am and 4 pm ($6, $4 concession). Surry Hills is a short walk east of Central Station or south from Oxford St. Catch bus No 301, 302 or 303 from Circular Quay.

Next door to Surry Hills is **Paddington**, an attractive residential area of leafy streets and tightly packed Victorian terrace houses.

It was built for aspiring artisans, but during the lemming-like rush to the outer suburbs after WWII the area became a slum. A renewed interest in Victorian architecture and the pleasures of innercity life led to its restoration during the 1960s and today these modest terraces swap hands for a decent portion of a million dollars.

Most facilities, shops, cafes and bars are on Oxford St but the suburb doesn't really have a geographic centre. Most of its streets cascade northwards down the hill towards Edgecliff and Double Bay. It's always a lovely place to wander around, but the best time to visit is Saturday when the **Paddington Village Bazaar** is in full swing on the corner of Newcombe and Oxford Sts.

At Moore Park, much of the former **RAS Showgrounds** has been converted into the new **Fox Studios** film and entertainment complex. As well as the film studio, the completed complex will include 16 cinemas, a shopping and dining precinct, an outdoor entertainment venue, and interactive film-oriented displays.

There are over 20 art galleries in Paddington; grab a copy of the blue *Guide*

NEW SOUTH WALES

KINGS CROSS

PLACES TO STAY		
1 Rucksack Rest	35 Plane Tree Lodge	46 Waterlily Cafe
2 Challis Lodge	39 Backpackers Connection	52 William's on William;
4 Macleay Lodge	41 Backpackers	Mamma Maria
6 De Vere Hotel;	Headquarters	
India Down Under	45 Barclay Hotel	**PUBS & CLUBS**
8 Manhattan Hotel	50 Cross Court Tourist Motel	34 Soho Bar
11 Palms Private Hotel	51 O'Malley's Hotel	37 EP1
12 Victoria Court Hotel		38 Barons
13 Eva's Backpackers	**PLACES TO EAT**	40 Piccolo's
14 Sydney Central	3 Cicada; Spring Cafe	44 Underground Cafe
Backpackers	7 Elizabeth Bay Deli	49 Kings Cross Hotel
15 Jolly Swagman	9 Japanese Noodles Shop	
16 Virgin Backpackers	17 Hwang So;	**OTHER**
21 Sebel Town House	Mere Catherine	5 Elizabeth Bay House
22 Pink House	18 Pad Thai	10 Wayside Chapel
25 Kingsview	23 Fountain Cafe	19 El Alamein Fountain
26 Funk House	24 Bourbon & Beefsteak	20 Car Market
29 Bernly Private Hotel;	27 Sushi Roll	28 Bureau de Change
Springfield Lodge	32 Star Bar & Grill	47 Backpackers World
30 Travellers Rest;	36 Roy's Famous Cafe;	48 Global Gossip
Potts Point House	Out of India	53 Thomas Cook
31 Original Backpackers	42 Hotel 59 & Cafe	
33 Highfield House	43 Bayswater Brasserie;	
	Darley Street Thai	

and Map to Art Galleries at the first one you stumble upon. There are free tours of the stately **Victoria Barracks** (☎ 9339 3000), on Oxford St, every Thursday at 10 am, including a performance by the military band. The Army Museum opens on Sunday between 10 am and 3 pm (admission is free).

EASTERN SUBURBS

A short walk north-east of the Cross is the harbour-front suburb of **Elizabeth Bay**. Elizabeth Bay House (☎ 9358 2344), 7 Onslow Ave, is one of Sydney's finest colonial homes. It's open daily except Monday from 10 am to 4.30 pm ($6, $3 concession).

Beautiful **Rushcutters Bay** is the next bay east. Its handsome harbourside park is just a five minute walk from the Cross and is the closest place for cooped-up backpackers to stretch their legs. The tennis courts (☎ 9357 1675) on Waratah St can be hired for $20 an hour. This is the yachting centre of Sydney and is one of the best places to learn to sail (see the Sailing & Boating section).

Further east is the manicured suburb of **Double Bay**, which is over-endowed with smart cafes and designer stores. The views from the harbour-hugging New South Head Rd as it leaves Double Bay, passes **Rose Bay** and climbs east towards wealthy **Vaucluse**, are up there with the best. Vaucluse House (☎ 9337 1957), in Vaucluse Park, is an attractive colonial villa open daily except Monday from 10 am to 4.30 pm ($6).

At the entrance to the harbour is **Watsons Bay**, a snug community with harbourside restaurants, a palm-lined park and a couple of nautical churches. It makes a great day trip if you want to forget you're in the middle of a large city. Nearby **Camp Cove** is one of Sydney's best harbour beaches, and there's a nude beach near South Head at **Lady Bay**. South Head has great views across the harbour entrance to North Head and Middle Head. **The Gap** is a dramatic cliff-top lookout on the ocean side (it's also Sydney's favourite suicide spot).

Bus Nos 324 and 325 from Circular Quay service the eastern suburbs via Kings Cross. Sit on the left side heading east to make the most of the views.

SOUTHERN BEACHES

The grande dame of Sydney's beaches is **Bondi**, which has a majesty all of its own. The focus is on the sand 'n' surf, but the suburb has a unique flavour blended from a mix of old Jewish and Italian communities, dyed-in-the-wool Aussies, New Zealand and UK expats, working travellers and resident surf rats bonded by their love for the beach. They'll be playing volleyball for gold here in the 2000 Olympics – a fact that doesn't delight all of the beach-loving locals.

Bondi has now shed much of its tired facade, a new lick of paint, some landscaping and a rash of new cafes having set it up to be 'rediscovered' by innercity trendies.

The ocean road is Campbell Parade, where most of the shops, cafes and hotels are. The Bondi Beach Market is held every Sunday at the Bondi Beach Public School, at the northern end of Campbell Parade. There are Aboriginal rock engravings on the golf course in North Bondi.

Catch bus Nos 380, 382 or 389 from the city to get to the beach or, if you're in a hurry, catch a train to Bondi Junction and pick up one of these buses as they pass through the Bondi Junction bus station.

Just south of Bondi is **Tamarama**, a lovely cove with strong surf. Get off the bus as it kinks off Bondi Rd onto Fletcher St, just before it reaches Bondi Beach. Tamarama is a five minute walk down the hill.

There's a superb beach hemmed in by a bowl-shaped park and sandstone headlands at **Bronte**, south of Tamarama. The cafes with outdoor tables on the edge of the park make it a great chill-out destination. Catch bus No 378 from the city or catch a train to Bondi Junction and pick the bus up there; sit on the left side heading to the beach for a breathtaking view as the bus descends Macpherson St. You can walk here along the wonderful cliff-top footpath from Bondi Beach or from Coogee via Gordon's Bay, Clovelly and the sun-bleached Waverley Cemetery.

Clovelly Bay is a narrow scooped-out beach to the south. As well as the saltwater baths here, there's a wheelchair-access boardwalk so the chairbound can take a sea dip.

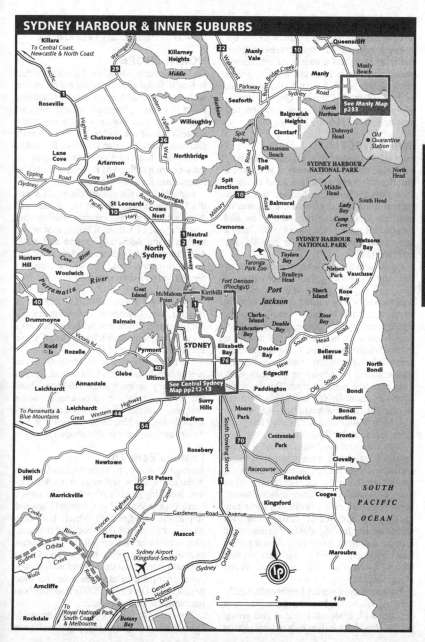

SYDNEY HARBOUR & INNER SUBURBS

Traditionally the poor cousin of Bondi, **Coogee** has recently been sprucing itself up. It has a relaxed air, few graces, a good sweep of sand and a couple of established hostels and hotels. You can reach Coogee by catching bus No 372 from Railway Square or No 373 from Circular Quay. Alternatively, take a train to Bondi Junction and pick up bus No 314 or 315 from there.

INNER WEST

West of the centre is the higgledy-piggledy peninsula suburb of **Balmain**. It was once a notoriously rough neighbourhood of dockyard workers but gentrification has transformed it into an arty, middle-class area of restored Victoriana flush with pubs and cafes. It's a great place for a stroll. Catch a ferry from Circular Quay or bus No 442 from the QVB.

Cosy, bohemian **Glebe** is south-west of the centre, bordering the northern edge of the University of Sydney. It has a large student population, a cruisy cafe-lined main street, a tranquil Buddhist temple, aromatherapy and crystals galore, and several decent hostels. A market is held at Glebe Public School, on Glebe Point Rd, on Saturday. It's a 10 minute walk from Central station along Broadway or you can walk from the city centre across Darling Harbour's Pyrmont Bridge and along Pyrmont Bridge Rd (20 minutes). Bus Nos 431 to 434 from Millers Point run via George St along Glebe Point Rd.

Bordering the southern flank of the university is **Newtown**, a melting pot of social and sexual subcultures, students and home renovators. King St, its relentlessly urban main drag, is full of funky clothes stores, bookshops and cafes. While it's definitely moving up the social scale, Newtown comes with a healthy dose of grunge, and harbours several live-music venues. The best way to get there is by train, but bus Nos 422, 423, 426 and 428 from the city all run along King St.

Predominantly Italian **Leichhardt**, south-west of Glebe, is becoming increasingly popular with students, lesbians and young professionals. Its Italian eateries on Norton St have a city-wide reputation. Bus Nos 436 to 440 run from the city to Leichhardt.

NORTH SHORE

On the northern side of the Harbour Bridge is **North Sydney**, a high-rise office centre with little to tempt the traveller. **McMahons Point** is a lovely, forgotten suburb wedged between the two business districts, on the western side of the bridge. There's a line of pleasant sidewalk cafes on Blues Point Rd, which runs down to Blues Point Reserve on the western headland of Lavender Bay. The reserve has fine city views.

Luna Park, on the eastern shore of Lavender Bay, is closed, but the big mouth still grins, anticipating redevelopment of the site.

At the end of Kirribilli Point, east of the bridge, stand **Admiralty House** and **Kirribilli House**, the Sydney residences of the governor-general and the prime minister respectively (Admiralty House is the one nearer the bridge).

East of here are the upmarket suburbs of **Neutral Bay**, **Cremorne** and **Mosman**, all with pleasant coves and harbourside parks perfect for picnics. Ferries go to all these suburbs from Circular Quay.

On the northern side of Mosman is the pretty beach suburb of **Balmoral**, which faces Manly across Middle Harbour. There are picnic areas, a promenade, three beaches, a couple of waterfront restaurants and water-sport hire facilities (see the Activities section later in this chapter).

Taronga Park Zoo

Taronga Park Zoo, in Mosman, has a superb harbourside setting and more than 4000 critters, including lots of native Australian ones. Ferries leave Wharf 2 at Circular Quay and stop at the Taronga Park Wharf. The zoo's rear entrance is near the wharf, but the complex perches on a steep hill, so if you want to avoid a tiring upward hike, catch a bus to the main entrance at the top and walk down. An alternative is to catch the cable car (due to reopen in December 2000) from the bottom entrance to the top one.

The zoo (☎ 9969 2777) is open daily from 9 am to 5 pm ($16); night visits are scheduled seasonally. A ZooPass, sold at the ferry ticket counters at Circular Quay, costs $21 and includes a return ferry ride, zoo admission and the bus to the top entrance.

MANLY

The jewel of the North Shore, Manly is on a narrow peninsula that ends at the dramatic cliffs of North Head. It boasts harbour and ocean beaches, a ferry wharf, all the trappings of a full-scale holiday resort and great sense of community. It's a sun-soaked place not afraid to show a bit of tack and brashness to attract visitors, and makes a refreshing change from the prim upper-middle-class harbour enclaves nearby.

The Manly Visitors Information Bureau (☎ 9977 1088), on the promenade at South Steyne, is open daily from 10 am to 4 pm. It has useful, free pamphlets on the 10km Manly Scenic Walkway and sells Manly Heritage Walk booklets for $3.50. There's a bus information booth at the entrance to the wharf. Both ferries and JetCat catamarans operate between Circular Quay and Manly. The JetCats seem to traverse the harbour before you get a chance to blink, while the stately Manly ferries do the trip in a cool 30 minutes and offer fantastic views of the city.

The ferry wharf is on Manly's harbour shore. A short walk along Manly's pedestrian mall, The Corso, brings you to the ocean beach lined by towering Norfolk pines. North and South Steyne are the roads running along the foreshore. A footpath follows the shoreline from South Steyne around the small headland to tiny **Fairy Bower Beach** and the picturesque cove of **Shelly Beach**.

The **Manly Art Gallery & Museum** (☎ 9949 2435) focuses on the suburb's special relationship with the beach. The museum is on West Esplanade, on the Manly Cove foreshore, and is open Tuesday to Sunday from 10 am to 5 pm; entry is $3.

The excellent **Oceanworld** is next door. The big drawcards are the sharks and

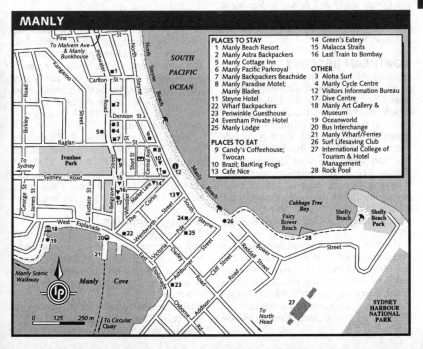

MANLY

PLACES TO STAY
1 Manly Beach Resort
2 Manly Astra Backpackers
5 Manly Cottage Inn
6 Manly Pacific Parkroyal
7 Manly Backpackers Beachside
8 Manly Paradise Motel;
   Manly Blades
11 Steyne Hotel
22 Wharf Backpackers
23 Periwinkle Guesthouse
24 Eversham Private Hotel
25 Manly Lodge

PLACES TO EAT
9 Candy's Coffeehouse;
   Twocan
10 Brazil; BarKing Frogs
13 Cafe Nice

14 Green's Eatery
15 Malacca Straits
16 Last Train to Bombay

OTHER
3 Aloha Surf
4 Manly Cycle Centre
12 Visitors Information Bureau
17 Dive Centre
18 Manly Art Gallery &
   Museum
19 Oceanworld
20 Bus Interchange
21 Manly Wharf/Ferries
26 Surf Lifesaving Club
27 International College of
   Tourism & Hotel
   Management
28 Rock Pool

NEW SOUTH WALES

stingrays, and the best time to visit is Monday, Wednesday or Friday at 11.30 am when divers enter the tanks to feed the sharks. An underwater perspex tunnel offers dramatic (but dry) close encounters with the fish, and there's a twice-daily seal show. Oceanworld opens daily from 10 am to 5.30 pm. Entry is \$14.50 (\$10 concession). Behind Oceanworld is the wonderful 10km-long Manly Scenic Walkway (see the 'Harbour Walks' boxed text).

North Head, at the entrance to Sydney Harbour, is about 3km south of Manly. Most of the dramatic headland is in Sydney Harbour National Park. The **Quarantine Station** represents an interesting slice of Sydney's social history; it housed suspected disease carriers from 1832 right up until 1984. To visit the station, book a guided tour (☎ 9977 6522). These depart Monday to Friday at 10.40 am, weekends 1.25 pm. Tours take 1½ hours and cost \$10 (\$7 concession). Night-time 'ghost tours' take place Wednesday and Friday to Sunday at about 7.30 pm. A three hour spook session costs \$17 (\$20 on Sunday). Catch bus No 135 from Manly Wharf.

NORTHERN BEACHES

A string of ocean-front suburbs sweeps north along the coast from Manly, ending after 30km at beautiful, well-heeled **Palm Beach** and the spectacular Barrenjoey Heads at the entrance to Broken Bay. The numerous beaches along the way include **Freshwater**, **Curl Curl**, **Dee Why**, **Collaroy** and **Narrabeen**. The most spectacular are **Whale Beach** and **Bilgola**, near Palm Beach; both have dramatic, steep headlands. Several of the northernmost beach suburbs also back onto **Pittwater**, a lovely inlet off Broken Bay and a favoured sailing spot.

Bus Nos 136 and 139 run from Manly to Freshwater and Curl Curl. Bus No 190 from Wynyard in the city runs to Newport and then north to Palm Beach. The Palm Beach Ferry Service (☎ 9918 2747) runs three times daily between Palm Beach and Patonga on the Central Coast (\$6 one way).

ACTIVITIES
Swimming
Sydney's harbour beaches offer sheltered swimming spots. But if you just want to frolic, nothing beats being knocked around in the waves that pound the ocean beaches, where swimming is safe if you follow instructions and swim within the 'flagged' areas patrolled by lifeguards. There are some notorious but clearly signposted rips even at Sydney's most popular beaches, so don't underestimate the surf just because it doesn't look intimidating. Efforts are made to keep surfers separate from swimmers. If you're worried about sharks, just remind yourself that Sydney has only had one fatal shark attack since 1937.

Outdoor pools in the city include the saltwater Boy Charlton pool in the Domain, on the edge of Woolloomooloo Bay; the Prince Alfred Park pool, near Central station; and the Victoria Park pool on Broadway, next to the University of Sydney.

Surfing
South of the Heads, the best spots are Bondi, Tamarama, Coogee and Maroubra. Cronulla, south of Botany Bay, is also a serious surfing spot. On the North Shore, there are a dozen surf beaches between Manly and Palm Beach; the best are Manly, Curl Curl, Dee Why, North Narrabeen, Mona Vale, Newport Reef, North Avalon and Palm Beach itself.

Shops such as the Bondi Surf Company (☎ 9365 0870), 72 Campbell Parade, Bondi Beach, and Aloha Surf (☎ 9977 3777), 44 Pittwater Rd, Manly, hire equipment. Expect to pay \$30 to \$40 for a board and a wetsuit for the day. Lessons are available.

Sailing & Boating
There are plenty of sailing schools in Sydney and even if you're not serious about learning the ropes, an introductory lesson can be a fun way of getting out on the harbour. Hiring a motorboat is even easier.

Sydney By Sail (☎ 9552 7561) offers a 90 minute introductory sail for \$49 departing daily from the National Maritime Museum in Darling Harbour.

The Elizabeth Bay Marina (☎ 9358 2057), close to Kings Cross, hires easy-to-operate five-metre boats with outboards for $65 for a half-day. They supply a map, instructions and can even whip up a picnic.

The EastSail Sailing School (☎ 9327 1166), at d'Albora Marina, New Beach Rd, Rushcutters Bay, runs a huge range of courses from introductory to racing level.

Northside Sailing School (☎ 9969 3972), at the southern end of the Spit Bridge in Mosman, also offers courses and rents sailboards and dinghies.

Balmoral Boatshed (☎ 9969 6006) offers tuition and rents sailboards ($25 to $35), catamarans and motor boats ($30) by the hour.

Pittwater and Broken Bay offer excellent sailing. Scotland Island Schooners (☎ 9999 2285), at Church Point, runs intensive two-day yachting courses with discounts for travellers and YHA members ($240 per person, cheaper for pairs and groups).

Diving

The best shore dives in Sydney are the Gordons Bay Underwater Nature Trail, north of Coogee; Shark Point, Clovelly; and Ship Rock, Cronulla. Popular boat dive sites are Wedding Cake Island, off Coogee; around the Sydney Heads; and off the Royal National Park.

Plenty of outfits will take you diving and many run dive courses, including Pro Dive (☎ 9264 6177), at 428 George St in the city, and 27 Alfreda St, Coogee (☎ 9665 6333), and Dive Centre Manly (☎ 9977 4355), at 10 Belgrave St, Manly. Days out start at around $50.

Canoeing & Kayaking

The NSW Canoe Association (☎ 9660 4597) provides information on canoe courses and hire, and also runs tours. Sydney Kayak Centre (☎ 9969 4590), at the southern end of Spit Bridge in Mosman, rents sea kayaks for $10 for the first two hours and $5 for each subsequent hour. Natural Wanders (☎ 9899 1001) has easy kayak tours of the harbour which pass under the bridge and stop in secluded bays. A four hour tour costs $75, including brunch.

Inline Skating

The beach promenades at Bondi, Manly and Centennial Park are the most favoured spots for skating. Manly Blades (☎ 9976 3833), 49 North Steyne, hires skates for $10 for the first hour and $5 for each subsequent hour, or $20 per day; Bondi Boards & Blades (☎ 9365 6555), 148 Curlewis St, Bondi Beach, has the same hourly rates and charges $28 a day. Protective gear is free and there's a free lesson every Tuesday afternoon. Total Skate (☎ 9380 6356), 36 Oxford St, Paddington, near Centennial Park, charges similar rates.

ORGANISED TOURS

Conventional city and country tour operators include Australian Pacific (☎ 13 1304) and Clipper Gray Line (☎ 9252 4499). A half-day city tour costs around $40, and a one day tour costs around $70. Tours of the Blue Mountains cost around $80, the Hunter Valley $95 and Canberra $85.

Maureen Fry (☎ 9660 7157) offers a variety of guided walking tours of Sydney for around $15. CTA Cycle Tours (☎ 1800 353 004) runs weekend day tours of Sydney for $45 ($40 YHA), including cycle and helmet hire and ferry transport.

Sydney Aboriginal Discoveries (☎ 9368 7684) offers a variety of interesting tours with an indigenous focus. Outings cost from $25 (concession) to $60; choices include harbour cruises, camping trips, walkabout tours, native food feasts, and Aboriginal philosophy meetings (adults only).

See 'The Olympic Games' special section for tours of Homebush Bay.

Cruises

There's a wide range of relatively inexpensive cruises on the harbour, from ferry boats and cruisers to paddle-steamers and sailing ships. You can book most at Australian Travel Specialists (☎ 9555 2700), at Circular Quay's Wharves 6 and 2; they're open on weekdays from 7 am to 9 pm and from 8 am to 9 pm on weekends. Captain Cook Cruises (☎ 9206 1111) also has a booking office at Wharf 6.

Sydney Transit Authority (STA) ferries offer some good-value cruises, such as the

NEW SOUTH WALES

2½ hour Ferry Cruise that departs Circular Quay at 1 pm on weekdays and 1.30 pm on weekends and visits Middle Harbour. Tickets cost $19 and can be purchased from the ticket office opposite Circular Quay's Wharf 4.

The Sydney Harbour Explorer is a hop-on/ hop-off service that stops at Circular Quay, the opera house, Watsons Bay, Taronga Zoo and Darling Harbour. Boats run two-hourly from 9.30 am until 3.30 pm and the fare is $20 ($15 concession).

For $52 you can take a two hour weekday lunch cruise on the *Bounty* (☎ 9247 1789), a replica of the ship lost by Captain Bligh. It departs Campbell Cove, in the Rocks, at 12.30 pm.

SPECIAL EVENTS

Call the City Events Infoline (☎ 9265 9007) for information on current events.

The massive Sydney Festival floods the city with art in January, including free outdoor concerts in the Domain. Chinese New Year is celebrated in Chinatown with fireworks in January or February. Surf lifesaving carnivals are held at Sydney's ocean beaches from mid-November to May.

The highlight of the month-long Gay & Lesbian Mardi Gras is the outrageous parade along Oxford St. The Mardi Gras culminates in an exclusive bacchanalian party at the Hordern Pavilion, in Moore Park, in early February.

The 12 day Royal Easter Show is an agricultural show and funfair held at Homebush Bay.

The 14 day Sydney Film Festival is held in June at the State Theatre and other cinemas. The Biennale of Sydney is an international art festival held between July and September in even-numbered years at the Art Gallery of NSW, the Powerhouse Museum and other venues.

The 14km City to Surf Run takes place on the second Sunday in August and attracts a mighty 40,000 entrants who run from Hyde Park to Bondi Beach.

Carnivale is an ethnic arts festival held in early spring. The Manly Jazz Festival is held over the Labour Day long weekend in early

October and the Kings Cross Carnival takes place in late October or early November.

Thousands of backpackers descend on Bondi Beach for a booze fest on Christmas Day, much to the consternation of the powers-that-be and the overworked lifesavers. Sydney Harbour is a fantastic sight on Boxing Day as hundreds of boats farewell the competitors in the gruelling Sydney to Hobart Yacht Race. The Rocks, Kings Cross and Bondi Beach are traditional gathering places for alcohol-sodden celebrations on New Year's Eve, although alcohol-free zones and a massive police presence are aimed to quell the rowdier elements.

Various Olympics Arts Festivals are scheduled in the lead up to the Olympics; 'Harbour of Life' will run concurrent with the Olympics in August 2000.

PLACES TO STAY

Sydney has a huge variety of accommodation, including a large selection of travellers' hostels. Prices listed below are summer rates – a time when prices rise and special deals vanish. At these times, expect hostel rates to increase by just the odd dollar; hotel rooms at beachside suburbs can increase by as much as 50%. A 'bed tax' of 10% has been applied to hotel and guesthouse (not hostel) beds in the city centre and inner suburbs to raise funds for the Olympics. During the games *all* bed prices are expected to go through the roof – expect to pay through the nose even for a humble dorm bed, if you can find one at all!

Bed & Breakfast Sydneyside (☎ 9449 4430) PO Box 555, Turramurra, 2074, arranges accommodation in private homes for $55 to $75 a night a single, or $70 to $110 a double.

To find long-stay accommodation, peruse the 'flats to let' and 'share accommodation' ads in the *Sydney Morning Herald* on Wednesday and Saturday. Hostel notice boards are also good sources of information.

Places to Stay – Budget

The average off-peak price for a dorm bed is around $17, but in the peak summer period they can rise to $22. Facilities vary from dorms with en suite, TV, fridge and cooking facilities to just a plain room with a couple of bunks. Some hostels have set hours for checking in and out, although all have 24-hour access once you've paid.

Things to consider when you're shopping around include whether a key deposit is required; whether alcohol is permitted; phone, Internet and satellite TV access; whether free pick-up is available, if visitors are allowed, and the standard of security on the premises.

Sydney also has some fine budget hotels and guesthouses, which work out only fractionally more expensive than hostels if you're travelling with friends. A refundable key deposit of around $10 is often required.

Camping Sydney's caravan parks are a long way out of town, but the following are within 25km of the city centre:

East's Lane Cove River Caravan Park (☎ 9888 9133, Plassey Rd, North Ryde) is 14km north and has van sites from $17 to $20, and cabins are $65 a double. *Lakeside Caravan Park* (☎ 9913 7845, Lake Park Rd, Narrabeen), 26km north, has camp sites/cabins from $20 to $70 a double – a seventh night free.

Sheralee Tourist Caravan Park (☎ 9567 7161, 88 Bryant St, Rockdale), 13km south, has camp sites for $20/120 per day/week and vans for $40/160 a double. *The Grand Pines Caravan Park* (☎ 9529 7329, 289 The Grand Parade, Sans Souci) is 17km south and has camp sites for $29 and vans/cabins from $50/70 to $70/130 a double.

Hostels The largest concentration of hostels is in Kings Cross, but there are clusters in other areas, including Glebe, Manly and Coogee.

City Centre *Sydney Central YHA* (☎ 9281 9111, fax 9281 9199), on the corner of Pitt St and Rawson Place, is opposite Central station. It's a big whizz-bang place with excellent facilities (pool, sauna, cafe) in a heritage building. Dorms start at $20; twins and doubles with en suite are a bargain $33

per person (YHA members only). Wheelchair-access rooms are available.

Nomad's Downtown City Backpackers (☎ 9211 8801), on the corner of Goulburn and George Sts, is a happening hostel with lots of activities (and the usual eye-boggling, chesty murals!). Rickety dorm beds start at $20. (See the Darling Harbour & Chinatown map.)

The super-civilised YWCA hostel, *Y on the Park Hotel* (☎ 9264 2451, fax 9285 6288, 5-11 Wentworth Ave) welcomes both genders. A dorm bed costs $25, but there's a maximum stay of three nights. Spotless singles/twins/triples cost $60/85/90, or $98/120/125 with en suite.

Kings Cross Area There are heaps of hostels in the Cross and little to distinguish between many of them. Eva's has one of the better reputations, followed by Backpackers Headquarters. The Pink House suits those who like their hostels a little more lived-in and cosy. The Jolly Swagman hostel has the best organised social life. There are also a lot of budget guesthouses and motel-style places offering reasonable accommodation.

Heading north along Victoria St from Kings Cross station, the first hostel you come to is *Plane Tree Lodge* (☎ 9356 4551, No 174). This is an average Kings Cross hostel, with a variety of rooms, each with TV and fridge. Rates start at $20 in a dorm; twins/doubles with en suite cost $45/50. Next down the street is the slightly cosier *Highfield House* (☎ 9326 9539, No 166), with three-bed dorms for $19 ($110 weekly) and singles/doubles for $37/52 ($220/310 weekly).

The *Original Backpackers* (☎ 9356 3232, No 162), set in a lovely Victorian building, is the original hostel in this part of the world. It's a clean but lived-in place with an excellent courtyard and a pleasant kitchen-dining area. Dorms are large and cost $20 ($120 weekly); twins/doubles are $50 ($300 weekly).

Travellers Rest (☎ 9358 4606, No 156) has clean dorms with fridge and TV for $17 ($110 weekly), rooms with shared bathroom for $38/40 ($230/240 weekly) and en suite doubles for $45 ($260 weekly). It's popular for long term stays and working travellers; the comfortable, well-equipped rooms have a fridge, a TV and a message-bank phone, and the owner/operators are friendly and helpful.

Potts Point House (☎ *9368 0733, No 154*) is also a cut above average. Bedding down in a cosy dorm is $20 ($110 weekly); doubles start at $45 ($260 weekly).

Virgin Backpackers (☎ *9357 4733, No 144*), the site of the old Jolly Swagman, is the new kid on the block. There are plans to incorporate a cafe and bar into the hostel when it's completed.

Eva's Backpackers (☎ *9358 2185, 6-8 Orwell St*) is a clean, friendly, well-run place, with a sociable dining room. Dorms cost $20 and doubles $48. It's so popular that it's often full, even in winter. Further up is the cheery *Sydney Central Backpackers* (☎ *9358 6600), 16 Orwell St)* – not to be confused with Sydney Central YHA in the city. Dorm beds are $18/108 per night/week, doubles $45/270. Over the road is the busy *Jolly Swagman* hostel (☎ *9358 6400, 14 Springfield Mall*). It has a good atmosphere, good security, Internet access (its Web site is www.jollyswagman.com) and 24-hour reception. Dorms cost $19/120 per day/week, doubles $45/270. Rooms have fridges and every bed has a reading light.

The secure, squeaky-clean *Backpackers Headquarters* (☎ *9331 6180, 79 Bayswater Rd*) has dorms from $19 (10 beds) or $20 (six beds) and is also often full.

One of the most popular hostels in the Cross is the mellow, homely *Pink House* (also known as Barncleuth House Travellers Hostel) (☎ *9358 1689, 6 Barncleuth Square*). It's east of Darlinghurst Rd, and has a lovely patio, a rear courtyard and a sociable atmosphere. Dorm beds cost $18 to $19 ($114 weekly) and twins are $20 to $21 per person ($126 weekly).

Funk House (☎ *9358 6455, fax 9358 3506, 23 Darlinghurst Rd*) is a relative newcomer but rates high on the fun scale (it's also a fully functional travel agency). It's a colourful, bustling place with dorm beds at $20 ($120 weekly), doubles $48.

Enter from Llankelly Place. If you'd prefer things a bit quieter, *Backpackers Connection* (☎ *9358 4844, 2 Roslyn St*) is an impressive hostel with $17 dorm beds and doubles for $44. Every room has its own bathroom and TV.

Rucksack Rest (☎ *9358 2348, 9 McDonald St, Potts Point*) is a quiet hostel. Dorm beds go for $17, twins and doubles around $40. If you stay a week, you only pay for six nights – a deal also available at *Forbes Terrace* (☎ *9358 4327, 153 Forbes St, Woolloomooloo*), four streets west of Victoria St. It's a clean and peaceful hostel with a good courtyard area, charging $18-20 for a dorm bed, $60 for twins/doubles.

South of the Centre The friendly *Kangaroo Bakpak* (☎ *9319 5915, 665 South Dowling St, Surry Hills*) has dorm beds for $18 ($100 weekly). Bus Nos 372, 393 and 395 run along Cleveland St from Central station. *Nomad's Backpackers* (☎ *9331 6487, 162 Flinders St, Surry Hills*) has beds in 10-bed dorms for $17, four-bed dorms for $20; double or twin rooms are $44. Weekly rates are available; the hostel is in the Captain Cook Hotel, where there's often live music.

The *Excelsior Hotel* (☎ *9211 4945, 64 Foveaux St, Surry Hills*) is a small pub only a few blocks from Central station with dorms for $19 ($108 weekly) and singles for $49 ($220 weekly). (The bands downstairs can be noisy.)

Two houses make up the *Alfred Park Private Hotel* (☎ *9319 4031, 207 Cleveland St*), just a short stroll from Central station. It has a pleasant courtyard and kitchen, and dorms with en suite, TV and fridge for $18. Singles/doubles cost $60, or $80 with en suite. Weekly rates are available, and the non-mauve house has better rooms.

Billabong Gardens (☎ *9550 3236, 5 Egan St, Newtown*) is a lovely, quiet hostel with a solar-heated pool and happy-looking guests. Clean dorms with en suite cost $19 ($115 weekly) and doubles from $49. Take a train to Newtown station, turn right into King St and Egan St is about four blocks along on the left.

Glebe Glebe Point YHA Hostel (☎ 9692 8418, 262 Glebe Point Rd) is large and squeaky clean. Five-bed dorms cost $19, four-bed $21 and twin rooms $50 (non-YHA add $3). The staff here have good tips about exploring Sydney, and they store luggage.

Glebe Village Backpackers (☎ 9660 8133, 256 Glebe Point Rd) is a ramshackle hostel in two big houses. Facilities range from scruffy to sparkling and there's a sociable atmosphere. Dorms cost from $19 and doubles $50.

Delightful **Wattle House** (☎ 9552 4997, 44 Hereford St) has dorm beds for $20 ($130 weekly) and twin or double rooms from $55. The **Alishan International Guesthouse** (☎ 9566 4048, 100 Glebe Point Rd) is a lovely, civilised guesthouse with a few dorm beds for $20 ($126 weekly).

Nomad's Forest Lodge (☎ 9660 1872, 117 Arundel St) is near the university above a small pub. The kitchen facilities are lacking, but there are good $5 pasta dinners available. Beds start at $17.

Bondi Bondi has a range of hostel accommodation, not all of it particularly appealing, but with the beach on your doorstep you're unlikely to spend much time staring at the paint peeling in your room.

This is a popular base for long-term working travellers so there are plenty of cheap flats available if you plan on sticking around for a while.

Indy's (☎ 9365 4900, 35a Hall St) is a social backpackers with loud murals you might not want to look at when drunk. Dorm beds are $19 ($119 weekly) and twins and doubles are $42 ($228). There's a good kitchen and courtyard and Internet access, and the staff have good work connections. Ask here about Indy's couples-only love shack further up the beach.

Bondi Lodge (☎ 9365 2088, 63 Fletcher St) is a short, sharp stroll up the hill from the southern end of the beach, but it's well placed to get to neighbouring Tamarama Beach. Dinner, B&B costs $30 in a dorm ($175 weekly) and from $60/40 per person in singles/doubles.

The **Bondi Beach Guest House** (☎ 9389 8309, 11 Consett Ave) is two blocks from the beach, and has unremarkable dorms for $20.

Coogee It's worth ringing before setting off to Coogee because some hostels have limited office hours. **Surfside Backpackers Coogee** (☎ 9315 7888), on the corner of Arden and Alfreda Sts, is conveniently opposite the beach and the main bus stop. Dorms start from $18 ($115 per week).

The popular **Coogee Beach Backpackers** (☎ 9315 8000, 94 Beach St) is a short but stiff walk up the hill at the beach's northern end. The hostel sprawls over three buildings, and has good common areas and a deck with great ocean views. Dorm beds cost $20. The same family also runs two smaller and simpler hostels with the same rates: **Sydney Beachside** (☎ 9315 8511, 178 Coogee Bay Rd) and the adjacent, purple-walled **Wizard of Oz Backpackers** (☎ 9315 7876, 172 Coogee Bay Rd).

The homely **Indy's** (☎ 9315 7644, 302 Arden St) is up the hill at the opposite end of the beach. A bed in four-bed dorms – some OK, some a bit musty – costs from $18 ($118 weekly), including breakfast.

In nearby Clovelly is **Packers at Clovelly** (☎ 9665 3333, 272 Clovelly Rd), a secure, motel-style place with twins/doubles for $20 per person ($110 weekly). All rooms have their own bathroom, TV and phone.

Manly This is the best place to stay if you want to be free of city hassles, experience Sydney's beach culture and stay within commuting distance of the city.

Manly Backpackers Beachside (☎ 9977 3411, 28 Raglan St) has modern dorms costing from $19. Doubles cost $50 ($55 with en suite). Nearby is the older **Manly Astra Backpackers** (☎ 9977 2092, 68 Pittwater Rd) with budget double rooms (couples only). **Manly Cottage Inn** (☎ 9976 0297, 25 Pittwater St) is a smallish hostel with average facilities. Dorms cost $18 ($110 weekly).

The renovated **Wharf Backpackers**, (☎ 9977 2800, 48 East Esplanade) is a large, alcohol-free hostel opposite the ferry terminal. It has an Internet lounge, and

NEW SOUTH WALES

dorms start at $17 ($105 weekly); twins are $46 ($300 weekly).

The **Manly Bunkhouse** (☎ 9976 0472, fax 9938 2553, 46 Malvern Ave) offers apartment-style accommodation. Each room has a small kitchen and bathroom but communal areas are lacking. Beds in dorms with en suite are $22 ($130 weekly).

The huge **Steyne Hotel** (9977 4977, The Corso) has squashy four-bed dorms for a steep $35 a night, including breakfast.

North Shore For a break from the city, the relaxed, northern beachside suburb of Avalon has the **Avalon Beach Hostel** (☎ 9918 9709, 59 Avalon Parade). There's an open-plan common area, but clean-freaks be warned – this place is sociable rather than scrubbed. Dorms cost from $18 a night ($110 weekly) and doubles are $44. Take bus No L90 from Wynyard Park, York St, and ask for Avalon Beach (1¼ hours, $4.60). Phone in advance, because it's often full.

Guesthouses & Budget Hotels
City Centre & the Rocks The **George St Private Hotel** (☎ 9211 1800, 700a George St) (see the Darling Harbour & Chinatown map) is the best of the budget innercity hotels. It's clean, equipped with cooking and laundry facilities, and doesn't have the slightest whiff of seediness. Spartan singles/doubles with shared bathroom cost $36/54, doubles with en suite and TV cost $75. There are weekly rates.

The nearby **CB Private Hotel** (☎ 9211 5115, 417 Pitt St) opened in 1908 and was once the largest hotel in the country. It's reasonably well maintained, but gets a lot of wear. Rooms with shared bathroom are $34/54 (cheaper by the week).

The **Sydney Central Private Hotel** (☎ 9212 1005, 75 Wentworth Ave) is a basic hotel with cooking and laundry facilities, just a short walk from Central station and Oxford St. Singles/doubles cost $35/55 with shared bathroom, or $65 with en suite. The small **Harbour View Hotel** (☎ 9252 3769), on the corner of Lower Fort and Cumberland Sts, is a community pub on the fringes of the Rocks. There's some noise

from trains on the bridge (and bands in the bar), but with clean rooms with views for $50/65 (including breakfast), it's good value and a great location.

Kings Cross Area A pleasant guesthouse near the Cross is the low-key, well-run **Challis Lodge** (☎ 9358 5422, 21-23 Challis Ave), which occupies a pair of cavernous terraces in Potts Point. Rooms with fridge and TV are $35/45; those with bathrooms are $45/55, and there are rooms with a balcony for $70. Rooms on the upper floors are considerably quieter and get better light.

Nearby **Macleay Lodge** (☎ 9368 0660, 71 Macleay St, Potts Point) has good-value, bright rooms with TV, fridge and shared bathroom from $35/40. En suite rooms start at $55.

Springfield Lodge (☎ 9358 3222, 9 Springfield Ave) has similar rooms but they're a tad depressing. Rooms with shared bathroom start at $35/45 ($210/270 weekly) and with en suite cost $60/70 ($360/420 weekly).

Nearby, the **Bernly Private Hotel** (☎ 9358 3122, 15 Springfield Ave) has uninspiring but acceptable modern rooms with TV and shared bathroom for $45/50. Those with en suite and phone are $75/85.

The **Cross Court Tourist Motel** (☎ 9368 1822, 201-3 Brougham St) is a terrace house offering tasteful rooms with shared bathroom from $45/58. Beds in a four-share dorm are $18 ($110 weekly). Rooms with en suite start at $75.

The **Palms Private Hotel** (☎ 9357 1199, 23 Hughes St) is a quiet guesthouse with a TV lounge and communal kitchen. Rooms with fridge and shared bathroom cost $40/50, doubles with en suite $70.

Newtown The clean, pleasant **Australian Sunrise Lodge** (☎ 9550 4999, 485 King St) has decent motel-style rooms with TV and fridge from $45/55, or $65 with en suite.

Bondi Thellelen Lodge (☎ 9130 1521, 11a Consett Ave) is a modest operation in a renovated suburban house two blocks back from the beach. It's reasonably clean, has a good communal kitchen and a friendly feel. Rooms cost from $45/49.

The *Biltmore Private Hotel* (☎ 9130 4660, 110 Campbell Parade) is a big rooming house with a hotch-potch of rooms – some with sea views, some poky and smelly, so check a few out before you commit. Dorms are $20 ($120 weekly). Rooms are $35/45 ($190/280 weekly).

Coogee The dilapidated but charming *Grand Pacific Private Hotel* (☎ 9665 6301), on the corner of Carr St, overlooks the southern end of the beach. Scungey old-style rooms with TV and fridge are $35/45 ($25/35 a night for stays of three nights or more). Some rooms have views.

Manly The *Eversham Private Hotel* (☎ 9977 2423, 27-29 Victoria Parade) is a huge, somewhat gloomy place more reminiscent of an Edwardian boarding school than accommodation at a beach resort. Scruffy singles/doubles/triples cost $28/46/69 ($123/150/225 weekly).

North Shore *Kirribilli Court Private Hotel* (☎ 9955 4344, 45 Carabella St, Kirribilli) has beds in spartan dorms for $15 ($80 weekly) and rooms with shared bathroom and kitchen for $30/40.

Tremayne Private Hotel (☎ 9955 4155, 89 Carabella St, Kirribilli) is a clean guesthouse with rooms with shared bathroom for $25/35 ($150/230 weekly).

Colleges Many colleges at the University of Sydney (☎ 9351 2222) and the University of NSW (☎ 9385 1000) are eager for casual guests during vacations. Most places quote B&B or full-board rates but it's often possible to negotiate a lower bed-only rate.

University of Sydney This is south-west of the city centre, close to Glebe and Newtown. The following is a sample of accommodation offered by colleges:

International House (☎ 9950 9800) has fully serviced B&B single rooms for $35, or full board for $45; weekly rates and twins are available. *St Johns College* (☎ 9394 5200)

has B&B in rooms with en suite from $55 to $67 daily, $220 to $270 weekly. *Women's College* (☎ 9516 1642) accommodates students and YHA members with single B&B for $36, dinner $42 and full board for $48; everyone else is charged $45/52/58. Twin rooms cost from $60/72/80.

Sancta Sophia College (☎ 9577 2100) has B&B singles for $50 ($55 with en suite).

University of NSW This is further from the centre but not far from Oxford St and the southern ocean beaches.

International House (☎ 9663 0418) offers full-board singles for $40 and *New College* (☎ 9662 6066) has singles from $40, or $35 for students.

Places to Stay – Mid-Range
Some mid-range hotels and guesthouses offer top-value facilities at little more than budget prices.

City Centre & The Rocks The *Sydney City Centre Apartments* (☎ 9233 6677, 7 Elizabeth St) offers reasonably-sized, fully-equipped, bedsit apartments, complete with washing machine and drier. Rates are $300 a week – but unfortunately there's a minimum nine-week stay.

The *Wynyard Hotel* (☎ 9299 1330), on the corner of Clarence and Erskine Sts, is a good-value pub with rooms with shared bathroom for $60/70. Another city pub, the *Grand Hotel* (☎ 9232 3755, 30 Hunter St), has similar rooms with TV and fridge for $70/90.

In the south of the city, *Westend Hotel* (☎ 9211 4822, 412 Pitt St) offers motel-style doubles for $100.

The *Mercantile Hotel* (☎ 9247 3570, 25 George St), in the Rocks, has pub rooms from $70/100, including breakfast.

The historic and sentinel-like *Palisade Hotel* (☎ 9247 2272, 35 Bettington St, Millers Point) has bright pub rooms with shared bathroom and views of the city, bridge, harbour and dockyard for $88 a double.

Kings Cross *O'Malley's Hotel* (☎ 9357 2211, 228 William St) is a friendly Irish pub, just downhill from the Coca-Cola sign. It has good rooms with fridge, TV and en suite from $80/85 including breakfast.

The *Barclay Hotel (☎ 9358 6133, 17 Bayswater Rd)* has an average selection of air-con rooms from $70/80, while the *Kingsview (☎ 9358 5599, 30 Darlinghurst Rd)* has air-con rooms for $75.

In Potts Point, the *De Vere Hotel (☎ 9358 1211, 46 Macleay St)* has air-con rooms from $100.

The oh-so-hip *L'Otel (☎ 9360 6868, 114 Darlinghurst Rd)* is on the Darlinghurst side of the huge William St-Victoria St-Darlinghurst Rd junction (see the Central Sydney map). It's a small, stylish hotel charging from $70 a double.

The *Lodge Motel (☎ 9328 0666, 38-44 New South Head Rd)*, in Rushcutters Bay, has small studio apartments with TV, kitchenette and en suite for $60 a double ($320 weekly).

Glebe The *Alishan International Guesthouse (☎ 9566 4048, 100 Glebe Point Rd)* is a guesthouse and upmarket hostel, with good common areas and a small garden. Rooms with en suite cost $80/85.

The *Rooftop Motel (☎ 9660 7777, 146 Glebe Point Rd)* charges from $80 for air-con rooms with TV, fridge, telephone and en suite.

The *Haven Inn (☎ 9660 6655, 196 Glebe Point Rd)* has motel-style rooms with en suite from $110. There's a heated swimming pool, spa and secure parking.

Bondi Like most other beachside suburbs, Bondi's hotels are prone to summer price rises.

The *Bondi Beachside Inn (☎ 9130 5311, 152 Campbell Parade)* is the kind of architectural monstrosity that gave Bondi a bad name, but inside it's a delightful place. The apartment-style rooms have TV, phone, kitchen, en suite and balcony. Standard doubles cost $98, some have good ocean views. Rooms are spacious enough to accommodate three people ($10 extra).

The *Hotel Bondi (☎ 9130 3271, 178 Campbell Parade)* is the peach-coloured layer-cake fronting the beach. It has small

single rooms for $45 with shared facilities (men only), and en suite doubles for $85, or $95 with an ocean view.

Plage Bondi (☎ 9387 1122, 212 Bondi Rd) is a 15 minute lungburster from the beach. The front rooms have amazing views. Single or double-occupancy apartments with more than adequate facilities cost $95 nightly, dropping to $80 by the week and $70 for stays of a fortnight or more.

Coogee The huge *Coogee Bay Hotel (☎ 9665 0000)*, on the corner of Arden St and Coogee Bay Rd, has air-con rooms with fridge, TV, telephone and en suite for $89/99, heritage suites from $109 to $159, and (quieter) renovated boutique rooms for $155.

Manly Like all beach suburbs, Manly is susceptible to price rises in summer and on weekends.

Manly Lodge (☎ 9977 8655, 22 Victoria Parade) offers B&B in good rooms with TV, fridge and en suite for $120 a double, including breakfast; a family room, which sleeps four, is $130 a night.

The *Steyne Hotel (☎ 9977 4977, the Corso)* has OK singles from $70 and twins/doubles from $95, including breakfast. Rooms with en suite are also available.

Motel-style rooms at *Manly Beach Resort (☎ 9977 4188, 6 Carlton St)* cost $95/105 for a single/double, including breakfast.

On Manly Cove is the *Periwinkle Guesthouse (☎ 9977 4668, 18-19 East Esplanade)*, an elegantly restored guesthouse with a good kitchen and rooms with en suite for $120, or $130 with harbour views.

The *Manly Paradise Motel (☎ 9977 5799, 54 North Steyne)* is on the beachfront. It has a rooftop pool and air-con motel double rooms for $115, or $125 with an oblique view of the ocean.

Watsons Bay If you want to enjoy the harbour in a quiet locale and still be within a short ferry ride of the city, try the harbourside *Watsons Bay Hotel (☎ 9337 4299, 1 Military Rd)* which has rooms for $50/80, including breakfast (but impending renovations mean rates may rise).

North Shore *St Leonards Mansions (☎ 9439 6999, 7 Park Rd, St Leonards)* has rooms with TV, cooking facilities and telephone for $50/70 with shared bathroom or $60/80 with en suite, including breakfast. From St Leonards station, turn left (west) along the Pacific Hwy and Park Rd is the second street on the left.

The oddly-named *Neutral Bay Motor Lodge (☎ 9953 4199)*, on the corner of Kurraba Rd and Hayes St in Neutral Bay, is actually a pleasant guesthouse with good rooms for $60/70.

Places to Stay – Top End

There are lots of hotels and serviced apartments charging between $100 and $200 a double, but many cater to business people so their rates might be lower on weekends. Serviced apartments sometimes sleep more than two people and with lower weekly rates they can be inexpensive if shared by a group.

The *Lord Nelson Hotel (☎ 9251 4044)*, on the corner of Kent and Argyle Sts in Millers Point, is a boutique pub on the edge of the Rocks. It has renovated rooms for $180. The boutique *Russell Hotel (☎ 9241 3543, 143 George St, the Rocks)* has good rooms with shared bathroom from $100/110 and with en suite from $140/150. *Trickett's Bed & Breakfast (☎ 9552 1141, 270 Glebe Point Rd)* is exceptionally pleasant. Homely double rooms (all with en suite) cost $140, including breakfast.

In the city centre, the *Sydney Vista Hotel (☎ 9290 1840, 7 York St)* has rooms from around $160. In the Cross, the *Sebel Town House (☎ 9358 3244, 23 Elizabeth Bay Rd)* charges from $169 on weekends, $179 during the week.

Aaron's Hotel (☎ 9281 5555 or 1800 023 071, 37 Ultimo Rd), in Haymarket, is close to Chinatown and Darling Harbour (see the Darling Harbour & Chinatown map). Doubles cost about $130, with frequent specials.

In Potts Point, the lovely Art Deco *Manhattan Hotel (☎ 9358 1288, 8 Greenknowe Ave)* has doubles from $145; it's worth enquiring about views. The comfortable, quiet *Victoria Court Hotel (☎ 9357 3200, 122*

Victoria St) has doubles from $135, including breakfast.

Beachside hotels include the *Swiss Grand Hotel (☎ 9365 5666)*, on the corner of Campbell Parade and Beach Rd, Bondi Beach (from $190); the *Holiday Inn (☎ 9315 7600, 242 Arden St)* in Coogee (from $169); and the *Manly Pacific Parkroyal (☎ 9977 7666, 55 North Steyne)* in Manly (from $190).

Ravesi's (☎ 9365 4422), on the corner of Campbell Parade and Hall St, Bondi Beach, is a classy boutique hotel indicative of the emerging smarter Bondi. Rooms start at $100 and climb to $275 depending on their angle to the ocean.

The international heavyweights include the *Regent (☎ 9238 0000, fax 9251 2851, 199 George St)*; the *Park Hyatt (☎ 9241 1234, fax 9256 1555, 7 Hickson Rd, the Rocks)*; and the *Ritz-Carlton (☎ 9362 4455, fax 9362 4744, 33 Cross St, Double Bay)*.

PLACES TO EAT

With great local produce, innovative chefs, inexpensive prices and BYO licensing laws, it's no surprise that eating out is one of the great delights of a visit to Sydney.

If you're going to explore Sydney's food options, Lonely Planet's *Out to Eat – Sydney* is the best value guide for any budget. *Cheap Eats in Sydney* ($8.95) and the *Sydney Morning Herald*'s *Good Food Guide* ($18.95) are also available.

City Centre

There's no shortage of places for a snack or meal in the city, especially on weekdays. They are clustered around the train stations, in shopping arcades and tucked away in the food courts to be found in just about every office building more than 20 storeys high.

Bodhi, in the Central station coach terminal, is a vegan cafe – perfect for a pre-bus-odyssey light meal.

Obelisk, near the Obelisk itself, has outdoor tables in the historic precinct, Macquarie Place. Breakfast starts at $5, bagels around $6.50. The *Customs House Bar* nearby has gourmet pies for $4.50 and hearty roasts for $10.50. *Deli on Market*, on the corner of Clarence and Market Sts, is a

NEW SOUTH WALES

large cafe serving muesli with fruit and yogurt for $5, and a range of wholesome, reasonably-priced lunches. **Parma Espresso Bar** *(203a Castlereagh St)* has cooked breakfasts for $5.50, tasty filled rolls for $4 and good takeaway coffee for $1.50.

The **Dendy Bar & Bistro** *(☎ 9221 1243, MLC Centre, Martin Place)* is an agreeable, comfy downstairs space serving risotto for $12, and wok-fried noodles for $8.50. There are pool tables, occasional live music and weekend dance parties. The bar is open until midnight (later on weekends). **Carruthers** *(235 Macquarie St)* has cheap vegetarian fare, salads and juices.

Kiosk on Macquarie, at the Macquarie St entrance to the Royal Botanic Gardens, is a nice spot for lunch on a sunny day. Cafe fare at the outdoor tables costs between $5 and $10.

Spanish Town consists of a cluster of seven or eight Spanish restaurants and bars on Liverpool St between George and Sussex Sts. **Casa Asturiana** *(77 Liverpool St)* is reputed to have the best tapas in the city (from $5). **Captain Torres** *(No 73)* has good seafood mains (from $15 to $20) and a great bar. **Vender** *(No 86)* is the only non-Spanish place in the strip. It's a groovy espresso bar serving coffee and $7 gourmet sandwiches until around 11 pm.

Planet Hollywood *(600 George St)*, opposite the cinemas, is overpriced and overcrowded.

Chinatown

Chinatown has expanded well beyond the confines of the officially designated pedestrian mall on Dixon St (see the Darling Harbour & Chinatown map). You can spend a small fortune at some outstanding Chinese restaurants or eat well for next to nothing in a food hall.

The best place to start is the **Sussex St Food Court**, with its bewildering array of Chinese, Malay, Vietnamese, Thai and Japanese food. At lunchtime it's the most hectic and bubbly food court in the city, and one of the best and most atmospheric places to eat. A full meal costs between $4 and $7. There are similar food courts in **Dixon**

House, on the corner of Dixon and Little Hay Sts, and the **Harbour Plaza**, on the corner of Dixon and Goulburn Sts.

Hingara *(82 Dixon St)* is a classic Cantonese eatery with most mains around $12. **BBQ King** *(18 Goulburn St)* is a sociable, high-turnover, meaty joint open until the wee hours; expect to pay between $8 and $16 for a main. **House of Guangzhou**, on the corner of Thomas St and Ultimo Rd, is a popular, established restaurant with most mains priced between $11 and $19.

If you're looking for quality, expect to pay a little more or choose from the cheaper dishes on the menu. **Marigold** *(4th & 5th floors, 683 George St)* and **East Ocean** *(421 Sussex St)* have great yum-cha. The **Regal**, on the corner of Liverpool and Sussex Sts, is a huge, chandeliered place with a lovely seasonal menu and $16 main courses. The **Golden Century** *(☎ 9212 3901, 393 Sussex St)*, the king of Sydney's Cantonese restaurants, is open till 4 am. Seafood mains are around $20.

Ippon *(404 Sussex St)* is a fun Japanese sushi bar where you choose your dishes as they trundle past on a conveyor belt. Pieces start at $2.

Darling Harbour

As well as having a couple of classier eateries, the Harbourside Shopping Centre has the food-court routine down pat, while the new Cockle Bay Wharf dining locale opposite has white tablecloths as far as the eye can see. The cartoonishly kitsch **Ettamogah Bar** *(Harbourside)* does meals of the burger ($4.50) and steak ($6) variety. Of the restaurants with outdoor tables and water views, **Jordon's** is well known for its seafood (mains are around $25).

The Health Tree, at Cockle Bay Wharf, is a takeaway with fresh juices, tasty salads for $3 to $7, and pastas for $6.50. **Wockpool**, in the IMAX building, is wonderful, expensive and *the* place to be seen wielding chopsticks.

The Rocks & Circular Quay

Restaurants and cafes in the Rocks are overtly aimed at tourists, but there are still some good deals available, especially in the pubs where most bar meals are still under $10.

The friendly **G'Day Cafe** *(83 George St)*, just north of Argyle St, has good-value cooked breakfasts from $4, and focaccia from $2. The cute **Gum Nut Tea Garden** *(28 Harrington St)*, near the junction with Argyle St, has a rear courtyard and serves breakfast for around $5, lunches from $6.50 and Devonshire tea on weekends. It's on Harrington St.

The la-de-dahling **MCA Cafe**, in the foyer of the Museum of Contemporary Art, Circular Quay West, has good coffee and food (lunch mains around $14), and a terrace overlooking the harbour and Opera House.

There are several average cafes and kiosks amid the ferry wharves notable mainly for being open 24 hours.

The **Sydney Cove Oyster Bar**, Circular Quay East, has one of the best views in the city. Mains are a tad expensive, but half-a-dozen oysters will set you back only $12.50, so crack open a bottle of Australian wine and toast the spectacular vista.

If you're looking for excellence, the Sydney Opera House's **Bennelong Restaurant** *(☎ 9250 7548)* is a culinary institution – and an architectural eye-popper. The space-age yet Art Deco **Rockpool** *(☎ 9252 1888, 107 George St)* and the well-heeled **Quay** *(☎ 9251 5600)*, in the Overseas Passenger Terminal, Circular Quay West, both have formidable reputations and require formidable amounts of cash. **Bel Mondo** *(☎ 9241 3700)*, in the Argyle Department Store, the Rocks, is similarly cash-splashy, but you can eat for under $15 in the attached **anti bar**.

Darlinghurst & East Sydney

Victoria St is the main cafe and restaurant strip in Darlinghurst (see the Central Sydney map). If you're just looking for a caffeine hit, **Bar Coluzzi** *(322 Victoria St)* is a Sydney institution, and **Tropicana** *(No 227)*, just over the road, is not far behind.

If you can't subsist on caffeine alone, the nearby **Backdoor Café** has fat toast and thin people. **La Bussola** *(No 324)* dishes up great pizzas from $8.50 to $15.50.

Fu-Manchu *(249 Victoria St)* is a groovy and gregarious noodle bar with famed soups for around $10. Next door is **Oh Calcutta!**, a quality Indian restaurant with mains from $10 and a balcony for balmy nights. Also here is **Fez**, on the corner of Liverpool and Victoria Sts, where you can mix and match mezze from $3.50.

For vegetarian food, try **Govinda's** *(☎ 9380 5155 or 9360 7853, 112 Darlinghurst Rd)*, a Hare Krishna restaurant just south of William St and Kings Cross. A $14.90 all-you-can-gobble smorgasbord also gives you free admission to the cushioned cinema upstairs.

The **Bandstand Cafe** *(Green Park)* has a fairly unadventurous lunch menu, but the setting is lovely.

Tum Tum Thai *(199 Darlinghurst Rd)* is an eat-in or takeaway place with scrumptious curries and stir-fries from $7.50 and queues out the door. **Fishface** *(No 132)* has some of the best affordable seafood in the city; all manner of marine life is seared with a hiss for around $14. **Eca Bar** next door is a wafer-thin, cheaper-than-it-looks trendoid cafe.

There's a second cluster of restaurants in Stanley St, East Sydney, just south of William St, between Crown and Riley Sts. This strip used to be an Italian monoculture but it's increasingly multicultural. The classic Italian cheapies are **Bill & Toni's** *(No 74)* and **No Names** *(No 81)*, above the Arch Coffee Lounge. **Pacifico** *(95 Riley St)* is an airy Mexican cantina just around the corner; enchiladas are $12.50.

Oxford St

The mish-mash of restaurants on Oxford St, east of Taylor Square, moves from Asia to southern Europe and from gold coin to gold card territory. The popular **Thai-Nesia** *(No 243)*, the Vietnamese **Vin Ha Long** *(No 233)*, and the Cambodian **Angkor Wat** *(No 227)* are $12 cheapies. At the nearby **Balkan Continental** *(No 209)*, carnivore-friendly mains start from $15, and at No 215 the **Balkan Seafood** restaurant is also good.

Metronome Cafe *(411 Bourke St)*, off Taylor Square, is a peaceful haven with a leafy outdoor area, a range of sweet treats, and delicious home-blended coffee.

The **Courthouse Hotel**, which dominates Taylor Square, has hearty pub fare in the upstairs bar for between $9 and $15. **Cafe 191**, which also fronts Taylor Square, is a prime people-watching spot.

The city end of Oxford St has a rash of nondescript cafes and fast-food Asian eateries, some relying on desperate clubbers and night owls, others on passing trade, so choose selectively. **Bach Hy** (No 139) is a good place to slurp a soup before or after glamming it up. The modish and super-busy **Thai Panic**, on the corner of Oxford and Crown Sts, has great curries and stirfries for $7.50 to $9.50.

The **Tandoori Palace** (No 86) is a fine budget Indian restaurant with mains for about $9. The reassuringly homely **Betty's Soup Kitchen** (No 84) has soup and damper for $5.50 and lamb stew for $8.80. Nearby, the cheerful **Don Don** (☎ 9331 3544, No 80) dishes delicious Japanese fare in generous portions. Tempura udon soup is $7.50.

There's a cluster of budget restaurants just to the south on Crown St. They include the cosy retro **Roobar** (No 253), which does great brekkies all day. **Fatz**, next door, manages to do new things with pasta ($12). The modest **Maltese Cafe** (No 310) has pastas under $5 and pastizzi snacks for 30c. Further down, the bohemian **Mali** (No 348a), one of Sydney's cutest cafes, has sandwiches, good coffee, and $3 breakfasts.

Kings Cross & Around

The Cross has a mixture of fast-food joints serving greasy fare designed mainly to soak up beer, tiny cafes servicing locals and travellers, and some swanky eateries among the city's best.

The low-key **William's on William** (242 William St), near the Coca-Cola sign, has eggs, bacon, chips and toast for $3.90 and pasta for $5. **Mamma Maria**, just down the hill, offers similar cheap fare. Other budget eateries include the legendary late-night pie cart **Harry's Cafe de Wheels** (Woolloomooloo Wharf); **Hwang So** (142 Victoria St), a cheap Korean BBQ place; and **Pad Thai** (Llankelly Place), where noodles and rice dishes cost between $5 and $8.

Sushi Roll, on Darlinghurst Rd, opposite Roslyn St, right in the thick of it, has nori rolls for $1.50 – they kept this author going!

At **Roy's Famous Cafe** (176 Victoria St), open breakfast through to supper, you can grab a booth and fill up on Mediterranean-style mains for around $12. **Out of India** (☎ 9357 7055), next door, does spicy meals for $10 to $13.

The two most prominent eateries in the Cross are the **Fountain Cafe**, at the junction of Darlinghurst Rd and Macleay St, a reasonable, plate-of-meat kind of place, and the surreal **Bourbon & Beefsteak**, next door, which is just for the tourists unless it's 4 am and you develop the munchies.

The **Japanese Noodles Shop** (87 Macleay St) has a small selection of noodles and soups for between $6 and $10. **India Down Under** (44 Macleay St) is a mid-priced restaurant with a good reputation.

Elizabeth Bay Deli, on the corner of Elizabeth Bay Rd and Greenknowe Ave, is a sunny little goldfish bowl of a cafe selling sandwiches, sweets and coffee.

For great coffee and inventive, tasty fare from around $6, try the diminutive and bustling **Spring Cafe** (Challis Ave).

Mére Catherine (146 Victoria St) is an unpretentious French restaurant, so intimate that you have to knock on the door to gain admittance. Main courses are around $25. The super-mod **Star Bar & Grill** (155 Victoria St), part of the famous Wockpool family, serves Chinese and Malaysian food; scallops are $14.

59 Hotel & Cafe (59 Bayswater Rd) has good smoothies and fresh juices, and hearty breakfasts for around $7.50. The **Waterlily Cafe** (No 6) has a friendly feel, and does great breakfasts; you can eat well here for under $10.

If you want to try some of Sydney's best restaurants, and can afford main courses of $25 or more, the **Bayswater Brasserie** (32 Bayswater Rd) is a welcoming institution with great food and impeccable service. **Darley Street Thai**, next door, has exotic, top-notch Thai food, and the lovely **Cicada** (29 Challis Ave) has kept Sydney's fashionable foodies entranced for a few years now.

Surry Hills

Crown St is the main thoroughfare through Surry Hills but it's a long street and the restaurants occur in fits and starts. It's worth a wander along, though, with interesting shops and eateries always springing up.

Prasits Northside Thai (No 395), near the corner with Foveaux St, is a nifty box-like Thai place where you can get great curries and stir-fries from $10. *Alt (553 Crown St)* is a funky little espresso bar with damn fine coffee and arty happenings.

A second smattering of eateries on Devonshire St includes the much-loved *Passion du Fruit*, on the corner of Devonshire and Cleveland Sts. Across the road is *Cafe Niki (554 Bourke St)*, a welcoming, wood-lined place with $4 fruit whips, $5 soups, and $7 open bagels. The vibrant *Rustic Cafe*, on the corner of Devonshire and Crown Sts, is a laid back, hearty Mediterranean eatery; mains are around $12. *Mohr Fish (No 202)* is a tiny designer fish and chip shop; seafood mains are around $17.

There are half-a-dozen nondescript Lebanese eateries around the corner of Cleveland and Elizabeth Sts, at the southern end of Surry Hills, where most dishes are between $4 and $6. *Abduls (565 Elizabeth St)* sells skewered food from $2.

Indian and Turkish places spice up Cleveland St between Crown and Bourke Sts. *Dhaba (466 Cleveland St)* has good northern Indian fare for under $10; *Maya* is a lovely Indian sweet shop almost next door. Just on the Redfern side of Crown St, *Casapueblo (☎ 9319 6377, 650 Bourke St)* does deftly-spiced and highly-praised Uruguayan food in an intimate atmosphere. There's a good vegetarian selection and nothing is over $15.50.

Paddington

Anastasia's Japanese Cosmopolitan (288 Oxford St) does mid-price Japanese and pasta dishes (under $12) and you can contemplate global cuisine in the rear garden. *Sloanes (No 312)* is an intimate, modern cafe offering light meals for $7.50, Mediterranean mains for $12.50 and breakfast all day.

Caffe Centaur (No 19) is a bookish, whisper-quiet coffee and dessert spot upstairs in the wonderful Berkelouw bookshop. The relaxed *Armand's le Cafe (No 100)* is an ambient French-Italian cafe with Aboriginal art on the walls and meals between $5 and $12.

La Mensa Cafeteria (No 257) is a bright 'n' breezy cafe/deli doing beautiful dishes for beautiful people.

The *Paddington Inn (No 338)* has a reputable bistro with mains for $12 to $15. The very lovely deli and cafe *Hot Gossip (No 436)* is one of the nicest hangouts in Paddington, with a good range of toothsome treats.

The *Light Brigade Hotel*, on the corner of Oxford and Jersey Sts, is a renovated pub with gourmet sandwiches for $6. The *Centennial Park Cafe*, a five minute walk inside the park from the Centennial Square entrance off Oxford St, serves pricey food in glorious surroundings.

Glebe

Glebe Point Rd was Sydney's original 'eat street' but it's managed to retain a laid-back, unfaddish atmosphere, good-value food and warm conversation.

IKU Wholefoods (25 Glebe Point Rd) serves super-cheap macrobiotic dishes and snacks. *Lolita's (No 29)* is a student hangout, with snacky stuff like bruscetta for $4.50. If you want to check your email while you munch, *Well Connected (No 35)* has good food and Internet access. *Badde Manors (No 37)* is the mellow neighbourhood favourite. Cafe fare and vegetarian meals are under $10. *Cafe Otto (No 79)* has a lovely front courtyard garden, but meals can get up around $15 – breakfasts are cheaper at around $5. Nearby, *Dakhni* is a traditional Indian place. Main dishes are either side of $10.

Figjam (No 197) has scary purple fluoro lights, but comfy cushions at the window seats; chai is $2, pasta around $6.

The tiny *Pudding Shop (No 144)* is a budget takeaway with delicious pies, quiches and sugar-fixes for under $4. *Craven (No 166)*, next to the old Valhalla cinema, is a reasonably inexpensive joint with that oh-so

Glebe, jumble-sale aura. It's a popular spot to kick back with a coffee, snack or meal.

Lien (No 331) has good value Thai, Vietnamese and Malaysian mains for around $7, while *Lilac (No 333)* has Chinese, Malaysian, Indonesian and vegetarian fare, mostly under $9. *That's It Thai (No 381)* is another of those popular eat-in/takeaway, closet-sized Thai places. Budget vegetarian and meat dishes are only $7 to $9.

The secret gem of Glebe is the *Blackwattle Canteen*, in the Blackwattle Studios in a converted wharf at the end of Glebe Point Rd, overlooking Rozelle Bay. It's among the studios of artists, sculptors and picture framers and has wonderful views, mega breakfasts and comfort food under $10.

Newtown

A swag of funky cafes and restaurants lining Newtown's King St offer an interesting introduction to the suburb's community life. The convivial *Green Iguana Cafe (No 6)* is a down-home vegetarian place with a rear courtyard, offering cheap cafe fare.

Cafe Solea (No 182) serves basic but tasty snacks, salads and frittatas for under $10 and there's free acoustic music most nights (there's a moneybox on your table). Serious coffee-heads make for *Has Beans (No 153a)*, a coffee shop and pasta place which sometimes hosts theatre nights and poetry readings. *Peasants Feast (No 121a)* does hearty old faves with a new twist. Entrees are $10, mains $15 and there's a good vegetarian selection. *Old Saigon (No 107)* is kookily decorated but the Vietnamese food is spot on; mains are $12.

Le Kilimanjaro (No 280) is a bustling, high-turnover African eatery with tempting mains for around $8.50. *Sumalee Thai (☎ 9565 1730, No 324)* is in the (heated) beer garden of the Bank Hotel. It's not cheap but the servings are massive and the food delicious.

The *Old Fish Shop (No 239)* is a wonderful spot for lunch (but beware the dangling garlic bulbs). *Cafe 381 (No 381)* is a loungeroomy, feral hangout. *MacDonna's (275 Australia St)*, just off King St, is a tiny cafe with loony decor and $5.50 vegie burgers.

Saray (18 Enmore Rd) is a low-key Turkish restaurant. The Turkish pizza ($7) is excellent.

Leichhardt

You can still get a cheap spag bol in Norton St, but the classic bistros are now rubbing shoulders with the classy, plus a few Greek, Chinese and Thai interlopers.

Bar Italia (169 Norton St) is everyone's old favourite. Almost everything is under $10 and the gelati is renowned. *L'Epoca Cafe (No 167)* has $7 snacks; chic *Elio (No 159)* is more expensive, with pasta mains around $15. *Portofino (No 166)* has pizzas and pastas for around $16. *Bar Galante (No 138)* has omelettes and focaccia for around $8. The friendly *Mezzapica (No 128)* is popular with local families.

Closer to Parramatta Rd, *La Cremeria (No 110)* scoops delicious home-made gelati from $2.50.

Bondi

The grill joints and takeaway greasebuckets are being squeezed away from the foreshore of Bondi by cafes, bistros and a slew of serious foodie joints. You can still eat well in Bondi for under $10, but might have to forgo a sea view. But you can always do as the locals do and take a steaming paper package down to the beach: the best fish and chips are at *Bondi Surf Seafood (128 Campbell Parade)*.

The lovely *Gusto* delicatessen *(16 Hall St)*, a block back from the beach, is a great spot to perch for a laid-back breakfast. *Le Paris-Go Cafe*, on the corner of Hall St and Consett Ave, is a chatty baguette hangout. The *Earth Food Store (81 Gould St)*, off Hall St, sells organic fruit 'n' vegies and does sustaining takeaways. *Thai Terrific (147 Curlewis St)* has cheap, tasty curries.

Closer to the surf, *Toriyoshi (224 Campbell Parade)* is a cheap Japanese eatery with yakitori sticks from $2.50. *Liberty Lunch (No 106)* is a breezy licensed cafe with mains from $15. *Hugo's (No 70)* has serious food for the white tablecloth brigade.

On Campbell Parade at the southern end of the beach, you'll find the *Sports Bar(d)*

(No 32), a busy drinking and shouting spot. Nearby is **Bondi Trattoria** *(No 34)*, a popular place with outdoor seating, ocean views and Mediterranean-influenced bistro fare around the $13 mark.

The beautiful people have colonised the northern end of the beach, too. **Jackie's**, on the corner of Warners and Wairoa Aves, is a classy cafe serving brekkies (weekends only) for around $8, but main dishes sneak up to $15. The slick **Raw**, opposite, serves bistro-style Japanese from $10 upward. Further north, **Diggers Cafe** *(232 Campbell Parade)* is cheaper, serving breakfasts from 7 am and soups ($6.50) and salads (from $7.50) until dark. The restaurant in the **Digger's Club** upstairs has $3 roast lunches.

There are lots of restaurants up Bondi Rd away from the beach. **Quaint** *(No 195)* has croissants and salads for around $7. **Laurie's Vegetarian** *(No 286)* is tucked in amid Thai, Indian and Italian cheapies. Delicious burgers, curries, pastas and stir fries start at $3.80.

Coogee

There are a number of cheap takeaways on Coogee Bay Rd, but you're better off hitting the cafes, which have healthier food, sunnier demeanours and outdoor tables. The exuberant **Congo Cafe** *(208 Arden St)* faces the beach. Pizzas, focaccias, bagels, melts and salads all cost $7 to $8. **La Casa**, a few doors along, has pasta or fish and chips for $9.

There are several bright, pleasant places on Coogee Bay Rd serving standard cafe fare for between $5 and $11. They include the nautical **Coogee Cafe** *(No 221)*, the more interesting **Globe** *(No 203)* (with $4 breakfasts) and **Cafe Blah Blah** *(No 198)* which has a small but well-thought-out menu of light, modern fare. If you want something more substantial, the **Coogee Bay Hotel**, on the corner of Arden St and Coogee Bay Rd, has a better-than-average pub brasserie with mains for around $13.

Bronte

For a beachside belly-filler, mix it with the locals at **Sejuiced** *(472 Bronte Rd)*. One of a string of goodish cafes in this strip by the park, it's a great place for sipping liquid vitamins, munching focaccia and drying off. If you can't get a table, polish off your shades and head to the nearby **Cafe Q** or the **Bogey Hole**.

Manly

The ocean end of The Corso is jam-packed with takeaways and outside tables. Manly Wharf and South Steyne have plenty of eateries, but you're often paying more for the view than the food.

If you want good value and don't need to see the ocean while you eat, head to the lovely **Candy's Coffeehouse** *(26 Belgrave St)*, which serves inexpensive food in a cosy, book-lined cafe more reminiscent of Glebe than a beachside suburb. The nearby **Twocan** serves jazzy Mod Oz – dinners are up around $20 but lunch can be had for around $10. **Last Train to Bombay** *(11 Belgrave St)* serves carefully prepared Indian food, mostly under $10.

Green's Eatery, in the mall section of Sydney Rd, adjoining The Corso, has a sunny aspect and serves light, health-conscious meals for around $5. For more spicy food, try **Malacca Straits**, on the corner of Sydney Rd and Whistler St, where Malay and Thai dishes cost $7 to $13.

Brazil *(46 North Steyne)* and **BarKing Frog**, next door, vie for the waterfront's trendiest food. It's all corn-fed-this and goat-cheese-that, but you can still eat for under $15. The South Steyne cafes and restaurants are overpriced, but if you're feeling groovy, **Cafe Nice**, on the corner South Steyne and Wentworth Sts, serves good coffee in steel cups.

North Sydney

The **North Sydney Noodle Market** is a praiseworthy attempt to capture the flavour of Asian street-food markets. It's held in the park on Miller St, between McClaren and Ridge Sts, North Sydney on Sunday lunchtimes during autumn and winter, and on Friday nights during spring and summer.

ENTERTAINMENT

The *Sydney Morning Herald* lift-out *Metro* is published on Friday and lists events in town for the coming week. Free newspapers, such as *Drum Media*, *3-D World*, *Revolver*, and the *Sydney City Hub* also have useful listings and are available from bookshops, bars, cafes and record stores.

Ticketek (☎ 9266 4800), 195 Elizabeth St, is the city's main booking agency for theatre, concerts, sports and other events. Phone bookings can be made weekdays from 7.30 am to 10 pm, Saturday 9 am to 4 pm, and Sunday 9 am to 8 pm. It also has agencies around town and publishes a bimonthly *Entertainment Guide*.

Halftix (☎ 9966 1622), at 201 Sussex St, near Cockle Bay Wharf, sells half-price seats to shows. Tickets are only available for shows that night, and they can't tell you where you'll be sitting. Halftix is open daily except Sunday. You can also book through the Web site at www.halftix.com.au.

Pubs

There are plenty of good pubs in Sydney's inner suburbs.

The Rocks Two interesting pubs in this district are the *Lord Nelson*, on the corner of Argyle Place and Kent St, which brews its own ale, and the friendly *Hero of Waterloo*, on the corner of Lower Fort and Windmill Sts.

Molly Bloom's Bar at the *Mercantile Hotel (25 George St)* is a nice place to sink a Guinness. The *Australian Hotel*, on the corner of Gloucester and Cumberland Sts, has renowned local brews on tap.

Darling Harbour The cartoonish *Ettamogah Bar*, Harbourside Shopping Centre, lays on the ocker to pull in the crowds.

Kings Cross The Cross has plenty of hotels, though many are in less than salubrious surroundings. The 24-hour *Kings Cross Hotel*, at the junction of William and Victoria Sts, is a rowdy backpacker favourite. It's the spooky-looking building in the shadow of the Coca-Cola sign.

O'Malley's, on the corner of William and Brougham Sts, is a convivial Irish pub which has live music every night (free

entry). The *Soho Bar (171 Victoria St)* is a discreetly trendy neighbourhood watering hole.

The *Bourbon & Beefsteak*, on the dogleg of Darlinghurst Rd, is a 24-hour institution still suffering a hangover from the Vietnam War. *Barons (upstairs, 5 Roslyn St)* is a snug late-night alternative with a loungeroom feel. There's also a strip of late-night hybrid bar-restaurant-clubs on Kellett St.

A five minute walk from the Cross is the huge *Woolloomooloo Bay Hotel (2 Bourke St, Woolloomooloo)*.

Darlinghurst The *Green Park Hotel*, on the corner of Liverpool and Victoria St, is the haunt of black-clad, pool-shooting, innercity groovers. The *Hard Rock Cafe (121 Crown St)* is for those who feel compelled to add to their souvenir T-shirt collection.

Kinselas (☎ 9331 3299, 383 Bourke St, Darlinghurst) is a large Art Deco building with a basement bar downstairs and a pool table (DJs playing cruisey sounds); there's a cocktail bar upstairs and possible nightclub to reopen.

On Oxford St, the cavernous shell of the *Burdekin Hotel (No 2)* attracts a lively, mixed crowd, especially on Friday and Saturday night. The *Lizard Lounge*, upstairs at the Exchange Hotel, No 34, is a hip melting pot of straights, gays and lesbians. *Q-Bar (upstairs at No 46)* is a hard-to-find pool hall cum bar-club that's open till the wee hours (watch the stairs when drunk).

See the Out & About in Gay Sydney aside for gay pubs and clubs near Oxford St.

Surry Hills There's a batch of decent pubs here, including the *Palace Hotel (122 Flinders St)*, the *Cricketers Arms (106 Fitzroy St)*, the *Hopetoun Hotel*, on the corner of Fitzroy and Bourke Sts, and *Forresters Hotel*, on the corner of Foveaux and Riley Sts. The *Bentley Bar*, on the corner of Crown and Campbell Sts, is a carpeted neighbourhood local.

Paddington The *Paddington Inn Hotel (338 Oxford St)* is a sociable local. The *Lord*

The Best Things in Life Are Free

There's plenty of free entertainment in Sydney for those who want to have fun without having to splash their hard-earned cash around. The Art Gallery of NSW has no admission charge for its permanent exhibitions, and most of the visual arts exhibitions at Customs House are free. The Powerhouse Museum has no admission charge on the first Saturday of the month.

Lunchtime offers a feast of free music, from bands who play regularly in the Martin Place amphitheatre to the 'Lunchbreak' series hosted by students from the Conservatorium of Music (1.10 pm Tuesday during term, at St Andrew's Cathedral next to the Town Hall). There are plenty of buskers and free weekend performances at Circular Quay, Playfair St in the Rocks and in Darling Harbour's Tumbalong Park.

There's a free Aboriginal dance performance at 12 pm Tuesday to Saturday at the Art Gallery of NSW.

The Paddington Village Bazaar is a spectacle in itself, and there are often performers strutting their stuff in Oxford St and Kings Cross. 'Speakers Corner', in the Domain, attracts the mad, the dangerous and the erudite on Sunday afternoons.

Tropfest (☎ 9368 0434) is a free, one day short-film festival in late February, which screens simultaneously at the Domain and in Darlinghurst's Victoria St (which is blocked off for the occasion). Entries follow a loosely-interpreted theme – for 2000 it's 'bugs'.

Don't forget the simple pleasures. It costs nothing to stroll across the Harbour Bridge, wander around the Royal Botanic Gardens, laze on the beach or frolic in the surf.

Saturday's *Sydney Morning Herald* lists freebies for the week ahead.

Dudley (236 Jersey St, Woollahra) is as close as Sydney gets to English pub atmosphere.

Glebe The eccentric *Friend in Hand (58 Cowper St)* has crab racing (Wednesday), poetry slams (Tuesday), live music (Friday and Sunday) and pool comps. The *Harold Park Hotel (115 Wigram Rd)* was once a music and comedy pub, but now concentrates on drinking; it has a sunny beer garden. The *Excelsior Hotel (101 Bridge St)* has music nightly from Tuesday to Sunday.

Bondi The *Icebergs Club (Nott Ave)* is an excellent place for a cheap beer and million-dollar ocean views. It's above the southern end of the beach; cover bands play on weekends. The *Bondi Pavilion* on Bondi Beach regularly has bands and DJs.

Clubs

Sydney's club scene is alive and kicking. The following are some of the more established venues.

Cauldron (207 Darlinghurst Rd, Darlinghurst) is a flashy retro and house club.

DCM (33 Oxford St, Darlinghurst); muscular and sweaty, mixed gay and straight.

Mister Goodbar (11 Oxford St, Paddington) is a cool basement club with superstrict door, while *EP1 (1 Earl Place, Kings Cross)* is a popular mainstream club with a backpacker night on Wednesday.

The huge, hip and happening *Home (Cockle Bay Wharf)* is a house music club with international guest DJs. *Underground Cafe (22 Bayswater Rd, Kings Cross)* is a keen house music club, with international guest DJs and cheap entry on Thursday.

Live Music

Sydney doesn't have a dynamic pub music scene, but you can still find live music most nights of the week. For detailed listings of venues and acts, see the listings in the papers mentioned in the Entertainment introduction.

Rock There's sometimes no charge to see young local bands, while between $5 and $12 is charged for more well known local acts, about $20 for top Australian bands, and around $50 or more for international performers. Venues worth considering are: **Enmore Theatre** (☎ 9550 3666, 130 Enmore Rd, Newtown), which hosts major Australian and overseas acts, as do the **Hordern Pavilion** (☎ 9331 9263, Moore Park), the **Metro** (☎ 9264 1581, 624 George St, city) and **Selinas** (Coogee Bay Hotel, Coogee Bay Rd, Coogee Bay).

The **Excelsior Hotel** (☎ 9211 4945, 64 Foveaux St, Surry Hills) has original live music every night and the **Hopetoun Hotel** (☎ 9361 5257), on the corner of Fitzroy and Bourke Sts, Surry Hills, is a comfy local with original music Thursday to Sunday.

Globe (☎ 9519 0220, 379 King St, Newtown) has DJs till late and live music Tuesday to Sunday nights.

The **Rose, Shamrock & Thistle Hotel** or the **'Three Weeds'** (☎ 9810 2244, 139 Evans St, Rozelle) has folk, blues and light rock, while the **Sandringham Hotel** (☎ 9557 1254, 387 King St, Newtown) is the breeding ground of Aussie pub rock.

Sydney Entertainment Centre (☎ 1900 957 333, Darling Harbour) is for the Elton Johns and Billy Joels of this world.

Out & About in Gay Sydney

Sydney has vibrant, vocal and well-organised gay and lesbian communities, which throw some spectacular parties and provide a range of social-support services. There are large gay and lesbian populations in Darlinghurst, Paddington and Surry Hills and growing communities in Newtown, Leichhardt and Alexandria. Light tans and, for men, heavy pecs are the rage, so hit the beach and the gym a few weeks before arriving.

Gay social life is predominantly focussed on Oxford St, where many cafes, restaurants and businesses are gay-owned and operated. Major entertainment venues include:

Albury Hotel, 6 Oxford St, Paddington (drag show heaven)
Barracks Bar, Taylor Square (men's bar with pool tables and music)
Stonewall Hotel, 175 Oxford St, Darlinghurst (friendly bar with upstairs lounge)
Midnight Shift, 85 Oxford St, Darlinghurst (1st-floor disco with trippy light show)
Oxford Hotel, 134 Oxford St, Darlinghurst (basement bar and 1st-floor cocktail lounge)

Other gay and lesbian haunts include the **Beauchamp Hotel**, 267 Oxford St, Darlinghurst (mainly men), the **Beresford Hotel**, 354 Bourke St, Surry Hills, and the **Flinders Hotel**, 63 Flinders St, Surry Hills (mainly men). In Newtown, try the **Bank Hotel**, 342 King St (mainly women), or the **Newtown Hotel**, 174 King St. There's a strong lesbian scene in Leichhardt – the **Leichhardt Hotel**, 126 Balmain Rd, is a starting point. Gay beach life is focussed on Lady Bay (nude) and Tamarama (also known as Glamarama).

The major social events of the year are the month-long Sydney Gay & Lesbian Mardi Gras, which culminates in an outrageous parade and dance party in March, and the Sleaze Ball, which takes place in early October. The parties for both events are held in Moore Park. Tickets are restricted to Mardi Gras members. Gay and lesbian international visitors wishing to attend the parties should contact the Mardi Gras office well in advance (☎ 9557 4332) – tickets usually sell out in January.

The free gay press includes the Sydney Star Observer and Capital Q, which can be found in shops and cafes in the inner east and west. Both papers have excellent listings of gay and lesbian organisations, services and events. The Australian Gay & Lesbian Tourism Association publishes a Tourism Services Directory listing all Australian members, including tour operators and accommodation. It's available by writing to PO Box 208, Darlinghurst, NSW 2010. Break Out Tours (☎ 9360 3616) is a helpful, gay-operated tour company offering trips to just about anywhere within Australia.

Jazz Sydney has a healthy and innovative jazz circuit. There are plenty of venues worth a swing.

The *Basement* (☎ 9251 2797, 29 Reiby Place, Circular Quay) is a good venue with a mix of local and international acts, as is the *Harbourside Brasserie* (☎ 9252 3000, Pier One, Walsh Bay).

Soup Plus (☎ 9299 7728, 383 George St, city) has live jazz at lunch and dinner time, as well as cheap food and a casual atmosphere. The *Strawberry Hills Hotel* (☎ 9698 2997), on the corner of Devonshire and Elizabeth Sts, Surry Hills, has a piano bar and jazzy duos, while at the *Tilbury Hotel* (☎ 9368 1955), on the corner of Forbes and Nicholson Sts, Woolloomooloo, there's Sunday afternoon jazz and funk.

Classical The best classical music venues are the *Concert Hall* (☎ 9250 7777, Sydney Opera House), the *Sydney Town Hall* (☎ 9265 9555) and the ABC's *Eugene Goosens Hall* (☎ 9333 1500, 700 Harris St, Ultimo). The *Sydney Conservatorium of Music* (☎ 9531 1222) is being re-vamped and will reopen in early 2001.

Musica Viva Australia (☎ 9698 1711) presents an ambitious program of Australian and international chamber music at various city venues.

Cinemas

Commercial cinemas line George St between Liverpool and Bathurst Sts. The average ticket price is $12 (students $9).

For art house and some commercial films, try independent cinemas such as the *Dendy* (☎ 9264 1577, 624 George St), in the MLC Centre in Martin Place, and another at 261 King St, Newtown, the *Palace Academy Twin* (☎ 9361 4453, 3 Oxford St, Paddington), the *Verona* (☎ 9360 6099, 17 Oxford St) and the *Chauvel Cinema* (☎ 9361 5398, Paddington Town Hall), on the corner of Oxford St and Oatley Rd. On the North Shore, try the Art Deco *Cremorne Hayden* (☎ 9908 4344, 180 Military Rd) and the *Manly Twin* (☎ 9977 0644), opposite Manly Wharf.

Places to catch independent films or cult reruns include the *Verona Cinema* and the

Movie Room (☎ 9360 7853, 112 Darlinghurst Rd), above Govinda's.

The *State Theatre*, in Market St, between Pitt and George Sts, hosts the Sydney Film Festival in June.

Theatre

The top theatre company is the Sydney Theatre Company (☎ 9250 1777), which has its own theatre at Pier Four, Hickson Rd, Walsh Bay. The similarly prestigious Sydney Dance Company and the acclaimed Bangarra Dance Theatre are also here.

The Drama Theatre and the contemporary Studio (☎ 9250 7777), at the Sydney Opera House, stage innovative performance pieces.

Mainstream theatres specialising in blockbusters and musicals include the *Capitol Theatre* (☎ 9320 9122), on the corner of George and Campbell Sts, the *Theatre Royal* (☎ 9320 9111, MLC Centre, King St), the *State Theatre* (☎ 9373 6655, 49 Market St) and the *Lyric Theatre* (☎ 9657 8500, Star City, Darling Harbour). If you like your musicals a little sweet, see what's happening at the *Footbridge Theatre* (☎ 9692 9955, Sydney University, Parramatta Rd).

There are invariably interesting productions at the *Belvoir Theatre* (☎ 9699 3444, 25 Belvoir St, Surry Hills), the *Seymour Centre* (☎ 9364 9400), on the corner of Cleveland St and City Rd, Chippendale, and the *Performance Space* (☎ 9319 5091, 199 Cleveland St, Redfern).

Comedy & Cabaret

The heart and home of Sydney comedy is the *Comedy Store* (☎ 9564 3900), on the corner of Parramatta Rd and Crystal St, Petersham. It's open Tuesday to Sunday and has a different show each night.

Best supporting role goes to the *Comedy Cellar* (☎ 9212 5882, 2 Bay St Broadway), a newish venue just north of the University of Sydney featuring a packed entertainment schedule including comedy, music and dance parties.

SPECTATOR SPORTS

Sydney is one of rugby league's world capitals. Games are played from April to

NEW SOUTH WALES

September; finals are played at the *Sydney Football Stadium*, Moore Park.

The *Sydney Cricket Ground*, Moore Park, is the venue for sparsely-attended state cricket matches, well-attended five-day Test matches and sell-out one-day World Series cricket matches. It's also the home ground of the high-flying Sydney Swans, NSW's only contribution to the Australian Football League. Aussie rules matches are played between March and September.

A spectator boat leaves the Sydney Flying Squadron at McDougall St, Milsons Point, on Saturday at 1.30 pm to follow the spectacular, honed-down 18-foot skiffs that race on the harbour between late September and April ($10).

The sporting year ends with the start of the Sydney to Hobart Yacht Race on Boxing Day. A huge fleet of spectator boats follows the racing yachts to the Heads as they set sail for the three to five day race to Tasmania.

SHOPPING

Shopping complexes in the city include the Queen Victoria Building, Piccadilly, Centrepoint, the Skygarden and Strand arcades, and Market City in Haymarket. David Jones and Grace Brothers are the biggest department stores. The hub of shopping is the Pitt St mall. For outdoor gear, head to the corner of Kent and Bathurst Sts, where Paddy Pallin is one of several outdoor suppliers in the area. Late-night shopping is on Thursday night, when most stores stay open until 9 pm.

Aboriginal Art

The Aboriginal & Tribal Art Centre (☎ 9247 9625) at Level One, 117 George St, the Rocks, has paintings and crafts. Prices range from $5 to $5000.

Desart (☎ 9388 7684), the resource and advocacy organisation representing 22 owner-operated Aboriginal art centres of central Australia, has a gallery at 4 Towns Road, Vaucluse. The Boomali Aboriginal Artists Cooperative (☎ 9698 2047) at 191 Parramatta Rd, Annandale, is an interesting Aboriginal-run gallery, showroom and resource centre.

Australiana

There are plenty of shops selling Australian arts, crafts and souvenirs in the Rocks and in Darling Harbour's Harbourside complex, but the city's markets (see the next entry) have the best bargains.

The Rocks Centre, on Playfair St in the Rocks, has one of the best selections of goods aimed at tourists. The Australian Conservation Foundation shop, 33 George St, caters for those shopping beyond cliches, and your bucks go to good causes. For bush gear, try RM Williams, 389 George St, or Thomas Cook, 790 George St.

Several leading Australian designers have shops on the upper floors of the Strand Arcade.

The Australian Wine Centre, in Goldfields House, 1 Alfred St, stocks wine from every Australian wine-growing region and can send wine overseas.

Markets

Sydney has lots of weekend 'flea' markets. The most interesting is the trendy Paddington Village Bazaar, held in the grounds of the church on the corner of Oxford and Newcombe Sts on Saturday.

The weekend Rocks Market, in George St in the Rocks, is more touristy but colourful nonetheless. The arty-farty Sunday Tarpeian Market is at a fantastic site, on the concourse of the Sydney Opera House.

There are bric-a-brac markets on Saturday at Glebe Public School, Glebe Point Rd, Glebe; St Andrews Church, Darling St, Balmain; and Bondi Public School, Campbell Parade, Bondi Beach. On Sunday there's one at the Fitzroy Gardens, Kings Cross.

The biggest innercity market is Paddy's Market (Friday to Sunday), in Market City. It's a smorgasbord of tack in a gloomy dungeon, but it's an interesting place to wander around if you're not allergic to fake Calvin Klein T-shirts and fluffy slippers.

GETTING THERE & AWAY

Air

Sydney's Kingsford-Smith airport is Australia's busiest and the most inadequate for handling demand, so expect delays. It's only 10km south of the city centre making access easy, but this also means that flights cease between 11 pm and 5 am due to noise regulations.

You can fly into Sydney from all the usual international points and from all over Australia. Both Qantas (☎ 13 1313) and Ansett (☎ 13 1300) have frequent flights to other capital cities and major airports – for standard one-way fares see the Australian Air Fares chart in the Getting Around chapter. Smaller airlines, linked to the major ones, fly within NSW.

Cheap international flights are advertised in the Saturday *Sydney Morning Herald*.

Bus

The private bus operators are competitive and service is efficient. Make sure you shop around for discounts – for example, Pioneer Motor Service (☎ 9281 2233) gives backpackers a 20% concession on services to Brisbane. Always compare private operator prices to the government's Countrylink network of trains and buses (☎ 13 2232), which has discounts of up to 40% on economy fares.

The Sydney coach terminal (☎ 9281 9366) deals with all the companies and can advise you on the best prices. It's on the corner of Pitt St and Eddy Ave, outside Central station. Coach operators have offices either in the terminal or nearby. Most buses stop in the suburbs on the way in and out of cities.

Brisbane It generally takes about 16 hours to reach Brisbane either along the coastal Pacific Hwy or inland via the New England Hwy. The standard fare is around $70. It's best to book in advance. Companies running the Pacific Hwy route include Greyhound Pioneer (☎ 13 2030) and McCafferty's (☎ 13 1499).

Some typical fares from Sydney to towns along the way are Port Macquarie $50 (seven hours), Coffs Harbour $57 (nine hours), Byron Bay $69 (12 hours) and Surfers Paradise $71 (15 hours). Not all buses stop in all main towns en route.

The backpacker-friendly Oz Experience (☎ 9368 1766) offers hop-on/hop-off four-day trips between Sydney and Brisbane for

$190. The Pioneering Spirit (☎ 1800 672 422) runs from Sydney to Brisbane ($215) via Byron Bay ($195), taking a leisurely three days. Dinner, breakfast and accommodation are included.

Ando's Outback Adventure (☎ 9559 2901) travels between Sydney and Byron Bay via a five day outback detour for $425 ($399 for backpacker card holders). Now run by Ando's nephew, this tour has received good feedback.

Canberra Murrays (☎ 13 2251) has three daily express buses to Canberra taking under four hours for $28. Greyhound Pioneer runs almost hourly to Canberra and also charges $28.

Melbourne It's a 12 to 13 hour journey to Melbourne if you travel via the Hume Hwy. McCafferty's and Firefly Express (☎ 9211 1644) charge $50, while most other companies charge around $60. Greyhound Pioneer runs along the Hume and the prettier, but much longer (up to 18 hours), coastal Princes Hwy for $60.

If that all sounds too rushed, the Wayward Bus (☎ 1800 882 823) offers flexible back-road packages and string out a trip to Melbourne over three days ($140).

Adelaide The cheapest way to get to Adelaide is with Firefly Express' $85 bus running Sydney-Melbourne-Adelaide, and you can break your journey in Melbourne. Countrylink's daily Speedlink service is the fastest option (☎ 13 2242). It takes just under 20 hours and involves catching a train to Albury, then a connecting bus to Adelaide. The fare is $103.

Elsewhere To the Snowy Mountains, Greyhound Pioneer runs to Cooma ($53) and Jindabyne ($68). The 53 hour trip to Perth costs $295. To Alice Springs it's $231 and takes 42 hours – check whether there's a wait in Adelaide.

Train

The government's Countrylink rail network is complemented by coaches. All interstate and principal regional train and bus services operate to and from Central station. Tickets must be booked in advance. Call the Central Reservation Centre (☎ 13 2232).

Three trains run daily to Canberra taking about four hours and tickets cost $42/58 in economy/1st class.

Two trains run between Sydney and Melbourne, one leaving in the morning and the other in the evening. The trip takes 10½ hours and the economy/1st class fare is $96/134; a 1st class sleeper is $229. Discounted tickets can bring the economy fare down to $59.

The nightly train to Brisbane takes about 13½ hours. Economy/1st class costs $96/134; a sleeper costs $229. There's also a daily morning train to Murwillumbah in northern NSW with connecting buses to either the Gold Coast or Brisbane (about 16 hours).

A daily Speedlink train/bus service between Sydney and Adelaide via Albury costs $130 economy and takes 20 hours. You can also travel on the twice-weekly *Indian Pacific* via Broken Hill, but this takes 26 hours. The economy fare is $162, an economy sleeper is $334 and a 1st class sleeper $480.

If you're going to Perth, one-way fares on the *Indian Pacific* are $424/888/1350 for an economy seat/economy sleeper/1st class sleeper – the journey takes about 65 hours. Sleeper fares increase significantly during September and October.

The *Ghan* to Alice Springs via Adelaide leaves Sydney weekly and costs $360/730/1095 for an economy seat/economy sleeper/1st class sleeper.

There's an extensive rail network within the state – see the NSW introductory Getting Around section for details.

Car
Rental There are Avis, Budget, Delta, Hertz and Thrifty branches, and a number of local operators, on William St. The larger companies' daily metropolitan rates are typically about $55 a day for a small car (Holden Barina), about $65 for a medium car (Toyota Corolla), or about $85 for a big car (Holden Commodore), all including insurance and unlimited kilometres. Some places require you to be over 23 years old.

There's no shortage of outfits renting older cars, which offer reasonable transport as long as your expectations are modest. Check for things like bald tyres and bad brakes before you sign, and check the fine print regarding insurance excess. Cut Price Rent-a-Car (☎ 9380 5122), 85 William St, is reputable and has adequate cars. A mid-80s sedan costs only $180 per week, if you're prepared to risk a $1000 excess.

Buying/Selling a Car or Motorcycle
Sydney is a good place for this; Parramatta Rd is lined with used car lots. There's a daily car market (☎ 9358 5000) at the Kings Cross Car Park, on the corner of Ward Ave and Elizabeth Bay Rd, which charges sellers $35 a week (the car must have a roadworthy certificate, or 'pink slip'). This place can help with paperwork and arrange third-party property insurance. Although it's a dismal spot, it's becoming something of a travellers' rendezvous. The Flemington Sunday Car Market (☎ 1900 921 122), near Flemington station, operates on Sunday and charges sellers $60. Its Web site is www.fscm.com.au.

Several dealers will sell you a car with an undertaking to buy it back at an agreed price, but make sure you read the small print and don't accept any verbal guarantees – get it in writing. Better Bikes (☎ 9718 6668), 605 Canterbury Rd, Belmore, sometimes has buy-back deals on motorcycles and can help arrange insurance.

Before you buy any vehicle, regardless of who the seller is, we strongly recommend that you have it thoroughly checked by a competent mechanic. The NRMA (☎ 13 2132) does this for members for $125; non-members $145. We've heard some real horror stories from readers who've failed to get their vehicles checked.

The Register of Encumbered Vehicles (REVS) (☎ 9600 0022) is a government organisation that can check to ensure the car you're buying is fully paid-up and owned by the seller.

CHRISTOPHER GROENHOUT

The Opera House and Sydney Harbour Bridge, Sydney

SIMON BRACKEN

Surf's up at Manly Beach, Sydney

GREG ELMS

'Girls' just wanna have fun at the Mardi Gras!

The Three Sisters, Blue Mountains, NSW

Snorkelling at Camp Cove, Sydney

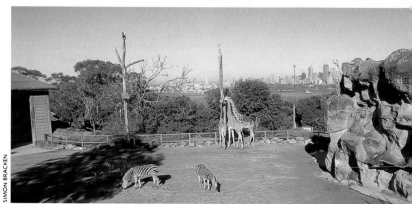

A giraffe's view of Sydney from Taronga Zoo

For more on buying and selling cars see that section in the Getting Around chapter.

GETTING AROUND

Securing the Olympics prompted Sydney to undertake much-needed transport improvements including new roads and expanded rail and ferry lines. For information on buses, ferries and trains, phone ☎ 13 1500 between 6 am and 10 pm daily.

To/From the Airport

Sydney airport is 10km south of the city centre. The international and domestic terminals are a 4km bus trip apart on either side of the runway.

The Airport Express is a special STA service operating every 8 minutes from Central station, between 6 am and 11 pm. Bus No 300 goes to the airport via Circular Quay and No 350 goes via Kings Cross. Airport Express buses have their own stops, extra-large luggage racks, and are painted green and yellow. The one-way fare is $6.50 and a return ticket, valid for two months, is $11. It's about 15 minutes from the airport to Central station; add another 15 minutes to reach Circular Quay or Kings Cross.

Kingsford Smith Transport (KST) (☎ 9667 0663) runs a door-to-door service between the airport and places to stay (including hostels) in the city, Kings Cross, Darling Harbour and Glebe. The fare is $6. When heading to the airport, book to be picked up at least three hours before you want to be collected. The Sydney Airporter (☎ 9667 3800) runs a similar service to and from the airport.

There are car rental agencies in the terminals. A taxi from the airport to Circular Quay should cost between $20 and $25. The new Eastern Distributor toll road, to be completed in June 2000, should reduce travelling time between the airport and the city (and will cost $3 for northbound traffic).

A rail link between the city and the airport is scheduled to be completed by May 2000.

Bus

Sydney's bus network extends to most suburbs. Fares depend upon the number of 'sec-tions' you pass through, so consult the driver. As a rough guide, short jaunts cost $1.30, and most other fares in the inner suburbs are $2.50. Regular buses run between 5 am and midnight, when Nightrider buses take over.

The major starting points for bus routes are Circular Quay, Argyle St in Millers Point, Wynyard Park and the Queen Victoria Building on York St, and Railway Square. Most buses head out of the city on George or Castlereagh Sts, and take George or Elizabeth Sts coming in. Pay the driver as you enter, or dunk your prepaid ticket in the ticket machines by the door.

The bus information kiosk on the corner of Alfred and Pitt Sts at Circular Quay, is open daily. There are other information offices on Carrington St and in the Queen Victoria Building on York St.

Special Bus Services The Sydney Explorer, a red STA tourist bus, navigates the inner city on a route designed to pass most central attractions. A bus departs from Circular Quay every 20 minutes between 8.40 am and 5.25 pm daily, but you can board at any of the 22 clearly marked, red bus stops on the route. Tickets are sold on board the bus and at STA offices, and entitle you to get on and off the bus as often as you like. They cost $28, so it's really only worthwhile if you don't want the hassle of catching ordinary buses.

The Bondi & Bay Explorer operates along similar lines, running a much larger circuit from Circular Quay to Kings Cross, Double Bay, Rose Bay, Vaucluse, Watsons Bay, the Gap, Bondi Beach and Coogee, returning to the city along Oxford St. Just riding around the circuit takes two hours, so if you want to get off at many of the 18 places of interest along the way you'll need to start early. The buses depart half-hourly from Circular Quay daily between 9.15 am and 4.15 pm; tickets cost $28.

Nightrider buses provide an hourly service after regular buses and trains stop running. They operate from Town Hall station and service suburban train stations. Return and weekly train tickets are accepted; otherwise most trips cost $3.60.

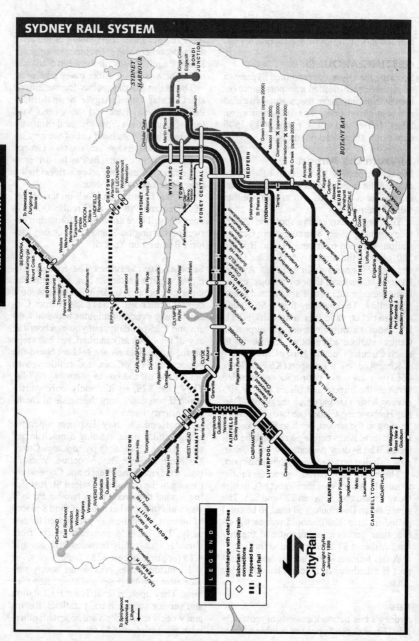

SYDNEY RAIL SYSTEM

NEW SOUTH WALES

LEGEND

Interchange with other lines

Suburban / Intercity train connections

Proposed line

Light Rail

CityRail

© Copyright CityRail
January 1999

Train

Sydney has a vast suburban rail network and frequent services, making trains much quicker than buses. The underground City Circle comprises seven city-centre stations. Lines radiate from the City Circle, but the rail network does not extend to the northern and southern beaches, Balmain or Glebe. All suburban trains stop at Central station, and usually one or more of the other City Circle stations as well (a ticket to the City will take you to any station on the City Circle). Trains run from around 5 am to midnight.

After 9 am on weekdays and at any time on weekends, you can buy an off-peak return ticket for not much more than a standard one-way fare. A trip anywhere on the City Circle or to a nearby suburb such as Kings Cross is $1.60 single or $2 return (off-peak), or $3.20 return (peak). A City Hopper costs $5.40 (off-peak) and gives you a day of unlimited rides in the central area after 9 am on weekdays and at any time on weekends; you can go north as far as North Sydney, south as far as Central and east as far as Kings Cross.

Staffed ticket booths are supplemented by automatic ticket machines at busy stations. If you have to change trains, it's cheaper to buy a ticket to your ultimate destination – but don't leave an intermediary station en route to your destination or your ticket will be invalid.

For rail information, ask at any station or drop by the rail information booth near the ferry ticket office at Circular Quay.

Light Rail

Sydney's snazzy, new 24-hour light rail (☎ 9660 5288) glides from Central station, through Haymarket, behind Darling Harbour, under the casino and past the Fish Markets to Wentworth Park. It's for the tourists at the moment, although the proposed extension to Lilyfield should make it a little more useful. A single ride costs $2 to $3, depending on distance; a day pass is $6.

Monorail

The monorail (☎ 9552 2288) circles Darling Harbour and the south-western quarter of the city centre, travelling at 1st-floor level. It operates between 7 am (8 am Sunday) and 10 pm (until midnight Thursday to Saturday). The entire loop takes 15 minutes, with a train roughly every three or four minutes. A single loop or a portion of a loop costs $3; a day pass costs $6. Unless you're heading for Darling Harbour, consider it a novelty rather than a mode of transport.

Ferry

Sydney's ferries are among the most enjoyable and sensible ways of getting around. Many people use ferries to commute so there are frequent connecting bus services. Some ferries operate between 6 am and midnight, although ferries servicing tourist attractions operate much shorter hours. Popular places accessible by ferry include Darling Harbour, Balmain, Hunters Hill and Parramatta to the west; McMahons Point, Kirribilli, Neutral Bay, Cremorne, Mosman, Taronga Zoo and Manly on the North Shore; and Double Bay, Rose Bay and Watsons Bay in the eastern suburbs.

There are four types of ferry: the regular STA ferries; fast, modern JetCats that go to Manly ($5.80); RiverCats that traverse the Parramatta River to Parramatta ($5.60); and small private operators. All ferries depart from Circular Quay. There's a ferry information office next to the ticket booths on the concourse behind Wharf 4 (☎ 9207 3166). Most regular harbour ferries cost $3.70, although the longer trip to Manly costs $4.60.

Privately operated ferries include the Rocket Express (☎ 9264 7377), which shuttles from Harbourmaster's Steps at Circular Quay West to the Casino and Darling Harbour every 20 minutes for $3.25; Hegarty's Ferries (☎ 9206 1167), which runs during the day from Wharf 6 at Circular Quay to wharves directly across the harbour at Milsons Point, Lavender Bay, McMahons Point, and Kirribilli ($2.45); and Doyles Ferries (☎ 9337 2007), which runs to Watsons Bay from Commissioners Steps between 11.30 am and 3 pm weekdays for $8.

NEW SOUTH WALES

NEW SOUTH WALES

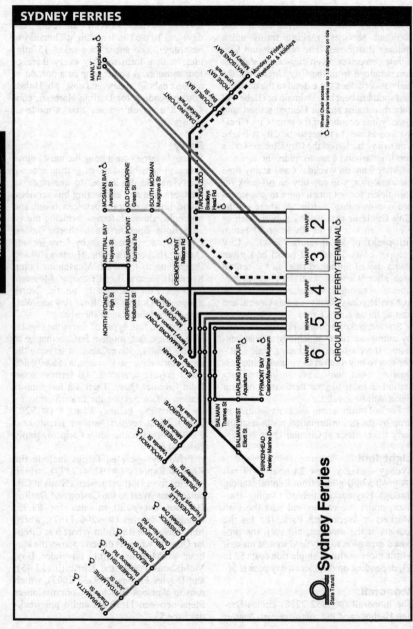

SYDNEY FERRIES

MANLY
The Esplanade ♿

WATSONS BAY
Military Rd
Vaucluse Bay
June Park
Rose Bay
ROSE BAY

DOUBLE BAY
Bay St

Monday to Friday
Weekends & Holidays

♿ Wheel Chair access
Ramp grade varies up to 1:8 depending on tide

DARLING POINT
McKell Park

MOSMAN BAY
Avenue St
OLD CREMORNE
Green St
SOUTH MOSMAN
Musgrave St

TARONGA ZOO
Bradleys
Head Rd

WHARF 2

WHARF 3

WHARF 4

NEUTRAL BAY
Hayes St
KURRABA POINT
Kurraba Rd

CREMORNE POINT
Milsons Rd

NORTH SYDNEY
High St
KIRRIBILLI
Holbrook St

MCMAHONS POINT
Henry Lawson Ave
MILSONS POINT
Alfred St South

WHARF 5

WHARF 6

CIRCULAR QUAY FERRY TERMINAL ♿

EAST BALMAIN
Darling St

BALMAIN
Thames St

DARLING HARBOUR
Aquarium ♿

PYRMONT BAY
Casino/Maritime Museum ♿

GREENWICH
Mitchell St
BIRCHGROVE
Louisa Rd

WOOLWICH
Valentia St

BALMAIN WEST
Elliott St

BIRKENHEAD
Hartley Marine Dve

HUNTERS HILL
Woolwich Rd

CHISWICK
Bortfield Dve
ABBOTSFORD
Great North Rd
MEADOWBANK
Bowden St
HOMEBUSH BAY
Bennelong Rd
RYDALMERE
John St
PARRAMATTA
Charles St

♿ Sydney Ferries
State Transit

Fare Deals

The SydneyPass offers three, five or seven days unlimited travel over a seven day period on all STA buses and ferries, and the red TravelPass zone (inner suburbs) of the rail network. The passes cover the Airport Express, the Explorers, the JetCats, River-Cats and three STA-operated harbour cruises. They cost $85 (three days), $115 (five days) and $135 (seven days). Passes are available from STA offices, train stations, and from Airport Express and Explorer bus drivers.

TravelPasses are designed for commuters and offer cheap weekly travel. There are various colour-coded grades offering combinations of distance and service. The Green TravelPass is valid for extensive train and bus travel and all ferries, except the Manly JetCat during the day; it costs $28 for a week. TravelPasses are sold at train stations, STA offices and major newsagents.

If you're just catching buses, get a Travel-Ten ticket which gives a sizeable discount on 10 bus trips. There are various colour codes for distances so check which is the most appropriate for your travel patterns. A red MetroTen (available from newsagents and STA offices) costs $17.60 and can be used to reach most places mentioned in this section.

Ferry Ten tickets are similar and cost from $19 for 10 inner-harbour (ie short) ferry trips, or $30 including the Manly ferry. They can be purchased at the Circular Quay ferry ticket office.

Several transport-plus-entry tickets are available, which work out cheaper than catching a ferry and paying entry separately. They include the ZooPass, AquariumPass and OceanPass (to Manly's Oceanworld aquarium).

Taxi

There are heaps of taxis in Sydney. The four big taxi companies offer a reliable service: Legion (☎ 13 1451), Premier Cabs (☎ 13 1017), RSL Taxis (☎ 13 1581) and Taxis Combined (☎ 8332 8888).

Water taxis are pricey but are a fun way of getting around the harbour. Companies include Taxis Afloat (☎ 9955 3222), Harbour Taxi Boats (☎ 9555 1155) and the Beach Hopper (☎ 0412 400 990), which will drop you off at any harbour beach within Sydney Harbour.

Bicycle

Bicycle NSW (☎ 9283 5200), 209 Castlereagh St, Sydney 2000, publishes a handy book *Cycling Around Sydney* ($10), which details routes and cycle paths.

Bicycle Hire Most cycle hire shops require a hefty deposit (up to $500) or a credit card.

Inner City Cycles (☎ 9660 6605), 31 Glebe Point Rd, Glebe, rents quality mountain bikes for $30 a day, $50 a weekend or $80 a week. Woolys Wheels (☎ 9331 2671), 82 Oxford St, Paddington, across from the Victoria Barracks, rents hybrid bikes for $30 a day (24 hours). Manly Cycle Centre (☎ 9977 1189), 36 Pittwater Rd, Manly, charges $10 an hour ($5 for each subsequent hour), $25 a day or $60 a week.

Around Sydney

There are superb national parks to the north and south of Sydney and historic small towns to the west, which were established in the early days of European settlement but survive today as pockets engulfed by urban sprawl.

BOTANY BAY

It's a common misconception that Sydney is built around Botany Bay. Sydney Harbour is actually Port Jackson and Botany Bay is 10 to 15km south on the fringe of the city. This area is a major industrial centre so don't expect too many unspoilt vistas. Despite this, the bay has pretty stretches and holds a special place in Australian history. This was Captain Cook's first landing point in Australia, and it was named by Joseph Banks, the expedition's naturalist, for the many botanical specimens he found here.

The **Botany Bay National Park** encompasses both headlands of the bay. At Kurnell, on the southern headland, Cook's landing place is marked by monuments. The 436 hectare park has bushland and coastal walking tracks, picnic areas and an 8km cycle track. The Discovery Centre (☎ 9668 9111) in the park describes the impact of European arrival, and has information on the surrounding wetlands. It's open on weekdays from 11 am to 3 pm, and to 4.30 pm on weekends. The park is open daily from 6.30 am to 7 pm. Entry costs $5 per car but pedestrians are not charged so you may as well park outside – the centre, monuments and most walking tracks are close to the entrance. From Cronulla train station (10km away), catch Kurnell Bus Co (☎ 9524 8977) bus No 987 ($5.30 return).

La Perouse, on the northern headland, is named after the French explorer who arrived in 1788, just six days after the arrival of the First Fleet. He gave the Poms a good scare because they weren't expecting the French to turn up quite so soon. Although the First Fleet soon sailed to Sydney Harbour, La Perouse camped at Botany Bay for six weeks before sailing off into the Pacific and disappearing. On the headland is a monument built in 1825 by the French explorer Bougainville in honour of La Perouse. The fabulous museum (☎ 9311 3379), in the old cable station, charts the history of La Perouse's fateful expedition; there's also an Aboriginal gallery with exhibits on indigenous history. It's open Tuesday to Sunday from 10 am to 4 pm and every day during school holidays. Entry costs $5.

Just off shore is **Bare Island**, a decaying concrete fort built in 1885 to discourage a feared Russian invasion. Entry is by guided tour only (☎ 9311 3379) which costs $7 ($5 concession).

There's no entry fee to this northern segment of the national park. Catch bus No 394 from Circular Quay or 393 from Railway Square.

ROYAL NATIONAL PARK

This coastal park of dramatic cliffs, secluded beaches, scrub and lush rainforest is the oldest gazetted national park in the world. It begins at Port Hacking, just 30km south of Sydney, and stretches 20km to the south. A road runs through the park with detours to the small township of Bundeena on

Port Hacking, to the beautiful beach at Wattamolla, and to windswept Garie Beach. The spectacular two day, 26km coastal walking trail running the length of the park is highly recommended. Garie, Era and Burning Palms are popular surfing spots; swimming or surfing at Marley is dangerous (Little Marley is safe). A walking and cycling trail follows the Port Hacking River south from Audley, and other walking tracks pass tranquil, freshwater swimming holes. You can swim in Kangaroo Creek but not the Port Hacking River. To do the coastal walks you'll need a permit, but they're granted for free when you phone the visitors centre.

There's a visitors centre (☎ 9542 0648) at the top of the hill at the park's main entrance, off the Princes Hwy. It's open daily from 8.30 am to 4.30 pm (closed 1 pm to 2 pm). You can hire rowboats and canoes at the Audley Boat Shed (☎ 9545 4967) for $12 an hour or $24 a day. Bikes cost $10 an hour, $24 a day.

Entry to the park costs $9 per car, but is free for pedestrians and cyclists. The road through the park and the offshoot to Bundeena are always open, but the detours to the beaches are closed at sunset.

Places to Stay

The only camp site accessible by car is at Bonnie Vale, near Bundeena, where sites cost from $10 for two people. Free bush camping is allowed in several other areas, but permits must be obtained beforehand from the visitors centre. Fires are not permitted except in designated picnic areas. If you camp at Era Beach in the south of the park, beware of deer breaking into your tent and foraging for food. The basic (no electricity or phone) and secluded *Garie Beach YHA* has beds for YHA members only for $7. You need to book and collect a key from the YHA Travel Centre (☎ 9261 1111) in Sydney.

The best place to stay on the edge of the park is the old *Imperial Hotel* (☎ 4267 1177, Clifton), perched dramatically on the cliff edge on the coast road from Wollongong. Bunkbeds in small dorms cost $25, double

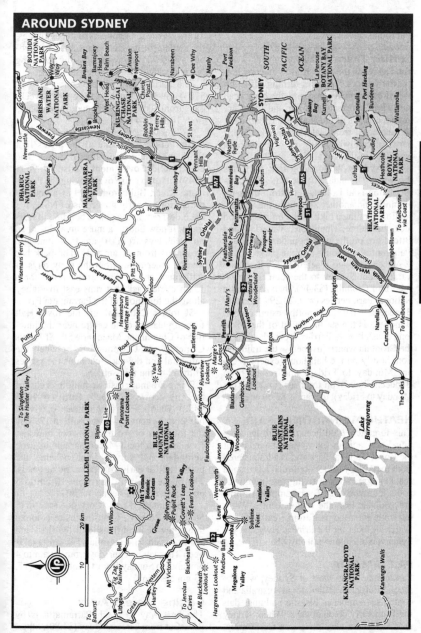

rooms cost $75 including breakfast, and several rooms have views.

Getting There & Away

You can reach the park from Sydney by taking the Princes Hwy and turning off south of Loftus. From Wollongong, the coast road north is a spectacular drive and there are fantastic views of the Illawarra Escarpment and the coast from Bald Hill Lookout, just north of Stanwell Park, on the southern boundary of the Royal National Park.

The Sydney-Wollongong railway forms the western boundary of the park. The closest station is at Loftus, 4km from the park entrance and another 2km from the visitors centre. Bringing a bike on the train is a good idea. Engadine, Heathcote, Waterfall and Otford are on the park boundary and have walking trails leading into the park.

A scenic way to reach the park is to take a train from Sydney to the southern beach suburb of Cronulla ($3.40), then a Cronulla National Park Ferries (☎ 9523 2990) boat to Bundeena in the park's north-eastern corner. Bundeena is the starting point of the 26km long coastal walk. Ferries depart daily from the Cronulla wharf, just below the train station, hourly on the half-hour (except 12.30 pm Monday to Friday) and return from Bundeena hourly on the hour (except 1 pm Monday to Friday); the fare is $2.60 one way.

HEATHCOTE NATIONAL PARK

This forgotten 2000 hectare heath land national park adjoins the western boundary of the Royal National Park and is administered from the Audley visitors centre. It has rugged scenery, great bushwalking and plenty of pools for swimming. Bush camping permits are available from the visitors centre. Walking trails enter the park from Heathcote and Waterfall, both on the Princes Hwy and the Sydney-Wollongong railway line.

PARRAMATTA

Parramatta, 24km west of Sydney, was the second European settlement in Australia and contains a number of historic buildings dating from early colonial days. When Sydney proved to be a very poor area for farming, Parramatta was selected in 1788 for the first farm settlement. Despite its rural beginnings, the settlement has been consumed by Sydney's westward sprawl and is now a thriving but undistinguished commercial centre.

The Parramatta visitors centre (☎ 9630 3703) is at 346 Church St. It's open on weekdays from 10 am to 5 pm, and on weekends from 10 am to 4 pm.

On the western edge of the city, **Parramatta Park** was the site of the area's first farm and contains a number of relics. The elegant **Old Government House** (☎ 9635 8149) sits atop a rise overlooking the Parramatta River. Built from 1799 as a country retreat for the early governors of NSW, it's the oldest remaining public building in Australia. It now houses a museum and is open on weekdays from 10 am to 4 pm, and weekends from 11 am ($5). The park has several other relics from the early days of settlement and is the starting point for a 15km cycle track that runs east to Putney along the foreshore of the Parramatta River.

St John's Cathedral and the **Town Hall** form a pleasant civic centre near the junction of Church and Macquarie Sts. St John's Cemetery, on O'Connell St between the cathedral and the park, contains the graves of many of the first settlers.

There are more historic buildings east of the city centre. **Elizabeth Farm** (☎ 9635 9488), 70 Alice St, is the oldest surviving home in the country. It was built in 1793 by the founders of Australia's wool industry, John and Elizabeth Macarthur, and its deep verandah and simple lines became the prototype for early Australian homesteads. The house is open daily from 10 am to 5 pm; entry is $6 ($3 concession).

Experiment Farm Cottage (☎ 9635 5655), 9 Ruse St, is an exquisite colonial bungalow built on the site of the first land grant issued in Australia. The cottage is open Tuesday to Thursday from 10 am to 4 pm, and on Sunday from 11 am to 4 pm ($5, $3 concession).

Getting There & Away

The best way to reach Parramatta is by RiverCat from Circular Quay ($4.80), otherwise catch a train from Central station ($2.80). By car, exit the city via Parramatta Rd and detour onto the Western Motorway tollway ($1.50) at Strathfield.

AROUND PARRAMATTA

There are two mainstream tourist attractions halfway between Parramatta and Penrith, further west. The **Featherdale Wildlife Park**, 217 Kildare Rd, Doonside, has plenty of native fauna. Featherdale is open daily from 9 am to 5 pm and costs $12. Take a train to Blacktown and bus No 725 from there. **Australia's Wonderland**, Wallgrove Rd, Eastern Creek, is a large amusement park complex with a wildlife park. It's open daily (admission $37; wildlife park only $13). Shuttle buses meet trains at Rooty Hill on weekends.

PENRITH

Penrith, on the serene Nepean River, is at the base of the forested foothills of the Blue Mountains. Despite being 50km west of the city centre, it's virtually an outer suburb of Sydney. The Penrith Tourist Office (☎ 4732 7671) is in the car park of the huge Panthers World of Entertainment complex on Mulgoa Rd. It's open daily from 9 am to 4.30 pm.

Cables Waterski Park (☎ 4732 1044), next to Panthers, offers cable-towed skiing ($25 for three hours), waterslides and pools. If you like water, but not necessarily dipping, you can take a cruise through the **Nepean Gorge** on the *Nepean Belle* paddle-steamer (☎ 4733 1274). There are lunch cruises ($28), dinner cruises (from $38) and Devonshire tea cruises ($16). There are fine views of the Nepean Gorge from the **Rock Lookout**, 5km west of the town of Mulgoa. Mulgoa is 10km south of Penrith on Mulgoa Rd. There's limited public access to the new regatta centre north of Penrith, purpose built for Olympic rowing, canoeing and rafting.

You can reach Penrith by train from Central station ($5.40) or by driving west along Parramatta Rd and taking the Western Motorway tollway at Strathfield ($1.50).

CAMDEN AREA

Camden is promoted as the 'birthplace of the nation's wealth' because it was here that John and Elizabeth Macarthur conducted the sheep-breeding experiments that laid the foundation for Australia's wool industry. Camden is on the urban fringe, 50km southwest of the city centre via the Hume Hwy. The Camden visitors centre (☎ 4658 1370), on Camden Valley Way, has free walking-tour leaflets.

The surrounding countryside has attractions aimed primarily at families and coach tourists, including the **Gledswood** historic homestead at nearby Narellan and the **Australiana Park** tourist complex next door.

The 400 hectare **Mount Annan Botanic Garden** is the native plant garden of Sydney's Royal Botanic Gardens and is midway between Camden and Campbelltown, to the east. It's open daily ($5 per car, $2 for pedestrians). Take a train to Campbelltown station ($4.60) and a Busways bus, Nos 894/5/6, from there.

South of Camden is the small town of **Picton**. The 1839 *George IV Inn* (☎ 4677 1415, 180 Argyle St) is one of the nicest places to stay around Sydney if you need to recharge your batteries. Basic singles/doubles/triples built around a courtyard cost $25/38/45. In nearby Thirlmere, the **Rail Transport Museum** (☎ 4681 8001) has a huge collection of steam trains. It's open daily ($8), and there are steam train rides on Sunday.

KU-RING-GAI CHASE NATIONAL PARK

This 15,000 hectare national park, 24km north of the city centre, borders the southern edge of Broken Bay and the western shore of Pittwater. It has that classic Sydney mixture of sandstone, bushland and water vistas, plus walking tracks, horse riding trails, picnic areas, Aboriginal rock engravings and spectacular views of Broken Bay, particularly from West Head at the park's north-eastern tip. There are several roads through the park and four entrances. Entry is $9 per car.

The Kalkari visitors centre (☎ 9457 9853) is on Ku-ring-gai Chase Rd, about 4km into the park from the Mt Colah entrance. It's open daily from 9 am to 5 pm. The road descends from the visitors centre to the picnic area at Bobbin Head on Cowan Creek.

NEW SOUTH WALES

Halvorsen (☎ 9457 9011) rents rowboats for $12 for the first hour and $4 for subsequent hours; motor boats that seat eight cost $43 for the first hour and $7 for subsequent hours. There are also boats for hire at the Akuna Bay marina on Coal & Candle Creek.

Recommended walks include the America Bay Trail and the Gibberagong and Sphinx tracks. The best places to see Aboriginal engravings are on the Basin Trail and the Garigal Aboriginal Heritage Walk at West Head. There's a mangrove boardwalk at Bobbin Head. It's unwise to swim in Broken Bay because of sharks, but there are netted swimming areas at Illawong Bay and the Basin.

Places to Stay

Camping is allowed at the *Basin* (☎ 9972 7378), on the western side of Pittwater. It's a 2.5km walk from the West Head road or a ferry ride from Palm Beach. It costs $10 for two people; book in advance and pay at the site. There is safe swimming in the lagoon at the Basin, and basic supplies are brought over by ferry from Palm Beach.

The *Pittwater YHA* (☎ 9999 2196) is on the shore of Pittwater, a couple of kilometres south of the Basin. It's noted for its idyllic setting and friendly wildlife. Dorms cost $16, and twins $20 per person. Nonmembers pay $3 more. Canoes and sailboats are available. Book in advance and bring food.

Getting There & Away

There are four road entrances to the park: Mt Colah, on the Pacific Hwy; Turramurra, in the south-west; and Terrey Hills and Church Point, in the south-east. Shorelink Buses (☎ 9457 8888) bus No 577 runs every 30 minutes from Turramurra station to the park entrance ($2.20) on weekdays; one bus enters the park as far as Bobbin Head. The schedule changes on weekends with fewer buses going to the entrance but more to Bobbin Head.

The Palm Beach Ferry Service (☎ 9918 2747) runs to the Basin hourly (except 12 noon) from 9 am to 5 pm for $7 one way. It also departs Palm Beach daily at 11 am for Bobbin Head via Patonga, returning at 3.30 pm. The one way fare is $13.

To reach the Pittwater YHA, take a ferry (☎ 9999 3492) from Church Point to Halls Wharf ($6 return). The hostel is a short walk from here. Bus No 156 runs from Manly to Church Point. From the city centre, bus No E86 is a direct peak-hour service, or catch bus No L88, L90 or 190 from Wynyard Park as far as Warringah Mall and transfer to No 156 from there.

HAWKESBURY RIVER

The mighty Hawkesbury River enters the sea 30km north of Sydney at Broken Bay. It's dotted with coves, beaches and picnic spots, making it one of Australia's most attractive rivers. Before reaching the ocean, the river expands into bays and inlets like Berowra Creek, Cowan Creek and Pittwater on the southern side, and Brisbane Water on the northern. The river flows between a succession of national parks – Murramarra and Ku-ring-gai Chase to the south; and Dharug, Brisbane Water and Bouddi to the north. Windsor (see the following section) is about 120km upstream.

An great way to get a feel for the river is to catch the *Riverboat Postman* (☎ 9985 7566) mail boat. It does a 40km round trip every weekday, running upstream as far as Marlow, near Spencer. It departs from Brooklyn at 9.30 am and returns at 1.15 pm. A shorter afternoon run on Wednesday departs at 1.30 and returns at 4 pm. It costs $28 ($22 concession). The 8.16 am train from Sydney's Central station ($4.60) will get you to Brooklyn's Hawkesbury River station in time to join the morning boat.

You can hire houseboats in Brooklyn, Berowra Waters and Bobbin Head. These aren't cheap but renting midweek during the low season is affordable for a group. Halvorsen (☎ 9457 9011), at Bobbin Head, has four-berth cabin cruisers for $450 for three days during the high season. No experience is necessary.

The settlements along the river have their own distinct character. Life in **Brooklyn** revolves totally around boats and the river. The town is on the Sydney-Newcastle railway line, just east of the Pacific Hwy. **Berowra Waters** is a quaint community further upstream, clustered around a free 24-hour winch ferry which crosses Berowra Creek. There are a couple of cafes overlooking the water and a marina, which hires outboard boats for $50 for a half-day. Berowra Waters is 5km west of the Pacific Hwy; there's a train station at Berowra, but it's a 6km hike down to the ferry.

Wisemans Ferry is a tranquil settlement overlooking the Hawkesbury River roughly halfway between Windsor and the mouth of the river. A free 24-hour winch ferry is the only means of crossing the river here. The historic *Wisemans Ferry Inn (☎ 4566 4301)* has cramped but clean rooms from $55 a double. The *Rosevale Farm Resort (☎ 4566 4207)* has camp sites for $7 per person and on-site vans from $35. It's a couple of kilometres north of the town, on the opposite bank of the river.

The **Yengo National Park**, a rugged sandstone area covering the foothills of the Blue Mountains, stretches from Wisemans Ferry to the Hunter Valley. It's a wilderness area with no facilities and limited road access. North of the river, a scenic road leads east from Wisemans Ferry to the Central Coast, following the river before veering north through bushland and orange groves. An early convict-built road leads north from Wisemans Ferry to tiny **St Albans**. The friendly, historic *Settlers Arms Inn (☎ 4568 2111)* here dates from 1836 and has rooms from $100 a double. There's a basic camp site opposite the hotel.

It may be unwise to swim in the Hawkesbury River between Windsor and Wisemans Ferry during the summer due to blue-green algae. Call the EPA Pollution Line (☎ 9325 5555) for information.

WINDSOR

Windsor, Richmond, Wilberforce, Castlereagh and Pitt Town are the five 'Macquarie Towns' established on rich agricultural land on the upper Hawkesbury River in the early 19th century by Governor Lachlan Macquarie. You can visit them on the way to or from the Blue Mountains if you cross the range on the Bells Line of Road – an interesting alternative to the Great Western Hwy.

The main visitors centre (☎ 4588 5895) is on Richmond Rd, between Richmond and Windsor, and is open daily (but closes early on weekends). Windsor has its own tourist information centre (☎ 4577 2310), in the 1843 Daniel O'Connell Inn on Thompson Square.

Windsor has some fine old buildings, notably those around the picturesque Thompson Square on the banks of the Hawkesbury River. The Daniel O'Connell Inn also houses the **Hawkesbury Museum of Local History**, which is open daily from 10 am to 4 pm ($2.50, $1.50 concession). The **Macquarie Arms Hotel** (1815) has a nice verandah fronting the square and is reckoned to be the oldest pub in Australia, but there are a few 'oldest pubs' around. Other old buildings include the convict-built **St Matthew's Church of England**, completed in 1822 and designed, like the **courthouse**, by the convict architect Francis Greenway. Windsor River Cruises (☎ 9831 6630) plies the Hawkesbury on Sunday and Wednesday (from $15).

If you want to stay overnight in Windsor, the lovely, historic *Clifton Cottage (☎ 4587 7135, 22 Richmond Rd)* is the best value at $45/65 for a spotless, old-fashioned single/double with excellent shared facilities.

You can reach Windsor by train from Sydney's Central station ($4.60), but public transport to other Macquarie Towns (apart from Richmond) is scarce. By car, exit the city on Parramatta Rd and head north-west on the Windsor Rd from Parramatta.

AROUND WINDSOR

The next largest of the Macquarie Towns is **Richmond**, which has its share of colonial buildings and a pleasant village-green-like park. It's 6km west of Windsor, at the end of the metropolitan railway line and at the start of the Bells Line of Road across the Blue Mountains. There's a NPWS office (☎ 4588 5247) open on weekdays, at 370 Windsor Rd.

At **Hawkesbury Heritage Farm** (☎ 4575 1457) theme park you'll find Rose Cottage (1811), probably the oldest surviving timber building in the country as well as native animals. It's in Wilberforce, 6km north of Windsor, and is open daily ($10). The pretty

Ebenezer Church (1809), 5km north of Wilberforce, is the oldest church in Australia still used as a place of worship.

Wilberforce is the starting point for the Putty Rd, a 160km isolated back road that runs north to Singleton in the Hunter Valley. The **Colo River**, 15km north along this road, is a picturesque spot popular for swimming, canoeing and picnicking. At *Colo Riverside Caravan Park* (☎ 4575 5253), right on the river bank, camp sites cost from $7 per person, and on-site vans are $28 a double. Canoes can be hired for $12 an hour ($20 for two hours).

Blue Mountains

The Blue Mountains, part of the Great Dividing Range, were initially an impenetrable barrier to white expansion from Sydney. Despite many attempts to find a route through the mountains – and a bizarre belief among many convicts that China, and freedom, was just on the other side – it took 25 years before a successful crossing was made by Europeans. A road was built soon afterwards which opened the western plains to settlement.

The first whites to venture into the mountains found evidence of Aboriginal occupation but few Aboriginal people. It seems likely that European diseases had travelled from Sydney long before the explorers and wiped out most of the indigenous people. The Blue Mountains National Park has some truly fantastic scenery, excellent bushwalks and all the gorges, gum trees and cliffs you could ask for. The foothills begin 65km inland from Sydney and the mountains rise up to 1100m. The blue haze which gave the mountains their name is a result of the fine mist of oil given off by eucalypts.

For the past century, the area has been a popular getaway for Sydneysiders seeking to escape the summer heat. Despite the intensive tourist development, much of the area is so precipitous that it's still only open to bushwalkers.

Be prepared for the climatic difference between the Blue Mountains and the coast – you can swelter in Sydney but shiver in Katoomba. It usually snows sometime between June and August, when the region has a Yuletide Festival, complete with Christmas decorations and dinners.

Bushfires in 1994 burned large areas of the Grose Valley but the Blue Gum Forest escaped almost intact.

Orientation

The Great Western Hwy from Sydney follows a ridge running east-west through the Blue Mountains. Along this less-than-beautiful road, the Blue Mountains towns merge into each other – Glenbrook, Springwood, Woodford, Lawson, Wentworth Falls, Leura, Katoomba (the main accommodation centre), Medlow Bath, Blackheath, Mt Victoria and Hartley. On the western fringe of the mountains is Lithgow – see the Central West section later in this chapter.

To the south and north of the highway's ridge, the country drops away into precipitous valleys, including the Grose Valley to the north, and the Jamison Valley south of Katoomba.

The Bells Line of Road is a much more scenic and less congested alternative to the Great Western Hwy. It's the more northerly of the two crossings, beginning in Richmond (see the Around Windsor section) and running north of the Grose Valley to emerge in Lithgow, although you can cut across from Bell to join the Great Western Hwy at Mt Victoria.

Information

There are Blue Mountains information centres open daily on the highway at Glenbrook (☎ 4739 6266) and at Echo Point in Katoomba (☎ 1300 653 408). The Blue Mountains Heritage Centre (☎ 4787 8877) is a NPWS visitors centre on Govetts Leap Rd, Blackheath, about 3km off the Great Western Hwy.

There are plenty of books on the Blue Mountains. For a general introduction, try the *Blue Mountains of Australia*. Lonely Planet's *Bushwalking in Australia* includes Blue Mountains treks. Cyclists can check out Robert Sloss' *Bushwalking-Hiking-*

Cycling in the Blue Mountains. Books and maps and individual walking-track guides are sold at visitors centres.

You can hire camping gear from Mountain Designs (☎ 4782 5999), 190 Katoomba St, Katoomba.

National Parks

The **Blue Mountains National Park** protects large areas to the north and south of the Great Western Hwy. It's the most popular and accessible of the three national parks in the area, and offers great bushwalking, scenic lookouts, breathtaking waterfalls and the chance to see Aboriginal stencils. **Wollemi National Park**, north of the Bells Line of Road, is the state's largest forested wilderness area and stretches all the way to Denman in the Hunter Valley. It has limited access and the park's centre is so isolated that a new species of tree, named the Wollemi pine, was only discovered in 1994.

Kanangra-Boyd National Park is southwest of the southern section of the Blue Mountains National Park. It has bushwalking opportunities, limestone caves and grand scenery, and includes the spectacular Kanangra Walls Plateau, which is surrounded by sheer cliffs and can be reached by unsealed road from Oberon or Jenolan Caves.

Entry to these national parks is free unless you enter the Blue Mountains National Park at Bruce Rd, Glenbrook, where it costs $5 per car; walkers are not charged.

Bushwalking

The roads across the mountains offer tantalising glimpses of the majesty of the area, but the only way to really experience the Blue Mountains is on foot. There are walks lasting from a few minutes to several days. The two most popular areas are Jamison Valley, south of Katoomba, and Grose Valley, northeast of Katoomba and east of Blackheath. The area south of Glenbrook is also good.

Visit an NPWS visitors centre for information or, for shorter walks, ask at one of the tourist information centres. It's very rugged country and walkers sometimes get lost, so it's highly advisable to get reliable information, not to go alone, and to tell someone where you're going. Many Blue Mountains watercourses are polluted, so you have to sterilise water or take your own. Be prepared for rapid weather changes.

Adventure Activities

The cliffs and gorges of the Blue Mountains offer excellent abseiling, climbing and canyoning. Mountain-bike touring is also popular. See the Katoomba Activities section for details.

Organised Tours

Wonderbus (☎ 9247 5151) runs backpacker-friendly day tours to the Blue Mountains for $65. Depending on seating availability, it's possible to arrange a one-night stopover in Katoomba and catch the tour back to Sydney the next day. Wildframe (☎ 9314 0658) runs reportedly good day tours with an ecological slant ($55). Book at the YHA Travel Centre (☎ 9261 1111) in Sydney.

Places to Stay

Accommodation ranges from camping grounds and hostels to guesthouses and luxury hotels. Katoomba is the main centre. Prices are fairly stable throughout the year, but most places charge more on weekends. Prices listed in the following sections are summer (peak) rates. If you intend to camp in the national parks, check with the NPWS first.

Getting There & Away

Katoomba is 109km from Sydney's city centre, but it's still almost a satellite suburb. Trains run approximately hourly from Central station. The trip takes two hours ($9.40 single), and there are stops at plenty of Blue Mountains townships on the way.

By car, leave the city via Parramatta Rd and detour onto the Western Motorway tollway ($1.50) at Strathfield. The motorway becomes the Great Western Hwy west of Penrith.

To reach the Bells Line of Rd, leave the city on Parramatta Rd and from Parramatta head north-west on the Windsor Rd to

Windsor. The Richmond Rd from Windsor becomes the Bells Line of Rd west of Richmond.

Getting Around

Mountainlink (☎ 4782 3333) runs between Katoomba, Medlow Bath, Blackheath and (infrequently) Mt Victoria, with some services running down Hat Hill Rd and Govetts Leap Rd, which lead respectively to Perrys Lookdown and Govetts Leap. The buses take you to within about 1km of Govetts Leap, but for Perrys Lookdown you have to walk a further 6km. Services are less frequent on weekends. In Katoomba, the bus leaves from the top of Katoomba St, opposite the Carrington Hotel.

The Blue Mountains Bus Company (☎ 4782 4213) runs between Katoomba, Leura, Wentworth Falls, and east as far as Woodford, and to the scenic railway and skyway. There's roughly one service an hour from Katoomba train station.

There are train stations in most Blue Mountains towns along the Great Western Hwy. Trains run roughly hourly between stations east of Katoomba and roughly two-hourly between stations to the west.

Thrifty (☎ 4784 2888), 80 Megalong St, Leura, rents cars from about $60 a day.

GLENBROOK TO KATOOMBA

From Marge's and Elizabeth's lookouts, just north of Glenbrook, there are good views east to Sydney. The section of the Blue Mountains National Park, south of Glenbrook, contains **Red Hand Cave**, an old Aboriginal shelter with hand stencils on the walls. It's an easy 7km return walk, south-west of the NPWS visitors centre.

The artist and author Norman Lindsay lived in **Springwood** from 1912 until he died in 1969. His home, at 14 Norman Lindsay Crescent (☎ 4751 1067), is now a gallery and museum, with exhibits of his paintings, cartoons, illustrations and sculptures. It's open daily from 10 am to 4 pm ($6, $2 concession).

Just south of the town of **Wentworth Falls**, there are great views of the Jamison Valley. You can see the spectacular 300m

Wentworth Falls from Falls Reserve, which is the starting point for a network of walking tracks.

Leura is a quaint tree-lined town full of country stores and cafes. Leuralla is an historic Art Deco mansion which houses a toy and model railway museum ($6). Sublime Point, south of Leura, is a great clifftop lookout. Nearby, Gordon Falls Reserve is a popular picnic spot, and from here you can take the clifftop path or Cliff Drive 4km west past Leura Cascades to Katoomba's Echo Point.

Places to Stay & Eat

There are NPWS *camping grounds* accessible by car at Euroka Clearing near Glenbrook, Murphys Glen near Woodford, and Ingar near Wentworth Falls. You need a permit to camp at Euroka Clearing (from $12.50) from the NPWS office in Richmond (☎ 4588 5247 Monday to Friday). The tracks to Ingar and Murphys Glen may be closed after heavy rain.

The new *Hawkesbury Heights YHA*, built to replace the old Springwood YHA razed in the 1994 bushfires, is surrounded by bush and gorgeous scenery. It's a 'green' hostel with solar power, an 'eco-friendly' toilet, a wood stove and six twin/double rooms. For rates and bookings, phone YHA NSW in Sydney (☎ 9261 1111).

Leura Village Caravan Park (☎ 4784 1552), on the corner of the Great Western Hwy and Leura Mall, has camp sites from $18, on-site vans from $40 and cabins from $50. There is plenty of guesthouse and expensive hotel accommodation; expect to pay from around $60 per person for guesthouse B&B.

Country-style cafes lining Leura Mall serve light meals for around $8. Try *Gracie's on the Mall* (No 174). *Baker's Cafe* (No 179) has sweet and savoury pastries to die for. *Le Gobelet* (No 131) is a traditional French noshery with mains from around $20.

KATOOMBA

• postcode 2780　　　• pop 17,700

Katoomba and the adjacent centres of Wentworth Falls and Leura form the tourist centre of the Blue Mountains. Despite the number of visitors and its proximity to Sydney, Katoomba retains an uncanny, otherworldy ambience, an atmosphere accentuated by its Art Deco and Art Nouveau guesthouses and cafes, its thick mists and occasional snowfalls. An alternative, new-agey scene has also developed: there are lots of yoga classes, meditation centres and incense burners. On a quiet day you can almost hear the chakras realigning.

Steep Katoomba St is the main drag. The major scenic attraction (and where you'll find the information centre) is **Echo Point**, near the southern end of Katoomba St, about a kilometre from the shopping centre. From here are some of the best views of the Jamison Valley and the magnificent **Three Sisters** rock formation.

To the west of Echo Point, at the junction of Cliff Drive and Violet St, are the **Scenic Railway** and **Scenic Skyway** (☎ 4782 2699). The railway runs to the bottom of the Jamison Valley (one-way $3, return $5), where the popular six-hour walk to the **Ruined Castle** rock formation begins. The railway was built in the 1880s to transport coal-miners and its 45° incline is one of the steepest in the world. The Scenic Skyway is a cable car that traverses Katoomba Falls gorge 200m above the valley floor ($5 return).

If you want to experience peak thrills from the safety of a cushioned seat, The Edge-Blue Mountains Maxvision Cinema (☎ 4782 8928), 235 Great Western Hwy, is a giant-screen cinema showing a stunning 38 minute Blue Mountains documentary, as well as feature films. Sessions cost $12.50 ($10.50 concession) for the daytime doco; feature films are just $6 on Tuesday.

Activities

There are several companies offering rock climbing, abseiling, canyoning and caving adventure activities. The Australian School of Mountaineering (☎ 4782 2014), 166b Katoomba St, offers introductory rock climbing ($99), abseiling ($89) and canyoning (from $89). High 'n Wild (☎ 4782 6224), opposite the train station, on the cor-

ner of Main and Katoomba Sts, offers half-day abseiling or rock climbing from $49.

Australian Outdoor Consultants (☎ 4782 3877), in Mountain Designs, 190 Katoomba St, and the Blue Mountains Adventure Company (☎ 4782 1271), 84a Main St, offer similar thrills at comparable prices.

Places to Stay – Budget
Camping *Katoomba Falls Caravan Park* (☎ 4782 1835, Katoomba Falls Rd) has camp sites for $10 per person and on-site vans from $36 for two people.

Hostels The *Katoomba YHA* (☎ 4782 1416), on the corner of Lurline and Waratah Sts, is in a pleasant old guesthouse. It's a clean place with excellent communal areas, and most rooms have bathrooms. Dorms cost from $14 and doubles are from $20 to $25 per person; nonmembers pay $3 more.

Nearby, *Katoomba Mountain Lodge* (☎ 4782 3933, 31 Lurline St) is a cosy, brick guesthouse charging from $16 for beds in squashy dorms, and $40/52 for OK singles/doubles with shared bathrooms ($45/70 on weekends).

Blue Mountains Backpackers (☎ 4782 4226, 190 Bathurst Rd) is a short walk from the train station. It's a friendly, lived-in hostel reminiscent of a large student house. Dorms are $16, and twins/doubles $43 (VIP/YHA members pay $3/$4 less), and there are camp sites too. *Hotel Gearin* and the *Katoomba Hotel* also have backpacker rooms (see the following section).

Hotels The *Katoomba Hotel* (☎ 4782 1106), on the corner of Parke and Main Sts, is a smoky Aussie local with unglamorous (but heated) singles/doubles for $25/45 midweek and $30/50 on weekends. A dorm bed is $12.

Hotel Gearin (☎ 4782 4395, 273 Great Western Hwy) is a local pub with decent rooms for $25/50 and dorms for $15. It's behind the train station.

Places to Stay – Mid-Range
Hotels & Motels The *Clarendon Guesthouse Motor Inn* (☎ 4782 1322), on the corner of Lurline and Waratah Sts, has both

old-fashioned and motel-style rooms from $48/68 midweek, and weekend dinner-and-show packages for around $100 per person. The old-time atmosphere is helped along by a log fire, games room, cocktail bar and cabaret-style entertainment.

The *Three Sisters Motel* (☎ 4782 2911, 348 Katoomba St), a 10 minute walk from the town centre, charges from $60/75 for a room midweek, and $95 for a room on weekends.

Lovely *Balmoral House* (☎ 4782 2264, 196 Bathurst Rd) claims to be the oldest guesthouse in the Blue Mountains. With log fires and a bar and restaurant downstairs,

it's certainly a beautiful building, full of period fittings and cosy little touches. B&B costs $99 per room midweek.

Places to Stay – Top End

One of the best hotels in the region is the well restored *Hydro Majestic Hotel* (☎ 4788 1002, Great Western Hwy, Medlow Bath), a superb relic of an earlier era. It's a few kilometres west of Katoomba. Rooms cost from $185/205 midweek, or $480/570 on weekends, including breakfast and dinner.

The equally grand *Carrington Hotel* (☎ 4782 1111, 10-16 Katoomba St) is a pala-

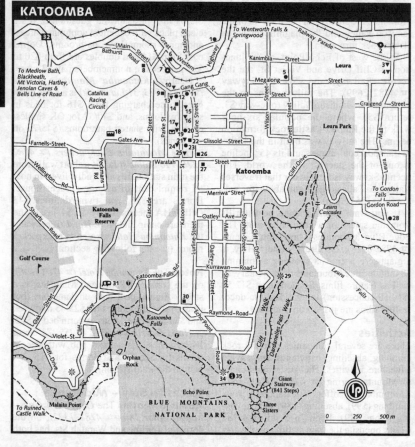

KATOOMBA

tial establishment that's recently been refurbished; rooms with shared bathrooms are $195 Sunday to Thursday, $225 Friday or Saturday; en suite rooms start from $275 midweek.

Places to Eat

The *Savoy (12 Katoomba St)* is an Art Deco establishment serving focaccia, nachos and pasta mains for around $9. *Carrington Bar & Bistro*, the pleasant pub opposite, has a mouth-watering range of gourmet wood-fired pizzas for around $15. *Cafe Zuppa (No 36)* is a relaxed, arty hang-out with a great atmosphere; another Art Deco gem, it serves decent coffee and interesting lunches for around $8.

The welcoming *Blues Cafe (No 57)* does huge vegetarian meals for around $8 – good cakes, too. The *Paragon (No 65)* is an Art Deco masterpiece serving delicious cakes and handmade chocolates. The rear cocktail bar looks like it's been poached from a 1930s ocean liner.

Siam Cuisine (No 172) is a low-key, budget Thai restaurant, with chicken laksa or satay vegetables for $6. For Indian food there's *The Ashram (No 189)*, a cheery place with entrees from $2 to $5, and curry main courses for $10.50.

Parakeet (No 195) is a sociable cafe serving breakfasts from 8 am, meals for around $8.50 and acoustic music on weekends. For good fast food and bad puns,

there's *Grillers in the Mist (No 208)*, a tiny seafood takeaway with cheap and inventive fishy snacks.

Tris Elies (☎ *4782 4026*) is a Greek restaurant next to the train station. Mains like moussaka and grilled snapper are $15 to $20, and weekend entertainment ranges from bouzouki to belly dancing. A mysterious corridor leads upstairs to the relaxed and quaintly eccentric *Avalon Cafe Restaurant* (☎ *4782 5532, 98 Main St)*. It's a lovely place for dinner, with tasty mains for around $14, and is also open for lunch Sunday, Thursday and Friday.

Getting Around

Bus The Blue Mountains Bus Company (☎ 4782 4213) runs a service between Katoomba train station, the Three Sisters Motel (five minutes walk from Echo Point), and the Scenic Railway and Scenic Skyway. There's a bus roughly every 45 minutes. Mountainlink (☎ 4782 3333) runs a service between Echo Point and Gordon Falls via Katoomba St and Leura Mall. There are roughly two services an hour midweek, less on weekends.

On weekends and public holidays, the hop-on/hop-off Blue Mountains Explorer Bus (☎ 4782 4807) does an hourly circuit of 18 attractions in the Katoomba and Leura area. The easiest place to catch the bus is Katoomba train station; tickets cost $18 ($16 concession).

NEW SOUTH WALES

KATOOMBA					
PLACES TO STAY		4	Baker's Cafe	7	Katoomba Train Station
6	Hotel Gearin	10	Tris Elies	11	Cycletech
8	Blue Mountains Backpackers; Balmoral House	13	Avalon Cafe Restaurant	12	High 'n Wild; Blue Mountains Adventure Company
9	Katoomba Hotel	15	Savoy		
14	Carrington Hotel; Carrington Bar and Bistro	16	Cafe Zuppa	18	Olympic Swimming Pool
		17	Paragon; Blues Cafe	20	Australian School of Mountaineering
		19	The Ashram		
22	Katoomba Mountain Lodge	21	Siam Cuisine	23	Australian Outdoor Consultants; Mountain Designs
26	Katoomba YHA	24	Parakeet Cafe		
27	Clarendon Guesthouse Motor Inn	25	Grillers in the Mist	28	Leuralla
				29	Honeymoon Lookout
30	Three Sisters Motel	**OTHER**		32	Scenic Skyway
31	Katoomba Falls Caravan Park	1	The Edge Blue Mountains Maxvision Cinema	33	Scenic Railway
				34	Three Sisters Lookout
PLACES TO EAT		2	Leura Train Station	35	Information Centre
3	Le Gobolet	5	Thrifty Car Rental		

Bicycle You can hire mountain bikes at the YHA hostel and Cycletech, 3 Gang Gang St, from $15 a half-day. Better bikes are available from Mountain Designs, 190 Katoomba St, from $15 a half-day. See Activities earlier for mountain-bike tours.

BLACKHEATH AREA

The little town of Blackheath is a good base for visiting the Grose and Megalong valleys. There are superb lookouts a few kilometres east of the town, such as **Govetts Leap** and **Evan's Lookout**. To the north-east, via Hat Hill Rd, are **Pulpit Rock**, **Perry's Lookdown** and **Anvil Rock**.

A clifftop track leads from Govetts Leap to Pulpit Rock, and there are several walks from Govetts Leap down into the Grose Valley. Get details on the walks from the nearby Heritage Centre. Perry's Lookdown is the beginning of the shortest route (four hours return) to the beautiful **Blue Gum Forest** in the valley bottom.

The **Megalong Valley**, south of Blackheath, is largely cleared farmland but it's still a beautiful place, with awesome sandstone escarpments. The road down from Blackheath passes through pockets of rainforest and you can walk the beautiful 600m Coachwood Glen Nature Trail. A couple of kilometres further is the small valley settlement of Werribee, where there are several horse riding outfits, including Werriberri Trail Rides (☎ 4787 9171) on Megalong Rd. Two-hour rides cost $35.

Blackheath is a short drive along the Great Western Hwy from Katoomba. It's also on the railway line from Sydney, two stops past Katoomba. From Blackheath, it's a 15 minute winding drive into the Megalong Valley via Shipley and Megalong Rds.

Places to Stay & Eat

The nearest NPWS camping ground is Acacia Flat, in the Grose Valley near the Blue Gum Forest. It's a steep walk down from Govetts Leap or Perry's Lookdown. You can also camp at Perrys Lookdown, which has a car park and is a convenient base for walks into the Grose Valley.

The **Blackheath Caravan Park** (☎ 4787 8101), in Prince Edward St, off Govetts Leap Rd, is about 500m from the Great Western Hwy. Camp sites cost from $7 per person and vans from $38.

Cosy **Gardners Inn** (☎ 4787 8347, 255 Great Western Hwy, Blackheath) is the oldest hotel in the Blue Mountains (1831). It charges $30 per person midweek and $35 on weekends. There's a bistro with cheap homemade pies, and a more upmarket steakhouse.

The **Lakeview Holiday Park** (☎ 4787 8534, 63 Prince Edward St) has cabins with en suite for $50 a double.

The **Wattle Cafe**, on the corner of the Great Western Hwy and Govetts Leap Rd, has $3 burgers, decent meals for $8 to $10 and a wood-heater to warm yourself by. The **Piedmont Inn**, on the highway near Gardners Inn, serves pizzas and fettucine from $6 to $10.

MT VICTORIA & HARTLEY

A few kilometres west of Blackheath is the pretty National Trust classified town of Mt Victoria. The museum at the train station is open on weekends and school holidays between 2 and 5 pm. Interesting buildings include the **Victoria & Albert guesthouse**, the 1849 **tollkeeper's cottage** and the **1870s church**.

The **Mt Vic Flicks** (☎ 4787 1577) is a lovely little cinema on Harley Ave, near the Victoria & Albert guesthouse. Movies ($5 to $10) are shown from Thursday to Sunday.

Off the highway at **Mt York** is a memorial to the explorers who first crossed the Blue Mountains. A short stretch of the original road crosses the mountains here.

About 11km past Mt Victoria, on the western slopes of the range, is the tiny, sandstone ghost town of **Hartley**, which flourished from the 1830s but declined when it was bypassed by the railway in 1887. There are several buildings of historic interest, including the 1837 courthouse and a quaint church and presbytery. There's a NPWS information centre (☎ 6355 2117) in the Farmers Inn. It's open daily between 10 am and 4.30 pm (closed between 1 and 2 pm) and tours of the town and courthouse ($4) are run from here.

Places to Stay

The *Imperial Hotel* (☎ *4787 1233*), on the corner of the Great Western Hwy and Station St, is a Blue Mountains institution. It's a fine old hotel, with dorm beds for $20 and rooms from $60/78 midweek, all including breakfast. It has a coffee shop with snacks and a bistro with good solid meals.

The nearby *Victoria & Albert* (☎ *4787 1241, 19 Station St)* is a lovely guesthouse that could be straight out of an Agatha Christie mystery. It offers comfortable B&B from $45 per person midweek (breakfast is outstanding). The stately *Manor House* (☎ *4787 1369, Montgomery St)* has luxurious B&B from $90 a single midweek.

JENOLAN CAVES

On the north-western fringe of the Kanangra-Boyd National Park, south-west of Katoomba, are the Jenolan Caves (☎ 6359 3311), the best-known limestone caves in Australia. One cave has been open to the public since 1867, yet parts of the system are still unexplored. Three 'arches' are open for independent viewing, but you can visit the nine caves by guided tour only – run between 10 am and 4 pm; there's a weekly evening tour at 8 pm. Tours last between one and two hours, and cost from $12. You have to pay for parking – expect crowds during holidays.

Places to Stay

You can camp near Jenolan Caves House for $10 per site. There's dorm accommodation at the *Gatehouse* (☎ *6359 3042)* for $15 ($20 on weekends). Ask in Trails Cafe. Set in a grassy clearing, *Binda Bush Cabins* (☎ *6359 3311)* is on the road from Hartley, about 8km north of the caves. Basic, clean cabins with bunks accommodate six people for $75 per night midweek and $90 on weekends and school holidays.

At *Jenolan Caves House* (☎ *6359 3322)* you can book a wide range of accommodation, from double rooms in a cottage for $65, to heritage-style doubles for $100 midweek.

Getting There & Away

The caves are on plenty of tour itineraries from Sydney and Katoomba. By car, turn off the Great Western Hwy at Hartley and they're a 45 minute drive along Jenolan Caves Rd. The Six Foot Track from Katoomba to Jenolan Caves is a fairly easy three day walk, but make sure you get information from an NPWS visitors centre.

BELLS LINE OF ROAD

This back road between Richmond and Lithgow is the most scenic route across the Blue Mountains. It's highly recommended if you have your own transport. There are fine views towards the coast from Kurrajong Heights on the eastern slopes of the range, orchards around Bilpin, and sandstone cliff and bush scenery all the way to Lithgow.

There are grass skiing and karting at **Kurrajong Heights Grass Ski Park** (☎ 4567 7260) on weekends and holidays for $16 for two hours. Roughly midway between Richmond and Lithgow is the exquisite **Mt Tomah Botanic Gardens**, the cool-climate annexe of Sydney's Royal Botanic Gardens. It's open daily ($5 per car, $2 for pedestrians); late October and late April are the most spectacular times to visit.

North of the Bells Line of Road, at the quaint town of **Mt Wilson**, are formal gardens and a nearby remnant of rainforest known as the **Cathedral of Ferns**. The **Zig Zag Railway** is at Clarence, 10km east of Lithgow. It was built in 1869 and was quite an engineering wonder in its day. Trains used to descend from the Blue Mountains by this route until 1910, when a series of tunnels made the line redundant. A section has been restored and several steam trains run daily. The fare is $13. Call ☎ 6351 4826 for timetable information.

North Coast

There are excellent beaches along the popular NSW north coast and several national parks offering wildlife, superb scenery and challenging bushwalks, including the 14 day Great North Walk that runs from Newcastle to Sydney: contact tourist offices and the Department of Land and Water Conservation (☎ 9228 6315, fax 9221 5980) for details.

The Pacific Hwy runs north along the coast into Queensland, passing a string of resorts, including Byron Bay – a surfing mecca and an established travellers' haunt. Scenic roads lead inland into the Great Dividing Range and onto the New England tableland.

SYDNEY TO NEWCASTLE

The area between Broken Bay and Newcastle is known as the Central Coast. It's a densely populated area of rampant suburban housing, superb beaches, inland waterways and national parks.

The largest town in the area is **Gosford** (population 55,000), an undistinguished settlement on the shores of Brisbane Water, some 85km north of Sydney. It's easily accessible by train from Sydney and Newcastle. A visitors information centre (☎ 4323 2353, thecoast@cctourism.com.au) is open daily, at 200 Mann St, near the train station. Gosford makes a sensible base from which to explore the region if you don't have transport because bus services radiate from here. The *Gosford Hotel* (☎ 4324 1634), on the corner of Mann and Erina Sts, has singles/doubles from \$40/55.

Brisbane Water National Park, a few kilometres south-west of Gosford, includes the northern inlets of the Hawkesbury River. It has Aboriginal engravings and good bushwalking, and is renowned for its spring wildflowers. The **Bouddi National Park**, 20km south-east of Gosford, extends north along the coast from the mouth of Brisbane Water and offers excellent coastal bushwalking and camping. Information about the area's parks is available from the NPWS, 207 Albany Street North, Gosford (☎ 4324 4911) and on its Web site, www.npws.nsw. gov.au.

There are several beach and riverside towns worth exploring. The National Trust classified township of **Pearl Beach**, south of Gosford on the eastern edge of the Brisbane Water National Park, is a quiet enclave with a lovely beach.

Terrigal, 15km east of Gosford, is like something out of an Australian soap opera – buzzing with activity and surfers carrying their boards down the main street, which runs alongside the beach. The *Terrigal Beach Backpackers Lodge* (☎ 4385 3330, 12 Campbell Crescent) is one block from the beach and has a relaxed seaside atmosphere. Dorms cost \$17, and rooms \$35/42.

The small township of **Brooklyn**, on the banks of the Hawkesbury, is a calm backwater offering fishing, boating, kayaking tours and bushwalking. The visitors centre is at the back of the *Hawkesbury Teahouse* (☎ 9985 7064, 5 Bridge St).

Further north is a series of large saltwater lakes, including **Tuggerah Lake**. The township of **The Entrance**, at the mouth of the lake, is a good place to stay to take advantage of the fine boating and fishing opportunities. Further north again, and just south of Newcastle, is **Lake Macquarie**, a saltwater lake four times the size of Sydney Harbour. It's a popular centre for sailing, water-skiing and fishing. The Lake Macquarie visitors centre (☎ 4972 1172, tourism@lakemac.nsw.gov.au) is on the old Pacific Hwy, before the bridge just north of Swansea.

The Sydney to Newcastle freeway is the major road link between the two cities, but it skirts the Central Coast. If you want to explore this area, it's best to take the Pacific Hwy between Gosford and Newcastle. You can reach the southern part of the Central Coast from Sydney's Palm Beach by catching the ferry to Patonga, which sails at least four times a day. There are four buses from Patonga to Gosford on weekdays run by Busways (☎ 4362 1030); it costs \$3.60.

NEWCASTLE

• postcode 2300   • pop 270,300

Newcastle, 167km north of Sydney at the mouth of the Hunter River, is the state's second-largest city and one of Australia's largest ports. It's a major industrial and commercial centre, and the export port for the Hunter Valley coalfields and for grain from the north-west.

For many, Newcastle conjures up images of belching smokestacks. It's an image that locals resent, and quite rightly. Newcastle is a relaxed and friendly place. The city centre has wide, leafy streets and some fine, early colonial buildings. There are beautiful clean surf beaches only a few hundred metres away.

Originally named Coal River, the city was founded in 1804 as a place for the most intractable of Sydney's convicts and was known as the 'hell of New South Wales'. Macquarie Pier, built by convicts, runs out to Nobbys Head, from where you get a great view of the city and huge tankers coming into port. Bogey Hole, a swimming pool cut into the rock on the ocean's edge below the pleasant King Edward Park, was built for Major Morriset, a strict disciplinarian. It was Australia's first ocean swimming pool and it's still a great place for a dip.

In late 1989 Newcastle suffered Australia's most destructive recorded earthquake. It killed 12 people and severely damaged property. In mid-1997 Newcastle was struck another blow when BHP announced it was to cease steel-making, with the loss of more than 2500 jobs. Still, spirits lifted when the Newcastle Knights won the 1997 NSW rugby league premiership.

Orientation

The city centre is a peninsula bordered by the ocean on one side and the Hunter River on the other. It tapers down to the long sand spit leading to Nobbys Head. Hunter St is the 3km-long main street, forming a pedestrian mall between Newcomen and Perkins Sts.

The train station, the long-distance bus stop, the post office, banks and some fine old buildings are at the north-eastern end of the city centre. Cooks Hill rises steeply behind the centre and offers good views. The city is worth a look but most travellers head for the lively inner western suburb of Hamilton, centred on Beaumont St.

There are good views over Newcastle's industrial landscape from Queens Wharf Tower and 360° views from the obelisk above King Edward Park.

Just across the river from the city centre is Stockton, a modest suburb with beaches and good views back to Newcastle city. It's minutes from the city by ferry but by road you have to wind through the docks, some dramatic industrial landscapes and over the bridge, a trip of about 20km.

Information

The tourist office (☎ 4974 2999, newtour@ hunterlink.net.au) is at Wheeler Place, just off Hunter St near Civic train station. It's open weekdays from 9 am to 4 pm and weekends from 10 am to 3 pm. It sells excellent heritage-walk maps and has information about transport and tours to the Hunter Valley and many other nearby attractions.

Pepperina bookshop, in Bolton St, 50m north of the Grand Hotel, is open daily, as is Cooks Hill Books, on the corner of Darby and Queen Sts. There's a left-luggage office at the train station, near the Watt St entrance ($1.50 per item). There is a laundrette (open daily) in Cleary St, just off Beaumont St.

Things to See & Do

The **Newcastle Regional Museum**, at 787 Hunter St, Newcastle West, is open Tuesday to Sunday from 10 am to 5 pm and daily in school holidays (admission is free). It has interesting exhibits covering science, history and technology and hosts temporary exhibitions. The **Fort Scratchley Military & Maritime Museum** is open Tuesday to Sunday from noon to 4 pm (admission is free). The tunnels under the fort are said to run all the way to King Edward Park.

The **Newcastle Regional Art Gallery** is on Laman St, next to Civic Park. The permanent collection contains pieces by famous Australian artists including Brett Whiteley, Sidney Nolan and Arthur Boyd, while the touring shows often have a more international flavour. Entry is free and it's open Tuesday to Sunday from 10 am to 5 pm.

Blackbutt Reserve (☎ 4952 1449) is a 182 hectare bushland reserve at New Lambton Heights, approximately 10km south-west of the centre, with bushwalks and aviaries, wildlife enclosures and fern houses. There is also a koala enclosure. It's open daily from 10 am to 5 pm (admission is free). Kotara train station is a short walk from the reserve, while the most direct buses from the city are Nos 232 and 363. A bus day pass costs $6, which will give you plenty of time to explore.

About 15km north-west of the centre, near Sandgate train station, the **Wetlands**

NEW SOUTH WALES

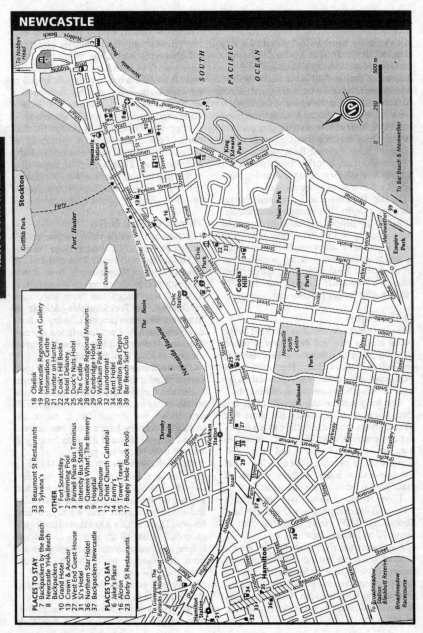

NEWCASTLE

PLACES TO STAY
7 Backpackers by the Beach
8 Newcastle YHA Beach
   Backpackers
10 Grand Hotel
13 Crown & Anchor
27 West End Guest House
31 SJ's Hotel
36 Northern Star Hotel
37 Backpackers Newcastle

PLACES TO EAT
6 Jake's Place
16 Alcron
23 Darby St Restaurants

33 Beaumont St Restaurants
35 Sylvana's

OTHER
1 Fort Scratchley
2 Swimming Pool
4 Parnell Place Bus Terminus
5 Intercity Bus Station
5 Queens Wharf; The Brewery
9 Hospital
11 Courthouse
12 Christ Church Cathedral
14 Fanny's
15 Tower Travel
17 Bogey Hole (Rock Pool)

18 Obelisk
19 Newcastle Regional Art Gallery
20 Information Centre
21 Hunter on Hunter
22 Cook's Hill Books
24 Hotel Delaney
25 Duck's Nuts Hotel
26 The Castle
28 Newcastle Regional Museum
29 Cambridge Hotel
30 Wickham Park Hotel
32 Laundromat
34 Kent Hotel
38 Hamilton Bus Depot
39 Bar Beach Surf Club

Ecopark (☎ 4951 6466) has lots of bird and wildlife as well as walks, canoe trails and picnic facilities. It's open daily from 9 am to 5 pm (admission is by a $2 donation).

Surf Beaches Newcastle's favourite surfing son is former world champ Mark Richards, and many surfers come to seek out the breaks where Richards cut his teeth. The main beach, **Newcastle Beach**, is just a couple of minutes walk from the city centre. It has an ocean pool and good surf. In March crowds gather here to witness the World Qualifying Series surf competition, Surfest, which attracts the world's top surfers to the city. Just north of here is **Nobbys Beach**, more sheltered from the southerlies and often open when other beaches are closed. At the northern end of Nobbys is a fast left-hander known as The Wedge. The most popular surfing break is about 5km south at **Bar Beach**, which is floodlit at night in summer. Nearby, **Merewether Beach** has two huge saltwater swimming pools. Bus 207 from the city runs to Merewether Beach every half-hour via Bar Beach.

Organised Tours
The *William the Fourth*, a replica of an old steamship, leaves Merewether St Wharf at 11 am and 2 pm on the third Sunday of the month ($20/11/5 families/adults/children) for cruises on the harbour. Newcastle's Famous Tram departs from Newcastle train station daily on the hour from 10 am till 3 pm. The 45 minute guided tour of Newcastle's historic sites costs $8/5 for adults/children.

Special Events
Beaumont St hosts its Jazz & Blues Festival in March, August sees the Newcastle Jazz Festival and the Newcastle Fringe Festival is held in late September.

Places to Stay – Budget
Camping *Stockton Beach Caravan Park* (☎ 4928 1393) is on the beach at Pitt St, Stockton. Stockton is handy by ferry but it's 20km away by road. Unpowered/powered sites are $13/16 a double and on-site cabins start at $40.

There are several caravan parks south of Newcastle, around Belmont and on the ocean at Redhead Beach.

Hostels *Backpackers Newcastle* (☎ 4969 3436, 42-44 Denison St, Hamilton) occupies a couple of fine old weatherboard houses. It's clean and friendly and near an interesting part of town. Dorm beds are $16 and doubles, located mostly at No 44, are $40. Surfboard hire is $5 and one of the managers is a keen surfer who gives lessons. Hamilton is about a kilometre from the city centre, but you can phone for a free pick-up from town. Broadmeadows train station, on the Sydney to Newcastle line, is 2km from the hostel and Hamilton station is also nearby. Any bus heading out of town along Hunter St can also drop you off nearby.

Closer to the centre of town, *Backpackers by the Beach* (☎ 4926 3472), on the corner of Pacific and Hunter Sts, occupies several storeys. It's close to Main Beach and Nobbys Beach, so the free use of surfboards and bikes is very handy. The place is sparse and clean, with dorms/doubles for $15/40. It's a short walk from both the Parnell Place bus terminal and the Newcastle train station.

Just up the road, *Newcastle YHA Beach Backpackers* (☎ 4925 3544, 20 Pacific St) opened in mid-1999 in a beautiful heritage building 100m from the beach. Dorms/doubles cost $16/44 and the managers can help arrange activities and tours of the area's attractions.

Hotels The *Crown & Anchor* (☎ 4929 1027), on the corner of Hunter and Perkins Sts, has bright singles/doubles/twins for $30/40/45 (rates are negotiable if you're in town for a few nights).

Places to Stay – Mid-Range
The *West End Guest House* (☎ 4961 4446), on the corner of Hunter and Stewart Sts, offers very stylish, clean and comfortable accommodation in its individually decorated rooms. The owners renovated the old pub themselves. A highlight is the roof-top

barbecue area. Dorm beds start from $16. Rooms are $40 for a single plus $10 for each extra person. It's 100m from Wickham train station.

The **Grand Hotel** (☎ 4929 3489), on the corner of Bolton and Church Sts, is a friendly neighbourhood pub across from the courthouse, hence the lawyers propping up the front bar. Rooms start at $50 (with TV and en suite).

The **Northern Star Hotel** (☎ 4961 1087, 112 Beaumont St) has motel-style single rooms for $45/55 and doubles for $56/70 without/with en suite.

Places to Eat

Beaumont St has the greatest concentration and variety of restaurants. The food available represents the variety of nationalities living in the area, and there's a wealth of Italian, Turkish and Asian cafes and restaurants. Down a small lane near the corner of Lindsay St (on the eastern side of Beaumont St), **Sylvana's** has all-you-can-eat vegetarian feasts for $10 on Monday and Tuesday nights. If it's Italian you're after, try **Caffé Giannotti**, **Café Trieste** or **Giovanni's** for great coffee and lunchtime focaccias. Bargain hunters will like the Chinese **Rickshaw Inn**, which serves two mains and fried rice for $4.50. The award-winning **Al-Oi Thai Express** restaurant has meals from $7.50.

Newcastle's other main restaurant strip is closer to the city on Darby St, south of King St. The choices include Vietnamese (**Lan's**), Thai (**Al-Oi**), Hawaiian (**Sunsets**), Italian (**Benvenuti**, with $5 pasta nights on Monday and Wednesday) and Indian (**Taj Takeaway**). **Splash** has fish and chips and the popular **Goldberg's Coffee House** serves great cakes and brews a mean coffee.

At the eastern end of town, a great place to relax, meet the locals, have a quiet beer and a meal (mains about $10) is the **Grand Hotel**, on the corner of Bolton and Church Sts.

If you feel like a blow-out, **Alcron** (☎ 4929 2423, 113 Church St) is Australia's oldest licensed restaurant and has fine views. Main courses range from $18 to $23.

Entertainment

Newcastle has a busy home-grown music scene, with live bands playing somewhere every night except Monday and Tuesday. There are gig guides in Thursday's *Newcastle Herald* or the weekly *Newcastle Post*, published on Wednesday. Try the **Cambridge Hotel** (Hunter St, West Newcastle). It was the home pub of top Aussie bands Screaming Jets and silverchair and still has live bands but is also the domain of groovers who don't mind a bit of disco or some 60s psychedelia. **Hunter on Hunter** (417 Hunter St) is a regular live venue and the **Ducks Nuts Hotel**, on the corner of Hunter and Steel Sts, (formerly the Family Hotel) has blues.

In Beaumont St, the **Kent Hotel** features plenty of jazz, the **Northern Star Hotel** has a bit of everything including jazz, African music and country and **SJ's Hotel** has original local bands and is often the venue for national touring bands.

Not far from the end of Beaumont St is the **Barracks** (139 Maitland Rd), an affable pub and Newcastle's main gay venue. South-east of the Barracks is the **Wickham Park Hotel** (61 Maitland Rd) – popular with kd lang fans.

The **Hotel Delaney**, on the corner of Darby and Council Sts, is a relaxed little pub with music most nights and the **Brewery** (Queens Wharf) has DJs and bands and brews its own beer.

The **Castle**, on the corner of King and Steel Sts, and **Fanny's**, in Wharf Rd, are Newcastle's most mainstream nightclubs, large and impersonal with plenty of dance music and some bands. They are open Wednesday to Saturday and entry is generally free before 10 pm and half price before midnight.

Getting There & Away

Air Aeropelican (☎ 13 1300) flies several times a day from Sydney to Belmont, south of Newcastle. The cheapest one-way fare is $44 (21-day advance).

Sydney Harbour Seaplanes (☎ 1800 803 558) flies between Rose Bay in Sydney and Newcastle (pulling up on the harbour between Queens and Merewether St wharves). There are four flights in each direction from

Monday to Friday ($100/190 single/return). Qantas (☎ 13 2327) has daily flights to Sydney (single/return $109/218, though specials can bring fares as low as $39 one way). Impulse (☎ 13 1381) flies between Newcastle and Port Macquarie ($179), Coffs Harbour ($228) and Brisbane ($298). Sunstate Airlines (☎ 13 1212) operates between Brisbane and Newcastle, sometimes via Coolangatta. Eastern, Sunstate and Impulse use the airport at Williamtown, north of Newcastle.

Bus Between Sydney and Newcastle you're better off taking the train, but heading up the coast from Newcastle buses offer a much better service. Nearly all long-distance buses stop on Watt St, near the train station. Cheapish fares from Newcastle include: Sydney $22, Port Macquarie $31, Byron Bay $59, Brisbane $60, all with McCafferty's (☎ 13 1499). Jayes Travel (☎ 4926 2000), at 285 Hunter St, near Darby St, and Tower Travel (☎ 4926 3199), at 245 Hunter St, on the corner of Crown St, can help with bookings.

Train Sydney suburban trains run from Central station to Newcastle about 30 times a day, taking nearly three hours. The one-way fare is $14.60; an off-peak return is $17.60. (Ring Cityrail on ☎ 13 1500.)

Other trains heading north on the lines to Armidale and Murwillumbah bypass central Newcastle, stopping at suburban Broadmeadow – just west of Hamilton. Frequent buses run from here to the city centre. An XPT from Central station to Broadmeadow takes about 2 hours and costs $22.

Car You can hire used cars from companies such as Cheep Heep (☎ 4961 3144), at 116 Maitland Rd, Islington, from $25 a day, including insurance. The regular car hire companies are also in town.

Getting Around
To/From the Airport Port Stephens Buses (☎ 4982 2940) stop at Williamtown airport, on the run to Nelson Bay. The trip takes 35 minutes and costs $4.40. Local bus No 348,

349, 350, 351, 358 or 359 stop outside Belmont airport (one hour ticket $2).

Taxis from Williamtown airport to the city centre cost around $32, and from Belmont airport to the city centre around $27.

Bus STA buses cover Newcastle and the eastern side of Lake Macquarie, offering various fare deals. An all-day pass costs $6 ($3 concession) and is valid on STA buses and ferries. Most services operate every half-hour. Bus information is available from Newcastle station, or call the Travel Information Centre (☎ 4961 8933) between 8.15 am and 4.30 pm. You can also pop into the Hamilton and Belmont bus depots.

Ferry There are ferries to Stockton from Queens Wharf approximately half-hourly, Monday to Thursday from 5.15 am to 11 pm. On Friday and Saturday they run until midnight and on Sunday they stop at 10 pm. The ferry terminus, on Queens Wharf, has a timetable. Fares cost $1.40/70c adults/ children one way.

Bicycle Bike-hire places come and go – the tourist office or the owners of Backpackers Newcastle will know if one is operating.

HUNTER VALLEY
The Hunter Valley has two curiously diverse products – wine and coal. If you're interested in winery tours, tastings and the associated pleasures of leisurely lunches, Sunday jazz and upmarket accommodation, then the area is certainly worth a visit. The heart of the valley vineyards is in the Pokolbin area near Cessnock, where some wineries date from the 1860s. Many of Australia's best-known wine names are in the Hunter, such as Lindemans Wines, McDonalds Rd, Pokolbin (☎ 4998 7684), Tyrell's Vineyards, Broke Rd, Pokolbin (☎ 4993 7000) and Wyndham Estate, Dalwood Rd, Dalwood via Branxton (☎ 4938 3444).

On the southern side of the valley rise the sandstone ranges of the Wollemi and Goulburn River national parks; the high, rugged ranges leading up to Barrington National Park border its northern side.

The main road through the Hunter Valley is the New England Hwy running north-west from Newcastle and climbing up to the New England tablelands near Murrurundi. There are more than 50 vineyards in the wide valley of the Lower Hunter, and nine more in the Upper Hunter. Generally they're open daily for tastings and sales, with slightly reduced hours on Sunday. Many have picnic and barbecue facilities.

Organised Tours

Hunter Vineyard Tours (☎ 4991 1659) has daily departures from Newcastle and other Hunter centres from $29 ($45 with lunch). Hunter Valley Day Tours (☎ 4938 5031) runs an award-winning Wine & Cheese Tasting Tour and rainforest tours with free hotel pick-ups in the Lower Hunter region for $90. Grapemobile (☎ 4991 2339) offers two-day bike rides through the wineries, with a support bus, accommodation and all meals for $179 per person. It also has day tours for $89 per person and rents bikes for $25 a day. Day tours with Pokolbin Horse Coach Tours (☎ 4998 7305) cost $49 during the week and $59 on weekends. For tours of the Upper Hunter, contact the Scone, Muswellbrook or Denman information centres.

Lower Hunter Wineries

The valley's wine-growing heartland is the rolling hill country north-west of **Cessnock**. The Cessnock Visitor Information Centre (☎ 4990 4477, info@winecountry.com.au) is the place to go for maps and brochures before you set out on a winery tour. It's on Aberdare Rd, on the way into town from Sydney, and is open daily.

Several wineries run tours, including McWilliams (weekdays at 11 am, $2); McGuigan Hunter Village (daily at noon); Wyndham Estate (weekdays at 11 am); Tyrrells (Monday to Saturday at 1.30 pm) and Tinkler's Farm (weekends at 11 am).

Places to Stay Cessnock is the main town and accommodation centre for the vineyards, although there is also pub accommodation in nearby Neath and Bellbird. Almost all places offering accommodation charge more at weekends and you might have to take a package (meals included). Cessnock's information centre can book accommodation and has information about off-peak specials.

There are a couple of caravan parks close to Cessnock. The *Valley Vineyard Tourist Park* (☎ 4990 2573, Mount View Rd) has camp sites for $12, on-site vans for $35 and cabins from $55 with en suite. *Cessnock Park* (☎ 4990 58190) is off Allandale Rd, north of Cessnock, and has camp sites for $7 per person, on-site vans from $30 and cabins from $50.

There is no hostel accommodation in Cessnock, but there are some good deals at the pubs. The *Black Opal Hotel* (☎ 4990 1070), at the southern end of Vincent St on the main shopping street, charges from $20 per person Monday to Thursday, and $25 Friday to Sunday. The *Wentworth Hotel* (☎ 4990 1364, 36 Vincent St) has rooms for $25 per person with breakfast.

Midweek motel prices include $59 for doubles at the *Cessnock Motel* (☎ 4990 2699) and the *Hunter Valley Motel* (☎ 4990 1722), both on Allandale Rd. Prices at these and other motels rise steeply at weekends.

There's a lot of accommodation out among the vineyards. Most charge well over $100 a night on weekends, but midweek there are a few places charging from around $70 a double. These include the *Hill Top Country Guest House* (☎ 4930 7111), in Talga Rd, off Lovedale Rd, about 11km north-east of Cessnock, and *Belford Country Cabins* (☎ 6574 7100, Hermitage Rd), north of the Hunter Estate.

Upper Hunter Wineries

The nearest town to the Upper Hunter wineries is **Denman**, a sleepy little place 25km south-west of Muswellbrook.

The Upper Hunter has fewer wineries, but it's worth visiting because the pace is slower and the scenery more beautiful than the Lower Hunter. The area's information centre (☎ 6547 2463) is on Denman's main street at the *Old Carriage Restaurant*, a cafe/restaurant in an old railway carriage next to the *Denham Café*. As well as the plentiful accommodation in nearby Muswellbrook and Singleton, there is camping, pub, motel and B&B accommodation in and around Denman.

The New England Hwy runs up the Hunter Valley through some old towns and attractive scenery. The **Goulburn River National Park**, at the upper end of the valley, follows the river as it cuts through sandstone gorges. This was the route used by Aboriginal people travelling from the plains to the sea and the area is rich in cave art and other sites. You can camp but there are no facilities. Access is from Sandy Hollow (near Denman) or Merriwa (on the Denman to Gulgong road). The Muswellbrook NPWS office (☎ 6543 3533, www.npws .nsw.gov.au), on the corner of Francis and Maitland Sts, has information.

Maitland Once a coal-mining centre, Maitland (population 50,000) is now promoted as the heritage centre of NSW and in April the city hosts its Heritage Month. Established as a convict settlement in 1818, it was at one time, along with Sydney and Parramatta, one of Australia's main settlements.

The information centre (☎ 4933 2611, maitland.tourism@hunterlink.net.au), on the corner of the New England Hwy and High St, has a couple of good heritage walk maps and is open daily from 9.30 am to 4 pm. There are frequent trains between Maitland and Newcastle.

High St follows the winding route of the original track through town and part of it is now the **Heritage Mall**. There are some beautiful old buildings on Church St including **Brough House** (open every afternoon), which houses the art gallery, and its neighbour, **Grossman House**, is the local history museum (open on weekend afternoons). The renovated *Imperial Hotel (☎ 4933 6566, 458 High St)* has singles/doubles for $35/50 with a self-service breakfast.

Morpeth, a few kilometres north-east of Maitland, was once the largest inland river port in Australia and is now full of interesting museums and antique shops. In May it hosts a two day jazz festival. The No 84 bus runs from Maitland station to Morpeth.

Singleton Founded in 1820, the coal-mining town of Singleton (population 12,500) is one of the oldest towns in the state. The **Singleton Historical Museum** (☎ 4972 1159), in Burdekin Park, is housed in the old lock-up (jail), built in 1862. It's open on weekends and public holidays from noon to 4 pm and on Tuesdays from 10 am to 1 pm. In the centre of town is the southern hemisphere's largest sundial, which was a bicentennial gift to the city. The old *Caledonian Hotel (☎ 6572 1356)*, on the highway near the town centre, and the *Imperial Hotel (☎ 6572 1290, John St)* have accommodation.

Muswellbrook Like other Hunter Valley towns, Muswellbrook (population 10,800) was founded early in Australia's white history and has some interesting old buildings surrounded by spreading residential areas. The information centre is on Hill St, just off the highway at the northern end of town (☎ 6541 4050).

Nearby, the historic *Eatons Hotel (☎ 6543 2403)* has singles/doubles for $20/30. It may be historic, but the clatter of gaming machines in the front bar and the betting-slip confetti on the floor dampen its appeal.

Scone With over 40 horse studs in the area, Scone dubs itself 'the horse capital of Australia'. Horse Week is held annually in May. At the information centre (☎ 6545 1526), open daily on the northern-side of town, large groups can arrange to visit studs or, alternatively, the studs have open days during the festival.

There are a few pubs on Kelly St, the main street, offering accommodation. Try the *Belmore Hotel (☎ 6545 2078)*, with rooms for $20/35, or the *Royal Hotel (☎ 6545 1722)*, with rooms for $25/50. *Airlie House Motor Inn (☎ 6545 1488)* has standard motel rooms starting at $69/79.

Your best bet is the rural *Scone Youth Hostel (☎ 6545 2072)*, in the old school house at pretty Segenhoe, 10km east of town. Dorm beds in this historic building are $13, doubles are $28 and family rooms $40. The owners will pick you up from

Scone ($5), or you can catch the school bus (50c) at 3.20 pm from the high school.

At **Burning Mountain**, off the highway 20km north of Scone, a coal seam has been burning for over 5000 years. On the scenic route between Scone and Aberdeen, **Lake Glenbawn** is a good place for swimming and fishing and cabins at the *Holiday Village (☎ 6543 7898)* can be rented from $55 a night.

Getting There & Around

Trains run from Sydney up the Hunter Valley en route to Armidale and Moree.

Keans Travel Express Coaches (☎ 1800 043 339) runs between Sydney and Tamworth via Cessnock ($22), Singleton ($26), Muswellbrook ($29) and Scone ($35) twice a day, Monday to Friday, and once a day on weekends. Rover Motors (☎ 4990 1699) runs between Newcastle and Cessnock ($8.50) frequently on weekdays, less often on Saturday and not at all on Sunday. Sid Fogg's (☎ 1800 045 952) runs up the valley on its route from Newcastle to Dubbo.

There's an interesting back route (with some unsealed roads) between Sydney and the Lower Hunter from Wisemans Ferry, passing through the pretty township of Wollombi, which has a small pub and a couple of accommodation possibilities. A great drive from Sydney to the Upper Hunter is on the Windsor to Singleton road, known as the Putty Road. (See the Around Windsor section earlier in this chapter.)

You can hire bicycles from Grapemobile (see Organised Tours earlier in this section).

NEWCASTLE TO PORT MACQUARIE
Port Stephens

This huge, sheltered bay is about an hour's drive north of Newcastle. The bay, which occupies a submerged valley, stretches more than 20km inland. It's a popular boating and fishing spot, and is well known for its resident **dolphins**. The bay is surrounded by bushland, and there is a sizeable **koala colony** living at Lemon Tree Passage, on the south side. There is a road to Lemon Tree Passage from the town of Salt Ash.

Development around Port Stephens is confined largely to the Tomaree Peninsula, which forms much of the southern shore. The tourist information centre (☎ 4981 1579, 1800 808 900, tops@hunterlink.net.au) in the main town, **Nelson Bay** (population 7000), is near the marina and will help with bookings for fishing and dolphin watching cruises or dive trips on the bay. Prodive (☎ 4981 4331) has dive courses for $295. Nearby, **Shoal Bay** has a long, sheltered beach and is a short walk from surf at Zenith Beach.

Back down the Tomaree Peninsula from Nelson Bay is the small resort town of **Anna Bay**, with good surf beaches nearby. Stockton Bight stretches 35km from Anna Bay to Newcastle, backed by the longest dune in the southern hemisphere.

On the northern side of Port Stephens, opposite Nelson Bay, are the small resort settlements of **Tea Gardens** and **Hawks Nest**, at the mouth of the Myall River.

Places to Stay There's a YHA hostel in the *Shoal Bay Motel (☎ 4984 2315)*, on the beachfront road. Dorm beds are $17 and there are family units from $20 per person (minimum two people); these rates can rise during school holidays.

The *Seabreeze Hotel (☎ 4981 1511)*, just uphill from the information centre, has motel-style doubles for $60 midweek and $70 on weekends. Cooked breakfast is $10.90.

Samurai Beach Bungalows (☎ 4982 1921) is on the corner of Frost Rd and Robert Connell Close, just east of Anna Bay, offering an opportunity for backpackers to go bush. The bungalows are dotted around a covered communal kitchen area. Dorm beds are $15 and doubles from $40 to $60. There's free use of surfboards and bicycles are free for long-stayers. Buses from Newcastle run past the door.

At **One Mile Bay**, *Melaleuca Surfside Cabins (☎ 4981 9422)* has been built by the owners and consists of a series of wooden cabins connected by walkways. All the facilities are wheelchair accessible and the place is set amid peaceful scrub. Cabins sleep five and cost $80 each or $20 per person. There's a $10 charge for camping here. Newcastle buses stop nearby at the One Mile Beach Caravan Park.

Animal lovers can stay close to the koalas at ***Larkwood Bed and Breakfast*** *(☎ 4982 4656, Oyster Farm Road, Lemon Tree Passage)*. Singles/doubles are $65/90, including a full breakfast.

Hawks Nest Beach Caravan Park *(☎ 4997 0239)* has just a narrow band of bush separating it from a good surf beach. Camp sites are $16 a double and cabins start at $35.

Getting There & Away Port Stephens Coaches (☎ 4982 2940) has a daily service to Sydney ($25) and there are plenty of buses to Newcastle ($8). If you're heading north up the coast, it's easier to backtrack to Newcastle and catch a long-distance bus from there. Great Lakes Coaches (☎ 1800 043 263) has three services from Newcastle to Tea Gardens on weekdays and one on weekends ($14).

Getting Around Port Stephens Ferries operates between Nelson Bay and Tea Gardens three times a day (adults/children $15/8 return). Bikes can be hired from Shoal Bay Bike Hire (☎ 4981 4121).

Barrington Tops National Park

Barrington Tops is a World Heritage wilderness area centred on the rugged Barrington Plateau, which rises to almost 1600m around Mt Barrington and Carey's Peak. The lower reaches of the park are covered by subtropical and temperate rainforest, while the slopes in between are dominated by ancient, moss-covered Antarctic beech forest. There are good walking trails, but be prepared for snow in winter and cold snaps at any time. Drinking water must be boiled. Hunter Valley Day Tours (☎ 4938 5031) runs eco-tours to Barrington Tops.

Places to Stay Camping is permitted at a number of sites. The main one is the ***Gloucester River Camping Area***, 31km from the Gloucester-Stroud road. The

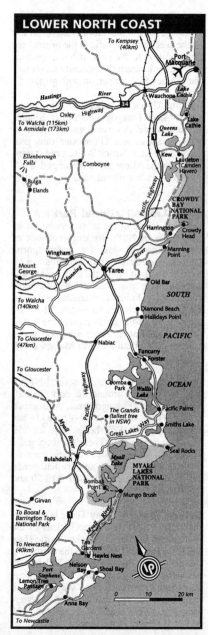

LOWER NORTH COAST

NEW SOUTH WALES

award-winning *Barrington Guest House* (☎ *4995 3212)*, 43km from Dungog on the southern edge of the park, is the nearest accommodation to the park. It has a spectacular setting beneath the plateau escarpment and charges $79 per person with meals.

Getting There & Away The park can be reached from Dungog, Gloucester, Singleton and Scone. An excellent tourist drive between Scone and Gloucester runs past Belltrees (writer Patrick White's old stamping ground). Allow three hours and don't attempt it in a conventional vehicle after rain.

Myall Lakes National Park

This park is one of the most popular recreation areas in NSW. Its large network of coastal lakes is ideal for water sports. Canoes, windsurfers and runabouts can be hired at **Bombah Point**, the park's main settlement, 11km from Bulahdelah. A car-ferry links Bombah Point to the coastal regions of the park from 8 am to 6 pm. The best beaches are in the north around the township of **Seal Rocks**. There are good walks through coastal rainforest at **Mungo Brush** in the south.

Places to Stay There are several NPWS camping grounds around the park, including a good one at Mungo Brush. At Bombah Point, *Myall Shores* (☎ *4997 4495)* has camp sites from $16, bungalows for $50 and cabins from $60. There's a shop and a restaurant. At Seal Rocks a basic caravan park (☎ 4977 6164) by an excellent beach has four-person camp sites for $10.50 and on-site vans from $32.

Getting There & Away There is road access to the park from Tea Gardens in the south, from Bulahdelah on the Pacific Hwy and from Forster-Tuncurry in the north. You can drive from Tea Gardens to Bulahdelah via the Bombah Point ferry. Seal Rocks is accessible from the Lakes Way, a scenic road between Bulahdelah and Forster-Tuncurry. Great Lakes Coaches (☎ 1800 043 263) services this route.

Forster-Tuncurry

• pop 17,000   • postcode 2428

Forster-Tuncurry are twin towns on either side of the sea entrance to Wallis Lake. Forster is the larger town and here you'll find the tourist information centre (☎ 6554 8799, tourglc@tpgi.com.au), on Little St, the lakefront road, open daily from 9 am to 5 pm. As well as the lake there are some excellent sea beaches in the area and right in town, though these are overlooked by a growing number of high-rise apartment buildings.

Places to Stay *Forster Beach Caravan Park* (☎ *6554 6269)* is right in the centre of town and a short walk from both the lake and the ocean. It has camp sites from $13.50 and on-site vans from $34 to $95 for a luxury cabin.

Try the friendly YHA-affiliated *Dolphin Lodge* (☎ *6555 8155, 43 Head St, Forster)*. It's clean and spacious and has a surf beach virtually at the back door. Dorm beds cost $14 and doubles $34, though prices rise during the summer holidays. Boards are free and bike hire is $10 a day.

In the low season there are some good deals on motels, with doubles for $35 or less, but around Christmas/January most are expensive – and booked out.

Getting There & Away Forster-Tuncurry is on the Lakes Way, which leaves the Pacific Hwy near Bulahdelah and rejoins it south of Taree. Great Lakes Coaches (☎ 1800 043 263) runs to Sydney ($39) and Newcastle ($24) daily, while Countrylink (☎ 13 2232) operates a combination of bus and train to Sydney three times a day for $42. McCafferty's (☎ 13 1499) calls in once a day at 9.30 am on its Mt Isa-Brisbane run.

Manning Valley

From Forster-Tuncurry the highway swings inland to **Taree**, a large town serving the farms of the fertile Manning Valley. Further up the valley is the timber town of **Wingham**, where you can visit Wingham Brush, a lovely 7 hectare vestige of the dense rainforest that once covered the valley. Small roads run north from Wingham to Wauchope, near Port

Macquarie, passing through some interesting towns and great scenery around Comboyne.

On the coast near Taree, **Old Bar** is one of several small resorts. **Crowdy Bay National Park** runs up the coast, and there is camping at **Diamond Head**, at the northern end of the park. You need to bring your own water.

North of the national park and accessible from the Pacific Hwy at Kew, **Camden Haven** is a collection of small towns clustered around the wide sea entrance of Queens Lake. Just north of here the coast road runs past **Bonnie Hills** and **Lake Cathie** (pronounced cat-eye), both with pretty beaches, good surf and caravan park accommodation, then enters the outer suburbs of Port Macquarie.

PORT MACQUARIE
• post code 2444   • pop 33,700

One of the larger resorts on the NSW north coast, Port Macquarie makes a good stopping point on the journey from Sydney (430km south). It was founded in 1821 and was a convict settlement until 1840.

Port, as it is known, has both a river frontage (the Hastings River enters the sea here) and a series of ocean beaches starting right in the town.

Orientation & Information
The city centre is at the mouth of the Hastings River, and Horton St, the main street, runs down to the water. West of the city centre, at the base of the Settlement Point Peninsula, is the big Settlement City shopping centre.

The information centre (☎ 1800 025 935, vicpm@midcoast.com.au) is on Clarence St and is open daily.

Things to See
The **Koala Hospital** is off Lord St, about 1km south of the town centre. Convalescent koalas are in outdoor enclosures and you can visit them daily (the best time is from 3 pm, when they are fed). The hospital is in the grounds of **Roto**, a historic homestead open on weekdays from 10 am to 4 pm and weekends from 9 am to 1 pm.

You can meet healthy koalas and other animals at **Kingfisher Park**, off the Oxley

Hwy ($7/5). **Billabong Koala Park** is further out, just past the Pacific Hwy interchange (adults/children $7.50/4).

Other than Roto, most surviving old buildings are near the city centre: **St Thomas' Church** (1828), on William St near Hay St; the **Garrison** (1835), on the corner of Hay and Clarence Sts; the **courthouse** (1869), across the road ($2); and the award-winning **Port Macquarie Historical Society Museum** (1830), nearby at 22 Clarence St, open daily ($4).

An old pilot cottage above Town Beach houses the small **Maritime Museum**, open Monday to Saturday from 11 am to 3 pm ($2). Nearby, a small **observatory** is at the beach end of Lord St. It's open Wednesday and Sunday, at 7.30 pm in winter and 8.15 pm in summer ($2).

Five kilometres south of the town centre on Pacific Drive, **Sea Acres Rainforest Centre** is a 30 hectare reserve protecting a pocket of coastal rainforest. There's an ecology centre with displays and a 1.3km boardwalk. Entry is $8.50 – worth every cent.

Activities
Water sports are top of the activity list. There are some good surf breaks, particularly at Town Beach and at Flynns Beach, which is patrolled on weekends and school holidays.

You can hire watercraft at several places on Settlement Point, such as Hastings River Boat Hire (☎ 6583 8811) at Port Marina (powered craft and canoes), and the Settlement Point Boatshed (☎ 6583 6300), next to the ferry departure point. Jordans Boating Centre (☎ 6583 1005) has yachts and windsurfers. Diving is available with Port Macquarie Dive Centre (☎ 6583 8483).

There are plenty of river cruises. The Pelican River Cruise (☎ 0418 652 171) puts on a BBQ cruise (Monday to Friday, $30) and a Weekend Explorer cruise (Saturday and Sunday, $15). Both cruises explore the Hastings River and backwaters.

Port Macquarie Camel Safaris (☎ 6583 7650) has beach rides for $22. East Coast Mountain Safaris (☎ 6584 2366) has 4WD tours of the rainforest hinterland, from $45/65 for a half/full day.

NEW SOUTH WALES

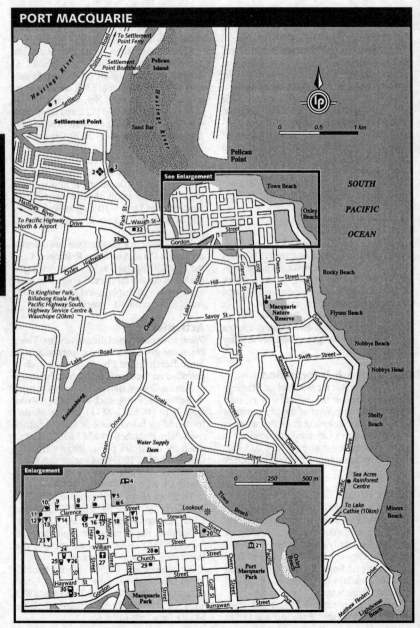

PORT MACQUARIE

To Settlement Point Ferry

Hastings River

Settlement Point Boatshed

Pelican Island

Settlement Road

● 7

Settlement Point

Hastings River

Sand Bar

Pelican Point

SOUTH

PACIFIC

OCEAN

0   0.5   1 km

2 ✦✦ ● 3

Hastings River

To Pacific Highway North & Airport

Park St

Waugh St

■ 32

See Enlargement

Town Beach

Oxley Beach

33 ●

Gordon   Street

Oxley Highway

34

To Kingfisher Park, Billabong Koala Park, Pacific Highway Service Centre & Wauchope (20km)

Hill Road

Lake Road

Savoy St

Grant St

Lord St

Owen St

Pacific Drive

Rocky Beach

Flynns Beach

34 ●
Macquarie Nature Reserve

Nobbys Beach

Koolenbung Creek

Lake Road

Koala Street

Granite Street

Kennedy Drive

Swift Street

Nobbys Head

Shelly Beach

Water Supply Dam

Ocean Street

Sea Acres Rainforest Centre ●

Pacific Drive

To Lake Cathie (10km)

Miners Beach

Enlargement

0   250   500 m

📷 4

10 ▼   9 ●   8 ●   ● 7   ▼ 5   ● 6

Clarence   Street

11 ▼   12 ▼   13 ▼   ▼ 14   ℹ 15   16 ▼ 17 ▼   18 ▼   19 ▼

Short St

Horton St

Hay St

Munster St

Murray St

Stewart St

Lookout ☀

Town Beach

23 ▼   24 ▼   🏛 22

25 ▼   ▼ 26   🏛 27

William Street

28 ●
29 ■

Church Street

Grant Street

Lord Street

Stewart Street

20 ● 🏛

21 🏛

Port Macquarie Park

30 ▼   ● 31

Hayward St

Gordon   Street

Macquarie Park

Burrawan Street

Owen Street

Golf St

Pacific Drive

Oxley Beach

Matthew Flinders Drive

Lighthouse Beach

Work of art in Silverton, NSW

Arching snow gum, Snowy Mountains, NSW

Green Cape Lighthouse, south of Eden, NSW

Charlotte Pass, Kosciuszko National Park, NSW

The Quoraburagun Pinnacles, Ben Boyd National Park, near Eden, NSW

The Walls of China, Mungo National Park, NSW

Places to Stay

Camping The most central caravan park is *Sundowner Breakwall Tourist Park* (☎ 6583 2755, 1 Munster St), near the river mouth and Town Beach. It has camp sites from $15 and on-site vans and cabins from $45. Prices rise sharply during school holidays. There are cheaper places near Flynns Beach and inland along the river or on the Oxley Hwy.

Hostels Backpackers are spoilt and pampered at Port Macquarie's three hostels. The newest one is *Ozzie Pozzie* (☎ 1800 620 020, 6583 8133, 36 Waugh Street), a few minutes' walk west of the city centre. The owners have gone to extraordinary lengths to lay it all on, including free bikes, fishing and surfing gear, barbecue nights, pick up from the bus, trips to the beach and information. The owners are friendly and laid-back, understanding the importance of a hammock in the courtyard. Dorms/twins/doubles start from $15/34/36.

Beachside Backpackers (☎ 6583 5512, 40 Church St) is a YHA associate. Dorm beds are $15, twin rooms $17 and family rooms $50. It's a short walk from the town centre and the closest hostel to the beach. There's free use of bikes and surfboards, and the owners meet the buses.

Lindel Port Macquarie Backpackers (☎ 6583 1791) occupies one of Port Macquarie's oldest houses. It's beside the Oxley Hwy on the way into town. There's a free pool table, lovely verandah with views over town and a swimming pool. Dorm beds cost from $16 and doubles/twins from $36. They meet buses arriving in town, there are free bikes, surfing and fishing gear, and the owner organises regular canoeing and fishing outings.

Hotels & Motels At the northern end of Horton St is the *Port Macquarie Hotel* (☎ 6583 1011). Singles/doubles costs $25/40 for, with an extra $5 for a room with en suite. Motel-style units overlooking the water cost $50/$65. Prices rise at peak times.

There are more than 30 motels. The cheapest, not surprisingly, are the ones furthest from the beaches, such as those on Hastings River Drive. In town, the pleasant *River Motel* (☎ 6583 3744, 5 Clarence St) is near the corner of School St and has off-season doubles from $50. Several nearby holiday apartments have similar deals.

Places to Eat

There are dozens of restaurants and cafes around the city centre, with something to suit every budget.

The *Fisherman's Co-op*, near the western end of Clarence St, sells seafood straight off the boats. If you want your seafood cooked, *Macquarie Seafoods*, on the corner of Clarence and Short Sts, does great fish and chips.

There's a good choice of Asian food. The *Yuen Hing*, on Horton St, does cheap

NEW SOUTH WALES

PORT MACQUARIE

lunches. *Noodle World (72 Clarence St)* has a $5.50 lunch specials.

Toro's Cantina (22 Murray St) is a Mexican place with main courses under $13 and backpacker discounts. For breakfast try *Eclipse*, a small place on Short St near the corner of William St. *Margo's Café*, in the historic Garrison building on the corner of Hay and Clarence Sts, has tables outside, good coffee and delicious, well priced meals. *Contasia (14 Clarence St)* has all-you-can-eat meals for $6 and *Carz Restaurant (☎ 6584 1446)*, near the river on Short St, has two-for-one dinners on Wednesday.

Entertainment
There are two nightclubs in town: *TC's* on William St, and *Down Under,* around the corner on Short St. The *RSL* club's big new complex at Settlement City has live bands on Friday and Saturday nights and free billiard tables. The *Port Macquarie Hotel* has a DJ on weekends in the back bar. *Finnians Irish Tavern,* behind the bus station on Gordon St, serves great Irish meals and is open until midnight every night.

Getting There & Away
The Oxley Hwy runs west from Port Macquarie through Wauchope and eventually reaches the New England tablelands near Walcha. It's a spectacular drive.

A vehicle ferry ($2) operates 24-hours a day across the river at Settlement Point, accessing two roads north. One is a very rough dirt road (4WD required) running along the coast, past Limeburners Creek Nature Reserve to Point Plomer (good surf) and Crescent Head – you can rejoin the highway at Kempsey. The second road – slightly better and gravelled – takes an inland route to meet the Crescent Head-Kempsey road.

Air Eastern Australia (☎ 13 1313) flies to Sydney at least three times a day for $187 one way. Impulse (☎ 13 1381) flies to Sydney for the same fare, and to Brisbane for $252 one way.

Bus Port Macquarie Bus Service (☎ 6583 2161) runs to Wauchope, 20km inland,

several times a day for $6.70. This service stops at Ritz Corner, at the corner of Clarence and Horton Sts. The long distance bus station is on Horton Street, however Greyhound Pioneer (☎ 13 2030) and McCafferty's (☎ 13 1499) stop at the Pacific Hwy Service Centre. Keans (☎ 1800 625 587) runs to Coffs Harbour ($20), Bellingen ($25) and Dorrigo ($27), Armidale ($40) and Tamworth ($57).

Train The nearest station is at Wauchope. The fare from Sydney to Port Macquarie ($62) includes the connecting Countrylink bus between Wauchope and Port (the train pulls into Wauchope at 1.21 pm).

Getting Around
Port Macquarie Bus Service (☎ 6583 2161) runs buses around the town. There are no super-cheap car rental outfits, only major rental firms. Thrifty (☎ 6584 2122) is on the corner of Horton and Hayward Sts. Graham Seer's Cyclery, at the Port Marina, rents bikes for $6 an hour, $20 for a day or $50 for five days.

PORT MACQUARIE TO COFFS HARBOUR
Wauchope
• postcode 2446   • pop 4700
Nineteen kilometres inland from Port Macquarie and on the Hastings River, Wauchope (pronounced 'war hope') is an old timber town. Wauchope's story is told at **Timbertown**, an interesting working replica of an 1880s town. It's open daily from 9.30 am to 4 pm. Entry is free but there are charges for the various activities once you're inside.

Wauchope has a range of accommodation including *Rainbow Ridge Hostel (☎ 6585 6134)*, a quiet YHA associate, 10km west of town on the Oxley Hwy. Dorm beds are $10 or you can camp for $5.

Kempsey Area
North along the Pacific Hwy from Wauchope is **Kempsey** (population 8600), a large town serving the farms of the Macleay Valley and also the home of the Akubra hat. The information centre (☎ 6563 1555,

ktic@midcoast.com.au) is off the highway at the southern end of town. Next door is the **Macleay River Historical Museum and Cultural Centre** ($3), both open daily. There is plenty of accommodation in town, but there's no reason to stick around. There are, however, some good spots on the coast.

Crescent Head (population 1175), a small town 20km from Kempsey, has a quiet front beach and a surf-washed back beach and is the surf long-boarding capital of Australia. The *Crescent Head Tourist Park* (☎ 6566 0261) is right on the beach and has camp sites from $13 and cabins from $44, but the new owners are strict and unfriendly. The *Bush and Beach Retreat* (☎ 6566 0235, 353 Loftus Rd) is 3.5km from Crescent Head. It's a big homestead set amid bush 1km from the beach along the bay from town. Bunk rooms are $20 a head and there's a pool and outdoor kitchen.

In town there are plenty of holiday apartments and some can be cheaper than cabins at the caravan park – contact either of the two estate agents on the main street (☎ 6566 0500 or 6566 0306), or the Crescent Head Accommodation Bureau (☎ 6566 0333). South of town, **Limeburners Creek Nature Reserve** has walking trails and two camp sites, with cabins at Barries Bay.

Stretching up the coast from Crescent Head to Smoky Cape is **Hat Head National Park**. Within the park is the quiet township of **Hat Head**, tucked beneath the headland. It has a beautiful sheltered beach, a few shops, a caravan park and holiday flats. There's a basic camp site in the park south of Hat Head and another camp site at the northern end of the park near the **Smoky Cape Lighthouse**. The lighthouse is the tallest and one of the oldest in NSW.

The pleasant resort town of **South West Rocks** (population 3514) is near the mouth of the Macleay River. Fishing and water sports are the main attractions. **Trial Bay Gaol** is on the headland 3km east of South West Rocks. This imposing edifice was a prison in the late 19th century and housed German internees during WWI. It's now a museum; open daily ($4). Trial Bay is named after the *Trial*, a brig that was stolen

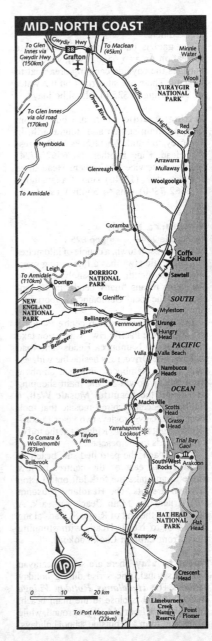

NEW SOUTH WALES

from Sydney by convicts in 1816 and wrecked here.

The gaol is part of the **Arakoon State Recreation Area** (☎ 6566 6168), which also manages the bayside camping area next to the gaol. There are sites right on the water for $10, rising to $25 in school holidays.

Getting Around There are buses from Kempsey train station and Belgrave St, in Kempsey, to South West Rocks and to Crescent Head. King Brothers (☎ 6562 4724) operates a service to Crescent Head three times a day ($5.40) and Cavanaugh's (☎ 6562 7800) runs to South West Rocks ($7.20).

Nambucca Heads

• postcode 2448   • pop 6250

This quiet resort town, a couple of kilometres off the Pacific Hwy, has a fine setting overlooking the mouth of the Nambucca River. The name means 'many bends' in the language of the local Gumbaingeri Aboriginal people.

The helpful information centre (☎ 6568 6954) is on the Pacific Hwy where you take the turning to Nambucca Heads. The road in, Riverside Drive, runs beside the wide estuary of the Nambucca and then climbs a steep hill to Bowra St, the main shopping street, and the beautiful **Mosaic Wall**, a 30m-long ocean inspired mosaic that took local artist, Guy Crosley, two years to complete. A right turn onto Ridge St at the top of the hill leads to the beaches.

Main Beach, the patrolled surf beach, is about 1.5km east of the centre. Follow Ridge St and take the fork left onto Liston St when it splits. The **Headland Museum** ($1) is near the Main Beach car park. A right fork at the end of Ridge St leads along Parkes St to North Head, with stunning views from **Captain Cook Lookout**.

Places to Stay There are several caravan parks. As usual, prices rise during holiday periods. The *Headlands Holiday Village* (☎ 6568 6547) is close to the main beach. Camp sites are from $14 all year round, while cabins start from $40 outside school holidays.

Nambucca Backpackers Hostel (☎ 6568 6360, 1800 630 663, Newman St) is a quiet hostel tucked away behind the town. It's a 1km walk through bush to the beach. Dorm beds are $15 and doubles are $34, with discounts for longer stays. The friendly managers meet the buses and can arrange outings in the area. They lend snorkel and fishing gear and boogie boards for no charge.

Dunaber House (☎ 6568 9434, 35 Piggott St) is a B&B close to all facilities. Their low-season prices start from $50 for a double. Breakfast is extra.

Scotts Guesthouse (☎ 6568 6386, 4 Wellington Drive) is a luxurious and stylish old weatherboard guesthouse overlooking the river with large rooms. It charges from $70 to $100 for a double, which includes breakfast.

Places to Eat The *RSL* has a prime site by the river at the foot of Bowra St and has $3 meals on Sundays and Thursdays. A popular hang-out is the *Beachcomber* exchange bookshop and cafe, just opposite the post office. *Matilda's*, on Wellington Drive, has three course specials for $17 from Wednesday to Friday. The *V-Wall Tavern*, at the end of Wellington Drive, serves bistro meals and the views from its balcony over the rivermouth are perfect. *Mahlbergs*, on Ridge St, serves good 'Mod Oz' Mediterranean food, but is closed Monday and Tuesday.

Getting There & Away Most long-distance buses stop on the highway at the Shell service station (southbound), or the Aukaka Caravan Park (northbound). The fare to Sydney with Premier is $45, to Byron Bay it's $41.

Newman's (☎ 6568 1296) has four buses a day to Coffs Harbour ($3). Joyces' (☎ 6655 6330) runs from Nambucca to Bellingen ($5). This local service leaves from opposite the police station on Bowra St and runs twice a day on weekdays.

Nambucca is on the main railway line north from Sydney ($69). The station is about 3km out of town – follow Bowra St north.

Bellingen

- postcode 2454   • pop 2700

This attractive small town sits on the banks of the Bellinger River just inland from the Pacific Hwy about halfway between Nambucca Heads and Coffs Harbour. The turning is north of Urunga. It's a lively country town and a centre for the area's artistic/alternative population. The information centre (☎ 6655 5711) is on the Pacific Hwy at Urunga.

Things to See & Do The main attraction is the setting in the lush Bellinger Valley. If you have your own transport, there are some great swimming holes to be discovered on the **Never Never River** at the aptly named **Promised Land**, about 10km north of town. Gambaarri Tours (see Things to Do in the Coffs Harbour section) runs a tour of the area.

A huge colony of flying foxes (grey-headed fruit bats) lives on **Bellingen Island**, near the caravan park, from December to March. They're an impressive sight when they head off in their thousands at dusk to feed. The island is a small remnant of subtropical rainforest that once covered the valley. Platypuses live in the river nearby.

There are plenty of craft shops, including the **Old Butter Factory**, on the eastern approach to town. It houses several workshops, a gallery and a cafe. The **Bellingen markets**, held at the park on Church St on the third Saturday of the month, have become a major regional event with more than 250 stalls, live music and other entertainment. The Global Carnival is a fantastic world music festival in October and there's a jazz festival in August.

Places to Stay The *Bellingen Caravan Park* (☎ 6655 1338) is across the river – turn onto Wharf St from the main street (the post office is on the corner), cross the bridge and follow the road around to the left, then turn left down Dowle St. You can walk from town. Camp sites start from $10 and on-site vans from $25.

Bellingen Backpackers (☎ 6655 1116) is a great place to hang out for a few days. It occupies a beautiful weatherboard house overlooking the river on Short St. Dorm beds are from $15 and doubles are $36. The pleasant owners will pick you up from Urunga by arrangement and organise trips to Dorrigo and other local spots. There are bikes for hire ($5 for as long as you stay).

Places to Eat Bellingen has a surprisingly large choice of restaurants for a town of its size. The *Carriageway Café*, on the main street, has meals as well as good coffee and cakes. There are several places on Church St, including the *Good Food Shop* with vegetarian takeaways, and the laid-back *Cool Creek Café*, which has live music most Friday nights. *Lodge 241*, a cafe cum gallery at the Dorrigo end of the main street, is great for breakfasts and lunches.

Getting There & Away Getting to Bellingen without your own transport can be a bit of a hassle. Keans (☎ 1800 625 587, 6543 1322) stops at Bellingen on its Port Macquarie-Tamworth run. Jessup's (☎ 6653 4552) operates two services a day to Coffs Harbour – school days only. Buses run between Bellingen and Coffs three times a day ($4.50).

Joyces' (☎ 6655 6330) runs the school bus on weekdays between Nambucca Heads, Urunga and Bellingen. The bus stop in Bellingen is on the corner of Church St and the main street.

The nearest train station is at Urunga.

Dorrigo

- postcode 2453   • pop 1110

It's a spectacular drive from Bellingen up to the quiet mountain town of Dorrigo. The road climbs 1000m through dense rainforest, with occasional breaks in the canopy offering great views down the Bellinger Valley to the coast. Dorrigo was one of the last places to be settled in the eastward push across the New England tablelands. It's a pleasant base for visiting the area's outstanding national parks. Island Continent (☎ 6655 2382) runs eco-tours to Dorrigo or will organise tours to suit your interests. The tour guide also works for the NPWS and has a good knowledge of the local area.

There is an information centre (☎ 6657 2486) at 36 Hickory St, open daily from 10 am to 4 pm.

Things to See & Do A few kilometres north of town, on the road to Leigh, are the picturesque **Dangar Falls**. The main attraction though is the magnificent subtropical rainforest of **Dorrigo National Park**, 2km east of town. It is the most accessible of Australia's World Heritage rainforests and well worth a visit. The Rainforest Centre (☎ 6657 2309), at the entrance, has information about the park's many walks and is open daily from 9 am to 5 pm. Camping is not allowed in the park. The turn-off to the park is clearly signposted on the Dorrigo-Bellingen road. See the New England section for information on other national parks in this area.

Places to Stay *Dorrigo Mountain Resort* (☎ 6657 2564), a caravan park with some substantial wooden cabins, is just out of town on the road to Bellingen. Camp sites cost from $10. There are on-site vans ($30) as well as self-contained cabins ($44). The historic *Commercial Hotel/Motel* (☎ 6657 2003, Cudgery St) has motel units for $28/36.

Getting There & Away Keans (☎ 1800 043 339) uses Dorrigo as a meal stop on its Port Macquarie-Tamworth run. It operates three times a week ($27), going via Coffs Harbour and Armidale. Hostels in Coffs Harbour, Bellingen and Nambucca all organise day trips to the Dorrigo National Park.

Urunga & Mylestom

Urunga, about 20km north of Nambucca, is a quiet little town at the mouth of the Bellinger and Kalang rivers. The rivers meet just 200m from the ocean, forming an impressive estuary that is popular for water sports. There is a surf beach just south of town at **Hungry Head**, but the best beach in the area is about 5km south of town at **Third Headland** – signposted off the Pacific Hwy along Snapper Beach Rd. The *Ocean View Hotel* (☎ 6655 6221), in Urunga, has

good rooms for $25/40 with breakfast. The front rooms have views over the estuary.

North of Urunga is the turn-off to Mylestom, also called North Beach. This quiet town is in a great location on the banks of the wide Bellinger River and also has ocean beaches. The *North Beach Caravan Park* (☎ 6655 4250) has camp sites for $10, on-site vans for $20 and cabins for $25. The good backpackers hostel, *Riverside Lodge* (☎ 6655 4245), on the main street across from the river as you enter town, has beds in two-bed 'dorms' from $15. The friendly owners can organise activities and they'll pick up guests from the train station or bus stop at Urunga; given a day's notice, they can pick you up from Coffs. There's free use of the lodge's bikes and kayaks.

COFFS HARBOUR

● postcode 2450   ● pop 60,000

Adrenalin junkies love Coffs Harbour for its huge variety of adventure sports. Everything from whale-watching to indoor rockclimbing is available and it is one of the cheapest places on the coast to get dive certified. The city's main street, Grafton St, is part of the Pacific Hwy and is pretty grotty. Fortunately it is not representative of the city's pleasant beaches and beautiful natural setting. The Beacon Hill lookout offers a fine panorama of the surrounding mountains, famous banana crops and spectacular coastline.

Orientation & Information

The city centre is around the junction of Grafton and High Sts. East of Grafton St, High St has been transformed into a rainforest mall. High St resumes on the other side of Grafton St and becomes the main road to the waterfront jetty area, a couple of kilometres east.

The information centre (☎ 6652 1522, 1800 025 650, tourism@coffscoast.com.au) is on the corner of Rose Ave and Marcia St.

Things to See & Do

The **North Coast Botanic Gardens**, at the end of Hardacre St (off High St), are well worth a visit. It's hard to believe that part of the site was once the town tip. These immaculately maintained gardens contain many endangered species and areas have been planted to re-create the region's different rainforest types. The gardens are also part of the popular **Coffs Creek Walk** that follows the creek upstream from the mouth of Coffs Creek to near the town centre.

Muttonbird Island, linked to the mainland by the harbour's northern breakwater, is home to more than 12,000 pairs of mutton birds (wedge-tailed shearwaters) from late August until April. The island is dotted with their nesting burrows; chicks emerge during December and January. Humpback whales can sometimes be seen off Muttonbird Island during their northbound migration in June and July and during their southern migration from September to November.

Fans of kitsch big things can take a walk through the **Big Banana**, on the northern outskirts of town, which is home to a new ice skating rink.

Beaches
The main beach is **Park Beach**, which is patrolled at weekends and during school holidays. There is a good beach at **Korora** and then a string of them up to Woolgoolga. Back in town, **Jetty Beach** is more sheltered and good for swimming when the surf is rough.

Activities
With excellent surfing at places such as Macauleys Headland and Diggers Beach, white-water rafting on the Nymboida and Goolang rivers, and great dive spots off the Solitary Islands, Coffs offers excellent outdoor activities.

Dive Depot (☎ 6652 2033) has a four day dive course for $150. Absolute Adrenalin (☎ 6651 9100), at 396B High St, represents individual outdoor activity operators. It has a range of packages offering everything from skydiving to white-water rafting, scuba diving, surfing, fishing, whale-watching and Harley-Davidson tours. Goforit Adventures (☎ 6650 0129) is another one-stop adventure shop. They may be a good place to start, although individual companies may be offering better deals at the time you visit. Some companies to consider are:

Adriatic III
(☎ 6658 4379) reef and game fishing and whale watching
Coffs City Skydivers
(☎ 6651 1167)
Dive Quest
(☎ 6654 1930)
East Coast Surf School
(☎ 6651 5515)
Endless Summer Adventures
(☎ 6658 0850) intermediate white-water rafting
Jetty Dive Centre
(☎ 6651 1611)
Liquid Assets
(☎ 6658 0850) sea kayaking and surf rafting
Mountain Trails
(☎ 6658 3333) 4WD tours
Skylink
(☎ 6658 0899) helicopter flights
Soaring Adventures
(☎ 6653 6331) glider flights
Valery Trails
(☎ 6653 4301) horse riding
Wildwater Adventures
(☎ 6653 4469)
WOW rafting
(☎ 6654 4066)
Wyndyarra Estate
(☎ 6653 8488) horse riding and carriage tours

Aboriginal Tours
Gambaarri Tours (☎ 6655 4195) runs cultural and historical trips to a number of Aboriginal sites on the coast and nearby rainforests costing from $45. Ring in advance as these tours are conducted according to demand, not schedule.

Places to Stay
Except in the hostels, prices rise by about 50% during school holidays and as much as 100% at Christmas/New Year.

Camping The huge *Park Beach Caravan Park (☎ 6648 4888, Ocean Parade)* is right next to the beach and has camp sites from $13, on-site vans from $28 and cabins from $34. There are lower weekly rates but not at peak times.

Coffs Harbour Tourist Park (☎ 6652 1694), on the highway a couple of blocks on from the Ex-Servicemen's Club, has camp sites from $12, on-site vans from $26 and

NEW SOUTH WALES

COFFS HARBOUR

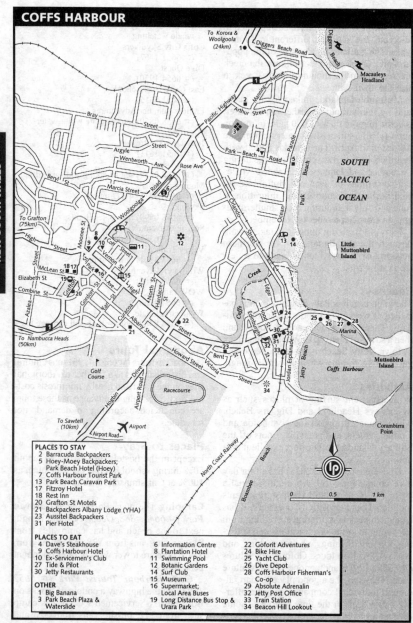

PLACES TO STAY
2 Barracuda Backpackers
5 Hoey-Moey Backpackers;
   Park Beach Hotel (Hoey)
7 Coffs Harbour Tourist Park
13 Park Beach Caravan Park
17 Fitzroy Hotel
18 Rest Inn
20 Grafton St Motels
21 Backpackers Albany Lodge (YHA)
23 Aussitel Backpackers
31 Pier Hotel

PLACES TO EAT
4 Dave's Steakhouse
9 Coffs Harbour Hotel
10 Ex-Servicemen's Club
27 Tide & Pilot
30 Jetty Restaurants

OTHER
1 Big Banana
3 Park Beach Plaza &
   Waterslide

6 Information Centre
8 Plantation Hotel
11 Swimming Pool
12 Botanic Gardens
14 Surf Club
15 Museum
16 Supermarket;
   Local Area Buses
19 Long Distance Bus Stop &
   Urara Park

22 Goforit Adventures
24 Bike Hire
25 Yacht Club
26 Dive Depot
28 Coffs Harbour Fisherman's
   Co-op
29 Absolute Adrenalin
32 Jetty Post Office
33 Train Station
34 Beacon Hill Lookout

cabins from $36. There are plenty of other places along the highway either side of town.

Hostels There are four good hostels and all can arrange discounts on just about every activity on offer.

Aussitel Backpackers Hostel (☎ 6651 1871, 312 High St) is about 1.5km from the town centre and 500m from the harbour. It is a lively place with dorm beds from $15 and double rooms from $36. It has disabled access and a pool. The enthusiastic management will help arrange white-water rafting, diving and surfing trips (as well as other activities), pick you up on arrival and provide rides to town or to the beach during the day or to the pub at night. Coffs Creek is over the road and canoes are free.

The town's YHA hostel, *Backpackers Albany Lodge YHA (☎ 6652 6462, 110 Albany St)*, is close to the city centre. Dorm beds are $15, doubles $34 and family rooms from $40; bikes and surfboards are free, there's a pool and a cosy lounge. The hostel's reception is open 18 hours a day and someone can usually pick you up – if arriving at night, phone in advance to ask. The hostel also arranges activities and excursions.

Hoey-Moey Backpackers (☎ 6652 3833, Ocean Parade), adjacent to the Park Beach Hotel (Hoey-Moey pub), has the best location – right behind Park Beach. It offers free bicycle hire, surfboards and pick-ups. The manager is keen to assist and several readers have recommended this hostel. Dorm beds cost $15, singles $25 and doubles $36. Rooms come with en suite and TV and there are cheap meals for hostel guests at the pub.

Barracuda Backpackers (☎ 6651 3514, 19 Arthur St) is in a suburban neck of the woods near the Park Beach Plaza Shopping Centre, which has a cinema and pub. Several readers have praised their helpfulness. It has a nice pool, a barbecue area and all the usual facilities. The owners will even help with finding fruit picking work in season. Dorms cost from $14 and doubles from $36.

Hotels & Motels The *Fitzroy Hotel (☎ 6652 3007, Moonee St)* is an old-style neighbourhood pub with rooms for $20 per person. Down near the harbour on High St, the *Pier Hotel (☎ 6652 2110)* has a few large, clean rooms from $20 per person, per night.

There's a string of motels on Grafton St on the southern approach to town, which outside school holiday periods charge around $45 to $55 a double. The *Rest Inn*, behind the Fitzroy Hotel, has low season rooms from $39. Another group of motels in the Park Beach area has similar rates.

Apartments There is a huge range of holiday apartments and houses. In the low season the cheapest two-bedroom apartments cost around $45 a night (less by the week) and $90 a night in the high season, although many places are only available by the week at this time. The information centre has a booking service (☎ 1800 025 650).

Places to Eat

Some of the best cheap eats can be found in the clubs, such as the *Ex-Servicemen's Club*, on the corner of Grafton and Vernon Sts, which charges $8.50 for a roast dinner and dessert.

There are simply too many snack places on the mall to list. Counter meals are served at the pubs along Grafton St, including the *Coffs Harbour Hotel*, on the corner of High St, which has great Thai meals from $7. *Dave's Steakhouse (99 Park Beach Rd)* has soup and steak specials for $14.50.

The main restaurant strip is at the jetty end of High St. There is an amazing variety of restaurants here including the excellent *Tahruah Thai Kitchen*, the *Fountain* Vietnamese, which has a banquet for $15, the *Fisherman's Katch*, which has three-course meals for $20, and the popular *Foreshores Café* which has breakfasts for $5.

There are several other restaurants along this part of High St offering various cuisines, but most of these are quite expensive. They include *Bush Turkey* (Australian cuisine) where you can try kangaroo, *Peter's Pepermill* (French), the *Royal Viking* (grill), the *Passionfish Brasserie* (multicultural), *Avanti* (Italian) and a couple of Indian restaurants. There are also $6 pub lunches at the *Pier Hotel*.

The harbour is the place to go for seafood. *Coffs Harbour Fishermen's Co-op* has a good takeaway section with a sushi and sashimi bar as well as fresh seafood. The nearby *Yacht Club* has $6 lunches on weekdays and *Tide & Pilot* offers fantastic views while you tuck into dishes like the amazing seafood platter ($57.50 for two).

Entertainment

There's something happening every night in Coffs Harbour, although the pickings are fairly slim early in the week. Thursday's edition of the *Coffs Harbour Advocate* has the week's listings.

The *Plantation Hotel*, on Grafton St, has free local bands from Thursday to Saturday and seven pool tables. The nearby *Saloon* bar and nightclub has pool tables and dance music from Wednesday to Saturday. Live bands play at the *Hoey-Moey* at Park Beach. Big-name touring bands play at the *Sawtell RSL Club*, 5km south of town. The hostels usually organise transport.

Getting There & Away

Air Coffs has a busy airport, on the south edge of town. Ansett and Eastern Australia (☎ 13 1313) fly to Sydney ($232). Impulse (☎ 13 1381) flies to Brisbane ($235).

Bus All the long-distance lines on the Sydney to Brisbane route stop at Coffs. The long-distance bus stop is at Urara Park, on the highway at the southern end of town; access is via Elizabeth St. Premier Motor Service (☎ 13 3410) stops here and has the cheapest fares. It has a ticket that allows unlimited stops between Sydney and Brisbane for $79. Its fares from Coffs include: Byron Bay $36, Brisbane $43, Nambucca Heads $24, Port Macquarie $34 and Sydney $65. All bookings can be made at the train station.

Local buses stop at the car park next to Woolworths on Park Ave. Ryans' buses (☎ 6652 3201) run several times daily, except Sunday, to Woolgoolga ($6.80) via beachside towns off the highway. Watson's Woolgoolga Coaches (☎ 6654 1063)

connects Coffs Harbour and Grafton on weekdays. The fare to Woolgoologa is $5.50 one way, Grafton $11 (see the Bellingen and Nambucca Heads sections for other local services).

Train The train station (☎ 6651 2757) is near the harbour at the end of High St. The fare to Sydney is $69 and to Brisbane $62.

Yacht Coffs is reportedly a good place to pick up a ride along the coast on a yacht or cruiser. Ask around or put a notice in the yacht club at the harbour. Sometimes the hostels know of boat owners who are looking for crew.

Getting Around

Coffs Harbour Coaches (☎ 6652 2877) and Sawtell Coaches (☎ 6653 3344) run several routes around town and out to Sawtell. The former does not run on Sundays.

The Coffs District Taxi Network (☎ 6658 8888) operates a 24-hour service. There's a taxi rank on the corner of High and Gordon Sts.

Bob Wallis World of Wheels (☎ 6652 5102), near the harbour on the corner of Collingwood and Orlando Sts, rents bikes.

All the main hire car companies have offices in Coffs Harbour. Coffs Rent-a-Car (☎ 6652 5022) hires cars from $39 a day.

COFFS HARBOUR TO BYRON BAY
Woolgoolga
• postcode 2456　　　• pop 3750

Twenty-six kilometres north of Coffs, Woolgoolga is a small resort with a fine surf beach. It has a sizeable Indian Sikh population whose *gurdwara* (place of worship), the **Guru Nanak Temple**, is just off the highway at the southern end of town.

The clean and friendly *Sunset Caravan Park* (☎ 6654 1499) backs onto the creek. It's a short stroll from town and has camp sites from $14 and cabins from $36.

For Indian food try the *Raj Mahal Restaurant* (☎ 6654 1149) or *Temple View*, near the temple.

North of Woolgoolga is **Arrawarra**, a quiet seaside town with yet another great beach and a pleasant caravan park close to the water. Further on, sleepy **Red Rock** is on a beautiful little inlet.

Long-distance buses run through Woolgoolga. There are local services to Coffs Harbour, Grafton and nearby beaches. See the Coffs Harbour section for services.

Yuraygir National Park

Yuraygir covers the 60km stretch of coast north from Red Rock to Angourie Point, just south of Yamba. The main attractions are fine beaches and bushwalking in the coastal heath. There are some great camping grounds along the coast, including the Illaroo Rest Area at **Minnie Water**. Minnie Water is signposted off the Pacific Hwy, 10km south of Grafton. Stan Young operates a diving and deep sea fishing charter from nearby Wooli (☎ 6649 7100).

The Solitary Islands

This island group, strung out along the coast from Yuraygir National Park, is a marine reserve at the meeting place of the warmer tropical currents and the more temperate southern currents, with some interesting varieties of fish attracted by the unusual conditions. It is a popular dive spot.

Grafton

• postcode 2460   • pop 17,500

Grafton is a graceful old country town on the banks of the mighty Clarence River. The town is noted for its fine street trees, particularly the spectacular jacarandas which carpet the streets with their mauve flowers at Jacaranda Festival time in late October. The town lies at the heart of a rich agricultural area. The wide Clarence delta is a patchwork of sugar-cane plantations.

On Fitzroy St is **Prentice House** (1880), now an art gallery. The nearby **Schaeffer House** (1900) is a historical museum, open in the afternoon from Tuesday to Thursday and Sunday.

The Pacific Hwy runs past Grafton, and the Clarence River Tourist Centre (☎ 6642 4677, crta@nor.com.au) is on the highway south of the town. The town centre is north of the Clarence River.

Places to Stay There's no shortage of motels and many pubs have accommodation. The *Crown Hotel/Motel* (☎ 6642 4000, Prince St) is a gorgeous place overlooking the river. At the time of writing it was establishing some backpacker accommodation for $12 per person. Pub rooms are $20/40 or $30/50 with en suite. Another nice pub in the same area is *Roches* (☎ 6642 2866, 85 Victoria St), where the spotless rooms are $24/30.

Getting There & Away Long-distance buses stop at the Shell service station on the highway in South Grafton, not far from the information centre. Fares with Premier (☎ 13 3410) include Sydney $49 and Byron Bay $34. Countrylink runs up the Gwydir Hwy to Glen Innes three times a week for $22. Watson's Woolgoolga Coaches (☎ 6654 1063) has three services a day between Grafton and Coffs ($11).

Most local-area buses leave from the Market Square shopping centre in the town centre, not far from the corner of King and Fitzroy Sts. A bus runs around town hourly (☎ 42 3111).

The train station is on the highway side of the river. The fare to Sydney is $75.

Grafton to Ballina

From Grafton the highway follows the Clarence River north-east, bypassing the pleasant little river port of **Maclean**. Maclean celebrates its Scottish early settlers with a Highland Gathering each Easter.

The fishing town of **Yamba** (population 4572), at the mouth of the Clarence River, is a growing resort with good beaches. The *Pacific Hotel* (☎ 6646 2466, Pilot St) has a great setting overlooking the main beach. It has backpackers' rooms for $17.50 per person. King Brothers Bus Service (☎ 6646 2019) runs five buses a day (less in school holidays and on weekends) from Grafton to Yamba via Maclean ($7). There are four ferries a day from Yamba to the town of **Iluka**, on the northern bank of the Clarence, for $3. They depart from the River St wharf in Yamba.

Just south of Yamba, **Angourie** is one of the coast's top spots for experienced surfers – but beware of the rips.

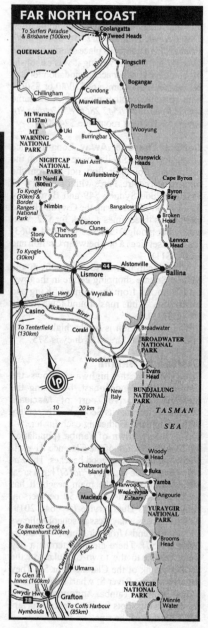

FAR NORTH COAST

NEW SOUTH WALES

Iluka is worth a detour off the highway to visit its World Heritage listed **Nature Reserve**, which contains the largest patch of littoral rainforest in NSW. There's a good camping ground at nearby Woody Head, within the Bundjalung National Park. Tent sites cost $10, plus $2 for each extra person, and cabins go for $30/40/60 for two/four/eight people. At peak times you might need to book (☎ 6646 6134).

Iluka is at the southern end of **Bundjalung National Park**, which stretches north to Evans Head between the highway and the coast. There are good surfing beaches, plus lots of wildlife. The park's extensive middens and old Aboriginal camp sites indicate it was a popular spot with the local Bundjalung people. The turn-off to Evans Head is at Woodburn or further along the highway at Broadwater.

Ballina

• postcode 2478   • pop 16,056

This town, at the mouth of the Richmond River, is a popular sailing and fishing spot and many find it a welcome break from the hype of Byron Bay. There are good beaches north of town and others south of town which are accessible via the Burns Point ferry to South Ballina.

Orientation & Information The Pacific Hwy runs through town, becoming River St, the long main road. The information centre (☎ 6686 3484, balinfo@balshire.org.au) is at the eastern end of River St, just past the old post office – now the courthouse. It's open daily from 9 am to 5 pm.

Beaches Popular **Shelly Beach** is the closest patrolled beach to town. To get there, head east out of Ballina along River St, cross the bridge over North Creek and take the first right after the Shaws Hotel turn-off. This road also passes **Lighthouse Beach** and the small beach curving around **Shaws Bay Lagoon**, which is a quiet place to swim.

River Cruises Ask at the information centre about river cruises. The MV *Bennelong* (☎ 0414 664 552) has a variety of cruises, including a day cruise up the river to Lismore for $55 ($20 children). You can buy lunch on board. These cruises leave from near the RSL Club.

Places to Stay *Ballina Lakeside Caravan Park (☎ 6686 3953)* has camp sites on the edge of Shaws Bay Lagoon for $11 and cabins for $35 for two people. Prices go up sharply during school holidays.

Ballina Travellers Lodge (☎ 6686 6737, 36-38 Tamar St) is a good, modern YHA hostel. Dorm beds are from $14 and twins/doubles are $48. There's a pool and nice barbecue area, free bikes and fishing gear. The lodge is also a motel and one of the few places to stay in town without highway noise. Doubles are $47 in the low season, rising to $85 around Christmas.

The *Flat Rock Camping Ground (☎ 6686 4848)*, just north of Ballina on the coast road to Lennox Head, has camp sites for $10. At Ballina Quays Marina (☎ 6686 4289), off the highway south of the Big Prawn, you can rent a houseboat which accommodates 10 people. The best deal is from Friday to Monday, which costs $480 during the low season. With over 100km of navigable river there's plenty of room to move.

Places to Eat *Shellys on the Beach*, above Shelly Beach, has outdoor tables, good food and wonderful views. It's open from 7.30 am. The huge modern *RSL* has a prime position on the riverbank, on the corner of Grant and River Sts. The club's downstairs bistro is great value and has seating on a deck overhanging the water. It's a good place to catch the sunset.

Cafe Fresco, at the Henry Rous Hotel in River St, has a large choice of snacks and light meals as well as good coffee. It's open until midnight every night.

Getting There & Away Most major bus lines stop at the Ballina Transit Centre, on the highway just south of town at the Big Prawn. Countrylink buses stop on Tamar St outside the Wigmore Arcade that runs through from River St.

Blanch's (☎ 6686 2144) has seven buses a day to Lennox Head ($4) and Byron Bay ($6.60), fewer on weekends, departing from Tamar St. Kirklands (☎ 6622 1499) runs buses to Evans Head ($11.60) and Lismore ($9). Both companies have services around town.

Lennox Head
• postcode 2478   • pop 4500

Lennox Head is a rapidly expanding small town on the coast road halfway between Ballina and Byron Bay. Lennox Head is also the name of the dramatic headland (a prime hang-gliding site) just south of town. Lennox has some of the best surf on the coast, particularly in winter.

Lake Ainsworth, just back from the beach, is popular for sailing and windsurfing. The water is stained brown by the tannin from the surrounding melaleuca trees. It acts as a water softener and is good for the skin and hair.

The *Lennox Point Hotel* often has bands on weekends.

Places to Stay *Lake Ainsworth Caravan Park (☎ 6687 7249)* has camp sites from $11 and cabins from $28 (bookings are essential for the high season).

Across the road is the YHA-affiliated *Lennox Head Backpackers Hostel (☎ 6687 7636)* – purpose-built, very clean and very friendly. Both Lake Ainsworth and the beach are nearby and you can have free use of a catamaran and a windsurfer, boards, bikes and other sporting equipment. Dorm beds are $17 and there are three doubles for $42.

BYRON BAY
• postcode 2481   • pop 6100

Byron Bay, a surfing mecca and meeting place for alternative cultures since the 1960s, is one of the most popular holiday spots on the east coast. Long-time locals bemoan tourism's impact – understandable when you can't cross the main street for the bumper-to-bumper traffic and you can't hear yourself think for the jangling of windchimes. Nonetheless, the beaches are superb, there are good music venues, restaurants and cafes and there's always the lush hinterland to escape to if you just can't stand the congestion and hype any longer.

Orientation & Information

Byron Bay is 6km east of the Pacific Hwy. Jonson St, which becomes Bangalow Rd, is the main shopping street.

Tourist information is handled by the Byron Environment Centre (☎ 6680 9279), in the old cottage outside the train station. Bus timetables are posted in the bus shelter. Next door, Byron Bus and Backpacker Centre (☎ 6685 5517) handles tour, bus and accommodation bookings, along with fares and other information. The local *Echo* and *Byron Shire News* newspapers have details on activities in the area and the weekly magazines *Phat* and *Go* in Thursday's *Northern Star* cover the music and entertainment scene.

Cape Byron

Cape Byron was named by Captain Cook after the poet Byron's grandfather, who had sailed round the world in the 1760s. One spur of the cape is the most easterly point of the Australian mainland. You can drive right up to the picturesque 1901 lighthouse, one of the most powerful in the southern hemisphere. There's a 3.5km walking track right round the cape from the Captain Cook Lookout, on Lighthouse Rd. It's circular, so you can leave bikes at the start. You've a good chance of seeing wallabies in the final rainforest stretch.

Humpback whales sometimes pass close by Cape Byron during their northern migration in June/July and the return trip from September to November. Dolphins are frequent visitors all year.

Beaches

The Byron area has a glorious collection of beaches, ranging from 10km stretches of empty sand to secluded little coves. **Main Beach**, immediately in front of the town, is a good swimming beach and sometimes has decent surf. The sand stretches 50km or more all the way up to the Gold Coast, interrupted only by river or creek entrances

and a few small headlands. West of Main Beach is **Belongil Beach**. In 1997 this beach was the setting for a rally in support of nude bathing after complaints from a local resident. The rally listened to reggae in the buff and witnessed enlightening comedy routines. **Tyagarah Beach**, further along the bay, is now a designated nudist beach but plenty of people get their kit off closer to town.

The eastern end of Main Beach, curving away towards Cape Byron, is known as **Clarks Beach** and can be good for surfing. The headland at the end of Clarks is called the Pass and the best surf is off here and at the next beach, **Wategos**. **Little Wategos Beach** is further round, almost at the tip of the cape. Dolphins are quite common, particularly in the surf off Wategos and Little Wategos.

South of Cape Byron, **Tallow Beach** stretches 7km down to a rockier shore around Broken Head, where a succession of small beaches (clothes optional) dot the coast before opening on to **Seven Mile Beach**, which goes all the way to Lennox Head a further 10km south. You can reach Tallow from various points along the Byron Bay-Lennox Head road.

The turn-off to the 'suburb' of **Suffolk Park** (with more good surf, particularly in winter) is 5km from Byron Bay. A further kilometre down the Byron-Lennox road is the turn-off to the Broken Head caravan park.

About 200m before the caravan park, the unsealed Seven Mile Beach Rd turns off south and runs behind the rainforest of the **Broken Head Nature Reserve**. Seven Mile Beach Rd ends after 5km (at the north end of Seven Mile Beach), but several tracks lead down from it through the forest to the Broken Head beaches – two good ones are **Kings Beach** (for which there's a car park 750m down Seven Mile Beach Rd) and **Whites Beach** (reached by a foot track after about 3.25km).

Activities

Adventure sports under water, on the water or in the air abound in Byron Bay. The waves are often quite mellow so it's a good place to wax up and have a go at surfing.

The marine park at Julian Rocks, 3km off shore, is a meeting point of cold southerly and warm northerly currents, which attracts a profusion of marine species and scores of divers each day.

The skies above Byron Bay are where you'll often see altitude junkies getting into hang-gliding and ultralight flying, while kite flying is popular for those who prefer to keep their feet on the ground.

For a true taste of Byron or to unwind after the thrill of leaping out of a plane or boat, it is worthwhile to indulge in some of the alternative therapies on offer such as floatation tanks, massage, crystal healing, clairvoyance or Reiki.

The hostels often have free surfboards for guests to use and they all have information about tour and activity operators. Many handle bookings for guests or you can arrange it yourself by phoning operators direct:

Bayside Scuba
  (☎ 6685 8333) dive courses and trips
Byron Bay Dive Centre
  (☎ 6685 7149) dive courses and trips
Byron Bay Hang-gliding School
  (☎ 015 257 699) tuition and tandem flights
Byron Bay Sea Kayaks
  (☎ 6685 5830)
Byron Bay Skydivers
  (☎ 6684 1323) tandem sky diving
Flight Zone
  (☎ 6685 8768) hang-gliding tuition and tandem flights
Flying Trapeze
  (☎ 6685 8000, Byron Beach Club) circus trapeze lessons
Leading Edge Kites
  (☎ 6685 5299) kite sales and rentals
Maddog Surf Centres
  (☎ 6685 6022) surfboard sales and rentals
Nexus Surf
  (☎ 6680 9999) two/three-day enviro-surf camps ($115/195)
Quintessence Healing Sanctuary
  (☎ 6685 5533, 8/11 Fletcher St)
Relax Haven
  (☎ 6685 8304, Belongil Beachouse) alternative therapy
Samadhi Floatation Centre
  (☎ 6685 6905, Eastpoint Arcade, Jonson St) alternative therapy
Skylimit
  (☎ 6684 3711) ultralight flights
Style Surfing
  (☎ 6685 5634) surf lessons
Sundive
  (☎ 6685 7755) dive courses and trips
Surfaris
  (☎ 1800 634 951) week-long north coast surf tours ($385), three-day tours ($195)

Organised Tours

Mick's Byron Bay to Bush Tours (☎ 6685 6889, 0418 662 684, bush@mullum.com.au) and Jim's Alternative Tours (☎ 6685 7720, 019 903 974) both run day tours of the spectacular north coast hinterland for $30. They also take groups to The Channon markets on the second Sunday of each month and to Bangalow on the fourth Sunday. Mick's tour includes a barbecue lunch at a rainforest farm and plenty of laughs along the way. Dreamtime Journey (☎/fax 6680 8505) runs Aboriginal cultural and historical day tours of the area for $49.

Places to Stay

Byron has lots of accommodation, particularly at the budget-end of the market, but beds can still prove hard to find in summer. Prices go up during school holidays and peak around Christmas and Easter.

Places to Stay – Budget

Camping At peak times you'll be lucky to find a site, and cabins are rented by the week.

The local council has four caravan parks, all by beaches. *First Sun Caravan Park (☎ 6685 6544)* is on Main Beach close to the town centre. Low-season camp sites start at $17. There's a range of cabins, the cheapest going for $60 in the low season to about $80 at the peak. *Clarks Beach Caravan Park (☎ 6685 6496)* is off Lighthouse Rd about 1km east of the town centre and has plenty of trees. Sites start at $15.50 and cabins at $53.

Down at Suffolk Park, on Tallow Beach, *Suffolk Park Caravan Park (☎ 6685 3353)* is a friendly place with shady sites from $11 and cabins from $42. They can probably squeeze in your tent when everywhere else is full. The small council-run caravan park at *Broken Head (☎ 6685 3245)* has a superb

NEW SOUTH WALES

NEW SOUTH WALES

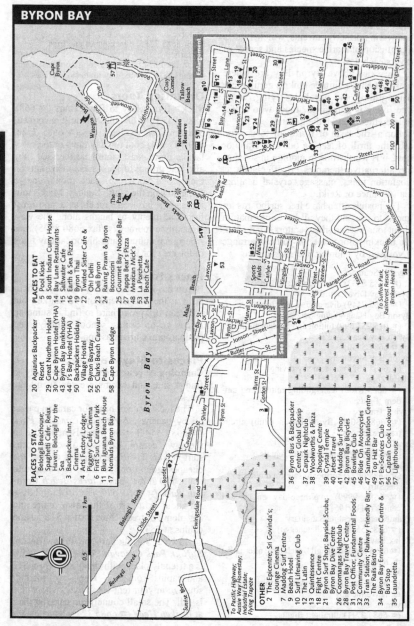

BYRON BAY

PLACES TO STAY
1 Belongil Beachouse;
   Spaghetti Cafe; Relax
   Haven; Belongil by the
   Sea
3 Backpackers Inn;
   Arts Factory Lodge;
4 Arts Factory Lodge;
   Piggery Cafe; Cinema
6 First Sun Caravan Park
11 Blue Iguana Beach House
17 Nomads Byron Bay
20 Aquarius Backpacker
   Resort
29 Great Northern Hotel
30 Cape Byron Hostel (YHA)
43 Byron Bay Bunkhouse
44 J's Bay Hostel (YHA)
50 Backpackers Holiday
   Village Hostel
52 Byron Baystay
55 Clarks Beach Caravan
   Park
58 Cape Byron Lodge

PLACES TO EAT
5 Pool Kiosk
8 South Indian Curry House
14 Bay Lane Restaurants
15 Saltwater Cafe
16 Earth & Sea Pizza
19 Byron Thai
22 Twisted Sister Cafe &
23 Ohi Delhi
24 Deli Byron
   Raving Prawn & Byron
   Bocconcini
25 Gourmet Bay Noodle Bar
27 Pappa Bear's Pizza
48 Mexican Mick's
53 La Porchetta
54 Beach Cafe

OTHER
2 The Epicentre; Sri Govinda's;
   Lounge Cinema
7 Maddog Surf Centre
9 Beach Hotel
10 Surf Lifesaving Club
12 The Latin
13 Quintessence
18 Flight Centre
21 Byron Surf Shop; Bayside Scuba;
   Byron Bay Dive Centre
26 Cocomangas Nightclub
28 Byron Bay Travel Centre
31 Post Office; Fundamental Foods
32 Community Centre
33 Train Station; Railway Friendly Bar;
   The Rails Bistro
34 Byron Bay Environment Centre &
35 Laundrette
36 Byron Bus & Backpacker
   Centre; Global Gossip
37 Carpark Nightclub
38 Woolworths & Plaza
   Shopping Centre
39 Crystal Temple
40 Maddog Surf Shop
41 Maddog Surf Centre
42 Byron Bay Bicycles
45 Bowling Club
46 Ride On Motorcycles
47 Samadhi Floatation Centre
49 Top Hat Bar
51 Ex-Services Club
56 Captain Cook Lookout
57 Lighthouse

To Pacific Highway;
Aussie Way Homestay;
Industrial Estate;
Flying Trapeze

location overlooking the southern end of Tallow Beach and is marginally cheaper than the others.

Hostels The hot competition between the town's numerous hostels is good news for budget travellers. Prices fluctuate depending on demand, peaking around Christmas/January, when you should book. At other times ask about special deals and weekly rates.

Backpackers Holiday Village Hostel (☎ 6685 8888, 116 Jonson St) is 300m from the bus stop. It's a clean, friendly, well-equipped place with a small pool and spa. Dorm beds cost from $18 and four person units with their own facilities start from $20 per person. Use of well-maintained bicycles, surfboards and boogie boards is free and there are plenty of them.

Backpackers Inn (☎ 6685 8231, 29 Shirley St) is near the beach and half a kilometre from the town centre. It's a modern hostel with a pool and all the usual features, including free bikes and boogie boards. To get to the beach, walk across the lawn, cross the railway line (carefully!) and climb a sand dune. Rates start at $17 for dorms and at $48 for doubles.

The *Cape Byron Lodge* (☎ 6685 6445, 78 Bangalow Rd) is clean, comfortable and well equipped. It's some way from the town centre at the southern end of Jonson St, but only about 10 minutes' walk to Tallow Beach. It has a small pool and is usually the cheapest hostel in town, with dorm beds starting at $12 and doubles at $35.

Byron Bay has two YHA-affiliated hostels. The impressive *Cape Byron Hostel* (☎ 6685 8788), on the corner of Byron and Middleton Sts, is close to the town centre and Main Beach. It's a big building with its own mini shopping centre and a heated pool. Prices are $19 for a dorm, $50 for a double or twin.

The other YHA affiliate is the purpose-built *J's Bay Hostel* (☎ 1800 678 195), on the corner of Carlyle and Middleton Sts. It's a friendly, laid-back place with helpful staff. There are several pleasant communal areas, a pool, and a fantastic kitchen. There

are facilities for disabled travellers and bikes and boogie boards for hire.

The *Belongil Beachouse Hostel* (☎ 6685 7868) is a great place to stay – well run, relaxed and friendly. It's off Childe St, just over the dunes from Belongil Beach and set amid well-established gardens; bike and boogie-board use is free. The cafe within the Belongil Beachouse complex, the *Spaghetti Cafe*, is a big plus, with excellent, healthy food served between 8 am and 10 pm. Dorm beds start at $17. Doubles with shared bathroom are $45, rising to $50. There are some upmarket doubles priced from between $70 to $125 and self-contained cottages from $80 to $160. Also within the complex is Relax Haven, a great place to unwind and pamper yourself with a massage or floatation therapy.

Belongil by the Sea (☎ 6685 8111), next to the Belongil Beachouse, has a cluster of cabins dotted around landscaped gardens with a large swimming pool (heated in winter). Prices start at $65 for two people for motel-style rooms or $90 for cabins.

Aquarius Backpacker Resort (☎ 1800 02 8909, Lawson St) is a well-appointed hostel. The small dorms each have their own en suite, TV and fridge. Dorm beds are $20, doubles are $50, with a $5 food voucher every day that's paid in advance.

Those with an alternative bent and a penchant for late nights will enjoy the atmosphere at the *Arts Factory Lodge* (☎ 6685 7709, Skinners Shoot Rd), with its permaculture gardens and creative furnishings. The huge choice of accommodation includes tent sites ($11) and teepees ($16) – not the most secure form of accommodation so don't leave your valuables lying around. Dorm beds are from $19 and doubles start at $48. Ideologically-sound food is available at the co-owned *Piggery Café* and there's a lounge *cinema* next door. The Arts Factory is about 10 minutes' walk from the town centre and beaches. Staff meet buses and bikes are free for an hour, as well as regular free minibuses to town.

The *Blue Iguana Beach House* (☎ 6685 5298), opposite the surf club on Bay St, has four-bed dorms for $18 per person during the week, rising to $22 at peak times. It has a deck and a nice barbecue area and free surf equipment.

The clean and pleasant *Nomads Byron Bay* (☎ 6685 8695, *Lawson St*) occupies the renovated former council chambers and has a pool and off-street parking. It charges $16/40 for dorms/doubles or $45 for a double with private bathroom. The boisterous *Byron Bay Bunkhouse* (☎ 6685 8311, *Carlyle St*) has 12/6-bed dorms for $12/15.

Places to Stay – Mid-Range
Hotels, Motels & Guesthouses The *Great Northern Hotel* (☎ 6685 6454, *Jonson St*) has singles/doubles for $40/50 in the low season, rising in summer. There are numerous motels lining the southern and western approaches to town.

The *Rainforest Resort* (☎ 6685 6139 or 6685 8679, *53-59 Broken Head Rd*) now incorporates the Wheel Resort, designed and run by wheelchair users for travellers with disabilities, and the River Oaks Guest House. The resort has two pools and walkways through extensive wetlands and Tallow Beach is nearby. Wheelchair-friendly cabins start at $85. Rooms in the guesthouse cost $65 in the low season and up to $150 at Christmas.

Byron Baystay (☎ 6685 7609, *30 Marvel St*) is a pleasant B&B in a pretty renovated house. Singles/doubles cost $35/65 in the low season and $120 a double in summer. *Aussie Way* (☎ 6685 6895, *6 Julian Rocks Rd, Sunrise Beach*) is another recommended homestay located in one of Byron's 'suburbs', about 20 minutes walk along the beach from town. Doubles/twins are $25 a night per person.

Apartments Holiday houses and apartments start from around $300 a week in the low season, $500 during school holidays and $900 over Christmas. Letting agents include The Professionals (☎ 6685 6552), on the corner of Lawson and Fletcher Sts, which handles bookings for two old cottages at the lighthouse on Cape Byron. A two bedroom cottage is $600 a week (low season), and a three bedroom cottage $660.

Rents rocket to $1500 and $1650 a week at Christmas.

Places to Eat
There is a wide choice of restaurants, cafes and takeaways serving good food, and vegetarians are particularly well catered for.

Overlooking Clarks Beach, the *Beach Café* isn't cheap but the views are superb. The *Cafe DOC*, at the Cape Byron Hostel complex, has good breakfast and coffee but slow service.

The *South Indian Curry House* (☎ 6685 6828, *2 Jonson St*) is a long-time favourite, with most main courses around $10. It's open nightly for dinner.

There's a string of restaurants in Bay Lane, behind the Beach Hotel, serving everything from Thai to gourmet fish and chips. The *Saltwater Café* (*13 Lawson St*) bakes its own bread and serves scrumptious rolls for lunch for about $8.

Fundamental Foods, next to the post office, has a huge range of goodies as well as organically grown fruit and vegetables. Further along Jonson St is the licensed *Mexican Mick's* (☎ 6680 9050, *109 Jonson St*). It's an old favourite and is still reasonably priced, with main courses under $16 and lots of snacks on the big menu. At the Railway Friendly Bar, the *Rails Bistro* opens for lunch and dinner. The food is innovative and not expensive.

Earth & Sea Pizza, on Lawson St, is a popular pizza place, as is the less expensive *La Porchetta*, further along Lawson St towards Clarks Beach. Opposite Earth & Sea are the *Twisted Sister Cafe* and the *Oh! Delhi* Indian restaurant and cocktail bar.

The Feros Arcade dog-legs between Lawson and Jonson Sts and has several options: *Deli Byron*, at the Lawson St entrance, is a nice leisurely morning spot, *Byron Bocconcini* is a good place to grab some lunch (simple sandwiches, Lebanese rolls and salads) and, next door, the *Raving Prawn* has an interesting modern menu.

Byron Thai, at the Bay Beach Motel on Lawson St, has an unusually large vegetarian selection. *Global Gossip*, next to the bus stop, is a good spot for coffee and emailing.

Entertainment

Byron Bay's nightlife is a major drawcard. The *Railway Friendly Bar*, next to the train station, has live music most nights. The *Beach Hotel*, on Bay St, and *Great Northern Hotel* have live bands Thursday to Saturday nights and sometimes on Sunday afternoons. Touring bands play at the latter. You can dance the night away at *Cocomangas* nightclub in Jonson St. The *Carpark* nightclub, in the Plaza Shopping Centre, has everything from jazz to trance depending on the night.

Top Hat bar, on Jonson St on the way out of town, is a more laid-back spot for a drink, with cabaret nights. The *Latin*, on Fletcher St, is open late for tapas, cocktails and a spot of latin dancing.

Getting There & Away

Air The closest airport is at Ballina, but most people use the much larger airport at Coolangatta on the Gold Coast in Queensland. It has frequent direct flights from both Sydney and Melbourne, but you still have to get down to Byron.

Bus Numerous buses run through Byron Bay. Kirklands' Lismore-Brisbane route passes through Byron Bay and stops at other useful places such as Coolangatta airport and Murwillumbah, Ballina, Tweed Heads. Blanch's (☎ 6686 2144) serves the local area with destinations such as Mullumbimby ($4) and Ballina ($6.60).

Fares with Premier (☎ 13 3410) are Brisbane $25, Sydney $67, Coffs Harbour $36 and Surfers Paradise $22.

Train Byron Bay is on the Sydney to Murwillumbah line, with a daily train in each direction, plus several rail/bus services. From Sydney ($85) the quickest service is the 7.05 am XPT, which reaches Byron Bay at 7.30 pm. The southbound train stops in town at 10 pm. To Coffs Harbour the fare is $38.

Car & Motorcycle Earth Car Rentals (☎ 6685 7472) has older cars from $35 a day (including 100km free) and new cars from $45. Jetset Travel (☎ 6685 6554) rents small current-model cars for $35 a day with 100km free or $45 a day unlimited kilometres.

Ride on Motorcycles (☎ 6685 6304), on Jonson St opposite Woolworths, hires motorcycles from $75 a day. You need a motorcycle licence, Australian or foreign.

Getting Around

Bicycle Hostels lend bikes of varying quality to guests. Byron Bay Bicycles (☎ 6685 6067), on Jonson St, has good single-speed bikes for $18 a day, including helmet, and geared bikes for $20 a day.

BYRON BAY TO TWEED HEADS

The Pacific Hwy continues north from the Byron Bay turn-off to the Queensland border at Tweed Heads. Just after the Mullumbimby turn-off is **Brunswick Heads**, a river-mouth town with a small fishing fleet and several caravan parks, motels and hotels.

A few kilometres north is the turn-off to the coastal town of **Wooyung**. The coast road from Wooyung to Tweed Heads makes a pleasant alternative to the Pacific Hwy. This stretch is known as the Tweed Coast and is much less developed than the Gold Coast to the north.

On the Tweed Coast are the small resorts of **Bogangar (Cabarita Beach)** and **Kingscliff**. Cabarita Beach has good surf and there's a great hostel, *Emu Park Backpackers Resort (☎ 6676 1190)*. It's one of the cleanest hostels around and the rooms are large. Dorm beds are $15 and there's a 'stay two nights, get the third night free' deal outside school holidays. Doubles cost $33, and the en suite double with TV is $40. Bikes and boards are free and the beach is a minute away. If you'd like to climb Mt Warning (1157m), the staff will drop you off there and pick you up after your climb for about $60 – not bad among several people. Guests staying more than one night can be picked up from Murwillumbah, Kingscliff or Coolangatta (Queensland).

Surfside (☎ 13 1230) has six buses a day from Tweed Heads to Cabarita Beach

($4.50) on weekdays – three on Saturday and three on Sunday – and frequent services to Kingscliff ($3.10).

Murwillumbah

• postcode 2484   • pop 7650

Murwillumbah is in a banana and sugar-growing area in the broad Tweed Valley. It's also the main town in this part of the north coast hinterland and there are several communes and 'back to the land' centres in the area. You're also within reach of Mt Warning and the spectacular border ranges.

The World Heritage Rainforest Centre and tourist information centre (☎ 6672 1340, info@tactic.nsw.gov.au) is on the Pacific Hwy, near the train station. The excellent **Tweed River Regional Art Gallery** is just up the road from the hostel. The **museum**, on Queensland Rd, is open Wednesday and Friday from 11 am to 4 pm, and every fourth Sunday of the month from 10 am to 3 pm ($2).

Places to Stay & Eat The associate-YHA *Mt Warning Backpackers of Murwillumbah (☎ 6672 3763, 1 Tumbulgum Rd)* is beside the Tweed River – you'll see it on the right as you cross the bridge into town. It's a friendly place with lots of activities, including free canoes and a rowing boat. It can also organise horse rides. Dorm beds are $15, doubles/twins $17 per person.

Several pubs have accommodation, including the *Imperial Hotel (☎ 6672 1036)*, on the main street across from the post office, with singles for $20 and doubles with/without en suite for $39/34.

Getting There & Away Murwillumbah is served by most buses on the Sydney to Brisbane coastal run. Premier (☎ 13 3410) leaves from near the train station to Sydney ($67) and Brisbane ($21). Marsh's Bus Service (☎ 6689 1220) runs to Uki ($4.80), Nimbin ($10.30) and Lismore ($14.20). Surfside runs to Tweed Heads ($4.80).

A daily train from Sydney ($91) connects with a bus to the Gold Coast and Brisbane.

TWEED HEADS

☎ 07 • postcode 2485 • pop 37,770

Sharing a street with the more developed Queensland resort of Coolangatta, Tweed Heads marks the southern end of the Gold Coast strip. The northern side of Boundary St, which runs along a short peninsula to Point Danger above the mouth of the Tweed River, is in Queensland. This end of the Gold Coast is much quieter than the resorts closer to Surfers Paradise.

The Tweed Heads visitors centre (☎ 5536 4244, info@tactic.nsw.gov.au) is at the northern end of Wharf St (the Pacific Hwy), just south of the giant Twin Towns Services Club. It's open daily from 9 am to 5 pm (until 1 pm on Saturday and closed on Sunday).

Things to See

At Point Danger the towering **Captain Cook Memorial** straddles the state border. The 18m-high monument was completed in 1970 (the bicentenary of Cook's visit) and is topped by a laser-beam lighthouse visible 35km out to sea. The replica of the *Endeavour*'s capstan is made from ballast dumped by Cook after the *Endeavour* ran aground on the Great Barrier Reef and recovered, along with the ship's cannons, in 1968. Point Danger was named by Cook after he nearly ran aground there, too.

On Kirkwood Rd in South Tweed Heads, the **Minjungbal Aboriginal Cultural Centre** (☎ 5524 2109) has exhibits on pre-contact history and culture. It's open daily from 9 am to 4 pm. Entry is $6.

Places to Stay

Accommodation in Tweed Heads spills over into Coolangatta and up the Gold Coast, where the choice is more varied. The cheaper motels along Wharf St are feeling the pinch as the highway bypasses Tweed Heads; you'll find doubles advertised for less than $40.

See the Coolangatta section of the Queensland chapter for places to stay across the border.

Places to Eat

The *Tweed Heads Bowls Club*, on Wharf St, has specials such as weekday roast lunches for under $5; the other clubs are also sources of cheap eats.

The *Fishermans Cove Restaurant* (☎ 5536 1646, 14 Griffith St) is known for its seafood and has main courses for around $20.

Getting There & Away

All long-distance buses stop at 29 Bay St, near Tweed Mall. Ticket sales are handled by Golden Gateway Travel (☎ 5536 6600). Coachtrans offers a same-day return to Brisbane for $22, $13 one way. Kirklands goes to Byron Bay for $14.20. Premier goes to Coffs Harbour for $49.

Surfside (☎ 13 1230) has frequent services to Murwillumbah ($4.80) and to Kingscliff ($3.10). It also has six buses a day to Cabarita Beach ($4.50) on weekdays – three on weekends. Buses leave from near the Tweed Mall.

There are several car-hire places that will get you moving from $20 a day, such as Tweed Auto Rentals (☎ 5536 8000), at the information centre on Wharf St.

Far North Coast Hinterland

The area stretching 60km or so inland from the Pacific Hwy in far northern NSW has spectacular forested mountains and a high population of alternative lifestylers. These settlers were attracted to the area by the Aquarius Festival at Nimbin in 1973 and have become a prominent, colourful part of the community.

The country between Lismore and the coast was once known as the Big Scrub, an incredibly inadequate description of an area that must have been close to paradise at the time of European incursion. Much of the 'scrub' was cleared for farming, after loggers had been through and removed the prized red cedar. These days the area is marketed as Rainbow Country.

A web of narrow roads covers the hinterland. If you're planning to explore the area, get the Forestry Commission's Casino area map ($5) – the information centres in Byron Bay and Nimbin both stock it.

Geography

The northern part of the hinterland was formed by volcanic activity (see Mt Warning later in this section) and is essentially a huge bowl almost completely rimmed by mountain ranges, with the spectacular peak of Mt Warning in the centre. The escarpments of the McPherson and Tweed ranges form the north-western rim, with the Razorback Range to the west and the Nightcap Range to the south-west. National parks, some of them World Heritage areas, protect unique and beautiful subtropical rainforests.

The country south of here is a maze of steep hills and beautiful valleys, some still harbouring magnificent stands of rainforest, others cleared for cattle-grazing and plantations – especially macadamia nuts and coffee.

Markets & Music

The alternative community can be seen in force at the weekend markets in the following list. The biggest markets are at The Channon, between Lismore and Nimbin, Byron Bay and Bangalow, 7km inland from Byron Bay.

Ballina
    3rd Sunday, Circus Ground, Canal Rd
Bangalow
    4th Sunday, Showground
Brunswick Heads
    1st Saturday of the month, behind the Ampol service station
Byron Bay
    1st Sunday, Butler St Reserve
The Channon
    2nd Sunday, Coronation Park
Lennox Head
    2nd and 5th Sundays, Lake Ainsworth foreshore
Lismore
    1st and 3rd Sundays, Lismore Shopping Square; 5th Sunday, Heritage Park
Mullumbimby
    3rd Saturday, Museum, Stuart St
Murwillumbah
    4th Sunday, Showground

Nimbin
　3rd Sunday, Community Hall, Cullen St
Uki
　3rd Sunday, Old Buttery

Many accomplished musicians live in the area and they sometimes play at the markets or in the town pub after the market (notably at Uki). Thursday's edition of the *Northern Star* includes a guide to the week's gigs and other activities. *Phat* magazine and the Byron *Echo* newspapers cover most musical and cultural events in the area.

LISMORE
☎ 02 • postcode 2480 • pop 28,400

Thirty-five kilometres inland from Ballina on the Bruxner Hwy to New England, is the main town of the state's far north. It's on the Wilson River, which forms the north arm of the Richmond River.

The Lismore Visitor & Heritage Centre (☎ 6622 0122, tourism@liscity.nsw.gov.au) is on the Bruxner Hwy – known as Ballina St through town – on the corner of Molesworth St, near the Wilson River. It has a rainforest display ($1) and the Big Scrub Environment Centre (☎ 6621 3278), on Keen St, sells topographic maps of the area.

The interesting **Richmond River Historical Society Museum** (☎ 6621 9993) is at 165 Molesworth St and is open weekdays ($2). The **Regional Art Gallery**, at 131 Molesworth St, is open Tuesday to Sunday (free). **Rotary Park** is an interesting 6 hectare patch of remnant rainforest that has survived while the town has grown around it. The park is dominated by towering hoop pines and giant fig trees. It's just off the Bruxner Hwy, about 3km east of the information centre. Access is from Rotary Drive.

Tucki Tucki Nature Reserve koala reserve is 16km south of Lismore on Wyrallah Rd. Initiation ceremonies were held at the Aboriginal **bora ring** nearby. **Lismore Koala Hospital** (☎ 6622 1233) is on Rifle Range Rd, near Southern Cross University, and is open daily.

The MV *Bennelong* (☎ 0414 664 552) runs a variety of cruises, including a day trip down the river to Ballina for $55 ($20 children).

Places to Stay
Lismore Backpackers (☎ 6621 6118, 14 Ewing St) occupies the old weatherboard Lismore hospital building. It's a cosy place close to the city centre with dorms from $14, singles/doubles from $20/32. Smoking and drinking are not permitted. The friendly managers can organise trips to places of interest in the area.

The *Northern Rivers Hotel* (☎ 6621 5797), at the junction of Terania and Bridge Sts, on the road out to Nimbin, has cheery, clean rooms for $20/30.

Places to Eat
The *Northern Rivers Hotel* (see Places to Stay) does unbelievably cheap meals, with roast lunches from $2 and dinners from $3. Opposite the Northern Rivers, philosophically as well as physically, is the vegan *20,000 Cows Café*, on Bridge St.

Dr Juice, on Keen St in the town centre, is open during the day for excellent juices and smoothies, plus vegetarian and vegan snacks for around $2. Next door is *Fundamental Health Foods*, a big health-food shop. *Mecca Café* has funky retro decor, booths and nice sandwiches and focaccias for under $8.

Getting There & Away
Hazelton (☎ 13 1713) has daily flights to Sydney and Sunstate (☎ 13 1313) flies to Brisbane three times a week.

Kirklands (☎ 6622 1499) is based here and runs buses around the immediate area as well as further afield. Destinations include Byron Bay ($10.50), Mullumbimby ($11.20), Murwillumbah ($14.70) and Brisbane ($28.70). There's also a service to Tenterfield in New England ($22) on weekdays. The XPT train from Sydney ($85) stops here.

NIMBIN
• postcode 2480 • pop 650

The Aquarius Festival of 1973 transformed the declining dairy town of Nimbin into a name synonymous with Australia's 'back to the land' counterculture movement. It remains a friendly and active alternative centre with many communes in the area, yet times have changed. Nowadays, you're just as likely to stumble over a syringe as a joint-but clip as you walk down Cullen St, the main street.

The weird and wonderful **Nimbin Museum** (admission by donation) is on Cullen St, near the Rainbow Cafe. It's not your average museum – it's a real hoot. There's a good market on the fourth Sunday of the month and you may catch a local band playing afterwards.

Nimbin Explorer (☎ 6689 1557) has two hour tours of the Nimbin area and its institutions ($18).

Many people come to the area to visit **Djanbung Gardens** (☎ 6689 1755), a permaculture education centre established by Robyn Francis – a disciple of permaculture guru Bill Mollison. Contact the centre for information about courses. The centre, five minutes walk from the town centre at 74 Cecil St, has guided tours on Tuesday and Thursday at 10 and 11 am on Saturdays.

The **Hemp Embassy** (☎ 6689 1842) has product displays and drug education. Entry is free and it is located past the caravan park.

Places to Stay

The council's basic caravan park (☎ 6689 1402) is near the bowling club – go down the road running past the pub. Camp sites start from $13 and on-site vans from $32.

Granny's Farm (☎ 6689 1333), a YHA-affiliated hostel, is a very relaxed place surrounded by farmland, with platypuses in the nearby creek. It also has a swimming pool. To get there, go north along Cullen St and turn left just before the bridge over the creek. Conventional dorm beds are $15 and doubles are $35. Other options are the teepee or 'pleasure dome' for $8 per person, and creekside camping from $6 per person. The friendly managers will sometimes give rides to places of interest.

Grey Gum Lodge (☎/fax 6689 1713), on the road into town from Lismore, is a stylishly renovated weatherboard house. There are five rooms and singles/doubles start at $25/45 with breakfast. There is a pool and, given enough notice, the friendly owners serve meals on the verandah.

Sundara (☎ 6633 7037), 20 minutes from Nimbin at Billen Cliffs, is an alternative lifestyle community which has cabins for guests (singles/doubles $20/30), alternative therapies, yoga, meditation and tai chi classes.

Places to Eat

The *Rainbow Café*, in the centre of town on Cullen St, is a famous Nimbin institution. Delicious cakes cost about $3 and there are vegetarian snacks and meals for around $6. It also does breakfast, as does the nearby *Rick's Café*, the closest thing you'll find to a standard country-town cafe. Across the street, *Choices* has healthy (and not-so-healthy) takeaways and light meals.

Just past the pub, under the school on Sibley St, the *Cage* serves great Indian and oriental lunches and dinners from $6.50.

Entertainment

If there's a dance at the town hall, don't miss the opportunity to meet the friendly people from the country around Nimbin. There's an annual Mardi Grass Festival at the end of April that culminates with the famous Marijuana Harvest Ball. The *Freemasons Hotel* often has music and the *Bush Theatre & Café*, at the old butter factory near the bridge at the northern end of town, has films on Friday, Saturday and Sunday.

Getting There & Away

The Nimbin Shuttle Bus (☎ 6680 9189) operates a daily service between Byron Bay and Nimbin for $12 one way. Marsh's Bus Service (☎ 6686 7324) runs through Nimbin on its morning school run from Murwillumbah to Lismore and again on the afternoon return. The one-way fare from Murwillumbah is $10.70 and the fare from Lismore is $6.50. Ask about backpacker discounts. Bookings can be made at Nimbin Tourist Connexion (☎ 6689 1764), on Cullen Street opposite the school. They can also help with WWOOFing work.

AROUND NIMBIN

The country around Nimbin is superb. The 800m-plus Nightcap Range, originally a flank of the huge Mt Warning volcano, rises north-east of the town and a sealed road leads to one of its highest points, **Mt Nardi**. The range is part of **Nightcap National Park**. The Mt Nardi road gives access to a variety of other vehicle and walking tracks along and across the range, including the historic Nightcap Track, a packhorse trail which was once the main route between Lismore and Murwillumbah. The views from **Pholis Gap** on the Googarna road, towards the western end of the range, are particularly spectacular.

The Tuntable Falls commune, one of the biggest, with its own shop and school and some fine houses, is about 9km east of Nimbin. The commune can be reached by the public Tuntable Falls Rd and you can walk to the 123m **Tuntable Falls** themselves, 13km from Nimbin.

The eastern region of the park covers the Terania Creek catchment area. A stunningly beautiful 700m walk leads to **Protesters' Falls**, named after the environmentalists whose 1979 campaign to stop logging was a major factor in the creation of the national park. There is free camping at Terania Creek, but you're supposed to stay only one night. No fires are allowed and swimming is prohibited.

Access to Terania Creek is via **The Channon**, a tiny town off the Nimbin-Lismore road that hosts one of the biggest of the region's markets on the 2nd Sunday of each month. A dance is sometimes held the night before the market and there's often music afterwards.

The *Channon Teahouse & Craftshop* is a pleasant place for a snack or light meal and has interesting handicrafts to browse through. It's open for lunch from Tuesday to Sunday. The *Channon Village Campsite* (☎ 6688 6321), near the market grounds, is basic but pretty and costs $5 per person. Four kilometres out of town, on the road to Terania Creek, *Terania Park Camping Ground* (☎ 6688 6121) has camp sites ($5) and on-site vans ($25).

Nimbin Rocks is an Aboriginal sacred site (not open to visitors) clearly visible west from the Lismore-Nimbin road just south of

Nimbin. **Hanging Rock Creek** has falls and a good swimming hole; take the road through Stony Chute for 14km, turn right at the Barker's Vale sign, then left onto Williams Rd; the falls are nearby on the right.

BANGALOW
● postcode 2471   ● pop 900

Ten minutes west of Byron Bay and 20 minutes drive from Lismore is the charming village of Bangalow. Although accommodation is a bit scarce, it is a lovely place to visit for its friendly country pub, good restaurants, heritage buildings and classy shops.

The Bangalow market, on the fourth Sunday of the month, is in a beautiful shady setting at the showgrounds and the annual Billy Cart Derby in May is a great community event and not to be missed. The swimming hole behind the village is a pleasant picnic spot and a good place to cool off. If you're in the area for Christmas Eve, Bangalow hosts a very festive street party when the whole town gets together to celebrate the occasion.

There are lots of lovely craft, clothing and antique shops in Byron St and interesting artist's studios nearby, such as Bangalow Pottery just over the hill on the road to Lismore.

Places to Stay & Eat
Right on the creek, a short stroll from the shops, the *Riverview Guest House* (☎ 6687 1317, 99 Byron St) has two double rooms with their own bathrooms for $120 a night including full breakfast. The *Bangalow Hotel* (☎ 6687 1314, Byron St) has two double rooms for $50, including a continental breakfast, and one single for $30, including breakfast.

The *Bangalow Hotel* is a fine spot for a beer and game of pool while *Ruby's* restaurant, inside the hotel, has an interesting menu with mains under $15. Further down Byron St, the main street, *Baci* and *Wild About Food* offer more upmarket dining but mains are still no more than $20. The *Urban Café*, near the bottom of the hill, is a popular spot for a leisurely coffee or breakfast.

MULLUMBIMBY

● postcode 2482   ● pop 2870

This pleasant little town, known locally as Mullum, is in subtropical countryside 5km off the Pacific Hwy, between Bangalow and Brunswick Heads. Perhaps best known for its marijuana – 'Mullumbimby Madness' – Mullum is a centre for a long-established farming community as well as for the alternative folk from nearby areas and the large sannyasin community, although it has nothing like Nimbin's cultural frontier mentality.

West of Mullum in the Whian Whian State Forest, **Minyon Falls** drop 100m into a rainforest gorge. There are good walking tracks around the falls; you can get within a couple of minutes' walk by conventional vehicle from Repentance Creek on one of the back roads between Mullum and Lismore. The eastern end of the historic Nightcap Track (see Around Nimbin) emerges at the north of Whian Whian State Forest.

Places to Stay & Eat

There are a couple of motels and, 12km north, *Maca's Main Arm Camping Ground* (☎ *6684 5211, Main Arm*) is an idyllic place, under the lee of hills lush with rainforest. It's nothing like a commercial caravan park but the facilities are quite good, with a kitchen, hot showers and a laundry. It costs $6 per person and you can hire tents from $6 a day. On-site vans are from $20. To get here, take Main Arm Rd and follow the 'camping' signposts.

In town, the *Commercial Hotel* (or Middle Pub) (☎ *6684 3229*), on the corner of Stuart and Burringbar Sts, has won an award for the best country pub accommodation. Singles/doubles cost $20/35.

The *Poinciana* (☎ *6684 4036, 55 Station St*) is a great outdoor restaurant shaded by a huge Poinciana tree. It has delicious light meals and salads for good prices, with huge burgers under $4. *Buon Appetito*, on Stuart St, has great pasta and pizzas to eat in or take away. The *Pizza Hive*, on Station St, has vegetarian meals as well as pizza. *Lu Lu's*, on Dalley St, is a very popular cafe which brews great coffee and offers snacks like pakoras with coriander sauce for $3.50.

Getting There & Away

Kirklands buses go through Mullum on their Lismore ($11.20) to Brisbane ($21.10) run. Mullumbimby Travel (☎ 6684 1089), in Stuart St, is the Kirklands agent.

Mullum is on the Sydney ($85) to Murwillumbah railway line.

There are two road routes to Mullum from the Pacific Hwy: one turns off just south of Brunswick Heads, and the other is the longer but prettier Coolamon Scenic Drive that leaves the highway north of Brunswick Heads near the Ocean Shores turn-off.

MT WARNING NATIONAL PARK

The dramatic peak of Mt Warning (1160m) dominates the district. It was named by Captain Cook as a landmark for avoiding Point Danger off Tweed Heads. The mountain is the former central magma chamber of a massive volcano formed more than 20 million years ago. The volcano once covered an area of over 4000 sq km, stretching from Coraki in the south to Beenleigh (Queensland) in the north, and from Kyogle in the west to an eastern rim now beneath the ocean. Erosion has since carved out the deep Tweed and Oxley valleys around Mt Warning, but sections of the flanks survive in the form of the Nightcap Range in the south and parts of the Border Ranges to the north.

The road into the park runs off the Murwillumbah-Uki road. It's about 6km to the car park at the base of the track leading to the summit. Much of the 4.5km walk is through rainforest. The final section is steep (to put it mildly), so allow five hours for a round trip. Take water. If you're on the summit at dawn you'll be the first person on the Australian mainland to see the sun's rays that day! The trail is well marked, but you'll need a torch if you're climbing at night (to reach the summit at dawn).

Places to Stay

You can't camp at Mt Warning but the *Mt Warning Park and Tourist Retreat* (☎ *6679 5120*), on the Mt Warning approach road, has camp sites ($12), on-site vans (from

$24) and cabins ($35). The vans and cabins cost less if you stay more than one night. There are kitchen facilities and a well-stocked kiosk – and lots of wildlife, including koalas, in the 120 hectare refuge. Platypus can be seen at dusk in the nearby Tweed River.

The *Mt Warning Forest Hideaway* (☎ 6679 7277, *Byrrill Creek Rd*), 12km south-west of Uki, has small units with cooking facilities for $60 for two people or $90 for four. Another option is the *Mt Warning Backpackers of Murwillumbah* (see that section for details).

Getting There & Away

A Marsh's (☎ 6689 1220) school bus runs from Murwillumbah to Uki, Nimbin and Lismore on weekdays. It leaves Knox Park in Murwillumbah at 7.10 am and can drop you at the start of the 6km Mt Warning approach road. The hostels at Murwillumbah and Cabarita Beach organise trips to the mountain.

BORDER RANGES NATIONAL PARK

The Border Ranges National Park covers the NSW side of the McPherson Range along the NSW-Queensland border and some of the range's outlying spurs. The Tweed Range Scenic Drive – gravel but useable in all weather – loops through the park about 100km from Lillian Rock (midway between Uki and Kyogle) to Wiangaree, north of Kyogle on the Woodenbong road. It has some breathtaking lookouts over the Tweed Valley to Mt Warning and the coast. The adrenalin charging walk out to the crag called the **Pinnacle** – about an hour from the road and back – is not for vertigo sufferers! The rainforest along **Brindle Creek** is also breathtaking, and there are several walks from the picnic area here.

There are a couple of camping grounds, basic but free, on the Tweed Range Scenic Drive: *Forest Tops*, high on the range, and *Sheepstation Creek*, about 6km further west and 15km from the Wiangaree turnoff. There might be tank water but it's best to bring your own.

New England

New England is the area along the Great Dividing Range stretching north from near Newcastle to the Queensland border. It's a vast tableland of sheep and cattle country with many good bushwalking areas and photogenic scenery and, unlike much of the northern-half of Australia, New England has four distinct seasons. If you're travelling along the eastern seaboard, it's worth diverting inland to New England to get a glimpse of the Australian lifestyle away from the coast. There's a lot less tourist hype for starters.

A diversion is easy enough thanks to the New England Hwy, which runs from Hexham, just north of Newcastle, to Brisbane. This route was developed as an inland alternative to the Pacific Hwy and is an excellent road, with far less traffic than on the coast. The scenery on the roads linking the New England Hwy with the coast is beautiful, particularly on the Oxley Hwy from Bendemeer (just north of Tamworth) to Port Macquarie, and on the Waterfall Way from Armidale to Bellingen via Dorrigo.

National Parks

The eastern side of the tableland tumbles over an escarpment to the coastal plains below, and along this edge is a string of fine national parks. Gorges and waterfalls are a common feature. The NPWS office in Armidale (☎ 6773 7211) has information on all the following parks.

Werrikimbe This remote, rugged World Heritage listed park straddles the escarpment north of the Oxley Hwy between Walcha and Wauchope. There are two main approaches to the park. The easiest is along the Forbes River road, which turns off the highway at Yarras, 45km west of Wauchope. This leads to the Plateau Beach Rest Area, the starting point for walks to the gorges of the Forbes and Hastings rivers – recommended for experienced bushwalkers only. The other approach to the park is along the Kangaroo Flat road, 55km east of Walcha.

Oxley Wild Rivers Consisting of several sections, this park east of Walcha and Armidale is crossed by deep gorges with some spectacular waterfalls – especially after rain. **Wollomombi Falls**, 39km east of Armidale, are among the highest in Australia with a 220m drop; **Apsley Falls** are east of Walcha at the southern end of the park. On the bottom of the gorges is a wilderness area, accessible from Raspberry Rd off the Wollomombi-Kempsey road.

New England & Cathedral Rock New England is a small park with a wide range of ecosystems. There are 20km of walking tracks and a wilderness area at the base of the escarpment. Access is from near Ebor and there are cabins and camp sites near the entrance at Point Lookout. Book these through the Dorrigo NPWS office (☎ 6657 2309). Cathedral Rock, off the Ebor-Armidale road, has photogenic granite formations.

Dorrigo See the North Coast section for information on this park.

Guy Fawkes River This is gorge country with canoeing and walking. **Ebor Falls**, near the town of Ebor on the road from Armidale to Dorrigo, are spectacular. Access to the park is from Hernani, 15km north-east of Ebor. From here it's 30km to the Chaelundi Rest Area, which has camp sites and water.

Gibraltar Range & Washpool Dramatic, forested and wild, these parks lie south and north of the Gwydir Hwy between Glen Innes and Grafton. Countrylink buses stop at the visitors centre – the start of a 10km track to the Mulligans Hut camping ground in Gibraltar Range, and at the entrance to Washpool (from where it's about 3km to camping grounds).

Bald Rock & Boonoo Boonoo Bald Rock is about 36km north-east of Tenterfield on an unsealed (but deceptively smooth – take it easy) road which continues into Queensland. Bald Rock is a huge granite monolith which has been compared to Uluru. You can walk to the top and camp near the base. Nearby is Boonoo Boonoo, with a 200m-drop waterfall and basic camping.

Getting There & Away
Airports at Armidale and Tamworth provide daily services to Sydney and Brisbane.

Several bus lines run through New England from Melbourne or Sydney to Brisbane. Keans (☎ 1800 625 587) runs between Tamworth and Port Macquarie via Coffs Harbour and Armidale; Kirklands (☎ 6622 1499) operates between Lismore and Tenterfield ($21); and Batterhams Express (☎ 1800 043 339) runs between Sydney and Tamworth via the Hunter Valley. Trains run from Sydney to Armidale, from where Countrylink buses run up to Tenterfield.

TAMWORTH
● postcode 2340   ● pop 35,100
Tamworth is the country-music centre of the nation, an antipodean Nashville. The town's population doubles during the 10 day country music festival in January, which culminates with the Australasian country music awards, Golden Guitars, on the Australia Day long weekend.

Guitar-shaped things are all the rage, starting with the information centre (☎ 6755 4300, tourism@tamworth.nsw.gov.au), on the corner of Peel and Murray Sts, where you can pick up a map of the Heritage Walk or the longer Kamilaroi Walking Track.

Country-music memorabilia around town includes a collection of photos at the Good Companions Hotel, the **Hands of Fame**, near the information centre and, at Tattersalls Hotel on Peel St, **Noses of Fame**!

The **Country Collection**, on the New England Hwy in South Tamworth, is hard to miss – out the front is the 12m-high **Golden Guitar**. Inside is a wax museum ($5). Also here is the **Longyard Hotel**, a major venue during the festival. Recording studios, such as Nashgrill (☎ 6762 1652) and Hadley Records & Yeldah Music (☎ 6765 7813), can be visited by arrangement.

Places to Stay
You'll be lucky to find a bed or camping ground spot anywhere during the country

music festival (unless you have booked years in advance).

The *Paradise Caravan Park* (☎ 6766 3120), on the corner of East and Peel Sts, is near the information centre and has camp sites for $11.50 and on-site vans for $31.

Country Backpackers (☎ 6761 2600, 169 Marius St), opposite the train station, is basic but clean and perfectly located with helpful managers. Dorms cost $15 with linen and breakfast, and doubles $35.

There are plenty of pubs in town with doubles for around $45. Just near the backpackers on Marius St, the *Tamworth Hotel* (☎ 6766 2923) is a gorgeous deco pub with singles/doubles for $32/52 with breakfast.

Many motels are enormous but few are cheap and charge around $45 at slow times. About 30km east of town near Kootingal, *Leconfield* (☎ 6769 4328) runs five-day jackaroo/jillaroo courses for $298 and 11-day courses for $495, everything included. The station owners will pick you up from Tamworth.

Getting There & Away

Eastern Australia (☎ 13 1313) has daily flights to Sydney for $186 and Impulse (☎ 13 1381) flies to Brisbane for $254. Most of the long-distance buses pull in at the information centre. Bus fares include $46 to Sydney and $20 to Armidale.

TAMWORTH TO ARMIDALE

North of Tamworth, in the **Moonbi Ranges**, is *Minbalup Hostel* (☎ 6766 9295), located in 1418 hectares of bushland. The owners pick up from Tamworth and run exploration expeditions around the property. It costs $20 for the first night and $16 thereafter.

The pretty town of **Uralla** (population 2460) is where bushranger Captain Thunderbolt was buried in 1870. Graffiti-splattered Thunderbolt's Rock, by the highway 7km south of town, was one of his hide-outs. There are several craft shops and the big McCrossin's Mill Museum ($3.50). A fossicking area is about 5km north-west of Uralla on the Kingstown road. The town of **Gostwyck**, a little piece of England, is 10km south-east of Uralla.

ARMIDALE
• postcode 2350   • pop 22,000

The regional centre of Armidale is a popular stopping point. The 1000m altitude means it's pleasantly cool in summer and frosty (but often sunny) in winter. The town is famous for its autumn colours, which are at their best in late March and early April.

The Beardy St pedestrian mall and some elegant old buildings make the town centre attractive. It's also a lively town, thanks to the large student population at the University of New England. Education is big business in Armidale; there are also three posh boarding schools, including The Armidale School (TAS), whose imposing buildings and grounds can be seen on the road to Grafton and Dorrigo.

The information centre (☎ 6772 4655, 1800 627 736, armvisit@northnet.com.au) is just north of the city centre, on the corner of Marsh and Dumaresq Sts. It has walking and driving-tour brochures and a free trolley tour of the city daily at 10 am. The bus station is in the same building.

The **Armidale Folk Museum** is in the city centre, on the corner of Faulkner and Rusden Sts, and is open daily from 1 to 4 pm (free). The excellent **New England Regional Art Museum** (free) is south of the centre, on Kentucky St. Just next door you'll find the excellent **Aboriginal Cultural Centre & Keeping Place**, which has changing exhibitions; you can visit from 10 am to 4 pm on weekdays or 1 to 4 pm on weekends ($3).

Saumarez Homestead, on the New England Hwy between Armidale and Uralla, is a beautiful, old house that still contains the effects of the rich pastoralists who built it.

The Armidale area is noted for its magnificent gorges and waterfalls – best viewed after rain. The best of them are **Wollomombi Falls**, 39km east of Armidale off the road to Grafton and Dorrigo, and **Dangar's Falls**, 22km south-east of Armidale off the Dangarsleigh road. Both have basic camping grounds.

Organised Tours

Waterfall Way Tours (☎ 6772 2018), based at Creekside Cottages, operates out of

Armidale taking small groups on natural history and interpretive tours of the World Heritage listed national parks between Armidale and Coffs Harbour. The tour operator has a degree in environmental science and is very knowledgeable about the local flora and fauna.

Places to Stay

The *Pembroke Caravan Park* (☎ 6772 6470, Grafton Rd) is about 2km east of town. It has camp sites from $12, single/double on-site vans from $20/25 and cabins between $32/37 and $42/48. It is also an associate-YHA hostel offering beds in a huge partitioned dorm for $15.50. Families might be offered an en suite cabin at YHA rates.

Much more convenient is Armidale's 'Pink Pub', the *Wicklow Hotel* (☎ 6772 2421), on the corner of Marsh and Dumaresq Sts, across from the bus station. It has comfortable pub rooms from $20/36. *Tattersalls Hotel* (☎ 6772 2247) is on the mall so it has little traffic noise. Rooms start at $25/40, more with en suite.

There are more than 20 motels but about the only places with doubles for under $50 are *Rose Villa Motel* (☎ 6772 3872) that charges from $43/45, and *Hideaway Motor Inn* (☎ 6772 5177) that charges from $42/45. Both are on the New England Hwy north of town.

Smith House (☎ 6772 0652) is a grand old building which used to house students but is now open to the public for $25/38. Three meals a day from the student dining room costs $12.

Creekside Cottages (☎ 6772 2018, 5 Canambe St) is a pretty B&B in an old homestead on 1.5 hectares by the creek. Rooms are $60/80 plus $5 for breakfast. Prices vary for those planning to accompany the owner on tours to the national parks between Armidale and Coffs Harbour (see the earlier Organised Tours section above).

Places to Eat

The central streets have a wide variety of eating places. The best place to start is the East Mall. *Café Yannis*, in the East Mall, is a popular place for breakfast ($8), lunch

and dinner (pastas and delicious salads under $10). *Jean-Pierre's BYO Café*, an odd combination of a country town cafe and a French restaurant, has snacks and meals. *Cafe Midale*, further along Beardy St, has breakfast and light meals from $6.50. *Rumours* serves breakfasts from $5, burgers from $7 and other meals such as nachos and focaccia. *Dalmatia*, on Marsh St near the mall, is open for lunch and dinner and has vegetarian feasts from $8.

Getting There & Away

Eastern Australia (☎ 13 1313) flies to Sydney ($190), as does Hazelton (☎ 13 1713) which has specials as low as ($79). Impulse (☎ 13 1381) flies to Brisbane ($243).

Countrylink (☎ 13 2232), McCafferty's and Greyhound Pioneer all service Armidale, and Keans (☎ 1800 625 587) runs down to Coffs Harbour and Port Macquarie, via Dorrigo. Fares from Armidale include Sydney $53, Brisbane $48, Tamworth $18, Dorrigo $16, Bellingen $23, Coffs Harbour $24 and Port Macquarie $40. Countrylink runs to Glen Innes for $11.

The train fare from Sydney is $69.

Getting Around

Bikes can be hired from the University of New England (☎ 6773 2316) for $9 a half day, $17 a day or $35 a week.

Realistic Car Rentals (☎ 6772 3004), on the corner of Rusden and Dangar Sts, has cars from $45 a day, including insurance and 100 free kilometres.

NORTH OF ARMIDALE

Guyra (population 2200), at an altitude of 1300m, is one of the highest towns in the state. **Mother of Ducks** is a waterbird sanctuary on the edge of town. The strange **balancing rock** can be seen by the highway 12km before Glen Innes at Stonehenge.

You're still at over 1000m at **Glen Innes** (population 6100), a good place to meet bushrangers a century ago. Buses stop at the information centre (☎ 6732 2397), on the New England Hwy.

The main street, Grey St, is worth strolling down for its old buildings. The area was settled by Scots, and Glen Innes regards itself as the Celtic capital of New England – there are bilingual street signs. The impressive **Standing Stones** can be seen on a hill above town.

At the junction of the New England and Bruxner highways, **Tenterfield** (population 3500) is the last big town before the Queensland border. The information centre (☎ 6736 1082) is on Rouse St, the main street, on the corner of Miles St. **Thunderbolt's Hideout**, where bushranger Captain Thunderbolt did just that, is 11km out of town.

The main attractions in the area are the Bald Rock and Boonoo Boonoo national parks – see the National Parks entry earlier in this section. The information centre can organise tours ($50) of these parks with Woollool Woollool Aboriginal Culture Tours.

Several pubs have accommodation, such as the *Exchange Hotel (☎ 6736 1054, Rous St)*, with rooms for $12/24.

TENTERFIELD TO CASINO

Known as the Upper Clarence region, the area is at the edge of what was once the Big Scrub and remnants of its former lush vegetation can still be seen. It's a quiet and beautiful area with some great accommodation for those who want to stay somewhere a bit off the beaten track.

The *Clarence River Wilderness Lodge (☎ 6665 1337)* is 42km up Paddy's Flat Rd, which leaves the highway 3km before the small town of **Tabulam**. The Lodge offers canoe expeditions, bush walking, bird watching and gold fossicking and the owners will pick-up from Tabulam by arrangement. It costs $7 a night to camp and $20 to stay in a cabin.

Close to the quaint town of **Bonalbo** is the *Gorge Station (☎ 6665 1285)*, on 1300 hectares of flora and fauna reserve. Horse trekking, canoeing, fishing and rainforest walks are just some of the activities at the Station. Cabin/bunkhouse accommodation costs $30/15. The turn-off to Bonalbo is on the Bruxner Hwy between Tabulam and Mummulgum.

Forgotten Country Eco Tours (☎ 6687 7545) runs three-day tours to the Upper

Clarence departing from Ballina and Byron Bay. Kirkland's (☎ 6622 1499) runs between Lismore and Byron Bay to Tabulam.

Casino (population 10,350) is more renowned for its title of Australia's Beef Capital than its attractions as a tourist destination. However if you're after an insight into a great agricultural tradition, Casino Beef Week runs between late May and early June. The information centre (☎ 6662 1572) is on the highway just after the bridge crossing the Richmond River.

South Coast

Though much less visited than the coast north of Sydney, the coast south to the Victorian border has beautiful scenery, excellent beaches, good surf and diving, attractive fishing towns, historic settlements and spectacular forests. The Princes Hwy runs along the coast from Sydney through Wollongong to the Victorian border. Although a longer and slower route to Melbourne than the Hume Hwy, it's infinitely more interesting and enjoyable. The Snowy Mountains, 150km from Sydney, can also be reached via the south coast.

There are literally thousands of excellent guesthouses, hotels, resorts and camping grounds in the area between Sydney and the Victorian border, as well as activities as diverse as scuba diving, hang-gliding, skydiving, motorcycle tours, horse riding, fishing, caving, bushwalking, scenic flights and island visits. The various district information centres are the best places to find details.

Getting There & Away

Hazelton (☎ 13 1713) flies to Merimbula and Moruya from Sydney; Kendell (☎ 13 1300, 6922 0100 in Wagga Wagga) flies to Merimbula from Melbourne.

Greyhound Pioneer travels the Princes Hwy. Fares from Sydney include Batemans Bay $38 (six hours), Narooma $47 (seven hours), Bega $54 (eight hours) and Eden $60 (nine hours). Sapphire Coast Express (☎ 4473 5517) runs between Batemans Bay and Melbourne ($61/110 one way/return) twice a week.

A Nowra-based company, Pioneer Motor Service (☎ 4423 5233), runs buses daily between Eden and Sydney ($49) and Eden and Melbourne ($40). For short hops between coastal towns it's much cheaper than the big lines. Countrylink (☎ 13 2242) serves Bega on its daily Eden-Canberra run ($36): Bega-Canberra ($29) and Bega-Eden ($8).

Murrays (☎ 13 2251) has daily buses from Canberra to Batemans Bay ($21.75) and south along the coast to Narooma ($32.95 from Canberra, $13.90 from Batemans Bay).

The railway from Sydney goes as far south as Bomaderry (Nowra) from $12.80/15.40 one way/return.

WOLLONGONG

● postcode 2500   ● pop 185,400

Only 80km south of Sydney, Wollongong is the state's third-largest city. Although an industrial centre that includes the biggest steelworks in Australia at nearby Port Kembla, Wollongong has some superb surf beaches and beautiful hinterland.

The name Illawarra, which is often applied to Wollongong and its surrounds, actually refers specifically to the hills behind the city (the Illawarra Escarpment) and the coastal Lake Illawarra to the south. The hills provide a fine backdrop to the city and great views over the coast.

Orientation & Information

Crown St is the main commercial street and between Kembla and Keira Sts is a two-block pedestrian mall. Keira St is part of the Princes Hwy. Through-traffic bypasses the city on the Southern Freeway.

The tourist information centre (☎ 4227 5545, 1800 240 737, fax 4226 6629, tourism@wollongong.nsw.gov.au), on the corner of Crown and Kembla Sts, opens daily. The post office is on Crown St. Wollongong East post office is near the tourist information centre.

The *SpidrWeb Cafe* (☎ 4225 8677, 67 Kembla St), the Illawarra region's first Internet cafe, is open Monday to Friday from

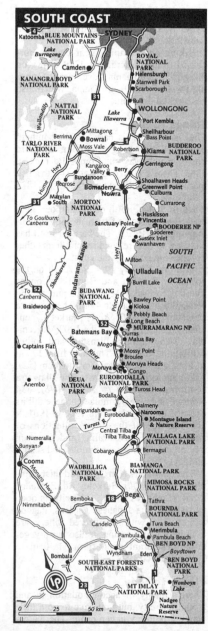

NEW SOUTH WALES

9 am to 5 pm and to noon on Saturday. The *Cyber Electric Cafe* is in the Mall at 105 Crown St.

Hiking and camping gear can be purchased from Bushcraft (☎ 4229 6748), on Stewart St, and Kiama Adventure & Camping (☎ 4233 2999), in Kiama, which also has a rental division.

Things to See
The fishing fleet is based in the southern part of Wollongong's harbour, **Belmore Basin**, which was cut from solid rock in 1868. There's a fish cooperative (with a fish market, cafe and restaurant) and an 1872 lighthouse.

North Beach, north of the harbour, generally has better surf than the South Wollongong City Beach. The harbour itself has beaches, which are good for children. Other beaches run north up the coast.

The **City Gallery** (☎ 4228 7500) on the corner of Kembla and Burelli Sts opens Tuesday to Friday 10 am to 5 pm, and on weekends from noon to 4 pm. The **Illawarra Museum** (☎ 4228 0158), 11 Market St, contains a reconstruction of the 1902 Mt Kembla town mining disaster and other exhibitions. It's open Thursday from 12 am to 3 pm, and weekends from 1 to 4 pm ($2).

For motoring enthusiasts, the **Illawarra Motoring Museum** (☎ 4228 7048), 634 Northcliffe Drive, Kembla Grange, exhibits cars and motorcycles from 1906 to 1961. It also has one of the finest collections of automobilia in Australia, and is open Wednesday, Sunday, and public and school holidays ($5).

The enormous **Nan Tien Buddhist Temple** (☎ 4272 0600), Berkeley Rd, Berkeley, a few kilometres south of the city, is open to visitors. The Japanese gardens, Pagoda and museum with its mirrored gallery, are definitely worth seeing. It also has a vegetarian restaurant open from 11.30am to 2pm. Meals cost $6.

Places to Stay
There's plenty of accommodation in and around the city, but you have to go a little way out before you can camp. There are a number of council-run caravan parks: the *Corrimal Holiday & Tourist Park* (☎ 4285 5688), on the beach about 6km north of town; the *Bulli* (☎ 4285 5677), near the beach on Farrell Rd, Bulli, 11km north; and *Windang* (☎ 4297 3166), on Fern St, Windang (with beach and lake frontage), 15km south, between Lake Illawarra and the sea. All charge about $15 for camp sites and from $55 to $145 for vans or cabins, with prices rising slightly during school and Christmas holidays.

Keiraleagh House (☎ 4228 6765, 60 Kembla St), north of Market St, is a large hostel with good single rooms without/with bath for $20/25. Dorm beds in the 'Stables' are $15, but these are not highly recommended.

Several pubs have accommodation, such as the central *Harp Hotel* (☎ 4229 1333, 124 Corrimal St), near Crown St, which charges $40/60 for rooms with TV and bathroom. It often has live bands.

The *Cabbage Tree Motel* (☎ 4284 4000, 1 Anama St), behind the Cabbage Tree Hotel in Fairy Meadow, 3.5km north of the city centre, has large rooms with two double beds at $50 midweek and $55 at weekends for two, plus $5 for each extra person. Most buses heading north from the Wollongong train station stop here.

The tranquil *Nan Tien Temple Pilgrim Lodge* (☎ 4272 0500), Berkeley Rd, Berkeley, offers quality non-smoking accommodation at reasonable rates. Singles are $30 for a Japanese-style futon mattress in a shared room. Singles and doubles in a motel-style room are $50/70.

Novotel Northbeach, (☎ 4226 3555, fax 4229 1705, 2-14 Cliff Rd) is Wollongong's only five-star hotel. Situated opposite the beach, it has two restaurants, a small gaming room and several bars. Double rooms cost from $195.

Places to Eat
There are plenty of cheap and cheerful cafes and good restaurants to be found in the city and along the beachfront. The *Thai Carnation* (☎ 4228 4102), on the corner of Crown and Corrimal Sts, is open for lunch and dinner with mains around $12. *Cafe on the Mall*,

NEW SOUTH WALES

WOLLONGONG

PLACES TO STAY
3 Novotel Northbeach
14 Keiraleagh House
24 Harp Hotel

PLACES TO EAT
1 Lagoon; Santorini
4 North Beach Gourmet
5 Coffee Cove
6 Beach House; Stingray Cafe
7 B&J's
8 Ocean View Chinese Restaurant
12 Fish Cooperative; Harbour Front
    Restaurant; Seaview Fish Market
    Nonabel Coffee Lounge

13 Boufflers Seafoods
15 Bon Appetit -
    Illawarra Master Builders Club
17 Plant Room
21 Cafe on the Mall
22 Il Faro
25 Thai Carnation
26 Cafe Suraz

OTHER
2 North Wollongong Train Station
9 Swimming Pool
10 Old Lighthouse
11 Breakwater Lighthouse
16 Bus Station

18 Wollongong Railway Station;
    Countrylink
19 Dicey Riley's
20 St Michael's Anglican
    Cathedral
23 Spidrweb Internet Cafe
27 Illawarra Museum
28 Local Bus Terminal;
    Entertainment Centre
29 Steelers Stadium
30 Oxford Tavern
31 Tourist Information
32 City Gallery
33 Cyber Electric Internet Cafe
34 Bushcraft

To Fairy Meadow,
Corrimal, Bulli
& Sydney

Fairy
Meadow
Beach

SOUTH

PACIFIC

OCEAN

Stuart
Park

Porter Street
Fairy Creek

Squires Way

Hanley Drive

Virginia Street

Bode Ave

Bessell St

Blacket St

North Beach

Bourke Street

Park St

Ocean St

Edward Street

Flinders Street

Cliff Road

Corrimal Street

Gipps Street

View St

Street

Gipps Street

Georges
Place

Benton
Park

Throsby Street

Denison Street

Belmore Street

Drive

Campbell Street

Keira Street

Church Street

Kembla Street

Smith Street

Thomas St

Marr St

Street

Wilson Street

0   250   500 m

Belmore
Basin

*Flagstaff
Point*

Endeavour Drive

Victoria Street

Market Street

Market Street

Crown
Lane

Mall

Crown Street

Burelli Street

Street

Street

Harbour Street

Hector Street

Marine Drive

City Beach

Wollongong

To Windang,
Kiama &
Nowra

Rawson St

Stewart Street

McCabe
Park

Ellen Street

Auburn Street

Gladstone Avenue

Station St

Atchison Street

Kenny Street

Keira Street

Bank Street

Church Street

Kembla Street

Corrimal Street

To Port Kembla
(8km)

South

on the corner of Church and Crown Sts, opens long hours for snacks and meals and has breakfasts from $7.20. *Cafe Suraz*, in Corrimal St, is known for its excellent muffins and cakes, and *Il Faro*, in Kembla St, is popular for its pasta and pizza.

The *Plant Room*, on Crown St near the corner of Gladstone Ave, opens during the day for coffee and snacks and at night offers a $15 buffet. It has a relaxed atmosphere, a cosmopolitan menu and live music some evenings.

In a delightful setting, overlooking the water at Belmore Basin, you will find *Bouffiers Seafoods*, the *Nonabel Coffee Lounge*, the *Seaview Fish Market* and the more up-market, but reasonably priced *Harbour Front Restaurant*, which is open for lunch and dinner.

The award winning and charmingly decorated *Lagoon Seafood Restaurant* (☎ 4226 1677), in Stuart Park opposite North Beach, is a must if you can afford it. Less expensive, and under the same ownership, is the *Santorini Coffee Shop* adjacent, which serves calorie-laden cakes, pizzas cooked in wood-fired ovens and light meals in a setting straight out of the Greek Islands.

Also at North Beach, grouped around Bourke St and Cliff Rd opposite the Novotel, are *B&J Cakes & Pastries*, *Coffee Cove*, *North Beach Gourmet* and the popular *Stingray Cafe*, which has Australian meals and wines. The *Beach House Seafood Restaurant* (☎ 4226 6730), above B&J's and the Stingray Cafe, has main meals from $19. The Chinese restaurant next door *Ocean View*, has a terrace overlooking the water; dishes are around $14.

Windjammers (☎ 4224 3123), at Novotel Northbeach, serves coffee, light and a la carte meals, and buffets which range from $16.50 for a continental breakfast to $45 for the deluxe seafood buffet.

Entertainment

There are many clubs and pubs with live entertainment. Young bands play at the *Harp Hotel*, on Corrimal St, and the *Oxford Tavern*, on Crown St. *Dicey Riley's*, also on Crown St, has Irish music. Information on performing arts, sporting facilities and indoor activities can be got from the tourist centre.

Getting There & Away

Bus The bus station (☎ 4226 1022) is on the corner of Keira and Campbell Sts. Premier Motor Services (☎ 13 3410) runs several daily services to Sydney ($11), and one to Canberra ($28) via Moss Vale and the Southern Highlands; Bega ($42), Eden ($47), Brisbane ($80) and Melbourne ($60). Greyhound Pioneer has daily buses to Sydney ($19), Melbourne ($60) and Brisbane ($90).

Train City Rail (☎ 13 1500) runs several daily trains to/from Sydney (about 90 minutes, $7.20 one way; off-peak day-return $8.60). A fair number continue south to Kiama, Gerringong and Bomaderry (Nowra).

From Port Kembla, Thursday to Sunday, a scenic tourist train known as the Cockatoo Run (☎ 1800 643 801) heads inland to Robertson in the Southern Highlands. The views as the train climbs the Illawarrra Escarpment are fabulous ($26 return).

Getting Around

Four local bus companies service the area: Rutty's (☎ 4271 1322), John J Hill (☎ 4229 4911), Dions (☎ 4228 9855), which runs past the university to Bulli, and Greens (☎ 4267 3884), which runs north to Helensburgh. The main stop is on Crown St, where it meets Marine Drive, next to the beach. You can reach most beaches by rail and trains are fairly frequent.

A cycle path runs from the city centre north to Bulli and south to Windang and you can hire bikes in Stuart Park on Sunday and holidays.

AROUND WOLLONGONG

The hills, known as the Illawarra Escarpment, rise dramatically behind Wollongong and there are walking tracks and lookouts on Mt Kembla and Mt Keira less than 10km from the city centre, but no buses go up there. You get spectacular views over the town and coast from the **Bulli Scenic Lookout** (pronounced 'bull-eye'), off the Princes Hwy, north of Wollongong.

The country is equally spectacular to the south, inland through the **Macquarie Pass National Park** to Moss Vale or through the Kangaroo Valley. The Fitzroy Falls and other attractions of mountainous **Morton National Park** can be reached by either route.

North of Wollongong are several excellent beaches. Those with good surf include **Sandon Point**, **Austinmer**, **Headlands** (only for experienced surfers) and **Sharkies**. The pubs at Clifton and Scarborough have meals, accommodation and spectacular views.

On the road to Otford and Royal National Park, the views from **Lawrence Hargrave Lookout**, at Bald Hill above Stanwell Park, are superb. Hargrave, a pioneer aviator, made his first flying attempts in the area in the early 20th century; today **Stanwell Park** is used for **hang-gliding**. Sydney Hang Gliding Centre (☎ 4294 4294) offers pilot courses and tandem flights from $145. South of Wollongong, **Lake Illawarra** is popular for water sports.

WOLLONGONG TO NOWRA
South of Lake Illawarra, **Shellharbour**, a popular holiday resort, is one of the oldest towns along the coast. It was a thriving port back in 1830, but it declined after construction of the railway. There are good beaches on Windang Peninsula north of town and good scuba diving off Bass Point to the south.

Kiama is a pretty seaside town famous for its blowhole, which can spout up to 60m high. Near the blowhole is the heritage **Pilot's Cottage Museum**. There are also good surf beaches and the scenic Cathedral Rock, at Jones Beach. *Blowhole Point Holiday Park* (☎ 4232 2707) is terrific if it's not too windy, with camp sites for $16 to $19. *Kiama Backpackers Hostel* (☎ 4233 1881), at 31 Bong Bong St (really!), is a laid-back place only 25m from the station and a minute from the beach. It has dorm beds for $15 and double rooms from $35.

The sub-tropical **Minnamurra Rainforest**, part of Budderoo National Park, is located 15km west of Kiama. Check out the size of the buttress roots and liana vines on some of the trees! There is a $7.50 entrance fee for cars. Kiama Coachlines (☎ 4232 1531) runs

one service there a day on weekdays leaving from the station in the morning, returning in the afternoon ($8 return).

Gerringong, 10km south of Kiama, has fine beaches and surf. In 1933, pioneer aviator Charles Kingsford-Smith took off for New Zealand from Seven Mile Beach – now a national park south of Gerringong. There is a council-run *Holiday Park* (☎ 4234 1340) at the north end of the beach with camp sites from $15 to $22. *Nesta House* (☎ 4234 1249), a hostel on Fern St, is 300m up the hill from Werri Beach. Dorm beds are $15.

The small town of **Berry** was an early settlement and today it has a number of National Trust classified buildings, a museum and many antique and craft shops. The *Hotel Berry* (☎ 4464 1011) is a pleasant country pub charging from $30/60 a single/double. The *Great Southern* (☎ 4464 1009) is a fun pub/motel absolutely crammed full of memorabilia, including a torpedo hanging from the ceiling, a motorcycle on the bar and two canoes on the roof. A small, adjacent building which houses an ATM, is covered in car hubcaps! Double rooms cost $60.

There are scenic roads from Berry to pretty **Kangaroo Valley**, where there's the Pioneer Farm Settlement (☎ 4465 1306), an old homestead with historic displays, and canoeing on the Shoalhaven and Kangaroo rivers.

Just west of Shoalhaven Heads, **Coolangatta** (no, not the Queensland Coolangatta, this one was the original) has a group of buildings that were constructed by convicts in 1822. They now form part of the *Coolangatta Estate* (☎ 4448 7131), with craft shops, a restaurant and double rooms from $91 midweek. The town also has Bigfoot, a strange vehicle that will carry you to the top of Mt Coolangatta for $10 on weekends and school holidays.

SHOALHAVEN
The coastal strip south of Gerringong to Durras Lake, just north of Batemans Bay, is a popular holiday destination known as Shoalhaven, which also stretches 50km inland to include Morton and Budawang national parks. Inland on the Shoalhaven

River, the twin towns of **Nowra** and **Bomaderry** form the main population centre. The region is popular for water sports, and white-water rafting is available – phone the **Shoalhaven Tourist Centre** (☎ 4421 0778, fax 4423 2950, 1800 024 261), on the highway in Bomaderry. The NPWS has an office (☎ 4423 2170, fax 4423 3122) at 55 Graham St, Nowra.

Five kilometres east of Nowra on the northern bank of the Shoalhaven River, is **Nowra Animal Park** (☎ 4421 3949). It's a pleasant place to meet some of Australia's native animals and you can camp in bushland here for $9 ($11 at peak times). *M&M's Guesthouse* (☎ 4422 8006, fax 4422 8007, 1A Scenic Drive) is a motorcycle friendly place closer to town, near the bridge on the Nowra side of the river. Dorm beds are $20, double rooms $45; rates include a light breakfast. The *White House & Coach House* (☎ 4421 2084, fax 4423 6876) has two and four-bed share rooms for $20 per person, or single/double federation-style rooms in the house (including light breakfast) for $45/65, three/four bed for $80/95.

Inland at Fitzroy Falls, just north of Kangaroo Valley, is the visitors centre (☎ 4887 7270) for **Morton National Park**. South of Morton the line of national parks (Budawang, Deua, Wadbilliga and South-East Forests) stretches to the Victorian border. These outstanding mountain wilderness areas are good for rugged bushwalking.

South of Nowra, **Booderee** (an Aboriginal word meaning 'bay of plenty'), formerly called Jervis Bay, is quite suburban, but **Huskisson**, one of the oldest towns on the bay, is still a pleasant place. There's a fascinating wetlands boardwalk (free) near the Lady Denman Heritage Complex, on the Nowra side of Huskisson.

Booderee National Park (☎ 14443 0977) takes up the south-eastern spit of land on the bay. It has good swimming, surfing and diving on bay and ocean beaches. There are camp sites at Green Patch (from $13) and Bristol Point (groups) and a more basic camping area at Caves Beach (from $8), where there's surf. For all camp sites you have to book through the visitors centre.

Entry to the park costs $5 per car for a week. Jervis Bay Botanic Gardens, located in the park near Cave Beach, are open Monday to Friday from 8 am to 4 pm and 10 am to 5 pm on Sunday and public holidays.

The historic township of **Milton** is situated on the highway 60km south of Nowra. This charming little place is full of historic homes. It conducts an annual scarecrow festival on the last Sunday of the Easter school holidays as part of the Ulladulla Blessing of the Fleet Festival.

Ulladulla is an area of beautiful lakes, lagoons and beaches. There's good swimming and surfing (try Mollymook beach, just north of town). Or you can take the bushwalk to the top of Pigeon House Mountain (719m) in the impressive Budawang Range.

The small *South Coast Backpackers* (☎ 4454 0500, 63 Princes Hwy), in Ulladulla near the top of the hill north of the shopping centre, has spacious five-bed dorms. Dorm beds cost $16, double rooms $37. They'll take guests to Murramarang National Park or Pigeon House and pick them up again for $15, or to Budderoo National Park for $25.

Fares from Ulladulla with Pioneer Motor Service include Sydney $24; Nowra $12; Merry Beach (at the northern end of Murramarang National Park) $7.40; the North Durras turn-off at East Lynne (for Pebbly Beach in Murramarang National Park) $8; Batemans Bay $9 and Eden $31.

Murramarang National Park (☎ 4478 6023) is a beautiful coastal park beginning about 20km south of Ulladulla and running all the way south to Batemans Bay. At lovely Pebbly Beach there's a camping ground (☎ 4478 6006), where sites cost $10 (plus the $7.50 per car day use fee). A kiosk operates during school holidays – when camp sites are scarce. Pebbly Beach is about 10km off the highway and there's no public transport there, but its charms include wild kangaroos and lorikeets which eat from your hand.

There's accommodation at settlements within the park and at **North Durras**, on the inlet to Durras Lake. *Durras Lake North Caravan Park* (☎ 4478 6072) has on-site vans set aside for backpackers at $10 per bed and camp sites from $6 per head.

BATEMANS BAY TO BEGA
Batemans Bay
- **pop 9568**

The fishing port of Batemans Bay is one of the south coast's largest holiday centres. The visitors centre (☎ 4472 6900, 1800 802 528) is on the Princes Hwy, near the town centre.

As well as many hotels, motels and resorts, the town has a lot of accommodation for backpackers. *Batemans Bay Tourist Park and YHA (☎ 4472 4972)* is on the Old Princes Hwy, just south of the town. It has dorm beds for $16 and double rooms for $18 per person. *Beach Road Backpackers (☎ 4472 3644, 92 Beach Rd)*, opposite the boat marina, 10 minutes' walk from the post office, is a friendly place with dorm beds for $17 and double rooms for $35.

About 60km inland from Batemans Bay, on the scenic road to Canberra is **Braidwood**, with its many old buildings and a thriving arts and crafts community. From here there's road access to superb bushwalking in the **Budawang Range**.

Moruya, 25km south of Batemans Bay, is a dairy centre, with oyster farming too. There's fairly unspoiled coast down the side roads south of Moruya. In **Eurobodalla National Park** there are beaches on both sides of a headland at Congo, where there's also a basic camping ground ($5). Bring your own supplies, including drinking water.

Narooma
- **pop 3389**

This seaside holiday town is popular for serious sport fishing in the nearby inlets and lakes. The information centre (☎ 4476 2881), on the beachfront, opens daily from 9 am to 5 pm. The NPWS office (☎ 4476 2798) is nearby on the corner of Field St and Princes Hwy.

About 10km off shore is **Montague Island**, a nature reserve with a historic lighthouse and many seals and fairy penguins. Ranger-guided tours cost $60 (children $45). The clear waters around the island are popular with divers, especially from February to June. The friendly *Bluewater Lodge – Narooma YHA (☎ 4476 4440, fax 4476 3492, 11 Riverside Drive, naryha@sci.net.au)*, near

Wagonga Inlet, has dorm beds for $16 and singles/doubles for $25/35.

Off the highway 15km south of Narooma, and perched on the side of **Mt Dromedary** (806m), is the delightful 19th century gold-mining boom town of **Central Tilba** (population 70!). Preserved as a unique part of Australian history, it is a centre for arts and crafts.

From the nearby town of **Tilba Tilba**, you can walk to the top of Mt Dromedary. The return walk (11km) takes about five hours, or you could ride up with Mt Dromedary Trail Rides (☎ 4476 3376); two/three-hour rides cost $40/$60. Umbarra Cultural Tours (☎ 4473 7232, fax 4473 7169) runs excellent tours to sites of Aboriginal significance, including Mt Dromedary, Mumbulla Mountain and **Wallaga Lake**. Tours cost $29 and $45.

South of Wallaga Lake and off the Princes Hwy, **Bermagui** (population 1196) is a fishing centre made famous 50 years ago by American cowboy-novelist Zane Grey. It's a handy base for visits to both Wallaga Lake and Mimosa Rocks national parks, and for **Wadbilliga National Park**, inland in the ranges. The main information centre (☎/fax 6493 4174) is on Wallaga Lake Rd, just near the bridge.

The friendly *Blue Pacific (☎ 6493 4921, 73 Murrah St)* has backpacker accommodation for $18 as well as regular holiday flats. It's up a hill off the road running along the beach north of the town centre. The turn-off is signposted just north of the fishing-boat wharf. Bega Valley Coaches (☎ 6492 2418) has a weekday service between Bermagui and Bega ($12.60).

More interesting than the inland highway, the largely unsealed coast road between Bermagui and Tathra runs alongside the excellent **Mimosa Rocks National Park** (☎ 4476 2888). There are basic camping grounds at Aragunnu Beach, Picnic Point and Middle Beach, and another with no facilities at Gillards Beach. Park entry is free, but camping costs $5; bring your own water.

Inland on the Princes Hwy is **Cobargo**, another unspoilt old town. The main 2WD access to Wadbilliga National Park is near here. It's a rugged wilderness which hasn't changed much in thousands of years.

Bega
• pop 4190

This sizeable town is near the junction of the Princes and Snowy Mountains highways. The information centre (☎/fax 6492 2045) is in a craft shop on Gipps St. The modern, mud-brick *Bega YHA Hostel* (☎ 6492 3103) is on Kirkland Crescent (off Kirkland Ave, which departs the highway about 1km west of the town centre). It's a friendly place where dorm beds cost $13 and doubles $34.

Countrylink's Eden to Canberra service passes through Bega daily (☎ 13 2242). Pioneer Motor Service runs north to Sydney, south to Eden. Greyhound Pioneer stops here on the run between Sydney and Melbourne, as does Sapphire Coast Express running between Batemans Bay and Melbourne.

SOUTH TO THE VICTORIAN BORDER

The coast here is quite undeveloped, and there are many good beaches and some awe-inspiring forests full of wildlife – and loggers.

Merimbula
• postcode 2548   • pop 4383

Merimbula is a big holiday resort and retirement town with an impressive 'lake' (actually a large inlet) and ocean beaches. Despite large-scale development, the setting remains beautiful and nearby **Pambula Beach** is quiet in a suburban way.

The tourist information centre (☎/fax 6495 1129), on the waterfront at the bottom of Market St, opens daily from 9 am to 5 pm. At the wharf on the eastern point is the small **Merimbula Aquarium** (☎ 6495 3227); it opens daily from 10 am to 5 pm ($8).

Near the surf beach, the spacious *Wandarrah YHA Lodge* (☎ 6495 3503, 8 Marine Parade) (follow the signs just south of the bridge) has dorm beds for $16, double rooms for $19 per person. Activities include minibus trips to nearby national parks and rainy day 'mystery tours'. *Mirimbula*

Divers Lodge (☎ 1800 651 861, fax 6495 3648, 15 Park St, diverslodge@acr.net.au), just off Main St, is the only other backpacker accommodation in town. Dorm beds and doubles in two-bedroom fully self-contained units cost from $15 per person, depending on the season and demand. The lodge, an accredited PADI resort, offers dive courses and whale watching.

Eden
• postcode 2551   • pop 3106

At Eden the road turns away from the coast and enters Victoria, where it runs through mighty forests. The town is an old whaling port on Twofold Bay, much less touristy than towns further up the coast. Eden Tourist Centre (☎/fax 6496 1953) on Imlay St opens weekdays and holidays from 9 am to 5 pm and weekends from 9 am to noon.

At the intriguing **Killer Whale Museum** (☎ 6496 2094) you can learn about the whaler who, in 1891, was swallowed by a whale and regurgitated, unharmed, 15 hours later. Well, almost unharmed. His hair turned white and fell out due to the whale's digestive juices. There's also the skeleton of a killer whale, Old Tom, the leader of a pod of killer whales that herded baleen and hump back whales into Twofold Bay where whalers were waiting to kill them. The museum opens daily from 9.15 am to 3.45 pm Monday to Saturday, and Sunday from 11.15 am to 3.45 pm; opening hours are longer during school holidays ($4).

Whales still swim along the coast in October and November. You can book **whale-spotting cruises** ($45, children $30) at the tourist centre.

The *Australasia Hotel* (☎ 6496 1600, 60 Imlay St) has backpackers' beds for $15, pub rooms for $25 per person and motel-style rooms for $35 per person.

Boydtown

Boydtown, south of Eden, was founded by Benjamin Boyd, a flamboyant early settler whose landholdings were once second in size only to the Crown's. His grandiose plans included making Boydtown the capital of Australia, but his fortune foundered and so did the town – later he did too, disappearing without trace somewhere in the Pacific. Some of his buildings still stand, and the *Seahorse Inn (☎ 6496 1361, Boydtown Park Rd)*, a guesthouse built by convict labour, is still in use. Double rooms range from $45 to $65 B&B, and there are live bands on the weekend. Camp sites cost $12.

Ben Boyd National Park & Around

To the north and south of Eden is Ben Boyd National Park – good for walking, camping, swimming and surfing, especially at Long Beach in the north. Edrom Rd is the main access road.

South of Ben Boyd National Park, **Nadgee Nature Reserve** continues down the coast, but it's much less accessible. **Wonboyn**, a small settlement on Wonboyn Lake at the northern end of the reserve, has a small store and *Wonboyn Cabins & Caravan Park (☎ 6496 9131)*, with camp sites from $10. Across the lake from Wonboyn, but with access from Green Cape Rd in Ben Boyd National Park, is *Wonboyn Lake Resort (☎ 6496 9162)*, with self-contained cabins from $60 for four people.

Inland from Wonboyn you can follow Imlay Rd (off the Princes Hwy) through **South-East Forests National Park**, which extends in pockets north to Wadbilliga National Park and south to the Victorian border.

Snowy Mountains

The Snowy Mountains, affectionately called the Snowies, form part of the Great Dividing Range which straddles the NSW-Victoria border. Mt Kosciuszko (pronounced 'kozzyosko' and named after a Polish hero of the American War of Independence), in NSW, is Australia's highest *mainland* summit (2228m). Much of the state's Snowies are within Kosciuszko National Park, an area of year-round interest: skiing in winter, bushwalking and vivid wildflowers in summer. The main ski resorts and the highest country are in the park,

west of Jindabyne. Thredbo, Perisher/Blue Cow and Smiggin Holes are the main downhill skiing areas. Charlotte Pass, Guthega and Mt Selwyn, further north, are smaller downhill areas.

The upper waters of the Murray River form both the state and national park boundaries in the south-west. The Snowy River, made famous by Banjo Paterson's poem *The Man from Snowy River* and the film based on it, rises just below the summit of Mt Kosciuszko. The Murrumbidgee River also rises in the national park.

You can take white-water rafting trips on the Murray River in summer when the water is high enough. Horse riding is also popular in summer and there are stables near Cooma, Adaminaby, Jindabyne, Tumut and Tumbarumba.

Getting There & Away

Cooma is the eastern gateway to the Snowy Mountains. The most spectacular mountain views are from the Alpine Way (sometimes closed in winter) running between Khancoban, on the western side of the national park, and Jindabyne. There are restrictions on car parking in the national park, particularly during the ski season – check with the NPWS or tourist information centres at Cooma or Jindabyne before entering.

Impulse (☎ 13 1381) flies daily to Cooma from Sydney; the standard economy fare is $282. There's no direct flight from Melbourne.

Greyhound Pioneer (☎ 13 2030) runs to Cooma (single/return $25/$48 from Canberra, $47/$90 from Sydney) and to Jindabyne ($40/$76 from Canberra, $60/$114 from Sydney), with some services continuing on to the resorts. Services are frequent in winter, but less so at other times. Several coach companies run ski specials in the winter from Sydney and Canberra.

Countrylink (☎ 13 2242) runs daily from Sydney, Canberra and Eden. To Melbourne, V-Line's Capital Link bus (☎ 13 6196) runs from Canberra via Cooma to Sale where it connects with a train to Melbourne on Tuesday and Friday, plus Sunday in the school holidays, for $49.

COOMA

• postcode 2630   • pop 9780

Cooma was the construction centre for the Snowy Mountains Hydro-electric Scheme, built by workers from around the world – see the boxed text. The **Avenue of Flags** in Centennial Park, next to Cooma Visitors Centre (☎ 1800 636 525), 119 Sharp St, flies the flags of the 28 nationalities involved. The **Snowy Mountains Hydro-electric Scheme Information Centre** (☎ 6453 2004, 1800 623 776), on the Monaro Hwy 2km north of town, has high tech-interactive exhibits and videos of this amazing project. Visits can be made to the three SMA power stations, including an underground experience and the dam at Tumut. The centre is open on weekdays from 8 am to 5 pm and weekends from 8 am to 1 pm. Its Web site is www.snowyhydro.com.au.

If you don't have time to take the town walk (maps are available from the visitors centre), at least walk down **Lambie St**, with its historic buildings and, on Vale St, see the imposing granite **Cooma Courthouse** and nearby **Cooma Gaol Museum** (☎ 6450 1357). Half a kilometre west, the **Southern Cloud Memorial** incorporates some of the wreckage of the *Southern Cloud*, an aircraft that crashed in the Snowies in 1931. The wreck was found in 1958.

There are several **horse riding** places in the area. Reynella (☎ 6454 2386), on Bolero Rd (turn off 8km south of Adaminaby), offers mainly longer treks and accommodation packages. San Michele (☎ 6454 2229), at Adaminaby, specialises in short rides.

Places to Stay

Prices are lower here than in Jindabyne or the ski resorts, but in winter it still pays to book well ahead – preferably in the summer!

The *Mountain View Caravan Park* (☎ 6452 4513), 6km west of Cooma towards Jindabyne, has camp sites for $10 ($14 with power) and on-site vans from $20 to $35.

The friendly *Bunkhouse Motel* (☎ 6452 2983), on the corner of Commissioner and Soho Sts, has dorm beds for $15 and singles/doubles for $25/40. Each dorm has its own kitchen and en suite.

All the pubs have accommodation. The *Australian Hotel* (☎ 6452 1844, 137 Sharp St), on the main street, has basic four-bed bunk rooms for $20 per person, or three-bed rooms with en suite for $65. The *Royal Hotel* (☎ 6452 2132), on the corner of Sharp and Lambie Sts, is quieter and has single/double rooms with shared facilities for $25/35.

In **Nimmitabel**, a small town on the highway 35km south-east of Cooma, the delightful *Royal Arms* guesthouse (☎ 6454 6422) has single/double rooms with shared facilities for $48/85, or doubles with en suite for $120.

Getting There & Away

All buses except the V/Line service (which stops near Centennial Park) stop at the Snowstop Village, on Sharp St, a few blocks east of the visitors centre. Snowliner Travel (☎ 6452 1422), on Sharp St opposite the visitors centre, handles bus bookings. See also the introductory Getting There & Away section to the Snowy Mountains.

JINDABYNE

• postcode 2627   • pop 4300

Fifty-six kilometres west of Cooma and a step nearer the mountains, Jindabyne is a modern town on the shore of the artificial Lake Jindabyne, which flooded the old town. In summer you can swim and rent boats. The magnificent, NPWS-operated Snowy Region Visitor Centre (☎ 6450 5600) is in the centre of town on Kosciuszko Rd, the main road in from Cooma. Check the notice board in Nugget's Crossing shopping centre for employment listings, cheap accommodation, car shares and second-hand ski gear.

Paddy Pallin (☎ 6456 2922) and Wilderness Sports (☎ 6456 2966) do guided walks and adventure activities in the Snowies, including mountain biking in summer.

Places to Stay

Winter sees a huge influx of visitors; prices soar, many places are booked out months ahead and overnight accommodation all but disappears. Prices also rise on Friday and Saturday nights throughout the year.

Snowy Mountains Hydro-electric Scheme

This huge project took more than 25 years to build, largely in mountainous terrain that had been barely explored, let alone settled. The Scheme was a major source of employment in post-war Australia, and much of the labour was recruited from war-ravaged Europe. Many of those who migrated to Australia to work on the Scheme were 'displaced persons' from Eastern Europe. Over 100,000 people worked on the project between 1949 and 1974.

The Scheme, however, didn't raise environmental concerns. It was begun at a time when the creation of 16 major dams and the diversion of six rivers was seen as an advance of civilisation rather than the drowning of a wilderness. It was a massive endeavour.

Today the Scheme provides electricity for Canberra, NSW, Victoria and South Australia and water from the diverted rivers irrigates the Murray and Murrumbidgee irrigation areas. It's estimated that if the electricity produced by the Scheme were produced by coal-fired turbines, five million tonnes of carbon dioxide would be released into the atmosphere each year.

Three power stations are open to visitors. Murray 1, near Khancoban and Tumut 2, near Cabramurra, have very good interactive displays and exhibits. Tumut 2 is only open for tours in the summer (except for groups of 10 or more, which can book all year round). Tumut 3, near Talbingo, has daily tours year round (hourly between 10 am and noon, then at 1.30 and 2.30 pm). Murray 1 Power Station is open from 9 am to 5 pm daily. Tours cost around $8 for adults and $5 for children/concession. The Snowy Mountains Scheme Information Centre (☎ 6453 2004, 1800 623 776) is in Cooma.

Turbines at Murray 2 Power Station, Khancoban

Photo courtesy of the Snowy Mountains Hydro-electric Authority

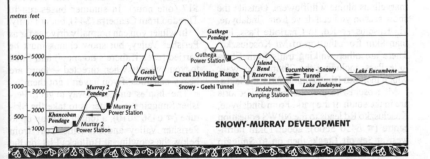

SNOWY-MURRAY DEVELOPMENT

Snowline Caravan Park (☎ *6456 2099, fax 6456 2180)*, at the intersection of the Alpine Way and Kosciuszko Rd, has camp sites from $15, as well as backpacker cabins from $11 to $20 per person. There are plenty of summer and winter activities at the park and they run a free pick-up service from bus stop. Self-contained cabins range from $34 to $150 (with spa).

The *Jindy Inn* (☎ *6456 1957, fax 6456 2057, 18 Clyde St)* is a friendly place with views of the lake. Single rooms with linen and en suite cost from a magic $20 in summer, and from $25 in winter. A guesthouse with moderate summer prices is the spotless *Sonnblick Lodge* (☎ *6456 2472, 49 Gippsland St)*, offering B&B for $30/60.

There's a fair range of motel-style places. *Banjo Patterson Inn* (☎ *6456 2372, fax 6456 1138, 1 Kosciuszko Rd)*, at the eastern edge of town, has good value doubles including breakfast from $85 in summer, $150 in the peak season.

Apartments & Lodges Many places offer ski-season accommodation. Letting agents include Jindabyne Real Estate (☎ 6456 2216, 1800 020 657). Fully equipped apartments sleeping six cost from around $400 a week in the low season and *from* $600 a week in the high winter season.

KOSCIUSZKO NATIONAL PARK

The state's largest national park (6900 sq km) includes caves, lakes, forest, ski resorts and Mt Kosciuszko. Most famous for its snow, the park is also popular in summer when there are excellent bushwalks and marvellous alpine wildflowers. Outside the snow season you can drive from Jindabyne, via Kosciuszko Rd, to Charlotte Pass, less than 8km from the top of Mt Kosciuszko. There are other walking trails from Charlotte Pass, including the 20km lakes walk which includes Blue, Albina and Club lakes.

Mt Kosciuszko and the main ski resorts are in the south of the park. From Jindabyne, Kosciuszko Rd leads to the NPWS education centre (☎ 6450 5666), about 15km northwest at **Sawpit Creek**, then on to Smiggin Holes, Perisher Valley (33km) and Charlotte

Pass, with a turn-off before Perisher Valley to Guthega. The Alpine Way also runs from Jindabyne to Thredbo (33km from Jindabyne) and around to Khancoban on the south-western side of the mountains, with accessibility subject to snow conditions.

Entry to the national park (and that includes all the ski resorts) costs $14 per car, *per day*. This makes the $60 annual pass a good investment – see the National Parks section at the start of this chapter. Motorcyclists pay $6 (annual $40) and bus passengers $6, but this is usually included in the bus fare.

Places to Stay

Bush camping is permitted in most of the park. *Kosciuszko Mountain Retreat* (☎ *6456 2224)*, up the road from the Sawpit Creek visitors centre, is a pleasant place in bushland. It has unpowered/powered camp sites from $12.50/18 to $19/27 in the high season and cabins from $53 to $163. Chalets with en suite start at $83 going up to $260 in the high season (there's a minimum two-night stay during the high season).

There's plenty of accommodation at the ski resorts, and there's a YHA hostel at Thredbo – see Thredbo Places to Stay.

Getting There & Away

Greyhound Pioneer is the main carrier in this area. There are plenty of services from Sydney and Canberra to Cooma and Jindabyne, from where shuttles will take you to the resorts in winter. Fares include: Jindabyne to Smiggin Holes, $17 (30 minutes), Perisher, $15 (45 minutes) and Thredbo, $17 (one hour). In summer buses run to Thredbo from Canberra ($44), but not daily.

In winter you can normally drive as far as Perisher Valley, but snow chains must be carried (even if there's no snow) and fitted to your wheels when directed – there are heavy penalties if you haven't got them.

The simplest and safest way to get to Perisher/Smiggins in winter is to take the Skitube (☎ 6456 2010), a tunnel railway up to Perisher Valley and Mt Blue Cow from below the snowline at Bullocks Flat, on the Alpine Way. A same-day return trip from

Bullocks Flat to either Mt Blue Cow or Perisher costs $25 (children $14) and there are deals on combined Skitube and lift tickets (one-day $75, children $42). You can hire skis and equipment at Bullocks Flat, and luggage lockers and overnight parking are also available. The Skitube runs a reduced timetable in summer.

SKIING & SKI RESORTS

Although the ski season in Australia starts on the long weekend at the beginning of June and ends in early October, in most years snow can only be guaranteed in July, August and September. However, to combat seasonal fluctuations in snowfall and to supplement nature's allocation, all resorts now have snow-making equipment.

The good news is that when the snow's on the ground and the sun's shining, the skiing can be great. You'll find all the fun (not to mention heart-in-the-mouth fear) you could ask for. Further, the open slopes of the Australian Alps are a ski-tourer's paradise and nordic (cross-country) skiing is very popular. The national park includes some famous trails – Kiandra to Kosciuszko, the Grey Mare Range, Thredbo or Charlotte Pass to Mt Kosciuszko's summit and the Jagungal wilderness. The possibilities for nordic touring are endless, and old cattle-herders' huts may be the only form of accommodation apart from your own tent.

There's also cross-country racing (classic or skating) in Perisher Valley. On the steep slopes of the Main Range near Twynam and Carruthers the cross-country downhill (XCD) fanatics get their adrenalin rushes. In winter, the cliffs near Blue Lake become a practice ground for alpine climbers. Various national and international downhill events and races are conducted at Perisher and Thredbo.

Snowboarding has taken the High Country by storm. Snowboard hire and lessons are widely available and the major resorts have developed purpose-built runs and bowls.

Australian ski resorts don't have quite the frenetic nightlife of many European resorts, but they compensate with lots of good bars and partying among the lodges.

Snow Reports

For general snow and road reports ring the various visitors centres or the recorded service (☎ 1900 912 370). Two resorts have their own snow report numbers – Thredbo (☎ 1900 934320) and Perisher Blue (☎ 1900 926 664). For cross-country skiing reports phone ☎ 1900 926 028. Most radio stations between Sydney and Melbourne also broadcast hourly reports.

Costs

Lift charges and lessons vary – see the following information on the various resorts. Skis, boots and stocks can be hired for around $35 a day at the resorts (less for longer periods). Off-mountain rentals are cheaper, but it can be a trade-off, as problems and adjustment are harder to fix. There are hire places in towns en route to the snow and many garages hire ski equipment as well as snow chains.

Accommodation

The cheapest (and most fun) way to get out on the slopes is to gather a bunch of friends and rent a lodge or apartment. Costs vary enormously, so check around. Bring as much food and drink as possible, as supplies in the resorts are expensive. Many travel agencies book accommodation and packages on the snowfields. Specialists include the Snowy Mountains Reservation Centre (aka Ski 'n' Save ☎ 6456 2633, 1800 020 622); Perisher Blue Snow Holidays (☎ 6456 1084, 1300 655 811); and Thredbo Resort Centre (☎ 6459 4294, 1800 020 589) that has a Web site, www.thredbo.com.au. The NSW Travel Centre (☎ 13 2077) in Sydney also makes bookings.

Accommodation is cheaper in towns like Jindabyne, and particularly Cooma, which is some distance below the snow line. Buses shuttle from Jindabyne and Cooma to resorts in the morning and back again in the late afternoon.

Thredbo
• elevation 1370m

Thredbo has the longest runs and some of the best skiing in Australia (the longest run

KOSCIUSZKO NATIONAL PARK

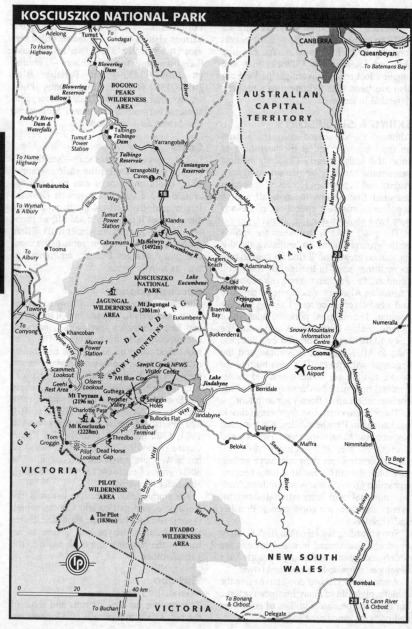

is 3km through 670m of vertical drop). Adult lift tickets cost from $64 per day up to $275 for a five day pass. Beginner/experienced skier lift and lesson packages cost from $64/$85 per day up to $250/340 for five days. Class lessons cost from $35. There is a purpose-built beginners area, Friday Flat, which has its own slow-speed quad chair lift.

Unlike the other resorts, Thredbo is still a good place to visit in summer. Known for its wildflowers, it's a popular bushwalking centre with many scenic tracks. The chair lift to the top of Mt Crackenback runs right through the summer ($18 return). From the top of the chair lift it's a 2km walk to a lookout point with good views of Mt Kosciuszko, or 7km to the top of the mountain itself. Take adequate clothing and be prepared for all conditions, even in summer – there is sometimes still snow on the ground until after Christmas.

Places to Stay The helpful *Thredbo YHA Lodge* (☎ 6457 6376) charges $16 a night ($19 per person twin share) outside the ski season. During the season it is $38 per person for a weekday or $283 for seven days. Although a ballot is held for winter places (entries close in April), it's worth checking for cancellations. There's plenty of room in the summer. The YHA Travel Centre (☎ 9261 1111) in Sydney is the best place to start making inquiries.

Although prices do drop in summer, there are no spectacular bargains. *House of Ullr* (☎ 6457 6210) is one of the cheaper places in Thredbo with doubles for $79 in summer and $295 per person in winter for a two day package including dinner and two breakfasts.

There's a pretty but quite basic free camping ground, *Thredbo Diggings*, between Jindabyne and Thredbo, near the Skitube at Bullocks Flat.

Perisher Blue
• elevation 1680m
Perisher Blue, which includes Perisher Valley, Smiggin Holes, Mt Blue Cow and Guthega, has 50 lifts which are accessible with one ticket. It has a great variety of alpine runs, a lot of valley and bowl skiing and is popular for cross-country skiing with around 1250 hectares of snow-covered terrain. There are purpose-designed snowboarding areas and night boarding sessions on the downhill runs. Snowboard instruction is available.

An adult day lift ticket costs $64, $275 for a five day pass (two and three day passes are also available). A combined lesson/lift pass costs $86 for a day, or $350 for five days. One-day lift and beginner's lesson costs $64, or $240 for a five day package. Packages offer over 50% discounts for Skitube. For information on the Perisher Blue area ring ☎ 6456 1084 or 1800 066 177. There is also a useful Web site at www.perisherblue.com.au.

There's a lot of accommodation in Perisher Valley and Smiggin Holes (4000 beds to be exact!), but it can be very expensive. One of the more reasonable places is *The Lodge* (☎ 6457 5341, fax 6457 5012), at Smiggin Holes, which charges $155 to $170 per person including full dinner and hot breakfast.

Charlotte Pass
• elevation 1780m
At the base of Mt Kosciuszko, this is the highest and one of the oldest, most isolated resorts in Australia. In winter you have to snowcat the last 8km from Perisher Valley ($23 each way). Five lifts service rather short but uncrowded runs, and this is good ski-touring country. Lift tickets cost $62. A Day Tripper pass costs $64 which includes snow transport, lift pass and lunch at the Chalet. Pick up is from the Charlotte Pass Village information desk (☎ 6457 5247), at the Perisher Skitube terminal.

The *Southern Alps Ski Club* (☎ 6457 5223) has lodges here (as well as at Perisher and Thredbo). The facilities are great; single en suite rooms start from $25 in summer.

The historic *Kosciusko Chalet* (☎ 6457 5245, fax 6457 5362) is the largest and grandest of the handful of lodges. Winter rates start from $391 per person for a two night package that includes three meals and transport, or $483 with a three day lift ticket.

NEW SOUTH WALES

Mt Selwyn
● elevation 1492m

Halfway between Tumut and Cooma, Mt Selwyn (☎ 6454 9488, 1800 641 064) is the only resort in the north of the park. It has 12 lifts and is ideal for beginners and families. Adult lift tickets cost $38 per day. Lift/lesson packages cost $56 for one day or $280 for five days. Selwyn is a day resort only, with accommodation available in Cabramurra (10 minutes), Adaminaby and Talbingo (both 40 minutes).

There are a number of caravan parks near Adaminaby. The *Alpine Tourist Park* (☎ 6454 2438), on the corner of the Snowy Mountains Hwy and Letts St, has sites for $14, on-site vans and cabins from $32 to $80 a double. The *Snow Goose Hotel/Motel* (☎ 6454 2202), on Baker St, has hotel rooms for $25 per person including breakfast, or $35 in winter. Motel rooms are $45 a double in summer or $85 in winter.

Adaminaby Bus Service (☎ 6454 2318) runs between Cooma and Mt Selwyn.

THE ALPINE WAY
From Khancoban on the western side of the ranges, this spectacular route runs through dense forest around the southern end of Kosciuszko National Park to Thredbo and Jindabyne. Two of the best mountain views are from Olsens Lookout, 10km off the Alpine Way on the Geehi Dam road, and Scammell's Lookout, just off the Alpine Way.

Khancoban has backpacker accommodation at the basic *Khancoban Backpackers & Fisherman's Lodge*, which has shared accommodation for $12 and single/double rooms for $17/25. Each extra person (up to six) costs $7. You need to supply your own bedding and cooking utensils. Book and check in at the nearby Khancoban Alpine Inn (☎ 6076 9471).

There's also backpacker accommodation at the *Snowgum Lodge* (☎ 6076 9522), on Mitchell Ave, for $15 per person in a single or twin room.

TUMUT AREA
The pretty town of Tumut is on the Snowy Mountains Hwy outside the north-western

side of the park. Tumut Visitors Centre (☎ 6947 1849) can tell you about visits to the various centres of the Snowy Mountains Hydro-electric Scheme. Australia's largest commercial trout farm is at nearby Blowering Dam. Canoeing and rafting can be arranged through the visitors centre.

Other places to visit are the stunning Buddong Falls, in the national park south of Talbingo, and the Yarrangobilly Caves (☎ 6454 9597), 70km south of Tumut. You can see the caves independently for $8 or take a tour for $10. As well as the beautiful country and reserve around the caves, there's a NPWS visitors centre and a thermal pool at a constant and pleasant 27°C.

In the fruit-growing area south of Tumut is Batlow where picking work is often available. Near the town is Hume & Hovell's Lookout, where the two explorers did indeed pause for the view in 1824. Paddy's River Dam, about 12km south-east, off the road to Tumbarumba, was built by Chinese gold-miners in the 1850s and there's a trail to the nearby waterfalls.

Continuing south you reach Tumbarumba, site of the early exploits of the bushranger Mad Dog Morgan. About 8km west of Tumbarumba, the Pioneer Women's Hut (☎ 6948 2635) is an interesting community museum open on Wednesday, weekends and public holidays.

South-West & the Murray

This is wide, rolling, sometimes hypnotic country with some of the state's best farming areas and some interesting history. The Murray River forms the boundary between NSW and Victoria – most of the larger towns are on the Victorian side. Part of this area is known as the Riverina because of the Murray and Murrumbidgee rivers and their tributaries.

Getting There & Away
The region is served by a number of airlines, including Hazelton (☎ 13 1713), Ansett and Kendell (both ☎ 13 1300).

Several roads run through the south-west – the Hume Hwy being the major one. There are quieter routes like the Olympic Way running through Cowra, Wagga Wagga and Albury. Routes to Adelaide include the Sturt Hwy through Hay and Wentworth. You'll also pass through the south-west if travelling between Brisbane and Melbourne on the Newell Hwy.

The region is crossed by major bus routes from Sydney and Brisbane to both Melbourne and Adelaide. The Melbourne to Sydney bus services run on the Hume and trains run close to it. Fearnes Coaches (☎ 1800 029 918) runs between Sydney and Wagga, Gundagai (both $40) and Yass ($35) and Goulburn ($25) and Mittagong ($20). Countrylink (☎ 13 2242) reaches most other towns in the area.

THE HUME HIGHWAY

The Hume is the main road between Australia's two largest cities. It's the fastest and shortest route and, although it's not the most interesting, there are attractive places and some worthwhile diversions along the way.

One of the simplest diversions is at the Sydney end – take the coastal Princes Hwy past Royal National Park to Wollongong. Just after Wollongong take the Illawarra Hwy up the picturesque Macquarie Pass to meet the Hume near Moss Vale. Further south you can leave the Hume to visit Canberra or continue beyond Canberra through the Snowy Mountains on the Alpine Way, rejoining the Hume near Albury.

The Hume is a divided freeway most of the way from Sydney to the Victorian border, with a few stretches of narrow, two-lane road carrying a lot of traffic.

SYDNEY TO GOULBURN

The large towns of **Mittagong** and **Bowral** adjoin each other along the Hume Hwy. The Southern Highlands Visitors Information Centre (☎ 4871 2888, fax 4871 3515) is in Mittagong. The **Tulip Time Festival**, held in the area at the end of September and early October, is a spectacular show of spring colour. Many private gardens are open to visitors at this time.

Four kilometres south of town, a winding 65km road leads west to the **Wombeyan Caves** (☎ 4843 5976) with their spectacular limestone formations. Self-guided and guided tours are available from $10 and $12. The drive up is through superb mountain scenery and there's a pretty camping ground at the caves.

Bowral was where cricketer Sir Donald Bradman, probably Australia's greatest sporting hero, spent his boyhood. There's a cricket ground and the **Bradman Museum** dedicated to 'the Don', which is open daily from 10 am to 4 pm. A little further south along the Hume is tiny **Berrima**, founded in 1829 and remarkably little changed since

KATE NOLAN

The 'Don', Sir Donald Bradman

then. It has the oldest continuously licensed pub in Australia and is full of art galleries and interesting antique and curio shops.

South of Berrima are the small town of **Bundanoon** and the large **Morton National Park** (☎ 4887 7270), with the deep gorges and high sandstone plateaus of the **Budawang Range**. There are several entry points to the park: two of the easiest are Fitzroy Falls (on the road between Moss Vale and Nowra) and Bundanoon. The pleasant *Bundanoon YHA Hostel* (☎ 4883 6010) occupies an old Edwardian guesthouse on Railway Ave. It has dorm beds for $16 and doubles for $40.

Bundanoon is on the railway line between Sydney ($22) and Canberra ($24) (and Melbourne $92). Countrylink buses run daily to Wollongong.

GOULBURN
• postcode 2580   • pop 24,000

Goulburn, founded in 1833, is at the heart of a prosperous sheep-grazing district famous for its fine merino wool – hence the three-storey-high **Big Merino** that towers over the Old Hume Hwy in town (the new highway bypasses the town).

Goulburn Visitors Centre (☎ 4823 0492, fax 4822 2692) is on Montague St, across from Belmore Park, and it has a walking-tour map. There are many fine old buildings, including the impressive **courthouse**, on Montague St. The **Old Goulburn Brewery** (☎ 4821 6071), Australia's oldest brewery built in 1836, was designed by convict/architect Francis Greenway, who also designed the Hyde Park Barracks in Sydney. It is a fascinating complex down on the river flats. As well as a working brewery, where you can sample *real* ale, it has mews accommodation for $35 a person, including light breakfast. There's plenty of other accommodation in town, in caravan parks, pubs and motels.

Yass
• postcode 2582   • pop 4840

Yass is closely connected with the early explorer Hume, after whom the highway is named. On Comur St, next to the tourist information centre (☎ 6226 2557, fax 6226

1509), the **Hamilton Hume Museum** has exhibits relating to him. Near Yass at Wee Jasper are **Carey's Caves** (☎ 6227 9622), open in the afternoon only from Friday to Monday (adults $8), and you can join the Hume & Hovell Walking Track here.

Check out *Backpackers Farmstay* at Boorowa in the Cowra section.

Just east of Yass the Barton Hwy branches off the Hume for Canberra. Transborder Express (☎ 6226 3788) has several daily buses ($10).

Gundagai
• postcode 2722   • pop 2060

Gundagai, 386km from Sydney, is one of the more interesting small towns encountered along the Hume. The tourist office (☎ 6944 1341, fax 6944 1409) on Sheridan St, is open on weekdays from 8 am to 5 pm and weekends from 9 am to noon and 1 to 5 pm. It houses **Rusconi's Marble Masterpiece**, a 21,000-piece cathedral model. The entry fee is only $1 and you get to hear a snatch of the tune, *Along the Road to Gundagai*. It was Frank Rusconi who made the Dog on the Tuckerbox memorial (see the boxed text).

The long wooden **Prince Alfred Bridge** (closed to traffic, but you can walk across it) spans the flood plain of the Murrumbidgee River. In 1852, Gundagai suffered

---

Dog on the Tuckerbox

Gundagai features in a number of famous songs, including *Along the Road to Gundagai*, *My Mabel Waits for Me* and *When a Boy from Alabama Meets a Girl from Gundagai*. Its most famous monument, the Dog on the Tuckerbox memorial, is 8km east of town just off the Hume Hwy. It's a sculpture of the dog who, in a 19th century bush ballad (and in a later poem by Jack Moses), 'sat on the tuckerbox, five miles from Gundagai', and refused to help while its owner's bullock team was bogged in the creek. A popular tale claims that in the original version the dog shat, rather than sat, on the tuckerbox.

Australia's worst flood disaster – 78 deaths were recorded, but probably over 100 people drowned. Gold rushes and bushrangers were part of the town's colourful early history. The notorious Captain Moonlight, leader of a gang of gay outlaws, was tried in Gundagai's **courthouse** (built in 1859) on Sheridan St, and is now buried in the town.

Other places of interest include **Gundagai Historical Museum** (☎ 6944 1995), on Homer St, and the **Gabriel Gallery** (☎ 6944 1722) of historic photos, on Sheridan St.

Places to Stay The *Gundagai River Caravan Park (☎ 6944 1702)*, on the river near the southern end of the Prince Alfred Bridge and next to the **golf course**, has camp sites for $10 and reasonable on-site vans for $20. The *Gundagai Caravan Village (☎ 6944 1057, June Rd)* is in town with camp sites for $12 and on-site vans for $29. The *Criterion Hotel (☎ 6944 1048, 172 Sheridan St)* has single/double accommodation for $20/38, including breakfast.

Holbrook
- postcode 2644   • pop 1320

Holbrook, the halfway point between Sydney and Melbourne, was known as Germanton until WWI, during which it was renamed after a British war hero. In Holbrook Park is a replica of the submarine in which the brave deeds that earned him the Victoria Cross took place. The large **Woolpack Inn Museum** (☎ 6036 2131), at 83 Albury St, opens daily ($3) and has tourist information.

ALBURY
- postcode 2640   • pop 42,500

Albury is on the Murray River just below the Hume Weir, and across the river from Wodonga, in Victoria. It's a good base for trips to the snowfields and High Country of both Victoria and NSW, the vineyards around Rutherglen (Victoria), and the tempestuous upper Murray River – the river becomes languid below Albury. It's also a good place to break the journey between Sydney and Melbourne.

Information
The large Gateway Information Centre (☎ 6041 3875, fax 6021 0322), with information on both NSW and Victoria, is on the highway in Wodonga. It opens daily from 9 am to 5 pm.

In summer bring insect repellent and/or a net as there are lots of mosquitoes.

Things to See & Do
In summer you can swim in the Murray River in **Noreuil Park** and from September to April (water levels permitting) you can take river cruises on the paddle-steamer *Cumberoona* (☎ 6021 1113) from $8.

The free **Albury Regional Museum**, on Wodonga Place in Noreuil Park, opens daily from 10.30 am to 4.30 pm. It contains material on migration, transport and Aboriginal culture. Also in the park is a tree marked by explorer William Hovell on his 1824 expedition with Hume from Sydney to Port Phillip. Charles Sturt departed for his 1838 exploration of the Murray from here. Albury Backpackers has half-day to seven-week **canoeing trips** on the Murray and you don't have to stay there to join one. There's a lot of good **horse riding** in the area and along the river.

Ettamogah Wildlife Sanctuary, 11km north on the highway and open daily ($5), has a collection of Aussie fauna. Most of the animals arrived sick or injured, so this is a genuine sanctuary. A few kilometres north, the grotesque **Ettamogah Pub** looms up near the highway – it's a real-life version of a famous Aussie cartoon pub.

The good **Jindera Museum**, 16km northwest of Albury in the town of Jindera, opens Tuesday to Sunday from 10 am to 3 pm ($5). Jindera is in an area known as **Morgan Country** because of its association with bushranger Mad Dog Morgan. Other pleasant little towns in this area include **Culcairn**, west of Holbrook, where the wonderful *Culcairn Hotel (☎ 6029 8501)* has rooms for $28/38.

Places to Stay
Albury Central Tourist Park (☎ 6021 8420), about 2km north of the centre on

North St, has camp sites for $7 per person, cottages from $40 and units from $32.

Albury Backpackers (☎ 6041 1822), on the corner of David and Smollett Sts, has dorm beds for $14 and doubles for $30. This friendly place makes a business of taking care of its guests. They hire bikes and organise snow skiing and fabulous canoeing trips on the Murray. They'll also help guests find farm work and fruit picking. There's a YHA hostel at *Albury Motor Village (☎ 6040 2999, 372 Wagga Rd)* (Hume Hwy), 4.5km north of the centre of town. Dorm beds cost $14, doubles $36.

There are some classic Australian pubs here. *Soden's Australia Hotel (☎ 6021 2400)*, on the corner of Wilson and David Sts, has single/double hotel rooms for $22/$36 and motel rooms for $38/$45. *Bradys Railway Hotel (☎ 6021 4700, 470 Smollet St)*, a block from the station, has rooms for $20/$34. The *New Albury Hotel (☎ 6021 3599, 491 Kiewa St)* has a great Irish bar, *Paddy's*, and a good restaurant. Rooms with en suite are $38/45.

Over the border in Victoria is *Herb & Horse (☎ 02-6072 9553)*, about 6km north of Granya, which in turn is 15km east of Tallangatta. It's run by a friendly family, popular with travellers, and is a great place to stay for a while. See the Wodonga to Corryong section of the Victoria chapter for details.

Places to Eat

Quite a cafe culture has sprung up along Dean St. *Cafe Gryphon* and *Electra* are art house cafes with good coffee and light meals. The large *Restaurant 2000* has an all-you-can-eat Chinese buffet. Lunch is $8.50 and $9.90 on Sunday, the dinner buffet is $12.50 midweek, a little more for the weekend menu. *La Porchetta* is a favourite for Italian food and the *Commercial Club* has the best value buffet in town at $8. The *Thai Lotus*, next door, is a popular and well-priced place and *The Kebab Place*, just north of Albury Backpackers, serves good, cheap nutritious food. The excellent *Bahn Thai (☎ 6041 5555, 592 Keiwa St)*, rather incongruously located in a delightful Victorian house, serves traditional Thai cuisine.

Getting There & Away

Ansett Express and Kendell (both ☎ 13 1300) and Hazelton (☎ 13 1713) fly from Albury to Melbourne ($143) and Sydney ($232).

Buses between Sydney and Melbourne stop at the train station. Most also stop at Viennaworld (a service station/diner), on the highway across from Noreuil Park. Countrylink (☎ 13 2242) runs to Echuca ($32), on the Murray River in Victoria. V/Line (☎ 13 6196) runs to Canberra ($46) and to Mildura ($55), along the Murray.

The nightly Sydney to Melbourne XPT train service stops in Albury. If you're travelling between the two capital cities it's much cheaper to stop over in Albury on a through ticket than to buy two separate tickets. The same applies to bus tickets.

WAGGA WAGGA
- **postcode 2650**   • **pop 57,000**

Wagga Wagga, on the Murrumbidgee River, is the state's largest inland city. Despite its size, the city retains a relaxed country town feel. The name is pronounced 'wogga' and is usually abbreviated to one word.

The long main street, Baylis St, which runs north from the train station, becomes Fitzmaurice St at the northern end. The Wagga Wagga Visitors Centre (☎ 6926 9621, fax 6926 9629) is on Tarcutta St. The excellent **Botanic Gardens**, about 1.5km south of the train station, has a small zoo with a free-flight aviary of native birds. There are two wineries worth a visit, the **Wagga Wagga Winery**, (☎ 6922 1221), on Oura Rd, and the **Charles Sturt University Winery and Cheese Factory** (☎ 6933 2435), entrance from Coolamon Rd. The **Museum of the Riverina** is in the old Council Chambers, on the corner of Morrow and Baylis Sts.

The **Wiradjuri Walking Track**, which includes some good lookouts, begins at the visitors centre and eventually returns there after a 30km tour of the area. There's a shorter 10km loop past the Wollundry Lagoon. The walks can be done in stages and the visitors centre has maps. From the **beach** near the Tourist Caravan Park you can go swimming and fishing.

On the Olympic Way, about 40km north of Wagga, the small town of **Junee** has some historic buildings, including some splendid pubs and the lovely Monte Cristo Homestead (☎ 6924 1637); the entrance fee is $7.50. Glass Buslines (☎ 6924 1633) runs a local service from Wagga to Junee on weekdays, picking up along Baylis St.

Places to Stay
There are several caravan parks around Wagga, with camp sites from $10; the information centre has full details.

Several pubs also have accommodation, including *Romano's Hotel* (☎ 6921 2013), on Fitzmaurice St, with good rooms from $30/38, some with en suite. The *Manor* (☎ 6921 5962, 38 Morrow St) is a small, well-restored guesthouse opposite the Memorial Gardens, near Baylis St. Rooms range from $35/80 to $80/150, including breakfast and its restaurant's main courses start at $10. There are plenty of motels, most starting around $50.

Places to Eat
Baylis/Fitzmaurice St has a surprisingly diverse range of places to eat. *Anatolia* is a popular kebab shop, and Dick Eyle's *Aussie Cafe* is good and opens for breakfast. The *Family Eating House* has all-you-can-eat meals at lunch and dinner for less than $10. *The Golden Season* (☎ 6921 1177) is a good value 'steak house' on the corner of Forsyth and Berry Sts, and the *Saigon Restaurant* (☎ 6921 2212, 89 Morgan St) is a friendly Vietnamese place where most dishes cost $8 to $11. *Bernie's*, at the Tourist Hotel in Fitzmaurice St, is a good vegetarian restaurant.

Getting There & Away
Kendell (☎ 6922 0100) and Hazelton (☎ 13 1713) have services connecting Wagga with Sydney, Melbourne and Brisbane. The standard economy one-way fare to Sydney is $186.

Countrylink buses leave from the train station but other long-distance services leave from the coach terminal (☎ 6921 1977) on the corner of Gurwood and Trail Sts, off Fitzmaurice St. You can make bookings here. Wagga is on the railway line between Sydney and Melbourne; the one-way fare to both is $66.

NARRANDERA
- **postcode 2700**   • **pop 5100**

Near the junction of the Newell and Sturt highways, Narrandera is in the Murrumbidgee Irrigation Area (MIA). The tourist information centre (☎ 6959 1766, fax 6959 2788) in Narrandera Park has a walking-tour map.

Lake Talbot is an excellent water sports reserve, partly a long, artificial lake and partly a big swimming complex. Bush (including a koala regeneration area) surrounds the lake and a series of walking trails make up the **Bundidgerry Walking Track**.

The **John Lake Centre** at the Inland Fisheries Research Station (☎ 6959 9036) opens on weekdays from 9 am to 4 pm and has guided tours (on which you can see a huge Murray cod) at 10.30 am ($5). To get there, turn off the Sturt Hwy 4km south-east of Narrandera.

South of Narrandera, on the Newell Hwy, is **Jerilderie**, immortalised by the bushranger Ned Kelly who held up the whole town for three days in 1879. Kelly relics can be seen in the **Telegraph Office Museum**, on Powell St. Close by, the **Willows**, a house dating from 1878, next to Billabong Creek, is a combination of museum, souvenir shop and cafe.

Places to Stay & Eat
There are a few pubs in town with accommodation and counter meals. The *Royal Mail Hotel* (☎ 6959 2007, 137 East St) has basic rooms at $10 per person, a Chinese restaurant and counter meals.

The *Historic Star Lodge* (☎ 6959 1768, 64 Whitton St) is a fine old hotel opposite the train station, which offers good B&B. Rooms cost $38/58, or $68 with en suite; there's also a restaurant here.

Getting There & Away
McCafferty's and Greyhound Pioneer both go to Sydney ($41) and Adelaide ($91). McCafferty's stops at the Mobil Roadhouse

on the Stuart Hwy, Greyhound stops at the Shell Autoport.

GRIFFITH

• postcode 2680   • pop 15,800

Griffith was planned by Walter Burley Griffin, the American architect who designed Canberra, and is the main centre of the MIA. Griffith Visitors Centre (☎ 6962 4145, fax 6962 7319) is on the corner of Banna Ave (the long main street) and Jondaryan Ave.

Things to See

On a hill north-east of the town centre, **Pioneer Park Museum** (☎ 6962 4196), on Remembrance Drive, is a re-creation of an early Riverina village and is worth seeing. It's open daily from 9 am to 4.30 pm ($5).

Descendants of the Italian farmers who helped to develop this area make up a large percentage of the population. Griffith produces 80% of the state's wine. You can visit eight **wineries** – the visitors centre has opening time details and a map.

Fruit-Picking

Many people come to Griffith looking for fruit-picking work. The grape harvest usually begins around mid-February and lasts six to eight weeks, while the citrus harvest begins in November and runs through to March. Few vineyards or other farms have accommodation, or even space to camp, so you'll need your own transport. Pickers Plus (☎ 6964 0800), at 20 Olympic St, and Employment National (☎ 13 3444) can help you find work.

Places to Stay

The small *Tourist Caravan Park* (☎ 6964 2144, 919 Willandra Ave), not far from the bus station, has camp sites for $15 and cabins for $48.

The *International Backpackers Hostel* (☎ 6964 4236, 112 Binya St), across the road from the Anglican Cathedral, is a friendly place that specialises in assisting international guests to find work. Dorm beds are $12 per person or $70 a week.

Pioneer Park (☎ 6962 4196) has shared accommodation in old shearers' quarters for $10 per person. The rooms are basic, but there's a good kitchen and lounge. Unfortunately it's a long, steep walk from the city centre and there is no public transport. It's often full at harvest time.

The *Area Hotel* (☎ 6962 1322, 209 Banna Ave) has single-bed rooms for one, two or three people for $35/$50/$70 with shared bathroom, but including continental breakfast.

Places to Eat

Italian food is the region's dominant cuisine. For good coffee and cake or pasta try *Bassano Caffe* (☎ 6964 4544, 453 Banna Ave). It's also open daily for breakfast. Nearby, and down some steps, *La Scala* (☎ 6962 4322, 455 Banna Ave) is the best of the Italian restaurants and opens Tuesday to Sunday from 6 pm. Pastas are $8 to $13. Close by on the other side of Banna Ave, the *Belvedere Restaurant* has more of a cafe atmosphere and it's also a busy takeaway pizzeria. *L'Oasis* (☎ 6964 5588, 150 Yambil St) is a very good restaurant offering varied cuisine. If you just want a hamburger, *Nibbles*, on Banna Ave, serves good old-fashioned hamburgers ($4 with the lot).

Getting There & Away

Hazelton (☎ 13 1713) flies between Griffith and Sydney daily for $228 one way.

All buses, except Countrylink (which stops at the train station), stop at the Griffith Travel & Transit Centre (☎ 6962 3419), 121 Banna Ave, at the Mobil service station opposite the visitors centre and the 'airplane on a stick'. The centre takes bookings for rail and coach, using Greyhound, McCafferty's, V-Line and Countrylink, with connections to regional coach lines. Typical prices are Sydney ($47), Melbourne ($49), Adelaide ($91), Canberra ($35), Brisbane ($115) and Wagga ($19). All services run daily.

AROUND GRIFFITH

West of Griffith, the last hills of the Great Dividing Range give way to endless plains.

Cocoparra National Park

Cocoparra, just east of Griffith, isn't a large park, but its hills and gullies provide some contrasts and there's a fair presence of wildlife. The camping ground is on Woolshed Flat in the north of the park, not far from Woolshed Falls. Bring your own water. Free bush camping is permitted away from the roads.

Leeton

• pop 7000

Leeton is the MIA's oldest town (1913) and, like Griffith, was designed by Walter Burley Griffin. While it remains close to the architect's original vision, a highway sprawl is developing.

Leeton Visitors Centre (☎ 6953 6481, fax 6953 2361), 8-10 Yanco Ave, opens on weekdays from 9 am to 5 pm and weekends from 9.30 am to 12.30 pm. Ask here about the tours of the rice mill and other food-processing plants. Lillypilly Estate and Toorak Wines are two **wineries** west of Leeton, open from Monday to Saturday for tastings and for tours on weekdays: 11.30 am at Toorak Wines, 4 pm at Lillypilly Estate.

Willandra National Park

This national park, on the plains 160km north-west of Griffith as the crow flies, has been carved from a huge sheep station on a system of usually-dry lakes. The World Heritage-listed park's 19,400 hectares represent less than 10% of the area covered by Big Willandra station in its 1870s heyday. The partially restored, 1918 homestead was the third to be built on the station.

There are several short walking tracks in the park and the Merton Motor Trail loops around the eastern half. The western half has no vehicular access but you can walk here – if you're *very* sure of what you're doing.

There's a camping ground near the homestead and with permission you can bush camp ($5). Shared accommodation in the 'men's quarters' costs $25 for up to four people in bunk rooms. A cottage which sleeps eight costs $40 for four people, plus $10 for each additional person. There is a $7.50 park entrance fee.

The main access to the park is off the Hillston to Mossgiel road, around 40km west of Hillston. It takes very little rain to close roads here – phone the park manager (☎ 6967 8159) or the NPWS office (☎ 6962 7755) at Griffith to check conditions.

Hay

• postcode 2711   • pop 3900

In flat, treeless country, Hay is at the junction of the Sturt and Cobb highways and is a substantial town for this part of the world. The Tourist & Amenities Centre (☎ 6993 4045, fax 6993 1288), 407 Moppett St, is just off Lachlan St (the main street). There are some fine swimming spots along the Murrumbidgee River, and interesting old buildings like the **Old Hay Gaol** and **Bishops Lodge**, a corrugated-iron mansion.

There are several caravan parks. The *Hay Plains Holiday Park* (☎ 6993 1875, 4 Nailor St) is in a quiet spot close to the river and town. Camp sites are $13, cabins range from $34 to $52. On the banks of the river 11km out on the Sturt Hwy, *Bidgee Beach Caravan Park* (☎ 6993 4808, mobile 014 452 304) has camp sites for $10 and vans for an amazing $12. Pets are welcome and boat hire available.

Most pubs also have accommodation. The big *Commercial Hotel* (☎ 6993 1504, 197 Lachlan St) has rooms for $20/30. The *New Crown Hotel/Motel* (☎ 6993 1600, 117 Lachlan St) charges $40/50 for air-con rooms with TV and private facilities.

DENILIQUIN

☎ 03   • postcode 2710   • pop 8500

Deniliquin is an attractive, bustling country town on a wide bend of the Edward River.

The Visitors Information Centre (☎ 03-5881 4150) is inside the **Peppin Heritage Centre**, on George St. The heritage centre has displays on rice growing and irrigation, and the history of wool-growing in the area. Merino sheep breeds developed around here have long been the mainstay of Australia's wool industry. The centre is open daily from 9 am to 4 pm (gold coin donation).

The visitors centre at the **Sun Rice Mill**, the largest rice mill in the southern hemisphere, is open on weekdays from 9 am to noon and 2 to 4 pm. The **Island Sanctuary** has pleasant walks among the river red gums and lots of animals, including over-friendly emus.

Places to Stay

There are several caravan parks, including *McLean Beach Caravan Park* (☎ *5881 2448*) at the north-western end of Butler St, by a good river swimming beach. Camp sites are $14, on-site vans $25 and cabins $45.

There are plenty of motels, but as trucks roll through town all night, choose one off the highway, such as the *Riverview Motel* (☎ *5881 2311*), Butler St, a few metres south of the McLean Beach Caravan Park, on the opposite side of the road. Singles/doubles/twins are $55/60/65.

The *Globe Hotel* (☎ *5881 2030, 28 Cressy St*) is good value, with rooms at $20 per person, including a cooked breakfast. The *Federal Hotel* (☎ *5881 1260*), on the corner of Cressy and Napier Sts, has rooms for $25/40 with a cook-your-own breakfast.

Getting There & Away

Long-distance buses stop at the Bus Stop Cafe on Whitelock St. Countrylink (☎ 13 2242) runs to Wagga ($39), from where trains run to Sydney and Melbourne. McCafferty's (☎ 13 1499) stops here on the run between Melbourne ($30) and Brisbane ($119). Victoria's V/Line (☎ 13 6196) also runs daily to Melbourne ($29).

ALONG THE MURRAY

Most of the major river towns are on the Victorian side – see the Victoria chapter. It's no problem to hop back and forth across the river, as in many places there are crossings between the roads which run along both sides. One of the places to cross the border is at the twin towns of Moama (NSW) and Echuca (Victoria). The information centre (☎ 5480 7555, 1800 804 446), which services both towns and the district, is located in Echuca right beside the bridge which crosses into NSW. This is the place to inquire about trips on the many paddle-steamers which ply these waters.

The Murray and Darling rivers were once main highways of communication and trade, with paddle-steamers splashing up and downstream from dawn till dusk.

The largest NSW town on the river is Albury (see earlier in this chapter). Downstream from here is **Corowa**, a wine-producing centre – the Lindemans winery has been here since 1860. **Tocumwal**, on the Newell Hwy, is a quiet riverside town with sandy river beaches and a giant fibreglass Murray Cod in the town square. The nearby airport is a gliding centre.

The old river port of **Wentworth** lies at the confluence of the Murray and Darling rivers, 30km north-west of Mildura. The information office (☎ 5027 3624) is on the main street. The riverboat MV *Loyalty* (☎ 5027 3330) runs two-hour cruises to the confluence from Monday to Friday, leaving the Wentworth & District Services Memorial Club at 1.45 pm. The fare is $14 or $17 with a meal.

You can see local history in the **Old Wentworth Gaol** (☎ 5027 3337) open daily from 10 am to 5 pm ($4.50) and across the road in the **Pioneer World Folk Museum** ($3.50). The **Perry Dunes** are large orange sand dunes 6km north of town, off the road to Broken Hill.

Central West

NSW's central west starts inland from the Blue Mountains and continues for about 400km, gradually changing from rolling agricultural land into the harsh far west. This region has some of the earliest inland towns in Australia. From Sydney, Bathurst is the gateway to the region, and from here you can turn north-west through Orange and Dubbo or south-west through Cowra and West Wyalong.

The Olympic Way runs from Bathurst through Cowra and Wagga Wagga to Albury and is an alternative Sydney-Melbourne route. The Newell Hwy, the most direct route between Melbourne and Brisbane, also passes through the central west. On long weekends accommodation all along the Newell is booked out.

Getting There & Away

Air The central west is well served by airlines. From Dubbo ($177 from Sydney with Eastern Australia or Hazelton) there are flights to other locations in the centre and far west of the state.

Bus Major companies have services through the region on routes between Sydney and Broken Hill or Adelaide, and from Brisbane to Melbourne or Adelaide. Local companies providing services include Rendell's Coaches (☎ 1800 023 328). Sid Fogg's (☎ 1800 045 952) runs from Newcastle to Dubbo ($48).

Train Direct trains run from Sydney to Lithgow ($22), Bathurst ($32), Orange ($39) and Dubbo ($57). There are connecting buses from Lithgow station to Cowra ($45 from Sydney), Forbes ($55) and Mudgee ($39).

LITHGOW

• postcode 2790   • pop 10,400

Lithgow is an industrial town on the western fringe of the Blue Mountains. The Lithgow Visitor Information Centre (☎ 6353 1859, lithinfo@list.com.au) is on the edge of town in the Old Bowenfels Station, 1 Cooerwull Rd, on the Great Western Hwy.

The gracious home, **Eskbank House**, is on Bennett St. It was built in 1842 and now houses a museum. It's open Thursday to Monday between 10 am and 4 pm. Admission costs $2. There are fine views from **Hassan Walls Lookout**, 5km south of town. About 40km north of Lithgow there's a disused railway tunnel, now full of glowworms. Further north **Newnes**, on the edge of the Wollemi National Park, is a ghost town with a pub that's still in business. On the way there, the **Gardens of Stone National Park** features Devonian limestone outcrops and Triassic sandstone escarpments. See the Blue Mountains section earlier in this chapter for information on the nearby Zig Zag Railway and the town of Hartley.

There are frequent trains between Lithgow and Sydney ($22).

BATHURST

• postcode 2795   • pop 29,355

Bathurst is Australia's oldest inland settlement and it was laid out on a grand scale. The streetscape is relatively intact and there are some impressive Victorian-era buildings, such as the 1880 **courthouse** on Russell St, which also houses the **historical museum** ($1). The tourist information centre (☎ 6332 1444, visitors@bathurst.nsw.gov.au) is at 28 William St.

South-west of the city centre is the 6.2km **Mt Panorama motor racing circuit**. It's the venue for one of Australia's best-known races, the 1000 Touring Car Race, a 1000km race for production cars held in October. You can drive around the circuit (it's a public road) and there's a small **motor racing museum** ($5) at Murray's Corner, open daily from 9 am to 4.30 pm.

Places to Stay & Eat

There are some good rooms at the hotels (pubs). The cheapest are at the *Railway Hotel (☎ 6331 2964, Havana St)*, where singles/doubles are $20/34 with breakfast. The *Edinboro Castle Hotel (☎ 6331 5020, William St)* has rooms for $25/40. The *Abercrombie (☎ 6331 1077)* and *Bathurst Explorers (☎ 6331 2966)* motels, on Stewart St, are the cheapest in town; rates start at $42.

For pizza or large servings of pasta (from $8), try *Uncle Joe's Pizza*, opposite the post office on Howick St. *Zeigler's Café*, on Keppel St, has an interesting modern menu and is not too expensive.

AROUND BATHURST

The **Abercrombie Caves** are 72km south of Bathurst. There are several guided tours each day.

There are some interesting old buildings at **Sofala**, Australia's oldest surviving gold town, 37km north of Bathurst. The fascinating old mining town of **Hill End** is 72km north-west of Bathurst. It was the scene of a gold rush in the 1870s and is classified as an historic site. The visitors centre (☎ 6337 8206) is in the old hospital, which also houses the **museum** ($2). There are two NPWS camping grounds; the *Village* and

Glendora. Both have facilities and charge $10. The *Royal Hotel (☎ 6337 8261)* has singles/doubles/family rooms for $30/45/60 with breakfast.

Rockley, 34km south of Bathurst, is another classified historic town. North-east of Bathurst is **Rylstone**, where there are sandstone buildings and Aboriginal rock paintings just outside the town (ask at the Rylstone Visitor Information Centre on Louee St).

MUDGEE
- postcode 2850   • pop 8200

Mudgee, about 120km north of both Lithgow and Bathurst, is a fine example of an old country town and is a pleasant place to stay. The tourist information centre (☎ 6372 5875, tourist@mudgee.nsw.gov.au) is at 64 Market St, near the old police station.

Wineries

There are many young wineries in the area run by enthusiastic people, and if you find the Hunter Valley too commercial, you'll enjoy these. Craigmoor Winery can hardly be called a newcomer. It has produced a vintage annually since 1858, making it the second-oldest continually operating winery in Australia. Most of the area's 20 wineries are open daily. In September there's a wine festival.

Places to Stay & Eat

Accommodation tends to fill up on weekends, and several hotels have above-average pub accommodation. The beautiful and historic *Lawson Park Hotel (☎ 6372 2183)*, on the corner of Short and Church Sts, charges $35/50 ($10 extra on weekends) with breakfast, while the *Federal Hotel (☎ 6372 2150, Inglis St)*, near the train station, charges $17/32 ($20/36 weekends).

Near the wineries to the north of town, *Hithergreen Lodge (☎ 6372 1022)*, about 5km out of town, has motel units from $55/65.

One of the best places for a coffee or snack is the *Tramp*; enter through an archway on Market St, near the corner of Church St. *Eltons*, on Market St, is also a great place for breakfast and lunch. The *Red*

Heifer Grill, at the Lawson Park Hotel, is recommended for lunch and dinner.

Getting There & Away

Air Link (☎ 13 1713) flies between Mudgee and Sydney ($160). Countrylink (☎ 13 2232) trains run from Sydney to Lithgow from where there are connecting buses to Mudgee ($39 from Sydney).

AROUND MUDGEE
Gulgong
- postcode 2852   • pop 2300

Gulgong, 30km north-west of Mudgee, is an old gold town once described as 'the hub of the world'. It was the boyhood home of the author Henry Lawson and the **Henry Lawson Centre**, on Mayne St, houses a collection of 'Lawsonia'; it's open Sunday to Friday from 10 am to noon and Saturday till 3 pm ($2).

The tourist information centre (☎ 6374 1202) is in the shire chambers. The huge **Gulgong Pioneer Museum**, on Herbert St, is one of the best country-town museums in the state ($4). It's open daily from 9 am to 5 pm.

The *Centennial Hotel (☎ 6374 1241, Mayne St)* has rooms with en suite for $35/40. Budget travellers may prefer the *Post Office Hotel (☎ 6374 1031)* which has basic rooms for $20/25. The best place in town for a snack is *Sindee's Café* which does a great burger.

Other Towns

At **Nagundie**, 11km north of Mudgee, there's a rock that is said to hold water year round – it's an old Aboriginal water hole and you can camp here. Further east, en route to the Goulburn River National Park and the Hunter Valley, **Merriwa** has a number of historic buildings, as has nearby **Cassilis**.

ORANGE
- postcode 2800   • pop 36,000

This important fruit-growing centre does not grow oranges! Rather, it was named after William of Orange. Pioneer poet Banjo Paterson (who wrote the words of *Waltzing Matilda*) was born here, and the foundations of his birthplace are in Banjo Paterson Park. Orange was considered as the site for the Federal capital before Canberra was eventually selected.

The visitors centre (☎ 6361 5226, ovc@ix.net.au) is on Byng St. The **museum**, on McNamara St, includes a 300-year-old tree carved with Aboriginal designs.

The autumn apple-picking season lasts for about six weeks; contact Centrelink (☎ 13 2850), on Anson St, if you're interested in casual work.

The council's *Colour City Showground Caravan Park (☎ 6362 7254, Margaret St)* is about 2km north-east of the city centre. Camp sites are $7.50 and cabins are $40.

The renovated *Hotel Canobolas (☎ 6362 2444)*, on Summer St at the corner of Lords Place, was once the largest hotel outside Sydney. Most double rooms have bathrooms, steam heat, a TV and a fridge and cost under $70. Singles/doubles with shared bathrooms are $28/45.

Australia's first real gold rush took place at **Ophir**, 27km north of Orange. The area is now a nature reserve and it's still popular with fossickers – you can buy a licence and hire a gold pan from the Orange visitors centre. **Mt Canobolas** (1395m) is a steep, extinct volcano 20km south-west of Orange. You can drive to the top or there are a couple of walking tracks.

Getting There & Away
Rendell's Coaches (☎ 1800 02 3328) runs to Dubbo ($30) and Sydney ($30) daily. There's also a service to Canberra ($35). Selwood's Coaches (☎ 6362 7963) also runs to Sydney daily ($30). Countrylink has daily trains to Orange from Sydney ($39) and Dubbo ($19).

DUBBO
• postcode 2830   • pop 36,701

Dubbo is a large agricultural town surrounded by sheep and cattle country. The information centre (☎ 6884 1422, 1800 674 443) is at the top end of Macquarie St, the main shopping street, on the corner of Erskine St. You can hire geared bikes from Wheelers (☎ 6882 9899), on the corner of Brisbane and Bultje Sts. The YHA hostel hires bikes to guests for $6 a day.

Things to See & Do
The **Old Dubbo Gaol** ($5), Macquarie St, is open daily from 9 am to 4.30 pm and has 'animatronic' characters telling the story of prison life. Also on Macquarie St is the **museum**, which is open daily from 10 am to 4.30 pm ($5).

Five kilometres south-west of town, the **Western Plains Zoo** (☎ 6882 5888) is the largest open-range zoo in Australia. The Bengal tigers and Asiatic lions alone are worth the price of admission. The zoo's rare black rhinoceroses were flown in from Zimbabwe as part of an international program designed to save these magnificent beasts from extinction.

You're better off walking around the 6km circuit or hiring a bike ($8 for four hours) than joining the crawling line of cars. The zoo is open daily from 9 am to 5 pm ($16/8.50 adults/children). There's a special zoo walk for an extra $2.50 that leaves from the zoo gates at 6.45am.

The slab homestead **Dundullimal** was built by a wealthy grazier in the 1830s. It's 2km beyond the zoo and is open daily ($5).

Places to Stay
The closest caravan park to the town centre is the small *Poplars (☎ 6882 4067)*, near the river at the western end of Bultje St. *Dubbo City (☎ 6882 4820)* is also on the river, but on the western bank and a fair distance from the centre.

Dubbo Backpackers (☎ 6882 0922, 87 Brisbane St) is a pleasant YHA hostel in a heritage home north of the railway line. From the bus station head west on Erskine St. Beds are $15. Guests get 10% off zoo tickets and the hostel can often arrange a lift out there, or you can hire a bike and ride ($6 a day). The hostel also organises trips to the huge Dubbo stockyards on sale days – an interesting insight into rural life.

Several pubs have accommodation, such as the good *Castlereagh Hotel (☎ 6882 4877)*, on the corner of Talbragar and Brisbane Sts, which has singles/doubles from $30/50, including a big cooked breakfast. Also good is the *Western Star (☎ 6882 4644, Erskine St)* where rooms cost $30/50.

There are more than 20 motels, mostly along Cobra St, although they tend to fill up quickly; book ahead.

For $180 per person, per night you can stay at the Western Plains *Zoofari Lodge* (☎ *1300 720 018*). For that price you get three meals, two-day entry to the zoo, three behind-the-scenes guided tours, bicycle hire and accommodation in luxury tented lodges.

Places to Eat

The *Dubbo Eating House*, on Macquarie St, has an all-you-can-eat smorgasbord lunch for $8 and dinner for $9.95. The *Ex-Services Club*, on Brisbane St, has big meals for under $12.50.

Scrubbers Steakhouse (☎ *6882 9766*), on Wingewarra St, is a small place serving light meals during the day (for around $8) and has $15 steaks at night.

To escape from the mixed-grill menus, head for the southern end of Macquarie St. You'll find trendy pancakes at *Jule's Crepes* and exceptional curries at the licensed *Darbar Indian Restaurant* (☎ *6884 4338*). The *Grapevine Café*, on Brisbane St, has a lovely courtyard and delicious breakfasts and lunches for under $10.

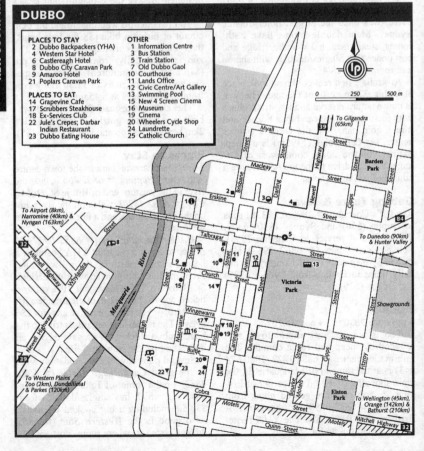

DUBBO

PLACES TO STAY
2 Dubbo Backpackers (YHA)
4 Western Star Hotel
6 Castlereagh Hotel
8 Dubbo City Caravan Park
9 Amaroo Hotel
21 Poplars Caravan Park

PLACES TO EAT
14 Grapevine Cafe
17 Scrubbers Steakhouse
18 Ex-Services Club
22 Jule's Crepes; Darbar Indian Restaurant
23 Dubbo Eating House

OTHER
1 Information Centre
3 Bus Station
5 Train Station
7 Old Dubbo Gaol
10 Courthouse
11 Lands Office
12 Civic Centre/Art Gallery
13 Swimming Pool
15 New 4 Screen Cinema
16 Museum
19 Cinema
20 Wheelers Cycle Shop
24 Laundrette
25 Catholic Church

Getting There & Away

The airfare from Sydney is $177 with Eastern or Hazelton airlines.

Dubbo is at the junction of the Newell Hwy (the main Melbourne-Brisbane route) and the Mitchell Hwy (the Sydney-Broken Hill/Adelaide route).

You can buy bus tickets at the bus station (☎ 6884 2411), on Erskine St, until late at night. Most of the major bus lines pass through, with Greyhound-Pioneer running to Sydney for $24. Sid Fogg's buses run to Newcastle three times a week for $48.

The Countrylink bus (☎ 13 2232) to Sydney costs $57.

COWRA

● postcode 2794   ● pop 9100

Cowra is a large country town in the fertile Lachlan Valley. It's best known for the mass break-out from a WWII prisoner-of-war camp by Japanese internees. Nearly 250 prisoners died in the failed escape attempt, many by suicide, and the tale is told in a book and film, both titled *Die Like the Carp*. The information centre (☎ 6342 4333, fax 6342 4563) is on the highway, west of the shopping centre across the bridge.

Things to See & Do

Australian and Japanese **war cemeteries** are 5km south of town and a memorial, 2km south-east of the cemeteries, marks the site of the break-out. Cowra's association with Japan is also commemorated in the superb **Japanese Garden**, on Bellevue Hill above the town centre. Large, beautiful and meticulously maintained, it's well worth visiting. The garden and the attached cultural centre open daily from 8.30 am to 5 pm ($7).

The Lachlan River flows through fertile and pretty farming country to the west of Cowra. The road to Forbes (turn off the Mid-Western Hwy about 5km south of Cowra) runs along the southern bank of the Lachlan and is a pleasant drive.

At Paynters Bridge, about 45km on from the turn-off, cross the Lachlan to **Eugowra**, a town in the shadow of bush-clad hills. Eugowra was held up by the bushranger Ben Hall in 1863 and there's a re-enactment every October.

You can also get here (and to Forbes) via the small town of **Canowindra** (also held up by Ben Hall), on a road running down the northern side of the Lachlan. Canowindra's curving main street, Gaskill St, has a number of old buildings. The **Age of Fishes Museum** (☎ 6344 1008) organises visits to nearby fossil sites, but the town's main attraction is **ballooning**. Several outfits offer flights; Balloon Aloft (☎ 6344 1797, 1800 028 568) charges $175 for a flight and champagne breakfast.

Places to Stay

Cowravan Park (☎ 6342 1058), by the river on Lachlan St south of Kendal St, has camp sites from $11 and cabins for $45. There are some beautiful old hotels on Kendal St, which are good for a drink and counter meals, but the accommodation can be a bit seedy. The best is the *Imperial Hotel* (☎ 6341 2588) which charges $25/35 or $40 twin share, including breakfast.

The *Cowra Holiday Park* (☎ 63422666), 4km out of town on the Bathurst Rd, is run by steam train enthusiasts. There's an interesting rail, rural and war relics museum, a small pool and tennis courts. Camp sites are $12, railway carriages are $45, on-site vans are $30 and cabins start from $45.

At Boorowa, 70km from Yass, 47km from Cowra, 115km from Canberra and four hours from Sydney, is the *Backpackers Farmstay at Woolpack Farm & Historic Homestead* (☎ 6385 8433, fax 6385 8410, Lachlan Valley Way, Boorowa). This award-winning historic homestead offers romance, seclusion and lots of activities in and around the adjoining 1000 hectare forest sanctuary. Package deals in the homestead start from $38 per person per night, for 10 days; camping is cheaper. The packages include accommodation, three meals (candle-lit dinners) and activities such as tennis, bush barbecues and stock mustering. Horse riding is $12 per day, but it's free, including lessons, on the first day. The homestead's Web site is www.backpackers~farmstay.com.au.

Getting There & Away

Greyhound Pioneer stops here on its run between Melbourne ($70) and Brisbane ($102). Countrylink (☎ 13 2242) goes to Bathurst ($66) and Cootamundra ($36). Rendell's Coaches (☎ 1800 023 328) runs daily to Canberra ($30).

FORBES

• postcode 2871   • pop 8500

Forbes is an oddly atmospheric place to wander around. It has wide streets and a number of grand 19th century buildings reflecting the wealth of its 1860s gold rush. Ben Hall is buried in the town's cemetery – his death is lamented in a bitter folk song, *The Streets of Forbes*. The information centre (☎ 6852 4155, fax 6852 4433), in the old train station off the highway north of town, opens daily from 9 am to 5 pm.

Forbes Museum (☎ 6853 4139), on Cross St, has Ben Hall relics and other memorabilia and opens daily from 3 to 5 pm June to September (2 to 4 pm October to May). One kilometre south, beside the Newell Hwy, **Lachlan Vintage Village** (☎ 6852 2655), a re-creation of a 19th century village, opens daily from 9.30 am to 5.30 pm.

There are several caravan parks, pubs and plenty of motels. The old but clean *Vandenberg Hotel (☎ 6852 2015)*, on Court St, has rooms for $20/$32.

Forbes has a lot of long-distance bus traffic, including Greyhound Pioneer and McCafferty's.

North-West

From Dubbo, roads radiate to various parts of the state. The Newell Hwy runs northeast/south-west and is the quickest route between Melbourne and Brisbane. The Castlereagh Hwy, forking off the Newell 66km from Dubbo at Gilgandra, runs north into the rugged opal country towards the Queensland border (its surfaced section ends soon after Lightning Ridge).

The Mitchell Hwy runs north-west to Bourke and Queensland via Nyngan, where the Barrier Hwy forks west to Broken Hill.

Getting There & Away

Eastern Australia (☎ 13 1313) and Ansett fly to several of the main towns. Those on the Newell Hwy are served by buses travelling to and from Brisbane, en route to Melbourne or Adelaide. Countrylink trains and/or buses (☎ 13 2232) connect most other towns in the area with Sydney. Fares from Sydney include Gunnedah $62, Coonabarabran $66 and Lightning Ridge $85.

NEWELL HIGHWAY
Gilgandra

This town is at the junction where the Newell and Castlereagh highways divide, and a road also cuts across to the Mitchell. It has a small **observatory** with an audio-visual of the moon landing and other space flights, plus a historical display ($8).

Coonabarabran (population 2500) is an access point for the spectacular granite domes and spires of the rugged **Warrumbungle National Park**, which offers great walking and rock climbing (permit required). There is an NPWS visitors centre (☎ 6825 4364) at the entrance to the park, about 35km west of Coonabarabran. Entry costs $5 per car. Camp sites are $10 with a maximum of two people per site. There's also an NPWS office in Coonabarabran (☎ 6842 1311).

One of the largest optical telescopes in the world is at **Siding Spring**, on the edge of the national park. If you want to spend $10 to look through a telescope, the **Skywatch Observatory** (☎ 6842 3303), on Timor Rd 2km from Coonabarabran, is open daily from 2 pm. Viewing times vary throughout the year.

Coonabarabran has several motels and caravan parks but during school holidays they can fill up. The *Imperial Hotel (☎ 6842 1023)*, a YHA associate, has dorm beds, singles and doubles for $14 per person.

In the country around the national park are a number of places to stay, including *Tibuc (☎ 6842 1740)*, an organic farm costing from $72 a night for two people.

Narrabri (population 6400) is a cotton-growing centre, with the enormous Australia Telescope 25km west on the Yarrie Lake road. **Mt Kaputar National Park**, 53km east of Narrabri via a steep, unsealed road, is good for walking, camping and climbing. **Moree** is a large town on the Gwydir River with some reputedly therapeutic hot baths.

CASTLEREAGH HIGHWAY

On the edge of the Western Plains is **Coonamble**, 98km north of Gilgandra. West of here are the extensive **Macquarie Marshes** with their prolific birdlife. The road continues north to **Walgett**, in dry country near the Grawin and Glengarry opal fields.

A few kilometres off the highway near the Queensland border, **Lightning Ridge** is a huge opal field and the world's only reliable source of black opals. Despite the emphasis on tourism, with underground opal showrooms etc, Lightning Ridge remains a mining community where any battler could strike it rich. There are motels (none cheap) and a few caravan parks with on-site vans. The *Tram-o-Tel* (☎ 6829 0448) has self-contained accommodation in old trams/caravans for $25/20 for the first person and $10 for every extra person.

MITCHELL HIGHWAY

From Dubbo the Mitchell Hwy passes through the citrus-growing centre of **Narromine**. **Warren**, further north and off the Mitchell on the Oxley Hwy, is an access point for the Macquarie Marshes, as is **Nyngan** where the Mitchell and Barrier highways divide. The huge marshes are breeding grounds for ducks, water hens, swans, pelicans, ibis and herons. Nyngan was the scene of fierce resistance by Aboriginal people to early European encroachment. The highway runs arrow-straight for 206km from Nyngan to Bourke.

Outback

You don't have to travel to central Australia to experience red-soil country, limitless horizons and vast blue skies. The far west of NSW is rough, rugged and sparsely populated. It also produces a fair proportion of the state's wealth, particularly from the mines of Broken Hill.

Always seek local advice before travelling on secondary roads west of the Mitchell Hwy. You must carry plenty of water, and if you break down *stay with your vehicle*.

BOURKE

- postcode 2840   • pop 2800

The town of Bourke, about 800km northwest of Sydney, is on the edge of the Outback – hence the expression 'back of Bourke' to describe anywhere remote. The area beyond Bourke is flat and featureless as far as the eye can see.

Bourke is on the Darling River as well as the Mitchell Hwy and it was once a major river port. Scores of paddle-steamers plied the river and in the 1880s it was possible for wool to be in London just six weeks after leaving Bourke – somewhat quicker than a sea-mail parcel today! The courthouse has a crown on its spire, signifying that its jurisdiction includes maritime cases.

The information centre (☎ 6872 2280) is at the train station on Anson St. Pick up a 'mud map' detailing drives to places like **Mt Gunderbooka**, where you'll find Aboriginal cave art and, in the spring, vivid wildflowers, and **Mt Oxley**.

Brewarrina (or Bree) is 95km east of Bourke. You can see **the Fisheries**, stone fish traps which the Ngemba Aboriginal people used to catch the fish to feed the intertribal gatherings they hosted. 'Brewarrina' means 'good fishing'. Nearby is the **Aboriginal Cultural Museum**.

Places to Stay

There are two caravan parks in Bourke. *Mitchell's* (☎ 6872 1791, *Brewarrina Rd*) is closest to town, while *Kidman's Camp* (☎ 6872 1612, *Cunnamulla Rd*) is a peaceful spot on the river 8km from town. Camp sites here are $12 and rooms are $30/40.

The best of Bourke's hotels is the *Port of Bourke* (☎ 6872 2544, *Mitchell St*), between Sturt and Richard Sts. It has rooms for $31/52.

The *Bourke Riverside Motel* (☎ 6872 2539, *Mitchell St*) has a pleasant setting behind the river. Rooms cost from $45/50.

Several stations in the Bourke area (a very large area!) offer accommodation. The information centre has details.

Getting There & Away

Air Link (☎ 13 1713) has five flights a week from Dubbo to Bourke ($179), which connect with Hazelton services from Sydney to Dubbo. Lachlan Travel (☎ 6872 2092), on Oxley St, sells tickets.

Countrylink buses (☎ 13 2232) run to Dubbo four times a week and connect with trains to Sydney ($85). It *might* be possible to go along on the bi-weekly mail run to Wanaaring and Brewarrina. The post office (☎ 6872 2017) can put you in touch with the contractors.

The road from Cobar to Bourke is sealed all the way.

BACK OF BOURKE – CORNER COUNTRY

There's no sealed road west of Bourke in NSW. If you cared to drive the 713km from Bourke to Broken Hill via Wanaaring and Tibooburra it would be mostly on lonely unsealed roads. The far western corner of the state is a semidesert of red plains, heat, dust and flies, but with interesting physical features and prolific wildlife. Running along the border with Queensland is the Dog Fence, patrolled every day by boundary riders who each look after a 40km section.

Tiny **Tibooburra**, the hottest place in the state, is right in the north-western corner and has a number of stone buildings from the 1880s and 90s. Sturt National Park starts right on the northern edge of town. You can normally reach Tibooburra from Bourke or Broken Hill in a conventional vehicle, except after rain (which is pretty rare!).

The NPWS office (☎ 08-8091 3308), open daily, also acts as an information centre.

A basic NPWS camping ground is 2km north of town at *Dead Horse Gully*. The camping fee is $5 for two people, park entry is free. You'll need to bring drinking water. In town, the *Granites Caravan Park* (☎ 08-8091 3305) has camp sites from $10, an on-site van for $26, cabins from $36 and single/double motel units for $42/52.

Both of the town's two fine old pubs, the *Family Hotel* (☎ 08-8091 3314) and the *Tibooburra Hotel* (☎ 08-8091 3310) – known as 'the Two-Storey' – have rooms and good counter meals.

South of Tibooburra, **Milparinka**, once a gold town, now consists of little more than a solitary hotel and some old sandstone buildings. In 1845 members of Charles Sturt's expedition from Adelaide, searching for an inland sea, were forced to camp near here for six months. About 14km northwest of the settlement you can see the grave of James Poole, Sturt's second-in-command, who died of scurvy.

Sturt National Park

Sturt National Park occupies the very northwestern corner of the state, bordering both SA and Queensland. The park has 300km of driveable tracks, camping areas and walks, particularly on the **Jump Up Loop** drive and towards the top of **Mt Wood**. It is recommended that you inform the ranger at Tibooburra where you are heading before venturing into the park. Park entry is free; car and camping costs $5 for two people.

At **Cameron Corner** there's a post to mark the place where Queensland, SA and NSW meet. It's a favourite goal for visitors and a 4WD is not always necessary to get there. In the Queensland corner, the staff at *Cameron Corner Store* (☎ 08-8091 3872) can advise on road conditions. You can also buy fuel here.

BARRIER HIGHWAY

The Barrier Hwy is the main route in the state's west – and just about the only sealed road. It heads west from Nyngan, from where it's 594km to Broken Hill. This provides an alternative route to Adelaide and it's the most direct route between Sydney and WA.

Cobar has a modern and highly productive copper mine, but it also has an earlier history as evidenced by its old buildings, like the Great Western Hotel with its endless stretch of iron lacework ornamenting the verandah. Pick up a town tour map at the information centre (☎ 6836 2448), which is in the excellent **museum** ($5) at the eastern end of the main street.

A weather balloon is released daily at 8.45 am from the meteorological station on the edge of town at Louth road.

There are important Aboriginal cave paintings at **Mt Grenfell**, 40km west of Cobar, then another 32km north of the highway. You can't camp here.

The *Cobar Caravan Park* (☎ 6836 2425) has camp sites for $10.50, on-site vans for $25 and cabins from $35. Several pubs have accommodation. The *New Occidental* (☎ 6836 2111) charges $15 per person with breakfast, while the *Great Western* (☎ 6836 2503) has motel-style rooms for $40/55, including breakfast.

Wilcannia is on the Darling River and was a busy port in the days of paddle-steamers. It's a much quieter place today but you can still see buildings from that era, such as the police station. There are a couple of motels charging around $60 a double. The pubs may provide meals but are best avoided unless you are an experienced bar-room brawler.

About 100km north-west of Wilcannia is **White Cliffs**, an opal-mining settlement. For a taste of life in a small outback community it's worth the drive on a dirt road. You can fossick for opals around the old diggings (watch out for unfenced shafts) and there are opal showrooms and underground homes (called dug-outs) open for inspection. The general store has a 'mud map' of the area and information.

As you enter White Cliffs you pass the high-tech dishes of the solar-energy research station, where emus often graze near the front. Tours of the station are held daily at 2 pm.

The *White Cliffs Hotel* (☎ 08-8091 6606) has basic rooms, but they have air-con and are good value at $20/30. A big cooked breakfast costs $8. Across the road from the post office is a small camping ground (☎ 08-8091 6627) where powered sites cost $10 and showers are $1. There's also a swimming pool.

PJ's Underground (☎ 08-8091 6626), 1.5km east of the post office on Turley's Hill, has doubles with breakfast for $85. Up on Smiths Hill is the *White Cliffs Underground*

Motel (☎ 1800 021 154). It's surprisingly roomy and the temperature is a constant 22°C, whether there's a heatwave or a frost on the surface. Singles/doubles cost $45/70 and $15 for each extra person. There is also an upmarket licensed restaurant.

The *Golf Club*, near the solar station, has Sunday roast lunches for $5.

Mootwingee National Park

This park in the Bynguano Range, 131km north of Broken Hill, teems with wildlife and is a place of exceptional beauty. It is well worth the two hour drive from Broken Hill on an isolated dirt road. You can also get here from White Cliffs but neither route should be attempted after rain. Entry to the park is $5 per car.

In the park is an Aboriginal tribal ground with important rock carvings and cave paintings. The major site is now controlled by the Aboriginal community and is off limits except on ranger-escorted tours. Inquire at the NPWS office in Broken Hill (☎ 08-8088 5933).

There are walks through the crumbling sandstone hills to rock pools, which often have enough water for swimming, and rock paintings can be seen in some areas. The *Homestead Creek* camping ground ($10) has bore water. Sites are available on a first in first served basis.

BROKEN HILL

☎ 08 • postcode 2880 • pop 23,900

Out in the far west, Broken Hill is an oasis in the semiarid wilderness. A mining town, it's fascinating not only for its comfortable existence in a rugged environment, but also for the fact that it was once a one-company town that spawned one equally strong union. It has also become a major centre for Australian art and artists.

There is now only one working mine in Broken Hill. See Mines later in this section for tour information.

History

The Broken Hill Proprietary Company Ltd (BHP) was formed in 1885 after Charles Rasp, a boundary rider, discovered a silver lode. Miners working on other finds in the area had failed to notice the real wealth. Other mining claims were staked, but BHP was always the 'big mine' and dominated the town. Charles Rasp amassed a personal fortune and BHP, which later diversified into steel production, became Australia's largest company.

Early conditions in the mine were appalling. Hundreds of miners died and many more suffered from lead poisoning and lung disease. This gave rise to the other great force in Broken Hill, the unions. Many miners were immigrants from various countries, but all were united in their efforts to improve conditions.

The town's first 35 years saw a militancy rarely matched in Australian industrial relations. Many campaigns were fought, police were called in to break strikes and, though there was a gradual improvement in conditions, the miners lost many confrontations. The turning point was the Big Strike of 1919 and 1920 that lasted for over 18 months. The miners won a 35-hour week and the end of dry drilling, responsible for the dust that afflicted so many of them.

The concept of 'one big union', which had helped to win the strike, was formalised in 1923 with the formation of the Barrier Industrial Council.

Today the world's richest deposits of silver, lead and zinc are still being worked, though zinc is of greatest importance in the Silver City, as Broken Hill is known. There's enough ore left to ensure about another six years of mining. Modern technology has greatly reduced the number of jobs, but while mining has declined, art has thrived.

Orientation & Information

The city is laid out in a grid and the central area is easy to get around on foot. Argent St is the main street.

The big, friendly Tourist Information Centre (☎ 8087 6077, fax 8088 5209), on the corner of Blende and Bromide Sts, opens daily. This is also where the buses arrive; there's a bus booking agency and a car-rental desk on the premises. The NPWS office (☎ 8088 5933) is on Argent St.

The Royal Automobile Association of South Australia (RAASA; ☎ 8088 4999), 261 Argent St, provides reciprocal service to other autoclub members. You can buy your South Australian Desert Parks Pass here (see the Outback section of the South Australia chapter).

There's a laundrette on Argent St just east of the West Darling Hotel.

In many ways Broken Hill is more a part of SA than NSW. It's 1170km from Sydney but only 509km from Adelaide; clocks are set on Adelaide (central) time, half an hour behind Sydney (eastern) time; and the telephone area code (08) is the same as SA's.

Mines

There's an excellent underground tour at **Delprat's Mine** from Monday to Saturday, where you don miners' gear and descend 130m for a tour lasting nearly two hours. It costs $23 (children $18). Children under six years of age are not allowed on the tour. To get there, go up Iodide St, cross the railway tracks and follow the signs – it's about a five minute drive.

Open daily, **Historic Day Dream Mine**, begun in 1881, is 28km from Broken Hill, off the Silverton Rd. A one hour tour costs $11 (all ages allowed), and sturdy footwear is essential. Contact the tourist information centre for bookings.

At **White's Mineral Art Gallery & Mining Museum**, 1 Allendale St, you can walk into a mining stope and see mining memorabilia and minerals. Follow Galena St out to the north-west for about 2km. It's open daily and the admission fee of $4 includes a tour.

Art Galleries

Broken Hill's red earth and harsh light has inspired many artists and a room in the **Broken Hill City Art Gallery** in the Entertainment Centre, on the corner of Blende and Chloride Sts, is devoted to their work. The gallery also houses the *Silver Tree*, an intricate silver sculpture commissioned by Charles Rasp.

There's also a plethora of private galleries, including the **Jack Absalom's Gallery** (☎ 8087 5881), 638 Chapple St, and the **Pro**

Signal Point, Lord Howe Island

Emus in Sturt National Park, NSW

The distinctive Northern Territory Parliament House, Darwin

Uluru at sunrise, NT

Jim Jim Falls, Kakadu National Park, NT

Hart Gallery (☎ 8087 2441), 108 Wyman St. Pro Hart, a former miner, is Broken Hill's best-known artist and a local personality. His gallery not only displays his own work, but also minor works of major artists (eg Picasso and Dali) and a superb collection of Australian art. Admission is $4. The **Ant Hill Gallery** (☎ 8087 2441), 24 Bromide St, features local and major Australian artists.

Royal Flying Doctor Service Base
You can visit the Royal Flying Doctor Service (RFDS; ☎ 8080 1777) base at the airport. The tour ($3) includes a film, and you can inspect the headquarters, aircraft and the radio room that handles calls from remote towns and stations. The centre is open from 9 am to 5 pm weekdays and 10 am to 4 pm on weekends (closed for lunch between noon and 1 pm). Tour bookings are made at the visitor information centre or by calling the RFDS.

School of the Air
On weekdays at 8.30 am you can sit in on broadcasts to kids in isolated homesteads at the School of the Air in Lane St. During school vacations a tape-recording is played for visitors. The one hour session costs $5/3 for adults/children. Book through the tourist information centre.

Other Attractions
The **Sulphide St Station Railway & Historical Museum** is in the Silverton Tramway Company's old station on Sulphide St. The tramway was a private railway running between Cockburn (South Australia) and Broken Hill via Silverton until 1970. It's open daily from 10 am to 3 pm ($2.50).

The **GeoCentre**, on the corner of Bromide and Crystal Sts, presents an interactive history of Broken Hill's geology. There are rock and mineral samples and displays on mining and metallurgy. It's open weekdays from 10 am to 5 pm and weekends from 1 to 5 pm ($3).

At **Photographic Recollections**, in the Central Power Station on Eyre St, interesting photographs depict the history and

culture of the area. The museum opens Monday to Friday from 10 am to 4.30 pm and 1 pm to 4 pm on weekends ($3).

The **Sculpture Symposium** was a project by 12 sculptors from several countries who carved sandstone blocks on a hilltop 9km from town. There are excellent views over the plains from here and it is a good place to watch one of Broken Hill's famous sunsets. Call at the tourist information centre for gate keys and directions.

Organised Tours
There are two-hour guided walks of Broken Hill from the Visitor Information Centre on Monday, Wednesday, Friday and Saturday at 10 am. Plenty of companies offer tours of the town and nearby attractions, some going further out to White Cliffs, Mootwingee National Park and other outback destinations. The tourist information centre has information and takes bookings.

Several outfits have longer 4WD tours of the area. Goanna Safaris (☎ 8087 6057) gets good reviews from travellers.

Places to Stay
There is lots of accommodation around including several motels. The tourist information centre has a list of them and their prices, but most start from $50.

Places to Stay – Budget
Camping & Hostels *Broken Hill City Caravan Park* (☎ 8087 3841), on Rakow St (the Barrier Hwy) about 3km west of the centre, has camp sites for $12, on-site vans from $29 and cabins from $32. *Lake View Caravan Park* (☎ 8088 2250, 1 Mann St), 3km north-east, has camp sites from $10, on-site vans for $26 and cabins for $35 and $45.

The *Tourist Lodge* (☎ 8088 2086, 100 Argent St) is an associate-YHA hostel with dorms for members/nonmembers for $14/16 and singles/doubles for $20/32 or $26/38 with air-con in the guesthouse. There is also a pool.

Hotels & Guesthouses High ceilings, wide corridors and huge verandahs come as

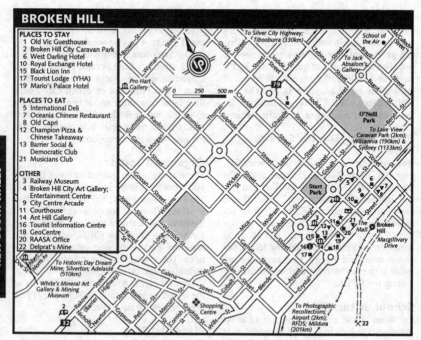

BROKEN HILL

PLACES TO STAY
1 Old Vic Guesthouse
2 Broken Hill City Caravan Park
6 West Darling Hotel
10 Royal Exchange Hotel
15 Black Lion Inn
17 Tourist Lodge (YHA)
19 Mario's Palace Hotel

PLACES TO EAT
5 International Deli
7 Oceania Chinese Restaurant
8 Old Capri
12 Champion Pizza &
    Chinese Takeaway
13 Barrier Social &
    Democratic Club
21 Musicians Club

OTHER
3 Railway Museum
4 Broken Hill City Art Gallery;
    Entertainment Centre
9 City Centre Arcade
11 Courthouse
14 Ant Hill Gallery
16 Tourist Information Centre
18 GeoCentre
20 RAASA Office
22 Delprat's Mine

standard equipment on pubs in this hot city. All places mentioned here have air-con.

The ***Black Lion Inn*** (☎ *8087 4801, 34 Bromide St*) is a congenial pub with singles/doubles with shared bathroom for $18/28. The elegant old ***Royal Exchange Hotel*** (☎ *8087 2308, 320 Argent St*) has rooms for $24/40 or $34/50 with bathroom, fridge and TV. The price includes a light breakfast.

Further west on the corner of Sulphide and Argent Sts, ***Mario's Palace Hotel*** (☎ *8088 1699*) is an impressive old pub (1888) covered in murals and featured in *Priscilla Queen of the Desert*. All rooms have fridges, TVs and tea/coffee-making facilities. Rooms are $30/40 or $40/50 with attached bathroom.

Old Vic Guesthouse (☎ *8087 1169, 230 Oxide St*) is an airy B&B with rooms for $30/45. ***The Base***, on the Barrier Hwy 8km east of the post office, was, until 1996, the Royal Flying Doctor base (now at the airport). It has large rooms for $30/48 (plus $10 per extra person). There are also large gardens with lots of wildlife and a convivial common room.

Places to Stay – Mid-Range
The ***Grand Guesthouse*** (☎ *8087 5305*), 50m from the station, has rooms with shared bathrooms for $45/$54 or $55/$64 with en suite (all include breakfast).

There are some beautiful cottages for rent. ***Broken Hill Historic Cottages*** (☎ *8087 5305, 472 Cummins Lane*) and ***Spicer's Holiday Cottage*** (☎ *8087 8488, 143 Knox St*) are both worth checking out. The cottages come complete with everything you could need, sleep up to six people (in three rooms) and cost $85 per night for up to six people.

Places to Eat
Broken Hill is a club town if ever there was one. The clubs welcome visitors and you usually just sign the visitors book at the

front door and walk in. Most of them have reasonably priced, reasonably good and very filling meals. The **Barrier Social & Democratic Club** (*'the Demo', 218 Argent St*) has meals, including breakfast (from 6 am, or 7 am on weekends), that will keep you going all day. The **Musician's Club** (*267 Crystal St*) is similar.

There are lots of pubs too – this is a mining town – but many don't cook after 8.30 pm or at all on a Sunday. Counter lunches cost around $5 and main courses in the evening around $10.

On Sulphide St, **Champion Pizza & Chinese Takeaway** (behind the Pizza Hut!), stays open late and does an all-you-can-eat Chinese buffet for $7 after 6 pm. The **Oceania Chinese Restaurant** (*423 Argent St*) is popular with $7 lunch specials and main courses from around $9.50, and the **Old Capri** (*415 Argent St*) is a small Italian place which makes home-made pasta. There's also a cluster of places at the eastern end of Argent St.

Entertainment

Maybe because this is a mining town, maybe because there are so many nights when it's too hot to sleep, but Broken Hill stays up late. There isn't a lot of formal entertainment, but on Thursday, Friday and Saturday pubs stay open until almost dawn.

The **Barrier Social & Democratic Club**, the 'Demo', runs a nightclub on Friday and Saturday nights. It also has live country cabaret. The **Black Lion Inn** is a bit of a party pub and good for a drink. It has a three-page cocktail list and two-for-one deals on some nights.

The traditional Australian game of Two-Up (gambling on the fall of two coins) is played at the **Musicians Club**, on Crystal St, on Friday and Saturday nights, and of course on Anzac Day. Broken Hill claims to have retained the atmosphere of a real two-up 'school', unlike the sanitised versions played in casinos.

Getting There & Around

Air Full economy one-way fares from Broken Hill include $174 to Adelaide with

Kendell (☎ 13 1300), $363 to Sydney with Hazelton (☎ 13 1713) and $446 to Melbourne (only via Adelaide on Ansett/Kendell). A $9 airport tax is added to all these fares.

Bus Greyhound Pioneer runs daily to Adelaide for $60, Mildura for $42 and Sydney for $96. Most buses depart from the tourist information centre, where you can book seats.

Train Broken Hill is on the Sydney to Perth railway line so the *Indian Pacific* passes through, as does the train between Sydney and Adelaide. Schedules change throughout the year so check with Great Southern Railway (☎ 13 2147). The economy fare to Sydney is $108 and Adelaide ($54), a student discount is available.

There's a slightly faster and marginally cheaper daily service to Sydney called Laser, a Countrylink bus departing Broken Hill daily at 4 am (groan) and connecting with a train at Dubbo, arriving in Sydney at 8.45 pm ($98). The Countrylink booking office at the train station is open on weekdays.

AROUND BROKEN HILL
Silverton

Silverton, 25km north-west of Broken Hill, is an old silver-mining town that reached its peak in 1885 when it had a population of 3000 and public buildings designed to last for centuries. In 1889 the mines closed and the population (and many of the houses) moved to Broken Hill.

Today it's an interesting little ghost town, which was used as a setting in the movies *Mad Max II* and *A Town Like Alice*. A number of buildings still stand, including the old gaol (now the museum) and the **Silverton Hotel** (☎ 8088 5313). The hotel is still operating and it has a display of photographs taken on the film sets. Don't leave this hotel without taking the infamous 'Silverton test'; ask at the bar. There are also a couple of art galleries. The information centre, in the old school, has a walking-tour map.

Bill Canard (☎ 8088 5316) runs a variety of **camel tours** from Silverton. You can take

NEW SOUTH WALES

a 15 minute tour for $5, one hour for $20 or a two hour sunset ride for $40 (children $20). There are also longer treks.

There's accommodation at *Penrose Park* (☎ 8088 5307), signposted to the right as you approach town from Broken Hill. Camp sites cost $3 per person, or you can bed down in a choice of 'bunkhouses' – $20 with kitchen, $15 without. There are coin-operated showers and water for washing, but bring or boil drinking-water.

The road beyond Silverton becomes bleak and lonely almost immediately. The **Mundi Mundi Plains** lookout, 5km north of town, gives an idea of just how desolate it gets. Further along, the **Umberumberka Reservoir**, 13km north of Silverton, is a popular picnic spot.

Menindee Lakes

This water storage development on the Darling River, 112km south-east of Broken Hill, offers a variety of water-sport facilities. **Menindee** is the closest town to the area. Burke and Wills stayed at *Maidens Hotel* (☎ 8091 4208) on their ill-fated trip north in 1860. The hotel was built in 1854 and still has accommodation for around $16 per person, including breakfast.

Kinchega National Park is close to town, and the lakes, overflowing from the Darling River, are a haven for birdlife. There are also many kangaroos and other native fauna. The visitors centre is at the site of the old Kinchega Homestead, about 16km from the park entrance, and the shearing shed has been preserved. There's accommodation at the shearers' quarters (book at the Broken Hill NPWS office) and there are plenty of camp sites along the river.

North of Menindee there are some good, free camp sites around Lakes Wetherell and Pamamaroo, but bone up on minimal impact camping strategies before you set up: this is a water catchment area.

MUNGO NATIONAL PARK

South-east of Menindee and north-east of Mildura is **Lake Mungo**, a dry lake that is the site of the oldest archaeological finds in Australia – human skeletons and artefacts dating back 45,000 years. Aboriginal people settled on the banks of these once fertile lakes and lived on the plentiful fish, mussels, birds and animals. After 25,000 years the climate changed, the lakes dried up and Aboriginal people adapted to life in a harsh semi-desert, with only periodic floods filling the lakes.

A 25km semicircle ('lunette') of huge sand dunes has been created by the unceasing westerly wind, which continually exposes fabulously ancient remains. The park also includes the dry lake-bed and the shimmering white cliffs known as the **Walls of China**. Remember, it's illegal in Australia to remove archaeological objects or to disturb human remains.

Mungo is 110km from Mildura and 150km from Balranald on unsealed roads. These towns are the closest places selling fuel. Mallee Outback Experiences (☎ 03-5021 1621) and Junction Tours (☎ 03-5027 4309) are two Mildura-based companies offering tours. Mallee Outdoor Experiences charges $45 for a day tour (Wednesday and Saturday).

Information

There's a visitors centre (not always staffed) by the old Mungo woolshed. The NPWS office (☎ 03-5023 1278), at Buronga near Mildura, also has information. A road leads across the dry lake bed to the Walls of China, and you can drive a complete 60km loop of the dunes – but not after rain.

Places to Stay

Accommodation fills up during school holidays. There are two camping grounds – *Main Camp* is 2km from the visitors centre and *Belah Camp* is on the eastern side of the dunes. Camping costs $5 a night for two. Shared accommodation in the old shearers' quarters costs $15 per person or $25 for a room to yourself ($15 if they're not full). Book through the NPWS office in Buronga.

On the Mildura road, about 4km from the visitors centre, is *Mungo Lodge* (☎ 03-5029 7297) where single/double/triple rooms cost from $68/78/88 or self-contained units with separate bedrooms cost $78/88/98. There's also a restaurant here.

Lord Howe Island

☎ 02   • postcode 2898   • pop 300

Beautiful Lord Howe is a tiny subtropical island 550km east of Port Macquarie and 770km north-east of Sydney. It's not a budget destination, although prices fall considerably in winter. Unless you've got a boat you'll have to fly there, and both food and accommodation are expensive. Most visitors take flight and accommodation packages.

The island is listed on the World Heritage Register. It's heavily forested and has beautiful walks, a wide lagoon sheltered by a coral reef and some fine beaches. It's small enough at 11km long and 2km wide for you to get around on foot or by bicycle. The southern end is dominated by towering Mt Lidgbird (777m) and Mt Gower (875m). You can climb Mt Gower in around eight hours (round trip) with a licensed guide. There's good fishing, diving and snorkelling in the lagoon and you can also inspect the sea life from glass-bottom boats. On the other side of the island there's surf at Blinky Beach.

A feature of Lord Howe during spring and summer (September to April) is the huge number of seabirds that nest here.

Information

The Lord Howe Island Visitor Centre (☎ 6563 2114) has lots of local information, while travel agencies are the best source of accommodation and package information. Try Pacific International Travel Centre (☎ 13 2747) or Fastbook Pacific (☎ 1300 361 153) in Sydney, or Oxley Travel (☎ 1800 671546) in Port Macquarie. Fastbook also has twin-island packages to Lord Howe and Norfolk islands from $1699 (12 nights).

Places to Stay & Eat

There's plenty of accommodation in lodges and self-contained apartments, but the only way to get a decent deal is to buy a package. Prices start from $599 for five nights in winter, rising to over $1000 in summer. Camping is not permitted on the island.

Some of the cheaper places include *Ocean View Lodge* and *Ebbtide*, while *Trader Nicks* and *Pinetrees*, which has a great fish

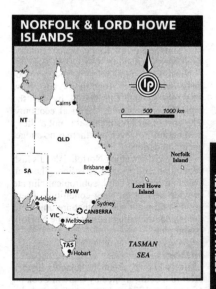

NORFOLK & LORD HOWE ISLANDS

fry ($25) on Monday evenings, are more upmarket.

Getting There & Away

Eastern Australia (☎ 13 1313) has four flights a week from Sydney, while Sunstate (☎ 13 1313) flies from Brisbane on Sundays. Most flights are booked as part of a package deal (see Information). Lord Howe Island Nature Tours (☎ 1800 806 820) runs eight-day nature-oriented packages for $1500 all inclusive, departing from Brisbane, Sydney, Coffs Harbour and Port Macquarie.

Getting Around

You can hire bicycles, motorcycles and cars on the island but a bicycle is all you need. There is a 25km/h speed limit throughout the island.

Norfolk Island

☎ international area code 6723
• postcode 2899   • pop 1800

Norfolk Island is a green speck in the middle of the Pacific Ocean, 1600km north-east of Sydney and 1000km north-west of the

New Zealand city of Auckland. It's the largest of a cluster of three islands emerging from the Norfolk Ridge, which stretches from New Zealand to New Caledonia.

Norfolk is a popular tourist spot, particularly with older Australians and New Zealanders, and tourism is by far the biggest contributor to the local economy. The cost of airfares means it is not a cheap destination, however, and there is no budget accommodation.

Many visitors enjoy Norfolk Island's lush vegetation and rugged coastline. The rich volcanic soil and mild, subtropical climate provide perfect growing conditions. There are 40-odd plant species that are unique to the island, including the handsome Norfolk Island pine.

History

Little is known about the island's history prior to it being sighted by Captain Cook on 10 October 1774 and named after the wife of the ninth Duke of Norfolk. Fifteen convicts were among the first settlers to reach the island on 6 March 1788, founding a penal colony that survived until 1814. The island was abandoned for 11 years before the colonial authorities decided to try again. Governor Darling planned this second penal settlement as 'a place of the extremest punishment short of death'. Under such notorious sadists as commandant John Giles Price, Norfolk became known as 'hell in the Pacific'. The second penal colony lasted until 1855, when the prisoners were shipped off to Van Diemen's Land (Tasmania) and the island was handed over to the descendants of the mutineers from the HMS *Bounty*, who had outgrown their adopted Pitcairn Island. About a third of the present population is descended from the 194 Pitcairners who arrived on 8 June 1856.

Visas

The island is a self-governing external territory of Australia; this has important ramifications in terms of passports and visas. Travelling to Norfolk Island from Australia means you will get an exit stamp in your passport and board an international flight. On arrival at Norfolk Island, you get a 30-day entry permit on presentation of a valid passport. To return to Australia you will need a re-entry visa, or a valid Australian passport.

Orientation & Information

The island measures only 8km by 5km. Vertical cliffs surround much of the coastline, apart from a small area of coastal plain (formerly swamp) around the historic settlement of Kingston. The only settlement of any consequence is the service town of Burnt Pine, at the centre of the island near the airport. Most of the northern part of the island is within the Norfolk Island National Park.

The Norfolk Islander Visitor Information Centre (☎ 22 147) is next to the post office on the main street (Taylors Rd) in Burnt Pine. The Communications Centre (Norfolk Telecom) is on New Cascade Rd.

The Commonwealth, with an ATM (☎ 22144), and Westpac banks are both in Taylors Rd and Eftpos is available in most shops.

Kingston

Kingston, built by convicts of the second penal colony, is the island's main attraction. Most of the buildings have been restored and the finest of these, along Quality Row, still house the island's administrators. Four of the buildings have been turned into small but excellent museums which are open daily from 11 am to 3 pm. Don't miss the convict cemetery, near the ocean at the far (eastern) end of Quality Row. There are some very poignant epitaphs on the headstones giving hints of the island's less pleasant past.

Other Attractions

Just south of Kingston is **Emily Bay**, a good sheltered beach; from here you can go out in glass-bottom boats to view the corals.

St Barnabas Chapel, west of Burnt Pine along Douglas Drive, is a magnificent chapel built by the (Anglican) Melanesian Mission, which was based on the island from 1866 to

1920. The **Bounty Folk Museum**, on Middlegate Rd, has a motley collection relating to Norfolk's three periods of settlement.

There are various walking tracks in **Norfolk Island National Park**, and good views from Mt Pitt (320m) and Mt Bates (321m). Mt Pitt was the higher of the two before the top was levelled to take a radio transmitter.

Organised Tours
Pinetree Tours (☎ 22 424) and Bounty Excursions (☎ 23 693), both in Burnt Pine, run tours around the island, including half-day introductory tours ($18) taking in all the major points of interest.

There's an exhausting array of tours and stage performances designed to showcase the island's convict history and links to the *Bounty* mutineers.

Places to Stay
Accommodation is expensive, but the cost is often disguised as most visitors come on package deals, which start at around $740 for five nights in winter and $900 in summer.

Accommodation ranges from a few family-run guesthouses to resort-style motels, but simple, self-contained apartments are more common. *Aunt Em's* (☎ 22 373, Taylors Rd) is a guesthouse with old-style charm. B&B costs $65/110 for a single/double. *Highlands Lodge* (☎ 22 741, Selwyn Pine Rd) is a good place nestled on the hillside below the national park with doubles from $148. *Channer's Corner* (☎ 22 532, Taylors Rd), on the

edge of Burnt Pine, has stylish apartments at $95 for two people.

Places to Eat
There are dozens of restaurants offering everything from humble fish and chips to upmarket a la carte. Competition is stiff and prices are reasonable. The *Brewery Bar & Bistro*, opposite the airport, has cheap counter meals ($6.50) and brews its own beer. The *Sports & Workers Club*, in Burnt Pine, is also good value. *Barney Duffy's* is a popular steakhouse in the main shopping area with mains for about $16 and, for a splurge, *James' Place* is the pick of the upmarket restaurants.

Getting There & Away
Flight West (☎ 1300 130092 or through Ansett ☎ 13 1300) has four flights a week from Brisbane and Sydney, while Norfolk Jet Express (☎ 1800 816 947) flies three times a week from Sydney and once a week from Brisbane. Most flights are booked as part of a package. Air New Zealand flies from Auckland (☎ 357 3000 in Auckland) from around NZ$600 return. Leaving Norfolk Island incurs a departure tax of $25.

Getting Around
Car hire can be organised at the airport for less than $20 a day. Petrol is expensive, but you'll struggle to use much. Cows have right of way on the island's roads, and there's a $300 fine for hitting one.

Northern Territory

The fascinating Northern Territory (NT) is the most barren and least populated area of Australia, with only 1% of the Australian population living in nearly 20% of the country's area. The populated parts of Australia are predominantly urban and coastal, but it is in the Centre – the Red Heart – that the picture-book, untamed and sometimes surreal Australia exists.

The Centre is not just Uluru (Ayers Rock). There are meteorite craters, eerie canyons, lost valleys of palms and noisy Alice Springs festivals. Where else is there an annual boat regatta on a dry river bed? The colour red is evident as soon as you arrive – in the soil, the rocks and in Uluru itself.

At the other end of 'The Track' – the Stuart Hwy, 1500km of bitumen that connects Alice Springs to the north coast – is Darwin, probably Australia's most cosmopolitan city. As you travel up or down that single link you'll notice another of the Territory's real surprises – the contrast between the Centre's aridity and the humid, tropical wetness of the Top End in the monsoon season. The wetlands and escarpments of Kakadu National Park are a treasure house of wildlife and Aboriginal rock painting.

The NT has a smaller population and a more fragile economy than other parts of Australia, and isn't classified as a state. It was formerly administered by New South Wales and then by South Australia, but it has been controlled by the Federal Government since 1911. Since 1978 the Territory has been self-governed, although Canberra still has more say over its internal affairs than over those of the states.

A motion that the NT should be granted statehood was narrowly defeated at a referendum in October 1998.

ABORIGINAL PEOPLE

Around 38,000 of the Territory's 190,000 people are Aboriginal.

The process of white settlement in the NT was just as troubled and violent as elsewhere

HIGHLIGHTS

Telephone code: ☎ 08
Population: 189,990
Area: 1.35 million sq km

- Taking a boat ride on the wetlands of Kakadu National Park

- Visiting Uluru (Ayers Rock) and Kata Tjuta (the Olgas) at Uluru-Kata Tjuta National Park

- Hiking in the spectacular Kings Canyon, Watarrka National Park

- Fishing for barramundi at Borroloola on the Gulf of Carpentaria

- Paddling a canoe up the Katherine Gorge, Nitmiluk National Park

- Taking an Aboriginal cultural tour at Manyallaluk, near Katherine

- Visiting the old gold mines in Tennant Creek

- Trekking the Larapinta Trail in the Western MacDonnell Ranges, near Alice Springs

- Delving into central Australian history at the Old Telegraph Station, Alice Springs

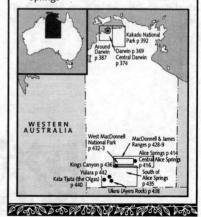

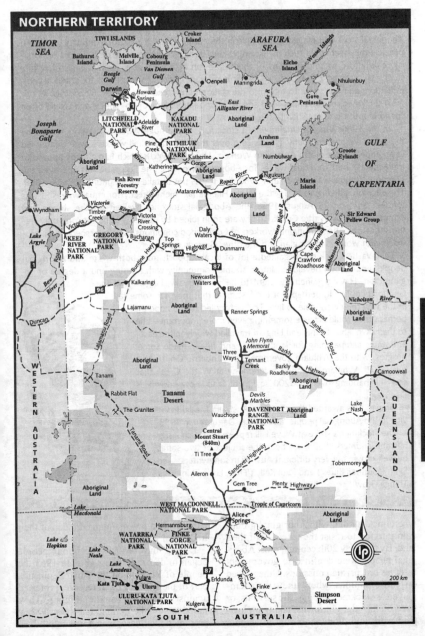

NORTHERN TERRITORY

TIMOR SEA

TIWI ISLANDS

Croker Island

ARAFURA SEA

Wessel Islands

Bathurst Island

Melville Island

Cobourg Peninsula

Van Diemen Gulf

Elcho Island

Beagle Gulf

Nhulunbuy

Oenpelli

Maningrida

Darwin

Howard Springs

Jabiru

Gove Peninsula

East Alligator River

Glyde R

LITCHFIELD NATIONAL PARK

Adelaide River

KAKADU NATIONAL PARK

Aboriginal Land

Joseph Bonaparte Gulf

Pine Creek

NITMILUK NATIONAL PARK

Arnhem Land

GULF

Daly River

Katherine

Katherine Gorge

Numbulwar

Groote Eylandt

OF

Aboriginal Land

Fish River Forestry Reserve

Mataranka

Roper River

Ngukurr

Maria Island

CARPENTARIA

Wyndham

Victoria River

Aboriginal Land

Sir Edward Pellew Group

Timber Creek

Victoria River Crossing

Daly Waters

Carpentaria

Borroloola

McArthur River

Lake Argyle

KEEP RIVER NATIONAL PARK

GREGORY NATIONAL PARK

Buchanan

Top Springs

Highway

Dunmarra

Highway

Cape Crawford Roadhouse

Aboriginal Land

Bow River

Barkly

Tablelands Hwy

Duncan

Kalkaringi

Newcastle Waters

Elliott

Nicholson River

Lajamanu

Aboriginal Land

Renner Springs

Tableland

Aboriginal Land

John Flynn Memorial

Ranken Road

Tanami

Three Ways

Barkly

Camooweal

WESTERN AUSTRALIA

Rabbit Flat

Tanami Desert

Tennant Creek

Barkly Roadhouse

Barkly Highway

The Granites

Wauchope

Devils Marbles

DAVENPORT RANGE NATIONAL PARK

Aboriginal Land

Lake Nash

QUEENSLAND

Tanami Road

Central Mount Stuart (840m)

Ti Tree

Sandover Highway

NORTHERN TERRITORY

Aboriginal Land

Aileron

Tobermorey

Lake Macdonald

Gem Tree

Plenty Highway

WEST MACDONNELL NATIONAL PARK

Tropic of Capricorn

Aboriginal Land

Lake Hopkins

Hermannsburg

Alice Springs

Todd River

Lake Neale

WATARRKA NATIONAL PARK

FINKE GORGE NATIONAL PARK

Old Ghan Rd

Lake Amadeus

Finke River

Yulara

Simpson Desert

Kata Tjuta

Uluru

Erldunda

Finke

ULURU-KATA TJUTA NATIONAL PARK

Kulgera

0   100   200 km

SOUTH   AUSTRALIA

Vincent Lingiari & the Wave Hill Stockmen's Strike of 1966

Aboriginal stockmen played a large role in the early days of the pastoral industry in the NT. Because they were paid such paltry wages (which often never even materialised) a pastoralist could afford to employ many of them, and run his station at a much lower cost. White stockmen received regular and relatively high wages, were given decent food and accommodation, and were able to return to the station homestead every week. By contrast Aboriginal stockmen received poor food and accommodation, little or no money, and would often spend months in the bush with the cattle.

In the 1960s Vincent Lingiari was a stockman on the huge Wave Hill station, owned by the British Vesteys company. His concern over the way Aboriginal workers were treated led to an appeal to the North Australian Workers' Union (NAWU), which had already applied to the Federal Court for equal wages for Aboriginal workers. The Federal Court approved the granting of equal wages in March 1966, but it was not to take effect until December 1968. The decision led Lingiari to ask the Wave Hill management directly for equal wages. It was refused, and, on 23 August 1966, the Aboriginal stockmen walked off the station and camped in nearby Wattie Creek. They were soon joined by others, and before long only stations that gave their Aboriginal workers not only good conditions but also respect, were provided with workers by Lingiari and the other Gurindji elders.

The Wattie Creek camp gained a lot of local support, from both white and Aboriginal people, and it soon developed into a sizable community with housing and a degree of organisation. Having gained the right to be paid equally, Lingiari and the Gurindji people felt, perhaps for the first time, that they had some say in the way they were able to live. This victory led to the hope that perhaps they could achieve something even more important – title to their own land. To this end Lingiari travelled widely in the eastern states campaigning for land rights, and finally made some progress with the Whitlam government in Canberra. On 16 August 1975, Whitlam attended a ceremony at Wattie Creek that saw the handing over of 3200 sq km of land, now known as Daguragu.

Lingiari was awarded the Order of Australia Medal for service to the Aboriginal people, and died at Daguragu in 1988.

The stockmen's strike at Wave Hill represented such a significant landmark that it has been the subject of two songs by well known but very different Australian songwriters – Ted Egan ('Gurindji Blues') and Paul Kelly ('From Little Things Big Things Grow').

KATE NOLAN

where in Australia, with Aboriginal groups vainly trying to resist the takeover of their land. By the early 20th century, most Aboriginal people were confined to government reserves or Christian missions. Others lived on cattle stations where they were employed as stockmen or domestic servants, or lived on the edges of towns, taking on low-paid work and often acquiring an alcohol habit. Only a few maintained much of their traditional way of life.

During the 1960s, Aboriginal people began to demand more rights. In 1963 the people of Yirrkala on the Gove Peninsula, part of the Arnhem Land reserve, protested against plans for bauxite mining. They failed to stop the mining, but the way they presented their case, which was to produce sacred objects and bark paintings that showed their right to the land under Aboriginal custom, was a milestone. In 1966 the Gurindji people on Wave Hill cattle station went on strike and asked that their tribal land, which formed part of the station, be returned to them. Eventually the Gurindji were given 3238 sq km in a government-negotiated deal with the station owners.

In 1976 the Aboriginal Land Rights (NT) Act was passed in Canberra. It handed over all reserves and mission lands in the Territory to the Aboriginal people, and allowed Aboriginal groups to claim government land with which they had traditional ties – provided the land wasn't already leased, or in a town, or set aside for some other special purpose.

Today, Aboriginal people own around 50% of the NT. Minerals on Aboriginal land are still government property – though the landowners' permission for exploration and mining is usually required and has to be paid for.

The NT land rights laws improved the lot of many Aboriginal people and gave a boost to the Outstation Movement that started in the 1970s. Aboriginal people began to leave the settlements and return to a more traditional, nomadic lifestyle on their own land. Ironically, equal-pay laws in the 1960s deprived Aboriginal people of a major source of work, as many cattle station owners reacted by employing white stockmen instead.

While white Australia's awareness of the need for reconciliation is on the increase, and more Aboriginal people are able to deal effectively with whites, there are still yawning gulfs between the cultures. Although the 1993 Native Title Act went some way towards reconciling the two sides, more recent developments over the Wik Decision (see the Government & Politics section in the Facts about Australia chapter) demonstrate that there is still a long way to go.

For these and other reasons it's usually hard for short-term visitors to make meaningful contact with Aboriginal people, who often prefer to be left to themselves. For this reason, tourism on Aboriginal land is generally restricted. This is gradually changing,

however, as more communities feel inclined to share their culture, and are able to do so on their own terms. The benefits to the communities are twofold: the more obvious is the financial gain; the other that introducing Aboriginal culture and customs to non-Aboriginal people helps alleviate the problems caused by the ignorance and misunderstandings of the past.

Permits

You need a permit to enter Aboriginal land, and in general one is granted only if you have friends or relatives working there, or if you're on an organised tour. Wandering at random through Aboriginal land to visit the communities is definitely not on. The exception to this rule is travel along public roads through Aboriginal land – though if you want to stop (other than for fuel or provisions) or deviate, you need a permit. If you stick to the main roads, there's no problem.

Three land councils deal with requests for permits; ask the permits officer of the appropriate council for an application form. The Central Land Council deals with all land south of a line drawn between Kununurra (WA) and Mt Isa (Queensland), the Northern Land Council is responsible for land north of that line, and the Tiwi Land Council deals with Bathurst and Melville islands.

Permits can take four to six weeks to be processed, although for Oenpelli they take just half an hour in Jabiru.

Northern Land Council
   (☎ 8920 5100, fax 8945 2633)
   9 Rowling St (PO Box 42921), Casuarina, Darwin, NT 0811
Tiwi Land Council
   (☎ 8981 4898)
   Unit 5/3 Bishop St, Stuart Park, NT 0820
Central Land Council
   (☎ 8951 6211, fax 8953 4345)
   33 Stuart Hwy (PO Box 3321), Alice Springs, NT 0871

Tours on Aboriginal Land

There are a number of tourist operations, some of them Aboriginal owned, running trips to Aboriginal land and communities. Arnhem Land offers the most options,

Aboriginal Events & Festivals

There are a number of regular festivals that are well worth attending. Although they are usually held on restricted Aboriginal land, permit requirements are generally waived for the festivals. Be aware also that alcohol is banned in many communities.

Barunga Wugularr Sports & Cultural Festival

For the four days over the Queen's Birthday long weekend in June, Barunga, 80km southeast of Katherine, becomes a gathering place for Aboriginal people from all over the Territory. There are traditional arts and crafts, as well as dancing and athletics competitions. No accommodation is provided so you'll need your own camping equipment, or visit for the day from Katherine. No permit is required.

Merrepen Arts Festival

In June or July, Nauiyu Nambiyu on the banks of the Daly River is the venue for the Merrepen Arts Festival. Several Aboriginal communities from around the district, such as Wadeye, Nauiyu and Peppimenarti, display their arts and crafts. No permit is required.

Yuendumu Festival

The Yuendumu community is located 270km north-west of Alice Springs, and Aboriginal people from the central and western desert region meet here over a long weekend in early August. There's a mix of sporting and cultural events, both traditional and modern. BYO camping gear. No permit is required.

Oenpelli Open Day

Oenpelli (Gunbalanya) is in Arnhem Land, across the East Alligator River not far from Jabiru. On the first Saturday in August an open day is held when there's a chance to purchase local artefacts and watch the sports and dancing events. No permit is required.

National Aboriginal Art Award

Each year (usually in September) an exhibition of works entered for this award is held at the Museum & Art Gallery of the Northern Territory in Darwin. It attracts entries from all over the country.

mainly because of its proximity to Kakadu. The tours there generally visit only the western edge of Arnhem Land, but take you to Oenpelli and other places that are normally off limits. Operations include Umorrduk Safaris and Davidson's Arnhem Land Safaris (see the Arnhem Land and Kakadu sections later for more details).

Other places in the Top End with similar operations include Bathurst and Melville islands, and the Litchfield and Katherine areas, while in the Centre they are in the Alice Springs area and at Uluru. See those sections and Aboriginal Cultural Tours under Darwin in this chapter for details.

CLIMATE

The climate of the Top End is best described in terms of the Dry and the Wet, rather than winter and summer. Roughly, the Dry lasts from April to September, and the Wet from October to March, with the heaviest rain falling from January onwards. April, when the rains taper off, and the period from October to December, with its uncomfortably high humidity and that 'waiting for the rains' feeling (known as the 'build-up'), are transition periods. The Top End is the most thundery part of Australia: Darwin has more than 90 'thunder days' a year, all between September and March.

In the Centre the temperatures are much more variable – plummeting below freezing on winter nights (June to August) and soaring into the 40s on summer days (November to March). Come prepared for both extremes, and for the occasional rainstorm at any time of the year. When it rains, dirt roads quickly become quagmires.

The most comfortable time to visit both the Centre and the Top End is June/July. The Top End does have its good points during the Wet – everything is green, the barramundi fishing is at its best, there are spectacular electrical storms and all the tourists have gone home. However, visiting at this time does present problems. The combination of heat and high humidity can be unbearable if you're not acclimatised, dirt roads are often impassable, swimming in the ocean is not recommended because of box jellyfish (stingers), and some national parks and reserves are either totally or partially closed.

INFORMATION

Surprisingly, the NT Tourism Commission (NTTC) doesn't have any tourist offices either within the Territory or elsewhere in Australia, although there are regional tourist offices in Darwin, Katherine, Tennant Creek and Alice Springs. See these sections later in this chapter.

If you want any predeparture information, contact the NTTC on ☎ 1800 621 336; or visit its Web site: www.nttc.com.au.

NATIONAL PARKS

The NT has some of Australia's best national parks. Most people are aware of the more famous ones, such as Uluru-Kata Tjuta, Kakadu and Nitmiluk (Katherine Gorge), but there are plenty of others that are equally appealing – such as Litchfield, West MacDonnell Ranges and Watarrka (Kings Canyon).

For information on Uluru-Kata Tjuta and Kakadu national parks contact the information offices in the parks themselves (see the Kakadu and Uluru-Kata Tjuta national park sections in this chapter for details).

Other parks, and natural and historic reserves are run by the Parks & Wildlife Commission of the NT, which has offices in Alice Springs, Katherine and Darwin, and information desks in the tourist offices in Darwin and Alice Springs. Parks & Wildlife puts out fact sheets on individual parks, and these are available from the offices or from the parks themselves.

ACTIVITIES
Bushwalking

There are interesting bushwalking trails in the NT, but take care if you venture off the beaten track. You can climb the ranges surrounding Alice Springs – remember to wear stout shoes and long pants, as the spinifex grass is very sharp. In summer, wear a hat and carry water, even on short walks. In the Top End, walking is best in the Dry, although shorter walks are possible in the Wet.

The Larapinta Trail, in the Western MacDonnell Ranges near Alice Springs, is well laid out with camp sites and other basic facilities along the way. At Watarrka there's the excellent Giles Track, a two day walk along the spectacular George Gill Range. Most other parks in the Centre have shorter walks. In the north there's plenty of potential in Gregory, Kakadu, Litchfield and Nitmiluk national parks – Nitmiluk has some good marked trails.

Willis' Walkabouts (☎ 8985 2134; walkabout@ais.com.au) is a Darwin-based commercial tour operator offering bushwalks in the Top End, Kimberley and the Centre. These range from three days to three weeks.

Swimming

Stay out of the sea from October to May, inclusive, when box jellyfish are most common. See the Health and Dangers & Annoyances sections in the Facts for the Visitor chapter.

Beware too of saltwater crocodiles in both salt and fresh waters in the Top End, though there are quite a few safe, natural swimming holes. Take local advice – and if in doubt, don't take a risk.

Fishing

Fishing is good, particularly for barramundi, a perch that often grows over 1m

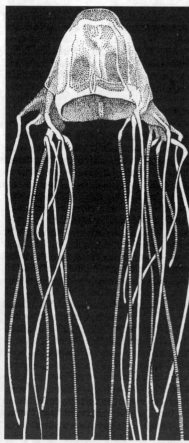

Deadly box jellyfish KATE NOLAN

long, puts up a great fight and is fantastic to eat. Barramundi is found both offshore and in estuaries, and there are fishing tours for the express purpose of catching it.

Companies that offer fishing tours include Big Barra Fishing Tours (☎ 8932 1473, bigbarra@octa4.nat.au), Land a Barra Tours (☎ 8932 2543) and Barra Bash (☎ 1800 632 225).

There are size and bag limits on barramundi and mud crabs, so be aware of these. For information contact the Recreational Fisheries Division (☎ 8999 4395) of the Department of Primary Industry & Fisheries in Darwin.

Fossicking

Fossicking is a popular pastime in the NT. Good locations include the Harts Range (70km north-east of Alice Springs) for beryl, garnet, quartz, tourmaline, zircon and many more; Tennant Creek for gold and jasper; Anthony Lagoon (215km east of the Stuart Hwy, north of Tennant Creek) for ribbonstone; Pine Creek for gold; and Brock's Creek (37km south-west of Adelaide River, south of Darwin) for topaz, tourmaline, garnet and zircon.

The Department of Mines & Energy publishes *A Guide to Fossicking in the Northern Territory*, available from its offices in Alice Springs (☎ 8951 5658), Tennant Creek (☎ 8962 1288) and Darwin (☎ 8999 5511). A fossicking permit is required, and these are available for $5 per month from the same offices.

GETTING THERE & AWAY

See the Alice Springs, Darwin and Uluru sections in this chapter for transport into the NT by air, bus, train and car.

GETTING AROUND
Air

Ansett (☎ 13 1300) and Qantas (☎ 13 1313) service the main centres in the Territory. There's also Airnorth (☎ 1800 627 474), which is affiliated with Ansett and links Darwin, Katherine, Bathurst Island, Jabiru, Oenpelli, Groote Eylandt, Gove Peninsula, Alice Springs and Tennant Creek. The NT Air Fares chart details regular fares.

Bus

Within the Territory, fairly good coverage is given by Greyhound Pioneer and McCafferty's. See the relevant Getting There & Away sections in this chapter for the various towns.

Backpackers Bus A good budget alternative for travel around the Top End – at least between Darwin, Kakadu, Katherine, Nitmiluk and Litchfield – is The Blue Banana

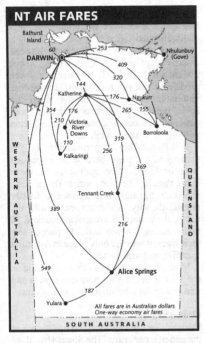

NT AIR FARES

Bathurst Island

DARWIN 60

253

Nhulunbuy (Gove)

409

320

144

Katherine

176 Ngukurr

354 176 265 155

210 Victoria River Downs

110 319 Borroloola

Kalkaringi

256

369

Tennant Creek

389

216

W E S T E R N   A U S T R A L I A

Q U E E N S L A N D

549

Alice Springs

187

Yulara

All fares are in Australian dollars
One-way economy air fares

SOUTH AUSTRALIA

(☎ 8945 6800, banana@octa4.net.au). It does a regular round trip – clockwise from Darwin via Kakadu to Katherine and back via Litchfield, stopping at several other attractions and points of interest en route. A ticket is valid for three months and allows you to jump on and off as you choose. Departures are on Thursday, Friday, Sunday and Monday from Darwin, and Saturday, Sunday, Tuesday and Wednesday from Katherine. The full round trip costs $170. Other options are Darwin to Katherine via Kakadu ($100), Katherine to Darwin via Litchfield ($90), a round trip from/to Darwin excluding Katherine ($140), and Jabiru to Katherine via Ubirr, Cooinda and Gunlom ($70). Prices do not include Kakadu National Park entrance fees.

Car

Off the beaten track, 'with care' is the thought to bear in mind, and all the usual precautions apply. You can get up-to-date

information on road conditions by phoning the Automobile Association of the NT (AANT) in Alice Springs (☎ 8953 1322) or in Darwin (☎ 8981 3837). It can also advise you on which roads require a 4WD year-round or just in the Wet.

Traffic may be fairly light, but watch out for the four great NT road hazards – speed (there are no speed limits on the open road), driver fatigue, road trains and animals. See the Car section in the introductory Getting Around chapter.

Hitching

Hitching is generally good, but once away from the main towns lifts can be few and far between. Three Ways, where the road to Mt Isa branches off to the Alice Springs road, is notorious for long waits for lifts. See the section on Hitching in the introductory Getting Around chapter.

Darwin & the Top End

DARWIN

● postcode 0800   ● pop 86,600

The capital of northern Australia comes as a surprise to many people. Instead of the hard-bitten, rough-and-ready town you might expect, Darwin is a lively, modern place with a young population, an easygoing lifestyle and a cosmopolitan atmosphere. However, despite the relative sophistication, Darwin is still something of a frontier town, with a fairly transient population.

From the traveller's point of view Darwin is a major stop. It's an obvious base for trips to Kakadu and other Top End natural attractions.

It's a bit of an oasis too – wherever you're travelling, there's a lot of distance to be covered, and having reached Darwin many people rest a bit before leaving.

History

It took a long time to decide on Darwin as the site for the region's centre, and even

NORTHERN TERRITORY

after the city was established growth was slow and troubled. Early attempts to settle the Top End were mainly due to British fears that the French or Dutch might get a foothold in Australia. Between 1824 and 1829 Fort Dundas on Melville Island and Fort Wellington on the Cobourg Peninsula, 200km north-east of Darwin, were settled and then abandoned. Fort Victoria, settled in 1838 on Cobourg's Port Essington harbour, survived a cyclone and an outbreak of malaria, but was abandoned in 1849.

In 1845 the explorer Leichhardt reached Port Essington overland from Brisbane, arousing prolonged interest in the Top End. The region came under the control of South Australia in 1863, and more ambitious development plans were made. A settlement was established in 1864 at Escape Cliffs on the mouth of the Adelaide River, not too far from Darwin's present location, but this was abandoned in 1866. Present-day Darwin was finally founded in 1869. The harbour had been discovered back in 1839 by John Lort Stokes aboard the *Beagle*, who named it Port Darwin after a former shipmate, the evolutionist Charles Darwin. At first the settlement was called Palmerston,

soon becoming unofficially known as Port Darwin, and in 1911 the name was officially changed.

Darwin's growth was accelerated by the discovery of gold at Pine Creek, about 200km south, in 1871. However, once the gold fever had run its course Darwin's development slowed down, owing to the harsh, unpredictable climate (including occasional cyclones) and poor communication with other Australian cities.

WWII put Darwin permanently on the map when the town became an important base for Allied action against the Japanese in the Pacific. The road south to the railhead at Alice Springs was surfaced, finally putting the city in direct contact with the rest of the country. Darwin was attacked 64 times during the war and 243 people lost their lives; it was the only place in Australia to suffer prolonged attack.

Modern Darwin has an important role as the door to Australia's northern region and as a centre for administration and mining.

Orientation

Darwin's centre is a fairly compact area at the end of a peninsula. The Stuart Hwy does

Darwin: Asian Gateway or Aussie Outpost?

While 20 years ago the common perception of Darwin from 'down south' was that it was a red-neck outpost, these days it is a vastly different place. The city is a melting pot of races, with anywhere between 45 and 60 ethnic groups represented, depending on whom you listen to. While some of them, such as the Vietnamese, are recent arrivals, many of the city's Asian residents are fourth generation Australians – and it's probably the only city in Australia to have had a Chinese lord mayor (two, in fact).

It comes as a surprise to many visitors that along with ethnic diversity comes a racial tolerance lacking elsewhere in Australia – there are no ethnic ghettos here – everyone just gets on with being a Territorian and what you are prepared to do seems to be far more important than where you've come from.

With such a strong Asian-oriented population and culture, it should come as no surprise that the city identifies strongly with Asia, at a time when the rest of the country is wringing its hands trying to work out exactly where – and even if – Australia fits in Asia.

With Australia looking increasingly to Asia for trade, business and tourism opportunities, Darwin sees itself as well placed to become Australia's main link with the region. To this end, major new port facilities are being developed and a railway to the south at last looks like getting off the drawing board. In the cultural sense Darwin is already an Asian gateway city; it may become so in reality when this new transport infrastructure is in place.

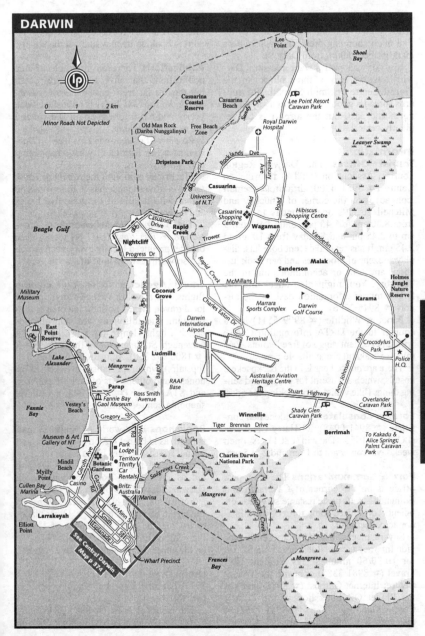

DARWIN

a big loop entering the city and finally heads south to end under the name Daly St. The main shopping area, Smith St and its mall, is about 500m from Daly St.

Most of what you'll want in central Darwin is within two or three blocks of the Transit Centre or Smith St mall. The suburbs spread a good 12 to 15km away to the north and east, but the airport is conveniently central.

Information

Tourist Offices The Darwin Region Tourism Association (DRTA) Information Centre (☎ 8981 4300, drtainfo@ozemail .com.au) is on the corner of Knuckey and Mitchell Sts. It's open Monday to Friday from 8.30 am to 5.45 pm, Saturday from 9 am to 2.45 pm and Sunday from 10 am to 2.45 pm. It has several decent booklets, displays dozens of brochures and can book just about any tour or accommodation in the Territory. You might also check out the DRTA tourist information desk at the airport (☎ 8945 3386).

Parks & Wildlife (☎ 8999 5511) has a counter in the DRTA Information Centre with an excellent range of free leaflets. Permits for Kakadu are available here.

There are notice boards in the backpackers hostels, which are useful for buying and selling things (like vehicles) or looking for rides.

Foreign Consulates The Indonesian consulate (☎ 8941 0048), 20 Harry Chan Ave (PO Box 1953, Darwin 0801), is open weekdays from 9 am to 1 pm and 2 to 5 pm.

Post & Communications The main post office is on the corner of Cavenagh and Edmunds Sts. Its poste restante service is efficient. You'll need some form of identification to collect mail.

Several places around the city centre provide Internet access. Rates are about $2/5/8 for 10/30/60 minutes. Try Student UNI Travel (☎ 8981 3388) opposite the Transit Centre; Internet Outpost (☎ 8981 0690) at the Planet OZ bookshop in the Transit Centre; Gondwana Tours (☎ 8941 7162) in the Transit Centre; and the NT Library

(☎ 8999 7177) in Parliament House, which offers 30 minutes free access but no email facility – book on the day and get there early.

Publications There are a couple of free publications that have some useful detail but they're far from comprehensive. *Darwin & the Top End Today* is published twice yearly and has information on Darwin and the surrounding area.

Possibly of more use is *This Week in Darwin*, as it has listings of what's happening on a weekly basis.

The Friday edition of the *Northern Territory News* newspaper has a *Your Weekend* liftout with details of theatres, live bands and cinemas.

The *Backpackers Information Guide – Northern Territory* (BIG-NT) is a free booklet produced locally every year, which is also worth getting hold of.

Travel Agencies To book or confirm flights, bus travel or virtually anything but local travel, there's no shortage of agents in Darwin. The following are centrally located: Flight Centre (☎ 8941 8002), 24 Cavenagh St; Jalan Jalan Tours & Travel (☎ 1800 802 250), Suite 35, 21 Cavenagh St (upstairs), which specialises in tickets to Indonesia and other parts of South-East Asia; and STA Travel (☎ 8941 2955), Galleria shopping centre, Smith St mall.

Bookshops Bookworld on Smith St mall is good, as is Planet OZ on Mitchell St next to the Transit Centre. For a large range of second-hand books as well as CDs and videos, Read Back Book Exchange is in Darwin Plaza off the Smith St mall.

For maps, the NT General Store on Cavenagh St has a good range. Other places to try include the Department of Lands, Planning & Environment's Maps NT shop on the corner of Bennett and Cavenagh Sts.

Useful Organisations The AANT (☎ 8981 3837) is in the MLC building on Smith St near the corner of Briggs St.

The National Trust (☎ 8981 2848) is at 52 Temira Crescent in Myilly Point. Pick up

Cyclone Tracy

The statistics of this disaster are frightening. Cyclone Tracy built up over Christmas Eve 1974 and by midnight the winds began to reach their full fury. At 3.05 am the airport's anemometer failed, just after it recorded a wind speed of 217km/h. It's thought the peak wind speeds were as high as 280km/h. Sixty-six lives were lost. Of Darwin's 11,200 houses, 50% to 60% were either totally destroyed or so badly damaged that repair was impossible, and only 400 survived relatively intact.

Much criticism was levelled at the design and construction of Darwin's houses, but plenty of places a century or more old, and built as solidly as you could ask for, also toppled before the awesome winds. The new and rebuilt houses have been cyclone-proofed with strong steel reinforcements and roofs that are firmly pinned down.

Most people say that next time a cyclone is forecast, they'll jump straight into their cars and head down the Track – and come back afterwards to find out if their houses really were cyclone-proof! Those who stay will probably take advantage of the official cyclone shelter.

a copy of its Darwin walking-tour leaflet (also available from the tourist office).

If you want to get involved in opposing the Jabiluka uranium mine or some other hot issue, the Environment Centre (☎ 8981 1984) is at 24 Cavenagh St. A noticeboard advises what's happening in the environmental arena.

Medical & Emergency Services The Federal Department of Health runs an International Vaccination Clinic (☎ 8981 7492) at 43 Cavenagh St. For emergency medical treatment phone the Royal Darwin Hospital on ☎ 8922 8888.

The Lifeline crisis line is ☎ 13 1114.

Dangers & Annoyances Don't swim in Darwin waters from October to May inclusive, when stingers are prevalent. Traps are

set for 'salties' (saltwater crocodiles) that venture into the harbour, but this doesn't mean they're all caught.

Town Centre

Despite its shaky beginnings and the destruction caused by WWII and Cyclone Tracy, Darwin still has a number of historic buildings. The National Trust produces an interesting booklet titled *A Walk through Historical Darwin*.

Old buildings include the **Victoria Hotel** on Smith St mall, originally built in 1894 and badly damaged by Tracy. On the corner of the mall and Bennett St, the stone **Commercial Bank** dates from 1884. The **old town hall**, a little further down Smith St, was built in 1883 but was virtually destroyed by Tracy, despite its solid Victorian construction. Today only its walls remain.

Across the road, **Brown's Mart**, a former mining exchange dating from 1885, was badly damaged but now houses a theatre. There's a **Chinese temple**, glossy and new, on the corner of Woods and Bennett Sts.

Christ Church Cathedral, on the Esplanade nearer the harbour, was also destroyed by the cyclone. It was originally built in 1902, but all that remained after Tracy was the porch, which had been added in 1944. A new cathedral has been built and the old porch retained.

The 1884 **police station** and **old courthouse** on the corner of Smith St and the Esplanade were badly damaged, but have been restored and are now used as government offices. A little further south along the Esplanade, **Government House**, built in stages from 1870, was known as the Residency until 1911, and has been damaged by just about every cyclone to hit Darwin. It is once again in fine condition.

Opposite Government House is a **monument** commemorating the submarine telegraph cable that once ran from Darwin to Banyuwangi in Java. This cable put Australia in instant communication with Britain for the first time.

Dominating the streetscape in this corner of the city is the garish **Parliament House**, opened in 1994 at a cost of $117 million. The interior is fortunately much more appealing and is worth a wander around. It also houses the excellent NT Library. The nearby **Supreme Court** building is chiefly of interest for the fine Aboriginal artwork on display inside.

Other buildings of interest along the Esplanade include **Admiralty House** on the corner of Knuckey St, and **Lyons Cottage**, across the road at 74 the Esplanade, which was the British-Australian Telegraph Residence. Today it is a museum housing displays on pre-1911 north Australian history. Entry is free, and it's open daily from 10 am to noon and 12.30 to 5 pm. Further along is the **Beaufort Darwin Centre**, housing a

luxury hotel, a couple of upmarket cafes and the **Darwin Entertainment Centre** (the latter on Mitchell St).

The Esplanade is fronted by the grassy expanse of **Bicentennial Park**, and a pleasant cliff-top pathway that runs along from Herbert to Daly Sts.

Aquascene

At Aquascene, Doctor's Gully, near the corner of Daly St and the Esplanade, fish come in for a feed every day at high tide. Half the stale bread in Darwin gets dispensed to a horde of milkfish, mullet, catfish and batfish. Some are quite big – the milkfish grow to

---

Darwin Walking Tour

First of all, Darwin's tropical climate doesn't lend itself to energetic exertions in the middle of the day, so this walk is most pleasant early in the morning or in the late afternoon.

The best place to start is the very heart of the city, the Smith St mall, with the historic Victoria Hotel towards its southern end. Heading south along Smith St brings you to the historic part of town with the **Old Town Hall**, the former mining exchange **(Brown's Mart)** and, on the corner of the Esplanade, the **former police station** and **courthouse**.

Turn right along the Esplanade at this corner and cross to the **Survivors' Lookout**, which is perched at the top of the cliff and has great views out over the harbour. The lookout has some interesting interpretive displays, complete with old WWII photos retelling some of the history of the Japanese bombing missions over Darwin.

If the heat's not getting to you, an interesting half-hour diversion from here is to descend the steps from the lookout, which take you down to Kitchener Drive at the base of the cliff and to the **WWII oil storage tunnels**.

Back on the Esplanade, continue along from the Survivors' Lookout and you'll soon come to **Government House** on the left, nestled in its immaculate tropical garden, and, on the right, the **Submarine Cable Monument** and the **Supreme Court** and **Parliament House** buildings. If you haven't yet visited Parliament House, this is a good opportunity to see the impressive interior and refresh with a drink from the Speaker's Corner Cafe, with great views out over the bay.

The Esplanade curves around Parliament House and then runs along the full length of the city centre, with the green expanse of **Bicentennial Park** on the left and a number of **historic buildings** (Hotel Darwin, Admiralty House and Lyons Cottage) on the right. In the park itself are a couple of monuments and one lookout over the bay, which gives great sunset viewing.

Once at the northern end of the park you can return to Smith St along Daly St, or follow a footpath which leads down to **Doctor's Gully**. This is really only worthwhile when it is fish feeding time at Aquascene, as there is little else to see here, although a signboard has some historic detail and old photos.

From Doctor's Gully a **boardwalk** leads up through a small patch of remnant vegetation, bringing you out on Mitchell St near the Banyan View Lodge, from where it's a only short walk back to the city centre.

over 1m and will demolish a whole slice of bread in one go. They take it right out of your hand – it's a great sight and children love it. Feeding times depend on the tides (call ☎ 8981 7837 for tide times). Entry is $4/2.50 for adults/children and the bread is free.

Botanic Gardens

The gardens' site north of the city centre was used to grow vegetables during the earliest days of Darwin. Tracy severely damaged the gardens, uprooting three-quarters of the plants. Fortunately, vegetation grows fast in Darwin's climate and the Botanic Gardens, with their noteworthy collection of tropical flora and the self-guided Aboriginal Plant Use walk, are well worth a look. There's a coastal section over the road, between Gilruth Ave and Fannie Bay. It's an easy bicycle ride to the gardens from the city centre.

Indo-Pacific Marine & Australian Pearling Exhibition

At the Wharf Precinct, this excellent aquarium is a successful attempt to display living coral and its associated life forms. Each small tank is a complete ecosystem, with only the occasional extra fish introduced as food for some of the carnivores such as stonefish or angler fish. It sometimes has box jellyfish, as well as more attractive creatures like sea horses, clown fish and butterfly fish. The living coral reef display is especially impressive.

Housed in the same building is the pearling exhibition, which details the history of the local pearling industry. The exhibition has excellent displays and informative videos.

The Indo-Pacific Marine is open daily from 9 am to 6 pm; entry costs $10 (children $4). Night shows, including a seafood buffet, are held on Wednesday, Friday and Sunday at 7.30 pm; these cost $45 ($22.50) and must be booked on ☎ 8981 1294. The pearling exhibition is open weekdays from 10 am to 5 pm (last entry 4.30 pm); admission costs $6/15 per adult/family.

Wharf Precinct

The Indo-Pacific Marine and Australian Pearling Exhibition are actually part of the Darwin Wharf Precinct, a tourist precinct which has turned what was basically the city's ugly old port facilities into something attractive.

Right at the outer end of the jetty is an old warehouse, now known as the Arcade, which houses a good food centre. The precinct also features the old oil-storage tunnels that were dug into the cliff face during WWII. The tunnels are open daily from 9 am to 5 pm during the Dry, and Tuesday to Sunday from 10 am to 2 pm during the Wet. Entry is $4.

Myilly Point Historic Precinct

At the northern end of Smith St is this small but important precinct of houses built in the 1930s. The buildings are elevated and feature asbestos-cement louvres and casement windows, so the ventilation could be regulated according to weather conditions. One building houses the National Trust office, while another is a gallery and cafe.

Museum & Art Gallery of the Northern Territory

This excellent museum and art gallery is on Conacher St at Fannie Bay, about 4km from the city centre. It's bright, well presented and not too big, but full of interesting displays. A highlight is the NT Aboriginal art collection. It's particularly strong on carvings and bark paintings from Bathurst and Melville islands and from Arnhem Land.

There's also a good collection on the art of the Pacific and nearby Asian nations, including Indonesian *ikat* (woven cloth) and gamelan instruments, and a sea gypsies' *prahu* (floating home) from Sabah in Malaysia.

Pride of place among the stuffed NT birds and animals undoubtedly goes to 'Sweetheart' – a 5m, 780kg saltwater crocodile, who became quite a Top End personality after numerous encounters with fishing dinghies on the Finniss River south of Darwin. Apparently he had a taste for outboard motors. He died when captured in 1979. You can also see a box jellyfish – safely dead – in a jar.

The museum has a good little bookshop and outside, but under cover, there is an

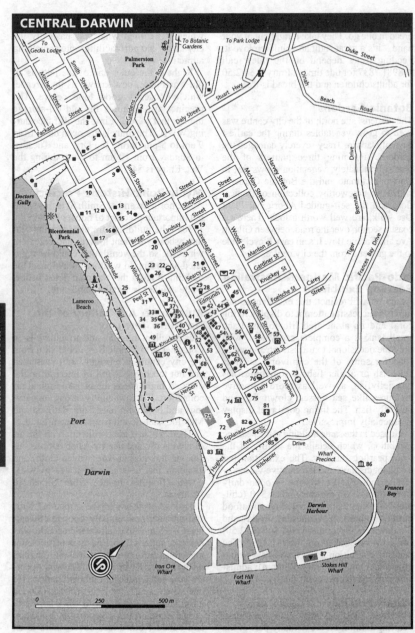

CENTRAL DARWIN

CENTRAL DARWIN

PLACES TO STAY
1 Alatai Holiday Apartments
2 Metro Inn
3 Asti Motel
5 Peninsula Apartment Hotel
6 Elke's Inner City Backpackers
7 Banyan View Lodge
10 Top End Hotel
11 Centra Darwin
12 Globetrotters Lodge
13 Fawlty Towers
17 Carlton Darwin
18 Frogshollow Backpackers
19 Mirrambeena Tourist Resort
25 Novotel Atrium
32 Melaleuca Lodge
33 Darwin City YHA
34 Holiday Inn
36 Chilli's Nomads
39 Value Inn
41 Darwin Central Hotel
58 Don Hotel
66 Rydges Plaza Darwin

PLACES TO EAT
4 Nirvana
23 Sizzler
29 Guiseppe's
31 Shenannigans
37 Rorke's Drift
38 Major's on Mitchell
40 Red Rooster
42 Swiss Cafe & Restaurant

44 Cafe Capri
46 Pancake Palace
56 Sugar Club
61 Hog's Breath Café
62 Rendezvous Cafe
65 Victoria Hotel & Arcade
67 Kitty O'Shea's Irish Bar & Cafe
68 Hanuman; Pente
87 The Arcade

OTHER
8 Aquascene
9 Hertz
14 Rent-a-Rocket
15 Nifty Rent-a-Car
16 Darwin Entertainment Centre
20 AANT
21 International Vaccination Clinic
22 McCafferty's
24 Leichhardt Memorial
26 Cinema
27 Main Post Office; Magic Wok
28 Time Nightclub; Squires Tavern
30 Night Market
35 Transit Centre
43 Supermarket
45 NT General Store
47 Paspalis Centrepoint; Singapore Airlines
48 Indigenous Creations

49 Lyons Cottage
50 Admiralty House
51 Darwin Regional Tourism Association Information Centre
52 Darwin Plaza
53 Galleria Shopping Centre
54 Ansett
55 Anthony Plaza
57 Rattle'n'Hum Nightclub
59 Chinese Temple
60 Garuda
63 Bookworld
64 Commercial Bank Building
69 Petty Sessions
70 Anzac Memorial
71 Parliament House
72 Telegraph Cable Monument
73 Supreme Court Building
74 Old Town Hall
75 Brown's Mart
76 City Bus Depot
77 Qantas
78 Maps NT
79 Indonesian Consulate
80 Deckchair Cinema
81 Christ Church Cathedral
82 Old Police Station; Courthouse
83 Government House
84 Survivors' Lookout
85 WWII Oil Storage Tunnels
86 Indo-Pacific Marine & Australian Pearling Exhibition

excellent maritime display with a number of vessels, including an old pearling lugger and a Vietnamese refugee boat.

Entry to the museum is free. It's open Monday to Friday from 9 am to 5 pm, and weekends from 10 am to 5 pm. Bus Nos 4 and 6 go close by, or you can get there on the Tour Tub (see Getting Around later in this section).

Fannie Bay Gaol Museum

Another interesting museum is a little further out of town on the corner of East Point Rd and Ross Smith Ave. This was Darwin's main jail from 1883 to 1979, after which a new maximum security lockup opened at Berrimah. You can wander round the old cells, see a gallows constructed for a hanging in 1952, and a minimum security section

used at various times for juvenile delinquents, lepers and Vietnamese refugees. The museum is open weekdays from 9 am to 5 pm and on weekends from 10 am to 5 pm; entry is free. Bus Nos 4 and 6 from the city centre go very close to the museum, and it's also on the Tour Tub route.

East Point Reserve

This spit of undeveloped land north of Fannie Bay is good to visit in the late afternoon when wallabies come out to feed, cool breezes spring up and you can watch the sunset across the bay. There are some walking and riding trails as well as a road to the tip of the point.

On the northern side of the point is a series of wartime gun emplacements and the **Military Museum**, devoted to Darwin's

WWII activities. It's open daily from 9.30 am to 5 pm (entry $8). Bus Nos 4 and 6 will take you 5km from the city centre to the corner of East Point Rd and Ross Smith Ave. From there it's 3km to the tip of the point, or you can take the Tour Tub.

Australian Aviation Heritage Centre

Darwin's aviation museum would be unspectacular were it not for the American B52 bomber. This truly mammoth aircraft, one of only two displayed outside the USA, dominates the other displays, which include the wreck of a Japanese Zero fighter shot down in 1942. The museum is on the Stuart Hwy in Winnellie, about 5km from the city centre. It is open daily from 9 am to 5 pm (entry $8). Bus Nos 5 and 8 run along the Stuart Hwy.

Crocodylus Park

This wildlife park in Berrimah showcases all things crocodilian. It is open daily from 9 am to 5 pm, with feeding at 10 am, noon and 2 pm (entry $15).

Activities

Beaches Darwin has plenty of beaches. Popular ones outside the stinger season include **Mindil** and **Vestey's** on Fannie Bay, **Casuarina** near the hospital and **Mandorah**, across the bay from the town (see the following Around Darwin section).

In north Darwin, there's a stinger net protecting part of **Nightcliff** beach off Casuarina Drive, and a stretch of the 7km Casuarina Beach further east is officially a nude beach. This is a good beach but at low tide it's a long walk to the water's edge.

Scuba Diving There are some opportunities for scuba diving in Darwin Harbour, largely thanks to the WWII wrecks that provide a habitat for a variety of marine life.

Cullen Bay DIVE! (☎ 8981 3049) at the Cullen Bay Marina takes divers out to wrecks in the harbour throughout the year. The cost is $54 for one dive, including equipment hire, which includes a protective suit to guard against stingers. It also does full open-water courses for $374.

Another company that does dives out of Darwin is Coral Divers (☎ 8981 2686) in Stuart Park.

Cycling Darwin has a network of excellent bicycle tracks. The main track runs from the northern end of Cavenagh St to Fannie Bay, Coconut Grove, Nightcliff and Casuarina. At Fannie Bay a side track heads out to the East Point Reserve. See Getting Around in this section for details of bicycle hire.

Abseiling & Rock-Climbing The Rock Climbing Gym (☎ 8941 0747), on Doctor's Gully Rd (near Aquascene), is open daily and charges $8 with no time limit. Harness and shoe hire is available.

Organised Tours

There are many tours in and around Darwin offered by a host of companies. The DRTA Information Centre on Mitchell St is the best place to find out what's available. Many tours go less frequently (if at all) in the Wet season. Some of the longer or more adventurous have only a few departures a year; inquire in advance if you're interested.

Aboriginal Cultural Tours If Darwin is your only chance to delve into Aboriginal culture, there are a few options. None of them is particularly cheap as they involve travel out of Darwin, usually by chartered plane. The four hour White Crane Dreaming tour, operated by Northern Gateway (☎ 8941 1394, oztravel@norgate.com.au), includes a 25 minute flight to the homelands of the Kuwuma Djudian people and a chance to sample bush tucker. The cost is $388 per person ($175 for children aged three to 12).

The Ngangikurrunggur people at Peppimenarti village south-west of Darwin host day tours operated by Peppi Tours (☎ 1800 811 633) at a cost of $314 fly in or $199 drive in. Tiwi Tours (☎ 8978 3904, tiwitours@ octa4.net.au) will fly you to Bathurst Island for the day, where you visit the Tiwi people, a *pukumani* burial site and a local craft outlet (see the Bathurst & Melville Islands section later for details on pukumani). The cost is $260/205 for adults/children.

City Sights Among the Darwin city tours, Darwin Day Tours' (☎ 8981 8696, larcdu@ ibm.net) five hour Sunset Tour takes in all the major attractions and finishes at sunset at East Point. The cost is $39/$27. Keetleys Tours (☎ 1800 807 868) does similar tours for $35/25.

The Tour Tub (☎ 8981 5233, nt4fish@ octa4.net.au) is an open sided minibus that tours the various Darwin sights throughout the day (see Getting Around in this section), and you can either stay on board and do a full circuit or get on and off at the various stops. The cost is $20/12.

The Darwin Road Runner Shuttle (☎ 8932 5577) is a similar service that allows 1½ hours at most of the sights and costs $18.

Harbour Cruises Darwin Hovercraft Tours (☎ 8981 6855) operates 1¼ hour, 35km hovercraft flights around the harbour from the Frances Bay Drive hoverport for $48/ 30, and these can be a lot of fun.

Tours Further Afield A number of operators do trips to the jumping crocodiles at Adelaide River and to the Territory Wildlife Park on the Cox Peninsula road. For Adelaide River try Adelaide River Queen Cruises (☎ 8988 8144), which does half-day trips at 7 am for $59/40 that include the two hour boat ride on the Adelaide River and a visit to Fogg Dam.

Darwin Day Tours (☎ 8981 8696, larcdu@ ibm.net) offers a variety of trips. A full-day Wildlife Spectacular Tour, which takes in the Territory Wildlife Park, Darwin Crocodile Farm, the Jumping Croc cruise and nearby Fogg Dam, costs $89/59. All prices include entry fees.

Lost Tours Wandering (☎ 8945 2962) has a full day, nature oriented tour that includes Fogg Dam, Adelaide River, Berry Springs, Howard Springs and sunset at Casuarina Beach for $60, including lunch and morning tea.

Special Events

Aside from the Beer Can Regatta in July/ August, with its sports and contests, there is the Festival of Darwin later in August. It's mainly an outdoor arts and culture festival that highlights Darwin's unique combination of large Asian and Aboriginal populations.

Darwinites are as fond of horse races as other Australians, and two big events at the Fannie Bay track are St Patrick's Day (17 March) and the Darwin Cup Carnival (July and August). The Royal Darwin Show takes place in July, and the Rodeo & Country Music Concert are in August.

Darwin is also the starting point for the Darwin to Ambon Yacht Race, which kicks off in July/August. The city is abuzz in the days leading up to it.

Places to Stay – Budget

Camping Camping grounds in Darwin tend to be a long way from the city centre, and some of the more conveniently situated caravan parks don't take tent campers.

Shady Glen Caravan Park (☎ 8984 3330), is 10km east of the city on the corner of Stuart Hwy and Farrell Crescent, Wimmellie. It offers cramped camping, old facilities and a minute pool. Camp sites are $16 ($19 with power) and on-site vans cost $46.

Lee Point, which is 15km north of the city, has the *Lee Point Resort* (☎ 8945 0535), a spacious park close to the beach. Facilities are excellent, although the shade trees are still a little small and the solar hot water doesn't last too long. Unpowered sites are $15 ($18 with power) and cabins with air-con, microwave and TV (but no kitchen or bathroom) cost $60.

Overlander Caravan Park (☎ 8984 3025, 1064 McMillans Rd, Berrimah) is 12km east of the city. Camp sites cost $10 ($15 powered). There are also basic cabins (no fan or air-con) that start at $86 a week.

Another out of town alternative is the *Palms Caravan Park* (☎ 8932 2891) 17km south-east of town on the Stuart Hwy at Palmerston. Camp sites are $16 ($18 with power), on-site vans are $40 and cabins start at $72.

Hostels – City Centre There's a host of choices in this bracket, most of which are on or near Mitchell St, a stone's throw from the Transit Centre. Most have a courtesy phone at the airport.

Competition is keen and standards are pretty high, so it's always worth asking about discounts for the first night (currently $2 at some hostels), for a weekly rate (usually seventh night free) if you plan to stay that long or if it's during the Wet when things are likely to be slack. The usual YHA/VIP and other discounts apply.

Facilities normally include communal kitchen and pool, but air-con is mostly only turned on at night. Free breakfasts are usually available.

Chilli's (*☎ 1800 351 313, 69A Mitchell St*) is part of the Nomads chain and is right next to the Transit Centre. There's no pool, but it has two outdoor spas, a breezy kitchen and meals area overlooking Mitchell St, a pool table and an air-con TV room. This is a well-run and clean place with very helpful staff. Dorms are $16, doubles are $44 and doubles with en suite are $46. Prices drop slightly during the Wet.

The *Darwin City YHA* (*☎ 8981 3995, 69 Mitchell St*) is at another part of the Transit Centre. It offers a pool, 24 hour reception, a games room, TV rooms and lockers for valuables. The choice includes four-bed dorms for $16 per person, doubles for $38 or $50 with en suite.

Fawlty Towers (*☎ 1800 068 886, 88 Mitchell St*) is a friendly place in one of the few surviving elevated tropical houses in the city centre. It has a shady backyard and swimming pool. A bed in a four-bed dorm costs $16, or there are doubles for $40.

Right across the road, *Globetrotters Lodge* (*☎ 1800 800 798, 97 Mitchell St*) is another popular place. All dorms have an attached bathroom and a fridge, and there's a pool, free breakfast, two kitchens, frequent barbecues and a very popular bar with cheap meals. A dormitory bunk is $16 in a four to seven-bed room. Doubles cost $44 with TV and en suite. Bike hire is available.

Across the road from the Transit Centre is the *Melaleuca Lodge* (*☎ 1800 623 543, 50 Mitchell St*), which boasts two pools, a good laundry and kitchen facilities, and free pancakes for breakfast. Dorm beds are $15

(in four to 10-bed rooms), or there are doubles with TV and fridge for $44 and triples for $50.

Frogshollow Backpackers (*☎ 1800 068 686, 27 Lindsay St*) is about 10 minutes walk from the Transit Centre. It's reasonably spacious, but cleanliness can be a problem and the staff less than helpful at times. There's a small swimming pool and spa in the garden. The charge is $16 a night in a four, eight or 12-bed dorm (air-con at night), and there are doubles with fridge and fan for $35 ($40 with air-con) and $44 with air-con and en suite.

Hostels – Elsewhere Outside the hustle, but still within walking distance of the action, there are a couple of budget choices north of Daly St. *Elke's Inner City Backpackers* (*☎ 1800 808 365, 112 Mitchell St*) is in a couple of renovated adjacent houses. There are a pool and spa between the two buildings, and it has much more of a garden feel to it than hostels right in the heart of the city. A bed in a four or six-bed dorm costs $17, or twins/doubles are $42/45.

Further out towards Mindil Beach is the *Gecko Lodge* (*☎ 1800 811 250, 146 Mitchell St*). This is a smaller hostel in an elevated house, with a pool, bike hire and free pancakes for breakfast. Dorm beds are $15, or singles/doubles cost $35/45. Reception is upstairs.

The big YWCA *Banyan View Lodge* (*☎ 1800 249 124, 119 Mitchell St*) takes women and men and has no curfew. Rooms have fans and fridges, and are clean and well kept; there are two TV lounges, a kitchen and an outdoor spa. The charge is $15 per person in a four-bed dorm with fridge, and singles/doubles cost $30/40 with fan or $32/45 with air-con. Weekly rates are also available.

Places to Stay – Mid-Range

Guesthouses Darwin has a number of good, small guesthouses, which can make a pleasant change from the hostel scene, especially if you're planning a longer stay.

Among those which aren't too far from the city centre is the friendly, quiet and airy *Park Lodge* (*☎ 8981 5692, 42 Coronation*

Drive) in Stuart Park, only a short cycle or bus ride from the centre. All rooms have fan, air-con and fridge; bathrooms, kitchen, sitting/TV room and laundry are communal. Singles/doubles cost $35/40, including a light breakfast. Numerous city buses, including Nos 5 and 8, run to this part of Darwin along the highway; get off near Territory Rent-a-Car.

Hotels Good value is the modern *Value Inn (☎ 8981 4733, kelly@downunder .net.au, 50 Mitchell St)*, opposite the Transit Centre. The rooms are comfortable but small, and have fridge, TV and bathroom. The price is $67 for up to three people.

The *Don Hotel (☎ 8981 5311, 12 Cavenagh St)* is also in the city centre; air-con rooms with TV and fans cost $63, including a light breakfast.

Apartments & Holiday Flats Prices in this range often vary between the Dry and the cheaper Wet. Many give discounts if you stay a week or more – usually of the seventh-night-free variety. Typically these places have air-con and swimming pools.

Good value and well located is the *Peninsular Apartment Hotel (☎ 1800 808 564, peninsularpts@octa4.net.au, 115 Smith St)*, just a short walk from the city centre. Studios have a double and a single bed, and cost $80 ($65 in the Wet), while the two-bedroom apartments accommodate four people and cost $130 ($95).

The *Alatai Holiday Apartments (☎ 1800 628 833, alatai@d130.aone.net.au)* are modern, self-contained apartments at the northern edge of the city centre on the corner of McMinn and Finniss Sts. Two-bed studio apartments cost $125 ($94 in the Wet), while two-bedroom apartments are $179 ($147). The resort has its own pool and an Asian restaurant.

Also in the city centre is the *Mirambeena Tourist Resort (☎ 1800 891 100, 64 Cavenagh St)*. This large place has 225 rooms, costing $114/124, and town houses that sleep up to four people for $199. It has a nice, tropical garden, complete with pool and spa, and a restaurant.

Motels Motels in Darwin tend to be expensive. Conveniently central is the *Asti Motel (☎ 1800 063 335, asti@octa4.net.au)* on the corner of Smith and Packard Sts, just a couple of blocks from the city centre. Rooms start at $90 ($68 in the Wet), and there are some four-bed family rooms for $105 ($89).

On the continuation of Cavenagh St beyond Daly St is the *Metro Inn (☎ 1800 891 128, midarwin@metroinns.com.au, 38 Gardens Rd)*. It's a comfortable, modern motel. Doubles cost $115; studio rooms with cooking facilities are $130 (these sleep three people). All rooms have bathroom, fridge and TV. There's also a pool, tennis court and a restaurant.

Places to Stay – Top End

Most of Darwin's upmarket hotels are on the Esplanade, making best use of the prime views across the bay. The modern *Carlton Darwin (☎ 1800 891 119, sales@carlton-darwin.com.au)* is part of the Darwin Entertainment Centre, and has rooms for $305; suites from $440.

Centra Darwin (☎ 8981 5388, 122 Esplanade) has singles/doubles for $138 ($119 in the Wet).

Close by is the *Novotel Atrium (☎ 8941 0755, h1478@accor-hotels.com.au)*, which does indeed have an atrium, complete with lush tropical plants, and rooms for $200 and up.

Also on the Esplanade is the *Holiday Inn (☎ 1800 681 686)*, with a range of choices: studios ($210), spacious hotel rooms ($195) or one/two/three-bedroom suites from $220/320/370.

One block back from the Esplanade, but still with fine views, is the city's only five star hotel, the *Rydges Plaza Darwin (☎ 8982 0000, 32 Mitchell St)*. It has all the facilities you'd expect, including some non-smoking floors. Rooms start at $265 for a single/double.

The latest addition to the scene is the *Darwin Central Hotel (☎ 8944 9000)* on the corner of Smith and Knuckey Sts. Doubles start at $215 ($166 in the Wet) and executive suites cost $239 ($189).

NORTHERN TERRITORY

Places to Eat

Dining out is not yet the obsession it has become in some other Australian cities, but Darwin's thriving tourist industry has spawned a rash of good and reasonably priced eateries. The standard is much better than virtually anywhere else in the Territory, so enjoy it while you're here.

A number of eateries around town, particularly pubs, offer discount meals for backpackers. Keep an eye out for vouchers at hostels.

Breakfast, Bakeries & Coffee All-night revellers and early starters can get a cooked breakfast at the 24 hour *Major's on Mitchell*, opposite the Transit Centre on Mitchell St.

The *Banyan Tree*, where the buses pull in at the rear of the Transit Centre, opens at 5.30 am and has cooked breakfasts as well as takeaways. *About Coffee*, also in the Transit Centre, opens at 10 am and has a good selection of breakfasts plus coffees. It sets up tables on the footpath on Mitchell St.

Salvatore's, on the corner of Knuckey and Smith Sts, opens early and has good Italian-style coffee.

For fresh bread and pastries there's the *My Linn* Vietnamese bakery at the Transit Centre, which opens early. In Anthony Plaza off the Smith St mall, *Le Pierrot* French bakehouse has quiche and vol-au-vents.

Budget & Takeaway There are a number of cheap eateries at the Transit Centre on Mitchell St, in the thick of all the backpackers hostels. Most are hole-in-the-wall outlets, but there are sheltered tables and stools out the back; the choice includes Mexican, Japanese, Chinese, Thai and vegetarian.

Coyote's Cantina (☎ 8941 3676) is an authentic Mexican place that's extremely popular with travellers and has a reputation that spans the country; there's both a hole in the wall and a sit-down restaurant upstairs (bookings essential on weekends).

The Mental Lentil is also popular and has very good vegetarian fare, including lentil burgers for $5.50, vegetable curry or dhal for $7, and lassis and fruit smoothies.

It would be hard to beat the meal deals at *Globetrotters Lodge* (97 Mitchell St) – $3.50 for nachos or lasagne, $4 for fish and chips, and $5 for a T-bone steak!

Rumpoles, in the Supreme Court building, is a good lunch-time cafe serving coffee, gourmet sandwiches and cakes.

Sizzler, on Mitchell St, is also popular, with queues out onto the footpath some nights. The reason is that it's very good value: for around $15 you can fill your plate from a wide range of dishes and have a dessert too. At lunch you can fill your plate several times over for as little as $5.90.

The city centre is also takeaway heaven, with outlets of *Red Rooster*, *KFC*, *McDonald's*, *Pizza Hut* and others.

Pubs Several watering holes along Mitchell St – two of them Irish – offer decent food at reasonable prices. *Shenannigans*, next to the YHA hostel, is Darwin's original Irish pub and offers traditional fare such as Irish stew. *Kitty O'Shea's Irish Bar & Café*, opposite the Darwin Plaza Hotel, is newer and roomier, and has similar dishes.

Rorke's Drift (46 Mitchell St) has good tucker for breakfast, lunch and dinner. Popular choices include huge serves of fish and chips for $10, and freshly baked pies, such as steak and stout or turkey and wild mushroom, for $7.50.

Restaurants The *Pancake Palace* (☎ 8981 5307) on Cavenagh St near Knuckey St is open daily for lunch and in the evening until 1 am. Conveniently close to many of Darwin's night spots, it has sweet and savoury pancakes from $8, as well as meaty offerings such as buffalo and barramundi crepes for around $15.

For something different you could try the *Swiss Cafe & Restaurant* (☎ 8981 5079), tucked away in the Harry Chan Arcade off Smith St. It serves good, solid European food, including popular favourites such as fondue, and is reasonably priced with main dishes for around $12 to $15.

Pente (☎ 8941 1444, 26 Mitchell St) is a relatively new place with a high standard; mains from $15.50 for pasta to $22.50 for barramundi; good pizzas from a wood-fired oven start at $12.

Meat eaters recommend the *Hog's Breath Cafe* (☎ 8941 3333), right opposite the Vic in the Smith St mall (see Entertainment later in this section). This popular American-style grill prides itself on its 18-hour tenderised rib steaks. There's also a wide range of burgers.

The licensed *Cafe Capri* (☎ 8981 0010, 37 Knuckey St) has a Mediterranean ambience and a good range of meat and pasta standards, plus burgers, bagels and kebabs. Pasta dishes are $10 to $13 and steaks around $18.

The *Sugar Club* (☎ 8981 9887, 21 Cavenagh St) is a cafe and bar with a pleasant, friendly ambience, and stays open till late nightly. It serves imaginative dishes, such as Mediterranean vegetables with curried lentil and mint couscous, as well as standard pasta and other mains ($15 to $20).

Guiseppe's (☎ 8941 3110, 64 Smith St) is a well established place that serves seafood as well as pasta ($14 to $16), pizza ($8 to $16) and other Italian standards.

Asian There are plenty of Asian eateries, although few stand out at the budget price end and others are decidedly expensive. One cheap exception is the excellent *Rendezvous Cafe* in the Star Village Arcade off the Smith St mall, a no-frills place with Thai and Malay food – the laksa has a legendary reputation. Darwin's best range of cheap Asian fare is at the Mindil Beach Market, though it's open only during the Dry (see Elsewhere in this section).

The *Hanuman* (☎ 8941 3500, 28 Mitchell St) is an award-winning, mainly Thai restaurant, although the menu includes some Indian and Malay dishes. It ain't cheap – expect to pay around $17 for a main course.

Another good choice is *Nirvana* (☎ 8981 2025), at the top end of Smith St past Daly St, which is open nightly for dinner only. It offers a good range of Thai, Malay and Indian standards – main courses are $15 to $17, but half serves are available so you can sample more dishes. This place also has live music (see Entertainment later in this section).

For Chinese, *The Magic Wok* (☎ 8981 3332), next to the main post office on Cavenagh St, offers a self-serve which you hand to the chef for cooking. It's $12.90 for one serve, $16.90 for all you can eat at lunchtime and $26 per person at dinner. It's not cheap, but it's good, fresh fare and a favourite among locals.

The more expensive hotels all have at least one major restaurant, and some of these can be fine places to eat – at fine dining prices.

Self-Catering There's a grotty Woolworth's *supermarket* on the corner of Smith and Knuckey Sts that's open daily. If you're heading out to Kakadu or Litchfield and have your own transport there's a better Woolie's at Palmerston on the way.

Elsewhere At the bustling *Mindil Beach Market* food stalls are set up on Thursday night from May to October and, to a lesser extent, Sunday night from June to September. Big crowds begin arriving from 5.30 pm with tables, chairs, rugs, grog and kids to settle under the coconut palms for sunset and decide which of the tantalising foodstall aromas has the greatest allure. It's difficult to know whether to choose Thai, Sri Lankan, Indian, Chinese, Malay, Brazilian, Greek or Portuguese – or something else. All prices are reasonable, at around $3 to $6 a serve. There are cake stalls, fruit-salad bars, arts and crafts stalls, and sometimes entertainment from a band or street theatre. Mindil Beach is about 2km from the city centre, off Gilruth Ave. Bus Nos 4 and 6 go past the market area.

Further along Fannie Bay the licensed *Cornucopia* at the Museum & Art Gallery has a good reputation. You can sit outside under the fans on the verandah close to the sea, or inside with the air-conditioning. It's open daily from 9 am until late.

Entertainment

Darwin is a lively city, with bands at several venues and a number of clubs and discos. More sophisticated tastes are also catered for, with theatre, film, concerts and a casino.

Your Weekend is a liftout in the Friday edition of the *NT News* that lists live music and other attractions. It's probably the best source of information on what's on around town.

Bars & Live Music You won't have to wander far down Mitchell St to find some form of distraction and it's as good a place as any to start.

Starting from the top, on the corner of Daly St there are two bars side by side, part of the Top End Hotel complex. The *Sportsmen's Bar* is a 'blokey' kind of place, with poker machines, TAB and televised sport. *Blah Blah Bar* next door has pool tables, pizzas and good bar food, plus a DJ from Wednesday to Saturday; it stays open till 4 am.

Backpackers are catered for at *Globetrotters Lodge (97 Mitchell St)*, where the bar features happy hours and there are fun nights such as karaoke. Another popular choice is *Rattle'n'Hum* on Cavenagh St, which has barbecue evenings, theme nights and happy hours. Both places have a good earthy atmosphere and stay open late nightly.

Shenannigans and *Kitty O'Shea's* are two pleasant Irish-style pubs on Mitchell St that serve Guinness and other delights; on Monday night there's an acoustic music session at Shenannigans to which all are welcome.

The decor at *Rorke's Drift*, also on Mitchell St, features memorabilia of the Zulu War and even a scale model of the famous engagement. It's a good, English-style pub with a beer garden that gets really jumping on Friday night.

Past Daly St on Smith St there's *Nirvana*, a good eatery (see Places to Eat earlier) that hosts live jazz/blues nightly. Entry is free and it's open until about 2 am, but you must eat as you drink; bar snacks are available at reasonable prices.

Live bands play upstairs at the *Victoria Hotel* (known simply as 'The Vic') from 9 pm Wednesday to Saturday, but it's also a good place for a drink in the early evening. Live music can also be heard on weekends at the *Billabong Bar* in the Novotel Atrium and at *Squires Tavern* on Edmunds St, which has a popular beer garden.

The *Jabiru Bar* in the Novotel Atrium is the venue on Friday evening for Crab Races. It's all very light hearted and there are prizes for the winners.

An All-Australian Game

The Alice and Darwin casinos offer plenty of opportunities to watch the Australian gambling mania in full flight. You can also observe a part of Australia's true cultural heritage, the all-Australian game of two-up.

The essential idea of two-up is to toss two coins and obtain two heads. The players stand around a circular playing area and bet on whether the coins will show either two heads or two tails when they fall. The 'spinner' uses a 'kip' to toss the coins and the house pays out and takes in as the coins fall – except that nothing happens on 'odd' tosses (one head, one tail) unless they're thrown five times in a row. In this case you lose unless you have also bet on this possibility.

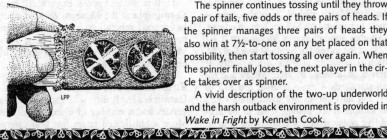

The spinner continues tossing until they throw a pair of tails, five odds or three pairs of heads. If the spinner manages three pairs of heads they also win at 7½-to-one on any bet placed on that possibility, then start tossing all over again. When the spinner finally loses, the next player in the circle takes over as spinner.

A vivid description of the two-up underworld and the harsh outback environment is provided in *Wake in Fright* by Kenneth Cook.

Nightclubs Next to Squires Tavern on Edmunds St is the *Time Nightclub*. It's probably the most popular nightspot in the city and claims to be Darwin's only dance club. It's open Monday, and Thursday to Saturday from 10 pm until 4 am.

Petty Sessions on the corner of Mitchell and Bennett Sts is a combination wine bar and nightclub. It's quite a popular place and stays open until 2 am. Another late night venue is *Caesars* nightclub at the Don Hotel on Cavenagh St.

Folk Music For something a bit more laid back there's the *Top End Folk Club* (☎ 8988 1301), which meets on the 2nd and 4th Friday of the month at the Rock, Doctors Gully. Visitors are welcome.

Also check what's on at *Shenannigans* and *Kitty O'Shea's* on Mitchell St for a bit of Guinness and reeling.

Jazz & Classical Music On Sunday afternoon during the Dry season there's *Jazz on the Lawns* at the MGM Grand Darwin casino. Entry is free, and food and alcohol are available. It's a pleasant way to watch the sunset.

The *Darwin Symphony Orchestra (DSO)* holds concerts of popular favourites periodically at the Darwin Entertainment Centre and other venues; check with the DRTA Information Centre for what's coming up.

Cinema The *Darwin Film Society* (☎ 8981 2215) has regular showings of offbeat/art house films at the Museum Theatrette, Conacher St, Bullocky Point. During the dry season the society runs the *Deckchair Cinema* (☎ 8981 0700) near Stokes Hill Wharf. Here you can watch a movie under the stars while reclining in a deckchair – there is usually sandfly and mosquito repellent on hand if you've forgotten to bring your own. Screenings are listed in the newspapers, or on flyers around town.

There's a commercial *cinema complex* on Mitchell St showing the latest releases, and *cinemas* at the Casuarina shopping square and in Palmerston.

Going for a Thong

Barefoot movie patrons are no longer turned away from Darwin's Cinema Centre, as the ticket counter sells rubber thongs, which are almost the Darwin equivalent of formal footwear!

Previously, due to health and safety reasons, movie patrons turning up at the cinema barefoot were refused entry. Sales are currently running at about half a dozen pairs of thongs per week.

Theatre The *Darwin Entertainment Centre* on Mitchell St houses the Playhouse and Studio Theatres, and hosts events from fashion award nights to plays, rock operas, pantomimes and concerts. Bookings and 24 hour information are available on ☎ 8981 1222.

The *Darwin Theatre Company* (☎ 8981 8424) often has play readings and other performances around the city.

The old *Brown's Mart* (☎ 8981 5522) on Harry Chan Ave is another venue for live theatre performances.

Casino Finally, there's the *MGM Grand Darwin* casino on Mindil Beach off Gilruth Ave – as long as you're 'properly dressed'. That means no thongs, and men wearing shorts will have to conform to the bizarre Aussie predilection for long socks!

Shopping

The city centre has a good range of outlets selling a range of art and crafts from the Top End – such as bark paintings from western Arnhem Land, and interesting carvings by the Tiwi people of Bathurst and Melville islands – and work from further afield in central Australia. Prices are generally very reasonable and if you have the bucks some very fine pieces are available. Taste and try – there's plenty to choose from.

Two long-established shops on Knuckey St are Raintree Aboriginal Fine Arts (☎ 8941 9933), at No 20, and Wadeye Arts & Crafts Gallery, at No 31.

Aboriginal Fine Arts, above Red Rooster on the corner of Mitchell and Knuckey Sts, has some very fine pieces, as does the excellent Framed, a gallery at 55 Stuart Hwy in Stuart Park near the entrance to the Botanic Gardens. Both are worth a browse just for pleasure, even if you can't afford the price tags.

Indigenous Creations is a chain with several outlets in Darwin; the one at the Transit Centre is called Cultural Images and there are two shops in the Smith St mall. Cultural Images offers didgeridoo lessons for $25 to $30 – inquire at the shop for details.

On Cavenagh St there's the Arnhemland Art Gallery (☎ 8981 9622), which has some fine bark paintings.

You can find Balinese and Indian clothing at Mindil Beach market (Thursday and Sunday evening – see Places to Eat). There's a Night Market on the corner of Mitchell St, open nightly from 5 to 11 pm, where you can buy T-shirts, didgeridoos and sarongs for every occasion.

Getting There & Away

Air Darwin is becoming increasingly busy as an international and domestic gateway.

International A popular international route is to/from Indonesia with Garuda, the Indonesian airline.

Garuda Indonesia (☎ 1300 365 331), Ansett (☎ 8982 3666) and Qantas (☎ 8982 3316) fly Darwin-Bali; Royal Brunei Airlines (☎ 8941 0966) flies twice a week between Darwin and Bandar Seri Begawan; and Malaysia Airlines (☎ 13 26 27) has twice-weekly flights to Kuala Lumpur.

Domestic Ansett and Qantas fly direct to Adelaide, Alice Springs, Brisbane, Broome, Kununurra and Sydney, but the number of flights is limited and there is very little discounting as it's not a heavy traffic route.

On a more local level, Airnorth (☎ 1800 627 474) flies daily to Katherine ($144), and Monday to Saturday to Tennant Creek ($319) and Alice Springs ($389); see the relevant sections in this chapter for details

of flights to various smaller settlements in the Top End.

Bus You can reach Darwin by bus on three routes – the Western Australian route from Broome, Derby, Port Hedland and Kununurra; the Queensland route through Mt Isa to Three Ways and up the Track; or straight up the Track from Alice Springs. Greyhound Pioneer has daily services on all these routes; McCafferty's doesn't operate services in Western Australia. On Queensland services you often have to change buses at Three Ways or Tennant Creek, and at Mt Isa. All buses stop at Katherine.

Fares can vary a bit among companies, but if one discounts a fare the others tend to follow suit quite quickly. Travel times are very similar, but beware of services that schedule long waits for connections in Tennant Creek or Mt Isa. Examples of fares include: around $101 one way to Darwin from Tennant Creek (13 hours), $176 from Mt Isa (21 hours), $374 from Brisbane (47 hours), $102 from Kununurra (12 hours), $145 from Alice Springs (20 hours), $202 from Broome (27 hours) and $436 from Perth (58 hours). In Darwin, Greyhound Pioneer (☎ 13 2030) operates from the Transit Centre at 69 Mitchell St; McCafferty's (☎ 13 1499) has its depot close by on the corner of Peel and Smith Sts.

The Blue Banana backpackers bus service (☎ 8945 6800) does a regular circuit from Darwin to Katherine, via Kakadu and Litchfield and a few other stops. It picks you up at your accommodation and discounts are available for YHA/VIP card holders. Darwin to Katherine via Kakadu costs $100; a return trip via Kakadu and Litchfield costs $170; a return trip to Darwin excluding Katherine is $140.

Car Darwin has numerous budget car-rental operators, as well as all the major national and international companies.

Avis
　(☎ 1800 672 099) 145 Stuart Hwy, Stuart Park
Britz:Australia
　(☎ 8981 2081) Stuart Hwy, Stuart Park
Budget
　(☎ 8981 9800) 69 Mitchell St

Mt Sonder at sunrise, West MacDonnell Ranges National Park, NT

RICHARD I'ANSON

On the main road through the West MacDonnell Ranges, central Australia, NT

JOHN HAY

Trephina Gorge, Eastern MacDonnell Ranges, NT

Nourlangie and Anbanbang Billabong, Kakadu National Park, NT

Balancing act at the Devil's Marbles Conservation Reserve, NT

Delta

(☎ 13 1390) Corner of Cavenagh and McLachlan Sts

Hertz

(☎ 8941 0944) Corner of Smith and Daly Sts

Nifty Rent-a-Car

(☎ 8981 2999) 86 Mitchell St

Territory Thrifty Car Rental

(☎ 8924 0000) 64 Stuart Hwy, Parap

For driving around Darwin, conventional vehicles are cheap enough, but most companies offer only 100km free and charge about 25c per additional kilometre; around Darwin 100km won't get you very far. Some companies offer 150km free, but you may be restricted to a 70km radius of the city. The prices invariably drop for longer rentals for both conventional and 4WD vehicles.

Nifty Rent-a-Car is about the cheapest, starting at $25 per day; Delta is another budget option with cars from $39, but these cheap deals don't include any free kilometres.

Territory Thrifty Car Rental is by far the biggest local operator and is probably the best value. Discount deals to look for include cheaper rates for four or more days' hire, weekend specials (three days for roughly the price of two) and one way hires (to Jabiru, Katherine or Alice Springs). Daily charges start at around $55 for a small car.

There are also plenty of 4WD vehicles available in Darwin, but you usually have to book ahead, and fees and deposits can be hefty. Larger companies offer one way rentals plus better mileage deals for more expensive vehicles.

The best place to start looking is probably Territory Thrifty, which has several different models. The cheapest, a Suzuki four-seater, costs $99 a day, plus 28c per kilometre over 100km. Territory also has camping equipment packages costing $25 per vehicle per day.

Britz:Australia has the largest range of 4WD campervans from around $130 per day with unlimited kilometres. Backpacker Campervans (☎ 1800 670 232) and Australian Camper Rentals (☎ 1800 808 365) both have budget-priced campervans with cooking facilities from $65 per day including unlimited kilometres – its 4WD campers start at $100 per day.

Most rental companies have agents in the city centre. Avis, Budget, Hertz and Territory Thrifty all have offices at the airport.

Getting Around

To/From the Airport Darwin's busy airport is only about 6km from the city centre. The taxi fare into the centre is about $15.

There is an airport shuttle bus (☎ 1800 358 945) for $6/10 one way/return, which will pick up or drop off almost anywhere in the city centre. When leaving Darwin book a day before departure.

Bus Darwin has a fairly good city bus service that operates from the small terminal (☎ 8924 7666) on Harry Chan Ave, near the corner with Smith St. Buses enter the city along Mitchell St and leave along Cavenagh St.

Fares are on a zone system – shorter trips are $1.20 or $1.60, and the longest cost $2.10. Bus No 4 (to Fannie Bay, Nightcliff, Rapid Creek and Casuarina) and No 6 (Fannie Bay, Parap and Stuart Park) are useful for getting to Aquascene, the Botanic Gardens, Mindil Beach, the Museum & Art Gallery, Fannie Bay Gaol Museum and East Point. Bus Nos 5 and 8 go up the Stuart Hwy past the airport to Berrimah, from where No 5 goes north to Casuarina and No 8 continues along the highway to Palmerston.

The Tour Tub (☎ 8981 5233) does a circuit of the city, calling at the major places of interest, and you can hop on or off anywhere. In the city centre it leaves from Knuckey St, at the end of the Smith St mall. The set fare is $20 for the day, and the buses operate hourly from 9 am to 4 pm. Sites visited include Aquascene (only at fish-feeding times), Indo-Pacific Marine and the wharf precinct, the MGM Grand Darwin casino, the Museum & Art Gallery, the Military Museum, Fannie Bay Gaol, Parap markets (Saturday only) and the Botanic Gardens.

A similar service operated by Galaxy Tours and Charters costs $18 per day, and also visits Crocodylus Park and Casuarina shopping centre.

The 24 hour Darwin City Shuttle service (☎ 8985 3666) will take you anywhere within 4km of the central business district (CBD) for a flat fare of $2.

Bicycle Darwin has a fairly extensive network of bike tracks. It's a pleasant ride to the Botanic Gardens, Fannie Bay, East Point or even, if you're feeling fit, all the way to Nightcliff and Casuarina. Many of the backpackers hostels have bicycles; the usual charge is $15 per day or $3 per hour.

AROUND DARWIN

All the places listed here are within a couple of hours travel from the city.

Howard Springs Nature Park

The springs, with crocodile-free swimming, are 35km east of the city. Turn left 24km down the Stuart Hwy, beyond Palmerston. The swimming hole, which is surrounded by forest, can get uncomfortably crowded because it's so convenient to the city. Nevertheless, on a quiet day it's a pleasant spot for an excursion and there are short walking tracks and lots of bird life.

Places to Stay The *Howard Springs Caravan Park* (☎ 8983 1169) on Whitewood Rd has unpowered ($12) and powered ($17) caravan sites only.

Arnhem Highway

The Arnhem Hwy branches off towards Kakadu 33km south of Darwin. After 10km along this road you come to the small town of **Humpty Doo**.

About 15km beyond Humpty Doo is the turn-off to **Fogg Dam Conservation Reserve**, a great place for watching water birds. Another 8km along the Arnhem Hwy is **Adelaide River Crossing**, where you can take a 1½ hour river cruise and see saltwater crocodiles jump for bits of meat held out on the end of poles. These trips cost $26 ($15 children) and depart at 9 and 11 am and 1 and 3 pm from May to August, and at 9 and 11 am and 2.30 pm from September to April. The whole thing is a bit of a circus really, but it's fun to see crocs

doing something other than sunning themselves on a river bank.

The **Window on the Wetlands** is a modern visitors centre atop Beatrice Hill, by the Arnhem Hwy just a few kilometres past the Fogg Dam turn-off. It's the headquarters for the proposed **Mary River National Park**, which encompasses important Mary River wetlands. The centre has some excellent 'touchy-feely' displays that give some great detail on the wetland ecosystem, as well as on the history of the local Aboriginal people and European pastoral activity. There are also great views out over the Mary River system. The centre is open daily from 7.30 am to 7.30 pm. Bush tucker sampling sessions are held twice a week during the Dry – check at Parks & Wildlife (see Tourist Offices in the previous Darwin section).

Mary River Crossing, 47km further on, is popular for barramundi fishing and camping. A reserve here includes lagoons that are a dry-season home for water birds, and granite outcrops that shelter wallabies.

The *Bark Hut Inn* (☎ 8978 8988), 2km beyond Mary River Crossing at **Annaburroo**, is another pleasant place for a halt. There's accommodation here but it's no great shakes. Camping costs $4 per person, or $14 for two with power, or there's basic accommodation at $22/35 for singles/doubles.

The turn-off to Cooinda (in Kakadu) is 19km beyond the Bark Hut. This is an unsealed road (known as the Old Jim Jim Rd), often impassable in the Wet; it's easier to continue along the sealed highway. The entrance to Kakadu National Park is 19km further along the highway.

There are Greyhound Pioneer and Blue Banana bus services along the Arnhem Hwy (see the Kakadu National Park Getting There & Around section later).

Mary River Wetlands

The Mary River wetlands, which extend north and south of the Arnhem Hwy, are scheduled to become part of the Mary River National Park. For the moment they consist of a number of reserves, including Mary River Crossing Reserve, Wildman River Reserve, Shady Camp, Mary River

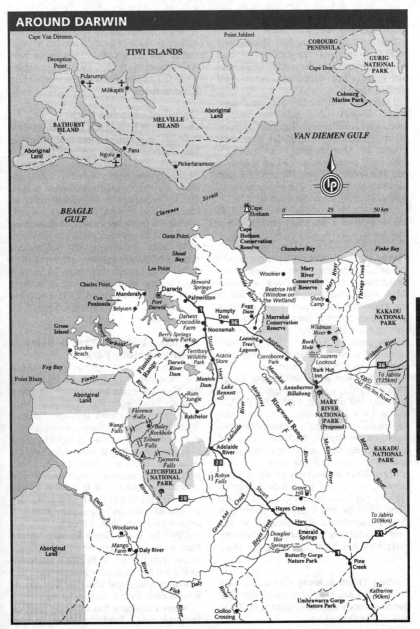

Conservation Reserve, Stuart's Tree Historical Reserve and Swim Creek.

This area offers excellent fishing and wildlife spotting opportunities, and because there is not much in the way of infrastructure it is far less visited than nearby, and similar, Kakadu.

There are a couple of private concessions within the park, which offer both accommodation (see Places to Stay) and trips on the river. From the Point Stuart Wilderness Lodge, 2½-hour wetland tours cost $25, with daily departures at 9.30 am and 4.30 pm. The Wildman River Wilderness Lodge runs two-hour river trips from North Rockhole daily at 9.30 am and 4 pm for $25.

Shady Camp Boat Hire (☎ 8978 8937) has self-drive 3.7m boats for $65/95 a half/full day.

Places to Stay There are basic camp sites at North Rockhole and Shady Camp. At the *Point Stuart Wilderness Lodge (☎ 8978 8914, nttours@adventuretours.com.au)*, a few kilometres off the main track, there are good grassy camping areas and a swimming pool. It costs $8 to camp, or there are dormitory beds for $20, and four-bed self-contained units from $85 for singles or doubles plus $20 per extra person.

The *Wildman River Wilderness Lodge (☎ 8978 8912, wildman.lodge@octa4.net .au)*, also off the main track, charges $76 and up for a double room, or $150 including meals. The lodge is beautifully positioned on the edge of the flood plains and has good facilities, including a swimming pool and a licensed dining room.

Mary River Houseboats (☎ 8978 8925) has a variety of vessels, including dinghies ($65/95 per half/full day), and six-berth (from $380 for two days) and eight-berth ($470) houseboats. The turn-off to the houseboat berth is 12km east of Corroboree Park, then it's 20km further to the Mary River.

Getting There & Away Access is via the Point Stuart Road, an often rough dirt road that heads north off the Arnhem Hwy 22km east of Annaburroo.

As the popularity of this area increases, so does the number of tour operators accessing the park. Already a number of companies operating out of Darwin, such as AKT Holidays (☎ 1800 891 121), combine a trip to Kakadu with a detour to the Mary River wetlands.

Darwin Crocodile Farm

On the Stuart Hwy, just a little south of the Arnhem Hwy turn-off, this crocodile farm has around 8000 saltwater and freshwater crocodiles. This is the residence of many of the crocodiles taken out of NT waters because they've become a hazard to people. But don't imagine they're here out of human charity. This is a farm, not a rest home, and around 200 of the beasts are killed each year for their skins and meat – you can find crocodile steaks or even crocodile burgers in a number of Darwin eateries.

The farm is open daily from 10 am to 4 pm. Feedings are the most spectacular times to visit and these occur daily at 2 pm, and on weekends at noon. Entry is $9.50/5 for adults/children.

Territory Wildlife Park & Berry Springs Nature Park

The turn-off to Berry Springs is 48km down the Track from Darwin, then it's 10km along the Cox Peninsula road to the Territory Wildlife Park. Set on 400 hectares of bushland this wildlife park (run by Parks & Wildlife) has some excellent exhibits featuring a wide variety of Australian birds, mammals, reptiles and fish, some of which are quite rare. There is a reptile house, superb walk-through aquarium, nocturnal house, aviaries and nature trails. It's well worth the entry fee ($12/6) and you'll need half a day to see it all. The park is open daily from 8.30 am to 4 pm (gates close at 6 pm).

Close by is the **Berry Springs Nature Park**, a great place for a swim and a picnic. There you'll find a thermal waterfall, spring-fed pools ringed with paperbarks and pandanus palms, and abundant bird life. It is open daily from 8 am to 6.30 pm.

A few kilometres further along the Cox Peninsula road is **Tumbling Waters**, another

Top End Crocs

There are two types of crocodile in Australia – the freshwater or 'freshie' (*Crocodylus johnstoni*) and the saltwater or 'saltie' (*C. porosus*) – and both are found in the northern part of the country, including the NT. After a century of being hunted, crocodiles are now protected in the NT – freshies since 1964 and salties since 1971.

The smaller freshwater crocodile is endemic to Australia and is found in freshwater rivers and billabongs, while the larger saltwater crocodile, found throughout South-East Asia and parts of the Indian subcontinent, can be found in or near almost any body of water, fresh or salt. Freshwater crocodiles, which have narrower snouts and rarely exceed 3m in length, are harmless to people unless provoked, but saltwater crocodiles, which can grow to 7m and more, can definitely be dangerous.

KATE NOLAN
Freshwater 'croc'

Ask locally before swimming or even paddling in any rivers or billabongs in the Top End – attacks on humans by salties happen more often than you might think. Warning signs are posted alongside many dangerous stretches of water. The beasts are apparently partial to dogs, and even from some distance can be attracted by the sound of dogs barking.

Crocodiles have become a major tourist attraction (eating the odd tourist certainly helps in this respect) and the NT is very big on crocodile humour. Darwin's shops have a plentiful supply of crocodile T-shirts and other paraphernalia.

KATE NOLAN
Saltwater 'croc'

good picnic and camping area, although there's no swimming due to the presence of salties. The road continues all the way to **Mandorah**, the last 30km or so being dirt. If you want to go directly to Mandorah, it's much easier to catch the ferry from Darwin!

Litchfield National Park

This 650 sq km national park, 140km south of Darwin, encompasses much of the Tabletop Range, a wide sandstone plateau mostly surrounded by cliffs. Four waterfalls, which drop off the edge of this plateau, and their surrounding rainforest patches are the park's main attractions. It's well worth a visit, although it's best to avoid weekends as Litchfield is a very popular day-trip destination for locals.

There are two routes to Litchfield Park, both about a two hour drive from Darwin. One, from the north, involves turning south off the Berry Springs-Cox Peninsula road; the second approach is from Batchelor into the east of the park. The two access roads join up so it's possible to do a loop from the Stuart Hwy.

Scrub typhus is spread by a tiny mite that lives in long grass and several cases – including one recent death – have been associated with Litchfield National Park. The danger is small, but cover up your legs and feet if you are going to walk in this habitat (most visitors won't encounter the problem). If you fall ill after a visit to the park, advise your doctor that you have been to Litchfield.

NORTHERN TERRITORY

If you enter the park from Batchelor it is 18km from the park boundary to the **Florence Falls** turn-off. The waterfalls lie 5km off the road along a good track. This is an excellent swimming hole in the dry season, as is **Buley Rockhole** a few kilometres away, where you can camp.

Eighteen kilometres beyond the turn-off to Florence Falls is the turn-off to **Tolmer Falls**, which are a 400m walk off the road. The 1.5km walking track here gives you some excellent views of the area.

It's a further 7km along the main road to the turn-off for the most popular attraction in Litchfield – **Wangi Falls** (pronounced 'wong-gye'), 2km along a side road. The falls flow year-round and fill a beautiful swimming hole. There are also extensive picnic and camping areas. From Wangi it's about 16km to the rangers' station near the park's northern access point.

Bush camping is also allowed at the pretty **Tjaynera (Sandy Creek) Falls**, in a rainforest valley in the south of the park (4WD access only). There are several other 4WD tracks in the park, and plenty of bushwalking possibilities.

As usual in the Top End, it's easier to reach and get around the park from May to October.

River Cruises About 4km north of the Wangi turn-off you can take a cruise on the Reynolds River or a scenic chopper flight over the park. A three hour cruise costs $20/8 for adults/children and helicopter flights are $55/45 for 15 minutes.

Visitors can take a cruise on McKeddies Billabong, an extension of the Reynolds River, for $20/10 – book at the Wangi kiosk.

Organised Tours There are plenty of companies offering trips to Litchfield from Darwin. Most day tours cost about $95, which normally includes a pick-up from your accommodation, guided tour of various sights, at least one swim, morning tea and lunch, and a billabong cruise. Readers have recommended Coo-ee Tours (☎ 8981 6116) and Goanna Eco Tours (☎ 8927 3880).

If you have energy to burn, Track'n Trek Adventures (☎ 1800 355 766) does a two day trip that includes mountain biking through certain sectors for $169.

KAKADU NATIONAL PARK

Kakadu National Park is one of the natural marvels not just of the NT, but of Australia. The longer you stay, the more rewarding it is.

Kakadu stretches more than 200km south from the coast and 100km from east to west, with the main entrance 153km east of Darwin, along a bitumen road. It encompasses a variety of superb landscapes, swarms with wildlife and has some of Australia's best Aboriginal rock art. It is on the World Heritage List for both its natural and cultural importance (a rare distinction), but this listing may be downgraded following the opening (in 1999) of a second uranium mine in the park.

The name Kakadu comes from Gagadju, a local Aboriginal language, and much of Kakadu is Aboriginal land, leased to the government for use as a national park. There are several Aboriginal settlements in the park and about one-third of the park rangers are Aboriginal people. Enclosed by the park, but not part of it, are a few tracts of land designated for other purposes – principally uranium-mining leases in the north-east.

Some of the southern areas are subject to a land claim under the Native Title Act by the Jawoyn people of the Katherine region. Should the claim be successful, the land will be leased back to Parks Australia North for continued use as a national park.

Geography & Vegetation

A straight line on the map separates Kakadu from the Arnhem Land Aboriginal land, which you can't enter without a permit. The circuitous Arnhem Land escarpment, a dramatic 100 to 200m-high sandstone cliff line that forms the natural boundary of the rugged Arnhem Land plateau, winds some 500km through eastern and south-eastern Kakadu.

Creeks cut across the rocky plateau and tumble off the escarpment as thundering waterfalls in the wet season. They then flow across the lowlands to swamp the vast flood plains of Kakadu, turning the north of the park into a kind of huge, vegetated lake. From west to east the rivers are the Wildman, the West Alligator, the South Alligator and the East Alligator. Such is the difference between dry and wet seasons that areas on river flood plains that are perfectly dry underfoot in September will be under 3m of water a few months later. As the waters recede in the Dry, some loops of wet-season watercourses become cut off, but don't dry up. These are billabongs, which are often carpeted with water lilies and act as a magnet for water birds.

The coastline has long stretches of mangrove swamp, important for halting erosion and as a breeding ground for marine and bird life. The southern part of the park is dry lowlands with open grassland and eucalypts. Pockets of monsoon rainforest crop up here, as in most of the park's other landscapes.

In all, Kakadu has over 1000 plant species, a number of which are still used by the local Aboriginal people for food, as well as for medicinal and other practical purposes.

Climate

The great change between the Dry and the Wet makes a big difference to visitors to Kakadu. Not only is the landscape transformed, but Kakadu's lesser roads often become impassable in the Wet, cutting off some highlights, such as Jim Jim Falls. The Aboriginal people recognise six seasons in the annual cycle.

The 'build-up' to the Wet (known as Gunumeleng) starts in October. Humidity increases, the temperature rises (to 35°C or more) and mosquitoes, always plentiful near water, proliferate to near-plague proportions. By November the thunderstorms have started, billabongs start to be replenished and the water birds disperse.

The Wet proper (Gudjuek) continues through January, February and March, with violent thunderstorms and an abundance of plant and animal life thriving in the hot, moist conditions. Around 1300mm of rain falls in Kakadu, most of it during this period.

Banggereng, in April, is the season when storms (known as 'knock 'em down' storms) flatten the spear grass, which during the course of the Wet has shot up to 2m in height.

Yekke, from May to mid-June, is the season of mists, when the air starts to dry out. It is quite a good time to visit – there aren't too many other visitors, the wetlands and waterfalls still have a lot of water, and most of the tracks are open.

The most comfortable time weatherwise is the late Dry, in July and August – Wurrgeng and Gurrung. This is when wildlife and birds are plentiful and they congregate around the shrinking billabongs and watercourses, but it's also when most tourists come to the park.

Wildlife

Kakadu has about 25 species of frog, 60 types of mammal, 51 freshwater fish species, 120 types of reptile, 280 bird species (one-third of all those native to Australia) and at least 10,000 kinds of insect. There are frequent additions to the list, and a few of the rarer species are unique to the park. Kakadu's wetlands are on the UN list of Wetlands of International Importance, principally because of their crucial significance to so many types of water bird.

You'll see only a tiny fraction of these creatures in a visit to the park since many are shy, nocturnal or few in number. Take advantage of talks and walks led by park rangers – mainly in the Dry – to get to know and see more of the wildlife. Cruises of South Alligator River and Yellow Water Billabong enable you to see the water life.

Reptiles Both Twin Falls and Jim Jim Falls have resident freshwater crocodiles, which are considered harmless, while there are plenty of the dangerous saltwater variety in the park. You're sure to see a few if you take a South Alligator or Yellow Water cruise.

Kakadu's other reptiles include lizards, such as the frilled lizard, and five freshwater turtle species, of which the most common is the northern snake-necked turtle. There are many snakes, including three highly poisonous species, but you're unlikely to see any.

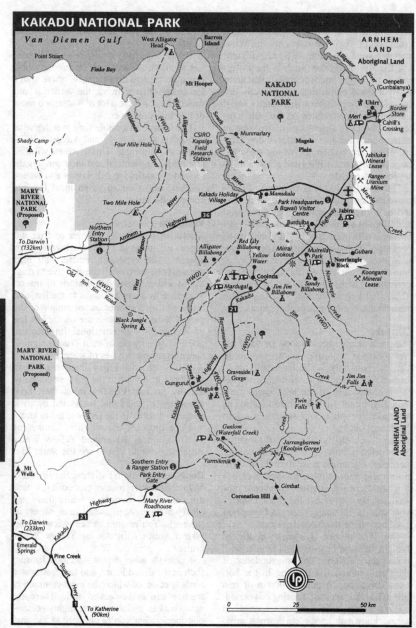

KAKADU NATIONAL PARK

Oenpelli pythons, probably unique to the Kakadu escarpment, were only discovered by science in 1977.

Birds Kakadu's abundant water birds, and their beautiful wetland setting, make a memorable sight. The park is one of the chief refuges in Australia for several species, among them the magpie goose, green pygmy goose and Burdekin duck.

Other fine water birds include pelicans, darters and the Jabiru stork, with its distinctive red legs and long, straight beak.

Herons, egrets, ibis and cormorants are common. You're quite likely to see rainbow bee-eaters and kingfishers (of which there are six types in inland Kakadu). Majestic white-breasted sea eagles are often seen near inland waterways too, and wedge-tailed eagles, whistling kites and black kites are common. At night you might hear barking owls calling – they sound just like dogs. The red-tailed black cockatoos are spectacular; you may also catch sight of brolgas and bustards.

Mammals Several types of kangaroo and wallaby inhabit the park, and the shy black wallaroo is more or less unique to Kakadu. You might be lucky enough to see a sugar glider in wooded areas in the daytime. Kakadu is home to 26 bat species and is a key refuge for four endangered varieties.

Fish You can't miss the silver barramundi, which creates a distinctive swirl near the water surface. It can grow to well over a metre in length and changes its sex from male to female at the age of five or six years.

Mining

In 1953 uranium was discovered in the region. Twelve small deposits in the southern reaches of the park were worked in the 1960s but were abandoned following the 1962 promulgation of the Woolwonga Aboriginal Reserve as a nature reserve.

In 1970 three huge deposits, Ranger, Nabarlek and Koongarra, were found, followed by Jabiluka in 1973. The Nabarlek deposit (in Arnhem Land) was mined in the late 1970s and the Ranger Uranium Mine started producing ore in 1981. Most of the Aboriginal people of the area were against the mining of uranium on traditional land, but were enticed with the double lure of land title and royalties.

The Jabiluka mine was the scene of widespread protest and sit-in demonstrations during the 1998 dry season. Things came to a head when a UN delegation inspected the mine site to assess whether the damage it was causing would endanger Kakadu's World Heritage listing. The delegation found that Jabiluka could degrade Kakadu's pristine environment – a decision that shook the Federal Government and is currently the subject of an appeal.

Aboriginal Art

Kakadu is an important repository of rock-art collections. There are over 5000 sites, which date from 20,000 years to 10 years ago. Two of the finest collections are the galleries at Ubirr and Nourlangie.

The paintings have been classified into three roughly defined periods: Pre-estuarine, which is from the earliest paintings up to around 6000 years ago; Estuarine, which covers the period from 6000 to around 2000 years ago, when the valleys flooded due to the rising sea levels caused by the melting polar ice caps; and Freshwater, from 2000 years ago until the present.

For the local Aboriginal people the rock-art sites are a major source of traditional knowledge, representing their historical archives, given that they have no written language. The youngest paintings, some executed as recently as the 1980s, connect the local community with the artists, while the older paintings are believed by many Aboriginal people to have been painted by spirit people and depict stories that connect the people with creation legends and the development of Aboriginal law.

The majority of rock-art sites open to the public are relatively recent, and some visitors feel somewhat cheated when they learn that the paintings were only done in the 1960s. Many people are also surprised to learn that the old paintings they are seeing have actually been touched up by Aboriginal people quite recently. In fact this was not uncommon, although the repainting could only be done by a specific person who had knowledge of the story being depicted. What also comes as a surprise to many people is the way the paintings in a particular site are often layered, with newer paintings being placed right over the top of older ones.

The conservation of the Kakadu rock-art sites is a major part of the park management task. As the paintings are all done with natural, water-soluble ochres, they are very susceptible to water damage from drip lines running across the rock. To prevent this sort of damage small ridges of clear silicon rubber have been made on the rocks above the paintings, so the water flowing down the rock is diverted to either side, or actually drips right off. Buffaloes also damaged the lower paintings as they loved to rub against the walls of the rock shelters. The dust raised by hundreds of tourists tramping past these sites on a daily basis didn't help either. Today most of the accessible sites have boardwalks that not only keep the dust down but also keep people at a suitable distance from the paintings.

Orientation

From where the Arnhem Hwy to Kakadu turns east off the Stuart Hwy, it's 121km to the park entrance and another 105km to Jabiru. The road is sealed all the way. The Kakadu Hwy (also sealed) to Nourlangie, Cooinda and Pine Creek turns south off the Arnhem Hwy shortly before Jabiru.

Eight kilometres east of South Alligator on the Arnhem Hwy, a short side road to the south leads to Mamukala, with views over the South Alligator flood plain, an observation building, bird-watching hides and a 3km walking trail.

From Mamukala it's 29km to the turn-off to one of the major sites in the park, Ubirr, 36km away in the northern part of the park near the East Alligator River. This road also gives access to Oenpelli, Arnhem Land and the Cobourg Peninsula, but note that a permit is needed to enter Arnhem Land (apply at the Northern Land Council office in Jabiru).

Information

The excellent Bowali Visitor Centre (☎ 8938 1121), on the Kakadu Hwy a few kilometres south of the Arnhem Hwy turn-off, is open daily from 8 am to 5 pm. Here you'll find informative and interesting displays, including a few to keep the kids happy: a theatrette showing a 25 minute audiovisual presentation on the park (screened on the hour), a cafe, a gift shop, and an excellent resource centre with a comprehensive selection of reference books. Another dozen or so videos featuring various documentaries made about Kakadu in the last few years are shown throughout the day (on the half-hour).

The Warradjan Aboriginal Cultural Centre near Cooinda gives an excellent insight into the culture of the park's traditional owners. The building itself is circular, symbolic of the way Aboriginal people sit in a circle when meeting or talking. The shape is also reminiscent of the *warradjan* (pig-nosed turtle), hence the name of the centre.

Unleaded and diesel fuel is available at Frontier Kakadu Village, Border Store, Jabiru and Cooinda. Jabiru also has a supermarket, post office and a Westpac bank. The Northern Land Council office here issues permits on the spot for the highly recommended trip to the excellent Injalak arts and crafts outlet in Oenpelli, a half-hour trip into Arnhem Land across the East Alligator River (see the Arnhem Land section later in this chapter).

Entry Fees Entry to the park is $15 (children under 16 free). This entitles you to stay in the park for 14 days. The fee is payable at the park gates as you enter.

A 'Territorian Ticket' ($60) covers one vehicle and all its occupants, as well as camping fees at the Mardugal, Muirella Park, Merl and Gunlom camping grounds. It's a good option if you plan to visit the park several times – and will get you into Uluru-Kata Tjuta as well – but it is available only to Australian residents and can't be used for a rented vehicle.

Ubirr

This spectacular rock-art site lies 39km north of the Arnhem Hwy. The turn-off to

Ubirr is 100km from the park entrance. The road is sealed but there are several creek crossings which make it impassable for conventional vehicles for most of the wet season – sometimes for 4WDs too. The rock-art site is open daily from 8.30 am until sunset between May and November, and 2 pm to sunset the rest of the year.

Shortly before Ubirr you pass the Border Store. Nearby are a couple of **walking trails** close to the East Alligator River, which forms the eastern boundary of the park here. There is a backpackers hostel and camp site (see Places to Stay in this section for details) nearby. Aboriginal-guided **Guluyambi River trips** are held on the East Alligator River here. The tours leave daily from the upstream boat ramp at 9 and 11 am and 1 and 3 pm, and last just under two hours. Entry is $25 for adults and $11 for children aged four to 14. A free shuttle bus runs between the boat ramp and the Border Store and Merl camping ground. During the Wet, Guluyambi operates half-day tours, leaving from Jabiru at 8 am and 12 pm daily. This tour includes a boat transfer across the picturesque Magela Creek and a bus drive on to Ubirr. The tour provides the only means for visitors to get to Ubirr when it is at its best. For information and bookings phone ☎ 1800 089 113.

A path from the Ubirr car park takes you through the main galleries to a lookout with superb views – a 1.5km return trip. There are paintings on numerous rocks along the path, but the highlight is the main gallery with a large array of well-executed and preserved x-ray-style wallabies, possums, goannas, tortoises and fish, plus a couple of *balanda* (white men) with hands on hips. Also of major interest is the Rainbow Serpent painting, and the picture of the Namarkan sisters, shown with string pulled taut between their hands.

The Ubirr paintings are in many different styles. They were painted over a period spanning 20,000 years ago to the 20th century.

Jabiru
- postcode 0886   - pop 1700

The township, originally built to accommodate Ranger Uranium Mine workers,

The Rainbow Serpent

The story of the Rainbow Serpent is common in Aboriginal tradition across Australia, although the story varies from place to place. In Kakadu the serpent is a woman, Kurangali, who painted her image on the rock wall at Ubirr, while on a journey through this area. This journey forms a creation path which links the places she visited: Ubirr, Manngarre, the East Alligator River and various places in Arnhem Land.

To the traditional owners of the park, Kurangali is the most powerful spirit. Although she spends most of her time resting in billabongs, if disturbed she can be very destructive, causing floods and earthquakes. One local story has it that she even eats people.

has shops and a public swimming pool. Six kilometres east is Jabiru airport and the Ranger Uranium Mine. There are minibus tours of the mine ($15) available three times a day through Kakadu Parklink (☎ 1800 089 113).

Nourlangie
The sight of this looming, mysterious, isolated outlier of the Arnhem Land escarpment makes it easy to understand why it has been important to Aboriginal people for so long. Its long, red, sandstone bulk – striped in places with orange, white and black – slopes up from surrounding woodland to fall away at one end in sheer, stepped cliffs, at the foot of which is Kakadu's best known collection of rock art.

The name Nourlangie is a corruption of *nawulandja*, an Aboriginal word that refers to an area bigger than the rock itself. The Aboriginal name of the rock is Burrunggui. You reach it at the end of a 12km sealed road that turns east off the Kakadu Hwy, 21km south of the Arnhem Hwy.

Other interesting spots nearby make it worth spending a whole day in this corner of Kakadu. The last few kilometres of the road are closed daily from around 5 pm.

From the main car park a circuit of about 2km takes you first to the **Anbangbang rock shelter**, which was used for 20,000 years as a refuge from heat, rain and frequent wet-season thunderstorms. From the gallery you can walk onto a lookout from where you can see the distant Arnhem Land cliff line, which includes Lightning Dreaming (Namarrgon Djadjam), the home of Namarrgon. There's a 12km marked trail the way round the rock; the Bowali Visitor Centre has a leaflet.

Heading back towards the highway you can take turn-offs to three other places of interest. The first, on the left about 1km from the main car park, takes you to **Anbangbang billabong**, with its picnic site and dense carpet of lilies. The second, also on the left, leads to a short walk up to **Nawulandja lookout** with good views back over Nourlangie Rock. The third turn-off, a dirt track on the right, takes you to another outstanding, although little visited, rock-art gallery, **Nanguluwur**.

A further 6km along this road, plus a 3km walk, is **Gubara (Baroalba Springs)**, an area of shaded pools in monsoon forest.

Jim Jim Falls & Twin Falls

These two spectacular waterfalls are along a 4WD dry-season track that turns south off the Kakadu Hwy between the Nourlangie and Cooinda turn-offs. It's about 60km to Jim Jim Falls (the last 1km on foot) and 70km to Twin Falls, where the last few hundred metres are through the water up a snaking, forested gorge – great fun on an inflatable air bed.

Jim Jim – a sheer 215m drop – is awesome after the rains, but its waters can shrink to nothing at the end of the Dry. Twin Falls doesn't dry up.

Note that the track to Jim Jim and Twin Falls is often still closed in late May and even into June.

Yellow Water & Cooinda

The turn-off to the Cooinda accommodation complex and the superb Yellow Water wetlands, with their large population of water birds, is 47km down the Kakadu Hwy from its junction with the Arnhem Hwy. It's then 4.5km to the Warradjan Aboriginal Cultural Centre (see Information earlier in this section), a further 1km to the Yellow Water wetland turn-off, and about another 1km again to Cooinda.

The boat trips on Yellow Water Billabong go six times daily (May through November) for two hours, and cost $30/17 for adults/children. This trip is one of the highlights of most people's visit to Kakadu. Early morning is the best time to go as the birds are most active. You're likely to see a saltwater crocodile or two. It's usually advisable to book your cruise the day before at Cooinda (☎ 8979 0111), particularly for the early departure.

Yellow Water is also an excellent place to watch the sunset, particularly in the Dry, when the smoke from the many bushfires that burn in the Top End at this time of year turns bright red in the setting sun. Bring plenty of insect repellent as the mosquitoes are voracious.

Cooinda to Pine Creek

Just south of the Yellow Water and Cooinda turn-off, the Kakadu Hwy heads south-west for 161km to Pine Creek, out of the park on the Stuart Hwy. On the way there is a turn-off to the very scenic falls and plunge pool at **Gunlom (Waterfall Creek)**, which featured in *Crocodile Dundee*. It's 37km along a good dirt road.

Walking

Kakadu is excellent but tough bushwalking country. Many people will be satisfied with the marked trails, which range from 1km to 12km long. For the more adventurous there are infinite walking possibilities, especially in the drier south and east of the park, but take great care and prepare well. Tell people where you're going and don't walk alone. You need a permit from the Bowali Visitor Centre (see Information in this section) to camp outside the established camp sites.

The Darwin Bushwalking Club (☎ 8985 1484) welcomes visitors and may be able to help with information. It has walks most weekends, often in Kakadu. Alternatively, you could join a Willis's Walkabouts guided bushwalk (see Organised Tours in this section).

Kakadu by Foot is a helpful guide to the marked walking trails in Kakadu. It is published by PAN ($1.95) and usually available from the Bowali Visitor Centre, although it can be in short supply.

Scenic Flights

Kakadu Air (☎ 1800 089 113) does a number of flights over Kakadu. A flight from Jabiru costs $65 for half an hour or $110 for an hour.

North Australian Helicopters (☎ 8972 1666) operates half-hour helicopter rides at $125 per person.

Organised Tours

There are hosts of tours to Kakadu from Darwin and a few that start inside the park. Two-day tours typically take in Jim Jim Falls, Nourlangie and the Yellow Water cruise, and cost from $220. Popular companies include Gondwana (☎ 1800 242 177) and Wilderness 4WD Adventures (☎ 1800 808 288, wildadv@downunder.net.au); you will certainly get a memorable trip and value for money with both outfits. Other operators that cater for younger travellers include Billy Can Tours (☎ 1800 813 484, billycan@ozemail.net.au), Hunter Safaris (☎ 1800 670 640, hunter.safaris@octa4 .net.au) and Backpacking Australia Tours (☎ 8945 2988).

Longer tours usually cover most of the main sights plus a couple of extras. Some combine Kakadu with Katherine Gorge. One of the most popular is the Blue Banana (☎ 8945 6800), which charges $150 for transport only and allows you to get on and off anywhere between Darwin and Katherine as often as you like for three months.

You can take 10-hour 4WD tours to Jim Jim and Twin falls from Jabiru or Cooinda ($120 during the Dry) with Kakadu Gorge & Waterfall Tours (☎ 8979 0111) or Lord of Kakadu Tours (☎ 8979 2567).

Willis's Walkabouts (☎ 8985 2134) are bushwalks guided by knowledgeable Top End walkers, following your own or preset routes of two days or more. Many of the walks are inside Kakadu. Prices vary, but $900 for a two week trip, including evening meals and return transport from Darwin, is fairly typical.

Into Arnhem Land A couple of outfits offer trips into Arnhem Land from Kakadu, although they only nip across the East Alligator River to Oenpelli. Aboriginal-owned Magela Cultural Heritage Tours (☎ 8979 2422) runs one-day tours from Jabiru for $150/100 for adults/children and Lord of Kakadu Tours (☎ 8979 2567) does a four hour fly/drive combo for $120.

Places to Stay & Eat

Prices for accommodation in Kakadu can vary tremendously depending on the season – prices during the Dry (given here) can be as much as 50% more than prices during the Wet.

Camping Some sites are run by the national parks. Others (with power) are attached to the resorts: *All Seasons Frontier Kakadu Village (☎ 8979 0166)*, South Alligator, costs $20/15 for two with/without power; *Gagadju Lodge Cooinda (☎ 8979 0145)* charges $11/9; and *Frontier Kakadu Lodge (☎ 8979 2422)*, Jabiru, charges $20/15.

A turn-off to the north, 20km into the park along the Arnhem Hwy, leads to camp sites at Two Mile Hole (8km) and Four Mile Hole (38km) on the Wildman River, which is popular for fishing. The track is not suitable for conventional vehicles except in the Dry, and then only as far as Two Mile Hole.

About 35km further east along the highway, a turn-off to the south, again impassable to conventional vehicles in the Wet, leads to camp sites at Red Lily (35km) and Alligator billabongs (39km), and on to the Old Jim Jim Road (69km).

The South Alligator River Crossing, with its popular boat ramp and picnic area, is 8km further along the highway, about 3km past the Frontier Kakadu Village.

The three main national parks camp sites are: *Merl*, near the Border Store; *Muirella Park*, 6km off the Kakadu Hwy a few kilometres south of the Nourlangie turn-off; and *Mardugal*, just off the Kakadu Hwy 1.5km south of the Cooinda turn-off. Only the Mardugal site is open during the Wet. The camp sites have hot showers, flushing toilets and drinking water, and the fee is $5 per person (collected on the site).

The national parks provide more basic camp sites in Kakadu, and at these there is no fee. To camp anywhere else you need a permit from the Bowali Information Centre.

South Alligator Just a couple of kilometres west of the South Alligator River on the Arnhem Hwy is the *All Seasons Frontier Kakadu Village* (☎ 8979 0166, fvillage@ allseasons.com.au). Sites in the grassed camping ground cost from $15, or $20 with power, and resort-style singles or doubles cost $176 ($139 in the Wet). The hotel has a restaurant and a basic shop (open from 7 am to 8 pm), as well as a swimming pool, restaurant and bar.

Jabiru The *Gagadju Crocodile Hotel* (☎ 1800 808 123) is probably most famous for its design – it's set out in the shape of a crocodile, although this is really only apparent from the air. There's nothing very exotic about the hotel itself, although it is comfortable enough. Prices start at $167 for a double.

The *All Seasons Frontier Kakadu Lodge* (☎ 8979 2422, flodge@allseasons.com.au) has four-bed rooms at $25 per person, or $100 for a whole room, and self-contained cabins for $179 ($132) plus tax. The only cooking facilities are a few barbecues, but the poolside bistro serves reasonable pub-style meals for around $14.

There's a cafe in the shopping centre and a bakery near the fire station.

Ubirr The basic *Hostel Kakadu* (☎ 8979 2232) behind the Border Store is the only place in Kakadu that offers budget accommodation (twin-share) and decent facilities. The budget accommodation at the resort hotels is a bit of an afterthought and there's not much in the way of cooking facilities. The hostel is open year-round (as long as

the road remains open) and costs $15 per person. There's a well equipped kitchen, lounge room and swimming pool. The Border Store has supplies and snack food, and is open daily during the Dry until 8 pm.

Cooinda This is by far the most popular place to stay, mainly because of the proximity of the Yellow Water wetlands and the early morning boat cruises. It gets mighty crowded at times, mainly with camping tours. The *Gagadju Lodge Cooinda* (☎ 8979 0145) has some comfortable units for $132, single or double, and much cheaper, more basic air-con 'budget rooms' – which are just transportable huts of the type found on many building sites, more commonly known in the Territory as 'demountables' or 'dongas'. For $25 per person they are quite adequate, if a little cramped (two beds per room). The only cooking facilities are barbecues.

The bistro here serves unexciting and overpriced barbecue meals, which you cook, at around $15, or there's the more expensive *Mimi Restaurant* if you want waiter service and a la carte.

Getting There & Around

Ideally, take your own 4WD. The Arnhem and Kakadu Hwys are both sealed all the way. Sealed roads lead from the Kakadu Hwy to Nourlangie, the Muirella Park camping area and to Ubirr. Other roads are mostly dirt and blocked for varying periods during the Wet and early Dry.

Greyhound Pioneer (☎ 13 2030) runs daily buses from Darwin to Cooinda via Jabiru. The buses stop at the Yellow Water wetland in time for the 1 pm cruise, and wait there for 1½ hours until the cruises finish. The buses leave Darwin at 6.30 am and Jabiru at 9.55 am, and arrive at Cooinda at 12.10 pm. Coming back they leave Cooinda at 2.30 pm and Jabiru at 4.20 pm, arriving in Darwin at 7 pm. The cost is $65, Darwin to Cooinda, including two stopovers.

Blue Banana The Blue Banana bus (☎ 8945 6800) runs to Kakadu, stopping at South Alligator, Jabiru, the Border Store/Ubirr,

Nourlangie Rock, Cooinda and Gunlom. You can alight at any or all of these stops.

The fare from Darwin to Kakadu and back via Litchfield is $140; Jabiru-Katherine via Ubirr, Cooinda and Gunlom is $70, and Darwin-Katherine via Kakadu is $100. A ticket is valid for three months.

BATHURST & MELVILLE ISLANDS

These two large, flat islands about 80km north of Darwin are the home of the Tiwi Aboriginal people. You need a permit to visit, and the only realistic option is to take a tour. Tiwi Tours (☎ 1800 183 630, tiwitours@octa4.net.au), a company which employs many Tiwi among its staff, is the main operator, and its tours are recommended. Aussie Adventure Holidays (☎ 1800 811 633) also run tours.

The Tiwi people's island homes kept them fairly isolated from mainland developments until this century, and their culture has retained several unique features. Perhaps the best known are the pukumani burial poles, carved and painted with symbolic and mythological figures, which are erected around graves. More recently the Tiwi have started producing art for sale – bark painting, textile screen printing, batik and pottery, using traditional designs and motifs.

The Tiwi had mixed relations with Macassan fishermen, who came in search of the *trepang*, or sea cucumber. A British settlement in the 1820s at Fort Dundas, near Pularumpi on Melville Island, failed partly because of poor relations with the locals. The main settlement on the islands is **Nguiu** in the south-east of Bathurst Island, which was founded in 1911 as a Catholic mission. On Melville Island the settlements are **Pularumpi** and **Milikapiti**.

Most Tiwi live on Bathurst Island and follow a nontraditional lifestyle. Some return to their traditional lands on Melville Island for a few weeks each year. Melville Island is also home to descendants of the Japanese pearl divers who regularly visited here early this century, and people of mixed Aboriginal and European parentage who were gathered here from around the

Territory under government policy half a century ago.

An all-day trip costs $260 and includes the necessary permit, a flight from Darwin to Nguiu, visits to the early Catholic mission buildings, morning tea with Tiwi women, swimming at Tomorapi Falls, a trip to a pukumani burial site and the flight back to Darwin from Melville. This tour is available from April to October. Tiwi Tours also offers two-day tours to the islands, staying at a tented camp.

ARNHEM LAND

The entire eastern half of the Top End is the Arnhem Land Aboriginal Land, which is spectacular, sparsely populated and the source of some good Aboriginal art. Apart from Oenpelli (just across the East Alligator River in Kakadu), the remote Gurig National Park (on the Cobourg Peninsula at the north-west corner) and Gove (the peninsula at the north-east corner), Arnhem Land is virtually closed to independent travellers.

Oenpelli

Oenpelli is a fairly nondescript Aboriginal community town, but it is well worth visiting for two reasons: the 17km dirt road from Kakadu traverses the wildly spectacular East Alligator River flood plain (and is probably as spectacular as anything within Kakadu itself), and the Injalak Arts & Crafts Association has really high quality Aboriginal artefacts at very reasonable prices. Injalak is both a workplace and shopfront for artists and craftspeople who produce traditional paintings on bark and paper, didgeridoos, pandanus weavings and baskets, and screen-printed fabrics. All sales benefit the community, and you can also be sure that you are buying authentic pieces. Injalak (☎ 8979 0190) is open daily except Sunday, and permits to visit can be obtained on the spot at the Northern Land Council office (☎ 8979 2410) at the Jabiru shopping centre.

Cobourg Peninsula

This remote wilderness includes the **Cobourg Marine Park**, which is owned by the local Aborigines and the **Gurig National Park**. Entry to the latter is by permit only.

The ruins of the early British settlement at Victoria can be visited on **Port Essington**, a superb 30km-long natural harbour on the northern side of the peninsula.

At **Black Point** there's a small store open daily, except Sunday, but only from 4 to 6 pm. It sells basic provisions, ice and camping gas. Be warned that credit cards are not accepted here and, as its operation has been erratic in recent years, phone the Black Point ranger station in advance to check its current status. Fuel (diesel, super, unleaded, outboard mix) is available at the jetty between 6 and 6.30 pm only.

Permits The track to Cobourg passes through part of Arnhem Land, and as the Aboriginal owners there restrict the number of vehicles going through (15 per week), you're advised to apply up to a year ahead for the necessary permit ($211 per vehicle for seven days). Permit application forms are available from the Cobourg Peninsula Sanctuary and Marine Park Board, PO Box 496, Palmerston NT 0831, or by phoning the Administration Office (☎ 8999 4555) or Ranger Station (☎ 8979 0244).

Places to Stay There are 15 shady camp sites about 100m from the shore at the *Smith Point Camping Ground*. Facilities include a shower, toilet and barbecues, but there's no electricity and generators are banned at night. The charge is $4 per site for three people, plus $1 for each extra person.

The fully equipped, four-bed *Cobourg Beach Huts* (☎ 8979 0263) at Smith Point cost $135 for the whole cottage, but you need to bring your own supplies. As with the store at Black Point, check in advance to see if the cottages are open.

The only other accommodation option is the *Seven Spirit Bay Resort* (☎ 8979 0277), set in secluded wilderness at Vashon Head and accessible only by air or boat. It charges $395/700 for single/double accommodation, but this includes three gourmet meals. Accommodation is in individual opensided, hexagonal 'habitats', each with semi-

outdoor private bathroom! Activities available (at extra cost) include day trips to Victoria Settlement, guided bushwalks and fishing.

Getting There & Away There's an airstrip at Smith Point, just a couple of kilometres or so from the camp site and Black Point, which is serviced by charter flights from Darwin.

The track to Cobourg starts at Oenpelli. It is recommended for 4WD vehicles exclusively, and only take a trailer if you are prepared to have it shaken to bits. The track is also closed in the Wet. The 288km drive to Black Point from the East Alligator River at Cahills Crossing (near Ubirr) takes about six hours and must be completed in one day.

Straight after the Wet, the water level at Cahills Crossing can be high, and you can only drive across the ford about an hour either side of the low tide. A tide chart is included with your permit, or the Bowali Visitor Centre in Kakadu has a list of tide times.

Eastern Arnhem Land

At **Nhulunbuy** (population 3720) there is a bauxite mining centre with a deep water export port. Free tours of the mine are conducted on Friday morning.

The Aboriginal people of nearby **Yirrkala** (population 520) made an important step in the land rights movement in 1963 when they protested at plans to mine on their traditional land. They failed to stop it, but forced a government inquiry and won compensation, and their case caught the public eye.

Groote Eylandt, a large island off the east Arnhem Land coast, is also Aboriginal land, with a big manganese mining operation. The main settlement here is **Alyangula** (population 670).

Getting There & Away You don't have to have a permit to fly into Nhulunbuy, which can be reached direct from Darwin for $260 or from Cairns for $355 with Qantas or Ansett. Travelling overland through Arnhem Land from Katherine requires a permit; contact the East Arnhem Regional Tourist Association (☎ 8987 2255).

You can hire vehicles in Nhulunbuy to explore the coastline (there are some fine beaches, but beware of crocodiles) and the local area. You need to get a permit to do this from the Northern Land Council in Nhulunbuy (a formality).

Organised Tours

There are a number of tours into Arnhem Land, but these usually visit only the western part.

The Aboriginal owned and operated Umorrduk Safaris (☎ 8948 1306, bbrookes@ozemail.com.au) has a two day tour from Darwin to the remote Mudjeegarrdart airstrip in north-western Arnhem Land. The highlight of the trip is a visit to the 20,000-year-old Umorrduk rock-art sites. The cost is $200 to $600 per person, and the trips operate from May through December.

Another operator with a very good reputation is Davidson's Arnhemland Safaris (☎ 8927 5240). Max Davidson has been taking people into Arnhem Land for years and has a concession at Mt Borradaile, north of Oenpelli, where he has set up his safari camp. Close by there are wetlands with excellent fishing and superb rock-art sites. The camp, which has a very informal and relaxed atmosphere, is open year-round and costs from $200 per person per day, which includes accommodation, all meals, guided tours and fishing. Transfers from Darwin can be arranged.

Venture North Australia (☎ 8927 5500) operates tours to remote areas that feature expert guidance on rock art. It also has a safari camp near Smith Point in Gurig National Park.

Other trips are available from Jabiru in Kakadu; see the Kakadu National Park section earlier.

Down the Track

It's just under 1500km south from Darwin to Alice Springs and, although at times it can be dreary, there is an amazing variety of things to see or do along the road and nearby.

Until WWII the Track really was just that – a dirt track connecting the Territory's two main towns, Darwin and 'the Alice'. The urgent need to supply Darwin, which was under attack from Japanese aircraft from Timor, led to a rapid upgrading of the road. Although it is now sealed and well maintained, short, sharp floods during the Wet can cut the road and stop all traffic for days at a time.

The Stuart Hwy takes its name from John McDouall Stuart, who made the first crossing of Australia from south to north. He was forced back twice but finally completed his epic trek in 1862. Only 10 years later the telegraph line to Darwin was laid along the route he had pioneered, and today the Stuart Hwy between Darwin and Alice Springs follows roughly the same path.

DARWIN TO KATHERINE

Some places along the Track south of Darwin (Howard Springs, Darwin Crocodile Farm and Litchfield National Park) are covered under Around Darwin earlier in this chapter.

Batchelor
• postcode 0845   • pop 645

This small town, 84km down the Track from Darwin, then another 14km west, once serviced the now-closed Rum Jungle uranium and copper mine. In recent years it has received a boost from the growing popularity of nearby Litchfield National Park. It has a swimming pool, open six days a week, and an Aboriginal residential tertiary college.

The **Batchelor Butterfly Farm** offers a pleasant diversion, with large walk-through enclosures decked with tropical vegetation full of butterflies bred on the farm.

Places to Stay The *Batchelor Caravillage* (☎ 8976 0166) on Rum Jungle Rd has cabins for $75, dorm beds for $13 or tent sites for $16. The friendly *Banyan Tree Caravan Park* (☎ 8976 0330) is halfway between Batchelor and Litchfield, and has on-site vans at $17 per person, camp sites are for $10 and meals are available.

Jungle Drums, next to the Butterfly Farm, should be open and have backpackers rooms; phone for an update ☎ 8976 0555.

The *Rum Jungle Motor Inn* (*☎ 8976 0123*) in Batchelor is expensive at $78/98 for singles/doubles.

Adelaide River

• postcode 0846   • pop 280

Not to be confused with Adelaide River Crossing on the Arnhem Hwy, this small settlement is on the Stuart Hwy, 111km south of Darwin. It has a well kept cemetery for those who died in the 1942-43 Japanese air raids. This stretch of the highway is dotted with WWII airstrips.

Adelaide River has a pub, the *Shady River View Caravan Park*, with tent sites for $12, and the *Adelaide River Inn*, with singles/doubles at $55/65 (*both ☎ 8976 7047*).

Old Stuart Highway

South of Adelaide River, a sealed section of the old Stuart Hwy loops to the south before rejoining the main road 52km on. It's a scenic trip without the hustle of the main highway, and it leads to a number of pleasant spots, but access to them is often cut in the Wet.

The beautiful 12m **Robyn Falls** are a short, rocky scramble 15km along this road. The falls, set in a monsoon-forested gorge, dwindle to a trickle in the dry season, but are spectacular in the Wet.

The turn-off to **Daly River** is 14km further on. To reach **Douglas Hot Springs Nature Park**, turn south off the old highway just before it rejoins the Stuart Hwy and continue for about 35km. The nature park here includes a section of the Douglas River, a pretty camping area and several hot springs – a bit hot for bathing at 40°C to 60°C, but there are cooler pools.

Butterfly Gorge Nature Park is about 17km beyond Douglas Hot Springs – you'll need a 4WD to get there. True to its name, butterflies sometimes swarm in the gorge. It's safe to swim in these places, although you may well see 'freshies' (freshwater crocodiles). There are camp sites with toilets and barbecues.

Daly River

• postcode 0822

Historic Daly River is 109km west of the Stuart Hwy. Most of the population belongs to the Naniyu Nambiyu Aboriginal community, about 6km away from the rest of the town. Visitors are welcome without a permit, although note that this is a dry community. Also here is Merrepen Arts, a resource centre that is also an outlet for locally made art and crafts. The associated Merrepen Arts Festival is held each year in June/July.

The main activity for visitors is getting out on the river and dangling a line. Boat hire is available at the Mango Farm and Woolianna tourist outfits. At the Mango Farm you can hire a dinghy with outboard motor and a full tank for $18 per hour (minimum of two hours), $65 for a half day and $100 for a full day.

Places to Stay There are a couple of accommodation options, including the *Woolianna on the Daly Tourist Park* (*☎ 8978 2478*), which has tent/van sites, and the *Mango Farm* (*☎ 8978 2464*), with tent/van sites and family units.

The *Daly River Roadside Inn* (*☎ 8978 2418*) has basic accommodation from $55.

Pine Creek

• postcode 0847   • pop 520

This small town, 245km from Darwin, was the scene of a gold rush in the 1870s and some of the old timber and corrugated iron buildings survive. The Kakadu Hwy goes north-east from Pine Creek to Kakadu National Park.

The old **train station** has been restored and houses a visitors centre and a display on the Darwin to Pine Creek railway, which opened in 1889 but is now closed. **Pine Creek Museum** (entry $2), on Railway Parade near the post office, has interesting displays on local history. It is usually open weekdays from 10 am to noon and 1 to 5 pm, and weekends from 10 am to 2 pm.

Ah Toys General Store is a reminder of the gold-rush days when Chinese heavily outnumbered Europeans.

Gun Alley Gold Mining (signposted) is an excellent little tourist operation with a talk on the history of gold in Pine Creek, a

North Australian Railway

In the 1880s the South Australian government decided to build a railway line from Darwin (Palmerston) to Pine Creek. This was partly to improve the conditions on the Pine Creek goldfields, as the road south from Darwin was often washed out in the Wet, but was also partly spurred by the dream of a transcontinental railway line linking Adelaide and Darwin.

The line was built almost entirely by Chinese labourers, and was eventually pushed south as far as Larrimah. It continued to operate until 1976, but was forced to close because the damage inflicted by Cyclone Tracy drained the Territory's financial resources.

Completion of the transcontinental link continued to be a subject of much discussion in the Territory. Then in February 1999 the dream came a little closer to reality. An agreement was signed between the NT government and the Aboriginal land owners, enabling the construction of the link between Darwin and Alice Springs to go ahead. It is envisaged it will take four years to construct and cost about $1 billion.

demonstration of some historic steam-powered crushing machinery, and a chance to find some 'colour' in a pan full of wash, all for $5.

Places to Stay There are three caravan parks in Pine Creek, but the best choice is *Kakadu Gateway Caravan Park* (☎ 8976 1166, Buchanan St), about 600m from Main Terrace, which has excellent facilities, meals and a range of accommodation. Camp sites are $16 ($18 with power), with a carport and en suite; budget singles/doubles start at $30/45; and there are also 'swag rooms' – empty, air-con carpeted rooms where you can store a bicycle and roll out your swag for $15/20.

Alternatives in town include the *Pine Creek Hotel* (☎ 8976 1288, Moule St), opposite the BP station, which has motel rooms

at $79 for singles/doubles and budget rooms for $30; and the *Pine Creek Diggers Rest Motel* (☎ 8976 1442, 32 Main Terrace), where self-contained units sleeping up to five people cost from $70 including tax.

Around Pine Creek
A well maintained dirt road follows the line of the old railway line east of the highway between Hayes Creek and Pine Creek. This is in fact the original 'north road', which was in use before the 'new road' (now the Old Stuart Hwy!) was built. It's a worthwhile detour to see the 1930s corrugated iron pub at **Grove Hill** (accommodation and meals available).

About 3km along the Stuart Hwy south of Pine Creek is the turn-off to **Umbrawarra Gorge Nature Park**, about 30km west along a dirt road (often impassable in the Wet). There's a camp site with pit toilets and fireplaces, and you can swim in crocodile-free pools 1km from the car park.

Edith Falls
At the 293km mark on the Track you can turn off to the beautiful Edith Falls, 19km east of the road at the western end of the Nitmiluk (Katherine Gorge) National Park. There's a camp site with showers, pit toilets and fireplaces ($5 per person). Swimming is possible in a clear, forest-surrounded plunge pool at the bottom of the falls. You may see freshwater crocodiles (the inoffensive variety), but be careful. There's a good walk up to rapids and more pools above the falls.

KATHERINE
• postcode 0851   • pop 7980
Apart from Tennant Creek, this is the only town of any size between Darwin and Alice Springs. It's a bustling place where the Victoria Hwy branches off to the Kimberley and Western Australia. The town's population has grown rapidly in recent years, mainly because of the establishment of the large Tindal air-force base just south of town.

Katherine has long been an important stopping point, as the river it's built on and named after is the first permanent running water north of Alice Springs. It's a mixed blessing really, because Katherine suffered devastating floods in January 1998 – not for the first time – that inundated the surrounding countryside and left their mark up to 2m high on buildings all over town.

The town includes some historic old buildings, but the main interest is the spectacular Katherine Gorge, 30km to the northeast. It's a great place to camp, walk, swim, canoe, take a cruise or simply float along on an air mattress.

Orientation & Information

Katherine's main street, Katherine Terrace, is the Stuart Hwy as it runs through town. Coming from the north, you cross the Katherine River Bridge just before the town centre. The Victoria Hwy to Western Australia branches off 300m on. After another 300m, Giles St, the road to Katherine Gorge, branches off in the other direction.

At the end of the town centre is the Katherine Region Tourist Association office (☎ 8972 2650, krta@nttech.com.au), open Monday to Friday from 8 am to 5 pm and weekends from 10 am to 3 pm. The bus station is over the road from the tourist office. There's a Parks & Wildlife office (☎ 8973 8770) on Giles St.

Mimi Aboriginal Art & Craft in the shopping complex on Lindsay St is an Aboriginal owned and run shop selling products made over a wide area, from the deserts in the west to the Gulf coast in the east.

Banyan Art Gallery, in the arcade off First St, has a good range of bark paintings and other crafts.

You are free to inspect the workshop at Katherine Didjeridoos at 21 First St and works are for sale. A plain or decorated 'didge' will set you back $100 to $300.

Things to See & Do

Katherine's old train station, owned by the National Trust, houses a display on railway history and is open Monday to Friday from 10 am to noon and 1 to 3 pm in the Dry.

The small Katherine Museum is in the old airport terminal building on Gorge Rd, about 1km from the centre of town. There's a good selection of old photos and other bits and pieces of interest, including the original Gypsy Moth biplane flown by Dr Clyde Fenton, the first Flying Doctor. It is open weekdays from 10 am to 4 pm and Sunday from 2 to 5 pm.

The School of the Air on Giles St offers an opportunity to see how remote outback kids are taught. There are guided tours on weekdays during the school term.

Katherine has a good public swimming pool beside the highway, about 750m south of the bus station. There are also some pleasant thermal pools beside the river, about 3km from town along the Victoria Hwy.

The 105 hectare Katherine Low Level Nature Park is 5km from town, just off the Victoria Hwy. It's a great spot on the Katherine River, taking in 4km of its shady banks, and the swimming hole by the weir is very popular in the Dry. In the Wet, flash floods can make it dangerous. Facilities provided here include picnic tables, toilets and gas barbecues.

Springvale Homestead, 8km south-west of town (turn right off the Victoria Hwy after 3.8km), claims to be the oldest cattle station in the NT. The stone homestead still stands by the river, about 8km from town, but it suffered terrible flood damage in 1998 and its future was uncertain at the time of writing.

Organised Tours

Tours are available from Katherine, taking in various combinations of the town, the gorge, Cutta Cutta Caves, Mataranka and Kakadu. Most accommodation places can book you on these and you'll be picked up from where you're staying – or ask at the tourist office or Travel North in the bus station.

There are excellent Aboriginal tours at Manyallaluk (see that section later for details), and Bill Harney's Jankanginya Tours (☎ 8971 0318) takes groups on their land, sometimes referred to as Lightning Brothers country. Here you learn about bush tucker, crafts and medicine, and hear some of the non-secret stories associated with the rock art of the area. Accommodation is in a basic bush camp.

For a trip along the Katherine River, Gecko Canoeing (☎ 1800 634 319, gecko@topend.com.au) has three-day guided tours for $435, including meals and safety gear.

Places to Stay

Camping There are several camping possibilities. Close to the Low Level Nature Park is the *Katherine Low Level Caravan Park* (☎ 8972 3962), a good place near the river. Tent sites are $14 for two, or $18 with power. Cabins cost $65.

Closer to town, on the Victoria Hwy, is the *Riverview Caravan Park* (☎ 8972 1011), which has reasonably comfortable cabins at $65 and tent sites at $14 ($17 with power). The thermal pools are five minutes walk away.

The *All Seasons Frontier Katherine* (☎ 1800 812 443, fkath@allseasons.com.au), 4km south of town on the Stuart Hwy, has powered camp sites with private bathrooms at $18, plus a pool, barbecue area and restaurant. It also has motel rooms for $114.

Hostels *Kookaburra Lodge Backpackers* (☎ 1800 808 211), on the corner of Lindsay and Third Sts, is just a few minutes walk from the Transit Centre. It consists of old motel units with between four and eight beds and costs $13 a night. There are some twin rooms for $40. It can get overcrowded at times, but it's a friendly and well run place. Kookaburra also does bike and canoe hire.

Just around the corner is the *Palm Court Backpackers* (☎ 8972 2722), on the corner of Third and Giles Sts. The air-con rooms are uncrowded, and have their own lockers, TV, fridge and bathroom. Costs are $13/15 per person in an eight/four-bed dorm; twins or doubles are $45. The staff work hard to make this a pleasant place and discounts are available for various services around town.

The *Victoria Lodge* (☎ 1800 808 875) is at 21 Victoria Hwy, not far from the main street. It's a good place with six-bed rooms at $14 per person and singles/doubles at $35/40.

Motels The best value is at *PGA Lodge* (☎ 8971 0266, 50 Giles St), where single/double motel rooms go for $35/45; budget singles are also available for $25. This place is popular with seasonal workers and it's often full.

The *Beagle Motor Inn* (☎ 8972 3998) on the corner of Lindsay and Fourth Sts is among the cheapest, with air-con rooms for $40/50.

Knotts Crossing Resort (☎ 8972 2511) on Giles St has a variety of accommodation. Self-contained cabins with a double and two single beds and en suite cost $65, standard motel rooms are $96.

Places to Eat

Eating out in Katherine comes a distant third to Darwin and Alice Springs, but since the flood purged the town several new places have sprung up and others got a much needed facelift.

For budget eating there are plenty of greasy choices at the Transit Centre's 24 hour *cafe*. The *Homestead Café* opposite Palm Court Backpackers opens early for breakfast.

Self-caterers should visit the large Woolworths' *supermarket*, at the southern end of Katherine Terrace, which is open daily. This is the cheapest place for hundreds of kilometres around to stock up for trips off the beaten track.

If you have transport, the *Kumbidgee Lodge Tea Room*, 10km out of town along the gorge road (Giles St), offers a hearty 'bush breakfast' in a pleasant outdoor setting for $8; cooked meals are available throughout the day for around $12.

Café Enio's (385 Katherine Terrace), next to the ANZ bank on the main street, is a popular lunch spot that does delicious foccacias, quiches and sandwiches, and has the best range of coffee in Katherine. Unfortunately, it's not open for dinner.

Café on First (17 First St), in the cinema complex, does reasonable snacks and light meals. It's one of the few places open for lunch on weekends.

Pizza outlets include *Nino's Pizza & Pasta Bar*, opposite the information centre, and *Popeye's* (32 Katherine Terrace), which has all-you-can-eat deals some nights for $7.

On the corner of Katherine Terrace and Murphy St (Victoria Hwy) is the *Mekhong Thai Cafe & Takeaway*. This is an unusual find in an outback town, with an extensive menu offering entrees at around $6 and main courses from $10 to $13.

The best tucker we found in Katherine was at *Katie's Bistro* at the Knotts Crossing Resort. The food is good, fresh and well prepared, and the menu changes regularly. Mains are in the $16 to $19 range.

Getting There & Away

Katherine airport is 8km south of town, just off the Stuart Hwy. You can fly to Katherine on weekdays from Darwin ($144) and Alice Springs ($369) with Airnorth (☎ 1800 627 474).

All buses between Darwin and Alice Springs, Queensland or Western Australia stop at Katherine, which means two or three daily to/from Western Australia, and usually four daily to/from Darwin, Alice Springs and Queensland. Typical fares from Katherine are Darwin $39, Alice Springs $133, Tennant Creek $65 and Kununurra $67.

The Blue Banana bus (☎ 8945 6800) has round trips from Katherine to Darwin via Litchfield National Park and Kakadu with many stops en route. Katherine to Darwin via Litchfield is $90 and the round trip is $170.

Avis (☎ 8971 0520), Territory Thrifty Car Rental (☎ 8972 3183) and Hertz (☎ 8971 1111) all have offices here.

NITMILUK (KATHERINE GORGE) NATIONAL PARK

Nitmiluk (Katherine Gorge) is 13 gorges, separated from each other by rapids. The gorge walls aren't high, but it is a remote, beautiful place. It's 12km long and has been carved out by the Katherine River, which begins in Arnhem Land. Further downstream it becomes the Daly River before flowing into the Timor Sea at a point 80km south-west of Darwin. The difference in water levels between the Wet and Dry is staggering. During the dry season the gorge waters are calm, but from November to March they can become a raging torrent.

Swimming in the gorge is safe except when it's in flood. The only crocodiles around are the freshwater variety and they're more often seen in the cooler months. The country surrounding the gorge is excellent for walking.

Information

The visitors centre and car park, where the gorge begins and cruises start, is 30km by sealed road from Katherine. The impressive visitors centre (☎ 8972 1886) has displays and information on the national park, which spreads over 1800 sq km to include extensive back country and Edith Falls to the north-west, as well as Katherine Gorge. There are details of a wide range of marked walking tracks starting here that go through the picturesque country south of the gorge, descending to the river at various points. Some of the tracks pass Aboriginal rock paintings up to 7000 years old. The visitors centre, which also has a cafe and souvenir shop, is open daily from 7 am to 7 pm.

You can walk to Edith Falls (76km, five days) or places along the way. For the longer or more rugged walks you need a permit from the visitors centre. The Katherine Gorge Canoe Marathon, organised by the Red Cross, takes place in June.

Activities

Canoeing Canoes can be hired at the boat ramp by the main car park, about 500m past the visitors centre. You can rent single and double canoes from Nitmiluk Tours (☎ 8972 1253) at the park. They cost $24/37 for adults/children for a half day, or $34/50 for a whole day. The price includes the use of a waterproof drum for cameras and other gear, a map, and life jackets if you feel the need.

This is a great way of exploring the gorge. You can also be adventurous and take the canoes out overnight, but you must book in advance as only a limited number of people are allowed to camp in the gorges.

Gorge Cruise Cruises depart daily. The two hour run goes to the second gorge and visits rock paintings for $29/12; it leaves at 9 and 11 am, and 1 and 3 pm. The four hour trip goes to the third gorge for $42/19, leaving at 9 and 11 am and 1 pm. Finally there's an eight hour trip that takes you to the fifth gorge, and involves walking about 4km. The cost is $73, and it departs daily at 9 am. The two and four-hour trips run all year, but the eight hour trip runs only from April to November.

It's a good idea to make a reservation the day before (☎ 1800 089 103 or ☎ 8972 1253).

Swimming There's a swimming jetty close to the boat ramp, not far from the visitors centre, although it's not suitable for small children.

Places to Stay
The popular *Gorge Caravan Park* (☎ *8972 1253)* has showers, toilets and fireplaces, and plenty of grass and shade. Wallabies and goannas are common visitors. Sites cost $14 ($18 with power); pay at the visitors centre.

Getting There & Away
The five-times-daily commuter bus costs $9/15 one way/return. It operates from the Transit Centre in Katherine and does accommodation pick-ups.

The Blue Banana bus stops at both Katherine Gorge and Edith Falls.

CUTTA CUTTA CAVES NATURE PARK
Guided tours of these limestone caverns, 24km south-east of Katherine along the Stuart Hwy, are held six times a day in the Dry and cost $6.75. Orange horseshoe bats, a rare and endangered species, roost in the main cave, about 15m below the ground. The rock formations outside the caves are impressive.

MANYALLALUK
Manyallaluk is the former 3000 sq km Eva Valley cattle station which abuts the eastern edge of the Nitmiluk National Park. These days it is owned by Top End Aboriginal people, some of whom now organise and lead very highly regarded tours.

The one day trip includes transport to/from Katherine, lunch, billy tea and damper, and you learn about traditional bush

tucker and medicine, spear throwing and playing a didgeridoo. The two day trip adds swimming and rock-art sites. The cost is $105/55 for adults/children for the day trip and $205/100 for the two day trip. For bookings and inquiries phone ☎ 1800 644 727.

The one day trip is available year-round on Monday, with extra trips on Wednesday and Saturday from October through March; the two-day trips operate on Monday from April through October. The trips start from Katherine, or with your own vehicle you can camp at Manyallaluk ($10 for two) and take the day tour from there, which costs $65/40. It is possible just to camp without taking the tour, but you are restricted to the camping area. There's a community store with basic supplies and excellent crafts at competitive prices. No permits are needed to visit the community, but alcohol is not permitted.

BARUNGA
Barunga is another Aboriginal community, 13km along the Arnhem Land track beyond the Manyallaluk turn-off. Entry to the community is by permit only, but every year over the Queen's Birthday long weekend in June the settlement really comes alive for the enjoyable Barunga Wugularr Sports & Cultural Festival.

Permits are not required to visit Barunga during the festival, but you'll need your own camping gear. Once again, this is a dry community so alcohol is officially not permitted.

KATHERINE TO WESTERN AUSTRALIA
It's 513km on the Victoria Hwy from Katherine to Kununurra in Western Australia.

As you approach the Western Australian border you start to see the boab trees found in much of the north-west of Australia. There's a 1½ hour time change when you cross the border. There's also a quarantine inspection post, and all fruit and vegetables must be left here. This only applies when travelling from the Territory to Western Australia.

Flora River Nature Park
This is an interesting and scenic little park that takes in 25km of the Flora River, and

includes some limestone tufa outcrops that form bars across the river and so act as dams, creating small waterfalls. It is still in the early stages of development, but Parks & Wildlife has just opened an all-weather camp site, complete with an amenities block. There's also a boat ramp and canoe ramps across the tufas.

The turn-off is 90km south-west of Katherine along the Victoria Hwy, and a further 45km north along a good dirt road.

Victoria River Crossing

The highway is sometimes cut by floods. If you stand on the Victoria River Bridge by the Victoria River Inn at the crossing in the Dry, it's hard to imagine that the wide river far below your feet can actually flow over the top of the bridge!

Timber Creek

• postcode 0852   • pop 560

From April to October, daily boat trips further west are made on the river from Timber Creek. You'll be shown fresh- and saltwater crocodiles, fish and turtles being fed – try some billy tea and crack a stock whip. The cost of a four hour morning tour is $40 ($25 children) and bookings can be made at Pike's Booking Centre in Timber Creek (☎ 8975 0850).

You can see a boab marked by an early explorer at Gregory's Tree Historical Reserve, west of Timber Creek.

Gregory National Park

This little visited national park to the south-west of Timber Creek covers 10,500 sq km and offers good fishing, camping and bushwalking. There's also the 90km 4WD **Bullita Stock Route**, which takes eight hours, although it's better to break the journey at one of the three marked camp sites. For more details contact the Parks & Wildlife office in Timber Creek (☎ 8975 0888), or the Bullita ranger (☎ 8975 0833).

Keep River National Park

Bordering Western Australia just off the Victoria Hwy, this park is noted for its sandstone landforms and has some excellent walking trails. You can reach the main points in the park by conventional vehicle during the Dry. Aboriginal art can be seen near the car park at the end of the road.

There's a rangers' station (☎ 9167 8827), 3km into the park from the main road, and there are camp sites with pit toilets at Gurrangalng (15km into the park) and Jarrnarm (28km).

MATARANKA

• postcode 0852   • pop 630

Mataranka is 103km south-east of Katherine on the Stuart Hwy. The attraction is the **Mataranka Thermal Pool**, 7km off the highway just south of the small town. The crystal clear thermal pool, in a pocket of rainforest, is a great place to wind down after a hot day on the road – though it can get crowded. There's no entry fee.

The pool is just a short walk from the Mataranka Homestead Resort which offers a variety of accommodation, including a camp site, a backpackers hostel, motel rooms and a restaurant – it's more relaxed than it sounds since you're a long way from anywhere else.

A couple of hundred metres away is the **Waterhouse River**, where you can walk along the banks or rent canoes and rowing boats for $5 an hour. Outside the homestead entrance is a replica of the Elsey Station Homestead, which was made for the filming of *We of the Never Never*, set near Mataranka. The replica houses the **Museum of the Never Never** with displays on the history of the Great Northern Railway, bush workshops and WWII, including a number of interesting photographs.

The **Elsey National Park** adjoins the thermal pool reserve and offers great camping, fishing and walking along the Waterhouse River. It's also far less touristed than the thermal pools.

Places to Stay & Eat

The hostel section at the *Mataranka Homestead Resort* (☎ 1800 089 103) is quite comfortable and has some single and twin rooms, though the kitchen is small. It costs $16 per person ($14 with a YHA card). Camping is

$14 for a site ($18 with power), and air-con motel rooms with private bathroom cost $82 and up. It has a store selling basic groceries, a bar with snacks and meals (not cheap), or you can use the camp site barbecues.

In Mataranka town, the *Old Elsey Roadside Inn* (☎ 8975 4512) has a couple of singles/doubles at $50/60, though *Territory Manor* (☎ 8975 4516) is a more luxurious place with swimming pool, restaurant and motel rooms at $82. Alternatively, you can camp for $18 (with power). Hefty discounts are offered during the Wet.

The *12-Mile Yards* camp site in Elsey National Park has good facilities and plenty of grass and shade. Camping costs $5 for adults.

Getting There & Around
Long-distance buses travelling up and down the Stuart Hwy call at Mataranka and the Homestead Resort.

MATARANKA TO THREE WAYS
Not far south of the Mataranka Homestead turn-off, the Roper Hwy branches east off the Stuart Hwy. It leads about 200km to **Roper Bar**, near the Roper River on the southern edge of Arnhem Land, where there's a store with a camp site and a few rooms – mainly visited by fishing enthusiasts. All but about 20km of the road is sealed.

About 5km south of the Roper junction is the turn-off to the **Elsey Cemetery**, not far from the highway. Here are the graves of characters like 'the Fizzer' who came to life in *We of the Never Never*.

Larrimah
• postcode 0852   • pop 20

Continuing south from Mataranka you pass through Larrimah – at one time the railway line from Darwin came as far as Birdum, 8km south of here, but it was abandoned after Cyclone Tracy. There's an interesting little **museum** housed in the former repeater station opposite the pub.

There are three camping grounds. The one on the highway at the southern end of town, *Green Park Tourist Complex* (☎ 8975 9937), charges $10 per site with power. Backpacker beds are $15 and a donga for

two is $40. There's a swimming pool and a few crocodiles in fenced-off ponds.

Daly Waters
Further south again is Daly Waters, 3km off the highway, an important staging post in the early days of aviation – Amy Johnson landed here. The historic *Daly Waters Pub* (☎ 8975 9927), with air-con motel-type rooms at $28/38 for singles/doubles, is not surprisingly the focus of local life. It's an atmospheric place, dating from 1893 and said to be the oldest pub in the Territory, and there's good food available. The pub also has a caravan park with tent sites at $6 ($10 powered), and there's another WWII airstrip with a restored hangar. The *Hi-Way Inn & Caravan Park* (☎ 8975 9925), on the Stuart Hwy, has rooms from $47/58 (expensive for what you get) and powered camp sites at $14.

Daly Waters to Three Ways
After Daly Waters, there's the fascinating ghost town of **Newcastle Waters**, a few kilometres west of the highway, and then the cattle town of **Elliott**. As you might expect, the land just gets drier and drier.

Further south is **Renner Springs**, and this is generally accepted as the dividing line between the seasonally wet Top End and the dry Centre.

About 50km before Three Ways and 4km off the road along a loop of the old Stuart Hwy is **Churchill's Head**, a large rock said to look like Britain's wartime prime minister, although it's hard to see any resemblance whatsoever. Soon after, there's a memorial to Stuart at **Attack Creek**, where the explorer turned back on one of his attempts to cross Australia from south to north, reputedly after his party was attacked by hostile Aborigines.

GULF COUNTRY
Just south of Daly Waters the single-lane, sealed Carpentaria Hwy heads east to Borroloola, 378km away near the Gulf of Carpentaria and one of the best barramundi fishing spots in the Territory. After 267km the Carpentaria Hwy meets the Tablelands Hwy, also sealed, at the **Cape Crawford**

Roadhouse. The Tablelands Hwy runs 404km south to meet the Barkly Hwy at **Barkly Homestead Roadhouse**; there's no petrol between these two roadhouses.

Borroloola

• postcode 0854   • pop 550

Borroloola is a small town close to the Gulf of Carpentaria. Tourism and cattle are the mainstays of the economy. The town's colourful past is preserved in the interesting displays housed in the **old police station**, which dates from 1886 and is open Monday to Friday from 10 am to noon. (At other times the key is available from the Borroloola Holiday Village.)

Offshore from Borroloola is **Barranyi National Park**, which is well worth a visit if you can arrange it, while 44km along the highway towards Cape Crawford are the picturesque **Caranbirini Waterhole** and **Bukalara Rock Formations**, both right by the road. There's a one hour walking trail around the base of the eerie formations. Good walking shoes are advised, and watch the spinifex which is sharp.

Places to Stay & Eat There's little shade at the *McArthur River Caravan Park* (☎ 8975 8734), on the main street, where powered sites cost $15 per night and unpowered sites cost $12 for two adults. Cabins are $65/75 for singles/doubles, but are usually full.

The *Borroloola Inn* (☎ 8975 8766) has air-con dongas from $45 for a twin. Its bistro restaurant serves a range of sensibly priced and generous meals, and the Sunday night carvery is excellent value.

The *Borroloola Holiday Village* (☎ 8975 8742) has air-con units with attached bath, cooking facilities, colour TV and phone (from $92 for a twin room). There are four economy rooms sleeping just one person each for $50, while budget beds in the bunkhouse cost $30.

A good option if you're in a group is to hire a houseboat on the McArthur River. *Borroloola Houseboats* (☎ 1800 658 529) are at the fishing club at King Ash Bay; four or eight-berth boats in the high/low season cost $1050/750 or $2050/1350 per week.

Getting There & Away Airnorth (☎ 1800 627 474) has three flights a week to Borroloola from Katherine ($265) and Darwin ($409).

THREE WAYS

Three Ways, 537km north of the Alice, 988km south of Darwin and 643km west of Mt Isa, is basically a bloody long way from anywhere – apart from Tennant Creek, 26km down the Track. This is a classic 'get stuck' point for hitchhikers.

The *Threeways Roadhouse* (☎ 8962 2744) at the junction is best avoided, but if you're stuck it has air-con singles/doubles at $32/50, or you can camp for $10 ($15 with power).

Just north of the junction is a rather ugly memorial to John Flynn, the founder of the Royal Flying Doctor Service.

TENNANT CREEK

• postcode 0860   • pop 3862

Apart from Katherine, this is the only town of any size between Darwin and Alice Springs. It's 26km south of Three Ways and 511km north of Alice Springs. A lot of travellers spend a night here, and there are one or two attractions, mainly related to gold mining, to tempt you to stay a bit longer.

To the Warumungu people, Tennant Creek is Jurnkurakurr, the intersection of a number of dreaming tracks.

There's a tale that Tennant Creek was first settled when a wagonload of beer broke down here in the early 1930s and the drivers decided they might as well make themselves comfortable while they consumed the freight. The truth is somewhat more prosaic: the town was established as a result of the small gold rush around the same time. One of the major workings was **Nobles Nob**, 16km east of the town along Peko Rd. It was discovered by a one-eyed man called Jack Noble who formed a surprisingly successful prospecting partnership with the blind William Weaber. This was the biggest open-cut gold mine in the country until mining ceased in 1985. Ore from other local mines is still processed and you can visit the open cut.

Information

The helpful visitors centre (☎ 8962 3388) is in the old Gold Stamp Battery on Peko Rd. It's open weekdays from 9 am to 5 pm, and Saturday (and Sunday during the tourist season) until noon.

Anyinginyi Arts is an Aboriginal shop on Davidson St specialising in arts and crafts from the Barkly Tablelands. Murranjirra Aboriginal Arts is another gallery on Paterson St, near the Transit Centre.

Things to See

Along Peko Rd you can visit the old **Gold Stamp Battery**, where gold-bearing ore was crushed and treated. The battery is still in working order and guided tours are given daily at 9.30 am and 5 pm from April to October, and cost $12. There's also an underground tour at 11 am for $12. Along the same road there is the **One Tank Hill lookout**.

The small **National Trust Museum**, on Schmidt St near the corner of Windley St, houses six rooms of local memorabilia and reconstructed mining scenes. It's open May to October daily from 3 to 5 pm; entry is $2.

Twelve kilometres north of town are the green-roofed stone buildings of the old **telegraph station**. This is one of only four of the original 12 stations remaining in the Territory (the others are at Barrow Creek, Alice Springs and Powell Creek). The station's telegraph functions ceased in 1935 when a new office opened in the town. Today it is owned by the government and maintained by Parks & Wildlife, and it's worth a wander around.

Activities

If you're into fossicking, head for **Moonlight Rockhole** fossicking area, about 60km west of town along the Warrego road. Note that a permit must be obtained from the Department of Mines & Energy (on the main street).

You can take part in a cattle drive or go horse riding at **Juno Horse Centre** (☎ 8962 2783). A four hour horseback cattle muster, including cooked breakfast and tea, costs $55 and trail rides of various length start at $30 per rider.

Organised Tours

Kraut Downs Station (☎ 8962 2820) runs informative half-day tours where you can learn about bush tucker and medicine, try whip-cracking and boomerang-throwing, and wash down a witchetty grub with billy tea and damper, all for $25.

Norm's Gold & Scenic Tours (☎ 0418 891 711) offers a 'Gold Fever Tour' for $25, where you can pan for gold and keep the proceeds, and afternoon trips to the Devil's Marbles ($50 including dinner).

Tours of the Dot Mine, an old gold mine dating from the 1930s, start each evening during winter at 7 pm and cost $14. For details phone ☎ 8962 2168.

The Tourist's Rest Tennant Creek Hostel (see Places to Stay) runs 'Devil's Deals' – trips out to the Devil's Marbles for $50, including a night's accommodation.

Places to Stay

Camping The *Outback Caravan Park* (☎ 8962 2459) is 1km east of town along Peko Rd. It has a swimming pool, tent sites at $13 a double ($17 with power) and on-site air-con cabins for $40 to $55 a double.

The other choice is the *Tennant Creek Caravan Park* (☎ 8962 2325) on Paterson St (Stuart Hwy) on the northern edge of town. It has powered sites at $6 per person, twin 'bunkhouse' rooms at $20 a double and air-con cabins at $55.

Hostels The *Safari Lodge Motel* (☎ 8962 2207) has a block of backpacker rooms across the road from its main building on Davidson St. A bed in these air-con rooms costs $12, and there are communal cooking facilities.

The other budget alternative is the *Tourist's Rest Tennant Creek Hostel* (☎ 8962 2719), in a shady location on the corner of Leichhardt and Windley Sts. Beds in air-con triple dorms cost $14 and twins/doubles are $30/32; YHA/VIP/Nomads discounts are available.

Hotels & Motels Tennant Creek's motels aren't cheap. The *Safari Lodge Motel* (☎ 8962 2207) in the centre of town on

Davidson St has singles/doubles from $40. The **Goldfields Hotel Motel** (☎ 8962 2030), just around the corner on the highway, has rooms for $45/65.

At the southern end of town the **Bluestone Motor Inn** (☎ 8962 2617) is the only place in this category with a swimming pool. Units cost $68 to $87.

Places to Eat

It comes as something of a surprise to find one of the most highly regarded restaurants in the Territory in the local squash centre! The **Dolly Pot Inn** on Davidson St is open daily from 11 am to midnight, and offers good-value meals such as steak and salad, and also features home-made waffles.

A popular place with locals for night-time takeaways is **Chompin Charlies** (114 Paterson St), near the Tennant Creek Hotel, which has good barramundi and chips for $3.50.

At the front of the Transit Centre building, **Priester's Café** opens for light meals and snacks whenever a bus pulls in; it's a nice enough place to kill time if you're just passing through. Next door to the Transit Centre is the recently opened **Top of the Town Café**, which is open all night until 5 or 6 am.

Rocky's Pizza & Pasta (☎ 8962 2522), next to the ANZ bank on Paterson St, has, yep, pizzas and pasta.

There's a **Chinese restaurant** in the Goldfields Hotel Motel. The Memorial Club on Memorial Drive welcomes visitors and has good, straightforward counter meals at its **Memories Bistro**, including a $5 lunch special.

TENNANT CREEK TO ALICE SPRINGS

About 90km south of Tennant Creek is the **Devil's Marbles Conservation Reserve**, a haphazard pile of giant spherical boulders scattered on both sides of the road. According to Aboriginal mythology they were laid by the Rainbow Serpent. There's also a basic Parks & Wildlife **camp site** here. At **Wauchope**, just south of the marbles, there's a **pub** (with accommodation) and **caravan park**.

After the Devil's Marbles there are only a few places of interest on the trip south to the Alice. Near Barrow Creek the **Stuart Memorial** commemorates John McDouall Stuart. Visible to the east of the highway is Central Mt Stuart.

At **Barrow Creek** itself there is another old telegraph repeater station. It was attacked by Aboriginal people in 1874 and the station master and linesman were killed – their graves are by the road. A great many Aboriginal people died in the inevitable reprisals.

There's also still a few hundred metres of the original line stretching north from the telegraph station. The **pub** here is a real outback gem, and the Barrow Creek Races in August are a colourful event that draw people in from all over the area.

The **Barrow Creek Hotel & Caravan Park** (☎ 8956 9753) has twin rooms in dongas for $25, singles/doubles for $25/35 and camp sites.

The road continues through **Ti Tree**, where there's the **Gallereaterie**, a small cafe and Aboriginal art outlet, usually with artists at work.

Alice Springs

● postcode 0870   ● pop 25,520

The Alice, as it is usually known, started off as a repeater station built in 1871 on the Overland Telegraph Line between Adelaide and Darwin, where the submarine cable from Java came ashore. The station was built near a permanent water hole in the bed of the normally dry Todd River. This was named after Charles Todd, Superintendent of Telegraphs back in Adelaide, and a spring near the water hole was named after Alice, his wife.

A town, named Stuart, was first established in 1888, a few kilometres south of the telegraph station as a railhead for a proposed railway line. Because the railway didn't materialise immediately, the town developed slowly. Not until 1933 did the town come to be known as Alice Springs.

Alice Springs' growth to its present size has been recent and rapid. When the name was officially changed in 1933 the population had only just reached 200. Even in the 1950s

Alice Springs was still a tiny town with a population in the hundreds. Until WWII there was no sealed road to it, and it was only in 1987 that the old road south to Port Augusta and Adelaide was finally replaced by a new, shorter and fully sealed highway.

Today, Alice Springs is a pleasant, modern town with good shops and restaurants. But while the appearance is modern, the underlying fact is that this is a fairly small rural town in a beautiful but harsh environment a bloody long way from anywhere. The realisation that the Outback is only a stone's throw away, as are some of the country's most spectacular natural wonders, does give the town a unique atmosphere that is a major draw for tourists.

Orientation

The centre of Alice Springs is a compact area just five streets wide, bounded by the Todd River on one side and the Stuart Hwy on the other. Anzac Hill forms the northern boundary to the central area, while Stuart Terrace is at the southern end. Many of the places to stay and virtually all of the places to eat are in this central rectangle.

Todd St is the main shopping street; from Wills Terrace to Gregory Terrace it is a pedestrian mall. Greyhound Pioneer buses pull in on the corner of Gregory and Railway Terraces; McCafferty's is opposite the CATIA office on Gregory Terrace.

Information

Tourist Offices The Central Australian Tourism Industry Association office (CATIA; ☎ 8952 5800, visinfo@catia .asn.au) is in the town centre on Gregory Terrace. The staff are helpful, and there's a range of brochures and maps. The office is open weekdays from 8.30 am to 5.30 pm, and on weekends from 9 am to 4 pm. This office issues permits to travel on the Mereenie Loop Rd in the Western MacDonnell Ranges. Parks & Wildlife (☎ 8951 8211) has a desk at the CATIA office, with a comprehensive range of brochures on all the parks and reserves in the Centre.

The *Centralian Advocate* is Alice Springs' twice weekly newspaper.

Post & Communications The main post office is on Hartley St, and there's a row of public phones outside.

Internet and email access is available at some of the backpackers hostels (Melanka's Internet Café charges $2 for 15 minutes and is open from 9 am to 9 pm) and at the Alice Springs Library, where the cost is $2 for 30 minutes.

Gay & Lesbian Travellers Alice has an established gay and lesbian community; for information on social activities and support phone ☎ 8953 2844.

Bookshops There are a couple of good bookshops. The Arunta Gallery on Todd St just south of the mall is one, and there's a branch of Dymocks in the Alice Plaza.

Useful Organisations The Department of Lands, Planning & Environment office (☎ 8951 5344) on Gregory Terrace is a good source for maps, as is the AANT (☎ 8953 1322) at 58 Sargent St, north of town.

Telegraph Station Historical Reserve

Laying the Overland Telegraph Line across the dry, harsh centre of Australia was no easy task, as the small museum at the old telegraph station, 2km north of town, shows. The station, one of 12 built along the telegraph line in the early 1870s, was constructed of local stone and operated until 1932.

Guided tours are given hourly between 8.30 am and 4.30 pm (☎ 8952 3993 to confirm times); there's also an informative self-guiding map. A free slide show is held three times weekly at 7.30 pm – check with Parks & Wildlife for details.

The station is open daily from 8 am to 7 pm in winter and until 9 pm in summer; entry costs $4.

The original **Alice Springs** here can be a great spot for a cooling dip (though it's often dry), and the grassy picnic area by the station has barbecues, tables and some shady gum trees – it's a popular spot on weekends.

It's easy to walk or ride to the station from the Alice – just follow the path on the

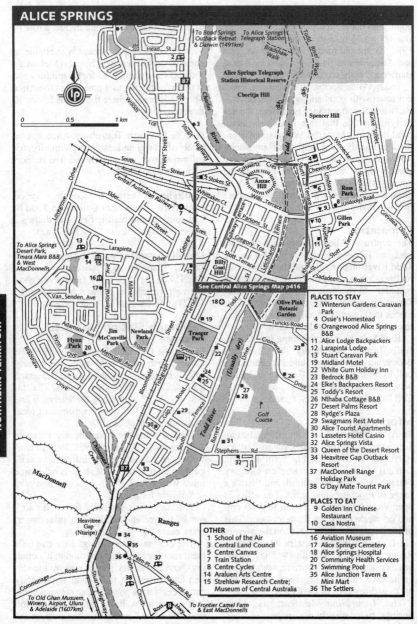

ALICE SPRINGS

0   0.5   1 km

See Central Alice Springs Map p416

PLACES TO STAY
2 Wintersun Gardens Caravan Park
4 Ossie's Homestead
6 Orangewood Alice Springs B&B
11 Alice Lodge Backpackers
12 Larapinta Lodge
13 Stuart Caravan Park
19 Midland Motel
22 White Gum Holiday Inn
23 Bedrock B&B
24 Elke's Backpackers Resort
25 Toddy's Resort
26 Nthaba Cottage B&B
27 Desert Palms Resort
28 Rydge's Plaza
29 Swagmans Rest Motel
30 Alice Tourist Apartments
31 Lasseters Hotel Casino
32 Alice Springs Vista
33 Queen of the Desert Resort
34 Heavitree Gap Outback Resort
37 MacDonnell Range Holiday Park
38 G'Day Mate Tourist Park

PLACES TO EAT
9 Golden Inn Chinese Restaurant
10 Casa Nostra

OTHER
1 School of the Air
3 Central Land Council
5 Centre Canvas
7 Train Station
8 Centre Cycles
14 Araluen Arts Centre
15 Strehlow Research Centre; Museum of Central Australia
16 Aviation Museum
17 Alice Springs Cemetery
18 Alice Springs Hospital
20 Community Health Services
21 Swimming Pool
35 Alice Junction Tavern & Mini Mart
36 The Settlers

western side of the riverbed; it takes about half an hour to ride.

Anzac Hill

At the northern end of Todd St you can make the short, sharp ascent to the top of Anzac Hill (or you can drive there). Aboriginal people call the hill Untyeyetweleye, the site of the Corkwood Dreaming, the story of a woman who lived alone on the hill. The Two Sisters ancestral beings (Arrweketye therre) are also associated with the hill.

From the top you have a fine view over modern Alice Springs and down to the MacDonnell Ranges that form the southern boundary of the town.

Old Buildings

Along Todd St you can see **Adelaide House**, built in the early 1920s and now preserved as the **John Flynn Memorial Museum**. Originally it was Alice Springs' first hospital. It's open Monday to Friday from 10 am to 4 pm, and Saturday until noon. Entry is $3 and includes a cup of tea or coffee. Flynn, who founded the flying doctor service, is also commemorated by the **John Flynn Memorial Church** next door.

There are a number of interesting old buildings along Parsons St, including the **Stuart Town Gaol** built from 1907 to 1908. It's open weekdays from 10 am to 12.30 pm, and on Saturday from 9.30 am to noon. The **Old Courthouse**, which was in use until 1980, is on the corner of Parsons and Hartley Sts, and now houses the fledgling **National Pioneer Women's Hall of Fame**. It is open daily from 10 am to 2 pm. Across the road on Parsons St is the **Residency**, which dates from 1926-27. It's now used for historical exhibits and is open weekdays from 9 am to 4 pm and weekends from 10 am to 4 pm.

Other old buildings include the **Hartley St School**, which now houses the National Trust office and has historical displays, and **Tuncks Store** on the corner of Hartley St and Stott Terrace.

Near the corner of Parsons St and Leichhardt Terrace, the old **Pioneer Theatre** is a

Mparntwe

The Alice Springs area is the traditional home of the Arrernte Aboriginal people, and to them it is Mparntwe. The heart of the area is the junction of the Charles (Anthelke Ulpeye) and Todd (Lhere Mparntwe) rivers, just north of Anzac Hill.

All the topographical features of the town were formed by the creative ancestral beings – the Yeperenye, Ntyarlke and Utnerrengatye caterpillars – as they crawled across the landscape from Emily Gap (Anthwerrke), in the MacDonnell Ranges south-east of town. Alice Springs today still has a sizeable Aboriginal community with strong links to the area.

former walk-in (not drive-in) cinema dating from 1944. These days it's a YHA hostel.

Royal Flying Doctor Service Base

The RFDS base is close to the town centre on Stuart Terrace. It's open Monday to Saturday from 9 am to 4 pm, and Sunday from 1 to 4 pm. The tours last half an hour ($5, children $2). There's a small museum and a souvenir shop.

School of the Air

The School of the Air, which broadcasts lessons to children living on remote outback stations, is on Head St, about 3km north of the town centre. During school terms you can hear a live broadcast (depending on class schedules). The school is open Monday to Saturday from 8.30 am to 4.30 pm, and Sunday from 1.30 to 4.30 pm; entry is by donation ($3).

Strehlow Research Centre

This centre, on Larapinta Drive, commemorates the work of Professor Ted Strehlow among the Arrernte people of the district (see the Hermannsburg section later in this chapter for information on the Hermannsburg Mission). The main function of the building is to house the most comprehensive collection of Aboriginal spirit items in the country. These were entrusted to Strehlow

NORTHERN TERRITORY

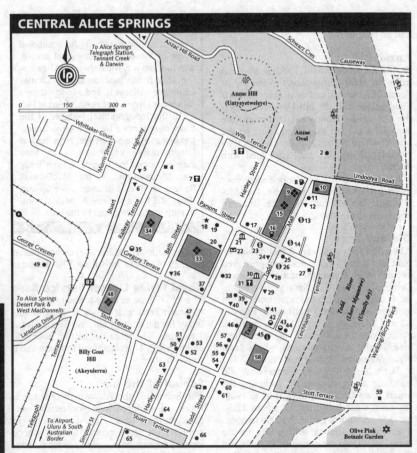

CENTRAL ALICE SPRINGS

To Alice Springs Telegraph Station, Tennant Creek & Darwin

0   150   300 m

Anzac Hill Road

Schwarz Cres

Causeway

Anzac Hill (Untyeyetweleye)

Anzac Oval

Whittaker Court

Wills Terrace

Undoolya Road

Morris Street

Stuart Highway

Railway Terrace

Bath Street

Hartley Street

Todd Street

Mall

Parsons Street

George Crescent

Gregory Terrace

Stott Terrace

To Alice Springs Desert Park & West MacDonnells

Larapinta Drive

Billy Goat Hill (Akeyulerra)

Hartley Street

Todd Street

Stuart Terrace

Leichhardt Terrace

Todd River (Lhere Mparntwe) (Usually dry)

Walking/Bicycle track

Telegraph Terrace

Simpson St

To Airport, Uluru & South Australian Border

Stott Terrace

Olive Pink Botanic Garden

---

for safekeeping by the local Aboriginal people years ago, when they realised their traditional life was under threat. Because the items are so important, and cannot be viewed by an uninitiated male or *any* female, they are kept in a vault in the centre. There is, however, a very good display detailing the works of Strehlow, and the culture of the Arrernte people. Strehlow's books about the Arrernte people are still widely read.

The building itself is something of a feature, with its huge rammed-earth wall. The centre is open daily from 10 am to 5 pm (entry $4).

Museum of Central Australia

Housed in the Strehlow Research Centre building, the Museum of Central Australia (☎ 8951 5532) has some fascinating collections, including some superb natural history exhibits, an interesting exhibition on meteorites (including the Henbury meteorites) and exhibits on Aboriginal culture.

The museum is open Monday to Friday from 9 am to 5 pm, and entry is $5.

Araluen Arts Centre

The Araluen Arts Centre on Larapinta Drive has a small gallery full of **Albert Namatjira**

CENTRAL ALICE SPRINGS

PLACES TO STAY
4 Desert Rose Inn
10 Todd Tavern; Pub Caf
27 Pioneer Hostel; Pioneer Theatre
59 Alice Springs Resort
62 Melanka's Lodge; Rattle 'n'
    Hum; Internet Cafe
64 Stuart Lodge

PLACES TO EAT
1 Hungry Jacks
5 Red Rooster
6 McDonald's
12 Al Fresco's Café
16 Stuart Arms Hotel
20 Hong Kong Chinese Restaurant
24 Puccini's Restaurant
28 Red Ochre Grill
29 Scotty's Tavern
36 Pizza Hut
39 Red Dog; La Cafetiere; Red
    Rock Café
40 Swingers
41 Café Mediterranean Bar
    Doppio; Camel's Crossing
    Mexican Restaurant
51 Overlander Steakhouse

54 KFC
56 Bojangles Restaurant; Territory
    Tucker
60 Dingo's
63 Oriental Gourmet

OTHER
2 Totem Theatre
3 Catholic Church
7 Anglican Church
8 Shell Service Station
9 Bi-Lo Supermarket
11 Cinema
13 Westpac Bank
14 ANZ Bank
15 Alice Plaza
17 Old Courthouse
18 Police Station
19 Stuart Gaol
21 The Residency
22 Main Post Office
23 Commonwealth Bank
25 Qantas
26 National Bank
30 Adelaide House
31 John Flynn Memorial
    Church

32 Hartley St School
33 Yeperenye Shopping Centre
34 Coles Supermarket
35 Greyhound Pioneer
37 Avis
38 Alice Springs Disposals
42 McCafferty's
43 Airport Shuttle Bus
44 Maps NT; Dept of Lands,
    Planning & Environment
45 CATIA (Tourist Office)
46 Minerals House
47 Arunta Gallery
48 K-Mart
49 Pioneer Cemetery
50 Hertz & Tuncks Store
52 Territory Thrifty Car Rental
53 Panorama Guth
55 Aboriginal Art & Culture
    Centre
57 Papunya Tula Artists
58 Library & Council Offices
61 CAAMA Shop
65 Royal Flying Doctor Service
66 Budget Rent a Car

paintings, and often other displays as well. The stained-glass windows in the foyer are the centrepiece. It's open weekdays from 10 am to 5 pm (entry $2).

Alice Springs Cemetery
Adjacent to the aviation museum, this cemetery contains a number of interesting graves. The most famous is that of **Albert Namatjira** – it's the sandstone grave on the far side. The headstone features a terracotta tile mural of three of Namatjira's dreaming sites in the MacDonnell Ranges. The glazes forming the mural design were painted on by Namatjira's granddaughter, Elaine, and the other work was done by other members of the Hermannsburg Potters.

Other graves in the cemetery include that of Harold Lasseter, who perished in 1931 while trying to relocate the rich gold reef he supposedly found west of Uluru 20 years earlier, and the anthropologist Olive Pink, who spent many years working with the Aboriginal people of the central deserts.

Pioneer Cemetery
This is the original Alice Springs cemetery, and today it lies almost forgotten and rarely visited on the light-industrial area on the western side of the railway line on George Crescent. The gravestones here tell some of the stories of the original settlers – including that of the young man who died at Temple Bar of 'foul air'.

Panorama Guth
Panorama Guth, at 65 Hartley St in the town centre, is a huge circular panorama which is viewed from an elevated observation point. It depicts almost all the points of interest around the Centre. The artist responsible, Henk Guth, also paints doe-eyed women with large breasts, if you like that sort of thing, but the real reason to come here is to see his extensive collection of Aboriginal artefacts and other relics of outback life.

It's open from Monday to Saturday from 9 am to 5 pm, and Sunday from 2 to 5 pm (entry $3).

Lasseter's Lost Reef

The gold prospector Lewis Hubert (Harold Bell) Lasseter (1880-1931) is immortalised as one of Australia's great hopefuls. We still know of him today because of Ion Idriess' romantic account *Lasseter's Last Ride* (1931); otherwise he would probably have faded into the red dust of the Petermann Range. Lasseter claimed to have found, sometime between 1897 and 1911, 'a vast gold bearing reef' in central Australia, some 23km in length. The diminutive Lasseter had supposedly been looking for rubies when he stumbled upon gold as thick as 'plums in a pudding'. In the remote, arid Petermann Range in Central Australia on the NT-SA border.

In 1930 the Central Australian Gold Exploration Company was formed, with Lasseter as a guide. The expedition was well equipped with an aeroplane, trucks and a wireless. But things started to go wrong: the aircraft crashed near Uluru (Ayers Rock) and Fred Blakeley, the expedition leader, abandoned it at the Rock. Lasseter, after an argument with another hopeful prospector Paul Johns, headed out alone to look for the reef.

Lasseter died of starvation in January 1931 near Shaws Creek and his body was found by Bob Buck in March; his diaries were retrieved and in them he claimed to have pegged the reef. Idriess used these diaries to write his book.

Subsequent attempts to find Lasseter's lost reef have been unsuccessful. His name is perpetuated in the Lasseter Hwy, which runs from the Stuart Hwy to Uluru.

Olive Pink Botanic Garden

Just across the Todd River from the town centre, and off Tuncks Rd, the Olive Pink Botanic Garden has a collection of native shrubs and trees that are typical of the 500km area around Alice Springs. This arid-zone botanic garden is open from 10 am to 6 pm. There are some short walks in the reserve, including the climb to the top of Annie Meyer Hill in the Sadadeen Range, from where there's a fine view over the town. The hill is known to the Arrernte people as Tharrarltneme and is a registered sacred site. Looking to the south, in the middle distance is a small ridge running east to west; this is Ntyarlkarle Tyaneme, one of the first sites created by the caterpillar ancestors, and the name relates that this was where the caterpillars crossed the river.

Frontier Camel Farm

About 5km along Palm Circuit is the Frontier Camel Farm, where you have the chance to ride one of the beasts. These strange 'ships of the desert', guided by their Afghani masters, were the main form of transport before the railways were built. There's a museum with displays about camels, and a guided tour and camel ride is held daily at 10.30 am (2 pm from April to October).

Also here is the **Arid Australian Reptile House**, which has an excellent collection of snakes and lizards.

The farm is open daily from 9 am to 5 pm. The cost of the camel tour is $10/5 for adults/children, including a visit to the reptile house.

Old Ghan Museum & Transport Hall of Fame

Transport buffs should like this centre is at the MacDonnell Siding, off the Stuart Hwy 10km south of Alice Springs. A group of local railway enthusiasts has restored a collection of *Ghan* locomotives and carriages on a stretch of disused siding from the old narrow-gauge *Ghan* railway track.

Also here is the Transport Hall of Fame, with a fine collection of old vehicles, including some very early road trains, and other transport memorabilia.

The centre is open daily from 9 am to 5 pm and entry is $4 to either museum.

There are also trips on the old *Ghan* on Wednesday, Friday and Sunday in winter to Mt Ertiva siding, 9km south of town. The trip starts at 10 am, takes 1½ hours and costs $13/7.50 for adults/children, including entry to both museums.

The Ghan

Australia's great railway adventure would have to be the *Ghan*. The *Ghan* went through a major change in 1982 and, although it's now a rather more modern and comfortable adventure, it's still a great trip.

The *Ghan* saga started in 1877 when it was decided to build a railway line from Adelaide to Darwin. It eventually took over 50 years to reach Alice Springs, and plans are still being made for the final 1500km to Darwin more than a century later (see the 'North Australia Railway' boxed text). The basic problem was that a big mistake was made right at the start, a mistake that wasn't finally sorted out until 1980: the line was built in the wrong place.

The grand error was a result of concluding that because all the creek beds north of Marree were bone dry, and because nobody had seen rain, there wasn't going to be rain in the future. In fact, the initial stretch of line was laid right across a flood plain and when the rain came, even though it soon dried up, the line was simply washed away. In the century or so that the original *Ghan* line survived it was a regular occurrence for the tracks to be washed away.

The wrong route was only part of the *Ghan*'s problems. At first it was built broad gauge to Marree, then extended narrow gauge to Oodnadatta in 1884. And what a jerry-built line it was – the foundations were flimsy, the sleepers were too light, the grading was too steep and it meandered hopelessly. It was hardly surprising that the top speed of the old *Ghan* was a flat-out 30 km/h!

Early rail travellers went from Adelaide to Marree on the broad-gauge line, changed there to narrow gauge as far as Oodnadatta, then had to make the final journey to Alice Springs by camel train. The Afghani-led camel trains had pioneered transport through the Outback and it was from these Afghanis that the *Ghan* took its name.

Finally, in 1929, the line was extended from Oodnadatta to Alice Springs. Though the *Ghan* was a great adventure, it simply didn't work. At the best of times it was chronically slow and uncomfortable as it bounced and bucked its way down the badly laid line. Worse, it was unreliable and expensive to run. And worst of all, a heavy rainfall could strand it at either end or even in the middle. Parachute drops of supplies to stranded train travellers became part of outback lore and on one occasion the *Ghan* rolled in 10 days late!

By the early 1970s the South Australian state railway system was taken over by the Federal government and a new line to Alice Springs was planned. The $145 million line was to be standard gauge, laid from Tarcoola, north-west of Port Augusta on the transcontinental line, to Alice Springs – and it would be laid where rain would not wash it out. In 1980 the line was completed in circumstances that would be unusual for any major project today, let alone an Australian one – it was ahead of time and on budget.

In 1982 the old *Ghan* made its last run and the old line was subsequently torn up. One of its last appearances was in the film *Mad Max III*.

Whereas the old train took 140 passengers and, under ideal conditions, made the trip in 50 hours, the new train takes twice as many passengers and does it in less than 24 hours. It's still the *Ghan*, but it's not the trip it once was.

KATE NOLAN

The old *Ghan*

NORTHERN TERRITORY

Alice Springs Desert Park

About 3km out of town along Larapinta Drive, the Desert Park (☎ 8951 8788) is a superb wildlife park built at the foot of the MacDonnell Ranges. The 1300 hectare park displays the ecosystems of central Australia and their traditional relationship with Aboriginal people. Features include walk-through enclosures, state-of-the-art interpretive displays and superb graphics.

It's best to kick off your tour with the 20 minute film (shown on the hour between 8 am and 5 pm), then take the 1.6km walking track through the major exhibits. The unique and endangered plants and animals of central Australia are a highlight of the park, and gems such as bilbies, mala, kowari and carnivorous ghost bats can be seen. There are **walk-through aviaries** housing desert parrots, such as the magnificent princess parrot, and a brilliant **nocturnal house** with a great assortment of creatures you wouldn't have a hope of seeing otherwise. Free-flying birds of prey are exhibited daily and ranger talks are held at various exhibits throughout the day.

There's a cafeteria and a la carte restaurant (see Places to Eat in this section).

Alice Springs Desert Park is open daily from 7.30 am to 6 pm. Entry is $12/30 per adult/family. Allow at least three hours to get the most out of the park.

Getting to/from the park is a problem if you don't have your own transport. The cheapest way to get there is by bike, but Desert Park Transfers (☎ 8952 4667) operates during park hours and does the return trip for $20 (students and children $14) including park entrance fee.

Activities

Cycling Alice Springs is a flat town which lends itself to getting around by bicycle, and there are a number of marked bike tracks. An excellent track leads up from town along the Todd River to the Old Telegraph Station and you can ride to Simpsons Gap along a designated track. This is an excellent way to get to Simpsons Gap, and the track meanders through pretty scrub country, well away from the road. Be sure to carry plenty of water whenever you go cycling.

Steve's Mountain Bike Tours (☎ 8952 1542) offers short trips through the MacDonnell Ranges near town from $30 for an easy hour to $85 for four to five hours for experienced riders.

Horse Riding Ossie's Outback Horse Treks (☎ 1800 628 211, ossies@topend.com.au) operates a variety of trail rides to suit all levels of experience. Three-hour morning, afternoon or sunset nature trail rides cost $65 per person including snacks and water; an all-day ride including barbecue lunch and billy tea costs $125; and an overnight ride, sleeping in a swag under the stars, costs $175.

Camel Rides Camel treks are another central Australian attraction. You can have a short ride for a few dollars at the Frontier Camel Farm (☎ 8953 0444), or take its longer Todd River Ramble, which is a one hour ride along the bed of the Todd River ($45/25 for adults/children).

Camel Outback Safaris (☎ 8956 0925), based at Stuart's Well 90km south of Alice Springs, also operates camel tours (see the Stuart's Well section later in this chapter).

Ballooning Sunrise balloon trips are also popular and cost from $120/55, which includes breakfast and a 30 minute flight. One-hour flights cost around $170/$80.

Balloon operators include Outback Ballooning (☎ 1800 809 790), Ballooning Downunder (☎ 1800 801 601) and Spinifex Ballooning (☎ 1800 677 893).

Organised Tours

The tourist office can tell you about all sorts of organised tours from Alice Springs. There are bus tours, 4WD tours, balloon tours, camel tours and a number of combinations that give you, say, a balloon flight and a camel ride for less than if you were to take the two separately.

Note that although many of the tours don't operate daily, there is at least one trip a day to one or more of the major attractions.

Most of the tours follow similar routes and you see much the same on them all, although the level of service and the degree of luxury will determine how much they cost. All the hostels can book tours, and they will also know which companies offer the best deals.

Town Tours Alice Wanderer Mini Town Tours (☎ 1800 669 111) can whizz you around some of the town's major sights in three hours for $60, including entry fees.

Aboriginal Culture Tours Rod Steinert Tours (☎ 8558 8377, rstours@cobweb .com.au) operates a variety of tours, including the popular Dreamtime & Bushtucker Tour ($76/38). It's a three hour trip in which you meet some Warlpiri Aboriginal people and learn a little about their traditional life. You can tag along on the same tour with your own vehicle for $64/32.

Oak Valley Day Tours (☎ 8956 0959) is an Aboriginal-owned and run organisation that makes day trips to Mpwellare and Rainbow Valley, both of cultural significance to the Aboriginal people. The cost is $110/80, which includes lunch and morning and afternoon tea.

MacDonnell Ranges Jim's Bush Tours (☎ 8953 1975) offers good-value day tours to the East and West MacDonnells. Itineraries vary, but the emphasis is less on driving than on walking. A day tour costs $55 ($49 for YHA/VIP holders and children), although you must bring your own lunch.

Full day 4WD tours to Finke Gorge run daily in winter by AAT King's (☎ 8952 1700, austour@aatkings.com.au) for $89 including lunch.

Uluru & Kings Canyon Sahara Outback Tours (☎ 8953 0881, sahara@saharatours .com.au) offers very good daily camping

---

Alice Events

The Alice has a string of colourful activities, particularly during the cool tourist months from May to August.

The **Camel Cup**, a series of camel races, takes place in mid-July.

The **Alice Springs Agricultural Show** takes place in early July, and the highlight is a fireworks display.

In August there's the **Alice Springs Rodeo**, when for one week the town is full of bow-legged stockmen, swaggering around in their 10-gallon hats, cowboy shirts, moleskin jeans and RM Williams Cuban-heeled boots.

In late September, there's the event which draws the biggest crowds of all – the **Henley-on-Todd Regatta**. Having a series of boat races on the Todd River is slightly complicated by the fact that hardly any water ever flows along the river bed. Nevertheless races are held for sailing boats, doubles, racing eights and every boat class you could think of. The boats are all bottomless, the crews' legs stick out and they simply run down the course!

The **Octoberfest** is held early in October, at the end of the regatta. It's held at the Memorial Club on Gap Rd and there are many frivolous activities, including spit the dummy, tug of war and stein-lifting competitions. There's a variety of cuisines on offer and a range of local and overseas beers for the beer enthusiast.

Through the cooler months there is also a string of country **horse races** at Alice Springs and surrounding settlements like Finke, Barrow Creek, Aileron or the Harts Range. They're colourful events and are the big turnouts of the year for the communities involved.

CLINT CURÉ

trips to Uluru (Ayers Rock) and elsewhere; these are popular with backpackers. It charges $240 for a two-day trip to the Rock and Kata Tjuta (the Olgas), or you can pay an extra $105 and spend one more day taking in Kings Canyon – well worthwhile if you have the time.

If your time is limited, Day Tours (☎ 8953 4664) will get you to the Rock and back for $155/120, including lunch and sunset viewing.

Places to Stay – Budget

Camping There are a number of camping options in Alice Springs. The *G'Day Mate Tourist Park* (☎ 8952 9589) on Palm Circuit, 3km south of town, offers camp sites for $14/16 without/with power and self-contained cabins that accommodate up to six people (from $44). Also on Palm Circuit is *Heavitree Gap Outback Resort* (☎ 1800 896 119), with camp sites for $14/16.

MacDonnell Range Holiday Park (☎ 1800 808 373) is on Palm Place, 4km from town. Camp sites cost $15/18 and on-site cabins $50/62. *Stuart Caravan Park* (☎ 8952 2547), 3km west from town on Larapinta Drive, has camp sites for $14/16, six-bed on-site vans for $39 (plus $6 each extra adult) and four-bed cabins for $50.

Wintersun Gardens Caravan Park (☎ 8952 4080), 3.5km north of town on the Stuart Hwy, has camp sites at $14/17, six-bed on-site vans for $38 for two people (plus $7 each extra adult) and six-bed cabins for $42 to $58 for two people (plus $7 for each extra adult).

Hostels There are plenty of hostels and guesthouses in Alice Springs. All places catering to backpackers have the usual facilities and services – pool, courtesy bus, travel desk, bicycle hire etc.

Right in the centre of town, on the corner of Leichhardt Terrace and Parsons St in the old Pioneer walk-in cinema, is the YHA *Pioneer Hostel* (☎ 8952 8855). It has beds in air-con dorms: $14 in a four or six share room and $18 per person for a twin; linen hire is $2 more. There's a swimming pool, and bicycles can be hired.

Also central is the popular *Melanka Lodge* (☎ 1800 815 066, 94 Todd St, melanka@ ozemail.com.au). This is a large, noisy, party place with a variety of air-con rooms, from eight-bed dorms at $13 to four-bed dorms at $14 and twin shares at $16 per person. There are also singles/doubles for $30/32, or motel rooms at $71/79 with TV, fridge and bathroom. There's a cafeteria with budget meals, an Internet cafe, bike hire and Rattle'n'Hum nightclub, one of the most popular travellers drinking spots in the Alice (see Entertainment later in this section).

Over the river and still just a short walk from the town centre, is the relaxed *Alice Lodge Backpackers* (☎ 1800 351 925, 4 Mueller St). This is a small, quiet and friendly hostel with a courtyard garden, barbecue, free breakfast and fridges in each room. Nightly rates are $13 in the bed dorm, $15 in a four-bed room and $16 per person in a double. There's a small kitchen and laundry facilities.

Also on this side of the river is *Ossie's Homestead* (☎ 1800 628 211, 18 Warburton St). B&B in the 12-bed dorm is $12, in a four-bed room $14 and in a double $32. There's a swimming pool and the usual facilities, as well as pet kangaroos. Ossie's also runs trail rides from $60 to $205.

Back on the other side of the river is *Toddy's Resort* (☎ 1800 806 240, 41 Gap Rd). This complex has laundry facilities and a communal kitchen for those not in the self-contained units. Toddy's has email access, a bar and cheap meals. Prices are $12 for six-bed dorms with shared facilities, $14 with TV and bathroom, and $36 for doubles ($48 with bathroom).

Right next door is *Elke's Backpackers Resort* (☎ 1800 633 354), a backpackers in an old apartment building consisting of two-bedroom, self-contained units. Beds (six to eight in a unit) cost $16 ($13 YHA/VIP); doubles are $45.

Places to Stay – Mid-Range

Hotels On the river, at 1 Todd St mall, is the *Todd Tavern* (☎ 8952 1255). It gets noisy when there are bands playing on weekends, but it's otherwise quite a reasonable place to stay. Rates are $40 for singles/doubles (some with bathroom) including a light breakfast.

At the southern end of Gap Rd, just before Heavitree Gap, is the large, upmarket *Queen of the Desert Resort* (☎ *1800 896 124*). A deluxe single/double with bathroom, fridge and TV costs $90/100; a budget room sleeping up to four costs $80. Backpackers are also catered for, although there are no kitchen facilities – a bed in a six-bed dorm costs $12.80 (no linen) or there's one four-bed dorm for $15 a bed (linen supplied). Facilities include a nightclub and good pool.

Stuart Lodge (☎ *1800 249 124*), on Stuart Terrace, is a nicely placed, cheap option run by the YWCA. Singles, twins/doubles and triples with shared bathrooms cost $35, $45 and $50, respectively. It's clean, quiet and well run.

Apartments & Holiday Flats There are very few apartments and flats for rent; in most cases the best you can do is a motel-type room with limited cooking facilities, which usually consists of an electric frying pan and a microwave oven.

Alice Tourist Apartments (☎ *1800 806 142*) is on Gap Rd. There are one and two-room, self-contained, air-con apartments for $72 a double, $104 for four people and $115 for six people. They consist of a main room with sleeping, cooking and dining facilities, and the larger flats have a second room with two or four beds. These are a good option for families.

The *White Gum Holiday Inn* (☎ *1800 896 131, 17 Gap Rd*) also has rooms with separate kitchen at $73 a double.

On Barrett Drive, next to the Plaza Hotel Alice Springs, the *Desert Palms Resort* (☎ *1800 678 037, despalms@saharatours .com.au*) has spacious rooms, each with limited cooking facilities, at $79 for two. There's a large swimming pool and nicely landscaped gardens.

Conveniently central is *Larapinta Lodge* (☎ *8952 7255, llodge@ozemail.com.au, 3 Larapinta Drive*), just over the railway line from the town centre. It has singles/doubles

for $67/77, with communal kitchen and laundry, and the obligatory swimming pool.

Motels Alice Springs has a rash of motels, and prices range from around $50 to $100 for a double room. There are often lower prices and special deals during the hot summer months.

The *Swagman's Rest Motel* (☎ *1800 089 612, 67 Gap Rd*) has singles/doubles for $63/73. The units are self-contained and there's a swimming pool.

The *Midland Motel* (☎ *1800 241 588, midland@topend.com.au, 4 Traeger Ave*) charges $65/75 and up for its rooms and also has a licensed restaurant.

B&B There are a few B&Bs in the Alice. The *Bedrock B&B* (☎ *8955 5288, 16 Range Crescent*) is east of the river not far from the golf course. It's a pleasant place with a landscaped garden, and doubles start at $150.

Nthaba Cottage B&B (☎ *8952 9003, nthaba@ozemail.com.au, 83 Cromwell Drive*) is also close to the golf course. The guest cottage has good facilities and costs $130 for a double.

Tmara Mara B&B (☎ *8952 7475, 1 Griffiths Place*), off Larapinta Drive west of the town centre, is close to the Desert Park. It's a modern place with one double room at $120.

Orangewood Alice Springs B&B (☎ *8952 4114, orangew@ozemail.com.au, 9 McMinn St*) is closer to the town centre, on the east bank of the river. It has four comfortable rooms, which cost from $140 for two.

About 25km north of Alice Springs, *Bond Springs Outback Retreat* (☎ *8952 9888, bondhmst@alice.aust.com*) offers accommodation in a comfortable, traditional homestead. A twin or double costs $250; a self-contained suite or cottage sleeping up to four costs $200.

Places to Stay – Top End
Most of the top-end accommodation is east of the river where there's space to spread out.

At the top of the range there's *Rydge's Plaza* (☎ *1800 675 212*), on Barrett Drive, with rooms from $190 to $420. The hotel is very well equipped, with facilities including heated pool, spa/sauna and tennis courts.

Almost next door is **Lasseters Casino** (☎ 1800 808 975, lasasp@lasseters.com.au), which has doubles from $180.

Another top-end option is the **Alice Springs Resort** (☎ 1800 805 055, 34 Stott Terrace) right by the Todd River, not far from the centre of town. Rooms go for $179, and it includes such luxuries as a heated pool.

Lastly there's the **Alice Springs Vista** (☎ 1800 810 664), stuck in the middle of nowhere at the foot of the MacDonnell Ranges on Stephens Rd. Its units go for $115. The resort has a pool, a tennis court and barbecue facilities.

Places to Eat

Alice has a reasonable range of eateries, but generally doesn't cater well for early risers or late-night diners.

Budget Dining & Self-Catering The thriving backpackers market in Alice ensures a cheap meal is usually easy to come by.

Rattle'n'Hum at Melanka's and **Toddy's Resort** both have cheap breakfasts and dinners – watch out for backpackers specials and special offer coupons around town.

If you're stocking up for a trip into the wilds, you can experience the joys of several large **supermarkets** around the town centre. All are open daily; Coles is open 24 hours and the Bi-Lo at the northern end of Todd St mall is generally the cheapest.

Cafes, Snacks & Takeaway There are numerous places for a sandwich or light snack along the Todd St mall and in the arcades running off it. Many have tables and chairs outside – ideal for breakfast on a cool, sunny morning.

La Cafetiere is at the southern end of the mall and is open for breakfast, burgers, sandwiches etc. Right next door are the **Red Dog** and **Red Rock Café**, very similar places with tables and umbrellas out on the footpath.

The big **Alice Plaza** has a number of lunchtime cafeteria-style eating places serving snacks, light meals, sandwiches and salads. There's another **food court** in the Yeperenye shopping centre on Hartley St.

Territory Tucker (80 Todd St) is a good takeaway joint. There are pies baked on the premises, including roo, camel and emu ($3.50), and novelty takeaways such as roo on a stick ($4.50) or kangaroo tail soup and damper ($4).

And of course Alice Springs has its share of popular takeaway outlets, such as **KFC**, **Hungry Jack's**, **Red Rooster**, **McDonald's** and **Pizza Hut**.

Pub & Counter Meals Far and away the most popular place is the **Pub Caf** at the Todd Tavern. The counter meals are tasty and there are special nights when you can get a meal for $5 to $8.

Scotty's Tavern is a small bar in the mall that has substantial meals for $12 to $16. Watch out for cheap meal deal coupons around town, which offer a burger with chips and a drink for $6.

The **Stuart Arms Hotel**, upstairs at the Alice Plaza, has a bar brunch menu and **Bojangle's** (80 Todd St) is a bistro in a colonial-style bar with a good range of hot meals.

Restaurants **Swingers** on Gregory Terrace (near the corner of Todd St) is something of an institution in the Alice, but although it opens early it's not open for dinner. The food is good and includes filled pita bread, focaccia and treats like laksa. It has a big noticeboard where you can check out what's happening around town.

Café Mediterranean Bar Doppio, in the small Fan Lane off the mall, opposite the Red Dog Café, has an excellent range of health food dishes and is open daily. You can BYO and most dishes cost between $5 and $10. The front window is covered with notices that may be of interest.

Next door is the **Camel's Crossing Mexican Restaurant**, which has a varied menu of both vegetarian and meat dishes. It's open nightly except Sunday, and a two course meal will set you back about $30.

There are a few good Italian options. **Puccini's Restaurant** is on the mall and claims to be the Territory's most-awarded restaurant. It serves excellent home-made pasta and char-grilled fish, but expect to pay around $18 to $20 for a main course.

Across the river from the town centre, on the corner of Undoolya Rd and Sturt Terrace, is the *Casa Nostra*, a long-standing, family-run pizza and pasta specialist. It is BYO, open nightly except Sunday and good value.

Good pasta with a choice of 26 sauces, plus a great range of pastries, cakes and *gelati* ice cream, can be enjoyed at the licensed *Al Fresco's Café*, in the cinema complex at the northern end of the mall.

For steaks try the *Overlander Steakhouse (72 Hartley St)*. It features 'Territory food' such as emu, crocodile, kangaroo and camel – and the 'Drover's Blowout' ($35) is a carnivore's delight! It's quite popular, but not cheap – main courses are about $17.50 to $25.

Both the Chinese restaurants on Hartley St are recommended. *Oriental Gourmet*, at No 80, is open only in the evening; the *Hong Kong Chinese Restaurant*, next to the Yeperenye shopping centre, is open nightly and also for lunch on weekdays except Tuesday.

Also recommended is the bright-yellow *Golden Inn (9 Undoolya Rd)*, just over the bridge from the town centre, where apart from the usual fare you can sample some Malaysian and Szechuan dishes.

The food is so-so at *Dingo's*, in the historic Country Women's Association (CWA) building on the corner of Stott Terrace and Todd St, but you can dine inside or out in a nice garden setting.

For very good upmarket dining in the town centre, the *Red Ochre Grill* on Todd St mall features 'creative native cuisine' for breakfast, lunch and dinner. Quality native plants and animals are imaginatively combined in dishes such as wallaby mignons and yam gnocchi; more conventional dishes are also available. Lunch char-grills cost around $19.50 and most main courses in the evening are $17 to $22.

Madigan's, out at the Alice Springs Desert Park, is another very good restaurant serving native foods. It's open Tuesday to Sunday for lunch and dinner.

Dining Tours A few interesting possibilities involve taking a ride out of town, although none could be considered good value and are best experienced for their novelty value. They include *The Camp Oven Kitchen (☎ 8953 1411)* and *Tuits Old Ghan Bush Kitchen Dinner Tour (☎ 8952 5443)* – the latter departs from MacDonnell Siding on Friday and Saturday at 7 pm and includes a 60 minute ride on the old *Ghan* ($75/60 with/without the train ride).

The popular *Take a Camel out to Breakfast/Dinner* tour combines a one hour camel ride with a meal at the Frontier Camel Farm (☎ 8953 0444). The cost is $55/35 for adults/children for breakfast and $80/60 for dinner.

Tailormade Tours *(☎ 8952 1731)* and Alice Limousine Tours *(☎ 8955 5595)* both operate evening *bush barbecues* complete with Australian bush songs. If you've never eaten food cooked on an open fire it may be worth the rather hefty price of $75.

Entertainment

Pubs, Live Music & Nightclubs Most backpackers drop into *Rattle'n'Hum* at Melanka's on Todd St – it's a good place for a beer and to meet other travellers, and there are occasionally live bands as well.

The *Todd Tavern*, by the river on the corner of Wills and Leichhardt Terraces, has a jam session on Monday night from 9 pm, which sometimes features better known bands. Friday night is another popular night.

For dance music you could try *Legends* at the Stuart Arms (Thursday, Friday and Saturday) or the *Alice Junction Tavern* on Palm Circuit, which has a disco on Friday and Saturday nights.

Live Performances The Alice has two long-running and popular shows with an outback flavour.

Local 'character' Ted Egan puts on a performance of tall tales and outback songs four nights a week at *The Settlers* on Palm Circuit. The show costs $15 (students $10). It's popular with tour groups and bookings are advised *(☎ 8952 9952)*.

NORTHERN TERRITORY

At 40 Todd St mall the *Sounds of Star-light Theatre* presents a musical performance evoking the spirit of the Outback with a didgeridoo and various Latin American instruments. Performances are held at 7 pm from Tuesday to Saturday between April and November. Bookings can be made through the theatre (☎ 8953 0826).

Shopping

There are plenty of shops along Todd St mall selling souvenirs and Aboriginal arts and crafts – including a forest of didgeridoos (an instrument not traditionally played in this part of the Territory). They haven't made it into the supermarkets yet, but if you're desperately short of time you can even buy a didgeridoo at the chemist!

Plenty of art galleries and craft centres specialise in Aboriginal creations – if you've got an interest in central Australian art or you're looking for a piece to buy, there are a couple of places where you can buy direct from the artists, such as the Papunya Tula Artists shop, on Todd St just south of the mall, or Jukurrpa Artists at 35 Gap Rd. Both places are owned and run by the art centres that produce the work.

Two of the better commercial outlets for Aboriginal art are Gallery Gondwana and the Original Aboriginal Dreamtime Gallery, both on Todd St mall.

The award-winning Aboriginal Art & Culture Centre, 86 Todd St, runs didgeridoo lessons, and has cultural displays and a gallery upstairs with some fine works.

The Central Australian Aboriginal Media Association (CAAMA) has a shop at 101 Todd St, just down from Dingo's, and is another very good outlet with reasonable prices.

Getting There & Away

Air You can fly to Alice Springs with Qantas (☎ 13 1313) or Ansett (☎ 13 1300). The two companies face each other on Todd St at the Parsons St intersection.

Alice Springs to Adelaide costs $414, Yulara (Uluru) $187, Darwin $392, Melbourne $575, Perth $555 and Sydney $577. You can also fly direct to Uluru from Adelaide, Sydney, Perth and Cairns. So if you're

planning to fly to the Centre and visit Uluru it would be more economical to fly straight to Uluru, then continue to Alice Springs. See Getting There & Away under the Uluru-Kata Tjuta section in this chapter for more details.

Bus Greyhound Pioneer (☎ 13 2030) on the corner of Gregory and Railway Terraces has daily services from Alice Springs to Yulara ($59), Darwin ($145) and Adelaide ($135). It takes about 20 hours from Alice Springs to Darwin (1481km) or Alice Springs to Adelaide (1543km). You can connect to other places at various points up and down the Track: Three Ways for Mt Isa and the Queensland coast; Katherine for Western Australia; Erldunda for Uluru; and Port Augusta for Perth.

McCafferty's (☎ 13 1499) at 91 Gregory Terrace also has daily departures to Adelaide ($135), Darwin ($145) and Yulara ($55).

Train You can get to Alice Springs on the *Ghan*, which departs from Melbourne and Sydney once a week each and Adelaide twice a week. From Melbourne it costs $270 for an economy seat, $528 for an economy sleeper and $895 for a 1st class sleeper (including meals) – it's cheaper going from the Alice to Melbourne. From Sydney the costs are $360/730/1095; and Adelaide to Alice Springs costs $182/374/574. You can also join the *Ghan* at Port Augusta in South Australia. Fares between Alice Springs and Port Augusta are $146/298/520.

Discounted fares are sometimes offered, especially in the low season (February through June). For bookings phone ☎ 13 2147.

It is also possible to put your car on the *Ghan*, which gives you transport when you arrive and saves the long drive from the south. The cost from Alice Springs to Adelaide is $220.

Car The basic thing to remember about getting to Alice Springs is that it's a long way from anywhere, although at least roads to the north and south are sealed. Coming in from Queensland it's 1180km from Mt Isa to Alice Springs or 529km from Three Ways (five hours), where the Mt Isa road meets the Darwin to Alice Springs road (the Stuart Hwy). Darwin to Alice Springs is 1476km (15 hours), to Yulara is 443km (4½ hours) and to Kings Canyon 331km (four hours).

These are outback roads, but you're not yet in the *real*, outer Outback, where a breakdown can mean big trouble. Nevertheless, it's wise to have your vehicle well prepared since getting someone to come out if you break down is likely to be very expensive. While fuel is readily available, make sure you know where the next service station is, and don't cut things too fine.

It's wise to carry drinking water and emergency food at all times, as even the Stuart Hwy can become impassable due to flooding. If it floods you'll have to wait for the water to recede, which can take several days in extreme circumstances.

Car Rental All the major hire companies have offices in Alice Springs; Avis, Budget, Hertz and Territory Thrifty also have counters at Alice Springs airport. Avis, Budget, Hertz and Territory all have 4WDs for hire.

Britz:Australia also has an office in Alice Springs.

Avis
  (☎ 8953 5533) 52 Hartley St
Britz:Australia
  (☎ 8952 8814) Corner of Stuart Hwy and Power St
Budget
  (☎ 8952 8899) 10 Gap Rd
Hertz
  (☎ 8952 2644) 76 Hartley St
Territory Thrifty Rent-a-Car
  (☎ 1800 891 125) Corner of Stott Terrace and Hartley St

Getting Around
Although there is a limited public bus system, Alice Springs is compact enough to get around on foot, and you can reach quite a few of the closer attractions by bicycle. If you want to go further afield you'll have to take a tour or rent a car.

To/From the Airport Alice Springs airport is 15km south of the town, about $20 by taxi.

An airport shuttle bus service (☎ 8953 0310) meets flights and takes passengers to all city accommodation and to the train station. It costs $9/15 single/return.

Bus Buses leave from outside the Yeperenye shopping centre on Hartley St – several routes are covered and the tourist office has timetables. Buses run approximately every 1½ hours from 7.45 am to 6 pm on weekdays and Saturday morning only. The fare for a short trip is $2.

The Alice Wanderer bus does a loop around the major sights – Frontier Camel Farm, the old *Ghan* Museum and Transport Hall of Fame, Royal Flying Doctor Base, the Strehlow Centre and Museum of Central Australia, Panorama Guth, Anzac Hill, School of the Air and the Old Telegraph Station. You can get on and off wherever you like; it runs every 70 minutes from around 9 am to 4 pm. The cost is $20 for a full day, and if you phone ahead (☎ 1800 669 111), you can be picked up from your accommodation prior to the 9 am departure.

The Alice Mini Bus (☎ 8955 1222) runs short trips between 8 am and midnight costing $6 for up to five people.

Bicycle Alice Springs has a number of bicycle tracks. A bike is a great way to get around town and out to the closer attractions, particularly in winter. The best place to rent a bike is from your hostel. Typical rates are $13 per day.

Centre Cycles (☎ 8953 2966) at 14 Lindsay Ave east of the town centre has 15-speed mountain bikes for $15 per day, or $50 per week. It's advisable to book ahead in winter.

The MacDonnell Ranges

Outside Alice Springs there are a number of places you can visit within a day or with overnight stops thrown in. Generally they're found by heading east or west along the roads running parallel to the MacDonnell Ranges, which are directly south of

Alice Springs. Places further south are usually visited on the way to Uluru.

The scenery in the ranges is superb. There are many gorges that cut through the rocky cliffs and their sheer walls are spectacular. In the shaded gorges there are rocky water holes, a great deal of wildlife (which can be seen if you're quiet and observant) and wildflowers in the spring.

You can get out to these gorges on group tours or with your own transport. Some of the closer gorges are accessible by bicycle or on foot. By yourself, the Centre's eerie emptiness and peace can touch you in a way that is impossible in a big group.

Getting There & Away

There is no public transport to either the Eastern or Western MacDonnells, so without your own transport you'll have to take a tour. Most places are covered by tours from the Alice.

EASTERN MACDONNELL RANGES

Heading south from Alice Springs and just through the Heavitree Gap, there is a sign for the Ross Hwy. The highway is sealed all the way to Ross River Homestead, 83km from Alice Springs. The dirt road out to Arltunga, about 100km from Alice Springs, is in pretty good condition. From there the road bends back north and west to rejoin the Stuart Hwy 50km north of Alice Springs, but this section is a much rougher road and sometimes requires a 4WD.

Emily & Jessie Gaps Nature Park

These two gaps are important to the Eastern Arrernte people as they are associated with the Caterpillar Dreaming trail.

Emily Gap, 16km out of town, is the next gap through the ranges east of the Heavitree Gap – it's narrow and often has water running through it. Known to the Arrernte as Anthwerrke, this is one of the most important Aboriginal sites in the Alice Springs area as it was from here that the caterpillar ancestral beings of Mparntwe (Alice Springs) originated. The gap is registered as a sacred site and there are some well preserved paintings to see on the eastern wall, although it often involves a swim to get to them.

Jessie Gap, 8km further on, like Emily Gap, is a popular picnic and barbecue spot.

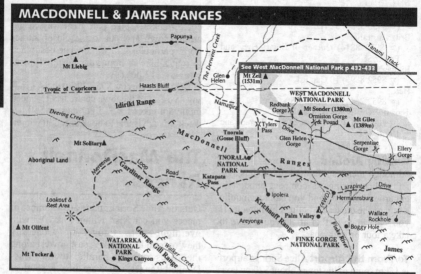

MACDONNELL & JAMES RANGES

Corroboree Rock Conservation Reserve

Shortly after Jessie Gap there's the Undoolya Gap, another pass through the range, then the road continues 43km to Corroboree Rock. There are many strangely shaped outcrops of rocks in the range and it's said to have been used by Aboriginal people as a storehouse for sacred objects. It is a registered sacred site and is listed on the National Estate. Despite the name, it is doubtful if the rock was ever used as a corroboree area, due to the lack of water in the vicinity.

Trephina Gorge Nature Park

About 70km out, and 8km north of the road, is Trephina Gorge. It's wider and longer than the other gaps in the range – here you are well north of the main MacDonnell Ranges and in a new ridge. There's a good walk along the edge of the gorge, and the trail then drops down to the sandy creek bed and loops back to the starting point.

Keen walkers can follow a longer trail (about five hours), which continues to the delightful **John Hayes Rockhole**, a few kilometres west of Trephina Gorge. Here the sheltered section of a deep gorge provides a series of water holes that retain water long after the more exposed places have dried up. You can clamber around the rockholes or follow the 90-minute Chain of Ponds marked trail which takes you up to a lookout above the gorge and then back through the gorge – perhaps you'll see why it is also called the Valley of the Eagles.

There's an excellent *camp site* at the gorge, and a smaller one (only two sites) at John Hayes Rockhole. There's a fee of $1 per adult for camping.

Ross River Homestead

From Trephina Gorge it's 13km on to the *Ross River Homestead* (☎ *8956 9711*). It's much favoured by coach tours, but is equally good for independent visitors. It's a friendly sort of place and there's lots to do, including walks in the spectacular surrounding countryside, excursions to other attractions, short camel rides or safaris, and horse riding – or simply lazing around with a cold one.

Air-con cabins with en suite cost $75 for two; four-bed dorms are $13 per person; or you can camp for $12 for two ($16 powered). There's also a restaurant, which has good food, and a very popular bar.

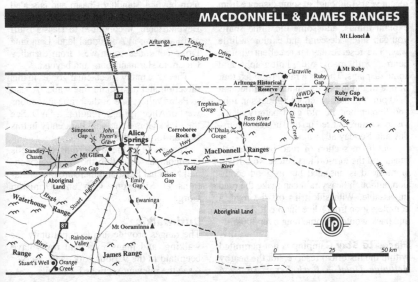

MACDONNELL & JAMES RANGES

N'Dhala Gorge Nature Park

N'Dhala Gorge is about 10km south of Ross River Homestead and has around 6000 ancient Aboriginal rock carvings, although they're generally not easy to spot. You may see rock wallabies. The track into N'Dhala is sandy and requires 4WD. It's possible to turn off before the gorge and loop around it to return to Alice Springs by the Ringwood Homestead road, but this also requires a 4WD.

There's a small *camp site* here with a toilet, but you need to bring your own water and firewood. The flies are friendly, too.

Arltunga Historical Reserve

At the eastern end of the MacDonnell Ranges, 110km north-east of Alice Springs, Arltunga is a gold-mining ghost town. Gold was discovered here in 1887 and 10 years later reef gold was discovered, but by 1912 the mining activity had petered out. Old buildings, a couple of cemeteries and the many deserted mine sites are all that remain. Alluvial (surface) gold has been completely worked out in the Arltunga Reserve, but there may still be gold further afield in the area, and in fact mining has recommenced in recent years (although at some distance from the old town). There are plenty of signs to explain things, and some old mine shafts you can safely descend and explore a little way. The reserve has an excellent visitors centre, with many old photographs and some displays. There's a ranger-guided tour of one of the mines on Sunday afternoon at 2.30 pm, and during school holidays in June and September the old gold battery at the visitors centre is fired up on Tuesday, Thursday and Sunday at 11 am.

The 40km section of road between Arltunga and the turn-off just before Ross River Homestead is unsealed but in good condition, although heavy rain can make the road impassable. With side trips off the road, a complete loop from Alice Springs to Arltunga and back would be something over 300km.

Places to Stay Camping is not permitted within the historical reserve, but the nearby *Arltunga Hotel & Bush Resort (☎ 8956 9797)* is a good place to stay. Camping costs $10. Meals, snacks and beer are also available at the atmospheric pub.

Ruby Gap Nature Park

Ruby Gap is another 44km to the east. It's on a rough track that takes a good couple of hours to traverse – definitely 4WD only. The sandy bed of the Hale River is purple in places due to the thousands of tiny garnets found here. The garnets were the cause of a 'ruby rush' to the area in the 19th century and a few miners did well out of it until the 'rubies' were discovered to be only garnets and virtually worthless. It's a remote and evocative place, and is well worth the effort involved to reach it.

There's excellent bush *camping* along the riverbank in the park, and there are some beautiful spots. However, this is a remote area and you need to be well equipped – bring your own water and collect firewood on the way in.

WESTERN MACDONNELL RANGES

Heading west from the Alice, Namatjira Drive turns north-west off Larapinta Drive 6km beyond Standley Chasm and is sealed all the way to Glen Helen, 132km from town. Beyond there, it continues to Haasts Bluff and Papunya, in Aboriginal land. Larapinta Drive continues south-west from Standley Chasm to Hermannsburg and beyond.

There are many spectacular gorges in this direction and also some fine walks. A visit to Palm Valley, one of the prime attractions west of Alice Springs, requires a 4WD. See the Finke Gorge National Park entry in this section for tour details.

The whole of the Western MacDonnells is encompassed within the West MacDonnell National Park, and there are ranger stations at Simpsons Gap and Ormiston Gorge.

Bushwalking

The ranges provide ample opportunity for walking, and many excellent trails have been laid in the various parks and reserves – see the relevant sections for details.

Anyone attempting an overnight walk is urged to register with the Voluntary Walker Registration Scheme (☎ 1300 650 730). A refundable deposit of $50 is requested (payable by credit card over the phone or cash at CATIA in the Alice) to offset the cost of a search should anything go wrong. More information can be obtained from Parks & Wildlife (☎ 8951 8211).

Larapinta Trail The Larapinta Trail is an extended walking track which, when completed, will offer a 13 stage, 220km trail of varying degrees of difficulty along the backbone of the Western MacDonnells, stretching from the telegraph station in Alice Springs to Mt Razorback, beyond Glen Helen Gorge. It will be possible to choose anything from a two day to a two week trek, taking in a selection of the attractions in the Western MacDonnells. At the time of writing, the following sections were open:

Section 1
    Alice Springs Telegraph Station to Simpsons Gap (24km)
Section 2
    Simpsons Gap to Jay Creek (23km)
Section 3
    Jay Creek to Standley Chasm (14km)
Section 8
    Serpentine Gorge to Ochre Pits (18km)
Section 9
    Ochre Pits to Ormiston Gorge (27km)
Section 10
    Ormiston Gorge to Glen Helen (12.5km)
Section 11
    Glen Helen to Redbank Gorge (29km)
Section 12
    Redbank Gorge to Mt Sonder (16km return)

Detailed trail notes and maps ($1 per section) are available from the Parks & Wildlife desk at the tourist office in Alice Springs, or contact the Parks & Wildlife office (☎ 8951 8211) for further details.

The problem lies in getting to the various trailheads, as there is no public transport out to this area. Jim's Bush Tours (☎ 8953 1975) can pick you up or drop you off for a fee, depending on distance. Trek Larapinta (☎ 1800 803 174, charlie@treklarapinta.com.au) offers transport and catering for one-day walks ($95), overnight walks ($160 for one night, $250 for two days/one night) or a three day/two night Mt Sonder special for $350.

Simpsons Gap

Westbound from Alice Springs on Larapinta Drive you soon come to the **Desert Wildlife Park & Botanic Gardens** (see the Alice Springs Desert Park section under Alice Springs) and **John Flynn's Grave**. The flying doctor's final resting place is topped by one of the Devils Marbles, brought down the Track from near Tennant Creek.

A little further on is the picturesque Simpsons Gap, 22km out. Like the other gaps it is an awesome example of nature's power and patience – for a river to cut a path through solid rock is amazing, but for a river that rarely ever runs to cut such a path is positively mind-boggling. There are often rock wallabies in the jumble of rocks on either side of the gap.

Standley Chasm

Standley Chasm is 51km out and is probably the most spectacular gap around Alice Springs. It is incredibly narrow – the near-vertical walls almost meet above you. Only for a scant 15 minutes each day does the late morning sun illuminate the bottom of the gorge – and this is obviously the time that most tourists visit; early or late in the day it is much more peaceful. The chasm is on Aboriginal land and entry is $4.

Namatjira Drive

Not far beyond Standley Chasm you can choose the northerly Namatjira Drive or the more southerly Larapinta Drive. West along Namatjira Drive another series of gorges and gaps in the range awaits you. **Ellery Creek Big Hole** is 93km from Alice Springs and has a large permanent water hole – just the place for a cooling dip, and there's a basic camp site close by. It's only 13km further to **Serpentine Gorge**, a narrow gorge with a pleasant water hole at the entrance.

The **Ochre Pits**, just off the road 11km west of Serpentine, were a source of painting material for the Aboriginal people. The various coloured ochres are weathered limestone, and the colouring is actually iron oxide stains.

The large and rugged **Ormiston Gorge** also has a water hole and it leads to the enclosed valley of **Ormiston Pound**. When the water holes of the Pound dry up, the fish burrow into the sand, going into a sort of suspended animation and reappearing after rain. There's some good, short walking trails around here.

Only a couple of kilometres further is the turn-off to the scenic **Glen Helen Gorge**, where the Finke River cuts through the MacDonnells. The road is gravel beyond this point, but if you continue west you'll reach the red-walled **Redbank Gorge**, which has permanent water, 161km from Alice Springs. Also out this way is **Mt Sonder**. At 1380m, it's one of the highest points in the NT.

Places to Stay & Eat There's no accommodation in the Western MacDonnells. There are, however, camp sites at Ellery Creek Big Hole, Ormiston Gorge and Redbank Gorge. Refurbishment of the tourist *Glen Helen Homestead* (☎ 8956 7489) at Glen Helen Gorge should be finished by the time this book is available.

Larapinta Drive

Taking the alternative road to the south from Standley Chasm, Larapinta Drive crosses the Hugh River and then Ellery Creek before reaching the turn-off for **Wallace Rockhole**, 17km off the main road and 117km from Alice Springs. This Arrernte Aboriginal community (☎ 8956 7993) offers camping ($14, on-site vans $40, cabins $95) and rock-art tours daily on demand for $7. Alcohol is prohibited here.

Back on Larapinta Drive, shortly before Hermannsburg, is the **Namatjira Monument**. Today the artistic skills of the central Australian Aboriginal people are widely known and appreciated. This certainly wasn't the case when Albert Namatjira started to paint his central Australian landscapes in 1934.

In 1957 Namatjira was the first Aboriginal person to be granted Australian citizenship. Because of his fame, he was allowed to buy alcohol at a time when this was otherwise illegal for Aboriginal people, but in 1958 he was jailed for six months for supplying alcohol to members of his family. He died the following year, aged only 57. (For further information on Albert Namatjira see the Aboriginal Art special section.)

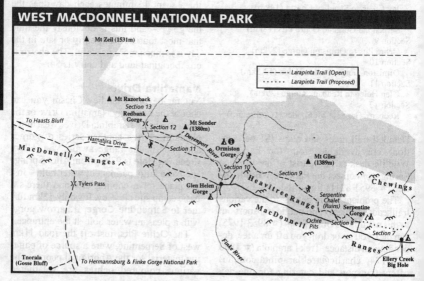

WEST MACDONNELL NATIONAL PARK

Larapinta Trail (Open)
Larapinta Trail (Proposed)

Albert Namatjira at Areyonga, 1952

WENDY HART

Hermannsburg
• postcode 0872   • pop 460

Only 8km beyond the Namatjira Monument you reach the Hermannsburg Aboriginal settlement, 125km from Alice Springs. The **Hermannsburg Mission** was established by German Lutheran missionaries in the middle of the 19th century. Many of the buildings are intact, and it's well worth a stroll through.

Although the town is restricted Aboriginal land, permits are not required to visit the mission or store, or to travel through. The *Kata-Anga Tea Rooms* serve excellent home-made pastries, and you can also get fuel (no credit cards) and basic provisions at the community store. The staff at the tea rooms also issue permits for travel on the Mereenie Loop Road (see Mereenie Loop Road entry in this section).

Hermannsburg's most famous resident was Professor Ted Strehlow (see the Strehlow Research Centre entry under Alice Springs).

Finke Gorge National Park

From Hermannsburg a 4WD trail follows the Finke River south to the Finke Gorge National Park, only 12km further on.

Palm Valley, in the park, is a gorge in which a variety of palm tree grows that is unique to this part of the MacDonnells – the central Australian cabbage palm *(Livistona mariae)*. This strangely tropical find in the dry Centre makes Palm Valley a popular day trip.

NORTHERN TERRITORY

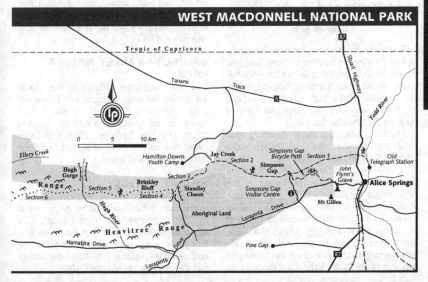

WEST MACDONNELL NATIONAL PARK

Tropic of Capricorn

Stuart Highway

87

Tanami Track

5

Todd River

0   5   10 km

Ellery Creek

Hamilton Downs Youth Camp

Jay Creek
Section 2

Simpsons Gap
Bicycle Path Section 1

Old Telegraph Station

Hugh Gorge

Range

Section 3

Simpsons Gap

John Flynn's Grave

Alice Springs

Brinkley Bluff

Standley Chasm

Simpsons Gap Visitor Centre

Section 5

Section 4

Mt Gillen

Section 6

Hugh River

Aboriginal Land

Larapinta Drive

Heavitree Range

Namatjira Drive

Drive

Pine Gap

87

Larapinta

KATE NOLAN

Cabbage palm

The track to the park crosses the sandy bed of the Finke a number of times and you need a 4WD to get through, not so much because of the risk of getting bogged down, but because of the high ground clearance needed to negotiate the numerous bars of rock on the track to the gorge.

There's a beautiful shady *camping* area ($12) with showers and flush toilets, and a couple of signposted walks.

If you are travelling by 4WD there's a track that traverses the full length of the picturesque Finke Gorge, much of the time along the bed of the (usually) dry Finke River. It's a rough but worthwhile trip, and the *camp sites* at Boggy Hole, about 2½ hours from Hermannsburg, make an excellent overnight stop. If you are in a hurry you can get from Palm Valley all the way to

Watarrka (Kings Canyon) National Park in less than eight hours via this route. Ask the rangers at Palm Valley or Kings Canyon for details.

Mereenie Loop Road

From Hermannsburg you can continue west to the Areyonga turn-off (no visitors), and then take the Mereenie Loop Road to Kings Canyon. This dirt road is suitable for robust conventional vehicles and offers an excellent alternative to the Ernest Giles Road as a way of reaching Kings Canyon.

To travel the loop road you need a permit from the Central Land Council as it passes through Aboriginal land. The permit includes the informative *Mereenie Tour Pass* booklet, which provides details about the local Aboriginal culture and has a route map. Permits are issued on the spot by the tourist office in Alice Springs, the service station at the Kings Canyon Resort and at the Kata-Anga Tea Rooms at Hermannsburg.

South to Uluru

You can make some interesting diversions off the road south from Alice Springs. There are also a number of attractions to the east of the Stuart Hwy, but to visit most of these requires a 4WD.

RAINBOW VALLEY NATURE PARK

The eerie sandstone bluffs of the James Range are the main attraction of this small park, which lies 22km off the Stuart Hwy along an unsignposted 4WD track 75km south of Alice Springs. There's a basic *camp site* but you will need to bring your own firewood and water.

STUART'S WELL

Camel Outback Safaris (☎ 8956 0925), a camel farm 90km south of the Alice, is run by Noel Fullerton, the 'camel king', who started the annual Camel Cup. For a few dollars you can try your hand at camel riding and extended safaris into Rainbow Valley and the outback are also available.

NORTHERN TERRITORY

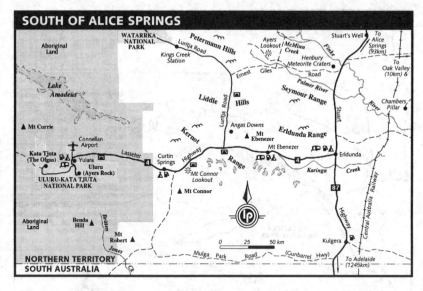

SOUTH OF ALICE SPRINGS

NORTHERN TERRITORY

ERNEST GILES ROAD

The Ernest Giles Road heads off to the west of the Stuart Hwy about 140km south of the Alice. This is the shorter (but rougher) route to Kings Canyon and is often impassable after heavy rain. The section from the Luritja Road to Kings Canyon is sealed.

Henbury Meteorite Craters

A few kilometres along Ernest Giles Road, west of the Stuart Hwy, a dusty, corrugated track leads to this cluster of 12 small craters. The biggest of the craters is 180m across and 15m deep. From the car park by the site there's a walking trail around the craters with signposted features.

There are no longer any fragments of the meteorites at the site, but the museum in Alice Springs has a small chunk which weighs a surprisingly heavy 46.5kg. It is illegal to fossick for or remove any fragments.

The site is administered by Parks & Wildlife, and there's a basic and very exposed *camp site* ($1 per person).

WATARRKA NATIONAL PARK

The road continues west from the craters to the Watarrka (Kings Canyon) National Park.

Kings Canyon, 323km from Alice Springs, is a spectacular gorge with natural features such as clusters of domed outcrops, and lush palms of the narrow gorge called the **Garden of Eden**. There are fine views and the walking trails are not too difficult. The walls of the canyon soar over 100m high, and the trail around the rim and to the Garden of Eden offers breathtaking views, although it is not for those who suffer from vertigo. There's a ranger station (☎ 8956 7488) 22km east of the canyon.

The Giles Track is a 22km walking track along the ridge to between the gorge and Kathleen Springs, 2.5km from the ranger station. It takes two days to walk, and you need to register with the rangers.

Organised Tours

Aboriginal Tours Lilla (☎ 8956 7909) is an Aboriginal-owned and run tour company that runs a couple of trips from the Kings Canyon Resort. Depending on demand, the four hour guided **King's Canyon Walk** departs at 7 am and an Aboriginal guide takes you on the canyon-rim walk. Inquire at reception.

The two-hour **Willy-Wagtail Tour** takes in cave paintings and an introduction to

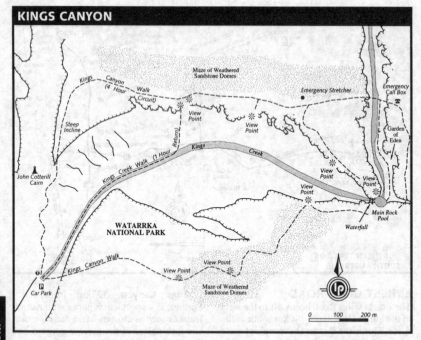

KINGS CANYON

Kings Canyon Walk (4 Hour) Circuit

Steep Incline

Kings Creek Walk (1 Hour)

Return

Maze of Weathered Sandstone Domes

View Point

View Point

Emergency Stretcher

Emergency Call Box

Garden of Eden

Kings Creek

John Cotterill Cairn

View Point

View Point

WATARRKA NATIONAL PARK

View Point

View Point

Main Rock Pool

Waterfall

Kings Canyon Walk

View Point

View Point

Maze of Weathered Sandstone Domes

Car Park

0   100   200 m

NORTHERN TERRITORY

Luritja traditions. It departs daily at 9 and 11 am and 4 pm, and the cost is $28/20 for adults/children.

Fifteen-minute helicopter flights are available from the resort (☎ 8956 7873), or from Kings Creek Station (see Places to Stay & Eat). They cost $150 for 33 minutes.

Canyon Tours Guided tours of the canyon-rim walk take place daily, leaving the resort at 7 am. The trips are run by AAT-King's (☎ 8952 1700) and cost $35/18.

Places to Stay & Eat

The closest accommodation available is at the ***Kings Canyon Resort*** (*☎ 1800 089 622, salesint@ayersrock.aust.com*), 6km west of the canyon. Camp sites cost $20, or $25 with power. There's a backpackers bunk house with beds in four-bed rooms at a hefty $35 each ($138 for the room), or more luxurious motel-type accommodation from $280. The resort has a swimming pool, a

bar, a cafe, a restaurant, a shop and (expensive) fuel.

Otherwise, there's the basic but friendly ***Kings Creek Station Camping Ground*** (*☎ 8956 7474*), on Ernest Giles Road just outside the national park's eastern boundary and about 35km from the canyon. The very pleasant camp site is set among large desert oaks, and camping costs $8 per person plus $1 per site for power. Fuel, ice and limited stores are available daily at the shop.

THE OLD GHAN ROAD

Following the 'old south road' which runs close to the old *Ghan* railway line, it's only 35km from Alice Springs to **Ewaninga**, with its prehistoric Aboriginal rock carvings. The carvings found here and at N'Dhala Gorge are thought to have been made by Aboriginal tribes who lived here earlier than the current tribes of the Centre.

The eerie, sandstone **Chambers Pillar** is carved with the names and visit dates of early explorers – and, unfortunately, some much less worthy modern-day graffitists. To the Aboriginal people of the area, Chambers Pillar is the remains of Itirkawara, a gecko ancestor of great strength. It's 160km from Alice Springs and a 4WD is required for the last 44km from the turn-off at Maryvale Station. There's a basic *camp site* but you need to bring water and firewood.

Back on the main track south, you eventually arrive at **Finke**, a small Apatula Aboriginal settlement 230km south of Alice Springs. When the old *Ghan* was running, Finke was a thriving little town; these days it seems to have drifted into a permanent torpor. There's a basic community store, which is also the outlet for the Apatula Arts Centre, and fuel is available on weekdays. Alcohol is prohibited.

From Finke you can turn west to join the Stuart Hwy at Kulgera (150km), or east to Old Andado station on the edge of the Simpson Desert (120km). Just 21km west of Finke, and 12km north of the road along a signposted track, is the **Lambert Centre**. Here stands a 5m-high replica of the flagpole found on top of Parliament House in Canberra. The reason? This point has been determined as Australia's geographical centre!

Uluru-Kata Tjuta National Park

ULURU (AYERS ROCK)

Australia's biggest drawcard, the world famous Uluru (Ayers Rock), is 3.6km long and rises a towering 348m from the surrounding sandy scrubland. It's believed that two-thirds of the Rock lies beneath the sand. Everybody knows how its colour changes as the setting sun turns it a series of deeper and darker reds before it fades into grey. A performance in reverse, with fewer spectators, is given at dawn.

The mighty Rock offers much more than pretty colours – the entire area is of deep cultural significance to the local Anangu Aboriginal people, and there are opportunities to delve into their culture. To Anangu

---

Grog

Please be aware that alcohol (grog) is a problem among some of the local Mutitjulu Aboriginal people living near Uluru. It is a 'dry' community and, at the request of the Aboriginal leaders, the liquor outlet in Yulara has agreed not to sell alcohol to Aboriginal people. For this reason you may be approached at Yulara by Aboriginal people who want you to buy grog on their behalf. The community leaders appeal to you not to do so.

---

the Rock is known as Uluru – the name also given to the national park that surrounds it. The Aboriginal people own the national park, although it is leased permanently to, and administered by, Parks Australia (the Federal Government's national parks body) in conjunction with the traditional owners.

There are plenty of walks and other activities around Uluru and the township of Yulara, and it is not at all difficult to spend several days here.

Information

The superb Uluru-Kata Tjuta National Park Cultural Centre (☎ 8956 3138) is 1km before the Rock on the road from Yulara. This excellent facility is open from 7 am to 5.30 pm in winter (to 6 pm in summer). It's worth putting aside at least one hour, preferably more, to have a good look around the Cultural Centre before visiting Uluru itself.

There are two main display areas, both with multilingual information: the Tjukurpa display features Anangu art and Tjukurpa; while the Nintiringkupai display focuses on the history and management of the national park.

The Cultural Centre also houses the Aboriginal-owned Maruku Art & Crafts shop (open from 8 am to 5.30 pm), and there's the opportunity to see artists at work and dancers performing. Everything is created in the surrounding desert region, and certificates of authenticity are issued with most artworks. It's about the cheapest

ULURU (AYERS ROCK)

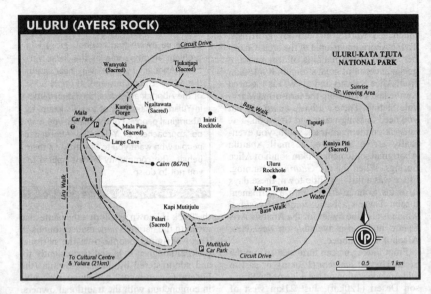

place in the Centre to buy souvenirs (carvings etc) and you're buying direct from the artists.

There's also the Aboriginal-run Ininti Store, which sells a surprisingly tasteful range of T-shirts and other souvenirs, plus snacks, books and videos (open from 7 am to 5.30 pm).

The Cultural Centre has a picnic area with free gas barbecues and the Anangu Tours desk (☎ 8956 2123), where you can book Aboriginal-led tours around Uluru.

There's also a visitors centre at Yulara. It's open daily from 8 am to 9 pm and is also a good source of information (see the Yulara section later in this chapter).

Entry to the national park costs $15 (free for children under 16) and this is good for a five day visit. Entry permits can be bought from the visitors centre at Yulara or from the park entrance on the road between Yulara and Uluru.

The park is open daily from half an hour before sunrise to sunset.

Aboriginal Cultural Tours

Owned and operated by Anangu from the Mutitjulu community, Anangu Tours (☎ 8956 2123) has a tour desk at the Cultural Centre

inside the park. See the Yulara Organised Tours section for details of trips offered by Anangu Tours.

Uluru Walks

There are walking trails around Uluru, and guided walks delving into the plants, wildlife, geology and mythology of the area. All the walks are flat and are suitable for wheelchairs.

Base Walk (10km) It can take five hours to walk around the base of Uluru at a leisurely pace, looking at the caves and paintings on the way, and often you'll have it pretty much to yourself. Full details of the Mala and Kuniya walks are given in the self-guided walks brochure available from the rangers' station for $1.

Note that there are several Aboriginal sacred sites around the base of Uluru. They're fenced off and clearly signposted and to enter these areas is a grave offence, not just for non-Aboriginal people but for 'ineligible' Aboriginal people as well.

Mala Walk (2km return) This walk starts from the base of the climbing point

Climbing Uluru

For years climbing the rock was considered a highlight of a trip to the Centre. It's important to note, however, that climbing Uluru goes against Aboriginal spiritual beliefs, and the Anangu would prefer that you didn't. The route taken by visitors is associated closely with the Mala Tjukurpa. The Anangu also feel responsible for all people on the rock, and are greatly saddened when a visitor to their land is injured or dies there.

Besides, they call the people climbing the 'Minga Mob'. You just have to look at them from a distance to get the joke – *minga* means ant.

Although the number of visitors to Uluru has risen steadily over the years, the number actually climbing the rock is declining, while sales of the ideologically sound 'I Didn't Climb Ayers Rock' T-shirts are on the rise.

and takes about 1½ hours at a very leisurely pace. The *tjukurpa* (traditional law) of the Mala (hare-wallaby people) is of great importance to the Anangu. You can do this walk on your own, or there are guided walks daily at 10 am from the car park (8 am October through April; no booking necessary).

Mutitjulu Walk (1km return) Mutitjulu is a permanent water hole on the southern side of Uluru. The tjukurpa tells of the clash between two ancestral snakes Kuniya and Liru (see 'The Rainbow Serpent' boxed text in the Top End section). The water hole is a short walk from the car park on the southern side.

Climbing Uluru

Those climbing Uluru should take care – numerous people have died while doing so, usually by having a heart attack but some by taking a fatal tumble. Avoid climbing in the heat of the day during the hot season. There is an emergency phone at the car park at the base of the climb, and another at the top of the chain, about halfway up the climbing route. The climb is actually closed between 10 am and 4 pm on days when the forecast temperature is more than 38°C.

The climb is 1.6km and takes about two hours up and back with a good rest at the top. The first part of the walk is by far the steepest and most arduous, and there's a chain to hold on to. It's often extremely windy at the top, even when it's not at the base, so make sure hats are well tied on.

KATA TJUTA (THE OLGAS)

Kata Tjuta (the Olgas), a collection of smaller, more rounded rocks, stands about 30km to the west of Uluru. Though less well known, the monoliths are equally impressive – indeed many people find them more captivating. Meaning 'many heads', Kata Tjuta is of tjukurpa significance.

The tallest rock, **Mt Olga**, at 546m, is about 200m higher than Uluru. There are a couple of walking trails, the main one being to the **Valley of the Winds**, a 7km circuit track (2½ to four hours). It's not particularly arduous, but be prepared with water and sun protection. There is also a short (2km return) signposted trail into the pretty **Olga Gorge** (Tatintjawiya).

There's a picnic and sunset viewing area with toilet facilities just off the access road a few kilometres west of the base of Kata Tjuta.

A lonely sign at the western end of the access road points out that there is a hell of a lot of nothing if you travel west – although, if suitably equipped, you can travel all the way to Kalgoorlie and on to Perth in Western Australia. It's 200km to Docker River, an Aboriginal settlement on the road west, and about 1500km to Kalgoorlie. See the Warburton Road information in the Getting Around chapter for details.

YULARA
● postcode 0872   ● pop 2080

Yulara, the service village for the national park, has effectively turned one of the world's least hospitable regions into an easy and comfortable place to visit. Lying just outside the national park, 20km from Uluru and 53km from Kata Tjuta, the complex, administered by the NT Government's

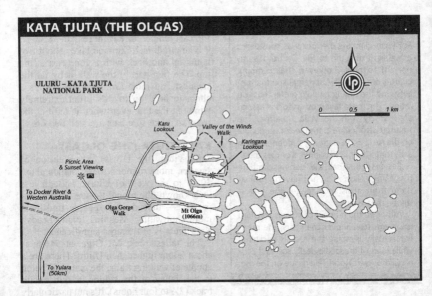

KATA TJUTA (THE OLGAS)

Ayers Rock Corporation, makes an excellent and surprisingly democratic base for exploring the area's renowned attractions. Opened in 1984, it supplies the only accommodation, food outlets and other services available in the region. The village incorporates the Ayers Rock Resort, and it combines flair with low, earth-toned buildings, fitting unobtrusively into the dunes.

By the 1970s it was clear that planning was required for the development of the area. Between 1931 and 1946 only 22 people were known to have climbed Uluru. In 1969 about 23,000 people visited the area. Ten years later the figure was 65,000 and now the annual rate is approaching 500,000!

Orientation & Information
In the spacious village area, where everything is within 15 minutes walk, there is a visitors centre, bank, post office, petrol station, newsagency, Royal Flying Doctor Service medical centre, craft gallery, camp sites, backpackers lodge, four hotels, apartments, two restaurants, a bistro, supermarket and even a pink police station!

The Tour & Information Centre (☎ 8956 2240) in the shopping square is open daily from 8.30 am to 9 pm; it's the place to book tours as all operators have desks here. There's also a central desk that can provide general information about the park itself.

The visitors centre (☎ 8957 7377), near the Desert Gardens Hotel, which contains good displays on the geography, flora, fauna and history of the region. It's open daily from 8.30 am to 7.30 pm.

The Resort Guide is a useful sheet available at the visitors centre and hotel desks. It lists facilities and opening times, and has a good map of Yulara on one side.

The shopping-square complex includes a supermarket, newsagency, post office and travel agency. You can get colour film processed at Territory Colour's same-day service. The only bank at Yulara is ANZ, but you can also use the EFTPOS facilities at the supermarket and the Mobil service station.

There's a childcare centre in the village for children aged between three months and eight years, which operates daily from 8 am to 5.30 pm. The cost is $18.50 for half a day or $40 for a full day. Bookings can be made on ☎ 8956 2097.

Activities

There are a number of activities in the resort, some conducted by the rangers and others organised by the resort.

The **Garden Walk** is a guided tour through the native garden of the Sails in the Desert Hotel. It takes place on weekdays at 7.30 am and is led by the hotel's resident gardener. This tour is free and there's no need to book.

Each evening there's the **Night Sky Show**, which is an informative look into local astrological legends, with the use of telescopes and binoculars (slide show on cloudy nights). The 1½ hour trips start at 8.30 and 10.15 pm, and bookings are required (☎ 1800 803 174). The cost is $25 (children $18) and you are picked up from your accommodation.

Frontier Camel Tours (☎ 8956 2444) has a depot at Yulara with a small museum and camel rides. Two popular rides are the Camel to Sunrise, a two hour tour that includes a saunter through the dunes before sunrise, billy tea and a chat about camels for $68 (breakfast box an additional $9.50); and the sunset equivalent, which costs the same. The sunrise trip can be combined with an Ayers Rock base tour ($100/83 for adults/children) and the sunset trip with a barbecue and Night Sky Show for $100/95.

Flights While the enjoyment of those on the ground may be diminished by the constant buzz of light aircraft and helicopters overhead, for those actually up there it's an unforgettable – and very popular – trip.

Three companies operate the trips and they collect you from wherever you're staying.

Rockayer (☎ 8956 2345) charges $69/57 for adults/children aged four to 14 for a 30 minute flight over the Rock and Kata Tjuta, or $190/160 for a 110 minute flight, which includes Lake Amadeus and Kings Canyon.

Ayers Rock Helicopters (☎ 8956 2077) and Professional Helicopter Services (PHS; ☎ 8956 2003) charge $70 for the 15 minute Uluru flight, and $150 for the 30 minute Uluru and Kata Tjuta flight. There are no child concessions on any helicopter flights, which make them an expensive proposition for families.

Organised Tours

There's a Tour & Information Centre at Yulara (☎ 8956 2240) where operators each have a desk. It's open from 8.30 am to 9 pm. If you arrive here from anywhere other than Alice Springs without a tour booked (see From Alice Springs later in this section) then you're limited to what's here.

Uluru Experience This company (☎ 1800 803 174) offers several possibilities. The five hour Uluru Walk includes the base walk and breakfast for $69/54 for adults/children; Spirit of Uluru is a four hour vehicle-based tour around the base of the Rock for the same price. The Olgas & Dunes Tour includes the walk into Olga Gorge and the sunset at the Olgas for $51/41. The Uluru Experience Pass lets you choose any two of the three tours above and also gives you a discount on the Night Sky Show (see the Activities section earlier for details).

AAT-King's To allow some flexibility with your itinerary, AAT-King's (☎ 1800 334 009) has a range of options that depart daily. Check with the desk at the visitor centre at Yulara for departure times.

A 'Rock Pass', which includes a guided base tour, sunset, climb, sunrise, Cultural Centre and Kata Tjuta (Olga Gorge only) tours, costs $154/77 for adults/children. The pass is valid for three days and includes the $15 national park entry fee.

If you don't want to climb the Rock the 24 hour Explorer Pass costs $119/60 and includes the Valley of the Winds (Olgas). Other combinations are available.

All these activities are also available in various combinations on a one-off basis: base tour ($37/19); sunrise tour ($34/17); climb ($34/17); sunset ($24/12); base and sunset ($52/26); sunrise and climb ($57/29); climb and base ($62/31); sunrise and base ($57/29); sunrise, climb and base ($76/38); and Olgas and Uluru sunset ($54/41). These prices do not include the park entry fee.

Another option is the Uluru Breakfast Tour, which includes breakfast at the Cultural

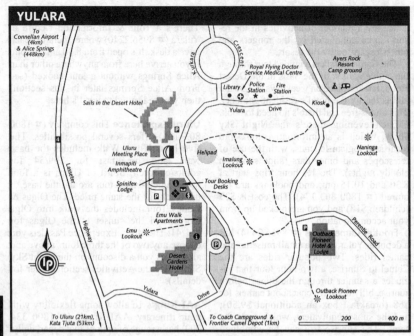

YULARA

To Connellan Airport (4km) & Alice Springs (448km)

Kurkara

Crescent

Ayers Rock Resort Camp ground

Royal Flying Doctor Service Medical Centre

Library
Police Station
Fire Station

Sails in the Desert Hotel

Kiosk

Yulara   Drive

Uluru Meeting Place

Helipad

Naninga Lookout

Inmapiti Amphitheatre

Imalung Lookout

Spinifex Lodge

Tour Booking Desks

Emu Walk Apartments

Emu Lookout

Desert Gardens Hotel

Outback Pioneer Hotel & Lodge

Perentie Road

Lasseter Highway

Yulara   Drive

Outback Pioneer Lookout

To Uluru (21km), Kata Tjuta (53km)

To Coach Campground & Frontier Camel Depot (1km)

0   200   400 m

Centre then hooks into the Anangu Tours' Aboriginal cultural walk for $81/41.

For Olgas viewing, there's the Morning Valley of the Winds Tour ($65/33) or you can do the three hour Valley of the Winds walk, then enjoy a relaxing barbecue with the sunset over the domes for $96/48. A combined Olgas and Uluru sunset costs $64/32.

Holiday AKT Another company operating from Yulara is Holiday AKT (☎ 8947 3900, akt@world.net). Its two day Touring Pass includes a half-day Olgas tour, Rock sunset, sunrise climb and base tour for $124/100.

Anangu Tours This tour company (☎ 8956 2123, lbanangu@bigpond.com) is owned and operated by Anangu from the Mutitjulu community. Its tour desk is at the Cultural Centre inside the park, but it also arranges transfers from Yulara.

The tours are led by an Anangu guide and an interpreter, and they offer a wonderful chance to meet and talk with Anangu. The Aboriginal Uluru Tour runs daily, costs $78/63 and takes approximately 4½ hours. Starting with sunrise over Uluru, it includes a restaurant breakfast, a base tour, a presentation on Aboriginal culture and law, and demonstrations of spear-throwing and bush skills.

The Kuniya Sunset Tour ($65/49) leaves at 2.30 pm (3.30 pm October to March) and includes a visit to Mutitjulu Waterhole and the Cultural Centre, finishing with viewing the sunset. Both tours can be combined over two days with an Anangu Culture Pass, which costs $120/95.

Self-drive options are also available for $39/20. You can join an Aboriginal guide at 8.30 am (7.30 in summer) for the morning walk or at 3 pm (4 pm) for the Kuniya Sunset Tour.

Bookings are essential for all tours.

From Alice Springs All-inclusive tours to Uluru by private operators start as low as about $300 for a three day camping trip, which includes Kings Canyon, although around $330 is the average. Companies such as Sahara Tours (☎ 8953 0881, sahara@ saharatours.com.au) and Northern Territory Adventure Tours (☎ 8981 4255, nttours@ adventuretours.com.au) are popular with the budget conscious.

Things to check out when shopping around for tours include the time it takes to get to the Rock and Kata Tjuta, and whether the return is done early or late in the day. Prices can vary with the season and demand, and sometimes there may be cheaper 'stand-by' fares available. Bus-pass travellers should note that the bus services to the Rock are often heavily booked – if your schedule is tight it's best to plan ahead.

Tours that include accommodation other than camping are generally much more expensive.

The passes offered by Greyhound Pioneer and McCafferty's are good value as they give you return transport to Yulara, plus various options at the Rock. They don't, however, include the park entry fee. See Getting There & Away in this section for more details.

Places to Stay

If there's anything to put a damper on your visit to Uluru, it's the high cost of accommodation and dining at Yulara – you're over a barrel so you'll just have to fork out the dough and grit your teeth. And, seemingly insatiable demand makes it advisable to book all accommodation, including dorm beds at the Outback Pioneer Hotel & Lodge and tent or van sites at the camping ground, especially during school holidays.

All accommodation, with the exception of the camping ground, should be booked through the central reservation office in Sydney (☎ 1800 089 622). There is also a 5% NT Bed Tax to be added.

Budget 'Cheap' is a relative term at Yulara and both the camp sites and dormitories are the most expensive in the Territory. The camping ground is fine but backpackers facilities are looking pretty tired.

The *Ayers Rock Resort Camp Ground* (☎ 8956 2055) charges $22 for two people on an unpowered site, or $26 with power. Most of the camp sites have manicured patches of green grass; the camping ground is set among native gardens and there's quite a bit of shade.

If you don't have your own tent, Elke's Backpackers Resort in the Alice has them for hire ($6/9 a day for two/three-person tents) and if you're not going back to the Alice the Greyhound bus driver can drop it back at Elke's for $5.

Facilities at the camp ground include a swimming pool, phones, laundry, free barbecues and amenities for the disabled.

The next cheapest option is dormitory accommodation at the *Outback Pioneer Hotel & Lodge* (☎ 8956 2170), across the dunes from the shopping centre. A bed in a segregated 20-bed dorm costs $27 (YHA members pay $21, dropping to $20 for the 2nd night and $18 for the 3rd and subsequent nights). The communal cooking facilities are in desperate need of upgrading and noticeably light on utensils. Baggage storage lockers cost $1 and linen is available for a $10 refundable deposit.

Also available are four-bed lodge cabin rooms for $30 per person ($27 for YHA members and $26/24 on 2nd/3rd nights).

Cabins & Units The *camping ground* has cabins sleeping up to six people for $126 per night. The price includes linen and cooking facilities, although bathrooms are shared. They get booked out pretty quickly during the cool winter months.

The *Outback Pioneer Hotel & Lodge* also has budget rooms, sleeping up to four in combinations of twin or double beds plus bunks. Each has TV, linen, fridge and tea/coffee-making facilities, but bathrooms are communal. The cost is $124. Out the back of this place there's a good lookout point for sunset views of the Rock.

Next up is the *Spinifex Lodge* (☎ 8956 2131) near the shopping square. It has 68 one-bedroom units that accommodate two to four people for $129 for a double. These are quite good value, with fridge, TV and microwave oven, although bathrooms are shared. There are guest laundry facilities.

Apartments Probably the best deal at Yulara is offered by the *Emu Walk Apartments* (☎ 8956 2100). It has one and two-bedroom flats that accommodate four and eight people, respectively. Each have a lounge room with TV and a fully equipped kitchen, and there's a communal laundry. They are also very central, being right between the visitors centre and the shopping square. The cost is $299 for the small apartments and $371 for the larger ones.

Hotels The most expensive part of the Outback Pioneer complex is known as the *Outback Pioneer Hotel & Lodge*, where a single or double room with attached bathroom costs $288.

At the opposite side of Yulara, the *Desert Gardens Hotel* (☎ 8956 2100) has 100 rooms with TV, phone, minibar and room service costing $322 for a standard single or double and $378 for deluxe rooms with a Rock view. The hotel has a pool and a restaurant.

At the top of the range is the *Sails in the Desert Hotel* (☎ 8956 2200), which has all the facilities you'd expect in a five star hotel, including in-house movies, 24 hour room service, spa, tennis court and art gallery. High-season rates start at $402 for a double, soaring to $485 with a Rock view and $709 for a deluxe suite.

Places to Eat

The range of eating options is pretty good, though self-catering is the only cheap option – the well-stocked *supermarket* at the shopping centre is open daily from 8.30 am to 9 pm.

Yulara Take-Away, also in the shopping centre, opens daily from 8.30 am to 7.30 pm and does reasonable fast food. There's a *bakery* here as well. The *Pioneer Kitchen* at the Outback Pioneer Lodge offers light meals and snacks from 8 am until 9 pm.

For sit-down dining there are licensed restaurants in the hotels and at the shopping centre. Prices are astronomical, yet you'll probably have to book for dinner.

Geckos Café (☎ 8956 2562) at the shopping centre offers a range of pasta ($15 to $20) and meat dishes ($20 to $25), and wood-fired pizzas ($14 to $19). The prices are way above the quality. Reservations are advised.

One of the most popular deals at Yulara is the *Pioneer Barbecue*, which takes place nightly at the Outback Pioneer Hotel & Lodge. For around $15 you can barbecue your choice of meat or fish and help yourself to a range of salads. A cheaper vegetarian dish is also offered, or you can just have the salads for $8.50.

For more conventional dining, the hotel also has the *Bough House* (☎ 8956 2170), which is open daily for breakfast, lunch and dinner. Its all-you-can-eat dinner buffet costs $35.

Upmarket a la carte dining can be enjoyed at the *Desert Gardens Hotel*, (breakfast and dinner only). Main courses are in the $20 to $25 range, and there's also a buffet for $37.

The last word in upmarket dining is the Sails in the Desert Hotel, which has the *Rockpool* poolside restaurant; the *Winkiku*, which features buffet meals; and the more sophisticated *Kuniya*, which is open for dinner only. Reservations for all three can be made by phoning ☎ 8956 2200.

Entertainment

All the hotels have at least one bar. There are no dress standards at the Outback Pioneer's *BBQ Bar*, which has is live music nightly. It's a good place to meet fellow travellers and takeaway alcohol can be bought here.

Getting There & Away

Air Connellan airport is about 5km from Yulara. You can fly direct from various major centres as well as from Alice Springs. Ansett has two flights daily for the 45 minute, $205 hop from the Alice to the Rock.

The numerous flights direct to Yulara can be money savers. If, for example, you were intending to fly into the Centre from Adelaide, it makes a lot more sense to travel Adelaide-Uluru-Alice Springs rather than Adelaide-Alice Springs-Uluru-Alice Springs. You can fly direct between Yulara and Perth

($547 one way), Adelaide ($587), Cairns ($537), Sydney ($576) and Darwin ($549) with Qantas or Ansett.

Bus Apart from hitching, the cheapest way to get to the Rock is to take a bus or tour. Greyhound Pioneer has daily services between Alice Springs and Uluru; McCafferty's on Sunday, Tuesday, Thursday and Friday, connecting at Erldunda, the turn-off from the Stuart Hwy. The 441km trip takes about 5½ hours.

The fare for one-way travel with McCafferty's is $55 from Alice Springs to Yulara; with Greyhound Pioneer it's $59 from the Alice.

There are also direct services between Adelaide and Uluru, although this actually means connecting with another bus at Erldunda. Adelaide to Yulara takes about 22 hours for the 1720km trip and costs $135.

Bus Passes McCafferty's has a Rock Pass, which is valid for three days and includes return transport from Alice Springs. Then at the Rock itself you join the following AAT-King's tours: guided base tour, Kata Tjuta and sunset tour, Uluru climb, Uluru sunrise and sunset. The pass doesn't include the park entry fee or accommodation, and costs $148. The only condition is that you must stay for two nights at your own expense. A variant costing of $219 allows you three of the AAT-King's trips plus Kings Canyon and on to the Alice, with no time limit.

Greyhound Pioneer has similar deals. If you already have a Greyhound Pioneer pass that gets you to Yulara, you can opt to do the two half-day tours at no extra cost.

Car If you don't have your own vehicle, renting a car in Alice Springs to go to Uluru and back can be expensive. You're looking at $70 to $100 a day for a car from the big operators, and this only includes 100km a day, each extra kilometre costing 25c.

Some companies offer one-way deals from Yulara to Alice Springs. For example,

Hertz offers two day rental with 700km free for $195 and three days with 1000km free for $295. Beware of extras such as insurance, but between four people it's cheaper than taking a bus there and back.

Territory Thrifty Car Rental in Alice Springs has a deal whereby a small car costs $70 per day, including 300km free per day; this is a more realistic option. On one of these deals if you spent three days and covered 1000km (the bare minimum), you'd be up for around $400, including insurance and petrol costs.

The road from the Alice to Yulara is sealed and there are regular food and petrol stops along the way. Yulara is 441km from the Alice, 241km west of Erldunda on the Stuart Hwy, and the whole journey takes about six to seven hours.

Major car rental companies Hertz (☎ 8956 2244), Avis (☎ 8956 2266) and Territory Thrifty Car Rental (☎ 8956 2030) are all represented at Yulara.

Getting Around
The resort sprawls a bit, but it's not too large to get around on foot, and there's a free shuttle bus that runs between all accommodation points daily, every 15 minutes from 10.30 am to 2.30 pm and 6.30 pm to 12.30 am. Walking trails lead across the dunes to little lookouts over the village and surrounding terrain.

A free shuttle bus operated by AAT-Kings meets all flights and drops at all accommodation points around the resort.

The National Park Several options are available if you want to go from Yulara to Uluru or Kata Tjuta in the national park. The ticket price includes a stop at the Cultural Centre, and you can then take a later bus to Uluru at no extra charge. The fare does not include the park entry fee.

Sunworth (☎ 8956 2152) runs shuttles to Uluru and return for $20 per person (sunset $15, sunrise $25). Morning/afternoon return services to Kata Tjuta cost $35/40.

Queensland

Queensland is Australia's holiday state. Whether you prefer neon-lit Surfers Paradise, a deserted beach, an island resort or excellent diving on the Great Barrier Reef, rainforest treks, the wide expanse of the Outback or remote national parks, you're certain to find something to suit your taste. Brisbane, the state capital, is a lively city. In the north, Cairns is a busy travellers centre and base for a whole range of side trips and activities. Between Brisbane and Cairns there are strings of towns and islands, offering virtually every pastime you can imagine connected with the sea. Inland, several spectacular national parks are scattered over the ranges and between the isolated towns and cattle stations. In the far south-west corner of the state you'll find one of the most isolated towns of all, Birdsville, on the famous Birdsville Track.

North of Cairns, the Cape York Peninsula remains a wilderness against which people still test themselves. You can get an easy taste of this frontier in Cooktown, Australia's first British settlement and once a riotous gold-rush town. Just inland from Cairns is the lush Atherton Tableland, with countless beautiful waterfalls and scenic spots. Further inland, on the main route across Queensland to the Northern Territory (NT), is the outback mining town of Mt Isa and, south-east of here, the town of Longreach with its Stockman's Hall of Fame.

Queensland started as a penal colony in 1824. The free settlers soon followed and Queensland became a separate colony independent of New South Wales (NSW) in 1859. Its early white settlers indulged in one of the greatest land grabs of all time and encountered fierce Aboriginal opposition. For much of the 19th century, what amounted to a guerrilla war took place along the frontiers of the white advance.

Traditionally, agriculture and mining have been the backbone of the Queensland economy: the state contains a substantial chunk of Australia's mineral wealth. More recently, vast amounts of money have been

HIGHLIGHTS

Telephone code: ☎ 07
Population: 3.46 million
Area: 1,727,000 sq km

- Diving and snorkelling on the incomparable Great Barrier Reef
- Taking a 4WD trip around beautiful Fraser Island
- Cruising the Whitsunday Islands
- Visiting Australia's northern tip – the rugged Cape York Peninsula
- Partying at the great nightlife centres of Cairns, Surfers Paradise and Brisbane
- Joining a whale-watching tour at Hervey Bay and spotting a platypus in the wild at the Eungella National Park

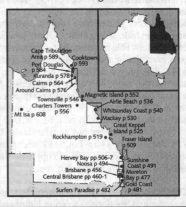

invested in tourism, which is on the verge of becoming the state's leading money earner.

ABORIGINAL PEOPLE & KANAKAS

By the turn of the 19th century, the Aboriginal people of Queensland had been comprehensively run off their lands, and the white authorities had set up reserves around the state for the survivors. A few of these reserves were places where Aboriginal people could live a self-sufficient life; others were strife-ridden places with people from different areas and cultures thrown unhappily together under unsympathetic rule.

It wasn't until the 1980s that control of the reserves was transferred to their residents, and that the reserves became known as 'communities'. These freehold grants, known as Deeds of Grant in Trust, are subject to right of access for prospecting, exploration or mining. This falls well short of the freehold ownership that Aboriginal people have in other parts of Australia, such as the NT.

Visitor interest has prompted opportunities to have some contact with Aboriginal culture – in addition to rock-art sites at various locations, you can visit a number of communities, including the Yarrabah community south of Cairns and the Hopevale community north of Cooktown, and take tours with Aboriginal content, such as at Mossman. At the Tjapukai Aboriginal Cultural Centre in Cairns, an award-winning Aboriginal dance group performs most days for tourists. Perhaps the most exciting event is the Laura Aboriginal Dance & Cultural Festival, held every second year in June on the Cape York Peninsula.

Another people on the fringes of Queensland society – though less so – are the Kanakas, descendants of Pacific Islanders brought in during the 19th century to work, mainly on sugar plantations, under virtual slave conditions. The business of collecting, transporting and delivering them was called blackbirding. The first Kanakas were brought over in 1863 for Robert Towns, the man whose money got Townsville going, and about 60,000 more followed until blackbirding stopped in 1905. You'll come across quite a few Kanakas in the coastal area north of Rockhampton.

GEOGRAPHY

Queensland has four distinct regions generally running parallel to the coast. First there's the coastal strip – the basis for the booming tourist trade. Along this strip there are beaches, bays, islands and, of course, the Great Barrier Reef. Much of the coastal region is green and productive with lush rainforests, endless fields of sugar cane and stunning national parks.

Next comes the Great Dividing Range, the mountain range that continues down through NSW and Victoria. The mountains come closest to the coast in Queensland and are most spectacular in the far north, near Cairns, and in the far south.

Then there are the tablelands – areas of flat agricultural land that run to the west. These fertile areas extend furthest west in the south, where the Darling Downs has some of the most productive grain-growing land in Australia.

Finally, there's the vast inland area, the barren Outback fading into the NT. Rain can temporarily make this desert bloom but basically it's an area of long, empty roads and tiny settlements.

There are a couple of variations from these basic divisions. In the far northern Gulf Country and Cape York Peninsula there are huge empty regions cut by countless dry riverbeds that can become swollen torrents in the wet season. The whole area is a network of waterways, sometimes bringing road transport to a complete halt.

The Tropic of Capricorn crosses Queensland about a third of the way up, running through the two major towns of Rockhampton and Longreach.

CLIMATE

The Queensland seasons are more a case of hotter and wetter or cooler and drier than of summer and winter. November/December to April/May is the wetter, hotter half of the year, while the real Wet, particularly affecting northern coastal areas, is January to March. Cairns usually gets about 1300mm of rain in these three months, with daily temperatures in the high 30s (°C). This is also the season for cyclones and, if one hits, the main road north, the Bruce Hwy, can be blocked by the ensuing floods.

In the south, Brisbane and Rockhampton get about 450mm of rain from January to March, and temperatures in Brisbane rarely

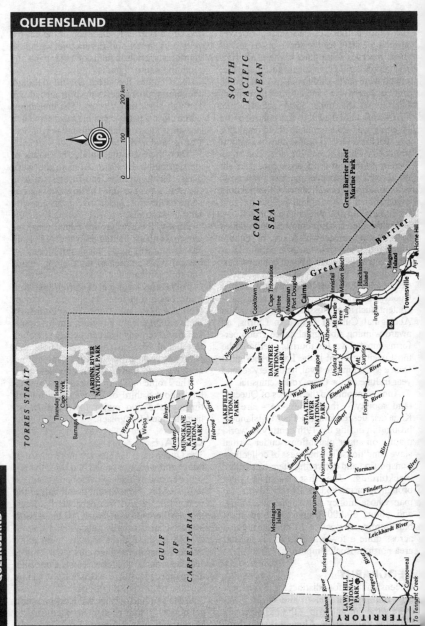

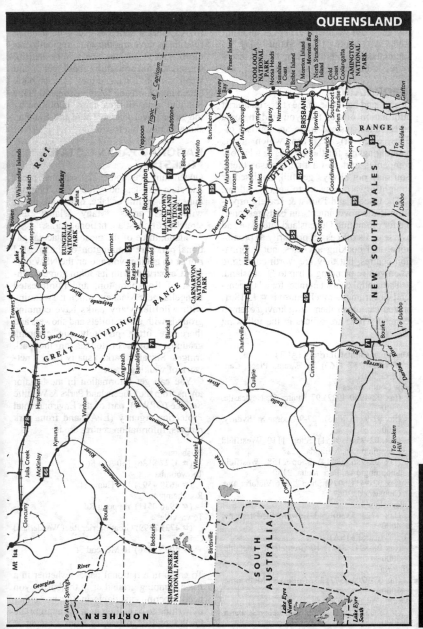

drop below 20°C. Queensland doesn't really get 'cold weather', except at night inland or upland from about May to September. Inland, of course, there's also a lot less rain than near the coast.

INFORMATION

Queensland has none of the state-run tourist information offices that you find in some other states. Instead there are tourism offices, often privately run, which act as booking agents for the various hotels, tour companies and so on that sponsor them. You may not always get full, unbiased or straightforward answers to your questions.

The Queensland Tourist & Travel Corporation is the government-run body responsible for promoting Queensland interstate and overseas. Its offices act primarily as promotional and booking agencies, not information centres, but they are worth contacting when you're planning a trip to Queensland.

The central contact number for all Queensland Government travel centres is ☎ 13 1801, or you can email them at qldtravl@ozemail.com.au. There are offices in the following places:

Australian Capital Territory (ACT)
    (fax 02-6257 4160) 25 Garema Place, Canberra, 2601
New South Wales
    (fax 02-4960 4922) 97 Hunter St, Newcastle, 2300
    (fax 02-9246 7046) 327-9 George St, Sydney, 2000
    (fax 02-9540 5051) Shop 1110, Westfield Shoppingtown, Miranda, 2228
    (fax 02-9865 8444) Shop 2158, Westfield Shoppingtown, Parramatta, 2150
    (fax 02-9411 6079) Shop 2, 376 Victoria Ave, Chatswood, 2067
Queensland
    (fax 3221 5320) 243 Edward St, Brisbane, 4000
South Australia (SA)
    (fax 08-8211 8841) 10 Grenfell St, Adelaide, 5000
Victoria
    (fax 03-9206 4577) 257 Collins St, Melbourne, 3000
Western Australia (WA)
    (☎ 08-9322 1800) Shop 6, 777 Hay St, Perth, 6000

The Royal Automobile Club of Queensland (RACQ) has a series of excellent, detailed road maps covering the state, region by region. RACQ offices are a very helpful source of information about road and weather conditions, and they can also book accommodation and tours. Also good is the Sunmap series of area maps, published by the state government. There are Sunmap shops in most big towns.

NATIONAL PARKS & STATE FORESTS

Queensland has some 220 national parks and state forests, and while some comprise only a single hill or lake, others are major wilderness areas. Many islands and stretches of coast are national parks.

Inland, three of the most spectacular national parks are: Lamington, on the forested rim of an ancient volcano on the NSW border; Carnarvon, with its 30km gorge southwest of Rockhampton; and rainforested Eungella, near Mackay, which is swarming with wildlife. Many parks have camping grounds with water, toilets and showers and there are often privately run camping grounds, motels or lodges on the park fringes. Sizeable parks usually have a network of walking tracks.

You can get information in most major towns from the Queensland Parks & Wildlife Service (QPWS), part of the Environmental Protection Agency (EPA), and from park rangers. Information centres are in:

Brisbane
    (☎ 3227 8186) 160 Ann St
Toowoomba
    (☎ 4639 4599) 158 Hume St
Rockhampton
    (☎ 4936 0511) Yeppoon Rd
Townsville
    (☎ 4721 2399) Great Barrier Reef Wonderland
Cairns
    (☎ 4052 3096) 10 McLeod St

To camp in a national park – whether in a fixed camping ground or in the bush – you need a permit, available in advance either by writing to or calling in at the appropriate QPWS or EPA office, or from a ranger at

Workers' Hostels

With casual labour and seasonal work being very much part of the working holiday scene in Queensland, there are a number of hostels, principally along the coast, which attract itinerant workers – and backpackers – in search of a job.

Most of these hostels are OK, if a little seedy, and the owners are usually helpful in finding work for people and are often involved in the industries themselves.

Unfortunately, some of the hostels exploit the people staying with them, who are often low on cash and desperate for work. Be wary of accepting accommodation or other services free in advance, as we have received many letters from travellers complaining that they are paid minimal wages – enough for food and board only.

In addition to this problem, it seems that some hostel owners are not averse to using threats to intimidate travellers into staying – 'a cross between Basil Fawlty and Charles Manson' was a description we received from a disgruntled backpacker about one overbearing hostel owner.

The best bet is to try to talk to other travellers who have stayed at a place and not to accept accommodation, transport or other services in lieu of pay.

---

the park itself. Camping in national parks and state forests costs $3.50 per person per night. Some camping grounds fill up at holiday times, so you may need to book well ahead; you can usually book sites six to 12 weeks ahead by writing to the appropriate office. Lists of camping grounds are available from QPWS offices.

The handy *National Parks in Queensland* booklets ($5) also have useful information about Queensland's national parks and state forests, including things to do, camping details and how to get there. These booklets are available from bookshops and QPWS offices. Also useful is the *Camping in Queensland* booklet ($6), which lists camp sites and facilities at all the national parks and state forests throughout Queensland.

ACTIVITIES
Bushwalking
This is a popular activity year-round. There are excellent bushwalking possibilities in many parts of the state, including several of the larger coastal islands such as Fraser and Hinchinbrook. National parks and state forests often have marked walking trails. Bushwalking favourites among the mainland national parks include Lamington in the southern Border Ranges, Main Range in the Great Divide, Cooloola (Great Sandy National Park) just north of the Sunshine Coast, and Wooroonooran south of Cairns, which contains Queensland's highest peak, Mt Bartle Frere (1657m). You can get full information from national park and state forest offices.

There are bushwalking clubs around the state and several useful guidebooks. Lonely Planet's *Bushwalking in Australia* includes three walks in Queensland, which range between two and five days in length.

Water Sports
Diving & Snorkelling The Great Barrier Reef provides some of the world's best diving and there's ample opportunity to learn and pursue this activity. The Queensland coast is probably the world's cheapest place to learn to scuba dive in tropical water – a five day course leading to a recognised open water certificate usually costs between $300 and $550 and you almost always do a good part of your learning out on the Great Barrier Reef. These courses are very popular and nearly every town along the coast has one or more dive schools. The three most popular places are Airlie Beach, Townsville and Cairns.

Important factors to consider when choosing a course include the school's reputation, the relative amounts of time spent on pool/classroom training and out in the ocean, and whether your open-water time is spent on the outer reef as opposed to reefs around islands or even just off the mainland (the outer reef is usually more spectacular). Normally you have to show you can tread water for 10 minutes and swim 200m before you can start a course. Most schools also require a medical, which usually costs extra (around $50); some tour operators will not take asthmatics. At the time of writing, the Queensland Health Department was reviewing its Code of Practice for Diving which diving companies must observe.

While school standards are generally high, each year a number of newly certified divers are stricken with 'the bends' and end up in the decompression chamber in Townsville. This potentially fatal condition is caused by bubbles of nitrogen which form in the blood when divers ascend too quickly to the surface – always ascend slowly and, on dives over 9m in depth, take a rest stop en route to the surface. With treatment most people make a full recovery, although your holiday budget may not if you don't have insurance that covers such a mishap.

For certified divers, trips and equipment hire are available just about everywhere. You usually have to show evidence of qualifications. You can snorkel almost everywhere too. There are coral reefs off some mainland beaches and around several of the islands, and many organisers of day trips to the Great Barrier Reef provide snorkelling gear free.

During the wet season, which is usually January to March, floods can wash a lot of mud out into the ocean and visibility for divers and snorkellers is sometimes affected.

The Pisces *Diving & Snorkelling Guide to Australia's Great Barrier Reef* is an excellent guide to all the dives available on the reef.

White-Water Rafting & Canoeing The
Tully and North Johnstone rivers between Townsville and Cairns are the big ones for white-water rafting. You can do day trips for about $130, or longer expeditions.

Coastal Queensland is full of waterways and lakes so there's no shortage of canoeing territory. You can hire canoes or join canoe tours in several places, including Noosa, Townsville and Cairns.

Swimming & Surfing Popular surfing and
swimming beaches are south of Brisbane on

the Gold Coast and north of Brisbane on the Sunshine Coast. North of Fraser Island the beaches are sheltered by the Great Barrier Reef so they're great for swimming, but no good for surf. The clear, sheltered waters of the reef hardly need to be mentioned. There are also innumerable good, freshwater swimming spots around the state.

Other Water Sports Sailing enthusiasts
will find many places that hire out boats and/or sailboards, both along the coast and inland. Airlie Beach and the Whitsunday Islands are possibly the biggest centres and you can find almost any type of boating or sailing you want there.

Fishing is one of Queensland's most popular sports and you can hire fishing gear or boats in many places.

Warning From around November to April,
avoid swimming on unprotected northern beaches where deadly box jellyfish may lurk. If in any doubt, check with locals. If you're still in doubt, don't swim. Great Keppel Island is usually safe, but don't swim any further north in the box jellyfish season. Also in northern waters, saltwater crocodiles are a hazard. They may be found close to the shore in the open sea or near creeks and rivers – especially tidal ones – sometimes at surprising distances inland.

Fossicking
There are lots of good fossicking areas in Queensland; see the *Gem Field* brochure published by the Queensland Tourist & Travel Corporation. It lists the places where you'll have a fair chance of finding gems and the types you might find. You'll need a 'miners right' before you set out.

GETTING THERE & AWAY
See the Brisbane Getting There & Away section for details on transport to Queensland.

GETTING AROUND
The peak tourist seasons are from mid-December to late January, 10 days either side of Easter, and June to mid-October. The low season is February and March.

Air

Ansett Australia (☎ 13 1300) and Qantas Airways (☎ 13 1313) fly to Queensland's major cities, connecting them to the southern states and to the NT. There are also a multitude of smaller airlines operating up and down the coast, across the Cape York Peninsula and into the outback. During the Wet season, such flights are often the only means of getting around the Gulf of Carpentaria or the Cape York Peninsula. These smaller airlines include Sunstate Airlines (book through Qantas) and Flight West Airlines (☎ 13 2392 within Queensland or ☎ 1800 777 879 from elsewhere in Australia, or book through Ansett).

Bus

Greyhound Pioneer Australia (☎ 13 2030) and McCafferty's Express Coaches (☎ 13 1499) have comprehensive bus networks throughout Queensland and cover all the major destinations. The busiest route is up the coast on the Bruce Hwy from Brisbane to Cairns – both companies offer various passes that cover all or part of this route. Youth Hostel Association (YHA) members receive a discount of between $15 and $20 on these passes. Greyhound Pioneer has the six month Whitsunday Pass for travel between Brisbane and Airlie Beach ($123), the three month Sunseeker, which takes you between Cairns and Sydney ($255), and the 30 day Traveller Pass from Brisbane to Cairns ($175).

McCafferty's has a number of passes that include Queensland, such as its three month Follow the Sun Pass allowing unlimited travel from Brisbane to Cairns for $210. See the Getting Around chapter for more details of passes.

The other major bus routes are the inland routes from Brisbane to Mt Isa (continuing into the NT); from Townsville to Mt Isa; and from Rockhampton to Longreach (McCafferty's only). Prices are fairly similar, although McCafferty's tends to be a dollar or two cheaper.

Train

The main railway line is the Brisbane to Cairns run. There are also inland services

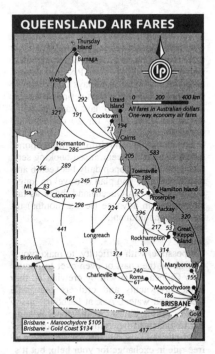

QUEENSLAND AIR FARES

Thursday Island
Bamaga
Weipa
292 Lizard Island
321 191 Cooktown
73 194
Cairns
Normanton 286
205 583
266 289 Townsville 185
Mt Isa 83 245 Hamilton Island
Cloncurry 420 226 Proserpine
298 309
224 396 Mackay
320
441 Longreach 217 53 Great Keppel Island
Rockhampton
Birdsville 223 374 363 314
Maryborough
Charleville 240 Roma 155
61 Maroochydore 186
451 325 BRISBANE
Gold Coast
417

0 200 400 km
All fares in Australian dollars
One-way economy air fares

Brisbane - Maroochydore $105
Brisbane - Gold Coast $134

from Brisbane to Charleville, from Rockhampton to Longreach, and from Townsville to Mt Isa. Local services include the *Gulflander* and the *Savannahlander* – see the Gulf Savannah section later in this chapter for details. The new *Tilt Train* service from Brisbane to Rockhampton is the world's fastest narrow-gauge railway service, capable of speeds over 200km/h but constrained by the present state of the track to a top speed of 170km/h.

Then there's the luxurious new *Great South Pacific Express*, Australia's version of the Orient Express, which runs between Cairns, Brisbane and Sydney. See the Cairns Getting There & Away section later in this chapter for more details.

Queensland trains are usually slower than buses but are similarly priced if you travel economy class.

The Sunshine Railpass is available for travel on the Queensland network in 1st/economy class. The cost is $388/267 for a

14 day pass, $477/309 for 21 days and $582/388 for 30 days. For travel on the *Queenslander* between Cairns and Brisbane there is a surcharge of $233, which includes meals and a sleeping berth. Roadrail Passes give you a set number of days of economy-class rail travel within a set period. The cost of these is $269 for 10 days travel in a 60-day period and $349 for 20 days travel within 90 days.

For bookings and information, phone Queensland Rail's centralised booking service (☎ 13 2232), open daily between 6 am and 8.30 pm. If you plan to travel on long-distance trains in Queensland, book as far as possible in advance (ie six months) to avoid disappointment.

Boat

It's possible, with difficulty, to make your way along the coast or even over to Papua New Guinea or Darwin by crewing on the numerous yachts and cruisers that sail Queensland waters. Ask at harbours, marinas or sailing clubs. Great Keppel Island, Airlie Beach, Townsville and Cairns are good places to try. Sometimes you'll get a free ride in exchange for your help, but it's more common for owners to ask you to pay a daily fee (say $20) for food etc.

Brisbane

• postcode 4000   • pop 1.6 million

For many years Brisbane was viewed by its southern cousins as something of a 'hicksville', an overblown country town. If there was ever any truth to that, there certainly isn't today. Since playing host to some major international events in the 1980s, including the 1982 Commonwealth Games and Expo 88, Brisbane has developed into a lively, cosmopolitan city with several interesting districts, a good street-cafe scene, a great park, a busy cultural calendar and a decent nightlife – some locals call it Bris Vegas.

The city began as a dumping ground for the worst convicts from the NSW colony. The tropical country to the north seemed a good place to banish them to. Accordingly,

in 1824, a penal settlement was established at Redcliffe on Moreton Bay, but it was soon abandoned due to lack of water and hostile Aborigines. The settlement was moved south and inland to the present site of Brisbane, where a town grew up.

Although the penal settlement was abandoned in 1839, Brisbane's future was assured when the area was thrown open to free settlers in 1842. As Queensland's huge agricultural potential and mineral riches were developed, so Brisbane grew. Today, it's the third largest city in Australia.

Although close to the coast, Brisbane is very much a river city. It's a scenic place, surrounded by hills and fine lookouts, with several impressive bridges spanning the Brisbane River. It also enjoys an excellent climate.

Several of Queensland's major attractions can be reached on day trips from Brisbane. The Gold and Sunshine coasts and their mountainous hinterlands are short bus rides from the city, and you can also visit the islands of Moreton Bay or head inland towards the Great Dividing Range and the Darling Downs.

Orientation

Brisbane is built along and between the looping meanders of the Brisbane River, about 25km upstream from the river mouth. The Roma St Transit Centre, where you'll arrive if you're coming in by bus, train or airport shuttle, is on Roma St, about 500m west of the city centre – which is focused on the Queen St Mall.

Most of the city's accommodation and eating options are clustered in the inner suburbs surrounding the city. Immediately north is Spring Hill, with some good mid-range options, while west of the centre is Petrie Terrace, with several budget hostels, and Paddington, an attractive residential suburb with good cafes and restaurants. North-east of the city, along Ann St, is Fortitude Valley, a fairly trendy area incorporating a small Chinatown and lots of cafes, restaurants and clubs. East beyond the Valley, as the locals call it, is New Farm, an upwardly mobile district of pricey eat-and-be-seen places.

South across the Victoria Bridge is South Brisbane, with the Queensland Cultural Centre and the South Bank Parklands; further south are Highgate Hill and the hip West End.

Information

Tourist Offices At the transit centre, on Level 3, is the privately run Brisbane Visitors Accommodation Service desk (☎ 3236 2020), which offers a booking and information service for backpackers. It operates weekdays from 7 am to 6 pm and weekends from 8 am to 5 pm. There's also an information desk on Level 2.

The Queen St Mall information centre (☎ 3229 5918), on the corner of Queen and Albert Sts, is good for information on things to see and do around town; it's open Monday to Thursday from 9 am to 5.30 pm, Friday to 8 pm, Saturday to 4 pm and Sunday from 10 am to 4 pm.

There's also the less useful Tourism Brisbane information desk (☎ 3221 8411) in the City Hall, on King George Square, and a Queensland Travel & Tourism Corporation centre (☎ 13 1801), on the corner of Adelaide and Edward Sts. It's more a booking office than an information centre, but staff may be able to answer some queries.

Money Exchange bureaus are open at Brisbane airport for all arriving flights.

Thomas Cook has three foreign exchange offices in the city centre. Its main branch is on level E of the Myer Centre in Elizabeth St; it's open weekdays from 8.45 am to 5.15 pm and Saturday from 9.30 am to 1 pm. The other branches are at 276 Edward St and on the 1st floor at 241 Adelaide St (opposite Qantas' international office).

American Express has its office at 131 Elizabeth St and is open weekdays from 9 am to 5.30 pm and on Saturday from 9 am to noon.

Most major city bank branches also provide specialist exchange bureaus.

Post & Communications The main post office is on Queen St and it's open weekdays from 7 am to 7 pm. At weekends there's a Post Shop, which also functions as a post office, on the 2nd level of the Myer Centre off the Queen St Mall; it's open from 10 am to 4 pm Saturday and Sunday.

The Central City Library, in the basement of the City Plaza complex behind City Hall, has Internet stations for hire at $4 per hour. It's open weekdays from 10 am to 6 pm and weekends from 10 am to 3 pm. The Hub (☎ 3229 1119) is an Internet cafe at 125 Margaret St in the city centre, and at the corner of Brunswick and Ann Sts down in the Valley there's Cafe Scene (☎ 3216 0624). There are Internet booths in the transit centre. Most backpacker hostels provide Internet access.

Bookshops The city's best is the Mary Ryan Bookshop, on Queen St Mall, one of a small, family run chain (other shops are in Paddington and New Farm). There's a good coffee bar in the basement of the city branch. Angus & Robertson Bookworld has shops on Post Office Square, in Adelaide St, and at the south-west end of the Queen St Mall. The largest range of travel guides and maps is to be found at World Wide Maps & Guides, at 187 George St (100m south-east of the Queen St Mall).

For second-hand titles try Archives Fine Books, spread over three shops at 40-42 Charlotte St, in the city centre. In the West End, check out Emma's Bookshop, a small, crammed place at 82A Vulture St, and Bent Books, just around the corner in Boundary St.

Medical Services The Travellers Medical & Vaccination Centre (☎ 3221 9066), on the 6th floor of the Qantas building at 247 Adelaide St, can handle all vaccinations and medical advice for travellers. There's also a 24-hour Travellers Medical Service (☎ 3211 3611), on the 1st floor at 245 Albert St above McDonald's, which offers travel vaccinations, women's health care and first-aid kits. The Brisbane Sexual Health Clinic (☎ 3227 8666) is at 484 Adelaide St.

Useful Organisations The RACQ (☎ 3361 2444) is in the GPO Building at 261 Queen St. The city council produces a series of brochures on Brisbane for visitors with a disability. These are available from the BCC Customer Services Centre at City Plaza behind the City Hall, or call the Disability Information Awareness Line (☎ 1800 177 120).

City Centre

Brisbane's **City Hall**, on the corner of Adelaide and Albert Sts, has gradually been surrounded by skyscrapers, but the observation platform still provides a great view across the city – a free lift runs weekdays from 8.30 am to 4.30 pm and Saturday from 10 am to 4.30 pm. There's also a free art gallery on the ground floor, open daily from 10 am to 5 pm.

There are many other attractive **historical buildings** dotted around the city centre, and Brisbane City Council publishes a series of *Heritage Trail* brochures that guide you around some of the most interesting. One worth taking a look at is the old **Treasury Building**, near the Victoria bridge on George St, which is now Brisbane's 24-hour casino.

A little further on, at 110 George St, is the **Sciencentre**, a hands-on science museum with interactive displays, optical illusions, a perception tunnel and a regular 20 minute

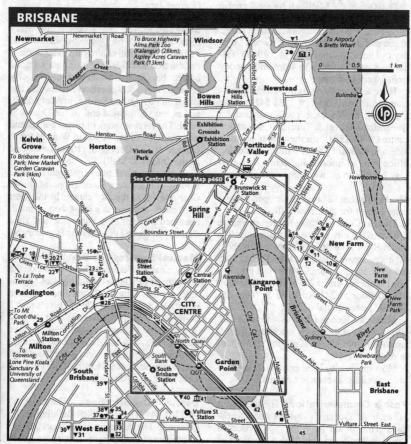

show in the theatre. It's open daily from 10 am to 5 pm ($7).

Continuing south-east on George St brings you to **Parliament House**, dating from 1868 and built in French Renaissance style. Free tours are given Monday to Friday five times a day (except when Parliament is sitting). The parliament building overlooks Brisbane's lush **Botanic Gardens**, to the north-east, which occupies 18 hectares in a loop of the river at the southern end of the city centre. The gardens are popular with in-line skaters, joggers, picnickers and lunching office workers, and they're open 24 hours a day (and lit at night). There are free guided tours of the gardens, leaving from the rotunda just south of the Albert St entrance, every day except Monday at 11 am and 1 pm.

Queensland Cultural Centre

This is an extensive cultural complex just across Victoria Bridge from the city centre and includes the city's main art gallery, museum and theatre complex.

The **Queensland Museum** contains a fairly lively and diverse set of collections, all of which are in some way relevant to Queensland. They include a dinosaur garden, exhibitions on whales, the history of photography and natural history, and an extensive collection of Melanesian artefacts. There's also a small aviation section with the *Avian Cirrus*, in which Queensland's Bert Hinkler made the first England to Australia solo flight in 1928. The museum is open daily from 9.30 am to 5 pm. Admission is free.

The **Queensland Art Gallery** has an impressive permanent collection of work by Australian artists and also features visiting exhibitions. It's open daily from 10 am to 5 pm and admission is free. There are free guided tours during the week at 11 am and 1 pm and on weekends at 11 am and 3 pm.

South Bank Parklands

Brisbane's South Bank has an excellent landscaped, riverside park with grassy areas, streams and a fantastic open-air **swimming pool** designed to resemble a lagoon, complete with a crescent of white sandy beach. There are also numerous cafes and restaurants, an IMAX theatre and a weekend market. It's always worth wandering down here at weekends during summer as there's usually some kind of performance, fair or food festival taking place.

In the plaza in the centre of the parkland, the **South Bank Wildlife Sanctuary** is a tropical conservatorium featuring hundreds of freely fluttering Australian butterflies, a

BRISBANE

PLACES TO STAY	PLACES TO EAT	OTHER
4 Centrepoint Backpackers	1 Breakfast Creek Hotel	2 Breakfast Creek Wharf
8 Atoa House Travellers' Hostel	17 Le Scoops	3 Newstead House
9 The Homestead	18 Hot Wok Cafe	5 Valley Pool
10 Allender Apartments	19 Jakarta Indonesian	6 Carazy Car Rentals
12 The Bowen Terrace	Restaurant	7 National Car Rentals
14 Globetrekkers' Hostel	20 Kari Tandoori	11 Village Twin Cinemas
16 Waverley B&B	21 3 F's Noodle Bar	13 New Farm Mountain Bikes
23 Aussie Way Backpackers	22 Paddo Tavern	15 Brisbane Arts Theatre
24 Banana Benders Backpackers	30 Kim Thanh	25 The Brisbane Underground
27 Brisbane City YHA; City	31 Soup Kitchen	26 La Boite Repertory Theatre
Backpackers Hostel	35 Cafe Babylon	29 Castlemaine Perkins XXXX
28 Yellow Submarine Backpackers	36 Caffe Tempo;	Brewery
32 Somewhere to Stay	Cafe Nouveau	37 Emma's Bookshop
33 Swagman's Rest	38 Qan Heng's	41 Queensland Maritime
34 Brisbane Backpackers Resort	39 Three Monkeys	Museum
43 Kangaroo Motel	Coffee House;	42 The Cliffs Rockclimbing Area
44 Kangaroo Point Holiday	Jazzy Cat Cafe	45 Brisbane Cricket Ground
Apartments	40 Captain Snapper	(The Gabba)

QUEENSLAND

Brisbane Walking Tour

As good a place as any to start is at the classically styled **City Hall**, where you should take the lift to the top of the bell tower for the view – this will give you some idea of the layout of the city centre.

On leaving, turn right out of the entrance, cross Adelaide St and head straight down Albert St to the **Queen St Mall**. This is the city's main shopping thoroughfare and it's nothing to write home about, but swing right and look up to the left at some of the facades – the former Carlton Hotel, the former Telegraph Building, the former York Hotel. Turn around and head down the mall to **Hoyts Regent Theatre**, which will be on your right, and pass through the foyer into the former booking hall, built in the days when movie houses were designed as temples to the glamour of the screen.

Retrace your steps along the mall to the junction with Albert St and head downhill, past the information centre. This time, keep your eyes on the ground and look for the bronze plaques set in the paving; these form part of a **literary trail** down Albert St, each plaque featuring a quote about Brisbane extracted from the work of one of the 32 featured writers. Albert St has a couple of good cafes and one of the better city pubs, Gilhooley's.

Take a left after Gilhooley's onto Charlotte St and continue across Edward St (notice the pattern in the street names: east-west are all women, north-south men). After about 150m, there's an entrance into the grounds of **St Stephen's Cathedral**. While the cathedral isn't particularly significant, pass around it and out onto Elizabeth St – then turn around for a great photo of the twin Gothic spires against a background of mirrored-glass office blocks.

Opposite the cathedral, on the north side of Elizabeth St, is an arched opening; follow it through. This walkway runs alongside the **post office**, built in the 1870s, which has a beautiful facade where you emerge on Queen St. (The newsagency you pass in the alleyway has Brisbane's best selection of overseas newspapers.) Next door and to the left of the post office (as seen from Queen St) is an amazingly imposing building, complete with carved gargoyles, which looks like it was lifted from a movie set of Gotham City – it only lacks Batman perched on top. During WWII this building, now known as **MacArthur Chambers**, was used as the headquarters of the commander-in-chief of the south-west Pacific, General MacArthur.

Walk on past the chambers, crossing Creek St, into the heart of Brisbane's central business district (CBD). At the junction with Wharf St, turning right would take you to the upmarket dining complexes of **Riverside Centre** and **Eagle St pier** (bizarrely, the latter is visually dominated by a McDonald's). Instead, turn left and walk two blocks up to Ann St. A left turn will take you past the Victorian-era **Central Station** and, opposite, the Greek Classical **Shrine of Remembrance**, from where it's 300m back to City Hall. To the right, Ann St runs through the heart of Fortitude Valley, just under a kilometre away.

Fortitude Valley is well worth exploring. Before the Valley you'll first pass **St John's Cathedral**, begun in 1901 and still under construction (this fact is proudly proclaimed on a billboard out front) and then the **Orient Hotel**, one of the city's oldest pubs and still a popular gig venue. Once you cross the slip road for the Story Bridge you're in the Valley's modest **Chinatown**, in Duncan St mall. One block after the dragon gateway of the Chinatown mall is the **Brunswick St Mall**, with several good cafes, a decent bar and **McWhirters Marketplace**, an eclectic shopping emporium.

To return to the city catch almost any of the buses from the stop on Ann St, just before the Story Bridge road junction.

glass-encased collection of insects and spiders, and an assortment of native reptiles, amphibians and birds. It's open daily from 9 am to 5 pm. Entry is $8/4.50 for adults/children.

The South Bank visitor information centre (☎ 3867 2051) is next to the sanctuary and opens daily from 8.30 am to 6 pm, later on Friday and Saturday nights. You can also phone ☎ 3867 2020 for a recorded message with details of the current entertainment program.

Queensland Maritime Museum

This museum, just south of South Bank, has a wide range of displays including an 1881 dry dock, an impressive collection of model ships, relics from old wrecks, and numerous boats such as the WWII frigate HMAS *Diamantina*. It's open from 9.30 am to 5 pm daily ($5/2.50).

Markets

The **Crafts Village** at South Bank is a handicraft market that sets up on Friday evenings and Saturday and Sunday until 5 pm. Over at the **Eagle St pier** there's a similar Sunday morning market also devoted to handicrafts. The two can be easily visited together using the City Cat. On Saturday, the **Fortitude Valley Market** in the Brunswick St Mall is a small affair comprising alternative art and craft stalls. There's usually live entertainment and plenty of streetside cafes in which to kick back and observe.

Mt Coot-tha Park

Located 8km west of the city centre, Mt Coot-tha has a great **lookout point** with views over Brisbane to the bay and Moreton and Stradbroke islands, the Glass House Mountains to the north and the mountains in the Gold Coast hinterland to the south. If you want to linger over the views, there's a good cafe and restaurant open every day for lunch and dinner.

There are some good walks around Mt Coot-tha and its foothills, like the one to JC Slaughter Falls on Simpsons Rd. There's also an **Aboriginal Art Trail**, a 1.5km walking trail that takes you past eight art sites with work by local Aboriginal artists, including tree carvings, rock paintings and a dance pit.

The very beautiful **Mt Coot-tha Botanic Gardens**, at the foot of the mountain, covers 52 hectares and includes over 20,000 species of plants, an enclosed tropical dome, an arid zone, rainforests and a Japanese garden. It's open daily from 8.30 am to 5.30 pm. There are free guided walks through the gardens daily except Sunday at 11 am and 1 pm.

Also within the gardens is the **Sir Thomas Brisbane Planetarium** (also known as the Cosmic Skydome), the largest planetarium in Australia. There are 45-minute shows from Wednesday to Friday at 3.30 and 7.30 pm, on Saturday at 1.30, 3.30 and 7.30 pm, and on Sunday at 1.30 and 3.30 pm ($8/4.50).

To get to the botanic gardens take the Mt Coot-tha bus No 471, which departs at 15/45 minutes past each hour from the corner of Adelaide and Albert St, close to King George Square. The bus operates daily between 9.15 am and 3.15 pm – the last bus back leaves at 3.50 pm. The ride takes about 15 minutes and the bus drops you off at the car park. The lookout is 3km from the botanic gardens – turn left out of the car park and start climbing. It's a tough walk.

Brisbane Forest Park

The Brisbane Forest Park is a 26,500 hectare natural bushland reserve stretching from the outskirts of Brisbane for more than 50km to the north and west. There's an **information centre** (☎ 3300 4855) at the Gap, at the start of the park, which is open daily from 9 am to 4.30 pm. The rangers run regular guided bushwalks and tours.

In the same spot is **Walk-About Creek**, a freshwater study centre where you can see fish, lizards, pythons and turtles at close quarters. It's open weekdays from 9 am to 4.30 pm and weekends from 10 am ($3.50). Upstairs, there's a good cafe/restaurant.

To get to the park from the city, follow Musgrave, Waterworks and Mt Nebo roads, or you can take bus No 385 to the Gap – it's about a 700m walk to the information centre. Note that the walking trails start elsewhere in the park and you'll need transport to reach them.

QUEENSLAND

CENTRAL BRISBANE

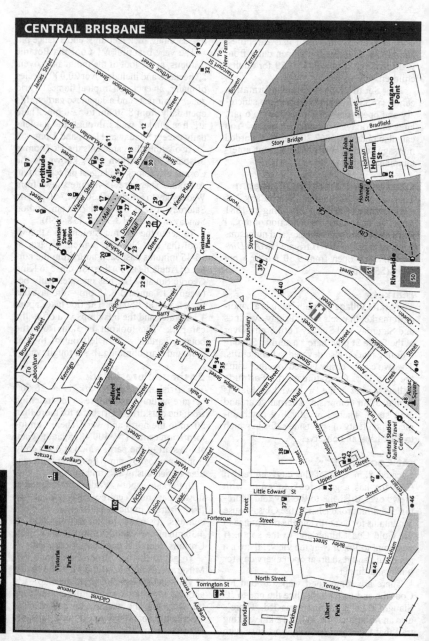

QUEENSLAND

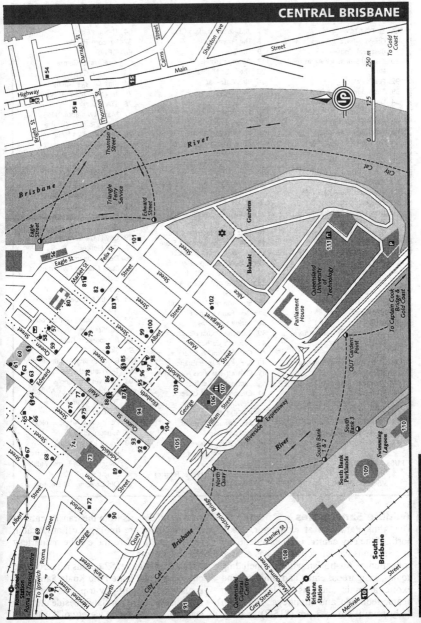

CENTRAL BRISBANE

QUEENSLAND

CENTRAL BRISBANE

PLACES TO STAY
2   Gregory Terrace Motor Inn
3   Balmoral House
30 Central Brunswick Apartment Hotel
32 Pete's Palace
33 Thornbury House B&B
34 Dahrl Court Apartments
35 Kookaburra Inn
42 Annie's Shandon Inn
43 Yale Inner-City Inn
44 Dorchester Self-Contained Units
45 Soho Club Motel
47 Astor Motel
54 Il Mondo Hotel
55 Ryan's on the River
65 Palace Backpackers; Downunder Bar & Grill
72 Explorers' Inn
101 Beaufort Heritage Hotel
106 Conrad International

PLACES TO EAT
4   Krishna's Cafe
10 Lucky's Trattoria
12 Tibetan Kitchen
14 California Cafe
15 Nile Cafe
17 Mellino's
21 Garuva Hidden Tranquility Restaurant & Bar
23 Enjoy Inn
24 Aloha Malaysian; Kim Lan Vietnamese
50 Riverside Centre
56 Eagle St Pier
62 Mekong Chinese Restaurant
66 Palace Cafe
83 Hungry Heart Bistro
95 Govinda's Restaurant
98 Pane e Vino

PUBS AND CLUBS
5   The Arena
6   Wickham Hotel
7   Red Room; Buffalo Club
8   The Healer
9   The Zoo
13 Dooley's Hotel
20 The Tube Nightclub
26 Ric's Cafe-Bar
28 The Empire
37 Options Nightclub
38 Sportsman's Hotel
40 Orient Hotel
52 Brisbane Jazz Club
53 Story Bridge Hotel
69 Jazz & Blues Bar; Travelodge
71 Transcontinental
81 The Gig
97 Gilhooley's

OTHER
1   Centenary Aquatic Centre
11 Integra Car Rentals
16 Cafe Scene Internet Cafe
18 24 Hour Convenience Store
19 McWhirters Marketplace
22 Outdoor, Camping & Adventure Sports Shops
25 Institute of Modern Art
27 Deck Bar
29 Bus Stop on Walking Tour
31 New Farm Laundrette
36 Spring Hill Baths
39 Brisbane Sexual Health Clinic
41 St John's Cathedral
46 Old Windmill & Observatory
48 Shrine of Remembrance
49 Qantas; Travellers Medical & Vaccination Centre
51 Customs House Gallery
57 Newsagency on Walking Tour
58 RACQ Office
59 MacArthur Chambers Walking Tour
60 Post Office Square
61 Angus & Robertson Bookworld
63 Queensland Travel & Tourism Corporation
64 Thomas Cook
67 Suncorp Theatre
68 QPWS
70 YHA Travel Centre
73 Brisbane City Hall
74 King George Square
75 Travellers Medical Service
76 STA Travel
77 Mary Ryan Bookshop
78 Hoyt's Regent Theatre
79 Night Owl 24 Hour Convenience Store
80 St Stephen's Cathedral
82 Metro Arts Centre
84 American Bookstore
85 American Express
86 Greater Union Cinema
87 Thomas Cook
88 Queen St Mall Information Centre
89 City Plaza Complex; Central City Library
90 Dendy Cinema
91 State Library; Riverfront Cafe
92 Ansett
93 Angus & Robertson Bookworld
94 Myer Centre; Underground Bus Station
96 Backpackers Travel Centre
99 Skatebiz
100 Brisbane Bicycle Sales & Hire
102 The Hub Internet Cafe
103 Archives Fine Books
104 World Wide Maps & Guides
105 Treasury Casino
107 Sciencentre
108 Performing Arts Complex
109 Suncorp Piazza
110 South Bank Visitor Information Centre; Crafts Village; South Bank Wildlife Sanctuary
111 Old Government House

Wildlife Sanctuaries

The **Alma Park Zoo** at Kallangur, 28km north of the city centre, is an excellent zoo in a spacious garden setting. It has a large collection of Australian wildlife, including koalas, kangaroos, emus and dingoes, and exotic animals such as Malaysian sun bears, leopards and monkeys. It's open daily from 9 am to 5 pm ($15/8). A daily 'zoo train' departs from the transit centre at 9 am (Caboolture line); get off at Dakabin (50 minutes) where there'll be a courtesy bus for the zoo.

Just a 35 minute, $2.60 bus ride from the city centre, the **Lone Pine Koala Sanctuary** is also an easy half-day trip. The sanctuary is set in attractive parklands beside the river and is home to a wide variety of Australian wildlife, of which the star attractions are the 130 or so koalas. They are undeniably cute and can be held. You can also picnic in a field of tame kangaroos. Talks about the animals are given throughout the day. Lone Pine is open daily from 8 am to 5 pm ($12.50/9/6.50 for adults/VIP or YHA card holders/children). Cityxpress bus No 581 leaves at 35 minutes past the hour from the Koala platform at the Queen St Mall underground bus station. Alternatively, the MV *Mirimar* (☎ 3221 0300) cruises up the Brisbane River to the sanctuary ($16/9 return; Lone Pine admission not included). It departs daily at 10 am from North Quay, next to Victoria Bridge, at the end of the Queen St Mall.

Activities
The Cliffs, on the south bank of the Brisbane River in Kangaroo Point, is an excellent **rock climbing** venue that is floodlit daily until midnight or later. Several operators offer climbing and abseiling instruction here, including Jane Clarkson's Outdoor Adventures (☎ 3870 3223). For beginners, there are abseiling sessions (three to four hours; $45 each for two people or $35 for three), and introductory rock climbing on Wednesday nights ($10 per person). Jane Clarkson also organises abseiling and climbing trips out of Brisbane.

Skatebiz (☎ 3220 0157), at 101 Albert St, hires out **in-line skates** from $10 for two hours.

Good **swimming pools** include the Valley Pool (☎ 3852 1231), on the corner of Wickham and East Sts in Fortitude Valley, open daily from 5.30 am (on Sunday from 7.30 am); the old Spring Hill Baths (☎ 3831 7881) in Torrington St; and the nearby Olympic-sized Centenary Aquatic Centre (☎ 3831 2665), on Gregory Terrace. Plus, of course, there's the 'lagoon' at the South Bank Parklands.

Organised Tours
City Tours The open-sided City Sights trambus shuttles around 18 of the city's major landmarks (including the South Bank

Parklands, the CBD, the Valley and Chinatown), departing every 40 minutes from 9 am to 12.20 pm and from 1.40 to 4.20 pm from Post Office Square in Queen St – you can get off and on whenever and wherever you want. One-day tickets cost $15 for adults – get them from City Hall or the tourist information centre on Queen St Mall. There's also a good, council-run two-hour City Heights tour, which goes to the Mt Coot-tha Lookout and botanic gardens. It departs daily at 2 pm from the City Hall City Sights bus stop on Adelaide St and costs $7.

Brewery Tours From Monday to Wednesday at 11 am, 1.30 and 4.30 pm, there are guided tours of the Castlemaine-Perkins XXXX brewery (☎ 3361 7597) on Milton Rd. Most hostels organise trips or you can go on your own but you must book. You also need to wear shoes. The tour lasts about an hour, costs $5 and you get four free beers at the end. The brewery is 1.5km south-west of the transit centre or take an Ipswich train (departing the transit centre and Central station every 15 minutes; $1.40) to Milton Rd station, right outside the brewery.

The Carlton Brewhouse (☎ 3826 5858), which produces Victoria bitter and Fosters, also conducts tours of its premises, which are a half hour south of the city centre. A bus departs the transit centre daily at 9.15 and 11.15 am and 1.15 pm. Tour times are 10 am, noon and 2 pm and the cost is $10 including beer, lunch and transfers.

River Cruises The *Club Crocodile River Queen I* and *II* (☎ 3221 1300) are restored wooden paddle-steamers that cruise the Brisbane River. There is a 1½ hour cruise at 12.45 pm ($30 including a buffet lunch), a Sunday afternoon-tea cruise at 3.30 pm ($20), and 2½-hour dinner cruises at 7.30 pm (Sunday at 6.30 pm) for $40 with buffet. The cruises depart from the Eagle St Pier, next to the Riverside Centre.

Other Tours Run by a former backpacking globetrotter, Rob's Rainforest Tours (☎ 019 496 607) offers several different day trips

QUEENSLAND

Brisbane from the Cat

Easily the best way to view Brisbane is from the river and the best way of getting about the river is on a City Cat. These large, blue catamaran ferries glide up and downstream all day from around 6 am until approximately 11 pm. A \$3.20 ticket will allow you to travel the whole route (from Bretts Wharf to the University of Queensland and back takes two hours), but if you step off you'll have to buy a new ticket. Alternatively, buy one of the various saver cards (see Getting Around in the Brisbane section) for as little as \$6 and you can hop on and off wherever you like.

Upriver from Riverside Riverside is the CBD stop at the north end of Elizabeth St, next to the Eagle St Pier complex. Heading upstream, the Cliffs of Kangaroo Point are off to the left, while over to the right the river is fringed by mangroves. As the City Cat passes under the Captain Cook Bridge, over to the left is the Maritime Museum. **QUT Gardens Point** is the place to get off to visit Parliament House and the city Botanic Gardens, after which there's a zigzag sprint across the river to **South Bank** for the parklands and back across to **North Quay** for the Casino and the Queen St Mall.

Upstream from North Quay is the longest uninterrupted stretch of the route, passing under three bridges and then cruising alongside the suburb of Auchenflower, on the right, and the grassy banks of South Brisbane, on the left. The lighthouse-like structure passed on the left is actually a scriving tower for the local gasworks. South Brisbane gives way to Orleigh Park, one of the city's most fashionable addresses.

Both **Guyatt Park** and **West End** service residential areas and there's nothing to get off for, but on the next bend is the City Cats' upstream terminus, **University of Queensland**, a place well worth spending a few hours. It's an attractive campus with some good museums, excellent sporting facilities, a bookshop, the Schonell Cinema and a good, cheap cafe. There's a helpful information office in a small building beside the main entrance.

Downriver from Riverside Heading downstream, the City Cat immediately passes under the Story Bridge, built from 1934 to 1940 and sharing some of the same design engineers as the Sydney Harbour Bridge. The river continues to loop around the peninsula of Kangaroo Point, a former shipbuilding area now the site of a major, upmarket residential development. Across the river, on the left, is the suburb of New Farm, serviced by the **Sydney St** stop. The City Cat then shuttles over to **Mowbray Park**, the stop for East Brisbane, and then back to **New Farm Park** – a large and quite beautiful park with a good cafe in the middle.

Just past the park the route passes through the old wharf area with huge brick warehouses lining the river to the left. The two stops on this stretch, **Hawthorne** and **Bulimba**, are for residential districts. After leaving Bulimba you can see over on the far bank a small, wooded headland; hidden within the trees is Newstead House, one of Brisbane's oldest residences, now a small museum. Across the creek from Newstead is the Breakfast Creek Hotel, an excellent place for lunch. The downriver terminus of the City Cat is **Bretts Wharf**. As you approach, look up to the left to see the white-painted verandas of what is perhaps Brisbane's most beautiful Queenslander house. From Bretts Wharf it's just a short walk to trendy, cafe-laden Racecourse Rd, or 1km back to Breakfast Creek.

The University of Queensland, Guyatt Park, North Quay, South Bank and Hawthorne stops all have disabled access.

out of Brisbane, taking travellers to the rainforests at Mt Glorious, Kondalilla Falls and the Glass House Mountains, and Lamington National Park. Several Lonely Planet readers have written in with high praise for the tours. The price per person is $48, which includes morning tea, a barbecue lunch and pickup and return to your hostel.

There are several other operators running similar trips, but in general their prices are considerably higher than Rob's.

Something a little more unusual that also offers good value is Araucaria Ecotours' (☎ 5544 1283, ecotoura@eis.net.au) three day wilderness trip into the Mt Barney National Park area. The tour starts in Brisbane every Wednesday morning (usually at the South Brisbane train station, but also at the transit centre by arrangement) and involves trekking through forests to examine flora and fauna, including stopping at a creek where a platypus often puts in an appearance. There are also possibilities to swim and snorkel in a creek and do some boating. However, the emphasis is firmly on the educational – the tours are led by Ronda Green, a qualified research wildlife ecologist who really knows her stuff. The cost is $160, including accommodation, but not meals.

Special Events

A major event on the arts calendar is the biennial Brisbane Festival of Music held in July on odd-numbered years. Another big event is the Ekka, or Royal National Agricultural Show, held at the exhibition grounds in early August. There's also Queensland Heritage Week in April, a 10 day international film festival in July/August, and Livid, an annual one day alternative rock festival, in October.

Places to Stay

Brisbane has plenty of hostels and backpackers' places, and there are also well-priced hotels, motels and self-contained apartment blocks within easy reach of the centre.

The Brisbane Visitors Accommodation Service (☎ 3236 2020), on the 3rd level of the transit centre, is a free booking service open on weekdays from 7 am to 6 pm and weekends from 8 am to 5 pm. This place has brochures and information on all the hostels and other budget options, and once you have decided where to stay, staff will arrange for someone to pick you up.

Brisbane's hostels are concentrated in three main areas: Petrie Terrace and Paddington, just west of the city centre; Fortitude Valley and New Farm, north-east of the city; and south of the city in South and East Brisbane and West End.

The main motel drags are Wickham St and Gregory Terrace, on the northern edge of the city, and Main St – especially the Kangaroo Point stretch – which is the link road to the southern Gold Coast Hwy.

Places to Stay – Budget

Camping The closest caravan park to the city centre is *Newmarket Gardens Caravan Park (☎ 3356 1458, 199 Ashgrove Ave)*, just 4km north, in Ashgrove. Several bus routes connect it with town and there's a train station nearby. Powered sites for two people are $17 and on-site vans go for $29/34 for two/three people. The park also has cabins for up to four people for $50.

Aspley Acres Caravan Park (☎ 3263 2668, 1420 Gympie Rd, Aspley), 13km north of the city, has camp sites from $10, on-site vans from $32 and cabins for $43. *Dress Circle Village (☎ 3341 6133, 10 Holmead Rd, Eight Mile Plain)* is 14km south of the city and has camp sites from $10 and on-site cabins from $50. In School Rd, Roachdale, 19km south of the city, are the *Gateway Junction Village (☎ 3341 6333)*, with camp sites for $22 and single rooms for $70, and the *Sheldon Caravan Park (☎ 3341 6166)*, with camp sites for $14 and double cabins for $40/50 without/ with linen.

Hostels – City Centre There's only one hostel in the city centre, the busy *Palace Backpackers (☎ 1800 676 340)*, on the corner of Ann and Edward Sts. It's as central as you can get and just five minutes walk from the transit centre. It occupies a Heritage-listed, former Salvation Army headquarters, which has been extensively modernised – facilities include a huge communal kitchen,

TV lounges, laundries, a tour desk, a job finders' club and a rooftop sundeck. Downstairs is the city's most popular backpackers' bar, Down Under (see Entertainment later in this section). The only drawback is that the partying has a tendency to spill over into the hostel corridors, and nights at the Palace can be far from quiet. Dorm beds cost from $15 (seven to nine per room) to $18 (three per room); singles/doubles are $30/40.

Hostels – Spring Hill The *Kookaburra Inn* (☎ 3832 1303, 41 Phillips St) is an old converted Queenslander with communal kitchens, bathrooms and laundry facilities. It's well located in a quiet, leafy street, not too far out of the city centre, and is especially popular with Japanese and European travellers. There are no dorms; singles/doubles cost $30/40 with cheaper weekly rates available.

Hostels – Petrie Terrace & Paddington Petrie Terrace isn't the most exciting of areas, but it is close to the transit centre and neighbouring Caxton St has plenty of good cafes, restaurants and bars.

There are three adjacent hostels on Upper Roma St, the first of which is the ever expanding *City Backpackers' Hostel* (☎ 3211 3221, 380 Upper Roma St). It's a fairly charmless, two storey hostel, but facilities are good and staff are friendly. A bed in a four to six bunk dorm costs $13, twins and doubles cost $32. The *Roma St Hostel*, right next door, is not recommended.

A little further along is the *Brisbane City YHA* (☎ 3236 1004, 392 Upper Roma St), with excellent facilities including a good on-site cafe, a tour booking desk and provision for the disabled. The cost for non-YHA members is $19 per person in a four to six bed dorm (no mixed dorms) or $46 for a twin room. There are also twins, doubles and triples with air-con and en suite for a little more.

One block south of Upper Roma St is *Yellow Submarine Backpackers* (☎ 3211 3424, 66 Quay St), occupying a brightly painted – yellow, naturally – old house. It's very homely and friendly with a pool, small

garden terraces and barbecue grills. Staff will also help you find work. Dorms (three or six beds to a room) cost $15 per night, twins and doubles $34.

Banana Benders Backpackers (☎ 3367 1157, 118 Petrie Terrace) is a short walk north. The outside is painted bright yellow and blue, so you can't miss it. It's a small, comfortable place in two sections and has good views from the back deck. The dorms are mostly four-share and cost $16 per person a night; doubles are $36. It's popular with long-term stayers and the friendly owners Chris and Ben can help you find work in town or on farms.

Down the side street past Banana Benders is *Aussie Way Backpackers* (☎ 3369 0711, 34 Cricket St). It's a beautiful, two storey timber house with a front balcony and a backyard pool – very clean, quiet and well set up. A bed in one of the three to five-bunk dorms costs $15 a night; there are also three single rooms for $24 and two doubles for $34.

Hostels – Fortitude Valley & New Farm *Balmoral House* (☎ 3252 1397, 33 Amelia St) is well located, with good facilities including a laundry, large kitchen and TVs in all rooms. The place is fairly quiet, so it's an excellent option if you want to be close to the cafes and nightlife in the valley, but also want a good night's sleep. A bed in a three or four bed dorm is $13; singles/doubles cost $30/44 with shared bathrooms or $40/45 with en suite.

Centrepoint Backpackers (☎ 1800 685 857), on the corner of Ann St and Commercial Rd, occupies the second floor of the Waterloo Hotel and is a 10 minute walk from Brunswick St. It's especially popular with working travellers and those looking for work. It has a 'Red Hot Chilli Packers' 24-hour job line (☎ 0414 744575), and if Peter O'Shea can't find you a job, you're not trying very hard.

The rest of the hostels are in New Farm, most of them a 10 minute walk from the Valley – itself a 15 minute walk from the city centre – but two regular bus services run along Brunswick St and into town.

Pete's Palace (☎ 3254 1984, 515 Brunswick St) is a small place that feels very much like a student house. Dorm beds (four to a room) cost from $11 and a basic double goes for $30.

The *Globetrekkers' Hostel* (☎ 3358 1251, 35 Balfour St) is a renovated 100-year-old timber house. It's small, tranquil and very friendly. A bed in a five bunk dorm costs $14 (there's a women's dorm); twins and doubles are $32. This place also allows travellers with mobile homes to park out the back and use the hostel facilities for $5 a night.

The *Bowen Terrace* (☎ 3254 0458, 365 Bowen Terrace), like the Globetrekkers, is family run and as such is well maintained, orderly and quiet. Singles cost from $25, while a large, well-furnished double with fridge and TV goes for $35.

The *Homestead* (☎ 3358 3538, 57 Annie St) is a large, modern place with reasonable facilities, and is popular with long-term stayers. It offers free use of bikes and free trips to Mt Coot-tha lookout. A bed in a six or eight bed dorm costs $14, singles go for $30, twins for $36 and doubles for $45.

Further down is the long-running *Atoa House Travellers' Hostel* (☎ 3358 4507, 95 Annie St), which occupies three adjacent Queenslander-style houses. Room size differs so the price does too. Have a look first to see if you like it. It has dorm beds for $11 a night, singles from $15, doubles and twins from $20, and self-contained flats for five people for $10 per person (good for students). The hostel has a spacious backyard with plenty of grass and shady trees, and if you have your own tent you can camp for $7 a night. It's a bit of a trek from here up to Brunswick St Mall and the bus stop.

Hostels – West End The *Brisbane Backpackers Resort* (☎ 3844 9956, 110 Vulture St) is a purpose-built backpackers' complex. Rooms have a TV, fridge and en suite, and there are five kitchens, a games room, a pool, a bar and a cafe serving cheap food. However, the place has an authoritarian air and is very soulless. Dorm beds cost $16, while singles and doubles go for $45. The *Swagman's Rest*, over the road at 145 Vulture St, is run by the same people as the Resort and shares the same reception. You may end up over here instead of the resort if dorms are crowded.

Somewhere to Stay (☎ 1800 812 398, 45 Brighton Rd) is 100m south, just uphill from Vulture Rd. It's a huge, rambling, wooden house with a lovely garden, a small pool and a nice tree-shaded deck. There's also a cheap cafe open for breakfast, lunch and evening meals. Dorm beds range from $12 to $17, with most rooms having a TV, fridge, private bathroom and balcony with a good view of the city. Singles cost $20 to $25, doubles and twins $30 and self-contained units $45.

Places to Stay – Mid-Range
Guesthouses & B&Bs If you can stomach the kewpie dolls and cuteness, *Annie's Shandon Inn* (☎ 3831 8684, 405 Upper Edward St, Spring Hill) is a friendly guesthouse with immaculate singles/doubles for $40/50, including a light breakfast. Four rooms with private bathroom go for $50/60. Next to Annie's, the *Yale Inner-City Inn* (☎ 3832 1663, 413 Upper Edward St) has rooms for $35/45 or $55 with private bathroom. The tariff includes a light breakfast. Rooms are small and the facilities are quite old, but the place is clean.

Still in Spring Hill, *Thornbury House B&B* (☎ 3832 5985, 1 Thornbury St) is a charming two storey timber Queenslander built in 1886 and attractively renovated in heritage style. There are four excellent double rooms for $90 and five smaller, attic-style single rooms for $55. A double en suite room costs $100.

About 2km west of the centre in Paddington, the *Waverley B&B* (☎ 3369 8973, 5 Latrobe Terrace) is also a renovated two storey Queenslander, with a family home upstairs and two guestrooms downstairs. It also has two excellent guest units at the rear with their own entrance. Rates are $60/90 or $380 a week for the self-contained apartments.

Apartments Not far north of the centre in Spring Hill, the *Dorchester Self-Contained Units* (☎ 3831 2967, 484 Upper Edward St)

QUEENSLAND

is a two storey block of self-contained, one-bedroom units costing $60/70/80 for singles/doubles/triples.

About 500m further north-east, the *Dahrl Court Apartments* (☎ 3832 1311, 45 Phillips St) has been recommended by several travellers. One-bedroom apartments here have a separate kitchen (with a small breakfast provided) and cost $65/75 for singles/doubles or $100 for four people. There's also a spacious, self-contained, basement apartment that sleeps up to 12 people for $25 a head.

On Brunswick St, close to all the cafes and nightlife, the new *Central Brunswick Apartment Hotel* (☎ 3852 1411, 455 Brunswick St) is gay and lesbian friendly and offers modern apartments from $85. Service is good, but the apartments on the Brunswick St side get a little noisy.

On the corner of Brunswick and Moreton Sts in New Farm, the *Allender Apartments* (☎ 3358 5832) is a two storey block of old cream-brick flats that have been refurbished. The studio units are beautiful – large and sumptuously furnished with a generous king-sized bed – and offer excellent value at $60 for a standard or $90 for a deluxe heritage apartment. It's too far to walk from here to the centre so you need to be prepared to take buses or, better still, have your own transport.

Motels The four-star *Gregory Terrace Motor Inn* (☎ 3832 1769, 397 Gregory Terrace) overlooks Victoria Park and is just across from the Centenary Aquatic Centre. Motel units cost $88 a double, and there are a couple of two-bedroom apartments that sleep up to eight people and cost $120 for two, plus $10 for each extra person.

Closer to the city, in Wickham Terrace, the recently renovated *Astor Motel* (☎ 3831 9522), near the junction with Upper Edward St, charges $89/95 for comfortable singles/doubles. A few minutes walk west, the *Soho Club Motel* (☎ 3831 7722, 333 Wickham Terrace) charges $49/58 for far more basic rooms.

At Kangaroo Point, the *Kangaroo Motel* (☎ 3391 1145, 624 Main St) has decent

rooms for $50/55. A stone's throw from the Gabba Cricket Ground, the *Kangaroo Point Holiday Apartments* (☎ 1800 676 855, 819 Main St) has good, one-bedroom apartments from $65 a night, with cheaper weekly rates.

Hotels One of the best accommodation deals in Brisbane is the *Explorers' Inn* (☎ 3211 3488, 63 Turbot St), a modern, three-star hotel in an old building on the edge of the city centre, just a few minutes walk from the transit centre. The facilities are good and the rooms, though a little cabin-like, are immaculate and good value at $69 for a double or twin.

In north Kangaroo Point, *Ryan's on the River* (☎ 3391 1011, 269 Main St) is very close to the landing stage for the city ferry. All rooms have some sort of river view and most go for $99.

Il Mondo (☎ 3392 0111, 25 Rotherham St) is in a quirky, post-modern building with a very attractive, semi-open-air cafe/restaurant on the ground floor. It has no river views but is still only a few minutes walk from the city ferry. Singles range from $59 to $75 and one-bedroom apartments go for $155.

Places to Stay – Top End
Brisbane's top-end hotels include the well-appointed *Beaufort Heritage Hotel* (☎ 3221 1999), on the corner of Edward and Margaret Sts, with rooms overlooking the river. The *Conrad International* (☎ 3306 8888), on the corner of George and Charlotte Sts, is a classy hotel in the Casino complex. Both offer package specials with substantial discounts (ie 30–40%) on the regular room rates of around $300.

Places to Eat
City Centre There are precious few restaurants in the city centre as it tends to empty out at night with the homeward migration of its office and shop workers, but the cafe scene has blossomed in recent years. There's no shortage of good budget eateries in the city and surrounding areas.

For breakfast, the best deal for the hungry is at the *Pane e Vino*, on the corner of

Albert and Charlotte Sts. The breakfast special here is an enormous plate of sausage, bacon, mushrooms, toast and two eggs (easily enough for two) plus coffee and juice for $8.50.

There's also the *Palace Cafe*, on Ann St, which offers a variety of breakfasts in the $4 to $8 range.

There are an abundance of cheap lunchtime eateries in the city centre catering for the hordes of office workers and shoppers. Probably the best variety and value is offered in the food courts found in the shopping malls – try the *Eatery*, in the basement of the Myer centre, off the Queen St Mall.

Another office workers' favourite, the *Hungry Heart Bistro (102-104 Edward St)*, has a variety of pastas, rice casseroles, noodles and the like served in generous portions for under $7. It's open weekdays only from 7 am to 4 pm.

For a big feed, the *Mekong Chinese Restaurant*, on Adelaide St just north of Edward St, does an all-you-can-eat lunch for $6.90, while the upstairs, Hare Krishna-run *Govinda's Restaurant (99 Elizabeth St)* offers all-you-can-eat vegetarian meals for $5. It's open weekdays for lunch and Friday and Sunday for dinner.

Blackjacks Casino Buffet (Treasury Casino, 21 Queen St) has a wide range of dishes and is good value at $12 for lunch and $15 for dinner.

The *Down Under Bar & Grill*, at Palace Backpackers, also has cheap lunches and evening meals served from 6 pm.

Gilhooley's, the Irish pub on Albert St, serves very good basic fare like stews, and Guinness and beef pie for around $8, plus other pricey dishes like steaks for about $16.

The city's premier dining spots are the *Eagle St Pier* complex and adjacent *Riverside Centre*. Both are home to several upmarket, credit-card crimping establishments of the kind best visited when somebody else is footing the bill. The two that are constantly talked about and always seem busy are *Il Centro (☎ 3221 6090)*, an impressive Italian joint, and *Pier Nine (☎ 3229 2194)*, a sophisticated oyster bar and seafood restaurant.

South Bank There are about a dozen restaurants and cafes in the South Bank Parklands. However, having something of a captive audience, they don't have to try too hard and a lot of the food is second rate and overpriced. A popular exception is *Captain Snapper*, a large seafood and steak restaurant that is constantly crowded. The food here is unadventurous but wholesome and the prices are reasonable.

At the Boardwalk on the southern edge of South Bank, *Chez Laila* has good-value breakfasts for $7.50 and high-quality Lebanese food for around $12 a dish. One of the best value eateries on the riverfront is the simple *Riverfront Cafe*, at the State Library. It has great rolls, sandwiches, coffee and snacks, and the tables on the outdoor courtyard overlook the river.

Petrie Terrace & Paddington Probably the best place for a decent, reasonably priced meal around here is the *City YHA hostel cafe* – you don't have to be staying at the hostel to eat there. Alternatively, the *Paddo Tavern*, on Given Terrace about 1km east of Petrie Terrace, does $2.45 lunches during the week.

Opposite the Paddo Tavern, the *3 F's Noodle Bar* is a good spot for a cheap feed, with most dishes less than $5.

Kari Tandoori (235 Given Terrace) is a charming Indian restaurant with great tandoori dishes and a bring your own (BYO) alcohol licence. It's open for dinner daily, and mains are around $11.

The *Jakarta Indonesian Restaurant (215 Given Terrace)* is a reasonably priced restaurant with an evocative bamboo decor. Rice, noodle and vegetarian dishes are $7 to $12, and seafood and meat dishes are from $10 to $13. It's open Tuesday to Sunday from 6 pm.

The *Hot Wok Cafe (257 Given Terrace)* is an above average Chinese restaurant offering creative, reasonably priced dishes for around $8. Its shaded rear deck is very pleasant.

A little further on, the popular *Le Scoops (283 Given Terrace)* is a Brisbane institution featuring an outdoor creperie serving up sweet and savoury crepes and pancakes. It opens for breakfast, lunch and dinner – the Sunday brunch is especially good.

Fortitude Valley The Valley is one of the best eating areas to explore, especially on Friday evening and Saturday when it's bustling with crowds of people wandering the streets, eating at outdoor tables and spilling out of the various pubs and bars. There's a good produce market and an international foodhall inside *McWhirters Marketplace*, on the corner of Brunswick and Wickham Sts.

Duncan St, between Ann and Wickham Sts, is Brisbane's Chinatown, home to a large number of Asian restaurants. For a cheap meal, two of the best, no-frills places we found were *Aloha Malaysian* and *Kim Lan Vietnamese*, next door to each other on Duncan St close to Wickham St. Both are always packed with locals. The menu in the Kim Lan is a large photo album of all its dishes!

The *Enjoy Inn*, opposite, is widely regarded as serving the best Cantonese food in town. During the week it's a little quiet and formal, but at weekends it gets really lively. Main courses cost $8 to $16, and it's open daily from noon to 3 pm and from 5 pm to midnight.

There are a cluster of eateries at the east end of the Brunswick St Mall, most of which have pavement seating. Of these *Mellino's (330 Brunswick St)*, a casual cafe that's open 24 hours a day, is the most reasonably priced – you can get pastas for $8.90 and a pizza for two for under $10. For a huge greasy breakfast, the *California*, on the corner of Brunswick and McLachlan Sts, is a cafe that opened in 1951 and retains many of the original fittings.

For a cheap lunch, the *Deck Bar*, on the corner of Brunswick and Ann Sts, has counter lunches for $3. Vegetarians may prefer to wander up to *Krishna's Cafe*, which is next to the Arena on Brunswick St, for a $4 lunch in a pleasant garden setting.

The *Garuva Hidden Tranquility Restaurant & Bar (☎ 3216 0124, 174 Wickham St)* is highly recommended, especially for a romantic dinner. You enter through a rainforest passageway before entering your own screened compartment. Dining sessions are for two hours and all dishes are $8.50. It's very popular so you need to book.

If you want really good Italian cooking we highly recommend *Lucky's Trattoria (683 Ann St)*. The pasta dishes here are fantastic – some of the best we've ever had, anywhere. It gets busy at weekends and you may have to wait for a table; no reservations are taken and it's BYO. Mains start at around $9.

The richly decorated *Tibetan Kitchen (☎ 3358 5906, 454 Brunswick St)* specialises in authentic Tibetan, Sherpa and Nepalese dishes. Most mains cost around $11, or you could try the 'Sherpa platter' for $14. It opens daily from 11 am to 2 pm and 5 to 9.30 pm.

West End Like the Valley, the West End has a fairly cosmopolitan range of cafes and restaurants, including quite a few budget places.

Three Monkeys Coffee House (58 Mollison St), just west of the roundabout, is a relaxed place with seductive pseudo-Moroccan decor, good coffee and cakes, and a wide range of food for $6 to $10. It is open daily from 10.30 am until midnight. Next door, the *Jazzy Cat Cafe* has a nice balcony and garden. Pizza and pasta mains average $11.

South on Boundary St are at least half a dozen trendy cafes. They include: *Caffe Tempo (181 Boundary St)*, a hip little eatery; *Cafe Nouveau (185 Boundary St)*, an attractive, Italian-style place with an outrageously pretentious menu featuring items such as 'Ming Dynasty fillet of pork' and 'Rebirth of Venus salad'; and *Cafe Babylon (142 Boundary St)*, across the road, a New Age cafe with ethnic decor, astrology evenings and tarot readers. One door up, the *Green Grocer* is a good health-food shop with a wide range of organic fruit and vegies, juices, wheat and gluten-free breads.

For something more down-to-earth, *Qan Heng's (151 Boundary St)* offers good Chinese and Vietnamese meals from $5.90 to $10, and has an all-you-can-eat lunch for $6.50.

On Hardgrave Rd, 400m west of Boundary St, there's a strip with more than 10 cafes and restaurants, all within 150m of each other. *Kim Thanh,* at No 93, is a large and noisy Chinese and Vietnamese BYO

Gorby at the Brekkie Creek

Brisbane's most famous pub, the Breakfast Creek Hotel, can now boast another steak-loving visitor – former president of the Soviet Union, Mikhail Gorbachev.

In town as a keynote speaker on the 'World Masters of Business Tour of Australia', a bizarre roadshow that also included Stormin' Norman Schwarzkopf, leader of 800,000 troops in the 1991 Gulf War, Gorby wanted an Australian steak, so his minders steered him to the Brekkie Creek. So it was that one Sunday lunchtime in May 1999, the raffle for the meat tray and two 'slabs' was briefly interrupted by the appearance of a Nobel Peace Prize winner. Gorby wound his way through the tables in the beer garden with their coloured beach umbrellas, strolled past the sign that says 'This way for big steaks' and sat down at a corner table in the pub's Spanish Garden Steak House.

Gorby ordered a well-done fillet steak with rice and coleslaw for $19.90 and washed it down with cabernet sauvignon shiraz. He then had a few laughs with the pub's other patrons, signed a football, and headed through the public bar to his waiting limousine.

Meanwhile, Stormin' Norman was choppered out to a luxury launch off the Gold Coast for a seafood lunch. On the tour they didn't socialise much.

---

with main courses from $7 to $9 and a good-value Vietnamese banquet menu.

Another good one is the *Soup Kitchen (166 Hardgrave Rd)*, a trendy Italian eatery fronted by an open-air courtyard. It's a cafe by day and a restaurant by night. It specialises in soups ($6 to $8) and pastas ($9.50 to $13.50), and also has interesting daily specials ($11.50 to $13.50). Around the corner is *Caravanserai (1 Dornoch Terrace)*, a former pawnbroker's shop converted into an attractive Turkish restaurant with an open kitchen in the centre. Main dishes range from $8.50 to $12.50. The place features belly dancing on Saturday nights.

Breakfast Creek On the north side of a bend in the Brisbane River, the famous *Breakfast Creek Hotel*, a great rambling building dating from 1889, is a real Brisbane institution. It's long been an ALP and trade union hang-out. In the public bar the beer is still drawn from a wooden keg. The pub's open-air Spanish Garden Steak House is renowned for its steaks and spare ribs, and a huge feed will set you back between $12 and $20; there are daily specials for about $6. It's open daily from noon to 3 pm and 5 to 9 pm. To get there take bus No 117 from Queen St or a City Cat to Bretts Wharf and then walk back along the river for about 1km.

Entertainment

Free entertainment papers – *Time Off*, *Rave* and the *Scene* (pick them up at record stores and some cafes) – have comprehensive listings of gigs, pubs, clubs and theatres. For what's on at the cinema, pick up the daily *Courier Mail*.

Pubs & Bars There's really only one good backpacker bar in Brisbane. The *Down Under*, underneath the Palace Backpackers at the top of Edward St in the city, is full-on seven nights a week, with cheap beer and promotions most nights, and loud, loud music. Dancing on the tables is encouraged and things keep going until the early hours. Other backpacker venues include the *Story Bridge Hotel*, in Kangaroo Point, and the *Transcontinental*, opposite the Roma St transit centre.

Since the early 1990s cafes have very much taken over as the places to drink at, especially in the more fashionable parts of town like Fortitude Valley and West End. This has resulted in the appearance of some curious hybrid bar/cafes like *Ric's Cafe-Bar (321 Brunswick St)*, well worth visiting for the retro-chic lounge decor and the free alternative music every night. The *Empire*, on the corner of Brunswick and Ann Sts, also has indie music upstairs at the Wunderbar on Friday and Saturday nights, and downstairs at the Press Club every Wednesday, Thursday and Sunday (free entry).

QUEENSLAND

More conventionally, *Dooley's Hotel*, also on Brunswick St in the Valley, is a large and excellent Irish pub with many pool tables in the upstairs bar.

Dooley's is just one of a growing number of Irish bars – there's also *Kelly's (521 Stanley St)*, in South Brisbane, and the very popular *Gilhooley's*, on Albert St, which is just about the best place for a drink in the city. Most of the other city pubs can be pretty rough and tend to have unwelcoming door policies.

Live Music Plenty of pubs, bars and clubs feature live music, with cover charges from $6 for local acts, but much more for touring bands. There's also a healthy alternative music scene, much of it free. According to our source at *Time Off*, the best gig venues in town are the *Zoo (☎ 3854 1381, 711 Ann St)*, in the Valley (more than one band, apparently, has rated this place as the best small venue in Australia), the *Arena (☎ 3252 5690, 210 Brunswick St)* and the *Red Room (☎ 3252 2565)* in the Buffalo Club at 14-20 Constance St.

Nightclubs Brisbane has a lively nightclub scene, if you know where to look. Mainstream clubs are mostly based in and around the city, and the alternative scene is centred on Fortitude Valley.

The city nightclubs attract a sort of letting-the-hair-down office crowd and play a lot of soul and dance music; they include the *Gig (22 Market St)*, *City Rowers*, at the Eagle St Pier, and *Friday's (123 Eagle St)*. Probably the best of the mainstream clubs is the *Brisbane Underground (61 Petrie Terrace)*.

Indie Temple, at Rosies Tavern in the city, is dedicated to live alternative original music. Over in the Valley, the *Tube (210 Wickham St)* has some good nights, too.

Gay & Lesbian Scene Brisbane has a lively gay and lesbian scene, covered by the free fortnightly *BrotherSister*. One of the city's busiest venues is the *Wickham Hotel (308 Wickham St)*, in the Valley, which provides entertainment (drag shows, strippers, promotions and great dance music) seven

nights a week. The *Sportsman's Hotel (130 Leichhardt St)*, in Spring Hill, is another mainstay of the scene with drag acts, talent quests and promotions. *Options (18 Little Edward St)*, also in Spring Hill, is a popular nightclub with live shows upstairs and a dance club downstairs.

Jazz & Blues The *Jazz & Blues Bar*, on the ground floor of the Travelodge (next to the transit centre), is the city's major venue for this kind of music with good local and international acts on stage from Tuesday to Saturday. The *Brisbane Jazz Club (1 Annie St, Kangaroo Point)*, down by the river, is where the jazz purists head on Saturday (trad and Dixie) and Sunday (big band) nights. For a Sunday afternoon jazz fix, check out the *Story Bridge Hotel* or *Snug Harbour Dockside*, both in Kangaroo Point.

For rhythm and blues, check the *Healer (☎ 3852 2575, 27 Warner St)*, in the Valley, a small venue in a converted church.

Cinemas The big, multi-screen, city-centre cinemas are *Hoyts Regent*, on the Queen St Mall, *Hoyts Myer Centre*, in the basement of the Myer Centre shopping mall, and *Greater Union*, with five screens, on Albert St, just south of the mall. They all show mainstream releases and tickets are $12 ($10 before 5 pm) or $7 all day Tuesday.

The *Dendy (346 George St)*, in the city centre, the *Classic (963 Stanley St, East Brisbane)* and the beautiful little *Metro (109 Edward St)*, also in the city centre, specialise in art house and independent films.

There's also the *Village Twin (701 Brunswick St, New Farm)*, which screens a combination of art house and mainstream releases. Tickets here are discounted on Tuesday, Wednesday and Thursday nights.

Theatre The *Performing Arts Complex (☎ 3840 7444)*, in the Queensland Cultural Centre in South Brisbane, features concerts, plays, dance performances and film screenings in its three venues.

Brisbane's other main theatre spaces include the *Suncorp Theatre (☎ 3221 5371, 179 Turbot St)*, with performances by the

Queensland Ballet and Queensland Theatre companies; the **Brisbane Arts Theatre** (☎ *3369 2344, 210 Petrie Terrace*), for amateur theatre; and the **La Boite Repertory Theatre** (☎ *3369 1622, 57 Hale St*), off Petrie Terrace.

Spectator Sports

You can see interstate cricket matches and international test cricket at the Brisbane Cricket Ground (the Gabba) in Woolloongabba, just south of Kangaroo Point. The cricket season runs from October to March.

During the other half of the year, rugby league is the big spectator sport. The Brisbane Broncos plays its home games at the ANZ Stadium in Upper Mt Gravatt. Brisbane also has an Australian Football League (AFL) club, the Brisbane Lions, based at the Gabba. Brisbane's major horse-racing tracks are at Doomben and Eagle Farm.

Getting There & Away

The easiest way to book all domestic flights and bus tickets is to use the Backpackers Travel Centre (☎ 3221 2225) at 138 Albert St. The manager, Debbie, and her crew are well up on the cheapest ways to get from A to B and back again.

Air Qantas has its travel centre (☎ 13 1313 for domestic flights, ☎ 13 1211 for international) at 247 Adelaide St in the city centre. Ansett (☎ 13 1300) has an office on the corner of Queen and George Sts. Both have frequent flights to the southern capitals and to the main Queensland centres.

Standard one way fares from Brisbane include Sydney ($317), Melbourne ($461), Adelaide ($551) and Perth ($752). Within Queensland, one way fares include Townsville ($396), Rockhampton ($314), Mackay ($363), Proserpine ($374), Cairns ($441) and Mt Isa ($451, Ansett only).

The little outback airline Flight West (☎ 13 2392) goes to Roma ($186 one way), Charleville ($240), Quilpie ($298), Barcaldine ($306), Blackall ($283), Longreach ($325), Winton ($344), Windorah ($339) and Birdsville ($417).

Bus Brisbane's transit centre, on Roma St about 500m west of the city centre, is the main terminus and booking office for all long-distance buses and trains. The centre has shops, banks, a post office, plenty of places to eat and drink, an accommodation booking service on the 3rd level and an information office on the 2nd level. Left-luggage lockers are on the 3rd level ($4 a day); there's also a cloakroom where you can store items longer term.

The bus companies have booking desks on the 3rd level of the transit centre. Greyhound Pioneer and McCafferty's run from Sydney to Brisbane. The coastal run along the Pacific Hwy takes about 17 hours; the inland trip along the New England Hwy takes a couple of hours less. The usual fare is around $70, but Premier Pioneer Motor Services (☎ 1300 368 100) often has cheaper deals.

Between Brisbane and Melbourne, the most direct route is the Newell Hwy, which takes about 24 hours. Again, Greyhound Pioneer and McCafferty's travel this route daily. The fare between Brisbane and Melbourne is about $130.

To Adelaide, the shortest route (via Dubbo) takes about 31 hours and costs about $148.

North to Cairns, Greyhound Pioneer and McCafferty's run five buses a day. The approximate fares and journey times to places along the coast are as follows:

destination	hours	one-way (A$)
Noosa Heads	3	15
Hervey Bay	5	32–38
Rockhampton	9	63
Mackay	13	94
Townsville	19	123
Cairns	24	144

McCafferty's and Greyhound Pioneer also run daily services to the Northern Territory – it's a 46 hour trip to Darwin ($374) via Longreach ($83; 17 hours) and Mt Isa ($112; 24 hours).

Train Countrylink has a daily XPT service between Brisbane and Sydney. The train runs overnight northbound and the south-bound train runs during the day. The trip takes 13½ hours and costs $98/142 in econ-omy/1st class, and $225 in a sleeper.

The speedy Brisbane-Rockhampton *Tilt Train* leaves Brisbane at 10.30 am, Sunday to Friday, returning from Rockhampton at 7.40 am, Monday to Saturday. Economy class fare is $70 for the seven hour trip. Brisbane to Maryborough West (for Fraser Island) takes 3½ hours and costs $39 in economy class.

The *Sunlander* departs three days a week for the 1681km journey to Cairns ($263/177/142 for 1st class sleeper/economy sleeper/seat; 30 hours), via Mackay and Townsville. The *Spirit of the Tropics* covers the Brisbane-Townsville route twice a week ($245/159/124; 24 hours).

The *Queenslander* does the Brisbane to Cairns run weekly. Travel is either 1st class, with sleeping berths and all meals included in the fares, or in economy seats. Sectors and fares include Brisbane-Mackay ($350/105; 16 hours), Brisbane-Townsville ($394/124; 21 hours) and Brisbane-Cairns ($439/142; 30 hours). For another $170, you can take your car with you from Brisbane to Cairns.

The luxurious *Great South Pacific Express* travels from Brisbane to Cairns, Cairns to Brisbane and Brisbane to Sydney approximately twice each month. For de-tails, see the Cairns Getting There & Away section later in this chapter.

The *Westlander* runs to Charleville via Roma twice a week; the trip takes 16½ hours and costs $178/81.

The popular *Spirit of the Outback* runs from Brisbane to Longreach via Rock-hampton twice weekly; it takes 24 hours and costs $235/159/124 for a 1st class sleeper/economy sleeper/economy seat.

For reservations, telephone Queensland Rail (☎ 13 2232) or call into its Railway Travel Centre (RTC; ☎ 3235 1331) beside Central station.

Car If you have a car, beware of the two hour parking limit in the city and inner sub-urbs – there are no signs, and the parking in-spectors are merciless.

The big rental firms have offices in Bris-bane and there are a number of smaller op-erators. One budget operator that we've received good reports on is Integra Car Rentals (☎ 1800 067 414), at 79 McLach-lan St, Fortitude Valley. It does one way rentals (Cairns, Sydney, Melbourne) and also has good value campervans. Others that might be worth checking include Car-azy Rentals (☎ 3257 1104), Ideal (☎ 3260 2307) and National (☎ 3854 1499).

Peter O'Shea (☎ 3392 0137) operates a well-established backpackers car market if you're buying or selling.

Getting Around

For all city bus, train and ferry information, ring the Trans-Info Service (☎ 13 1230); it operates daily from 6 am to 10 pm. The RTC is at Central station, and bus and ferry information is also available at the Queen St information centre and in the bus station in-formation centre, under the Queen St Mall.

To/From the Airport Brisbane's airport is north-east of the city, with the new inter-national/domestic terminal about 15km away. Coachtrans runs the Skytrans (☎ 3236 1000) shuttle bus between the tran-sit centre and the airport, with services about every half hour between 5 am and 8.30 pm ($7.50). Coachtrans also operates the Airporter (☎ 5588 8777) direct services from the airport to the Gold Coast ($29), while Suncoast Pacific (☎ 3236 1901) has a direct service to the Sunshine Coast.

A taxi to the city centre costs about $20.

Bus The red City Circle bus No 333 does a clockwise loop along George, Adelaide, Wharf, Eagle, Mary, Albert and Alice Sts every five minutes on weekdays between 8 am and 5.45 pm ($1.40).

In addition to the normal city buses, there are Cityxpress buses that run between the suburbs and the city centre, and Rockets, which are fast peak-hour commuter buses. From the transit centre you need to walk into the city centre to pick up some buses. Most above-ground bus stops in the city are colour-coded to help you find the right one.

The underground bus station beneath the Myer Centre is used mainly by Cityxpresses and buses to/from the south of the city.

In the city centre, buses cost $1.40 a trip. If you're going to be using public transport a lot on any single day, it's worth getting an Off-Peak Saver card for $6, which gives unlimited travel on buses, ferries and City Cats on weekdays between 9 am and 3.30 pm and after 7 pm, and all weekend. Alternatively, the Day Rover card at $8 gives the same thing but without the time limitations. If you want to go a long way, the South East Explorer cards range from $8 for unlimited travel in the city to $20 for a Zone 3 pass to Noosa Heads or the Gold Coast.

Buses run every 10 to 20 minutes Monday to Friday till about 6 pm, and on Saturday morning. Services are less frequent at other times, and cease at 7 pm on Sunday, and 11 pm on other days.

Train The fast Citytrain network has seven lines: to Ipswich, Beenleigh and Cleveland in the south and Pinkenba, Shorncliffe, Caboolture and Ferny Grove in the north. All trains go through Roma St, Central and Brunswick St stations and a journey in the central area is $1.50.

Boat Brisbane has a fast and efficient ferry service along and across the Brisbane River in the form of the City Cats. The City Cats are large blue catamarans that zip along the river between Queensland University in the west and Bretts Wharf in the east. Stops along the way include North Quay (for the Queen St Mall), South Bank, Riverside (for the CBD) and New Farm Park. They run every 20 minutes on weekdays from 6 am until around 10.30 pm, on Friday and Saturday until midnight, and on Sunday until 8.30 pm. City Cats are also wheelchair accessible.

In addition, there are three cross-river ferries, the most useful being between Eagle St and Kangaroo Point and Riverside and Kangaroo Point.

Fares range from $1.40 for cross river trips to $3.20 for the length of the route. Off-Peak, Day Rover and SE Explorer cards are valid on ferries and City Cats.

Bicycle Brisbane has some excellent bike tracks, particularly around the Brisbane River. Pick up a copy of the city council's *Brisbane Bicycle Maps* brochure from information centres, which includes good bike route maps.

A good way to spend a day is to ride the riverside bicycle track from the city Botanic Gardens out to the University of Queensland. It's about 7km one way and you can stop for a beer at the Regatta pub in Toowong.

Brisbane Bicycle Sales & Hire (☎ 3229 2433), at 87 Albert St in the city centre, hires out mountain bikes for $9 an hour or $20 a day.

Bicycles are allowed on city trains, except on weekdays during peak hours (7 to 9 am and 3 to 6.30 pm). You can also take bikes on City Cats and ferries for free.

Moreton Bay

Moreton Bay, at the mouth of the Brisbane River, is reckoned to have some 365 islands. The two that most people head for are Moreton Island, in particular to participate in the dolphin feeding at the Tangalooma resort, and North Stradbroke, for its great beaches and surfing. Manly, a mainland coastal suburb, is also a good spot to kick back for a few days – there's a good hostel and free yachting on Wednesday.

THE BAYSIDE

The first white settlement in Queensland, **Redcliffe** is 35km north of Brisbane.

The local Aboriginal people called the place Humpybong, or 'Dead Houses', and the name is still applied to the peninsula. Redcliffe is now an outer suburb of Brisbane and a popular retirement place. South of Redcliffe, **Sandgate** is another long-running seaside resort, now also more of an outer suburb.

Coastal towns south of the Brisbane River mouth include Wynnum, Manly, Cleveland and Redland Bay. **Manly** is an attractive seaside suburb with the largest marina in the southern hemisphere after Fremantle. Every Wednesday there are yacht races out in the bay and quite a few of the captains are happy to take guests on board free of charge. Inquire at one of the yacht clubs along the waterfront or at **Nomads Moreton Bay Lodge** (*☎ 3396 3020, 45 Cambridge Parade*), in the heart of Manly Village. It is a well set up backpackers' hostel surrounded by cafes and restaurants and across the road from a pub. Dorms cost $14 and doubles from $45. The hostel can also arrange sailing trips and one to four-day tours to Moreton Island, and help to find work in the area.

Cleveland is the main access point for North Stradbroke Island (see Getting There & Away later in this section). There's an 1864 lighthouse at Cleveland Point as well as an 1853 courthouse, which is now a restaurant.

SOUTH & NORTH STRADBROKE ISLANDS

The two Stradbroke islands used to be one, but in 1896 a storm cut the sand spit that joined them. Today, South Stradbroke is virtually uninhabited but it's a popular day trip from the Gold Coast.

North Stradbroke – or 'Straddie' – is a larger island with a permanent population and, although it is a popular escape from Brisbane, it's still relatively unspoilt (that said, the Christmas and Easter holidays can get pretty hectic). It's a sand island and, despite some heavy sand-mining operations, there's plenty of vegetation and beautiful scenery, especially in the north.

Dunwich, Amity Point and Point Lookout, the three small centres on the island, are all in the north and connected by sealed roads. Most of the southern part of the island is closed to visitors due to the mining and the only road into this swampier, more remote area is a private mining-company road.

The Stradbroke Island visitor information centre (*☎ 3409 9555*) is near the ferry terminal in Dunwich; it's open weekdays from 8.45 am to 4 pm and weekends until 3 pm.

Activities

Water Sports Straddie's best beaches are around Point Lookout, where there's a series of points and bays around the headland and endless stretches of white sand.

There are some excellent surfing breaks here, and you can hire surfboards and boogie boards from various places. You can also sandboard – surf down dunes just behind Main Beach. It's great fun and costs $25 for two hours – call Blair at Straddy Adventures (*☎ 3409 8414*) for information and booking. Straddy Adventures also offers sea kayaking and snorkelling trips ($39; three hours) with a chance of spotting dolphins, turtles, manta rays and even humpback whales from June to November.

The island is also famous for its fishing, and the annual Straddie Classic, held in August, is one of Australia's richest and best-known fishing competitions.

Diving & Snorkelling The Scuba Centre (*☎ 3409 8715*), adjacent to the Stradbroke Island Guesthouse, offers snorkelling for $39 inclusive of the boat trip and all the gear. The same people also run diving courses, and for certified divers they have all-inclusive single dives and double dives for $63/98.

Bushwalking A sealed road runs across from Dunwich to **Blue Lake**; a 2.7km walking track will take you from the road to the lake. You can swim in the freshwater lake or nearby **Tortoise Lagoon**, or walk along the track and watch for snakes, goannas, golden wallabies and birds. **Brown Lake**, about 3km along the Blue Lake road from Dunwich, also offers deep freshwater swimming and is more easily accessible.

Alternatively, you could walk south from Point Lookout along Main Beach then 2.5km inland to Blue Lake – 11km one way in all. There's also a shorter beach walk to **Keyhole Lake**.

If you want to hike the 20km across the island from Dunwich to Point Lookout, a number of dirt track loops break the monotony of the bitumen road. A pleasant diversion is to **Myora Springs**, surrounded by lush vegetation and walking tracks, near the coast about 4km north of Dunwich.

Organised Tours

Stradbroke Island Tours (*☎ 3409 8051*), based in Point Lookout, runs good 4WD

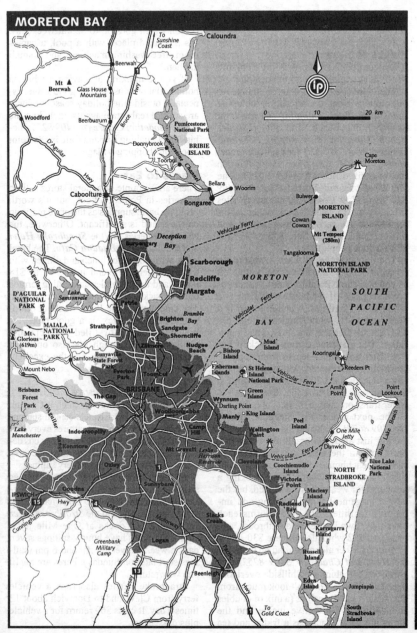

tours of the island including a fishing trip or half-day tour ($28).

Places to Stay

All accommodation is at Point Lookout, which is strung along 3km of coastline.

There are some good council-run camping grounds along the foreshore, including the *Adder Rock Camping Ground,* at Rocky Point Beach, and the *Cylinder Beach Caravan & Camping Ground.* Camp sites are $10, ($3 for each additional person) plus $4 for power. Book through the council office (☎ 3409 9025). The *Stradbroke Island Tourist Park (☎ 3409 8127),* on East Coast Rd, has camp sites from $10 to $15, beds in backpacker cabins for $15 (or $10 each for three people), and self-contained cabins from $48 to $53 (or $60 for four people).

The *Stradbroke Island Guesthouse (☎ 3409 8888)* is the first place on the left as you come into Point Lookout. It's an impressive place of 64 beds, well kept and with modern facilities. A bed in a four bed dorm costs $16, while singles/doubles are $38. There's free use of a surf ski and sand-sailer. The guesthouse runs a pickup bus from Brisbane, which leaves from opposite the transit centre every Monday, Wednesday and Friday at 2.20 pm, and also stops at hostels; you need to book, and there's a water transport charge of $8.

The next place, the *Straddie Hostel (☎ 3409 8679),* is also on the main road, on the left just after the Stradbroke Hotel (the only pub on the island). It's a neat two storey beachhouse that's popular with surfers and beach lovers. It was looking a bit worse for wear when we visited, but the new management is redecorating and improving facilities. The large dorms each have their own kitchen and bathroom, and beds cost $12 while doubles are $30.

A little further along the road on the right, the *Headland Chalet (☎ 3409 8252)* is a cluster of 11 cabins on a hillside overlooking Main Beach. It doesn't look much from the outside, but the cabins (a mix of doubles and twins) are attractive inside and the views are great. Each has a fridge and tea

and coffee-making gear. The cost is $20 per person which goes up to $25 at weekends. It's a relaxed place, with a pool, a games room, free washing machines and a small kitchen.

If you're thinking of staying a while, a holiday flat or house can be good value, especially outside the holiday seasons. There are several real estate agents, including the *Accommodation Centre (☎ 3409 8255),* behind the Laughing Buddha Cafe in the Point Lookout Shopping Village.

Places to Eat

There are a couple of general stores selling groceries in Point Lookout, but it's worth bringing basic supplies as the price mark-up on the island is significant. Otherwise, the two best eateries are the *Stradbroke Hotel* and the *Laughing Buddha Cafe.* The hotel has a bistro, open for lunch and dinner, with a fairly extensive menu in the $6 to $18 range, and there's a pleasant dining terrace out the back overlooking Cylinder Beach. The cafe, part of the Point Lookout Shopping Village complex, is a good place for breakfast (plenty of filled focaccia and similar snacks), though it's also open for dinner from 6 to 8 pm. Try the excellent Penang curry for $12.

Getting There & Away

To get to Straddie you can catch a Citylink train from any of Brisbane's central stations to Cleveland (one hour; departures every half hour from 5 am) for $3.20. A courtesy bus departs from Cleveland train station to the ferry terminal 15 minutes before every sailing.

At Cleveland, two water-taxi companies shuttle across to Straddie: Stradbroke Ferries (☎ 3286 2666) goes to Dunwich (the island's main town) and the *Stradbroke Flyer* (☎ 3286 1964) docks at One Mile jetty. Both companies have hourly sailings seven days a week between 5 am and 6 pm (sailings start later on Sunday). Fares are $6/10 one way/return.

Stradbroke Ferries also runs a vehicle ferry from Cleveland to Dunwich about 12 times a day. It costs $69 return for a vehicle plus passengers.

People staying at the Stradbroke Island Guesthouse can also take advantage of their courtesy bus.

Getting Around
North Stradbroke Island Bus Service (☎ 3409 7151) runs 10 minibus services a day between the three main centres; Dunwich to Point Lookout costs $4.40 ($8 return). They meet all the ferries. Ask the driver for a handy timetable.

MORETON ISLAND
North of Stradbroke, Moreton Island is less visited and still almost a wilderness. Apart from a few rocky headlands it's all sand, with Mt Tempest – towering to 280m – the highest coastal sandhill in the world. It's a strange landscape, alternating between bare sand, forest, lakes and swamps, with a 30km surf beach along the eastern side. The island's birdlife is prolific, and at its northern tip is a **lighthouse**, built in 1857. Sandmining leases on the island have been cancelled and 96% of the island is now a national park.

Moreton Island has no sealed roads, but 4WD vehicles can travel along beaches and a few cross-island tracks – seek local advice about tides and creek crossings. The QPWS publishes a map of the island, which you can get from the QPWS office at False Patch Wrecks, between Cowan Cowan and Tangalooma.

Tangalooma, halfway down the western side of the island, is a popular tourist resort at an old whaling station. The main attraction at here is the wild dolphin feeding, which takes place each evening – usually about eight or nine dolphins swim in from the ocean and take fish from the hands of volunteer feeders. The feeding is carefully regulated and accompanied by commentary. The dolphin feeding is free, but you must be an overnight guest of the resort – there is nothing, however, stopping campers coming to watch. Call the Dolphin Education Centre (☎ 3408 2666) between 1 and 5 pm for more details.

The only other settlements, all on the west coast, are **Bulwer** near the north-west tip, **Cowan Cowan** between Bulwer and Tangalooma, and **Kooringal** near the southern tip. The shops at Kooringal and Bulwer are expensive, so bring what you can from the mainland.

Without your own vehicle, walking is the only way to get around, and you'll need several days to explore the island. There are some trails around the resort area, and there are quite a few decommissioned 4WD roads with good walks. It's about 14km from Tangalooma or the Ben-Ewa camping ground on the west side to Eagers Creek camping ground on the east, then 7km up the beach to Blue Lagoon and another 6km to Cape Moreton at the north-eastern tip. There's a strenuous track to the summit of **Mt Tempest**, about 3km inland from Eagers Creek; the views from the top are worth the effort.

About 3km south and inland from Tangalooma is an area of bare sand known as the **Desert**, while the **Big Sandhills** and the **Little Sandhills** are towards the narrow southern end of the island. The biggest lakes and some swamps are in the northeast, and the west coast from Cowan Cowan past Bulwer is also swampy.

Organised Tours
Sunrover Expeditions (☎ 3203 4241) has good 4WD day tours ($105 with lunch) three times a week from Brisbane and three-day camping tours of the National Park ($300 all inclusive). It also offers a three day camping trip for $185 and a three day lodge accommodation package for $205, both leaving Brisbane on Friday. Another recommended tour company is Dream Island 4 × 4 Tours (☎ 3824 0786), with day tours for $99 and three-day camping trips for $189.

Places to Stay
QPWS camp sites, with water, toilets and cold showers, are at Ben-Ewa and False Patch Wrecks, both between Cowan Cowan and Tangalooma, and at Eagers Creek and Blue Lagoon on the island's east coast. Sites cost $3.50 per person per night. For information and camping permits, contact the QPWS (☎ 3227 8186), at 160 Ann St in Brisbane, or the ranger at False Patch Wrecks (☎ 3408 2710).

QUEENSLAND

There are a few holiday flats or houses for rent at Kooringal, Cowan Cowan and Bulwer. A twin room at the *Tangalooma Resort* (☎ 3268 6333) costs from $180 per night.

Getting There & Away

The *Tangalooma Flyer* (☎ 3268 6333), a fast catamaran operated by the Tangalooma Resort, leaves from a dock at Holt St, off Kingsford-Smith Drive, Pinkenba, every day at 10 am (a courtesy bus departs Brisbane's transit centre for the wharf at 9.15 am). The catamaran costs $26 one way or $30 day return. You have to book.

The *Moreton Venture* (☎ 3895 1000) is a vehicular ferry which runs six days a week from Lytton (at the southern side of the Brisbane River mouth) to Tangalooma or to Reeders Point. The return fare, including driving permit, is $125 for a 4WD (including passengers); pedestrians are charged $20 return.

Another ferry to the island is the *Combie Trader* (☎ 3203 6399), with daily services between Scarborough and Bulwer (except Tuesday). Return fares are $135 for a 4WD and four people, and $20 return for pedestrians. The ferry also does day trips on Monday, Friday, Saturday and Sunday for $20 return.

ST HELENA ISLAND

Little St Helena Island, only 6km from the mouth of the Brisbane River, was a high-security prison from 1867 to 1932 and is now a national park. There are remains of several prison buildings and the first passenger tramway in Brisbane, which, when built in 1884, had horse-drawn cars. Sandy beaches and mangroves alternate around the coast.

St Helena Island Guided Tours (☎ 3262 7422) runs day trips ($37 including lunch or $30 BYO) from the Hamilton Game Fishing Wharf every Sunday and two or three other days a week, from 9 am to 4 pm. ABSea Cruises (☎ 3396 3994) operates its *Cat o' Nine Tails* catamaran daily, leaving from Manly Harbour. The $43 return fare includes lunch, a four hour tour and entry to the national park. You can reach Manly from central Brisbane in about 40 minutes by train (Cleveland Line).

Gold Coast

● pop 365,000

The Gold Coast is a 35km strip of beaches running north from the NSW/Queensland border. It's the most commercialised area in Australia and is virtually one continuous development culminating in the high-rise crassness of the Surfers Paradise resort.

This coast has been a holiday spot since the 1880s, but developers only started taking serious notice of Surfers, as the locals call it, after WWII. These days more than two million visitors a year come to the Gold Coast. Accommodation ranges from backpacker hostels to resort hotels, and there's quite a range of things to do – good surf beaches, excellent eating and entertainment possibilities and a hinterland with some fine natural features. There are also a huge variety of artificial 'attractions' and theme parks, although most are very commercial and fairly expensive.

Orientation

The whole coast from Tweed Heads in NSW up to Main Beach, north of Surfers Paradise, is developed, but most of the real action is around Surfers Paradise itself. Tweed Heads and Coolangatta at the southern end are older, quieter, cheaper resorts. Moving north from there you pass through Kirra, Bilinga, Tugun, Currumbin, Palm Beach, Burleigh Heads, Miami, Nobby Beach, Mermaid Beach and Broadbeach – all lower-key resorts.

Southport, the oldest town in the area, is north and just inland from Surfers Paradise, behind the sheltered expanse of the Broadwater, which is fed by the Nerang and Coomera rivers. The Gold Coast Hwy runs right along the coastal strip, leaving the Pacific Hwy just north of Coolangatta and rejoining it inland from Southport.

The Gold Coast airport is at Coolangatta. Most buses to the Gold Coast travel the full length of the strip.

Information

The Gold Coast Tourism Bureau (☎ 5538 4419), on the Cavill Ave Mall in Surfers

Paradise, is open weekdays from 8.30 am to 5.30 pm, Saturday from 9 am to 5 pm and Sunday from 9 am to 3.30 pm.

In Coolangatta, there's a tourist information booth (☎ 5536 7765) at the Beach House Plaza on Marine Parade, open weekdays from 8 am to 2 pm and 3 to 4 pm, and Saturday from 8 am to 3 pm.

For information on the area's national parks, flora and fauna, there's a QPWS information centre (☎ 5535 3032) by the Burleigh Heads National Park entrance on the Gold Coast Hwy, open daily from 9 am to 4 pm.

Most of the backpackers hostels have email facilities. The Email Centre (☎ 5538 7500), at 51 Orchid Ave, Surfers Paradise, charges from $2 for 15 minutes. It also has cheap overseas phone calls and is open from 10 am to midnight. On the Southport Mall beside the Australia Fair shopping centre, the Sugar Shack Internet Cafe (☎ 5532 4495) is open daily from 9 am to 8 pm.

SOUTHPORT & MAIN BEACH

Sheltered from the ocean by The Spit, Southport was the original town on the Gold Coast, but it's now modern, residential and rather nondescript. There is little to see or do in Southport, but it makes a pleasant, quiet base from which to explore.

Between Southport and Surfers Paradise is Main Beach, and north of that The Spit, which is a narrow, 3km-long tongue of sand dividing the ocean from The Broadwater. On the Broadwater side of The Spit are three waterside complexes next to each other – **Fisherman's Wharf** is the departure point for most pleasure cruises, and has a pub, a restaurant, a swimming pool and several shops.

Immediately south of Fisherman's Wharf are the **Palazzo Versace**, Versace's first Australian hotel, the **Marina Mirage**, an upmarket shopping and dining complex, and **Mariners' Cove**, a collection of cheaper eating places. Further north on The Spit is **Sea World** (see Theme Parks later in this section). The beach at the northern end of The Spit is not developed and is good for relatively secluded sunbathing.

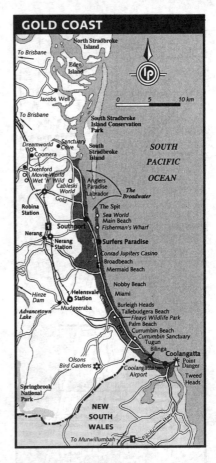

GOLD COAST

North Stradbroke Island
To Brisbane
Eden Island
Jacobs Well
To Brisbane
South Stradbroke Island Conservation Park
0   5   10 km
Dreamworld
Sanctuary Cove
Coomera
South Stradbroke Island
SOUTH PACIFIC OCEAN
Oxenford
Movie World
Wet 'n' Wild
Cableski World
Anglers Paradise
Labrador
The Broadwater
Robina Station
Gold
Nerang
Southport
Sea World
Main Beach
Fisherman's Wharf
The Spit
Nerang Station
Surfers Paradise
Conrad Jupiters Casino
Broadbeach
Mermaid Beach
Nobby Beach
Helensvale Station
Miami
Hinze Dam
Mudgeeraba
Burleigh Heads
Tallebudgera Beach
Advancetown Lake
Fleays Wildlife Park
Palm Beach
Currumbin Beach
Currumbin Sanctuary
Tugun
Bilinga
Olsons Bird Gardens
Coolangatta
Springbrook National Park
Coolangatta Airport
Point Danger
Tweed Heads
NEW SOUTH WALES
To Murwillumbah
Pacific Hwy

SURFERS PARADISE

- postcode 4217   • pop 16,000

Surfers Paradise has come a long way since 1936, when there was just the new Surfers Paradise Hotel, a little hideaway 9km from Southport. The hotel has been swallowed up by a shopping/eating complex called the Paradise Centre, one of several such developments that constitute the highly commercialised centre of this vibrant, if tacky, beachside resort. The popularity of Surfers Paradise these days rests not so much on the sand and surf (which is better down the coast), but on the shopping and nightlife

QUEENSLAND

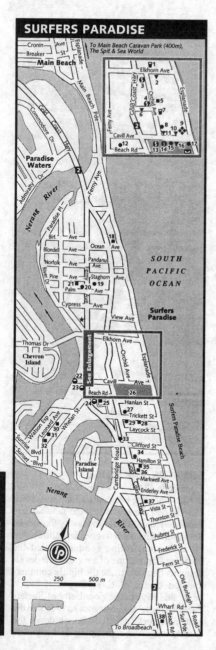

SURFERS PARADISE

PLACES TO STAY

5	Diamonds Resort
18	Surf & Sun Backpackers
21	Cheers Backpackers
25	Nomads Islander Resort
28	Trickett Gardens Holiday Apartments
30	Backpackers in Paradise
31	Sleeping Inn Surfers
32	Couple O' Days Accommodation
35	Mardi Gras International Backpackers Resort
36	Silver Sands Motel
37	Admiral Motor Inn
38	Surfers Paradise Backpackers Resort

PLACES TO EAT

2	Thai Kitchen & Noodles
6	Centre Arcade; New Seoul; Malaysian Kitchen; Raku Gaki
10	Gold Star
11	La Porchetta
16	Healthy Squeeze

OTHER

1	Nellie Kelly's
3	Currency Exchange Bureau
4	American Express
7	Cocktails & Dreams; The Party; Shooters Bar; Email Centre; Bourbon Bar
8	Aquabus Booking Kiosk
9	Raptis Plaza
12	Ansett
13	Thomas Cook Foreign Exchange
14	Gold Coast Tourism Bureau
15	24 Hour Convenience Store
17	Surfers Beach Hut Beach Hire
19	Bungee Rocket & Flycoaster
20	South Pacific Rentals
22	Tiki Village Wharf
23	Bus Stop for Southport
24	Surfers Paradise Transit Centre
26	Paradise Centre
27	24 Hour Convenience Store
29	Qantas
33	Hoyts Cinema Centre
34	Half-Price Car Rental

and its proximity to attractions like the Gold Coast theme parks.

For backpackers it's probably the most partying place in Queensland after Cairns, and hostel staff work hard to whip up a good-time groove on virtually every night of the week. Despite all this, at most times of the year you will not have to go very far north or south to find a relatively open, blissful stretch of white sand.

The town is extremely small and its heart consists of two or three streets: Cavill Ave, with a pedestrian mall at its beach end, is the main thoroughfare, while Orchid Ave, one block in from the seafront Esplanade, is the nightclub and bar strip.

SOUTHERN GOLD COAST

Just south of Surfers Paradise at Broadbeach, the **Conrad Jupiters Casino** is a Gold Coast landmark – it was Queensland's first legal casino (see Entertainment later in this section for details). The **Burleigh Heads National Park**, on the north side of the mouth of Tallebudgera Creek, is a small but diverse forest reserve with walking trails around and through the rocky headland, as well as a lookout and picnic area. On the northern side is one of Australia's most famous surfing point breaks.

There are three excellent wildlife sanctuaries in this area but if you're going to visit only one we recommend making it the **Currumbin Sanctuary** (☎ 5598 1645). It's a large bushland park flocked by technicoloured lorikeets and other birds, with tree kangaroos, koalas, emus and lots more Australian fauna. The sanctuary is off the Gold Coast Hwy, half a kilometre south of Currumbin Creek; it is open daily from 8 am to 5 pm ($16). If you're travelling by the Surfside bus, get off at stop No 20.

Fleays Wildlife Park (☎ 5576 2411), 2km inland along the Tallebudgera Creek in West Burleigh, also has a fine collection of native wildlife (it claims the first platypus to be bred in captivity) and 4km of walking tracks through mangroves and rainforest. It's open daily from 9 am to 5 pm ($9.50). About 9km inland, **Olson's Bird Gardens** (☎ 5533 0208) is another attractive subtropical garden with over 1000 exotic birds in enclosures. The gardens are open every day from 9 am to 5 pm ($7.50).

The twin towns of **Coolangatta** and **Tweed Heads** mark the southern end of the Gold Coast. Tweed Heads is in NSW, but the two places merge into each other. At **Point Danger**, the headland at the end of the state border, there are good views from the Captain Cook memorial.

THEME PARKS

The Gold Coast's theme parks are a major drawcard for tourists. While they are generally quite expensive, the ticket price usually covers all rides and shows, so for a full day's entertainment they can be worthwhile and good fun.

Sea World (☎ 5588 2222), on The Spit in Main Beach, is the longest running Gold Coast theme park. The main draws are the animal performances, which include twice-daily dolphin and sea lion shows, and shark feeding. In addition to these there are rides including a corkscrew rollercoaster, a monorail, a pirate ship, a water park with slides and an adventure route called the Bermuda Triangle. Sea World is open daily from 9.30 am to 5 pm ($44/28 for adults/children).

Movie World (☎ 5573 8485), otherwise known as 'Hollywood on the Gold Coast', is a re-creation of the Warner Brothers film studio in Hollywood, and claims to be Australia's number one tourist attraction. Warner Bros cartoon characters wander around keeping the kids happy, and there are stunt shows, movie sets, a Batman ride and the Lethal Weapon ride, an inverted, suspended rollercoaster that has you spending most of the 105 second ride upside down. The place is open every day from 9.30 am to 5.30 pm ($44/28).

Wet 'n' Wild (☎ 5573 2255), just south of Movie World, is a fun water-sports park – probably the country's best. It has a couple of great raft slides, a twister (in which you pelt down a water-sprayed, enclosed, tightly spiralling tube), a speed slide on which people have clocked up to 70km/h, and a 1m-wave pool. Wet 'n' Wild also screens 'Dive-In Movies' every Saturday night from September to April (and every night during January) – you get to watch a film while floating on a rubber tube in the wave pool. Wet 'n' Wild is open every day from 10 am to 4.30 pm in winter, 5 pm in summer and 9 pm in late December and January ($25/17).

Dreamworld (☎ 5588 1111), a little way north at Coomera, is a Disneyland-style creation with 11 theme areas, a wildlife sanctuary and various thrill rides including the Tower of Terror, on which you plummet from a height of 38 storeys reaching a speed of 160km/h. It's open daily from 10 am to 5 pm ($34/29). At **Cableski World** (☎ 5537 6300), 12km north of Surfers Paradise near Sanctuary Cove, you can water-ski by being towed around a large network of lakes by overhead cables; day passes (10 am to 5 pm) are $30, night passes $18 (7 to 9 pm).

ACTIVITIES
Water Sports & Surfing Aussie Bob's (☎ 5591 7577), at the Marina Mirage in Main Beach, and Surfers Beach Hut Beach Hire, at the beach end of the Cavill Ave Mall, rent out a wide range of gear including jet skis, fishing boats and sailboards, and can take you parasailing, water-skiing and more. Prices for jet-skiing are about $50 to $60 per half hour (jet skis normally take two, so that's $30 per person) and for parasailing $35 per person; you're usually up for about 10 to 15 minutes.

You can also sea kayak from the north end of The Spit to South Stradbroke Island, snorkelling en route and possibly encountering dolphins. Trips depart twice daily at around 8.30 am and 2 pm, depending on the tides. Trips last about three hours; the price of $40 includes pickups. Call ☎ 5527 5785 for bookings.

Bungee Jumping At Bungee Down Under (☎ 5531 1103), on The Spit by Sea World, first-time jumpers pay $70, while for experienced jumpers it's $50. Backpackers pay $55 on Monday. In Surfers, a former car park just off Ferny Ave is home to a bungee rocket, which is basically a giant catapult in which you take the place of the projectile. To be shot 50m into the air in one second and experience up to six times the force of gravity costs $25 per person. There's also something called a flycoaster and you get to play Peter Pan, swung from a hoist 20m up ($29). Photos and video of your facial distortions are available.

Horse Riding Numinbah Valley Adventure Trails (☎ 5533 4137) has three-hour horse riding treks through beautiful rainforest and river scenery in the Numinbah Valley, 30km south-west of Nerang, costing $45 per person or $50 with pickups from the Gold Coast. You'll need to book.

Gum Nuts Horse Riding Resort (☎ 5543 0191), on Biddaddaba Creek Rd near Canungra, also has half-day riding treks for $35 ($40 in the afternoon), and a full day trek with lunch for $65. The price includes Gold Coast pickups.

Other Activities Off The Edge (☎ 1800 686 406) offers downhill mountain biking out in the hinterland forests. There are a variety of routes, from those for the timid to slopes for those with a death wish – and to cut out the tiresome bit a van takes you back uphill each time. The cost is $30 for backpackers including pickups. The same company also offers a 'triple challenge', which begins with some trail biking, moves on to powerboating and then peaks with your choice of a bungee jump, jet ski or parasail. The cost is $130, including a meal and a beer.

ORGANISED TOURS
Hinterland Trips We've had plenty of good feedback for Off The Edge (☎ 1800 686 406), which does an excellent day trip (four person minimum) out to the Springbrook Plateau, taking in some hiking, walks behind waterfalls, swimming and a barbecue lunch with wine – the price, including pickups, is excellent value at $29 for backpackers.

Cruises During the summer months, cruises on offer from Surfers Pardise include two-hour harbour and canal trips (about $22) and cruises to South Stradbroke Island (about $45 including lunch). Boats depart from Marina Mirage or Fisherman's Wharf on The Spit, or from the Tiki Village Wharf down at the river end of Cavill Ave. Operators change from season to season, so ask at your accommodation what's available and what they've had good word on.

The Aquabus (☎ 5539 0222) is good; it's a semiaquatic vehicle that departs five times daily from Cavill Ave, in Surfers Paradise, and makes a 75 minute tour up Main Beach and The Spit, and sails back on the Broadwater. The fare is $24 and you can book from the kiosk on Cavill Ave.

SPECIAL EVENTS

Various life-saving carnivals and ironman and ironwoman events are held on the coast during summer, and there's also the Surfers Paradise International Triathalon each April. June sees the Wintersun Festival held over 10 days at Coolangatta, and the Gold Coast International Marathon is run in July. In mid-October the whole town comes to a standstill for the IndyCar motor race between the high rises of Surfers Paradise. There's a four-day Tropicarnival to coincide with the event, but if you want access to the race it will cost from $25 to $45 for a day pass.

PLACES TO STAY

Backpacker hostels aside, all accommodation rates are seasonal; tariffs given here rise by as much as 50% during the school holidays and 100% at Christmas time.

Most backpackers choose to stay as close to the centre of Surfers Paradise as possible, but some of the hostels a bit further out run regular shuttle buses.

Budget motels line the Gold Coast Hwy and advertise cheap deals in flashing neon signs. Holiday apartments can be excellent value, especially for a group of three or four. Many of the apartments have a two night minimum stay, increasing to seven nights during the peak holiday seasons.

Places to Stay – Budget

Camping There are caravan/camping parks all the way along the Gold Coast from Main Beach to Coolangatta. Most of the foreshore parks are run by the local council and are quite good. The closest to Surfers Paradise is the *Main Beach Caravan Park* (☎ *5581 7722, Main Beach Parade)*, near the southern end of The Spit, with camp sites from $15. The riverside *Broadwater Tourist Park* (☎ *5581 7733)*, just off the Gold Coast Hwy in Southport, has camp sites from $17. It also has on-site villas for $85 a night.

In Burleigh Heads, the *Burleigh Beach Tourist Park* (☎ *5581 7755)*, just back from the beach, has sites from $16.50.

Hostels – Southport *Trekkers* (☎ *5591 5616, 22 White St)*, about 1km south of Southport's transit centre, is a strong candidate for south-east Queensland's best hostel. It's clean, well cared for and has a comfortable, homely feel. Accommodation is in three or four-bed dorms, or twins with their own TV. The staff organise trips to nightclubs in Surfers Paradise every evening. Beds are $17, while twin rooms are $40.

Over on Main Beach in the Mariners' Cove complex, the YHA-affiliated *British Arms Hostel* (☎ *1800 680 269)* is right on the wharf. It's a little bit spartan, but the management is working hard to liven things up with free beers on check-in, twice weekly barbecues and various other activities. Dorm beds for non-YHA members are $17 and doubles are $40.

Hostels – Surfers Paradise One full-on, party-oriented place is the large *Cheers Backpackers* (☎ *1800 636 539, 8 Pine Ave)*. It's well set up with a decent pool, an excellent bar area and large barbecue courtyard. Beds in dorms of either two, four or six beds cost $16. Doubles and twins go for $34.

Another partying place, *Surf & Sun* (☎ *5592 2363, 3323 Gold Coast Hwy)* looks very barracks-like from the outside, but inside it's comfortable and it's close to the beach. All rooms have TV and en suite. It's $17 a night in a four bed dorm or $20 each in a double.

For facilities the *Surfers Paradise Backpackers Resort* (☎ *1800 282 800, 2835 Gold Coast Hwy)* is unbeatable – a decent-sized pool, a small gym and sauna, a pool room, bar, tennis court, free laundry and basement parking. The only drawback is that the hostel is some way south of the centre; there is, however, a courtesy bus. A dorm or unit bed costs $17, doubles are $40.

A bit closer to the centre is the *Mardi Gras International Backpackers Resort* (☎ *1800 801 230, 28 Hamilton Ave)*, a modern hostel with good facilities including a bar and restaurant. All rooms have a bathroom, TV and balcony. Service is friendly and it's close to the beach and nightlife. Beds are $16 a night in a three bed room, $20 per person in a twin and $23 in a double.

QUEENSLAND

The closest hostel to the Surfers Paradise transit centre is *Nomads Islander Resort* (☎ *1800 074 393, 6 Beach Rd)*, set up in an older wing of the Islander Resort Hotel. Guests can use the resort's facilities and it's very close to the centre. There's a 10 bed dorm in the old first-aid room in the basement. Beds here go for $16, or $18 in a four to six bed dorm. If you want to stay above ground, apartments for two go for $44.

Just south of the transit centre, on Whelan St, there are three hostels. *Backpackers in Paradise* (☎ *1800 268 621, 40 Whelan St)* is pretty basic, but all rooms have bathrooms, dorm beds are cheap at $12 a night, and staff are friendly. *Sleeping Inn Surfers* (☎ *1800 817 832, 26 Whelan St)* is modern, well-furnished and clean, and good for anyone who wants privacy and comfort. Dorms are $15, doubles are $38. We've had mixed reports on a *Couple O' Days Accommodation* (☎ *1800 646 586, 18 Whelan St)* and we suggest you check your room and make sure that you're happy with it before paying as the reception displays conspicuous 'no refund' notices. Dorm beds are $12.

Hostels – Coolangatta The *Sunset Strip Budget Resort* (☎ *5599 5517, 199 Boundary St)* has motel-style singles/doubles/triples for $30/40/60, all with shared bathrooms. There's a TV lounge, kitchen and dining area and a large pool. Guests also have free use of surf and boogie boards.

The *Coolangatta YHA* (☎ *5536 7644, 230 Coolangatta Rd, Bilinga)* is just north of the airport and about 3km from central Coolangatta. For nonmembers, a bed in a six or eight bed dorm costs $19 and doubles are $36. It's a newish building, with good facilities including a pool, but it's not convenient for anything except plane spotting.

Places to Stay – Mid-Range
Surfers Paradise The *Silver Sands Motel* (☎ *5538 6041, 2985 Gold Coast Hwy)* has attractively refurbished units and a small pool, with doubles starting at $55. Close by, the *Admiral Motor Inn* (☎ *5539 8759, 2965 Gold Coast Hwy)* has rooms starting from $60.

The *Trickett Gardens Holiday Apartments* (☎ *5539 0988, 24-30 Trickett St)* is a low-rise block of good one and two-bedroom apartments that range from $92 to $116 for two people, $124 to $132 for four.

Diamonds Resort (☎ *5570 1011, 19 Orchid Ave)* is a small, cheap resort in the heart of Surfers Paradise, with motel units and apartments from $75 to $95.

There are quite a few cheap motels just south of Surfers Paradise along the highway at Mermaid Beach. The *Red Emu Motel* (☎ *5575 2748, 2583 Gold Coast Hwy)* has doubles from $45, while the *Mermaid Beach Motel* (☎ *5575 1577, 2395 Gold Coast Hwy)* has clean units from $40.

Southern Gold Coast In Burleigh Heads, the *Hillhaven Holiday Apartments* (☎ *5535 1055, 2 Goodwin Terrace)* has the prime position in Burleigh – next to the national park and with great views along the coast. Old but comfortable refurbished apartments start from $130 per night (for two bedrooms), with good discounts for longer stays (eg $190 for two nights, and $330 a week if you stay six weeks).

In Coolangatta, *The Shipwreck Beach Motel* (☎ *5536 3599)*, on the corner of Musgrave and Winston Sts, has motel units ranging from $45 to $80 a night, as well as self-contained one-bedroom units from $60 to $120 and two-bedroom units from $90. *On the Beach Holiday Units* (☎ *5536 3624, 118 Marine Parade)* is a complex of older-style units on the foreshore. The place is a little shabby but some of the units are extremely roomy and the location, across from the beach, is excellent. Beach view doubles are $60, those at the back $50.

PLACES TO EAT
Surfers Paradise The large number of Asian visitors ensures there's plenty of cheap, authentic Japanese, Korean, and Malaysian fare available. One of the best value spots we found is the Centre Arcade, 331 Gold Coast Hwy. Upstairs, the *Raku Gaki* is a good Japanese restaurant with daily lunch specials for $9. On the ground floor, the *Malaysian Kitchen* serves a tasty *laksa* for $7 and the

New Seoul, a Korean place, does a lunch special of a main meal, rice and *kimchi* for $8. It gets very busy in the evenings.

There are plenty of choices in and around the Cavill Ave Mall. A good value breakfast spot is *Healthy Squeeze*, with fresh juices and daily specials. If you just want to fill up cheaply then there are a couple of all-you-can-eat Chinese food places, including *Gold Star*, just east of the junction with Orchid Ave, which charges $6.90 at lunch and dinner. There are more, good budget eateries in the Raptis Plaza Arcade, including Thai and Vietnamese, a carvery and a bakery.

At the southern end of Orchid Ave, *La Porchetta (3 Orchid Ave)* is a popular, cheap pasta, pizza and steak house. A large pizza costs $7. Around the corner on Elkhorn Ave, the *Thai Kitchen & Noodles* serves a decent satay with noodles for $6.50.

Southern Gold Coast In Burleigh Heads, the *Pagoda Buffet*, on the Gold Coast Hwy in the centre of town, has all-you-can-eat Asian buffets for $6.50 for lunch and $8.50 for dinner. *Earth 'n' Sea*, in the Old Burleigh Theatre Arcade on Goodwin Terrace, has highly acclaimed pizzas made from lots of natural ingredients. A small one is $11. *Montezuma's* is a licensed Mexican eatery with mains from $9 to $14. There are also a couple of good cafes fronting the arcade.

In Coolangatta, the most pleasant places to eat are the two Surf Life Saving Clubs, one at Greenmount Beach, the other at Rainbow Bay. They serve well-priced lunches and dinners and you can eat out on the deck overlooking the beach. For a tasty, folded Turkish pizza, try *Cafe Fez Turkish Pizza & Kebab House (122 Griffith St)*. It has a BYO license too. *Sushi Train* has a branch across the road that's good for a Japanese snack.

ENTERTAINMENT

Nightclubs Orchid Ave, in Surfers Pardise, is the Gold Coast's main bar and nightclub strip. Many of the backpackers' hostels organise nights out at the clubs, usually with free admission and cheap drinks and food. The starting place most nights is *Bourbon Bar*, a fairly gloomy basement bar popular for its cut-price beer and especially busy on Thursday, which is karaoke night. *Shooters* is an American-style saloon with pool tables, big-screen videos and occasional live entertainment. It gets particularly busy on Sunday when it offers a free meal and free pool to groups from hostels – otherwise it's $5 to get in.

The other two major backpacker-friendly places are *Cocktails & Dreams* and the *Party*, two nightclubs, one above the other, linked by an internal staircase. They have different themes most week nights.

Nellie Kelly's, on Elkhorn Ave, is a large Irish bar which attracts an older, more sedate crowd.

Cinemas Cinemas include: *Hoyts (☎ 5570 3355)*, on the corner of the Gold Coast Hwy and Clifford St, a multi-screen complex within the Pacific Fair shopping centre at Broadbeach; the *Mermaid 5 (☎ 5575 3355, 2514 Gold Coast Hwy)*, at Mermaid Beach; and the *Coolangatta Cinema Centre (☎ 5536 8900)*, level two at Showcase on the Beach complex in Griffith St.

Other Entertainment *Conrad Jupiters Casino*, just off the Gold Coast Hwy at Broadbeach, is open 24 hours a day and has more than 100 gaming tables, including blackjack, roulette, two-up and craps, as well as hundreds of poker machines. Admission is free but you have to be over 18 years of age. There's a dress code of 'neat casual' – basically, long socks if you're wearing shorts, no sleeveless T-shirts and no ripped jeans.

GETTING THERE & AWAY

Air Ansett and Qantas fly direct from the major cities including Sydney ($317), Melbourne ($461), Adelaide ($485) and Perth ($752).

Bus The Surfers Paradise transit centre, on the corner of Beach and Cambridge Rds, is where you'll arrive if you're coming by bus. Inside are the booking desks of the bus companies, a cafeteria, left-luggage lockers ($4 a day) and the In Transit (☎ 5592 2911) backpackers' accommodation booking desk.

McCafferty's, Greyhound Pioneer, Kirklands and Coachtrans all have frequent services to Brisbane ($13 or $14), Byron Bay ($18 or $19) and Sydney ($71 to $79); Greyhound and McCafferty's also have one service a day each to Noosa ($27 or $28), changing at Brisbane.

The trip to Brisbane takes about 1½ hours from Surfers Paradise and just over two hours from Coolangatta.

Train The Gold Coast is served by the Helensvale, Nerang and Robina stations, which have direct links to Brisbane's Roma St and Central stations. None are particularly close to any of the main Gold Coast centres, but Surfside buses run regular shuttles from the train stations down to Surfers Paradise and beyond, and to the theme parks. The one way Brisbane-Nerang fare is $7.80, while the Surfside shuttle to/from Surfers Paradise is $3.50.

GETTING AROUND
To/From the Airport Coachtrans (☎ 5588 8747) meets every Qantas and Ansett flight into Coolangatta airport, with transfers to Coolangatta ($7 one way), Burleigh Heads ($8), Surfers Paradise ($9) and Main Beach ($10).

Bus Surfside Buslines (☎ 5536 7666) runs a frequent service 24 hours a day up and down the Gold Coast Hwy, between Southport and Tweed Heads and beyond. You can buy individual fares, get a Day Rover ticket for $10, or a weekly one for $30.

Car, Bicycle & Moped There are dozens of car-rental firms around with flyers in every hostel, motel and hotel. A few of the cheaper ones (around $25 a day) are Red Back Rentals (☎ 5592 1655), in the transit centre at Surfers Paradise, Half-Price Car Rentals (☎ 5570 3560), on the corner of Hamilton Ave and the Gold Coast Hwy, and Rent-A-Bomb (☎ 5538 8222), at 8 Beach Rd.

South Pacific Rentals (☎ 5592 5878), at 102 Ferny Ave, across from the bungee jumping, hires out mopeds for $40 for two hours or $75 for 24 hours.

Red Back Rentals also has bikes for $15 a day and Surfers Beach Hut Beach Hire, at the beach end of the Cavill Ave Mall, has them for $15 a half day or $20 for a full day.

GOLD COAST HINTERLAND
The mountains of the **McPherson Range**, about 20km inland from Coolangatta and stretching about 60km back along the NSW border to meet the Great Dividing Range, are a paradise for walkers. The great views and beautiful natural features are easily accessible if you have a car, and there are plenty of wonderfully scenic drives. Otherwise, there are several places offering tours and day trips from the coast. Expect a lot of rain in the mountains from December to March, and winter nights can be cold.

Tamborine Mountain
Just 45km west of the Gold Coast, this 600m-high plateau is on a northern spur of the McPherson Range. Patches of the area's original forests remain in nine small national parks. There are gorges, spectacular waterfalls including Witches Falls and Cedar Creek Falls, walking tracks and great views inland or over the coast. However, because of its proximity to the coast, this area is more developed and commercialised than the ranges further south.

The main access roads are from Oxenford, on the Pacific Hwy, or via Nerang from the coast. There's a QPWS information centre (☎ 5545 1171) in North Tamborine. Some of the best lookouts are in **Witches Falls National Park**, south-west of North Tamborine, and at **Cameron Falls**, north-west of North Tamborine. **Macrozamia Grove National Park**, near Mt Tamborine township, has some extremely old macrozamia palms.

Springbrook National Park
This forested 900m-high plateau is, like the rest of the McPherson Range, a remnant of the huge volcano once centred on Mt Warning in NSW. It's a lovely drive from the Gold Coast, reached by a sealed road via Mudgeeraba.

The national park is in three sections: Springbrook, Mt Cougal and Natural Bridge.

The vegetation is cool-temperate rainforest and eucalypt forest, with gorges, cliffs, forests, waterfalls, an extensive network of walking tracks and several picnic areas.

At the **Gwongorella picnic area**, just off the Springbrook road, the lovely Purling Brook Falls drop 109m into rainforest. Downstream, Waringa Pool is a beautiful summer swimming hole. There's a good camping ground beside the picnic area, and readers have recommended the tearooms as a good place for Devonshire tea with scones.

The **Natural Bridge section**, off the Nerang to Murwillumbah road, has a 1km walking circuit leading to a rock arch spanning a water-formed cave that is home to a huge colony of glow-worms.

There are rangers' offices and information centres at Natural Bridge and Springbrook, where you can pick up a copy of the national park's walking tracks leaflet. Camping permits for Gwongorella are available from the ranger at Springbrook (☎ 5533 5147, weekdays from 3 to 4 pm). Springbrook township has a general store, a YHA hostel, tearooms, craft shops and several guesthouses. See Organised Tours earlier in the Gold Coast section for details of trips to Springbrook from the coast.

Places to Stay There's a great YHA hostel, the *Springbrook Mountain Lodge* (☎ 5533 5366, 317 Repeater Station Rd), and it picks up from the Gold Coast for $10 return (two person minimum). It can also drop you off at the park for some great walks. It costs $19 for a member in a dorm and $22 in a twin or double. Nonmembers pay $25. Chalets cost $40 per person during the week or $60 on weekends.

Lamington National Park

West of Springbrook, this 200 sq km park covers more of the McPherson Range and adjoins the Border Ranges National Park in NSW. It includes thickly wooded valleys, 1100m-high ranges, plus most of the Lamington Plateau. Much of the vegetation is sub-tropical rainforest. There are beautiful gorges, caves, superb views, waterfalls, pools and lots of wildlife. Bowerbirds are quite common and pademelons, a type of small wallaby, can be seen late in the afternoon.

The two most popular and accessible sections, **Binna Burra** and **Green Mountains**, can be reached via sealed roads from Canungra. The 24km Border Trail walk links the two.

The park has 160km of walking tracks, ranging from a 'senses trail' for blind people at Binna Burra to a tree-top canopy walk along a series of suspended bridges at Green Mountains. Walking trail maps and brochures are available from the QPWS offices at Binna Burra (☎ 5533 3584) and Green Mountains (☎ 5544 0634), both open weekdays only from 1 to 3.30 pm.

Places to Stay The *Binna Burra Camp Ground* (☎ 5533 3758) has a great setting and good facilities; tent and van sites cost $9 per person, while on-site tents cost $36 a night for two. The *Binna Burra Mountain Lodge* (☎ 5533 3622) is a good mountain retreat with two types of rustic cabins costing from $99 to $165 per person per night, which includes all meals, free hiking and climbing gear, and activities like guided walks, bus trips and abseiling.

O'Reilly's Guesthouse (☎ 5544 0644), at Green Mountains, is a fantastic place to splurge if you can afford it. It was built in the 1930s and retains much period charm, plus it's smack in the middle of the national park. Beds cost from $75 in comfortable, old-style (shared bathroom) rooms to $120 per person in a spacious room with en suite and balcony. If you want breakfast and dinner at the guesthouse, add another $44 per person. There's also a kiosk, and a QPWS camping ground about 600m away, with sites for $3.50 per person per night.

You can bush camp in Lamington but permits are limited. You can get information from the QPWS offices at Burleigh Heads or Brisbane, but camping permits must be obtained from the ranger at Green Mountains.

Getting There & Away The Binna Burra bus service (☎ 5533 3622) operates daily between Surfers Paradise and Binna Burra ($16 one way; one hour), departing from

Surfers Paradise at 8.30 am and from Binna Burra at 2.30 pm – book ahead.

Allstate Scenic Tours (☎ 3285 1777) has services daily (except Saturday) departing Brisbane at 9.30 am for Binna Burra and O'Reilly's ($20; three hours, or $35 for a return day trip), and returning at 3.15 pm.

Mountain Coach Company (☎ 5524 4249) has a daily Green Mountains service picking up along the Gold Coast ($35 return).

Mt Lindesay Hwy

This road runs south from Brisbane, across the Great Dividing Range west of Lamington and into NSW at Woodenbong. **Beaudesert**, in cattle country 66km from Brisbane and 20km south-west of Tamborine Mountain, has a pioneer museum, a tourist centre on Jane St, and several motels.

West of Beaudesert is the stretch of the Great Dividing Range known as the **Scenic Rim**. Further south, **Mt Barney National Park** is undeveloped but popular with bushwalkers and climbers. It's in the Great Dividing Range just north of the state border. You reach it from the Rathdowney to Boonah road. There's a tourist office (☎ 5544 1222) on the highway at Rathdowney.

Sunshine Coast

The stretch of coast from the top of Bribie Island to Noosa Heads is known as the Sunshine Coast. It's a popular holiday area, renowned for fine beaches, good surfing and fishing. Although it doesn't have the high-rise jungle and neon-lit strips of the Gold Coast, it is still quite commercial and has been heavily developed.

Noosa Heads is the most fashionable and exclusive town on the coast, with an excellent national park and great beaches. Maroochydore is also quite popular. North of Noosa is the Cooloola National Park and Rainbow Beach, an access point for Fraser Island.

Getting There & Away

Bus Greyhound Pioneer and McCafferty's buses travel along the Bruce Hwy, but both have only one service a day each way from Brisbane to Noosa and Maroochydore. The main Sunshine Coast operator is Suncoast Pacific (☎ 3236 1901). It runs frequent direct services from the Brisbane transit centre and Brisbane airport to Noosa ($21; three hours) via Maroochydore ($18; two hours).

From Cooroy and Nambour on the highway, Tewantin Bus Services (☎ 5449 7422) runs regular buses across to Noosa, continuing to Maroochydore, while Sunshine Coast Coaches (☎ 5443 4555) has daily services south from Maroochydore and inland across to Landsborough and Nambour.

Train The most convenient stations for the Sunshine Coast are Nambour and Cooroy. There are services daily to these places from Brisbane and from the north.

CABOOLTURE

• postcode 4510   • pop 26,800

This region, 49km north of Brisbane, once had a large Aboriginal population. Nowadays it's a prosperous dairy centre.

It also has two interesting attractions. Seven kilometres east (signposted off the road to Bribie Island), the **Abbey Museum** is a world social history museum with a small but well-presented collection of ancient artefacts, weaponry, pottery and costumes. The collection was previously housed in the UK, Cyprus, Egypt and Sri Lanka. It's open Tuesday, Thursday, Friday and Saturday from 10 am to 4 pm; entry is $5.

The **Caboolture Historical Village**, on Beerburrum Rd, 2km north of the town, has more than 50 early Australian buildings in a bush setting. It is open daily from 9.30 am to 3 pm ($6).

GLASS HOUSE MOUNTAINS

About 20km north of Caboolture, the Glass House Mountains are a dramatic visual starting point for the Sunshine Coast. They're a bizarre series of volcanic crags rising abruptly out of the plain to a height of around 300m. They were named by Captain Cook and, depending on whose story you believe, he either noted the reflections of the glass-smooth sides of the mountains, or he thought they looked like the glass furnaces in his native Yorkshire.

The mountains are great for scenic drives, bushwalking and rock climbing. The main access is via the Forest Drive, a 22km-long series of sealed and unsealed roads that wind through the ranges from Beerburrum to the Glass House Mountains township, with several spectacular lookout points en route.

There are four small national parks within the range, and each has walking/climbing trails of varying levels of difficulty: Mt Ngungun is an easy two hour walk to the summit; Mt Beerwah and Mt Tibrogargan are steep and difficult three-hour climbs; and Mt Coonowrin is popular with experienced rock climbers. Contact the ranger (☎ 5494 3983) at Maleny for more information.

Another attraction in this area is the **Australia Zoo** (☎ 5494 1134), on the Glass House Mountains Tourist Route at Beerwah. It's the home of TV's crocodile hunters Steve and Terri Irwin. It's open daily from 8.30 am to 4 pm ($13). With over 550 animals on-site, there are plenty of feeding demonstrations. The crocodile feeding is a highlight.

Mt Tibrogargan Relaxapark (☎ 5496 0151), 1.5km north of Beerburrum, has a shop, walking trails and information on walks and wildlife; camp sites are $11, onsite vans cost from $22 and self-contained units from $35.

CALOUNDRA
• postcode 4551   • pop 28,500

At the southern end of the Sunshine Coast, Caloundra has some decent beaches and excellent fishing, but compared with places further north, it's a bit faded these days. It's still a popular holiday town with families, and has numerous caravan parks and holiday flats, but no backpackers' hostel. Bulcock Beach, good for windsurfing, is just down from the main street, overlooking the northern end of Bribie Island.

The **Queensland Air Museum** (☎ 5492 5930), at Caloundra aerodrome, is open daily from 10 am to 4 pm ($5). **Aussie World & the Ettamogah Pub** is on the Bruce Hwy, just north of the Caloundra turn-off.

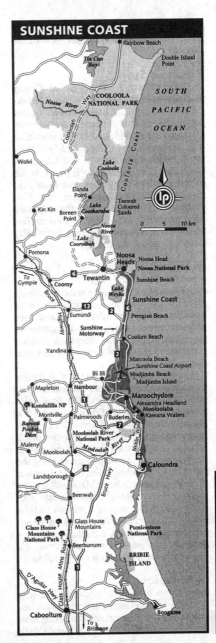

QUEENSLAND

There's a helpful tourist office (☎ 5491 0202) on Caloundra Rd, 2km west of the town centre.

Places to Stay

If you're driving, the *Dicky Beach Family Holiday Park* (☎ 5491 3342), on Beerburrum St next to Dicky Beach, is well located and the beach is nicer than the one in town. Camp sites cost $14, and cabins from $36. The *Hibiscus Holiday Park* (☎ 5491 1564), on the corner of Bowman and Landsborough Park Rds, is close to Bulcock beach and the centre; camp sites cost from $16, on-site vans from $29 and cabins from $34. Opposite the bus terminal, the *City and Surf Motel* (☎ 5491 2511, 6 Cooma Terrace) has good units ranging seasonally from $50 to $68 for doubles.

MAROOCHY

• pop 40,000

North from Caloundra, the coast is built-up most of the way to the triple towns of **Mooloolaba**, **Alexandra Headland** and **Maroochydore**, which sprawl together to form Maroochy – the Sunshine Coast's biggest and most heavily developed urban conglomeration.

Maroochydore, the main town, is a busy commercial centre and popular tourist spot, with an ocean beach and the Maroochy River, which has lots of pelicans and a few islands. Alexandra Headland has a pleasant beach and good surfing off a rocky point. Mooloolaba has the brightest atmosphere, the best beach and a strip of shops along the beachfront, including cafes, restaurants and the odd nightspot. Also at Mooloolaba is the **Wharf**, a riverfront development with shops, eateries, a tavern, a marina and the excellent **Underwater World**, a large oceanarium with a transparent tunnel leading underneath and performing-seal shows. It's open daily from 9 am to 6 pm ($18.90).

Information

The Maroochy tourist information centre (☎ 5479 1566) is near the corner of Aerodrome Rd (the main road connecting Maroochydore and Mooloolaba) and Sixth Ave; it's open weekdays from 9 am to 5 pm and weekends from 9 am to 4 pm.

Activities

As in Caloundra, the main attractions here are the excellent beaches. There are numerous surf shops along the coast where you can hire surf and boogie boards. In-line skates and bicycles (both $15 a half day, $20 a day) can be hired from Maroochy Skate Biz (☎ 5443 6111), on the foreshore at 160 Alexandria Parade in Alexandra Headland.

Places to Stay

The best caravan/camping parks are the foreshore parks run by the local council. They include *Cotton Tree Caravan Park* (☎ 5443 1253), on the Esplanade, and the *Seabreeze Caravan Park* (☎ 5443 1167), behind the information centre. Camp sites cost from $12 and powered sites from $14 (no on-site vans).

There are three hostels in Maroochydore – ring from the bus station for a pickup. The best is possibly the *Cotton Tree Beachouse* (☎ 5443 1755, 15 The Esplanade), a comfortable, rambling old timber guesthouse overlooking the river. There are free surfboards and boogie boards and free jet-skiing sessions twice a week. Dorm beds cost $14, singles/doubles or twins $30/32. It's a friendly place, just five minutes walk from the bus station.

The *Suncoast Backpackers' Lodge* (☎ 5443 7544, 50 Parker St) is a modern hostel with free bikes, surfboards and boogie boards, and dorm beds for $14 and doubles for $34. *Maroochydore YHA Backpackers* (☎ 5443 3151, 24 Schirmann Drive) is buried in a residential estate a couple of turns off Bradman Ave. It's a bit institutional and has mainly six to eight-bed dorms from $16 a night with a few doubles for $36. It also provides free canoes, surfboards, boogie boards and fishing gear.

There are dozens of motels and holiday units but generally they are expensive. *Tallows Lodge Holiday Units* (☎ 5443 2981, 10 Memorial Ave) is close to the beach and has self-contained units for $55 for two people. Alternatively, there's a strip of cheap motels on Brisbane Rd, the main road south out of Mooloolaba.

Places to Eat

For cheap eating, about the best option is the *food court* at the Sunshine Plaza shopping centre, where about 20 outlets offer a huge variety of foods at budget prices. Alternatively, over at the Wharf in Mooloolaba, *Friday's* is a popular tavern/bar and eatery with great specials on T-bone steaks – from $7.95. There's also a branch of the *Hog's Breath Cafe* at the Wharf. For good cafes and places where you can get a decent salad or pasta, try the extension of Alexandra Parade, east of the junction with Brisbane Rd.

Back in Maroochydore, *Hathi Indian Restaurant (25 Aerodrome Rd)* has all-you-can-eat Indian smorgasbords for $15 a head and main courses in the $8 to $10 range. Next door, the *Som Tam Thai* is recommended. It has vegetarian mains for less than $10.

Getting There & Away

Long-distance buses stop at the Suncoast Pacific Bus Terminal (☎ 5443 1011), on First Ave in Maroochydore, just off Aerodrome Rd (near KFC).

NOOSA

• postcode 4567   • pop 20,000

A surfers' mecca since the early 1960s, Noosa (officially Noosa Heads) has so far managed to avoid the blitzkrieg development that has afflicted the Gold Coast. It remains a low-key resort for the fashionable, as well as a popular stopoff for travellers moving up or down the coast. It has good beaches, some fine cafes and restaurants, a very accessible national park close by, and just a little to the north, the walks, waterways and beaches of the Cooloola National Park.

Orientation

Noosa is actually a string of small, linked centres stretching back from the mouth of the Noosa River and along its maze of tributary creeks and lakes. The most popular resort area and the liveliest part of town is

Noosa Heads, centred on the trendy shopping and dining zone of Hastings St. Three kilometres south-west – inland along the Noosa River – is Noosaville, which is where most of the river tours depart from. The river here is seawater and fringed with occasional sandy beaches. Gympie Terrace, which runs along the river, has a string of eating and drinking places and is quite lively most evenings.

A kilometre south of Noosa Heads, over the hill, is Noosa Junction, another shopping and eating area, from where a main road leads east to Sunshine Beach, the quietest and most residential of the four main areas, but also the place with the best beaches and surf.

Information

The tourist information centre (☎ 5447 4988), in Hastings St, is open daily from 9 am to 5 pm. There are also several less useful, privately run tourist information offices, which double as booking agents for accommodation, trips and tours.

The best bookshop in the area is Written Dimensions, next to the cinema on Sunshine Beach Rd in Noosa Junction. A few doors away, at the back of a small arcade, is the Book Exchange, a second-hand place. Down on Hastings St in Noosa Heads there's a Dwyer's Bookstore in the Laguna Arcade and a Mary Ryan Bookshop in the Bay Village Mall.

You can check your email at Backpacking Round Queensland, 9 Sunshine Beach Rd, in Noosa Junction. It also acts as booking agent for Commando Kev's popular Fraser Island Tours.

Noosa National Park

The spectacular cape at Noosa Head marks the northern end of the Sunshine Coast. This small but lovely national park extends for about 2km in each direction from the headland and has fine walks, great coastal scenery and a string of bays on the north side with waves that draw surfers from all over. Alexandria Bay, on the eastern side, has the best sandy beach.

The main entrance, at the end of Park Rd, has a car park, an information centre and

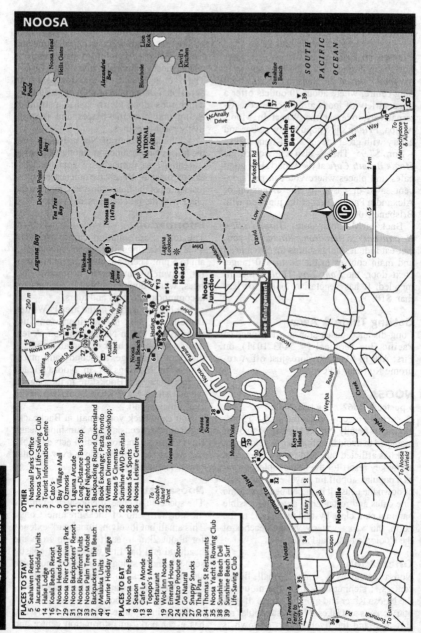

NOOSA

PLACES TO STAY
5 Seahaven Resort
6 Jacaranda Holiday Units
14 Halse Lodge
16 Koala Beach Resort
17 Noosa Heads Motel
29 Noosa River Caravan Park
31 Noosa Backpackers' Resort
32 Noosa Riverfront Units
33 Noosa Palm Tree Motel
37 Backpackers on the Beach
40 Melaluka Units
41 Sunrise Holiday Village

PLACES TO EAT
4 Noosa on the Beach
8 Season
13 Cafe Le Monde
18 Toppo's Mexican
   Restaurant
19 Wok Inn Noosa
20 Emerald House
24 Matzo Produce Store
25 Go Natural
27 Snappy Snacks
30 Thai Pan
34 Thomas St Restaurants
35 Noosa Yacht & Rowing Club
38 Sunshine Beach Deli
39 Sunshine Beach Surf
   Life-Saving Club

OTHER
1 National Parks Office
2 Noosa Surf Life-Saving Club
3 Tourist Information Centre
7 Cato's
9 Bay Village Mall
10 Ozmosis
11 Laguna Arcade
12 Long-Distance Bus Stop
15 Reef Nightclub
21 Backpacking Round Queensland
22 Book Exchange; Pasta Pronto
23 Written Dimensions Bookshop;
   Noosa 5 Cinemas
26 Sunshine 4WD Rentals
28 Noosa Sea Sports
36 Noosa Leisure Centre

picnic areas (with goannas and koalas), and is also the starting point for five great walking tracks ranging from 1km to 4km in length. You can drive up to the Laguna Lookout from Viewland Drive in the Noosa Junction, or walk into the park from McAnally Drive or Parkedge Rd in Sunshine Beach.

Activities

Total Adventures (☎ 5474 0177), based at Noosa Leisure Centre, Wallace Drive, Noosaville, runs a good range of activities including abseiling and rock-climbing trips, mountain bike tours and canoeing trips up the Noosa River. It also offers sea kayaking from September to June.

Catamarans and surf skis can be hired from the Noosa Main Beach. Most of the surf shops rent boards, including Ozmosis (☎ 5447 3300), in Hastings St, which has mini-malibu boards for hire for $30 a day ($200 deposit). There are lots of places along the Noosa River in Gympie Terrace, Noosaville, where you can rent out fishing dinghies, barbecue pontoons, catamarans, jet skis, canoes and surf skis.

Other activities on offer include horse riding with Clip Clop Treks (☎ 5449 1254), camel safaris with Camel Company Australia (☎ 5442 4402), paraflying with Fly High (☎ 5449 9630), joy flights in the Red Baron biplane (☎ 5474 1200) and hot-air ballooning (☎ 5495 6714).

Organised Tours

There are a number of operators offering trips from Noosa up to Fraser Island via the Cooloola National Park and the Teewah Coloured Sands.

Fraser Explorer Tours (☎ 5449 8647) has trips daily to Fraser Island for $80 per person – it's possible (and recommended) to extend your stay on Fraser Island to two days for $145. Sunlover Holidays (☎ 5474 0777) also operates daily Fraser Island tours for $105.

For the more adventurous, Commando Kev (☎ 4127 9126) offers good-value three-day camping safaris to Fraser Island departing twice a week ($185, including driver and guide, all meals and camping gear).

Off Beat Tours (☎ 5473 5135) runs excellent rainforest day tours to Conondale National Park for $95, including pickups and gourmet lunch.

Several companies run boats up the Noosa River into the Everglades area: the Everglades Water Bus Co (☎ 1800 688 045) has a four hour cruise departing daily at 12.30 pm (from $45); Noosa River Tours (☎ 5449 7362) has a daily 10 am departure, returning at 3 pm ($50); and Everglades Express (☎ 5449 9422) offers a four hour cruise, departing twice daily ($45).

There are plenty of other tours on offer – check with the tourist centre.

Places to Stay – Budget

Although it has a reputation as a resort for the rich and fashionable, Noosa has a wide range of accommodation, from caravan parks and backpackers' hostels to resort hotels and apartments. With the exception of the hostels, accommodation prices can rise by 50% in busy times and by 100% in the December to January peak season.

Camping The *Sunrise Holiday Village* (☎ 5447 3294, David Low Way), overlooking Sunshine Beach, has camp sites from $12 to $15, on-site vans from $30 to $45 and cabins from $35 to $55. Unfortunately facilities and maintenance are not what they might be. Better is the *Noosa River Caravan Park* (☎ 5449 7050), on Russell St, Noosaville, at Munna Point, with riverfront camp sites from $12 and a good camp kitchen.

Hostels All of Noosa's hostels have courtesy buses and do pickups from the long-distance bus stop – all, that is, except the YHA *Halse Lodge* (☎ 1800 242 567), which doesn't need to, being only 100m away. It's a fine, 100-year-old heritage-listed building with polished wooden floors, a colonial-type dining room and big verandahs. The only drawback is that the place is a little austere – no partying here. Dorm beds cost $17 to $18 (six and four-bed dorms), but the spartan doubles are way overpriced at $45.

A 10 minute walk uphill from the beach, *Koala Beach Resort* (☎ 1800 357 457, 44

Noosa Drive, Noosa Junction) is the place to go for noise and beery evenings. It's a converted motel with good facilities including a pool and bar. A place in a six bed dorm costs $16 and doubles are $36.

The *Noosa Backpackers' Resort (☎ 1800 626 673, 9 William St)*, in Noosaville, is a relaxed place with a good courtyard, a pool and a small bar. Like the above two places there are cheap meals available, free use of boogie and surf boards, and a variety of trips and tours on offer. Dorm beds are $16, doubles $36.

In Sunshine Beach, *Backpackers on the Beach (☎ 1800 240 344, 26 Stevens St)* is a little remote, but it is almost on top of Noosa's best stretch of beach. Beds cost $14 a night. Also at Sunshine Beach, the *Melaluka Units (☎ 5447 3663, 7 Selene St)* benefits from being right by the beach. It has two and three-bedroom holiday units with beds for $18 plus a one bedroom unit for $40.

Places to Stay – Mid-Range

The best places to stay are those along the beach around Hastings St – they're also the most expensive. A one bedroom beachfront apartment costs at least $200 a night. *Seahaven Resort (☎ 1800 072 013, 13 Hastings St)* has streetside studios from $100 a night. Its $200, one bedroom beachfront apartment sleeps four. On the other side of Hastings St, the *Jacaranda Holiday Units (☎ 5447 4011)* has motel-style units that sleep up to three from $80 a night, and self-contained one-bedroom units sleeping up to five for $120.

About 1km back, the *Noosa Heads Motel (☎ 5449 2873, 2 Viewland Drive)*, in Noosa Junction, is a good option, with four comfortable self-contained units in a shady garden setting, a pool and a barbecue area. The units sleep up to six and range from $59 to $120.

One of the best areas for cheaper accommodation is along Gympie Terrace, the main road through Noosaville. *Noosa Riverfront Units (☎ 5449 7595, 277 Gympie Terrace)* has good budget units from $50 for a studio or from $79 ($325 per week) for two bedrooms. The *Noosa Palm*

Tree Motel (☎ 5449 7311, 233 Gympie Terrace) has eight motel-style units and eight self-contained units from $55/90 to $60/100 for singles/doubles in the low/high season.

Places to Eat

Hastings St For a cheap lunch on Hastings St, the Bay Village *food court* has a pizza and pasta bar, a bakery, a Chinese kitchen, a kebab shop and a deli. You can eat reasonably well here for around $5.

In the Noosa On The Beach complex, just west of the tourist information centre, the *Appetizer*, a greasy, stand-up place, does Aussie breakfast for $5 and snacks like burgers and fish and chips from around $4. In the same complex but on the beachfront, the *Beach Cafe* is a good spot for breakfast, with a menu including muesli with fresh fruit ($4.80) or bacon and eggs ($5.90).

Possibly the best value restaurant on Hastings St remains the ever-popular *Cafe Le Monde*, east of the roundabout. Dining is out front in a large covered courtyard with a menu that attempts to please everyone. We tried Thai, Italian and Aussie dishes and all were excellent, served in enormous portions and at pretty good prices – $12 to $20 for our mains. On the beachfront in the Noosa On The Beach complex, *Bistro C (☎ 5447 2855)* is a stylish place with a full menu, but it also does excellent cocktails if you just want to drink. *Season (☎ 5447 3747)* is a popular, new BYO restaurant using only fresh, seasonal produce in creative dishes.

Noosa Junction A few doors past KFC, the *Emerald House* is a cheap Chinese restaurant with most dishes for about $7.50. Across the road, *Snappy Snacks* serves breakfast until 3 pm for $3.

Pasta Pronto (2/25 Sunshine Beach Rd), near the Book Exchange in an arcade towards the cinemas, has excellent homemade pastas, with main courses for around $14. It has daily lunch specials for $7.50.

The *Matzo Produce Store (4 Sunshine Beach Rd)* is a very cool place for a sandwich and caffe latte for under $10. It also has Internet access.

On the roundabout, *Wok Inn Noosa* is a cheerful noodle bar where you create your own dishes. A couple of doors away up the hill, *Topopo's Mexican Restaurant* is a colourful cantina with main courses for around $10, combo dishes for around $20 and margaritas and sangria by the glass or jug – drink prices tend to be low to attract the crowds from Koala Beach Resort over the road. On Wednesday all meals are $9.50.

Back on Sunshine Beach Rd, *Go Natural* is a health-food shop with plenty of sandwich and salad-type lunch options.

Noosaville Next door to the Noosa Backpackers' Resort in William St, the *Thai Pan* Thai restaurant is very good, with competitive prices. It's BYO and opens nightly for dinner.

Thomas St, in Noosaville, has a number of surprisingly good restaurants on both sides of the street. They include the innovative *Max's Native Sun Cuisine*, with 300 different duck recipes, *Raymondos Gourmet Pizza*, *A Taste of Spice* Malaysian restaurant, with mains for $10.90, and the popular *Albertos*.

On Gympie Terrace, just before you cross the river, the *Noosa Yacht & Rowing Club* is a two storey riverfront building open every day for lunch and dinner and on Sunday for breakfast. The food here is cheap and hearty with most meals around the $8 to $12 mark and a Monday to Friday lunch special for $5. The crowd is mostly a family/geriatric mix.

Sunshine Beach If you're staying in Sunshine Beach, there's a general store, a fruit and vegie shop and a couple of eateries in the small shopping centre in Duke St – of these the *Sunshine Beach Deli* is a decent gourmet deli with vegetarian dishes, home-made pastries and burgers and hot sandwiches. Down at the beach, the *Sunshine Beach Surf Life-Saving Club* serves bistro meals and has a courtyard overlooking the ocean.

Entertainment
The bar and club scene in Noosa is not particularly great. If you are staying at *Koala Beach Resort* then you're sorted, as that's pretty much the liveliest place most evenings. Alternatively, downstairs at the Noosa Reef Hotel, on Noosa Drive, the *Reef Nightclub* opens from Thursday to Sunday nights till late. The pub occasionally has live bands and Sunday afternoon sessions. Otherwise most folk tend to sit and sip in cafe-bars like *Cato's*, on Hastings St.

Noosa's main nightclub is the *Rolling Rock*, upstairs in the Bay Village Mall off Hastings St. It's open every night until around 3 am, with a 'smart casual' dress code and cover charges from $5 to $10. Nearby and run by the same operator, the *NYC* is a quieter, more sophisticated cocktail bar with an outdoor courtyard.

The *Noosa 5 Cinemas (☎ 5447 5300)*, in Noosa Junction, is a plush, comfortable place that screens latest-release movies. Tickets are cheaper before 6 pm and Tuesday is budget day.

Getting There & Around
Long-distance buses stop at the bus terminal near the corner of Noosa Drive and Noosa Parade, just back from Hastings St. Advance tickets are available from the booking desk inside the Avis office, across the road from the bus stop.

Sunbus (☎ 13 1230) runs frequent daily services up and down the coast between Noosa and Maroochydore, and has local services linking Noosa Heads, Noosaville, Noosa Junction, etc. It also runs a special service every half hour on Saturday to the Eumundi Markets.

If you want to drive up the Cooloola Coast beach to the Teewah Coloured Sands, Double Island Point, Rainbow Beach or Fraser Island, Sunshine 4WD Rentals (☎ 5447 3702), beside the Noosa Junction post office, rents out four-seater Suzuki Sierras from $105 a day and seven-seater Nissan Patrols from $150 a day.

Bikes can be hired from several places. Sierra Mountain Bike Hire (☎ 5474 8277), based in the Budget Rent-a-Car office in the Bay Village Mall, Hastings St, charges $12 per day, and Koala Bike Hire (☎ 5474 2733), has mountain bikes from $15 a day and a delivery service.

QUEENSLAND

COOLOOLA COAST

Stretching for 50km between Noosa and Rainbow Beach, the Cooloola Coast is a remote strip of long sandy beaches backed by the Great Sandy National Park. Although this stretch is undeveloped, at times it is so popular with campers you might be excused for thinking otherwise.

The Cooloola Way, a gravel road, runs from Tewantin all the way up to Rainbow Beach (via Boreen Point and the national park). From Tewantin, the Noosa River Ferry operates daily from 6 am to 10 pm (Friday and Saturday until midnight) and costs $4 per car one way. On the other side are Lake Cooroibah and the beaches of Laguna Bay, and, if you have a 4WD, at low tide you can continue right up the beach to Rainbow Beach and Wide Bay, passing the Teewah Coloured Sands and the rusting *Cherry Venture*, a 3000 tonne freighter swept ashore by a cyclone in 1973.

Lake Cooroibah

There are several good camping grounds between Lake Cooroibah and the coast, including the low-key *Lake Cooroibah Resort* (☎ 5447 1225), with a bar/restaurant, tennis courts, horse riding, camp sites ($4 per person), on-site tents ($25 for two) and cabins ($35/40/60 for 4/5/6). Also based here is the Camel Company Australia (☎ 5442 4402), offering two-hour **camel treks** for $35, or half-day treks (Thursday only; $60), overnight safaris ($150) and six-day safaris to Fraser Island ($1100 all-inclusive).

Boreen Point

On the western shores of Lake Cootharaba, Boreen Point is a relaxed little place with a caravan park, a motel and a few holiday units.

The historic *Apollonian Hotel* (☎ 5485 3100), in Laguna St, has a garden setting, shady verandahs, simple double rooms from $30 and it serves meals. The *Jetty* restaurant (☎ 5485 3167), in Booreen Parade, has a lovely setting overlooking the lake and serves lunches daily and dinners on Friday and Saturday.

Great Sandy National Park (Cooloola)

North of Noosa, the Great Sandy National Park covers over 54,000 hectares, with the Noosa River running through the centre. It's a varied wilderness area with long sandy beaches, mangrove-lined waterways, forest, heaths and lakes, all of it featuring plentiful birdlife and lots of wildflowers in spring.

You can drive through the park, although the best way to see Cooloola is from a boat. Boats can be hired from Tewantin and Noosaville, or there are various operators offering cruises from Noosa – see Organised Tours in the Noosa section earlier in this chapter.

Five kilometres north of Boreen Point, at Elanda Point, there's a lakeside camping ground. Several walking trails start here, including the 46km Cooloola Wilderness Trail and a 7km trail to the QPWS visitor centre (☎ 5449 7364) on Kinaba Island.

Places to Stay The unconventional and totally laid-back riverside wilderness camp *Gagaju* (☎ 5474 3522, 118 Johns Drive, Tewantin) is in forest bordering the park. It's built from scavenged timber (furniture and bunks included). Possible activities include free canoeing and mountain biking, bushwalking and, in season, cane toad golf – cruel it may sound, but we're assured that it's totally environmentally friendly. There's just one communal dorm with beds for $11, or you can pitch your own tent for $7. Shower and toilet facilities are basic; bring your own food. Gagaju does free pickups from Noosa.

There are also about 10 camping grounds in the park, many of them by the river. The main ones are *Fig Tree Point*, at the north of Lake Cootharaba, and *Harry's Hut*, about 4km upstream. *Freshwater* is the main camp on the coast; it's about 6km south of Double Island Point.

SUNSHINE COAST HINTERLAND

The mountains of the Blackall Range rise just in from the coast, and this scenic hinterland area has mountain towns, guesthouses and B&Bs, national parks with rainforests and waterfalls, art and craft galleries, and lots of tourists.

Nambour is the main commercial centre for the region. It's an attractive town, but it has little of interest for travellers. Six kilometres south, the **Big Pineapple** is one of Queensland's kitschy 'big things'. As well as the 15m-high fibreglass fruit there's a train ride through a plantation, a macadamia orchard tour and a themed boat ride, which together cost $15.50 for adults. It's all very tacky but interesting and very popular.

Further north, locals and visitors flock to the **Eumundi Village Market** every Wednesday and Saturday morning. Eumundi is a charming little rural centre and the original home of Eumundi Lager (now brewed on the Gold Coast). Buses run from Noosa to Eumundi roughly every half hour on Saturday morning. West of town, you can fossick for thunder eggs (fossils, stones or mineral concretions supposed to have been cast to earth by lightning) at **Thunder Egg Farm**.

The scenic Mapleton to Maleny road runs right along the ridge line of the Blackall Range. **Mapleton Falls National Park** is 4km west of Mapleton and **Kondalilla National Park** is 3km off the Mapleton to Montville stretch of the road. Both have rainforest. At Mapleton Falls, Pencil Creek plunges 120m, while the Kondalilla Falls drop 80m into a rainforest valley. This is a great area for exploring – there's lots of birdlife and several walking tracks in the parks.

Midway between Mapleton and Maleny, **Montville** is a very popular tourist spot, with lots of craft shops and restaurants.

The **Maleny Folk Festival**, held annually over the five days leading up to New Year's Eve, is the closest thing Australia has to Woodstock.

SOUTH BURNETT REGION

Further inland, the South Burnett region includes Australia's most important peanut-growing area. The thing to do here is visit the **Bunya Mountains National Park**. The Bunyas are isolated outliers of the Great Dividing Range, which rise abruptly to over 1000m and are accessible by sealed road from Dalby or Kingaroy. They are covered with a variety of vegetation, from rainforest to heathland, and if you haven't already seen wallabies in the wild then this is where to go for guaranteed sightings. There are three camping grounds, plus a network of walking tracks to numerous waterfalls and lookouts. The ranger (☎ 4668 3127) is at Dandabah, at the entrance to the park.

Darling Downs

West of the Great Dividing Range in southern Queensland stretch the rolling plains of the Darling Downs, some of the most fertile agricultural land in Australia. Towns such as Toowoomba and Warwick are among the most historic in the state. South of Warwick, the scenic Granite Belt region has Queensland's only wine-growing district and some fine national parks. Other regional attractions include the historic Jondaryan Woolshed, west of Toowoomba, and the Miles Historical Village.

West of the Darling Downs, the population becomes more scattered as the crop-producing areas give way to sheep and cattle country.

Getting There & Away
Air Flight West flies daily from Brisbane to Roma ($186) and Charleville ($240).

Bus McCafferty's operates the following bus services that pass through Darling Downs: from Brisbane to Longreach ($83; 17 hours) along the Warrego and Landsborough Hwys via Ipswich, Toowoomba ($15; two hours), Miles ($30; 5½ hours), Roma ($41; seven hours) and Charleville ($52; 10 hours); and inland from Brisbane via Toowoomba and Goondiwindi ($36; five hours) to Melbourne.

McCafferty's also has an inland service from Brisbane to Sydney that goes along the New England Hwy via Warwick ($24; 2¾ hours) and Stanthorpe ($30; 3½ hours). There are also McCafferty's buses between Toowoomba and the Gold Coast ($21), and between Brisbane and Rockhampton ($56) via Toowoomba and Miles.

QUEENSLAND

Train The *Westlander* runs twice a week from Brisbane to Charleville via Ipswich, Toowoomba and Roma. One-way fares are $81 for an economy seat, $115 for an economy sleeper and $178 for a 1st class sleeper. There are connecting bus services from Charleville to Quilpie and Cunnamulla.

IPSWICH TO WARWICK

Virtually an outer suburb of Brisbane, Ipswich was a convict settlement as early as 1827 and an important early Queensland town. It still contains many fine old houses and public buildings, and these are described in the excellent *Ipswich City Heritage Trails* leaflet available from the tourist office (☎ 3281 0555), on the corner of D'Arcy Place and Brisbane St.

South-west of Ipswich, the Cunningham Hwy to Warwick crosses the Great Dividing Range at **Cunningham's Gap**, with 1100m peaks rising either side of the road. **Main Range National Park**, which covers the Great Dividing Range for about 20km north and south of Cunningham's Gap, is great walking country, with a variety of walks starting from the car park at the crest of the gap. Much of the range is covered in rainforest. There's a camping ground and an information office by the road on the western side of the gap; contact the ranger (☎ 4666 1133) for permits.

WARWICK

- postcode 4370   • pop 13,000

Warwick, 162km south-west of Brisbane, is the oldest town in Queensland after the capital. It's a busy farming centre noted for its roses, numerous historic buildings built of local sandstone and its rodeo (held over the last weekend in October).

The Warwick tourist information centre (☎ 4661 3122), at 49 Albion St, is a good one, with plenty of material on neighbouring towns too; it's open weekdays from 9 am to 5 pm and weekends from 10 am to 2 pm.

Warwick's major attraction is **Pringle Cottage & Museum**, on Dragon St, dating from 1863. It is open daily except Tuesday and entry costs $3.50.

The *Warwick Tourist Park* (☎ 4661 8335, 18 Palmer Ave), off the New England

Hwy on the northern outskirts of town, has unpowered/powered sites for $12/15 and dormitory accommodation for $10 per person. The *Criterion Hotel* (☎ 4661 1042, 84 Palmerin St) is a huge old country pub with clean and simple rooms opening up onto a broad front verandah costing $15 per person. Of the dozen or so motels in town the *Centre Point Mid-City Motor Inn* (☎ 4661 3488, 32 Albion St) is the most central; it charges $60 a double.

STANTHORPE & THE GRANITE BELT

South of Warwick is the Granite Belt, an elevated plateau of the Great Dividing Range, 800 to 950m above sea level. It's known for fruit and vegetable production and wine making, and there are around 20 wineries in the area, most of which are open to visitors.

Stanthorpe is the region's main centre and it has a good range of accommodation, a historical museum and an art gallery. It celebrates being Queensland's coolest town with a Brass Monkey Festival every July. The tourist information office (☎ 4681 2057) is in the Civic Centre, on the corner of Marsh and Lock Sts, open on weekdays from 9 am to 5 pm and weekends to 4 pm.

The *Central Hotel* (☎ 4681 2044), on the corner of High and Victoria Sts, has good singles/doubles for $20 per person ($25 with a continental breakfast) while *Stanthorpe Backpackers & Top of the Town Caravan Village* (☎ 4681 4888) specialises in finding fruit and vegetable-picking work for travellers – ring ahead to see what's available. Beds in a four share dorm are $15 a night ($80 a week), caravans are $14 per person and camp sites are $13 a night for two.

From the highway 26km south of Stanthorpe, a sealed road leads 9km east up to **Girraween National Park**, an area of 1000m-high hills, huge granite outcrops, and valleys. The park has a visitors centre (☎ 4684 5157), two camping grounds with hot showers and several walking tracks of varying length. Girraween adjoins Bald Rock National Park over the border in NSW. It can fall below freezing on winter nights up here, but summer days are warm.

GOONDIWINDI

- postcode 4390   • pop 5000

West of Warwick, Goondiwindi is on the NSW border and the Macintyre River. Known as the home of the great racehorse Gunsynd, it's an attractive town and a popular stop at the end of the Newell Hwy between Melbourne and Brisbane. There's a small museum in the old customs house and a wildlife sanctuary at the Boobera Lagoon. The municipal tourist office (☎ 4671 2653) is on McLean St near the bridge, a block from the post office. It's open from 9 am to 5 pm.

If you plan on staying the night here the best value is *O'Shea's Royal Hotel-Motel (☎ 4671 1877, 48 Marshall St)*, which has motel-style singles/doubles for $48/57 and some cheaper hotel rooms.

TOOWOOMBA

- postcode 4350   • pop 92,000

On the edge of the Great Dividing Range and the Darling Downs, 138km inland from Brisbane, Toowoomba is a gracious city with pleasant parks, tree-lined streets and many early buildings. The local tourist information centre (☎ 4639 3797) is inconveniently located some 1.5km south-east of the centre on James St, at the junction with Kitchener St. It's open weekdays from 8.30 am to 5 pm and weekends from 9 am to 5 pm.

It's odds on that the staff at the centre will direct you to visit sights such as: the **Cobb & Co Museum**, 27 Lindsay St, which has a large collection of old horse-drawn carriages and buggies and is open 10 am to 4 pm daily ($4); the **Toowoomba Regional Art Gallery**, 531 Ruthven St; and the **Ju Raku En Japanese Garden**, a beautiful spot but several kilometres south of the centre at the University of Southern Queensland in West St – you need a car to get there.

The best budget accommodation in town is *Gowrie House (☎ 4632 2642, 112 Mary St)*, with rooms for $20 per person. *Jeffery's Rainforest Motel-Caravan Park (☎ 4635 5999, 864 Ruthven St)*, a couple of kilometres south of the centre, has excellent, modern self-contained singles/doubles from $44/53.

TOOWOOMBA TO ROMA

At **Jondaryan**, 45km west of Toowoomba, you can visit the 1859 Jondaryan Woolshed (☎ 4692 2229), a historic tourist complex with rustic old buildings and daily shearing and blacksmithing demonstrations ($10). There's also a hostel here in authentically spartan shearers' quarters, with beds for $10 and camp sites for $8.

At Miles, 167km further west, the **Miles Historical Village** is also worth a visit; it's open daily from 8 am to 5 pm ($9). There's an information centre at the village with the same opening hours.

There are two caravan parks in town, a pub – the *Hotel Australia (☎ 4627 1106, 55 Murilla St)* – and four motels. The most central motel is the *Golden West Motor Inn (☎ 4627 1688, 50 Murilla St)*, with singles/doubles from $50/64.

ROMA

- postcode 4455   • pop 7000

An early Queensland settlement and now the centre for a huge sheep and cattle-raising district, Roma also has some curious small industries. There's enough oil in the area to support a small refinery, which produces just enough petroleum for local use. Gas deposits are much larger, and Roma supplies Brisbane through a 450km pipeline. The local information centre (☎ 4622 4355) sits in the shadow of the Historic Oil Rig, an authentic drilling rig from the 1920s, at the eastern entrance to town. It's open daily from 9 am to 5 pm.

Fraser Coast

The focal point of this stretch of coast is the majestic Fraser Island – at 120km long it's the world's largest sand island. Hervey Bay, the major access point for the island, has grown into a busy tourist centre, while the southern access point is the sleepy and attractive Rainbow Beach.

Along the Bruce Hwy are the rural centres of Gympie, where you turn off for Rainbow Beach, and Maryborough, where you turn off for Hervey Bay. Further north, Bundaberg is the largest town in the area and mostly famous as the home of the distinctive Bundaberg rum.

GYMPIE
● postcode 4570   ● pop 17,000

Gympie came about as the result of an 1867 gold rush and became one of Queensland's richest goldfields, mined right up until 1920. A week-long Gold Rush Festival is held in Gympie every October. The Country Music Muster in August is also pretty big.

There's a tourist office (☎ 5482 5444) beside the Bruce Hwy on the southern outskirts of town, open daily from 9 am to 4.30 pm. It also incorporates a QPWS office where you can get permits and information for Fraser Island and the Cooloola National Park.

Nearby is the interesting and extensive **Gympie & District Historical & Mining Museum**, open daily from 9 am to 5 pm ($6). A few kilometres north of the town, on Fraser Rd, is the **Woodworks Forestry & Timber Museum**, open weekdays from 9 am to 4 pm ($2.50).

Gympie has several motels and caravan parks, and it's on the main bus and train routes north from Brisbane.

RAINBOW BEACH
● postcode 4581   ● pop 1000

This little settlement on Wide Bay, 70km north-east of Gympie, is the southern access point for Fraser Island and the northern access point for the Great Sandy National Park. The centre of town, which is little more than a cluster of shops, a post office and a caravan park, is on Rainbow Beach road at the point where it stops dead on the clifftops. Down below are kilometres of good beach with few people around, while 1km south-east is the 120m-high **Carlo Sandblow** and beyond it the coloured sand cliffs which gave the town its name.

The privately run Rainbow Beach tourist information centre (☎ 5486 3227), at 8 Rainbow Beach Rd, has a list of walks in the area. In a 4WD it's possible to drive most of the way to Noosa, 70km south, along the beach. See the Cooloola Coast section earlier in this chapter for more details.

From Rainbow Beach it's a 13km drive north along the beach to Inskip Point, where ferries leave for Fraser Island (see Fraser Island later in this section for details).

The place for information on Fraser Island and Great Sandy National Park is the Rainbow Beach information centre, actually the QPWS office (☎ 5486 3160), situated off to the right of the main road as you enter Rainbow Beach. This is also the place to get vehicle and camping permits. It's open daily from 7 am to 4 pm.

Organised Tours
Rainbow Beach Backpackers runs a free trip south along the beach every morning for guests. Surf & Sand Safaris (☎ 5486 3131) runs four-hour 4WD trips south along the beach taking in Double Island Point, the wreck of the *Cherry Venture* and the Coloured Sands for $40 a head. Sun Safari Tours (☎ 5486 3154) runs day trips to Fraser Island costing $65 for adults.

Places to Stay
Rainbow Beach Backpackers (☎ 5486 3288, 66 Rainbow Beach Rd) is the first place on the left as you enter town. It charges from $10 per person in a dorm or $25 for a double, though rooms are sparse and facilities are poor. Camp sites are $5 a head. A more comfortable option is the modern, motel-style *Rocks Backpacker Resort (☎ 1800 646 867)*, on Spectrum St. It's close to the shops, and has a pool, games room and bar with cheap meals. Dorm beds are $12 to $15 in eight-bed dorms and doubles are $35 to $45.

The *Rainbow Beach Holiday Village & Caravan Park (☎ 5486 3222)*, on Rainbow Beach Rd, is a good foreshore camping and caravan park that has a backpackers' section with three-bed cabin-tents for $10 per person. Camp sites start from $14, powered sites from $16, on-site vans from $27 and cabins cost from $50 to $80.

Getting There & Away
Polley's Coaches (☎ 5482 9455), in Gympie, runs bus services between Gympie and Rainbow Beach every weekday. Buses

leave Gympie at 6 am and 1.45 pm, and Rainbow Beach at 7.30 am and 3.45 pm.

Another way to Rainbow Beach is to hitch along the beaches up from Noosa. If you have a 4WD vehicle you can drive this way too.

MARYBOROUGH
• postcode 4650   • pop 26,000

Maryborough's early importance as an industrial centre and port on the Mary River led to the construction of a series of imposing Victorian buildings. The greatest concentration of these is along Wharf St and includes the impressive **post office** (1869).

Maryborough's most interesting feature is the National Trust classified **Brennan & Geraghty's Store**, at 64 Lennox St. This historic store was run by the same family for 100 years and has been preserved intact with original stock, trading records and other fascinating stuff – well worth a look. It is open daily from 10 am to 3 pm ($3).

There are several motels and caravan parks in the town, plus budget accommodation in some of the old hotels.

HERVEY BAY
• postcode 4655   • pop 40,000

The once-sleepy settlement of Hervey Bay has grown at an astronomical rate in the last decade and is now a major stopover on the backpacker circuit. The main attractions are Fraser Island, for which Hervey Bay is the main access point, and whale-watching trips in the bay.

The town consists of five small settlements strung along a north-facing 10km stretch of coast. Of the five areas, Pialba is the main business and shopping centre but Scarness and Torquay have most of the accommodation and eating places.

Fraser Island is 12km across the Great Sandy Strait from Urangan, with Big and Little Woody islands in between. River Heads, the departure point for the main Fraser Island ferries, is 15km south of Urangan – although the Kingfisher foot passenger ferry goes from Urangan harbour, as do the whale-watching boats.

Information
Competition for the tourist dollar is fierce in Hervey Bay, so keep this in mind when seeking information about Fraser Island and whale watching trips. Take your time and shop around to find the trip that suits you.

There are numerous privately run information centres and tour booking offices scattered along the Esplanade. They rent out bikes and provide Internet access, as well as having lots of tour information. They include Hervey Bay Tourist & Visitors Centre (☎ 1800 649 926), at 412 Esplanade and the Fraser Coast Holiday Centre (☎ 1800 627 583), at 463 Esplanade.

If you're driving, drop into Village Pottery (☎ 4124 4987), 63 Old Maryborough Rd in Pialba, on your way into town. Potters Lyn and Joe Edie run a helpful information centre and there's a good cafe next door.

Things to See & Do
The **Hervey Bay Nature World**, near the corner of Maryborough Rd and Fairway Drive in Pialba, has native fauna including wedge-tailed eagles and koalas, and introduced species, such as camels and water buffaloes. It's open daily from 9 am to 5.30 pm ($10).

Vic Hislop's Great White Shark Expo, on the corner of Charlton Esplanade and Elizabeth St in Urangan, has a collection of photos, newspaper articles, jaw bones and three great white sharks kept in a freezer with viewing portals. It also continuously screens a couple of shark documentaries. The centre is open daily from 8.30 am to 6 pm ($10; $8 for backpackers).

Urangan Pier, a little further along Charlton Esplanade, is 1.4km long. Once used for sugar and oil handling, it's now a popular fishing spot.

One kilometre east of the pier at Dayman Point is **Neptune's Reef World**, a small and old-fashioned aquarium with coral displays, fish, seals, turtles and a shark. There are touch tanks where turtles and stingrays can be petted, a seal display at 10.30 am and shark feeding at 3 pm. It is open every day from 9.30 am ($12). From the point, there are good views over to Woody and Fraser islands.

QUEENSLAND

The Whales of Hervey Bay

Up to 3000 humpbacks enter the waters of Hervey Bay every year on the return leg of their annual migration, during which they swim some 5000km from Antarctic waters up to the warmer waters off eastern Australia. They come in clusters of two or three (known as pods) with the numbers usually peaking in early September.

No-one is quite sure why the whales make the diversion into the bay, but one theory is that it might be a kind of pit stop that gives the whales a chance to rest up after a stressed period of birthing and mating. A few weeks in the calm, warm waters may also give the new calves more time to develop the protective layers of blubber necessary for survival in the icy Antarctic waters.

The rest and recovery theory certainly seems to be borne out by the behaviour of the whales, who are positively playful some days. It's not uncommon for the animals to swim up to boats and cruise alongside within touching distance of the excited, camera-wielding whale-spotters on board. Often one great eye will be clear of the water, raising the question of who is actually watching whom?

ANN JEFFREE

Diver's Mecca (☎ 1800 351 626), at 403 Esplanade, has a cheap PADI open water **diving course** for $149 that includes four boat dives (two around shipwrecks).

Organised Tours

Boat tours to watch the humpback whales on their annual migration operate out of Hervey Bay every day, weather permitting, between mid-July and late October. Sightings are guaranteed from August 1 to November 1. Which boat you go with depends on what kind of experience you want. The smaller boats take between 32 and 50 passengers and tend to go out twice a day for four hours each time, once in the early morning and once in the afternoon; the sea tends to be calmer in the first part of the day. Prices for half-day tours are $50 to $75 with substantial reductions for children. We recommend the MV *Seaspray* (☎ 1800 066 404), smallest and fastest of all the whale-watching boats.

The larger boats run full-day trips. This doesn't necessarily mean more time spent with the whales as some of these boats can take two or three hours, or more, to cruise out to Platypus Bay, where the whales swim. Amenities are better though, with most boats including a lunch of some kind and all having a bar. The boat that was most often recommended to us was the MV *Bay Runner* (☎ 4125 3188), which charges $62 for a seven hour trip.

Bookings for boats can be made through your accommodation or one of the information centres.

Places to Stay – Budget

Camping There are at least a dozen caravan parks in Hervey Bay. Some of the best are the council-run *Pialba Caravan Park* (☎ 4128 1399), *Scarness Caravan Park* (☎ 4128 1274) and *Torquay Caravan Park* (☎ 4125 1578), all along the Esplanade. All of these places charge the same rates – camp sites start from $12 and powered sites from $14. These prices increase during the holiday season.

Hostels Hervey Bay has a growing number of backpackers' hostels, spread between Scarness and Urangan. All do pickups from the main bus stop and most organise trips to Fraser Island as well as booking whale-watching tours and other activities.

Many readers have recommended *Fraser Escape Backpackers* (☎ 1800 646 711, 21 Denman Camp Rd) for its good-value accommodation and Fraser Island camping trips. It's a friendly place, with a small pool, a cafe with cheap meals and free bicycle use. A bunk in a six bed dorm in a converted overnight van is $6, $10 per person or $30 a double in a modern cabin with kitchen and bathroom. You can also pitch your tent for $5.

Just up the road, *Olympus Backpacker Villas* (☎ 1800 063 168, 184 Torquay Rd) is a modern hostel with eight two-storey apartments. Each is very spacious, with two bathrooms, balcony, kitchen and TV lounge (dorms $13, twins and doubles $36). On-site facilities include a pool, Internet access, a pool table and video hire.

Next door, the *Friendly Hostel* (☎ 4124 4107, 182 Torquay Rd) is a small, quiet place with three units, each with three bedrooms, a TV lounge, kitchen and bathroom.

The place is spotless and comfortable, and certainly lives up to its name. Beds are $12 per person in a three bed dorm or $14 per person twin-share.

The most partying places are the attractively laid out *Koala Backpackers* (☎ 1800 354 535, 408 Esplanade), across the road from the beach, and the far less appealing *Beaches Hervey Bay Backpackers* (☎ 1800 655 501, 195 Torquay Terrace). Both have pools and bars and have games and entertainment most nights. Rooms at both are no more than adequate – Koala has six-bed dorms for $13 per person, or self-contained twins/doubles for $15 per person. Beaches charges $9 for a place in an eight bed dorm.

The YHA-associated *Colonial Backpackers' Resort* (☎ 4125 1844/1800 818 280), also called the Colonial Log Cabin, is on the corner of Boat Harbour Drive and Pulgul St and is set in 4.5 hectares of bushland. It's near the boat harbour where the whale-watching and some Fraser Island boats depart from. Accommodation is in wooden cabins. Three-bed dorms cost $16 per person for non-YHA members and twins are $19 per person (both with shared facilities). Doubles with en suite and kitchen go for $38. Self-contained cabins cost $50 for two people, but will take up to six people for $8 extra per person. Facilities include an on-site restaurant/bar, two tennis courts, a volleyball court and one of Queensland's few hostel pools large enough to actually swim in.

Boomerang Backpackers (☎ 4124 6911, 335 Esplanade) specialises in doubles and twins with two bedrooms to a unit, each unit with its own kitchen, bathroom and lounge. Rates are $28 per double, or there are some private units where you get the whole thing to yourself for $35 a double. Boomerang also has about 20 dorm beds, which cost from $11 a night.

Other options include *Fraser Magic Backpackers* (☎ 1800 063 168, 369 Esplanade), which, despite being relatively new, is already fairly run-down and has a gloomy atmosphere (dorms $12, doubles $30).

Fraser Lakes Beachside Hostel (☎ 4128 9286, 264 Charles St) is in Hervey Bay's old hospital, a beautiful 100-year-old

QUEENSLAND

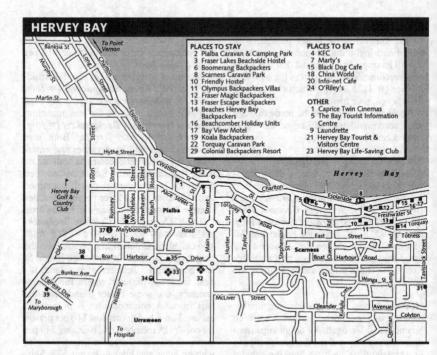

HERVEY BAY

PLACES TO STAY
2 Pialba Caravan & Camping Park
3 Fraser Lakes Beachside Hostel
6 Boomerang Backpackers
8 Scarness Caravan Park
10 Friendly Hostel
11 Olympus Backpackers Villas
12 Fraser Magic Backpackers
13 Fraser Escape Backpackers
14 Beaches Hervey Bay
     Backpackers
16 Beachcomber Holiday Units
17 Bay View Motel
19 Koala Backpackers
22 Torquay Caravan Park
29 Colonial Backpackers Resort

PLACES TO EAT
4 KFC
7 Marty's
15 Black Dog Cafe
18 China World
20 Info-net Cafe
24 O'Riley's

OTHER
1 Caprice Twin Cinemas
5 The Bay Tourist Information
     Centre
9 Laundrette
21 Hervey Bay Tourist &
     Visitors Centre
23 Hervey Bay Life-Saving Club

building with polished wooden floors. Good-value accommodation comprises mostly twins ($8 per person) and doubles with queen-size beds ($10 each). It's a quieter place for those who don't want to party all night.

Motels & Apartments Some of these places offer fantastic value and can work out much cheaper than a hostel, particularly if there's a group of you. *Beachcomber Holiday Units* (☎ 4124 2152, 384 Esplanade) has well-worn, comfortable self-contained units consisting of a double bedroom, bathroom, kitchen and living room with fold-out double bed for $40.

The nearby *Bay View Motel* (☎ 4128 1134, 399 Esplanade) offers similar for the same price, but is a little less homely.

Places to Eat

The *Colonial*, *Koala* and *Beaches* hostels have cheap restaurants. Otherwise, the food focus in Hervey Bay is the Esplanade, in Torquay.

The cheapest deal has to be at *Marty's*, a pub on the corner of the Esplanade and Queens Road: it does a special of a T-bone steak, chips and salad, plus a pot of beer for $6.50. Other meals are served, all in the $6.50 to $8.50 range.

China World (402 Esplanade), on the corner of Tavistock St, has an all-you-can-eat deal for $7 at lunch and $9.50 in the evening. Dishes on the standard menu are also very good, most of which are in the $7.50 to $11.50 range. It's open until 9 pm only.

O'Riley's (446 Esplanade) is a relaxed BYO pancake, pizza and pasta joint with savoury crepes and pasta under $10, large pizzas in the $10.95 to $19.50 range (enough for two) and a range of dessert pancakes from $4 to $6. It is open daily for dinner and on weekends also serves breakfast.

The *Black Dog Cafe*, on the corner of Esplanade and Denman Camp Rd, has some

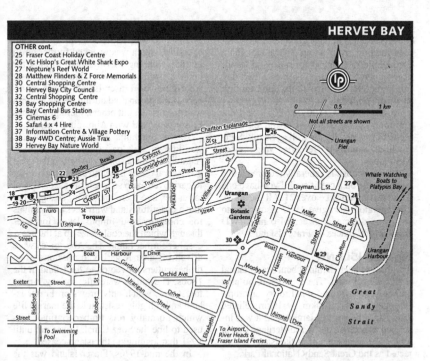

HERVEY BAY

OTHER cont.
25 Fraser Coast Holiday Centre
26 Vic Hislop's Great White Shark Expo
27 Neptune's Reef World
28 Matthew Flinders & Z Force Memorials
30 Central Shopping Centre
31 Hervey Bay City Council
32 Central Shopping Centre
33 Bay Shopping Centre
34 Bay Central Bus Station
35 Cinemas 6
36 Safari 4 x 4 Hire
37 Information Centre & Village Pottery
38 Bay 4WD Centre; Aussie Trax
39 Hervey Bay Nature World

interesting sushi, teriyaki and noodle dishes, mostly under $10. It is closed Tuesday.

For good breakfasts all day, try the *info-net cafe (417 Esplanade)*. It also has plenty of excellent sandwich, pasta and vegetarian options. Dishes are under $10 and Internet use costs $2 for 10 minutes, $4 for 30.

Getting There & Away
Sunstate and Flight West have daily flights between Brisbane and Hervey Bay. The one way fare is $157. Hervey Bay airport is off Booral Rd, Urangan.

Queensland Rail's *Tilt Train* and the *Spirit of Capricorn* both stop at Maryborough West. A bus to Hervey Bay always meets the train. The fare from Brisbane is $37 one way, plus $4.50 for the bus.

Hervey Bay is on a main bus route. It's about 4½ hours from Brisbane ($32 to $38 depending on carrier), and about 5½ hours from Rockhampton ($55). Wide-Bay Transit Coaches (☎ 4121 3719) runs between Maryborough West and Hervey Bay, with nine trips on weekdays and three on Saturday.

Getting Around
Getting around Hervey Bay is a major problem. Distances from the main accommodation areas to the Bay Central bus station and the harbour are prohibitive for walking and there's no decent bus service – Maryborough-Hervey Bay Coaches (☎ 4121 3719) does run local services weekdays and on Saturday mornings, but the buses on each route run at intervals of up to two hours or more. Taxis (☎ 13 1008) are expensive and have to be ordered. If you're staying in a hostel you'll probably be using its courtesy buses, otherwise get a bike – many hostels have them for guests' use, or you can hire them from the tourist information places on the Esplanade for $10 for a half day, $15 for a full day.

4WD The Bay 4WD Centre (☎ 1800 687 178), 54 Boat Harbour Drive in Pialba, and

Safari 4X4 Hire (☎ 1800 689 819), 55 Old Maryborough Rd, have good, reliable vehicles ranging from about $90 a day for a Suzuki Sierra to $130 for a Toyota Landcruiser, which usually involves a two day minimum. Safari also rents out camping kits from $5 a day.

Aussie Trax (☎ 1800 062 275), 56 Boat Harbour Drive, Pialba, has old ex-army jeeps from $90 a day as well as Suzuki Sierras and Landrover Defender Wagons for $130 a day.

A $500 deposit is generally required – this can be made on a credit card if you have one – and drivers must be over 21. All the above hire operators also give 4WD instruction to first-time drivers. You can also hire 4WD from several places on Fraser Island.

FRASER ISLAND

The thing to keep in mind about Fraser Island is that it's all sand. There's no soil, no clay and only two or three small rocky outcrops. It's one gigantic, 120km by 15km foliated sand bar – the world's largest, and it was inscribed as such on the World Heritage List in 1993. The northern half of the island is protected as the Great Sandy National Park.

Fraser Island is a delight for those who love fishing, walking, exploring by 4WD or for those who simply enjoy nature. Some of the sandblows (large drifting dunes) are magnificent, while much of the island is densely forested with an amazing variety of tree and plant types, many of which are only to be found on Fraser Island. There are also about 200 lakes, some of them superb for swimming – which is just as well since the sea is a definite no-go; there are lethal undertows as well as man-eating sharks. Other wildlife is in abundance, including 40 different mammal species and more insects and reptiles than you want to know about.

You can camp on Fraser Island or stay in accommodation. The island is sparsely populated and, although more than 20,000 vehicles a year pile on to it, it remains wild. A network of sandy tracks crisscrosses the island and you can drive along great stretches of beach – but it's 4WD only; there are no paved roads.

History

The island takes its name from the captain of a ship, which was wrecked further north in 1836. Making its way south to look for help, a group from the ship fell among Aborigines on Fraser Island. Some members of the group died during the two month wait for rescue, but others, including James Fraser, survived with Aboriginal help.

To the Butchulla Aborigines, the island was known as K'gari (which translates as 'Paradise') after a spirit who helped the great god Beeral create the earth and other worlds. K'gari loved earth so much she asked Beeral to let her live there and so he changed her into a beautiful island with trees and animals for company and limpid lakes for eyes through which she could gaze up at the heavens, her former home. The Aborigines were driven off their K'gari onto missions when timber cutters moved on to the island in the 1860s. The cutters were after satinay, a rainforest tree, which only grows on Fraser Island and is highly resistant to the marine life which normally rots timber. Satinay was used to line the Suez Canal. It was not until 1991 that logging on the island ceased.

In the mid-1970s, Fraser Island was the subject of a bitter struggle between conservationists and industry – in this case a sand-mining company. The decision went to the conservationists.

Information

There's a visitors centre on the east coast of the island, at Eurong (☎ 4127 9128), and ranger's offices at Dundubara and Waddy Point. These places all have plenty of leaflets detailing walking trails and the flora and fauna found on the island.

At Central station (the old forestry depot) there's a small display on the history of exploration and logging on the island.

General supplies are available from stores at Eurong, Happy Valley and Cathedral Beach, but as you might expect, prices are high. There are also public telephones at these sites.

Permits You'll need a permit to take a vehicle onto the island and another to camp.

The most convenient place to get permits is the River Heads general store (which also sells sensational home-made pies), just half a kilometre from the ferry to Wanggoolba Creek. Vehicle permits cost $30, or $40 if the permit is purchased on the island. Camping costs $3.50 per person per night – you don't need to pay this if you're staying in cabin accommodation or camping in one of the island's private camping grounds.

Permits can also be obtained from the EPA offices in the area (Rainbow Beach, Maryborough and Gympie included), or from the Hervey Bay City Council (☎ 4125 0222), in Tavistock St, Torquay.

Things to See & Do

Starting from the south at Hook Point, you cross a number of creeks to get to Dilli Village, the former sand-mining centre, and beyond that Eurong. Four kilometres beyond Eurong is a signposted walking trail to the beautiful **Lake Wabby**, possibly the highlight of the island. The deepest of Fraser Island's lakes, it's surrounded on three sides by eucalypt forest while on the other is a massive sandblow whose steep slope crashes into the lake. From the beach, Lake Wabby is a 45 minute walk (rewarded by a swim in the lake), or you can drive a further 2.6km north along the beach to take a scenic route up to a lookout on the inland side of the lake – this is well worth doing as the lake seen from the lookout is spectacular.

A popular inland area for visitors is the south-central lake and rainforest country around Central station and McKenzie, Birrabeen and Boomanjin lakes. **Lake McKenzie** is unbelievably clear. Known as a 'window' lake, the water is part of the water table, and so has not flowed over land. It's a wildly disorienting experience to snorkel here, to look down through a face mask and then suddenly have the bottom drop away to a depth of 15m and yet still be visible.

Two signposted vehicle tracks lead inland from Happy Valley: one goes to **Lake Gara-wongera**, then south to the beach again at Poyungan Valley (15km); the other heads to **Yidney Scrub** and some lakes before returning to the ocean beach north of the wreck of

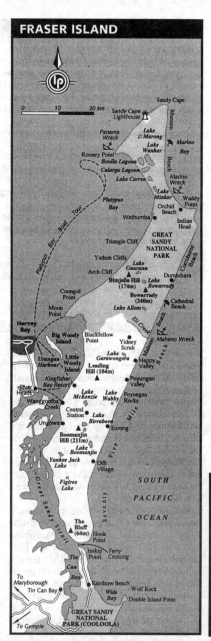

FRASER ISLAND

QUEENSLAND

Stay Close to Your Children

There are a lot of attractions on Fraser Island. The biggest one for dingoes is campers who leave their belongings and food scattered around. Then there are the idiots who coo 'nice doggie' as they hold out food for the dingoes.

Let's face it – dingoes aren't stupid. Especially the Fraser Island dingoes – the purest examples of Australia's native dog. They are cunning wild animals looking for opportunities to scavenge what they can from humans. It sure beats eating swamp wallabies, their natural prey here.

Signs on the island display warnings including a picture of a dingo with the caption:

'If you are not dingo-smart, I could become threatening, which you think is aggression, and I could be killed. Please don't do this to me!'

The signs also read: 'Enjoy the beauty of dingoes, but keep your distance and always stay close to your children'.

Unfortunately, the message doesn't always get through, and we heard some horror stories about careless visitors getting mauled by packs of dingoes. Probably the best advice is in the letter we received below:

You should warn people NOT TO FEED and NOT TO PLAY with the DINGOES. This has been happening and recently the wild dogs have become increasingly brazen, stalking people in packs. Children are at risk of being attacked. It's a beautiful place, but make sure you carry a big stick.

Andrew Kane

the *Maheno* (45km). The latter route will take you to some fine lakes and good lookout points among the highest dunes on the island.

After the settlements of Eurong and Happy Valley, you cross **Eli Creek**, the largest stream on the east coast. Wooden boardwalks go 400m up the creek and it's pleasant to enter the water up here and drift back down to the beach. About 65km from Hook Point are the remains of the *Maheno*, a former passenger liner blown ashore here by a typhoon in 1935 as it was being towed to a Japanese scrapyard.

Not far north of Happy Valley you enter the national park and pass the **Cathedrals**, 25km of coloured sand cliffs. Dundubara has a ranger's hut and probably the best camping ground on the island. Then there's a 20km stretch of beach before you come to the rock outcrop of **Indian Head**, the best vantage point on the island. Climb up onto the headland and scan the waters below for sharks, manta rays, dolphins and, in season, whales further out.

Beyond Indian Head are Middle Rocks, Waddy Point and **Orchid Beach**, and it's a further 30km of beach up to **Sandy Cape**, the northern tip, with its lighthouse a few more kilometres to the west.

Organised Tours

While the freedom that comes with racking your own (rented) 4WD over tree stumps and thundering along beaches at low tide is extremely satisfying, the major part of Fraser Island's allure is its geology, plantlife and animals. It takes someone who knows their stuff to bring it to life. Several operators offer one, two or three-day tours led by well-informed guides. (See also the Noosa and Rainbow Beach sections earlier in this chapter for tours from those places.)

Top Tours (☎ 1800 063 933) and Fraser Venture Day Tours (☎ 4125 4444) do day trips to Fraser Island for $70. Kingfisher Bay (☎ 1800 072 555) is slightly more expensive with tours at $85 for adults and

$45 for children. Each outfit follows a different route, but a typical tour, conducted in a hulking 4WD bus with a ranger guide, might take in a trip up the east coast to the *Maheno* wreck and the Cathedrals, plus Central station and a couple of the lakes in the centre of the island. Most day tours to Fraser Island allow you to split the trip and stay a few days on the island before coming back.

Air Fraser Island (☎ 4125 3600) flies out of Hervey Bay airport and lands on the island's east coast beach. You can do a day trip for $35 per person (once down you're left to amuse yourself for the day until it's time to fly back), or for $85 per person a day's hire of a 4WD is included; there are also two-day tours for around $150 per person, which includes return flights, a tent and one day's 4WD hire.

Top Tours has a two day trip for $150, including a night's accommodation at Happy Valley. Fraser Venture Tours offers a similar trip, with a night at the Eurong Beach Resort for $145, or a three day tour for $195. In both cases accommodation is four-share and a sleeping bag is required.

Kingfisher Bay also has a three day 'Cool Dingo Wilderness Adventure'. This is the one that we tried out and we can wholeheartedly recommend it. It takes in all the island's major sites and includes opportunities for bush walking, swimming and snorkelling. The $245 package also includes three meals a day (the breakfast is fantastic), twin or quad accommodation and use of all facilities at the luxury Kingfisher Bay Resort.

For backpackers, self-drive tours to Fraser Island organised by the Hervey Bay backpackers' hostels are popular and cost around $105 per person for a three day trip. This doesn't include food or fuel but all the gear is organised for you. These trips are an affordable and (usually) fun way to see the island, but you'll probably be in a group of eight and, like relatives, you can't choose who you go with.

Fraser Escape 4x4 Tours (☎ 1800 646 711) offers self-drive, guided tours, where backpackers do the driving and the guides

tag along. At $180 per person all-inclusive, it's good value, especially when a $105 self-guided tour usually ends up costing around $160 when you add food, permits, fuel and camping gear.

Sand Island Safaris (☎ 1800 246 911) offers a three day guided tour for $215 with accommodation at Eurong Beach Resort. Tours leave Hervey Bay every Tuesday and Friday.

Places to Stay & Eat
Come well equipped since supplies on the island are limited and only available in a few places. Be prepared for mosquitoes and horseflies.

The QPWS and Forestry Department operate 11 *camping grounds* on the island, some accessible only by boat or on foot. Those in the north at Dundubara, Waddy Point and Wathumba and in the south at Central station, Lake Boomanjin and Lake McKenzie have toilets and showers. You can also camp on some stretches of beach. To camp in any of these public areas you need a permit.

The *Dilli Village Recreation Camp* (☎ 4127 9130) is 200m from the east coast and 24km from Hook Point. A four bed cabin with shower and kitchen costs $45 per night, or there are cabins without kitchens or bathrooms for $10 per person. You can also camp here for $3 per person.

The *Cathedral Beach Resort & Camping Park* (☎ 4127 9177) is 34km north of Eurong. Camp sites cost $20 for two people and cabins cost $95 for up to four people – note that they don't take backpacker groups here.

Just south of Happy Valley, the low-key *Yidney Rocks Cabins* (☎ 4127 9167) is right on the edge of the beach. The cabins are old but comfortable; the nightly rate is $65 for up to six people or $80 for up to eight. The recently upgraded *Eurong Beach Resort* (☎ 4127 9122), 35km north of Hook Point on the east coast, has beds in four-bunk cabins for $12 or A-frame cottages for $90 for four people plus $5 per extra person (maximum eight). There are also more expensive motel units and two-bedroom apartments. Day-trippers and campers are welcome in the restaurant. The $10 lunch buffet is good value (for Fraser Island that is).

The **Fraser Island Retreat** (*☎ 4127 9144*), at Happy Valley, has good self-contained timber lodges for $160/175 a night for doubles/triples and a family lodge for $195.

The impressive and luxurious **Kingfisher Bay Resort** (*☎ 1800 072 555*), on the west coast, has 'Wilderness Cabins', which contain a refrigerator, a dining area, bathrooms and four quad rooms plus one twin from $30 per person. There are also hotel rooms from $225 per double, two-bedroom villas for four/five people from $750 for three nights, and three-bedroom villas for six from $960 for three nights. The resort has restaurants, bars and shops and, architecturally, it's worth a look even if you're not staying here. There's also a day-trippers' section near the jetty, with the Sandbar bar and brasserie.

Getting There & Away

Vehicle ferries (known locally as barges) operate between the southern end of Fraser Island and Inskip Point, north of Rainbow Beach, and between the west coast of the island and River Heads, south of Urangan. The *Rainbow Venture* (*☎ 5486 3227*) makes the 10 minute crossing from Inskip Point to Hook Point on Fraser Island regularly each day from about 7 am to 4.30 pm. The price is $55 return for a vehicle and driver, plus $1 per passenger, and you can get tickets on board. Walk-on passengers pay $10.

The *Fraser Venture* (*☎ 4125 4444*) makes the 30 minute crossing from River Heads to Wanggoolba Creek on the west coast of Fraser Island. It departs daily from River Heads at 9 and 10.15 am and 3.30 pm. It returns from the island at 9.30 am and 2.30 and 4 pm. On Saturday there is also a 7 am service from River Heads, which returns at 7.30 am from the island. The barge takes 27 vehicles, but booking is advisable. The return fare for vehicle and driver is $60, plus $3 for each extra passenger. Walk-on passengers pay $12 return.

The Kingfisher Bay Resort (*☎ 4125 5155*) also operates two boats. The vehicle barge does the 45 minute crossing from River Heads to Kingfisher Bay daily. Departures from River Heads are at 7.15 and 11 am and 2.30 pm, and from the island at 8.30 am and 1.30 and 4 pm. The return fare is $65 for a vehicle and driver, plus $5 for extra people.

The *Kingfisher 2 Fastcat* is a passenger catamaran that crosses from the Urangan boat harbour to Kingfisher Bay daily at 8.30 am, noon and 4 and 6 pm, for a return fare of $30. Ask about the 'Day Away' package – good value because it includes lunch for the same price.

There's also a ferry, the *Fraser Dawn*, from Urangan to Moon Point on the island, but this is an inconvenient place to land as it's a long drive across to the other side.

Getting Around

The only thing stopping you taking a conventional (non-4WD) vehicle onto the island is that you probably won't get more than half a kilometre before you get bogged in sand. Small 4WD sedans are OK, but you may have ground-clearance problems on some of the inland tracks – a 'proper' 4WD gives maximum mobility.

Some of the hostels tell travellers that the only way to get to and around Fraser Island is on one of their trips. Not true. If you'd rather do your own thing, you could quite easily get a group together. A 4WD and camping gear can be hired from various places, permits are readily available and ferries are frequent.

When you hire a 4WD, make sure the hire operators are members of the Fraser Coast 4WD association. They ensure vehicles are well maintained and give you an avenue of complaint if something goes wrong.

A 4WD can be hired on the mainland (see the Hervey Bay section earlier in this chapter) or on the island (around $175 a day) through Kingfisher Bay 4WD Hire (*☎ 4120 3366*), Happy Valley 4WD Hire (*☎ 4127 9260*) and Shorty's Off Road Rentals (*☎ 4127 9122*), at Eurong.

Driving on the island requires a good deal of care to protect yourself and the fragile environment. Plan your trip reckoning on covering roughly 20km an hour on

CHRIS MELLOR

Botanic Gardens, Brisbane, Qld

CHRIS MELLOR

Brisbane Town Hall, Qld

ROSS BARNETT

The Brisbane River reflects the lights of the city, Qld

MITCH REARDON

There are no rose gardens on a Queensland cattle station

Noosa from Laguna Lookout, Qld

Stockman's Hall of Fame, Longreach, Qld

Making progress, Simpson Desert, Qld

Frilled lizard championships, Eulo, Qld

inland tracks and 50km an hour on the eastern beach.

CHILDERS
● postcode 4660   ● pop 1560

Childers, a historic township on the Bruce Hwy, has quite a few pretty Victorian-era buildings. The town is also the turn-off for the lovely Woodgate Beach and Woodgate National Park.

The *Palace Backpackers Hostel* (☎ 4126 2244, 72 Churchill St), in the centre of Childers, is a converted historic two storey pub. It's a workers' hostel geared to fruit picking and the management will find guests work. The facilities are good, with a big communal kitchen, walk-in fridge, big TV room, games and clean showers. All beds cost $14 per night or $90 per week, including transport to and from work. We've had reports about rent disputes here, so make sure you receive a receipt when you pay.

BUNDABERG
● postcode 4670   ● pop 44,000

Bundaberg attracts a steady stream of travellers looking for harvest work, picking everything from avocados to zucchinis, and the hostels here can often help you find work – but ring before you come to check on the work situation. It's a reasonably attractive town 15km inland from the coast, most famous for its Bundaberg rum, as the southernmost access point for the Great Barrier Reef and departure point for Lady Elliot and Lady Musgrave islands.

Orientation & Information
The excellent Bundaberg tourist information centre (☎ 1800 060 499) is on Bourbong St, the town's main drag, about 1km west of the centre. It's open daily from 9 am to 5 pm. The Cosy Corner Internet Cafe, in Barolin St opposite the post office, is open daily and charges from $2 for 15 minutes.

Things to See
The main thing everybody does here is take a tour of the **Bundaberg Rum Distillery** (☎ 4150 8684), on Avenue St in East Bundaberg, about 2km east of the town centre.

Mon Repos Turtle Rookery

Australia's most accessible turtle rookery is at Mon Repos Beach, 15km north-east of Bundaberg. Four types of turtle – loggerhead, green, flatback and leatherback – have been known to nest here, but it's predominantly the loggerhead that lays its eggs here. The rookery is unusual, since turtles generally prefer sandy islands off the coast. The nesting season runs from early November through to the end of March, and you're most likely to see the turtles laying their eggs at about midnight when the tide is high. From mid-January to March, the young begin to emerge and make their way quickly to the sea. Observation of the turtles is controlled by the QPWS Information Centre (☎ 4159 2628), which is open daily during the season from 7 pm to 6 am; entry costs $4.

During the season, the QPWS operates a 24-hour hotline (☎ 4159 1652) with recorded information about the turtles.

KATE NOLAN

Tours are run weekdays between 10 am and 3 pm and weekends till 2 pm ($5), and include a sample of the product.

Bundaberg's attractive **Botanic Gardens** is 2km north of the centre on Gin Gin Rd. Within the gardens reserve are rose gardens, walking paths, a historical museum and **Hinkler House Museum**, dedicated to the life of the aviator Bert Hinkler, who was born in Bundaberg and in 1928 made the first solo flight between England and Australia. Hinkler's former home was transported here from Southampton, England, and rebuilt to house a collection of memorabilia and information on the aviation pioneer. Nearby is the

Bundaberg & District Historical Museum.
Both museums are open daily from 10 am to
4 pm, and both charge $2.50 admission.

Activities

Salty's (☎ 1800 625 476), at 200 Bourbong
St, and Bundaberg Aqua Scuba (☎ 4153
5761), on Targo St next to the bus station,
offer PADI open-water diving courses for
$149, including four shore dives. Bargara
Beach Dive (☎ 4159 2663), in Bargara,
13km from town, offers a course including
four boat dives for $225.

Places to Stay & Eat

All of the hostels in Bundaberg specialise in
finding harvesting work for travellers. They
all offer discounts for weekly stays, but
make sure that you will find work before
forking out lots of rent – a week in Bundaberg is a long time if you're not working.

The *Bundaberg Backpackers & Travellers Lodge* (☎ 4152 2080), on the corner
of Targo and Crofton Sts, is diagonally opposite the bus terminal. It's clean and modern with a friendly atmosphere; a bed in a
four bed dorm costs $18 a night, including
transport to and from work.

Another good option is the *Nomads
Bundaberg Workers and Diving Hostel*
(☎ 4151 1422, 64 Barolin St), an old Queenslander with motel units out the back. It's a
friendly place offering a free, light breakfast,
a pool and colour TV. Dorm beds cost $17 a
night and doubles and twins $18 per person.

City Centre Backpackers (☎ 4151 3501,
216 Bourbong St), in the former Grosvenor
Hotel, has two sections: three to eight-bed
bunk rooms upstairs and six-bed motel units
out the back. Bunk beds cost $13 or a bed
in one of the motel units costs $15. It also
has three doubles for $32.

Across the road is *Federal Guesthouse*
(☎ 4153 3711, 221 Bourbong St), in a big,
old, wooden building leased from the pub
downstairs. While it has plenty of character
it's also extremely dirty and facilities are
poor. Dorms in a room with 10 beds are $14
or $15 in a room with four beds.

The *Lyelta Lodge & Motel* (☎ 4151
3344, 8 Maryborough St) has motel-style

rooms for $34 and a guesthouse section
with singles/doubles with shared bathrooms
for $25/30.

For a cheap pub feed, head for the refurbished (downstairs anyway) *Grand Hotel*,
on the corner of Bourbong and Targo Sts, or
the *Club Hotel*, on the corner of Bourbong
and Tanotitha Sts. The Club Hotel has a
small garden dining area entered off Tanotitha St. Both places do basic dishes like
roasts and chops for $5, served noon to 2
pm. The Grand Hotel also has a surprisingly good coffee bar.

Numero Uno (163 Bourbong St) is a
popular Italian bistro with good pastas
under $12, pizzas under $10 and mains
from $12 to $15.

Getting There & Away

Air services are by Sunstate (daily from
Brisbane, Gladstone, Rockhampton,
Mackay and Townsville) and Flight West
(daily from Brisbane and Gladstone). The
one way Brisbane-Bundaberg fare is $200.

The main bus stop is Stewart's coach terminal (☎ 4153 2646), at 66 Targo St. One-
way bus fares from Bundaberg include
Brisbane ($43), Hervey Bay ($19), Rockhampton ($42) and Gladstone ($33).

Bundaberg is also a stop for trains between Brisbane and Rockhampton or
Cairns.

Capricorn Coast

This central coastal area of Queensland
takes its name from its position straddling
the Tropic of Capricorn. Rockhampton is
the major population centre in the area, and
just off the coast lies Great Keppel Island, a
popular getaway. Offshore from Gladstone
are the Southern Reef Islands, the southernmost part of the Great Barrier Reef,
while south of Gladstone are the laid-back
townships of Agnes Water and Town of
1770, the state's northernmost surf beach.

Inland, the Capricorn hinterland has the
fascinating gem fields region and the spectacular Carnarvon and Blackdown Tableland national parks.

SOUTHERN REEF ISLANDS

The southernmost part of the Great Barrier Reef, known as the Capricornia section, begins 80km north-east of Bundaberg around Lady Elliot Island. The coral reefs and cays in this group dot the ocean for about 140km up to Tryon Island east of Rockhampton.

Several cays in this part of the reef are excellent for snorkelling, diving and just getting back to nature – though reaching them is generally more expensive than reaching islands nearer the coast. Access is from Bundaberg, Gladstone or Rosslyn Bay near Rockhampton. A few islands are

important breeding grounds for turtles and sea birds.

On the four national park islands where camping is allowed (Lady Musgrave, Masthead, Tryon and North West), campers must be totally self-sufficient. Numbers of campers are limited, so it's advisable to apply well ahead for a camping permit. You can book six months ahead for these islands instead of the usual six to 12 weeks for other Queensland national parks. Contact the QPWS (☎ 4972 6055) in Gladstone. If you get a permit you'll also receive information on any rules, such as restrictions on

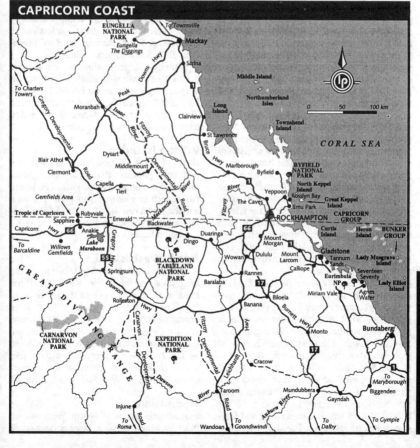

CAPRICORN COAST

the use of generators and how to avoid harming the wildlife.

Lady Elliot Island

Eighty kilometres north-east of Bundaberg, Lady Elliot Island is a 0.4 sq km vegetated coral cay at the southern end of the Great Barrier Reef. It is very popular with divers and snorkellers, and has the advantages of superb diving straight off the beach, as well as numerous shipwrecks, coral gardens, bommies and blowholes to explore. The *Lady Elliot Island Resort* (☎ 1800 072 200) is the only accommodation. It has basic tent-cabins and timber lodges costing $75 per person for two or three people or $59 per person for four, and more expensive motel-style Reef Units ($145 per person). For breakfast, lunch and dinner, add $49 per person.

Whitaker Air Charters flies guests to the resort for $145 return. From Bundaberg or Hervey Bay, you can pay $185 for a day trip, which includes the flight, lunch and snorkelling gear etc.

Lady Musgrave Island

This 0.15 sq km cay in the Bunker Group is an uninhabited national park about 100km north-east of Bundaberg. The island sits at the western end of a huge lagoon, which offers some excellent snorkelling and diving opportunities. There's a national park *camping ground* on the western side of the island, but there are no facilities apart from bush toilets. Campers – a maximum of 50 at any one time – must be totally self-sufficient. You'll need to bring your own drinking water and a gas or fuel stove.

The MV *Lady Musgrave* (☎ 1800 072 110) operates day trips from Port Bundaberg marina daily (except Friday/Sunday) at 8.30 am. The cost is $114, which includes government tax, lunch, snorkelling gear and a glass bottomed-boat ride. The trip takes 2½ hours and you have about four hours on the island.

The MV *Spirit of 1770* (☎ 4974 9077) has day trips to Lady Musgrave Island from the Town of 1770 (90 minutes to get there, six hours on the island) costing $110 for adults, with lunch and snorkelling and fishing gear. Cruises depart Tuesday, Thursday,

Saturday and Sunday at 8 am – more often during holiday periods. It also does camping drop-offs for $100 per person one way (including lunch), and rents out camping gear and dinghies.

Heron Island

Only 1km long and 0.17 sq km in area, Heron Island is 72km east of Gladstone. The *Heron Island Resort* (☎ 4978 1488), owned by P&O, covers the north-eastern third of the island; the rest is national park but you can't camp there. The resort has room for more than 250 people, with nightly tariffs ranging from $165 per person in the bunk rooms to $224 per person in the suites, including all meals – though there are cheaper stand-by rates. There are no day trips – resort guests pay another $150 return in the *Reef Adventurer* fast catamaran from Gladstone.

Although large sections of coral have been killed by silt as a result of dredging for a new, longer jetty at the island, Heron Island is still something of a mecca for divers. The resort offers lots of dive facilities and trips and has its own dive school.

Wilson Island

North of Heron, Wilson Island is a national park and a popular day trip for Heron guests looking for a break from diving. The island has superb snorkelling and great beaches, and the resort runs day trips for $45 including a good barbecue lunch. There is no accommodation.

North West Island

At 0.9 sq km, North West Island is the biggest cay on the Barrier Reef. It's all national park, and it is one of the major nesting sites for green turtles, with nesting occurring between November and February. It's a popular destination for campers, but there's a limit of 150 people and you must be totally self-sufficient (including a fuel stove). Book with the Department of Environment office (☎ 4972 6055) in Gladstone.

Tryon Island

Immediately north of North West Island, this tiny, beautiful, six hectare national park is another important nesting area for sea birds and green turtles. There is a camping ground but the island is currently closed to visitors to allow for revegetation. Check with the Department of Environment office in Gladstone (☎ 4972 6055) for the latest.

AGNES WATER & TOWN OF 1770

• postcode 4677   • pop 2000

These two coastal towns are among the state's less commercialised seaside destinations. Fast-growing Agnes Waters boasts the northernmost surf beach in Queensland, while the Town of 1770 is perhaps the most beautiful and tranquil spot on the whole south-east Queensland coast. There are few shops here, just one pub, a couple of caravan parks and a few cabins and B&Bs. Most people come here for the fishing or boating, or to visit the neighbouring national parks. Things do get a little hectic at Christmas and Easter and you'll need to book ahead to secure accommodation at these times.

Access is from Miriam Vale, on the Bruce Hwy, or south from Bundaberg. All the roads are now sealed.

The Discovery Centre (☎ 4974 7002) is a helpful, privately run information centre in Agnes Waters, at the turn-off to the Town of 1770. It's open daily from 8.30 am to 5 pm, later during busy periods.

1770 Environmental Tours (☎ 4974 9422), at the marina on Captain Cook Drive, runs enjoyable trips in its LARCs (large amphibious vehicles) *Sir Joseph Banks* and *Dr PC Solander*. It does full-day environmental tours of Round Hill Creek, Bustard Head and Eurimbula National Park. Tours operate on Wednesday and Saturday (more often during the peak season) and cost $80.

Places to Stay

The *Agnes Water Caravan Park* (☎ 4974 9193), on Jeffery Court on the foreshore, has camp sites from $10 and cabins from $40, while the riverfront *Seventeen Seventy Camping Ground* (☎ 4974 9286) has sites for $14, but no on-site vans. The *Captain Cook Holiday Village* (☎ 4974 9219), on Captain Cook Drive, is another excellent camping and caravan park in a great bush setting, 300m from the beach. Camp sites cost $12 and backpacker beds $15. There are also self-contained timber bungalows and cabins that sleep up to seven people.

Four kilometres inland from Agnes Water, *Hoban's Hideaway* (☎ 4974 9144, 2510 Round Hill Rd) is a friendly, well-run B&B in an attractive, colonial-style timber homestead. The guests' section contains three immaculately presented double bedrooms with en suites, a loungeroom, a dining room, an outdoor patio, a barbecue area and pool. Singles/doubles cost $85/95, including breakfast.

Getting There & Away

Barbours Bus & Coach (☎ 4974 9030) runs from Agnes Water to and from Bundaberg every Monday and Thursday. It leaves Endeavour Plaza in Agnes Water at 7.35 am and departs from the Barolin St Post Office in Bundaberg at 2 pm. The fare is $15 one way or $20 return.

GLADSTONE

• postcode 4680   • pop 39,000

Twenty kilometres off the Bruce Hwy, Gladstone is one of the busiest ports in Australia, handling agricultural, mineral and coal exports from central Queensland. From a visitor's point of view though, it's a pretty dull place. The town's otherwise attractive estuary setting is marred by a scattering of industrial plants.

Gladstone's marina is the main departure point for boats to Heron, Mast Head and Wilson islands on the Great Barrier Reef.

The Gladstone visitor information centre (☎ 4972 9922), at the marina, is open on weekdays from 8.30 am to 5 pm and on weekends from 9 am to 5 pm. The EPA office (☎ 4972 6055) is a good source of information. It's open for business at Level 3 in the Centrepoint building, 136 Goondoon St, on weekdays from 8.30 am to 5 pm.

Gladstone Backpackers (☎ 4972 5744, 12 Rollo St) is a small, extremely friendly place close to the marina and the town's main street. The owner, Bob, is the local QPWS snake catcher and he usually has a

QUEENSLAND

reptile or two in the garage. Dorms have three or four beds which go for $15 a night; doubles are $35. The hostel offers free use of bicycles and will pick up guests from the bus stop, train station or marina.

Most coast buses stop at Gladstone and it's on the Brisbane to Rockhampton rail route. You can also fly there with Sunstate or Flight West.

ROCKHAMPTON
● postcode 4700   ● pop 57,500

Rockhampton, the administrative and commercial centre of central Queensland, sits astride the Tropic of Capricorn, marking the beginning of the tropical north. The city was founded as a port in 1855 and there was a small, early gold rush, but cattle soon became the big industry and today Rockhampton regards itself as the 'beef capital' of Australia.

Rockhampton has several tourist attractions, including a good art gallery, an Aboriginal cultural centre and excellent parks and gardens, but it is mainly an access point for Great Keppel Island – boats leave from Rosslyn Bay about 50km away. Nearby are the spectacular limestone caves in the Berserker Range to the north, the old gold-mining town of Mt Morgan (38km south-west), the Koorana Crocodile Farm near Emu Park, and the very popular Myella Farm Stay (see Around Rockhampton later in this chapter).

Orientation

Rockhampton is about 40km from the coast, straddling Queensland's largest river, the Fitzroy. The long Fitzroy Bridge connects the old downtown area with the newer suburbs to the north.

The Bruce Hwy skirts the town centre and crosses the river upstream from the Fitzroy Bridge.

Information

The Capricorn Information Centre (☎ 4927 2055) is on the highway 3km south of the centre, beside the Tropic of Capricorn marker. More convenient is the helpful Rockhampton Information Centre (☎ 4922 5339), in the impressive old Customs House on Quay St. It's open weekdays from 8.30

am to 4.30 pm and weekends from 9 am to 4 pm. The EPA office (☎ 4936 0511) is 7km north of the centre on the Yeppoon road.

Things to See

There are some fine old buildings in town that date back to the gold-rush days, particularly on Quay St. You can pick up tourist leaflets that map out town walking trails.

The **Rockhampton City Art Gallery**, on Victoria Parade, is open on weekdays from 10 am to 4 pm and on Sunday from 2 to 4 pm (free). On the Bruce Hwy, 6km north of the centre, is the **Dreamtime Cultural Centre** (☎ 4936 1655), an Aboriginal heritage display centre. It's open daily from 10 am to 3.30 pm, with tours at 10.30 am and 2 pm ($11/5 adults/children). The impressive **Botanic Gardens**, on Spencer St in the south of the city, were established in 1869 and have an excellent tropical collection and a small and poorly-maintained zoo (free). North of the centre the **Kershaw Gardens** has a good collection of Australian native plants.

Get-About Tours (☎ 4934 8247) offers town tours including the Botanic Gardens and Dreamtime centre, and trips to the Berserker Range, Mt Morgan and the Koorana Crocodile Farm (from $54).

Places to Stay

Camping The small *Municipal Riverside Caravan Park* (☎ 4922 3779), in Reaney St just across the bridge from the city centre, has camp sites for $11.50. The pleasant *Southside Holiday Village* (☎ 4927 3013), across the Bruce Hwy from the Capricorn Information Centre, offers camp sites from $13 and on-site cabins from $35.

Hostels The *Rockhampton City YHA* (☎ 4927 5288, 60 MacFarlane St) is close to the McCafferty's bus terminal (Greyhound will also drop you nearby), and it has good facilities and a friendly atmosphere. Six-bed dorms cost $16/18 and twins $17/20 for members/nonmembers, and there is a spacious lounge and kitchen. The hostel is a 20 minute walk north of the centre, but it does courtesy pickups from the McCafferty's, Greyhound and train stations. You can

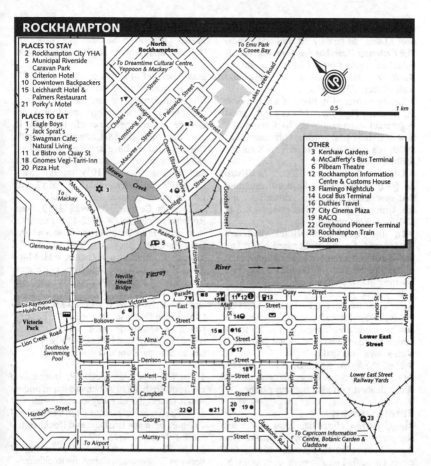

ROCKHAMPTON

PLACES TO STAY
2 Rockhampton City YHA
5 Municipal Riverside Caravan Park
8 Criterion Hotel
10 Downtown Backpackers
15 Leichhardt Hotel & Palmers Restaurant
21 Porky's Motel

PLACES TO EAT
1 Eagle Boys
7 Jack Sprat's
9 Swagman Cafe; Natural Living
11 Le Bistro on Quay St
18 Gnomes Vegi-Tarri-Inn
20 Pizza Hut

OTHER
3 Kershaw Gardens
4 McCafferty's Bus Terminal
6 Pilbeam Theatre
12 Rockhampton Information Centre & Customs House
13 Flamingo Nightclub
14 Local Bus Terminal
16 Duthies Travel
17 City Cinema Plaza
19 RACQ
22 Greyhound Pioneer Terminal
23 Rockhampton Train Station

book the popular YHA hostel on Great Keppel Island here.

Downtown Backpackers (☎ 4922 1837), on the corner of East and Denham Sts (above the Oxford Hotel), is fairly basic, but it's central and cheap. The cost in dorms or twins is $13.50 per person – inquire at the hotel.

Hotels & Motels On Quay St beside the Fitzroy Bridge, the *Criterion Hotel* (☎ 4922 1225) is one of Rockhampton's most magnificent old buildings. Budget single/double rooms with shared bathroom cost $21/36 and period-style suites are $46/50 with air-con.

At the top end of the local hotels, the *Leichhardt Hotel* (☎ 4927 6733), on the corner of Denham and Bolsover Sts, has plush modern rooms from $99 a double.

Porky's Motel (☎ 4927 8100, 141 George St) is quite central and, despite the dodgy name, has respectable rooms for $39/44, plus $8 for each extra adult. You'll find dozens of motels on the Bruce Hwy as you come into Rockhampton from either the north or south.

Places to Eat
The *Swagman Cafe* (8 Denham St) does cooked breakfasts from $5 as well as burgers

QUEENSLAND

and sandwiches, and two doors down *Natural Living* has healthy lunches and salads. The *Criterion Hotel* has hearty and excellent-value bar meals from $7.50 to $12 and the *Bush Inn Steakhouse* serves steak and seafood from $10 to $18.

On the corner of William St and Denison St, *Gnomes Vegi-Tarri-Inn* is a very good vegetarian restaurant in the back room of a new-age shop. Main meals with salads start at $9; it's open from Monday to Saturday for lunch and dinner.

Close to the Customs House, *Le Bistro on Quay St* is a classy licensed restaurant that specialises in modern Australian cuisine, with modern Australian prices – $18 to $24 for a main course.

In the Leichhardt Hotel, *Palmers Restaurant* is a stylish licensed bistro and bar with a very reasonable lunchtime buffet (including Spanish tapas dishes) for $10. Evening mains start at $15.

If you're watching your waist, *Jack Sprat's*, by the bridge on Fitzroy St, is an unusual low-fat cafe, with lunches like quiche, tacos and lasagne in the $5 to $8 range. You can even wash down your meal with a soya milkshake.

Near the YHA, *Eagle Boys (☎ 13 1433, 145 Musgrave St)* delivers pizzas, and has cheap deals if you pick up your pizza.

Entertainment

The *Criterion Hotel* has local musicians and groups in its easy going Newsroom Bar from Wednesday to Saturday nights (no cover charge). The *Flamingo*, on Quay St between William and Derby Sts, is the biggest and most popular nightclub.

The *Pilbeam Theatre (☎ 4927 4111)*, at the Rockhampton Performing Arts Complex (ROKPAC) on Victoria Parade, is the main venue for theatre and music, while the *City Cinema Plaza*, on Denham St, charges $5 for all shows.

Getting There & Away

Air Qantas/Sunstate and Ansett have flights to the centres along the coast, while Flight West has a daily coastal hop to Brisbane ($323) and Mackay ($224). Sunstate charges

$314 and $217 for the same routes. Duthies Travel (☎ 4927 6288), on the corner of Bolsover and Denham Sts, handle bookings.

Bus The McCafferty's terminal (☎ 4927 2844) is just north of the bridge off Queen Elizabeth Drive; the Greyhound Pioneer terminal is at the Mobil roadhouse in George St, near the corner of Fitzroy St. It also stops near the McCafferty's terminal. Both companies have services to Mackay ($39; four hours), Cairns ($95; 16 hours) and Brisbane ($63; 10½ hours). McCafferty's goes to Emerald ($29; daily), and Longreach ($53; three times a week).

Young's Coaches (☎ 4922 3813) and Rothery's Coaches (☎ 4922 4320) operate loop services to Yeppoon and Rosslyn Bay, Emu Park and back ($6.30/$7 one way). Young's Coaches also has buses to Mt Morgan ($6.30) daily except Sunday. Buses leave from the Kern arcade on Bolsover St, between Denham and William Sts, but stop near the YHA hostel if you call ahead.

Yeppoon Backpackers runs a free bus between Rockhampton and Yeppoon (☎ 1800 636 828). Greyhound Pioneer Aussiepasses can also be used for this route.

Train The new, high-speed *Tilt Train* travels from Brisbane to Rockhampton in under seven hours; the one way economy fare is $67. The weekly *Spirit of Capricorn* takes 10 hours between Brisbane and Rockhampton for the same fare.

The *Sunlander* and *Queenslander* travel between Brisbane and Cairns via Rockhampton. One-way economy fares are $67 to Brisbane and $108 to Cairns. The *Spirit of the Tropics* stops here on its way to Townsville.

The slow *Spirit of the Outback* runs twice-weekly between Brisbane, Rockhampton, Emerald and Longreach, ($72 for an economy seat from Rockhampton). Book with the Queensland Rail Travel Centre at the train station (☎ 4932 0453), 1km south-east of the centre.

AROUND ROCKHAMPTON

The Berserker Range, which starts 26km north of Rockhampton, is noted for its spectacular limestone caves and passages. A couple of kilometres from the Caves township, **Olsen's Capricorn Caverns** (☎ 4934 2883) has the most impressive caves, and is open daily from 8.30 am with six different tours including a one hour 'cathedral tour' ($11), and adventure tour ($15). There's also a pool, walking trails and barbecue areas, and you can camp for $10. Nearby, the family-run **Cammoo Caves** has self-guided tours daily from 8.30 am to 5 pm ($7).

About 25km south-west of Rockhampton and 22km east of Baralaba is *Myella Farm Stay* (☎ 4998 1290), a working cattle station which offers the full 'City Slickers' experience – horse riding, cattle mustering, helping out with the fence repairs etc. It's run by a hospitable family and receives consistently good reports from travellers. You stay in a recently renovated timber farmhouse and rates start at $130 per person for two days and one night, which includes all meals and activities. Ring for directions.

Mt Morgan
• postcode 4714   • pop 2490

The open-cut gold and copper mine at Mt Morgan, 38km south-west of Rockhampton on the Burnett Hwy, was worked (off and on) from the 1880s until 1981. Mt Morgan is a registered heritage town with a well-preserved collection of period buildings. The tourist office (☎ 4938 2312) is housed in an attractive old train station.

The interesting **Mt Morgan Historical Museum**, on the corner of Morgan and East Sts, is open daily from 10 am to 1 pm (Sunday until 4 pm); entry is $4. Mount Morgan Mine Tours (☎ 4938 1081) has day tours that include the town sights, the mine, and a cave with dinosaur footprints on its ceiling, departing daily at 9.30 am and 1 pm ($18.50). They also pick up from Rockhampton.

There's a good caravan park on the southern outskirts, and budget accommodation in several of the pubs. The *Miners' Rest Motel Units* (☎ 4938 2350), 1km south of the centre on Coronation Drive, has cottages from $45 a double.

Young's Bus Service (☎ 4922 3813) has daily buses from Rockhampton to Mt Morgan (except Sunday); the fare is $6.30 one way. McCafferty's also passes through here on its inland Rockhampton-Brisbane run.

YEPPOON
• postcode 4703   • pop 17,000

Yeppoon is a relaxed seaside township 38km north-east of Rockhampton. It's the main resort on the Capricorn Coast and it makes a pleasant alternative to Rockhampton if you're breaking your journey on the way to Great Keppel Island. The boats leave from Rosslyn Bay 7km south and there are some good beaches north of town.

The Capricorn Coast Information Centre (☎ 1800 675 785) is at the Ross Creek Roundabout at the entrance to the town. On Australia Day, Yeppoon holds a popular nudist boat regatta.

If you have transport, the drive from Yeppoon to Byfield, 40km north, passes through some appealing state forests; there are some good picnic and camping grounds en route.

Places to Stay

On the hill behind town, the *Yeppoon Backpackers* (☎ 1800 636 828, 30 Queen St) is an easy-going place in a comfortable old timber house. It has good facilities and a large backyard with a pool and good views of town. Four-bed dorms cost $16 per person and doubles are $34 (VIP and YHA discounts apply). The hostel does free pickups from Rockhampton and the ferry terminal at Rosslyn Bay.

Of the numerous motels and holiday flats in town, *Como Holiday Units* (☎ 4939 1594, 32 Anzac Parade) is friendly and it's opposite the beach. Self-contained one and two-bedroom units cost $60 a double, plus $10 for each extra adult.

YEPPOON TO EMU PARK

There are beaches dotted all along the 19km coast from Yeppoon south to Emu Park. **Cooee Bay**, a couple of kilometres from Yeppoon, holds the World & Australian Cooeeing Contest & Carnival each August.

Rosslyn Bay Boat Harbour, about 7km south of Yeppoon, is the departure point for

QUEENSLAND

The Great Barrier Reef

Facts & Figures The Great Barrier Reef is 2000km in length. It starts slightly south of the Tropic of Capricorn, somewhere out from Bundaberg or Gladstone, and ends in the Torres Strait, just south of Papua New Guinea. It is not only the most extensive reef system in the world, but the biggest structure made by living organisms. At its southern end the reef is up to 300km from the mainland, while at the northern end it runs nearer the coast, is much less broken up and can be up to 80km wide.

In the 'lagoon' between the outer reef and the coast, the waters are dotted with smaller reefs, cays and islands. Drilling on the reef has indicated that the coral may be more than 500m thick. Most of the reef is about two million years old, but there are sections dating back 18 million years.

What is It? Coral is formed by a small, primitive animal, a marine polyp of the family *Cnidaria*. Some polyps, known as hard corals, form a hard surface by excreting lime. When they die, the hard 'skeletons' remain and these gradually build up the reef. New polyps grow on their dead predecessors and continually add to the reef. The skeletons of hard corals are white; the reef's colours come from living polyps.

Coral needs a number of preconditions for healthy growth. The water temperature must not drop below 17.5°C – thus the Great Barrier Reef does not continue further south into cooler waters; the water must be clear to allow sunlight to penetrate; and it must be salty. Coral will not grow below a depth of 30m because sunlight does not penetrate sufficiently. Nor does it grow around river mouths: the Great Barrier Reef ends near Papua New Guinea because the Fly River's enormous water flow is both fresh and muddy.

One of the most spectacular sights of the Great Barrier Reef occurs for a few nights after a full moon in late spring or early summer, when vast numbers of corals spawn at the same time. The tiny bundles of sperm and eggs are visible to the naked eye and the event has been likened to a gigantic underwater snowstorm.

Reef Types What's known as the Great Barrier Reef is not one reef but about 2600 separate ones. Basically, reefs are either fringing or barrier. You will find fringing reefs off sloping sides of islands or the mainland coast. Barrier reefs are further out to sea: the 'real' Great Barrier Reef, or outer reef, is at the edge of the Australian continental shelf, and the channel between the reef and the coast can be 60m deep. In places, the reef rises straight up from that depth. This raises the question of how the reef built up when coral cannot survive below 30m. One theory is that it gradually grew as the sea bed subsided. Another theory is that the sea level gradually rose, and the coral growth was able to keep pace.

Reef Inhabitants There are about 400 different types of coral on the Great Barrier Reef. Equally colourful are the many clams that appear to be embedded in the coral. Other reef inhabitants include about 1500 species of fish, 4000 types of mollusc (clams, snails etc), 350 echinoderms (sea urchins, starfish, sea cucumbers etc, all with a five-arm body plan), and countless thousands of species of sponge, worm and crustacean (crabs, shrimps etc).

Reef waters are also home to dugong (the sea cows believed to have given rise to the mermaid myth) and are breeding grounds for humpback whales, which migrate every winter from Antarctica. The reef's islands form important nesting colonies for many types of sea bird, and six of the world's seven species of sea turtle lay eggs on the islands' sandy beaches in spring or summer.

QUEENSLAND

The Great Barrier Reef

Crown-of-Thorns Starfish One reef inhabitant that has enjoyed enormous publicity is the crown-of-thorns starfish, notorious because it appears to be chewing through large areas of the reef. It's thought that the starfish develop a taste for coral when the reef ecology is upset; for example, when the supply of bivalves (oysters, clams), which comprise its normal diet, is diminished. It's believed this starfish arrived from Japan in ship ballast.

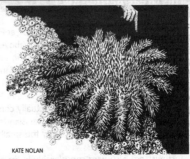

KATE NOLAN

Dangerous Creatures Hungry sharks are the usual idea of an aquatic nasty, but the Great Barrier Reef's most unpleasant creatures are generally less dramatic. For a start, there are scorpion fish with highly venomous spines. The butterfly cod is a very beautiful scorpion fish that relies on its colourful appearance to warn off possible enemies. In contrast, the stonefish lies hidden on the bottom, looking just like a rock, and is very dangerous if stepped on.

Stinging jellyfish are a danger only in coastal waters and only in certain seasons. The deadly 'sea wasp' is, in fact, a box jellyfish (see Warning in the Activities section at the start of this chapter). As for sharks, there has been no recorded case of a visitor to the reef islands meeting a hungry one.

Viewing the Reef The best way of seeing the reef is by diving or snorkelling. Otherwise you can view it through the floor of glass-bottom boats or the windows of semisubmersibles, or descend below the ocean surface inside 'underwater observatories'. You can also see a living coral reef and its accompanying life forms without leaving dry land, at the Great Barrier Reef Wonderland aquarium in Townsville.

Innumerable tour operators run day trips to the outer reef and to coral-fringed islands from towns on the Queensland coast. The cost depends on how much reef-viewing paraphernalia is used, how far the reef is from the coast, how luxurious the vessel is that takes you there, and whether lunch is included. Usually, free use of snorkelling gear is part of the package. Some islands also have good reefs and are usually cheaper to reach; you can stay on quite a few of them.

The Great Barrier Reef Marine Park Authority (GBRMPA) is the body looking after the welfare of most of the reef. Its address is PO Box 1379, Townsville, Queensland 4810 (☎ 4750 0700). It has an office in the Great Barrier Reef Wonderland complex in Townsville.

Islands There are three types of island off the Queensland coast. In the south, before you reach the Great Barrier Reef, are several large vegetated sand islands, including North Stradbroke, Moreton and Fraser islands. These are interesting to visit, although not for coral. Strung along the coast, mostly close to shore, are continental islands, such as Great Keppel, most of the Whitsundays, Hinchinbrook and Dunk. At one time, these would have been the peaks of coastal ranges, but rising sea levels submerged the mountains. The islands' vegetation is similar to that of the adjacent mainland.

The true coral islands, or cays, are on the outer reef or isolated between it and the mainland.

Continued next page

QUEENSLAND

The Great Barrier Reef

Continued from previous page

Green Island near Cairns, the Low Isles near Port Douglas, and Heron Island off Gladstone, are all cays. Cays are formed when a reef is above sea level, even at high tide. Dead coral is ground down by water action to form sand and, in some cases, vegetation eventually takes root. Coral cays are low-lying, unlike the often hilly islands closer to the coast. There are about 300 cays on the reef, and 69 are vegetated.

The islands are extremely variable so don't let the catchword 'reef island' suck you in. Most of the popular resort islands are actually continental islands and some are well south of the Great Barrier Reef. Many continental islands have fringing reefs as well as other attractions for which a tiny coral cay is simply too small; there may be hills to climb, bushwalks and secluded beaches.

The islands also vary considerably in their accessibility. For example, Lady Elliot is a $145 return flight, whereas others cost only a few dollars by ferry. If you want to stay on an island rather than make a day trip from the mainland, this too can vary widely in cost. Accommodation is generally in the form of expensive resorts, where most visitors will be on various all-inclusive package holidays. But there are a few exceptions to this rule, and on many islands it's possible to camp. A few islands have proper camping areas with toilets and fresh water on tap; on others you'll even have to take drinking water with you.

For more information on individual islands, see the Capricorn Coast, Whitsunday Coast, North Coast and Far North Queensland sections of this chapter. Also good is Lonely Planet's *Islands of Australia's Great Barrier Reef*.

---

ferries to Great Keppel Island and other Keppel Bay islands. There's a free day car park at the harbour, or the Kempsea lock-up car park (back on the main road) charges $5.50 a day ($7 under cover; $4 for motorcycles).

South of Rosslyn Bay are three headlands with fine views – **Double Head**, **Bluff Point** and **Pinnacle Point**. After Pinnacle Point the road crosses **Causeway Lake**, a saltwater inlet where you can rent canoes and sailboards. Further south at **Emu Park** there are more good views and the 'Singing Ship' – a series of drilled tubes and pipes that emit whistling or moaning sounds when there's a breeze blowing. It's a memorial to Captain Cook.

Koorana Crocodile Farm is 5km off the Emu Park to Rockhampton road. The turnoff is 15km from Emu Park. The farm has hundreds of crocs and is open daily from 11.30 am, with 1½-hour tours at 1 pm ($12/6).

Most towns along this stretch of coast have caravan and camping parks, and there are numerous motels and holiday flats.

GREAT KEPPEL ISLAND

Although it's not actually on the reef, Great Keppel is the equal of most islands up the coast. Known as *wappaburra* (resting place) to the local Aboriginal people, the island covers 14 sq km and boasts 18km of very fine white-sand beaches, as well as some good fringing coral reefs. You can easily spend several days exploring the island and there are some interesting bushwalks if you get tired of the beach.

The Great! Keppel Island Resort is beyond the reach of the average shoestring traveller, but unlike many of the resort islands, Great Keppel has some good budget accommodation alternatives. It's also one of the cheapest and easiest Queensland islands to reach. Daytrippers to the island have access to a pool, bar and restaurant at the resort, and they can hire all sorts of water sports gear.

Things to See & Do

Great Keppel Island's beaches are among the best of any on the resort islands. The main **Fisherman's Beach** has a broad strip of fine white sand, but it can become crowded with resort vehicles when the ferries come in. Better choices are **Putney Beach** to the north, or **Long Beach**, just south of the airstrip. The water is clear and warm and there is good coral at several points around the island. **Monkey Beach**, a 30 minute walk/scramble around the headland south of the resort, has good snorkelling.

There are also good bushwalking tracks. The longest track goes across to the lighthouse near **Bald Rock Point** on the far side of the island, but it's quite hard going (2½ hours one way). The **Mt Windham** circuit walk (1½ hours) has pleasant views over the island.

There's an **underwater observatory** by Middle Island, close to Great Keppel. A confiscated Taiwanese fishing junk was sunk next to the observatory to provide a haven for fish.

The Beach Shed on Putney Beach and Keppel Watersports on Fisherman's Beach both hire out sailboards, catamarans, motorboats and snorkelling gear, and can take you water-skiing or parasailing. Keppel Reef Scuba Adventures (☎ 4939 5022), on Putney Beach, offers two dives with all gear supplied

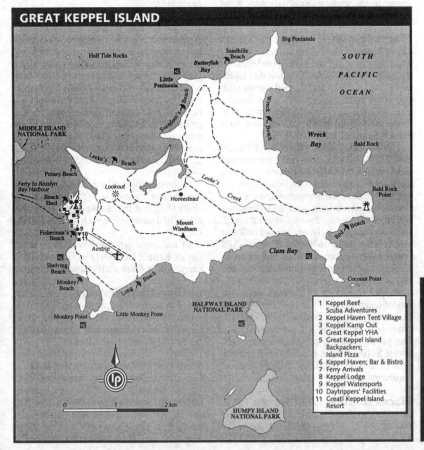

GREAT KEPPEL ISLAND

1 Keppel Reef Scuba Adventures
2 Keppel Haven Tent Village
3 Keppel Kamp Out
4 Great Keppel YHA
5 Great Keppel Island Backpackers; Island Pizza
6 Keppel Haven; Bar & Bistro
7 Ferry Arrivals
8 Keppel Lodge
9 Keppel Watersports
10 Daytrippers' Facilities
11 Great! Keppel Island Resort

QUEENSLAND

for $100 ($80 for introductory dives), and five-day diving courses for $420.

Organised Tours

Keppel Tourist Services (☎ 4933 6744) runs various catamaran cruises. Its island cruise departs daily from Rosslyn Bay at 9.15 am and from Fisherman's Beach at 10 am, and spends three hours at a pontoon off the northern tip of the island before cruising back. It costs $70 from Rosslyn Bay ($65 from Great Keppel) and includes boom netting (riding on a net trailed behind a boat), snorkelling, a glass-bottom boat trip and lunch. There's a cruise to the underwater observatory from Fisherman's Beach at 12.15 pm daily ($10).

Places to Stay – Budget

Great Keppel Island Backpackers (☎ 4939 8655) is a friendly, old-style hostel close to the ferry drop-off point. Comfortable eight-bed dorms are $15 and six-bed cabins with their own bathroom are $90 for a double, plus $10 per extra adult. The hostel provides snorkelling gear and offers two-hour sea-kayaking trips for $20.

The popular *Great Keppel YHA Hostel (☎ 4927 5288)* has camp-o-tels (permanent tents with beds and lighting) with up to four beds for $15 per person and doubles/twins for $34/36 for members/nonmembers. The hostel has snorkelling gear and organises activities such as bushwalks. Book through the Rockhampton YHA or the head office in Brisbane (☎ 3236 1680). Its $79 deal ($89 nonmembers) is good value: one night in Rockhampton, two nights on the island and bus and boat transfers.

Keppel Haven (☎ 4939 1907) has a variety of budget accommodation. Four-bed safari tents are $10 and $12 per person, bunkhouse cabins are $22 per person (up to four people) and self-contained six-bed cabins are $110 a double, plus $30 per extra person. Communal facilities include fridges, barbecues and basic kitchen equipment.

Places to Stay – Mid-Range

Next door to Keppel Haven is *Keppel Kamp Out (☎ 4939 2131)*, which is geared to the 18 to 35 age bracket. The cost of $60 per person per day ($54 stand-by usually available) includes twin share tents, three meals and activities such as water sports, parties and video nights.

Keppel Lodge (☎ 4939 4251) has four good motel-style units that sleep up to five and cost from $90 a double, plus $30 per extra adult; there's a large communal lounge and kitchen and a barbecue area.

The *Great! Keppel Island Resort (☎ 1800 245 658)* is popular with young people and promotes itself as 'the active resort'. All-inclusive daily costs start at $280 per person, but stand-by rates of $154 per person are available.

Places to Eat

If you want to cook it's best to bring a few basic supplies. Otherwise, the reasonably pricey kiosk at *Keppel Haven* has a few groceries, or you can get staples like soup noodles at *Great Keppel Island Backpackers*. The *Keppel Haven Bar & Bistro* does lunches and evening meals (burgers $8, grills $15 to $18) and it shows films in the evenings. Near the YHA, the friendly *Island Pizza* makes good pizzas ($10 to $26), pasta and submarines. It's open Wednesday to Sunday.

In the day-trippers' area, the *Keppel Cafe* has burgers, sandwiches ($5) and fish and chips ($7), and the *Anchorage Char Grill* has grilled steak or fish with salad and chips for $13.

In the evenings, the *Wreck Bar* in the Great! Keppel Island Resort is the place to party, with a disco until the early hours.

Getting There & Away

Air Whittacker Air flies at least four times a day between Rockhampton and Great Keppel Island ($53 one way). Book through the Great! Keppel Island Resort.

Boat Two companies run ferries to Great Keppel from Rosslyn Bay Harbour. Keppel Tourist Services (☎ 4933 6744) operates three catamarans, which leave Rosslyn Bay at 7.30, 9.15 and 11.30 am and 3.30 pm, and return from Great Keppel at 8.15 am, 2 pm and 4.30 pm. There's an extra service on

Friday at 6 pm, returning at 6.40 pm. The fare is $27 return.

The *Freedom Flyer* (☎ 4833 6244) departs from the Keppel Bay Marina in Rosslyn Bay at 9 and 11 am and 3 pm, returning from Great Keppel at 10 am and 2 and 4 pm. The return fare is $27.

OTHER KEPPEL BAY ISLANDS

There are 18 continental islands dotted around Keppel Bay, all within 20km of the coast. You may get to visit **Middle Island**, with its underwater observatory, or **Halfway** or **Humpy** islands if you're staying on Great Keppel Island. Most of the islands have clean, white beaches and several (notably Halfway Island) have excellent fringing coral reefs. You can maroon yourself on several national park islands, including Middle and Miall islands, though you'll need to take all your own supplies, including water. You can get information and permits from the EPA regional office in Rockhampton (☎ 4936 0511) or the QPWS rangers' office at Rosslyn Bay Harbour (☎ 4933 6595).

North Keppel Island National Park is the second largest of the group and one of the most northerly. It covers 6.3 sq km and there's a popular *camping spot* at Considine Beach on the north-west coast, which has well water for washing, and toilets. Take drinking water, insect repellent and a fuel stove.

Just south of North Keppel Island, tiny **Pumpkin Island** has five cabins (☎ 4939 2431) that accommodate either five or six people each from $120 per cabin. There's water and solar power, and each cabin has a stove, fridge and a bathroom with shower. Camping costs $12 per person.

The Keppel Bay Marina (☎ 4933 6244) can organise a water taxi for camping drop-offs from Rosslyn Bay to the islands; it costs $120 per trip (one way).

CAPRICORN HINTERLAND

The Capricorn Hwy runs inland, virtually along the Tropic of Capricorn, across the central Queensland highlands to Barcaldine, where it meets the Landsborough/

Matilda Hwy. You can continue north-west from here to connect with the Townsville to Mt Isa road.

The area was first opened up by miners looking for gold and copper around Emerald and sapphires around Anakie, but cattle, grain crops and coal provide its main living today. Carnarvon National Park, south of Emerald, is one of Queensland's most spectacular.

Getting There & Away

McCafferty's has a service from Rockhampton to Longreach three times a week, calling at all towns along the Capricorn Hwy. The twice weekly *Spirit of the Outback* train follows the same route.

Blackdown Tableland National Park

The Blackdown Tableland is a spectacular 600m sandstone plateau that rises suddenly out of the flat plains of central Queensland. This impressive national park features stunning panoramas, waterfalls, great bushwalks, Aboriginal rock art, plus some unique wildlife and plant species.

There's a self-registration *camping ground* at South Mimosa Creek, about 10km into the park. Bookings can be made with the ranger at Dingo (☎ 4986 1964). You'll need to bring water, a gas stove for cooking and a bag for your rubbish.

The turn-off to the Blackdown Tableland is 12km west of Dingo and 35km east of the coal-mining centre of Blackwater. The 25km gravel road can be unsafe in wet weather and isn't suitable for caravans at any time – the last 7km are incredibly steep and slippery.

Coal Mines

A few of the massive open-cut coal mines in this region offer free tours lasting about 1½ hours; book ahead. For the Peak Downs (☎ 4968 8233) mine near Moranbah, free buses depart Moranbah town square at 10 am on Thursday, and the tour takes about 2½ hours (call ☎ 4941 7243 to book). Tours of Blair Athol mine (☎ 4983 1866), near Clermont, start on Tuesday at 9 am.

QUEENSLAND

Gemfields

West of Emerald, about 270km inland from Rockhampton, the gemfields around Anakie, Sapphire and Rubyvale and the Willows Gemfields are known for sapphires, zircons, amethysts, rubies, topaz, jasper, and even diamonds and gold. To go fossicking, you need a 'fossicking licence', sold from the Emerald courthouse or on the gemfields. If you're just passing through, you can buy a bucket of 'wash' (dirt) from one of the fossicking parks and hand-sieve and wash it ($4). You can also explore several tourist mines, including the excellent **Silk 'n' Sapphire** mine, 1.5km north of Rubyvale, which has underground tours for $30 for two hours, and hands-on sapphire mining for $60 for a half day.

Anakie, 42km west of Emerald just off the Capricorn Hwy, has a pub, a caravan park and an information centre (☎ 4985 4525). A sealed road leads north to **Sapphire** (10km) and **Rubyvale** (7km further on), which is the main town for the fields. There's a pub, a general store, a post office and a few gem shops and galleries.

Between Rubyvale and Sapphire, *Sunrise Cabins & Camping* (☎ 4985 4281) has camp sites for $8.50 or rustic stone cabins with shared kitchen from $27/33 a single/double, plus $3 for each extra person (maximum six). You can get information, licences and maps, and hire fossicking gear here.

Ramboda Homestead (☎ 4985 4154), on the highway near the turn-off to Sapphire, is a B&B farmstay that charges from $27/64 for a single/double room and offers dinner for $15 per person; it does pickups from Anakie. There are also caravan/camping parks at Anakie, Rubyvale and Willows Gemfields.

Clermont

• postcode 4721   • pop 2390

North of Emerald is Clermont, with the huge Blair Athol open-cut coal mine. Clermont is Queensland's oldest tropical inland town, founded on copper, gold, sheep and cattle. It was the scene of goldfield race riots in the 1880s, and there was a military takeover of the town in 1891 after a confrontation between striking sheep shearers and non-union

labour. The town has a couple of pubs and a caravan park with on-site vans.

Springsure

• postcode 4722   • pop 670

Springsure, 66km south of Emerald, has an attractive setting with a backdrop of granite mountains and surrounding sunflower fields. There's a small **historical museum** by the windmill at the southern entrance to town, a motel and a caravan park. The **Virgin Rock**, an outcrop of Mt Zamia on the northern outskirts, was named after early settlers claimed to have seen the image of the Virgin Mary in the rock face.

Ten kilometres south-west, at Burnside, is the **Old Rainworth Fort**, built following the Wills Massacre of 1861 when Aboriginal people killed 19 settlers on Cullin-la-ringo Station north-west of Springsure. This was Australia's worst massacre of white people by Aborigines.

Carnarvon National Park

Rugged Carnarvon National Park, in the middle of the Great Dividing Range, features dramatic gorge scenery and many Aboriginal rock paintings and carvings. The national park has several sections, but the impressive Carnarvon Gorge is all that most people see as the rest is pretty inaccessible.

Carnarvon Gorge is stunning partly because it's an oasis surrounded by drier plains and partly because of the variety of its scenery, which includes sandstone cliffs, moss gardens, deep pools, and rare palms and ferns. There's also a lot of wildlife. Aboriginal art can be viewed at two main sites – the **Art Gallery** and **Cathedral Cave**.

From Rolleston to Carnarvon Gorge, the road is bitumen for 20km and unsealed for 75km. From Roma via Injune and Wyseby, the road is bitumen for about 200km, then unsealed and fairly rough for the last 45km. After rain, both roads are impassable.

Three kilometres into the Carnarvon Gorge section there's an information centre and a scenic *camping ground*. The main walking track starts beside the information centre and follows Carnarvon Creek through the gorge, with detours to various points of interest such as the Moss Garden (3.6km from the camping ground), Ward's Canyon (4.8km), the Art Gallery (5.6km) and Cathedral Cave (9.3km). You should allow at least half a day for a visit here, and bring lunch and water with you as there are no shops.

To get into the more westerly and rugged Mt Moffatt section of the park, there are two unsealed roads from Injune: one through Womblebank Station, the other via Westgrove Station. There are no through roads from Mt Moffatt to Carnarvon Gorge or to the third and fourth remote sections of the park – Salvator Rosa and Ka Ka Mundi. Mt Moffatt has some beautiful scenery, diverse vegetation and wildlife, and **Kenniff Cave**, an important Aboriginal archaeological site. It's believed Aboriginal people lived here as long as 20,000 years ago.

Places to Stay The *Oasis Lodge* (☎ 4984 4503), near the entrance to the Carnarvon Gorge section of the park, offers 'safari cabins' from $170 a night per person, including full board and organised activities ($115 from January to March, without activities). There's a general store with fuel.

You need a permit to camp at the national park *camping ground* or in any of the more remote camping areas, and it's advisable (essential during school holidays) to book by phoning the Carnarvon Gorge rangers (☎ 4984 4505). Sites cost $3.50 per person per night and you'll need a fuel stove.

You can also camp at *Big Bend camping area*, 500m upstream from Cathedral Cave – a 12km walk up the gorge. If you camp here, you can explore the side gorges unhurriedly.

In the Mt Moffatt section, camping is allowed at four sites but you need to be completely self-sufficient and a 4WD is advisable; phone the Mt Moffatt rangers for details (☎ 4626 3581).

Whitsunday Coast

The Whitsunday Islands, which lie just off the coast between Mackay and Bowen, are famous for their clear, aquamarine waters,

lush forests and secluded island resorts. This is one of the most beautiful parts of the coast, and there's plenty to do, including dive courses, cruises to and around the islands, snorkelling, fishing, sailing and bush camping on the islands.

Mackay is a major regional centre, while the main access point for the islands is Airlie Beach, which is a very popular travellers hangout, mainly because many companies offering dive courses and boat trips to the islands operate from here.

MACKAY

- postcode 4741   • pop 74,000

Mackay is surrounded by a sea of sugar cane and boasts the world's largest sugar-loading terminal, Port Mackay. Sugar has been grown here since 1865, and today Mackay processes a third of Australia's sugar crop.

As a tourist destination, Mackay is nothing special, yet the town centre is spacious and leafy and there is a surprisingly lively cafe and bar scene. There are also some good beaches a bus ride away and Mackay is an access point for the national parks of Eungella and Cape Hillsborough, for Brampton and Carlisle islands, and for the Great Barrier Reef.

Orientation

Mackay is divided by the broad Pioneer River, but most places of interest are in the old city centre on the south side of the river. Victoria St, the main street, is an attractive thoroughfare with a central plantation. The bus station is a few hundred metres west of the centre on Milton St; the train station and airport are both about 3km south of the centre signposted from the Bruce Hwy. The harbour and marina are 6km north, and the best beaches are about 15km north.

Information

Mackay's tourist office (☎ 4952 2677), in a replica of the old Richmond Sugar Mill 3km south of the town centre on the Bruce Hwy, publishes the handy *Mackay the Natural North* brochure. It's open weekdays from 8.30 am to 5 pm and on weekends from 9 am to 4 pm.

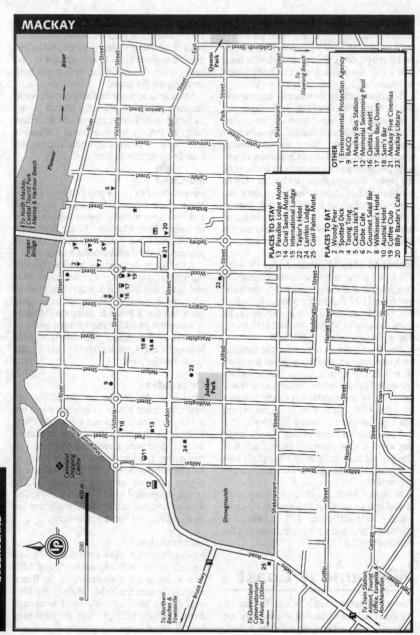

MACKAY

QUEENSLAND

To North Mackay,
Central Tourist Park,
Marina & Harbour Beach

To Illawong Beach

Queens Park

Goldsmith Street

Caneland
Shopping
Centre

Jubilee
Park

Showgrounds

To Queensland
Conservatorium
of Music (300m)

To Train Station,
Airport, Tourist
Office, Eungella &
Rockhampton

To Northern Beaches
& Townsville

Bruce Hwy

Nebo Rd

Field St

George St

0   200   400 m

PLACES TO STAY

13 Paradise Lodge Motel
14 Coral Sands Motel
15 International Lodge
22 Taylor's Hotel
24 Larrikin Lodge
25 Cool Palms Motel

PLACES TO EAT

2 Woody Pear
3 Spotted Dick
4 Toong Tong
5 Cactus Jack's
6 Globe Cafe
7 Gourmet Salad Bar
8 Wilkinson's Hotel
10 Austral Hotel
19 Coffee Club
20 Billy Baxter's Cafe

OTHER

1 Environmental Protection Agency
9 RACQ
11 Mackay Bus Station
12 Memorial Swimming Pool
16 Qantas; Ansett
17 Saloon Bar; Doors
18 Sam's Bar
21 Mackay Five Cinemas
23 Mackay Library

The RACQ (☎ 4957 2918) is at 214 Victoria St, and the EPA office (☎ 4951 8788) is on the corner of Wood and River Sts.

On Sydney St, there's Internet/email access at the Globe Cafe for $5 per half hour.

Things to See & Do

Mackay has weathered several major cyclones, but a lot of interesting old buildings have survived. The tourist office's brochure *A Heritage Walk in Mackay* can guide you around 21 historic sites in town. There are botanic gardens and an orchid house in **Queens Park**, towards the eastern end of Gordon St, and good views over the harbour from **Mt Basset** and the **Rotary Lookout** on Mt Oscar, in North Mackay.

The **Town Beach**, 2km from the centre at the eastern end of Shakespeare St, is shallow and muddy; **Illawong Beach**, a couple of kilometres further south, is only slightly better. More pleasant is the sandy **Harbour Beach** 6km north, although the best beaches are about 16km north at Blacks Beach, Eimeo and Bucasia.

In the cane-crushing season (July to December) the **Farleigh Sugar Mill** (☎ 4957 4727), Armstrong St, Farleigh, 12km northwest of Mackay along the Bruce Hwy, has two-hour tours on weekdays at 1 pm ($12), but you'll need to book. You can also take two-hour tours of the **Polstone Sugar Farm** (☎ 4959 7298), 16km west on Homebush Rd, on Monday, Wednesday and Friday at 1.30 pm ($12). Follow the Peak Downs Hwy, which branches off the Bruce Hwy near the information office.

The **Illawong Fauna Sanctuary** (☎ 4959 1777), an excellent fauna park at Mirani, in the Pioneer Valley on the road to Eungella, has kangaroos, birds, crocodiles (fed at 2.15 pm) and koalas (10.30 am and 4.30 pm); it's open daily ($10/5 for adults/children). There's also a children's playground, a swimming pool and homestay accommodation.

Organised Tours

Roylen's Cruises (☎ 4955 3066) runs fast catamaran trips from Mackay Harbour to Credlin Reef on the outer reef, where Roylen's has a pontoon with an underwater observatory. Trips depart on Sunday, Wednesday and Friday ($100 including lunch and a semisubmersible boat ride); you can hire snorkelling or diving gear. Roylen's also has five-day island cruises that include Brampton, Hamilton, South Molle and Daydream islands.

Jungle Johno Tours (☎ 4959 1822) has day trips to Eungella and Cape Hillsborough national parks for $55. Natural North/Reeforest Tours (☎ 4959 8360) has day trips to the Illawong Fauna Sanctuary ($59/39) and Eungella National Park and Finch Hatton Gorge ($65).

The Illawong Fauna Sanctuary has three-day outback tours to the gemfields around Sapphire ($275).

Places to Stay

Camping The modern *Beach Tourist Park* (☎ 4957 4021, 8 Petrie St), 4km south of Mackay at Illawong Beach, has camp sites for $14, camp-o-tels for $20 and on-site cabins from $42.

The *Central Tourist Park* (☎ 4957 6141, 15 Malcomson St), in North Mackay, has camp sites from $10 and cabins from $25 a double.

Hostels Close to the bus station, *Larrikin Lodge* (☎ 4951 3728, 32 Peel St) is a small YHA-associate hostel in an airy timber house, with a small pool. The hostel is quite straightforward, but it's well run and has a good atmosphere. Dorm beds cost $15 and twins/doubles are $32.

Hotels & Motels *Taylor's Hotel* (☎ 4957 2500), on the corner of Wood and Alfred Sts, has single rooms (only) for $20. The friendly *International Lodge* (☎ 4951 1022, 40 Macalister St) is quite central and has good budget singles/doubles from $40/48. Nearby, the *Coral Sands Motel* (☎ 4951 1244, 44 Macalister St) has a good pool and restaurant, with rooms from $58/66.

The *Paradise Lodge Motel* (☎ 4951 3644, 19 Peel St), near the bus station, has units for $53/60. There are about a thousand motels strung along Nebo Rd (the Bruce Hwy) south of the centre. The closest of these, the *Cool Palms Motel* (*☎ 4957 5477, 4 Nebo Rd*) has rooms from $38/40.

Places to Eat

Mackay's city centre seems to have a pub on every corner, so finding a counter meal is not a problem. Close to the bus terminal, the friendly Austral Hotel, on the corner of Victoria and Peel Sts, has the tropical-style *Coco's* with mains in the $10 to $16 range and $4.50 lunches in the corner bar (weekdays only).

In the centre, Wilkinson's Hotel, on the corner of Victoria and Gregory Sts, has the trendy *Rangoon Rowing Club* upstairs, with noodles/pasta from $10 and other mains from $14 to $20.

Nearby on Sydney St, the *Spotted Dick* is a funky bar and diner in a renovated pub. This place is straight out of 70s Las Vegas, though the menu is pretty much the standard grill fare; steaks are $14 to $18, pizzas are about $10, and you can build your own burger for $7.

The *Coffee Club*, on Wood St, is another hip licensed bar, bistro and coffee house, with pizza/pasta options from $9 and other mains from $11 to $18.

For a more formal meal, the *Woody Pear* (*7 Wood St*) is a cosy little BYO restaurant that grows its own herbs. It's open for dinner Tuesday to Saturday.

The lively *Cactus Jack's*, just east of the centre on Victoria St, has Mexican meals from $10 to $15 and it's licensed. *Toong Tong* (*10 Sydney St*) is a well presented Thai restaurant with mains from $10 to $14 and cheap lunches for $7.50.

At No 36 Sydney St, the *Globe Cafe* is an old-fashioned Art Deco place with great quiche and coffee and Internet access for $5 per hour. The narrow and popular *Gourmet Salad Bar* (*23 Wood St*) is another good lunchtime option with rolls and sandwiches from $2 as well as very cheap salads and cakes.

For breakfast, *Billy Baxter's Cafe*, next to the post office on the corner of Gordon and Sydney Sts, has bacon and eggs on pancakes ($7) and good coffee – it's also open for meals at night.

Entertainment

The popular *Sam's Bar*, upstairs in the former Australian Hotel on the corner of Wood and Victoria Sts, is a laid-back meeting place, with pool tables, balconies overlooking the street and regular live bands. Nightclubs include the *Saloon Bar (99 Victoria St)* and the upstairs *Doors (85 Victoria St)*. There's also live music at the *Austral Hotel* on weekends.

The *Queensland Conservatorium of Music* (*☎ 4957 3727, 418 Shakespeare St*) has jazz and classical performances – call to find out what's on.

The *Mackay Five Cinemas (30 Gordon St)* shows mainstream releases.

Getting There & Away

Air Ansett's office is on the corner of Victoria and Gregory Sts; Qantas is nearby at 105 Victoria St. Both airlines have flights to Brisbane ($363 one way), Townsville ($226) and Rockhampton ($217), and connecting flights to other state capitals.

Flight West flies to Cairns ($330) and Sunstate flies to Proserpine ($91). Hamilton Island Aviation (*☎ 4946 8249*) has flights to Hamilton Island ($95 one way, $130 same-day return).

Bus Greyhound Pioneer and McCafferty's buses stop at the Mackay bus station (*☎ 4951 3088*) on Milton St. Major stops along the coast include Cairns ($75; 11 hours), Townsville ($49; eight hours), Airlie Beach ($25; two hours) and Brisbane ($94; 15 hours).

Train The *Sunlander* and *Queenslander* (both from Brisbane to Cairns) stop at Mackay. A sleeper to/from Brisbane on the *Sunlander* costs $130/199 in economy/1st class; a seat to/from Cairns is $77. The 1st class only *Queenslander* costs $350 to/from Brisbane. The train station is at Paget, about 3km south of the centre.

Getting Around

It costs about $10 for a taxi from Mackay airport to the city. Avis, Budget and Hertz have counters at the airport.

Local bus services are operated by Mackay Transit Coaches (☎ 4957 3330). The Taxi Transit Service (☎ 4951 4990) takes people to the northern beaches for $3.45 one way.

AROUND MACKAY
Brampton & Carlisle Islands

These two mountainous national park islands are in the Cumberland Group, 32km north-east of Mackay. Both are about five sq km in area and are joined by a sand bank, which you can walk across at low tide. Carlisle's highest point is 389m Skiddaw Peak, and Brampton's is 219m Brampton Peak. Both islands have forested slopes, sandy beaches, good walks and fringing coral reefs with good snorkelling.

The *Brampton Island Resort (☎ 4951 4499)* is a good mid-range family resort with rates from $180 per person per day twin share, including breakfast, tennis, golf and water sports; there is also a restaurant and a cafe. Transfers from Mackay cost $60 return, or you can fly there from Mackay for $75 one way with Transtate Airlines (☎ 13 1528).

Carlisle Island is uninhabited, but there's a QPWS *camp site* across from the Brampton Island Resort. The easiest way to reach the island is to take the Brampton Island transfer boat and walk across the sand bar. There are no facilities so you must be totally self-sufficient (although you could always pop across to the resort for a beer or a bite).

Most other islands in the Cumberland Group and the Sir James Smith Group to the north are also national parks; if you fancy a spot of Robinson Crusoeing and can afford to charter a boat or a seaplane, Goldsmith and Scawfell islands are good bets. Contact the EPA offices in Mackay (☎ 4951 8788) or the QPWS Seaforth office (☎ 4959 0410) for all camping permits and information.

Newry & Rabbit Islands

The Newry Island Group is a cluster of rocky, wild-looking continental islands just off the coast about 40km north-west of Mackay. Newry Island, 1km long, has a small and very low-key *resort (☎ 4959 0214)*, where camping costs $5 per site, a bunk is $12 and cabins, which sleep up to five and have their own bathrooms and cooking facilities, cost $20 per person (maximum charge $60). The resort has a restaurant and bar, and will pick up guests from Victor Creek, 4km west of Seaforth, for $15 return.

Rabbit Island, the largest of the group at 4.5 sq km, has a national park *camping ground* with toilets and a seasonal rainwater tank. It also has the only sandy beaches in the group. From November to January sea turtles nest here. Contact the Mackay EPA office (☎ 4951 8788) or the QPWS Seaforth office (☎ 4959 0410) for permits and information.

Eungella National Park

Eungella (pronounced '*young*-gulla', meaning 'Land of Clouds') National Park covers nearly 500 sq km of the Clarke Range, climbing to 1280m at Mt Dalrymple. The area has been cut off from other rainforest areas for roughly 30,000 years and it has at least six life forms that exist nowhere else: the Eungella honeyeater (a bird), the orange-sided skink (a lizard), the Mackay tulip oak (a tall, buttressed rainforest tree) and three species of frog, including the Eungella gastric brooding frog, which has the unusual ability to incubate its eggs in its stomach and give birth by spitting out the tadpoles!

Most days of the year you can be pretty sure of seeing platypuses close to the Broken River bridge and camping ground in this large national park, 84km west of Mackay. The best times to see the creatures are immediately after dawn and at dusk; you must remain patiently still and silent.

The main access road from Mackay takes you through the narrow Pioneer Valley, with a turn-off near Finch Hatton township to **Finch Hatton Gorge**. The last section of the 12km drive to the gorge is quite rough and involves several creek crossings. At the gorge, there's a swimming hole, picnic areas and a walking trail to the spectacular Araluen Falls (1.6km) and Wheel of Fire Falls (2.6km).

Eungella, 28km past Finch Hatton, is a sleepy mountain township with a guesthouse and a couple of tearooms. At **Broken River**, 5km south of Eungella, there's a

QUEENSLAND

rangers' office, a camping ground, picnic area, swimming hole and kiosk. Several excellent walking tracks start from around the Broken River picnic area. There's a platypus-viewing platform near the bridge. At night, the rufous bettong, a small kangaroo, is quite common. Brushtail possums and gliders are also seen here and the birdlife is prolific. Park rangers sometimes lead wildlife watching sessions, or night spotlighting trips to pick out nocturnal animals.

Places to Stay A couple of kilometres from the Finch Hatton Gorge is the *Platypus Bush Camp* (☎ 4958 3204), a simple bush retreat with a lovely forest setting by a creek. You can camp ($5 per person) or sleep in a slab-timber hut ($45 for up to three people); there are communal cooking shelters, hot showers and toilets. Bring your own food and linen. If you phone from Finch Hatton village, someone will pick you up.

In Eungella township, the *Eungella Chalet* (☎ 4958 4509) is an old-fashioned guesthouse perched on the edge of the mountain. It's fairly straightforward, but it has spectacular views, a pool, a bar, a restaurant and a hang-gliding platform. Singles/doubles cost $30/45 and en suite

rooms cost $65. Out the back, they have three-bed timber cabins from $80.

There's a good QPWS *camping ground* ($3.50 per person per night) at Fern Flats, near Broken River; for bookings (recommended during school holidays) and permits contact the ranger on ☎ 4958 4552.

Broken River Mountain Retreat (☎ 4958 4528), beside the bridge, has motel-style timber cabins from $58 ($68 weekends) and four-bed self-contained units from $78 a double, plus $10 for extra adults ($98 weekends).

Getting There & Away There are no buses to Eungella, but Jungle Johno Tours runs day trips from Mackay and will do camping drop-offs – see the Mackay Organised Tours section earlier in this chapter for details.

Cape Hillsborough National Park

This small coastal park, 54km north of Mackay, includes rocky Cape Hillsborough (300m high), and Andrews Point and Wedge Island, which are joined by a causeway at low tide. There are beaches and some good short walking tracks. The scenery ranges from cliffs, rocky coast, dunes and scrub to rainforest and woodland. Kangaroos hang

---

A Sweet Success

Sugar is easily the most visible crop from Mackay and north past Cairns, up the Queensland coast. Sugar was a success almost from the day it was introduced to the region in 1865, but its early days had a distinctly unsavoury air as the plantations were worked by Pacific Islander people, referred to as Kanakas, who were often forced from their homes to work on Australian cane fields. 'Blackbirding', as this virtual slave trading was known, was not stamped out until 1905.

Today, cane growing is highly mechanised and visitors can inspect crushing plants during the harvesting season (roughly July to October). The most spectacular part of the operation is the firing of the cane fields, when rubbish is burnt off by night fires. Mechanical harvesters cut and gather the cane, which is then transported to the sugar mills, often on narrow-gauge railway lines laid through the cane fields. The cane is shredded and passed through a series of crushers. The extracted juice is heated and cleaned of impurities and then evaporated to form a syrup. Next, the syrup is reduced to molasses and low-grade sugar. Further refining stages end with the sugar loaded into bulk containers for export.

Sugar production is a remarkably efficient process. The crushed fibres, known as bagasse, are burnt as fuel; impurities separated from the juice are used as fertilisers; and the molasses is used either to produce ethanol or as stock feed.

out on the beaches and wallabies, sugar gliders and turtles are also quite common. There's a rangers' office and information centre (☎ 4959 0410) on the foreshore, and a good picnic and barbecue area nearby.

Places to Stay At the end of the Cape Hillsborough road, the *Cape Hillsborough Resort (☎ 4959 0152)* has camp sites from $10, four-bed units from $30 a double and motel-style rooms from $54.

There's a small QPWS self-registration *camping ground* ($3.50 per site) at Smalleys Beach. Facilities include toilets, water and picnic shelters.

AIRLIE BEACH
• postcode 4802   • pop 3030

This small but popular resort town, 25km north-west of Proserpine off the Bruce Hwy, is the gateway to the Whitsunday Islands. Airlie Beach has a reputation as a backpacker party place, but it also attracts a diverse bunch of boaties and other tourists, mostly lured by the extensive pleasure-boating opportunities off the coast. The whole town revolves around tourism, and there is an excellent range of budget to mid-range accommodation, plenty of good eateries and a loud, lively nightlife.

Despite its name, Airlie Beach doesn't have any great beaches, but most people come to town to sail around the Whitsunday Islands or learn to scuba dive with one of the local schools. A wide assortment of travel agents and tour operators are based here, and most boats to the islands leave from Shute Harbour, 8km east of Airlie Beach, or from the Abel Point Marina, 1km west. Whale-watching boat trips, between July and September, are another attraction.

Information

There's a tourist office (☎ 07-4945 3711) on the Bruce Hwy at Proserpine, near the turn-off to Airlie Beach.

In Airlie Beach nearly everything of importance is on the main road, Shute Harbour Rd, including the registered Airlie Beach Tourist Information Centre (☎ 1800 819 366). There are also numerous privately run 'information centres' (ie booking agencies). Destination Whitsunday (☎ 1800 644 563), on the corner of Airlie Esplanade and Shute Harbour Rd, is quite well regarded. Most places have Internet/email access for around $5 per half hour.

The EPA office (☎ 4946 7022), 3km past Airlie Beach towards Shute Harbour, is open weekdays from 8 am to 5 pm (at varying hours on weekends), and handles camping bookings and permits for the Conway and Whitsunday Islands national parks.

Things to See & Do

The **Wildlife Park** has a large collection of Australian native animals and various daily shows including crocodile feeding; it's open daily from 8.30 am to 5 pm ($15). The park is 8km west of town – a courtesy bus does pickups from Airlie Beach. Also here is a bungee setup ($49) and a pool with water-slides ($5 all day).

The **Vic Hislop Great White Shark and Whale Expo** (☎ 4946 6928), on Waterson Rd, is one of two centres set up by the controversial shark hunter Vic Hislop (the other is in Hervey Bay). The show is basically a propaganda campaign against the great white shark, and the displays – including shark jaws, newspaper articles and photographs – are suitably gruesome. The expo has an 1818kg shark in a glass-fronted freezer. It's open daily from 9 am to 6 pm ($14).

The beaches at Airlie are fairly uninspiring, but you can hire catamarans, windsurfers, and other water sports gear from booths on the beach. Thrill seekers can also try tandem skydiving ($239) and parasailing ($40) – book through your accommodation or one of the agents in Airlie Beach.

Brandy Creek Trail Rides (☎ 4946 6665) offers three-hour rides through a nearby forest ($41) and will pick you up from your accommodation. Fawlty's 4WD Tropical Tours (☎ 4946 6733) offers half-day rainforest tours ($35).

Diving

Four outfits in and around Airlie Beach offer four to six-day scuba-diving certificate courses. You can get your certification

QUEENSLAND

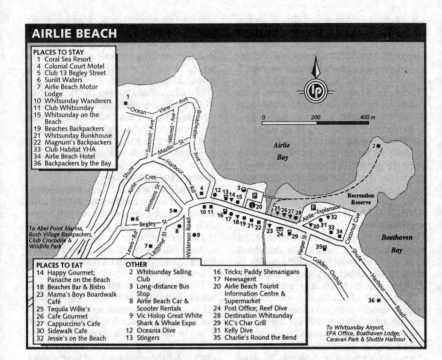

AIRLIE BEACH

PLACES TO STAY
1 Coral Sea Resort
4 Colonial Court Motel
5 Club 13 Begley Street
6 Sunlit Waters
7 Airlie Beach Motor Lodge
10 Whitsunday Wanderers
11 Club Whitsunday
15 Whitsunday on the Beach
19 Beaches Backpackers
21 Whitsunday Bunkhouse
22 Magnum's Backpackers
33 Club Habitat YHA
34 Airlie Beach Hotel
36 Backpackers by the Bay

PLACES TO EAT
14 Happy Gourmet; Panache on the Beach
18 Beaches Bar & Bistro
23 Mama's Boys Boardwalk Café
25 Tequila Willie's
26 Cafe Gourmet
27 Cappuccino's Cafe
30 Sidewalk Cafe
32 Jessie's on the Beach

OTHER
2 Whitsunday Sailing Club
3 Long-distance Bus Stop
8 Airlie Beach Car & Scooter Rentals
9 Vic Hislop Great White Shark & Whale Expo
12 Oceania Dive
13 Stingers
16 Tricks; Paddy Shenanigans
17 Newsagent
20 Airlie Beach Tourist Information Centre & Supermarket
24 Post Office; Reef Dive
28 Destination Whitsunday
29 KC's Char Grill
31 Kelly Dive
35 Charlie's Round the Bend

Airlie Bay

Recreation Reserve

Boathaven Bay

To Abel Point Marina, Bush Village Backpackers, Club Crocodile & Wildlife Park

To Whitsunday Airport, EPA Office, Boathaven Lodge, Caravan Park & Shuttle Harbour

for as little as $159, but you may spend most of the course in the pool or the classroom. Better, more expensive courses cost from $325 to $545, combining tuition on the mainland with three or four days diving on the Great Barrier Reef. All the firms also offer diving trips for certified divers.

Dive companies are only as good as their instructors, however, and the staff turnover is pretty high throughout the diving industry. It's worth talking to the tourist office and other backpackers to get a feel for which companies are currently offering the best service. The main companies in Airlie Beach are: Reef Dive (☎ 1800 075 120), Kelly Dive (☎ 1800 063 454) and Oceania Dive (☎ 1800 075 035). The Dive Academy (☎ 1800 331 316) is based at Abel Point Marina.

Special Events
Airlie Beach is the centre of activities during the Whitsunday Fun Race (for cruising yachts) each September. The festivities include a Miss Figurehead competition, where the contestants traditionally compete topless.

Places to Stay – Budget
Camping There are three good caravan parks east of Airlie Beach along the road to Shute Harbour. The *Island Gateway Holiday Resort* (☎ 4946 6228), about 1.5km east of Airlie Beach, has camp sites ($14), caravans ($30) and cabins (from $42). The *Shute Harbour Gardens Caravan Park* (☎ 4946 9388), 2.5km east, has camp sites for $10 and cabins for $50 per night. The *Flame Tree Tourist Village* (☎ 1800 069 388), 6km east, has camp sites for $14, caravans from $35 and five-bed cabins from $60 a double, plus $10 per extra person.

You can also camp at the central *Koala Beach Resort*, a hostel, for $8/12 for one/ two people.

QUEENSLAND

Hostels Airlie Beach is a major stopover on the backpackers' circuit and there are hostels to suit everyone, whether you want to party or just kick back with a good book. At the long-distance bus stop there's a row of booths where the hostel reps tout for trade when the buses arrive. All the hostels out of the city centre run courtesy buses to and from Airlie Beach. It's quite common for hostels to charge around $8 for the first night if you are prepared to pay for two nights up front.

Right in the city centre, **Beaches Backpackers** (☎ 4946 6244, 362 Shute Harbour Rd) is a big place with a party attitude, a pool and a popular bar and restaurant. It's not a place for light sleepers, but the facilities are good, with six-bed (not bunk) units with their own bathroom, balcony, TV and air-con. Beds cost $14 a night ($13 VIP).

Also in the city centre on Shute Harbour Rd, **Magnum's Backpackers** (☎ 4946 6266) is another huge party hostel. It's set out in a pleasant tropical garden with two pools. Beds in five-share units with air-con, TV and bathroom cost $12 ($10 if you book multiple nights). The hostel's Bar and Grill is popular in the evenings.

Sandwiched between Magnum's and Beaches is **Whitsunday Bunkhouse** (☎ 1800 683 566). This converted motel isn't particularly flash, and lacks both a pool and other outdoor areas. It's a cheap option with beds in eight-bed units with kitchenettes for $10 and doubles for $35.

Club 13 Begley St (☎ 4946 7376) has great views over the bay from the hill just above the city centre. This modern multi-level place consists of five three-bedroom apartments, each with two bathrooms (some with spa), cooking and laundry facilities. Beds cost $16 ($15 VIP/YHA), doubles cost $38 and breakfast is included. This place gets good reports from travellers.

Back on Shute Harbour Rd, **Club Whitsunday** (☎ 4946 6182) is a comfortable converted motel, with clean six-bed dorms with a bathroom and small kitchen area for $15 per person, and doubles for $35 (breakfast included). Despite its central location, this place is surprisingly quiet, and the staff are friendly and helpful.

Nearby is the **Koala Beach Resort** (☎ 4946 6001), part of the Whitsunday Wanderers Resort. Dorm beds cost $16 ($15 VIP), or there are twins and doubles for $40. The units sleep up to six people, are air-con and fully self-contained.

At the opposite end of Shute Harbour Rd is **Club Habitat YHA** (☎ 4946 6312), yet another motel converted to backpacker accommodation. It's a friendly place, with a pool, good communal kitchen and lounge. It costs $15 per night in a four to six bed unit with bathroom, and en suite twin rooms are $35; nonmembers pay an extra $3.

Just out of town on the way to Shute Harbour is **Backpackers by the Bay** (☎ 4946 7267, Lot 5, Hermitage Drive). It's a small, relaxed hostel with a nice atmosphere, and is generally quieter than those in the centre. The facilities here are good, and the nightly cost in a small four bed dorm is $16 ($14 VIP, $15 YHA). Doubles cost $36.

The **Bush Village Backpackers' Resort** (☎ 4946 6177, 2 St Martin's Lane), 1.5km west of Airlie Beach in Cannonvale, is a small place with a bar, pool, pleasant garden setting and comfy four-bed cabins, all with cooking facilities, fridge, bathroom and TV. Bunks cost $15 to $20, twins/doubles are $38 ($45 with air-con and TV), including breakfast.

Places to Stay – Mid-Range
Hotels & Motels The **Airlie Beach Hotel** (☎ 4946 6233), on Shute Harbour Rd, has standard, unexciting motel units from $65/80 a single/double.

Of the motels, the central **Colonial Court Motel** (☎ 4946 6180), on the corner of Shute Harbour Rd and Broadwater Ave, has doubles from $55, and the **Airlie Beach Motor Lodge** (☎ 4946 6418), on Lamond St, has doubles from $65 and self-contained units from $75.

Apartments & Resorts In the centre, **Whitsunday on the Beach** (☎ 4946 6359, 269 Shute Harbour Rd) has small, brightly renovated four-bed studio apartments from $75 to $85.

Up the hill on the corner of Begley St and Airlie Crescent, **Sunlit Waters** (☎ 4946 6352)

QUEENSLAND

has budget studio flats for $55 a double, plus $15 for extras. *Boathaven Lodge* (☎ 4946 6421, 440 Shute Harbour Rd), just east of the centre, has neat, renovated studio units overlooking Boathaven Bay from $50 a double, plus $10 for extra adults.

Whitsunday Wanderers (☎ 4946 6446), on Shute Harbour Rd, has four pools, two spas, tennis courts, landscaped gardens, a bar and restaurant, and Melanesian-style units for $45 to $55 per person, depending on the season.

Places to Stay – Top End
Club Crocodile (☎ 1800 075 125) in Cannonvale, 2km west of Airlie Beach, has modern units around a central courtyard, two swimming pools, a gym, tennis courts and a heated spa, and costs $145 per person including 'tropical' breakfast.

The *Coral Sea Resort* (☎ 1800 075 061, 25 Ocean View Ave) overlooks the ocean from a low headland and has double units from $140 ($195 with ocean views).

Places to Eat
Most of the eating possibilities are on or just off Shute Harbour Rd in Airlie Beach. If you're preparing your own food there's a small supermarket on the main street near the long-distance bus stop, and a large shopping centre at Cannonvale.

Beaches Bar & Bistro is almost always crowded with both travellers and locals, and has salads, pasta and burgers ($5 to $7), grill mains from $9 to $12 and nightly special events. *Magnum's Bar & Grill* covers similar ground, with bistro meals, theme nights, pool tables and a video screen.

The *Happy Gourmet* (263 Shute Harbour Rd) is a great place for lunch, with delicious filled rolls, sandwiches and home-made cakes. *Cafe Gourmet*, at No 289, also has good rolls and sandwiches plus smoothies and juices.

In a breezy arcade near the corner of Shute Harbour Rd and Airlie Esplanade, *Cappuccino's Cafe* has focaccias ($6), pasta ($9 to $11) and serious coffee. The *Sidewalk Cafe*, on the Airlie Esplanade, has great fish and chips ($4) while *Jessie's on the Beach* does good breakfast deals for $3.65.

The open-air *Mama's Boys Boardwalk Cafe*, next to Magnum's, is popular in the evenings, and the steaks ($8) and burgers ($5) are good value. *Panache on the Beach* is a very pleasant open-air place with pasta from $12 to $14 and other mains from $19 to $26.

If you must have Mexican, *Tequila Willie's* is open for lunch and dinner and is good value at $9 for main courses and $14 to $18 for grills. Willie's also has a small Internet cafe.

Entertainment
The bars at *Beaches Bar & Bistro* and *Magnums Bar & Grill* manage to draw a large crowd most nights, with special events and party games (prizes include free beer and complimentary cruises). Several of the bars and cafes, including *KC's Char Grill* and *Charlie's Round the Bend*, have live music most nights.

There are a couple of nightclubs on Shute Harbour Rd: *Stingers*, upstairs in an arcade near the Happy Gourmet cafe, and *Tricks*, upstairs next to the newsagency. *Paddy Shenanigans*, underneath Tricks, is a fairly standard Irish-themed place, but it has a good range of imported beers including Guinness.

Getting There & Away
Air The closest major airports are at Proserpine and Hamilton Island (Ansett only).

There are a few operators based at Whitsunday airport, a small airfield about 6km past Airlie Beach towards Shute Harbour. Island Air Taxis (☎ 4946 9933) flies to Hamilton ($50) and Lindeman ($60) islands. Heli Reef (☎ 4946 9102), Coral Air Whitsunday (☎ 4946 9130) and Island Air Taxis do joy flights over the reef.

Bus Most Greyhound Pioneer and McCafferty's buses make the detour from the highway to Airlie Beach, stopping in the main car park between the shops and beach. Buses run to/from all the main centres along the coast, including Brisbane ($107; 18 hours), Townsville ($36; 4½ hours), Mackay ($25; two hours), and Cairns ($61; 11 hours).

Whitsunday Transit (☎ 1300 655 449) runs local bus services to Proserpine ($6.50) and Shute Harbour ($8.50); buses operate daily from 6 am to 7 pm. It also meets all flights at Proserpine airport and goes on to Airlie Beach ($11) and Shute Harbour ($13).

Boat The Whitsunday Sailing Club is at the end of Airlie Esplanade. There are notice boards at the Abel Point Marina showing when rides or crewing are available. Ask around Airlie Beach or Shute Harbour.

Getting Around
Several car-rental agencies operate locally; Avis, Budget and National all have agencies on Shute Harbour Rd. Airlie Beach Car and Scooter Rentals (☎ 4946 6110), which is on the corner of Begley St and Waterson Rd, has cars and scooters for hire from $45 a day. Whitsunday Taxis can be booked on ☎ 13 1008.

CONWAY NATIONAL PARK
The road between Airlie Beach and Shute Harbour passes through Conway National Park, which stretches north and south along the coast. The southern end of the park separates the Whitsunday Passage from Repulse Bay, named by Captain Cook who strayed into it thinking it was the main passage.

Most of the park consists of rugged ranges and valleys covered in dense rainforest, but there are a few walking tracks in the surrounding area. The 2.4km walk up to **Mt Rooper lookout**, north of the road, gives good views of the Whitsunday Passage and islands. Another pleasant walk is along Mandalay Rd, about 3km east of Airlie Beach, up to **Mandalay Point** (actually outside the national park).

To reach the beautiful **Cedar Creek Falls**, turn off the Proserpine-Airlie Beach road on to Conway Rd, 8km from Proserpine. It's then about 15km to the falls – the roads are well signposted. At the end of Conway Rd, 27km from the turn-off, is the small settlement of **Conway**, with a beach and a caravan park.

Whitsundays
Curiously, the Whitsundays are misnamed – Captain Cook didn't really sail through them on Whit Sunday. When he returned to England, it was found that his meticulously kept log was a day out because he had not allowed for crossing the International Date Line! As he sailed through the Whitsundays and further north, Cook was unaware of the existence of the Great Barrier Reef, although he realised that something to the east of his ship was making the water unusually calm. It wasn't until he ran aground on the Endeavour Reef, near Cooktown, that he finally found out about the reef.

WHITSUNDAY ISLANDS
The 74 Whitsunday Islands are probably the best-known Queensland islands, and one of Australia's pleasure-boating capitals. They were named by Captain Cook when he sailed through here on 3 June 1770. The islands fall into four groups – the Molle Islands, Whitsunday Islands, Lindeman Islands and Repulse Islands – scattered along both sides of the Whitsunday Passage, and all within 50km of Shute Harbour.

The Whitsundays are mostly continental islands – the tips of underwater mountains – and many of them have fringing coral reefs, though the Great Barrier Reef is at least 60km from the mainland. Most of the islands are hilly and wooded and the passages between them are certainly beautiful enough to warrant a boat trip if you have the time.

A few are developed with tourist resorts, but most are uninhabited and several offer the chance of some back-to-nature beach camping and bushwalking. All but four of the Whitsundays are predominantly or completely national park (the exceptions are Dent Island, and the resort islands of Hamilton, Daydream and Hayman). The other main resorts are on South Molle, Lindeman, Long and Hook islands.

Most people staying in the resorts are on package holidays and, with the exception of the cabins on Hook Island, resort

QUEENSLAND

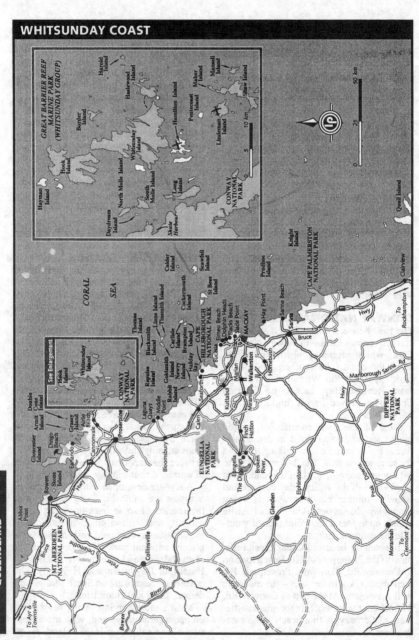

WHITSUNDAY COAST

GREAT BARRIER REEF MARINE PARK (WHITSUNDAY GROUP)

Harold Island

Hayman Island

Hook Island

Border Island

Haslewood Island

Maher Island

Maxwell Island

Shaw Island

Daydream Island

North Molle Island

South Molle Island

Whitsunday Island

Hamilton Island

Pentecost Island

Lindeman Island

Long Island

Shute Harbour

CONWAY NATIONAL PARK

CORAL SEA

See Enlargement

Hook Island

Whitsunday Island

CONWAY NATIONAL PARK

Quail Island

Knight Island

CAPE PALMERSTON NATIONAL PARK

Prudhoe Island

Hay Point

Sarina Beach

Sarina

Bruce

To Rockhampton

Clairview

Calder Island

Scawfell Island

St Bees Island

Cockermouth Island

Brampton Island

Carlisle Island

Keswick Island

Linne Island

Tinsmith Island

Thomas Island

Blacksmith Island

Goldsmith Island

Newry Island

Rabbit Island

Middle Island

Repulse Island

Laguna Quays

CAPE HILLSBOROUGH NATIONAL PARK

Halliday Bay

Seaforth

Kuttabul

Calen

Bloomsbury

Proserpine

Cannonvale Beach

Airlie Beach

Shute Harbour

Double Cone Island

Armit Island

Grassy Island

Dingo Beach

Earlando

Gloucester Island

Stone Island

Bowen

Abbot Point

MT ABERDEEN NATIONAL PARK

Collinsville

Bucasia
Eimeo Beach
Dolphin Heads
Blacks Beach
Slade Point
MACKAY
Racecourse
Te Kowai
Mirani
Marian
Walkerston
Homebush
Hampden

Manborough Sarina Rd

Finch Hatton
Broken River
Eungella
The Diggings

EUNGELLA NATIONAL PARK

Elphinstone

Glenden

DIPPERU NATIONAL PARK

Moranbah

To Clermont

To Ayr & Townsville

Bruce Hwy

Delmotte

Peter

River

Bowen

Collinsville

Road

Developmental

Peak Downs

Bowen

Elphinstone

0   5   10 km

0   25   50 km

accommodation is beyond the reach of the shoestring traveller. However, there are usually more affordable stand-by rates for most resorts – check with the booking agencies in Airlie Beach.

Camping on the Islands

Although accommodation in the island resorts is mostly expensive, it's possible to camp on many of the islands. There are QPWS camp sites on North Molle, South Molle, Long, Planton, Denman, Tancred, Hook (two sites and a privately run camping ground), Whitsunday (three camping areas), Henning, South Repulse, Lindeman, Shaw (two sites) and Thomas islands.

Self-sufficiency is the key to camping at these sites; some have toilets, but only a few have drinking water, and then not always year-round. You're advised to take five litres of water per person per day, plus three days supply extra in case you get stuck. You must also have a fuel stove as wood fires are banned.

The EPA office (☎ 4946 7022) in Airlie Beach publishes a leaflet that describes the various sites, and can provide detailed information on what to take and do. You can book sites and get camping permits ($3.50 per person per night) here.

Getting There & Away

For information on boat transport, talk to the rangers or contact one of the many booking agencies in Airlie Beach. Sea Trek (☎ 4946 5255) will drop you off at Long, North Molle, South Molle, Denman or Planton Islands for $35 return (minimum of two people). Alternatively, for $50 to $65 return per person, regular day-trip boats will drop you off at the end of a cruise and pick you up again on an agreed date.

Long Island

The closest resort island to the coast, Long Island has three resorts and is nearly all national park. The island is about 11km long, but no more than 1.5km wide, and it has good rainforest, 13km of walking tracks and some fine lookouts.

At Happy Bay in the north, the *Club Crocodile Resort* (☎ 1800 075 125) is a modern mid-range resort fronting a long expanse of tropical island beach. The resort has two pools, a cafe, a restaurant, tennis courts, water sports and so on, as well as the obligatory disco. There are three levels of rooms ranging from $145 to $190 a double (including transfers).

Two kilometres south, the small *Long Island Palm Bay Hideaway* (☎ 4946 9233) is a low-key, old-fashioned resort with Melanesian style *bures* (cabins), all with verandahs, kitchenettes and bathrooms. The resort is a pleasant reminder of days gone by and offers a simple, relaxing stay. Prices are very contemporary, however, with doubles between $156 and $224. Breakfast is $10, lunch $17 and dinner $29.

At the southern end of the island is *Whitsunday Wilderness Lodge* (☎ 4946 9777), a low-key, ecofriendly resort with eight comfortable beachfront cabins. The cost is around $1290 per person, per week, including transfers and daily guided boat and walking trips.

South Molle Island

At 4 sq km, South Molle is the largest of the Molle group of islands and it is virtually joined to Mid Molle and North Molle. It has long stretches of beach and is crisscrossed by walking tracks. The highest point is 198m Mt Jeffreys, but the climb up Spion Kop is also worthwhile. You can spend a day walking on the island for the cost of the $16 ferry trip.

South Molle is mainly national park but there's the *South Molle Island Resort* (☎ 1800 075 080) in the north, where the boats come in. The resort has straightforward motel-style rooms, a small golf course, a gym, tennis courts and water sports gear. Nightly costs start at $114 per person (single or double), which includes all meals and activities. There's also a QPWS *camping ground* at Sandy Bay (bring your own water).

If you like the idea of having an island to yourself, the tiny islands of Denman, Planton and Tancred are close to Shute Harbour, and they all have QPWS camping sites (no facilities).

Hook Island

The second largest of the Whitsundays, Hook Island is 53 sq km and rises to 450m at Hook Peak. It's mainly national park and has numerous beaches, with QPWS *camping areas* at Maureens Cove and Bloodhorn Beach (bring your own water).

The *Hook Island Wilderness Resort* (☎ 4946 9380) is the only true budget resort in the Whitsundays. It's a simple and basic lodge with 12 adjoining bunk units; a bunk costs $20 a night and doubles are $60. It also has camp sites for $13 per person, and there's a casual restaurant serving cheap breakfasts, lunches and dinners, as well as communal cooking and bathroom facilities.

The island also has an unimpressive underwater observatory ($7). The launch trip from Shute Harbour to the resort is $25 return.

The beautiful, fjord-like Nara Inlet on Hook Island is a very popular deep-water anchorage for visiting yachts.

Whitsunday Island

The largest of the Whitsundays, this island covers 109 sq km and rises to 438m at Whitsunday Peak. There's no resort, but 6km-long Whitehaven Beach on the south-east coast is the longest and finest beach in the group (some say in the country), with good snorkelling off its southern end. There are good QPWS *camping areas* with water supplies at Dugong, Sawmill and Joes beaches, all on the west side of the island.

Daydream Island

Tiny Daydream Island, about 1km long and a few hundred metres wide, is the nearest resort island to Shute Harbour. At the northern end is the 300 room *Daydream Island International Resort* (☎ 1800 075 040), a modern, family oriented resort. Rooms start at $155 per person including meals, transfers, use of tennis courts, a gym, pools, water sports gear etc.

Daydream Island has a good day-trippers' section at the southern end, with a pool, bar and cafe, and water sports gear for hire. The return trip from Shute Harbour costs $24.

Hamilton Island

- postcode 4803   • pop 1500

The most heavily developed resort island in the Whitsundays, Hamilton Island is about 5 sq km and rises to 200m at Passage Peak. It is more like a town than a resort, with its own airport, a 200 boat marina, shops, restaurants, bars and accommodation for more than 2000 people, including three high-rise tower blocks. If your pockets are deep enough, Hamilton offers helicopter joy rides, game fishing, parasailing, cruising and scuba diving. It also has nine restaurants, squash courts and a hill-top fauna reserve with wombats, crocodiles and koalas. Double rooms cost from $184 a night, ranging up to $1200 a night for your own private villa. Meals cost $15 for breakfast, $45 for breakfast and dinner. For reservations phone ☎ 1800 075 110.

Hamilton can make an interesting day trip from Shute Harbour ($45 return for the launch only), and you can use all of the resort facilities.

The airport is used mainly by people jetting between resort islands, with launches and helicopters laid on to whisk them off to their chosen spots. Ansett flies non-stop between Hamilton and Brisbane ($320 one way), Cairns ($583), Melbourne ($545) and Sydney ($455). Hamilton Island Aviation has flights between Hamilton and Whitsunday airport near Airlie Beach ($50/75 one way/day return), and Mackay ($95/130).

Hayman Island

The most northerly of the Whitsundays, Hayman Island is 4 sq km and rises to 250m above sea level. It has forested hills, valleys and beaches, but it has become such an exclusive resort island that day-trip operators no longer call there. The nearest you'll probably get is some of the reefs or small islands nearby such as Black Island (also called Bali Hai) or Arkhurst, Langford or Bird islands.

The *Hayman Island Resort* (☎ 1800 075 175), fronted by a wide, shallow reef that emerges from the water at low tide, is a luxurious five star hotel dripping with style. Rooms range from $490 for Palm Garden rooms to $1500 a night for a suite, all including breakfast.

Lindeman Island

One of the most southerly of the Whitsundays, Lindeman Island covers 8 sq km, rising to 210m at Mt Oldfield. It's a little far from Shute Harbour to justify a day trip, but, if you have more time, the island has lots of little beaches and secluded bays and is mostly national park with 20km of walking trails. You can get across to some of the small islands off the coast. There's a QPWS *camp site* at Boat Port.

The *Club Med Resort* (☎ 1800 807 973), in the south, has a pool, several restaurants, a bar, a golf course, tennis and lots of water-based activities. Nightly tariffs range from $199 plus a one-off $50 membership, including all meals and most activities. The internationally famous Club Med style is very evident here, with a heavy emphasis on fun, fun, fun. Transfers are $45 (return) with Whitsunday Allover (☎ 4946 6900).

You can also fly there with Island Air Taxis ($50 one way, $65 day return) from Whitsunday airport on the mainland.

Getting Around

Air Hamilton and Lindeman islands are the only islands with airports. Island Air Taxis (☎ 4946 9933) flies from Airlie Beach to Hamilton ($50) and Lindeman ($60) islands. Heli Reef (☎ 4946 9102), Coral Air Whitsunday (☎ 4946 9130) and Island Air Taxis do joy flights over the reef.

Boat There's a bamboozling array of boat trips heading out to the islands. Fantasea Cruises (☎ 4946 5111) and Whitsunday Allover (☎ 1300 366 494) are the two major operators for transfers to the islands – most of their boats depart from Shute Harbour. Island transfers cost from $16 to $38 return, depending on the distance involved; you can also buy tickets that combine visits to two or more islands.

In addition, there are literally dozens of different cruises and pleasure trips heading out to the islands and reefs; these depart from either Shute Harbour or the Abel Point Marina near Airlie Beach.

Depending on how much time and money you have, there are day trips to the islands or reefs from $50 to $120; overnight cruises from $120; two-night/three-day trips from $250; or self-skippered charter yachts from about $275 per day (sailing experience required).

All of the boats and trips are different, so it's worth speaking to a couple of the booking agents to find out which trip will suit you, whether it's a leisurely sailing cruise to an uninhabited island or a high-speed trip to the outer reef for diving. Most trips include activities such as snorkelling and boom netting, with scuba diving as an optional extra. It's worth asking how many people will be on your boat.

Most of the cruise operators do bus pickups from Airlie Beach. You can bus to Shute Harbour or there's car parking in Shute Harbour car park, or the lock-up car park by the Shell service station (a few hundred metres before the harbour). Both places charge $9 for 24 hours.

Roylen's Cruises has weekend trips from Mackay to Hamilton and other islands – see the Mackay section earlier in this chapter for details.

BOWEN

● postcode 4805   ● pop 8990

Bowen, founded in 1861, was the first coastal settlement north of Rockhampton. Although overshadowed by Mackay to the south and Townsville to the north, Bowen developed into a thriving fruit and vegetable growing centre. Most travellers come here looking for seasonal picking work.

The Bowen Historical Museum, at 22 Gordon St, has displays relating to the town's early history. It's open weekdays and Sunday morning. Just north of Bowen, a string of sandy beaches, some of them quite secluded, dot the coast around the cape.

There's a helpful tourist office at 34 Williams St (☎ 4786 4494).

Places to Stay

There are three 'workers hostels' in Bowen that specialise in finding seasonal picking (mainly tomatoes) for travellers. All three are fairly basic, and have buses that do pickups and run workers to and from work (sometimes free, Barnacles is $4). It's a competitive scene, and all the hostels have cheaper weekly rates; it's worth ringing around before you come, to find out what's available.

Barnacles Backpackers (☎ 4786 4400, 16 Gordon St) has two sections, with dorm beds for $13 and doubles for $26. It can get quite crowded here, though there's a bistro that opens during the picking season to relieve the pressure on the kitchens.

The long-running **Bowen Backpackers** (☎ 4786 3433, 56 Herbert St) is nearby, on the main road through town. It has a good reputation for finding fruit-picking work, although the owners may get very annoyed if, after finding you work, you move elsewhere, such as the (cheaper) caravan park. The nightly cost is $13 in 10-bed dorms.

The other backpacker in town is **Trinity's Backpackers** (☎ 4786 4199, 93 Horseshoe Bay Rd). It's fairly seedy, even by workers-hostel standards, but it's certainly cheap, with beds in five or 10-share units for $11.

Getting There & Away

The long-distance bus stop is outside the Traveland travel agency (☎ 4786 2835) on William St, near the centre. There are buses along the coast to Rockhampton ($70; 7½ hours), Airlie Beach ($19; one hour) and Townsville ($27; 2½ hours). The *Sunlander* and *Queenslander* trains also stop at Bowen (at Bootooloo Siding, 3km south of the centre). The fare from Brisbane is $139 in an economy sleeper.

North Coast

AYR TO TOWNSVILLE

Ayr (population 8700) is on the delta of one of Queensland's biggest rivers, the Burdekin. It is the major commercial centre for the rich farmlands and cane fields of the Burdekin Valley. On Wilmington St, the Ayr Nature Display has exhibits of butterflies, moths and beetles; it's open daily from 8 am to 5 pm ($2.50). South across the Burdekin River is Home Hill, where you can visit the bizarre **Ashworth's Fantastic Tourist Attraction** with its tacky souvenir shop, pottery gallery and collection of fossils, gemstones and rocks.

Between Ayr and Townsville is the turn-off to the **Australian Institute of Marine Science**, on Cape Ferguson. You can visit it on weekdays from 9 am to 3 pm, and from March to November there are free guided tours every Friday at 10 am.

About 60km north-west of Ayr and 86km south of Townsville there's a turn-off from the Bruce Hwy to the **Bowling Green Bay National Park**. It's 6km from the highway to the park, where there's a good *camping ground* (firewood provided) and a ranger station (☎ 4778 8203) near Alligator Creek. There are two walking trails (17km and 8km return) and the creek has good swimming holes. Alligator Creek tumbles down between two rugged ranges that rise steeply from the coastal plains. The taller range peaks in Mt Elliot (1432m), whose higher slopes harbour some of Queensland's most southerly tropical rainforest. There's no public transport to the park, and the main gate is closed between 6.30 pm and 6.30 am.

TOWNSVILLE

• postcode 4810   • pop 109,900

The fourth largest city in Queensland, Townsville is the city port for the vast inland agricultural and mining regions of northern Queensland. The city takes its name from Robert Towns, a Sydney-based sea captain and financier, who founded the town in 1864. Like many places in Queensland, Townsville developed mainly on the back of Chinese and Kanaka labour.

As well as the port, Townsville has a major armed forces base and the James Cook University. It's the start of the main highway from Queensland across to the NT, and the only departure point for Magnetic Island (20 minutes away by ferry). The Great Barrier Reef is about 1¼ hours away by fast catamaran.

From a travellers' point of view, Townsville hasn't really got a lot going for it. The city's main attractions are the excellent aquarium at the Great Barrier Reef Wonderland and as an access point for Magnetic Island.

QUEENSLAND

Red rock formations, Sybella creek near Mt Isa, Qld

Seascape with anthias

Lamington National Park, Qld

Cape York Peninsula, Qld

Lady Elliot Island, Qld

Imperial Hotel, Eumundi, Qld

Diver photographers over the Great Barrier Reef, Qld

Remains of a mining smelter in historic reserve, Chillagoe, Qld

Pandora's Box

Sent to recapture the mutineers from the *Bounty*, the HMS *Pandora* is probably Australia's most famous shipwreck. The historic vessel struck the reef off Cape York in 1791, while returning 14 mutineers to face trial in England.

Under the orders of Captain Edward Edwards, the prisoners were left on the ship to drown, still imprisoned in their tiny cell, a wooden cage known as 'Pandora's Box'. All would have perished but for the heroic actions of boatswain's mate William Moulter, who released the mutineers as he fled the sinking ship.

Thirty-one crew members and four mutineers were lost, but the British authorities showed no mercy to the survivors. On their return to England, the mutineers were tried on board HMS *Duke* and six were sentenced to death by hanging.

The wreck of the *Pandora* was rediscovered in 1977, and archaeologists have now made more than 1700 dives to the site. The artefacts recovered are displayed in the Museum of Tropical Queensland in Townsville.

In recent years redevelopment of the Flinders St East and Palmer St heritage areas, on opposite sides of Ross Creek, has given the Townsville city centre a real lift.

Orientation

Townsville centres on Ross Creek and is dominated by 290m-high Castle Hill, which has a lookout at the top. The city sprawls a long way, but the centre is fairly compact and you can easily get around on foot.

The transit centre, the arrival and departure point for long-distance buses, is on Palmer St, just south of Ross Creek. The city centre is immediately to the north of the creek, over the Dean St bridge. Flinders St Mall stretches to the left from the northern side of the bridge, towards the train station. To the right of the bridge is the Flinders St East area, which contains many of the town's oldest buildings, plus cafes, restaurants, the Great Barrier Reef Wonderland and the Sunferries City terminal (there's another terminal on Sir Leslie Theiss Drive on the breakwater).

Information

Townsville Enterprises' main tourist information office (☎ 4778 3555) is on the Bruce Hwy, 8km south of the city centre. There's a more convenient information booth (☎ 4721 3660) in the middle of Flinders St Mall, between Stokes and Denham Sts. It's open Monday to Saturday from 9 am to 5 pm and Sunday to 12.30 pm.

The RACQ (☎ 13 1111) is at 635 Sturt St, close to the city centre. The main post office can be found on the corner of Flinders St Mall and Denham St. There's also an EPA information office (☎ 4721 2399) at the Wonderland, open from Monday to Friday from 9 am to 5 pm.

The Internet Den, near McDonald's in the mall, charges $9 per hour for Internet/email access, and you can also use the Internet at the Mary Who bookshop on Stanley St ($5 per half hour).

Great Barrier Reef Wonderland

Townsville's top attraction is at the end of Flinders St East beside Ross Creek. Although the impressive Reef HQ aquarium is the highlight, there are several other sections including a theatre, a museum, shops and the Great Barrier Reef Marine Park Authority office.

Reef HQ Billed as a 'living reef experience', the main attraction at this newly renovated aquarium is a vast living-coral reef, which provides a home to hundreds of fish, sharks, rays and other marine life. To maintain the natural conditions needed to keep this community alive, a wave machine simulates the ebb and flow of the ocean, circular currents keep the water in motion and marine algae are used in the purification system. There are also numerous smaller tanks, hands-on reef displays, a slide show and a turtle research station and captive-breeding facility, which you can tour. It's open daily from 9 am to 5 pm ($14.80/6.50 adults/children).

QUEENSLAND

QUEENSLAND

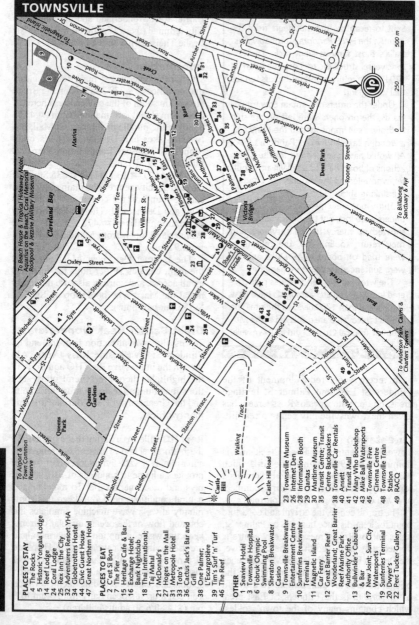

TOWNSVILLE

PLACES TO STAY
4 The Rocks
5 Historic Yongala Lodge
6 Reef Lodge
24 Coral Lodge
25 Rex Inn the City
32 Adventurers Resort YHA
34 Globetrotters Hostel
44 Civic Guest House
47 Great Northern Hotel

PLACES TO EAT
2 C'est Si Bon
7 The Pier
15 Heritage Cafe & Bar
16 Exchange Hotel;
     Bank Nightclub
18 Thai International;
     Taj Mahal
21 McDonald's
27 Hoges on the Mall
31 Metropole Hotel
33 Toto's
36 Cactus Jack's Bar and
     Grill
38 One Palmer;
     L'Escargoliere
39 Tim's Surf 'n' Turf
46 The Reef

OTHER
1 Seaview Hotel
3 Townsville Hospital
6 Tobruk Olympic
     Swimming Pool
8 Sheraton Breakwater
     Casino
9 Townsville Breakwater
     Entertainment Centre
10 Sunferries Breakwater
     Terminal
11 Magnetic Island
     Car Ferry
12 Great Barrier Reef
     Wonderland; Great Barrier
     Reef Marine Park
     Authority Office
13 Bullwinkel's Cabaret
     & Bar
17 New Joint; Sun City
     Watersports
19 Sunferries Terminal
20 Dwyer's
22 Perc Tucker Gallery
23 Townsville Museum
26 Internet Den
28 Information Booth
29 Qantas
30 Maritime Museum
35 Transit Centre; Transit
     Centre Backpackers
38 Townsville Car Rentals
40 Ansett
41 Transit Mall
42 Mary Who Bookshop
43 Mike Ball Watersports
45 Townsville Five
     Cinema Centre
48 Townsville Train
     Station
49 RACQ

Omnimax Theatre This is a cinema with angled seating and a dome-shaped screen for a three-dimensional effect. Hour-long films on the reef and various other topics such as outer space alternate through the day from 10.30 am to 4.30 pm. Admission to one film is $10/5.

Museum of Tropical Queensland The museum is being extended to include artefacts recovered from the historic wreck of the *Pandora* (see the boxed text 'Pandora's Box'). The museum will also include displays on the natural history of north Queensland and Aboriginal culture. It will open daily from 9 am to 5 pm ($9).

Other Museums & Galleries

The **Townsville Museum**, on the corner of Sturt and Stokes Sts, has a permanent display on early Townsville and the North Queensland independence campaigns. It's open daily from 10 am to 3 pm (to 1 pm on weekends). Entry is $2.

The **North Queensland Military Museum** is in an 1890s fort in the grounds of the Jezzine Army Barracks, beyond the northern end of The Strand; it is open Monday, Wednesday and Friday mornings. There's also a **Maritime Museum**, on Palmer St, beside Ross Creek; it is open weekdays from 10 am to 4 pm and weekends from 1 to 4 pm ($3). The **Perc Tucker Gallery**, at the Denham St end of the Flinders St Mall, is a good regional art gallery, with free entry every day.

Parks, Gardens & Sanctuaries

The **Queens Gardens**, on Gregory St 1km from the town centre, contain sports fields, tennis courts and Townsville's original Botanic Gardens, dating from 1878. The entrance to these lovely gardens is on Paxton St. The new botanic gardens, **Anderson Park**, are 6km south-west of the centre on Gulliver St, Mundingburra.

The **Billabong Sanctuary**, 17km south on the Bruce Hwy, is a popular wildlife sanctuary. It's open daily from 8 am to 5 pm, with various shows, including crocodile, koala and giant eel feeding, throughout each day. Admission costs $18/9. See Organised Tours later in the Townsville section for tours to the sanctuary.

The **Palmetum**, about 15km south-west of the city centre off University Rd, is a 25 hectare botanic garden devoted to native palms, ranging from desert to rainforest species, in their natural environments.

The 32 sq km **Town Common Reserve**, 5km north of the centre off Cape Pallarenda Rd, covers mangrove swamps, salt marsh, dry grassland and pockets of woodland and forest. It isn't particularly attractive but it's a refuge for water birds, such as the magpie geese that herald the start of the wet season, and stately brolgas, which gather in the Dry. Early morning is the best time to see them.

Other Attractions

The **Flinders St Mall** is the retail heart of the city. It's bright and breezy with fountains, plantations and crowds of shoppers. Every Sunday morning, the busy **Cotter's Market** is held in the mall, with a wide range of crafts and local produce on offer.

East of the mall you can stroll along **Flinders St East** beside the creek, which features many 19th century buildings and some of Townsville's best restaurants. The Sheraton Townsville Hotel & Casino and the Townsville Breakwater Entertainment Centre are out on a breakwater at the mouth of Ross Creek, but it's a long walk through a series of car parks to get there. More pleasant is the walk north-west along **The Strand**, a long, beachfront drive with a marina, gardens, some awesome banyan trees, the Tobruk Olympic swimming pool and an artificial waterfall. At the top end of The Strand is the **Coral Memorial Rockpool**, a large artificial swimming pool on the edge of the ocean.

If you're feeling energetic, the panoramic views from the top of **Castle Hill** are well worth the 2km scramble to the summit; the walking path begins at the end of Victoria St.

Activities

Diving & Snorkelling Townsville has four or five diving schools, including one of Australia's best – Mike Ball Watersports (☎ 4772 3022), at 252 Walker St. Certificate courses

QUEENSLAND

start weekly and cost either $295 for five days with two separate day trips to the reef, or $535 for six days with three days/three nights on the reef.

Pro-Dive (☎ 4721 1760), another well-regarded dive school, has an office in the Great Barrier Reef Wonderland. Pro-Dive's weekly five day course costs $480, with two nights and three days on the reef. You can get deals on accommodation if you book a dive course through your hostel.

Certified divers can explore the wreck of the *Yongala*, a passenger liner that sank off Cape Bowling Green in 1911; 122 lives were lost. Mike Ball and Pro-Dive run two-day/multi-dive trips out to the *Yongala* (from around $410), or you can take a day trip to the wreck with Sun City Watersports (☎ 4771 6527), at 121 Flinders St East, for $160.

Pure Pleasure Cruises (☎ 4721 3555), at Great Barrier Reef Wonderland, has five day trips a week out to Kelso Reef. The cost of $124 (children $64) includes lunch and snorkelling gear; scuba dives are an optional extra.

Other Activities Risky Business (☎ 4725 4571) has abseiling and rock climbing ($54) and 'skyseiling' (like a huge flying fox, $79). Coral Sea Skydivers (☎ 4725 6780) will let you throw yourself out of a plane for $217 (tandem dive, from 2430m); freefall courses cost $400.

Organised Tours

Based at the Great Barrier Reef Wonderland Centre, Detours (☎ 4721 5977) offers tours in and around Townsville, including a city sights tour (weekdays, two hours, $24), tours to the Billabong Sanctuary (daily, 3½ hours, $32), or Charters Towers (Monday and Friday, eight hours, $69), and cruises to Dunk and Bedarra Islands (Tuesday, Thursday and Sunday, $98).

Places to Stay – Budget

Camping There are two good caravan parks about 3km from the centre. The better choice is the *Rowes Bay Caravan Park* (☎ 4771 3576), opposite the beach on Heatley Parade in Rowes Bay. Camp sites are

$13 and on-site cabins start from $42. The *Town & Country Caravan Park* (☎ 4772 1487, 16 Kings Rd)*, in West End, has camp sites for $12, on-site vans from $30 and cabins from $45.

Hostels Townsville's hostel scene is probably the best example of large operators jumping on the budget accommodation bandwagon. There are far more beds here than Townsville can hope to fill, and as a result, the standard of hostels here is lower than in many towns along the coast. All the places in town offer VIP discounts ($1).

On the south side of Ross Creek there are at least three hostels that are conveniently close to the transit centre and the upmarket Palmer Street area. The huge *Adventurers Resort YHA* (☎ 4721 1522, 79 Palmer St) is a multilevel complex with over 300 beds, a shop and a swimming pool. The facilities are quite good, but because of its size it tends to feel impersonal. Accommodation in a four bunk dorm costs $14 for YHA members, singles/doubles cost $24/32. Nonmembers pay an extra $2 per person.

Townsville's other huge offering is the *Transit Centre Backpackers* (☎ 1800 628 836)*, which is upstairs on top of the transit centre. It's big, clean and charmless, but it's certainly convenient for the buses. It has dorm beds for $15 and rooms for $26/34. Its free evening city tour is popular.

Between these two places is the smaller *Globetrotters Hostel* (☎ 4771 3242, 45 Palmer St)*. It's a cheerful, old-style hostel with all the usual facilities – kitchen, lounge, pool, laundry – and it's clean and well run. Beds in six-bed dorms cost $15 per night, singles cost $28 and twins are $18 per person.

The other hostels are on the north side of Ross Creek, in and around the city centre. Best of this bunch is the *Civic Guest House* (☎ 4771 5381, 262 Walker St)*. This clean and easy-going hostel has beds in three or four-bed dorms for $15, in six-bed dorms with bathroom and air-con for $17, and pleasant rooms from $35/39. Its courtesy bus does pickups and there's a free barbecue on Friday night.

The **Reef Lodge** (☎ 4721 1112, 4 Wickham St) is a small, fairly run-down place that mainly caters to long-term tenants, but it's convenient for Flinders St East. Dorm beds start at $13 and rooms at $28/32.

Hotels The **Great Northern Hotel** (☎ 4771 6191, 500 Flinders St), across the road from the train station, is a good old-fashioned pub with clean, simple singles/doubles for $20/30, and a few doubles with private bathrooms for $35; the food downstairs is good.

Places to Stay – Mid-Range

Guesthouses On the hill overlooking the centre, the **Coral Lodge** (☎ 4771 5512, 32 Hale St) is a neat, friendly guesthouse with air-con singles/doubles from $45/50 and self-contained units from $60, including a light breakfast.

The **Rocks** (☎ 4771 5700, 20 Cleveland Terrace) is a superb, renovated historic home with great views over the bay. All the rooms have period furnishings and are great value at $78 to $98, including breakfast.

Motels & Apartments Cheaper motels include: the **Tropical Hideaway Motel** (☎ 4771 4355, 74 The Strand), with doubles from $55; the central **Rex Inn the City** (☎ 4771 6048, 143 Wills St), with rooms from $79; and the **Beach House Motel** (☎ 4721 1333, 66 The Strand), with singles/doubles for $62/68.

The **Historic Yongala Lodge** (☎ 4772 4633, 11 Fryer St) has modern self-contained rooms from $79 a double and heritage-style units from $89, as well as a good Greek restaurant at the front.

The high-rise **Aquarius on the Beach** (☎ 4772 4255, 75 The Strand) has excellent self-contained suites (only), complete with great views, from $105 for two.

Places to Eat

Flinders St East is the main area for eateries, and it offers plenty of choice. The **Heritage Cafe & Bar** is a modern, cosy place with light meals (pasta etc) from $12 to $15, other mains are slightly more.

The elegant **Thai International Restaurant**, upstairs at No 235, has fine soups for $6, a good range of vegetarian dishes from $6 to $9 and other mains from $10 to $14. Downstairs is the **Taj Mahal**, an Indian and Persian restaurant with vegetarian dishes from $11 to $15, others are $17 to $19.

On the same street, the Exchange Hotel has the pleasant **Thai Exchange** (mains $9 to $14), **Melton Black's Bistro** (grill mains from $15) on the balcony, and the casual **Portraits Wine Bar**, with bistro-type meals.

Still in Flinders St, but on the Mall, is **Hoges on the Mall**, a family restaurant with main meals for $10 to $18, and breakfast from $3.

The **Sheraton Breakwater Casino** has amazingly cheap (and low-glamour) meals for the punters – $7.50 gets you a roast and vegies. If your numbers come up, the **Pier**, an upmarket seafood restaurant on stilts on Sir Leslie Thiess Drive, is a good place to celebrate. Lunchtime mains start at $20 and evening meals are from $20 to $25.

Many of the pubs also do decent counter meals. The **Great Northern Hotel**, on the corner of Flinders and Blackwood Sts, has an excellent bistro with mains from $10 to $12 and good bar meals from $5 to $8. Nearby, the **Reef** (491 Flinders St) is an excellent Thai BYO, with vegetarian and meat dishes for $9/$10, and seafood dishes for $14.

The **Seaview Hotel**, on the corner of The Strand and Gregory St, is another popular pub, and it has a pleasant beer garden. **C'est Si Bon**, on Eyre St near Gregory St, is a good little gourmet deli with salads, sandwiches and other home-made goodies.

The Historic Yongala Lodge is fronted by a **Greek restaurant** in a lovely 19th century building with period furnishings, memorabilia and finds from the Yongala shipwreck. Main meals cost from $18 to $25.

South of the river, Palmer St also has some good pubs and eateries. On the corner of Palmer and Dean Sts, **One Palmer**, is a chic licensed cafe (mains $14 to $18), with a simple BYO French restaurant, **L'Escargotière**, next door.

Cactus Jack's Bar & Grill (☎ 4721 1478, 21 Palmer St) is a lively licensed Mexican place with main courses in the $10 to $15 range; you'll need to book on weekends. Close to the Globetrotters Hostel at No 51, *Toto's* is a smart Italian restaurant with pasta from $9 to $12 and other mains from $15. There's an evening backpacker menu for $10. The *Metropole Hotel*, next to the Adventurers Resort YHA, has good bistro meals in its rear beer garden.

The popular *Tim's Surf 'n' Turf*, on Ogden St, has views of the river, but the huge (700g) steaks are the main attraction ($13). Other mains like chicken parmigiana and beef schnitzel range from $9 to $11.

Entertainment

Townsville's lively nightlife also centres on Flinders St East. The *New Joint*, at No 237, is a loud sports bar, with live music at weekends. *Portraits Wine Bar*, at the Exchange Hotel at No 151, attracts an older, more sophisticated crowd. Nearby at No 169 is the *Bank*, the city's most upmarket nightclub; it's open nightly till late, with a small cover charge and dress regulations. *Bullwinkle's Cabaret & Bar*, on the corner of Flinders St East and Wickham St, is another popular nightclub.

Close by is *Dwyer's*, an Irish bar with live music on Wednesday, Friday and Saturday – and Guinness, of course.

Along The Strand, the popular *Seaview Hotel*, on the corner of Gregory St, has its own nightclub, *Francine's*, and live music in the beer garden.

The *Townsville Five Cinema Centre*, on the corner of Sturt and Blackwood Sts, shows mainstream current releases, with $6 films all day Tuesday. The impressive *Townsville Breakwater Entertainment Centre (☎ 4771 4000)* is the main venue for concerts, the performing arts and other cultural events.

If you have the right clothes and fancy trying your luck on the spin of the wheel, the *Sheraton Breakwater Casino* is at the end of Sir Leslie Thiess Drive, beyond Flinders St East.

Getting There & Away

Air Ansett and Qantas have daily flights between Townsville and all the major cities, including Cairns ($205), Brisbane ($396) and Alice Springs ($458). Ansett and Qantas have offices in the Flinders St Mall.

Sunstate/Qantas has flights within Queensland to Mackay ($226), Proserpine ($185), Rockhampton ($309), Gladstone and Bundaberg, while Flight West flies to Mt Isa ($298), often with stops at smaller places on the way, plus Mackay ($226) and Rockhampton ($309).

Bus All long-distance buses operate from the transit centre on Palmer St. Greyhound Pioneer and McCafferty's have frequent services along the coastal Bruce Hwy. Destinations include Brisbane ($123; 20 hours), Rockhampton ($73; nine hours), Mackay ($47; 4½ hours), Airlie Beach ($36; four hours), Mission Beach ($34; 3½ hours) and Cairns ($36; six hours). There are also daily services inland to Mt Isa ($84; 12 hours) via Charters Towers ($19; 1¾ hours), continuing on to the NT.

Train The Brisbane-Cairns *Sunlander* travels through Townsville three times a week. From Brisbane to Townsville takes 24 hours ($148/$226 for an economy/1st class sleeper). Other destinations include Proserpine ($36 for an economy seat; four hours), Rockhampton ($77 for a seat, $107/$172 for an economy/1st class sleeper; 12 hours) and Cairns ($41, or $29 on a stand-by ticket; 7½ hours). The faster and more luxurious *Queenslander* does the Brisbane-Cairns run once a week – the Brisbane-Townsville fare is $344, which includes all meals and a sleeping compartment.

The *Inlander* heads inland twice-weekly from Townsville to Mt Isa ($125/192 for an economy/1st class sleeper; 18 hours) via Charters Towers ($20 for an economy seat; three hours).

Car The larger car-rental agencies are all represented in Townsville. Of the smaller operators, Townsville Car Rentals (☎ 4772 1093), at 12 Palmer St, (near the transit centre) is reliable, with cars and scooters from $45/30 per day.

Getting Around

To/From the Airport Townsville airport is 5km north-west of the city at Garbutt; a taxi to the centre costs $10. The Airport Shuttle (☎ 4775 5544) services all main arrivals and departures. The shuttle costs $6/10 one way/return and will drop you off or pick you up almost anywhere fairly central.

Bus Sunbus runs local bus services around Townsville. Route maps and timetables are available in the Transit Mall (near the Flinders St Mall tourist office).

Taxi For a taxi in Townsville, call Townsville Taxi (☎ 13 1008).

MAGNETIC ISLAND
• postcode 4819   • pop 2500

Tourists first came to Magnetic Island from the mainland more than 100 years ago, making it one of Queensland's oldest island resorts. While it's a popular destination, it has a nice, old-fashioned feel, and with a little effort, you can have a tropical beach all to yourself. About half of the island is national park, and there are some excellent bushwalks and abundant wildlife. It's also cheap and easy to get to, being only 8km from Townsville (15 minutes by ferry).

Magnetic Island was named by Captain Cook, who thought his ship's compass went funny when he sailed by in 1770. It's one of the larger reef islands, at 52 sq km, and it's dominated by 494m Mt Cook. The island is surrounded by the Great Barrier Reef Marine Park, and so there are restrictions on fishing and collecting in some areas.

There are several small towns along the coast and the island has quite a different atmosphere to the purely resort islands along the reef – it's almost an outer suburb of Townsville, with many of the 2500 residents commuting to the mainland by ferry.

Orientation & Information

Magnetic Island is roughly triangular in shape. Picnic Bay, the main town, has the ferry pier and is at the southern corner. A sealed road follows the eastern side of the island up to Horseshoe Bay. There's also a rough track along the west coast; the north coast is for walking only.

The Island Travel Centre (☎ 4778 5155) has an information centre and booking office between the end of the pier and the mall in Picnic Bay. You can book local tours and accommodation, organise domestic and international travel arrangements, and there's email access at $6 for 30 minutes. The EPA office (☎ 4778 5378) is on Hurst St in Picnic Bay.

Picnic Bay

Picnic Bay is the main settlement and the stop for the ferries. The mall along the waterfront has a good selection of shops and eateries, and you can hire bikes, cars, scooters and mokes here. Picnic Bay has several places to stay, and the main beach, patrolled by a life-saving club, has a stinger-free enclosure.

There's a lookout above the town and just to the west of Picnic Bay is **Cockle Bay**, with the wreck of the *City of Adelaide*. Heading around the coast in the other direction is **Rocky Bay**, where there's a short, steep walk down to its beautiful beach. The popular **Picnic Bay Golf Course** is open to the public.

Nelly Bay

Heading north along the coast is Nelly Bay, which has a good beach with shade and a reef at low tide. At the far end of the bay there are some pioneer graves. The north end of the bay is marred by the half-finished Magnetic Quay Development, which was abandoned some years ago after the developers went broke.

Arcadia

Around the headland, **Geoffrey Bay** has a broad beach and a reef at the southern end of the bay. The low-tide reef walk around the headland is now discouraged by the EPA (allowing tourists to walk on the reef was never exactly environmentally friendly!).

Overlooking the bay is the town of Arcadia, with shops, more places to stay and the Arcadia Hotel Resort (with live bands at weekends and a public pool). Just around

QUEENSLAND

the next headland is the very pleasant **Alma Bay** beach.

Radical Bay & the Forts

The road runs back from the coast to the junction of the road to Radical Bay. You can go straight to Horseshoe Bay, or take the central track via the Forts, a WWII military post with good views over the island. The area is a good place to spot koalas.

Alternatively, turn right to Radical Bay via a rough vehicle track, with walking tracks leading off it to secluded Arthur and Florence bays, and the old **Searchlight Station** on the headland between the two bays.

From Radical Bay you can walk across the headland to beautiful **Balding Bay** (an unofficial nude bathing beach) and **Horseshoe Bay**.

Horseshoe Bay

Horseshoe Bay, on the north coast of the island, has a few shops, accommodation and a long stretch of beach. There's a fairly desolate **Koala Park**, which is quite a long drive off the main road, and a **mango plantation**, signposted off the main road, which offers tours and light lunches. At the beach there are boats, sailboards and canoes for hire. From here, you can walk to Maud Bay, to the west, or to Radical Bay.

Activities

The EPA produces a leaflet for Magnetic Island's excellent bushwalking tracks. Possible walks include: Nelly Bay to Horseshoe Bay (6km, two hours one way); Picnic Bay to West Point (8km, 2½ hours); Horseshoe Bay road to Arthur Bay (2km, 30 minutes); Horseshoe Bay to Florence Bay (2.5km, one hour); Horseshoe Bay to the Forts (2km, 45 minutes); Horseshoe Bay to Balding Bay (3km, 45 minutes); and Horseshoe Bay to Radical Bay (3km, 45 minutes).

Magnetic Island Pleasure Divers (☎ 4778 5788), at the Arcadia Resort, offers a basic

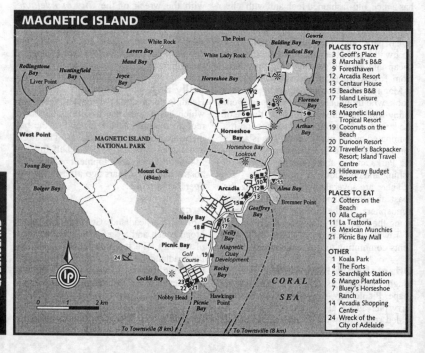

MAGNETIC ISLAND

PLACES TO STAY
3 Geoff's Place
8 Marshall's B&B
9 Foresthaven
12 Arcadia Resort
13 Centaur House
15 Beaches B&B
17 Island Leisure Resort
18 Magnetic Island Tropical Resort
19 Coconuts on the Beach
20 Dunoon Resort
22 Traveller's Backpacker Resort; Island Travel Centre
23 Hideaway Budget Resort

PLACES TO EAT
2 Cotters on the Beach
10 Alla Capri
11 La Trattonia
16 Mexican Munchies
21 Picnic Bay Mall

OTHER
1 Koala Park
4 The Forts
5 Searchlight Station
6 Mango Plantation
7 Bluey's Horseshoe Ranch
14 Arcadia Shopping Centre
24 Wreck of the City of Adelaide

five day dive course for $149 or a more comprehensive course costing $249. Bluey's Horseshoe Ranch, at Horseshoe Bay, offers trail rides for $18 an hour or $45 for a half-day trot.

On the beach at Horseshoe Bay you can hire a variety of water sports equipment and boats by the hour.

Places to Stay – Budget

Although half the island is national park, there are no designated park camping areas. The only camping possibilities are at the hostels.

Hostels There's a good selection of back-packers' hostels on the island and it's a competitive scene, with several hostels sending vehicles to meet the ferries at Picnic Bay. There are also package deals on accommodation and transport (see Getting There & Away in this section).

Picnic Bay Immediately opposite the ferry jetty, *Travellers Backpacker Resort* (☎ 1800 000 290) is a big modern hostel in a converted hotel. It's a popular place with good facilities (air-con and bathrooms in all rooms and dorms), and there's a bar and nightclub. Beds in six-bed dorms are $16; singles/doubles are $20 per person. Close by, the *Hideaway Budget Resort* (☎ 4778 5110, 32 Picnic St) is a clean, renovated place with a small kitchen, pool, a TV room and laundry facilities. A bed in a twin or double room costs $16 per person, or there are dorm beds for $14. There's a VIP discount, and air-con for $4 extra.

Nelly Bay The *Magnetic Island Tropical Resort* (☎ 4778 5955), on Yates St, just off the main road, is a good budget resort that caters to backpackers, with a swimming pool, an inexpensive restaurant and a pleasant garden setting. A bed in a four to six bed timber cabin with attached bath costs $16. Whole cabins start from $45 for a double plus $10 for each extra adult.

At the southern end of Nelly Bay is *Coconuts on the Beach* (☎ 1800 065 696), which promotes itself as a backpacker party

place. You can camp here for $9 per person (no shade), or stay in tent-type dorms ($12) or in permanent tents a little further away from the noisy bar for $16 per person. VIP/YHA discounts are available.

Arcadia *Centaur House* (☎ 4778 5668, 27 Marine Parade) is a rambling, old-style hostel opposite the beach. The atmosphere is quiet and relaxed, though the place has become a little run-down in recent years. Dorm beds cost from $11 to $15; double rooms cost $36, with $1 off for VIP/YHA members.

Also in Arcadia is *Foresthaven* (☎ 4778 5153, 11 Cook Rd). This hostel has seen better days and is fairly spartan, although the peaceful bush setting is nice. Accommodation is in old-fashioned but adequate two and three-bed units which have their own kitchen. Dorm beds cost $14, twins/doubles cost $34, or there are self-contained rooms from $25 per person. The friendly owners speak German and French.

Horseshoe Bay One of the island's most popular places for young travellers is *Geoff's Place* (☎ 4778 5577), although maintenance and service are suffering these days. There are extensive grounds and you can camp for $8 per person or share a four or eight bed A-frame cedar cabin for $16 (eight-bed cabins have their own bathroom). There's a communal kitchen and a bar, and basic meals cost around $7. The hostel's courtesy bus shuttles between here and Picnic Bay to meet the ferries.

Places to Stay – Mid-Range

There are plenty of pubs, motels, holiday flats and even a couple of B&Bs. Rates for these places vary seasonally, and in the school holiday periods you'll probably need to book.

In Picnic Bay, the pleasant *Dunoon Resort* (☎ 4778 5161), on the corner of Granite St and the Esplanade, has self-contained units from $89.

The impressive *Island Leisure Resort* (☎ 4778 5511, 4 Kelly St), in Nelly Bay, has a pool, tennis court and gym, and units from

QUEENSLAND

$94. In Arcadia, the *Arcadia Resort* (☎ 4778 5177) has motel units from $60/70.

There are also two B&Bs in Arcadia. The friendly *Marshall's B&B* (☎ 4778 5112, 3 Endeavour Rd) is a relaxed place with singles/doubles from $38/55. *Beaches B&B* (☎ 4778 5303, 39 Marine Parade) is a stylish timber cottage with a pool and separate guest wing. Doubles cost $65.

Places to Eat
Picnic Bay The Picnic Bay Mall, along the waterfront, has a small supermarket and a good selection of eating places. Nearest to the jetty, the *Picnic Bay Pub* has decent counter meals. Further along, the *Green Frog Cafe* is good for breakfasts or light lunches.

The licensed *Maxine's*, at the far end of the Esplanade, is a bit more upmarket and has steaks, and Thai and Malaysian mains from $17 to $25.

Nelly Bay Just off Kelly St, *Mexican Munchies* (☎ 4778 5658) runs the gamut from enchiladas to tacos, and is open daily from 6 pm. Main courses are $12 to $15, and you need to book in advance. In the small shopping centre on the main road are *Possums Cafe*, a bakery and a supermarket.

Arcadia The *Arcadia Resort* has bistro meals from $10 to $12 and there's also a more expensive restaurant section. On Wednesday evenings, the resort has popular cane-toad races. Toads are auctioned at the start of each race ($8 should get you a steed) and the first toad out of the circle wins the stake (normally a cash prize plus freebies like cruises and T-shirts), though you have to kiss your toad to claim the winnings.

On the beach at Alma Bay, the BYO *La Trattoria* has a great setting overlooking a pretty little bay, and serves Greek meals and pasta in the $15 to $17 range. Close by, on Hayles Ave, is the friendly *Alla Capri*, a licensed Italian place, with pasta for $8 and other mains from $8 to $15.

In the small Arcadia shopping centre on Hayles Ave, the *Bakehouse* is open early and is a good place for breakfast coffee and croissants. Next door is *Banister's Seafood*,

which is a good fish and chips place with an open-air dining area; it's BYO.

Horseshoe Bay *Cotters on the Beach* is a relaxed licensed restaurant with lunches from $6 and steak, chicken and seafood dinners from $10 to $17. Next door, the *Bounty Snack Bar* has takeaways and there's a small general store where you can buy groceries.

Getting There & Away
Sunferries (☎ 4771 3855) operates the passenger ferry between Townsville and Magnetic Island, with about 10 services a day between 6.20 am and 7.15 pm. Ferries leave from the Sunferries City terminal on Flinders St East, also stopping at the breakwater terminal on Sir Leslie Thiess Drive. The trip takes about 20 minutes and costs $7/13 one way/return. There's a large car park at the breakwater terminal.

You can also buy package deals, which include return ferry tickets and accommodation. One-night packages start at $29. Check with the hostels in Townsville for deals.

The Capricorn Barge Company (☎ 4772 5422) runs a vehicular ferry to Arcadia from the south side of Ross Creek on weekdays four times a day and on weekends three times a day. It's $98 return for a car and up to six passengers, $31 return for a motorcycle and $12 return for walk-on passengers.

Bicycles are carried free on all ferries.

Getting Around
Bus The Magnetic Island Bus Service operates between Picnic Bay and Horseshoe Bay 11 to 20 times a day, meeting all ferries and stopping at all accommodation places. Some bus trips include Radical Bay, others the Koala Park. You can get individual tickets ($1.50 to $3.50) or a day pass ($9).

Car, Moke & Moped Moke Magnetic (☎ 4778 5377), in an arcade off the Picnic Bay Mall, and Holiday Moke Hire (☎ 4778 5703), based in the Jetty Cafe in the Picnic Bay Mall, have Mokes from $35 a day ($3 more if you're under 25) plus 30c per kilometre. Both companies also have Suzuki Sierras, Mazda 121s and other vehicles.

Roadrunner Scooter Hire (☎ 4778 5222) has an office in an arcade off the Picnic Bay Mall. Day hire of mopeds is $25, half-day hire $19, and 24-hour hire $30.

Bicycle Magnetic Island is ideal for cycling, and mountain bikes are available for rent at several places, including the Esplanade in Picnic Bay, Foresthaven in Arcadia and on the waterfront in Horseshoe Bay. Bikes cost $12 for a day, and $8 for half a day.

NORTH COAST HINTERLAND

The Flinders Hwy heads inland from Townsville and runs due west for almost 800km to Cloncurry, via the gold-mining town of Charters Towers.

Ravenswood
• postcode 4816   • pop 200

At Mingela, 83km from Townsville, a sealed road leads 40km south to Ravenswood, a living ghost town which dates back to the gold-rush days. Although many of the buildings were demolished or fell down years ago, some interesting **old buildings** linger amid the scattered red-earth hills, including the old post office, two historic pubs and the restored courthouse, police station and cell block compound, which houses a fascinating mining and historical museum (open 10 am to 3 pm), staffed by the gregarious Woody.

In recent years a couple of companies have recommenced mining operations here, breathing new life back into the town.

The impressive *Imperial Hotel (☎ 4770 2131)*, on Macrossan St, is built in the flamboyant style known as 'goldfields brash' and has a great public bar, a dining room with home-cooked meals and B&B from $35. There's also a free council camping ground.

Eighty kilometres past Ravenswood, the big **Burdekin Falls Dam**, completed in 1987, holds back more than 200 sq km of water.

Charters Towers
• postcode 4820   • pop 9400

This picturesque town, 130km inland from Townsville, was fabulously rich during the gold rush, and unlike many gold rush towns, it still has a remarkable number of fine old villas and public buildings. It's possible to make a day trip here from Townsville and get a glimpse of outback Queensland on the way.

The gleam of gold was first spotted in 1871 in a creek bed at the foot of Towers Hill by an Aboriginal boy, Jupiter Mosman. Within a few years, the surrounding area was peppered with diggings and a large town had grown. In its heyday (around the end of the 19th century), Charters Towers had almost 100 mines and a population of 30,000 – and it even had its own stock exchange. The town came to be known as 'The World' and Mosman St, then the main street, had 25 pubs.

Despite its heritage appearance, Charters Towers is very much a living rural community, with cattle and mining as the main industries. There has even been a gold revival since the 1980s as modern processes have allowed companies to work deposits found in previously uneconomical areas. The town is very proud of its history, and even the local police station was renovated in heritage style following lobbying by concerned residents.

Information The helpful tourist office (☎ 4752 0314), in a renovated wooden building between the historic City Hall and Stock Exchange buildings, is open daily from 9 am to 5 pm. Pick up the free *Guide to Charters Towers* booklet and a copy of the National Trust's walking tour leaflet.

The National Trust of Queensland (☎ 4787 2374) has an office in the Stock Exchange Arcade on Mosman St. You can access the Internet at the Municipal Library, on Gill St, for $5 (one hour maximum); book with the librarian.

Things to See & Do On Mosman St, a few metres up the hill from the corner of Gill St, is the picturesque **Stock Exchange Arcade**, built in 1887 and restored in 1972. At the end of the arcade, opposite the National Trust office, is the interesting **Assay Room & Mining Museum** ($1). Further up Mosman St, the recently restored **ABC Bank Building** (1891) is now the World Theatre.

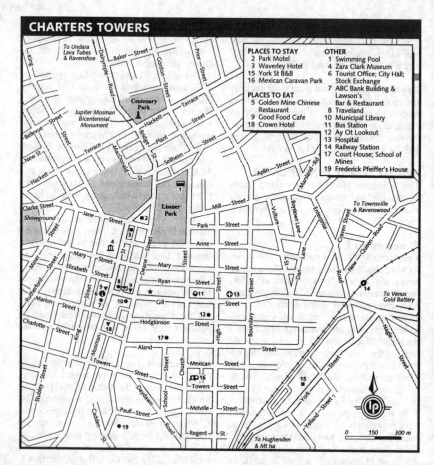

CHARTERS TOWERS

PLACES TO STAY
2 Park Motel
3 Waverley Hotel
15 York St B&B
16 Mexican Caravan Park

PLACES TO EAT
5 Golden Mine Chinese Restaurant
9 Good Food Cafe
18 Crown Hotel

OTHER
1 Swimming Pool
4 Zara Clark Museum
6 Tourist Office; City Hall; Stock Exchange
7 ABC Bank Building & Lawson's Bar & Restaurant
8 Traveland
10 Municipal Library
11 Bus Station
12 Ay Ot Lookout
13 Hospital
14 Railway Station
17 Court House; School of Mines
19 Frederick Pfeiffer's House

The cinema is next door, behind Lawson's Bar & Restaurant.

At 62 Mosman St, the **Zara Clark Museum** is well worth a visit, with an interesting collection of memorabilia, antiques, photos and a military display. It's open daily from 10 am to 3 pm ($3).

One of the finest of the town's old houses is Frederick Pfeiffer's, on Paull St, which is now a private Mormon chapel. Pfeiffer was a gold miner who became Queensland's first millionaire.

Another fine old mansion is **Ay Ot Lookout**, a restored house now owned by Leyshon Mining, one of the gold mining companies in the area. The ground floor is open to the public. The timber building was constructed using a technique known as 'balloon framing', where the walls lack external cladding and so do not have a cavity where rats and other vermin might breed.

Five kilometres from town is the **Venus Battery**, where gold-bearing ore was crushed and processed from 1872 until as recently as 1972. The battery has been restored to working order and is open daily from 9 am to 3.30 pm, with guided tours at 10 am and 2 pm ($3).

There are several historical tours of the town, which you can book through the tourist information offices, including a one hour walking tour ($8), a 1½ hour guided driving tour ($10) and daily tours around the heritage World Theatre ($3).

Special Events During the Australia Day weekend in late January, more than 100 cricket teams and their supporters converge on Charters Towers for the Goldfield Ashes. The town also hosts one of Australia's biggest annual country music festivals, on the May Day weekend, and has a major rodeo every Easter.

Places to Stay South of Gill St, the *Mexican Caravan Park* (☎ 4787 1161, 75 Church St) is fairly central and has camp sites for $9 and on-site cabins from $28, plus a swimming pool and store.

The cheapest accommodation in town is in pub rooms. Best of the bunch is the *Waverley Hotel* (☎ 4787 2591), on the corner of Jane and Mosman Sts. It's one of the quieter places, with clean, cheerful singles/doubles for $20/30.

A few kilometres south of the centre, *York St B&B* (☎ 4787 1028, 58 York St) is a renovated timber house built in the 1880s, with pleasant breezy verandahs and a swimming pool. Air-con doubles are $65, or simpler miners' rooms are $24 for a single, all with breakfast.

The *Park Motel* (☎ 4787 1022, 1 Mosman St) has pleasant grounds and a good restaurant, and units cost from $58/66.

You can stay at or visit a number of cattle stations in the area including *Bluff Downs* (☎ 4770 4084), 1½ hours drive away. It costs $100 per person to stay in the homestead, including meals and activities, or $30 in dorms. You can visit or stay at *Plain Creek* (☎ 4963 5228), 180km from Charters Towers on the Emerald road.

Places to Eat Nearly all the pubs have decent meals. The *Crown Hotel*, on Mosman St, is a good cheapie, with a lunchtime roast and vegies for $4. The best deal in town is the all-you-can-eat smorgasbord at the licensed *Golden Mine Chinese Restaurant*, on Mosman St; it's $6 for lunch, $7 for dinner. The *Good Food Cafe*, on Gill St opposite the library, is a gourmet cafe with home-cooked meals, smoothies, burgers and other snacks.

Lawson's Bar & Restaurant, in a nicely restored heritage building next to the ABC Bank building on Mosman St, is an attractive, casual eatery with burgers from $8 and mains for $14 to $18 ($18 to $24 evenings).

Getting There & Away McCafferty's has daily bus services from Townsville to Charters Towers ($19; 1¾ hours), continuing on to Mt Isa ($79; 10 hours). Greyhound Pioneer also serves Townsville ($15) and Mt Isa ($82). Buses for all companies depart from the Caltex service station, at 105 Gill St. Traveland (☎ 4787 2622), at 13 Gill St can issue tickets.

The train station is on Enterprise Rd, 1.5km east of the centre. The twice weekly *Inlander* also runs from Townsville to Charters Towers ($20 for an economy seat; three hours) and continues on to Mt Isa ($115/177 in an economy/1st class sleeper; 17 hours).

TOWNSVILLE TO MISSION BEACH
Paluma Range National Park
The Mt Spec-Big Crystal Creek section of this national park, which straddles the 1000m-plus Paluma Range west of the Bruce Hwy, has Australia's most southerly pocket of tropical rainforest.

There are two access routes; both leave the Bruce Hwy about 62km north of Townsville (47km south of Ingham). The southern route is a narrow and spectacular road that winds up along the southern edge of the park, passing Little Crystal Creek (with a waterfall and good swimming beside a stone bridge) and McClelland's Lookout, where there are three good walking trails, on the way to the sleepy mountain village of Paluma (18km). The northern route leads to Big Crystal Creek (4km), which has good swimming, a barbecue area and a camp site – to book (compulsory, as key must be collected and deposit paid), contact the EPA in Ingham (☎ 4776 1700) or Townsville (☎ 4721 2399). Bowerbirds are relatively common in the park.

The **Jourama Falls section** of the park, which contains the Seaview Range, is six unsealed kilometres off the highway, 91km north of Townsville (24km south of Ingham). In the centre, Waterview Creek has good swimming holes, several lookouts, a picnic area and a self-registration camping ground; book with the ranger (☎ 4777 3112). You can walk to the waterfalls (600m) and the falls lookout (1.2km).

Ingham
• postcode 4850   • pop 5010

Ingham, a major sugar-producing town, celebrates its Italian heritage with the Australian-Italian Festival each May.

There's a good tourist centre (☎ 4776 5211) on the corner of Lannercost St and Townsville Rd. The EPA office (☎ 4776 1700), at the end of an arcade at 11 Lannercost St, deals with information for Paluma Range, Lumholtz (Wallaman Falls) and Hinchinbrook and Orpheus islands. The *Hotel Hinchinbrook (☎ 4776 2227, 83 Lannercost St)* has simple twin rooms for $25 and good bistro meals from $6.

Around Ingham

There are a number of places to visit around Ingham. At the Wallaman Falls section of the **Lumholtz National Park**, 50km west of Ingham on a tributary of the Herbert River, the Wallaman Falls cascade for 278m – the longest single drop in Australia. The falls are most spectacular in the wet season. You can usually reach them by conventional vehicle along an unsealed road; there's a QPWS *camping area* with a swimming hole nearby.

Only 7km east of Ingham is the **Victoria Mill**, the largest sugar mill in the southern hemisphere. Free tours are given in the crushing season (about July to December). **Lucinda**, a port town 24km from Ingham, is the access point for the southern end of Hinchinbrook Island. It also has a 6km jetty used for shipping sugar.

Orpheus Island

Lying off the coast near Ingham, Orpheus Island is a narrow 13 sq km granite island surrounded by coral reefs. The second largest of the Palm group, it's a quiet, secluded island with good camping, snorkelling and diving. Orpheus is mostly national park and is heavily forested, with lots of birdlife; turtles also nest here. Bush camping is allowed in two places (permits obtainable from Townsville or Ingham), but take your own water and fuel stove. Also on the island are a giant-clam research station and a small resort with rooms for $400-plus per person.

Campers can get there by charter boat from Dungeness (north of Lucinda) for about $120 return per person – contact the Lucinda Reef & Island Charter Service (☎ 4777 8220) for details.

Cardwell
• postcode 4849   • pop 1400

Dating from 1864, Cardwell is one of north Queensland's earliest towns, and it is the only town on the highway between Brisbane and Cairns that is actually on the coast. It's more or less a one street place.

Information The QPWS Centre (☎ 4066 8601), beside the main jetty at 142 Victoria St, has information and permits for Hinchinbrook Island and other national parks in the area. It's open weekdays from 8 am to 4.30 pm, weekends till noon.

If you are travelling south from Cardwell, most fruit and some vegetables must be surrendered to the officers at the fruit-fly inspection point here, who also have the right to search your vehicle.

Things to See & Do Cardwell is the main departure point for Hinchinbrook and other islands, but there are also numerous points of interest around town. The **Cardwell Forest Drive** starts from the centre of town and is a 26km round trip, taking you to some excellent lookouts, swimming holes, walking tracks and picnic areas.

Most of the coastal forest north of Cardwell is protected as the **Edmund Kennedy National Park**. There's a boardwalk walking track at the southern end of the park. The creeks here are home to estuarine crocodiles, so swimming isn't advised.

The **Murray Falls**, which have fine rock pools for swimming and a walking track and barbecue area, are signposted 22km west of the highway, about 27km north of Cardwell.

Between Cardwell and Ingham the Bruce Hwy briefly climbs high above the coast with tremendous views over the winding, mangrove-lined waterways known as the Everglades, which separate Hinchinbrook Island from the coast.

Places to Stay The well set up *Kookaburra Holiday Park (☎ 4066 8648, 175 Bruce Hwy)*, which includes the YHA *Hinchinbrook Hostel*, is 800m north of the centre. The hostel has dorm beds for $15 and doubles for $32, camp sites for $7.50 per person and on-site vans, cabins and units from $32. Facilities include a pool and free use of bikes. It has a good package deal for Hinchinbrook Island (see Getting There & Away in the Hinchinbrook Island National Park section, following).

Further north (behind the 'big crab'), the *Cardwell Backpackers' Hostel (☎ 4066 8014, 178 Bowen St)* is a fairly seedy workers' hostel with dorm beds and double rooms. Cardwell also has several other caravan parks, a pub, motels and holiday units.

Getting There & Away All buses between Townsville and Cairns stop at Cardwell. The fare is about $20 from either place. Cardwell is also on the Brisbane to Cairns railway.

Hinchinbrook Island National Park

This island is a spectacular and unspoiled wilderness area, with granite mountains rising dramatically from the sea and a varied terrain of lush tropical forest on the mainland side, and long sandy beaches and thick mangroves lining the eastern shores. All 399 sq km of the island is a national park and rugged Mt Bowen, at 1121m, is the highest peak. There's plenty of wildlife, especially pretty-faced wallabies and the iridescent-blue Ulysses butterfly.

Hinchinbrook is very popular with bushwalkers and naturalists and has some excellent walking tracks. The highlight is the **Thorsborne Trail** (also known as the East Coast Trail), a 32km walking track from Ramsay Bay to Zoe Bay with its beautiful waterfall, and on to George Point at the southern tip. It's a three to five day walk, although you can walk shorter sections if you don't have that much time. This is the real bush experience, however. You'll need to draw water from creeks as you go (all water should be chemically purified or boiled before drinking), keep your food out of reach of the native bush rats, and keep an eye out for estuarine crocodiles in the mangroves! Take plenty of insect repellent.

There's an expensive but low-key *resort (☎ 4066 8585)* on the northern peninsula, Cape Richards, with rooms for 60 people from $215 per person, including meals.

There are seven QPWS *camping grounds* along the Thorsborne Trail, plus others at Macushla and Scraggy Point in the north. Fires are banned so you'll need a fuel stove, and all rubbish must be carried out for disposal on the mainland. There is a limit of 40 people allowed on the main trail at any one time, so it's necessary to book ahead, especially for holiday periods. Pick up the informative *Thorsborne Trail* and *Hinchinbrook to Dunk Island* leaflets from the Queensland Parks and Wildlife Centre in Cardwell (☎ 4066 8601), the main office for Hinchinbrook permits.

Getting There & Away Hinchinbrook Island Ferries (☎ 1800 682 702), at 131 Bruce Hwy in Cardwell, has a daily ferry to the northern end of the Thorsborne Trail from June to November and three services a week December through May. Boats leave Cardwell at 9 am, returning around 4.30 pm. The cost is $45/69 one way/return. If you want to walk the trail, you'll need to arrange your southern boat pickup with Hinchinbrook Wilderness Safaris (☎ 4777 8307). The cost is $50, which includes transport back to Cardwell.

QUEENSLAND

The YHA Hinchinbrook Hostel in Cardwell has a good **Hinchinbrook Passport** package for $169, which includes two nights accommodation at the hostel, a day cruise to Hinchinbrook Island, a scenic island flight and a half-day trek through the Cardwell State Forest. Call ☎ 4066 8648 for information and bookings.

Tully
- postcode 4854   • pop 2500

The wettest place in Australia, Tully has an average rainfall of over 4000mm a year, and the Tully River is the setting for whitewater rafting trips. There's a tourist office on the highway, and the basic but friendly *Savoy Backpackers (☎ 4068 2700, 4 Plumb St)* costs $14 a bed; it can often find fruit-picking work for travellers. There's also a caravan park and a motel, although nearby Mission Beach is a much more appealing place to stay.

MISSION BEACH
- postcode 4852   • pop 3470

This small stretch of coast is a very popular stopover on the backpacker circuit. The name Mission Beach actually covers a string of small settlements – Mission, Wongaling and South Mission beaches, Bingil Bay and Garners Beach – along a 14km coastal strip east of Tully.

This is a good base for visits to Dunk Island and the Barrier Reef, white-water rafting trips on the Tully River and walks through the rainforest.

Mission Beach is named after an Aboriginal mission that was founded here in 1914, but destroyed by a cyclone in 1918. There's a memorial to the explorer Edmund Kennedy at Tam O'Shanter Point, which was the starting point for Kennedy's tragic overland expedition to Cape York in 1848. All but three of the party's 13 members died, including Kennedy, who was killed by Aboriginal people.

Information
There's a tourist centre (☎ 4068 7099) on Porters Promenade in Mission Beach. It's open on weekdays from 9 am to 5 pm and on weekends from 10 am to 2 pm. Next door is the Wet Tropics Visitor Centre (☎ 4068 7179), open daily from 10 am to 4 pm, which has information on the local environment and conservation of cassowaries.

Zola's Books, in the cluster of shops at Mission Beach, has email facilities and new and second-hand books. The hugely popular *Mudfest*, held in June, is a celebration of youth culture, with local and big-name bands, dance and new-age arts and crafts.

Activities
Bushwalking The rainforest around Mission Beach is a haven for cassowaries but unfortunately the population of these large flightless birds has been depleted by road accidents and the destruction of rainforest by logging and cyclones. The rainforest comes right down to the coast in places and there are some impressive walks, including Lacey's Creek Walk (30 minutes), the Bicton Hill Lookout (1½ hours), the Licuala Walking Track (two hours), and the Edmund Kennedy Walking Track (three hours).

Mission Beach Rainforest Treks (☎ 4068 7137) runs guided walks through the forests. The four hour morning walk costs $28 and the 2½ hour night walk is $18.

White-Water Rafting & Sea Kayaking
Raging Thunder (☎ 1800 079 092) and R'n'R (☎ 1800 079 039) charge $123 from Mission Beach for trips on the Tully River (you'll save several hours travel time by doing these trips from here rather than Cairns).

Sunbird Adventures (☎ 4068 8229) has morning sea-kayaking and snorkelling trips for $35. Coral Sea Kayaking (☎ 4068 9154) runs day trips out to Dunk Island for $69.

Diving & Snorkelling Certified divers can explore the shipwreck of the *Lady Bowen*, which sank in 33 metres of water in 1894 (this is for experienced divers only). Quick Cat Dives (☎ 0419 785 809) has trips to the wreck for $130, including gear and two dives, plus outer reef trips for $120.

Mission Beach Dive Charters (☎ 4068 7277) also visits the wreck for $185 all inclusive. Friendship Cruises (☎ 4068 7262) has day trips out to the reef with snorkelling and a ride in a glass-bottom boat ($66). Boats leave from Clump Point jetty, just north of Mission Beach.

Other Activities Jump the Beach (☎ 4068 7655) offers tandem skydives from $199, or there's water sports gear for hire on the beach at Castaways.

Organised Tours
The MV *Lawrence Kavanagh* (☎ 4068 7211) does day trips to Dunk Island ($22) and a combined Dunk-Bedarra trip with a barbecue lunch ($54). You can also cross over to Dunk Island on this vessel – it leaves from the northern end of Mission Beach.

Places to Stay
Camping In Mission Beach, there's a council-run *camping ground* on the foreshore with sites for $8, or the well-equipped *Hideaway Holiday Village* (☎ 4068 7104) opposite has camp sites from $16 and on-site cabins from $49. At South Mission Beach, the *Beachcomber Coconut Village* (☎ 4068 8129) has camp sites from $15.50 and on-site cabins from $43 a double.

Hostels All three hostels have courtesy buses and do pickups from both bus stops.

The *Treehouse* (☎ 4068 7137), a YHA-associate hostel, is at Bingil Bay, 6km north of Mission Beach. This popular and very laid-back hostel is in an impressive timber stilt house with good views over the surrounding rainforest. There's a pool, bikes for hire and an airy verandah. Beds in six-bed dorms cost $16, twins/doubles are $40, or you can camp for $10.

The other hostels are both at Wongaling Beach, 5km south of Mission Beach. Opposite the beach, *Scotty's Mission Beach House* (☎ 4068 8676, 167 Reid Rd) is friendly and fun-oriented and has a good pool. Beds in large dorms are $15 ($14 VIP) and doubles cost $35 or $40 with bathroom and air-con. At the front of the hostel is a bar and grill, which specialises in steaks and has seafood, roasts, curries and vegetarian dishes from $5 to $20.

Mission Beach Backpackers Lodge (☎ 4068 8317, 28 Wongaling Beach Rd) is a modern, well-equipped place with a pool and garden. There are two buildings, one has spacious dorms with beds for $16 ($15 VIP), the other has very good double rooms for $33 to $40. This easy-going hostel is a five minute walk from the beach.

Motels & Apartments There's a scattering of motels, holiday units and resorts along the coast. The *Waters Edge* (☎ 4068 8890, 32 Reid Rd), in Wongaling Beach, has passable self-contained holiday units on the waterfront that sleep up to eight. Prices start at $40 a double.

The *Clump Point Eco Village* (☎ 4068 7534), on the foreshore a few kilometres north of Mission Beach, has lush gardens and a great tropical feel. Good timber bungalows that sleep up to five start at $118 a night.

If you're flush, the *Horizon Resort* (☎ 4068 8154), at South Mission Beach, is a very stylish resort with rooms from $175 a double, though cheaper deals are available.

Places to Eat
Mission Beach proper has a good selection of eateries. The tiny *Port o' Call Cafe*, beside the bus stop, has breakfasts, homemade meals and good coffee. In the arcade just across Campbell St, *The Seafood Place* has good fish and chips and burgers.

There are more eateries across the road. *Butterflies* is a friendly Mexican place with entrees from $8 and mains from $12 to $15. Next door is *Food*, a modern brasserie with mains from $15 to $20 and vegetarian dishes, such as lasagne, for $15. The cosy *Friends* is a popular open-air BYO with mains for about $18, and further down David St is an Italian bistro called *Piccolo Paradiso*, with pizza and pasta from $7 to $12 and other mains for $14 to $16. Right by the beach, the *Shrubbery Taverna* has Greek-themed entrees from $4 and mains from $10.

In Wongaling Beach, the *Mission Beach Resort Hotel* has a bistro and cheap bar meals. If you're preparing your own food,

QUEENSLAND

there are supermarkets in Mission Beach and Wongaling Beach.

Getting There & Around

McCafferty's buses stop outside the Port o' Call Cafe in Mission Beach; Greyhound Pioneer stops at the Mission Beach Resort in Wongaling Beach. The average fare is $12 from Cairns and $34 from Townsville.

Coral Coaches does five runs a day between Mission Beach and Cairns for $25, ($10 as far as Innisfail). Bookings are required (☎ 4031 3555).

Mission Beach Bus Service does regular runs from Bingil Bay to South Mission Beach between 8.30 am and 5 pm, with limited evening services. The maximum fare is $4 ($2 evenings). There are also buses to the Lacey Creek and Licuala Walks ($2.50 each way).

DUNK ISLAND & THE FAMILY ISLANDS

Dunk Island is an easy and affordable day trip from Mission Beach. It's 4.5km off the coast, and has walking tracks through rainforest and good beaches.

The P&O-owned *Dunk Island Resort* (☎ 4068 8199), at Brammo Bay on the northern end of the island, has rooms from $165 per person. There's a take-away food kiosk and you can hire catamarans, sailboards and snorkelling gear. You can get permits for the QPWS *camping ground* close to the resort from the resort's watersports office (☎ 4068 8199). Dunk Island is noted for prolific birdlife (nearly 150 species) and many butterflies. There are superb views over the entrances to the Hinchinbrook Channel from the top of 271m Mt Kootaloo. Thirteen kilometres of walking tracks lead from the camping ground area to headlands and beaches.

South of Dunk are the seven tiny Family Islands. To stay at the exclusive *Bedarra Island Resort* (☎ 4068 8233) costs a mere $1000/1290 a day all-inclusive. Five of the other Family Islands are national parks. You can bush camp on Wheeler and Combe islands (permits available at Cardwell; take your own water).

Getting There & Away

Dunk Island Express Water Taxis (☎ 4068 8310) has seven daily services from Wongaling Beach to Dunk and back ($22 return). You can also cross over on MV *Lawrence Kavanagh* (see Organised Cruises in the Mission Beach section).

You can fly to Dunk Island from Cairns with Transtate (☎ 13 1528) for $120.

MISSION BEACH TO CAIRNS

Eight kilometres north of El Arish, you can turn off the Bruce Hwy and take an interesting alternative route to Innisfail via the sugar-cane townships of Silkwood and Mena Creek, 20km south-west of Innisfail. At **Mena Creek**, Paronella Park (☎ 4065 3225) is a rambling tropical garden set among the ruins of a Spanish castle built in the 1930s. This place is quite bizarre and well worth a visit – it's open daily from 9 am to 5 pm and costs $10. It also has a *caravan park* next door with sites from $12 and on-site cabins from $32.

At **Mourilyan**, 7km south of Innisfail, there's the Australian Sugar Museum, open daily from 9 am to 5 pm, and the Innisfail tourist office (☎ 4063 2000). An export terminal on the coast east of Mourilyan handles the sugar produced in Innisfail, Tully and Mourilyan.

Innisfail

* postcode 4860   * pop 8990

At the junction of the North and South Johnstone rivers, this solid and prosperous sugar city has a large Italian population. The Italians arrived early this century to work the cane fields, and in the 1930s there was even a local 'mafia' called the Black Hand.

Points of interest include a **Chinese Joss House**, on Owen St, the **Historical Society Museum**, at 11 Edith St, and the **Johnstone River Crocodile Farm**, 4km east on the Flying Fish Point road ($10).

The *River Drive Van Park* (☎ 4061 2515) is on River Ave, and there are numerous pubs and motels.

The four hostels in town cater mainly for people working on the local banana plantations. *Endeavour* (☎ 4061 6610, 31 Glady

St), **Backpackers Innisfail** *(☎ 4061 2284, 73 Rankin St)* and **Innisfail Budget Backpackers** *(☎ 4061 7833, 125 Edith St)* all have dorm beds for $13 and can help arrange banana-picking work.

Pick of the bunch is the **Codge Lodge** *(☎ 4061 8055, 63 Rankin St)*, a spacious, relaxed place in a renovated house. It's friendly, well equipped and has cable TV. It also has a pool and river views from the back balcony. Dorm beds are $17, singles/doubles are $20/35.

From Innisfail, the Palmerston Hwy winds up to the Atherton Tableland, passing through the rainforest of the **Wooroonooran (Palmerston) National Park**, which has creeks, waterfalls, scenic walking tracks and a self-registration *camping ground* at Henrietta Creek, just off the road.

Innisfail to Cairns

Between Innisfail and Cairns, the Bruce Hwy skirts the edge of the Bellenden Ker range, which includes Queensland's highest peak, **Mt Bartle Frere** (1657m). Most of the area is protected as **Wooroonooran National Park**. You can hike to the top of Bartle Frere from **Josephine Falls**, 8km from the highway about 22km north of Innisfail. It's a popular picnic spot, with some great swimming holes and natural waterslides, although heed the warnings about the very slippery rocks.

The Mt Bartle Frere Hiking Track leads from the car park to the Bartle Frere summit. The ascent is for fit and experienced walkers – it's a 15km, two-day return trip, and the weather can change suddenly.

The *Plantation Village Resort (☎ 4067 4133)*, on Evans Rd, Bramston Beach, is a good budget resort with camp sites ($12), motel units (from $59) and self-contained cabins (from $49), plus a restaurant, pool and tennis courts.

Seven kilometres inland from Babinda, **Babinda Boulders** is a good picnic place with a swimming hole, barbecues, walking trails and a self-registration *camp site*. From the boulders you can walk the **Goldfield Track**, which leads 10km to the **Goldsborough Valley State Forest Park**, across a saddle in the Bellenden Ker range.

Gordonvale, 33km north of Babinda, has two Sikh *gurdwaras* (places of worship). The winding Gillies Hwy leads from here up onto the Atherton Tableland. During the cutting season (July to November), Cairns Wonderland Tours (☎ 4033 6103) runs tours of the Mulgrave Sugar Mill ($15, or $25 with transfers from Cairns).

Four kilometres north is a turn-off to the **Yarrabah Aboriginal Community**, where you'll find the Menmuny Museum (open weekdays from 8.30 am to 4 pm), an interpretive boardwalk (1.2km) and daily dance performances ($10). On the way you can detour to the Cairns Crocodile Farm (feeding and tours are at 11 am and 2 pm, $11).

Far North Queensland

Queensland's far north is one of the most popular tourist destinations in Australia, especially in winter when sun-starved southerners flock here in droves.

Cairns, with its international airport, is the major centre for the region. It's a place where most travellers spend a few days before heading off: north to the superb rainforests of Daintree and Cape Tribulation and the historic town of Cooktown; west to the cool air of the Atherton Tableland; or east to the islands and the Great Barrier Reef.

CAIRNS
• postcode 4870   • pop 118,800

The 'capital' of the far north, Cairns is firmly established as one of Australia's top travel destinations. It is a centre for a whole host of activities – not only reef trips and scuba diving, but white-water rafting, canoeing, horse riding, bungee jumping and skydiving. On the downside, Cairns' rapid tourist growth has destroyed much of the city's laid-back tropical atmosphere. It also lacks a beach, but there are some good ones not far north.

Cairns began life in 1876 as a beachhead amongst the mangroves, intended as a port for the Hodgkinson River goldfield 100km inland. Initially it struggled under rivalry

QUEENSLAND

CAIRNS

PLACES TO STAY

1 Costa Blanca Apartments
2 Floriana Guesthouse
3 JJ's Backpackers
4 Captain Cook Backpackers Hostel
5 Calypso Inn
8 Cairns Backpackers Inn
9 Castaways
10 Pacific Cay Holiday Units
11 Concord Holiday Units
12 Castle Holiday Flats
13 Bel-Air by the Sea
14 Caravella's 149
16 Tracks Hostel
17 Poinsettia Motel
18 Parkview Backpackers
23 YHA on the Esplanade; Chapel Bar
24 Hostel 89
25 Bellview
26 Jimmy's on the Esplanade
28 Royal Harbour Tradewinds
29 Caravella's Backpackers 77
30 Radisson Plaza Hotel

31 International Hostel;
   Rattle 'n' Hum Pub
53 Great Northern Hotel
54 Pacific International Hotel
77 Macleod St YHA Hostel
80 Travellers Oasis
81 Dreamtime Travellers' Rest
82 Ryan's Rest Guesthouse
83 Gone Walkabout Hostel
86 Tropic Days

PLACES TO EAT

6 Cock & Bull Tavern
22 The Meeting Place; Tusa Dive
32 Night Markets; Internet Outpost
35 Old Ambulance Cafe Bistro
38 Silver Dragon Chinese Restaurant
61 Venus Cafe
62 Beethoven Cafe
63 Sawasdee
64 La Fettucine; Gypsy Dee's
66 Red Ochre Grill
67 John & Diana's Breakfast &
   Burger House
70 Tiny's Juice Bar
71 Yama Japanese Restaurant

OTHER

7 Hospital
15 Cheap Car Rental Companies
19 Theatre
20 Jolly Frog Rentals/Dollar
21 Beach Nightclub
27 Gulf Savannah Tourist
   Organisation

33 Global Gossip
34 Cairns Library
36 Adventure Equipment
37 Cairns Five Cinemas
39 Walker's Bookshop
40 Cairns Dive Centre
41 Air Niugini; Tropical Arcade
42 Johno's Blues Bar
43 Pro-Dive
44 Cairns Regional Gallery
45 Tropical North Queensland
   Information Centre
46 STA Travel
47 Wool Shed
48 Qantas & Sunstate Airlines
49 City Place Amphitheatre;
   Sydney's Place
50 Cairns Museum
51 Lake St Transit Centre
52 Palace Independent Cinema
55 Reef Teach
56 Thomas Cook
57 Orchid Plaza; Australia
   Post Shop; American Express
58 Tropo's Nightclub;
   Central Arcade; Fox & Firkin
59 Underdog
60 Tropical Paradise Travel
   & White Car Coaches
65 Northern Disposals
68 Harris Bros
69 Rusty's Bazaar
72 Reef Casino
73 Great Adventures Booking Office
74 Trinity Wharf; Transit Centre
75 Playpen International Nightclub;
   Millennium Club; Court
   Jester Bar
76 Environmental Protection Agency
78 Train Station
79 Cairns Central Mall
84 Down Under Dive
85 Deep Sea Divers Den

QUEENSLAND

from Smithfield, 15km north, and Port Douglas, founded in 1877 after Christie Palmerston discovered an easier route to the goldfield. Fortunately for Cairns, Smithfield was washed away by a flood in 1879 (it's now an outer suburb of Cairns) and Cairns was chosen as the starting point for the railway line to the Atherton Tableland during the 1880 'tin rush'.

Cairns marks the end of the Bruce Hwy and the railway line from Brisbane, and is at its climatic best – and busiest – from May to October; in summer the high humidity can be draining.

Orientation

The centre of Cairns is quite compact and most places of interest are contained in the area between the Esplanade and Wharf, McLeod and Aplin Sts. The main departure points for reef trips are Great Adventures Wharf, Marlin Jetty and the Pier Marina, all just off Wharf St (the southern continuation of the Esplanade). Further south along Wharf St is Trinity Wharf (a cruise-liner dock with shops and cafes) and the transit centre, where long-distance buses arrive and depart.

Back from the waterfront is City Place, a pedestrian mall at the meeting of Shields and Lake Sts. Cairns train station is hidden inside the Cairns Central mall on McLeod St.

Cairns is surrounded by mangrove swamps to the south and north. The sea in front of the town is shallow and at low tide it becomes a long sweep of mud, with lots of interesting water birds.

Information

Tourist Offices The helpful Tropical North Queensland Information Centre, at 51 the Esplanade, provides unbiased tourist information. It's open daily from 8.30 am to 5.30 pm.

You will see dozens of privately run 'information centres' (basically tour-booking agencies) in Cairns, but each will be pushing the tours that give them the best commission. The sales pitch can be quite heavy-handed in some of these places, but it's worth holding out until you find a deal

that suits you. The hostel tour desks often have discount deals for their guests.

The Community Information Service (☎ 4051 4953), upstairs in the Tropical Arcade off Shields St, has more offbeat information, like where you can find health services or do t'ai chi.

Post & Communications The main post office, on the corner of Grafton and Hartley Sts, has a poste restante service. For general business (stamps etc), there's also an Australia Post shop in Orchid Plaza on Lake St.

Many hostels now offer email/Internet access. Global Gossip, at 125 Abbott St, is probably the cheapest of the many Internet cafes; the first five minutes are free, and it's 15c per minute thereafter. Internet Outpost, in the Night Markets arcade off the Esplanade, opens at 5 am (Internet access is $3 per hour).

Bookshops Proudmans, in the Pier complex, and Walker's Bookshop, at 96 Lake St, sell a good range of reading material. For maps, try Northern Disposals, at 47 Sheridan St.

Useful Organisations The RACQ office (☎ 4033 6433), at 520 Mulgrave Rd, Earlville, is a good place to get maps and information on road conditions, especially if you're driving up to the Cape York Peninsula or across to the Gulf of Carpentaria.

The EPA office (☎ 4052 3096), at 10 McLeod St, is open on weekdays from 8.30 am to 4.30 pm; it deals with camping permits and information on the region's national parks, including the permit for camping on Fitzroy Island.

Things to See & Do

Cairns' main attraction is as a base for getting to the places that surround it, but there are several local attractions. The impressive **Cairns Regional Gallery** is housed in a cleverly restored historic building on the corner of Abbott and Shields Sts, and features theme exhibitions, works by local artists and loans from major galleries. It is open daily from 10 am to 6 pm ($6/3 adults/students, free on Friday).

QUEENSLAND

Most of Cairns' older buildings have been engulfed by the booming developments of the 1980s and 90s. The oldest part of town is the **Trinity Wharf** area, but even this has been redeveloped. There are still some imposing neoclassical buildings from the 1920s on Abbott St, and the frontages around the corner of Spence and Lake Sts date from 1909 to 1926.

A walk along the **Esplanade Walking Trail**, with views over to rainforested mountains across the estuary and cool breezes in the evening, is very agreeable.

Housed in the 1907 School of Arts building, on the corner of Lake and Shields Sts, the **Cairns Museum** has some interesting historic displays on the far north, including Aboriginal artefacts, the construction of the Cairns to Kuranda railway and the old Palmer River and Hodgkinson goldfields. It's open daily (except Sunday) from 10 am to 3 pm ($3).

The colourful markets at **Rusty's Bazaar**, on Sheridan St between Spence and Shields Sts, are great for people-watching and for browsing among the dozens of stalls, which sell fruit and vegies, arts and crafts, clothes and more. The markets are held on Friday night and Saturday and Sunday mornings; Saturday is the busiest and best time.

The **Pier Marketplace** is a glossy shopping plaza with expensive boutiques, souvenir shops, a foodhall, cafes and restaurants. On weekends the **Mud Markets** are held here, with a wide range of stalls selling food and local arts and crafts. Also here is the impressive **Undersea World** aquarium, which is open daily from 8 am to 8 pm; entry is steep at $10 but there are often 20% discount vouchers available from the various hostels. The best time to visit is when the sharks are being fed (four times daily).

Three kilometres north-west of town are the **Flecker Botanic Gardens**, on Collins Ave in Edge Hill. Over the road from the gardens, a boardwalk leads through a patch of rainforest to **Saltwater Creek** and the two small **Centenary Lakes**. Collins Ave turns west off Sheridan St (the Cook Hwy) 3km from the centre of Cairns. The gardens are 700m from the turning. Near the gardens is

the entrance to the **Whitfield Range Environmental Park**, one of the last remnants of rainforest around Cairns. Two long walking tracks give good views over the city and coast. You can get there with Sunbus or the Cairns Explorer.

Also in Edge Hill, the **Royal Flying Doctor Service** visitors centre and regional office, at 1 Junction St, is open to visitors on weekdays from 8.30 am to 5 pm and weekends from 9 am to 4.30 pm ($5).

The **Tjapukai Aboriginal Cultural Centre**, an award-winning Aboriginal dance troupe, has a theatre complex beside the Skyrail terminal at Smithfield, just off the Captain Cook Hwy about 15km north of the city centre. This multi-million dollar complex incorporates four sections – a cultural village, a 'creation theatre', an audio-visual show and a traditional dance theatre. Performances include a re-enactment of a traditional corroboree, boomerang and spear-throwing and the telling of Dreamtime stories. The complex is open daily from 9 am to 5 pm; entry costs $24/12 for adults/children, or $36/18 with return bus transfers from Cairns. Allow at least two hours.

Activities

As a rule, bookings for tours and trips are made by phone (either direct or through agents or hostels) and the tour companies pick up from your accommodation.

Diving & Snorkelling Cairns is one of the scuba-diving capitals of the Barrier Reef, which lies about an hour offshore. It's one of the better places to learn to dive as the local dive schools have purpose-built training facilities; elsewhere you may find yourself using a swimming pool at a local hotel.

There are a wide range of courses on offer, from no-frills four-day courses (which combine pool training with a few day trips to the reef) to five or six-day courses that give you several days living on a boat and multiple reef dives, including at least one night dive. Unless you are particularly short on time or money, it's worth paying a little more for one of the longer courses; you'll have more fun, see more of the reef, and you'll usually end up a better and more confident diver.

Reputable dive schools in Cairns include: Down Under Dive (☎ 1800 079 099), 287 Draper St; Deep Sea Divers Den (☎ 4031 2223), 319 Draper St; Cairns Dive Centre (☎ 1800 642 591), 121 Abbott St; Pro-Dive (☎ 4031 5255), on the corner of Abbot and Shields Sts; and Tusa Dive (☎ 4031 1248), corner of Aplin St and Esplanade. All of these places have hostel pickups and can be booked through the hostel tour desks.

Expect to pay about $250 for a four day course with day trips to the reef, $350 to $400 for four days with an overnight stay, and $450 upwards for five and six-day courses. Discounts are often available. You'll also need a medical (about $30).

If you want to learn more about the reef before you dive, Reef Teach offers an entertaining and educational lecture at Boland's Centre, 14 Spence St, Monday to Saturday from 6.15 to 8.30 pm, and it's highly recommended. The cost is $10.

White-Water Rafting, Kayaking & Canoeing Three of the rivers flowing down from the Atherton Tableland make for some excellent white-water rafting. Most popular is a day in the rainforested gorges of the Tully River, 150km south of Cairns. The river can get pretty crowded, with as many as 20 craft queuing up to shoot each section of rapids, yet despite this, most people are exhilarated at the end of the day. Day trips on the Tully leave daily year-round; Raging Thunder (☎ 1800 079 092), 52 Fearnley St, and R 'n' R (☎ 1800 079 039), 48 Abbott St, charge $133, including pickups from Cairns, or there are cheaper half-day trips on the Barron River ($75), which runs down to Cairns from Kuranda. If you have more time, there are two-day ($390), four-day ($730) or five-day ($845) expeditions on the remote North Johnstone River, which rises near Malanda and enters the sea at Innisfail.

Foaming Fury (☎ 4032 1460), 21 Berry St, offers white-water rafting ($118) on the Russell River south of Wooroonooran National Park, and half-day trips on the Barron River for $75.

The Adventure Company (☎ 4051 4777) has one-day wilderness canoe paddles on the Musgrave River ($89) and three-day sea-kayaking tours out of Mission Beach ($498).

Other Activities At Smithfield, 15km north of the city centre, you can bungee jump from a steel tower with sensational views with AJ Hackett (☎ 4057 7188; $95 including transfers).

Blazing Saddles (☎ 4093 4493) offers half-day horse trail rides for about $70, including pickups from Cairns. Dan's Tours (☎ 4033 0128) has full-day mountain bike tours to Cape Tribulation ($115). Skydive Cairns (☎ 4035 9667) has tandem skydiving ($228). For air travel at a more leisurely pace there are three ballooning outfits with half-hour (about $115) and one-hour flights (about $180), including transfers and breakfast. Contact Raging Thunder (☎ 1800 079 092), Hot Air (☎ 1800 800 829) or Champagne Balloon Flights (☎ 1800 677 444).

Northern Air Adventures (☎ 4035 9156) has half-hour flights over Green Island and Arlington and Upton reefs ($50), or one-hour flights that also include Batt Reef ($90).

Organised Tours

There are literally hundreds of tours available out of Cairns, some of which are aimed at backpackers and are very good value. You can make bookings through your accommodation or at one of the many booking agencies in town.

Cairns Half-day trips around the city sights or two-hour cruises from Marlin Jetty up along Trinity Inlet and around Admiralty Island start from around $25.

Atherton Tableland On the Wallaby (☎ 4050 0650) runs lively guided tours of the tableland waterfalls and wildlife-spotting canoeing trips, both for $55. Its overnight trips, which include rainforest walks, mountain biking, canoeing and accommodation at the *On the Wallaby Hostel* in Yungaburra, are great value, with two/three days for $89/105.

Jungle Tours (☎ 1800 817 234) also runs good guided day trips for backpackers for $60. Uncle Brian's quirky tours (☎ 4050 0615) have received good reports from travellers and a day trip is $60.

Reef & Rainforest Connections (☎ 4099 5599) has day tours to the historic mining town of Chillagoe ($115).

Daintree & Cape Tribulation Cape Tribulation is one of the most popular destinations for day trips and there are dozens of operators offering tours. Most operators use 4WD vehicles, but don't be misled into thinking that you can't do this trip yourself by car – the road is bitumen most of the way.

Jungle Tours (☎ 1800 817 234) offers fun trips up to Cape Tribulation, usually with a cruise on the Daintree River thrown in, for $88 (no lunch). If you have time, you'd be better off taking one of its longer packages – $84 for two days and $96 for three days, which includes accommodation at Crocodylus Village and/or PK's Jungle Village. Dan's Tours (☎ 4033 0128) has full-day mountain bike trips to Cape Tribulation ($115).

Cooktown Wild Track Safaris (☎ 4055 2247) runs good 4WD day trips to Cooktown from Cairns and Port Douglas, via the Bloomfield Track, for $199, travelling up by 4WD and returning by plane. Overnight trips are $299, including accommodation.

Barrier Reef & Islands There are dozens of options available for day trips to the reef. It's worth asking a few questions before you book, such as how many passengers the boat takes, what's included in the price and how much the 'extras' (such as wetsuit hire and introductory dives) cost. It's also worth asking which reefs you will be visiting; as a general rule, the further out you go, the better the diving.

Great Adventures (☎ 1800 079 080) is the major operator with the biggest boats and a wide range of combination cruises, including a day trip to either Norman or Moore reefs. You get about three hours on a pontoon at the reef, lunch, snorkelling

gear and a ride in a semisubmersible, glass-bottom boat.

Compass (☎ 1800 815 811) has popular day trips to Hastings Reef and Michaelmas Cay for $55, including boom netting, snorkelling gear and lunch. Certified divers can take two dives for an extra $45. Other operators include Noah's Ark Cruises (☎ 4051 0677), with day trips for $49, and the MV *Super Cat* (☎ 1800 079 099; $65).

Falla (☎ 4031 3488), *Passions of Paradise* (☎ 4050 0676) and *Seahorse* (☎ 4041 1919) are all ocean-going yachts that 'sail' out to Upolo Cay, Green Island and Paradise Reef daily for $60, which includes lunch and snorkelling gear.

There are many, many other boats and operators, so shop around.

Undara Lava Tubes Undara Experience (☎ 4097 1411), in conjunction with Australian Pacific (☎ 13 1304), has two-day trips out to the Undara Lava Tubes for $312, including accommodation, meals and a tour of the vast lava tubes, which were hollowed out by underground lava flows nearly 190,000 years ago.

Cape York See the Cape York section later in this chapter for details of tours from Cairns to Cape York.

Places to Stay
Cairns has a huge range of accommodation, catering for everybody from backpackers to those with more upmarket tastes. There are plenty of hostels, as well as cheap guesthouses and holiday flats. Prices go up and down with the seasons, and lower weekly rates are par for the course. Prices given here for the more expensive places can rise 30% or 40% in the peak season, and some of the hostels will charge a dollar or two less in the quiet times. A VIP or YHA card will get you few dollars discount in most of the main hostels.

Places to Stay – Budget
Camping There are about a dozen caravan parks in and around Cairns, but none are really central. Almost without exception

they take campers as well as caravans. The closest to the centre is the *City Caravan Park* (☎ 4051 1467), about 2km north-west on the corner of Little and James Sts, with camp sites from $14, on-site vans from $40 and cabins from $45.

Out on the Bruce Hwy, about 8km south of the centre, is the *Cairns Coconut Caravan Village* (☎ 4054 6644) with camp sites from $19, on-site cabins from $45 and units from $75. If you want to camp by the beach, the *Yorkeys Knob Beachfront Van Park* (☎ 4055 7201), about 20km north, has camp sites and on-site vans.

Hostels Cairns is the backpacking capital of Queensland and has more than 20 hostels, ranging from the huge pack-'em-in type to the smaller, quieter owner-operated places. Most have fan-cooled bunk rooms with shared bathrooms, kitchens, laundries, lounge and TV rooms, and a swimming pool. Many also offer private rooms with their own facilities. Unfortunately, you have to beware of theft in some hostels – use lock-up rooms and safes if they're available. There have also been reports of female travellers being harassed, but most of the main hostels now offer female-only dorms.

There are two main areas for accommodation. If you want to be in the thick of things, the greatest concentration of hostels is around the Esplanade, but there's another big group of hostels just north of the town centre.

Esplanade Heading north along the Esplanade from the corner of Shields St, the first place you come to is the *International Hostel* (☎ 4031 1424, 67 Esplanade), a big, multilevel place with about 200 beds. This place is popular with party-goers, but the atmosphere is impersonal and it lacks communal areas. Beds in four to eight-bed dorms with fan are $16, twin rooms are $25 and doubles range from $30 to $40 with either air-con and TV or private bathroom. You also get a free meal at the Rattle 'n' Hum pub next door.

Caravella's Backpackers 77 (☎ 4051 2159), at No 77, is one of the longest established Cairns hostels. It's a big rambling

place with a large pool and air-con throughout, and it's recently been renovated. Bed prices remain reasonable at $16 in four-bed dorms or $34 for spacious doubles ($45 with a private bathroom). The price includes a free evening meal. There are security patrols in the evenings.

Jimmy's on the Esplanade (☎ 4031 6884), at No 83, is a reasonably modern place with six-bed air-con units with their own bathrooms. There's a pool, kitchen and a good tour desk; dorm beds cost $16, doubles are $40 or $50 with your own bathroom.

Next door, the *Bellview* (☎ 4031 4377) is a good quiet hostel with beds in clean four-bed dorms for $16 and singles/twins from $27/36; all rooms have air-con. The kitchen is good and there's a small pool, a laundry, and a good, cheap cafe. It also has motel-style units from $49 a double.

Hostel 89 (☎ 1800 061 712), at No 89, is immaculately clean, but it doesn't have much atmosphere. Security is tight, though, with a locked grille at the street entrance, and there's a good tour desk and a pool. Beds in three or four-bed dorms are $18, and singles/doubles are from $36/44, all air-conditioned.

At No 93 is *YHA on the Esplanade* (☎ 4031 1919). There are two blocks, one with spacious, airy five-bed dorms with their own bathrooms, the other with small twins and doubles. Some rooms have air-con. Dorm beds cost $17 and doubles $38; nonmembers pay an extra $3.

Three blocks further on, the large *Caravella's 149* (☎ 4031 5680, 149 Esplanade) offers similar facilities to Caravella's 77. It has a good pool and plenty of outdoor areas. You pay $16 for a bed in a six share dorm with air-con, $15 in a four share dorm with fan, or from $10 in larger dorms. Air-con doubles cost $34, and all prices include an evening meal.

Bel-Air by the Sea (☎ 4031 4790, 155-157 Esplanade) has four renovated Queenslanders with a variety of rooms, and a pool and hot tub. Beds in four to six-bed dorms are $14 ($16 with air-con) and air-con doubles and twins are $36. There are also four six-bed flats for $14 per person, and a small cafe with cheap breakfasts.

QUEENSLAND

Around Town Three blocks back from the Esplanade, *Parkview Backpackers (☎ 1800 652 215, 174 Grafton St)* is a friendly and laid-back place where you can relax by the pool and listen to music. It's in a rambling old timber building with a large tropical garden; beds in four to eight-bed dorms cost from $14, twins and doubles cost $30, and there's a free meal.

Tracks Hostel (☎ 4031 1474), on the corner of Grafton and Minnie Sts, is spread out over five slightly tired-looking buildings, but many people like the atmosphere. It runs regular trips out to the northern beaches. Dorm beds cost from $14 and doubles are $30, all including an evening meal.

Captain Cook Backpackers Hostel (☎ 4051 6811, 204 Sheridan St) is a huge converted motel with lots of beds, two pools, a bar, and a restaurant and a huge statue of Captain Cook out front. The facilities here are looking a little tired, but it's still a popular backpacker resort. Dorm beds cost $15, doubles range from $32 to $38, or $44 in motel-style units with cooking facilities. Breakfast is included and evening meals are free if you buy a jug of beer or wine.

The *Calypso Inn (☎ 1800 815 628)*, on Digger St behind the Cock & Bull tavern, is a friendly, low-key hostel in a renovated Queenslander. The downstairs area has a pool, bar and restaurant in a tropical garden. Dorm beds are $15 and doubles are $34.

JJ's Backpackers (☎ 4051 7642, 11 Charles St) is a small block of apartments converted into a hostel, with dorm beds for $14 and doubles for $32, plus a small pool. This place is not as clean as it could be.

Castaways (☎ 4051 1238, 207 Sheridan St) is a small place in a converted motel. It lacks good outdoor areas, but the staff are helpful and there's a small pool. Dorms are $15, and single/double rooms are $27/32. All rooms are fan cooled and have a fridge, and prices include a free evening meal in one of the town centre restaurants.

A little further out, the *Cairns Back-packers Inn (☎ 1800 681 889, 242 Grafton St)* is spread out over three Queenslanders and has good facilities, lots of outdoor areas

and a nice pool. Four-bed dorms cost $15 per person and twins/doubles are $34.

The YHA *McLeod St Youth Hostel (☎ 4051 0772, 20-24 McLeod St)* has dorm beds for $17 and twins/doubles for $36/38. Nonmembers pay $3 extra. Standards here are high, and there are car parking spaces.

The *Up-Top Down Under (☎ 4051 3636, 164-170 Spence St)*, 1.5km from the town centre, is a spacious and quiet place with a large, well-equipped kitchen, two TV lounges (smoking and non-smoking) and a pool. Dorm beds are $15 and singles/doubles $28/32, all with shared bathroom.

Sunny Grove (☎ 4051 4513, 42 Grove St) is a brightly decorated weekly hostel that caters mainly for backpackers working in Cairns. Twin share rooms start from $70 per person per week.

Guesthouses There are a number of family run guesthouses west of the train station that offer a quieter, more intimate experience. These are probably the nicest places to stay in Cairns. The inconvenience of being out of the centre is minimal as there are courtesy buses that make regular runs into town.

Tropic Days (☎ 4041 1521, 28 Bunting St) has a quiet location and is set in an immaculately maintained tropical garden. It's run by a friendly young couple, and has good facilities and a great pool. Beds in three to four-bed dorms (no bunks) are $15, comfortable doubles are $35, with a free meal in town.

Dreamtime Travellers' Rest (☎ 4031 6753, 4 Terminus St) is another friendly guesthouse run by an enthusiastic young couple. It's in a brightly renovated timber Queenslander and has a nice pool, double rooms from $35 and three or four-bed (no bunks) rooms for $15 per person.

Down the road, *Ryan's Rest (☎ 4051 4734, 18 Terminus St)* has a similar setup. It's a quiet and personal family run place with breezy verandahs and good double rooms upstairs for $35, twins for $17 per person and a triple room for $15 per person.

A block west of the station, *Gone Walk-about Hostel (☎ 4051 6160, 274 Draper St)* is small, popular and well run, with a friendly atmosphere. Set in two attractively renovated old houses, it has beds in four-bed dorms for $14, singles for $20 and doubles and twins for $32. There's a small pool and a garden, but it's not a place for late partying.

Close to the train station, *Traveller's Oasis* (☎ 4052 1377, 8 Scott St) comprises two renovated Queenslanders and has a quiet laid-back atmosphere. Beds in clean, colourful dorms cost $15 per person; rooms cost $20/36.

The Art Deco *Floriana Guesthouse* (☎ 4051 7886, 183 Esplanade) has four self-contained units with polished timber floors, TVs, en suites and kitchenettes. This place is excellent value at $55 to $70 for up to four. The old building next door has 24 simple doubles, some with air-con and others with ocean views, which cost from $28 to $48 (bookings advised).

Places to Stay – Mid-Range
Hotels & Motels The *Great Northern Hotel* (☎ 4051 5151, 69 Abbott St) is a very central, modern hotel with reasonable rates. Singles cost from $65, with doubles/twins from $75.

Budget motels around the centre include the *Poinsettia Motel* (☎ 4051 2144, 169 Lake St), which has decent budget rooms from $45/50.

Apartments Holiday flats are well worth considering, especially for a group of three or four people who are staying a few days or more. Expect pools, kitchens, air-con and laundry facilities in this category.

Just back from the water, the *Castle Holiday Flats* (☎ 4031 2229, 209 Lake St) is one of the cheapest places, and it has a small pool. Self-contained one/two-bedroom flats cost from $60/80 per night.

On the waterfront, the *Costa Blanca Apartments* (☎ 4051 3114, 241 Esplanade) aren't particularly flashy, but they're comfortable enough and sleep up to four people. They range from $45 to $85 a double, plus $5 per extra person. There's a guest laundry and a big pool.

There's a string of motels and holiday units along Sheridan St – these include the

Pacific Cay (☎ 4051 0151), at No 193, with one/two-bedroom units from $50/80, and the *Concord Holiday Units* (☎ 4031 4522), at No 183, with one-bedroom units for $77 a double, plus $10 per extra person.

Places to Stay – Top End
If a balcony view and room service are more to your taste, Cairns has a number of luxury international hotels, with suitably luxurious price tags. The *Radisson Plaza Hotel at the Pier* (☎ 1800 333 333) probably has the prime location in town – right on top of the Pier Marketplace, overlooking Trinity Inlet. This place has the usual array of classy restaurants and bars and there's a rainforest waterfall in the foyer. Prices start at $195 a double.

Another high profile place is the *Royal Harbour Tradewinds* (☎ 4080 8888), which looms over the Esplanade between Shields and Aplin Sts. It's housed in a stylish Art Deco building and all rooms have ocean views. Rates start at $160 for a double, but for a real taste of luxury you can hire out the Imperial Suite for $500 a night.

The *Pacific International Hotel* (☎ 1800 079 001, 43 Esplanade) is also noteworthy – a swish, modern hotel overlooking the Reef Casino. Rates start at $145 for a double. *18-24 James St* (☎ 4051 4644) at, funnily enough, 18-24 James St, is an exclusively gay and lesbian hotel with four-share rooms for $55 per person or singles/doubles for $95/120, all including a tropical breakfast.

Places to Eat
Cairns has an abundance of eateries, so you shouldn't have too much trouble finding somewhere to satisfy your particular gastronomic craving and/or your budget.

Restaurants The BYO *La Fettucini* (43 Shields St) is a narrow bistro with great home-made pasta for $12 and Italian mains for about $18. Next door is the dim and exotic *Gypsy Dee's*, with a bar, live acoustic music nightly and mains in the $12 to $18 range. On the corner of Shields and Sheridan Sts, the *Red Ochre Grill* is a stylish restaurant with innovative Aussie bush tucker, but it's not cheap, with mains ranging from $17 to $25.

The *Silver Dragon (102 Lake St)* Chinese restaurant has a good buffet lunch deal for $4.90.

The friendly *Sawasdee (89 Grafton St)* is a tiny BYO Thai restaurant with lunch specials from $7.50 and dinner mains from $12 to $16. Across the road, the *Venus Cafe* is a narrow and groovy eatery with vegetarian-friendly world cuisine from $7.50 upwards.

For Japanese food, try *Yama*, on the corner of Spence and Grafton Sts – it has good-value lunches and dinners.

The Pier Marketplace has a couple of good eating options, including a good international food hall and *Johnny Rocket's*, an American-style burger joint. On the 1st floor is *Donnini's*, a smart licensed restaurant with some of the best Italian food in town; gourmet pizzas cost $9 to $16, pasta $12 to $16 and Italian mains about $17.

Pubs Most of the hostels give away vouchers for cheap (or free) meals at various nightclubs, pubs and bars around town.

On the Esplanade, next to the International Hostel, *Rattle 'n' Hum* serves traditional English/Irish pub grub for around $10 in a lively but relaxed atmosphere.

The hugely popular *Wool Shed*, on Shields St in the mall, has good meals in the $5 to $10 range. Many of the hostels offer coupons for free meals here, and there's a bus that runs around to the hostels to pick up hungry travellers. The *Underdog*, on the corner of Spence and Grafton Sts, is another popular bar with cheap meal (and drink) deals.

On the corner of Digger and Grove Sts, the *Cock & Bull Tavern* is an excellent English-style tavern with draught beers and hearty, stodgy tucker in the $8 to $10 range – just the spot for homesick Poms, and far enough from the touristy centre of town to have the atmosphere of a 'local'.

Cafes The Esplanade, between Shields and Aplin Sts, is basically wall-to-wall eateries open all hours and with plenty of variety – Italian and Chinese food, steaks, burgers,

kebabs, pizzas, seafood and ice cream. The *Night Markets*, in the thick of it, is a somewhat soulless hawker-style food court, but with plenty of choice. Better is the *Meeting Place*, around the corner in Aplin St, with Japanese, Thai, Chinese and Australian meals in the $7 to $14 range.

The *Beethoven Cafe (105 Grafton St)* is a popular breakfast place, with excellent German pastries, filled croissants and coffee. *Sidney's Place*, on the corner of Lake and Shields Sts in the pedestrian City Place mall, has pavement seating and good tropical breakfasts for $4.50. The somewhat downmarket *John & Diana's Breakfast & Burger House (35 Sheridan St)* also has cooked breakfasts for $5 or less.

The very popular *Tiny's Juice Bar*, on Grafton St near Spence St, has a great range of fruit and vegetable juices as well as filled rolls and lentil and tofu burgers at good prices.

The *Old Ambulance Cafe Bistro* is a chic new place in, as the name suggests, the old ambulance station, and has great coffee and filled croissants. Next to the Cairns Regional Gallery, *Perrotta's* is a breezy cafe and bistro with lunchtime sandwiches and salads from $6, and dinner mains from $12.

Entertainment

The free and widely available magazine *Barfly* covers music gigs, movies, pubs and clubs – and it's quite an entertaining read in itself.

Pubs & Live Music Free lunchtime concerts are held daily at the *City Place Amphitheatre*, in the mall on the corner of Lake and Shields Sts.

The long-running *Johno's Blues Bar*, upstairs on the corner of Shields St and the Esplanade, has blues, rock and rhythm and blues bands every night until late; the cover charge is about $5.

Live bands perform regularly in quite a few pubs in Cairns, including the *Underdog Hotel*, the *Fox & Firkin*, on the corner of Spence and Lake Sts, and the *Big Kahuna Bar*, overlooking the bay from the Pier Marketplace.

In Shields St, *Gypsy Dee's* has live acoustic, jazz and blues music at night (see Places to Eat earlier in the Cairns section).

Chapel is a low-key bar with live acoustic music on some nights. It's on the 1st floor close to the YHA on the Esplanade hostel.

Nightclubs & Bars Cairns' nightclub scene is notoriously wild and promiscuous, especially in the early hours of the morning – it has been said that if you can't get lucky here you may as well stop trying!

The phenomenally popular *Wool Shed* is right in the heart of the action, with party games, backpacker theme nights and other wild stuff. This place is heaving most nights, so it's worth coming early to beat the crowds.

Other nightclub options include the *Beach* nightclub, on the corner of Abbott and Aplin Sts, with a huge video screen, foam parties and competition nights such as Mr Backpacker, and *Tropo's Nightclub*, on the corner of Spence and Lake Sts.

The converted warehouse complex on the corner of Lake and Hartley Sts houses the *Playpen International*, a huge nightclub that often has big-name bands, the *Millennium Club* and the more upmarket *Court Jester Bar*, which tends to attract an older crowd.

Cinemas & Theatre The *Cairns Five Cinemas (108 Grafton St)* screens mainstream releases, or there's the *Central Cinemas* in Cairns Central mall. Near City Place, the *Palace Independent Cinema (☎ 4031 3607, 86 Lake St)* shows an interesting program of foreign and art films. The *Cairns Civic Theatre (☎ 4050 1777)* is the main venue for theatre and concerts.

Other Entertainment Cairns' big *Reef Casino* is on the block bordered by the Esplanade, and Wharf, Abbott and Spence Sts. Inside it's thoroughly characterless, the decor is glitzy and tacky and the place has no atmosphere – basically it's a big, gaudy, poker machine venue.

Shopping

Many artists live in the Cairns region, so there's a wide range of local handicrafts available at the various markets, including the weekend Mud Markets at the Pier Marketplace, the (expensive) stalls in the rear of the Night Markets food hall on the Esplanade, and Rusty's Bazaar.

Harris Bros, on the corner of Shields and Sheridan Sts, has a good range of Aussie clothing, boots and Akubra hats.

Getting There & Away

Air Qantas has an office on the corner of Shields and Lake Sts. STA Travel (☎ 4031 4199), at 9 Shields St, is a good discount agent.

Ansett and Qantas have daily flights between Cairns and all the major Australian destinations, including Melbourne ($677 one way), Sydney ($599), Brisbane ($441), Townsville ($205), Darwin ($470), Alice Springs ($490), Perth ($709) and Adelaide ($661).

For shorter hops within Queensland, Sunstate flies to Lizard Island ($194) and Thursday Island ($321); Ansett flies to Weipa ($191) and Mt Isa ($289); Flight West flies to Cooktown ($73) and Bamaga ($292) and has a service through the Gulf Savannah; and Transtate (☎ 13 1528) flies direct to Dunk Island ($120), Cooktown ($73) and Mt Isa ($391).

Cairns airport also has regular flights to and from North America, Papua New Guinea and Asia. Air Niugini (☎ 4051 4177) is at 4 Shields St; the Port Moresby flight costs $402 one way and goes at least once daily. Qantas also flies to Port Moresby (Tuesday, Friday and Sunday), Singapore (daily, from $859) and Hong Kong (Thursday, from $1039).

Bus Greyhound Pioneer, McCafferty's and Coral Coaches operate from the transit centre at Trinity Wharf. Most backpackers' hostels have courtesy buses that meet the arriving buses.

Greyhound (☎ 13 2030) and McCafferty's (☎ 13 1499) both run at least five buses a day up the coast from Brisbane and Townsville to Cairns. Journey times and fares are: Brisbane, $144, 27 hours; Rockhampton, $98, 15 hours; Mackay, $78, 11 hours; and Townsville, $38, six hours. Greyhound also has daily buses to Cape Tribulation ($28) via Port Douglas ($16), with a service through to Cooktown three times a week ($78).

Coral Coaches (☎ 4031 7577) has daily buses to Port Douglas ($16) and Cape Tribulation ($28). It also has regular services to Cooktown, via the inland road ($47) or coastal road ($52), and to Karumba ($122) on the Gulf of Carpentaria, via the Undara Lava Tubes ($42). There's a service to Weipa once a week ($130).

White Car Coaches (☎ 4051 9533) has services to Kuranda and the Atherton Tableland; buses leave from Tropical Paradise Travel, at 51 Spence St.

Train If money is no object, you can travel to Brisbane and Sydney in style on the *Great South Pacific Express*, an Orient Express-style service with luxury cabins, a bar and two restaurants. It's more of a tour than a train ride; there's even an excursion to the Great Barrier Reef on the Cairns-Brisbane leg. Twin share from Cairns to Sydney start at a cool $3720 per person ($2430 as far as Brisbane). Call Traveltrain Holidays (☎ 1800 627 655) for departure dates.

Three normal trains run between Cairns and Brisbane – the *Sunlander* (three times a week), the *Queenslander* and the *Spirit of the Tropics* (both weekly). The 1631km trip from Brisbane takes 32 hours. The luxurious *Queenslander* leaves Brisbane on Sunday and Cairns on Tuesday; the fare is $389 including sleeping berth and all meals (1st class only). For another $270 you can put your car on the train too. The economy/1st class fare for a sleeper on the *Sunlander* or *Spirit of the Tropics* is $165/253. Call Queensland Rail for bookings and inquiries (☎ 13 2232).

Car & Motorcycle A hire vehicle is a great way to explore the area around Cairns, whether it's doing the beach crawl up to Port Douglas and Cape Tribulation or exploring the Atherton Tableland. The major rental firms have desks at the airport and offices in town, and there are dozens of smaller local operators offering good deals. Generally, small cars are about $45 per day with 300km free.

Note that most Cairns rental firms specifically prohibit you from taking their cars on the road to Cooktown, to Chillagoe or up the Cape Tribulation road. If you ignore this prohibition, you risk losing your deposit and/or a hefty fine, so if you're planning to tackle one of these routes you'll need to hire a 4WD. Several companies in town rent 4WDs for about $95 a day with up to 300km free, including Marlin Truck & 4WD Rentals (☎ 4031 3094) and Britz:Australia (☎ 4032 2611) – minimum hire periods apply.

Boat The daily Quicksilver (☎ 4099 5500) fast-catamaran service links Cairns, leaving from Marlin Jetty, with Port Douglas. The trip takes 1½ hours and costs $20/30 one way/return.

Getting Around

To/From the Airport The approach road to the Cairns airport (domestic and international flights) leaves the main highway about 3.5km north of the centre. The old Cairns airport (local flights) is reached from a second turning about 1.5km further north.

The Australia Coach shuttle bus (☎ 4031 3555) meets all incoming flights and runs a regular pickup and drop-off service between the airport and town; the one way fare is $4.50. Black & White taxis (☎ 13 1008) charge about $10.

Bus Sunbus runs the (expensive) local bus services in and around Cairns. Schedules for most of them are posted at the main city stop (known as the Lake St transit centre) in City Place. Buses run from early morning to late evening. Useful destinations include: Yorkeys Knob and Holloways Beach (routes 1C, 1D and 1H); Trinity and Clifton beaches (1, 1A); and Palm Cove (1, 1X). All are served by the 24 hour night service (N) on Friday and Saturday. Heading south, bus No 1 goes as far as Gordonvale.

The Cairns Explorer (☎ 4033 5244) is a daily air-con service that plies a circular route around the city. It leaves the Lake St transit centre every hour from 9 am to 4 pm (Monday to Saturday from October to April), and a day ticket costs $25. Stops include the Pier Marketplace, the mangrove boardwalk near the airport and the botanic gardens.

Bicycle Most of the hostels and car-hire firms, plus quite a few other places, have bikes for hire so you'll have no trouble tracking one down. Expect to pay about $10 a day.

ISLANDS OFF CAIRNS

Off the coast from Cairns are Green Island and Fitzroy Island. Both attract hordes of day-trippers (some say too many), and both have resorts owned by the cruise company Great Adventures, which in turn is owned by the Japanese corporation Daikyo.

South of Cairns, the Frankland Islands Group is a cluster of undeveloped national park islands. You can do day trips to these islands or camp.

Green Island

Green Island, 27km north-east of Cairns, is a coral cay 660m long by 260m wide. Although the island is a national park, a multimillion dollar resort takes up a substantial proportion of the island. Nevertheless, a 10 minute stroll from the resort to the far end of the island will remind you that the beach is beautiful, the snorkelling good and the fish prolific.

The resort has a separate section for daytrippers, with impressive facilities, including a pool, a bar, several eateries and water sports gear for hire. Marineland Melanesia is worth a visit ($7.50), with its aquarium of fish, turtles, stingrays and crocodiles, and a bizarre collection of Melanesian artefacts.

The five-star *Green Island Reef Resort* (☎ *1800 673 366)* has room for 92 guests who each pay $400-plus a night.

Getting There & Away Great Adventures (☎ 4051 0455) has regular services to Green Island by fast catamaran ($40 return). Other operators include the Big Cat (☎ 4051 0444), with a day cruise for $42 (lunch $8).

JUDITH KÜNZLE

The parrot fish is a common sight on the reef

Fitzroy Island

Six kilometres off the coast and 29km east of Cairns, Fitzroy is a continental island with coral-covered beaches, which are good for snorkelling, but not ideal for swimming and sunbaking, although Nudey Beach (1.2km and 45 minutes return) is pleasant. Snorkellers will find good coral only 50m off the beach in the resort area, and the island has its own dive school. There are some fine walks, including one to the island's high point.

The *Fitzroy Island Resort (☎ 1800 079 080)* has hostel-style bunk rooms with shared kitchen, bathroom and laundry facilities for $28 per person including linen, and 'villa units' for $240/340 for singles/doubles including activities, breakfast and dinner. There's also a QPWS camping ground (permits available through EPA in Cairns). Sites cost $10 a night for up to five people, but only one tent per site is allowed. Both campers and day-trippers have access to the resort facilities, which include a pool, snack bar, a bar, a couple of shops and a laundrette.

Getting There & Away Great Adventures (☎ 4051 0455) and Sunlover Cruises (☎ 1800 810 512) have return trips for $30.

Frankland Islands

Frankland Island Cruise & Dive (☎ 1800 079 039) has day trips to these untouched national park islands, costing $125 including lunch and snorkelling gear. If you fancy camping on a remote tropical island, camping drop-offs are $140 per person (permit required).

ATHERTON TABLELAND

Inland from the coast between Innisfail and Cairns, the land rises sharply then rolls

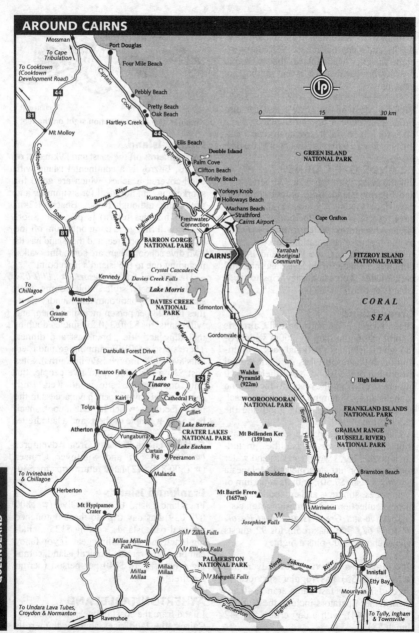

AROUND CAIRNS

Mossman
Port Douglas
To Cape
Tribulation
Four Mile Beach
To Cooktown
(Cooktown
Development Road)
Captain
Cook
Pebbly Beach
Pretty Beach
Oak Beach
Hartleys Creek
Mt Molloy
Ellis Beach
Highway
Double Island
Palm Cove
Clifton Beach
Trinity Beach
Yorkeys Knob
Holloways Beach
Machans Beach
Strathford
Cairns Airport

GREEN ISLAND
NATIONAL PARK

Barron River
Clohesy River
Kuranda
Freshwater
Connection

BARRON GORGE
NATIONAL PARK

CAIRNS

Cape Grafton

Yarrabah
Aboriginal
Community

FITZROY ISLAND
NATIONAL PARK

To Chillagoe

Crystal Cascades
Davies Creek Falls
Lake Morris
Kennedy

DAVIES CREEK
NATIONAL PARK

Mareeba
Granite Gorge

Edmonton

Gordonvale

CORAL
SEA

Malgrave River

Danbulla Forest Drive
Tinaroo Falls
Lake Tinaroo
Kairi
Tolga
Atherton
Yungaburra
Curtain Fig
Peeramon
Malanda

Cathedral Fig
Gillies

Lake Barrine
CRATER LAKES
NATIONAL PARK
Lake Eacham

Walshs
Pyramid
(922m)

WOOROONOORAN
NATIONAL PARK

Mt Bellenden Ker
(1591m)

High Island

FRANKLAND ISLANDS
NATIONAL PARK

GRAHAM RANGE
(RUSSELL RIVER)
NATIONAL PARK

Herberton
Mt Hypipamee
Crater

Babinda Boulders
Babinda
Bramston Beach

To Irvinebank
& Chillagoe

Mt Bartle Frere
(1657m)

Mirriwinni

Josephine Falls

Millaa Millaa
Falls
Zillie Falls
Ellinjaa Falls

PALMERSTON
NATIONAL PARK

North Johnstone River

Millaa
Millaa
Mungalli Falls

Innisfail
Etty Bay
Mourilyan

To Undara Lava Tubes,
Croydon & Normanton
Ravenshoe

Palmerston Highway

To Tully, Ingham
& Townsville

0   15   30 km

QUEENSLAND

gently across the lush Atherton Tableland towards the Great Dividing Range. The tableland's altitude, more than 1000m in places, tempers the tropical heat, and the abundant rainfall and rich volcanic soil combine to make this one of the greenest places in Queensland. In the south are the state's two highest mountains – Bartle Frere (1657m) and Bellenden Ker (1591m).

Vast tracts of tropical rainforest once covered the region, but logging in the early years of this century reduced the forests to isolated pockets, most of them clinging to the steep coastal slope. Nevertheless, some impressive areas of jungle remain, providing a haven for wildlife such as the rare Lumholtz's tree-climbing kangaroo.

The pioneers of the 1870s were lured here by gold, and later tin, forging some impressive roads and railways through the difficult terrain, but logging and farming soon became the main activities.

Getting There & Around

The historic train ride and the Skyrail cableway from Cairns to Kuranda are major attractions, and there are bus services to the main towns from Cairns, although having your own vehicle is the ideal way to get around. There are also some good tours on offer from Cairns.

From south to north, the three major roads from the coast are: the Palmerston Hwy from Innisfail to Millaa Millaa; the Gillies Hwy from Gordonvale to Yungaburra and Atherton; and the Kennedy Hwy from Cairns to Kuranda and Mareeba. The Peninsula Developmental Rd heads north from Mareeba towards Cooktown, with a turning at Mt Molloy to Mossman.

Kuranda

• postcode 4872   • pop 670

Famed for its markets, this mountain town is surrounded by spectacular tropical scenery. Unfortunately, Kuranda's charms have long since been discovered by the masses, and the place is flooded with tourists on market days. Many of the stalls and shops sell mainly trashy souvenirs, although there are still quite a few good arts, craft and produce stalls.

Things to See & Do The **Kuranda Markets** are held every Wednesday, Thursday, Friday and Sunday, although things quieten after about 2 pm. On other days, Kuranda reverts to its normal sleepy character.

Within the market area, **Birdworld** ($8) is a large canopied garden with a lake, waterfalls and over 30 species of birds; it's open daily from 9 am to 4 pm. Also within the market is Sky Screamer, a kind of giant swing ($35).

The **Australian Butterfly Sanctuary** ($10) is open daily from 10 am to 3 pm and has regular guided tours. On Coondoo St, the **Kuranda Wildlife Noctarium** ($9), where you can see nocturnal animals such as gliders and fruit bats, is open daily from 10 am to 4 pm.

Nearby, the Ark is a tasteless shopping mall in the shape of a ship, with a restaurant, an Internet cafe and a shooting gallery where you can work out your aggressive tendencies for $20 (no licence required).

Over the footbridge behind the train station, Kuranda Riverboat & Rainforest Tours (☎ 4093 7476) runs 45-minute riverboat cruises ($10) and has one-hour guided rainforest walks daily at 12.30 and 1.30 pm ($10).

On Thongon St, the **Aviary** ($9) has a free-flight enclosure with dozens of species of parrots and finches.

There are several signed walks through the market, and a short walking track through **Jumrum Creek Environmental Park**, off the Barron Falls road, 700m from the bottom of Thongon St. The park has a big population of fruit bats.

Further down, the Barron Falls road divides: the left fork takes you to a lookout over the falls, while a further 1.5km along the right fork brings you to Wrights Lookout where you can see back down the Barron Gorge National Park to Cairns.

Outside town on the road to Cairns, **Rainforestation** is a wildlife park with rainforest tours in amphibious vehicles, a zoo and an Aboriginal dance troupe ($29).

Places to Stay The leafy *Kuranda Van Park* (☎ 4093 7316) is a few kilometres out of town on the Kuranda Heights Rd, off the road directly opposite the Kuranda turn-off

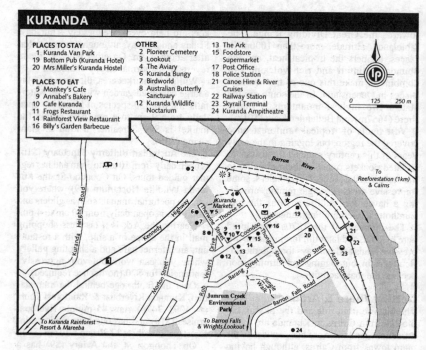

KURANDA

PLACES TO STAY
1 Kuranda Van Park
19 Bottom Pub (Kuranda Hotel)
20 Mrs Miller's Kuranda Hostel

PLACES TO EAT
5 Monkey's Cafe
9 Annabel's Bakery
10 Cafe Kuranda
11 Frogs Restaurant
14 Rainforest View Restaurant
16 Billy's Garden Barbecue

OTHER
2 Pioneer Cemetery
3 Lookout
4 The Aviary
6 Kuranda Bungy
7 Birdworld
8 Australian Butterfly Sanctuary
12 Kuranda Wildlife Noctarium

13 The Ark
15 Foodstore Supermarket
17 Post Office
18 Police Station
21 Canoe Hire & River Cruises
22 Railway Station
23 Skyrail Terminal
24 Kuranda Ampitheatre

---

on the Kennedy Hwy. It has camp sites for $13 and on-site cabins from $45.

Near the train station, the agreeably rustic **Kuranda Backpackers Hostel** (☎ 4093 7355, 6 Arara St), also known as Mrs Miller's, is a rambling old timber building with a huge garden, a small saltwater pool and an enlightening graffiti room. Dorm beds are $14 and doubles are $32 (VIP/YHA $1 less).

Tentative Nests (☎ 4093 9555, 26 Barron Falls Rd), about 2km from town, offers unusual accommodation in tented platforms in the rainforest. The cost is $60 per person with breakfast, and transfers to/from Cairns are $5.

The **Bottom Pub/Kuranda Hotel** (☎ 4093 7206), at the corner of Coondoo and Arara Sts, remains doggedly downmarket and has a pool and basic motel-style singles/doubles with ceiling fans from $39/49.

A couple of kilometres out of town, back on the Kennedy Hwy towards Mareeba, the upmarket **Kuranda Rainforest Resort** (☎ 4093 7555) has a bar, restaurant, swimming pool and tennis courts. Two-bedroom cabins with en suite (and some with cooking facilities) cost from $125 a double.

Places to Eat Some of the best food is found in the market's food stalls – fresh juices, Thai stir-fries, Indian curries etc – just follow your nose! There's a supermarket in Coondoo St if you're self-catering.

The Bottom Pub has the very pleasant **Garden Bar & Grill** in its backyard, with a swimming pool, shady lawns, burgers for $5 and other grills from about $8.

Monkey's Cafe/Restaurant, on Therwine St near the markets, is an intimate BYO cafe, open for dinner from 5 pm. **Billy's Garden Barbecue** offers barbie favourites like steak and teriyaki chicken from $11. **Frogs Restaurant**, on Coondoo St, is another good local eatery. There's live music here on Sunday nights.

The *Rainforest View Restaurant* is a large place with balconies looking right into the rainforest, and buffet meals from $11 to $15.

Cafe Kuranda, on the corner of Coondoo and Therwine Sts, does sandwiches, snacks and takeaways. Nearby is *Annabel's Bakery*.

Getting There & Away Getting to Kuranda is half the fun, whether you come via the scenic railway or the cableway through the rainforest. It's worth trying both options on a return trip, though you'll have to take the train if you have a backpack in tow.

The Kuranda Scenic Railway (☎ 4052 6249) winds 34km from Cairns to Kuranda. This line, which took five years to build, was opened in 1891 and goes through 15 tunnels, climbing more than 300m in the last 21km. The trains operate daily and cost $25/40 one way/return.

The Skyrail Rainforest Cableway (☎ 4038 1555) is a 7.5km gondola cableway that runs from Smithfield, a northern suburb of Cairns, to Kuranda, with two stops along the way. It operates daily from 8 am to 3.30 pm (last departure from Kuranda at 2.30 pm); fares are $27/42. A number of day-tour packages combine travel on both the train and the cableway for about $66.

White Car Coaches has buses five times daily (twice on weekends) from outside Tropical Paradise Travel (☎ 4051 9533), at 51 Spence St, Cairns ($7 one way).

Mareeba
● postcode 4880　　● pop 6870

From Kuranda, the Kennedy Hwy runs west across the tableland to Mareeba, the centre of a tobacco and rice-growing area, then continues south to Atherton in the centre of the tableland. Mareeba has a wide range of accommodation and in July hosts one of Australia's biggest rodeos.

The new Information Centre & Museum (☎ 4092 5674), near the Kuranda turn-off, is open daily from 8 am to 4 pm.

Chillagoe
● postcode 4871　　● pop 500

Set in attractive arid country 140km west of Mareeba, the old mining town of Chillagoe is close enough to make a day trip from Cairns, but far enough out to have the feel of a real outback town. All but the last 34km of the route is along sealed roads, and it should not present a problem for conventional vehicles during the dry season. Around town are impressive limestone caves, rock pinnacles, Aboriginal rock art, ruins of smelters from early this century and a museum.

The rangers run guided tours through the various caves of the **Chillagoe-Mungana Caves National Park**, leaving daily at 9 and 11 am and 1.30 pm ($5 to $7.50) – contact the EPA office (☎ 4094 7163) on Queen St for more details. If you have a torch, the rangers can direct you to other caves with self-guiding trails.

Places to Stay On Queen St, *Chillagoe Tourist Park* (☎ 4094 7177) has camp sites ($10), on-site cabins ($40) and units ($50). The old *Post Office Hotel* (☎ 4094 7119, 37 Queen St) has basic air-con rooms for $15 per person, and the *Chillagoe Caves Lodge* (☎ 4094 7106, 7 King St) has budget singles/doubles from $25/35 and motel units from $42/50, plus a restaurant.

One kilometre north of town, the *Chillagoe Bush Camp & Ecolodge* (☎ 4094 7155) is a former miners' village with beds from $20, doubles/triples from $40/45 and home-cooked meals.

Getting There & Away White Car Coaches (☎ 4091 9533) has buses from Cairns to Chillagoe ($37) three times a week, with a change at Mareeba ($16), or you can take a day tour from Cairns ($115) with Reef & Rainforest Connections (☎ 4099 5599).

Atherton
● postcode 4883　　● pop 5690

Atherton is a pleasant, prosperous town, though it's not really much of a tourist destination. The main attraction is the bizarre **Crystal Caves** (☎ 4091 2365), a geological museum in an artificial cave setting straight out of the *Flintstones*. Entry is $10. Railco (☎ 4791 4871) runs steam-train trips to Herberton ($25 return; 1½ hours one way) on Wednesday, Saturday and Sunday.

Atherton Backpackers (☎ 4091 3552, 37 *Alice St*), on the hill above town, has good dorm beds from $14 and singles/doubles for $17/30.

Lake Tinaroo

From Atherton or nearby Tolga it's a short drive to this large lake created for the Barron River hydroelectric power scheme. It's open year-round for barramundi fishing. The main settlement on the lake is Tinaroo Falls, a small hamlet in the shadow of the Tinaroo Dam Wall at the north western corner of the lake. In town is a petrol station, a motel and the *Lake Tinaroo Holiday Park* (☎ 4095 8232), with camp sites ($6 per person) and on-site cabins (from $38/42 for singles/doubles). Right by the dam, *Cafe Pensini's Deckbar & Bistro* is a good spot for a snack.

From the dam, the unsealed **Danbulla Forest Drive** winds through the **Danbulla State Forest** beside the lake, finally emerging on the Gillies Hwy 4km north-east of Lake Barrine. The road passes several self-registration lakeside camping grounds, run by the Department of Natural Resources (☎ 4095 8459). The road is sometimes impassable for conventional vehicles after heavy rain. **Lake Euramoo**, about halfway along, is in a double volcanic crater; there's a short botanical walk around the lake. There is another crater at **Mobo Creek**, a short walk off the drive. Finally, 6km from the Gillies Hwy, a short walk will take you down to the **Cathedral Fig**, a gigantic strangler fig tree.

Yungaburra
- postcode 4872   - pop 985

This pretty village is 13km east of Atherton along the Gillies Hwy. It's right in the centre of the tableland, has some good restaurants and accommodation and, if you have transport, it's a good base from which to explore the lakes, waterfalls and national parks nearby. The atmospheric central streets of the town have been classified by the National Trust.

Three kilometres out of Yungaburra, on the Malanda road, is the strangler fig known as the **Curtain Fig** for its aerial roots, which form a 15m-high hanging screen.

Places to Stay & Eat The excellent *On the Wallaby* (☎ 4095 2013, 37 *Eacham Rd*) is a small backpackers' hostel with comfortable dorm, double and twin rooms upstairs and good living areas downstairs. It offers activities like mountain biking and night canoeing, and the cost is $16 per person, or you can camp in the yard for $9. It has a good $89 package which includes transfers from Cairns, accommodation and tours.

The *Lake Eacham Hotel* (☎ 4095 3515, 29 *Gordonvale Rd*) is a fine old timber pub with a magnificent dining room and comfy singles/doubles upstairs for $45/50. The best of the motels is the (non-smoking) *Kookaburra Lodge* (☎ 4095 3222), on the corner of Oak St and Eacham Rd, with bright modern units from $65 a double. There's a pool and a tiny dining room with three-course meals for about $20.

Gumtree Getaway (☎ 4095 3105) is a B&B farm just outside town on the Atherton road, with doubles for $98 ($118 at weekends).

There are three good restaurants: the chalet-style *Nick's Swiss-Italian Restaurant*, with occasional live piano playing; the charming little *Burra Inn*, opposite the pub, with country-style mains for about $18; and *Eden House*, a swish licensed place with mains like barramundi from $20.

Lakes Eacham & Barrine

These two lovely crater lakes are off the Gillies Hwy, east of Yungaburra. Both are reached by sealed roads and are great swimming spots. There are rainforest walking tracks around their perimeters – 6.5km around Lake Barrine, and 4km around Lake Eacham.

The *Lake Barrine Teahouse* (☎ 4095 3847) serves Devonshire teas and snacks, and offers 45-minute cruises ($8.50) between 10.15 am and 3.35 pm daily. Lake Eacham is quieter and more beautiful – an excellent place for a picnic or a swim, and there's a small floating pool for kids.

Both lakes are national parks and camping is not allowed. However, there are camp sites at *Lake Eacham Tourist Park* (☎ 4095 3730), 2km down the Malanda road from

Lake Eacham. *Chambers Wildlife Rainforest Lodge* (☎ *4095 3754)*, on Eacham Close, has self-contained one-bedroom apartments sleeping one to four people for $85 for two.

Malanda
• postcode 4885   • pop 860

About 15km south of Lake Eacham is Malanda, a busy dairy centre that claims to have the longest milk run in Australia – all the way to Darwin and the north of WA. On the Atherton road on the outskirts, the **Malanda Falls** drop into a big old swimming pool, with picnic facilities, a walking trail and the **Malanda Environmental Centre**, which has excellent displays on the geology of the tableland.

Places to Stay There's a caravan park by the falls, and the huge old *Malanda Hotel* (☎ *4096 5101)*, in English St, has pub rooms for $16 per person and motel-style singles/doubles for $25/38; it also serves good bistro meals.

The *Honeyflow Homestead* (☎ *4096 8173)* is 7km from town on the Gordonvale road. It is a heritage homestead set in beautiful gardens, and costs $155 for a double, including dinner and breakfast.

Fairdale Farmstay (☎ *4096 6599, Lot 1 Hillcrest Rd)* is a working dairy farm 3km south of town. It has a four bed cottage, or rooms in the homestead, for $85 a double including meals, plus $10 per extra person. It has good activities for children.

Millaa Millaa
• postcode 4886   • pop 320

The 16km 'waterfall circuit' near this small town, 24km south of Malanda, passes some of the most picturesque falls on the tableland. You enter the circuit by taking Theresa Creek Rd, 1km east of Millaa Millaa on the Palmerston Hwy. **Millaa Millaa Falls**, the first falls you reach, are the most spectacular and have the best swimming hole.

Continuing around the circuit, you reach **Zillie Falls** and then **Ellinjaa Falls** before returning to the Palmerston Hwy just 2.5km out of Millaa Millaa. A further 5.5km down the

Palmerston Hwy there's a turning to **Mungalli Falls**, 5km off the highway, where the *Mungalli Falls Outpost* (☎ *4031 1144)* has cabins ($40 a double, with shared facilities) and a teahouse, and runs horse trail rides.

Millaa Millaa has a pub and a caravan park, and the Eacham Historical Society Museum is on the main street.

Mt Hypipamee National Park
The Kennedy Hwy between Atherton and Ravenshoe passes the eerie Mt Hypipamee crater. It's a scenic 800m (return) walk from the picnic area, past **Dinner Falls**, to this narrow, 138m-deep crater with its evil-looking lake far below.

Herberton
• postcode 4872   • pop 990

On a slightly longer alternative route between Atherton and Ravenshoe is this old tin-mining town, which holds the colourful Tin Festival each September. On Holdcroft Drive is the Herberton Historical Village, with about 30 old buildings that have been transported here from around the tableland.

Ravenshoe
• postcode 4872   • pop 870

Ravenshoe is on the western edge of the tableland at an altitude of 915m. It was once a thriving timber town, but things are pretty quiet around here nowadays. It has an excellent Visitors Centre (☎ *4097 7700)*, a caravan park, a couple of pubs and a motel.

On weekends at 2.30 pm, you can take a 7km ride on the Millstream Express, a historic steam train ($25). The **Little Millstream Falls** are 2km south of Ravenshoe, just before the intersection of the Tully Gorge road and the Kennedy Hwy. The attractive **Millstream Falls** are 3km west of the junction along the highway. The falls are about 1km from the road and are the widest in Australia although only 13m high (no swimming).

Kennedy Highway
Beyond Ravenshoe, the small mining town of **Mt Garnet**, 47km west, comes alive one weekend every May when it hosts one of

Queensland's top outback race meetings. If you're heading west there is a staffed fruit-fly quarantine inspection post 4km from town; all fruit and some vegetables must be deposited here, and vehicles may be searched.

About 60km past Mt Garnet, the Kennedy Hwy (Australia's Hwy 1) passes through **Forty Mile Scrub National Park**, where the semi-evergreen vine thicket is a descendant of the vegetation that covered much of the Gondwana super-continent 300 million years ago – before Australia, South America, India, Africa and Antarctica drifted apart. Just past the park is the turn-off to **Undara Lava Tubes** (a must-see) and the Gulf Savannah.

CAIRNS TO PORT DOUGLAS

The Bruce Hwy, which runs nearly 2000km north from Brisbane, ends in Cairns, but the sealed coastal road continues another 110km north to Mossman and Daintree. This final stretch, the Captain Cook Hwy, is a treat because it often runs right along the shore and there are some superb beaches.

Heading out of Cairns towards the airport you'll find an interesting and informative elevated **mangrove boardwalk** 200m before you reach the airport. Explanatory signs give some insight into the surprising ecological complexities of mangrove communities.

Kamerunga Rd, off the Captain Cook Hwy just north of the airport turn-off, leads inland to the **Freshwater Connection**, a railway museum complex and the start of the Kuranda Scenic Railway. It's 10km from the centre of town. Just beyond Freshwater Connection is a turn-off south along Redlynch Intake Rd to **Crystal Cascades**, a popular destination, 22km from Cairns, with waterfalls and swimming holes.

North along the Captain Cook Hwy are the Cairns northern beaches, which are really a string of suburbs. In order, these are Machans, Holloways, Yorkeys Knob, Trinity, Kewarra and Clifton beaches and Palm Cove. **Holloways Beach** has a good foreshore caravan park. **Trinity Beach** is perhaps the best for a short trip from Cairns, with pleasant beaches, a pub and a cluster of

eateries and upmarket resorts along the beachfront. There's a *caravan park* on the main road into town.

Further north, **Palm Cove** is an exclusive little resort town with fancy hotels, expensive boutiques and restaurants. The very good council-run *Palm Cove Camping Area*, on the foreshore, has camp sites from $10. On the highway, Wild World ($18) has lots of crocodiles and snakes, tame kangaroos and Australian birds, and has shows daily.

Around the headland past Palm Cove and Double Island, **Ellis Beach** is a lovely spot. Off the highway by the beach, the *Ellis Beach Leisure Park* (☎ 4055 3538) has a good camping ground and a restaurant/bar complex with live music most Sunday afternoons. There's an unofficial nudist area at the southern end of the beach.

Soon after Ellis Beach is **Hartleys Creek Crocodile Farm**, with a collection of Australian wildlife. Most of the enclosures are a bit shoddy, but skill and spectacle make it an interesting 'animal place'. When they feed Charlie the crocodile in the 'Crocodile Attack Show' (3 pm) you know for certain why it's not wise to get bitten by one! The park is open daily ($14.50).

The secluded *Turtle Cove Resort* (☎ 4059 1800), off the highway 45km north of Cairns, is a popular gay resort. Prices start from $125 for a double, including breakfast.

Shortly before Mossman there's a turn-off to fashionable Port Douglas. The turn-off to Cape Tribulation is just before Daintree village. From Cape Tribulation it's possible to continue up to historic Cooktown by 4WD along the controversial Bloomfield Track (see the boxed text 'Queensland's Wet Tropics World Heritage Area'). Alternatively, there's the partly surfaced inland road from Cairns, but both roads to Cooktown can be impassable after periods of heavy rain.

PORT DOUGLAS
- postcode 4871 • pop 3640

Port Douglas has a reputation as a reef resort for the rich and fashionable, with a host of multi-million dollar resort complexes and expensive eateries, but there are now several budget options for those who want to see how the other half live.

Port, as it's known locally, was a rival for Cairns in the early days of far north Queensland's development with a population of 12,000, but when Cairns eventually got the upper hand, the town became a sleepy little backwater. So it might have stayed but for the efforts of Christopher Skase, an Australian entrepreneur who backed the development of the Sheraton Mirage complex in the mid-1980s. Within a few years, Skase's model resort had burgeoned into a huge money-making machine, though Skase himself fled to Majorca leaving behind debts of over one billion dollars. For several years now, a series of suspicious 'medical conditions' have saved Skase from deportation to face criminal charges in Australia.

Today, in addition to the multi-million dollar resorts, Port Douglas has a fast catamaran service from Cairns, an exclusive golf course, marina and shopping complex, and operators providing all the usual reef and rainforest activities. Yet, despite the development, Port Douglas still has a good deal of its original charm, with attractive palm-lined avenues and a long and surprisingly peaceful beach. You can make trips to the Low Isles, the Great Barrier Reef, the Mossman Gorge and Cape Tribulation.

Orientation & Information

It's 6km from the highway along a long, low spit of land to Port Douglas. The Sheraton Mirage resort occupies a long stretch of Four Mile Beach. The main road in, Davidson St, ends in a T-intersection with Macrossan St; to the left is the town centre with most of the shops and restaurants. The beach is to the right, and there are fine views over the coastline and sea from Flagstaff Hill lookout.

There are several tour booking agents, including the helpful Port Douglas Tourist Information Centre (☎ 4099 5599), at 23 Macrossan St, and Port Douglas Accom-Holiday Rentals (☎ 4099 4488), on the corner of Macrossan and Owen Sts. Cyberworld, behind the Salsa Bar & Grill on Macrossan St, has Internet access for $6 per half hour.

Things to See

On the pier off Anzac Park, **Ben Cropp's Shipwreck Museum** is quite interesting and open daily from 9 am to 5 pm ($5). At the **Rainforest Habitat**, where the Port Douglas road leaves the main highway, an enclosed canopy houses an artificial rainforest with elevated timber boardwalks, with at least 30 bird and butterfly species. It's a good introduction to the rainforest, although it's not cheap at $16 per person.

Port's **Sunday Markets**, held in Anzac Park at the northern end of Macrossan St, feature dozens of stalls and tents, selling fruit and vegies, clothing, crafts and more.

Diving

Several companies offer learn-to-dive courses here. The Discover Dive Centre (☎ 4099 6333), at 15 Grant St, has a four day course for $425; Poseidon (☎ 4099 4772), at 34 Macrossan St, has a similar four day course for $475; Quicksilver (☎ 4099 5050), based at the Marina Mirage & Shopping Centre, has a five day course for $439. Most of the boats heading out to the reef offer dives for certified divers.

Organised Tours

Reef Trips Quicksilver's huge fast cats do daily trips to Agincourt Reef, on the outer reef, for $135, which includes snorkelling gear, a semisubmersible boat ride, underwater observatory viewing and lunch. For certified divers, two 40-minute dives cost $94 with all gear provided. Numerous smaller boats including *Wavelength* and *Poseidon* offer similar but much more personalised reef, snorkelling and diving trips starting at about $100.

Low Isles There are also cruises out to the Low Isles, a fine little coral cay surrounded by a lagoon and topped by an old lighthouse. Several of the smaller boats, such as *Sail Away*, *Willow* and *Shaolin*, offer good day trips from $85 to $120, which generally include lunch, snorkelling gear and boom netting. *Wavelength* has good half-day trips to the Low Isles for $62. All boats operate from the Marina,

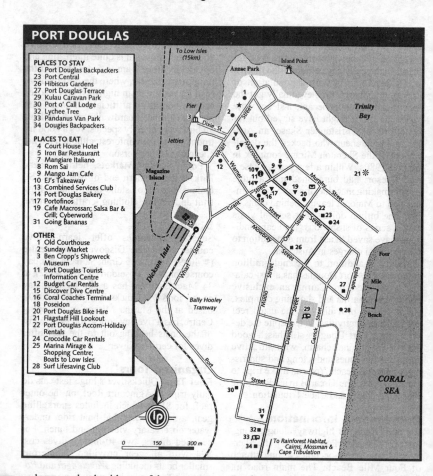

PORT DOUGLAS

To Low Isles
(15km)

Island Point

Anzac Park

Trinity
Bay

Pier

Dixie St

Jetties

Magazine
Island

Dickson Inlet

Bally Hooley
Tramway

CORAL
SEA

Four

Mile

Beach

To Rainforest Habitat,
Cairns, Mossman &
Cape Tribulation

0   150   300 m

PLACES TO STAY
6   Port Douglas Backpackers
23 Port Central
26 Hibiscus Gardens
27 Port Douglas Terrace
29 Kulau Caravan Park
30 Port o' Call Lodge
32 Lychee Tree
33 Pandanus Van Park
34 Dougies Backpackers

PLACES TO EAT
4   Court House Hotel
5   Iron Bar Restaurant
7   Mangiare Italiano
8   Rom Sai
9   Mango Jam Cafe
10 EJ's Takeaway
13 Combined Services Club
14 Port Douglas Bakery
17 Portofinos
19 Cafe Macrossan; Salsa Bar &
    Grill; Cyberworld
31 Going Bananas

OTHER
1   Old Courthouse
2   Sunday Market
3   Ben Cropp's Shipwreck
    Museum
11 Port Douglas Tourist
    Information Centre
12 Budget Car Rentals
15 Discover Dive Centre
16 Coral Coaches Terminal
18 Poseidon
20 Port Douglas Bike Hire
21 Flagstaff Hill Lookout
22 Port Douglas Accom-Holiday
    Rentals
24 Crocodile Car Rentals
25 Marina Mirage &
    Shopping Centre;
    Boats to Low Isles
28 Surf Lifesaving Club

and you can book with one of the agents on Macrossan St.

Other Tours There are numerous operators offering day trips to Cape Tribulation, some via Mossman Gorge, from about $90. A two day 4WD Cooktown loop with Wild Track Safaris (☎ 4055 2247) is $299 including accommodation. Many of the tours out of Cairns also do pickups from Port Douglas; book with one of the agencies in town.

Bike N Hike (☎ 4099 4000), on Macrossan St, does excellent mountain bike day trips to the Mowbray Valley for $82.

Reef & Rainforest Connections (☎ 4099 5599) has day tours to many attractions in the area from Port Douglas and Cairns, including Kuranda (from $52) and Chillagoe ($115).

Places to Stay – Budget
Camping Port Douglas has two good caravan parks. The *Kulau Caravan Park (☎ 4099 5449, 24 Davidson St)* is the closest to the centre and a short walk from the beach. It has camp sites from $15 and on-site cabins from $43. About a kilometre from the centre, the *Pandanus Van Park (☎ 4099 5944, 107*

QUEENSLAND

Davidson St) has camp sites from $14 and on-site cabins from $55.

Hostels The *Port o' Call Lodge (☎ 4099 5422)*, on Wharf St, is a YHA-associate hostel and has modern four-bed units with private bathrooms for $18 per person ($19 for nonmembers) and air-con motel units from $76 a double. There's a pool, cooking facilities, bar and a good budget restaurant, and a free courtesy coach to and from Cairns every Monday, Wednesday and Saturday.

The Nomads backpacker resort, *Dougies Backpackers (☎ 1800 996 200, 111 Davidson St)* close by, is well-maintained with good facilities including a pool, bar and a large kitchen. Dorm beds cost $17, twins/doubles start at $45 and camp sites are $14. All rooms are air-con and you can hire bikes.

Port Douglas Backpackers (☎ 4099 4883, 8 Macrossan St) lacks communal areas, but it's central and cheap. Dorm beds in air-con rooms cost $15 and doubles are $35.

Places to Stay – Mid-Range
Of the cheaper motels, *Port Central (☎ 4051 6722, 36 Macrossan St)* has good double/twin rooms from $59.

Port Douglas Terrace (☎ 4099 5397, 17 Esplanade) has self-contained one and two-bedroom apartments ranging from $130 to $198 (the more expensive ones with sea views).

The *Lychee Tree (☎ 4099 5811, 95 Davidson St)* has good one and two-bedroom units, which sleep from one to four people, starting from $90 a double.

Places to Stay – Top End
Hibiscus Gardens (☎ 4099 5315), on the corner of Mowbray and Owen Sts, is a modern resort with stylish Balinese decor and a large pool. Studio units start at $180 for a double.

At the top of the range are the *Sheraton Mirage Resort (☎ 1800 818 831)*, on Davidson St, with an amazing swimming pool and five-star hotel rooms from $490 a night, and the *Radisson Reef Resort (☎ 4099 5577)*, on

Port Douglas Rd, with hotel rooms starting from $165 a night and villas from $205.

Places to Eat
Port Douglas has a great range of cafes and restaurants, mostly along Macrossan St, although few places cater for budget travellers.

Close to the tourist information centre are *EJ's Takeaway*, with good fish and chips, and burgers, and the *Port Douglas Bakery*, with cakes and sandwiches. *Cafe Macrossan (42 Macrossan St)* is another good snack place, and next door is the trendy and popular *Salsa Bar & Grill*.

The *Court House Hotel*, on the corner of Macrossan and Wharf Sts, has an outdoor eating area with cheap bistro meals from $8. The *Combined Services Club*, a great old tin and timber building on the waterfront, also has good pub grub from $7 to $10.

The *Iron Bar Restaurant (5 Macrossan St)* is decked out like an outback woolshed and specialises in Aussie tucker, and across at No 24 the *Mango Jam Cafe* is a lively and popular bar/restaurant with tasty gourmet pizzas ($10), pasta, salads and lots more.

On Grant St near Macrossan St, the BYO *Rom Sai* has Thai and Japanese mains from $10 to $14, while *Portofinos (31 Macrossan St)* is a licensed bistro with pasta, curries and vegetarian options like baked mushrooms from $10 to $15.

The relaxed *Mangiare Italiano (18 Macrossan St)* has pizzas from $14 to $18.

Port's best known restaurant is the bizarre *Going Bananas (☎ 4099 5400, 87 Davidson St)*. The decor is quite bizarre – a sort of post-cyclone tropical forest look – and the service is often equally strange. The interesting menu includes mains like crocodile ribs, from $20 to $30, and it's well worth the splurge (bookings advisable).

Entertainment
On Macrossan St, the *Court House Hotel* has live bands in the beer garden on weekends. The nearby *Iron Bar Restaurant* has live music in the back bar and cane-toad races on Tuesday and Thursday nights.

Upstairs in the Marina Mirage & Shopping Centre complex are *FJ's Nightclub* and the **Waterfront Bar**, with three bars and regular live bands.

The bar at **Going Bananas** is a popular watering hole, or you could always pop into the **Sheraton Mirage Resort** for a drink – it's worth a look.

Getting There & Away

Bus The Coral Coaches terminal (☎ 4099 5351) is on Grant St. Coral Coaches covers the Cairns to Cooktown coastal route via Port Douglas, Mossman, Daintree, Cape Tribulation and Bloomfield. There are about eight buses a day between Cairns and Port Douglas ($16; 1½ hours), about 13 buses a day from Port Douglas to Mossman ($6; 30 minutes), twice-daily buses to Daintree village ($14; one hour) and Cape Tribulation ($20; 2½ hours), and buses to Cooktown via the (coastal) Bloomfield Track on Tuesday and Saturday ($45; about six hours), plus Thursday from June to October. Greyhound Pioneer passes through daily on its way to Cape Tribulation ($20).

Coral Coaches usually lets you stop over as often as you like along the route, so it can be as good as any tour.

Boat The daily *Quicksilver* (☎ 4099 5500) fast catamaran service between Cairns and the Marina at Port Douglas costs $20/30 one way/return.

Getting Around

Budget (☎ 4099 4690) is at 7 Warner St. Cheaper local operators include Network (☎ 4099 5111), at 11 Warner St, and Crocodile Car Rentals (☎ 4099 5555), which specialises in 4WD hire.

Port Douglas is very compact, and the best way to get around is by bike. You can hire bikes at the Port o' Call Lodge and Dougies Backpackers (about $1 per hour), while Port Douglas Bike Hire (☎ 4099 5799), at 40 Macrossan St, rents out mountain bikes for $12 a day. Call ☎ 4099 5345 for a taxi.

MOSSMAN

● postcode 4873   ● pop 1920

Mossman is Australia's most northerly sugar town and a centre for tropical fruit growing,

but the main point of interest is beautiful **Mossman Gorge**, 5km west. There are some excellent swimming holes and rapids and a 3km walking circuit through rainforest. Kuku-Yalanji Dreamtime Tours (☎ 4098 2595) offers award-winning Aboriginal tours that focus on the traditional foods and medicines growing in the gorge ($15 from Mossman or $37 with pick up from Port Douglas). Coral Coaches runs buses to the gorge from Mossman and Port Douglas.

Places to Stay & Eat

You can't camp at the gorge, but there's a creekside caravan park next to the swimming pool in Mossman. The old green and cream *Exchange Hotel* (☎ 4098 1410), in the centre of town, has clean singles/doubles for $20/30 and a few dorm beds for $10. The *Demi-View Motel* (☎ 4098 1277, 41 Front St) has budget rooms for $55/65, and *White Cockatoo Cabins* (☎ 4098 2222), 1km south of the centre, has good self-contained cabins from $65 a double.

Palms Cafe, opposite the Exchange Hotel, is the most convenient eatery.

DAINTREE

The highway continues 36km beyond Mossman to the quaint village of Daintree, passing the turn-off to the Daintree River ferry after 24km.

Established as a logging town, with timber cutters concentrating on the prized red cedars that were so common in this area, Daintree is now known as a centre for river cruises along the beautiful Daintree River. It's a quiet little backwater, with a couple of shops and cafes and several good B&Bs. The Timber Museum, Gallery & Shop is worth a look, although the pieces for sale carry astronomical price tags.

Organised Tours

There are at least six operators offering river trips on the Daintree from various points between the ferry and Daintree village. It's certainly a worthwhile activity. Birdlife is prolific, and in the cooler months (April-September) crocodile sightings are common, especially on sunny days when the tide

Queensland's Wet Tropics World Heritage Area

Nearly all of Australia was covered in rainforest 50 million years ago, but by the time Europeans arrived, only about 1% of the rainforest was left. Today, logging and clearing for farms have reduced that amount to less than 0.3% – about 20,000 sq km – of which more than half is in Queensland.

The biggest area of surviving virgin wet tropical rainforest covers the ranges from south of Mossman up to Cooktown. It's called the Greater Daintree.

Throughout the 1980s, a series of battles over the future of the forests was waged between conservationists, the timber industry and the Queensland government. The conservationists argued that – apart from the usual reasons for saving rainforests, such as combating the greenhouse effect and preserving species' habitats – this forest region has special value because it's such a diverse genetic storehouse. The timber industry's case, aside from jobs, was that only a small percentage of the rainforest was used for timber – and then not destructively, since cutting is selective and time is left for the forest to regenerate before it is logged again.

The 1983 fight over the controversial Bloomfield Track, from Cape Tribulation to the Bloomfield River, drew international attention to the fight to save Queensland's rainforests. The greenies may have lost that battle, but the exposure of the blockade indirectly led to a Federal government move in 1987 to nominate Queensland's wet tropical rainforests for World Heritage listing. The area was listed in 1988, with a ban on commercial logging in the area.

Stretching from Townsville to Cooktown, the Wet Tropics World Heritage Area covers 9000 sq km of the coast and hinterland, and includes the Atherton Tableland, Mission Beach, Mossman Gorge, Jourama Falls, Mt Spec and the Daintree-Cape Tribulation area. The scenery is diverse and spectacular, ranging from coastal mangroves and eucalypt forest to some of the oldest rainforest in the world.

A 1993 survey found that 80% of north Queenslanders now support the wet tropics area. Part of the reason for the turnaround has been ecotourism – the buzzword of the 1990s and north Queensland's green gold mine. With reef and rainforest-related tourism now easily eclipsing sugar production as the Far North's biggest industry, the rainforests have become a vital part of the area's livelihood. The challenge now is to learn how to manage and minimise the environmental impact of the enormous growth in tourism and population.

---

is low as they love to sun themselves on the exposed banks.

The longest-established operator is Daintree Connection (☎ 1800 658 833), with 1½-hour cruises from Daintree Village ($18), one-hour cruises from the Daintree River ferry crossing ($15) and popular 2½-hour cruises to the mouth of the Daintree, including a walk along the beach at Cape Kimberley ($25). Other big operators include Daintree Rainforest River Trains (☎ 1800 808 309), based beside the Daintree River ferry crossing, with one-hour cruises for $12 and 1½-hour cruises for $20, and the more low-key Daintree River & Cruise Centre (4km beyond the ferry

turn-off on the Mossman to Daintree road), with one-hour cruises for $12 and 1½-hour cruises for $15.

There are several operators that offer more personalised tours for smaller groups. Chris Dahlberg's Specialised River Tours (☎ 4098 6169), based at the Red Mill B&B in Daintree village, takes groups of up to 12 people, and Chris is an enthusiastic birdwatcher and knowledgeable guide. His two-hour trips depart at 6.30 am in winter and 6 am in summer and cost $30. Electric Boat Cruises (☎ 1800 686 103) takes groups of 12 in very quiet electric-powered boats for 1½-hour cruises ($25, including breakfast) or one-hour cruises throughout the day ($15).

Places to Stay

Close to the boat ramp in Daintree Village, the run-down *Daintree Riverview Caravan Park* (☎ 4098 6119) has camp sites for $12 and on-site vans from $35. If you have transport, a better camping option is the *Pinnacle Village Holiday Park* (☎ 4098 7566), at Wonga Beach, about 15km from Daintree on the Mossman road, with camp sites for $14 and units from $45.

The excellent *Red Mill House B&B* (☎ 4098 6233), in Stewart St in the centre of town, has a variety of comfortable rooms, lovely spacious gardens and a pool. Singles/doubles cost from $30/60, including breakfast on the balcony. It's not suitable for young children.

There's also the impressive *Daintree Eco Lodge* (☎ 4098 6100), on Daintree Rd, with classy timber lodges starting at $315/330.

Kenadon Homestead Cabins (☎ 4098 6142), on Dagmar St, has also been recommended. The cost is $70 for a double, plus $10 for each extra person (maximum of five).

Places to Eat

In Daintree village, *Jacanas Restaurant* is a casual cafe with sandwiches, burgers and main meals from $10, while across the road, the *Big Barramundi* has an outdoor eating area with light snacks and meals such as tasty barbecued barramundi with salad ($13). There's also the excellent *Baaru House* restaurant at the Daintree Eco Lodge.

CAPE TRIBULATION AREA

After crossing the Daintree River by ferry, there's another 34km of (mostly sealed) road, with a few hills and creek crossings, to Cape Tribulation. Unless there has been exceptionally heavy rain, conventional vehicles can make it easily, with care.

Cape Tribulation was named by Captain Cook after his ship ran onto the Endeavour Reef just north of the cape. The captain's frustration was imprinted on a variety of local landmarks like Mt Sorrow and Weary Bay, which Cook also named at the time.

In recent times, people have been much more appreciative of this beautiful stretch of coast. In the 1970s, Cape Tribulation attracted a sizeable hippy community, which included self-sufficient communities like Cedar Bay, about 30km north of the cape. The 20th century has caught up with Cape Tribulation, but the area still retains some of its relaxed, jungle-outpost feel.

Numerous tour companies come up here, or there are regular buses from Cairns and Port Douglas. Note that accommodation at Cape Tribulation is often booked out during peak periods – ring before you arrive to make sure there's a bed!

Approaching Cape Tribulation from the south, the last bank is at Mossman. You can get fuel at two or three places between Mossman and Cooktown along this coastal route.

Getting There & Away

See the Cairns and Port Douglas sections earlier in this chapter for details of bus services and tours. There are some excellent tour deals out of Cairns and Port Douglas that include accommodation at the Cape Tribulation hostels.

It's quite easy to hitch because, beyond the Daintree ferry, all vehicles have to head to Cape Tribulation – there's nowhere else to go!

Daintree River to Cape Tribulation

The Daintree River ferry is the gateway to Cape Tribulation. Ferries operate every few minutes from 6 am to midnight and cost $7 for a car, $3 for a motorbike and $1 for a pedestrian.

Three kilometres beyond the ferry, Cape Kimberley Rd leads down to Cape Kimberley beach, 5km away. About 9km from the ferry, just after you cross the spectacular heights of Alexandra Range (and lookout), is the Daintree Rainforest Environmental Centre (☎ 4098 9171) – an excellent information centre with interactive displays, a forest boardwalk and a 24m tower, which stretches up into the jungle canopy. It's open daily from 8.30 am to 5 pm ($10).

About 12km from the ferry you reach Buchanan Creek Rd, which is the turn-off for **Cow Bay** (5.5km) and Crocodylus Village.

CAPE TRIBULATION AREA

PLACES TO STAY
1   Cape Trib Beach House
5   PK's Jungle Lodge
6   Ferntree Rainforest Resort
8   PK's Jungle Village
11   Coconut Beach Rainforest Resort
12   Noah Beach Camping Area
16   Heritage Lodge
18   Lync-Haven
20   Crocodylus Village
22   Cow Bay Hotel
24   Rainforest Retreat
27   Club Daintree

PLACES TO EAT
4   Boardwalk Takeaway; PK's Jungle Lodge
14   Cafe on Sea Kiosk
23   Latitudes 16.12°

OTHER
2   Cape Tribulation Parking Area
3   Bat House
7   Ranger Station
9   Dubuji Rainforest Boardwalk
10   Mason's Store
13   Marrdja Botanical Walk
15   Cooper Creek Wilderness Cruises
17   Wundu Trailrides
19   Cow Bay Airstrip
21   Matt Lock's Service Station & General Store
25   Daintree Rainforest Environmental Centre
26   Alexandra Range Lookout

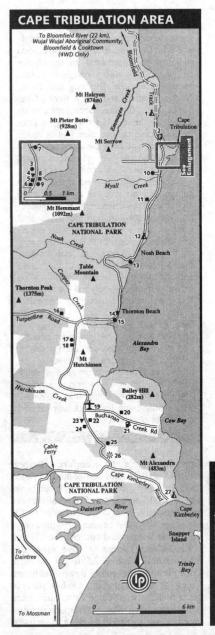

Further on, the road strikes the shore at
Thornton Beach, near the mouth of Cooper
Creek. Cooper Creek Wilderness Cruises
(☎ 4098 9052) offers croc-spotting trips
through the mangroves, with a one hour
morning cruise ($15) and a 1½ hour night
cruise ($16). The **Marrdja Botanical Walk**,
at Noah Creek, is an interesting 800m
boardwalk through rainforest and mangroves. **Noah Beach**, with a QPWS camping ground, is 8km before Cape Tribulation.

Places to Stay & Eat At Cape Kimberley
beach, *Club Daintree* (☎ 4090 7500) is a
beachfront camping park, with camp sites
for $15 for two people and four-bed cabins
from $98 a night.

On the Cape Tribulation road near the
turn-off, the *Cow Bay Hotel* (☎ 4098 9011)
has meals and motel units for $60 a double.

QUEENSLAND

Ferals in the Forests

Ferals, who pursue an alternative lifestyle and who live deep in the dark rainforests of Far North Queensland, are the hippies of the 1990s – with a couple of fundamental differences. The long hair, flares, tie-dyed clothes and peace signs of the 1960s and 70s have been replaced by shaven or dreadlocked hair, ragged rainbow-coloured clothes, bare feet or heavy work boots, and body piercing galore. And instead of peace, love and understanding, ferals espouse radical environmentalism.

Ideologically, ferals reject contemporary culture and see city life as the ultimate nightmare. They consider the mass-production, mass-consumption doctrines that drive modern society to be totally unsustainable in the long term. Rather than seeing themselves as dropouts, ferals consider their lifestyle to be the way of the future, and that their rejection of materialism is the only way modern society will ever progress to a point where life on earth is sustainable.

Ferals live in communal, seminomadic tribal groups. Most of them are vegetarians who live off unemployment benefits and avoid using mass-produced goods or fossil fuels. They see themselves as the protectors of the forests they live in. You'll often see them wandering barefoot around places like Cairns and Mossman, where they come to collect supplies and their unemployment benefits.

Opposite there's the *Rainforest Retreat* (☎ 4098 9101), with self-contained motel units from $70 a double and a 20 bed bunkhouse for $15 per person. There's also a pool and restaurant. Next door, *Latitudes 16.12°* is an open-fronted restaurant with everything from burgers and curries to coral trout.

Crocodylus Village (☎ 4098 9166) is a YHA-associate hostel 2.5km off the main Cape Tribulation road, down Buchanan Creek Rd. This is probably the best place to get a feel for what Cape Tribulation once must have been like, with spacious, elevated canvas cabins in a quiet and secluded rainforest setting. There's a pool, a small store, a cafe and a bar. Beds in 16 to 20-bed dorms cost $15 ($16 nonmembers). There are also cabins with a double bed, six bunks and bathrooms for $55 a double, plus $10 per extra person. You can hire bikes and the hostel runs guests down to Cow Bay beach. The hostel also organises activities, including guided forest walks, half-day horse rides ($45), a three hour sunrise paddletrek ($40) and a two day sea-kayaking trip to Snapper Island ($159 with everything supplied).

About 3km north of the Cow Bay turn-off is *Lync-Haven* (☎ 4098 9155), a 16 hectare property with walking trails, plenty of wildlife, a cafe/restaurant, camp sites for $8.50 per person and self-contained, six-berth cabins for $85 a double, plus $10 for each extra person.

On the Turpentine Rd, which runs inland along the left bank of Cooper Creek near Thornton Beach, the secluded *Heritage Lodge* (☎ 4098 9138) is a small, sophisticated resort with a classy restaurant, a great swimming hole and stylish cabins from $155 a double, including breakfast.

At Thornton Beach, the *Cafe on Sea Kiosk* is a laid-back beachfront bar/cafe, with good meals from $5 to $12 and takeaways. Further north on the beachfront is the self-registration *Noah Beach Camping Area*, with 16 shady sites, toilets and water – permits can be booked through the rangers at Cape Tribulation (☎ 4098 0052).

Cape Tribulation

Cape Tribulation is famed for its superb scenery, with long beaches stretching north and south from the low, forest-covered cape. If you want to do more than relax on the beach, there are some good rainforest walks including the Dubuji Rainforest Boardwalk, just south of PK's, or there are numerous activities, which you can book from where you're staying. Paul Mason's Cape Trib Guided Rainforest Walks (☎ 4098 0070), based at Mason's Store, has four-hour daytime walks ($23), 2½-hour night walks ($25) and 4WD trips.

The other attraction in Cape Tribulation is the reef, which is only 45 minutes away by fast launch. The boats leave early in the morning so you should book the evening before; they'll pick you up from where you're staying. The popular MV *Jungle Diver* (☎ 4051 5888) offers fun trips to the reef for $74 including lunch and snorkelling; two dives are $45 (book early). The catamaran *Rum Runner IX* (☎ 1800 686 444) has reef cruises for $99 ($79 standby); two dives are $60.

About halfway between Crocodylus and Cape Tribulation, Wundu Trailrides (☎ 4098 9156) offers three-hour horse rides ($45).

The **Bat House**, north of PK's, is a fruit-bat rehabilitation centre and it offers the chance to see these impressive creatures close up. It's open daily from 11.30 am to 3.30 pm ($2).

Places to Stay & Eat Close to the excellent Myall Beach, *PK's Jungle Village* (☎ 4098 0040) is very well set up with comfortable log cabins, a pool, a very lively bar and a restaurant with cheap meals. Beds in eight-bed cabins are $18 ($17 VIP), doubles are $52, or you can camp for $8. PK's has a (deserved) reputation as a party place, but there's quieter accommodation across the road at *PK's Jungle Lodge*, with comfortable, permanent tents with fan for $57 a double/twin. Next door the *Boardwalk Takeaway* has good burgers and snacks. PK's offers similar tours to Crocodylus, including an interesting tropical fruit-tasting farm tour ($8).

Just south of PK's, the plush *Ferntree Rainforest Resort* (☎ 4098 0000) has luxury cabins, two pools, a restaurant and bar. Prices start at $210 for two people.

Three kilometres north, the *Cape Trib Beach House* (☎ 4098 0030) has a forest setting near a secluded beach. Camp sites/dorms are $8/18 per person. There are also 10 en suite cabins.

Three kilometres south of the cape, the *Coconut Beach Rainforest Resort* (☎ 4098 0033) has stylish units with all the mod cons from $215 a double and villas from $315 a night (or $139 and $199 on stand-by).

Daintree Dreaming (☎ 4098 0008) offers homestays in four private houses with views over the jungle or Coral Sea. Prices vary from $90 to $200 for a double (cheaper if you stay a few days) and the properties have full facilities. Call for details.

CAPE TRIBULATION TO COOKTOWN

Heading north from Cape Tribulation, the spectacular Bloomfield Track (4WD only) continues through the forest as far as the **Wujal Wujal Aboriginal community**, 22km north on the far side of the Bloomfield River crossing. Even for 4WD vehicles, a number of amazingly steep sections of the Bloomfield Track can be impassable after heavy rain.

From Wujal Wujal another dirt road – rough but usually passable in a conventional vehicle in the Dry – heads 46km north through the tiny settlements of **Bloomfield**, **Rossville** and **Helenvale** to meet the main Cooktown road (also dirt), 28km before Cooktown.

Places to Stay & Eat

The *Bloomfield Beach Camping* (☎ 4060 8207), 11km north of the Bloomfield River crossing, has a pleasant setting, camp sites for $8 per person, a bar and restaurant, and it's a short walk from the beach. The *Bloomfield Wilderness Lodge* (☎ 4035 9166) is close to the mouth of the Bloomfield River and aims to make holes in fat wallets, with package deals from $723 per person twin share for three nights, including air transfers, meals and activities.

Signposted 33km north of the Bloomfield River, the simple *Home Rule Rainforest Lodge* (☎ 4060 3925) has a lovely, peaceful setting, with a bar, good cooking facilities and cheap meals. It has bunk rooms for $15 per person and camping for $6 per person. There's a two hour walk to a nearby waterfall, and horse riding is available. Ring from Rossville for a pickup.

Nine kilometres north at Helenvale, the *Lion's Den Hotel* (☎ 4060 3911) is a colourful, 1875 bush pub with corrugated tin walls and a slab-timber bar. It has cheap meals and you can stay in spartan singles/doubles for $18/25, or camp out the back by the river ($4).

CAIRNS TO COOKTOWN – THE INLAND ROAD

The 'main' road up from Cairns loops through Kuranda, Mareeba, Mt Molloy, the tungsten mining town of Mt Carbine, Palmer River and Lakeland, where the road up to Cape York Peninsula splits off. Most of the second half of this 341km road is un-sealed and often corrugated.

In **Mt Molloy**, the *National Hotel* (☎ *4094 1133*), in Main St, has cheap accommodation. James Venture Mulligan, the man who started both the Palmer River and Hodgkinson River gold rushes, is buried in the Mt Molloy cemetery. At the **Palmer River** crossing there's a cafe/petrol station and a camping ground. The 1873 to 1883 Palmer River gold rush occurred in very remote country about 70km west of here, throwing up boom towns like Palmerville and Maytown, though very little of either remains today.

Shortly before Cooktown, the road passes through the sinister **Black Mountain National Park**, a range of hills made up of thousands of granite boulders. It's said that, between the huge rocks, there are ways under the hill from one side to the other, but people have died trying to find them. Black Mountain is known to Aboriginal people as Kalkajaka – 'Place of the Spears'. The colour comes not from the rocks, but from lichen growing on them.

COOKTOWN
- postcode 4871   • pop 1410

Cooktown can claim to have been Australia's first British settlement. From June to August 1770, Captain Cook beached his barque *Endeavour* here, during which time the chief naturalist, Joseph Banks, collected 186 species of Australian plants from along the banks of the Endeavour River and wrote the first European description of a kangaroo.

While Cook had amicable contacts with the local Aboriginal people, race relations in the area turned sour a century later when Cooktown was founded as the unruly port for the 1873 to 1883 Palmer River gold rush, 140km south-west. Battle Camp, about 60km inland from Cooktown, was the site of a major battle between whites and Aboriginal people.

In 1874, before Cairns was even thought of, Cooktown was the second-biggest town in Queensland. At its peak there were no less than 94 pubs, almost as many brothels, and the population was over 30,000! As many as half of the inhabitants were Chinese, and their industrious presence led to some wild race riots.

After the gold rush ended, cyclones and a WWII evacuation came close to killing Cooktown. The opening of the excellent James Cook Historical Museum in 1970 started to bring in some visitor dollars, although Cooktown's population is still only around 1300 and only three pubs remain.

The effort of getting to Cooktown is rewarded not only by the atmosphere but by some fascinating reminders of the area's past. With a vehicle, you can use the town as a base for visiting the waterfalls and national parks in the area, the Quinkan rock-art galleries near Laura or even Lakefield National Park.

Orientation & Information

Cooktown is on the inland side of a headland sheltering the mouth of the Endeavour River. Charlotte St runs south from the wharf, and along it are the three pubs, a post office, a heritage bank and several cafes and restaurants.

The Cooktown Travel Centre (☎ 1800 001 770) in the Charlotte Street Centre, opposite the West Coast Hotel, provides tourist information. There's Internet/email access at the Cooktown Library on Helen St.

Things to See

Charlotte St has a number of interesting monuments, including one to the tragic Mary Watson (see the Lizard Island section later in this chapter), opposite the Sovereign Resort. A little further towards the wharf is a pleasant park containing memorials to the explorer Edmund Kennedy and to Captain Cook. Behind these are the old town well and a cannon, which was sent from Brisbane in 1885 along with three cannonballs, two rifles and one officer in response to Cooktown's plea for defences

QUEENSLAND

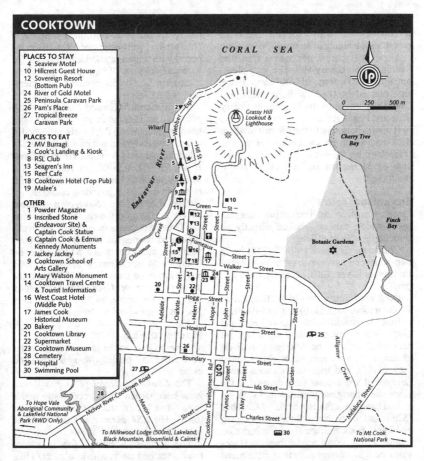

COOKTOWN

PLACES TO STAY
4 Seaview Motel
10 Hillcrest Guest House
12 Sovereign Resort
(Bottom Pub)
24 River of Gold Motel
25 Peninsula Caravan Park
26 Pam's Place
27 Tropical Breeze
Caravan Park

PLACES TO EAT
2 MV Burragi
3 Cook's Landing & Kiosk
8 RSL Club
13 Seagren's Inn
15 Reef Cafe
18 Cooktown Hotel (Top Pub)
19 Malee's

OTHER
1 Powder Magazine
5 Inscribed Stone
(*Endeavour* Site) &
Captain Cook Statue
6 Captain Cook & Edmun
Kennedy Monuments
7 Jackey Jackey
9 Cooktown School of
Arts Gallery
11 Mary Watson Monument
14 Cooktown Travel Centre
& Tourist Information
16 West Coast Hotel
(Middle Pub)
17 James Cook
Historical Museum
20 Bakery
21 Cooktown Library
22 Supermarket
23 Cooktown Museum
28 Cemetery
29 Hospital
30 Swimming Pool

against a feared Russian invasion! At the north end of the park by the waterside is a statue of Captain Cook and an inscribed stone, marking the spot where the *Endeavour* was careened.

The delightful **James Cook Historical Museum**, in a handsome 1880s convent on Helen St near Furneaux St, has some excellent displays relating to all aspects of Cooktown's past: Aboriginal people, Cook's voyages, the Palmer River gold rush and the Chinese community. The museum is open daily from 9.30 am to 4 pm and costs $5. The **Cooktown Museum**, a block away on Walker St, isn't really worth the admission price – it's more of a souvenir shop.

On Charlotte St, the **Jackey Jackey** has a window display of interesting historical photos, and across the road is the **School of Arts Gallery**.

The **Cooktown Cemetery**, on the McIvor River-Cooktown Rd, is worth a visit, with many interesting graves, including those of Mary Watson and the 'Normanby Woman' – believed by many to have been a north European who survived a shipwreck as a child and lived with Aboriginal people for years until 'rescued' by whites.

QUEENSLAND

The 1874 **powder magazine**, a short walk around the northern tip of the headland, is the oldest brick building in far north Queensland.

There are spectacular views from the lookout up on **Grassy Hill**. The very pleasant **Botanic Gardens**, off Walker St, were first planted in 1886. Walking trails lead from the gardens to the beaches at Cherry Tree and Finch bays.

It's a 1½ hour trek to the summit of 431m Mt Cook, which has even better views. The trail starts by the Mt Cook National Park sign on Melaleuca St, beyond the swimming pool.

Organised Tours

Cooktown offers an interesting range of tours which can be booked directly or through the tourist office.

Cooktown Cruises (☎ 4069 5712) has a two-hour scenic cruise up to the head of the Endeavour River ($20), departing daily at 2 pm.

Cooktown Tours (☎ 4069 5125) offers 1½-hour town tours ($16) and half-day trips to Black Mountain and the Lion's Den Hotel ($45); both depart daily at 9 am. There are also 4WD trips to the Aboriginal rock-art galleries at Laura and Lakefield National Park ($100), and trips to Coloured Sands (an area of spectacular sand dunes) via the Hopevale Aboriginal Community ($75).

You can also get to Hopevale by local bus ($20 return, daily except Sunday at 7.30 am and 3 pm). Book with the Tourist Information Centre. You'll need a permit from the Hopevale Aboriginal Community to visit Coloured Sands ($10).

Reel River Sportsfishing (☎ 4069 5346) offers lure-fishing trips on weekends and during school holidays (a charter for two people costs $75/140 per person for a half/full day).

Places to Stay

There are two good caravan parks: the *Tropical Breeze Caravan Park* (☎ 4069 5417), on the McIvor River-Cooktown Rd, and the *Peninsula Caravan Park* (☎ 4069 5107), in the bush at the end of Howard St. Both have camp sites, on-site vans and units.

Pam's Place (☎ 4069 5166), on the corner of Charlotte and Boundary Sts, is a comfortable, well-equipped YHA-associate hostel with a pool, a good kitchen, and TV lounge. Bunks are $15 a night and doubles/triples are $20/18 per person (YHA members pay $1 less).

The pleasant *Milkwood Lodge* (☎ 4069 5007), about 1km out of town on the Cooktown Developmental Rd, has six airy wooden cabins with bathroom and kitchenette for $80 a double, including breakfast. *Hillcrest Guest House* (☎ 4069 5305), on Hope St, is a friendly old place with rooms with shared facilities from $30/45, including breakfast.

The impressive *Sovereign Resort* (☎ 4069 5400), on the corner of Charlotte and Green Sts, has a superb pool and well-appointed rooms for $100/112, and two-bedroom apartments for $140. Also on Charlotte St, the *Seaview Motel* (☎ 4069 5377) has good units from $55/65, and the modern *River of Gold Motel* (☎ 4069 5222), on the corner of Hope and Walker Sts, has singles/doubles from $70.

Places to Eat

The *Reef Cafe*, on the main street, is a decent takeaway place with good fish and chips.

The *Cooktown Hotel* (Top Pub) has a great beer garden with decent bistro meals from $8 to $12 (probably the best value in town). The *RSL Memorial Club*, near the post office also has pub meals.

The licensed *Seagren's Inn* is an upmarket seafood place, with local catches like barramundi and red-claw yabbies (crayfish) from $15 to $20. Across the road, *Malee's*, opposite the Cooktown Hotel, is an excellent Thai BYO, with soups for $10 and mains around the $13 mark (closed on Monday).

For something different, eat aboard the MV *Burragi*, a former Sydney Harbour ferry now permanently moored near the jetty. It's both licensed and BYO, and mains cost around $18. Close by, the *Cook's Landing Kiosk* has snacks and light meals.

The *Sovereign Resort* has a swish balcony restaurant overlooking the river, with evening mains from $19.

Getting There & Away

Air Transtate Airlines (☎ 13 1528) has daily flights between Cairns and Cooktown for $73/94 (one way/return).

Bus Coral Coaches (☎ 4031 7577) travels from Cairns to Cooktown via the Cooktown Developmental Rd on Wednesday, Friday and Sunday ($47; 6½ hours) and via the Bloomfield Track on Tuesday and Saturday ($52; 8½ hours), plus Thursday from June to October. Greyhound also covers the coastal route three times weekly ($78).

Getting Around

Endeavour Car Hire (☎ 4069 6100) and Cooktown Car Hire (☎ 4069 5007), at the Milkwood Lodge, rent out small 4WD jeeps from $90 a day, with 150km free. For a taxi phone ☎ 4069 5387.

LIZARD ISLAND

Lizard Island, the furthest north of the Barrier Reef resort islands, is about 100km from Cooktown. It was named by Joseph Banks after the numerous lizards he saw there. Captain Cook surveyed the reef from Cook's Look, the highest point on the island, trying to find a way out through the reef to the open sea.

A tragedy occurred on the island in 1881 when a settler's wife, Mary Watson, took to sea in a large metal pot with her son and a Chinese servant after Aboriginal people killed her other servant while her husband was away fishing. The three eventually died of thirst on a barren island to the north, Mary leaving a diary of their terrible last days. Their tragic story is told at the Cooktown museum.

Lizard Island is dry, rocky and mountainous, with superb beaches, great swimming and snorkelling, the remains of the Watsons' cottage, a pricey resort, a research station and a camping ground. There are plenty of bushwalks and birdlife, and great views from Cook's Look.

Places to Stay

Watson's Bay has a small QPWS *camping ground*. It has a fireplace, pit toilet and a hand-pumped water supply 250m away. Camping permits are available from the EPA (☎ 4052 3096) in Cairns, and you must take all supplies. You'll also need charcoal, as all wood on the island, including driftwood, is protected and light planes are prohibited from carrying stove fuels.

At the exclusive *Lizard Island Resort* (☎ 4060 3999), singles/doubles cost from $890/1080 per day, including all meals and use of the facilities. Because of its isolation, the resort has been a favourite retreat for celebrities for many years.

Getting There & Away

Sunstate Airlines flies from Cairns for $194 one way, and Aussie Airways (☎ 1800 620 022) has a good day trip from Cairns for $299 per person, including lunch and snorkelling gear. Marineair Seaplanes (☎ 4069 5860) has day trips from Cooktown for $195 and does camping drop-offs costing $400 one way for up to four people.

Cape York Peninsula

The Cape York Peninsula is one of the wildest and least populated parts of Australia. The Tip, as it is called, is the most northerly point on the mainland of Australia, and islands dot the Torres Strait between here and Papua New Guinea, only 150km away.

Getting up to the Tip along the rough and rugged Peninsula Developmental Rd is still one of Australia's great road adventures, though it's a trip for the tough and experienced. Don't be fooled into thinking you can make it all the way to the top in a conventional vehicle; the roads here are all dirt, and even at the height of the Dry there are some difficult river crossings. Several tour operators offer this adventure to those who can't or don't want to go it alone.

Of the numerous books on the peninsula, Ron and Viv Moon's *Cape York – An Adventurer's Guide* is the most comprehensive. Lonely Planet's *Outback Australia* and

CAPE YORK PENINSULA

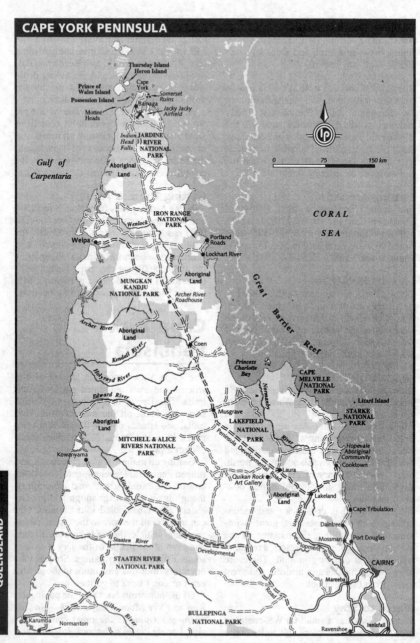

Queensland guides have extensive information for travellers to Cape York.

Information & Permits

Visits to the RACQ and the EPA offices in Cairns are well worthwhile before you head north. You don't need a permit to visit Aboriginal or Torres Strait Islander communities, but you do to camp on Aboriginal land (which is effectively most of the land north of the Dulhunty River). Designated camping grounds are provided in a number of areas, including Seisia, Umagico, Pajinka and Punsand Bay. Camping elsewhere in the area requires a permit from the Injinoo Community Council (☎ 4069 3252) or Pajinka Wilderness Lodge. You can write to the Injinoo Community Council, PO Box 7757, Cairns, Queensland 4870. Apart from Bamaga, most of the mainland Aboriginal communities are well off the main track north, and do not have any facilities or accommodation for travellers.

Organised Tours

Local Aboriginal people run tours of the Quinkan rock-art sites; for further information call ☎ 1800 633 933.

A number of companies operate 4WD tours from Cairns to Cape York. The trips generally range from six to 16 days, and take in Cooktown, Laura, the Quinkan rock-art galleries, Lakefield National Park, Coen, Weipa, Indian Head Falls, Bamaga, Somerset, Cape York itself and Thursday Island.

Travel on standard tours is in 4WDs with five to 12 passengers. Accommodation is in tents and all food is supplied. Reliable 4WD tour operators include Oz Tours Safaris (☎ 1800 079 006), Australian Outback Travel (☎ 4031 6900), Heritage 4WD Tours/Kamp Out Safaris (☎ 4038 2628) and Wild Track Adventure Safaris (☎ 4055 2247), the last being among the most experienced operators with an excellent reputation.

Most of the companies offer a variety of alternatives, such as to fly or sail one way, and travel overland the other. Expect to pay about $1000 to $1400 for a seven day fly/drive tour and anywhere from $1500 to $2500 for a 12 to 14 day safari.

Cape York Motorcycle Adventures (☎ 4059 0220) offers a five day trip for $1550 ($1150 with your own bike) or a 12 day trip for $3200 ($1950). Prices include fuel, all meals and equipment.

Getting There & Away

Air Sunstate and Flight West fly from Cairns to Thursday Island for $321. Flight West also flies to Bamaga ($292) and Ansett has a flight to Weipa for $191.

Cape York Air (☎ 4035 9399) operates the Peninsula Mail Run, claimed to be the longest in the world, visiting remote cattle stations and towns every weekday. Passengers pay from $195 to $390 for round trips, depending on the length of the journey. It also has two-day scenic tours of Cape York and the Torres Straits Islands for $550.

Bus There are no bus services all the way to the top, but, from June to October, Coral Coaches (☎ 4098 2600) operates a weekly service between Cairns and Weipa ($130 one way; 13½ hours).

Car Every year, more and more hardy travellers equipped with their own 4WD vehicles or trail bikes make the long haul to the top of Cape York. Apart from being able to say you have been as far north as you can get in Australia, you get to test yourself against some pretty wild country into the bargain.

The travelling season is from mid-May to mid-November, but it fluctuates depending on how early or late the Wet season is. From August to September, conventional vehicles can usually reach Coen and even, with care and skill, get across to Weipa on the Gulf of Carpentaria, but it's *very* rough going. During the Wet nothing moves by road at all. If you want to continue north to the Tip, you'll need a well-equipped 4WD. Ask about the road conditions further up as you go. If the locals won't drive along a section of the route, it's usually for a good reason!

The major problem is the many river crossings; even as late as June or July the rivers will still be swift-flowing and they frequently alter course. The rivers often have very steep banks. The Great Dividing

Range runs right up the spine of the peninsula and rivers run east and west off it. Although the rivers in the south of the peninsula flow only in the Wet, those further north flow year-round.

The ideal setup for a Cape York expedition is two 4WD vehicles travelling together – one can haul the other out where necessary. You can also make it to the top on motorcycles, floating the machines across the wider rivers. Beware of crocodiles!

Several Cairns operators hire out 4WDs and equipment for Cape York expeditions, including Marlin Truck & 4WD Rentals (☎ 4031 3094) and Britz:Australia (☎ 4032 2611) – minimum hire periods apply.

Boat Jardine Shipping (☎ 4035 1900) operates a twice weekly barge service from Cairns to Thursday Island ($250/400 one way/return) and Bamaga ($750 per vehicle) although passengers are taken only once a week.

Gulf Freight Services (bookings only ☎ 1800 640 079) operates weekly barge services between Weipa and Karumba ($285 to $385 per vehicle depending on direction, and $250 per passenger).

LAKELAND & LAURA

The Peninsula Developmental Road turns off the Cairns to Cooktown Development Rd at Lakeland. Facilities here include a general store with food, petrol and diesel, a small caravan/camping park and a hotel-motel. From Lakeland it's 734km to Bamaga, almost at the top of the peninsula. The first stretch to Laura is not too bad, just come corrugations, potholes, grids and causeways – the creek crossings are bridged. It gets worse.

About 48km from Lakeland is the turnoff to the Quinkan Aboriginal rock-art galleries at Split Rock, located in spectacular sandstone country. The art was executed by Aboriginal tribes whose descendants were decimated during the Palmer River gold rush of the 1870s. The galleries contain some superb examples of well-preserved rock paintings dating back 14,000 years. Entry to the park costs $3 per person (honesty box).

Laura, 12km north of Split Rock, has a general store with food and fuel, a place for minor mechanical repairs, a post office, a Commonwealth Bank agency, a pleasant pub and an airstrip.

At *Jowalbinna Bush Camp* (☎ 4060 3236), 40km west of Laura and accessible by 4WD, the Trezise Bush Guide Service offers excellent guided full/half-day walks to the magnificent rock-art sites in the area for $80/55 per adult. Visitors can stay at the bush camp ($7 per person to camp or $60 for two people in a cabin). You can also reach Jowalbinna using Coral Coaches' (☎ 4098 2600) weekly Cairns to Weipa bus service. The Adventure Company (☎ 4051 4777) has a three day package from Cairns, which includes two nights at Jowalbinna, meals and guide services ($455).

The major event is the Laura Aboriginal Dance & Cultural Festival, held every second year (odd numbers) on the last weekend of June. All the Cape York Aboriginal communities assemble for this festival, which is a great opportunity for outsiders to witness living Aboriginal culture.

Lakefield National Park

The main turn-off to Lakefield National Park is just past Laura and it's only about a 45 minute drive from Laura into the park. Conventional vehicles can get as far as the ranger station at New Laura, and possibly well into the northern section of the park during the dry season.

Lakefield is the second largest national park in Queensland and the most accessible of those on the Cape York Peninsula. It's best known for its wetlands and prolific birdlife. The park's extensive river system drains into Princess Charlotte Bay on its northern perimeter. This is the only national park on the peninsula where fishing is permitted, and a canoe is a good way to investigate the park. Watch out for the crocs! There's a good *camp ground* with showers and toilets at Kalpowar Crossing – for permits see the rangers at New Laura (☎ 4060 3260) or Lakefield (☎ 4060 3271), further north in the park. The *Lotus Bird Lodge* (☎ 1800 674 974), on Violet Vale Station, offers exclusive accommodation in individual cottages for $165 per person for full board.

The wide sweep of Princess Charlotte Bay, which includes the coastal section of Lakefield National Park, is the site of some of Australia's biggest rock-art galleries. Unfortunately, this stretch of coast is extremely hard to reach except from the sea.

LAURA TO ARCHER RIVER ROADHOUSE

North from Laura, the roads deteriorate further. At the 75km mark, there's the Hann River crossing and the *Hann River Roadhouse (☎ 4060 3242)*. Another 62km on is Musgrave, with its historic *Musgrave Telegraph Station (☎ 4060 3229)*, built in 1887. The station has accommodation for $25/40 for singles/twins as well as camp sites, a pay phone, a cafe and an airstrip, and you can get petrol, diesel, food and beer here.

Coen, 108km north of Musgrave, is virtually the capital of the peninsula with a pub, two general stores, a hospital, school and police station. You can get mechanical repairs done here. Coen has an airstrip and a racecourse, where picnic races are held in August. The peninsula closes down for this event. The *Exchange Hotel (☎ 4060 1133)* has pub rooms for $35/50 and units for $55, and the delightful Mrs Taylor's *Homestead Guest House (☎ 4060 1157)* has rooms for $30/50 and home-cooked meals.

Beside the Archer River, 65km north of Coen, the *Archer River Roadhouse (☎ 4060 3266)* has great burgers as well as beer, fuel and groceries, and can handle minor mechanical repairs. There are camp sites, or units for $35/50.

Northern National Parks

Three national parks can be reached from the main track north of Coen. To stay at any of them you must be totally self-sufficient. Only a few kilometres north of Coen, before Archer River Roadhouse, you can turn west to the remote **Mungkan Kandju National Park** – the ranger station (☎ 4060 3256) is in Rokeby, about 75km off the main track. Access is for 4WDs only, and visitors are required to inform the ranger when they leave

the park. This little-visited park covers a large area including the McIlwraith Range and the junction of the Coen and Archer rivers. There are no facilities, but bush camping is permitted at a number of river sites (contact the ranger for permits). Contact the EPA office in Coen (☎ 4060 1137) for more information.

Around 21km north of the Archer River Roadhouse, a turn-off leads 135km through the **Iron Range National Park** to the tiny coastal settlement of Portland Roads. Although still pretty rough, this track has been improved. If you visit the national park, register with the ranger (☎ 4060 7170) on arrival. It has the rugged hills of the Janet and Tozer ranges, beautiful coastal scenery as well as Australia's largest area of lowland rainforest, with some animals that are found no further south in Australia. Bush camping is permitted.

The **Jardine River National Park** includes the headwaters of the Jardine and Escape rivers, where the explorer Edmund Kennedy was fatally speared by Aboriginals in 1848.

WEIPA

• postcode 4874   • pop 2200

Weipa is 135km from the main track. The southern turn-off to it is 47km north of the Archer River crossing. You can also get to Weipa from Batavia Downs, which is 48km further up the main track. The two approaches converge about halfway along.

Weipa is a modern mining town that works the world's largest deposits of bauxite (the ore from which aluminium is processed). The mining company, Comalco, runs regular tours of its operations from May to December. The town has a wide range of facilities including a motel, a hotel and a camping ground.

In the vicinity, there's interesting country to explore, good fishing and some pleasant camping sites.

NORTH TO THE JARDINE

Back on the main track, after Batavia Downs, there are almost 200km of rough road and numerous river crossings (the Wenlock and the Dulhunty being the two major ones) before you reach the Jardine

QUEENSLAND

River ferry crossing. Between the Wenlock River and the Jardine ferry there are two possible routes: the more direct but rougher old route (Telegraph Track, 155km), and the longer but quicker new route (193km), which branches off the old route about 40km north of the Wenlock River. Don't miss **Indian Head Falls**, one of the most popular camping and swimming spots on the Cape. It's signposted off the main road about 90km before Jardine River crossing.

The Jardine River ferry, operated by the Injinoo Community Council, operates daily from 8 am to 5 pm. The $80 return fare includes permits and fees for camping on Aboriginal land, and helps maintain camp sites in the Cape.

Stretching east to the coast from the main track is the **Jardine River National Park**. The Jardine River spills more fresh water into the sea than any other river in Australia. It's wild impenetrable country.

THE TIP

The first settlement north of the Jardine River is **Bamaga**, home to the peninsula's largest Torres Strait Islander community. The town has postal facilities, a hospital, a Commonwealth Bank agency, a supermarket, a garage which does repairs and sells fuel. It's only about 40km from Bamaga to the very northern tip. **Seisia**, on the coast 5km north-west, has the *Seisia Village Resort* (☎ *4069 3243*), with camp sites, budget units and air-con motel rooms.

North-east of Bamaga, off the Cape York track and about 11km south-east of the Cape York, is **Somerset**, which was established in 1863 as a haven for shipwrecked sailors and a signal to the rest of the world that this was British territory. It was hoped that it might become a major trading centre, a sort of Singapore of north Queensland, but its trading functions were moved to Thursday Island in 1879, and there's nothing much left now, though the fishing is good and there are lovely views.

At **Cape York**, 400m from the Tip, *Pajinka Wilderness Lodge* (☎ *4062 2100*) is a luxury resort with cabin-style rooms ranging from $250 to $270 per person, including all

meals. It also has a small camping ground with a kiosk, toilets and showers ($8). The scenic **Punsand Bay Private Reserve** (☎ *4069 1722*), on the western side of the cape, provides more modest accommodation. Camp sites cost $8 per person; cabins and permanent tents are from $95 to $125 per person, including meals.

TORRES STRAIT ISLANDS

The Torres Strait Islands have been a part of Queensland since 1879, the best-known of them being Thursday Island. The 70 other islands are sprinkled from Cape York in the south almost to New Guinea in the north, but only 17 are inhabited and all but three are set aside for islanders.

Torres Strait Islanders came from Melanesia and Polynesia about 2000 years ago, bringing with them a more material culture than that of the mainland Aboriginal people.

It was a claim by a Torres Strait Islander, Eddie Mabo, to traditional ownership of Murray Island that eventually led to the High Court handing down its ground-breaking Mabo ruling. The court's decision in turn became the basis for the Federal government's 1993 Native Title legislation (see Government & Politics in the Facts about Australia chapter).

Thursday Island is hilly and just over 3 sq km in area. At one time it was a major pearling centre and the cemeteries tell the hard tale of what a dangerous occupation it was. Some pearls are still produced here from seeded 'culture farms', which don't offer much employment to the locals.

Thursday Island is a rough-and-ready but generally easy-going place, and its main appeal is its cultural mix – Asians, Europeans and Pacific Islanders have all contributed to its history.

Places to Stay

Options include the *Jumula Dubbins Hostel* (☎ *4069 2122*), with singles for $19 (if there's space – ring ahead); the *Federal Hotel* (☎ *4069 1569*) from $55/80 a single/double; and the *Jardine Motel* (☎ *4069 2555*), with rooms for $130/160. Accommodation is also available on Horn Island at the swish *Gateway Torres Strait Resort* (☎ 4069 2222) for $96/122, and at the *Wongai Hotel* (☎ 4069 1683) for $65.

Getting There & Around
Sunstate/Qantas and Flight West fly between Cairns and Thursday Island. The airport is actually on nearby Horn Island – a ferry links the two islands (hourly, $5). Several smaller airlines operate flights around the other islands in the strait.

Peddell's Ferry & Tour Bus Service (☎ 4069 1551) operates ferry services from Seisia, Pajinka and Punsand Bay on the mainland to Thursday Island daily except Sunday.

Gulf Savannah

The Gulf Savannah is a vast, flat and sparsely populated landscape of bushland, saltpans and savannah grasslands, all cut by a huge number of tidal creeks and rivers that feed into the Gulf of Carpentaria. During the Wet, the dirt roads turn to mud and even the sealed roads can be flooded, so June to September is the safest time to visit this area.

Two of the settlements in the region, Burketown and Normanton, were founded in the 1860s, before better-known places on the Pacific coast such as Cairns and Cooktown. Pioneers flooded in, hoping to produce a western port for produce from further east and south in Queensland, but these days the Gulf has more cattle and crocodiles than people. However, the fishing is excellent, and the tough, hot environment is the very vision of rural Australia.

This remote area's main attraction is the superb Riversleigh fossil field, which is part of Lawn Hill National Park, north of Mt Isa.

For tourist information, advice on road conditions and general inquiries, contact the Gulf Savannah Tourism Organisation, 74 Abbott St, Cairns (☎ 4051 4658).

Organised Tours
The Savannah Guides is a network of professionals who staff guide posts at strategic locations throughout the Gulf. They are people with good local knowledge who have access to points of interest, many of which are on private property and would be difficult to visit unaccompanied. Contact the Savannah Guides Headquarters (☎ 4031 7933) in Cairns for more information.

Getting There & Around
Air Transtate Airlines (☎ 13 1528) flies a few times a week between Cairns and various places in the Gulf, including Normanton ($286), Karumba ($312) and Burketown ($376).

Bus Coral Coaches (☎ 4031 7577) has a service three times a week between Cairns and Karumba ($122; 12 hours) via Undara ($42), Georgetown ($64), Croydon ($87) and Normanton ($110). Ruby Charters Coaches (☎ 4743 0576) has a weekly bus service from Mt Isa to Normanton ($54) and Karumba ($62).

Train The *Savannahlander*, a tiny 1950s locomotive, runs weekly between Cairns, Mt Surprise and Forsayth ($85, or $35 from Mt Surprise to Forsayth; two days), leaving Cairns every Wednesday and returning from Forsayth every Friday. The famous *Gulflander* (☎ 4745 1391) is a weird-looking, snub-nosed vintage train that travels the 153km between Croydon and Normanton ($35; four hours), leaving Normanton every Wednesday and returning from Croydon every Thursday. You can put your car on the train for $110.

There are bus services from Cairns that connect with both trains.

Car & Motorcycle There are two main roads into the Gulf region. The Gulf Developmental Rd takes you from the Kennedy Hwy, south of the Atherton Tablelands, across to Normanton (450km, about 300km of which is sealed), while the Burke Developmental Rd runs north from Cloncurry to Normanton (378km, sealed all the way) via the Burke & Wills Roadhouse. There is also a sealed road between Julia Creek and the Burke & Wills Roadhouse.

QUEENSLAND

Other roads through the region are unsealed. If you're driving on any of these roads, make sure you seek advice on road conditions and fuel stops, and carry plenty of water with you.

GULF DEVELOPMENTAL ROAD
Undara Volcanic National Park
The massive volcanic tubes here were formed around 190,000 years ago after the eruption of a single shield volcano (a flat, shield-shaped volcano formed by fluid lava flows). Huge lava flows drained towards the sea, forming a surface crust as they cooled. Meanwhile, molten lava continued to flow through the centre of the tubes, eventually leaving hollow basalt chambers. They form the largest lava tube system in the world, and are a must-see if you are in the region.

The *Undara Lava Lodge's* (☎ *4097 1411*) resident guides run full-day tours ($85 including lunch), half-day tours ($68 including lunch, $58 without) and two-hour introductory tours ($21). The lodge has three accommodation options: camp/caravan sites ($5 per person); semipermanent tents ($15 per person); and charmingly restored old railway carriages ($69 per person). Breakfast and dinner are available for $40 more. There's a restaurant and bar but no shops here so, if you're self-catering, you'll need to bring supplies. There are good barbecue and cooking facilities in the camping area.

The turn-off to Undara is 17km past the start of the Gulf Developmental Rd and from there it's another 15km of good dirt road to the lodge. If you're travelling by bus, the lodge will pick you up from the turn-off.

Undara to Croydon
About 39km past the Undara turn-off, **Mt Surprise** is an overnight stop for the *Savannahlander* train, and has a curiosity museum, a caravan park, two roadhouses and the *Mt Surprise Hotel* (☎ *4062 3118*), which has basic singles/doubles for $20/35.

The **Elizabeth Creek** gem field, 42km north-west of Mt Surprise and accessible by conventional vehicle in the Dry, is Australia's best topaz field. Information on the field is available at the Mt Surprise service station (☎ 4062 3153).

South and west of Mt Surprise are the old mining townships of Einasleigh and Forsayth, which you can visit on the *Savannahlander*. If you're driving, there's also a (poorly marked) road off the Gulf Developmental Rd midway between Mt Surprise and Georgetown – it's a slow and bumpy 150km loop through the towns and back to the main road.

Einasleigh is a ramshackle little place with a collection of mostly derelict tin buildings. **Forsayth** isn't much bigger, although it is perhaps a little more alive. The *Goldfields Hotel* (☎ *4062 5374*) has air-con rooms for $60 per person, including breakfast and dinner.

Forty-five kilometres south of Forsayth is the scenic **Cobbold Gorge**, where the *Cobbold Camping Village* (☎ *4062 5470*) has boat cruises led by the Savannah Guides. Options include a budget tour ($25; three hours) and full-day tours ($80). Camping is $5.

Croydon
- postcode 4871   • pop 220

Connected to Normanton by the *Gulflander* train, this old gold-mining town was once the biggest in the Gulf Savannah. It's reckoned that at one time there were 5000 gold mines in the area and reminders of them are scattered all around the countryside.

By the end of WWI the gold had run out and the town became something of a ghost town, but there are still some interesting **historic buildings** here, including the old shire hall, the courthouse, the mining warden's office and the Club Hotel.

The *Club Hotel* (☎ *4745 6184*) has beds on the upstairs verandah for $15, pub singles/doubles for $28/38 and motel units for $33/48; meals are available.

Normanton
- postcode 4890   • pop 1330

Normanton was set up as a port for the Cloncurry copper fields, but then became Croydon's gold-rush port, its population peaking at 3000 in 1891. Today it's the Gulf's major town, a bustling little centre

QUEENSLAND

with good barramundi fishing and a handful of historic buildings. These include the train station, a lovely Victorian-era building that houses the *Gulflander* train when it's not travelling to Croydon and back.

Accommodation includes a *caravan park* (☎ *4745 1121, Brown St*), the *Albion Hotel* (☎ *4745 1218)* with beds in miners' huts for $20 (often booked out) or motel-style units for $40/50, and the *Gulfland Motel* (☎ *4745 1290)*, with singles/doubles for $55/67.

Karumba
• postcode 4891   • pop 1040

Karumba, 69km from Normanton by sealed road and right on the Gulf of Carpentaria at the mangrove-fringed mouth of the **Norman River**, is a prawn, barramundi and crab-fishing centre. You can charter boats for fishing trips from here, and there's a regular vehicular barge between Karumba and Weipa.

The town has quite an interesting history. At one time it was a refuelling station for Qantas flying boats, which used to connect Sydney and the UK.

Most of the accommodation places cater for fishing enthusiasts. The *Karumba Lodge Hotel* (☎ *4745 9143)* charges $65/75 for singles/doubles and the *Gulf Country Caravan Park* (☎ *4745 9148)* has on-site cabins ($30/45).

NORMANTON TO CLONCURRY
South of Normanton, the flat plains are interrupted by a solitary hill beside the road – Bang Bang Jump-up. The *Burke & Wills Roadhouse* (☎ *4742 5909)*, 195km south of Normanton, has four air-con singles/doubles for $30/40 and a few camp sites for $4 per person. **Quamby**, 43km north of Cloncurry, was originally a Cobb & Co coach stop. The historic *Quamby Hotel* (☎ *4742 5952)* has air-con rooms for $20 per person, and a pool.

NORMANTON TO THE NT BORDER
The historic Gulf Track stretches from Normanton across to Roper Bar in the NT. Although the entire route is along unsealed

roads, a 4WD vehicle isn't normally required during the dry season.

Camp 119, the northernmost camp of the Burke and Wills expedition of 1861, is signposted 37km west of Normanton. Also of interest are the spectacular **Leichhardt Falls** and **Floraville Station**, both about 160km west of Normanton.

With a population of about 230, **Burketown** is probably best known for its isolation. It's in the centre of a cattle-raising area, close to the Albert River and about 25km south of the Gulf of Carpentaria. Some of Nevil Shute's novel *A Town Like Alice* is set here.

Burketown is an excellent place for birdwatching, and is also one of the places where you can view the phenomenon known as 'Morning Glory' – weird tubular cloud formations extending the full length of the horizon, which roll in from the Gulf of Carpentaria in the early morning. This only happens from September to November.

The town's focal point is the *Burketown Pub* (☎ *4745 5104)*, a great old pub housed in the former customs house, with upstairs singles/doubles from $40/50 and motel-style units from $65/85. There's also a caravan park (no on-site vans).

Escott Lodge (☎ *4748 5577)*, 17km north-west of Burketown, is a working cattle station and fishing resort with camp sites, and rooms from $45/70; meals are available.

In pioneer times, **Hell's Gate**, 175km west of Burketown, was the last outpost of police protection for settlers heading north to Katherine, and was the scene of frequent ambushes as Aboriginal people tried to stop their lands being overrun. The *Hell's Gate Roadhouse* (☎ *4745 8258)* has meals, camp sites, 4WD tours (for groups of five or more) and four air-con rooms from $50 a double, including breakfast. There's also an airstrip and Savannah Guide station (☎ 4745 8258).

BURKETOWN TO CAMOOWEAL
This road is the most direct route to Lawn Hill National Park, although for conventional vehicles the mostly sealed route via

the Burke & Wills Roadhouse provides much easier access to the park.

The *Gregory Downs Hotel* (☎ 4748 5566), 117km south of Burketown, is at the main turn-off to Lawn Hill National Park. The pub sells fuel and has motel-style singles/doubles for $50/60 and camp sites on the river bank. There's a great swimming hole here, and every Labour Day in May the pub hosts the Gregory River Canoe Races – great fun if you're in the area.

Lawn Hill National Park

Amid arid country 100km west of Gregory Downs, the Lawn Hill Gorge is an oasis of gorges, creeks, ponds and tropical vegetation that the Aboriginal people have enjoyed for perhaps 30,000 years. Their paintings and old camping sites abound and two rock-art sites have been made accessible to visitors. There are freshwater crocodiles – the inoffensive variety – in Lawn Hill Creek.

In the southern part of the park, the amazing World Heritage listed **Riversleigh fossil field** contains fossils ranging from 25 million to a mere 50,000 years old, making it one of the world's pre-eminent fossil sites. The fossils include everything from giant snakes to carnivorous kangaroos, though fossicking is forbidden. If you can't get out to the park, the Riversleigh Fossils Interpretive Centre, in Mt Isa, displays fossils from here.

There are 20km of walking tracks, and a *camping ground* with showers and toilets at Lawn Hill; it's extremely popular and sites must be booked well in advance (especially March to September) with the park rangers (☎ 4748 5572) or the EPA office in Mt Isa (☎ 4743 2055). *Adel's Grove Kiosk* (☎ 4748 5502), 10km east of the park entrance, has basic food supplies, camp sites and fuel, as well as a Savannah Guide station (☎ 4748 5502). About 30km north of Adel's Grove on a track to Doomadgee, *Bowthorn Homestead* (☎ 4745 8132) has rooms for $75 per person including all meals, or charges $6 in the camp site by the river.

Getting to the park poses a few problems simply because it is a long way from anywhere. The last 230km or so from Mt Isa – after you leave the Barkly Hwy – are unsealed and often impassable after rain. A 4WD vehicle is recommended, though it is not always necessary in the dry season.

Outback

Heading west from the Queensland coast across the Great Dividing Range, the land becomes drier and the towns smaller and further apart.

The outback, although sparsely settled, is well serviced by major roads. The Flinders Hwy connects northern Queensland with the NT, but is in many places a narrow and badly deteriorated strip of bitumen. West of Cloncurry it becomes the Barkly Hwy. The Capricorn Hwy runs along the Tropic of Capricorn from Rockhampton to Longreach; and the Landsborough and Mitchell Hwys run from the NSW border south of Cunnamulla to Mt Isa.

Once off these major arteries, road conditions deteriorate rapidly, services are far apart and you need to be fully self-sufficient, carrying spare parts, fuel and water. With the correct preparation, it's possible to make the great outback journeys down the tracks that connect Queensland with SA (the Strzelecki and Birdsville Tracks) and the NT (the Plenty and Sandover Hwys).

Getting There & Away

Air The major towns of the outback are serviced by Flight West Airlines. Ansett has flights to Mt Isa from Cairns ($289) and Brisbane ($451), while Airlines of South Australia (☎ 08-8642 3100) flies on Saturday from Port Augusta (SA) to Birdsville ($255 one way), Bedourie and Boulia.

Bus McCafferty's (☎ 13 1499) operates three major bus routes through the outback: from Townsville to Mt Isa (and on to the NT); from Rockhampton to Longreach; and from Brisbane to Mt Isa (via Longreach). Greyhound Pioneer (☎ 13 2030) also does the Townsville to the NT run.

Train There are three train services heading inland from the coast, all running twice

ANN JEFFREE

An icon of outback Australia

weekly: the *Spirit of the Outback* from Brisbane to Longreach (via Rockhampton), the *Westlander* from Brisbane to Charleville (with connecting buses to Cunnamulla and Quilpie), and the *Inlander* from Townsville to Mt Isa.

CHARTERS TOWERS TO CLONCURRY

As a scenic drive, the Flinders Hwy is probably the most boring route in Queensland,

although there are a few points of interest along the way to break the monotony. The highway was originally a Cobb & Co coach run, and along its length are a series of small towns that were established as stopovers for the coaches. **Pentland**, 105km west of Charters Towers, and **Torrens Creek**, 50km further on, both have pubs, fuel and camping grounds. At **Prairie**, 200km west of Charters Towers, is the friendly and historic *Prairie Hotel* (☎ *4741 5121*).

Hughenden, a busy commercial centre on the banks of the Flinders River, bills itself as 'the home of beauty and the beast'. The 'beast' is imprisoned in the **Dinosaur Display Centre**, on Gray St – a replica of the skeleton of *Muttaburrasaurus*, one of the largest and most complete dinosaur skeletons found in Australia.

The 'beauty' is the **Porcupine Gorge National Park**, an oasis in the dry country north of Hughenden. It's about 70km along the mostly unsealed, often corrugated Kennedy Developmental Rd to **Pyramid Lookout**. You can camp here and it's an easy 30 minute walk down into the gorge, with some fine rock formations and a permanent creek. Few people come here and there's a fair bit of wildlife. The Kennedy Developmental Rd eventually takes you to Undara and the Atherton Tableland, a rough but scenic trip.

Back in town, the *Allan Terry Caravan Park* (☎ *4741 1190*), opposite the train station, has camp sites for $9 and on-site vans from $25. The town swimming pool is next door. The *Grand Hotel* (☎ *4741 1588*), on the corner of Gray and Stanfield Sts, has timber-lined singles/doubles for $16/32 (more with air-con).

Keep your eyes open for wild emus and brolgas on the Hughenden to Cloncurry stretch. **Richmond**, 112km from Hughenden, and **Julia Creek**, 144km further on, are both small towns with motels and caravan/camping parks. From Julia Creek, the (bitumen) Wills Developmental Rd turns off north to Normanton (420km) and Karumba (494km) on the Gulf of Carpentaria. You can also reach Burketown (467km) this way; see the Gulf Savannah section earlier in this chapter for more information on these towns.

QUEENSLAND

CLONCURRY

• postcode 4824   • pop 2460

The centre for a copper boom in the last century, 'the Curry' was the largest copper producer in the British Empire in 1916. Today it's a pastoral centre, and the town's major claim to fame is as the birthplace of the Royal Flying Doctor Service (RFDS).

The **John Flynn Place** museum and art gallery, in Daintree St, houses interesting exhibits on mining, the RFDS and the School of the Air. It is open weekdays from 7 am to 4 pm and weekends from 9 am to 3 pm ($5).

Cloncurry's **Mary Kathleen Park & Museum**, on the east side of town, is partly housed in buildings transported from the town of Mary Kathleen and includes relics of the Burke and Wills expedition and a big collection of local rocks and minerals. The Burke Developmental Rd, north from Cloncurry, is sealed all the way to Normanton (375km) and Karumba (446km).

Places to Stay

You can camp in the *Cloncurry Caravan Park* (☎ 4742 1313), on the Flinders Hwy, or there's the *Wagon Wheel Motel* (☎ 4742 1866, 54 Ramsay St), with budget singles/doubles from $49/59. On the eastern edge of town is the *Gilbert Park Tourist Park* (☎ 4742 2300), with modern self-contained units from $55.

CLONCURRY TO MT ISA

This 124km stretch of the Barkly Hwy has a number of interesting stops. At **Corella River**, 43km west of Cloncurry, there's a memorial cairn to the Burke and Wills expedition, which passed here in 1861. Another kilometre down the road is the **Kalkadoon and Mitakoodi Memorial**, which marks an old Aboriginal tribal boundary (see the boxed text 'Last Stand of the Kalkadoons').

The turning to **Lake Julius**, Mt Isa's reserve water supply, is 36km beyond Mary Kathleen. It's 90km of unsealed and bumpy road north to the lake, which is a popular spot for fishing, canoeing, sailing and other water sports. The *Lake Julius Recreation Camp* (☎ 4742 5998) has camp sites ($2.60

Last Stand of the Kalkadoons

Before the coming of the Europeans, the arid and rocky hill country to the north of Mt Isa was home to the Kalkadoons, one of the fiercest and most warlike of the Aboriginal tribes. They were one of the last tribes to resist white settlement, and from the mid-1870s they conducted a guerilla-type war, frequently ambushing settlers and police.

In 1884 the authorities sent Frederick Urquhart, the Sub-Inspector of Police, to the region to take command. In September of that year, Urquhart gathered his troops and, heavily armed, rode to the rocky hill that came to be known as Battle Mountain. The Kalkadoons, with only their spears for weapons, stood no chance against the carbines of the troopers and were all but wiped out in a bloody massacre that marked the end of Aboriginal resistance in the region.

A memorial beside the Barkly Hwy, 42km west of Cloncurry, is inscribed with the words:

> You who pass by are now entering the ancient tribal lands of the Kalkadoon/Mitakoodi, dispossessed by the European. Honour their name, be brother and sister to their descendants.

---

per person), dorm beds ($5.50 per person) and there are self-contained units ($32.60 for up to four).

Battle Mountain, north of the Lake Julius dam wall, was the scene of the last stand of the Kalkadoon people in 1884. About 30km north-east of the lake is the tiny township of **Kajabbi**, where the historic *Kalkadoon Hotel* (☎ 4742 5979) has Saturday night barbecues, annual yabbie races (April) and budget accommodation.

MT ISA

• postcode 4825   • pop 21,750

The mining town of Mt Isa owes its existence to an immensely rich copper, silver, lead and zinc mine. The skyline is dominated by the 270m-high exhaust stack from the lead smelter. 'The Isa', as the town is known locally, is a rough and ready but prosperous town, and the job opportunities here have attracted people from about 60 different ethnic groups. There's plenty to see in town, and you can tour the mine.

The first Mt Isa deposits were discovered in 1923 by the prospector, John Campbell Miles, who gave Mt Isa its name – a corruption of Mt Ida, a goldfield in Western Australia. Since the ore deposits were large and low-grade, working them required the sort of investment only a company could make. Mt Isa Mines was founded in 1924 but it was during and after WWII that Mt Isa really took off, and today it's the Western world's biggest silver and lead producer. The ore is transported 900km to Townsville by rail.

Orientation & Information

The town centre is fairly compact and it's separated from the sprawling mining area to the west by the Leichhardt River.

The Riversleigh Fossils Interpretive Centre & Tourist Office (☎ 4749 1555), in Centenary Park on Marian St, is open weekdays from 8 am to 4.30 pm and on weekends from 9 am to 2 pm. Greyhound Pioneer has an office and depot here.

Book Country is an excellent bookshop in an arcade at 27 Simpson St. The Mt Isa Newsagency, on Miles St, has Internet/email access for $5 per half hour.

The Mine

Mt Isa's major attraction offers two different tours; both are very popular, and you'll need to book in advance with the tourist office (☎ 4749 1555).

The four hour underground tour, for which you don a hard hat and miner's suit, takes you down into some of the 4600km of tunnels. Tours leave Monday to Friday at 7.30 and 11.30 am and cost $35. There's a maximum of nine on each tour, and you must be over 16 years of age.

The two-hour surface tours (by bus) are run by Campbell's Tours and Safaris, and drivers pick up from various places on request. It's well worth the $15 charge, especially as the bus takes you right through the

major workshops and mine site, and the price includes a visit to the John Middlin Mining Display & Visitor Centre. The tours depart weekdays at 11 am. Mt Isa Mines also runs the visitor centre, on Church St. It has audio-visuals, photographic displays and a 'simulated underground experience'. It's open weekdays from 9 am to 4 pm and weekends from 9 am to 2 pm (shorter hours during summer); entry costs $4.

Other Attractions

The Frank Aston Museum is a partly underground complex on a hill at the corner of Shackleton and Marian Sts. This rambling place has a diverse collection ranging from old mining gear to ageing flying doctor radios, and displays on local Aboriginal culture. It's open daily from 9 am to 4 pm ($5).

At the tourist office, the Riversleigh Fossils Interpretive Centre features an important collection of fossils spanning 25 million years, which have revealed much about the evolution of Australia's unique wildlife. The fossils were found on a station near Lawn Hill National Park, 250km north-west of Mt Isa (the site now has World Heritage listing) and the centre has dioramas featuring some of the creatures discovered. You can also tour the fossil-treatment laboratory. It's open daily from 8.30 am to 4.30 pm ($5).

Next to the tourist office, the Kalkadoon Tribal Centre & Culture-Keeping Place is run by elders from the local Kalkadoon community and has a small collection of artefacts ($1).

You can visit the RFDS base on the Barkly Hwy, weekdays from 9 am to 5 pm and on weekends from 10 am to 2 pm. The $3 admission includes a film. The School of Distance Education, which brings education by radio to children in remote places, is at the Kalkadoon High School, on Abel Smith Parade. It's open for public tours at 9 and 10 am on school days ($2).

Mt Isa has a big, clean swimming pool on Isa St, next to the tennis courts. Lake Moondarra, 16km north of town, is a popular recreational area with boating and barbecue facilities.

QUEENSLAND

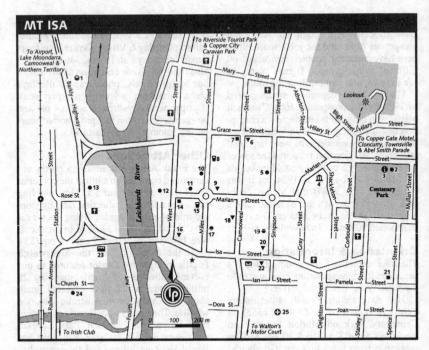

MT ISA

Mt Isa's August rodeo is among the biggest in Australia.

Organised Tours

There are several interesting tours which can be booked through the tourist office (☎ 4749 1555). Campbell's Tours and Safaris (☎ 4743 2006) runs a three day camping safari to Lawn Hill National Park and the Riversleigh fossil sites ($340 with all meals and equipment supplied).

Look-About Trips (☎ 4743 9523) does day tours to Kajabbi and Lake Julius ($60), a night town tour ($10) and a half-day town tour ($15). Air Mt Isa (☎ 4743 2844), the local mail run operator, will take tourists on its twice-weekly runs ($320 per person, bookings required). It also does a day tour of Riversleigh from $300 per person.

Places to Stay – Budget

On the Leichhardt River, a couple of kilometres north of the centre, the *Riverside*

Tourist Park (☎ 4743 3904, 195 Little West St) has camp sites for $12 and cabins from $58. The *Copper City Caravan Park* (☎ 4743 4676, 185 Little West St) also has camp sites from $12, on-site vans from $35 and cabins from $45. Both have swimming pools.

The *Moondarra Caravan Park* (☎ 4743 9780), about 4km north of town on the road to Lake Moondarra, has shady camp sites by the river bank for $13 for two people.

The clean and quiet *Travellers Haven* (☎ 4743 0313), about 500m from the centre on the corner of Spence and Pamela Sts, is the main budget accommodation option. All rooms have air-con and a fridge, with bunk beds in small dorms from $14 ($13 VIP) and singles/doubles from $26/34. There's a good pool, bikes for hire, and its courtesy coach does pickups.

Places to Stay – Mid-Range

The *Boyd Hotel* (☎ 4743 3000), on the corner of West and Marian Sts, has basic

MT ISA

PLACES TO STAY
7   Burke & Wills Motor Inn
14 Boyd Hotel
21 Travellers Haven

PLACES TO EAT
6   Buffs
9   Flamenco Cafe
16 Eagle Boys
18 Los Toros Mexican Restaurant
20 Red Lantern Chinese Restaurant
22 The Tavern

OTHER
1   Campbell's Coaches Terminal
2   Kalkadoon Tribal Centre & Culture-Keeping Place
3   Riversleigh Fossils Interpretive Centre & Tourist Office
4   Frank Aston Museum
5   Book Country
8   Switches Nightclub
10 Mt Isa Newsagency
11 Cinema Mt Isa
12 Civic Centre
13 Royal Flying Doctor Service
15 Mt Isa Hotel
17 Ansett
19 RACQ
23 Swimming Pool
24 John Middlin Mining Display & Visitor Centre
25 Hospital

singles/doubles for $35/55 with shared facilities.

Walton's Motor Court (☎ 4743 2377, 23 Camooweal St), just south of the centre, and the **Copper Gate Motel** (☎ 4743 3233, 97 Marian St), near the eastern entrance to town, have singles/doubles for $50/60.

If you're looking for something more up-market, the **Burke & Wills Motor Inn** (☎ 4743 8000), on the corner of Grace and Camooweal Sts, is an impressive modern motel with its own restaurant and pool; rooms cost from $92 to $120.

Places to Eat

Mt Isa's clubs are among the best places to eat. The **Irish Club**, 2km south of the centre on the corner of Buckley and Nineteenth Aves, is excellent value, with smorgasbord lunches for $8 and dinners for $13, and

bistro meals from $6 to $12. On the corner of Camooweal and Grace Sts, **Buffs** also has good meals costing from $8 to $14. Visitors to the clubs sign in as honorary buffaloes or Irish persons, and dress regulations apply.

The **Tavern**, on Isa St, has good pub food with cheap counter meals in the public bar, and bistro meals from $10. The **Flamenco Cafe**, on Marian St, also has burgers, sandwiches and 20 flavours of ice cream.

For pizzas (takeaway or home delivery) there's **Eagle Boys** (☎ 13 1433, 8 West St).

The very popular **Los Toros Mexican Restaurant** (79 Camooweal St) is a lively cantina-style eatery with main courses in the $12 to $16 range. It's licensed and open nightly except Monday.

For Chinese food try the **Red Lantern**, on the corner of Isa and Simpson Sts.

Entertainment

Switches Nightclub, on Miles St, is a big upmarket nightclub, open Wednesday to Saturday until 3 am; there's a $5 cover charge and dress regulations apply.

There are live bands in the **Boyd Hotel** most weekends. Also popular are the **Kave** nightclub, in the Mt Isa Hotel, and **Buffs**, on Grace St. The **Irish Club** (☎ 4743 2577) has a good entertainment program, with a mixture of live music, disco and karaoke on weekends.

The **Civic Centre** (☎ 4744 4244) has theatre and cabaret acts. **Cinema Mt Isa** (☎ 4743 2043), on Marian St, screens latest releases.

Getting There & Away

Air Ansett has an office at 8 Miles St, with daily flights to Brisbane ($451) and Cairns ($289).

Transtate Airlines (☎ 13 1528) has a regular service between Mt Isa and Cairns ($391, weekdays), stopping off at various towns in the Gulf Savannah including Normanton ($266) and Karumba ($260), and a direct service to/from Cairns three times a week.

Bus The Campbell's Coaches terminal (☎ 4743 3685), at 27 Barkly Hwy, is the main depot for McCafferty's buses, while

Greyhound Pioneer buses stop at the rear of the Riversleigh Fossil Centre & Tourist Office on Marian St. Both companies have daily services between Townsville and Mt Isa ($84; 9½ hours), continuing on from Mt Isa to Tennant Creek in the NT ($75; 7½ hours). From Tennant Creek you can head north to Darwin ($176 from Mt Isa) or south to Alice Springs ($153). McCafferty's also has daily buses south to Brisbane ($112; 24 hours) through Winton ($52) and Longreach ($59).

Ruby Charters Coaches (☎ 4743 0576) goes to Normanton ($54) and Karumba ($62) once a week from the Riversleigh Fossils Centre.

Train The air-con *Inlander* operates twice weekly between Townsville and Mt Isa, via Charters Towers, Hughenden and Cloncurry. The full journey takes about 18 hours and costs $192/125 in a 1st class/economy sleeper.

MT ISA TO THREE WAYS
Established in 1884 as a service centre for the vast cattle stations of the Barkly Tablelands, **Camooweal** is 188km from Mt Isa and 13km east of the NT border. It has a couple of historic buildings – in particular, **Freckleton's General Store** is worth a visit – as well as a pub and a couple of roadhouses (with extremely expensive fuel).

From Camooweal, you can head north to the Lawn Hill National Park and Burketown (see Gulf Savannah earlier in this chapter for details). Eight kilometres south of town is the **Camooweal Caves National Park**, where there is a network of unusual caves and caverns with sinkhole openings. There are no facilities here, and you'll need proper caving equipment to explore the caves.

There's nothing much for the whole 460km of the journey to the Three Ways junction in the NT. The next petrol station west of Camooweal appears 270km along at *Barkly Homestead* (☎ 08-8964 4549). You can camp at the homestead for $4 per person and there are also motel-style single/double rooms for $62/72.

MT ISA TO LONGREACH
Fourteen kilometres east of Cloncurry, the Landsborough Hwy turns off south-east to McKinlay (91km), Kynuna (165km), Winton (328km) and Longreach (501km).

McKinlay is a tiny settlement that probably would have been doomed to eternal insignificance had it not been used as a location in the amazingly successful movie *Crocodile Dundee*. The **Walkabout Creek Hotel** (☎ 4746 8424), which featured in the film, is cluttered with photos and other *Crocodile Dundee* memorabilia. Camp sites are $10 and air-con singles/doubles are $38/46.

Kynuna, another 74km south-east, isn't much bigger than McKinlay. The **Blue Heeler Hotel** (☎ 4746 8650) is another renowned old outback pub, which for some reason has its own surf life-saving club! It's a good spot for a feed and there are pub rooms from $30, motel-style units from $50, and camp sites in the Jolly Swagman Van Park for $12. The nearest beach may be almost 1000km away, but the pub hosts a surf life-saving carnival every August, complete with surfboard relays, a tug of war and a beach party at night.

The turn-off to the **Combo Waterhole**, which Banjo Patterson is said to have visited in 1895 before he wrote *Waltzing Matilda*, is signposted off the highway about 12km east of Kynuna.

Winton

• postcode 4735   • pop 1140

Winton is a sheep-raising centre and also the railhead from where cattle are transported after being brought from the Channel Country by road train. It's a friendly, laid-back place with some interesting attractions and characters, and if you're not in a hurry it's a good place for a stopover.

Winton's biggest attraction is the **Waltzing Matilda Centre** on Elderslie St, beside the post office. There's a surprising amount here for a museum devoted to a song, though, predictably, most of the displays are dedicated to Banjo Patterson. The centre also houses the **Qantilda Museum**, which has displays on the founding of Qantas at Winton in 1920. It's open daily from 9 am to 4 pm ($13). Across the road are the **Jolly Swagman** statue – a tribute to Banjo Patterson and the unknown swagmen who lie in unmarked graves in the area – and the **Winton Swimming Pool**.

The **Royal Theatre**, out the back of the Stopover Cafe in the centre of town, is a wonderful open-air theatre with canvas-slung chairs, corrugated tin walls and a star-studded ceiling. Films are screened every Saturday night and, from April to September, on Wednesday night as well.

There are a couple of operators offering tours from Winton – see the South of Winton section, following.

The Waltzing Matilda Centre (☎ 4657 1466) handles information inquiries. Winton's major festival is the nine day Outback Festival, held every second year (odd numbers) during the September school holidays.

Places to Stay & Eat The *Matilda Country Caravan Park* (☎ 4657 1607, 43 Chirnside St) has camp sites from $10 and on-site vans and cabins from $25 to $50.

In the town centre, the *North Gregory Hotel* (☎ 4657 1375, 67 Elderslie St) has clean budget air-con rooms for $45 a double. Opposite the Qantilda Museum, the *Matilda Motel* (☎ 4657 1433) has units from $40/53.

The *North Gregory Hotel* has good bistro meals off the char-grill in its beer garden. You can also have a Chinese meal or a beer in the Qantas Board Room Lounge at the *Winton Club*, where the fledgling airline's first meeting was held back in 1921. The club is one block back from the Waltzing Matilda Centre, on the corner of Oondooroo and Vindex Sts.

Getting There & Away Winton is on Mc-Cafferty's Brisbane to Mt Isa bus route. There are also connecting bus services between Winton and Longreach that meet up with the *Spirit of the Outback* train.

South of Winton

The *Carisbrooke Station* (☎ 4657 3984), 85km south-west of Winton, has a wildlife sanctuary, Aboriginal paintings and bora rings (circular ceremonial grounds). The station offers day tours (with advance notice) from Winton or the homestead ($110 per person, minimum of four) and has a self-contained unit for $60, shearer's quarters for $25 per person and camping $7.

At **Lark Quarry Environmental Park**, 115km south-west of Winton, dinosaur footprints 100 million years old have been perfectly preserved in limestone. It takes about two hours to drive from Winton to Lark Quarry in a conventional vehicle but the dirt road is impassable in wet weather – you can get directions at the Winton Shire Council offices (☎ 4657 1188) at 78 Vindex St. Alternatively, Diamantina Outback Tours (☎ 4657 1514) runs day trips from Winton to Lark Quarry for $75 per person (minimum of four).

LONGREACH

• postcode 4730   • pop 3770

This prosperous outback town was the home of the Queensland & Northern Territory Aerial Service – better known as Qantas – earlier this century, but these days it's just as famous for the Australian Stockman's Hall of Fame & Outback Heritage Centre, one of the biggest attractions in outback Queensland.

Longreach's human population is vastly outnumbered by the sheep population, which numbers over a million; there are a fair few cattle too.

The tourist office (☎ 4658 3555), a replica of the first Qantas booking office, is on the corner of Duck and Eagle Sts, opposite the post office. It is usually open daily from 9 am to 5 pm (Sunday to 1 pm). Longreach holds Australia's largest sheep-shearing contest in July.

Stockman's Hall of Fame & Outback Heritage Centre

The centre is in a beautifully conceived building, 2km east of town on the road to Barcaldine. The excellent displays are divided into periods from the first white settlement through to today, and cover all aspects of the pioneering pastoral life. The hall was built as a tribute to the early explorers and stockmen, and also commemorates the crucial roles played by the pioneer women and Aboriginal stockmen, although the section on the latter is pathetically brief.

It's well worth setting aside at least half a day to visit the hall of fame, as it gives a fascinating insight into the development of outback Australia. Admission is $15 ($10 students), valid for two days, and the centre is open daily from 9 am to 5 pm.

It's a pleasant half-hour walk or a $6 taxi ride to the hall of fame.

Other Attractions

The Qantas Founders Outback Museum is housed in the original Qantas hangar, which still stands at Longreach airport (almost opposite the hall of fame), and was the first aircraft 'factory' in Australia – six DH-50 biplanes were assembled here in 1926. The museum features, among other exhibits, a

Captain Starlight

Longreach was the starting point for one of Queensland's most colourful early crimes when, in 1870, Harry Redford and two accomplices stole 1000 head of cattle and walked them 2400km to SA, where they were sold. Redford's exploit opened up a new stock route south and, when he was finally brought to justice in 1873, he was found not guilty by an adoring public. Ralph Bolderwood's classic Australian novel *Robbery Under Arms* later immortalised Redford as 'Captain Starlight'.

full-scale replica of the first aircraft owned by the airline, an Avro 504K. It is open daily from 9 am to 5 pm ($6).

You can also visit the **School of Distance Education**, towards Ilfracombe on the Matilda Hwy, and the rather ordinary **Powerhouse Museum**, with local memorabilia and exhibits on the electricity industry.

Organised Tours

The Outback Travel Centre (☎ 4658 1776), at 115 Eagle St, offers a variety of tours including a full-day tour that takes in the hall of fame, an outback station and a dinner cruise along the Thomson River, for $49.

You can also take an attractive sunset dinner cruise along the Thomson River with Yellowbelly Express (☎ 4658 2360) or Billabong Boat Cruises (☎ 4658 1776) for $25.

Queensland Helicopters offers scenic flights from the Longreach Aerodrome from $25 per person; book through the tourist office.

Places to Stay

The *Royal Hotel (☎ 4658 2118, 111 Eagle St)* has a few backpacker beds for $15 and basic air-con singles/doubles for $20/35. There's also accommodation at the *Central (☎ 4658 2263)* and *Lyceum (☎ 4658 1036)* pubs on Eagle St, with basic rooms from $20/30.

The *Gunnadoo Caravan Park (☎ 4658 1781)*, east of town on the corner of the highway and Thrush Rd, has camp sites for $12 and self-contained cabins from $50.

Aussie Betta Cabins (☎ *4658 2322*), on the highway about halfway to the hall of fame, has modern self-contained cabins from $59 a double, plus $10 for extra persons.

Hallview Lodge B&B (☎ *4658 3777*) is a comfortable, renovated, air-con timber house on the corner of Womproo and Thrush Rds. It has rooms with en suite and breakfast for $45/62 and does pickups from the train and bus terminals.

For a group or family, the *Old Time Cottage* (☎ *4658 1550, 158 Crane St*) is a fully self-contained old-style cottage with established garden. It has air-con, sleeps six and costs $60 a double, plus $6 per extra person.

Motels are not cheap. The *Commercial Hotel/Motel* (☎ *4658 1677, 102 Eagle St*) has basic hotel rooms for $25/35 and motel rooms for $45/55.

Places to Eat

There's a *cafe* out at the hall of fame and there are also several *cafes*, *takeaways* and a *bakery* on Eagle St, in the centre of town.

The pub meals are about as dreary as you'll find – this is what Australian food used to be like everywhere! Perhaps the best is *Starlight's Hideout Tavern*, also on Eagle St, with bistro meals of a sort.

On the corner of Galah and Swan Sts, the *Bush Verandah Restaurant* is a little licensed place with rustic decor and country-style cooking (mains $16 to $20, open Wednesday to Saturday).

Getting There & Away

Flight West has daily flights from Longreach to Brisbane ($325) and also flies twice a week to Winton ($85) and Townsville ($224).

McCafferty's buses stop at the back of Longreach Outback Travel (☎ *4658 1776*) at 113 Eagle St. There are daily services to Winton ($24; two hours), Mt Isa ($59; 7½ hours) and Brisbane ($83; 17 hours), and three a week to Rockhampton ($53; nine hours).

The *Spirit of the Outback* train runs twice a week between Longreach and Rockhampton (14 hours, $72 economy seat); there are connecting bus services between Longreach and Winton ($26).

LONGREACH TO WINDORAH

The Thomson Developmental Rd is the most direct route for people wanting to cut across towards Birdsville from Longreach. The first half of the trip is a narrow sealed road to **Stonehenge**, a tiny settlement in a dry and rocky landscape with half a dozen tin houses and a pub. The *Stonehenge Hotel* (☎ *4658 5944*) sells fuel and has doubles for $40.

The second half of the route is over unsealed roads of dirt, gravel and sand. **Jundah**, 65km south of Stonehenge, is an administrative centre with a pub and a general store.

LONGREACH TO CHARLEVILLE

Ilfracombe

• postcode 4727   • pop 350

This small town, 28km east of Longreach, modestly calls itself 'the Hub of the West' and boasts a train station, a general store, a swimming pool, a golf course and a pub. Along the highway you'll see the **Ilfracombe Folk Museum**, a scattered collection of historic buildings, farming equipment and carts and buggies. The charming little *Wellshot Hotel* (☎ *4658 2106*) is well worth a visit and has cheap meals and clean singles/doubles from $25/40.

Barcaldine

• postcode 4725   • pop 1900

Barcaldine (pronounced 'bar-*call*-din'), at the junction of the Landsborough and Capricorn Hwys 108km east of Longreach, gained a place in Australian history in 1891 when it became the headquarters of a major shearers' strike. The confrontation led to the formation of the Australian Workers' Party, the forerunner of today's Australian Labor Party (ALP). The **Tree of Knowledge**, a ghost gum near the train station, was the meeting place of the organisers and stands as a monument to workers and their rights. There's a tourist office (☎ *4651 1724*) beside the train station.

Barcaldine's **Australian Workers Heritage Centre**, built to commemorate the role of workers in the formation of Australian social, political and industrial movements, is one of the most impressive attractions in the Outback. Set in landscaped gardens, its excellent

QUEENSLAND

displays include a circular theatre-tent, an old one-teacher schoolhouse and a replica of Queensland's Legislative Assembly. It's open daily from 9 am to 5 pm (on Sunday from 10 am); entry costs $7.

The **Barcaldine & District Folk Museum**, on the corner of Gidyea and Beech Sts, has an eclectic collection of memorabilia and is open daily ($3). On the corner of Pine and Bauhinia Sts is **Mad Mick's Funny Farm**, a ramshackle farmlet with historic buildings, a fauna park, art studios, a doll collection, and billy tea and damper. It's open most days from April to September ($7).

Places to Stay & Eat The *Homestead Caravan Park* (☎ *4651 1308)*, in Box St, has camp sites for $10, on-site vans for $25 and cabins for $30 to $60. The owners run a couple of good day trips. The *Commercial Hotel* (☎ *4651 1242, 67 Oak St)* has singles/doubles from $17.50/30 and good bistro meals. *Charley's Coffee Lounge*, next door, has home-cooked meals.

The *Landsborough Lodge Motel* (☎ *4651 1100)*, on the corner of Box and Boree Sts, is the best of the four motels, with a licensed restaurant and shaded pool area. It has doubles from $65.

Blackall

- postcode 4472   • pop 2100

South of Barcaldine is Blackall, supposedly the site of the mythical Black Stump. The **Blackall Woolscour**, 4km north-east, is the only steam-driven scour (wool cleaner) left in Queensland. Built in 1908, it operated up until 1978. Although the machinery is not operating, the woolscour is open for personalised tours daily from 8 am to 4 pm ($5).

In town, the **Jackie Howe Memorial Statue** is a tribute to the legendary shearer from Warwick.

CHARLEVILLE

- postcode 4470   • pop 3500

At the junction of the Mitchell and Warrego Hwys, Charleville is a major outback centre. The town was an important centre for early explorers and, being on the Warrego River, it is something of an oasis.

There's a visitors information centre (☎ 4654 3057) on Sturt St, on the southern edge of town. Almost opposite is the CDEP, an Aboriginal workshop with limited artefacts and an expert didgeridoo player.

The **Historic House Museum** is housed in the 1880 Queensland National Bank building at 91 Albert St. South-east of the centre on Park St, the Department of Environment operates a captive breeding program where you can see several endangered species, including the yellow-footed rock wallaby and the bilby.

You can also visit the **RFDS** base, the **School of the Air** and the **Skywatch** observatory at the meteorological bureau, which has high-powered telescopes through which you can study the heavens ($8). Book through the tourist office or your accommodation.

Places to Stay & Eat There are a couple of caravan parks and three motels, but the best place to stay is at *Corones Hotel* (☎ *4654 1022)*, a grand old country pub on the corner of Wills and Galatea Sts. Basic pub rooms go from $10 per person twin share, while restored heritage-style singles/doubles are great value at $35/45. Next to the pub, `Poppa's Caffe* has excellent food and coffee.

CUNNAMULLA

- postcode 4490   • pop 1600

The southernmost town in western Queensland, Cunnamulla is on the Warrego River, 120km north of the Queensland-NSW border. It's another sheep-raising centre, noted for its wildflowers. Accommodation options include a caravan park, a pub and a motel.

THE CHANNEL COUNTRY

The remote and sparsely populated southwest corner of Queensland, bordering the NT, SA and NSW, takes its name from the myriad channels that crisscross it. In this inhospitable region it hardly ever rains, but water from the monsoon further north pours into the Channel Country along the Georgina, Hamilton and Diamantina rivers and Cooper Creek. The mass of water floods towards the great depression of Lake Eyre in SA, eventually drying up in water holes or salt pans.

Only rarely (the early 1970s and 1989 in this century) does the vast amount of water reach Lake Eyre and fill it. For a short period after each wet season, the Channel Country becomes fertile, and cattle are grazed here.

Getting There & Around

Some roads from the east and north to the fringes of the Channel Country are sealed, but during the October to May wet season even these can be cut, and dirt roads become quagmires. The summer heat is unbearable, so a visit is best made in the cooler winter, from May to September. Visiting this area requires a sturdy vehicle (4WD if you want to get off the beaten track) and some outback driving experience. Always carry plenty of drinking water and petrol, and if you're heading off the main roads notify the police.

The main road through this area is the **Diamantina Developmental Rd**. It runs south from Mt Isa through Boulia to Bedourie and then east through Windorah and Quilpie to Charleville. It's a long and lonely 1340km, a little over half of which is sealed.

Mt Isa to Birdsville

It's 295km south from Mt Isa to Boulia, and the only facilities along the route are at **Dajarra**, which has a pub and a roadhouse.

Boulia is the 'capital' of the Channel Country. Burke and Wills passed through here on their long trek; there's a museum in a restored 1888 stone house in the little town. Near Boulia, the mysterious Min Min Light, a sort of earthbound UFO, is sometimes seen. It's said to resemble the headlights of a car and can hover a metre or two above the ground before vanishing and reappearing in a different place.

The *Australian Hotel-Motel* (☎ 4746 3144), in Herbert St, Boulia, has singles/doubles for $30/45.

The sealed Kennedy Developmental Rd runs east from Boulia, 360km to Winton. The *Middleton Hotel* (☎ 4657 3980), 192km west of Winton, is the only fuel stop on route. It has accommodation in caravans for $15 per person.

It's 200km (unsealed) south from Boulia to **Bedourie**, the administrative centre for the huge Diamantina Shire Council. The town's *Royal Hotel* (☎ 4746 1201), in Herbert St, hasn't changed much since it was built in 1880; it has accommodation for $45 per person. The *Simpson Desert Roadhouse* (☎ 4746 1291), also in Herbert St, has a general store, a restaurant, motel units for $65/80 and a caravan park.

Twenty-three kilometres south of Bedourie is the intersection of the Diamantina Developmental Rd (which turns east towards Windorah, 400km away) and the Eyre Developmental Rd, which takes you 170km south to Birdsville.

Birdsville
● postcode 4482   ● pop 100

This tiny settlement is the remotest place in Queensland and possesses one of Australia's most famous pubs – the Birdsville Hotel. Only 12km from the SA border, Birdsville is at the northern end of the 481km Birdsville Track, which leads down to Marree in SA. In the late 19th century Birdsville was quite a busy place as cattle were driven south and a customs charge was made on each head of cattle leaving Queensland. With Federation, the charge was abolished and Birdsville became a near ghost town. In recent years the growing tourism industry has revitalised the town. Its big event is the annual Birdsville Races on the first weekend in September, when up to 6000 racing and boozing enthusiasts make the trip to Birdsville.

Birdsville gets its water from a 1219m-deep artesian well, which delivers the water at over 100°C.

Don't miss the **Birdsville Working Museum**. Inside this big tin shed is one of the most impressive private museums in Australia, with a fascinating collection of drover's gear, shearing equipment, wool presses and much more. It's open daily and private tours cost $5.

Birdsville's facilities include a couple of roadhouses, a general store, a hospital and a caravan park. The *Birdsville Hotel* (☎ 4656 3244), in Adelaide St, dates from 1884, but it has been impressively renovated, and has modern motel-style singles/doubles out the back for $50/70.

Birdsville Track

To the south, the Birdsville Track passes between the Simpson Desert to the west and Sturt's Stony Desert to the east. The first stretch from Birdsville has two alternative routes. Ask for local advice about which is better. The Inside Track – marked 'not recommended' on most maps – crosses the Goyder Lagoon (the 'end' of the Diamantina River) and a big Wet will sometimes cut this route. The longer, more easterly Outside Track crosses sandy country at the edge of the desert. You can contact the Birdsville police (☎ 4656 3220) for advice on road conditions.

Simpson Desert National Park

West of Birdsville, the waterless Simpson Desert National Park is Queensland's biggest at 5000 sq km. Conventional cars can tackle the Birdsville Track quite easily, but the Simpson requires a 4WD and far more preparation. Official advice is that crossings should only be tackled by parties of at least two 4WD vehicles and that you should have a radio to call for help if necessary. Permits are required before you can traverse the park. They are available from the police station in Birdsville (☎ 4656 3220) or Department of Environment and Heritage (DEH) offices. For more information, contact the DEH offices in Longreach (☎ 4658 1761) or Birdsville (☎ 4656 3272).

Birdsville to Charleville

The Birdsville Developmental Rd heads east from Birdsville, meeting the Diamantina Developmental Rd after 275km of rough gravel and sand – watch out for cattle grids and sudden dips at the many dry creek crossings. Betoota, the sole 'town' between Birdsville and Windorah, closed in late 1997 and now motorists have to carry enough fuel to cover the 384km distance.

Windorah is either very dry or very wet. The town's general store sells fuel and groceries and the *Western Star Hotel* (☎ 4656 3166) has air-con singles/doubles for $30/35. There's also a caravan park (of sorts).

Quilpie is an opal-mining town and the railhead from which cattle are transported to the coast. It has a good range of facilities, including two pubs, a motel and several service stations. From here it's another 210km to Charleville.

South of Quilpie and west of Cunnamulla are the remote **Yowah Opal Fields** and the town of **Eulo**, which hosts the World Lizard Racing Championships in August/September. **Thargomindah**, 130km west of Eulo, has a pub and a motel. From here camel trains used to cross to Bourke in NSW. **Noccundra**, another 145km further west, was once a busy little community. It now has only a hotel and a population of eight. If you have a 4WD you can continue west to Innamincka on the Strzelecki Track in SA, via the site of the **Dig Tree**, where Burke and Wills camped in their ill-fated 1860-61 expedition (see Innamincka in the Outback section of the SA chapter).

South Australia

South Australia (SA) is the driest state – not even Western Australia (WA) has such a large proportion of semidesert. It is also the most urbanised. Adelaide, the capital, once had a reputation as the wowsers' capital and is often referred to as 'the city of churches'. Although the churches are still there, times have changed. Today the city's cultural spirit is epitomised by the biennial Adelaide Festival of Arts, while the death of wowserism is nowhere better seen than in the Barossa Valley Vintage Festival, also held every two years. Another example of SA's relatively liberal attitude is that it was the first Australian state to have a legal nudist beach – Maslin Beach, just a short drive south of Adelaide.

SA is renowned for its vineyards and wineries. The Barossa Valley, just north of Adelaide, is probably Australia's best known wine-producing area, but there are also the fine Clare Valley, Coonawarra and McLaren Vale districts.

Further north, the rugged Flinders Ranges offer spectacular scenery and superb bushwalking, while the vast Outback has some of the most inhospitable yet fascinating semidesert country in Australia. The long drive west across the Nullarbor Plain runs close to dramatic cliffs along the Great Australian Bight, with whale-watching at Head of Bight.

That still leaves the mighty Murray River, the wild south-east coast, laid-back Kangaroo Island and the diverse Eyre, Yorke and Fleurieu peninsulas. All have plenty to offer the visitor.

The first British settlers landed at Holdfast Bay (today Glenelg) on 28 December 1836 and the Province of SA was proclaimed later that same day. Colonel William Light chose a site about 10km inland for the capital – he designed and surveyed the city, which the colony's first governor, Captain John Hindmarsh, named after the wife of the then British monarch, William IV. At first, progress in the independently managed colony was slow and

HIGHLIGHTS

Telephone code: ☎ 08
Population: 1,480,000
Area: 984,277 sq km

- Soaking up the cosmopolitan atmosphere of Rundle Street's lively cafe scene
- Watching southern right whales from the cliffs at Victor Harbor or Head of Bight
- Canoeing the quiet backwaters of the Murray River National Park
- Sampling the local drop on a tour of one of the state's great wine-producing areas
- Listening to the night silence from a lonely sand ridge by the Oodnadatta Track
- Experiencing the lunar landscapes and frontier atmosphere of Coober Pedy and Andamooka
- Walking the rugged ramparts of the northern Flinders Ranges

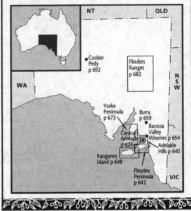

only British government funds saved it from bankruptcy. It was self-supporting by the mid-1840s and self-governing by 1856.

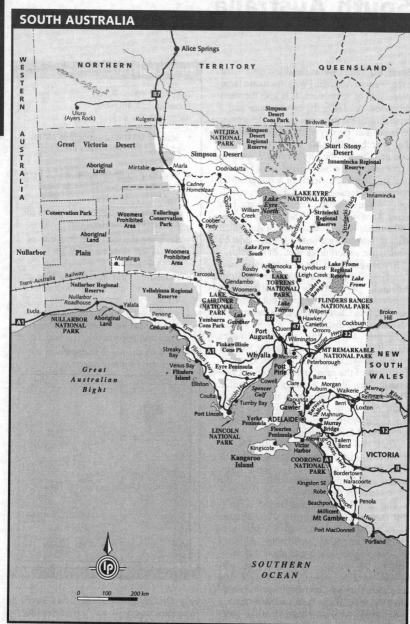

ABORIGINAL PEOPLE

It is estimated that there were 12,000 Aboriginal people in SA at the beginning of the 19th century. In the decades following white settlement, many were either killed by the settlers or died from starvation and introduced diseases. Except in the north-west, which was mainly unsuitable for pastoral development, they were usually forcibly dispossessed of their traditional lands. As a result, there was a general movement to missions and other centres where they could find safety and obtain food rations.

Today, most of the state's 21,000 Aboriginal people live in urban centres such as Adelaide and Port Augusta. In 1966 SA became the first state to grant Aboriginal people title to their land. The early 1980s saw most of the land lying west of the Stuart Hwy and north of the railway to Perth being transferred to Aboriginal ownership.

Survival in Our Own Land, edited by Christobel Mattingley & Ken Hampton, has been exhaustively researched and has beautifully written individual and historical accounts by Nungas (South Australian Aboriginal people). It is available from good bookshops in Adelaide.

GEOGRAPHY

South Australia is sparsely settled, with over 80% of its population living in Adelaide and a handful of major rural centres. The state's productive agricultural regions are found in the south: the Fleurieu Peninsula near Adelaide, the Mid-North, the Eyre and Yorke peninsulas, the South-East and the Murray River irrigation centres. As you travel further north or west the terrain becomes increasingly drier and more inhospitable; the Outback, which takes up over three-quarters of the state's area, is largely semidesert.

The state's topography mainly consists of vast plains and low relief. Over 80% of the land area is less than 300m above sea level, and few points rise above 700m. The only hills of any real significance are the Mt Lofty and Flinders ranges, which form a continuous spine running 800km from south-east of Adelaide into the interior.

South Australia's most important watercourse by far is the Murray River, which rises in the Australian Alps and meets the sea at Lake Alexandrina. The state's low and unreliable rainfall has resulted in water from the Murray being piped over long distances to ensure the survival of many communities, including Adelaide. In fact, around 90% of South Australians depend either wholly or partly on the river for their water supply. The continuing deterioration of the Murray's water quality and flow rates is thus a major concern to the state.

INFORMATION

The South Australian Tourism Commission (SATC) and regional tourism associations produce an excellent range of regional brochures and newspapers. These are available from SATC travel centres, which can also supply tour and accommodation costs and so on, and make bookings. The central contact number for all SATC travel centres is ☎ 1300 366 770, or you can email them at sthaustour@tourism.sa.gov.au. Its Web site is www.tourism.sa.gov.au and its offices are located at:

Queensland
(☎ 07-3229 8533)
Level 1, 245 Albert St, Brisbane 4000
South Australia
(☎ 8303 2033)
1 King William St, Adelaide 8000
Western Australia
(☎ 08-9481 1268)
1st Floor, Wesley Centre, 93 William St, Perth 6000

Information SA (☎ 8204 1900, fax 8204 1909), at 77 Grenfell St Adelaide, is a handy resource centre with brochures and other publications covering a vast range of topics – from museums, industries and legislation to cycling and trekking routes. It's open weekdays only from 9 am to 5 pm.

NATIONAL PARKS

South Australia has over 300 conservation reserves including national parks, recreation parks, game reserves and regional reserves. In fact, around 22% of the state's

SOUTH AUSTRALIA

land area is under some form of official conservation management. The largest areas are in the outback – some parks here consist entirely of vast salt pans, but there are many with a range of ecosystems and great scenery. Two of Australia's better-known national parks are in SA – Flinders Chase National Park on Kangaroo Island and the Flinders Ranges National Park in (where else?) the Flinders Ranges.

The day-to-day management of the state's conservation areas is handled by National Parks & Wildlife SA (a division of the Department of Environment, Heritage & Aboriginal Affairs). For general information, contact the Environment Shop (☎ 8204 1910, fax 8204 1919) at 77 Grenfell St in Adelaide. It's open weekdays only from 9 am to 5 pm.

If you intend visiting the state's parks you should inquire about the Four Week Holiday Parks Pass ($15). It covers the cost of entry and camping permits at a number of the most popular parks, excluding the desert parks (you need a separate pass for these areas). The Environment Shop has details on the various passes and their retail outlets – they also sell them.

ACTIVITIES
Bushwalking
Close to Adelaide there are many walks in the Mt Lofty Ranges, including those at Belair National Park, Cleland and Morialta conservation parks and the Para Wirra recreation park.

In the Flinders Ranges there are excellent walks in the Mt Remarkable and Flinders Ranges national parks, and further north in the Gammon Ranges National Park and adjoining Arkaroola-Mt Painter Wildlife Sanctuary. The 1200km **Heysen Trail** winds south from near Blinman, in the central Flinders Ranges, to Cape Jervis on the tip of the Fleurieu Peninsula.

Several bushwalking clubs in the Adelaide area organise weekend walks in the Mt Lofty and Flinders ranges, and a number of Adelaide operators offer guided walks. Good places for information are the outdoor shops on Rundle St, such as Paddy

---

Heysen Trail

One of the world's great long-distance walks, the Heysen Trail, extends over 1200km from Cape Jervis at the tip of the Fleurieu Peninsula to Parachilna Gorge in the northern Flinders Ranges. En route it travels along the Mt Lofty Ranges, through the Barossa Valley wine region and the old copper town of Burra, then heads into the Flinders Ranges. Here it scales Mt Remarkable and Mt Brown before continuing on to Wilpena Pound and beyond.

The trail was named in honour of Sir Hans Heysen (1877-1968), South Australia's best-known landscape artist. Sir Hans emigrated to Adelaide from Germany at the age of seven, and sold his first painting nine years later. Unlike many artists he became famous in his own lifetime, winning a number of prestigious awards. His favourite subjects were the Australian gum tree and the rural landscapes of the Mt Lofty and Flinders ranges.

Overall, the Heysen Trail presents a remarkable challenge, but you can also follow short sections on day trips or longer. Due to fire restrictions, the trail is closed between November and April.

Good maps detailing each of the 15 sections are available for $6.50 from Information SA and the Environment Shop, both at 77 Grenfell St in Adelaide. Other city outlets include the outdoor gear shops on Rundle St, and speciality map shops.

Pallin (☎ 8232 3155) and the Scout Outdoor Centre (☎ 8223 8224).

Women of the Wilderness (☎ 8227 0155) at the YWCA, 17 Hutt St, runs courses and organises outdoor activities for women, such as bushwalking, canoeing and surfing.

Water Sports
Canoeing & Sailing The Murray River and the Coorong (south of Murray Bridge) are popular for canoeing trips. Visitors can hire equipment and join trips organised by canoeing associations. There is good sailing

all along Adelaide's shoreline in the Gulf St Vincent, where there are a number of sailing clubs.

Diving There are some good diving possibilities around Adelaide. Off Glenelg there's an artificial reef centred on a sunken barge; at Port Noarlunga (18km south) you can shore dive on the Marine Reserve or boat dive on the *HA Lum*, a sunken fishing boat.

Despite the effects of stormwater run-off, the reefs off Snapper Point and Aldinga (42 and 43km south respectively) are still good. You can snorkel at Snapper Point, but the Aldinga Reef is better for scuba diving.

At Second Valley (65km south of Adelaide) the water is generally clear and the caves are accessible, while 23km further on at Rapid Bay you can dive from the jetty and see abundant marine life. Other good areas include most jetties around the Yorke Peninsula, the reefs off Port Lincoln and the wrecks and drop-offs around Kangaroo Island. Any of the scuba-gear shops in Adelaide will be able to give you pointers on places to dive around the state.

Swimming & Surfing There are fine swimming beaches right along the South Australian coast. The Adelaide suburbs of Seacliff, Brighton, Somerton, Glenelg, West Beach, Henley Beach, Grange, West Lakes, Semaphore, Glanville and Largs Bay all have popular city beaches. Further south there are several beaches with reasonable surf in the right conditions – Seaford and Southport have reliable if small waves. Skinny-dipping is permitted at Maslin Beach, 40km south of the city.

You have to get over to Pondalowie Bay on the Yorke Peninsula for the state's most reliable large waves. Other worthwhile surfing spots can be found along the Eyre Peninsula between Port Lincoln and the Ceduna area; Cactus Beach, near Penong west of Ceduna, is world-famous for its surf. Closer to Adelaide, and near Victor Harbor on the Fleurieu Peninsula, there's often good surf at Waitpinga Beach, Middleton and Port Elliot.

GETTING THERE & AWAY

See the Adelaide Getting There & Away section later for details on transport to SA. If you are travelling to WA you can't take honey, plants, fruit or vegetables past the Australia quarantine checkpoint at Border Village; there's a similar checkpoint at Ceduna for those heading east. If you're travelling to or from Victoria there are checkpoints on the Mallee Hwy at Pinnaroo and on the Sturt Hwy between Mildura and Renmark. There's another at Oodla-Wirra, on the Barrier Hwy from Broken Hill.

GETTING AROUND
Air

Kendell Airlines (book through Ansett on ☎ 13 1300) is the main regional operator with flights from Adelaide to Mt Gambier, Kangaroo Island, Port Lincoln, Ceduna, Coober Pedy and Broken Hill (in New South Wales (NSW)). See the air fares chart below for prices.

Bus

As well as the major interstate companies, services within the state are provided by

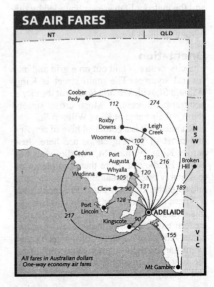

SA AIR FARES

NT — QLD

Coober Pedy — 112 — 274

Roxby Downs — Leigh Creek

Woomera — 100 — N S W

Ceduna — Port Augusta — 80 — 180 — 216 — Broken Hill

Wudinna — Whyalla — 105 — 120

Cleve — 90 — 131 — 189

Port Lincoln — 128

217

Kingscote — 90 — ADELAIDE

155 — V I C

All fares in Australian dollars
One-way economy air fares

Mt Gambier

Premier Stateliner (☎ 8415 5555) and a handful of smaller local companies.

Train

Apart from suburban trains and several tourist trains, SA does not have any intrastate passenger trains. You can, however, get on and off the *Indian Pacific* (Sydney to Perth), *The Ghan* (Sydney and Melbourne to Alice Springs via Adelaide) and the *Overland* (Adelaide to Melbourne) at various points along the line (see Train in the Getting Around chapter, and Adelaide's Getting There & Away section later).

Adelaide

• postcode 5000   • pop 1,070,000

Adelaide is a solid, even gracious, city: when the early colonists built they generally used stone and plenty of style. The solidity goes further than architecture, however, as Adelaide is still very much an 'old money' place.

It's also civilised and calm in a way no other Australian capital city can match. What's more, it has a superb setting. The city centre is surrounded by green parkland and the metropolitan area is bounded by the hills of the Mt Lofty Ranges, which crowd it against the sea.

Orientation

The city centre is laid out on a grid and has several squares. The main street is King William St, with Victoria Square at the city's geographical centre. Most cross streets change their name at King William St.

Rundle Mall is a colourful hive of activity and most of the big shops are here. Just across King William St, Rundle Mall becomes Hindley St. Here there are plenty of reasonably priced restaurants and snack bars, and a number of glitzy bars and dance clubs.

These days, however, Hindley St is looking decidedly weary and Rundle St (the eastern extension of Rundle Mall) has become Adelaide's cosmopolitan heart and avant-garde artists' quarter. Here you'll find the best in al fresco dining, retro clothing and *haute grunge*.

The next street north of Hindley St is North Terrace. The casino and suburban train station are just to the west of King William St, and there's a string of magnificent public buildings, including the art gallery, museum, state library and university, to the east.

Continue north and you're in the North Parklands, with its Festival Centre; King William Rd then crosses the Torrens River into North Adelaide.

Maps You'll find a comprehensive selection of maps at Mapland, 300 Richmond Rd, Netley and, in the city, at the Land Information Centre (25 Pirie St) and The Map Shop (16A Peel St).

Information

Tourist Offices The SATC travel centre (☎ 8303 2033, 1300 366 770) is at 1 King William St on the corner of North Terrace. It's open weekdays from 8.45 am to 5 pm, and on weekends and public holidays from 9 am to 2 pm. The centre has a wide range of information specific to tourism, including regional brochures.

Another good source is the information booth at the King William St end of Rundle Mall.

Money There are plenty of banks and Automatic Teller Machines (ATMs) in the city centre. Adelaide's out-of-hours options for changing foreign currencies include American Express at 13 Grenfell St, and the general office on the fifth floor of the Myer department store on Rundle Mall. The latter has the best hours – from 9 am to 5 pm Monday to Saturday (to 9 pm Friday), and from 11 am to 5 pm on Sunday.

Post & Communications The main post office is in the city centre on King William St. It opens weekdays from 8 am to 6 pm weekdays and Saturday morning, and has public telephones (coin and card), a public fax service, and poste restante and philatelic sections.

Adelaide has a couple of Internet cafes. Most central is the Ngapartji Multimedia

Centre (☎ 8232 0839) at 211 Rundle St. Open daily, it has 20 terminals and charges $5 for 30 minutes. There's free Internet access at the State Library (see the Libraries entry). In fact, every public library in the state has free Internet access – you don't have to be a member, but you do have to book.

Internet Resources Useful Web sites include the SATC's (www.tourism.sa.gov.au), which (naturally) has plenty of tourist information. The state government's site (www.sa.gov.au) is more comprehensive, and www.saweb.com.au/saweb/directory/index.html is a search engine for South Australian sites.

Bookshops Adelaide has numerous good new and second-hand bookshops. Imprint Booksellers, at 80 Hindley St, has quality literature, biographies and a gay and lesbian section. Mary Martin's Bookshop, an Adelaide institution, is at 249 Rundle St East, while Dymocks is at 136 Rundle Mall and Angus & Robertson is next door at No 138. Try the excellent Europa Bookshop, at 238 Rundle St East, for its selection of foreign-language novels, travel books and maps.

The Royal Automobile Association of South Australia (RAA) has an excellent little bookshop with a good selection of titles including travel within the state, bushwalking, natural and social history, and Aboriginal culture.

The Conservation Council, at 120 Wakefield St, has a good selection of books on conservation and environmental issues.

Murphy Sisters Bookshop, at 240 The Parade, Norwood, specialises in feminist and lesbian works, and has a section on Aboriginal studies. The sisters also own Sisters by the Sea, Shop 1, 14 Semaphore Rd, Semaphore.

For cheap second-hand books try the Central and Orange Lane markets (see the Markets section for details).

Libraries As well as a huge selection of books and other printed material, the State Library complex on North Terrace has interesting exhibitions and displays including memorabilia of local cricket legend Sir Donald Bradman. Its newspaper reading room has publications from around the world – these come by surface mail, so don't expect yesterday's (or even last week's) editions. There's also free Internet access, but you have to book (☎ 8207 7248).

The library opens from 9.30 am till 8 pm weekdays (5 pm on Thursday) and noon until 5 pm weekends. It's closed on public holidays.

Cultural Centres If you're interested in learning more about the first South Australians, Tandanya at 253 Grenfell St is an Aboriginal cultural institute containing galleries, art and craft workshops, performance spaces, a cafe and a good gift shop. It opens daily from 10 am to 5 pm; admission is $4.

Women Travellers The Women's Information Service (☎ 8303 0590) at Station Arcade, 136 North Terrace (opposite the train station), operates weekdays from 8 am to 6 pm and Saturday from 9 am to 5 pm. It can give information, advice and referrals on just about anything of interest to women.

Gay & Lesbian Travellers Gayline (☎ 1800 182 233, 8362 3223) operates nightly between 7 and 10 pm, and on weekends from 2 to 5 pm. It offers counselling and general information, including social activities and gay-friendly service providers.

Adelaide Gay Times (☎ 8232 1544) publishes *Adelaide gt*, a fortnightly newspaper that makes an excellent all-round reference for travelling gays and lesbians. Call them to get details of outlets near you. They also publish the useful *Lesbian & Gay Adelaide Map*, showing venues and services of interest in the city area.

Disabled Travellers The Disability Information & Resource Centre (☎ 8223 7522/TTY 8223 7579), at 195 Gilles St, can provide advice on accommodation venues, tourist destinations and travel agencies that cater for people with disabilities.

SOUTH AUSTRALIA

CENTRAL ADELAIDE

PLACES TO STAY
1 Greenways Apartments
19 Hyatt Regency Adelaide
21 Princes Arcade Motel
41 Austral Hotel
45 Hindley Parkroyal Hotel
47 City Central Motel
49 Holiday Inn Apartments
54 YMCA
58 Cannon St Backpackers
59 Cumberland Arms Hotel
61 Adelaide City Backpackers;
    Adelaide Travellers Inn
62 Sunny's Backpackers Hostel
63 Backpack Australia
65 Metropolitan Hotel
68 Hilton International
    Adelaide
79 Adelaide Backpackers Inn
81 East Park Lodge
85 Adelaide YHA Hostel
86 Clarice Motel
87 Adelaide Backpackers Hostel;
    Rucksackers Riders
    International
88 Apartments on the Park
90 Moore's Brecknock Hotel

PLACES TO EAT
9 Union Complex
24 Pasta Palace
25 Ceylon Hut;
    Fast Eddy's Café
26 Parlamento
28 Terrace Eats
29 London Tavern
30 Food Affair
31 Amalfi
33 Cafe Tapas
36 Alfresco Gelateria; Piatto;
    Scoozi
37 Boltz Cafe
39 Raj Tandoor
46 Pancake Kitchen;
    Ming's Chinese Restaurant
48 Food 4 Life
53 The Volga Restaurant
70 Chinatown
71 Rock Lobster Cafe
73 Ming Palace
74 Paul's
76 Star of Siam
75 Mamma Getta Restaurant
82 La Trattona
84 Hawker's Corner

OTHER
2 Light's Vision
3 Old Adelaide Gaol
4 Elder Park
6 Adelaide Festival Centre
7 Government House
8 Adelaide Railway Station
9 Migration Museum
10 University of Adelaide
11 Royal Adelaide Hospital
12 University of South Australia
13 University of South Australia
14 South Australian Museum
15 State Library of SA;
    Royal SA Society of Arts
16 Parliament House
17 Old Parliament House
18 Adelaide Casino
20 Newmarket Hotel
22 Lion Arts Centre
23 Holy Trinity Church
27 STA Travel Centre
32 Paddy Pallin
34 Ayers Historic House Museum
35 Exeter Hotel
38 Universal Wine Bar
40 Ngapartji Multimedia Centre
    (Internet Access)
42 City Arcade
43 American Express
44 Edmund Wright House
50 Information SA;
    The Environment Shop
51 RAA
52 Tandanya (Cultural Centre)
55 Adelaide Town Hall
56 Old Treasury Building
57 Main Post Office
60 St Mary's Convent
64 Central Bus Station
66 Conservation Council
67 St Francis Xavier
    Cathedral
69 Central Market
72 Mars Bar
77 Supreme Court
78 Magistrates Court
80 Earl of Aberdeen Hotel
83 YHA office
89 Disability Information Centre

Medical Services The Traveller's Medical & Vaccination Centre (☎ 8212 7522) is at 29 Gilbert Place. It opens daily except Sunday at 9 am, closing at 1 pm on Thursday and Saturday, 5 pm on Tuesday and Friday, and 7 pm on Monday and Wednesday.

Emergency The emergency number for ambulance, fire and police is ☎ 000. Crisis Care (☎ 13 1611) offers an after hours emergency counselling and referral service.

Useful Organisations The RAA (☎ 8202 4500) is at 41 Hindmarsh Square. The Youth Hostel Association (YHA) office (☎ 8231 5583) is at 38 Sturt St.

SA-FM, a local radio station, has a 'community switchboard', which provides current information on everything from forthcoming concerts, art shows and festivals, to fire ban days, surfing conditions and beach reports: call ☎ 8271 1277 daily between 9 am and 5 pm.

Museums

On North Terrace, the free **South Australian Museum** is an Adelaide landmark with huge whale skeletons in the front window. Although primarily a natural history museum, it has a large and superb display featuring the Ngarrindjeri people of the lower Murray and Coorong – included is the story of Ngurunderi (a Dreamtime spirit ancestor) and how the Murray was created. There are also good coffee and souvenir shops. The museum opens daily from 10 am to 5 pm; admission is free.

The excellent **Migration Museum**, at 82 Kintore Ave, is dedicated to the migrants who came from all over the world to make SA their home. Many interesting displays explain how the state's rich multicultural society has evolved. It's open weekdays from 10 am to 5 pm, and weekends and public holidays from 1 to 5 pm.

The **Museum of Classical Archaeology**, on the 1st floor of the Mitchell Building (in the University of Adelaide grounds on North Terrace) has a small but representative collection of antiquities dating from the 3rd millennium BC (Egypt and Mesopotamia) to the European Middle Ages. It's open weekdays from noon to 3 pm, with a short recess in summer. Admission is free.

The **Maritime Museum**, 126 Lipson St, Port Adelaide, has several old ships, including the *Nelcebee*, the third-oldest ship on Lloyd's register. There's also an old lighthouse and a computer register of early migrants. It's open daily from 10 am to 5 pm; admission is $8.50. Bus Nos 151 or 153 will get you there from North Terrace, or you can take the train.

Next door, and open the same hours, the **Port Dock Station Railway Museum** features a huge collection of railway memorabilia. Admission is $6.

The **Investigator Science & Technology Centre** ($7.50), at the Wayville Showgrounds off Goodwood Rd, takes an entertaining look at science. It is usually open daily from 10 am to 5 pm, but may be closed while exhibitions are changed (check first on ☎ 8410 1115). To get there, take bus No 212, 214, 216, 296 or 297 from King William St.

Also interesting is the **Old Adelaide Gaol** (in use from 1841 to 1988), at Gaol Rd, Thebarton. On weekdays you can do self-guided tours ($5) between 11 am and 4 pm; guided tours ($6) are conducted on Sunday and public holidays between 11.30 am and 3.30 pm. Features include the hanging tower and various gaol artefacts.

Art Galleries

On North Terrace, next to the museum, the free **Art Gallery of South Australia** has a marvellous collection of Australian and overseas works – its display of Australian art is the world's largest. The gallery opens from 10 am to 5 pm daily, and there are guided tours on weekdays at 11 am and 2 pm, weekends at 3 pm. There's a good art bookshop on the premises.

The gallery of the **Royal South Australian Society of the Arts,** in the Institute Building on the corner of North Terrace and Kintore Ave, hosts major exhibitions. It's open weekdays from 11 am to 5 pm and weekends from 2 to 5 pm, and admission is free.

Adelaide Walking Tour

There are several good walks in and around the city centre. This tour, of about 4km, takes you on a loop starting at the intersection of King William Rd and North Terrace. It includes solidly evocative reminders of Adelaide's more halcyon past, as well as the botanical gardens and attractive parkland along the River Torrens. Most places mentioned here are described in more detail elsewhere in this chapter. Allow a full day for more than just a quick look.

One of the city's major thoroughfares, **North Terrace**, is a broad boulevard lined with some of South Australia's finest public buildings. The earliest were constructed during the 1830s, but most are a legacy of the copper, wheat and wool booms that took place from the early 1840s through to around 1880.

Right on the corner with King William Rd, and outside the wrought-iron gates of **Government House** (1838–40), is the **South African War Memorial** with its impressive statue. Heading east from here you'll see the stone wall surrounding the grounds of Government House on your left; on the right, the **London Tavern** is a great place to enjoy a refreshing drink at the end of the tour.

On the near corner with Kintore Ave is the **National War Memorial**. The **Institute Building** on the opposite corner dates from 1836, which makes it the oldest building on North Terrace; it houses major art exhibitions as well as memorabilia associated with cricketing legend Sir Donald Bradman. It's a few steps down the avenue to the **State Library** and a few more to the excellent **Migration Museum**.

Continuing along North Terrace, the **South Australian Museum** has fine Aboriginal and natural history displays; if you're tired already there's a very pleasant coffee shop here. Next door is the **Art Gallery of South Australia**, where you'll have no trouble filling a couple of hours admiring its many magnificent exhibits.

Keep walking east and you pass the imposing facade of the **University of Adelaide**, founded in 1874 with a grant made from the profits of copper mining. It was the first university in Australia to admit women to degree courses. The much smaller **University of South Australia** is next door on the corner with leafy Frome Rd. If you want, you can shorten the tour here by turning left (north) on Frome Rd to the **Zoological Gardens**.

A little farther along North Terrace and on the left is **Ayers Historic House** (1846). The elegant bluestone home of early premier Sir Henry Ayers is now part museum, part restaurant. Continue on this southern side to the grand old **Botanic Hotel** at the corner with East Terrace.

The main gates to the 20 hectare **Adelaide Botanic Garden** are on North Terrace, directly opposite the Botanic Hotel. From here, a network of paths links various highlights including a **tropical rainforest conservatory** and a **historic palm house** (1877). There's also a good kiosk where you can grab a drink and sandwich.

Head generally north through the botanic garden to **Plane Tree Drive**, then turn left. Leave the road at the elbow bend and continue straight ahead (west) to Frome Rd, where you turn right. The **zoo entrance** is just in front by the River Torrens.

From the zoo, pleasant walks meander through the parks and gardens that line both banks of the river as far as **King William Rd**. Having reached this busy thoroughfare you turn left (south) past the **Festival Centre** to North Terrace, and come to the end of this tour.

Grand City Buildings

Close to the city centre, **Ayers Historic House** (1846), 288 North Terrace, was the residence of Sir Henry Ayers, seven times SA's premier. The elegant bluestone mansion is open Tuesday to Friday from 10 am to 4 pm, and weekends and public holidays from 1 to 4 pm. Admission is $5 and there are tours (bookings ☎ 8223 1234).

At 59 King William St, **Edmund Wright House** (1876) was originally constructed for the Bank of South Australia in an elaborate Renaissance style with intricate decoration. It's open daily from 9 am to 4.30 pm and admission is free, but you can't really see much apart from the old banking chamber. You'll also find the State History Centre here, with good information on state historical societies.

The imposing **Adelaide Town Hall**, built between 1863 and 1866 in 16th century Renaissance style, looks out onto King William St between Flinders and Pirie Sts. The faces of Queen Victoria and Prince Albert are carved into the facade. There are free tours on Tuesday, Wednesday and Thursday (bookings ☎ 8203 7563). The **main post office** building across the road is almost as impressive.

Government House, on North Terrace, was built between 1838 and 1840, with further additions in 1855. It's not generally open to the public, but ring ☎ 8203 9800 for details of open days. The earliest section is one of the oldest buildings in Adelaide. **Parliament House**'s facade includes 10 marble Corinthian columns. Building commenced in 1883 but was not completed until 1939. When parliament isn't sitting it is open to the public Monday to Friday at 10 am and 2 pm (☎ 8237 9100).

Holy Trinity Church, also on North Terrace, was the first Anglican church in the state; it was built in 1838. Other early churches are **St Francis Xavier Cathedral**, on Wakefield St, (around 1856) and **St Peter's Cathedral**, in Pennington Terrace, North Adelaide (1869-76).

St Francis Xavier Cathedral is beside Victoria Square, where you will also find a number of other important early buildings: the **Magistrate's Court** (1847-50); the **Supreme Court** (1869); and the old **Treasury building** (1839), which has a small museum.

Festival Centre

The Adelaide Festival Centre is on King William St close to the Torrens River. Looking vaguely like a squared-off version of the Sydney Opera House, it performs a similar function, with a variety of auditoriums and theatres but a far greater range of activities.

While the centre is visually uninspiring, it does have a marvellous riverside setting; people picnic on the grass in front of the theatre and there are several places to eat. You can hire pedal boats nearby, or enjoy free concerts (see the Entertainment section) and exhibitions.

Botanic Garden & Other Parks

The central city is completely surrounded by green parkland. The Torrens River, itself bordered by park, separates Adelaide from North Adelaide, also surrounded by parkland.

On North Terrace, the 20 hectare **Adelaide Botanic Garden** has pleasant artificial lakes and is only a short stroll from the city centre. The gardens open weekdays from 8 am to sunset, and on weekends and public holidays from 9 am to sunset. Free guided tours taking about 1½ hours leave from the kiosk on Tuesday, Friday and Sunday at 10.30 am. A stunning conservatory ($3) which recreates a tropical rainforest environment is open from 10 am to 4 pm daily.

Rymill Park, in the East Parklands, has a boating lake and a 600m-long jogging track. The South Parklands contain the **Veale Gardens**, with streams and flowerbeds, and the Japanese **Himeji Gardens**. To the west are a number of sports grounds, while the **North Parklands** border the Torrens and surround North Adelaide. The **Adelaide Oval**, the site of interstate and international cricket matches, is north of the Torrens River in this area of the parklands.

Light's Vision

On Montefiore Hill, north of the city centre across the Torrens River, is a statue of Colonel William Light, Adelaide's founder. He's said to have stood here and mapped out his visionary plan. In the afternoon there's a nice view from here of the city's gleaming office towers rising above the trees, with the Adelaide Hills making a scenic backdrop.

Adelaide Zoo

On Frome Rd, the zoo holds about 1500 exotic and native mammals, birds and reptiles, and also has a children's zoo. Its South-East Asian rainforest exhibit is a major drawcard.

The zoo is open daily (including Christmas Day) from 9.30 am to 5 pm; admission is $10. A different way of getting there is to take a cruise on the *Popeye* ($5), which departs daily (weather permitting) every 20 minutes from Elder Park in front of the Festival Centre. You can also catch bus Nos 272 or 273 from Grenfell St (get off at stop 2) or take a pleasant walk along the Torrens from Elder Park.

Markets

Close to the centre of town, the Central Market, off Victoria Square between Grote and Gouger Sts, is a great place for self-catering travellers. You can buy fresh produce direct from the producer, so things are generally quite a bit cheaper than in the shops. It's open Tuesday (7 am to 5.30 pm), Thursday (11 am to 5.30 pm), Friday (7 am to 9 pm) and Saturday (7 am to 3 pm). The best time to get there for real bargains is just after lunch on Saturday, when unsold produce is disposed of at give-away prices.

The much smaller Orange Lane Market in Norwood is more casual and will appeal to those who lead alternative lifestyles – it's the place to go for Indian fabrics, second-hand clothing, massage, tarot readings, palmistry, remedies, bric-a-brac and junk. You'll find it on the corner of Edward St and Orange Lane (off Norwood Parade) on weekends and public holidays from 10 am to 6 pm.

Haigh's Chocolates

Haigh's is generally considered to make Australia's finest chocolates at its factory at 154 Greenhill Rd, Parkside, just south of the city. The visitor centre opens weekdays from 8.30 am to 5.30 pm, and Saturdays from 9.30 am to 4.45 pm; free tours run daily at 2.30 pm except Saturday.

To get there from the city, take bus Nos 190, 191, 191B or 192 from King William St. Get off at stop 1 on Unley Rd, just across Greenhill Rd.

Suburban Historic Buildings

On Jetty St, Grange (west of the city centre), is **Sturt's Cottage**, the home of the early Australian explorer. It's open Friday to Sunday and public holidays from 1 to 5 pm (4 pm in winter) ($3). Take bus No 130 or 137 from Grenfell St and get off at stop 29A.

In Springfield (7km south-east of the city), magnificent **Carrick Hill**, at 46 Carrick Hill Drive, is built in the style of an Elizabethan manor house and set in an English-style garden. It's open Wednesday to Sunday and public holidays from 10 am to 5 pm ($8), and there are free guided tours at 11.30 am and 2.30 pm. Catch bus No 171 from King William St and get off at stop 16.

Mother Mary MacKillop Sites

This Australian saint-to-be lived in Adelaide for 16 years and there are a number of sites associated with her (for more information about Mother Mary MacKillop see the following boxed text). They include **St Mary's Convent**, at 253 Franklin St, Adelaide, where she was excommunicated, and **St Ignatius Church**, on Queen St, Norwood, where she assisted at mass during her excommunication period.

Another is **St Joseph's Convent**, at 286 Portrush Rd, Kensington where you find the **Mary MacKillop Centre**. The centre has historic photos and artefacts, as well as a leaflet describing eight significant pilgrimage sites. It's open weekdays (except Wednesday) from 10 am to 4 pm and Sunday from 1 to 4 pm.

Glenelg

Glenelg has Adelaide's most popular beach, and is one of the state's favourite summer seaside holiday destinations. For this reason there's a large choice of accommodation, including a couple of backpacker hostels.

There's a tourist centre (☎ 8294 5833 or 1800 500 054) behind the town hall, close to the jetty. In the same premises, Beach Hire rents out deckchairs, umbrellas, wave skis and body boards; it's open from September to April only and the opening times vary, but if it's sunny, it'll be open.

On MacFarlane St, the **Old Gum Tree** marks the spot where the proclamation of

A Champion of the Poor

Mary MacKillop (or McKillop) was born of Scottish immigrant parents in Fitzroy, Melbourne, in 1842 and became a schoolteacher at the age of 21. Three years later she moved to Penola in South Australia (SA) to take charge of a Catholic school that had been taken over by the Jesuit priest Father Julian Tenison Woods. At that time the district had many poor and struggling families whose children were denied an education. Mary and Father Woods agreed that all children, regardless of their parents' social or financial position, should have the right to attend school. So they established Australia's first 'free' school, where fees were paid only by those who could afford to pay.

The new school was opened in 1866, jointly founded by MacKillop and Father Woods. The Order of the Sisters of St Joseph of the Sacred Heart was the first Australian order of nuns whose primary purpose was to educate and care for the poor.

Mary took her vows in Adelaide on 25 August 1867. A year later, there were 30 sisters in SA running eight Josephite schools, an orphanage and a home for 'fallen' women. The following year they opened their first school in Queensland. These remarkable achievements were testament to the vision and determination of the order's co-founders.

Unfortunately, however, Mary's single-mindedness soon brought her into conflict with SA's Catholic religious hierarchy. Several previous allies turned against her, and there were a number of complaints that the sisters were incompetent. It didn't help that one of her worst enemies was the Bishop of Adelaide's most influential advisor.

Finally, in September 1871, the attacks culminated in Mary's excommunication and the virtual disbandment of the Josephites. Cleared of any wrongdoing by a Commission of Inquiry, she was reinstated two years later by Pope Pius IX, who gave his approval of the Josephites.

Despite this happy outcome, Mary continued to find powerful enemies among the colonial clergy, but at the same time she had many influential friends both there and in the wider community. This was partly due to the egalitarian spirit she imparted to the Order – every person should be respected and valued as an individual regardless of colour, creed or social status.

By 1890, the Josephites had established schools or charitable homes in most Australian colonies and New Zealand (NZ), and Mary's health was beginning to suffer from years of overwork and worry. In 1891 she almost died from a severe case of bronchitis. More bouts of ill health followed until, while in NZ in 1902, she suffered a disabling stroke. She died in Sydney in 1909, aged 67 years.

By the time of Mary's death, the Order had founded 117 schools and 11 charitable homes, mainly in Australia and NZ. Many of these institutions are still operating today, while around 1300 Josephite sisters continue the Order's work of providing education and social services to anyone in need.

The case for Mary to be declared 'blessed' (or beatified) was first made in 1925, but it was not until 1973 that her cause was formally introduced by the Vatican. Her beatification was finally approved by Pope John Paul II in 1993 – this being the first of two stages on the path to sainthood. It is a fitting tribute to an outstanding Australian.

South Australia was read in 1836. Governor Hindmarsh and the first colonists landed on the beach nearby.

On the south-west bank of the Patawalonga (River Sturt) across the water from

Glenelg Scuba Diving is a full-size replica of **HMS Buffalo**, which carried the original free settlers of Adelaide out from England in 1836. The original *Buffalo* was built in 1813 in India and wrecked off New Zealand in

1840. On board, you'll find an upmarket seafood restaurant.

A vintage tram runs from Victoria Square in the city centre right to Glenelg Beach, taking about 25 minutes (see the following Getting Around section for details).

Ice Skating & Indoor Skiing

Adelaide's ice-skating rink at 23 East Terrace, Thebarton, is open daily. There are two ice rinks and a 150m-long slope surfaced with artificial snow where you can ski, toboggan and snowboard. Take bus Nos 151 or 153 from North Terrace and get off at stop 2.

Organised Tours

There is a huge variety of tours available in and around Adelaide. Most of the hostels have travel or tour agencies specialising in backpacker deals.

For $23 you can get a day pass on the Adelaide Explorer (☎ 8364 1933), a road-registered tram replica, which does a continuous circuit of a number of attractions, including Glenelg. The tour takes 2¾ hours and you can get on and off en route; daily departures are at 9 and 10.20 am, and 12.15, 1.35 and 3 pm, and they leave from 38 King William St.

Premier Stateliner (☎ 8415 5566) has a range of half-day tours in luxury coaches for $25 which include the city sights, Hahndorf and the Cleland Wildlife Park (both in the Adelaide Hills). They also have reasonably priced day tours, including the Barossa Valley and Murray River.

Busway (☎ 8262 6900) has a very good daily Barossa winery tour, including lunch and a visit to four/six wineries for $35/45 ex-Adelaide. Prime Mini Tours (☎ 8293 4900) also does a good Barossa day tour (four wineries and lunch for $38). Groovy Grape (☎ 8395 4422) is another operator worth trying, while Ecotrek (☎ 8383 7198) and Rolling On (☎ 8358 2401) have cycling tours of the Barossa on weekends.

Bound-Away Tours (☎ 8371 3147) offers a day tour of the Adelaide Hills and Fleurieu Peninsula for $39, not including lunch. Among other highlights, you visit Hahndorf and a McLaren Vale winery. They also do a full-day trip to the Murray, including a six hour houseboat cruise with barbecue lunch ($74).

We've also had good reports on Bee-init Tours (☎ 8332 1401). Their offerings include a three hour 'city and hills' trip for $28 and a day trip to Victor Harbor and the Murray Mouth.

Further Afield Competition is fierce on the Kangaroo Island run. If you're short on time, Kangaroo Island Sealink (☎ 13 1301), the Penneshaw Youth Hostel (☎ 8553 1284) and Kangaroo Island Ferry Connections (☎ 8553 1233) have day tours ex-Adelaide from around $150. These options include the bus run to Cape Jervis and the ferry across to Penneshaw, and return.

For budget travellers wanting to stay longer, Daniel's Tours (☎ 1800 454 454; we've had several very good reports about this operator), the Penneshaw Youth Hostel and Kangaroo Island Ferry Connections have two-day packages ex-Adelaide from around $200. Kangaroo Island Air & Sea Adventures (☎ 8231 1744) in Adelaide has a range of packages.

There are several tours to the Flinders Ranges. Wallaby Tracks Adventure Tours (☎ 8648 6655) does two/three-day packages for $249/279 ex-Adelaide. Its trips include bush camping, visits to Aboriginal sites and a Wilpena Pound bushwalk.

Special Events

One of the nation's premier cultural events, the Adelaide Festival of the Arts, takes place in February/March of even-numbered years. Accommodation fills up and things generally go a little crazy as a vast horde of culture vultures descends on the city for a 17 day feast of drama, dance, music, literary readings and visual arts. Each festival features exclusive Australian and international performances, and has several world premieres. For information, contact the Festival Centre (☎ 8216 4444, fax 8216 4455, ausfest@adelaide.on.net).

The Adelaide Fringe, which takes place at the same time, celebrates innovation in the arts. Once a relatively minor event, the

Fringe is now just as big as the Adelaide Festival of the Arts. It's possibly even more popular – in 1998, 335 companies from 14 countries performed or exhibited their work to an attendance of 857,000. Contact the Fringe on ☎ 8231 7760, fax 8232 5080, buzz@adelaidefringe.com.au.

Also huge is the WOMADelaide festival of world music and dance, which happens in Botanic Park over three days and nights in February of odd-numbered years. Check what's coming on ☎ 8271 1488, fax 8271 9905, apadmin@artsprojects.com.au.

Places to Stay

Many caravan park, hotel and motel prices rise between Christmas and the end of January, when accommodation is extremely scarce – some also put their prices up in other school holiday periods. Unless otherwise stated, all prices given here are off-peak.

Places to Stay – Budget

Camping There are quite a few caravan parks around Adelaide. The following are within 10km of the city centre – check the tourist office for others. All prices given are for two people.

Adelaide Caravan Park (☎ 8363 1566, *Bruton St, Hackney*) is 2km north-east of Adelaide and has on-site vans from $38, cabins from $58 and camp sites from $20.

Windsor Gardens Caravan Park (☎ 8261 1091, 78 Windsor Grove, Windsor Gardens) is 7km north-east of Adelaide. Camp sites are from $10 and cabins cost $35 ($50 for three or four adults).

At the outstanding *West Beach Caravan Park* (☎ 8356 7654, Military Rd, West Beach), 2km north of Glenelg, camp sites start at $14, on-site vans $38 and cabins $53.

Marineland Holiday Village (☎ 8353 2655, Military Rd, West Beach) has two-bedroom villas for $95, two-bedroom units for $75 and cabins from $49. There are no camp sites.

Hostels There are a number of backpacker hostels, with the standard varying from excellent to ordinary. Competition is fierce, and as a result all sorts of freebies (free tours, free

breakfasts, free apple pie, free coffee and so forth) are offered to tempt you through the door, particularly in the winter off season. Almost all can book tours for you.

City Most hostels offer a free pick-up/drop off service from the airport, bus station or train station. Several are within easy walking distance of the bus station on Franklin St.

When you leave the terminal, turn left onto Franklin St and on the next corner you'll find *Sunny's Backpackers Hostel* (☎ 1800 225 725, 139 Franklin St). Dorm beds are priced from $15 and twin share/doubles are $17 per person; off-street parking is available. There's a licensed travel agent on the premises (open at 6 am). Parties are discouraged – there's a backpacker hotel nearby (the Hampshire Hotel) if you feel like raging.

Right opposite the bus station, the large (150 beds) and somewhat cavernous *Cannon St Backpackers* (☎ 8410 1218, 1800 069 731, 110 Franklin St) has bunk beds from $12 and singles/doubles for $28/34. It isn't what you'd call intimate, but it's clean and friendly and has good facilities, including undercover parking, cheap meals, a popular bar and a licensed travel agency. You can also hire bicycles for $12 a day.

Backpack Australia (☎ 1800 804 133, bpa_adelaide@hotmail.com, 128 Grote St) is about 50m from the Central Market. Dorm beds cost from $14, single rooms are $17 and twins and doubles are $15 per person, but facilities are cramped. The owners of this hotel also own the nearby Hampshire Hotel, which has some memorable parties – stay at the hostel rather than the hotel if you want a quiet time.

The comfortable *Cumberland Arms Hotel* (☎ 1800 355 599, 205 Waymouth St) has a variety of options, from $12 in an 11 bed dorm to $16 per person in a double room. There is no kitchen, but cheap meals are available in the bar.

Just around the corner, *Adelaide City Backpackers* (☎ 8212 2668, 239 Franklin St) is in a lovely old two storey house. The dorms are reasonably spacious, if gloomy, with bunk beds from $15; private rooms cost from $20 per person. It has an appealing bar, but parties are not encouraged (there are pubs nearby). You can get cheap meals and there's a pleasant outdoor area to eat them in.

Most of the other hostels are clustered in the south-eastern corner of the city centre. You can get there on bus Nos 191 or 192 from Pulteney St or take any bus going to the South Terrace area (Nos 171 and 172 to Hutt St; 201 to 203 to the corner of King William St and South Terrace), although it's not really that far to walk.

The very pleasant and well appointed *Adelaide YHA Hostel* (☎ 8223 6007, adelyha@ chariot.net.au, 290 Gilles St) has dorm beds for $14 and twin rooms for $42 for members (linen extra). The reception is closed daily between 11.30 am and 4 pm. In terms of facilities and standards this is one of the best – if not *the* best – of Adelaide's hostels. There's a tour office and limited off-street parking.

Nearby is the *Adelaide Backpackers Hostel* (☎ 8223 5680, 1800 677 351, 263 Gilles St) where dorm beds cost from $14, and double rooms are $32; some rooms have air-con and others ceiling fans. Bicycles are for hire at $9 for a half day.

Right next door, *Rucksackers Riders International* (☎ 8232 0823, 257 Gilles St) is very popular with Japanese motorcyclists and bicycle travellers. The rooms in this attractive 110-year-old bluestone villa are heated day and night in winter; dorm beds cost from $12; twin rooms from $14 per person.

Two streets closer to the city centre, the *Adelaide Backpackers Inn* (☎ 8223 6635, 1800 247 725, abackinn@tne.net.au, 112 Carrington St) is a converted pub with dorm beds from $15. Their annexe across the road at No 109 is more upmarket, with a good kitchen and small but comfortable single/ double/triple rooms for $25/40/45. There's a licensed travel agent on the premises, and limited off-street parking.

Next door, the *Adelaide Travellers Inn* (☎ 8232 5330, 1800 633 747, 112 Carrington St) has been getting some repairs and renovations in recent times. It's another popular place with Japanese visitors. Dorm beds are $11, double and twin rooms are $15 per person, and there is a travel agency and limited off-street parking.

The three storey *East Park Lodge* (☎ 8223 1228, 1800 643 606, eastpark@dove.net.au, 341 Angas St) was built 90 years ago as a Salvation Army hostel for young country ladies. The building is labyrinthine, but it has good facilities (including car, motorcycle, mountain bike, canoe and windsurfer hire, and a small in-ground swimming pool). It enjoys the nicest location of any of Adelaide's hostels, with the leafy East Parklands just a few steps away. Dorm beds cost $14 and rooms are $25/35.

The *YMCA* (☎ 8223 1611, adelaidey@ ymcasthaust.asn.au, 76 Flinders St) is more central and takes guests of either sex. This is another good hostel, with dorms costing $15 and singles/twins $25/35 (members get a 10% discount). There are gyms and squash courts on the premises and you can book into the hostel 24 hours a day.

Glenelg There are a couple of hostels near the beach in Glenelg. The friendly *Glenelg Beach Resort* (☎ 8376 0007, 1800 066 422, info@glenelgbeachresort.com.au, 7 Moseley St) is just around the corner from the tram terminus. It has dorm beds (not bunks) from $13 and private rooms with fridges for $22/32 a single/double. The kitchen is pokey, but there's a cheap licensed cafe on the premises. It's a good place for entertainment with its public bar, live acts and games area.

Hotels The following provide basic pub-style accommodation with common facilities.

The *Metropolitan Hotel* (☎ 8231 5471, 46 Grote St) is opposite the Central Market. It charges $20 per person.

The *Austral Hotel* (☎ 8223 4660, 205 Rundle St) has rooms for $25/35. There's a trendy bar downstairs and several good restaurants, cafes and bars nearby.

Moore's Brecknock Hotel (☎ 8231 5467, 410 King William St) has rooms for $30/50, including a light breakfast. This is a popular Irish pub, with Irish folk groups performing on Friday nights.

Holiday Flats & Apartments There are many holiday flats and serviced apartments; most quote weekly rather than daily rates.

The *Glenelg Seaway Apartments* (☎ 8295 8503, 18 Durham St), about a minute's walk from the Glenelg tram stop, offers backpacker rooms with kitchen for $30 per person; its self-contained apartments are $50 off-peak ($60 peak) for couples. This place is good value and the owner, Vladimir, is very friendly and helpful. Off-street parking is available.

Colleges At the University of Adelaide, *St Ann's College* (☎ 8267 1478) operates as a hostel from the second week in December to the end of January; beds are $16 ($20 if you need linen). At other colleges, accommodation generally includes meals and is much more expensive.

Places to Stay – Mid-Range

Hotels & Motels The *St Vincent* pub-hotel (☎ 8294 4377, 28 Jetty Rd), near the tram terminus at Glenelg, charges from $33/50 for singles/twins with shared facilities ($45/65 for singles/doubles with private facilities). These rates include a light breakfast.

The *City Central Motel* (☎ 8231 4049, 23 Hindley St) has small rooms, but they're clean and comfortable. Singles/doubles cost $52/59, and off-street parking can be arranged.

A little further from the action, the *Princes Arcade Motel* (☎ 8231 9524, 262-266 Hindley St) has basic units from $45/50. Off-street parking is available.

The *Clarice Motel* (☎ 8223 3560, 220 Hutt St) has basic twin rooms with shared facilities for $28/45, and motel units for $49/59/69; prices include a light breakfast.

In a grand old town house opposite a park, the *Princes Lodge Motel* (☎ 8267 5566, 73 Lefevre Terrace), in North Adelaide, has pleasant rooms from $30/58, including a light breakfast. It's within walking distance of the city, and handy to the restaurants and cafes on O'Connell and Melbourne Sts.

Festival Lodge (☎ 8212 7877, 140 North Terrace), opposite the casino, has rooms from $68/80. There's no on-site parking, but the motel negotiates reduced rates with a nearby car park.

Although there are motels all over Adelaide, it's worth noting that there's a 'motel alley' along Glen Osmond Rd, leading into the city centre from the south-east. This is quite a busy road so some places are noisy. Worth mentioning is *Powell's Court* (☎ 8271 7033, 2 Glen Osmond Rd), in Parkside, about 2km from the city. One-bedroom units cost $52/58/68/78, and there's a three bedroom unit sleeping up to nine – it costs $120 for the first six people and $5 per extra adult. All units have kitchens.

Holiday Flats & Apartments In North Adelaide and close to the inner city, *Greenways Apartments* (☎ 8267 5903, bpsgways@camtech.net.au, 45 King William Rd) has basic but comfortable one, two and three-bedroom apartments. For two people, a one bedroom unit costs $77 per night up to three nights ($73 after three nights, $70 after seven nights).

Apartments on the Park (☎ 8223 0500, 1800 882 774, 274 South Terrace, reservations@majesticapartments.com.au) is a more upmarket place diagonally across from the Himeji Gardens in the South Parkland. Studios are $99 and two-bedroom apartments are $120 – both prices are for singles and doubles.

Places to Stay – Top End

Hotels All of Adelaide's major hotels offer a variety of rates depending on factors such as the view and the season. Weekend room-only rates are cheaper – these rates are indicated below. All rates are for one or two persons.

The *Hindley Parkroyal* (☎ 8231 5552, 65 Hindley St) offers luxury accommodation from $150. Alternatively, rooms at the *Hilton International Adelaide* (☎ 8217 2000, 233 Victoria Square) start at $135.

Opposite the casino, and with panoramic views from above the 5th floor, the *Stamford Plaza* (☎ 8461 1111, 150 North Terrace) has rooms from $125. With a handsome pile of chips from the casino you could indulge yourself at the *Hyatt Regency Adelaide* (☎ 8231 1234, North Terrace), where rooms start at $240.

Places to Eat

With around 700 restaurants and a huge variety of cuisines on offer, dining out in Adelaide is a culinary adventure. A high proportion of restaurants is licensed.

The Advertiser newspaper often publishes a useful reference to the constantly changing food scene. Check its front counter at 121 King William St, and at larger newsagencies.

Rundle St Between Rundle Mall and North Terrace, *Terrace Eats* is a large, casual dining area in the basement of the Myer Centre. Its numerous eateries include Mexican, Asian, Italian and English. From here there's access through to the evocative *London Tavern* at the North Terrace end, which does pub-style meals.

Amalfi (☎ 8223 1948, 29 Frome St), just off Rundle St, has excellent Italian cuisine and a great menu. It's often difficult to get into, but hang around as it's worth the wait.

Café Tapas (☎ 8223 7564, 242 Rundle St) is a good Spanish bar and restaurant. Imagine tucking into treats such as 'kid goat braised in Moroccan spices with an apricot and walnut infused couscous'.

For something even spicier, *Taj Tandoor (☎ 8359 2066, 253 Rundle St)* is one of Adelaide's best Indian restaurants. Main courses start at $10.

Just up the street is 'little Italy'. The *Alfresco Gelateria* at No 260 is a good place for a gelato, cappuccino and a variety of sweets. *Scoozi* at No 272 is a huge cosmopolitan cafe noted for its wood-oven pizzas. In between is *Piatto*, with more pasta and pizza. The tables on the pavement outside these places are popular on balmy nights.

At No 286 is *Boltz Cafe, (☎ 8232 5234)*, another al fresco place. It specialises in modern Australian fare with Asian and Mediterranean influences. The upstairs bar has stand-up comedians on Thursday night.

Hindley St Although Hindley St has gone to seed in recent years, there are still some good eateries to be found here.

On Gilbert Place, which dog-legs between Hindley and King William Sts, the

---

No Smoking, Please!

In South Australia it's against the law to smoke in any enclosed public area where meals are eaten. This includes hotel dining rooms – apparently you can smoke in bars provided counter meals aren't being consumed there at the time. The law is strictly enforced in Adelaide and penalties are severe.

If you're desperate you can nip outside for a fag – not a pleasant option on a cold, wet night – or, in fine weather, eat at a pavement table. To find out more – or to complain, or offer congratulations – ring ☎ 1300 363 703.

Pancake Kitchen is open 24 hours a day and has main-course specials from $8. Next door, the *Penang Chinese Restaurant* is open Monday to Saturday from 11 am until 10 pm. Mains here are a little cheaper.

Cafe Boulevard (15 Hindley St) is a pleasant coffee lounge with hot meals for under $8 and cheap and delicious sweets.

The *Ceylon Hut (27 Bank St)*, just off Hindley St, has tasty curries from $12.

Abdul and Jamil's friendly *Quiet Waters*, in the basement at No 75, is a Lebanese coffee lounge serving predominantly vegetarian dishes. Takeaways are available and if you want to eat in it's BYO. There's also a belly dancer on Wednesday night.

Across the street at No 76, *Fast Eddy's Café* is open 24 hours and does a range of meals and snacks. It's licensed, so if you've been up all night you can enjoy a beer with your burger for breakfast.

On the 1st floor at No 79, *Food for Life*, a Hare Krishna restaurant, has vegetarian food (all you can eat) for $5, including dessert. It's open Monday to Saturday from noon to 3 pm.

Pasta Palace, at No 90, is another institution. It specialises in Italian (what else?) and claims that its food is 'justa like mamma used to make'.

North Terrace If you're not on a strict budget, the *Pullman Adelaide Casino*

Restaurant has very good smorgasbord lunches and dinners for around $25 to $30. It's closed Monday and Tuesday.

Parlamento, (☎ 8223 1948, 140 North Terrace), on the corner of Bank St, is one of the city's better pasta places and has a great atmosphere. Main courses start under $10.

At No 150, the *Pasta Hound* in the Fox & Hounds Pub (part of the Stamford Plaza Hotel) is similarly priced. The pub has live jazz from Monday to Thursday from 7 pm.

Food Affair, at the Gallerie Shopping Centre, which runs from North Terrace through to Gawler Place and John Martins on Rundle Mall, has numerous international eateries.

Gouger St This is another street of restaurants, many of which have become local institutions.

Tacked on to the western end of Central Market is *Chinatown*, which has a large collection of mainly Asian-style eateries; one group of kitchens shares a busy communal eating area.

The very popular *Mamma Getta Restaurant*, at No 55, is an authentic Italian place with most dishes around $8. At No 67 the *Star of Siam* (☎ 8231 3527) serves delicious Thai food.

Paul's, at No 79, serves some of the best fish and chips in town, while across the road at No 76 is the award-winning fish restaurant *Stanley's* (☎ 8410 0909). The *Rock Lobster Cafe* (☎ 8212 5885), at No 108, is more upmarket and well worth the splurge.

Ming's Palace (☎ 8231 9970) at No 201 serves good Chinese food, with Peking duck a speciality.

Around Town Other streets with plenty of good restaurants and cafes include Hutt St in the city and Melbourne and O'Connell Sts in North Adelaide.

The trendy *Equinox Bistro*, at the University of Adelaide, is in the Union Complex, above the Cloisters off Victoria Drive. It's open weekdays from 10 am to 10 pm (8 pm in university holiday periods) and has main courses from just $5. The *Union Cafeteria* on the ground floor is even cheaper.

Also good value is *Hawker's Corner*, on the corner of West Terrace and Wright St. It's open daily, except Monday, for lunch and dinner and has Chinese, Vietnamese, Thai and Indian food. It's popular with overseas students – in fact, there's a student hostel on the premises.

The *Volga* (☎ 8232 0441, 116 Flinders St) is Adelaide's only Russian restaurant. It's a friendly place, with Roma (Gypsy) violinists on Friday and Saturday nights and beluga caviar for those with expensive palates. Main meals (without the caviar) range from $10 to $21.

La Trattoria (☎ 8212 3327, 346 King William St) is an Adelaide institution for pizza and pasta. Mains cost from $10, and there are cheaper lunchtime specials.

Adelaide is very well supplied with hotels offering counter meals, particularly at lunchtime. Just look for the telltale blackboards outside. You won't have to search for long to find one with meals around $5, particularly now that most have poker machines – many offer good-sized meals at ridiculous prices to get people through the door.

In North Adelaide, the *British Hotel (58 Finniss St)* has a great beer garden where you can grill the food yourself at the barbecue. Large steak meals are around $15 ($2 to $3 less if you cook your own).

Entertainment

Bookings for performances at the *Festival Centre* and other Adelaide venues can be made through Bass on ☎ 13 1246. There are numerous Bass outlets around town, including one at the Festival Centre (open Monday to Saturday from 9 am to 6 pm) – look in the *White Pages* telephone book for others.

Pubs & Music There are lots of pubs that feature entertainment. Check *The Guide* in Thursday's *The Advertiser* newspaper or phone the radio station SA-FM (☎ 8272 1990) for a recorded rundown of who's playing what, and where. The free music paper *Rip it Up* is worth picking up for its listings. For theatre and gallery reviews check the free monthly *Adelaide Review*. You'll find both publications at record shops, hotels, cafes and night spots around town.

The only pub brewing its own beer is the *Port Dock Brewery Hotel (10 Todd St)* in Port Adelaide. It produces four distinctive beers – overseen by a German brewing specialist – and an alcoholic lemonade.

There's the usual rock pub circuit. The *Earl of Aberdeen Hotel* on Carrington St at Hurtle Square is a very nice, very trendy place with lots of character and usually a rock band on Friday and Saturday nights. It's close to the backpackers hostels in the south-east of the city centre.

On Rundle St, the *Austral Hotel* and the *Exeter Hotel*, at Nos 205 and 246 respectively, often have bands and DJs. They're popular with business folk and office workers during the day (both pubs have interesting lunchtime menus), while at night they're university student hang-outs. Try them if you're looking for a place for a drink before heading out to eat.

Also good for a pre-dinner drink is the *Universal Wine Bar (285 Rundle St)*. It's got a great atmosphere, with plenty of iron filigree, and the doors fold back on summer nights so you can catch the breeze.

Adelaide's most popular club is *Heaven Nightclub*, in the grand old Newmarket Hotel on the corner of West and North Terraces. Open every night, it has DJs on Wednesday to Saturday nights. The pub also has *Joplins Nightclub*, which has live bands nightly and is popular with the older set.

Also worth mentioning is *The Planet (77 Pirie St)*, with DJs from Wednesday to Saturday nights.

The *Mars Bar (120 Gouger St)* is a popular gay and lesbian dance club. It opens nightly from 10 am until late.

In the Union Complex at the University of Adelaide, the *UniBar (☎ 8303 5856)* often features big-name and upcoming rock bands during lunchtimes, afternoons and evenings – usually Friday. It's also a venue for avant-garde performances and social activities. You'll find it off Victoria Drive and above the Cloisters, and visitors are welcome.

The Festival Centre has free concerts on Saturday evenings in January and Sunday afternoons in February, March, June, July and August.

Cinemas Adelaide has a number of multi-screen cinema complexes – Greater Union's *Megaplex Marion*, in the huge Westfield Marion shopping centre at Oaklands Park, has 30 screens. Check the entertainment pages in *The Advertiser* newspaper for listings of what's showing around town.

The major venue for alternative films is *Palace East End Cinemas (274 Rundle St)*. It's open daily and shows Australian, foreign-language, classic and art-house films on its four screens – Monday is cheap night ($7 tickets).

Right next door is the *IMAX Cinema*, with the state's largest screen (350 sq m). It shows a variety of 2D and 3D films daily.

Casino The *Adelaide Casino* is housed in the grand old train station on North Terrace and boasts a magnificent foyer – some visitors reckon that this the best part of the place. There's a wide range of gambling facilities (including a two-up game, naturally), three bars and two restaurants. The casino opens daily from 10 am to 4 am (to 6 am from Friday to Sunday and on public holidays). Smart casual dress is required.

Most of the pubs around town have poker machines.

Shopping

Rundle St is a good place for retro clothes and boutiques; the Orange Lane market is worth checking for second-hand and alternative clothing (see the earlier Markets section for details).

Tandanya, at 253 Grenfell St, has a range of Aboriginal arts and crafts.

High-quality craftwork is produced and sold at the Jam Factory Craft & Design Centre, in the Lion Arts Centre on the corner of Morphett St and North Terrace. It also has a shop at 74 Gawler Place in the city centre.

Getting There & Away

Air Adelaide is connected by regular air services to all Australian capitals. Many flights from Melbourne and Sydney to the Northern Territory (NT) go via Adelaide, so the Darwin route is often heavily booked. Qantas (☎ 13 1313) has its main travel centre at 144 North Terrace, while Ansett's (☎ 13 1300) is 305 Greenhill Rd, Eastwood.

Standard one-way fares from Adelaide include: Alice Springs $414; Sydney $391; Hobart $392; and Perth $582. See the Australian Air Fares chart in the Getting Around chapter for fares to other destinations.

Bus Most interstate and all intrastate services go from Adelaide's central bus station at 101-111 Franklin St. The major carriers – Greyhound Pioneer, McCafferty's and Premier Stateliner – have their offices here. Left-luggage lockers are available.

Greyhound Pioneer (☎ 13 2030) has services between Adelaide and all major cities. The fare to Melbourne is $45 (11 hours), Sydney $96 (22 hours), Perth $199 (34 hours) and Alice Springs $135 (20 hours). There's a 10% discount for backpackers.

McCafferty's (☎ 13 1499) also has a backpacker discount and charges similar rates to Greyhound Pioneer, except it doesn't go to WA.

The Victorian V/Line bus service (☎ 8231 7620) runs daily between Adelaide's central bus station and Bendigo – from Bendigo you catch the train to Melbourne. The fare from Adelaide to Melbourne is $49.

Firefly Express (☎ 8231 1488, 1800 631 164) is at 110 Franklin St opposite the central bus station. It runs to Melbourne every evening at 8.30 pm ($45) and on to Sydney for $80 ex-Adelaide.

See the introductory Getting Around chapter for other alternatives to the major bus lines between Adelaide and interstate.

Premier Stateliner (☎ 8415 5555) and other South Australian operators are at the central bus station. Premier Stateliner is the largest local operator, with services from Adelaide to such places as Ceduna, Coober Pedy (with Greyhound Pioneer), Moonta, Mount Gambier, Port Augusta, Port Lincoln, Victor Harbor and Wilpena Pound. For details of regional services see the Getting There & Away sections later in this chapter.

Train There are two stations in Adelaide: the terminal for suburban trains on North Terrace; and the interstate terminal on Railway Terrace, Keswick, just south-west of the city centre. All train services into SA are operated by Great Southern Railway (inquiries and bookings ☎ 13 2147).

The *Overland* travels to/from Melbourne daily except Saturday and Wednesday. It takes about 12 hours and costs $64 for an economy seat and $199 in a 1st class sleeper.

The fastest service between Sydney and Adelaide is Speedlink – a daily bus and train connection taking about 20 hours. You travel from Sydney to Albury on the XPT train, and then from Albury to Adelaide on a V/Line bus. An economy/1st class seat is $130/160 – all bus seats are economy.

Alternatively, the *Indian Pacific* between Sydney and Perth via Adelaide and Broken Hill travels twice weekly each way. From Sydney to Adelaide (26 hours) costs $162 for an economy seat, $334/480 for an economy/1st class sleeper. From Adelaide to Perth (36 hours) costs $262 for an economy seat and $554/870 for an economy/1st class sleeper. Sleeper fares increase significantly during September and October.

The *Ghan* between Adelaide and Alice Springs runs twice weekly each way throughout the year, taking 19 hours. The fare is $182 in an economy seat and $374/574 in an economy/1st class sleeper.

Car & Motorcycle The *Yellow Pages* lists over 30 vehicle rental companies in Adelaide, including all the major national companies.

Those with cheaper rates include:

Access Rent-a-Car	☎ 1800 812 580
Action Rent-a-Car	☎ 8352 7044
Airport Rent-a-Car	☎ 8443 8855
Delta	☎ 13 1390
Rent-a-Bug	☎ 8234 0911
Smile Rent-a-Car	☎ 8234 0655

Show & Go (☎ 8376 0333), at 236 Brighton Rd, Somerton Park, has motor scooters for $59 per day (driver's licence required) and motorcycles from 250cc ($69) to 1000cc (from $89). A full motorcycle licence is required for all bikes.

Getting Around

To/From the Airport Adelaide airport is 7km west of the city centre. An airport bus service (☎ 8381 5311) operates between city hotels and some hostels on weekdays at least half-hourly from around 7 am to 9.30 pm, and on weekends and public holidays hourly for $6. From Victoria Square to the domestic terminal takes about 30 minutes; slightly less to the international terminal. If you're catching a flight on one of the smaller regional airlines let the driver know, as the drop-off point is different. You don't have to be staying at the hotel to catch the bus.

Remember, too, that most of the hostels will pick you up and drop you off if you're staying with them. A taxi costs about $15 from the city centre.

Budget, Hertz, Avis and Thrifty have hire-car desks at the airport.

To/From the Train Station The airport-to-city bus service calls into the interstate train station at Keswick on its regular run; it costs $3 from the station to the city centre. See To/From the Airport (earlier) for details.

Public Transport Adelaide has an integrated transport system covering metropolitan buses and trains, as well as the Glenelg tram. This is operated by TransAdelaide (TA) (☎ 8210 1000) – the TA Information Bureau, where you can get timetables and free guides and brochures on services, is on the corner of King William and Currie Sts.

Tickets purchased on board the buses on weekends, and on weekdays before 9 am and after 3 pm, cost $2.80; tickets purchased weekdays between 9 am and 3 pm cost $1.60. They are valid for two hours from the commencement of the first journey. (Tickets can be purchased on board some trains and at staffed railway stations.)

For travellers, the best deal is the day-trip ticket, which permits unlimited travel for the whole day and costs $5.40. They can be prepurchased on buses and trams, and at staffed railway stations.

There are two free Bee Line bus services. No 99B runs in a loop from the Glenelg tram terminus at Victoria Square, up King William St and around the corner to the train station. It leaves the square every five to eight minutes weekdays from 7.47 am to 6 pm; every 15 minutes on Friday to 9.20 pm and on Saturday from 8.37 am to 5.37 pm.

No 99C runs around the margins of the Central Business District from the train station, passing the Central Market en route. It leaves the station every 15 minutes on weekdays between 7.54 am and 6.09 pm (9.09 pm Friday) and every 30 minutes on Saturday between 8.39 am and 5.09 pm.

The 1929 Bay Tram rattles its way along a single line out to the Glenelg beach from Victoria Square in the city.

Bicycle Adelaide is a relatively cyclist-friendly city, with good cycling tracks and bicycle lanes on many main routes. Bicycle SA (☎ 8410 1406) can give advice on the local cycling scene.

Linear Park Mountain Bike Hire (☎ 0411 596 065) is at Elder Park, near the Popeye landing just below the Festival Theatre; it's on the Linear Park Bike & Walking Track, a 40km sealed path that wends its way mainly along the Torrens River from the beach to the foot of the Adelaide Hills. Bicycles are $8 per hour or $20 for the day, including helmets – groups of four or more get a 25% discount.

Flinders Outdoor Leisure (☎ 8359 3344), at 235 Pirie St, and Adelaide Bike Hire (☎ 8293 2313) also rent bikes. The latter will deliver and collect their bikes for free anywhere within 15km of the main post office.

Some hostels hire out mountain bikes.

Adelaide Hills

Only 30 minutes drive from the city centre are the scenic Adelaide Hills, part of the Mt Lofty Ranges and a popular day-trip destination from Adelaide. Apart from the gentle beauty of the hills themselves, with their huge gum trees and landscapes, there's great bushwalking (over 1000km of trails), several forested conservation parks, and historic townships such as Hahndorf and Strathalbyn. There are also several good wineries.

The Adelaide Hills Visitor Centre (☎ 8388 1185, 1800 353 323, fax 8388 1319) is at 41 Main St in Hahndorf; it opens daily from 9 am to 5 pm.

NATIONAL PARKS & SCENIC DRIVES

To visit the northern hills area, leave the city via North Terrace, Botanic Rd and then Payneham Rd and continue on to Torrens Gorge Rd. This scenic route takes you through Birdwood and north to the Barossa Valley. However, you might prefer to head south at Birdwood and travel through Hahndorf, returning to Adelaide via the South Eastern Freeway. Alternatively, leave Payneham Rd and take McGill Rd through **Morialta Conservation Park**, near Rostrevor, which has walking trails, waterfalls and a rugged gorge.

Continue south via Norton Summit and Summertown to the popular **Cleland Wildlife Park**. The park has numerous species of Australian fauna and is open daily from 9.30 am to 5 pm; entry is $8. You can have your photo taken with a koala daily from 2 to 4 pm, at a cost of $8. Take bus No 822 from outside Harris Scarfe department store in Grenfell St in Adelaide or visit on one of the day tours that operate from the city.

From the wildlife park you can walk through the bush (2km) or drive up to **Mt Lofty Summit** (727m), which has a good restaurant and beautiful views over the city. From here continue south for 1.5km to the stunning **Mt Lofty Botanical Gardens** (open weekdays from 8.30 am to 4 pm, and weekends from 10 am to 5 pm).

Further south is Crafers, from where you can head back to the city via the freeway. Alternatively, head west to **Belair National Park**, which has more walking trails and picnic facilities. The grand lifestyle of SA's colonial gentry is on display here at **Old Government House**, built in 1859 as the governor's summer residence. The park opens daily from 8.30 am to sunset and entry costs $5 per car. You can get here from

Adelaide on bus No 195 from King William St (get off at stop 27) or take the train to Belair station on the edge of the park.

To the south-east, **Warrawong Sanctuary** (☎ 8370 9422) on Stock Rd, near Mylor, has a variety of native wildlife, including some rare species. Dawn and sunset guided walks must be booked and cost $15 – there's accommodation in luxury tents for $99 a night including dinner, breakfast and guided walks. To reach the sanctuary from Adelaide, turn off the freeway at Stirling and follow the signs from the Stirling roundabout.

Places to Stay

There are 'limited access' YHA hostels (for members only) in the Mt Lofty Ranges at Para Wirra, Norton Summit, Mt Lofty, Mylor and Kuitpo. These hostels are all on the Heysen Trail (see Activities in the introduction to this chapter) and cost between $8 and $12. You must book in advance and obtain a key from the YHA office (☎ 8231 5583) in Adelaide.

Fuzzies Farm (☎ 8390 1111), at Norton Summit 15km east of the city, is a unique opportunity to learn practical skills in a friendly farm environment. You can join in a wide variety of activities such as animal care, organic gardening, land management, building construction and wood crafts. The setting is great, as are its cafe and self-contained bushland cabins; the daily rate for helpers is $10 including city transfers, all meals and laundry. Stays of at least one week are preferred, and bookings are essential. Budget package tours are also available.

Getting There & Away

Public transport is limited to a couple of bus runs operating from the central bus station in Adelaide. For details see the various town sections.

BIRDWOOD
• postcode 5234   • pop 580

The **National Motor Museum**, in the historic Birdwood Mill, has Australia's largest collection of vintage and classic cars and motorcycles. It's open daily from 9 am to 5 pm and admission is $8.50.

You can get to Birdwood (30km east-north-east of Adelaide) by driving up through the scenic **Torrens Gorge** to Gumeracha, 7km before Birdwood. Just before you get to Gumeracha is the award-winning **Chain of Ponds Wines**, open daily for tastings.

ABM Coachlines (☎ 8347 3336) runs from Adelaide to Birdwood on weekdays for $7.50.

HAHNDORF
● postcode 5245   ● pop 1660

The oldest surviving German settlement in Australia, Hahndorf, 29km south-east of Adelaide, is a popular day trip. Settled in 1839 by Lutherans who left Prussia to escape religious persecution, the town took its name from the ship's captain, Hahn; *dorf* is German for 'village'. Hahndorf still has an honorary *Burgermeister* (mayor). These days it's a major tourist attraction, with more stuffed koalas than you can shake a eucalyptus leaf at.

There are many old German-style buildings in town. The **German Arms Hotel**, at 50 Main St, dates from 1862 and is one of the best pubs in the hills for atmosphere and good food.

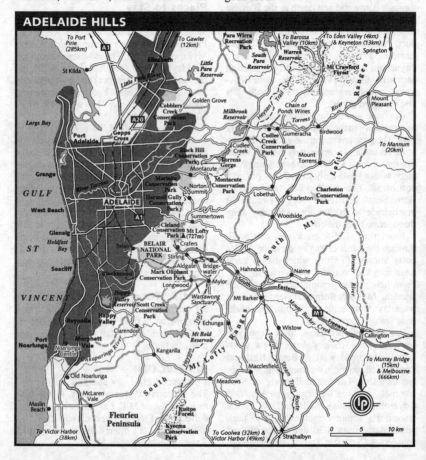

ADELAIDE HILLS

At 68 Main St, the **Hahndorf Academy** was established in 1857 and houses an art gallery, craft shop and museum – it has several original sketches by Sir Hans Heysen, a famous landscape artist who lived in Hahndorf for many years. See the boxed text 'Heysen Trail', under Activities earlier in this chapter.

The Cedars

Tours through Sir Hans' studio and house, The Cedars (1858), are conducted daily, except Saturday, at 11 am, 1 and 3 pm ($7 house and studio, or $4 studio only). You'll see a number of the artist's original works here.

Places to Stay & Eat

The friendly McMullen family has emergency accommodation for a maximum of three backpackers in their home at 54 English St (☎ 8388 7079). They charge $20 per person ($15 second night) including linen and breakfast.

The *Hahndorf Resort* (☎ 8388 7921) is 1.5km out of town on Main St. Camp sites cost from $11, cabins from $46 and motel singles/doubles from $79/89. The only other alternatives are several fairly expensive motels.

Hahndorf has many good restaurants and several feature German food. They include the *German Arms Hotel* as well as the *German Cake Shop*, both on Main St. *Karl's German Coffee House Restaurant (17 Main St)* is recommended by locals for authentic German cuisine.

Getting There & Away

Hills Transit (☎ 8339 1191) runs several times daily from the central bus station in Adelaide ($4.50).

STRATHALBYN

• postcode 5255   • pop 2600

Just over 40km south-east of Adelaide on the Angas River, this picturesque town was settled in 1839 by Scottish immigrants. It has many interesting old buildings, a number of which are classified as having heritage significance. They include the magnificent **St Andrew's Church**, which is unusually large and decorative for a country church.

The tourist office (☎/fax 8536 3212) on South Terrace is open from 9.30 am to 4 pm daily.

A walking-tour pamphlet ($2) lists historic buildings and sites of interest in the township. The old courthouse and police station are now a National Trust **museum** telling the history of the town and its Celtic influence; entry costs $2 and it's open weekends and school and public holidays from 2 to 5 pm.

Strathalbyn is about 12 minutes' drive from the wineries at **Langhorne Creek**.

Places to Stay

The *council caravan park* (☎ 8536 3681) in the showgrounds on Coronation Rd has grassed camp sites for $10 and on-site vans from $22.

The modest *Robin Hood Hotel* (☎ 8536 2608, 18 High St) charges $30/45 a single/double for its basic rooms, including a light breakfast. Alternatively, the much more upmarket *Victoria on the Park Hotel* (☎ 8536 2202, 16 Albyn Terrace) has motel units from $58/65.

Getting There & Away

Hills Transit (☎ 8339 1191) runs from Adelaide on weekdays ($6).

Between June and November inclusive, SteamRanger (☎ 8391 1223) runs a tourist train on alternate Sundays from Mt Barker to Strathalbyn and return for $18. It spends around 2½ hours in the town.

Fleurieu Peninsula

South of Adelaide is the Fleurieu Peninsula, with attractions close enough to be visited on day trips from the city. The coast has a number of excellent swimming and surfing beaches, while inland there's rolling farmland, a handful of conservation areas and the vineyards of the McLaren Vale area.

There are also several small historic towns such as Port Elliot, Goolwa and Willunga.

The peninsula was named by Frenchman Nicholas Baudin, after Napoleon's minister for the navy who financed Baudin's expedition to Australia. In the early days, settlers on the peninsula ran a smuggling business. In 1837 a whaling station was established at Encounter Bay and this became the colony's first successful industry.

GULF ST VINCENT BEACHES

There's a series of fine swimming beaches along the Gulf St Vincent coast of the peninsula. They extend all the way from **Christies Beach** through **Port Noarlunga**, **Seaford** and **Moana** to **Maslin Beach**. Further south, beyond **Aldinga Beach** and **Sellicks Beach**, the coastline is rockier but there are still good beaches at **Carrickalinga** and **Normanville**.

Yankalilla, just in from the coast near Normanville, has gained recent fame thanks to the image of Jesus and the Virgin Mary that has mysteriously appeared on a wall of the Anglican church. Cynics will tell you that it's just rising damp. This picturesque little town is also where the first country **schoolhouse**

was established by Mother Mary MacKillop (1867) after she became a nun.

The coast road ends at **Cape Jervis** at the tip of the peninsula, where vehicle ferries travel back and forth across Backstairs Passage to Kangaroo Island, 13km away. There's a good swimming beach here if you're early for the ferry – the beach is 2km by road to the north of the ferry.

Along the south coast near Cape Jervis is the **Deep Creek Conservation Park**, with walking tracks including the Heysen Trail, and bush camping areas.

Inman Valley, on the main road between Yankalilla and Victor Harbor, is a pretty spot in a prime dairying area. It's an access point for the Heysen Trail.

Places to Stay

On the main road, about 3.5km before the ferry landing, the friendly *Old Cape Jervis Station Homestead* (☎ 8598 0233) has several options from $20 per person – you get a

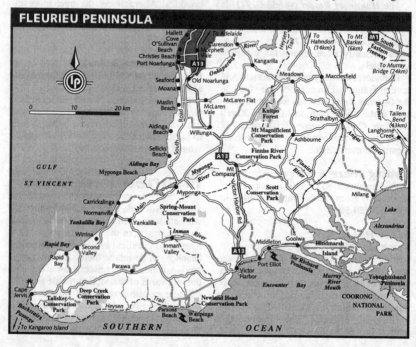

FLEURIEU PENINSULA

bed in the historic shearers' quarters, with use of the kitchen. Alternatively, the *Cape Jervis Tavern* (☎ 8598 0276) in town has self-contained rooms for $50/55 a single/double.

There are *caravan parks* in Normanville, Second Valley and the Wirrina Resort They all have camp sites, on-site vans and cabins.

The *Old School House* (☎ 8558 8376) in Inman Valley, 16km west of Victor Harbor, has an attractive setting and bunk beds for $12. Maps of the Heysen Trail are available from the hostel manager.

Getting There & Away

Adelaide Sightseeing (☎ 8231 4144) runs once daily to Cape Jervis from Adelaide, charging $12 to Yankalilla and $14 to Cape Jervis. Smart Car (☎ 8554 3788) offers a casual shuttle service from Victor Harbor to Cape Jervis. One-way tickets cost from $15.

MCLAREN VALE WINE REGION

Adelaide has sprawled so far that the small town of **Morphett Vale** is now an outer suburb. Among its historic buildings is St Mary's (1846), the first Roman Catholic church in the state. **Old Noarlunga** is a tiny old historic township only 10 minutes drive from McLaren Vale.

Interesting **heritage walks** (☎ 8384 7918) are conducted on various days in Morphett Vale, Old Noarlunga, Port Noarlunga and Reynella. They take 1½ to two hours and cost $9; times are flexible.

The helpful McLaren Vale & Fleurieu Visitor Centre (☎ 8323 9944, fax 8323 9949 information@mclarenvale.aust.com) on Main Rd at the northern end of McLaren Vale is open daily from 10 am to 5 pm.

Wineries

The peninsula has a string of wineries around **McLaren Vale** (population 2000), as well as Reynella, Willunga and Langhorne Creek. The area is particularly well suited to red wines, but a trend towards white wine consumption in the 1970s prompted growers to diversify.

There are around 45 wineries with cellar-door sales in the area. The first winery was established in Reynella in 1838 – some of the existing wineries date to the 19th century and have fine old buildings. Most are open daily from 10 am to 5 pm. The Visitor Centre has full details and a useful map of the wineries.

Each winery has its own appeal, whether it be a superb setting or just a good, full-bodied drop of the home product. The following are suggestions to help with your explorations.

Chapel Hill, Chapel Hill Rd, McLaren Vale south, has a magnificent hilltop location with views over the Gulf St Vincent. This is a small vineyard producing sophisticated white and red wines.

d'Arenberg, Osborne Rd, McLaren Vale, has produced consistently good wines since 1928. Its restaurant offers a fine view of the valley.

Noon's, Rifle Range Rd, McLaren Vale south, specialises in full-bodied reds. This winery is in a pleasant rural setting beside a small creek, and there are barbecue facilities.

Woodstock, Douglas Gully Rd, McLaren Flat, is a small winery with a restaurant and tranquil garden setting. It's well known for its tawny port and botrytis sweet wines.

The McLaren Vale **Wine Bushing Festival** takes place over a week in late October/ early November each year. It's a busy time of wine tastings and tours, and the whole thing is topped by a grand feast.

The **Sea & Vines Festival** in June and the **Continuous Picnic** in October are weekend-long celebrations of food, wine and music. During these events you can sample offerings from the McLaren Vale wineries on a free bus service, which picks up and drops off imbibers en route.

A great way to visit a few wineries is on a camel with the Bush Safari Co (☎ 8543 2280). Several tours are available, including a one day trek for $85 – they don't operate in winter. Alternatively, Sea & Vine Tours (☎ 8384 5151) will take you around in their minibus ($45 ex-Adelaide) or private hire car ($75) – each price include a winery lunch.

Another option is to cycle. There's a cycle/ walking track along the old railway line from McLaren Vale to Willunga, 6km to the south. Cyclomobile Bicycle Hire (☎ 8326 3427) hires out mountain bikes for $15 a half day, and they'll deliver and collect anywhere within the McLaren Vale area.

Willunga, in the south of the Southern Vales winery area, is a lovely old town with numerous interesting buildings from the colonial era. It's a major centre for Australian almond growing, and hosts the **Almond Blossom Festival** in July.

There are fine views, kangaroos and walks in the **Mt Magnificent Conservation Park**, 12km east of Willunga. This is another access point for the Heysen Trail.

Places to Stay & Eat

The friendly *McLaren Vale Lakeside Caravan Park* (☎ 8323 9255), in a pretty rural setting off Field St, has camp sites from $13, on-site vans from $32 and self-contained cabins from $48.

In Willunga, to the south of McLaren Vale, the *Willunga Hotel* (☎ 8556 2135, High St) has pub rooms from $20/35 for singles/doubles. It's also one of the best places in town for meals.

Emu Retreat (☎ 8556 2467, Hahn Rd) is in a rich farming area halfway between Willunga and Aldinga Beach. It offers backpacker beds for $20 including a substantial breakfast, and the manager can arrange a variety of outdoor activities, including rock climbing and surfing.

There are some good restaurants in and around McLaren Vale, including several wineries. Perhaps best of all is the historic *Salopian Inn*, just out of town on the Willunga Rd; it has a fascinating menu featuring fresh local produce (main courses start at $20). You'll need to book (☎ 8323 8769) as it's small and popular.

Getting There & Away

Premier Stateliner (☎ 8415 5555) has up to three buses a day from Adelaide to McLaren Vale ($5) and Willunga ($5.50) on its Victor Harbor run. Transit Regency Coaches (☎ 8381 5311) departs several times each weekday from the Noarlunga Centre train station for McLaren Vale and Willunga.

VICTOR HARBOR

- postcode 5211   • pop 9000

The main town on the peninsula, and 84km south of Adelaide, Victor Harbor looks out onto Encounter Bay, where Flinders and Baudin had their historic meeting in 1802. There's a memorial to the 'encounter' up on the steep headland known as The Bluff at the southern end of the bay, about 4km south of the Victor Harbor post office.

Victor Harbor was founded as a sealing and whaling centre. The first whaling station was established here at Rosetta Harbor, below The Bluff, in 1837 and another followed soon after on Granite Island. Operations ceased in 1864 due to a dramatic decline in whale numbers.

Information

The tourist office (☎ 8552 5738, fax 8552 5476) is at the mainland end of the Granite Island causeway. It's open daily from 10 am to 4 pm (9 am to 5 pm in summer).

Things to See & Do

Historic buildings include **St Augustine's Church of England** (1869), the **Telegraph Station** (1869) and the **Fountain Inn** (1838). Now a National Trust museum, the **Old Custom House & Station Master's Residence** (1866) is part of the **Encounter Coast Discovery Centre** on Flinders Parade opposite the causeway. The centre has interesting displays on local history and is open daily from 10 am to 4.30 pm (less in winter). Admission is $4.

Victor Harbor is protected from the angry Southern Ocean by **Granite Island**, which is connected to the mainland by a causeway. You can ride out there on a double-decker tram pulled by Clydesdale draught horses ($4 return). It's an easy climb to the top of the hill, where there are good views across the bay.

Granite Island is a rookery for little penguins. The **Penguin Interpretive Centre** (☎ 8552 7555) on the island has excellent audio-visual displays. It also operates one-hour **guided walks** every evening to watch the penguins come home from fishing. Walks cost $5 and leave from the centre at dusk.

Between June and October you might be lucky enough to see a **southern right whale** swimming near the causeway. Victor Harbor is on the migratory path of these splendid

Southern Right Whales

Southern right whales are so called because they were once considered by whalers to be the 'right' whales to hunt – large quantities of oil and fine whalebone meant a tidy profit from each carcass.

Southern rights once roamed the seas in prolific numbers, but unrestrained slaughter last century reduced the population from 100,000 to just a few hundred by 1935. Although considered an endangered species, they are fighting back and the population worldwide may be as high as 4000. From June to October inclusive many southern rights migrate to the warmer waters along Australia's southern coast to breed. Around 100 whales are born each year in South Australian waters, and you can observe them from lookouts at places such as Port Elliot, Victor Harbor, Port Lincoln and Head of Bight.

The South Australian Whale Centre, on Railway Terrace in Victor Harbor, operates a whale information network. To report a sighting, call ☎ 8552 5644; or for current information on where the whales are, call ☎ 1900 931 223.

The centre has an informative booklet ($4) that tells you all about whale-watching. You can write to the centre at PO Box 950, Victor Harbor, SA 5211 (whale@webmedia.com.au). Its Web site is www.webmedia.com.au/whales/.

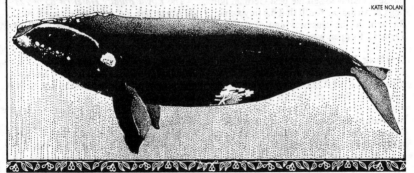

KATE NOLAN

animals and you can observe them from several points around the bay, including The Bluff. You'll need binoculars with a magnification power of seven or more.

If you want to learn more about whales, the **South Australian Whale Centre** at the causeway end of Railway Terrace is the place to go. It operates a 'whale information network' that covers sightings and strandings on the South Australian coast. It's open daily from 9 am to 5 pm (often staying open later in summer) and entry costs $6 (see the boxed text for further details).

Places to Stay

There are a number of caravan parks, hotels, motels and B&Bs in and around Victor

Harbor; details are available from the tourist office.

The *Victor Harbor Beachfront Caravan Park* (☎ 8552 1111, 114 Victoria St) has camp sites from $12, basic cabins from $40 and self-contained cabins from $50.

The *Anchorage at Victor Harbor* (☎ 8552 5970, victor@anchorage.mtx.net, 21 Flinders Parade) has bunk beds in backpacker dorms for $15; comfortable rooms in a heritage-listed guesthouse cost from $35/50 a single/double.

Also offering a good standard, the *Grosvenor Junction Hotel* (☎ 8552 1011, 40 Ocean St) has dorm beds for $20 and pub rooms for $25/49. The most central of the motels is the *City Motel* (☎ 8552 2455,

SOUTH AUSTRALIA

51 Ocean St), next to the post office, with rooms from $55/65.

Places to Eat
The *Original Fish & Chip Shop* in the town centre on Ocean St is popular, but the best of the local seafood takeaways is *Pa's Place* (next to the Yilki Store) – it's along the coast about 3km south of the town centre. Both also have sit-down meals.

The atmosphere at the *Grosvenor Junction Hotel* is nothing flash but you can get a decent cheap feed there. For more formal dining the *Hotel Victor* on The Esplanade is best. Also worth trying is the *Anchorage at Victor Harbor*, which has a good licensed cafe.

For a different eating experience, *Klaus's Wurst Haus*, run by the ebullient Klaus himself, claims to sell the best German hot dogs in Australia. You'll find his tiny van in the park on the causeway end of Railway Terrace; it's open weekends only.

Getting There & Away
From June to November inclusive, Steam-Ranger (☎ 8391 1223) runs a tourist train on alternate Sundays from Mt Barker (in the Adelaide Hills) to Victor Harbor via Strathalbyn and Goolwa and return for $35. It spends about three hours in town before making the return journey.

Every Sunday, and more frequently over school holidays and Easter, the steam Cockle Train travels the scenic Encounter Coast between Goolwa and Victor Harbor. The return fare is $15, and tickets can be purchased at the stations in Goolwa, Port Elliot and Victor Harbor.

Premier Stateliner (☎ 8415 5555) has two to three services daily from Adelaide for $12.

At the time of writing, a 23km sealed cycle path was being constructed along the coast from The Bluff to the Murray Mouth.

Getting Around
Motor scooters can be hired from Victor Leisure (☎ 8552 1875) at the Shell service station, 105 Victoria St, for $25 per hour. Victor Bike Hire (☎ 8552 4458), at 12 Flinders Parade, rents out mountain bikes and tandems for $30 per day.

PORT ELLIOT
• postcode 5212   • pop 1200
Port Elliot, established in 1854 as the seaport for the Murray River trade, is on Horseshoe Bay, a part of Encounter Bay. **Horseshoe Bay** has a safe swimming beach and a nice clifftop walk. Nearby surf beaches include **Boomer Beach** on the western edge of town and **Middleton Beach**, to the east. The Southern Surf Shop, a few doors west from the Royal Family Hotel, rents surfing gear and can provide information on surfing conditions.

Places to Stay & Eat
You can camp ($13) or stay in cabins (from $48) at the *Port Elliot Caravan & Tourist Park* (☎ 8554 2134) on Horseshoe Bay.

The *Royal Family Hotel* (☎ 8554 2219, 32 North Terrace) has single/double rooms for $25/35; counter meals start at $7, and there's an excellent bakery across the road.

Getting There & Away
Premier Stateliner (☎ 8415 555) has up to three services daily from Adelaide to Port Elliot ($12).

GOOLWA
• postcode 5214   • pop 3000
On Lake Alexandrina near the mouth of the Murray River, Goolwa initially grew with the developing trade along the river. As large ships were unable to get up to Goolwa, a railway line (the first in the state) was built from there to nearby Port Elliot. In the 1880s a new railway line to Adelaide from Murray Bridge spelt the end for Goolwa as a port town.

The tourist office (☎ 8555 3488, fax 8555 3810), open daily from 9 am to 5 pm, is on the waterfront near the centre of Goolwa in the **Signal Point River Murray Interpretive Centre**. The centre contains interesting exhibits on the early history of life on the river ($5). Walking-tour pamphlets of Goolwa are available.

The **museum** on Porter St is open daily except Monday and Friday from 2 to 5 pm ($2). It's well worth a visit for its displays on early settlement and farming.

The **Sir Richard Peninsula** has a long stretch of sandy beach leading to the mouth of the Murray. You can drive along it (4WD only), but there's no way across to the Coorong beach on the other side.

The MV *Aroona* and PS *Mundoo* both have a variety of cruises on the lower Murray from $12, while the MV *The Spirit of the Coorong* and MV *Wetlands Explorer* do longer trips into the Coorong. More amusing is a trip with the Coorong Pirate (☎ 018 812 000), a large and irredeemably ocker gentleman who runs fun trips from $6. His tours leave on the hour from 10 am to 3 pm (October to April only).

A free vehicle ferry from Goolwa to **Hindmarsh Island** operates 24 hours seven days a week.

Places to Stay

The closest caravan park to town is the basic *Goolwa Camping & Tourist Park* (☎ 8555 2144, 40 Kessell Rd), a 15 minute walk away. It has camp sites from $10, on-site vans from $25 and cabins from $45.

Right on the river about 1km out of town, the *South Lakes Motel* (☎ 8555 2194, Barrage Rd) has units with kitchen facilities from $54/59 a single/double.

In the middle of town, the *Corio Hotel* (☎ 8555 1136, Railway Terrace)' has pub rooms for $25/50, which includes a light breakfast.

Graham's Castle (☎ 8555 2182, Castle St), an amazing rambling structure built in 1868, is a hostel-style place about 2km from the town centre and 500m from the beach. Basic twin rooms cost $12/24, and they'll pick you up from the town centre if you give them a ring on arrival.

Now decommissioned, the *PS Murray River Queen* (☎ 8555 1733) is permanently moored at the town wharf. You can stay in its old crew quarters for $15 (there's a communal stoveless kitchen) or in a twin room with private facilities for $40/46.

On Hindmarsh Island, *Narnu Farm* (☎ 8555 2002) has rustic cottages from $70 for singles/doubles. Guests are encouraged to take part in farm activities, such as feeding the animals and hand-milking the cows.

Getting There & Away

Premier Stateliner has daily buses to Adelaide ($12). See the earlier Victor Harbor section for details of steam trains that pass through Goolwa.

Kangaroo Island

Separated from the mainland about 9500 years ago, Kangaroo Island is Australia's third-largest island (after Tasmania, and Melville Island off Darwin). About 150km long and 30km wide, the island offers peaceful scenery, a varied coastline including towering cliffs, swimming and surf beaches, lots of native wildlife and good fishing. There is also a number of shipwrecks off the coast, many of which are of interest to scuba divers.

The island was unoccupied by Aboriginal people at the time of European settlement; stone implements have been discovered, however, and these suggest human occupation more than 11,000 years ago. Archaeologists are uncertain as to what caused the demise of these early inhabitants, but it's thought they disappeared about 2250 years ago.

Kangaroo Island has a rough-and-ready early European history with sealers, whalers and escaped convicts all playing their often ruthless part. Many of the place names on the island are French – the first thorough survey of its coast was carried out by the French explorer Nicholas Baudin on two visits in 1802 and 1803. The island was named by Matthew Flinders in 1802 after his crew slaughtered many kangaroos here and enjoyed a welcome feast of fresh meat.

Kangaroo Island's geographical isolation from the mainland has been a boon to its native wildlife: it is free from dingoes, rabbits and foxes. Because of this, a number of threatened native Australian animals, such as the koala and platypus, have been introduced to ensure their survival.

Information

The Kangaroo Island Gateway Visitor Information Centre (☎ 8553 1185, fax 8553 1255,

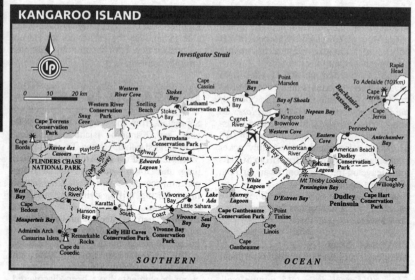

KANGAROO ISLAND

tourki@ozemail.com.au) is just outside Penneshaw on the road to Kingscote. Check out its Web site at www.tourkangarooisland.com.au. It's open weekdays from 9 am to 5 pm and weekends and public holidays from 10 am to 4 pm.

The main National Parks & Wildlife Service (NPWS) office is at 37 Dauncey St in Kingscote (☎ 8553 2381). It is open weekdays from 8.45 am to 5 pm.

The Island Parks Pass ($20), which can be purchased only on the island, covers all NPWS entry and camping fees on the island and entitles holders to free NPWS tours (see Organised Tours). Passes can be obtained from any of the island's seven NPWS.

Fire restrictions are in force from 1 December to 30 April. Only gas fires may be lit in national parks, and on days of total fire ban, all fires are prohibited (including gas fires). Penalties for lighting a fire illegally are severe.

Organised Tours

The NPWS operates a range of economical guided tours and walks in areas of conservation and historical significance, and most of these are free for Island Parks Pass holders.

The Pass does not cover the penguin walks at Kingscote and Penneshaw.

At **Seal Bay**, 55km south-west of Kingscote, guided tours to the sea-lion colony are conducted daily every 45 minutes between 9 am and 4.15 pm (later in summer). Tours at the **Kelly Hill Caves Conservation Park**, 79km from Kingscote, take place daily between 10 am and 4.30 pm (3.30 pm in winter).

Rangers also conduct tours of the historic lighthouses at **Cape Borda**, 103km from Kingscote on the western extremity of the island, and **Cape Willoughby**, 28km southeast of Penneshaw at the island's eastern end; see the sections on Flinders Chase and Penneshaw for times.

Package Tours Several tour operators offer packages ex-Adelaide – see Adelaide's Organised Tours section.

Bus Tours Tours designed for backpackers and other budget travellers are run by Kangaroo Island Sealink, the Penneshaw Youth Hostel and Kangaroo Island Ferry Connections. You can expect to pay anywhere between $70 and $85 for a day tour that includes lunch and a visit to Seal Bay and Flinders Chase.

There are also more personalised 4WD tours, fishing charters, yacht cruises, walking tours and visits to such places as a eucalyptus oil distillery and a sheep's milk dairy.

Diving Tours Operating from the Penneshaw Youth Hostel, Adventureland Diving runs one-day ($150) to five-day ($690) diving packages, including accommodation. It also offers abseiling, canoeing, rock climbing and scuba diving for beginners, as well as dive charters (licensed divers only).

At Western River, Kangaroo Island Diving Safaris (☎ 8559 3225) has one to five-day diving tours for similar prices to Adventureland Diving, not including accommodation. These give you a chance to dive with fur seals and see 30cm-long leafy sea dragons.

Places to Stay
There is plenty of accommodation on the island, including backpacker hostels, guesthouses, caravan parks and a burgeoning number of B&Bs; contact the visitor centre in Penneshaw for details.

The NPWS has a number of historic cottages for rent in the national parks. These range from basic huts ($10 per person) to the more upmarket lightkeepers' cottages (from $30 per person) at Cape Willoughby, Cape Borda and Cape du Couedic.

Kangaroo Island Ferry Connections (☎ 8553 1233, 1800 018 484) in Penneshaw has a range of combined accommodation and car-hire packages. Staff can book self-contained properties around the island starting at $55 for a double (car hire extra).

In addition to those at the main townships, small and mainly basic caravan parks are located at Emu Bay, Stokes Bay, Vivonne Bay and near Rocky River.

Getting There & Away
Air The following airlines have daily services to Kangaroo Island, all landing at Kingscote. Prices given are for one-way economy fares:

Emu Air	(☎ 1800 182 353)	$80
Kendell Airlines	(☎ 13 1300)	$90

Emu Air has a free shuttle service into Kingscote.

Ferry Departing from Cape Jervis, Kangaroo Island Sealink (☎ 13 1301) operates two vehicular ferries that run all year, taking 45 minutes to Penneshaw. One-way fares are $30 for passengers, $5 for bicycles, $20 for motorcycles and $65 for cars.

Sealink's bus service from Adelaide's central bus station to Port Jervis connects with ferry departures. The one-way fare is $14 and bookings are essential.

Getting Around
To/From the Airport An airport bus runs from Kangaroo Island airport to Kingscote for $10. The airport is 14km from the town centre.

To/From the Ferry Landings The Sealink Shuttle (☎ 13 1301) connects with most ferries and links Penneshaw with American River ($6.50) and Kingscote ($11). You have to book.

Car & Motorcycle Most of the island's rural roads are unsealed. Many are narrow, and have loose gravel surfaces and sharp corners, not to mention dust and wandering wildlife. Drive carefully.

Car Rental There are three car-hire companies, all based at Kingscote: Budget (☎ 553 3133); Hertz/Kangaroo Island Rental Cars (☎ 8553 2390, 1800 088 296); and Koala Car Rentals (☎ 8553 2399).

Very few of Adelaide's car-rental outlets will allow their vehicles to be taken across to Kangaroo Island. Three that do are Smile Rent-a-Car (☎ 8234 0655), Thrifty (☎ 8211 8788) and Access Rent-a-Car (☎ 8223 7466).

Scooter/Motorcycle Rental In Kingscote you can hire scooters from the Country Cottage Shop (☎ 8553 2148) at 6 Centenary Ave, for $45 a day. However, you can't take the scooters on unsealed roads.

Bicycle The number of unsealed roads and the relatively long distances between settlements can make cycling hard work. If you're still game, bicycles can be hired from Bernard O'Connor (☎ 8553 0169) for $20 a day. Bernard can also arrange tours/group support.

KINGSCOTE
• postcode 5223　　• pop 1440

Kingscote, the main town on the island, was the first white settlement in SA. Although Europeans had been on the island for many years, Kingscote was only formally settled in 1836. It was all but abandoned just a few years later, when most settlers had moved to the mainland.

There are branches of the ANZ and BankSA in town. BankSA has an ATM and there are plenty of EFTPOS outlets, some of which will let you withdraw cash.

Things to See & Do
The **tidal pool** about 500m south of the jetty is the best place in town to swim. However, most locals head out to **Emu Bay**, 18km away.

Hope Cottage on Centenary Ave was built in 1857. It is now a good museum ($2.50), with some interesting memorabilia including a eucalyptus-oil distillery and an old lighthouse. It's open daily from 2 to 4 pm ($3).

Pelican feeding takes place every evening at 4 pm (5 pm during daylight saving) at the wharf near the town centre. A number of these wonderful beaked battleships usually turn up for the free tucker, as does a Pacific gull or two. A donation of $2 is requested.

Each evening at 7.30 and 8.30 pm (8.30 and 9.30 pm during daylight saving) rangers take visitors on a **Discovering Penguins walk**. They leave from the Penguin Burrow at the Ozone Hotel and the walk costs $5 – wear sturdy footwear and leave your camera flash behind.

Island Pure is a **sheep dairy** and cheese factory on Gum Creek Rd, near Cygnet River. You can visit daily (from 1 to 5 pm) to watch the sheep being milked and to taste delicious cheeses and yogurt.

Most people find the working **eucalyptus oil distillery** at Emu Ridge, on Wilsons Rd between Kingscote and American River, is well worth a visit. It's the only enterprise of this type left in the state, and you can check it out daily between 9 am and 2 pm.

Places to Stay & Eat
The **Kingscote Caravan Park** (☎ 8553 2325, The Esplanade) has camp sites from $12, on-site vans from $30, self-contained cabins from $45 and flats from $55 – the rates are for up to four people. The owners also operate the caravan park at Emu Bay.

On the foreshore at Brownlow, about 3km west of the town centre, the **Nepean Bay Tourist Park** (☎ 8553 2394, First St) has camp sites from $11, on-site vans from $28 and cabins from $33.

The friendly **Kangaroo Island Central Backpackers Hostel** (☎ 8553 2787, 19 Murray St) has dorm beds for $14 and twin and double rooms for $37. While the facilities are well maintained, the kitchen is minuscule and the dorms are crowded.

Overlooking the tidal pool, **Ellson's Seaview Guesthouse** (☎ 8553 2030, ellsons@kin.on.net, Chapman Terrace) is an old-style guesthouse with luxurious budget rooms for $35/44/51 for singles/doubles/triples. It has a good restaurant and is only a short walk to the handful of cafes and takeaways in the town centre.

The **Queenscliffe Family Hotel** (☎ 8553 2254, 57 Dauncy St) and the **Ozone Hotel** (☎ 8553 2011, Kingscote Terrace) are both in the town centre – the latter is the more upmarket of the two, charging upwards of $80 for singles and doubles. Otherwise there are several motels.

AMERICAN RIVER
• postcode 5221　　• pop 300

Between Kingscote and Penneshaw, this small settlement takes its name from the American sealers who built a boat here in 1804. The town is on a small peninsula and shelters an inner bay, named **Pelican Lagoon** by Flinders, which is now a bird sanctuary. You can watch **pelican-feeding** daily at 4.30 pm down on the wharf.

Places to Stay & Eat

Linnetts Island Club (☎ 8553 7053, The Esplanade) has a range of options including camp sites (from $15) and very basic twin rooms with share facilities from $20 per person.

At *Casuarina Holiday Units (☎ 8553 7020, 9 Ryberg Rd)*, next to the post office, basic self-contained units sleeping up to five cost from $50 for two people and $10 per extra adult.

PENNESHAW

• postcode 5222   • pop 300

Looking across Backstairs Passage to the Fleurieu Peninsula, Penneshaw is a quiet resort town with a white sandy beach at **Hog's Bay**. It's the arrival point for ferries from Cape Jervis.

There's no bank in town, but Sharpys has an ANZ agency, Servwel has the BankSA agency and the post office is an agent for the Commonwealth Bank. All have EFTPOS cash withdrawal facilities.

Things to See & Do

In the evenings rangers take visitors to view the little penguins that nest along the shore near town – you'll generally see more penguins here than at Kingscote. Tours ($6 adults, $16 family) depart from the 'Penguin Rookery' on the foreshore near the ferry terminal, leaving at 7.30 and 8.30 pm (an hour later during daylight saving). Take sturdy shoes and leave your camera flash behind.

The **Penneshaw Maritime & Folk Museum** has some interesting memorabilia on local history. It opens Monday, Wednesday and Saturday from 10 am to noon and 3 to 5 pm ($2).

Penneshaw is situated on Dudley Peninsula, a knob of land at the eastern end of the island. The peninsula has several points of interest outside the town itself: **Pennington Bay** has surf; the sheltered waters of **Chapman River** are popular for canoeing; and the **Cape Willoughby Lighthouse** (first operated in 1852) has 45-minute tours daily between 10 am and 2 pm (later between September and April).

Places to Stay

The visitor centre issues camping permits for bush sites at Chapmans River, Browns Beach and American River.

The basic but clean *Penneshaw Youth Hostel (☎ 8553 1284, 1800 686 620, adv.host@kin.on.net, North Terrace)* has dorm beds for $14 and twin rooms for $16 per person. It has a cafe on the premises, and the owners run bus and diving tours and packages.

The *Penguin Walk YHA Hostel (☎ 8553 1233, kifc@kin.on.net, Talinga Terrace)* near the ferry terminal charges much the same rates as the Penneshaw Youth Hostel, but is a much more upmarket place. Its dorms (maximum six beds) are quite pleasant and spacious; each has its own bathroom and cooking facilities. The twin rooms have share facilities and there's a communal kitchen.

Alternatively, the *Penneshaw Caravan Park (☎ 8553 1075, Talinga Terrace)* has shady camp sites and on-site caravans next to the beach.

NORTH COAST

There are several fine, sheltered beaches along the north coast. Near Kingscote, **Emu Bay** has a beautiful, long sweep of sand. Other good beaches include **Stokes Bay**, **Snelling Beach** and **Western River Cove**.

FLINDERS CHASE NATIONAL PARK

Occupying the western end of the island, Flinders Chase is one of SA's most significant national parks. There is plenty of mallee scrub, but also beautiful tall forests with koalas, echidnas and possums; the kangaroos and emus have become so fearless they'll brazenly badger you for food – the picnic area at Rocky River is fenced to protect visitors from these freeloaders.

On the north-western corner of the island, **Cape Borda** has a lighthouse that was built in 1858. There are guided tours on weekdays from 11 am to 3.15 pm (to 2 pm in winter and 4 pm in the summer school holidays). At nearby **Harvey's Return** is a small, poignant cemetery on the clifftop.

Just south of Cape Borda is the **Ravine des Casoars**, with one of the island's most pleasant walking trails (8km return). This lovely spot was named by Baudin after the dwarf emus he saw there – the species became extinct soon after European settlement.

In the south-eastern corner of the park, **Cape du Couedic** is wild and remote, with towering cliffs. A picturesque lighthouse built in 1906 tops the cape; you can follow the path from the car park down to **Admirals Arch** – a large natural archway formed by pounding seas. New Zealand fur seals are often seen here.

At Kirkpatrick Point, a couple of kilometres east of Cape du Couedic, **Remarkable Rocks** is a cluster of large, weather-sculpted granite boulders on a huge dome swooping 75m down to the sea.

Places to Stay

In Flinders Chase you can camp at the Rocky River park headquarters and in other designated areas, with a permit. Watch out for the kangaroos: they can rip their way into tents looking for food and can cause a lot of damage.

Facilities are much better at the *Western KI Caravan Park* (☎ 8559 7201) on the South Coast Rd just a few minutes drive east from Rocky River. There are plenty of wild koalas here as well.

On West Hwy, a 10 minute drive from Rocky River, friendly *Flinders Chase Farm* (☎ 8559 7223) has bunk beds in a self-contained farmhouse for \$15.

There are a number of historic cottages available for hire in the park; see Places to Stay at the beginning of this section.

SOUTH COAST

The south coast is rough and wave-swept compared with the north. At **Hanson Bay**, close to Cape du Couedic, there's a colony of fairy penguins. A little further east you come to **Kelly Hill Caves Conservation Park**, a series of limestone caves 'discovered' in the 1880s by a horse named Kelly, which fell into them through a hole in the ground; see Organised Tours at the start of this section.

ANN JEFFREE

They're Australian sea lions, not seals, at Seal Bay

Vivonne Bay has a long and beautiful beach. There is excellent fishing but bathers should take great care; the undertows are fierce and swimmers are advised to stick close to the jetty or the river mouth. **Seal Bay** is another sweeping beach, with a large colony of Australian sea lions; see Organised Tours at the start of this section.

Near Seal Bay and close to the south coast road is **Little Sahara**, a series of enormous, white sand dunes.

Places to Eat

Historic *Kaiwarra Cottage (South Coast Rd)* near the Seal Bay turn-off has light meals and Devonshire teas.

Just outside the boundary of Flinders Chase, *Tandanya (South Coast Rd)* has an upmarket restaurant and does takeaways.

Barossa Valley

About 55km north-east of Adelaide, this is Australia's best known wine-producing district – it crushes about a quarter of the Australian vintage of 500,000 tonnes. The valley is gently sloping and measures about 25km long and five to 11km wide.

The Barossa still has a German flavour from its early days, which started with the original settlement in 1842. Fleeing religious persecution in Prussia and Silesia, these first settlers weren't actually wine makers, but fortunately someone soon came along and recognised the valley's potential. The name is actually a misspelling of Barrosa in Spain, close to where Spanish sherry comes from. Prior to WWI, place names in the Barossa probably sounded even more Germanic, but during the war many names were patriotically anglicised. When the fervour died down some were changed back.

You must get off the main road to begin to appreciate the Barossa Valley. Take the scenic drive between Angaston and Tanunda, the palm-fringed road to Seppeltsfield and Marananga, or wander through the sleepy historic hamlet of Bethany.

Information

The Barossa Wine & Visitor Centre (☎ 1800 812 662, fax 8563 0616, bwta@dove.net.au), at 66-68 Murray St in Tanunda, is open weekdays from 9 am to 5 pm and weekends and public holidays from 10 am to 4 pm. It includes an interpretive centre ($2) designed to educate visitors about wine. For more information see its Web site at www.dove.net.au/~bwta/bwta.html.

Wineries

The Barossa has over 50 wineries; almost all are open to the public and offer free wine tastings. Get a copy of the regional tourist guide for full details of locations and opening hours.

The following are some well known – and some not so well known – wineries.

Bethany Wines, Bethany Rd, Bethany, is a small family-operated winery in a scenic location. Its white port is highly recommended.

Branson Wines, near Greenock, is one of the valley's newest small wineries. It's already earning a fine reputation for its semillon and full-bodied reds.

Chateau Yaldara, at Lyndoch, was established in 1947 in the ruins of a 19th century winery and flour mill. It has a notable antique collection, which can be seen on conducted tours ($4).

Orlando, at Rowland Flat, between Lyndoch and Tanunda, was established in 1847 and is one of the oldest wineries in the valley.

Peter Lehmann Wines, Para Rd, Tanunda is set by the Para River. You can buy a bottle at the cellar door and enjoy it on a picnic in the grounds.

Rockford Wines is another small winery. It's noted for its full-bodied wines and intimate tasting room – a restored stone stable.

Saltram Wine Estate, near Angaston, was established in 1859. It's set in beautiful gardens.

Seppelts, in Seppeltsfield, was founded in 1852. The old bluestone buildings are surrounded by gardens and date palms, and there's a Grecian mausoleum on the main access road. The extensive complex includes a picnic area with gas barbecues. Guided tours cost $4.

Yalumba, in Angaston, was founded in 1849 and is Australia's largest family-owned wine company. The marble winery is topped by a clock tower and surrounded by gardens.

Special Events

The colourful Barossa Vintage Festival is the valley's big event. Taking place over seven days starting on Easter Monday in odd-numbered years, it features processions, brass bands, tug-of-war contests between the wineries, traditional dinners and, of course, a lot of wine tasting.

In October there's the two week International Barossa Music Festival featuring rock, jazz and classical music by big-name performers. Barossa Under the Stars, held in February, has night picnics and top entertainment.

Other festive occasions include the German Oompah Fest in January and the Hot-Air Balloon Regatta in May.

Getting There & Away

There are several routes from Adelaide, with the most direct being via Main North Rd through Elizabeth and Gawler. More picturesque routes go through the Torrens Gorge, then via either Williamstown or Birdwood. If you're coming from the east and want to tour the wineries before hitting Adelaide, the scenic route via Springton and Eden Valley to Angaston is the best bet.

The Barossa Adelaide Passenger Service (☎ 8564 3022) has three daily return bus services between the valley and Adelaide on weekdays (fewer on weekends and public holidays). Fares from Adelaide are Lyndoch $8, Tanunda $10.50, Nurioopta $11 and Angaston $12.

SOUTH AUSTRALIA

BAROSSA VALLEY WINERIES

1 Wolf Blass	12 Saltram Wine Estate	22 Old Barn Wines
2 The Willows Vineyard	13 Yalumba	23 Basedow Wines
3 Elderton Wines	14 Tarchalice Winery	24 Barossa Wine & Visitor Centre
4 Penfolds; Tarac	15 Hardy's Siegersdorf	25 Turkey Flat Vineyards
5 Branson Wines	16 Chateau Dorrien	26 Bethany Wines
6 Greenock Creek Cellars	17 Stanley Brothers	27 Krondorf
7 Seppelts	18 Richmond Grove Barossa Winery	28 Charles Melton Wines
8 Gnadenfrei Estate; Viking Wines	19 Peter Lehmann Wines	29 Rockford Wines
9 Heritage Wines	20 Langmeil Winery	30 St Hallett Wines
10 Kaesler Estate	21 Veritas	31 Grant Burge Wines
11 Barossa Cottage Wines		

32 Orlando	
33 Liebichwein	
34 Miranda Wines	
35 Jenke Vineyard Cellars	
36 Charles Cimicky Wines	
37 Chateau Yaldara	
38 Kies Family Wines	
39 Kellermeister Wines	
40 Barossa Settlers	
41 Twin Valley Estate	
42 Mountadam Winery	

The *Bluebird* tourist train (☎ 8212 7888) goes to Tanunda from Adelaide's suburban train station on Tuesday, Thursday and Sunday mornings at 8.50 am, returning at 3.50 pm; tickets cost $40 one way and $55 return.

A number of day tours to the valley operate from Adelaide; see under Organised Tours in the Adelaide section for some ideas.

Getting Around
Valley Tours (☎ 8563 3587) has a good, informative day tour of the Barossa for $37. Visits to various wineries and a winery lunch are included.

Balloon Adventures (☎ 8389 3195) does one-hour flights in a hot-air balloon, departing daily from Tanunda (weather permitting). The trip includes a champagne breakfast and costs $210.

The Barossa is good for cycling, with many interesting routes from easy to challenging. Bicycles can be rented from the Zinfandel Tea Rooms and the Tanunda Caravan and Tourist Park in Tanunda, the Bunkhaus Travellers Hostel in Nuriootpa, and the caravan park in Lyndoch. (The bicycle path between Nuriootpa and Tanunda runs past the Bunkhaus Travellers Hostel.)

LYNDOCH
• postcode 5351   • pop 960
Coming up from Adelaide via Gawler, Lyndoch, at the foot of the scenic Barossa Range, is the first valley town. About 7km south-west of town, the Barossa Reservoir has the famous **Whispering Wall**, a concrete dam wall with amazing acoustics; normal conversations held at one end can be heard clearly at the other end, 150m away.

Places to Stay & Eat
The friendly *Barossa Caravan Park (☎ 8524 4262)* is 2km from town on the Gawler road. It has camp sites from $10, on-site vans from $25 and cabins from $45.

The *Kersbrook Youth Hostel (bookings YHA Adelaide ☎ 8231 5583)*, 20km south of Lyndoch, is in the grounds of a National Trust property called Roachdale; beds cost $9 for members.

In the centre of town, the German-style *Lyndoch Bakery & Restaurant* is a wonderful spot for lunch. Nearby, the *Lyndoch Hotel* has good value counter meals.

TANUNDA
• postcode 5352   • pop 3100
In the centre of the valley is Tanunda, the most Germanic of the towns. You can still see early cottages around **Goat Square** on John St – this was the site of the original *ziegenmarkt*, a meeting and market place laid out as the original centre of Tanunda in 1842.

At 47 Murray St, the **Barossa Valley Historical Museum** has exhibits on the valley's early settlement; it's open daily from 11 am to 5 pm (Sunday from 1 to 5 pm).

You can watch artisans making kegs and other wooden items at the free **Keg Factory** on St Hallett Rd. It's open daily from 9 am to 5 pm.

Halfway between Tanunda and Nuriootpa on Barossa Valley Hwy is the **Kev Rohrlach Technology & Heritage Centre** ($8). This is a truly amazing collection with seemingly everything from aerospace rockets to steam engines. It's open daily from 11 am to 4 pm (Sunday from 10 am to 5 pm).

Three kilometres from Tanunda on the Gomersal road, **Norm's Coolies** – trained sheepdogs – go through their paces at the Breezy Gully Farm on Monday, Wednesday and Saturday at 2 pm ($6). The performance is worth seeing.

There are fine old Lutheran churches in all the valley towns but Tanunda has some of the most interesting. The **Tabor Church** dates from 1849; the 1868 **St John's Church** has life-size wooden statues of Christ, Moses and the apostles Peter, Paul and John.

From Tanunda, turn off the main road and take the scenic drive through Bethany and via **Menglers Hill** to Angaston. It runs through beautiful, rural country featuring large gums; the view over the valley from Menglers Hill is superb as long as you make sure to ignore the dreadful statues in the foreground.

SOUTH AUSTRALIA

Places to Stay & Eat

The *Tanunda Caravan & Tourist Park* (☎ 8563 2784, Barossa Valley Hwy) has camp sites for $11, on-site vans from $27 and cabins from $35.

There's also the reasonable *Tanunda Hotel* (☎ 8563 2030, 51 Murray St), which charges $54/60 a single/double for rooms with private facilities ($44/50 without). Otherwise there are two or three expensive motels and several B&Bs.

Two excellent, reasonably priced German-style eateries on Murray St are the *Zinfandel Tea Rooms*, at No 58, (it does breakfast and lunch) and the *Heidelberg Café*, at No 8, (lunch and dinner).

For something cheaper try the *Tanunda Club (45 MacDonnell St)*, which sells hearty dinners for $6. There's also the *Siegersdorf Wine Co & Restaurant (Barossa Valley Hwy)*, about halfway to Nuriootpa. It does three-course lunches for $10 and dinners for $12 – cheaper than most pubs in the state, yet the food is better.

NURIOOTPA

• postcode 5355   • pop 3500

At the northern end of the valley is the Barossa's commercial centre, Nuriootpa. There are several pleasant picnic areas along the Para River, as well as some nice river walks close to the town centre.

Places to Stay

The attractive *Barossa Valley Tourist Park* (☎ 8562 1404, Penrice Rd) has camp sites from $12 and cabins from $30.

The *Bunkhaus Travellers Hostel* (☎ 8562 2260, Nuraip Rd) is set on a family vineyard, 1km from town on the Barossa Valley Hwy to Tanunda (look for the keg on the corner). It's a very pleasant and welcoming place with dorm beds from $12 plus a cottage for four people (a double bed costs from $36). Mountain bikes can be hired here and Jan, the friendly proprietor, will be pleased to help you plan your day.

About halfway between Nuriootpa and Greenock, *Karawatha Guesthouse* (☎ 8562 1746) is a friendly, down-to-earth place charging $45/70 a single/double for bed and breakfast. This is one of the valley's few 'hosted' B&Bs (ie you eat with the owners).

ANGASTON

• postcode 5353   • pop 2000

On the eastern side of the valley, this town was named after George Fife Angas, one of the area's pioneers. Magnificent **Collingrove Homestead**, built by his son in 1856, is owned by the National Trust; it's open weekdays from 1 to 4.30 pm and during festivals from 11 am to 4.30 pm (entry $4; see the following Places to Stay entry).

The **Bethany Art Gallery**, at 12 Washington St, is worth visiting for its arts and crafts.

Places to Stay

In the centre of town, the *Barossa Valley Hotel* (☎ 8564 2014, 41 Murray St) and the *Angaston Hotel* (☎ 8564 2428, 59 Murray St) both charge $25 per person for basic pub-style rooms, including a light breakfast.

Good for a splurge is the historic *Collingrove Homestead* (☎ 8564 2061), about 7km from town on the Eden Valley road. Antique-furnished rooms in the old servants' quarters cost $160 per double, including a cooked breakfast.

BETHANY & AROUND

South-east of Tanunda, **Bethany** was the first German settlement in the valley. Old cottages still stand around the Bethany reserve; *The Landhaus* claims to be the world's smallest licensed restaurant – it seats 12 and bookings are essential (☎ 8563 2191).

Just south-east of the Barossa in the Eden Valley is **Springton**. On the main road at the Adelaide side of town you'll find the Herbig Tree – a hollow gum tree that was home to a pioneer family from 1855 to 1860.

Mid-North

The area between Adelaide and Port Augusta is generally known as the Mid-North. It includes some of the most productive farming land in the state, and is noted for its wheat and fine wool. As well, good wines are produced in the Clare Valley. There are a number of small historic towns, such as Auburn, Burra, Kapunda and Mintaro, whose streetscapes have changed little over the past 100 years.

Two main routes from Adelaide run through the Mid-North. One runs to Gawler then on through Burra to Peterborough. From there you can head west to Port Augusta, north-west to the Flinders Ranges or continue along the Barrier Hwy to Broken Hill in NSW.

The second route heads through Port Wakefield and on to Port Augusta on the Spencer Gulf. You can then travel north-east to the Flinders Ranges, south-west to the Eyre Peninsula, north to Alice Springs or west towards the Nullarbor and WA.

KAPUNDA
- postcode 5373   • pop 2000
About 80km north of Adelaide and just outside the Barossa Valley, historic Kapunda is off the main roads that head north. However, you can take a pleasant back route from the Barossa Valley through the town and join the Barrier Hwy a little further north.

A rich deposit of copper was found here in 1842 and Kapunda became the first mining town in Australia. At its peak in 1861 it had 11 hotels and was the colony's major commercial centre outside Adelaide. Large-scale operations ceased in 1878 and the mines closed altogether in 1912.

The Kapunda & Light Information Centre (☎ 8566 2902), on Main St, is open daily – check times as they depend on the availability of volunteers.

On the edge of town, a lookout offers views over the old open-cut mines and mine chimneys. There's a 1.5km walking track with information signs through the old mining area.

On Hill St in the town centre, Bagot's Fortune is a mining information centre with interesting displays. It opens weekends and public holidays from 1 to 4 pm ($2). Next door in the big old Baptist church, the Kapunda Museum is one of the state's best folk museums. It opens daily from 1 to 4 pm ($3).

'Map Kernow' (or, in old Cornish, 'Son of Cornwall'), an 8m-high bronze statue, stands at the Adelaide end of town as a tribute to pioneer miners.

Places to Stay
The classic *Sir John Franklin Hotel* (☎ 8566 3233, Main St) has basic pub rooms for $25/45 for singles/doubles. Diagonally opposite, the *North Kapunda Hotel* (☎ 8566 2205) also has rooms.

Alternatively, the attractive *Dutton Park Caravan Park* (☎ 8566 2094, Baker St) has camp sites from $11 and self-contained cabins for $40.

In the centre of town, *Bergnor's Vault* (☎ 8566 3355, bergnor@bigpond.com.au, 45 Main St) is a friendly B&B place charging $60 for singles/doubles, including a hearty breakfast.

AUBURN
- postcode 5451   • pop 330
This little township, 24km south of Clare, has some beautifully preserved old buildings, particularly on St Vincent St. A brochure – available from the post office and Pethericks Antiques – takes you on a 3km walk to 24 historic sites. Auburn was the birthplace of CJ Dennis, one of Australia's best known colonial authors.

The *Rising Sun Hotel* (☎ 8849 2015, Main North Rd) does good meals and has elegant rooms with private facilities for $40/65 for singles/doubles. Almost next door, *Tatehams* (☎ 8849 2030) has a gourmet restaurant and wonderful heritage-style rooms for $100/140.

CLARE
- postcode 5453   • pop 2600
At the heart of the Clare Valley wine region, this attractive town 135km north of Adelaide is so far free of many of the tourist trappings characteristic of the Barossa Valley. It was settled in 1842 and named after County Clare in Ireland.

The tourist information centre (☎ 8842 2131, fax 8842 1117), in the town hall on Main St, is open daily from 9 am to 5 pm (Sunday and public holidays 10 am to 4 pm).

Clare itself has a number of interesting buildings, including an impressive Catholic church. The police station and courthouse date from 1850 and are preserved as a **National Trust museum**; it's open weekends and public holidays from 10 am to noon and 2 to 4 pm ($2).

Established in 1851 by Jesuit priests, **Sevenhill Cellars**, at Sevenhill about 7km south of Clare, was the valley's first winery. It still produces communion wine, as well as a very good Verdelho. The marvellous **St Aloysius Church** adjoins the winery and dates from 1875.

There are many other wineries in the valley, including the award-winning Leasingham Winery (1894) on Clare's southern outskirts. Opening times vary, but the regional guide, available at the tourist centre, has all the relevant details.

Special Events

One of the Clare Valley's major events is the Clare Valley Gourmet Weekend, a festival of wine, food and music put on by local wineries over the Adelaide Cup weekend in May. Another is the Clare Valley Spring Garden Festival, which features some of the valley's best private gardens. It's held on a weekend in early November. The colourful Romeria del Rocio Spanish Festival takes place over four days in April.

Places to Stay

The attractive and friendly *Clare Caravan Park (☎ 8842 2724, Main North Rd)*, 4km south of the Clare post office, is the closest camping ground to town. It has camp sites from $11 ($8 if you're travelling solo), on-site vans for $30 and cabins from $40.

On Main St, the *Taminga Hotel (☎ 8842 2808)* has basic singles/doubles for $20/32. The *Clare Hotel (☎ 8842 2816)* on Main North Rd – an extension of Main St – has single pub rooms for $17 and rooms with private facilities for $45/50.

Bentley's Hotel/Motel (☎ 8842 2815, 191 Main North Rd) has a variety of options from backpacker beds for $10 to motel units for $55 singles and doubles.

Bungaree Station (☎ 8842 2677) 12km north of Clare has beds in its historic shearers' quarters for $15. This working farm has

many historical exhibits and you can do self-conducted cassette tours if you're staying there (tours cost $8 including morning or afternoon tea).

Geralka Farm (☎ 8845 8081), on the Spalding road 25km north of Clare, is another working farm that caters for visitors. You can camp (from $11) or stay in on-site vans (from $28).

In Mintaro, a small heritage town 18km south-east of Clare, the historic *Martindale Hall (☎ 8843 9088)* is an imposing mansion that offers B&B from $65 per person.

There are several motels in Clare and numerous B&Bs throughout the valley.

Getting There & Away

The Mid-North Passenger Service (☎ 8826 2346) bus goes daily except Saturday and Monday from Adelaide to Auburn ($13) and Clare ($17).

Getting Around

You can wander on foot or by bicycle past some of the district's finest wineries on the **Riesling Trail**, which meanders through the valley from Auburn to Clare. Clare Valley Cycle Hire (☎ 8842 2782), at 32 Victoria Rd in Clare, has bicycles for $15/20 per half/full day.

BURRA

• postcode 5417   • pop 1200

This pretty little town is bursting at the seams with historic sites. It was a copper-mining centre from 1847 to 1877, with various British ethnic groups forming their own distinctive communities (the Cornish being the most numerous).

The district, Burra Burra, takes its name from the Hindi word for 'great' by one account, and from the Aboriginal name of the creek by another.

Information

The Burra Visitor Centre (☎ 8892 2154, fax 8892 2555, bvc@capri.net.au), on Market Square, is open daily from 9 am to 5 pm. It can sell you the *Discovering Historic Burra* booklet, which describes numerous sites on an 11km heritage trail.

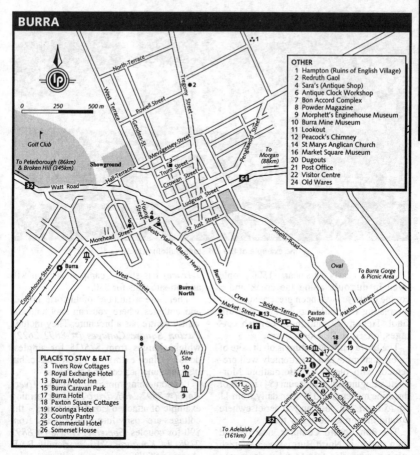

BURRA

0   250   500 m

Golf Club

To Peterborough (86km) & Broken Hill (345km)

Showground

North Terrace

West Terrace

Powell Street

Tregony Street

Genders St

Mevagessey Street

Truro Street

Crowan Street

Pengillwy Street

To Morgan (88km)

Hall Terrace

Watt Road

Young Street

Ludgvan Street

St Just Street

Morehead Street

Bests Place (Barier Hwy)

Smelts Road

Coppethouse Street

Burra

West Street

Burra North

Burra Creek

Market Street

Bridge Terrace

Paxton Square

Paxton Terrace

Oval

To Burra Gorge & Picnic Area

Mine Site

Upper Thames St

Commercial Street

Kingston Bridge

Chapel St

Church Street

Kintore Street

Ostock Street

To Adelaide (161km)

OTHER
1 Hampton (Ruins of English Village)
2 Redruth Gaol
4 Sara's (Antique Shop)
6 Antique Clock Workshop
7 Bon Accord Complex
8 Powder Magazine
9 Morphett's Enginehouse Museum
10 Burra Mine Museum
11 Lookout
12 Peacock's Chimney
14 St Marys Anglican Church
16 Market Square Museum
20 Dugouts
21 Post Office
22 Visitor Centre
24 Old Wares

PLACES TO STAY & EAT
3 Tivers Row Cottages
5 Royal Exchange Hotel
13 Burra Motor Inn
15 Burra Caravan Park
17 Burra Hotel
18 Paxton Square Cottages
19 Kooringa Hotel
23 Country Pantry
25 Commercial Hotel
26 Somerset House

The booklet forms part of the *Burra Passport*, which gives entry to eight National Trust sites and the town's four main museums. The passport costs $10 per person if you just want to visit the eight National Trust sites ($18 including the museums).

Things to See & Do

Burra has many substantial stone buildings, tiny Cornish cottages and numerous other reminders of the mining days. The visitor centre can arrange tours of the town – a two hour tour costs $20 and visits eight major National Trust sites.

The **Market Square Museum**, across from the visitor centre, has a shop, post office and a house as it might have looked between 1880 and 1930. It's open Friday, weekends and public holidays from 1 to 3 pm ($4).

The 33 attached cottages on **Paxton Square** were built for Cornish miners in the 1850s. One of the cottages, **Malowen Lowarth**, has been furnished in 1850s style. It's open on Saturday from 1 to 3 pm and Sunday and public holidays from 10.30 am to 12.30 pm ($4). The other cottages are available for accommodation (see the later Places to Stay & Eat entry).

RICHARD I'ANSON

A fine example of the old stone buildings in Burra

In Burra's early days nearly 1500 people lived in **dugouts** along the creek and a couple of these have been preserved. Other interesting old buildings include **Redruth Gaol**, Tregony St, and more **Cornish cottages**, on Truro St, North Burra.

The **Burra Mine Museum** is on the site of an original mine and is extremely well presented, with plenty of information. Morphett's Enginehouse Museum ($4) is part of the mine museum and is open daily from 11 am to 1 pm, but you can wander elsewhere around the mine site at any time.

The **Bon Accord Complex**, near the old train station in North Burra, was a Scottish mining enterprise that found underground water instead of copper. Not to be deterred, the canny Scots sold the site to the town, and the property supplied Burra's water until 1966. The site is now an interpretive centre, open daily from 12.30 to 2.30 pm ($4).

On the Morgan road, and about 3km from town, Burra Trail Rides (☎ 8892 2627) has a variety of **horse rides** in the scenic Burra Hills. These include two to three-day sheep droving trips for $90 a day.

Places to Stay & Eat

Down by the peaceful Burra Creek, the *Burra Caravan Park* (☎ 8892 2442, Bridge Terrace) has shaded camp sites from $10 and on-site vans for $30.

There are a number of historic houses and cottages where you can stay, and the visitor centre has a brochure. They include *Paxton Square Cottages* (☎ 8892 2622), which charges from $25/35 for singles/doubles (linen extra) – it's pretty basic, but it's clean and has cooking facilities.

For something more comfortable, *Tivers Row* (☎ 8892 2461, Truro St) is a charming example of attached Cornish cottages – the cottages are cosily furnished and cost from $90 for couples. *Somerset House* (☎ 8892 2198, 14 Kangaroo St) is a friendly B&B charging $50/80.

Several old hotels offer pub-style accommodation. Typical is the *Burra Hotel* (☎ 8892 2389, Market Square), which has rooms with ceiling fans for $30/50, including a cooked breakfast.

The more upmarket *Burra Motor Inn* (☎ 8892 2777, Market St) has large single/double/triple rooms overlooking the creek for $54/64/74.

Most of the hotels sell good-value counter meals and have more formal dining rooms. Alternatively, the *Country Pantry*, in Commercial St, near the visitor centre is good for lunches.

Getting There & Away

Greyhound Pioneer's Adelaide to Sydney service passes through Burra daily ($20 from Adelaide) – the visitor centre is the agency. The Mid-North Passenger Service (☎ 8826 2346) passes through Burra ($17) on Wednesday and Friday on its Adelaide to Orroroo run.

PORT PIRIE

● postcode 5540   ● pop 15,100

Port Pirie, 231km north of Adelaide (84km south of Port Augusta), is an industrial centre with a huge lead-smelting complex, which handles the output from Broken Hill.

The tourist office (☎ 8633 0439, 1800 000 424, fax 8632 1136, fretwell@a1.com.au) is at the **Tourism & Arts Centre** on Mary Ellie St. It is open on weekdays from 9 am to 5 pm, Saturday from 9 am to 4 pm and Sunday from 10 am to 3 pm.

The Arts Centre has an A-class exhibition hall and hosts some excellent touring exhibitions; ask to see its exquisite silver tree fern. It opens the same hours as the tourist office.

In the town centre on Ellen St, the interesting **National Trust museum** ($2) includes Port Pirie's first train station, the old customs house and the old police station. It's open Monday to Saturday from 10 am to 4 pm, and Sunday from 1 to 4 pm.

Places to Stay & Eat

The tourist office has details of Port Pirie's five motels and three hotels.

The very formal *Port Pirie Caravan Park (☎ 8632 4275, Beach Rd)* has camp sites from $8, on-site vans for $25 and cabins from $42.

Beds are $15 in the basic *Central Hotel (☎ 8632 1031, 30 Alexander St)*. The *Newcastle Hotel (☎ 8632 2365, 18 Main Rd)* and the more upmarket *International Hotel (☎ 8632 2422, 40 Ellen St)* charge around $25/40 a single/double for their rooms.

The *Abaccy Motel (☎ 8632 3701, 46 Florence St)* is the cheapest (and most basic) of the motels. It charges $45/55/60 for singles/doubles/triples.

Locals recommend *Annie's Coffee Shop (15 Jubilee Place)* and *Café Florence*, in

Norman St, for light meals. A pie cart is parked near the museum from 10 pm on Thursday, Friday and Saturday night.

MT REMARKABLE NATIONAL PARK

This steep, rugged park covers 16,000 hectares and straddles the southern Flinders Ranges between Melrose and Wilmington. From **Wilmington** (population 250) you can drive into the park and enjoy some nice bushwalks, including the Heysen Trail. One short walk you can do is through colourful **Alligator Gorge**, whose walls are only 2m apart in places.

The entry fee to the Alligator Gorge area is $5 per car. There's no vehicle-based camping here, but there is a large and attractive bush camping area at Mambray Creek on the other (western) side of the range. Camping permits ($12 per car including entry fee) can be obtained from the rangers' office (☎ 8634 7068) at Mambray Creek.

Hancocks Lookout, just north of the park and on the way to Horrocks Pass from Wilmington, offers excellent views of Spencer Gulf. The 7km detour (one way) is well worth it.

Basic rooms cost $25/45 a single/double at the *Wilmington Hotel (☎ 8667 5154)*. The town also has two caravan parks.

MELROSE

● postcode 5483   ● pop 200

This tiny town, 265km north of Adelaide, was established in 1853 and has a beautiful setting at the foot of Mt Remarkable (956m). There are some interesting old buildings here, including the police station and courthouse. The latter now houses a **museum**, open daily from 2 to 5 pm ($2). **Mt Remarkable Hotel** was built in 1859 and its exterior looks as if it has scarcely changed since.

Places to Stay

The *Melrose Caravan Park (☎ 8666 2060)* has great bush sites for $10, on-site vans for $30 and cabins for $40. Beds in a well appointed bunkhouse cost $10.

Alternatively, the *Mt Remarkable Hotel (☎ 8666 2119, Stuart St)* and the nearby

North Star Hotel (☎ 8666 2100) both have rooms. The latter's are actually in a National Trust-owned property across the road from the pub.

PETERBOROUGH
- postcode 5422   • pop 2300

Peterborough is another agricultural service town. There are several worthwhile attractions, mostly of a historic nature.

The tourist office (☎ 8651 2708), in an old railway carriage near the town hall, is generally open daily from 10 am to 3 pm.

Steamtown, at the western end of Main St, is a working railway museum. You can also visit a **gold battery** built in 1897 – it's used to crush gold-bearing ore from mines to the north-east. Ask at the tourist office if you want to check these places out.

Tiny **Terowie** (population 200), 23km south of Peterborough, is worth the short detour off the Barrier Hwy. The town was originally linked by broad-gauge train line to Adelaide and by narrow-gauge line to Peterborough – the railway yards provided hundreds of jobs, as goods had to be transferred from carriages on one line to the other. At its peak, the population exceeded 2000 people.

In 1967 the broad-gauge line was extended to Peterborough, sounding the death knell for Terowie. The town is worth a visit as much for its lingering air of a bygone age, as for its wonderful, though sadly deteriorating, historic streetscape.

Places to Stay
The *Budget Travellers' Hostel* (☎ 8651 2711, 86 Railway Terrace), behind the train station, has beds from $13.

Alternatively, the friendly *Peterborough Caravan Park* (☎ 8651 2545, 36 Grove St) has grassy camp sites from $10, on-site vans for $25 and cabins from $33.

OTHER MID-NORTH TOWNS
Other towns include **Carrieton**, where a major rodeo is held towards the end of December each year. **Bruce** and **Hammond** are old railheads, which have virtually faded away to ghost towns.

Orroroo, an agricultural centre, has the fascinating Yesteryear Costume Gallery, a restored settlers' cottage, and Aboriginal rock carvings at Pekina Creek.

Heading south from Melrose you come to tiny **Murraytown**, where there's a pub and very little else.

Continuing on, you can turn west through the scenic Germein Gorge to **Port Germein**. Here you find the very friendly *Casual Affair* (☎ 8634 5242), a pleasant coffee shop, gallery and craft centre with some backpackers' accommodation – beds in a tranquil, Japanese-style room cost $10. Meals are available and you can hire bicycles.

Alternatively, go straight ahead from Murraytown to **Wirrabara**. On the outskirts of the nearby Wirrabara Forest is a *YHA youth hostel* with beds costing $12 for members – ring the YHA office in Adelaide on ☎ 8231 5583 for contact details. There are some nice walks in the forest, which is on the Heysen Trail.

South-East

The Dukes Hwy provides the most direct route between Adelaide and Melbourne (729km), but you wouldn't take it if you wanted to see interesting country – although there are some worthwhile detours.

The Princes Hwy runs close to the coast and has greater appeal. Along here you can visit the Coorong (an extensive coastal lagoon system), call in at quiet fishing and holiday towns, detour into the Coonawarra wine belt and see the crater lakes at Mt Gambier.

Getting There & Away
Premier Stateliner (☎ 8415 5555) runs from the central bus station, Adelaide to Mt Gambier daily ($39). You can either go along the coast via the Coorong, stopping at Meningie ($19), Kingston ($30), Robe ($34) and Beachport ($36); or inland via Bordertown ($29), Naracoorte ($36) and Penola ($37).

COORONG NATIONAL PARK
The Coorong is a narrow lagoon curving along the coast for 145km from Lake

KATE NOLAN

Flocks of pelicans live on the Coorong

Alexandrina to near Kingston SE. A complex series of salt pans, it is separated from the sea by the huge sand dunes of the Younghusband Peninsula. There is vehicle access through the dunes and onto the surf beach in several places.

This area is home to vast numbers of water birds. *Storm Boy*, a film about a young boy's friendship with a pelican, and based on a novel of the same name by Colin Thiele, was shot on the Coorong. These wonderful birds are very evident in the park, as are ducks, waders and swans.

Coorong Nature Tours (☎ 8574 0037) has a good reputation for its nature-based trips. Tours ex-Meningie start at $60 for a half day and $110 for a full day – pick-ups in Adelaide can be arranged.

Places to Stay

The park has plenty of bush camp sites, but you need a permit ($5 per car per night). These can be purchased from numerous outlets in the area including both roadhouses at Salt Creek and the NPWS office (☎ 8575 1200) on the Princes Hwy in Meningie. General park information can also be obtained here.

Camp Coorong (☎ 8575 1557), on the highway 10km south of Meningie, is run by the Ngarrindjeri Lands & Progress Association. The Cultural Museum here has information about the Ngarrindjeri Aboriginal people. There are several tours on which you can learn about traditional lifestyles and visit a midden site. Self-contained units

and bunkhouse beds are available, but you have to book.

Alternatively there are several caravan parks and motels scattered along the Princes Hwy between Meningie and Salt Creek.

KINGSTON SE
- postcode 5275   • pop 1400

Near the southern end of the Coorong, Kingston SE is a small holiday and fishing port. It is a centre for rock-lobster fishing, and the annual **Lobsterfest**, held in the second week of January, is celebrated with live bands and exhibitions.

The Australian obsession with gigantic fauna and flora is apparent in **Larry the Big Lobster**, which looms over the highway on the Adelaide approach to town. Larry fronts a tourist information centre and cafe. You can buy freshly cooked rock lobster at the jetty during the lobster season (October through April).

From Kingston SE conventional vehicles can drive 16km along the beach to the **Granites**, while with a 4WD you can – depending on the tides – continue on past the Coorong to the Murray Mouth.

Places to Stay & Eat

The friendly *Kingston Caravan Park* (☎ 8767 2050, Marine Parade) has camp sites from $10, on-site vans for $26 and cabins from $30.

The small and homely *Backpackers Hostel* (☎ 8767 2107, 21 Holland St) is in a private home. Mrs Derr, the manager, charges $12 for dorm bunks, including use of her kitchen.

Standard pub rooms cost $16/28 a single/double at the *Crown Inn Hotel* (☎ 8767 2005, Agnes St) and $20/30 at the *Royal Mail Hotel* (☎ 8767 2002, Hansen St). Both offer counter meals.

ROBE
- postcode 5276   • pop 750

Robe, a charming holiday and fishing port dating from 1845, was one of the state's first settlements. Its citizens made a fortune in the late 1850s when the Victorian government instituted a £10-per-head tax on

Chinese gold miners. Many Chinese circumvented the tax by getting to Victoria via Robe; 10,000 arrived in 1857 alone. The **Chinamen's Wells** in the region are a reminder of that time.

The tourist office (☎ 8768 2465) is in the public library at the Smillie and Victoria Sts intersection. It's open weekdays from 10 am to 5 pm and Saturday morning from 10 am to 12.30pm.

There are numerous interesting old stone buildings in Robe, including the 1863 **customs house** on Royal Circus, which is now a nautical museum. The tourist office has a leaflet ($1) that takes you on a walk around many of the buildings.

There's a safe swimming beach opposite the town centre. **Long Beach**, about 2km from town off the Kingston SE road, is good for windsurfing and board surfing.

Wilsons of Robe is an excellent **arts and crafts shop** on the main street.

Places to Stay

Robe is a hugely popular summer holiday destination. There's plenty of accommodation, but you'll be lucky to find any vacancies in peak periods.

Places to Stay – Budget

About a kilometre out of town on the Kingston SE road, the **Lakeside Tourist Park** (☎ 8768 2193, Main Rd) is in a beautiful setting with resident ducks and peacocks. Camp sites cost from $13, on-site vans from $34 and cabins from $45.

A little further out, the aptly named **Bushland Cabins** (☎ 8768 2386, Nora Creina Rd) is very peaceful and has lots of wildlife. It has limited backpacker beds for $13, bush camp sites for $10 and basic self-contained cabins for $36 for two – the cabins sleep up to six ($6 for each extra person).

At the southern end of Long Beach, the **Long Beach Caravan Park** (☎ 8768 2237) has tent sites, on-site vans and self-contained cabins.

Places to Stay – Mid-Range

The historic **Caledonian Inn** (☎ 8768 2029, Victoria St) has basic rooms for $30/50 for singles/doubles, including a light breakfast, and motel-style units within a stone's throw of the beach for $80/100. Its restaurant is one of the best in Robe.

Overlooking Guichen Bay, the **Robe Hotel** (☎ 8768 2077, Mundy Terrace) has rooms from $50/70 with private facilities ($35/50 without). Some of the front rooms have private balconies with sea views.

Robe also has a number of B&Bs (some in historic homes) and generally expensive motels. The tourist office has details.

BEACHPORT

● postcode 5280   ● pop 440

If you have a yen for peace and solitude, you'll love this quiet little seaside town south of Robe with its long jetty, aquamarine sea and historic buildings. It's a lobster-fishing port, and during the season (October to April) you can buy freshly cooked lobsters at the jetty.

The **Old Wool & Grain Store Museum** ($2) is in a National Trust building on the main street. It has relics of Beachport's whaling days and rooms furnished in 1870s style. The **Aboriginal Artefacts Museum** on McCourt St has an extensive collection; admission is $1.50. Ask at the council office for keys to both buildings.

There's good board surfing at the local surf beach, and windsurfing is popular at **Lake George**, 5km north of the township. The hypersaline **Pool of Siloam** is a pretty swimming lake among sand hills on the outskirts of town.

Places to Stay & Eat

The **Beachport Caravan Park** (☎ 8735 8128, Beach Rd) is very ordinary but has a great location near the beach. Much nicer is the **Southern Ocean Tourist Park** (☎ 8735 8153, Somerville St), which has camp sites for $12 and cabins from $45.

Right on the beach and near the jetty, the friendly **Beachport Backpackers** (☎ 8735 8197) is in the old harbourmaster's house (1880). It has a cosy log fire on winter evenings and there's a spacious kitchen. Dorm beds cost $15; mountain bikes and surf boards are available for guests' use.

Bompa's (☎ 8735 8333, Railway Terrace), near the jetty, has comfortable rooms with share facilities from $55 for doubles, with a light breakfast.

MILLICENT

• postcode 5280   • pop 5120

At Millicent, 50km north-west of Mt Gambier, the 'Alternative 1' route through Robe and Beachport rejoins the main road.

At the Mt Gambier end of George St, the tourist centre (☎/fax 8733 3205) is open daily from 9.30 am to 4.30 pm. It has a good quality **craft shop** and there's an excellent National Trust **museum** ($4) in the complex with many interesting displays.

The **Canunda National Park**, with its giant sand dunes and rugged coastal scenery, is 13km west of town. It features 4WD tracks (in summer you can drive all the way from Southend to Carpenter's Rocks) and pleasant walks. You can camp near Southend – contact the ranger at Southend (☎ 8735 6053) for details and permits.

In **Tantanoola**, 21km to the south-east, the stuffed 'Tantanoola tiger' is on display at the Tantanoola Tiger Hotel. This beast, actually an Assyrian wolf, was shot in 1895 after a lot of publicity. It was presumed to have escaped from a shipwreck, but why a ship would have a wolf on board is not quite clear!

The **Tantanoola Caves** are on the Princes Hwy 8km away. The visitor centre (☎ 8734 4153) runs tours ($6) of the show cave every hour from 9.15 am to 4 pm daily (more often over the summer school holidays and Easter). They're the only caves in SA with wheelchair access.

MT GAMBIER

• postcode 5290   • pop 22,000

The major town and commercial centre of the South-East, Mt Gambier is 486km from Adelaide. It is built on the slopes of the extinct volcano from which it takes its name.

Information

For details on local attractions contact the Lady Nelson Visitor Information & Discovery Centre (☎ 8724 9750, 1800 087 187, fax 8723 2833, theladynelson@mountgam

biertourism.com.au) on Jubilee Hwy East. It's open daily from 9 am to 5 pm.

Allow at least an hour to look through the discovery centre ($6), which features a replica, complete with sound effects and taped commentary, of the historic brig *Lady Nelson*. It also has interesting natural history displays, and an audio-visual that acknowledges the devastating impact of European settlement on local Aboriginal people.

Things to See & Do

There are three craters, two of which have lakes. The beautiful **Blue Lake** is the best known, although from about March to November the lake is more grey than blue – in November it mysteriously changes back to blue again.

Blue Lake is about 85m deep at its deepest point and there's a 5km scenic drive around it. The lakes are a popular recreation spot and have been developed with boardwalks (over Valley Lake), a wildlife park, picnic areas and walking trails.

In the evenings you can visit the floodlit sunken gardens in the **Umpherston Sinkhole** and watch the possums feeding. You can also do daily tours ($4) down to the water table in the **Engelbrecht Cave**, a popular cave-diving spot. Both are in the town area.

Places to Stay & Eat

Mt Gambier has six caravan parks and all offer camp sites, on-site vans and cabins. You can get details from the information & discovery centre.

Off Margaret St, *The Jail (☎ 8723 0032, 1800 626 844, turnkey@seol.net.au, Langlois Drive)* is a backpacker hostel with dorm beds for $15 and twin rooms (these are old cells) for $16 per person. Otherwise the *Blue Lake Motel (☎ 8725 5211, 1 Kennedy Ave)*, just off the highway, has small twin rooms, including a kitchen, for $12 per person.

The *Mount View Motel (☎ 8725 8478, 14 Davison St)* charges $33 for singles and $38/40 for doubles/twins in its standard rooms ($3 more with kitchenettes). Few other motels in town come anywhere near these prices.

There are a number of grand old hotels in the town's busy centre and all offer accommodation and meals. The *Federal Hotel (☎ 8723 1099, 76 Commercial St East)* and the *Commercial Hotel (☎ 8725 3006, 76 Commercial St West)* charge $17/30 for singles/doubles – the latter also has backpacker beds for $12. The *South Australia Hotel (☎ 8725 2404, 78 Commercial St East)* charges $20/30.

Other than the pubs, the best value in town for a big feed is the *Barn Steakhouse*, about 2km out on Nelson Rd. It serves huge meals, as does *Charlies Family Diner* in the Western Tavern on Jubilee Hwy West – several cuisines are available here.

Getting There & Away

Air Both Kendell Airlines (☎ 13 1300) and O'Connors Air Services (☎ 13 1313) have daily return flights from Mt Gambier to Adelaide and Melbourne. One-way fares to both cities are $155.

Bus Premier Stateliner buses depart daily except Saturday for Adelaide (six hours; $39) from the Shell Blue Lake service station, 100 Commercial Rd West (☎ 8725 5037).

V/Line (☎ 1800 817 037) runs daily to/from Melbourne ($48) – you take the bus from Mt Gambier to Ballarat, where you hop on the train for Melbourne.

PORT MACDONNELL
• postcode 5291   • pop 660

South of Mt Gambier, this rock-lobster fishing centre was once the second most important port in the state, hence the surprisingly large and handsome 1863 **customs house**. The **Maritime Museum** features artefacts from local shipwrecks. **Dingley Dell**, the home of colonial poet Adam Lindsay Gordon, is open from Friday to Wednesday from 10 am to 4 pm (to 2 pm on Thursday); admission costs $5.

The area has some fine walks, including the path to the top of **Mt Schank**, an extinct volcano. Closer to town, the rugged coastline to the west is worth a visit, while **Piccaninnie Ponds** is a popular cave diving and snorkelling spot.

NARACOORTE
• postcode 5271   • pop 4710

Settled in the 1840s, Naracoorte is one of the oldest towns in the state and one of the largest in the south-east.

The tourist office (☎ 8762 1518) is at the award-winning **Sheep's Back Museum** on MacDonnell St. The museum, which is housed in an old flour mill, has interesting displays on the wool industry. It's open daily from 10 am to 4 pm ($5).

On Jenkins Terrace, the **Naracoorte Museum & Snake Pit** ($8) has an eclectic and interesting collection, including local venomous snakes – there are daily feeding demonstrations between October and April. It's open daily from 10 am to 5 pm (Sunday from 2 to 5 pm), but is closed from mid-July to the end of August.

The **Naracoorte Caves Conservation Park** (☎ 8762 2340) is 12km south-east of Naracoorte off the Penola road and is open daily from 9 am to 5 pm. Its limestone caves featured in David Attenborough's *Life on Earth* series. They have earned World Heritage listing, thanks to the Pleistocene fossil deposits in **Victoria Fossil Cave**.

The excellent **Wonambi Fossil Centre**, which houses a re-creation of the rainforest environment that covered this area 200,000 years ago, has life-size reconstructions of some of the animals whose bones have been found here. These are computer controlled and are said to be very lifelike.

There are four show caves: the fossil cave, **Alexandra Cave** (the main attraction), **Blanche Cave** and the **Wet Cave**. The Wet Cave can be seen on a self-guided tour. For the others, ranger-guided tours run from 9.30 am to 3.30 pm.

The **Bat Cave**, from which bats make a spectacular departure on summer evenings, isn't open to the public, but infra-red TV cameras allow you to see inside.

All the above activities, including the Bat Cave and Wonambi Fossil Centre, are charged on a sliding scale – one tour costs $8, two cost $14, and so on.

Adventure tours to undeveloped caves in the area (wear sneakers or sandshoes and old clothes) start at $20 for novices and $30 for advanced explorers (a minimum of three persons applies to both). You can hire overalls and kneepads for $5.

There are 155 bird species (79 are waterbirds) at the **Bool Lagoon Game Reserve**, 24km to the south of Naracoorte which, with the adjoining **Hacks Lagoon Conservation Park**, is the region's largest surviving wetland. A spectacular time to visit is during the ibis nesting season (September to January), when you can watch the action from bird hides. Bird-watching tours are available with Bourne's Birds (☎ 8764 7551) and these are highly recommended. Both reserves are open 24 hours daily.

Places to Stay & Eat

The attractive *Naracoorte Holiday Park (☎ 8762 2128, 81 Park Terrace)*, close to the town centre, has camp sites from $13, on-site vans for $35 and cabins from $41.

The *Naracoorte Caves* and *Bool Lagoon* have basic camping areas where sites cost $12 per car.

Naracoorte's three hotels all have good value meals.

COONAWARRA & PENOLA

The compact (25 sq km) wine-producing area of Coonawarra, renowned for its reds, is just north of Penola. Over 20 wineries offer cellar-door sales, most on a daily basis.

There are numerous heritage buildings in historic **Penola** (population 1200), which has won fame for its association with the Sisters of St Joseph of the Sacred Heart. This was the order co-founded in 1867 by Mother Mary MacKillop, who is to be canonised as Australia's first saint (see the earlier boxed text 'A Champion of the Poor'). Penola has been named as a significant MacKillop pilgrimage site.

The tourist centre (☎ 8737 2855, fax 8737 2206), on Arthur St, is open weekdays from 9 am to 5 pm and on weekends and public holidays from noon to 4 pm.

On Petticoat Lane, the **Mary MacKillop Interpretative Centre** is open daily from 10 am to 4 pm ($3). It features the 1867 **Woods-MacKillop Schoolhouse**, which has memorabilia associated with Mary MacKillop and

Father Julian Tenison Woods. In 1866 they co-founded the first school in Australia to welcome children from lower socioeconomic backgrounds. Classes were held in a stable at first, but moved to the schoolhouse when it opened the following year.

In dramatic contrast to the tiny historic **cottages** on Petticoat Lane, the lavish lifestyle of the colonial squattocracy is on display at **Yallum Park**. This opulent, two storey mansion (built in 1880) is on the Millicent road about 8km from town. You can do tours by arrangement (☎ 8737 2435).

Places to Stay

Beds cost $7 (linen extra) at *Whiskas Woolshed (☎ 8737 2428, 0418 854 505)*, 12km south-west of Penola and off the Millicent road. This place is pretty basic, but each bedroom has oil heating and there's a good kitchen and laundry. Andy, the genial owner, is a real character and it's worth stopping there just to meet him.

In the centre of town, *McKay's Trek Inn (☎ 8737 2250, 1800 626 844, trekin@penola.mtx.net.au, 38 Riddoch St)* is a comfortable place with bunk beds for $16, including linen and a light breakfast. You get a free night's accommodation if you break the record around the hostel's rock climbing circuit. Mountain bikes are available free to guests.

Over 20 restored historic cottages in the Penola district offer accommodation, with prices starting at $70 for twin share. Penola also has two hotels and a caravan park.

Getting There & Away

Premier Stateliner buses depart daily, except Saturday, for Adelaide ($37) and Mt Gambier ($8) from the Penola Supermarket in Church St.

DUKES HIGHWAY

The last town on the South Australian side of the border is **Bordertown** (population 2350). The town is the birthplace of former Australian prime minister Bob Hawke, and there's a bust of Bob outside the town hall. On the left as you enter from Victoria there is a wildlife park, with various species of

Australian fauna, including rare white kangaroos dozing behind a wire fence.

Keith (population 1100) has the vast Ngarkat group of conservation parks 16km north. Also worth visiting is the **Padthaway** wine-growing area, 62km south of Keith on the Naracoorte road – there are cellar-door sales at the historic Padthaway Homestead.

Murray River

Australia's greatest river starts in the Snowy Mountains, in the Australian Alps, and for most of its length forms the boundary between NSW and Victoria. It meanders for 650km through SA, first heading west to Morgan and then turning south towards Lake Alexandrina.

En route, the river is tapped to provide domestic water for Adelaide as well as country towns as far away as Whyalla and Woomera. Between the Victorian border and Blanchetown, irrigation has turned previously unproductive land into an important wine-making and fruit-growing region. This area is generally known as the Riverland.

The Murray has a fascinating history. Before the advent of railways, it was Australia's Mississippi, with paddle-steamers carrying trade from the interior down to the coast. Several of these shallow-draught vessels have been restored and you can relive the past on cruises of a few hours or several days. They include the huge stern-wheeler PS *Murray River Princess*, which regularly makes its stately passage up and down the river from Mannum.

Accommodation

There's plenty of conventional accommodation along the Murray, including a hostel in Berri. Alternatively, you can rent a fully self-contained houseboat and set off to explore the river.

Houseboats can be hired in most towns. However, they're very popular from October to April, so for these months it's wise to book well ahead. The Houseboat Hirers Association (☎ 8395 0999, fax 8263 5373, hbc@ kern.com.au) in Adelaide can give advice

and arrange a boat for you. Prices vary hugely, but in the high season you can expect to pay from around $25 per person per night depending on such factors as size of boat and duration of hire. Prices are usually considerably cheaper in winter.

Alternatively, there are numerous bush camp sites among huge river red gums scattered along the river, particularly east of Morgan.

Getting There & Away

Premier Stateliner (☎ 8415 5555) has daily services from Adelaide to the Riverland towns. The fare to Berri, Loxton and Renmark is $28.

Greyhound Pioneer and McCafferty's run daily through the Riverland en route to Sydney but can't drop off until past Renmark. Their fare to Sydney from Renmark is $79.

RENMARK
● **postcode 5341** ● **pop 8100**
In the centre of the Riverland irrigation area and 254km from Adelaide, prosperous Renmark resulted from the first of the great irrigation projects that revolutionised the Riverland.

The tourist office (☎/fax 8586 6704) is on Murray Ave, beside the river. It's open weekdays from 9 am to 5 pm, Saturday from 9 am to 4 pm and Sunday and public holidays from noon to 4 pm. Part of the building is an interpretive centre, which includes the recommissioned 1911 paddle-steamer *Industry* ($2).

Renmark River Cruises (☎ 8595 1862) offers **cruises** for $16 on the MV *River Rambler* departing from the town wharf daily at 2 pm. It also does dinghy trips, as do Bush & Backwaters 4WD Tours (☎ 8586 5344).

Angoves Wines, on Bookmark Rd, and Renmano Wines, on Industry Rd, have cellar door sales and **tastings**.

Upstream from town, the huge **Chowilla Regional Reserve** (part of the sprawling Bookmark Biosphere Reserve) is great for bush camping, canoeing and bushwalking. Access is along the north bank from Renmark. For details contact the NPWS office (☎ 8595 2111) on Vaughan Terrace in Berri.

Places to Stay

Renmark Riverfront Caravan Park (☎ 8586 6315, Sturt Hwy) is idyllically situated on the river about 1km east of town. Camp sites cost from $5, on-site vans/cabins from $27/48. It rents out canoes from $7.50 an hour. Further along the river beside the Paringa Bridge, the *Riverbend Caravan Park (☎ 8595 5131, Sturt Hwy)* has similar options.

Camping in the *Chowilla Regional Reserve* costs $5 per car per night – contact the NPWS office in Berri for a permit.

BERRI

• postcode 5343   • pop 7100

At one time a refuelling stop for wood-burning paddle-steamers, this town takes its name from the Aboriginal *berri berri*, meaning 'big bend in the river'.

The tourist office (☎ 8582 1655, fax 8582 3201), on Vaughan Terrace, opens weekdays from 9 am to 5 pm (Saturday to 11.30 am).

The **lookout**, on the corner of Vaughan Terrace and Fiedler St, has good views over the town and river. On Riverside Ave is a **monument** to Jimmy James, a famous Aboriginal tracker.

The **Willabalangaloo Reserve** ($4) is a flora and fauna reserve with walking trails, a museum and a historic paddle-steamer. It's open Thursday to Monday from 10 am to 4 pm (daily during school holidays).

Berri Estates at Glossop, 7km west of Berri, is one of Australia's biggest wineries. It's open for tastings and cellar-door sales daily, except Sunday, from 9 am to 5 pm.

Road access to the beautiful Katarapko Creek section of the **Murray River National Park** is through Berri or Winkie (near Glossop). This is another great area for bush camping, canoeing and bird-watching – for details contact the NPWS office (☎ 8595 2111) on Vaughan Terrace.

You can hire canoes from Lyons Motors (☎ 8582 1449) on Riverview Drive from $5 per hour and $25 per day; transport can be arranged.

Places to Stay

The *Berri Riverside Caravan Park (☎ 8582 3723, Riverview Drive)* has camp sites from $11, on-site vans from $31 and cabins from $38. Air-con twin and double rooms in its backpacker quarters cost $20.

Berri Backpackers (☎ 8582 3144, Sturt Hwy) on the Barmera side of town is one of the best-equipped hostels you'll find anywhere – but it's only for international visitors. Among other facilities it has a swimming pool, sauna, tennis court and volleyball court, as well as bicycles and canoes for guests' use. The manager has excellent contacts if you want seasonal work in local orchards and vineyards. Dorm beds are $15 each ($90 per week).

At the *Berri Resort Hotel (☎ 8582 1411, Riverview Drive)* pub rooms with private facilities cost from $48/53 for singles/doubles. It also has more upmarket accommodation from $82/88.

Bush camping in the *Katarapko Creek* area costs $5 per car per night – contact the NPWS office for a permit.

The *Berri Club*, across from Berri Backpackers, has great-value meals from Thursday to Sunday nights.

LOXTON

• postcode 5333   • pop 3320

From Berri, the Murray makes a large loop south of the Sturt Hwy, with Loxton at its base. From here you can canoe across to the Katarapko Creek section of the Murray River National Park, which occupies much of the area within the loop (see the Berri section, above, for more details).

The tourist office (☎ 8584 7919, fax 8584 6225), at the roundabout on Bookpurnong Terrace, is open weekdays from 9 am to 5 pm, Saturday from 9.30 am to 12.30 pm and Sunday and public holidays from 1 to 4 pm.

Loxton's major attraction is the **Historical Village**, with over 40 fully furnished buildings from days gone by. It's open daily from 10 am to 4 pm (weekends 5 pm); admission is $5.

The **Australian Vintage** winery, on Bookpurnong Rd, is open for tastings daily except Sunday from 10 am to 5 pm.

Riverland Canoeing Adventures (☎ 8584 1494), on Alamein Ave, towards Renmark, rents single kayaks for $15 a day and double kayaks and canoes for $25 a day. Various forms of transport, maps and camping equipment can also be hired.

Places to Stay & Eat

The *Loxton Riverfront Caravan Park* (☎ 8584 7862) is at Habels Bend, 2km from town. It has camp sites from $11, on-site vans for $25, cabins from $32 and you can hire canoes ($8/25 per hour/day).

The *Loxton Hotel/Motel* (☎ 8584 7266, East Terrace) has pub singles/doubles for $20/25 and more upmarket rooms from $41/46. It has a good bistro plus counter meals.

BARMERA

• postcode 5345   • pop 4500

On the shores of Lake Bonney, Barmera was on the old overland stock route from NSW. The ruins of **Napper's Old Accommodation House**, built in 1850 at the mouth of Chambers Creek, are a reminder of that era, as is the **Overland Corner Hotel** on the Morgan road, 19km north-west of town. Built in 1859, it's now owned by the National Trust and has a small museum and walking trails. You can also stay here – see Places to Stay.

The tourist office (☎ 8588 2289, fax 8588 2777, brmtrvl@www.murray.net.au) is at the top of the main street, next to the roundabout, and is open weekdays from 9 am to 5.30 pm and Saturday until noon.

Lake Bonney, which has sandy beaches, is popular for swimming and water sports. There's a nudist beach at **Pelican Point**.

You'll find a game reserve at **Moorook** and another across the river from **Kingston-on-Murray** – the latter backs onto the Overland Corner Hotel. Both reserves have nature trails and are good spots for bird-watching and canoeing. For camping permits, contact the Berri NPWS office (☎ 8595 2111).

Riverland Safaris (☎ 8588 2869) offers various guided tours, including winery visits and fishing and yabbying trips.

Places to Stay

There are several caravan parks in the area, with the closest to the town centre being the *Lake Bonney Holiday Park* (☎ 8588 2234, Lakeside Drive). It has camp sites from $12,

cabins from $25 and self-contained cottages from $45.

The comfortable *Barmera Hotel/Motel* (☎ 8588 2111, Barwell Ave) has basic rooms for $20/30 for singles/doubles and rooms with private facilities from $38. Out at the historic *Overland Corner Hotel* (☎ 8588 7021), old-fashioned double rooms cost $36/50, including breakfast.

WAIKERIE

• postcode 5330   • pop 1800

A citrus-growing centre, the town takes its name from the Aboriginal word for 'anything that flies', after the teeming birdlife on the nearby lagoons and river.

For tourist information go to the **Orange Tree** (☎ 8541 2332) on the Sturt Hwy on the Barmera side of town – look out for the large, green fibreglass sphere with red spots. It sells a comprehensive range of local fruit and nut products, and is open weekdays from 9 am to 5.30 pm and weekends from 10 am to 4 pm.

You can take **joy flights** in a glider at the Waikerie International Soaring Centre (☎ 8541 2644). Twenty minutes costs $50.

Places to Stay

The *Waikerie Hotel/Motel* (☎ 8541 2999, McCoy St), in the town centre, has pub rooms at $35/45 for singles/doubles, and you can eat in the front bar or bistro.

Down by the river on the west side of town, the *Waikerie Caravan Park* (☎ 8541 2651, Ramco Rd) has camp sites for $10 and cabins from $30.

Basic bush camping is available at *Eremophila Park* (☎ 8589 3023), a private nature park off the Sturt Hwy 20km east of town. Sites in woodland cost $4 per person.

MORGAN

• postcode 5320   • pop 1350

In its prime, this was one of Australia's busiest river ports, with wharves towering 12m high. There's a car ferry across the Murray here. A leaflet details a heritage walk that includes PS *Mayflower*, the state's oldest operating paddle-steamer. The **Port of Morgan Historic Museum**, by the river below the town centre, has exhibits on the paddle-steamer trade; it opens according to demand.

Places to Stay
Down by the ferry landing, the *Morgan Riverside Caravan Park* (☎ 8540 2207) has camp sites from $10, on-site vans for $27 and cabins from $35. It rents out canoes for $6/20 per hour/day.

Opposite each other on Railway Terrace, the *Commercial Hotel* (☎ 8540 2107) and *Terminus Hotel/Motel* (☎ 8540 2006) have basic pub rooms for $15 per person.

SWAN REACH
- postcode 5354   • pop 230

This sleepy old town, 70km south-west of Waikerie, has picturesque river scenery but not many swans – there are lots of pelicans, however. Just downstream the Murray makes a tight meander known as **Big Bend**; the lookout beside the Walker Flat road, 9km from town, gives you a great view of its towering yellow cliffs.

MANNUM
- postcode 5238   • pop 2030

The *Mary Ann*, Australia's first riverboat, was built here in 1853 and made the first paddle-steamer trip up the Murray. There are many relics of the pioneering days, including the fully restored 1897 paddle-steamer *Marion* – it's now a floating museum ($3) moored at the tourist office (☎ 8569 1303). Both are open weekdays from 9 am to 4 pm and weekends from 11 am to 3 pm.

The **Purnong Rd Bird Sanctuary** is a great spot to see water birds; it starts at the Mannum Caravan Park and you drive along it for several kilometres on the main road to Purnong. **Cascade Waterfalls**, 9km from Mannum on Reedy Creek, are worth a visit. Although the falls only flow during winter, the rugged scenery and large river red gums can be enjoyed at any time.

River Cruises
The grand paddle-steamer *Murray River Princess* does two, three and five-night cruises from Mannum. Contact Captain Cook Cruises (☎ 1800 804 843) for times and prices – their weekend cruises start at around $350 per person twin-share.

The PS *Marion* often does short cruises on weekends; check at the tourist centre for an operating schedule.

The MV *Lady Mannum* also does short cruises; check times with Lady Mannum Cruises (☎ 8569 1438) in the main street.

Places to Stay
Mannum Caravan Park (☎ 8569 1402, Purnong Rd), on the town side of the ferry crossing, has camp sites from $11 and self-contained cabins from $45. Beds in a well appointed bunkhouse with kitchen cost $13 – internationals only, please. You can camp for free on the other side of the river near the ferry and use the shower facilities ($2.50) between noon and 6 pm at the caravan park.

Getting There & Away
ABM Coachlines (☎ 8347 3336) runs to Mannum from Adelaide via Birdwood on weekdays for $11.50.

MURRAY BRIDGE
- postcode 5253   • pop 13,500

SA's largest river town, only 82km south-east of Adelaide, is named for its 1km-long bridge; built in 1879, it was the first to span the Murray. It's a popular area for fishing, swimming, water-skiing and barbecues.

The tourist office (☎ 8532 6660, fax 8532 5288), on South Terrace, is open on weekdays from 8.30 am to 4.30 pm, and weekends and public holidays from 10 am to 2 pm (to 3.45 pm on Saturday).

Things to See & Do
Dundee's Wildlife Park ($7) is 4km out on the Wellington road. Open 10 am to 5 pm daily, it has many gorgeous parrots and other native birds, as well as juvenile crocodiles in a tropical hot house.

On 1000 hectares 20km west of town, the open-range **Monarto Zoological Park** has Australian and international exhibits, including herds of zebras and giraffes. It's open daily from 9 am to 5 pm. Entry costs $10, which includes a bus ride through the park (departing 10.30 am to 3.30 pm).

River Cruises

Both MV *Barrangul* and PS *Captain Proud* have a restaurant on board and do day and short cruises – check at the tourist office for times.

The PS *Proud Mary* departs from Murray Bridge on two and five-night cruises. Contact Proud Australia Holidays (☎ 8231 9472) in Adelaide for times and prices.

Places to Stay & Eat

The *Avoca Dell Caravan Park* (☎ 8532 2095, Murray Drive), across the river from town and north of the bridge, has camp sites from $12 and cabins from $38.

In the centre of town, the friendly *Balcony Guesthouse* (☎ 8531 1411, 6 Sixth St) has various options including basic backpacker rooms for $18 per person ($25 standard rate), including a light breakfast. If you want to go more upmarket, it has rooms with four-poster beds and private facilities from $55/70.

The *Murray Bridge Community Club*, at Sturt Reserve, and the *Happy Gathering* Chinese restaurant, on the corner of First and Seventh Sts, are recommended for good value meals. The *Italian Club (Lincoln Rd)* is a fair way out but worth trying on Thursday night – all the pasta you can eat for $8.

Getting There & Away

Buses to Adelaide cost $11 with the Murray Bridge Passenger Service (☎ 8532 6660); they leave daily from outside the tourist office, where tickets can be purchased. If you are travelling from Adelaide, bookings need to be made with Premier Stateliner (☎ 8415 5555).

Tickets to Mt Gambier cost $39 with Premier Stateliner. It's $45 to Melbourne with Greyhound Pioneer and McCafferty's.

TAILEM BEND

• postcode 5260   • pop 1600

Tailem Bend's major attraction is Old Tailem Town, a fascinating re-creation of a pioneer village with many old buildings; it is open daily from 10 am to 5 pm ($10).

You can take a ferry across the Murray to Jervois from where it's 11km to the pretty hamlet of Wellington, near where the river enters Lake Alexandrina. Here you'll find the Old Wellington Court House Museum (open daily) and the historic Wellington Hotel, where you can sit on the lawn and watch the river go by. Aboriginal middens can be seen 2km south-east of the township.

Tailem Bend has two hotels, a motel and two caravan parks.

Yorke Peninsula

Yorke Peninsula is a popular holiday area within easy driving distance of Adelaide. There are pleasant beaches along both sides, while Innes National Park, on the tip, has good fishing, surfing and diving. The economy was originally based on the so-called 'Copper Triangle' centred on Kadina. As the copper mines declined, agriculture developed. Most of the land now grows barley and other grains.

The main tourist office for Yorke Peninsula is in the old train station in Moonta (☎ 8825 1891, fax 8825 2930, tourism@kadina.mtx.net.au). It's open daily from 9 am to 5 pm.

Getting There & Away

Premier Stateliner (☎ 8415 5555) operates a daily bus from Adelaide to Kadina, Wallaroo, Moonta, Port Hughes and Moonta Bay. It takes about three hours to Moonta and costs $15.50.

The Yorke Peninsula Passenger Service (☎ 8391 2977) runs daily from Adelaide's central bus station to Yorketown. The route alternates between the east coast and down the centre of the peninsula. Fares from Adelaide are: Ardrossan $18.50, Port Vincent $24, and Edithburgh and Warooka (both $25).

WEST COAST

The west coast, facing onto Spencer Gulf, has several quiet swimming beaches and small resorts. These are off the main road from Wallaroo, which runs inland through small farming communities.

The west coast of the 'foot' (from Corny Point down to Innes National Park) has

Adelaide and the Torrens River after a storm, SA

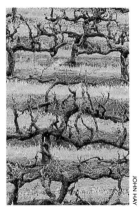

Coriole vineyard, Barossa Valley

Dog fence, Camerons Corner

Veale Garden waterspout, SA

King George Cove, on the north coast of Kangaroo Island, SA

Wilpena Pound, Flinders Ranges National Park, SA

The Remarkable Rocks on the dramatic coast of Kangaroo Island, SA

Red dunes in the Strzelecki Desert near Lake Eyre, SA

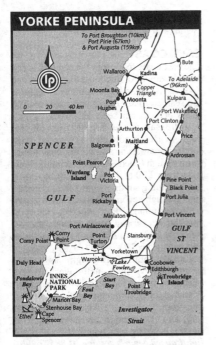

YORKE PENINSULA

To Port Broughton (10km),
Port Pirie (67km)
& Port Augusta (159km)

Bute

Wallaroo Kadina

To Adelaide
(96km)

Moonta Bay   Copper
             Triangle   Kulpara
Port   Moonta
Hughes   Port Wakefield

0   20   40 km   Port Clinton

                Arthurton

SPENCER   Balgowan Maitland   Price

Point Pearce

Wardang   Port
Island   Victoria   Pine Point
                               Black Point
GULF   Port
             Rickaby   Port Julia

            Minlaton   Port Vincent

Port Minlacowie   *GULF*
Corny   Point   *ST*
Point   Point   Turton
Corny Point   Stansbury *VINCENT*

            Yorketown

Daly Head   Warooka   Lake   Coobowie
                      Fowler Edithburgh
Pondalowie INNES   Troubridge
Bay   NATIONAL   Sturt   Island
           PARK   Bay   Point
        Foul   Troubridge
'Ethel' Bay
     Marion Bay
   Stenhouse Bay   *Investigator*
'Ethel' Cape
        Spencer   *Strait*

some good surfing breaks, fine coastal
scenery and a couple of bush camping areas.

In the early 1860s, copper was discovered in the Moonta-Kadina-Wallaroo area
and soon a full-scale mining rush was on.
Most miners were from Cornwall in England, and the area still has a strong Cornish
flavour – it was often referred to as **Little
Cornwall**. The boom peaked around the turn
of the century, but in the early 1920s a
slump in copper prices and rising labour
costs closed all the peninsula's mines. The
lack of development since then has largely
preserved the historic streetscapes.

In celebration of its Cornish heritage, the
Kernewek Lowender Festival is held here
over several days in May of odd-numbered
years. It's a chance to try Cornish pasties or
watch a wheelbarrow race, and if you drink
enough traditional beer you may see a
piskey – a mischievous sprite believed, by
superstitious Cornish people, to bring good
fortune.

Kadina

● postcode 5554   ● pop 4500

The largest town on the peninsula, Kadina
was once the main copper-mining centre. A
booklet available from the Moonta tourist
office takes you on a tour of the town's numerous historic sites.

The **Kadina Heritage Museum** ($4) fea-
tures Matta House (1863), the restored home
of the Matta Matta mine manager. There's
also the Matta Matta mine, old farming machinery and a blacksmith's shop, among
other displays. It is open Wednesday and
weekends from 2 to 4.30 pm (from 10 am on
public and school holidays).

The **Wallaroo Mine** is 1km west of the
town and off the Wallaroo road. It takes
half an hour to stroll around the area, which
includes numerous deep shafts and the impressive ruin of a stone engine house.

Also interesting is the **Banking & Currency Museum** ($3), in an old bank on
Graves St. It is open daily, except Friday and
Saturday, from 10 am to 5 pm (closed during June). You can buy and sell coins here.

Places to Stay & Eat The *Kadina Caravan
Park (☎ 8821 2259, Lindsay Terrace)* has
camp sites from $13 and on-site vans for $32.

The *Wombat Hotel (☎ 8821 1108, 19 Taylor St)* charges $19 per person, while the *Kad-
ina Hotel (☎ 8821 1008)*, a block away at No
29, has singles/doubles with private facilities
for $35/50. Both include a light breakfast.

The town's three pubs do meals, and there
are several bakeries, cafes and restaurants.

Wallaroo

● postcode 5556   ● pop 2250

This port town was a major centre during
the copper boom. The 'big stack', one of the
great chimneys from the copper smelters
(built in 1861), still stands, but today the
port's main function is exporting agricultural products.

In the old post office, on Jetty Rd, there's
the fascinating **Heritage & Nautical Museum** ($3), open on Wednesday, weekends
and public and school holidays. It tells
about the square-rigged sailing ships that
serviced this area from England, and has a

detailed history of Caroline Carleton, who wrote the words to 'Song of Australia'.

A booklet detailing a town heritage walk can be obtained from the tourist desk (☎ 8823 2020) in the new post office on the corner of Irwin St and Owen Terrace.

Places to Stay & Eat On the beach near the jetty, the basic *Office Beach Caravan Park* (☎ 8823 2722) has camp sites from $12, on-site vans for $27 and cabins from $32.

The *Weerona Hotel* (☎ 8823 2008, 4 John Terrace) has singles/doubles for $20/30. Alternatively, the *Sonbern Lodge Motel* (☎ 8823 2291, 18 John Terrace) charges $40/55 for rooms with private facilities ($24/38 without) in its charming, older lodge section.

The town's five hotels have counter meals and there are several takeaways, bakeries and tearooms.

Moonta

• postcode 5558   • pop 2300

In the late 19th century the copper mine at Moonta, 18km south of Wallaroo, was the richest mine in Australia. At its peak, the town's grand old school had 1100 pupils on its rolls, but these days it's an excellent **folk museum** ($3), open daily, except Sunday, from 1.30 to 4 pm. The museum is part of the **Moonta Heritage Site**, on the eastern outskirts of town, which you can explore with a self-guiding booklet from the tourist office in the old train station. Nearby is a fully restored **miner's cottage** and garden.

A section of the underground workings at the **Wheal Hughes** mine (this isn't one of the early mines) is open to the public – tours cost $12 and you book at the tourist office.

Places to Stay & Eat Right on the beach, 3km from town, the *Moonta Bay Top Tourist Park* (☎ 8825 2406, Tossell St) has camp sites from $13 and self-contained cabins from $47.

The *Royal Hotel* (☎ 8825 2108, 2 Ryan St) has basic rooms for $25/40, including a light breakfast.

There are numerous places to eat. Recommended is the *Cornish Kitchen (Ellen St)*, a great place for homemade Cornish pasties and lunches.

EAST COAST

The east coast road from the top of Gulf St Vincent down to Stenhouse Bay near Cape Spencer is generally within one to 2km of the sea. En route, tracks and roads lead to sandy beaches and secluded coves.

Ardrossan is the largest town on this coast. It has an interesting National Trust folk museum featuring the famous stump-jump plough (open Sunday and public holidays from 2.30 to 4 pm) on Fifth St.

Continuing south, the next 50km of road runs through several small seaside resorts, including tranquil **Port Vincent**. Here you find the *Tuckerway Youth Hostel* (☎ 8853 7285, 14 Lime Kiln Rd), with good facilities and beds from $10.

Further south, **Edithburgh** has a tidal swimming pool in a small cove; from the clifftops you can look across to **Troubridge Island** and its prominent lighthouse. A 2½ hour tour, including a historical commentary, can be taken to the island ($20) – overnight stays are available in the old *lighthouse keeper's cottage* (☎ 8852 6290).

Near Marion Bay, on the coast road, is *Hillocks Drive* (☎ 8854 4002), a large farm where you can enjoy some wonderful coastal scenery, native wildlife and wildflowers (July to November). Bush camping is $5 per car, and elderly on-site vans are from $22. For day visitors there's a $3 entry fee.

Yorketown (population 750) is the district's business and administrative centre. It's a pleasant, friendly place and you may find accommodation here when the seaside resorts are full over summer.

INNES NATIONAL PARK

The southern tip of the peninsula, marked by Cape Spencer, is part of the Innes National Park. The park has spectacular coastal scenery as well as good fishing, reef diving and surfing. You'll go a long way to find quieter emus! There's a $5 entry fee per vehicle. **Stenhouse Bay**, just outside the park, and **Pondalowie Bay**, within the park, are the principal settlements. Pondalowie

Bay is the base for a large lobster-fishing fleet and also has a fine surf beach. Beaches in the park are swimmable, but you should keep an eye on the swell and wind direction.

In the park is the wreck of the steel barque *Ethel*, a 711-tonne ship that ran aground in 1904. All that remains are the ribs of the hull rising forlornly from the sands – her anchor is mounted in a memorial on the clifftop above the beach. Just past the Cape Spencer turn-off, a sign on the right directs you to the ruins of the **Inneston Historic Site**. Inneston was a gypsum-mining community abandoned in 1930.

Places to Stay
With a permit (from $5 to $15 per car per night, depending on facilities), you can camp in a number of places in the park, or stay in basic huts (from $22 per hut). The NPWS office in Stenhouse Bay (☎ 8854 4040, fax 8854 4072) can provide details.

Getting There & Away
There is no public transport to the end of the peninsula. The Yorke Peninsula Passenger Service will take you to Warooka or Yorketown, from where you could try to hitch.

Eyre Peninsula

The wide, triangular Eyre Peninsula points south between Spencer Gulf and the Great Australian Bight. It's bordered in the north by the Eyre Hwy from Port Augusta to Ceduna. The coastal run is in two parts: the Lincoln Hwy south-west from Port Augusta to Port Lincoln; and the Flinders Hwy north-west to Ceduna. It's 468km from Port Augusta direct to Ceduna via the Eyre Hwy; via the coast road it's 763km.

The coast is an extremely popular summer holiday area with many good beaches, sheltered bays and pleasant little port towns. On the wild western side are superb surf beaches, spectacular coastal scenery and important breeding grounds for the southern right whale, the Australian sea lion and the great white shark – some scenes in the film *Jaws* were shot here.

Eyre Peninsula is also a major agricultural region, while rich iron-ore deposits in the Middleback Ranges are processed and shipped from the busy port of Whyalla. The peninsula takes its name from Edward John Eyre, the hardy explorer who, in 1841, made the first overland crossing between Adelaide and Albany, WA.

Getting There & Away
Air Kendell Airlines (☎ 13 1300) flies daily from Adelaide to Port Lincoln ($128) and Whyalla ($131), and daily except Saturday to Ceduna ($217).

Airlines of SA (☎ 13 1313) flies from Adelaide to Port Augusta ($120) weekdays and Port Lincoln ($95) daily.

Whyalla Airlines (☎ 1800 088 858) has daily services from Adelaide to Cleve ($90), Wudinna ($105) and Whyalla ($95).

Bus Premier Stateliner (☎ 8415 5555) has daily services from Adelaide to Port Augusta ($29), Whyalla ($33), Port Lincoln ($58), Ceduna ($68) and Streaky Bay ($61).

Train See the following section on Port Augusta for details of train services.

PORT AUGUSTA
● postcode 5700   ● pop 14,600
Matthew Flinders was the first European to set foot in the area, but the town of Port Augusta was not established until 1854. Today, this busy city is the gateway to the outback region of SA. It's also a major crossroads for travellers.

From here, roads head west across the Nullarbor to WA, north to Alice Springs in the NT, south to Adelaide and east to Broken Hill in NSW. The railway line between the east and west coasts and the Adelaide to Alice Springs route both pass through Port Augusta.

Information
The tourist information centre (☎ 8641 0793, 1800 633 060, fax 8642 4288, info@flinders.outback.on.net) is in the Wadlata Outback Centre at 41 Flinders Terrace – this is the major information source for the Flinders

Ranges and the outback, but also has a good selection of material on the Eyre Peninsula. It's open weekdays from 9 am to 5.30 pm and weekends from 10 am to 4 pm. Check out its Web site at: www.flinders.outback.on.net.

Open the same hours, the Wadlata Outback Centre is a very interesting interpretative centre ($7), with numerous exhibits tracing the Aboriginal and European history of the Flinders Ranges and the outback. It's well worth a look.

Things to See & Do

There are tours ($2) of the **School of the Air**, at 59 Power Crescent, on weekdays at 10 am. You can also tour the **Royal Flying Doctor Service**, at 4 Vincent St, on weekdays between 10 am and 3 pm; admission is by donation.

Another good educational tour, available on weekdays only, takes you around the huge **Northern Power Station** (☎ 8641 1633) on Power Station Rd – it has the added advantage of being free. Tours of the complex depart at 11 am and 1 pm; closed footwear, long trousers and long-sleeved shirts are essential.

Off the Stuart Hwy, the **Australian Arid Lands Botanic Garden** covers 250 hectares on the northern edge of town. There are several walks and a pleasant information centre and coffee shop.

Other attractions include the **Curdnatta Art & Pottery Gallery** in Port Augusta's first train station, at 101 Commercial Rd, near the Wadlata Outback Centre. The **Homestead Park Pioneer Museum** ($2.50) features an original log-cabin homestead from the Flinders Ranges. It's on Elsie St and is open daily from 10 am to 5 pm.

The **Apex Camel Cup** is held over a weekend in late August or early September at the Port Augusta Racecourse.

Places to Stay

There are plenty of places to stay in Port Augusta, and the tourist centre has details. Following are some budget places.

The *Port Augusta Holiday Park* (☎ 8642 2974), at the junction of the Stuart and Eyre Hwys, has camp sites for $16 and on-site

vans/cabins from $37/39. A four bed bunk house costs $12 per person – there's a campers' kitchen adjacent.

Port Augusta Backpackers (☎ 8641 1063, 17 Trent Rd) has bunk beds for $15. It's conveniently located just off Hwy 1, but the building and facilities are decidedly weary, and security is poor. In short, we don't recommend it.

A much better standard is offered by the *Hotel Flinders* (☎ 8642 2544, 39 Commercial Rd), in the town centre, and the *Pampas Motel* (☎ 8642 3795, 76 Stirling Rd), 2km out. Both have backpacker beds for $15; the former does cheap meals and the latter has a kitchen.

Getting There & Away

Air Airlines of SA (bookings ☎ 13 1313) flies weekdays to Adelaide ($120) and Leigh Creek ($100), and Wednesday and Thursday to Woomera ($80). Twin-share packages are $970 ex-Adelaide and $740 ex-Port Augusta.

On Saturday (returning Sunday) the mail plane flies to Boulia in outback Queensland, stopping at Innamincka and Birdsville on the way; to go, check details with Airlines of SA, mail run inquiries ☎ 8642 3100.

Bus The bus station for Premier Stateliner and Greyhound Pioneer is at 23 McKay St, in the town centre.

Premier Stateliner (bus station ☎ 8642 5055) runs to Adelaide ($29), Coober Pedy ($62), Wilpena Pound ($25), Whyalla ($12), Port Lincoln ($41), Ceduna ($54) and other places on the Eyre Peninsula.

Greyhound Pioneer travels to Perth ($199), Alice Springs ($147), Darwin ($270) and Sydney ($123). McCafferty's travels to Alice Springs, Darwin and Sydney for the same prices.

Train The *Ghan* and *Indian Pacific* trains pass through Port Augusta.

Sydney is 32 hours away. A standard economy ticket costs $196, while a holiday/1st-class sleeper costs from $397/574.

It takes 33 hours to Perth; an economy seat is $233 and a holiday/1st-class sleeper is from $496/762.

To Alice Springs takes 16 hours and costs $146 for an economy seat and $298/520 for a holiday/1st class sleeper.

It's four hours to Adelaide from Port Augusta ($34).

Refer to the Train section of the Getting Around chapter for booking details.

WHYALLA
• postcode 5600   • pop 23,400

The largest city in the state after Adelaide, Whyalla is a major steel-producing centre with a deep-water port.

Information
The tourist centre (☎ 8645 7900, fax 8645 3620, ic3tour@plain.sa.gov.au) is on the Lincoln Hwy on the northern side of town. It's weekdays from 8.45 am to 5.10 pm, Saturday from 9 am to 4 pm and Sunday from 10 am to 4 pm.

Things to See & Do
There are interesting tours of the **BHP steel works** on Monday, Wednesday and Saturday at 9.30 am. They start from the tourist centre and cost $8. Long trousers, long-sleeved shirts and closed footwear are essential.

Next door to the tourist centre is the **Maritime Museum**, featuring the 650-tonne, WWII corvette HMAS *Whyalla* ($6). It's open daily from 10 am to 4 pm.

The **Whyalla Wildlife & Reptile Sanctuary** ($6), on the Lincoln Hwy near the airport, is definitely worth a visit; it's open daily at 10 am and there are many exhibits, including around 50 native mammal species.

On Ekblom St, there are historical exhibits in the **Mt Laura Homestead Museum** ($4). It's open Sunday, Monday and Wednesday from 2 to 4 pm and Friday from 10 am to noon.

Places to Stay & Eat
The *Whyalla Foreshore Caravan Park* (☎ 8645 7474, Broadbent Terrace) has camp sites for $11, on-site vans for $24 and cabins from $28. Prices are similar at the friendly *Hillview Caravan Park* (☎ 8645 9357), off the Lincoln Hwy 5km south of town, except its cabins cost from $43.

Hotels in the city centre have rooms with private facilities from $25/40 for singles/doubles – the tourist centre can provide all details of local pubs and motels.

Memories Coffee Lounge (31 Playford Ave) has a good atmosphere and is recommended for light meals.

COWELL
• postcode 5602   • pop 700

Cowell is a pleasant little town near a large jade deposit – you can purchase a wide range of jade products from the Jade Motel, on the Lincoln Hwy at the northern end of town. Oysters are farmed locally – they're sold at several places for as little as $5 a dozen.

Places to Stay
Close to the town centre, the *Cowell Foreshore Caravan Park (☎ 8629 2307, The Esplanade)* charges $11 for camp sites, from $30 for on-site vans and from $35 for cabins.

Alternatively, there are two classic pubs on Main St; the *Franklin Harbour Hotel (☎ 8629 2015)* and the nearby *Commercial Hotel (☎ 8629 2181)*. Both charge $20/30 for singles/doubles.

Schultz Farm (☎ 8629 2194), run by kindly Mr and Mrs Schultz, has spacious rooms for $45 for doubles, including a cooked breakfast. It's on Smith Rd about 1km south-west of town.

COWELL TO PORT LINCOLN
The first township on the road south from Cowell is **Elbow Hill** (15km down the Lincoln Hwy). There's not much here, but the beaches at nearby **Point Gibbon** (6km) are magnificent with huge, white sand dunes behind a beautiful coastline.

The very hospitable *Elbow Hill Inn (☎ 8628 5012)* does light lunches and gourmet dinners, and has a great atmosphere. It has limited accommodation starting at $70 for doubles.

Back on the coast, **Arno Bay** is another small beach resort with a pub and caravan park.

South again is **Port Neill**, a pleasant little seaside town with a vintage vehicle museum. Further south is **Tumby Bay**, with its long, curving white-sand beach, a National Trust museum and a number of old buildings around the town. Hales Mini Mart (☎ 8688 2584) has tourist information.

The **Sir Joseph Banks Islands**, 15km offshore, form a marine conservation park. A couple of islands have sea-lion colonies, and there are many attractive bays and reefs plus a wide variety of sea birds, including Cape Barren Geese. Cruises can be arranged; contact Hales Mini Mart in Tumby Bay or the tourist office in Port Lincoln.

PORT LINCOLN
- postcode 5606   • pop 13,000

Port Lincoln, at the southern end of the Eyre Peninsula, is 662km from Adelaide by road but only 250km as the crow flies. The first settlers arrived in 1839 and the town has grown to become the tuna-fishing capital of Australia.

Information
The helpful and efficient Port Lincoln Visitor Information Centre (☎/fax 8683 3544, 1800 629 911) is at 66 Tasman Terrace (the foreshore). It's open daily from 9 am to 5.30 pm.

Contact the NPWS office (☎ 8688 3111, fax 8688 3110), at 75 Liverpool St, for information on Lincoln and Coffin Bay national parks.

There are some good surfing and diving spots near the town. For information about the best areas, contact the Port Lincoln Skin-Diving & Surfing Centre (☎ 8682 4428) at 1 King St. Licensed divers can hire scuba equipment here.

Things to See & Do
Celebrating the tuna industry, the **Tunarama Festival** is held over the Australia Day weekend in January. There's tuna and wheatsheaf tossing, keg rolling, slippery pole climbing, a boat-building race, stalls and bands.

Port Lincoln is well situated on Boston Bay. There are a number of historic buildings, including the **Old Mill** on Dorset Place (1846) – it has a lookout affording good views over the bay – and the **Port Lincoln Hotel** (1840) at 20 Tasman Terrace. On the Flinders Hwy, **Mill Cottage** ($2 with guided tour) is a historic homestead built in 1866; it's open daily, except Monday, from 2 to 4.30 pm.

There are boat charters and yacht cruises to various off-shore islands – most can be booked through the information centre. Thirty-one kilometres offshore is **Dangerous Reef**, a major breeding area for the great white shark – cruises to the reef start at $55 (minimum numbers apply). Book through the Information Centre or at Westward Ho Holiday Units (☎ 8682 2425). Sightings of sharks are rare, but you'll probably see plenty of sea lions. Alternatively – if money is no object, and you've plenty of time – you can go **cage diving** here and (hopefully) observe a great white or two that way.

Land trips include a town tour ($25), a day tour of the town and Whalers Way ($65) and a 4WD day tour incorporating Coffin Bay ($80).

Places to Stay & Eat
There are a number of hotels, motels and holiday flats in and around town; the information centre has details.

The popular **Kirton Point Caravan Park** *(☎ 8682 2537, Hindmarsh St)* is 3km east of the town centre. It has camp sites from $6 per person and cabins from $25, as well as nice views over the bay.

Cheapest of the five hotels in the city centre is historic **Port Lincoln Hotel** *(☎ 8682 1277, 16 Tasman Terrace)*, with singles/doubles with private facilities for $25/45 ($20/35 without). Close by is the **Great Northern Hotel** *(☎ 8682 3350, 24 Hallett Place)*, with basic pub rooms for $20/38.

Westward Ho Holiday Units *(☎ 8682 2425, 112 London St)* has flats from $45/55. If there's six of you and you have your own bedding, you can get a flat for $63 outside holiday periods.

There are plenty of eating establishments in the city centre. One of the most popular is **Bugs Restaurant** on Eyre St, which has delicious pasta, pizza and seafood.

AROUND PORT LINCOLN
Cape Carnot, better known as Whalers Way, is 32km south of Port Lincoln and features

beautiful and rugged coastal scenery. A permit ($15 plus key deposit), valid for 24 hours, enables you to visit this spectacular area and also camp if you want to. Permits can be obtained from most petrol stations or the information centre in Port Lincoln.

These places also sell entry permits ($8) to **Mikkira Koala Sanctuary**, on the road to Whalers Way.

Sleaford Bay's beautiful beaches are a 3km detour off the road to Whalers Way.

Also south of Port Lincoln is the **Lincoln National Park**, again with a magnificent coastline, including quiet coves and pounding surf beaches. Entry to the park costs $5 per car, and it'll cost another $5 per night if you're going to camp – you can obtain permits at the entry station. Most of the park's vehicle tracks are suitable for conventional vehicles but you will need a 4WD to visit tranquil **Memory Cove** – the Information Centre in Port Lincoln has keys to the gate on this track.

PORT LINCOLN TO STREAKY BAY
Coffin Bay
Ominous-sounding Coffin Bay (it was named by Matthew Flinders to honour Sir Isaac Coffin) is a sheltered stretch of water with many quiet beaches and good fishing. The main centre is the holidayville of Coffin Bay (usual population 200).

From here you can visit wild coastal scenery along the ocean side of **Coffin Bay Peninsula**, which is entirely taken up by a national park. Access for conventional vehicles is limited within the park – you can get to scenic **Point Avoid** quite easily, but otherwise you need a 4WD. Entry to the park costs $5 per car – you pay this at the park entry station.

Birdlife, including some unusual migratory species, is a feature of the **Kellidie Bay Conservation Park**, just outside Coffin Bay township.

Places to Stay The *Coffin Bay Caravan Park* (☎ 8685 4170, Shepperd Ave) has camping ($10) on-site vans ($25) and basic cabins ($38). The pub does counter meals and there's a couple of takeaways.

Bush camping (generally with difficult access) is allowed at several places on the peninsula; permits cost $5 per car.

Coffin Bay to Point Labatt
Just past **Coulta**, 40km north of Coffin Bay, there's good surfing at **Greenly Beach**. **Locks Well**, about 15km south of **Elliston** (a small resort and fishing town on peaceful Waterloo Bay), is one of several good salmon-fishing spots along this wild coast. Elliston itself has two caravan parks, a pub and a motel.

Just north of Elliston, take the 7km detour to **Anxious Bay** and **Salmon Point** for some great ocean scenery – en route you pass **Blackfellows**, which has some of the strongest waves on the west coast. From here you can see distant **Flinders Island**, where there's a sheep station and tourist accommodation.

At **Venus Bay** there are quiet beaches, plenty of pelicans and a couple of small caravan parks. The **Venus Bay Conservation Park** has fine coastal scenery and birdlife.

Shortly before Streaky Bay, the turn-off to **Point Labatt** takes you to one of the few permanent colonies of sea lions on the Australian mainland. You can view them from the clifftop above the colony – take binoculars.

STREAKY BAY
● postcode 5680 ● pop 1000
This attractive little town takes its name from the 'streaks' of seaweed Flinders saw in the bay. The main tourist information outlet is in the Shell Auto Mart (☎ 8626 1126), at 15 Alfred Terrace. It's open daily from 8 am to 6 pm and has the cast of a 5.5m great white shark on display out the back.

The National Trust museum ($2), on Montgomerie Terrace, features a fully furnished pioneer hut and has many other interesting exhibits. It's open Tuesday and Friday from 2 to 4 pm and at other times by prior arrangement. Open the same hours, the **Powerhouse Museum**, opposite the Shell Auto Mart, has a large collection of restored engines.

Curious granite outcrops known as inselbergs are found at numerous places on the peninsula. One of the most impressive is a group known as **Murphy's Haystacks**, near the highway about 20km south-east of Streaky Bay. **Back Beach**, 4km west of Streaky Bay, is good for surfing; there's some grand cliff scenery around the coast here.

There are oyster farms here as well as further along the coast at sleepy **Smoky Bay**. You can get fresh oysters from several outlets from as little as $5 a dozen.

Places to Stay & Eat

About one kilometre west of town, the *Foreshore Tourist Park (☎ 8626 1666)* has ungrassed camp sites (from $11) and cabins (from $34) by a safe swimming beach. The adjoining kiosk does good takeaways.

Right in the centre of town, the comfortable *Streaky Bay Community Hotel/Motel (☎ 8626 1008, 35 Alfred Terrace)* has rooms with share facilities for $25/30 and rooms with TV and private bathroom for $48/57, both in the pub section.

Near the jetty at Smoky Bay, the friendly *Smoky Bay Caravan Park (☎ 8625 7030)* has camp sites from $9 and basic cabins from $20.

CEDUNA

• postcode 5690   • pop 3600

Just past the junction of the Eyre and Flinders Hwys, Ceduna marks the end of the Eyre Peninsula and the start of the long, lonely drive across the Nullarbor Plain into WA. The town was founded in 1896, although there had been a whaling station on St Peter Island, off nearby Cape Thevenard, back in 1850.

The tourist office is in Traveland Ceduna (☎ 8625 2780, 1800 639 413, fax 8625 3294), at 58 Poynton St (the main street); it's open weekdays from 9 am to 5 pm and Saturday from 9 to 11.30 am. After a few days of fruitlessly waiting for a lift you might find yourself paying it a visit to buy an onward ticket.

The National Trust's **Old Schoolhouse Museum**, on Park Terrace, has pioneer exhibits as well as artefacts and newspaper clippings from the British atomic weapons program at Maralinga. Entry costs $3 and

it's open daily except Sunday – check at the tourist office for times.

There are many beaches and sheltered coves around Ceduna, with good surfing and fishing. **Laura Bay Conservation Park**, off the road to Smoky Bay 20km south-west of Ceduna, has mangroves and tidal flats that attract many species of seabirds and waders.

Places to Stay

The best of the four caravan parks here is the attractive *Ceduna Foreshore Caravan Park (☎ 8625 2290, South Terrace)*, near the town centre. It has camp sites from $13 and cabins from $35 (extra adults $3).

We've had good reports about the friendly, helpful management of *Greenacres Backpackers (☎ 8625 3811, 017 165 346, 12 Khulmann St)*, near the Greyhound Pioneer bus station (the Pine Grove Motel). Beds in small dorms and private rooms – a couple have fans – cost $15, including a substantial dinner.

The comfortable *Ceduna Community Hotel/Motel (☎ 8625 2008, O'Loughlin Terrace)* has pub rooms with private facilities for $35/37 for singles/doubles ($25/29 without). Don't leave any valuables in your car if it's parked in the street overnight – not that you should do this anywhere else, either.

CEDUNA TO THE WA BORDER

It's 480km from Ceduna to the WA border and the only places with tourist facilities are at Penong (73km from Ceduna), Nundroo (151km), the Yalata Roadhouse (202km), the Nullarbor Hotel/Motel (294km) and the Border Village. Wheat and sheep paddocks line the road to Nundroo, after which you're in attractive mallee until 50km beyond Yalata. Here the trees start to become sparser until petering out in a sea of shrubby bluebush 20km later. This is the true Nullarbor (derived from the Latin for no trees) and you travel through it for the next 40km or so – elsewhere the plain is north of the highway.

Turn off the highway at **Penong** (population 200), and a 20km dirt road gets you to Point Sinclair. Here you'll find the famous **Cactus Beach**, which has some of Australia's best surfing breaks. The area is private property but you can camp for $6; bring your own drinking water in summer.

The turn-off to the almost ghost town of **Fowlers Bay** is 34km beyond Penong. There's a small caravan park here and good fishing.

Further west is **Head of Bight**, where southern right whales come in close to shore during their breeding season from June to October. Between 20 and 30 calves are born here each year, and you'll usually see several adult whales swimming close to the cliffs. There are excellent lookout points, but it's best if you have binoculars. This area of sea is included in the huge Great Australian Bight Marine Park.

Head of Bight is on Aboriginal land – you can get entry permits ($7) and whale information from the Yalata Roadhouse and at the warden's hut on the way in to the viewing area. The signposted turn-off is 78km west of Yalata, and 14km east of the Nullarbor Hotel/Motel.

You can also inspect the **Murrawijinie Cave**, a large overhang behind the Nullarbor Hotel/Motel. West of here there are several signposted coastal lookouts along the top of the 80m-high **Bunda Cliffs**.

Watch out for kangaroos, camels and wombats if you're driving through here at night.

Places to Stay & Eat

There are basic caravan parks, motel-style accommodation, restaurants and fuel sales at the *Nundroo Hotel/Motel* (☎ 8625 6120), *Yalata Roadhouse* (☎ 8625 6807), *Nullarbor Hotel/Motel* (☎ 8625 6271) and *Border Village* (☎ 08 9039 3474) – the latter is on the WA-SA border.

In Penong, the *Penong Hotel* (☎ 8625 1050) has basic pub rooms.

Flinders Ranges

Rising from the northern end of Gulf St Vincent and running north for 400km into the arid Outback, the Flinders Ranges offer some of the most spectacular and rugged scenery in SA. It's a superb area for bushwalks, wildlife or taking in the ever-changing colours of the Outback. In the far north, the ranges are hemmed in by sand ridges and barren salt lakes.

As in many other dry regions of Australia, the vegetation here is surprisingly diverse and colourful. In the early spring, after good rains, the country is carpeted with wildflowers. In summer the days can be searingly hot but the nights usually cool down to a pleasant temperature. Winter and early spring are probably the best times to visit, although there are attractions at any time of the year.

In 1802, when Matthew Flinders landed near Port Augusta, several Aboriginal tribes lived in the region. You can visit some of their sites: the cave paintings at Yourambulla (near Hawker) and Arkaroo (near Wilpena); and the rock carvings at Sacred Canyon (near Wilpena) and Chambers Gorge.

Bushwalking is one of the main attractions of the area, but this is wild, rugged country and care should be taken before setting out. Wilpena Pound, the Arkaroola-Mt Painter Wildlife Sanctuary and Mt Remarkable National Park all have excellent walks, many of them along marked trails. The Heysen Trail starts in Parachilna Gorge, near Blinman, and winds south through the ranges from there.

Information

The main tourist information outlet is in the Wadlata Outback Centre, at 41 Flinders Terrace, Port Augusta (see the earlier section on the Eyre Peninsula).

The NPWS head office for the northern and central Flinders Ranges is in Hawker (☎ 8648 4244, fax 8648 0092), in the same building as the post office. For the southern Flinders (ie south of Quorn) contact the NPWS office in Port Augusta (see the later Outback section).

You'll need a good map of the area as there are many back roads and a variety of road surfaces. According to local experts, the most accurate touring map is put out by Westprint; the RAA's map is also very good.

Organised Tours

A number of operators, including Premier Stateliner and Adelaide Sightseeing, visit

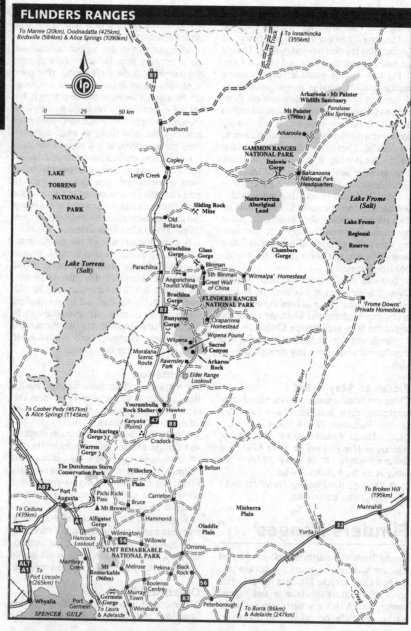

FLINDERS RANGES

To Marree (20km), Oodnadatta (425km),
Birdsville (584km) & Alice Springs (1090km)

To Innamincka
(355km)

Strzelecki Track

0   25   50 km

Arkaroola - Mt Painter
Wildlife Sanctuary

Mt Painter
(790m)

Paralana
Hot Springs

Arkaroola

Lyndhurst

Copley

GAMMON RANGES
NATIONAL PARK
Italowie
Gorge

Balcanoona
National Park
Headquarters

LAKE
TORRENS
NATIONAL
PARK

Leigh Creek

Lake Frome
(Salt)

Sliding Rock
Mine

Nantawarrina
Aboriginal
Land

Old
Beltana

Lake Frome
Regional
Reserve

Lake Torrens
(Salt)

Parachilna
Gorge

Glass
Gorge

Chambers
Gorge

Parachilna

Blinman
Sth Blinman

'Wirrealpa' Homestead

Angorichina
Tourist Village

Great Wall
of China

Brachina
Gorge

FLINDERS RANGES
NATIONAL PARK

'Frome Downs'
(Private Homestead)

Bunyeroo
Gorge

Oraparinna
Homestead

Wilpena

Wipena Pound

Wilpena Creek

Moralana
Scenic
Route

Sacred
Canyon

Rawnsley
Park

Arkaroo
Rock

Elder Range
Lookout

To Coober Pedy (457km)
& Alice Springs (1145km)

Yourambulla
Rock Shelter

Hawker

Siccus River

Kanyaka
(Ruins)

Buckaringa
Gorge

Warren
Gorge

Cradock

The Dutchmans Stern
Conservation Park

Willochra
Plain

Belton

To Broken Hill
(195km)

Stuart Highway

Quorn

Pichi Richi
Pass

Carrieton

Minburra
Plain

Port
Augusta

Bruce

Hammond

Mannahill

To Ceduna
(439km)

Alligator
Gorge

Wilmington

Oladdie
Plain

Yunta

Barrier Highway

Hancocks
Lookout

Willowie

Orroroo

Mambray
Creek

Mt
Remarkable
(960m)

MT REMARKABLE
NATIONAL PARK

Melrose

Pekina

Black
Rock

To
Port Lincoln
(265km)

Murray
Town

Booleroo
Centre

Whyalla

Port
Germein

Germein
Gorge

To Laura
& Adelaide

Wirrabara

Peterborough

To Burra (86km)
& Adelaide (247km)

SPENCER GULF

the Flinders from Adelaide, and there are others departing from Port Augusta, Quorn, Hawker, Wilpena Pound and Arkaroola.

Small operators offering more adventurous 4WD trips include: Gawler Outback Tours (☎ 8278 4467) based in Adelaide; and Intrepid Tours (☎ 8648 6277, intrepid@ dove.net.au) and Wallaby Tracks Tours (☎ 8648 6655, 1800 639 933, headbush@ dove.net.au) based in Quorn. Both do a range of tours departing from Quorn and Port Augusta (day trips are around $80), while Wallaby Tracks also has packages ex-Adelaide. Treckabout Australia (☎ 8396 2833), of Adelaide, operates at the top end of the market.

Note that most tours operating to the Flinders Ranges are ex-Adelaide. Many visitors unwisely leave booking a trip until they get to the ranges, where they discover that there's not a lot on offer.

Accommodation

Hotels, motels and caravan parks as well as many cottages and farms offer all sorts of accommodation in the Flinders Ranges. Sadly there are no cheap beds at Wilpena Pound itself – to stay here you will need your own camping gear, unless you're prepared to fork out for an expensive motel room. The closest budget accommodation to Wilpena Pound is at Rawnsley Park, 10km south – see the Wilpena Pound section.

Getting There & Away

Air Airlines of SA (☎ 13 1313) flies weekdays from Adelaide to Port Augusta ($120) and Leigh Creek ($180).

Bus Premier Stateliner (☎ 8415 5555) has services daily from Adelaide to Port Augusta ($29) and twice weekly to Wilpena Pound ($52) via Quorn ($37) and Hawker ($48).

Car There are good sealed roads all the way north to Wilpena Pound. From there the roads are quite good, and although there are quite good when they're dry, they can be closed by heavy rain. Check with NPWS offices for current information. The Marree road skirting the western edge of the Flinders Ranges is sealed to Lyndhurst.

Probably the most interesting way to get to Arkaroola is to go to Wilpena Pound and on to South Blinman, then head east to Wirrealpa Homestead, where you swing north via Chambers Gorge to meet the Frome Downs road south of Balcanoona.

For recorded information on road conditions in the Flinders Ranges and other outback areas of SA, phone ☎ 1300 361 033.

Getting Around

If you have a vehicle you can make a loop that takes you around an interesting section of the central part of the ranges. From Port Augusta go north-east through the Pichi Richi Pass to Quorn and Hawker and on up to Wilpena Pound. Continue north through the Flinders Ranges National Park past Oraparinna Homestead, then veer west through Brachina Gorge to the main Leigh Creek road. You can then either head straight back to Hawker, or make a detour via the Moralana Scenic Route. The section via Brachina Gorge is a self-guided geology trail with information signs en route – pick up a leaflet from the Wilpena visitor centre.

Alternatively, from Wilpena Pound you can loop north into the Flinders Ranges National Park past Bunyeroo Gorge, meeting up with the Brachina Gorge road. You can then either return to Wilpena via Oraparinna Homestead, or head west to the Hawker to Leigh Creek road.

QUORN

• **postcode 5433**   • **pop 1000**

The picturesque 'gateway to the Flinders' is about 330km north of Adelaide and 50km north-east of Port Augusta. It became an important railway town after the completion of the Great Northern Railway in 1878, and it still retains the atmosphere of its pioneering days.

The tourist office (☎ 8648 6419, fax 8648 6001, tourism@flindersrangescouncil.sa.gov .au) is next to the council chambers in Seventh St – it is open daily, except public holidays, from 9 am to 5 pm. At the time of writing, the office planned to relocate to the nearby train station in late 1999.

The railway closed in 1957, but part of the line to Port Augusta has been reopened as a tourism venture. A vintage train – often pulled by a steam engine – makes a 32km round trip from Quorn to the scenic **Pichi Richi Pass** for $24. It runs from April to October inclusive, mainly during school holiday periods and at other times on alternate Sundays and public holidays. Ask the tourist office for a timetable.

Ask at the train station about tours ($5) of the **railway workshop** – usually conducted on days when the train is running. Here you'll find a large and fascinating collection of locomotives, carriages, freight wagons, brake vans and sundry items.

The town has several good art galleries. The **Junction Art Gallery**, on a farm off the Yarah Vale Gorge road, about 20km north of town, is a very friendly place with high-quality arts and crafts, and bushwalking. A little further out on the same road, **Warren Gorge** has good rock climbing and pleasant picnic sites.

There are several good walks in Pichi Richi Pass out on the Port Augusta road, including the **Waukerie Creek Trail** and the Heysen Trail. Closer to town are walks at **Dutchman's Stern** and **Devil's Peak** – both are within easy cycling distance of Quorn.

Places to Stay & Eat

The *Quorn Caravan Park (☎ 8648 6206, Silo Rd)*, just behind the old train station, has camp sites from $11, on-site vans for $28 and cabins with air-con for $46. It also has magnificent gum trees, although the screeching corellas in them aren't so inspiring first thing in the morning.

In the old hospital, *Andu Lodge (☎ 1800 639 933, headbush@dove.net.au, 12 First St)* is a very good hostel with excellent facilities and a quiet, comfortable atmosphere. Beds in spacious dorms cost $15, and there are singles/twins/doubles for $28/36/38. You can hire mountain bikes ($20 a day) and Mick, the owner, will tell you about the bushwalks and rides around town. He also does backpacker-friendly tours. Transfers to and from Port Augusta can be arranged for $6 each way.

The *Transcontinental Hotel (☎ 8648 6076, 15 Railway Terrace)* is the pick of the town's four hotels for accommodation. It's a friendly place with standard rooms (no air-con) for $29/49, including breakfast.

Quorn's four pubs sell counter and dining-room meals, usually starting at about $6. There's a very good restaurant in the *Quorn Mill Motel* at the west end of Railway Terrace and another at the old *Willows Brewery* in Pichi Richi Pass.

KANYAKA

About 40km north of Quorn, on the way to Hawker, are the impressive ruins of the old Kanyaka settlement, founded in 1851. Up to 70 families lived here, tending the settlement's 50,000 sheep, but it was finally abandoned in 1888 as a result of drought and overgrazing.

From the homestead ruins you can drive along the creek to the old woolshed, then walk about 1.5km to picturesque **Kanyaka Waterhole**, which is overlooked by the so-called **Death Rock**.

If you're coming from Wilpena Pound, don't be confused by the sign that indicates the old Kanyaka town site – the clearly marked turn-off for the ruins is about 4km further on.

HAWKER

● postcode 5434   ● pop 490

Hawker is 55km south of Wilpena Pound. For tourist information, chat with the helpful staff at Hawker Motors (the Mobil service station), on the corner of Wilpena and Cradock Rds.

There are Aboriginal rock paintings 12km west of Hawker at the **Yourambulla Rock Shelter**, a hollow in the rocks high up on the side of Yourambulla Peak, a half hour walk from the car park. The **Jarvis Hill Lookout** is about 6km south-west of Hawker and affords good views over Hawker and north to Wilpena Pound.

The **Moralana Scenic Route** is a round-trip drive from Hawker, taking in the magnificent scenery between the Elder and Wilpena Pound ranges. It is 24km to the Moralana turn-off, then 28km along an unsealed road that joins up with the sealed Hawker to Leigh Creek road. From here it's 46km back to Hawker.

Both the town's caravan parks offer **4WD tours**. Fray Cultural Tours (☎ 8648 4182) has a range of one to six-day **Aboriginal-guided tours** to cultural sites between Hawker and Arkaroola.

Places to Stay

The *Hawker Caravan Park* (☎ 8648 4006, *Chaceview Terrace*), on the northern outskirts of town, off Wilpena Rd, has lawned camp sites for $12, on-site vans for $30 and deluxe cabins from $65 – all units have air-con. About a kilometre from town on the Leigh Creek road, the friendly *Flinders Ranges Caravan Park* (☎ 8648 4266) has similar options for similar prices – it has a very good campers' kitchen.

The *Hawker Hotel/Motel* (☎ 8648 4102, *Elder Terrace*) has pub-style rooms (some with air-con) for $30/40 a single/double and motel units for $50/60. The *Outback Chapmanton Motel* (☎ 8648 4100, 1 *Wilpena Rd*) charges $55/65 for its motel units and holiday flats.

Travellers recommend the *Elder Terrace Café* for its imaginative menu and reasonable prices. It's open daily for breakfast, lunch and dinner.

WILPENA POUND

The best known feature of the ranges and the main attraction in the 94,500 hectare **Flinders Ranges National Park**, is the large natural basin known as Wilpena Pound. Covering about 80 sq km, it is accessible only by the narrow gap through which Wilpena Creek exits the pound. On the outside, the **Wilpena Wall** soars almost sheer for 500m; inside, the basin slopes relatively gently away from the encircling ridge top.

There is plenty of wildlife in the park, particularly euros (hill kangaroos), red and grey kangaroos, and birds – everything from rosellas, galahs and budgerigars to emus and wedge-tailed eagles. You may even see endangered yellow-footed rock wallabies, whose numbers are increasing

---

Flinders Ranges Dreaming

The almost palpable 'spirit of place' of the Flinders Ranges has inspired a rich heritage of Aboriginal 'dreaming' stories. Many of these legends – some secret, but some related by Adnyamathanha elders – explain the creation of the landscape, and the native birds and animals that inhabit it.

Arkaroola comes from Arkaroo, the name of a giant serpent ancestor. Suffering from a powerful thirst, Arkaroo drank Lake Frome dry, then carved out the sinuous Arkaroola Creek as he dragged his bloated body back into the ranges. He went underground to sleep it off, but all that salty water had given him a bellyache. The rumblings from his belly explain the 30 to 40 small earth tremors that occur in this area each year.

Another story relates that the walls of Wilpena Pound (Ikarra) are the bodies of two serpents (Akurra). They'd coiled up around an initiation ceremony, then created a whirlwind and devoured most of the participants.

In another story the bossy eagle Wildu, seeking revenge on his nephews who had tried to kill him, built a great fire. All the birds, which were originally white, were caught in the flames and emerged blackened and burnt. The magpies and willie wagtails were partially scorched, but the crows were entirely blackened and have remained so until this day.

---

now that populations of foxes and rabbits are being controlled. **Brachina Gorge** is a good spot to see these beautiful animals.

Sacred Canyon, with its many petroglyphs (rock carvings), is to the east. To the north and still within the national park are striking scenic attractions, such as **Bunyeroo Gorge**, Brachina Gorge and the **Aroona Valley**. There are several bush-camping areas, all accessible by conventional vehicle. The 20km **Brachina Gorge Geological Trail** (you follow it in your car) features an outstanding geological sequence of exposed sedimentary rock.

Entry to the park costs $5 per car (you don't need to buy an entry permit if you're camping); pay at the visitors centre (☎ 8648 0048) in the Wilpena tourist village, near the pound entrance. The centre, which has plenty of tourist information on the district, is open from 8 am to 5 pm daily.

Bushwalking

If you're planning to walk for more than about three hours, fill in the log book at the visitors centre – and don't forget to 'sign off' when you return. Searches are no longer initiated by the rangers, so make sure someone responsible knows the details of your walk.

There are a number of marked walking trails (sections that incorporate parts of the Heysen Trail are indicated by red markers) and these are listed in a NPWS leaflet ($1). Topographical maps (scale 1:50,000) are available for $8.50 from the visitor centre.

Solo walks are not recommended and you must be adequately equipped – particularly with drinking water and sun protection, especially during the summer months.

Most of the walks start from the visitors centre, which is near the main camp site. The St Marys Peak walk is probably the most interesting, but there are plenty of others worth considering. They vary from short walks suitable for people with small children, to longer ones taking more than a day.

You should allow a day for the walk to St Marys Peak and back, whether you do it as an up-and-down or a round trip. Up and down, it's faster and more interesting to take the route outside Wilpena Pound as the scenery this way is much more spectacular. The climb up to the Tanderra Saddle is fairly steep and the final stretch from there to the summit is a real scramble. However, the views are some of the best in SA, with the white glimmer of Lake Torrens off to the west, the beautiful Aroona Valley to the north, and the pound spread out below your feet.

Descending from the peak, you can either head back down on the same direct route or take the longer round-trip walk through Wilpena Pound. This is the same track you take to get to Edeowie Gorge. Alternatively, you can take your time and stay at the

Cooinda bush-camping area within the Pound.

Arkaroo Rock is at the base of the Wilpena Range, about 10km south of Wilpena off the Hawker road. It takes about half an hour to walk from the car park to the rock shelter, where there are well preserved Aboriginal paintings. The walk itself is worth the effort.

Organised Tours

The following tours can be booked through the visitors centre.

You can take a scenic flight from Wilpena for $50/60/85 for 20/30/45 minutes, or go further afield (costs increase if there are fewer than three passengers).

Nearby Arkaba station has a 4WD tour costing $55/75 for a half/full day. You see some spectacular country on this trip.

Places to Stay & Eat

Unless you've got a tent, there is no cheap accommodation at Wilpena. The camping ground at the Wilpena Pound Resort has sites from $11, while bush camping within the national park costs $5 per car per night. You pay all camping fees at the visitor centre.

Otherwise, the *Wilpena Pound Resort* *(☎ 1800 805 802)* has all mod cons including a swimming pool and motel-style units from $93/98 a single/double – good discounts may be available during December and January.

Groceries and last-minute camping requirements are available at the store in the visitor centre. You can get counter lunches at the resort, which also has a good restaurant.

Off the Hawker road, about 20km south of Wilpena and close to the Pound's outer edge, the friendly owners of *Rawnsley Park* *(☎ 8648 0030)* have camp sites from $10, on-site vans for $36 and cabins with air-con from $44. There are several good bushwalks on offer, and you can also do trail rides and 4WD tours.

BLINMAN

● postcode 5730   ● pop 50

From the 1860s to the 1890s this was a copper-mining centre, but today it's just a quaint hamlet on the circular route around the

Flinders Ranges National Park. It's a useful starting point for visits to many of the scenic attractions in the area.

From Blinman, you can take up to eight-day camel treks ($985) through remote station country; phone ☎ 8543 2280 for details.

About a kilometre to the north of town is the historic **Blinman copper mine**, which has walking trails and interpretive signs.

Alpana Station, 5km south of Blinman, has 4WD tours, guided walks and budget accommodation in the shearing quarters (☎ 8648 4864), charging $15 per bed, for a minimum of four people. The *Blinman Hotel (☎ 8648 4867)* has a real outback pub flavour – rooms with private facilities cost $45/70 a single/double ($35/60 without). They also have camp sites (dusty ones) and a bunkhouse with a kitchen ($13).

AROUND BLINMAN
Dramatic **Chambers Gorge**, 64km to the north-east of Blinman towards Arkaroola, features a striking gallery of Aboriginal rock carvings. From Mt Chambers you can see over Lake Frome to the east and all the way along the Flinders Ranges from Mt Painter in the north to Wilpena Pound in the south.

The beautiful **Aroona Valley** and the **Aroona Homestead** ruins, to the south of Blinman in the Flinders Ranges National Park, are reached from **Brachina Gorge** further south.

An inspiring scenic drive links Blinman with Parachilna, to the west, where there's a great pub (the Prairie Hotel). This route takes you through **Parachilna Gorge** and past some lovely picnic and camping spots – the gorge marks the northern end of the Heysen Trail.

North of Parachilna, on the Marree road, you turn east at the Beltana Roadhouse to get to historic **Old Beltana** (8km). This small settlement almost became a ghost town, but is now inhabited by interesting people seeking to escape the rat race. It's a fascinating spot and the roadhouse (☎ 8675 2744) has information on the area.

Places to Stay & Eat
Angorichina Tourist Village (☎ 8648 4842), in Parachilna Gorge, boasts a magnificent setting with steep hills all around. It has camp sites from $8, backpacker beds for $13, on-site vans for $30 and units from $48.

A number of stations in the area offer budget accommodation in their shearers' quarters; some close down over summer. *Angorichina Station (☎ 8648 4863)* is the agent for several properties near Blinman. *Gum Creek Station (☎ 8648 4883)*, 15km south, is another worth checking out.

At tiny Parachilna there's the friendly *Prairie Hotel (☎ 8648 4844, ab@flinders .outback.on.net)*, a real oasis of luxury in the harsh outback. There's a range of accommodation options – camp sites from $10, basic cabins from $40 and very tastefully appointed single/double rooms with private facilities from $70/80 – it has a great menu featuring Australian bush tucker.

Nearby, the *Old Schoolhouse (☎ 8648 4676)* has bunks and cooking facilities for $12 per person (camping $5 per person).

LEIGH CREEK
• postcode 5731   • pop 1400
North of the Beltana Roadhouse, Leigh Creek's huge open-cut coal mine supplies Port Augusta power station. The township was developed in 1980 when the original settlement was demolished to make way for mining. Landscaping has created a very pleasant, leafy environment in dramatic contrast to the stark surroundings. Flinders Power offers free 2½-hour tours of the mining operations; ring ☎ 8675 4320.

The *Leigh Creek Caravan Park (☎ 8675 2025, Acacia Rd)* near the town centre has good amenities but the ground is like concrete. Camp sites cost $10/15.

From Leigh Creek, you can visit the scenic **Aroona Dam** (10km to the west), the **Gammon Ranges National Park** and **Arkaroola** (respectively 100 and 130km to the east). For information on the Gammon Ranges National Park contact the ranger at Balcanoona on ☎ 8648 4829, or the NPWS office in Hawker.

ARKAROOLA
The 61,000 hectare Arkaroola-Mt Painter Wildlife Sanctuary sprawls across rugged

and spectacular country near the northern end of the Flinders Ranges. For bookings and information contact the Arkaroola Travel Centre in Adelaide (☎ 1800 676 042, admin@arkaroola.on.net) or ring the resort direct on ☎ 8648 4848.

The resort has a garage that sells fuel and does mechanical repairs.

There are a number of tours, including the highly recommended, half day 4WD **Ridgetop Tour** ($60) through wild mountain scenery. Another excellent tour ($22) allows you to view the heavens through a high-powered telescope at the **Arkaroola Astronomical Observatory**.

Dirt roads and tracks lead to rock pools at the **Barraranna Gorge** and **Echo Camp**, and to water holes at Arkaroola and **Nooldoonooldoona**. Further on are **Bolla Bollana Springs** and the ruins of a copper smelter. You can take a guided or tag-along tour, or do your own thing on most of the sanctuary's 100km of graded tracks. Most places of interest are accessible to conventional vehicles, with some hiking involved.

Mt Painter is a magnificent landmark and you pass close to it on the ridge-top tour. There are fine views from **Freeling Heights** across Yudanamutana Gorge and from **Siller's Lookout** over the salt flats of Lake Frome. **Paralana Hot Springs** is the 'last hurrah' of Australia's geyser activity. It's geologically interesting but otherwise not worth a special trip.

Places to Stay & Eat
The resort has a good range of accommodation. Camp sites in the dusty caravan park and down along the creek (much nicer) cost $10, as do beds in spartan huts. Cabins without air-con cost from $29 twin share and motel units with air-con cost from $49 for singles and doubles. There's a small shop (where you can buy basic supplies) and a good restaurant.

Outback

The area north of Eyre Peninsula and the Flinders Ranges stretches into the vast,

empty spaces of SA's outback. Although sparsely populated and often difficult to travel through, it has much of interest. However, without 4WD or camels, it's often not possible to stray far from the few main roads. Entry permits are required for large parts of the north-west (which are either Aboriginal land or the Woomera Prohibited Area).

Information
The main tourist information outlet is in the Wadlata Outback Centre at 41 Flinders Terrace, Port Augusta (see the earlier section on the Eyre Peninsula).

For information on national parks and an update on the park permit system, contact the NPWS office (☎ 8648 5310, 1800 816 078, fax 8648 5301), at 9 MacKay St in Port Augusta.

National Park Permits To visit most of the outback's conservation areas you need a Desert Parks Pass, which costs $60 per vehicle. It's valid for a year and includes an excellent information book and detailed route and area maps.

Desert Parks Passes are widely available and the NPWS office in Port Augusta can tell you about outlets. They include: all state NPWS regional offices, Adelaide (RAA and the Environment Shop), Alice Springs (Shell Todd service station), Birdsville (Birdsville Auto, near the service station), Coober Pedy (Underground Books), Hawker (Hawker Motors), Innamincka (Trading Post), Marree (Marree General Store), Mt Dare Homestead, Oodnadatta (Pink Roadhouse), Port Augusta (Wadlata Outback Centre) and William Creek (William Creek Hotel).

If you just want to visit Cooper Creek in the Innamincka Regional Reserve, Lake Eyre in the Lake Eyre National Park or Dalhousie Springs in the Witjira National Park, you need only buy a day/night permit for $15 per vehicle. These are available from Mt Dare Homestead, the Pink Roadhouse in Oodnadatta, the William Creek Hotel, the Marree General Store and the rangers at Innamincka and Dalhousie Springs.

ROUTES NORTH

The Stuart Hwy is sealed all the way from Port Augusta to Darwin. It's a long, often boring drive and the temptation to get it over with quickly has resulted in many high speed collisions between cars and cattle, sheep, kangaroos and wedge-tailed eagles. Take care, particularly at night.

If you want to travel to the NT by a more adventurous route there's the **Oodnadatta Track**. This option takes you from Port Augusta through the Flinders Ranges to Leigh Creek, Lyndhurst, Marree and Oodnadatta before joining the Stuart Hwy at Marla, about 180km south of the Territory border. For most of the way it runs close to the defunct 'Old Ghan' train line.

The road is sealed as far as Lyndhurst, then you're on dirt (and often rough and dusty dirt, at that) all the way to Marla. There are several routes across to the Stuart Hwy: from Lake Eyre south via Roxby Downs to Pimba; from William Creek west to Coober Pedy; and from Oodnadatta either south to Coober Pedy or west to Cadney Homestead (a roadhouse on the Stuart Hwy). With a 4WD you can keep going up the old railway line from Oodnadatta to Alice Springs, visiting Witjira National Park and Old Andado Homestead on the way.

Two other routes of interest in the outback are the **Birdsville** and **Strzelecki** tracks (see the relevant sections later in this chapter). These days the tracks have been so much improved that it's usually quite feasible to travel them in any car that's in good condition and has reasonable ground clearance.

For more information on these roads check with the state automobile associations. *Outback Central & South Australia*, published by the Department of Environment, Heritage & Aboriginal Affairs, is an excellent tourist map with a lot of interesting information. Westprint does a good *Simpson Desert South-Lake Eyre* map that covers all three tracks. For more detail on outback travel, see Lonely Planet's *Outback Australia*.

The South Australian outback includes much of the **Simpson Desert** and the harsh, rocky landscape of the **Sturt Stony Desert**.

There are also huge salt lakes that fill with water every once in a long while. **Lake Eyre**, used by Donald Campbell for his attempt on the world's land-speed record in the 1960s, filled up for a time in the 1970s. It was full again in 1989 – only the third occasion since Europeans settled this area over 130 years ago.

When soaking rain does fall on this usually dry land the effect can be amazing – flowers bloom and plants grow at a breakneck pace in order to complete their life cycles before the drought returns. There is even a species of 'water-holding' frog that goes into suspended animation, remaining in the ground for years on end, only to pop up when the rains come again.

On a much more mundane level, roads can either be washed out or turned into glue-like mud. Venture into the wrong place after heavy rain and you may be stuck for days – or even weeks.

Note that fuel outlets, repair facilities and spare parts are often extremely limited, so be prepared in case of breakdown. See the Outback Travel entry in the Getting Around chapter for more information.

WOOMERA

● postcode 5720 ● pop 1000

During the 1950s and 1960s Woomera was used to launch experimental British rockets and conduct tests in an abortive European project to send a satellite into orbit. The Woomera Prohibited Area, into which rockets are still fired, occupies a vast stretch of land in the centre of the state.

Woomera is now an 'open town', but it is just a shadow of its former self. While rocket research still goes on, these days the town's main role is to service the mostly US personnel working at the Joint Defence Facility at Nurrungar, a short distance south. At the time of writing, this was due to close and Woomera's future doesn't look promising.

A small **heritage centre** (☎ 8673 7042), in the middle of town has interesting displays that tell you about Woomera's past and present roles and what may happen in the future. Outside is a collection of old military aircraft, rockets and missiles. The centre is open daily from 9 am to 5 pm (closed in summer).

Ask at the heritage centre about tours of the rocket range.

Places to Stay & Eat

The *Woomera Travellers' Village* (☎ 8673 7800), near the town entrance, has backpacker accommodation ($15/20 for singles/doubles with ceiling fans; $17/24 with air-con), grassed camp sites ($5 per person), on-site vans (from $25 for doubles), cabins (from $45) and budget motel units ($45).

Alternatively, the *Eldo Hotel* (☎ 8673 7867, *Kotara Ave*) has air-con rooms with share facilities from $33 per person, as well as more upmarket units. You can also get counter meals here from about $7.

Getting There & Away

Air Airlines of SA (☎ 13 1313) flies from Adelaide daily except Friday and weekends for $180.

Bus Woomera is 7km off the Stuart Hwy from the scruffy little settlement of Pimba, 175km north of Port Augusta. The long-distance buses pass through Woomera daily.

ROXBY DOWNS & ANDAMOOKA

• postcode 5722   • pop 470

Roxby Downs (population approximately 3500) is a modern, pleasantly landscaped town in sandy semidesert 92km from the Stuart Hwy via Woomera. There has to be a good reason for a town like Roxby to be in such a harsh area. In this case it's the nearby **Olympic Dam mine**, which produces uranium, copper, silver and gold from a huge mass of ore only discovered in 1975.

From April to October inclusive there are daily tours of the mine (surface only), metallurgical plant and township. These take 2½ hours, cost $26 and leave at 9.45 am from the Olympic Dam Tours office (☎ 8671 0788) next to the BP service station in town. The operators also run tours of Andamooka and Woomera.

About 25km by sealed road from Roxby Downs, **Andamooka** (population 470) is a

rough-and-ready opal-mining town with a strong frontier flavour. The contrast between this barren place and leafy Roxby is breathtaking.

For general information call in to the post office in the centre of town – it's by Duke's Bottlehouse. There are various tours, including a guided walk ($10) around local points of interest.

Places to Stay & Eat

Roxby Downs The *Roxby Downs Caravan Park* (☎ 8671 1000, *Pioneer Drive*) near the town centre, has grassed camp sites for $11 and on-site vans for $34, otherwise there's the *Roxby Downs Motor Inn* (☎ 8671 0071, *Richardson Place*) in the town centre where singles/doubles are $95.

Andamooka You can camp (from $14) or stay in an on-site van or cabin without air-con (both $30) at the dusty *Andamooka Caravan Park* (☎ 8672 7117, *94 Government Rd*), in the town centre. There's not much shade here – not that there is anywhere else, for that matter.

Duke's Bottlehouse (☎ 8672 7007, *275 Opal Creek Blvd*) has motel units for $45/65

RICHARD I'ANSON

Welcome to camel country

a single/double. Alternatively, the *Andamooka Opal Hotel/Motel* (☎ 8672 7078), on the corner of Watkins Ave and Chicago Square, charges from $55/65.

The best place in town to eat is the *Tuckerbox Restaurant*, next to Duke's Bottlehouse, which sells hearty meals for reasonable prices.

Getting There & Away

Air Kendell Airlines (☎ 13 1300) flies daily to Roxby Downs from Adelaide ($216) and from Roxby Downs to Coober Pedy ($112).

Bus Premier Stateliner has buses to Adelaide daily except Saturday to Roxby Downs ($63).

GLENDAMBO
• postcode 5710   • pop 20

Glendambo, 113km north of Pimba and 252km south of Coober Pedy, was created in 1982 as a service centre on the Stuart Hwy to replace the township of Kingoonya, which was bypassed. Glendambo has a good pub, motel, two roadhouses and a caravan park. Fuel is available from 6 am to midnight.

The *Glendambo Tourist Centre* (☎ 8672 1030) has bars, a restaurant and motel units from $72/74 a single/double plus $12 for each extra person.

Right next door is the *BP Roadhouse & Caravan Park* (☎ 8672 1035), which has grassy camp sites for $12. Its on-site vans (no air-con) cost $25 plus $5 for each additional person, and there's a very basic bunkhouse where bunk beds cost $12.

If you're heading north, remember that there are no refuelling stops between here and Coober Pedy.

COOBER PEDY
• postcode 5723   • pop 3000

On the Stuart Hwy, 535km north of Port Augusta, Coober Pedy is the 'opal capital' of Australia, if not the world. The lure of opal has brought people from all over the world to live here – about 40 nationalities are represented.

The name 'Coober Pedy' is Aboriginal and is said to mean 'white fellow's hole in the ground'. This aptly describes the place, as about half the population lives in dugouts to shelter from the extreme climate: daytime summer temperatures can soar to over 50°C and the winter nights are freezing cold. Apart from the dugouts, there are over 250,000 mine shafts in the area. Walk carefully and keep your eyes open!

Coober Pedy is in an extremely inhospitable environment and the town's appearance reflects this; water is expensive and the rainfall scanty, so even in the middle of winter the town looks dried out and dusty. It's not as ramshackle as it used to be, but even so you could never describe it as attractive. In fact, the town looks a bit like the end of the world – which is probably why much of *Mad Max III* was filmed here.

There are plenty of opal shops, but banking facilities are limited: there are several EFTPOS cash-withdrawal facilities, a Westpac branch with ATM, and a Commonwealth Bank agency in the post office – the latter two are in the main street (Hutchison St).

While Coober Pedy is a friendly enough place, it has a reputation for being pretty volatile. Since 1987 the police station has been bombed twice and the courthouse once, the most successful restaurant was demolished by a blast and hundreds of thousands of dollars worth of mining equipment has gone the same way. More recently, two police cars were blown up!

Information

The tourist office (☎ 1800 637 076, fax 8672 5699) is in the council offices, diagonally opposite the Ampol Roadhouse as you enter town along Hutchison St from the Stuart Hwy. It's open weekdays from 9 am to 5 pm only. Otherwise Underground Books (☎ 8672 5558), on Post Office Hill Rd, is very good for information on the local area and the Outback in general.

Dugout Homes

Many of the early dugout homes were simply worked-out mines; now, however, they're usually cut specifically as residences. Several are open to visitors – it

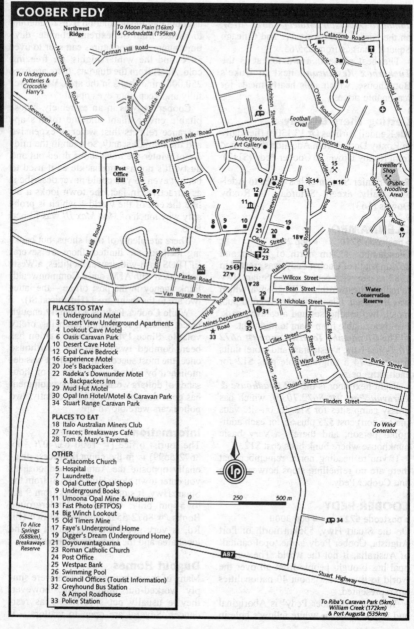

COOBER PEDY

PLACES TO STAY
1 Underground Motel
3 Desert View Underground Apartments
4 Lookout Cave Motel
6 Oasis Caravan Park
10 Desert Cave Hotel
12 Opal Cave Bedrock
16 Experience Motel
20 Joe's Backpackers
22 Radeka's Downunder Motel
  & Backpackers Inn
29 Mud Hut Motel
30 Opal Inn Hotel/Motel & Caravan Park
34 Stuart Range Caravan Park

PLACES TO EAT
18 Italo Australian Miners Club
27 Traces; Breakaways Café
28 Tom & Mary's Taverna

OTHER
2 Catacombs Church
5 Hospital
7 Laundrette
8 Opal Cutter (Opal Shop)
9 Underground Books
11 Umoona Opal Mine & Museum
13 Fast Photo (EFTPOS)
14 Big Winch Lookout
15 Old Timers Mine
17 Faye's Underground Home
19 Digger's Dream (Underground Home)
21 Doyouwantagoanna
23 Roman Catholic Church
24 Post Office
25 Westpac Bank
26 Swimming Pool
31 Council Offices (Tourist Information)
32 Greyhound Bus Station
  & Ampol Roadhouse
33 Police Station

To Moon Plain (16km)
& Oodnadatta (195km)

Northwest Ridge

German Hill Road

To Underground
Potteries &
Crocodile
Harry's

Seventeen Mile Road

Northwest Ridge Road

Russell Street

Oodnadatta Road

Catacomb Road

McKenzie Close

O'Neil Road

Hutchison Street

Hospital Road

Football Oval

Umoona Road

Seventeen Mile Road

Underground Art Gallery

Post Office Hill

Post Office Hill Road

Ain Street

Brewster Street

Crowders Gully Road

Jeweller's Shop
(Public Noodling Area)

Old Water Tank Road

Flat Hill Road

Cameon Drive

Oliver Street

Paxton Road

Van Brugge Street

Wright Road

Club Road

Italian Street

Willcox Street

Bean Street

St Nicholas Street

Water Conservation Reserve

Mines Department Road

Giles Street

Hocking Street

Robins Blvd

Eyre Street

Ward Street

Burke Street

Stuart Street

Flinders Street

To Wind Generator

To Alice Springs (688km), Breakaways Reserve

0   250   500 m

LP

To Riba's Caravan Park (5km),
William Creek (172km)
& Port Augusta (535km)

A87

Stuart Highway

seems all you have to do to charge admission is create an eccentric enough abode!

Opal Mining

The town survives on opals, which were first discovered here by a teenage boy in 1915. Keen fossickers can have a go themselves, the safest area being the **Jeweller's Shop** opal field in the north-east corner of town – fossicking through the mullock, or waste dumps is known as 'noodling'.

There are literally hundreds of working mines around Coober Pedy but there are no big operators. When somebody makes a find, dozens of miners home in like bees around a honey pot. Looking at all the vacant ground between the various 'fields' makes you wonder just how much opal is still down there!

Other Attractions

Coober Pedy has a number of other attractions. The most prominent is the **Big Winch**, at the northern end of Italian Club Rd, which has a lookout over the town and a display of cut and uncut opal.

There are numerous reputable – and some not so reputable – opal outlets in town; it's best to shop around and be wary of anyone offering discounts over 30% (this is a sign that the opal may be overpriced). Some of the best buys are found at the **Opal Cutter** on Post Office Hill Rd.

The **Old Timers Mine** is an early mine and underground home, with many interesting displays. It is open daily from 9 am to 5 pm for self-guided tours and is well worth the $5 entry fee.

The **Umoona Opal Mine & Museum** is right in the centre of town; opal was still being pulled out of here until mining within the town limits was banned some years ago. It has a very good information centre ($5), which includes early and modern dugout homes, an old mine, Aboriginal displays and an excellent 18 minute documentary on opal and opal mining. It's open daily from 8 am to 7 pm.

A couple of kilometres north-west of town is **Underground Potteries**, which has some fine products – you can often yarn to the potters and watch them working; it's open Monday to Saturday from 8.30 am to 6 pm.

Three kilometres further on is **Crocodile Harry's** ($2). This amazing dugout home has featured in a number of documentaries, the movies *Mad Max III* and *Ground Zero* and the mini-series *Stark*, so you can expect something different. Harry – a Latvian baron who emigrated to Australia after WWII – spent 13 years in northern Queensland and the NT hunting crocodiles.

Organised Tours

Several operators run tours that will take you into an opal mine, underground home and various other places in and around town. The tour offered by Radeka's Downunder Motel ($25) is popular with backpackers; the Desert Cave Hotel has a more upmarket tour ($36).

The Opal Quest tour (ask at Underground Books) is the only one to enter a working mine and give hands-on mining experience. This interesting two hour tour costs $25.

Also good is an informative 'star tour' ($15) where you explore the heavens from the Moon Plain – an appropriate venue. Book at Radeka's for this one.

On Monday and Thursday you can travel with the mail truck along 600km of dirt roads as it does the round trip from Coober Pedy to Oodnadatta and William Creek. This is a great way to get off the beaten track and visit small, remote outback communities. It costs $75 and doesn't include lunch. For details, call ☎ 1800 069 911 or contact Underground Books.

Places to Stay – Budget

Camping There are three caravan parks in town and another further out. None are visually inspiring – there's no lawn but plenty of dust, and the ground is as hard as nails. Showers are usually extra (typically 20c per minute).

Central to the action is the *Opal Inn Caravan Park (☎ 8672 5054, Hutchison St)*, which has camp sites for $9. The *Oasis Caravan Park (☎ 8672 5169, Seventeen Mile Rd)* is a short walk from the town centre and boasts the best shade and shelter.

SOUTH AUSTRALIA

Opals

Australia is the opal-producing centre of the world, and South Australia is where most of the country's opals come from. Opals are hardened from silica suspended in water, and the colour is produced by light being split and reflected by the silica molecules.

Opals are cut in three different fashions: solids can be cut out of the rough into cabochons (domed-top stones); triplets consist of a layer of opal sandwiched between an opaque backing layer and a transparent cap; and doublets are simply an opal layer with an opaque backing. In Queensland, opals are often found embedded in rock; these are sometimes polished and left in the surrounding rock.

An opal's value is partly determined by its colour and clarity – the brighter and clearer the colour the better. The type of opal is also an indicator of value: black and crystal opals are the most valuable, semiblack and semicrystal are in the middle and milk opal is the least valuable. The bigger the pattern, the better. Flaws (such as cracks) have a detrimental effect on value.

Shape is important – a high dome is better than a flat opal – as is size. As with the purchase of any sort of gemstone, don't expect to find great bargains unless you clearly understand what you are buying.

Camp sites here cost $5.50 per person, and there are basic twin rooms with air-con for $26. It has an undercover swimming pool in a big old storage tank.

The *Stuart Range Caravan Park (☎ 8672 5179, Hutchison St)* is the largest and has the best facilities, including a swimming pool; its cabins are more like motel rooms, and there are some backpacker beds ($10). The park is about 1km from town and on the main entrance off the Stuart Hwy.

Riba's (☎ 8672 5614) is a very friendly place on the William Creek road, 5km from town. It has above-ground sites costing $4.50 per person – you can camp underground for $8 – and showers are free. There's an interesting one hour evening mine tour for $10, which includes the above-ground camping fee.

Hostels There are four backpacker places, all underground. The *Backpackers' Inn* at Radeka's Downunder Motel (☎ 8672 5223, 1800 633 891, Oliver St) offers the best standard. Bunks in open alcoves cost $14, including linen and showers – if you want privacy, its renovated twins and doubles (from $35) with share facilities are very pleasant. The Inn's facilities include a very good kitchen, a bar, a restaurant and a laundry. You can book in between 7.30 am and 1 am, and if offers free transfers from the airport and bus station.

Also on Oliver St, *Joe's Backpackers (☎ 8672 5163)* has apartment-style two-bedroom, bunkhouses, each sleeping up to 10. Beds cost $14, including linen and showers, but there's no laundry (the laundrette is a short walk away on Post Office Hill Rd). They also do free transfers.

The very basic *Opal Cave Bedrock (☎ 8672 5028, Hutchison St)* has four-bed alcoves opening off a wide central passageway – curtains provide a measure of privacy here. Beds cost $12, including linen and showers. It's a fair hike to the toilets and showers out the front, particularly for the males, and kitchen facilities are limited.

The *Umoona Opal Mine (☎ 8672 5288, Hutchison St)*, in the town centre, has beds in basic, two-bunk private rooms for $10 each, including shower (linen is $5 extra). There are only limited kitchen facilities.

Hotels The *Opal Inn Hotel/Motel (☎ 8672 5054, Hutchison St)*, in the town centre, has basic pub rooms with air-con for $25/35 and motel rooms from $40/45/50 for singles/doubles/triples.

Places to Stay – Mid-Range

Motels & B&Bs There are a number of hotels and motels, some underground and some with big air-cons. Most are expensive! Listed here are the cheaper places.

Radeka's Downunder Motel (☎ 8672 5223, Oliver St) has an underground family room sleeping six for $90; its motel units are very comfortable and single/double/triples cost $50/70/75.

The *Opal Dreaming Underground Cottage*, 4km out at Black Point, has stunning views of wide open spaces. It charges $70 for two people – this place is very well appointed, but doesn't have a flush toilet. Book at the Underground Art Gallery in Hutchison St (☎ 8672 5985).

While it is not the cheapest, the underground *Experience Motel* (☎ 8672 5777, Crowders Gully Rd) is probably the homeliest place in town. It has a backpacker room sleeping six for $100, and very pleasing standard rooms costing $90 for singles and doubles with private facilities ($80 without).

Places to Stay – Top End
The luxurious *Desert Cave Hotel* (☎ 8672 5688, reserve@desertcave.com.au, Hutchison St) has rooms above and below ground for $148 for singles and doubles.

Places to Eat
Cheap eats are not that easy to come by, but you can get reasonably priced counter meals in the saloon bar of the *Opal Inn* – Thursday and Friday are 'specials' nights ($7). The *Italo Australian Miners Club (Italian Club)*, on Italian Club Rd, has similarly priced specials on Wednesday and Saturday nights.

There are a couple of Greek places: *Tom & Mary's Taverna* and *Traces* on Hutchison St in the town centre. Both are popular in the evenings and Traces stays open until late. Both do platters that make an economical meal for three or four people.

The *Breakaways Café*, under Traces, is popular for lunches. Another place worth trying on this street is the *Opal Run Restaurant*, next to the Westpac bank, which charges from around $10 for mains.

There are several takeaways and coffee lounges in the main street, as well as an up-market restaurant in the *Desert Cave Hotel*.

Getting Around
The Opal Cave (next to the Opal Cave Bedrock hostel) rents out mountain bikes for $8 a day, while the Desert Cave Hotel

(☎ 8672 5688) has an agency for Thrifty – one-way rentals can be arranged.

Getting There & Away
Air Kendell Airlines (☎ 13 1300) flies daily from Adelaide ($274). The Desert Cave Hotel handles reservations and operates the airport shuttle bus ($5 one way). Most hostels will meet you if you ring ahead.

Bus It's 413km from Coober Pedy to Kulgera, just across the border into the NT, and from there it's another 275km to Alice Springs.

To Coober Pedy, Greyhound Pioneer charges $76 from Adelaide and $75 from Alice Springs, stopping at the Ampol Roadhouse on Hutchison St.

McCafferty's, which stops at Radeka's Downunder Motel, charges $76 from Adelaide and $69 from Alice Springs.

AROUND COOBER PEDY
Breakaways Reserve
The Breakaways Reserve is a stark but very colourful area of mesa hills and scarps off the Stuart Hwy about 35km north of Coober Pedy. Here you find the white-and-yellow formation known as the **Castle**, which featured in the films *Mad Max III* and *The Adventures of Priscilla, Queen of the Desert*. Entry is subject to a permit ($2 per person), which you can get from the tourist office or Underground Books.

An interesting loop of 70km of mainly unsealed road from Coober Pedy takes in the Breakaways, the Dog Fence (it's supposed to keep dingoes to the north, away from the sheep) and the Moon Plain. Underground Books has a leaflet and 'mud map' ($1) – the route is generally OK for conventional vehicles.

MARLA
● postcode 5724　　● pop 150

In the mulga scrub, about 180km south of the NT border, Marla replaced Oodnadatta as the official regional centre when the Ghan railway line was re-routed in 1980. The rough-and-ready **Mintabie** opal field is on Aboriginal land, 35km west.

RICHARD I'ANSON

Locals help to make sure you don't get lost in the Outback.

Fuel and provisions are available in Marla 24 hours a day; there's also an EFTPOS cash-withdrawal facility.

The *Marla Travellers Rest* (☎ 8670 7001) has camp sites for $10, basic air-con cabins sleeping two for $19/28 a single/double (linen extra) and spacious motel rooms from $59/65. There's a choice of takeaway, a la carte and restaurant meals.

On the Stuart Hwy, 85km south of Marla and 151 km north of Coober Pedy, *Cadney Homestead* (☎ 8670 7994) has camp sites for $12, basic air-con cabins sleeping two for $25 (linen extra) and motel rooms for $77 singles and doubles.

If you're heading for Oodnadatta, turning off the highway at Cadney Homestead gives you a shorter run on dirt roads than the routes via Marla or Coober Pedy. En route you pass through the aptly named **Painted Desert**. You can visit this interesting area weekdays with the mail run from Cadney Homestead – the tour takes six hours and costs $50 per person, including lunch and a

one hour walk in the Painted Desert. There are camp sites and cabins at *Copper Hills Homestead* (☎ 8670 7995) about 32km east of Cadney Homestead.

MARREE
● postcode 5733   ● pop 80

Sleepy Marree was a major centre for the Afghan camel trains that serviced the Outback from the 1870s into the 1930s. There are still a couple of date palms, an incongruously large pub, and relics of the old *Ghan* train.

The township is at the southern end of the Birdsville and Oodnadatta tracks, and has a good range of services including EFTPOS (in both minimarkets). The place really fires up during the **Marree Australian Camel Cup**, held on the first Saturday in July of odd-numbered years.

Ask at the Oasis Cafe about scenic flights over **Lake Eyre** and **Marree Man**, the huge outline of an Aboriginal warrior that people unknown etched into the desert sands in 1998.

Places to Stay

The *Oasis Caravan Park* (☎ *8675 8352* , in the town centre, has lawned camp sites from $5 per person, and self-contained cabins with air-con for $20 per person.

Outside town at the turn-off to Birdsville, the somewhat dustier *Marree Caravan & Campers Park* (☎ *8675 8371)* has camp sites from $5 per person, on-site vans from $25, and twin rooms with air-con for $12/20 for singles/doubles. There's a campers' kitchen, and you can get fuel and tyres here.

Alternatively, the rather grand old *Great Northern Hotel (☎ 8675 8344)* in the town centre has old-style pub rooms ranging from $30/50 singles/doubles to $80 for a family room sleeping five. It has counter meals daily.

WILLIAM CREEK

● postcode 5351   ● pop 10

On the Oodnadatta Track, about halfway between Oodnadatta and Marree, the weatherbeaten *William Creek Hotel* (☎ *8670 7880*) is a fair dinkum outback pub, with more character than you'll find in a host of Adelaide hotels. Ask here about camel treks and scenic flights over nearby Lake Eyre.

The pub sells fuel, tyres and meals. It has modest motel-style units with air-con for $45/60 a single/double and a bunkhouse with no air-con for $12 per person. Dusty camp sites cost $3 per person.

At Coward Springs, about 150km west of Marree (70km south of William Creek), is a small, very basic *camping ground* (☎ *8675 8336)* with toilets and showers. You can do camel treks here in the cooler months, and there's a warm-water spa.

OODNADATTA

● postcode 5734   ● pop 200

Oodnadatta (like Marree, it lost much of its population when the Old Ghan Railway closed down) is at the point where the road and the old railway line diverged. It was here that, in 1912, the Reverend John Flynn, founder of the Royal Flying Doctor Service, established the Australian outback's first hospital.

One of the town's most distinctive features is the **Pink Roadhouse**, an excellent place to ask advice about track conditions and attractions in any direction. The owners, Adam and Lynnie Plate, have spent a great deal of time and effort putting road signs and kilometre pegs over a huge area in this district – even in the Simpson Desert you'll come across signs erected by this dedicated pair! They have no doubt saved many a 4WD traveller hours of searching for the right track. The roadhouse is also the place to buy a permit if you intend camping at Dalhousie Springs.

The old train station has been converted into an interesting little **museum**. It is kept locked but pick up the key from the pub, store or roadhouse.

The local Aboriginal community owns the town's only pub and the general store.

Places to Stay

The *Oodnadatta Caravan Park* (☎ *8670 7822)*, attached to the Pink Roadhouse, has plenty of accommodation including camp sites from $13, a self-contained backpacker cabin sleeping seven for $10 each, and basic motel-style rooms for $40. Most units have air-con.

The *Transcontinental Hotel (☎ 8670 7804)* has air-con singles/doubles with shared facilities for $30/55. You can get meals at the pub (dinner only) and at the roadhouse.

BIRDSVILLE TRACK

Years ago cattle from the south-west of Queensland were walked down the Birdsville Track to Marree where they were loaded onto trains. Motor transport took over from the drovers in the 1960s and these days the cattle is trucked out in road trains. It's 520km between Marree and Birdsville, just across the border.

Although conventional vehicles can usually manage the track without difficulty, it's worth bearing in mind that traffic is anything but heavy – particularly in summer. Petrol, diesel and minor mechanical repairs are available at the **Mungeranie Roadhouse** (☎ 8675 8317), about 205km from Marree

(315km from Birdsville). It also has camping, rooms and meals.

The track is more or less at the meeting point between the sand dunes of the Simpson Desert to the west and the desolate wastes of Sturt Stony Desert to the east. There are ruins of a couple of homesteads along the track and artesian bores gush out boiling-hot salty water at many places.

At Clifton Hill, about 200km south of Birdsville, the track splits with the main route going around the eastern side of Goyders Lagoon.

The last travellers to die on the track were a family of five. They took a wrong turning, got lost, ran out of petrol and perished from thirst.

STRZELECKI TRACK

These days the Strzelecki Track can be handled by conventional vehicles. It starts at Lyndhurst, about 80km south of Marree, and runs 460km to the tiny outpost of Innamincka. The discovery of natural gas deposits near Moomba has brought a great deal of development and improvement to the track, although the amount of heavy transport means the surface is often rough.

The new Moomba-Strzelecki Track is better kept but is longer and less interesting than the old track, which follows Strzelecki Creek. Accommodation, provisions and fuel are available at Lyndhurst and Innamincka, but there's nothing in between.

INNAMINCKA

● postcode 5731   ● pop 15

At the northern end of the Strzelecki Track, Innamincka is on Cooper Creek, where the Burke and Wills expedition of 1860 came to its tragic and hopeless end. Near here is the famous **Dig Tree**, as well as the memorials and markers where Burke and Wills died and where King, the sole survivor, was found.

There is also a memorial where Howitt, who led the rescue party, set up his depot on the creek. The dig tree is actually across the border in Queensland. The word 'dig' is no longer visible, but the expedition's camp number can still be made out.

Cooper Creek flows only after heavy soaking rains fall over central Queensland, but there are permanent water holes. The area had a large Aboriginal population prior to white settlement, and relics such as middens and grinding stones are common.

Westprint's *Innamincka-Coongie Lakes* map is a good source of information on the Innamincka area. For a moving account of the Burke and Wills expedition, read Alan Moorehead's *Cooper's Creek*.

You can get fuel and provisions at the Innamincka Trading Post. The old **Australian Inland Mission hospital** now houses the NPWS ranger's office (☎ 8675 9909) and displays on the surrounding **Innamincka Regional Reserve**.

Places to Stay & Eat

The *Innamincka Hotel* (☎ 8675 9901) has motel-style rooms sleeping up to five for $40/60 a single/double (extra persons $10 each). It does takeaways and has counter meals in the evenings – its Wednesday night 'Beef-and-Creek' and Sunday night roasts are both good value at $10 for all you can eat.

The *Innamincka Trading Post* (☎ 8675 9900) has three very modest two-bedroom cabins sleeping up to four for $40/60/85/100.

There are plenty of good places to camp among the coolabahs along Cooper Creek, but there are no facilities whatsoever – see the ranger for a permit if you want to camp within the Innamincka Regional Reserve. For a donation to the Progress Association you can use the shower, toilet and laundry facilities (sorry, no washing machines here) outside the Trading Post.

THE GHAN

See the Northern Territory chapter for details of the famous Ghan railway line from Adelaide to Alice Springs.

Tasmania

Tasmania is Australia's only island state, a fact that was a major influence on its development and made it an ideal location for penal settlements. Its isolation has also helped preserve its rich colonial heritage and much of its wilderness (with a few notable exceptions).

The first European to see Tasmania was the Dutch navigator Abel Tasman, who arrived in 1642 and named it Van Diemen's Land, after the governor of the Dutch East Indies. In the 18th century, Tasmania was sighted and visited by a series of European sailors, including captains Tobias Furneaux, James Cook and William Bligh, all of whom believed it to be part of the Australian mainland.

European contact with the Tasmanian coast became more frequent after the First Fleet arrived at Sydney Cove in 1788, mainly because ships heading to the colony of New South Wales (NSW) from the west had to sail around the island.

In 1798 Lieutenant Matthew Flinders circumnavigated Van Diemen's Land, proving it to be an island. He named the rough stretch of sea between the island and the mainland Bass Strait, after George Bass, the ship's surgeon. The discovery of Bass Strait shortened the journey to Sydney from India or the Cape of Good Hope by a week.

In 1803 Risdon Cove, on the Derwent River in Tasmania, became the site of Australia's second colony. One year later the settlement was moved to the present site of Hobart. Although convicts were sent with the first settlers, penal settlements were not built until later: at Macquarie Harbour in 1822, at Maria Island in 1825 and at Port Arthur in 1830. For more than three decades, Van Diemen's Land was the most feared destination for British convicts.

In 1856 transportation to Van Diemen's Land was abolished and the colony's first parliament elected. Also in 1856, in an effort to escape the stigma of its dreadful penal reputation, Van Diemen's Land officially

HIGHLIGHTS

Telephone code: ☎ 03
Population: 471,885
Area: 67,800 sq km

- Trekking through Cradle Mountain-Lake St Clair – one of the world's last temperate wilderness areas
- Exploring convict history among the ruins of Port Arthur
- Strolling along Hobart's waterfront and sipping a coffee at Salamanca Place
- Enjoying the hospitality and history of the sandstone garrison towns along the Midland Hwy
- Dipping a toe in Wineglass Bay on the very beautiful Freycinet Peninsula
- Climbing the Nut and finding a fossil on Tassie's 'top end'

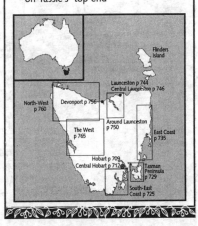

became known as Tasmania, after its first European visitor.

Reminders of the island's convict days and early colonial history are everywhere. There are the penal settlement ruins at Port Arthur, many convict-built bridges, a host

TASMANIA

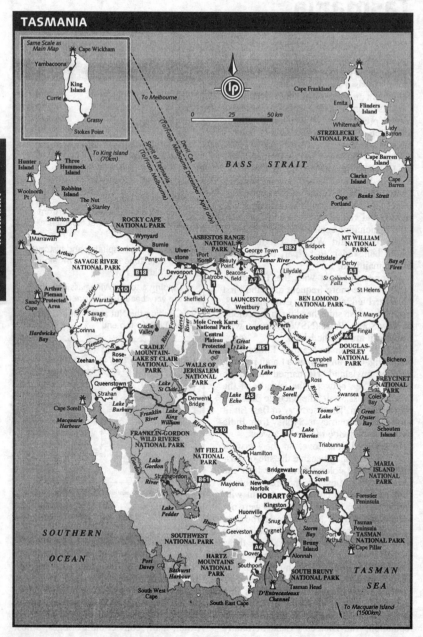

TASMANIA

Same Scale as Main Map

Cape Wickham

Yambacoona

King Island

Currie

Grassy

Stokes Point

To King Island (70km)

To Melbourne

To Macquarie Island (1500km)

Hunter Island

Three Hummock Island

Robbins Island

The Nut

Stanley

Woolnorth Pt

Smithton

Marrawah

A2

ROCKY CAPE NATIONAL PARK

Wynyard

Somerset

Burnie

Penguin

Ulverstone

Port Sorell

ASBESTOS RANGE NATIONAL PARK

George Town

Cape Frankland

Emita

Flinders Island

Whitemark

Lady Barron

STRZELECKI NATIONAL PARK

Cape Barren Island

Clarke Island

Cape Barren

Banks Strait

Cape Portland

BASS STRAIT

Devil Cat

Spirit of Tasmania (To/From Melbourne)

Spirit of Tasmania December - April only)

SAVAGE RIVER NATIONAL PARK

Arthur River

B18

A10

Arthur Pieman Protected Area

Sandy Cape

Hardwicke Bay

Waratah

Savage River

Corinna

Zeehan

Rosebery

Queenstown

Strahan

Cape Sorell

Macquarie Harbour

Lake Burbury

Cradle Valley

CRADLE MOUNTAIN-LAKE ST CLAIR NATIONAL PARK

Lake St Clair

FRANKLIN-GORDON WILD RIVERS NATIONAL PARK

Franklin River

Lake King William

Gordon River

Lake Gordon

Strathgordon

B61

Lake Pedder

SOUTHWEST NATIONAL PARK

Port Davey

Bathurst Harbour

South West Cape

South East Cape

SOUTHERN OCEAN

Sheffield

Deloraine

Mole Creek Karst National Park

Central Plateau Protected Area

WALLS OF JERUSALEM NATIONAL PARK

Great Lake

B51

Arthurs Lake

Lake Echo

A5

Derwent Bridge

A10

Bothwell

MT FIELD NATIONAL PARK

Maydena

Derwent River

New Norfolk

Hamilton

Beauty Point

Beaconsfield

A7

A8

Tamar River

LAUNCESTON

Westbury

Longford

Perth

Evandale

Mersey River

River Forth

Latrobe

Mt William National Park

Bridport

B82

Scottsdale

Lilydale

Derby

St Columba Falls

Bay of Fires

A3

St Helens

BEN LOMOND NATIONAL PARK

South Esk River

St Marys

Fingal

A4

Campbell Town

DOUGLAS-APSLEY NATIONAL PARK

Bicheno

Macquarie River

Ross

Swansea

FREYCINET NATIONAL PARK

Coles Bay

Great Oyster Bay

Schouten Island

Lake Sorell

Tooms Lake

Oatlands

Lake Tiberias

Triabunna

MARIA ISLAND NATIONAL PARK

Bridgewater

Richmond

Sorell

A3

A9

Forestier Peninsula

HOBART

Kingston

Huonville

Snug

Geeveston

Cygnet

Huon River

A6

Dover

Southport

HARTZ MOUNTAINS NATIONAL PARK

Storm Bay

Bruny Island

Alonnah

SOUTH BRUNY NATIONAL PARK

Tasman Head

D'Entrecasteaux Channel

Port Arthur

Tasman Peninsula

TASMAN NATIONAL PARK

Cape Pillar

TASMAN SEA

0   25   50 km

of beautifully preserved Georgian sandstone buildings, and more than 20 historic towns and villages classified by the National Trust.

Tasmania is also renowned world wide for its pristine wilderness areas, and for the pivotal role it played in world environmental and conservation movements during a period of 20 years or so from the late 1960s onwards.

In the 1989 state elections, Tasmania's Green Independents gained 18% of the vote and held the balance of power in parliament. Until recently, they were a key force in Tasmanian state politics, but in the 1998 election the number of seats in each electorate was reduced from seven to five and, as a result, their numbers in parliament were reduced.

ABORIGINAL PEOPLE

Since European settlement the story of Australia's Aborigines has been an unhappy one, and nowhere has it been more tragic than in Tasmania.

Tasmania's Aborigines became separated from the mainland over 10,000 years ago when sea levels rose as a result of the thawing of the last ice age. From that time on, their culture diverged from that of the mainland population. While the mainland people developed more specialised tools for hunting, such as boomerangs and spearthrowing holders, the Tasmanian people continued to use simpler tools, such as ordinary spears, wooden waddies and stones. They lived by hunting, fishing and gathering, sheltered in bark lean-tos and, despite Tasmania's cold weather, went naked apart from a coating of grease and charcoal.

European settlers found Tasmania fertile and fenced off sections of land to make farms. As the Aborigines lost more and more of their traditional hunting grounds, battles erupted. By 1806 the killing on both sides was out of control. In 1828 martial law was proclaimed by Lieutenant-Governor Arthur, and Aboriginal tribes were forced out of the settled districts and their traditional homeland (see the boxed text 'Lieutenant-Governor Arthur's Proclamation').

TASMANIANA LIBRARY, STATE LIBRARY OF TASMANIA

The 'last' Tasmanian Aborigine

Between 1829 and 1834 all remaining Aborigines were resettled in a reserve on Flinders Island – to be 'civilised' and Christianised. Most of them died of despair, homesickness, poor food or respiratory disease. Of the 135 who went to the island, only 47 survived to be transferred to Oyster Cove in 1847. Within 32 years the entire Aboriginal population at Oyster Cove had perished.

European sealers had been working in Bass Strait since 1798 and, although they occasionally raided tribes along the coast, their contact with Aboriginal people was mainly based on trade. Aboriginal women were also traded and many sealers settled on the Bass Strait islands with these women and had families.

By 1847 an Aboriginal community, with a lifestyle based on both Aboriginal and European ways, had emerged on the Flinders and other islands in the Furneaux group, and although the last full-blooded Tasmanian Aborigine died in the 19th century, the strength of this community helped save the race from total extinction. Today, thousands of descendants of members of this community still live in Tasmania.

TASMANIA

Lieutenant-Governor Arthur's Proclamation

In 1828, following an escalation in violence between set-tlers and Aborigines in Van Diemen's Land that came to be known as the Black War, Lieutenant-Governor Arthur issued a proclamation giving soldiers the right to shoot on sight any Aborigine found in an area of European settle-ment. Shortly afterwards, white people formed a human chain called the Black Line, which moved through settled areas of the colony, forcing its Aboriginal inhabitants from their homelands.

The incorrectly titled lithograph, *Governor Davey's Proclamation to the Aborigines 1816,* is an example of 19th century colonial propaganda. Similarly, were history not written by the victors, the Black War would surely have been called the White War after those who aimed to dis-possess the original inhabitants of Van Diemen's Land, just as the Black Line would have been known as the White Line.

HAND COLOURED LITHOGRAPH; REX NAN KIVELL COLLECTION, NATIONAL LIBRARY OF AUSTRALIA

GEOGRAPHY

Tasmania's population is concentrated mainly on the north and south-east coasts, where the undulating countryside is rich and fertile. The coast and its bays are ac-cessible and inviting. In winter, the mid-lands region looks very English, while the sparsely populated lakes country in the cen-tral highlands is serenely beautiful.

By contrast, the south-west and west coasts are wild and virtually untouched. For much of the year raging seas batter the west coast and rainfall is high. Inland, the rich forests and mountains of Tasmania's west and south-west form one of the world's last great wilderness areas, almost all of it na-tional park with World Heritage listing.

INFORMATION
Tourist Offices

There are privately run Tasmanian Travel & Information Centres (TTICs) in Hobart, Launceston, Devonport and Burnie. On the mainland there are government-run Travel Centres in:

Australian Capital Territory
(☎ 1800 354 564, fax 02-6209 2155)
165 City Walk, Canberra 2601

New South Wales
(☎ 1800 060 448, fax 02-9202 2055)
149 King St, Sydney 2000
Queensland
(☎ 1800 672 169, fax 07-3405 4140)
239 George St, Brisbane 4000
South Australia
(☎ 1800 675 972, fax 08-8400 5588)
1 King William St, Adelaide 5000
Victoria
(☎ 1800 632 641, fax 03-9206 7947)
259 Collins St, Melbourne 3000
Western Australia and Northern Territory
(☎ 1800 806 846) or contact SA office

These travel centres provide information on just about everything you need to know about Tasmania, and book accommodation, tours and airline, boat and bus tickets. Tourism Tas-mania publishes an invaluable free news-paper called *Tasmanian Travelways* that has comprehensive statewide listings of accom-modation, activities, public transport, con-necting transport facilities and vehicle hire, all with an indication of current costs.

The travel centres also stock the monthly magazines *This Week in Tasmania* and *Treasure Islander.* The annual *Tasmania Visitors Guide,* which has a good fold-out touring map of Tasmania, is also free and particularly useful.

The *Touring Map* and *Visitors Map* are excellent road maps of Tasmania, while the *Tasmanian Towns Street Atlas* ($24.95) is probably the best source of maps of individual towns and cities. They are available at Royal Automobile Club of Tasmania (RACT) offices, bookshops and visitor centres around the state, and at the Tasmap counter at Service Tasmania (☎ 6233 3382), 134 Macquarie St, Hobart.

Money

Automatic teller machines (ATMs) are scarce outside Hobart, Launceston and major towns across the north coast. However, many businesses across the state have EFTPOS, enabling you to pay for purchases with your key card or credit card; you can usually make small cash withdrawals with purchases.

Post & Communications

Post offices are open from about 9 am to 5 pm Monday to Friday (slightly longer in Hobart and Launceston). There are also many postal agencies in general stores and newsagencies.

All Tasmanian telephone numbers have eight digits and the area code for the state is 03. However, although there is a single area code for the entire state, calls outside your immediate area are treated as STD calls and timed and charged a fee per minute according to the distance you are calling.

NATIONAL PARKS

A greater percentage of land is national park or scenic reserve in Tasmania than in any other Australian state. In 1982 Tasmania's three largest national parks – Franklin-Gordon Wild Rivers, Cradle Mountain-Lake St Clair and South-West – and much of the Central Plateau were placed on the UNESCO World Heritage List. This listing acknowledged that these parks comprise one of the last great temperate wilderness areas left in the world. Today, about 20% of Tasmania is World Heritage Area protected from logging, hydro-electric power schemes and, with a few simple rules, ourselves.

An entry fee is charged for all of Tasmania's national parks; a pass is needed whether there is a collection booth or not. There are a number of passes available at park entrances, from many bus and tour operators, from some local stores and from Service Tasmania (☎ 6233 3382), at 134 Macquarie St, Hobart. A 24 hour pass to any number of parks costs $9 per car (for up to eight people) or $3 per person. The best value for most will be the two month holiday pass, which costs $30 per vehicle or $12 per person for bushwalkers, cyclists and motorcyclists, and provides entry into all parks. An annual pass for cars is $42.

The Parks and Wildlife Service (PWS ☎ 6233 6191), which can be reached at GPO Box 44A, Hobart, has an excellent Web site at www.parks.tas.gov.au.

ACTIVITIES

For excellent information about adventure tourism in Tasmania, pick up a free copy of Networking Tasmanian Adventures magazine at visitors centres and RACT offices around the state. A Web site with the same name at www.tasmanianadventures.com.au was being put together at the time of writing.

Bushwalking

The most well known of Tasmania's many superb bushwalks is the Overland Track in Cradle Mountain-Lake St Clair National Park (see The West later in this chapter). Among the many wonderful shorter walks Tasmania has to offer are the Organ Pipes and Zig-Zag tracks on Mt Wellington close to Hobart, the Tarn Shelf in Mt Field National Park west of Hobart, Hartz Peak south of Hobart and Wineglass Bay in Freycinet National Park on the East Coast.

On long walks, it's important to remember that in any season a fine day can quickly deteriorate, so warm clothing, waterproof gear, a tent and a compass are vital. The PWS (see National Parks earlier in this chapter) publishes *Welcome to the Wilderness – Bushwalking Trip Planner for Tasmania's World Heritage Area*, which has sections on planning, minimal-impact bushwalking and wilderness survival. It includes an equipment check list, which is essential reading. The PWS will send you this information, including a *Bushwalking Code*, free of charge, or you can pick it up from Service Tasmania, 134 Macquarie St, Hobart, or from any rangers' offices in the national parks.

Tasmap produces an excellent series of maps available at visitors centres, Service Tasmania, the Tasmanian Map Centre (☎ 6231 9043), at 96 Elizabeth St, Hobart, outdoor-equipment shops, Wilderness Society shops and newsagencies throughout the state.

Lonely Planet's *Bushwalking in Australia* has a large section on some of Tasmania's best walks.

Many excellent shops sell bush gear, while several youth hostels hire out equipment and/or take bushwalking tours. In the former category are Paddy Pallin in Hobart and Launceston, Mountain Design in Hobart, Allgoods in Launceston and the Backpackers' Barn in Devonport. Goshawk Gear in Hobart sells good second-hand clothing and equipment.

Water Sports

Swimming The north and east coasts have many sheltered white sand beaches that are excellent for swimming. On the west coast, there's some pretty ferocious surf and the beaches are unpatrolled.

Some pleasant beaches near Hobart tend to be polluted, so it's better to head for Kingston, Blackmans Bay or Seven Mile Beach.

Surfing Tasmania has plenty of good surf beaches. Close to Hobart, the best spots are Clifton Beach and the surf beach en route to South Arm. The southern beaches of Bruny Island, particularly Cloudy Bay, are also good. The east coast from Bicheno north to St Helens has good surf when conditions are favourable. The greatest spot of all is Marrawah on the west coast, though you'll need your own transport to get there.

Scuba Diving On the east coast and around King and Flinders islands there are some excellent scuba-diving opportunities.

Equipment can be rented in Hobart, Launceston, and towns on the north and east coasts; dive courses in Tasmania are considerably cheaper than those on the mainland. Dive Tasmania offers diving tours throughout the state – contact Gary Myors on ☎ 0417 013 518 or email at dive@tasadventures.com.

Sailing If you are planning a sailing trip to or around Tasmania, ring Paul Kerrison (☎ 6273 4192), the commodore of the Cruising Yacht Club of Tasmania, for advice. There are many good anchorages in the D'Entrecasteaux Channel, which is wide, deep and a beautiful place to sail. A berth at the Royal Hobart Yacht Club (☎ 6223 4599) is $15 a night, with the first night free. The Hobart Ports Corporation (☎ 6235 1000) charges by the week (around $40 or $50).

Rafting, Canoeing & Kayaking Rafting, rowing and canoeing are all popular pastimes. The most challenging river to raft is the Franklin (see the Franklin-Gordon Wild Rivers National Park section later in this chapter). Most of the tour operators that run rafting trips on the Franklin also offer trips on the Picton, upper Huon, Weld and Leven rivers. Ocean kayaking is another very popular activity on the east coast – see the Hobart, Kettering and Port Arthur sections later in this chapter.

Fishing

Many Tasmanian rivers and lakes offer superb trout fishing. A licence is required to fish in Tasmania's inland waters, and there are bag, season and size limits on a number of fish (see the *Fishing Code* brochure that you receive when you purchase your licence). Licences cost $45 for the full season, $35 for 14 days, $20 for three days and $12 for one day. They are available from many sports shops, post offices, petrol stations and visitors centres.

The lakes in the centre of the state are the best known spots for both brown and rainbow trout. Rod fishing in salt water is allowed all year without a permit, although size restrictions and bag limits apply.

Hop farm near New Norfolk, Tasmania

Cascade Brewery, Hobart, Tasmania

Constitution Dock and the Franklin Wharf, Hobart, Tasmania

PAUL SINCLAIR

Near Cradle Mountain, Tasmania

JOHN HAY

Mt Roland, near Sheffield, north-west Tasmania

CHRIS MELLOR

Spikey Bridge, near Swansea, on the east coast of Tasmania, was built by convicts in 1843.

RICHARD I'ANSON

Wineglass Bay, Freycinet National Park, Tasmania

Caving

Tasmania's caves are regarded as some of the most impressive in Australia. See the Mole Creek and Hastings sections later in this chapter for details.

Rock Climbing & Abseiling

Dry weather is desirable for rock climbing, and Tasmania's weather is often wet. Nevertheless, rock climbing and abseiling are very popular.

Some excellent cliffs have been developed for rock climbing, particularly along the east coast where the weather is usually best. The Organ Pipes on Mt Wellington (above Hobart), the Hazards at Coles Bay and cliffs on Mt Killiecrankie on Flinders Island provide excellent climbing on firm rock. Many visitors, having seen photos or footage of the magnificent rock formations on the Tasman Peninsula, head straight for that region, but while the coastal cliffs there are indeed spectacular, it should be noted that it may be impossible to climb them if the ocean swell is too big. At Adamsfield, on the road to Strathgordon, there are lots of bolted, steep, overhanging climbs on conglomerate rock and also opportunities for bouldering.

The really keen climbers drag all their gear onto the huge cliffs of Frenchmans Cap on the western side of the state and wait for a break in the rain.

If you want to climb or abseil with an experienced instructor, try Aardvark Adventures Tasmania (π 018 127 714), Freycinet Adventures (π 6257 0500), the Climbing Company (π 6234 3575), at the Climbing Edge indoor climbing venue, or Summit Sports (π 0418 362 210). And if you're after something different, ask Phil at Aardvark about abseiling down the silos in Battery Point or the massive wall of the Gordon Dam in the south-west.

Skiing

There are two minor ski fields in Tasmania: Ben Lomond, 60km from Launceston; and Mt Mawson, in Mt Field National Park. Downhill skiing is best at Ben Lomond – see that section later in this chapter for details.

ACCOMMODATION

Youth hostels and/or backpacker facilities are in most major towns, and there are plenty of caravan parks, most of which have camp sites, on-site vans and en suite cabins. Tasmania also has a huge number of B&Bs, including everything from restored convict-built cottages to bedrooms in family homes. Rates range from $60 to $120 a double.

Despite the variety of places to stay, Tasmania's major tourist centres are often fully booked in summer, so it's wise to make reservations well in advance for January. B&B and motel accommodation is at its most expensive in summer, but at other times put your bargaining skills to use.

GETTING THERE & AWAY
Air

The airlines that fly to Tasmania are Qantas Airways and Southern Australia Airlines (π 13 1313), Ansett Australia (π 13 1300), Kendell Airlines (π 1800 338 894), Island Airlines (π 1800 818 455) and King Island Airlines (π 9580 3777).

Qantas has direct or connecting flights to Hobart and Launceston from most Australian state capitals. Ansett used to have direct or connecting services to Hobart and Launceston, but by the time this book is published, the associated company Kendell will operate the vacated routes. The other airlines operate from various airports in Victoria. Most flights are to Hobart, Launceston, Devonport, Burnie/Wynyard, Flinders Island or King Island.

Air fares to Tasmania are constantly changing, but you can get some good deals by booking well in advance or travelling in winter.

Hobart The standard Qantas one way economy fare from Melbourne is $260 (the rock-bottom low-season return is around $199). From Sydney the standard one way fare is $376 (rock-bottom low-season return $293) and from Brisbane $504 (rock-bottom low-season return $379).

Launceston Qantas flies to Launceston from Melbourne for $225 one way (the

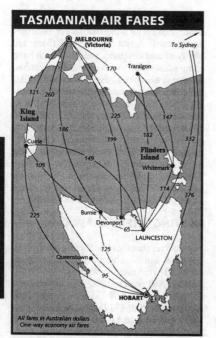

TASMANIAN AIR FARES

MELBOURNE (Victoria)

To Sydney

Traralgon

170

121 260

King Island

225

147

186

199 182

332

Currie

149

Flinders Island

105

Whitemark

114

376

225

Burnie

Devonport

65

LAUNCESTON

Queenstown

125

95

HOBART

All fares in Australian dollars
One-way economy air fares

rock-bottom low-season return is $179). From Sydney it's $332 one way ($269 rock-bottom low-season return). Some of the smaller airlines flying out of Melbourne use the city's second-string airports (Essendon and Moorabbin) and have lower base rates but offer fewer discounts. Island Airlines' full economy fare from Traralgon, in country Victoria, to Launceston is $182, or $261 via Flinders Island.

Devonport & Burnie/Wynyard There are flights from Melbourne to Devonport and Burnie/Wynyard (the airport is in Wynyard) with Kendell Airlines ($199 and $186 respectively, one way) and Southern Australian Airlines ($199 and $186).

The Islands Kendell Airlines flies to King Island, and Par Avion and Island Airlines fly to Flinders Island. Fewer discounts are available to these destinations and, as you will need accommodation, the best deal is

to buy a fly-drive package that includes accommodation. See the Bass Strait Islands section at the end of this chapter for details.

Boat

The *Spirit of Tasmania*, which operates between Melbourne and Devonport, can accommodate 1300 passengers and over 600 vehicles. It has nine decks and is more like a floating hotel than a ferry. The public areas of the ship and four cabins have been designed to cater for wheelchairs.

It departs from the TT-Line terminal (☎ 13 2010, reservations@tt-line.com.au) at Melbourne's Station pier on Monday (7.30 pm), Wednesday and Friday (6 pm) and from the terminal on the Esplanade in Devonport on Saturday (4 pm), Tuesday and Thursday (6 pm), arriving 13 to 14½ hours later. Additional sailings are often scheduled for the December/January holiday period.

Fares depend on whether you're travelling in the peak holiday (roughly late December to late January and Easter), shoulder (February to April, except Easter, and October to November) or off-peak (May to September) season. Contact TT-Line for precise dates. One way fares cost $106 ($136 peak season) in hostel-style accommodation (20-bed cabins) to $232 ($317 peak season) for suites. Student discounts apply to cabins but not to hostel-style accommodation. All fares include an evening buffet dinner and continental breakfast, but you can also choose to eat (and pay) at the more formal restaurant.

The cost for accompanied vehicles depends on the size of the vehicle and is currently subsidised by a federal government rebate. The standard size is 5m or less, for which the one way rate in 1999 was $30 ($40 peak season). Motorcycles cost $25 ($30) and bicycles $20 ($25).

Over the Christmas to Easter period 2000 to 2002, a 200 car, 550 passenger fast catamaran, the *Devil Cat*, operates between George Town on the Tamar River near Tasmania's central north coast and Melbourne, taking six hours to make the crossing weather permitting. It leaves Melbourne's Station Pier Tuesday, Thursday and Saturday at 8.30 am and arrives in Georgetown at

2.30 pm. It departs Georgetown Wednesday, Friday and Sunday at 2 pm and arrives in Melbourne at 8 pm. The return peak season fare for an adult is $260. For a standard vehicle it's $80 and for an adult accompanying a vehicle it is $410. Ring the TT-Line (☎ 13 2010) for more information.

TT-Line (☎ 1800 811 580, fax 1800 636 110 for its package-tour information) offers a Backpacker's Value Pack available to full-time students and members of YHA, VIP and Z Card. This covers return hostel accommodation on the *Spirit of Tasmania*, five days travel on scheduled services of Tasmanian Wilderness Travel (TWT) and a 20% discount on travel over the same five days on Tasmanian Redline Coaches (TRC). Prices vary according to the season and the year: the high season price is around $250.

There is also an infrequent ferry service between Bridport in Tasmania and Port Welshpool in Victoria (see the following Getting Around section).

GETTING AROUND

Tasmania is decentralised and its population very small. While public transport is adequate between most larger towns and popular tourist destinations, many people who wish to visit more remote and interesting sights find air and bus schedules frustrating and prefer to hire a car.

Air

Island Airlines (☎ 1800 818 455), Tasair (☎ 1800 062 900) and Par Avion (☎ 1800 646 411) fly intrastate. Approximate prices one way from Launceston are $65 to Burnie/Wynyard, $114 to Flinders Island and $149 to King Island. Flights from Burnie/Wynyard to King Island cost around $105 one way. Par Avion flies between Hobart and Melaleuca in the south-west for $95 one way and between Hobart and Burnie/Wynyard for $125 one way.

Bus

Tasmania has a good bus network connecting all major towns and centres, but weekend services are infrequent and this can be inconvenient for the traveller with limited

time. There are more buses in summer than in winter.

The main bus companies are TRC (☎ 1300 360 000) and TWT (☎ 1300 300 520), and they cover most of the state between them. Both have depots in the major centres of Hobart, Launceston and Devonport as well as agents in the stopover towns. To give you some idea of the costs, a one way trip between Hobart and Launceston costs $19.50, between Hobart and Queenstown $36.20, and between Launceston and Bicheno $19.

TWT has a 7/10/14/30 day stand-by pass (called a Wilderness Pass) that must be used within 10/14/20/40 days and costs $129/159/169/230. The pass is valid on all scheduled services and can also be used to obtain a 20% discount on many TRC services. Passes can be bought from mainland Tasmanian Information Centres, YHA offices and STA Travel offices, or directly from TWT.

If you are intending to buy a Wilderness Pass, ask for timetables in advance or check TWT's Web site at www.tassie.net.au/wildtour and plan your itinerary exhaustively before making your purchase. This is the only way to ensure that you will be able to get where you want to go within the life of the pass.

All bus fares and conditions quoted in this chapter should be used as a guide only, as both change frequently.

Car & Campervan

Although you can bring cars from the mainland to Tasmania, renting may be cheaper, particularly on short trips. Tasmania has a wide range of national and local car-rental agencies, and the rates are considerably lower here than on the mainland.

Tasmanian Travelways lists many of the rental options, but before you decide on a company, ask about any kilometre limitations and find out what the insurance covers. Also ensure that there are no hidden seasonal adjustments. It is, however, quite normal for smaller rental companies to ask for a bond of around $300.

Large international firms such as Avis, Budget and Hertz have standard rates for

TASMANIA

cars, from about $50 or $60 per day for high-season multi-day hire of a small car. By booking in advance and choosing smaller cars, rates can be as low as $45 per day for one week's hire (outside the holiday season).

Small local firms such as Advance (☎ 1800 030 118), Selective (☎ 6234 3311), Rent-a-Bug (☎ 6231 0300) and Jim's (☎ 6236 9779) rent older cars for as little as $25 or $30 a day, depending on the length of time and season. You can usually collect your car from the airport or ferry terminal.

Tasmanian Travelways also has a listing of campervan rental companies. Autorent-Hertz (☎ 1800 030 500) has campervans for around $926 a week for five people in the low season or $1674 a week in the high season. Savings can be made by going to the smaller operators but must be weighed against the rental conditions and general condition of the vehicle – make sure you are familiar and confident with both before you sign.

Warning While driving around the state watch out for the wildlife. If possible, avoid driving between dusk and dawn, as this is when marsupials are most active. Also be wary of 'black ice', an invisible layer of ice over the bitumen, especially on the shaded side of mountain passes.

Bicycle

Tasmania is a good size for exploring by bicycle and you can hire bikes throughout the state. If you plan to cycle between Hobart and Launceston via either coast, count on it taking 10 to 14 days. For a full circuit of the island, you should allow 14 to 28 days. Get a copy of *Bicycling Tasmania* by Ian Terry & Rob Beedham to help plan your trip. If you are planning a circuit, consider following the Giro Tasmania, which is detailed on the excellent 'giro' page of Bicycling Tasmania's Web site at www.netspace.net.au/~smithp.

If you bring a bike over on the *Spirit of Tasmania* it will cost you $20 to $25 each way, depending on the season. Airlines charge $10 to carry a bicycle from Melbourne to Hobart or Launceston.

Hitching

If you travel by thumb in Tasmania, wrap up in winter and keep a raincoat handy. A good number of the state's roads are still unsurfaced and the traffic can be very light, so although these roads often lead to interesting places, you normally have to give them a miss if you're hitching. See Hitching in the Getting Around chapter.

Hobart

● postcode 7000   ● pop 128,600

Hobart is Australia's second-oldest city and its southernmost capital. Straddling the mouth of the Derwent River and backed by towering Mt Wellington, Hobart combines the benefits of a modern city with a rich colonial heritage and a serene natural beauty. The attractive Georgian buildings, the busy harbour and the easy-going atmosphere make Hobart one of the most enjoyable and engaging of Australia's cities.

The first inhabitants of the area were the semi-nomadic Aboriginal Mouheneer tribe. The first European colony in Tasmania was founded in 1803 at Risdon Cove, but a year later it was decided that a site about 10km below Risdon and on the opposite shore was a better place to settle. Hobart began as a village of tents and wattle-and-daub huts with a population of 262 (178 of whom were convicts).

Hobart Town, as it was known until 1881, was proclaimed a city in 1842. Very important to its development was the Derwent River estuary, one of the world's finest deep-water harbours; many merchants made their fortunes from the whaling trade, shipbuilding and the export of products such as merino wool and corn.

Orientation

Being fairly small and simply laid out, Hobart is an easy city to find your way around. The streets in the city centre, many of which are one way, are arranged in a grid around the Elizabeth St Mall. The Tasmanian tourist information centre, Qantas and the

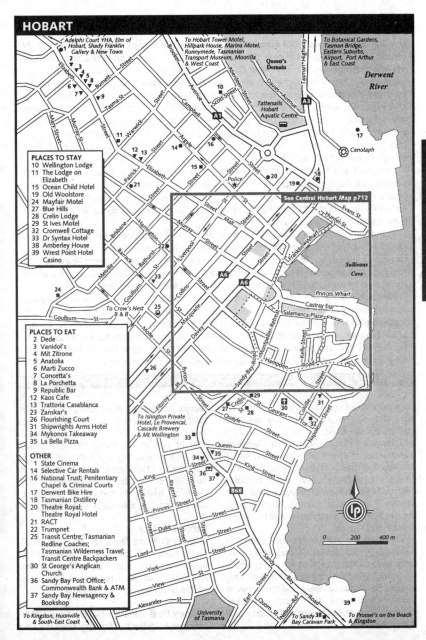

HOBART

See Central Hobart Map p712

PLACES TO STAY
10 Wellington Lodge
11 The Lodge on
   Elizabeth
15 Ocean Child Hotel
19 Old Woolstore
24 Mayfair Motel
27 Blue Hills
28 Crelin Lodge
29 St Ives Motel
32 Cromwell Cottage
33 Dr Syntax Hotel
38 Amberley House
39 Wrest Point Hotel
   Casino

PLACES TO EAT
2 Dede
3 Vanidol's
4 Mit Zitrone
5 Anatolia
6 Marti Zucco
7 Concetta's
8 La Porchetta
9 Republic Bar
12 Kaos Cafe
13 Trattoria Casablanca
23 Zanskar's
26 Flourishing Court
31 Shipwrights Arms Hotel
34 Mykonos Takeaway
35 La Bella Pizza

OTHER
1 State Cinema
14 Selective Car Rentals
16 National Trust; Penitentiary
   Chapel & Criminal Courts
17 Derwent Bike Hire
18 Tasmanian Distillery
20 Theatre Royal;
   Theatre Royal Hotel
21 RACT
22 Trumpnet
25 Transit Centre; Tasmanian
   Redline Coaches;
   Tasmanian Wilderness Travel;
   Transit Centre Backpackers
30 St George's Anglican
   Church
36 Sandy Bay Post Office;
   Commonwealth Bank & ATM
37 Sandy Bay Newsagency &
   Bookshop

*To Hobart Tower Motel,
Hillpark House, Marina Motel,
Runnymede, Tasmanian
Transport Museum, Moorilla
& West Coast*

*To Botanical Gardens,
Tasman Bridge,
Eastern Suburbs,
Airport, Port Arthur
& East Coast*

Derwent River

Queen's Domain

Tattersalls Hobart Aquatic Centre

Cenotaph

Sullivans Cove

Princes Wharf

Franklin Wharf

Castray Esp

Salamanca Place

To Crow's Nest B & B

To Islington Private Hotel, Le Provencal, Cascade Brewery & Mt Wellington

University of Tasmania

To Kingston, Huonville & South-East Coast

To Sandy Bay Caravan Park

To Prosser's on the Beach & Kingston

0   200   400 m

TASMANIA

Hobart Walking Tour

This walk starts at **Salamanca Place**, the tourist precinct of Hobart. While waterside activity has moved away from this once bustling area, restoration work has saved and preserved one of Hobart's best vistas. The sandstone Georgian warehouses were built from about 1835, replacing earlier wooden structures in what was called New Wharf. At street level, the majority of the warehouses are now speciality and craft shops, restaurants, cafes and bars.

A gap in the warehouses leads to the **Kelly Steps** (1839), which link the waterfront area with residential **Battery Point**. These stone stairs were built on private land owned by Captain James Kelly, by all accounts a larger-than-life character in early Hobart Town. You can take the steps to Kelly St, which is lined with small cottages (1850s), but continue our walk along Salamanca Place past the silos.

At Runnymede St, either continue straight ahead to pretty Princes Park or turn right and wander past the wonderful **Lenna of Hobart** (1880). Now an upmarket hotel, this splendid neoclassical building was once a private residence. Continuing up Runnymede, you come to **Arthur Circus**, a circle of quaint Georgian houses (some squeezed in by sacrificing plenty of living space) around a small village green.

Runnymede St ends at Hampden Rd, the main thoroughfare through Battery Point. To the right there are antique shops and restaurants that you can peruse, but first consider the option of heading left and following narrow Secheron Rd which ends at **Secheron House** (1831). This attractive, understated sandstone house was built for Surveyor General George Frankland and in its time would have had a wonderful, uninterrupted river view from the balcony.

Back along Hampden Rd it's time for a spot of window shopping, antique browsing and planning the evening meal. There are numerous interesting buildings for the period-architecture buff, but the highlight would have to be **Narryna** (1834). This two storey Georgian house is now home to the **Van Diemen's Land Folk Museum**. Just beyond Narryna, Hampden Rd meets busy Sandy Bay Rd; veer right and continue along Sandy Bay Rd to **St David's Park.** This was Hobart Town's original cemetery, which became an overgrown eyesore and was turned into a park in 1926.

---

main post office are all on Elizabeth St. The main shopping area extends west from the mall on Elizabeth St.

Salamanca Place, the row of Georgian warehouses, is along the waterfront, while just south of this is Battery Point, Hobart's delightful, well-preserved early colonial district. If you follow the river around from Battery Point you'll come to Sandy Bay, the site of Hobart's university and the Wrest Point Hotel Casino.

The northern side of the city centre is bounded by the recreation area known locally as the Domain (short for the Queen's Domain), which includes the Royal Tasmanian Botanical Gardens and the Derwent River. From here the Tasman Bridge crosses the river to the eastern suburbs and the airport.

Maps The best maps of Hobart are the *Hobart Street Directory* and the Hobart maps in the *Tasmanian Towns Street Atlas*, available at Service Tasmania (☎ 6233 3382), 134 Macquarie St, and newsagents. The Tasmanian Map Centre (☎ 6231 9043), at 96 Elizabeth St, the TTIC and the RACT (☎ 6232 6300), on the corner of Murray and Patrick Sts, also stock street maps.

Information

Tourist Offices The TTIC (☎ 6230 8233), on the corner of Davey and Elizabeth Sts, is open weekdays from 8.30 am to 5.15 pm and from 9 am to 4 pm on weekends and public holidays.

Money Banks, many of which have ATMs, are open Monday to Thursday from 9.30 am

Hobart Walking Tour

Captain James Kelly and Lieutenant Governor David Collins are buried here. Behind the Supreme Court buildings, at the bottom end of the park, retaining walls now house the headstones that were removed. The inscriptions make an interesting, if sobering, insight into colonial life.

Across Salamanca Place from St David's Park is **Parliament House** (1835). Originally, this building was the Customs House for Hobart Town. It became Parliament House in 1856. Stroll through the manicured gardens of Parliament Square, in front of Parliament House, to **Waterman's Dock**. From here you can walk along the waterfront of **Sullivans Cove**.

Just beyond Waterman's Dock are the terminals for harbour ferries and cruises. The large **Elizabeth St Pier** now houses upmarket accommodation and restaurants.

Cross the drawbridge over the entrance to **Constitution Dock**. This place really comes alive when yachties celebrate the finish of the famous Sydney to Hobart yacht race around New Year and also during the Royal Hobart Regatta in February.

Moored along the north-eastern side of the dock are several inexpensive **fish and chips barges**, behind them is **Mures Fish Centre (Upper and Lower Deck)**, one of Hobart's gastronomic landmarks, and **Victoria Dock**, home to much of Hobart's fishing fleet.

Beyond Victoria Dock, and making a photogenic backdrop to the fishing fleet, are the warehouses (1836) of **Hunter St**, including the University of Tasmania's Centre for the Arts (which houses the Plimsoll Gallery, open from noon to 5 pm daily), and the former IXL jam factory. The history of this dockside area is pictorially described on 'pedestals' on the Hunter St footpath beside Victoria Dock and at the north-western end of Hunter St, at the intersection with Davey St. You can stand above the archaeological site and read about the tragic fire that destroyed the former red-light district of Wapping.

You might also sample the wares at the **Tasmania Distillery**, in the Gasworks complex, 150m to the north of Hunter St along Davey St.

From the corner of Hunter and Davey Sts it's a short walk back along the docks to either Salamanca Place or Elizabeth St and the Mall.

---

to 4 pm and until 5 pm Friday. There are also multi-bank ATMs at Waterman's Dock, in Salamanca Place and at Antarctic Adventure in Salamanca Square.

Post & Communications The main post office is on the corner of Elizabeth and Macquarie Sts. It's open weekdays from 8 am to 5.45 pm. The Sandy Bay post office, in King St opposite the Purity supermarket, is open weekdays from 9 am to 5 pm and Saturday from 9.30 am to 1 pm.

Internet access is available at the State Library (☎ 6233 7529), 91 Murray St; Drifters Internet Cafe in The Galleria, 33 Salamanca Place; at Southern Internet Services, Ground Floor, Marine Board Building, 1 Franklin Wharf; Trumpnet, 117 Harrington St (☎ 1300 361 220); and at some hostels.

Bookshops Fullers, at 140 Collins St, the Hobart Book Shop, at 22 Salamanca Square, and the Sandy Bay Newsagency & Bookshop, 197 Sandy Bay Rd, are the places to go if you are looking for quality literature, travel guides and books about Tasmania in general. The Tasmanian Map Centre, at 96 Elizabeth St, specialises in guide books.

Medical Services The Travellers Medical & Vaccination Centre (☎ 6223 7577, fax 6224 8077) is at 270 Sandy Bay Rd, Sandy Bay.

Emergency The Royal Hobart Hospital can be contacted on (☎ 6222 8308), police are on (☎ 6230 2111) and for fire, accident and other emergencies dial ☎ 000.

TASMANIA

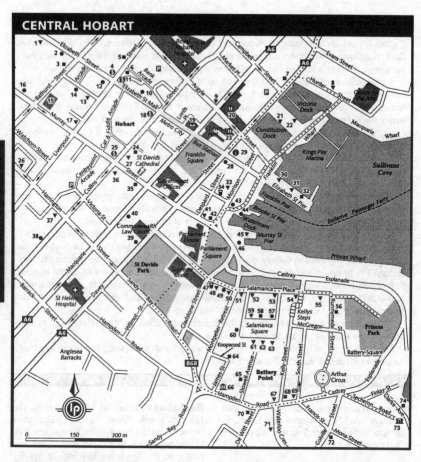

CENTRAL HOBART

Useful Organisations The Tasmanian YHA office (☎ 6234 9617) is at 28 Criterion St, and is open Monday to Friday from 9 am to 5 pm.

The Wilderness Society's head office (☎ 6234 9366) is at 130 Davey St and its shop is in The Galleria, Salamanca Place; the National Trust shop is in the same arcade.

Salamanca Place

The row of beautiful sandstone warehouses on the harbour front at Salamanca Place is a prime example of Australian colonial architecture. Dating back to the whaling days of the 1830s, these warehouses were the centre of Hobart Town's trade and commerce. Today they have been tastefully developed to house galleries, restaurants, nightspots and shops selling everything from vegetables to antiques. Every Saturday morning a large open-air **market** is held here.

Battery Point

Behind Princes Wharf is the historic core of Hobart, the old port area known as Battery Point. Its name comes from the gun battery that stood on the promontory by the

CENTRAL HOBART

TASMANIA

guardhouse (1818). During colonial times this area was a colourful maritime village.

Don't miss **Arthur Circus** – a small circle of quaint cottages built around a village green – or **St George's Anglican Church**. The *Battery Point and Sullivan's Cove Trail of Discovery* pamphlet is available at the TTIC.

At the time of writing it was expected that the speed limit in Battery Point would be reduced to 40km/hour.

Van Diemen's Land Folk Museum

The oldest folk museum in Australia is housed in Narryna, a fine Georgian home at 103 Hampden Rd, Battery Point. Dating from 1836, it stands in beautiful grounds and has a large and fascinating collection of relics from Tasmania's early pioneering days. It's open Tuesday to Friday from

10.30 am to 5 pm and at weekends from 2 to 5 pm. Entry is $5/2 for adults/children.

Maritime Museum of Tasmania

The fascinating Maritime Museum has an extensive collection of photos, paintings, models and relics depicting Tasmania's, and particularly Hobart's, colourful shipping history. By the time this book goes to print, it should be housed in new premises in the Carnegie Building in lower Argyle St (near Constitution Dock). It's open daily from 10 am to 4.30 pm ($4).

Tasmanian Museum & Art Gallery

The excellent Tasmanian Museum & Art Gallery, at 5 Argyle St, (enter via Macquarie St) incorporates Hobart's oldest building, the Commissariat Store (1808). The museum section features a Tasmanian Aboriginal display and relics from the state's colonial heritage, while the gallery has a good collection of Tasmanian colonial art. Entry is free and it's open daily from 10 am to 5 pm. Free guided tours depart Wednesday to Sunday at 2.30 pm.

Cascade Brewery

Australia's oldest brewery, on Cascade Rd close to the city centre, is still in use and produces some of the finest beer in the country – although no doubt others would argue differently! There are two-hour tours daily at 9.30 am and 1 pm ($7.50); bookings are essential (☎ 6224 1144). The brewery is on the south-western edge of the city centre; bus Nos 43, 44, 46 and 49 leave from the Elizabeth St side of Franklin Square and go right by it – alight at stop 17.

Interesting Buildings

One of the things that makes Hobart so unusual among Australian cities is its wealth of old and remarkably well-preserved buildings. There are more than 90 buildings in Hobart that are classified by the National Trust and 60 of these, featuring some of Hobart's best Georgian architecture, are on Macquarie and Davey Sts. An excellent booklet on both new and old buildings, *An Architectural Guide to the City of Hobart*, is available from the National Trust for $3.20.

Close to the city centre is **St David's Park**, which has gravestones that date from the earliest days of the colony. Opposite is **Parliament House**. Hobart's prestigious **Theatre Royal**, at 29 Campbell St, was built in 1837 and is the oldest theatre in Australia.

There's a **royal tennis court** on Davey St, one of only three in the southern hemisphere, which you can look into on the Footsteps Walking Tour – see the Organised Tours section later in this chapter for details. (Royal, or 'real', tennis is an ancient form of tennis played in a four-walled indoor court.) The historic **Penitentiary Chapel & Criminal Courts** are on the corner of Brisbane and Campbell Sts; the National Trust runs tours of the buildings daily between 10 am and 2 pm ($6). Ghost tours

($10) are also available but bookings are essential (☎ 0417 361 392).

Runnymede, at 61 Bay Rd, New Town, is a gracious colonial residence dating from the early 1830s. Now managed by the National Trust, it is open daily from 10 am to 4.30 pm ($6). To get there take bus No 15 or 20 from Stop H in the Metro City bus station (Elizabeth St) and alight at the Old New Town station.

Other Attractions

The **Allport Library & Museum of Fine Arts** is based in the State Library, at 91 Murray St. It has a collection of rare books on Australasia and the Pacific region – and you can visit on weekdays from 9.30 am to 5 pm (free).

Other museums include: the **Tasmanian Transport Museum**, in Glenorchy, which is Australia's first public museum, open weekends only, from 1 to 4.30 pm; the **Lady Franklin Gallery**, on Lenah Valley Rd (weekends only from 1 to 4.30 pm); the military museum at **Anglesea Barracks**, on Davey St (Tuesday from 9 am to 12.30 pm); and the **Moorilla Museum of Antiquities**, at Moorilla Estate Vineyard, 655 Main Rd, Berriedale, which features a mummy case from 600 BC (Wednesday to Sunday from 10 am to 4 pm). At the vineyard you can eat at the restaurant, sample some excellent wines and, occasionally, enjoy an outdoor concert.

Antarctic Adventure, in Salamanca Square is a combination of theme park and science centre, and is open daily from 10 am to 5 pm ($16/8). The displays incorporate large amounts of written information, but children will find the planetarium and the simulated downhill skiing entertaining. Nearby in Salamanca Square, and open similar hours, is **Time Warp House**, which bills itself as Australia's first retro entertainment centre ($8/4).

Just by the Tasman Bridge are the small but beguiling **Royal Tasmanian Botanic Gardens**, which are free and open from 8 am daily. They boast the largest collection of mature conifers in the southern hemisphere. After you've see the plants outside, you can explore their world in more detail in the interactive Botanical Discovery Centre ($6/3/12 for adults/children/family).

Hobart is dominated by 1270m-high **Mt Wellington**, which has many fine views and walking tracks. The *Mt Wellington Walks* map (available at the TTIC) has details. To get there (without taking a tour), take bus No 48 or 49 from Franklin Square on Elizabeth St; it will take you to Fern Tree at the base of the mountain and from there it's an often stunning 13km walk to the top. From December to mid-February, there may be buses to the top – ring the Metro (☎ 13 2201) for details.

There are also wonderful views from **Mt Nelson**, which is a good alternative when Mt Wellington is in cloud.

Cycling

If you fancy a ride beside the Derwent, hire a bike from Derwent Bike Hire, at the Cenotaph in the Regatta Grounds ($7 an hour). You can also take a $35 organised ride from the top of Mt Wellington with Brake Out Cycling Tours (☎ 6239 1080).

Kayaking

You can hire ocean kayaks from Aardvark Adventures Tasmania (☎ 018 127 714) and the Roaring 40°s Ocean Kayaking Company (☎ 1800 653 712). In summer, ocean kayaking on the Derwent at twilight is popular.

Sailing

The Derwent River and D'Entrecasteaux Channel are wonderful sailing waters. If you are a capable sailor you can hire a yacht from Yachting Holidays (☎ 6224 3195, 0417 550 879). If you are not a sailor, you can take a cruise on the *Prudence* (☎ 6223 4568), a Huon pine vessel usually moored at Waterman's Dock.

Organised Tours

Cruises Several boat cruise companies operate from the Brooke St Pier and Franklin Wharf and offer a variety of cruises in and around the harbour. The 4½ hour Cadbury's Cruise, run by the Cruise Company (☎ 6234 9294; $33/16), departs at 10 am on weekdays and cruises slowly to the Cadbury Schweppes factory in Claremont, where you disembark and tour the premises.

Harbour cruises are also available and vary from one to three hours. The MV *Cartela* (☎ 6223 1914), for example, has $26 lunch and dinner cruises.

Guided Walks A two hour guided walk ($15) departs from the TTIC at 10 am daily from September to May; a two hour Hobart Historic Pub Tour ($35 with four drinks, $19 with one) departs from the TTIC Sunday to Thursday at 5 pm; a tour of the Hobart Rivulet ($7), which runs beneath the central business district, departs from the Hobart City Council offices, on the corner of Davey and Elizabeth Sts, at 4 pm on Thursday; and the Footsteps Walking Tour of Battery Point ($10) is available on demand – ring ☎ 6224 0996.

Bus Tours Day and half-day bus tours in and around Hobart are operated by Tasmanian Tours & Travel/Tigerline (☎ 6231 2200, 1300 653 633). Typical half-day tours include trips to Richmond ($35) and the City Sights and Mt Wellington ($25). Full-day tours include Port Arthur ($45), the Huon Valley ($69) and Bruny Island ($95). TWT (☎ 1300 300 520) runs day trips to places such as Mt Field National Park ($59), Tasmanian vineyards ($85), the Tamar Valley ($85) and Freycinet National Park ($59), and also offers some of longer tours.

Another company offering similar coach tours of and from Hobart is Experience Tasmania (☎ 6234 3336). It also runs twilight and evening tours of the city sights, a sunrise tour of Mt Wellington, a coach tram tour, and a combined coach tram tour and cruise.

Scenic Flights Scenic flights are run by Par Avion (☎ 1800 646 411) and Tasair (☎ 1800 062 900) from Cambridge airport, 15km from the city. Par Avion charges $190 an hour for up to three people and also offers day tours of the south-west wilderness for $240.

Motorcycle Tours Tours in a Harley-Davidson sidecar are offered by Harley Tours of Hobart (☎ 6224 1565).

Special Events

Hobart's premier festival is the Hobart Summer Festival from late December to late January. The docks are at their most festive for 10 days or so around the finish of the annual Sydney to Hobart Yacht Race and New Year. Highlights include a New Year's Eve party for revelling yachties, locals and visitors alike, and the Taste of Tasmania, a Tasmanian food and wine extravaganza.

The Royal Hobart Regatta, in early February, is a major aquatic carnival.

The Australian Wooden Boat Festival, held at the docks each November in even-numbered years, features vessels from around Australia and celebrates Tasmania's vibrant boat-building heritage.

Hobart has a thriving literary scene and its Salamanca Readers' and Writers' Festival in August draws participants from around the country.

The first biennial Tasmanian cultural festival is planned for 2001.

Places to Stay

The best area of Hobart to stay in is Battery Point; unfortunately, but understandably, prices here are high and vacancy rates low. Accommodation in the affluent neighbouring suburb of Sandy Bay is also generally expensive. Sandy Bay Rd is long and winding, as is the suburb, so if you don't want to be too far from town, check distances from the city before making a booking.

Away from the water on the other side of the city centre, but still reasonably close to town, are the adjoining suburbs of North Hobart and New Town, where you'll find good B&Bs and some moderately priced motels within walking distance of a cluster of lively restaurants and cafes. Also bordering the city centre are West Hobart, from where you can get some wonderful views of the city lights at night, and the quirky little suburb of Glebe, on the edge of the Domain parkland.

If you are visiting in January and are particular about accommodation, you really should book at least nine months ahead.

Places to Stay – Budget

Camping Approximately 3km from the city is *Sandy Bay Caravan Park* (☎ 6225 1264, 1 Peel St), with powered sites ($12 a double), on-site vans ($35) and cabins ($55). To get there, take Metro bus No 54, 55 or 56 from Franklin Square or walk along Sandy Bay Rd for 40 minutes. Other caravan parks are further out.

Hostels In the centre of town is the rambling *Central City Backpackers* (☎ 6224 2404, 138 Collins St), with excellent facilities and friendly staff. It's $16 or $18 for a dorm bed, $20 per person in a twin, and $32/40 a single/double.

At the TRC depot is the *Transit Centre Backpackers* (☎ 6231 2400, 199 Collins St), with beds for $13 and a very large communal area; it's open from 9 am to 10 pm.

The *New Sydney Hotel* (☎ 6234 4516, 87 Bathurst St) charges $14 for backpacker beds, while the *Ocean Child Hotel* (☎ 6234 6730), on the corner of Argyle and Melville Sts, charges $12.

In Battery Point, the *Hobart Town Guesthouse* (☎ 6224 8331, 1 Stowell Ave) has dorm beds for $14 a night with a continental breakfast. Basic singles/doubles with shared facilities are $25/40 with breakfast.

Hobart's YHA hostel, *Adelphi Court* (☎ 6228 4829, 17 Stoke St, New Town), is

---

Wild Winds on the Westcoaster

The Westcoaster yacht race starts in Melbourne and heads down Tasmania's wild and windy west coast. With few harbours for shelter, it is indeed one of the toughest yachting events around. The race concludes over the same days as its more famous counterpart, the Sydney to Hobart yacht race. Constitution Dock, in Hobart, is definitely the place to be around New Year, when yachts fill the harbour and there is much celebrating.

2.5km from the city and reasonably close to the lively North Hobart restaurant and cafe strip. It's an excellent hostel with good facilities. It charges $14 a dorm bed, $38 a twin room with shared facilities and $42/48 for an en suite room. Take Metro bus No 15 from stop H in Elizabeth St to stop 8. Any bus leaving stop E in Elizabeth St will take you to stop 13, which is close to Stoke St. The TRC airport bus stops at the hostel.

Hotels & Motels In the middle of town are the *Brunswick Hotel* (☎ 6234 4981, 67 Liverpool St), which has singles/doubles for $30/50 with a continental breakfast, and the *Alabama Hotel* (☎ 6234 3737, 72 Liverpool St), which charges $28/44.

There are plenty of motels in Hobart, but the inexpensive ones are often rather a long way out. The *Marina Motel* (☎ 6228 4748, 153 Risdon Rd, Lutana) is reasonably central. Its rooms cost from $39/49.

Places to Stay – Mid-Range

Guesthouses & B&Bs Near the Adelphi Court YHA hostel is *Hillpark House* (☎ 6228 7094, 344 Park St, New Town), which has singles/doubles with private bathrooms for $70/90, including a cooked breakfast.

A couple of good mid-range B&Bs close to town are *Crows Nest* (☎ 6234 9853, 2 Liverpool Crescent, West Hobart), which has lovely views and charges from $55/75, and *Wellington Lodge* (☎ 6231 0614, 7 Scott St, Glebe), which has views over the city and charges $75/95.

Hotels & Motels Near the docks is the *Customs House Hotel* (☎ 6234 6645, 1 Murray St), which has good views of the waterfront from some rooms and charges $50/65 for singles/doubles ($70 for en suite doubles) with a continental breakfast.

The *Prince of Wales Hotel* (☎ 6223 6355), on Hampden Rd, Battery Point, provides good accommodation with private facilities for $60/70, including breakfast. The *Shipwrights Arms Hotel* (☎ 6223 5551, 29 Trumpeter St, Battery Point) is a more attractive hotel, but its rooms ($40/60 with shared facilities) are less inviting than those at the Prince.

At the city end of Sandy Bay is the *Dr Syntax Hotel* (☎ 6223 6258, 139 Sandy Bay Rd), which has large rooms with en suite for $43/59 (breakfast extra).

Two good Battery Point motels, walking distance from the city and docks, are *Blue Hills* (☎ 6223 1777, 96A Sandy Bay Rd) and *St Ives Motel* (☎ 6224 1044, 86 Sandy Bay Rd). They charge around $90 a double.

Within walking distance of the city centre is the pleasant, suburban *Mayfair Motel* (☎ 6231 1188, 17 Cavell St, West Hobart), which has singles/doubles from $80/95.

Around the corner from the Adelphi Court hostel is the *Hobart Tower Motel* (☎ 6228 0166, 300 Park St, New Town). Its rooms are attractive for the price ($65/69), but the nearby Brooker Ave is noisy.

Apartments Hobart has a number of self-contained holiday flats with fully equipped kitchens. *Knopwood Holiday Flat* (☎ 6223 2290, 6 Knopwood St, Battery Point) is a three bedroom upstairs flat overlooking Salamanca Place that charges $70 a double and $20 for each extra person. Its view has been obstructed by new buildings considerably in the past few years, but the position and the garden are still drawcards. Further from the docks is *Crelin Lodge* (☎ 6223 1777, 1 Crelin St, Battery Point), which charges $80 a double.

Places to Stay – Top End

Guesthouses & B&Bs *Barton Cottage* (☎ 6224 1606, 72 Hampden Rd), which dates back to 1837, has B&B for $95/110 for singles/doubles. *Cromwell Cottage* (☎ 6223 6734, 6 Cromwell St), dating from the late 1880s, has B&B for $85/110, while *Colville Cottage* (☎ 6223 6968, 32 Mona St), set in lovely gardens, has B&B for $95/115. The modern *Jarem Waterfront B&B* (☎ 6223 8216, 8 Clarke Ave) has singles with private bathrooms for $95 and doubles with en suite for $120. The breakfast menu changes regularly.

In North Hobart is the *Lodge on Elizabeth* (☎ 6231 3830, 249 Elizabeth St), an old mansion charging $115 a double, while a bit further up the road is the *Elms of Hobart*

TASMANIA

(☎ 6231 3277, 452 Elizabeth St), which is more luxurious and charges $112/130.

Near the Casino is the grand *Amberley House (☎ 6225 1005, 391 Sandy Bay Rd)*, which has rooms with en suite for $106/120 (breakfast extra).

Hotels *Country Comfort Hadleys Hotel (☎ 6223 4355, 34 Murray St)* is one of Hobart's best older-style hotels. Singles or doubles with en suite cost $105.

Top-end, international-standard accommodation is available at the *Hotel Grand Chancellor (☎ 6235 4535, 1 Davey St)*, which charges from $220 a double in peak season, though reductions apply for advance bookings. *Wrest Point Hotel Casino (☎ 6225 0112, 410 Sandy Bay Rd)*, 3km south of the city centre, has rooms for $100 in the motel and $218 in the tower.

Lenna of Hobart (☎ 6232 3900, 20 Runnymede St, Battery Point) is an ideally situated mansion steeped in history that charges from $140 a double. More intimate but further from the city centre is the charming *Islington Private Hotel (☎ 6623 3900, 321 Davey St, South Hobart)*, which has rooms for $75/140 with breakfast.

Apartments Two upmarket complexes that have opened in recent years are the *Old Woolstore (☎ 6235 5355, 1 Macquarie St)*, which has retained the facade of the original Sullivans Cove building, and the *Oakford on Elizabeth Pier (☎ 6220 6600)*, right at the end of the pier. Both offer high standard, modern accommodation for between $130 and $160 a double.

Places to Eat
Restaurants Some of the best Indian curries in town are those at the *Tandoor & Curry House (☎ 6234 6905, 101 Harrington St)*.

Elizabeth St in North Hobart has a reputation for good-value ethnic cuisine. At No 321 is *Anatolia*, a Turkish restaurant where you can bring your own (BYO) alcohol. Just down from there *La Porchetta* serves pizza and pasta (it's part of the Melbourne chain). For more pasta and Italian dishes try *Trattoria Casablanca*, at No 213, or *Concetta's*,

at No 340. *Vanidol's*, at No 353, is a BYO restaurant open Tuesday to Sunday. It has an excellent mixed menu of Thai, Indian and Indonesian cuisines. At No 369 is another BYO Asian restaurant, *Dede*, which has delicious sticky rice balls for $5 and mains for between $10 and $15.

Also in Elizabeth St, North Hobart, is *Mit Zitrone (☎ 6234 8113)*, probably the trendiest restaurant in town. Its entrees and cakes live up to their reputation (highly recommended are the twice-cooked eggs).

The suburban *Le Provencal (☎ 6224 2526, 417 Macquarie St, South Hobart)* has wonderful, hearty provincial French fare with an emphasis on couscous ($17). Down on the Elizabeth St pier, *A Splash of Paris (☎ 6224 2200)* has good food and great views of the water, but can be very noisy if crowded.

Understandably, Salamanca Place boasts a few swish eateries. Italian cuisine can be found at *Maldini* while *Panache*, which is licensed to serve alcohol, is a cafe/restaurant with an outdoor eating area by the adjoining rock walls. For Japanese food, try the licensed *Mikaku*, at No 85. *Syrup (☎ 6224 8249)* above Knopwood's Retreat, *Blue Skies (☎ 6224 3747, Murray St Pier)* and *Rockerfeller's (☎ 6234 3490, 11 Morrison St)* are nearby informal eateries.

Behind the Customs House Hotel is *Areeba! (7 Despard St)*, a Mexican restaurant and bar. Innovative Mexican and Santa Fe style cuisine distinguish this place from run-of-the-mill Mexican restaurants.

In Hampden Rd, Battery Point, is the bustling *Da Angelo Ristorante (☎ 6223 7011)*, which serves pasta and pizza for $10. Come early or book as it's often full.

The *Upper Deck* restaurant, at Mures Fish Centre, Victoria Dock, is licensed and has great harbour views and excellent seafood. Over at Murray St Pier *Sisco's on the Pier* prepares local seafood with modern Mediterranean flair. Also on the waterfront, the licensed *Drunken Admiral (17 Hunter St)* is open every evening and has good seafood and a great atmosphere.

Prosser's on the Beach (☎ 6225 2276, Beach Rd, Lower Sandy Bay) is a taxi ride from the city but serves some of the best seafood in town in attractive, unpretentious premises overlooking the water.

For Chinese food, try *Flourishing Court* (☎ *6223 2559, 252 Macquarie St)*, the *Golden Bamboo (*☎ *6234 2282, 116 Elizabeth St)* or the *Asian Restaurant (*☎ *6225 1718, 410 Sandy Bay Rd)* at Wrest Point.

Pubs In the city, the *Brunswick Hotel (67 Liverpool St)* has meals from $4. The *New Sydney (87 Bathurst St)* is popular for cheap, filling counter meals, while *Montgomery's (87 Macquarie St)* has bar meals for $9 or $10 and snacks for $4.50. The *Customs House Hotel (1 Murray St)* serves excellent bar meals for under $10, and there is also a reputable restaurant on the premises (children's meals available). The place to go in North Hobart is the *Republic Bar (299 Elizabeth St)*, while in Battery Point the *Prince of Wales* and the *Shipwright's Arms (29 Trumpeter St)* have good meals.

Cafes In the centre of town is the stylish, licensed *Kafe Kara (119 Liverpool St)*, open from 8 am to 3 pm weekdays and from 9 am to 3 pm on Saturday. Another gem just around the corner is *Cumquat (10 Criterion St)*, open weekdays from 9 am until customers leave after dinner.

Upstairs in Fullers Bookshop is the *Afterword Cafe (140 Collins St)*, open from 9 am to 5 pm Monday to Saturday and from 10 am to 4 pm Sunday. It's a good option on Sunday, when it's one of the few pleasant cafes in the centre of town that is open.

A little to the west of the centre is the inexpensive *Zanskar's (39 Barrack St)*, a popular alternative place to relax over a vegetarian meal, a game of Scrabble or a letter home; it's open from 10 am to 9 pm daily.

T-42° is a popular cafe and wine bar that serves tempting, reasonably priced meals'.

The *Retro Cafe*, in Salamanca Place, has to be *the* Hobart corner. The food is hearty, the atmosphere and decor vibrant; it's open daily from 8 am to 6 pm. Towards Parliament House is the equally popular but relatively sedate *Zum Cafe*, which has a more interesting menu. In the other direction, towards

the silos, is *Maldini*, which has great coffee and cakes, while further along, inside the Salamanca Arts Centre, is the *Foyer* espresso bar. Retro, Zum and Maldini all have outdoor tables. Nearby is the *Vietnamese Kitchen*, with cheap Asian fare.

Behind Salamanca Place, beside a fountain in a pleasant, sunny square with plenty of outdoor tables, is the capacious *All Bar One*, a wine bar with a cafe section that serves wood-fired gourmet pizzas. Across the square is the *Salamanca Bakehouse*, a rather plain bakery that has the advantage of being open 24 hours a day. Also in this square is the *Machine Laundry Cafe* (nothing tastes so good as brunch consumed knowing that tedious domestic tasks are being completed as you eat).

If you happen to be rubbernecking in Battery Point and need to rest your legs, drop in to the rustic *Jackman & McRoss (57-59 Hampden Rd)*, a bakery cafe open weekdays from 7.30 am to 7 pm and weekends from 7.30 am to 5 pm. Nearby is *Mummy's Cafe (38 Waterloo Crescent)*, where you can get a snack late at night every day except Monday. It's been transformed recently into a thriving, modern cafe/restaurant – a far cry from the Mummy's of old.

Near North Hobart is *Kaos Cafe (273 Elizabeth St)*, which enjoys a good reputation. It's open weekdays from noon to midnight, Saturday from 10 am to midnight, and Sunday from 10 am to 10 pm.

On the other side of the city, near the main library on the campus of the University of Tasmania (via Churchill Ave), is *Lazenby's (*☎ *6226 1858)*, where cheap, hot lunches and dinners are served in a bright, licensed cafe. Unfortunately, opening times vary with term dates and catering commitments.

The historic *Mount Nelson Signal Station Tea House*, on the summit of Mt Nelson, has spectacular panoramic views of Hobart and the surrounding area. It serves lunches and morning and afternoon teas.

Fast Food Constitution Dock has a number of floating takeaway *seafood stalls* (you can't miss them). Nearby is *Mures Lower Deck*, where you can get good quality takeaway fish and chips (the blue eye is usually excellent) and other seafood dishes.

In the city centre are the appropriately named *Little Bali (84A Harrington St)*, *Little Salama* (next door) and *Little Italy (152 Collins St)* takeaways.

For Japanese, try the excellent *Toshi's Kitchen*, in Salamanca Square, where you can get two pieces of sushi for $4.

You can get takeaway pizzas in Sandy Bay at *La Bella (172 Sandy Bay Rd)* or in Battery Point at *Da Angelo Ristorante (47 Hampden Rd)*. On Elizabeth St, North Hobart, are *Marti Zucco* and *Concetta's*, both of which sell takeaway pasta and pizzas.

If you need something to soak up the slops after the pubs shut, head for *Mykonos (165 Sandy Bay Rd, Sandy Bay)*, which sells fish and chips etc until the early hours of the morning.

Entertainment

The *Mercury* newspaper has details on most of Hobart's entertainment in its Thursday insert, 'Pulse'.

The *New Sydney Hotel (87 Bathurst St)* has low-key live music most nights. *Irish Murphy's* is a popular Salamanca Place pub with live bands from Wednesday to Sunday. The pleasant *Brooke St Bar & Cafe* has views of the docks, as does the *Customs House Hotel*.

Round Midnight (39 Salamanca Place), above *Knopwood's Retreat*, is open until the early hours of the morning Tuesday to Saturday. *Knopwood's Retreat* itself is a popular place to drink late on Friday nights.

Club Surreal, at the St Ives Hotel on the corner of Sandy Bay Rd and St George's Terrace, Battery Point, is popular.

There are plenty of bars at the *Wrest Point Hotel Casino*, which also has a disco.

A pub in North Hobart with Irish beer and live music is the *Republic Bar*, in the Elizabeth St shopping centre.

Also in North Hobart is the *State Cinema (☎ 6234 6318, 373 Elizabeth St)*, which screens art house films, while in the city there's the large *Village* complex *(☎ 6234 7288, 181 Collins St)*, which shows the mainstream releases.

Shopping

Fine grain, oily texture and distinctive aroma distinguish Huon pine, a slow-growing timber that features heavily in Tasmanian souvenir shops. The Salamanca Place art and craft stores show what a lathe and a fertile imagination can produce, and even more wood turning permutations can be found at the Saturday morning open-air market.

Getting There & Away

Air For information on flights to/from Hobart see the Getting There & Away section at the beginning of this chapter. Qantas (☎ 13 1313) has an office in the Elizabeth St Mall.

Bus The main bus companies operating from Hobart are TRC (☎ 1300 360 000) and TWT (☎ 1300 300 520), both based at the Transit Centre at 199 Collins St. See the Getting Around section at the start of this chapter for general information about their services.

Car There are a large number of car-rental firms in Hobart. Some of the cheaper ones are Rent-a-Bug (☎ 6231 0300), at 105 Murray St, and Selective Car Rentals (☎ 6234 3311), at 132 Argyle St.

Hitching To hitch north, first take a Bridgewater or Brighton bus from opposite the main post office in Elizabeth St. To hitch along the east coast, take a bus to Sorell first.

Getting Around

To/From the Airport The airport is in Hobart's eastern suburbs, 16km from the city centre. TRC runs a shuttle service between the city centre (via Adelphi Court YHA and some other accommodation places on request) and the airport for $7. A taxi to or from the airport should cost around $23.

Bus The Metro main office (☎ 13 2201) is at 9 Elizabeth St, inside the post office. Most buses leave from this area of Elizabeth St, known as the Metro city bus station, or from around the edges of the nearby Franklin Square. If you're planning to bus around Hobart it's worth buying Metro's user-friendly timetable ($1). For $3.10 you can get a Day Rover ticket that can be used all day at weekends and between 9 am and 4.30 pm and after 6 pm on weekdays.

Taxi Taxi Combined Services can be reached on ☎ 13 2227. City Cabs' phone number is ☎ 13 1008 and Arrow Taxis' is ☎ 13 2211.

Bicycle Adelphi Court hostel (☎ 6228 4829) hires out bicycles for $20 per day, Derwent Bike Hire (☎ 0419 008 357) charges $100 a week and Brake Out (☎ 6239 1080) charges $20 a day. Jim's Car Rentals (☎ 6236 9779) also hires out bicycles; its rate is $15 a day.

Boat The *Wrest Point Wanderer* (☎ 6223 1914) runs a ferry service that departs from the Brooke Street Pier daily at 90 minute intervals from 10.30 am to 3 pm and visits the Botanical Gardens ($2.50), Bellerive ($5), Wrest Point Casino ($7.50) and Battery Point ($9.50). The round trip is $12, and you can get on and off as many times as you like. The same boat operates the Bellerive Ferry Service, which runs primarily to get residents to and from work.

The Southern Shipping Company (☎ 6356 1753) runs a small passenger and car ferry from Bridport in the North-East to Flinders Island and (infrequently) on to Port Welshpool in Victoria.

Antarctica At the time of writing, the Australian Shipping Company was planning to offer three cruises a year to Antarctica from Hobart – check with TTIC for details.

Around Hobart

Getting There & Around
The Metro (☎ 13 2201) runs regular services to Taroona, Kingston and Blackmans Bay, New Norfolk ($4.30) and Richmond ($6). There are also various tours to Richmond (see the Richmond Getting There & Away section later in this chapter). TWT (☎ 1300 300 520) has a daily service to Mt Field National Park from Hobart during summer (December to March, $25 one way); day tours are also available.

TAROONA
Ten kilometres from Hobart on the Channel Hwy is Taroona's **Shot Tower**, completed in 1870. From the top of the 48m-high tower there are fine views over the Derwent River estuary. Lead shot was once produced here by dropping down molten lead, which, on its way, formed perfect spheres. Take care with children as the railing around the deep stairwell would not save them from falling.

The tower, small museum, craft shop and beautiful grounds are open daily from 9 am to 5 pm ($4/2). There is also a tearoom serving 'convictshire' teas. Take bus No 60 from Franklin Square near Elizabeth St and get off at stop 45.

From Taroona Beach you can walk around to Kingston Beach (4.5km) along the **Alum Cliffs Track**; at some points the track runs close to rock cliffs and you get good views of the Derwent.

KINGSTON
• postcode 7050   • pop 14,000
The town of Kingston, 11km south of Hobart, is the headquarters of the **Commonwealth Antarctic Division**. The centre is open weekdays from 9 am to 5 pm and admission to its fine display is free.

Kingston Beach is a popular suburban swimming and sailing spot, with attractive wooded cliffs at each end of a long arc of white sand. Behind the clubhouse at the southern end is the start of a short, pretty walk to a much smaller and more secluded beach called **Boronia**, which has a deep rock pool. Further south by road are **Blackmans Bay**, which has a blowhole, and the pretty little beach at **Tinderbox**, where you can go snorkelling along an underwater trail marked with submerged information plates.

Places to Stay & Eat
You can stay opposite Kingston Beach in very plain motel style units at the *Beachside Hotel* (☎ 6229 6185), on the corner of Beach Rd and Osborne Esplanade, for $45/55 a single/double. *Tranquilla Guesthouse*

(☎ 6229 6282, 30 Osborne Esplanade) has rooms for $45/79, while *On the Beach (☎ 6229 3096, 38 Osborne Esplanade)* has a self-contained unit for $80 a double.

Even though the *Echo Cafe* is on Beach Rd rather than opposite the water, it's the perfect place for a coffee or lunch between swims or walks along the esplanade. Nearby, you can get a curry at *Goa Curry* (open Tuesday to Sunday from 5 pm to 9 pm), where the Thai green chicken ($9) packs a reasonable punch.

NEW NORFOLK

• postcode 7140   • pop 5300

Set in the lush countryside of the Derwent Valley, New Norfolk is an interesting historical town. It was first settled in 1803 and became an important hop-growing centre, which is why the area is dotted with old oast houses used for drying hops. Also distinctive are the rows of tall poplars planted to protect crops from the wind.

Originally called Elizabeth Town, New Norfolk was renamed after the arrival of settlers (1807 onwards) from the abandoned Pacific Ocean colony on Norfolk Island.

Things to See & Do

The **Oast House**, on Hobart Rd, is a museum devoted to the history of the hop industry, with a tearoom and a fine-arts gallery. It's open Wednesday to Sunday from 9.30 am to 6 pm ($3.50). The building is worth seeing, even if only from the outside.

St Matthew's Church of England, built in 1823, is Tasmania's oldest existing church, while the **Bush Inn** is said to be the oldest continuously licensed hotel in Australia. The **Old Colony Inn**, at 21 Montagu St, is a museum of colonial furnishings and artefacts with a tearoom serving home-made snacks. It's open from 9 am to 5 pm ($1, free for children).

For $44 (children $22) you can take a 30 minute **jet-boat ride** on the Derwent River rapids. Book at the Devil Jet office (☎ 6261 3460), which is behind the Bush Inn.

In 1864 rainbow and brown trout were bred, for the first time in the southern hemisphere, in the **salmon ponds** at Plenty, 9km

west of New Norfolk. The ponds, museum and restaurant on Salmon Ponds Rd are open daily ($5/3).

Places to Stay

Camp sites ($8), on-site vans ($30) and cabins ($40) are available at *New Norfolk Caravan Park (☎ 6261 1268)* on the Esplanade, 1.5km north of town. It's a great place if you want to fish in the river.

The *Bush Inn (☎ 6261 2011, 21 Montagu St)* has plain singles/doubles from $28/48, including a cooked breakfast. The *Old Colony Inn (☎ 6261 2731)*, also in Montagu St, has just one double room for $70 (watch the doors). On the other side of the river, *Rosie's Inn (☎ 6261 1171, 5 Oast St)* provides B&B for $90 a double.

The nicest place is *Tynwald (☎ 6261 2667)*, overlooking the river by the Oast House. It's a three-storey house dating back to the 1830s and oozing character. Rooms cost from $125, which includes a cooked breakfast.

MT FIELD NATIONAL PARK

Mt Field, 80km from Hobart, was declared a national park in 1916, which makes it one of Australia's oldest. The park is well known for its spectacular mountain scenery, alpine moorland, dense rainforest, lakes, abundant wildlife and spectacular waterfalls. To get to the magnificent 40m **Russell Falls** it's an easy 15 minute walk (the path is suitable for wheelchairs). There are also easy walks to Lady Barron, Horseshoe and Marriotts Falls as well as much longer bushwalks, of which the Tarn Shelf walk is one of the most beautiful. When the snowfall is sufficient, cross-country and gentle downhill skiing is possible at **Mt Mawson**.

The abundance of wildlife that can be viewed here at dusk make this a memorable place to stay overnight with children.

Places to Stay

Lake Dobson Cabins, 15km into the park, has three very basic six-bunk cabins for $20 a double. Book at the rangers' office (☎ 6288 1149). There's also a self-registration camping ground just inside the park; tent/

powered sites are $5/7 per person and a park entry permit is required.

The *National Park Youth Hostel* (☎ 6288 1369) is 200m past the turn-off to the park on Lake Dobson Hwy and charges $13/16 for members/non-members a night. The nearby *Russell Falls Holiday Cottages* (☎ 6288 1198), also on the Lake Dobson Hwy, has four one or two-bedroom fully equipped cottages for $50 a double.

RICHMOND
● postcode 7025   ● pop 760
Richmond is just 24km from Hobart and, with more than 50 buildings dating from the 19th century, is Tasmania's premier historic town. Straddling the Coal River on the old route between Hobart and Port Arthur, Richmond was once a strategic military post and convict station.

Things to See & Do
The much-photographed **Richmond Bridge**, built by convicts in 1823, is the oldest road bridge in Australia.

The northern wing of **Richmond Gaol** was built in 1825, five years before the settlement at Port Arthur, and is the best preserved convict jail in Australia. It is open daily from 9 am to 5 pm ($4/1.50).

Other places of interest include **St John's Church** (1836), the oldest Catholic church in Australia; **St Luke's Church of England** (1834); the **courthouse** (1825); the **Bridge Inn** (1817); and the **Richmond Arms Hotel** (1888). There's also a model village (designed from original plans) of Hobart Town as it was in the 1820s. It's open daily from 9 am to 5 pm ($6/3.50).

The **Lark Distillery**, a working distillery open from 10 am to 5 pm daily, produces malt whisky and liqueurs distilled from native ingredients such as pepperberry.

Places to Stay & Eat
The *Richmond Cabin & Tourist Park* (☎ 6260 2192), on Middle Tea Tree Rd, has camp sites ($12 for two people), on-site vans ($32) and cabins ($48).

The cheapest B&B is the *Richmond Country Guesthouse* (☎ 6260 4238), on an attractive rural property on Prossers Rd, 4km north of town. It has singles/doubles for $45/70; you'll feel like you are a part of the family.

Red Brier Cottage (☎ 6260 2349, 15 Bridge St) is not historic, but it's spacious and attractive and charges $116 a double.

Prospect House (☎ 6260 2207) is a superb two-storey Georgian country mansion just outside Richmond, on the Hobart road. Accommodation costs $122/144. Nearby is *Daisy Bank Cottages* (☎ 6260 2390), where there are two very attractive units in a converted sandstone barn for $110 or $130 a double.

Mrs Currie's House (☎ 6260 2766, 4 Franklin St) is a beautiful central B&B with rooms for $96/116.

You can get something to eat and drink at the *Richmond Wine Centre*, on Bridge Rd. This new building is set back from the street and is a good place for breakfast and lunch. There are also several tearooms with light meals; try *Ma Foosies* or *Ashmore House Cafe*, in the main street, for some country service.

Getting There & Away
If you have your own car, Richmond is an easy day trip from Hobart. Tasmanian Tours & Travel/Tigerline (☎ 6231 2200, 1300 653 633) has bus tours most days. The Metro (☎ 13 2201) runs regular buses during the week ($6) and sometimes has weekend services in summer.

South-East Coast

South of Hobart are the scenic timber and fruit-growing areas of the Huon Peninsula, D'Entrecasteaux Channel and Port Esperance, as well as beautiful Bruny Island and the Hartz Mountains National Park. Once mainly an apple growing region, the area has now diversified and produces a range of other fruits, Atlantic salmon and wines, as well as catering to the growing tourism industry. With the abundance of fresh local produce, some of the hotels turn out fabulous meals.

Around the end of February and during March fruit picking work is available, but competition for jobs is stiff.

Organised Tours

The Bottom Bits Bus (☎ 1800 777 103) offers an all-inclusive three day tour of this entire area for $175. TWT has a half day tour to Hastings Caves ($59).

Getting There & Around

Bus The region south of Hobart has two distinct areas: the peninsula, which includes Kettering and Cygnet, and the coastal strip followed by the Huon Hwy from Huonville to Cockle Creek.

The Metro (☎ 13 2201) runs several buses on weekdays from Hobart to Kettering ($5.40). One bus each weekday runs from Hobart to Snug and inland across to Cygnet.

TWT (☎ 1300 300 520) has services from Hobart through Huonville ($6.30), Franklin ($7.50) and Geeveston ($9.40) to Dover ($12.50).

From December to March on Tuesday, Thursday and Saturday, TWT runs buses along the Huon Hwy from Hobart through Huonville, Geeveston and Dover all the way to the end of the road at Cockle Creek ($45).

There is no regular public transport from Geeveston to the Hartz Mountains.

Car The views from the highway between Hobart and Woodbridge are lovely, particularly on sunny days when the contrast between the lush green of the pastures and the deep blue of the channel waters is dazzling. If you then take the road from Woodbridge to Gardners Bay on the way to Cygnet, you will be rewarded with stunning water views on both sides of the ridge.

Further south, some sections of the side route from Surges Bay through Police Point and on to Dover are gravel, but this should not deter you, as the road is in good condition and the views are great. The 19km road from Lune River to Cockle Creek has been surfaced with very coarse gravel, which can put pressure on older vehicles. Check your tires before you start out and make sure your spare is in good condition.

KETTERING

- **postcode 7155**   • **pop 300**

The small port of Kettering, on a sheltered bay 34km south of Hobart, is the terminal for the Bruny Island car ferry. The nearby town of **Snug** has a walking track to Snug Falls (one hour return).

The Roaring 40s Ocean Kayaking Company (☎ 1800 653 712) has an office in the same building as the visitors centre, near the ferry departure point, and has a range of kayaking options, including evenings and weekends.

Reports of the food at the *Oyster Cove Inn* are mixed, but the views are undeniably gorgeous. Accommodation is available for $20 to $35 per person.

The *Old Kettering Inn* (☎ 6267 4426) is a perfectly positioned B&B in which only one bedroom (with en suite and private lounge overlooking the marina) is rented out ($89 a double).

Just out of town, *Herons Rise Vineyard* (☎ 6267 4339) has private, luxury accommodation for $125 a double.

At the excellent Bruny D'Entrecasteaux Visitors Centre (☎ 6267 4494), at the ferry terminal you can purchase ferry tickets and get all the latest information on accommodation and services on the island. The licensed *cafe* here is surprisingly pleasant, so don't be put off by the bland exterior.

BRUNY ISLAND

- **pop 550**

Bruny Island is almost two islands, joined by an isthmus where mutton birds and other waterfowl breed. It is a peaceful and beautiful retreat. The sparsely populated island is renowned for its varied wildlife, including fairy penguins and many reptile species.

The island's coastal scenery is superb and there are plenty of fine swimming and surf beaches, good sea and freshwater fishing, and signposted walking tracks within the stunning **South Bruny National Park**.

The island was sighted by Abel Tasman in 1642 and later visited by Furneaux, Cook, Bligh and Cox between 1770 and 1790, but was named after Rear-Admiral Bruni D'Entrecasteaux, who explored and

SOUTH-EAST COAST

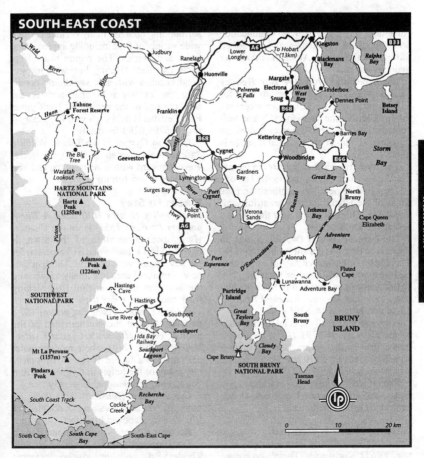

TASMANIA

surveyed the area in 1792. Initially the Aboriginal people were friendly towards the Europeans, but relations deteriorated after the sealers and whalers arrived. The island itself remained little changed until the car ferry started in 1954.

Tourism, an important part of the island's economy, is still low key. There are no large resorts, just interesting cottages and guest-houses, most of which are self-contained. Supplies can be bought at Adventure Bay, South Bruny, and there are a few small shops at the other settlements, but it's best to stock up on food before boarding the ferry. Man-

agers often don't live next door to their rental cottages, so it's best to book. The Bruny D'Entrecasteaux Visitors Centre in Kettering is the central booking office for all accommodation on Bruny Island. A car or bike is necessary to get around the island, unless you travel on the daily mail bus (see Getting There & Around later in this section).

The island's history is recorded in the **Bligh Museum of Pacific Exploration**, at Adventure Bay ($4/2). Also of historical interest is South Bruny's **lighthouse**, which was built in 1836 and is the second oldest in Australia.

Places to Stay & Eat

Adventure Bay is the main accommodation area, but there are places to stay dotted throughout the island. Alonnah is the other main settlement.

The appealing *Adventure Bay Holiday Village* (☎ 6293 1270) has camp sites for $10, powered sites for $13, backpacker cabins for $45, on-site vans for $50 and self-contained cabins for $90 (prices quoted are doubles). Meals can be arranged if notice is given.

There are free *bush camp sites* in the national park (park passes required). The one at Jetty Beach, near the lighthouse on the south of the island, is on a beautiful sheltered cove. Other sites are near the isthmus and at Cloudy Bay.

The *Lumeah Hostel* (☎ 6293 1265), in Adventure Bay, has dormitory beds for $14. This hostel offers activities and can organise transport from Hobart or Kettering.

Cottages can be rented from $70 a double: near Adventure Bay are *Rosebud* (☎ 6293 1325) and *Mavista* (☎ 6293 1347).

For something really special, try *Morella Island Retreats* (☎ 6293 1131), on the entrance road to Adventure Bay. It has two stylish cottages for $170 and $195 a double with breakfast.

The *Hotel Bruny* has standard pub meals, and the *Penguin Tea Room*, at Adventure Bay, has good meals.

Getting There & Around

There are frequent daily ferry services – ring ☎ 6273 6725 for details. There's no charge for foot passengers; a car costs $18 return except on public holidays and public holiday weekends, when it's $23; bicycles cost $3. At least two buses a day connect with the ferry and will stop at the terminal on request.

For $5 you can catch the mail bus, which travels around the island. Inquire at the Bruny D'Entrecasteaux Visitors Centre.

CYGNET

• postcode 7112　　• pop 980

Named 'Port de Cygne Noir' (Port of the Black Swan) by Rear-Admiral D'Entrecasteaux after the many swans seen on the bay, this town is now known as Cygnet. The surrounding area has many orchards with a wide variety of fruit including apples, stone fruits and berries. The region also offers some excellent fishing, bushwalking and good beaches with safe swimming conditions, particularly at **Verona Sands** on the southern end of the peninsula. The Cygnet Folk Festival is held each year in January – ring ☎ 6295 0280 for details.

Close to Cygnet is the **Talune Wildlife Park & Koala Garden** ($7/2.50), the **Hartz-view Vineyard** with wine tastings, and The Deepings **wood-turning** workshop.

Places to Stay

Huon Valley (Balfes Hill) YHA & Backpackers (☎ 6295 1551) is on the Channel Hwy, about 5km north of the town. It charges $15 for bunks and $18 a person for the new rooms with en suite. The spacious new communal area has lovely views, and the host can help you find fruit-picking work and organise day trips.

In town is a basic *camping ground* ($7 a double). Also at the northern end of the main street is *Howard's Cygnet Central Hotel* (☎ 6295 1244), where modern motel units are $50 a double. If you are fruit picking, many of the hotels in Cygnet will rent you a room at a reasonable weekly rate.

Cygnet Guest House (☎ 6295 0080, 89 Mary St) has attractive singles/doubles for $70/79 with a cooked breakfast.

Accommodation is available out of town at *The Deepings* (☎ 6295 1398), on Nichols Rivulet Rd, and the lovely upmarket *Hartzview Vineyard Homestead* (☎ 6295 1623, 70 Dillons Rd, Gardners Bay).

Places to Eat

The *Old School House Coffee Shop*, in the centre of town, has good light lunches. *The Red Velvet Lounge*, in the main street, is a wonderful wholefood cafe in an old weatherboard place set well back from the road. Next door is the *Old Bank Teashop*. The modern *Howard's Cygnet Central Hotel*, at the northern end of the main street, has cheap counter meals daily in its spacious bistro.

HUONVILLE

• postcode 7109 • pop 1600

Named after Huon de Kermadec, who was second in command to D'Entrecasteaux, this small, busy town on the picturesque Huon River is another apple growing centre. The valuable softwood, Huon pine, was also first discovered here. You can take **jet-boat rides** or hire **pedal boats** from Huon River Jet Boats (☎ 6264 1838), which is also the visitors centre.

At Grove, 6km north, is an **apple museum** and Doran's **jam factory**; at the latter, you can see jam being made and eat at the cafe (the spiced apple butter is a taste sensation).

GEEVESTON

• postcode 7116 • pop 800

This town was founded by the Geeves family and their descendants still live here. It is an important base for the timber industry as well as the gateway to the Hartz Mountains National Park.

The town's main attraction is the **Esperance Forest & Heritage Centre**, in the main street, which is open daily from 9.30 am to 5 pm, or 10 am to 4 pm in the low season ($4/2.50). It has comprehensive displays on all aspects of forestry. The centre also incorporates the helpful and efficient South-West Visitor Centre (☎ 6297 1836).

If you have your own transport, head out of town to the **Tahune Forest Reserve**, but first pick up a copy of the map and information brochure from the visitors centre. There are several lookouts and walks along the way, with a good picnic ground and a Huon pine walk at the reserve on the banks of the Huon River. On the way back to Geeveston take the one way Arve Loop Rd to see the Big Tree, indeed a very large *Eucalyptus regnans*.

HARTZ MOUNTAINS NATIONAL PARK

This national park, classified as part of the World Heritage Area, is very popular with weekend walkers and day-trippers as it's only 84km from Hobart. The park is renowned for its rugged mountains, glacial lakes, gorges, alpine moorlands and dense rainforest. The area is subject to rapid changes in weather, so even on a day walk take waterproof gear and warm clothing. The usual park entry fee applies.

There are some great views from the **Waratah Lookout** (24km from Geeveston) – look for the jagged peaks of the Snowy Range and the Devils Backbone. There are good walks in the park, including tracks to Hartz Peak (three hours return) and Lake Osborne (40 minutes return).

DOVER

• postcode 7117 • pop 500

This picturesque fishing port, 21km south of Geeveston on the Huon Hwy, has some fine beaches and excellent bushwalks. Last century, the processing and exporting of Huon pine was Dover's major industry, and sleepers made here were shipped to China, India and Germany. If you have your own car and are heading further south, it's a good idea to buy petrol and food supplies here. **Yacht cruises** are available from the South West Passage Cruising Company (☎ 6298 1062).

Places to Stay

The *Dover Beachside Caravan Park* (☎ 6298 1301), on Kent Beach Rd, has camp sites ($10), hostel bunks ($12.50), on-site vans ($30) and en suite cabins ($55). The *Dover Hotel* (☎ 6298 1210), on the Huon Hwy, has single/double hotel rooms for $40/60 with breakfast, and plain motel rooms, one with views of the water, for $75 a double. The large unit called the 'housefront', also with water views, is $95 a double.

The nearby *Dover Bayside Lodge* (☎ 6298 1788), opposite the water, offers B&B in plain rooms with en suites for $75 a double with water views, or $60 a double without. One room has wheelchair access.

3 Island Holiday Apartments (☎ 6298 1396), on Station St, has units with reasonable facilities for $65 a double. The much more modern *Driftwood Cottages* (☎ 6298 1441), opposite the water on Bay View Rd, has apartments with all facilities for $120. Also on Bay View Rd, *Beach House* and *Cove House* are self-contained units ($160 a double) owned by the same people.

For somewhere special, try *Riseley Cottage (☎ 6298 1630, 170 Narrows Rd, Strathblane)*, signposted off the highway south of Dover. It's on a hill overlooking the water in a bush setting and provides singles/doubles with en suite and a cooked breakfast for $65/85 a night, which is great value.

Places to Eat
The *Dover Hotel* has a blackboard menu featuring local produce.

The Gingerbread House, on the main bend as you come into town, is a pleasant bakery and cafe open daily except Monday.

HASTINGS
• postcode 7109   • pop 300

The spectacular **Hastings Cave & Thermal Pool** attracts visitors to this once-thriving logging and wharf town, 21km south of Dover. The cave is found among the lush vegetation of the **Hastings Caves State Reserve**, 10km inland of Hastings and well signposted from the Huon Hwy. Daily tours of the cave ($10/5, including admission to the thermal pool – tickets available from the kiosk) leave at 11 am and 1, 2 and 3 pm, with extra tours daily from December to April.

About 5km before the cave is a **thermal swimming pool** ($2.50/1.50), filled daily with warm water from a thermal spring. Near the pool there's a kiosk and a restaurant. The 10 minute sensory walk near the pool is suitable for blind people and well worth doing.

The hostel at Lune River runs Huon Magical Mystery Tours (☎ 6298 3117), which offers **wild cave tours** of Mystery Creek Cave.

LUNE RIVER
A few kilometres south-west of Hastings is Lune River, the site of Australia's most southerly youth hostel. From here you can take a scenic 6km ride on the **Ida Bay Railway** to the lovely beach at Deep Hole Bay. The train runs on Sunday year-round at noon and 2 and 4 pm. The 1½ hour ride costs $12/6.

The most southerly drive you can make in Australia is along the secondary gravel road from Lune River to **Cockle Creek** and beautiful **Recherche Bay**. This is an area of spectacular mountain peaks and endless beaches – ideal for camping and bushwalking. This is also the start (or end) of the challenging South Coast Track, which, with the right preparation and a week or so to spare, will take you all the way to Port Davey in the south-west. See Lonely Planet's *Bushwalking in Australia* for track notes.

The *Lune River Youth Hostel (☎ 6298 3163)* charges $12 a night. It's a cosy hostel and there's certainly plenty to do – ask the managers about hiring mountain bikes or kayaks, or about bushwalking, fishing and caving. Don't forget to bring plenty of food with you as the hostel only has basic supplies. The hostel runs a shuttle bus connecting with the TWT Dover service; bookings are essential.

Tasman Peninsula

The Arthur Hwy runs from Hobart through Sorell and Copping to Port Arthur, 100km away. The peninsula is famous for the convict ruins at Port Arthur and for its magnificent 300m-high cliffs, delightful beaches, beautiful bays and stunning bushwalks.

The main information centre for the region is the Eaglehawk Neck Visitor Information Centre (☎ 6250 3722), at the Officers Mess restaurant and store, 443 Pirates Bay Drive.

Near Eaglehawk Neck are the incredible coastal formations of the **Tessellated Pavement**, the **Blowhole**, the **Devils Kitchen**, **Tasmans Arch** and **Waterfall Bay**. South of Port Arthur is **Remarkable Cave**.

The **Tasman National Park** was proclaimed in 1999 and national park fees now apply to all but the shortest walks. Some spectacular walks include Waterfall Bluff (1½ hours return), Cape Raoul (1½ hours to the lookout, five hours to the cape) and Cape Huay (five hours). *Tasman Tracks*, available from bookshops and walking shops, provides detailed notes.

You can also visit the remains of the **penal outstations** at Koonya, Premaydena and Saltwater River, and the ruins of the dreaded **Coal Mines Station**. The **Tasmanian Devil**

Park, at Taranna, is open daily ($11/5.50). The **Bush Mill**, on the Arthur Hwy, features a steam railway and pioneer settlement ($14/6).

Organised Tours

Seaview Lodge (☎/fax 6250 2766) offers daily $20 lantern-lit night tours of the coal mines and basement cells at Saltwater River, including spotlighting of fauna and some role-play.

Places to Stay

The biggest camping area is at lovely *Fortescue Bay* (☎ 6250 2433), 12km from the highway. Basic sites are also available at pretty *Lime Bay*, at Saltwater River, beyond the Coal Mines Station Historic Site. Fees apply to both.

Seaview Lodge Host Farm (☎ 6250 2766), signposted off the main road at Koonya, has fantastic views: bunks are $15 each, double rooms $35. School groups often stay here in the off season.

At Tarrana, at *Teraki Cottages* (☎ 6250 3436) try the tiny but well-presented cabins at $60 a double, or the historic *Norfolk Bay Convict Station* (☎ 6250 3487), at $100 a double.

The remaining options mentioned here are in scenic Eaglehawk Neck. The *Eaglehawk Neck Backpackers* (☎ 6250 3248) is on the northern side of the isthmus, down the Old Jetty Rd to the west. It's a small and friendly hostel charging $12 a night. The managers hire out bicycles, which are ideal for visiting the remoter parts of the peninsula. There is also a small camping ground on the site.

For great views the *Lufra Holiday Hotel* (☎ 6250 3262), perched above the Tessellated Pavement, is hard to beat. It charges $80 a double for en suite rooms with a continental breakfast.

Further along this road towards a lookout is the turn-off to *Wunnamurra Waterfront* (☎ 6250 3145) and *Osprey Lodge Beachfront B&B* (☎ 6250 3629). Both are in attractive, private gardens and overlook the bay. B&B in rooms with en suite is $80 to $94 a double at Wunnamurra and $90 to $110 a double at Osprey Lodge.

TASMAN PENINSULA

Places to Eat

At Eaglehawk Neck, the *Officers Mess* provides takeaways and meals in a large cafe, the bistro at the *Lufra Hotel* serves lunch and dinner seven days a week, and the licensed *Eaglehawk Cafe*, overlooking Norfolk Bay, serves breakfast, lunch and dinner daily.

Getting There & Around

TWT (☎ 1300 300 520) has a weekday service from Hobart that stops at all the main towns on the Tasman Peninsula.

Another way to visit the area is to join a coach tour run by Tasmanian Tours & Travel/Tigerline (☎ 6231 2200).

PORT ARTHUR

In 1830, Governor Arthur chose the Tasman Peninsula as the place to confine prisoners who had committed further crimes in the colony. He called the peninsula a 'natural penitentiary' because it was connected

Windgrove

Windgrove, at Roaring Beach near Nubeena on the Tasman Peninsula, is a peaceful coastal property owned by Peter Adams, a creator of beautiful wooden benches that sell for upwards of $10,000. Peter attempts to produce works that express a link between art, ecology and theology and in November and May each year displays them in 40 hectares of revegetated coastal heath as part of the Australian Open Garden Scheme. In time, Peter hopes to develop Windgrove as an artists' retreat. Meanwhile, if you are in the area when his property is open, you should take the time to follow the signs from the main road to this garden gallery: there is no better artists' space in the state.

to the mainland by a strip of land less than 100m wide, called Eaglehawk Neck. To deter convicts from escaping, ferocious guard dogs were chained in a line across the isthmus and a rumour circulated that waters on either side were infested with sharks.

Between 1830 and 1877, about 12,500 convicts served sentences at Port Arthur. For some of them it was a living hell, but those who behaved often lived in better conditions than they had endured in England and Ireland.

The historic township of Port Arthur became the centre of a network of penal stations on the peninsula and was much more than just a prison town. It had fine buildings and thriving industries including timber milling, shipbuilding, coal mining, brick and nail production and shoemaking.

Australia's first railway literally 'ran' the 7km between Norfolk Bay and Long Bay: convicts pushed the carriages along the tracks. A semaphore telegraph system allowed instant communication between Port Arthur, the penal outstations and Hobart. Convict farms provided fresh vegetables, a boys' prison was built at Point Puer to reform and educate juvenile convicts, and a church (today one of the most readily recognised tourist sights in Tasmania) was erected.

Port Arthur was again the scene of tragedy in April 1996, when a lone gunman opened fire on visitors and staff at the historic site, killing 35 people, either there or close by, and injuring several others. The gunman was finally captured after he had burned down a local guesthouse; he is now in prison.

The well presented historic site of Port Arthur is Tasmania's premier tourist attraction. Following the shootings, a new visitor and interpretation centre and cafe/restaurant has been built at the site, and you can visit all the restored buildings, including the Lunatic Asylum (now a museum) and the Model Prison, for $16/8/38 for adults/children/families. The ticket is valid for the day of purchase and the following day, and entitles you to admission to the museum, a guided tour of the settlement and a cruise on the harbour circumnavigating, but not stopping at, the Isle of the Dead. The site is open daily from 8.30 am to dusk.

Organised Tours
The guided tours (included in the site entry fee) are well worthwhile and leave hourly from the visitors centre (☎ 6250 2539) between 9.30 am and 3.30 pm. An Isle of the Dead Landing Cruise costs $7, and seaplane flights are also available.

Ninety-minute ghost tours (☎ 1800 659 101) leave from outside the visitor centre at dusk and, at $12, are good value.

For a fun and different outlook on Port Arthur and the surrounding coast, Baidarka Experience (☎ 6250 2612) runs two-hour and half-day ocean kayak tours.

Places to Stay
The peaceful, attractive *Port Arthur Caravan and Cabin Park (☎ 6250 2340)* is 2km before Port Arthur at Garden Point. It costs $12 to camp, $13 for the hostel and $70 a double for a cabin. You can pay historic site entry fees at the reception office and follow a track around the shoreline from here to Port Arthur.

The *Port Arthur Youth Hostel (☎ 6250 2311)* is very well positioned on the edge of the historic site and charges $13 a night. To get there, continue half a kilometre past the Port Arthur turn-off and turn left at the sign for the hostel into the street known as both Safety Cove Rd and Remarkable Cave Rd. You can buy your historic site entry ticket at the hostel.

If you don't mind staying some distance from the town, try **Anderton's Accommodation** (☎ 6250 2378, 20 Safety Cove Rd), 2.5km south of Port Arthur ($70 a double), which has been recommended by Lonely Planet readers. Also on Remarkable Cave Rd, but closer to the site, is the **Port Arthur Motor Inn** (☎ 6250 2101), with doubles for $110, and **Port Arthur Villas** (☎ 6250 2239), with self-contained units for $95 a double.

Places to Eat

At the historic site, there's a large **cafe/restaurant** in the visitors centre, which you can visit without paying the entry fee, and a **cafe** in the Museum. Takeaways are available at the **General Store**, snacks and country-style meals at the **Bush Mill**. For more formal dining, try the **Port Arthur Motor Inn**, which often has specials on the menu. **The Fox and Hounds** serves counter lunches and a la carte dinners daily.

Midlands

English trees and hedgerows give Tasmania's midlands a definite English feel. The agricultural potential of the area contributed to Tasmania's rapid settlement, and coach stations, garrison towns, stone villages and pastoral properties soon sprang up as convict gangs constructed the main road between Hobart and Launceston. Fine wool, beef cattle and timber milling put the midlands on the map and these, along with tourism, are still the main industries.

The course of the Midland Hwy (called the Heritage Hwy in many tourist publications) has changed slightly from its original route and many of the historic towns are now bypassed, but it's definitely worth making a few detours to see them.

Getting There & Around

TRC (☎ 1300 360 000) runs up and down the Midland Hwy, and you can be dropped off at any of the main towns provided you are not travelling on an express service. The fare from Hobart to Launceston is $19.50. Fares from Hobart/Launceston are: Oatlands $10.90/14.10; Ross $14.60/9.80; Campbell Town $16.50/8.50.

There's a secondary road from Campbell Town, through the excellent fishing and bushwalking area around **Lake Leake** (32 km), to Swansea (67 km) on the east coast. Some TRC buses travel this route and can drop you at the Lake Leake turn-off, 4km from the lake. Another highway, the A4, runs from Conara Junction, 11km north of Campbell Town, east to St Marys. Buses running from Launceston to Bicheno follow the A4, as do buses from Hobart and Launceston to St Helens.

From December to March, TWT (☎ 1300 300 520) has a service between Lake St Clair and Launceston that goes via Bronte Park, Miena, Great Lake and Deloraine. Bookings are essential. For details of services from Hobart to Lake St Clair and beyond, see The West section later in this chapter. The Metro (☎ 13 2201) has a weekday 4 pm bus from Hobart to Bothwell ($9.20).

OATLANDS

● postcode 7120   ● pop 540

The Central Tasmanian Tourism Centre (☎ 6254 1212), at 77 High St, is the visitor centre for Oatlands, which has the largest collection of Georgian architecture in Australia, and the largest number of buildings dating from before 1837. In the main street alone, there are 87 historic buildings, the oldest of which is the 1829 convict-built **courthouse**. Much of the sandstone for these early buildings came from the shores of **Lake Dulverton**, now a wildlife sanctuary, which is beside the town. Unfortunately, at the time of writing the lake had been dry for some time.

Also at the time of writing, **Callington Mill**, the restoration of which was Tasmania's main Bicentennial project, was still not open to the public but the government was again attempting to attract developers.

An unusual way of seeing Oatlands' sights is to go on one of Peter Fielding's

(☎ 6254 1135) ghost tours. The tours start at 8 pm (9 pm in summer; $8/4).

Places to Stay & Eat

There's plenty of accommodation in Oatlands, although much of it is the more expensive colonial type. The *Oatlands Youth Hostel (☎ 6254 1320, 9 Wellington St)* is a couple of hundred metres off the main street and charges $12 a night. The *Midlands Hotel (☎ 6254 1103, 91 High St)* charges $35/45 for singles/doubles with continental breakfast. The *Oatlands Lodge (☎ 6254 1444, 92 High St)* has B&B for $85 a double. For information about cottage accommodation ($125 a double), ring *Waverly Cottages (☎ 6254 1264)*.

Blossom's Cottage Restaurant, on the main street, is a good place for meals.

ROSS

● postcode 7209   ● pop 280

This ex-garrison town, 120km from Hobart, is steeped in colonial charm and history. It was established in 1812 to protect travellers on the main north-south road and was an important coach staging post. The visitors centre is the Tasmanian Wool Centre (☎ 6381 5466).

Things to See & Do

This appealing town is known for its convict-built **Ross Bridge**, the third-oldest bridge in Australia. Daniel Herbert, a convict stonemason, was granted a pardon for his detailed work on the 184 panels that decorate the arches.

In the heart of town is a crossroads that can lead you in one of four directions: 'temptation' (represented by the Man O' Ross Hotel); 'salvation' (the Catholic church); 'recreation' (the town hall); and 'damnation' (the old jail).

Historic buildings include the Scotch Thistle Inn; the old barracks, restored by the National Trust; the Uniting Church (1885); St John's Church of England (1868); and the post office (1896).

The **Tasmanian Wool Centre**, a museum and craft shop in Church St, is open daily from 9 am to 5.30 pm in the high season and until 4 pm the rest of the year. Admission to the display is $4, a **town tour** is $3, and a combined ticket is $6.

The Ross bridge, built by convicts in 1836

Places to Stay & Eat

The *Ross Caravan Park* (☎ *6381 5462)* has tent/powered sites for $10/14 and units that share the park facilities for $25 a double. The *Man O-Ross Hotel* (☎ *6381 5240)* has singles/doubles for $40/60 and serves counter meals daily.

The *Ross Bakery Inn* (☎ *6281 5246)* has B&B for $55/89, which includes breakfast baked in the 100-year-old wood-fired oven in the adjacent *Ross Village Bakery* (a good place for lunch). For cottage accommodation, ring *Colonial Cottages of Ross* (☎ *6381 5354)*. *Somercotes Historic Estate* (☎ *6381 5231)*, south of town, has B&B in 1820s cottages on an attractive property for $110/120.

CAMPBELL TOWN

● postcode 7210   ● pop 800

Another former garrison settlement, Campbell Town is 12km north of Ross. It boasts many examples of early **colonial architecture**, including the convict-built Red Bridge (1836), the Grange (1847), St Luke's Church of England (1835), the Campbell Town Inn (1840), the building known as the Foxhunters Return (1829), and the old school (1878).

LAKE COUNTRY

The sparsely populated Lake Country, on Tasmania's Central Plateau, is a region of glacial lakes, crystal-clear streams, waterfalls and a variety of wildlife. It's also known for its fine trout fishing and its ambitious hydro-electric schemes, which have seen the damming of rivers, the creation of artificial lakes, the building of power stations (both above and below ground) and the construction of massive pipelines.

Tasmania has the largest hydro-electric power system in Australia. The first dam was constructed on Great Lake in 1911. Subsequently, the Derwent, Mersey, South Esk, Forth, Gordon, King, Anthony and Pieman rivers were also dammed. If you want to inspect the developments, go to the Tungatinah, Tarraleah and Liapootah power stations on the extensive Derwent scheme between Queenstown and Hobart.

On the western edge of the Central Plateau is the **Walls of Jerusalem National Park**,

which is a focal point for mountaineers, bushwalkers and cross-country skiers. There's excellent fishing at **Lake King William**, on the Derwent River, south of the Lyell Hwy, as well as at **Lake Sorell**, **Arthurs Lake** and **Little Pine Lagoon**. Unfortunately, **Lake Crescent** has been closed to fishing indefinitely, due to carp infestation.

At Waddamana, on the road which loops off the Lake Hwy between Bothwell and Great Lake, there's the **Waddamana Power Museum** (☎ 6259 6175). It has an interesting display of the state's early hydro history, and is open weekdays from 10 am to 4 pm, Sunday and public holidays to noon (free).

BOTHWELL

● postcode 7030   ● pop 360

Bothwell, in the beautiful Clyde River valley, is a sleepy historic town with 53 buildings recognised or classified by the National Trust. Of particular interest are the beautifully restored **Slate Cottage** of 1835; a **bootmaker's shop**, fitted out as it would have been in the 1890s; **Thorpe Mill**, a flour mill from the 1820s; the delightful **St Luke's Church** (1830); and the **Castle Hotel**, first licensed in 1821.

Although Bothwell is probably best known for its proximity to great trout fishing, it also has Australia's oldest golf course, still in use today and open to members of any golf club. There is also the **Australasian** (no less!) **Golf Museum**, in the Visitor Information Centre in the **Old School House** (1887).

Places to Stay

The *caravan park* is small and ugly but cheap (tent sites are $3 a double, powered sites $6 – check in at the council chambers). *Bothwell Grange* (☎ *6259 5556)* has pleasant B&B for $100 a double. *'Nant' Highland House* (☎ *6259 5506)* is an entire cottage on a working farm for $80 a double with breakfast. At *Mrs Wood's Farmhouse* (☎ *6259 5612)* at Dennistoun, 8km from town, accommodation in a basic cabin in paddocks is $25 a person.

At Swan Bay, near Miena, the *Great Lake Hotel* (☎ *6259 8163)* has a wide range of accommodation.

East Coast

Tasmania's scenic east coast is known for its long sandy beaches, fine fishing, peacefulness and mild, sunny climate.

Exploration and settlement of the region, found to be most suitable for grazing, proceeded rapidly after the establishment of Hobart in 1803. Offshore fishing, and particularly whaling, also became important industries, as did tin mining and timber cutting. Many of the convicts who served out their terms in the area stayed on to help the settlers lay the foundations of the fishing, wool, beef and grain industries, which are still significant in the region today.

The best features are the major national parks of Maria Island and Freycinet. The spectacular scenery around Coles Bay is not to be missed, and Bicheno and Swansea are pleasant seaside towns in which to spend a few restful days.

Banking facilities on the east coast are limited and in some towns the banks are only open one or two days a week. There are agencies for the Commonwealth Bank at all post offices. There are also EFTPOS facilities in the main coastal towns and at Coles Bay and St Marys.

Getting There & Around
Bus TRC (☎ 1300 360 000) and TWT (☎ 1300 300 520) are the main bus companies servicing this area.

TRC runs at least one service each weekday (and Sunday from January to Easter Sunday) from Hobart to Swansea ($26.40) and Bicheno ($31.50) and return via the Midland Hwy and inland linking roads. There are similar runs to the same towns from Launceston and return. You must change buses in Campbell Town, where you will have to wait anything from a couple of minutes to 1½ hours depending on the service. TRC also runs services every day except Saturday from Hobart/Launceston to St Helens ($31.70/19.20) and returning via St Marys ($29.40/15.50 one way).

TWT has a service from Hobart to Swansea ($16.50) via Richmond ($4.10), Orford ($11) and Triabunna ($11.70) on weekdays except public holidays. It has an additional service from Hobart to all these towns, except Richmond, and on to Bicheno ($20.30) and St Helens ($29.40) on Wednesday, Friday and Sunday all year and Monday from 1 December to early April.

TWT also has a service between Launceston and Bicheno ($19) via Avoca ($8.50), Fingal ($11.50) and St Marys ($13.70). This runs on Wednesday, Friday and Sunday, and there is also a Monday service in summer.

Neither major bus company services the Freycinet Peninsula. For this route you must rely on Bicheno Coach Service (☎ 6257 0293), which runs from Bicheno to Coles Bay (see the Coles Bay & Freycinet National Park section later in this chapter for details). This service connects with all TRC services at the Coles Bay turn-off. It will also meet TWT services, provided you book. The TRC fare from Hobart to the Coles Bay turn-off is $30.20.

Because services are limited at weekends, it might take a little longer to travel between towns than you anticipate.

Bicycle Cycling along the east coast is one of the most enjoyable ways of seeing this part of Tasmania. Traffic is usually light and the hills are not too steep, particularly if you follow the coastal highway from Chain of Lagoons to Falmouth.

If you plan to cycle between Swansea and Coles Bay, there's an informal boat service for cyclists and hikers (☎ 6257 0239) from Dolphin Sands across the Swan River to Swanwick, 6km north of Coles Bay, which will save you 65km. The approximate cycling time from Swansea to Dolphin Sands is one hour. The service operates from October to late April, weather permitting. Ring first.

ORFORD
● postcode 7190   ● pop 460

Orford is a small seaside resort on the Prosser River (named after an escaped prisoner who was caught on its banks). The area has good fishing, swimming and some excellent walks. **Spring Beach**, 4km south of town (turn right instead of crossing the bridge), is a pretty place for a barbecue.

Places to Stay

There's plenty of accommodation in Orford, although no real backpacker places. On the Tasman Hwy, the *Blue Waters Motor Hotel* (☎ 6257 1102) has singles/doubles for $35/50, while the *Island View Motel* (☎ 6257 1114) has rooms for $52/64.

More lavish and expensive is the *Eastcoaster Resort* (☎ 6257 1172), on Louisville Point Rd, a few minutes drive north of Orford. It has motel rooms from $80/99 and one to three-bedroom cabins (four with spas) for $100 to $140. You can catch the catamaran to Maria Island from here.

Spring Beach Holiday Villas (☎ 6257 1440), 4km south of town on Rheban Rd opposite the beach, has modern, self-contained units with views of Maria Island for $100.

MARIA ISLAND NATIONAL PARK

Maria Island is popular with bird-watchers; it's the only national park in Tasmania where you can see 11 of the state's native bird species. Forester kangaroos, Cape Barren geese and emus are a common sight during the day.

This peaceful island features some magnificent scenery, including fossil-studded sandstone and limestone cliffs, beautiful sandy beaches, forests and fern gullies. Brochures are available from the ranger's office on the island, close to where the ferry docks, for the Bishop & Clerk Mountain Walk and the historical Fossil Cliffs. The marine life around the island is also diverse and plentiful, and for those with the equipment, the scuba diving is spectacular.

From 1825 to 1832 **Darlington** was Tasmania's second penal colony (the first was Sarah Island near Strahan). The remains of the penal village, including the commissariat store (1825) and the mill house (1846), are remarkably well preserved and easy to visit; in fact, you'll probably end up staying in one of the old buildings. There are no shops on the island so bring your own supplies. A current national park pass is required.

Places to Stay

The rooms in the penitentiary at Darlington and some of the other buildings have been

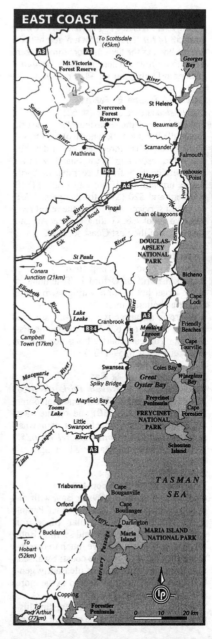

EAST COAST

TASMANIA

converted into bunkhouses called the *Parks, Wildlife & Heritage Penitentiary Units* (☎ *6257 1420)*. They cost $8 a night, but it's wise to book as the beds are sometimes taken by school groups. There is also a *camping ground* at Darlington for $4 per adult.

Getting There & Away

The *Eastcoaster Express* (☎ 6257 1589) is operated by the Eastcoaster Resort, Louisville Point Rd, 4km north of the Orford post office. It has three services a day between the resort and Maria Island, with an extra service daily from December to April. The return fare is $17 for day visitors ($10 children) and $20 ($13) for campers. TWT east coast services will stop at the resort provided you book (see Getting There & Around at the start of the East Coast section).

TRIABUNNA

• postcode 7190   • pop 1000

Just 8km north of Orford is Triabunna, a much larger but less interesting town at the end of a sheltered inlet.

There is an attractive and well stocked visitors centre (☎ 6257 4090) on the Esplanade. You can charter boats for fishing and cruising (☎ 6257 1137).

Places to Stay & Eat

The *Triabunna Caravan Park* (☎ *6257 3575)*, on the corner of Vicary and Melbourne Sts, has camp sites ($10) and on-site vans ($25 double). The peaceful but somewhat shabby *Triabunna Youth Hostel* (☎ *6257 3439, 12 Spencer St)* charges $12 a night.

SWANSEA

• postcode 7190   • pop 450

On the shores of Great Oyster Bay, with superb views across to the Freycinet Peninsula, Swansea is a popular place for camping, boating, fishing and surfing. Both Swansea and Bicheno have much to recommend them as bases on the coast; Swansea, settled in the 1820s, seems pleasantly genteel and almost rural compared to the more lively Bicheno.

Swansea has a number of interesting historic buildings, including the original **council**

chambers, which are still in use, and the lovely red-brick **Morris' General Store**, built in 1838. The community centre dates from 1860 and houses a **museum of local history** and the only oversized billiard table in Australia. The museum is open Monday to Saturday ($4).

The **Swansea Bark Mill & East Coast Museum**, at 96 Tasman Hwy, is also worth a look. The restored mill displays working models of equipment used in the processing of black-wattle bark, a basic ingredient used in the tanning of heavy leathers. The adjoining museum features displays of Swansea's early history, including some superb old photographs. It's open daily from 9 am to 5 pm ($5/2.75).

Places to Stay & Eat

The *Swansea Cabin & Tourist Park* (☎ *6257 8177)*, in Shaw St, just by the beach, is very clean and has good services. Camp sites cost $12 and cabins are $55 to $70 a double.

The *Swansea Youth Hostel* (☎ *6257 8367, 5 Franklin St)*, in a lovely spot near the sea, charges $13. The *Swan Inn* (☎ *6257 8899, 1 Franklin St)* has budget rooms right on the beach for $50 a double.

There are many excellent mid-range and upmarket accommodation options in and around town, including the friendly *Oyster Bay Guest House* (☎ *6257 8110)*, in Franklin St, almost opposite the youth hostel. Built in 1836, it has colonial singles/doubles for $55/95 with a cooked breakfast. It incorporates the *Shy Albatross Restaurant*, which has an Italian and seafood menu.

Freycinet Waters Beachside Cottage (☎ *6257 8080, 16 Franklin St)* is a bright and breezy B&B with definite seaside ambience charging $65/80. *Braeside* (☎ *6257 8110, 21 Julia St)*, away from the water and the main road, offers very pleasant B&B for $75/95.

Schouten House (☎ *6257 8564, 1 Waterloo Rd)* offers upmarket B&B from $105 for doubles. It is often booked by visitors who've come especially to eat at *Fidler's* restaurant, which is in the same building. The restaurant specialises in seafood and game and has an inviting cocktail bar and an excellent wine list.

Kabuki by the Sea (☎ 6257 8588) is 12km south of town, above some of the best coastline on the Tasman Hwy. B&B in self-contained units is $85/120, and Japanese food is served in the restaurant.

COLES BAY & FREYCINET NATIONAL PARK

The small township of Coles Bay is dominated by the spectacular 300m-high pink granite outcrops known as the **Hazards**. The town is the gateway to many white sand beaches, secluded coves, rocky cliffs and excellent bushwalks in the Freycinet National Park.

The park, incorporating Freycinet Peninsula, beautiful Schouten Island and the Friendly Beaches (on the east coast north of Coles Bay), is noted for its coastal heaths, orchids and other wildflowers and for its wildlife, including black cockatoos, yellow wattlebirds, honeyeaters and Bennetts wallabies. Walks include a 27km circuit of the peninsula plus many other shorter tracks, one of the most beautiful being the return walk to **Wineglass Bay** (2½ to three hours). On any walk remember to sign in (and sign out) at the registration booth at the car park. A current national parks pass is also required.

On the road in to Coles Bay, look for **Moulting Lagoon Game Reserve**, which is a breeding ground for black swans and wild ducks.

Freycinet Adventures/Coastal Kayaks (☎ 6257 0500) offers various ocean kayaking, rock-climbing and abseiling tours, while Freycinet Experience (☎ 6223 7565) offers a four day walk along the Peninsula.

Information

The post office/store/information centre is open daily and sells groceries, basic supplies and petrol. It also has a newsagency and boat hire. The Iluka Holiday Centre, on Muir's Beach, has its own minisupermarket, takeaway food, bistro and petrol. At the time of writing the construction of a visitors centre and the redevelopment of the camping grounds in the park were being proposed.

Places to Stay & Eat

The national park *camping ground (☎ 6257 0107)* stretches along Richardsons Beach and has sites for $10 for two people. Bookings can be made at the rangers' office, but during peak periods, such as school holidays, it is essential to book well in advance. Facilities are basic – pit toilets and cold water.

The scenery at the *camp sites* of Wineglass Bay (one to 1½ hours), Hazards Beach (two to three hours) and Cooks Beach (about 4½ hours) is well worth the walk. There's little reliable drinking water at any of these sites, and little elsewhere on the peninsula, so you'll need to carry your own.

The *Coles Bay Caravan Park (☎ 6257 0100)* is 3km by road from Coles Bay at the western end of Muir's Beach. Sites cost $11 for two and on-site vans are $30.

Freycinet Backpackers (☎ 6257 0100), part of the aforementioned caravan park, has dormitory-style accommodation for $14 per person. *Iluka Backpackers* is the YHA hostel in Coles Bay and is in the Iluka Holiday Centre. Clean and pleasant dorm accommodation costs $13 and linen can be hired.

The *Iluka Holiday Centre (☎ 6257 0115)*, on Muir's Beach, has camp sites ($12), on-site vans ($35) and cabins ($50 to $85). Linen is $5 extra. The nearby *Iluka Tavern* has counter lunches and dinners daily and gives YHA members a 10% discount.

The *Coles Bay Youth Hostel*, actually in the national park, is mainly used by groups and must be booked at the YHA head office in Hobart (☎ 6234 9617). Keys are obtained from the Iluka Holiday Centre.

Jessie's Cottage (☎ 6257 0143), on the Esplanade by the general store, is $100 a double for a one bedroom unit, $120 for a two bedroom unit.

Surrounded by the national park is *Freycinet Lodge (☎ 6257 0101)*, at the southern end of Richardsons Beach. Rooms cost from $155 to $200 a double, and there are some with disabled access. You can eat here in the licensed restaurant or the cheaper bistro, both of which have magnificent views. Alternatively, on a clear, moonlit night you can walk along the beach for about 20 minutes to Coles Bay, where you can eat at *Madge*

TASMANIA

Malloy's (☎ *6257 0399, 3 Garnet Ave).*
Seashells Seafood Takeaway, opposite, sells
fish and chips, crayfish rolls etc.

Getting There & Away

Bus Bicheno Coach Services runs a bus service from Coles Bay to Bicheno, meeting
TWT and TRC services at the Coles Bay
turn-off (see Getting There & Around at the
start of the East Coast section). From June
to October there are up to three services on
weekdays, up to two on Saturday and one on
Sunday. From November to May extra services are scheduled but only run if needed.

Some services only run if bookings exist
and it is wise to book at least the night before. The fare each way is $5 ($6 to the
walking tracks car park). The bus will pick
you up from your accommodation if requested. In Bicheno, buses depart from the
Bicheno Take-Away and Caravan Park in
Burgess St; in Coles Bay they leave from
the general store.

It's more than 5km from the town to the
national park walking tracks car park, and
Bicheno Coach Services has a shuttle bus
running from Monday to Saturday, two or
three times a day if required. Bookings are
advised and the cost is $2/3 one way/return.
Park entry fees apply.

BICHENO

• postcode 7215   • pop 750

In the early 1800s, whalers and sealers used
Bicheno's narrow harbour, called the
Gulch, to shelter their boats. They also built
lookouts in the hills to watch for passing
whales. These days, fishing is still one of
the town's major occupations, and if you
are down at the Gulch around lunch time,
when all the fishing boats return, you can
buy fresh crayfish, abalone, oysters or anything else caught that night straight from the
boats.

Tourism is also very important to
Bicheno and it has a helpful information
centre in the main street at which you can
book tours (penguins, glass-bottom boat,
fishing etc) and hire bikes ($15 a day).
Bicheno has beautiful beaches and is a
lovely spot to visit for a few days.

Things to See & Do

An interesting 3km **foreshore walk**, from
Redbill Point to the blowhole, continues
south around the beach to Courlands Bay.
You can also walk up to the **Whalers Lookout** and the **Freycinet Lookout** for good
views.

At nightfall you may be lucky enough to
see the **fairy penguins** at the northern end of
Redbill Beach, but if you want to avoid
overly disturbing the birds and learn a little
about their habits, go on the tour organised
at the information centre.

The Dive Centre (☎ 6375 1138), opposite
the Sea Life Centre, runs courses, and you
can hire or buy diving equipment from its
shop.

The **Sea Life Centre** is open daily from 9
am to 5 pm and features Tasmanian marine
life swimming behind glass windows.
There's also a restored trading ketch, but at
$4.50 for admission, the centre is rather
overpriced and a bit depressing. Seven
kilometres north of town is the 32-hectare
East Coast Birdlife & Animal Park, which is
open daily from 9 am to 5 pm ($7.50).

Just a couple of kilometres north of the
animal park is the turn off to the **Douglas-
Apsley National Park**. The park was proclaimed in 1989 and protects a large and
undisturbed dry eucalypt forest. It has a
number of waterfalls and gorges, and birds
and animals are prolific. There's road access
to the **Apsley Gorge**, in the south of the park,
where there's a water hole with excellent
swimming. You can walk the north-south
trail through the park in a couple of days.

Places to Stay

The *Bicheno Cabin & Tourist Park* (☎ *6375
1117*), in Champ St, has camp sites for $12
and on-site vans from $40. The *Bicheno
Take-Away and Caravan Park* (☎ *6375
1280, 4 Champ St*) has camp sites ($8), on-
site vans ($28) and hostel beds in the *Waubs
Harbour Backpackers* ($14).

A more comfortable option is the *Bicheno
Hostel* (☎ *6375 1651, 11 Morrison St*) which
charges $13 per person. It is centrally lo-
cated and much newer than the *Bicheno
Youth Hostel* (☎ *6375 1293*), whose lovely

location 3km north of town, on the beach opposite Diamond Island, is its only redeeming feature. It's $11 a night, and bookings during the summer period are recommended.

The *Silver Sands Resort* (☎ 6375 1266), in a great location at the end of Burgess St, has budget rooms, but you have to ask for them. Otherwise, you'll pay $70 to $95 a double for rooms overlooking the bay. Cheap meals are also available.

Bicheno Hideaway (☎ 6375 1312), 3km south of town and down a side road, is secluded and tranquil. It has three arc-shaped holiday units with great ocean views. The hosts speak six European languages and rates are $80 a double.

In town and set in bushland between the two lookout hills is *Bicheno Holiday Village* (☎ 6375 1171), where A-frame holiday units are $128 a double.

The *Bicheno Gaol House* (☎ 6375 1430, Burgess St) is the town's oldest building (1845) and offers colonial accommodation for $115 a double. *Maple Cottage* (☎/fax 6375 1172, 160 Tasman Hwy) charges $105 a double. Both places can provide for a cooked breakfast.

Places to Eat

There are the usual coffee shops and takeaways in the main shopping centre. Cheap meals are available at the *Silver Sands Resort*.

In Burgess St is *Cyrano* restaurant, which specialises in seafood and French cuisine. On the Tasman Hwy, the *Longboat Tavern* has good counter meals and *Waubs Bay House* has fresh seafood.

Getting There & Away

The TWT bus stop to/from Hobart and Launceston is at the Four Square Store in Burgess St. The TRC bus stop to/from Hobart and Launceston is at the Bicheno General Store (Value Plus) in Foster St, and Bicheno Coach Service buses to/from Coles Bay stop at the Bicheno Takeaway and Caravan Park in Burgess St. See Getting There & Around in the East Coast and Coles Bay & Freycinet National Park sections earlier in this chapter for more details.

ST MARYS

● postcode 7215   ● pop 600

St Marys is a charming little town, 10km inland from the coast, near the Mt Nicholas range. There's not much to do except enjoy the peacefulness of the countryside, visit a number of waterfalls in the area, and take walks in the state forest.

Places to Stay & Eat

The *Seaview Farm Hostel* (☎ 6372 2341), on a working farm, is surrounded by state forest. It's at the end of a dirt track, 8km from St Marys on Germantown Rd, and commands magnificent views of the coast, ocean and mountains. Bunks are $13.50, doubles $35.

The *St Marys Hotel* (☎ 6372 2181) has singles/doubles at $25/40 and serves counter meals.

To the south, beside the highway to Bicheno in Elephant Pass, is the famous *Mount Elephant Pancake Barn*, with splendid views and delicious pancakes of all varieties. The sign out the front says it all: 'Good food – fresh coffee. Relax. No Arts, No Crafts, No Souvenirs.' It's open daily from 8 am to 6 pm.

Getting There & Away

See Getting There & Around at the start of the East Coast section. Broadby's (☎ 6376 3488) runs a service from St Helens to St Marys return on weekdays (see Getting There & Around at the start of the North-East section).

North-East

It is remarkable that the north-east receives so little attention from visitors: it is conveniently and seductively close to the wines and restaurants of the Pipers Brook and Pipers River vineyards, yet it boasts some of the most secluded and magnificent white sand beaches in the state. Encompassing the pretty seaside town of St Helens, the evocatively named Bay of Fires, Mt William National Park, Eddystone Point, the historic mining town of Derby and the grand St Columba

Falls, north-eastern Tasmania's appeal may well endure beyond that of many of the more popular tourist destinations you visit in your journey around the state.

Organised Tours
North-East Adventure Tours (☎ 6353 2340) offers day and half-day 4WD tours of many of the region's sights and will pick up within a 50km radius of Ringarooma (near Scottsdale).

Getting There & Around
Bus TRC (☎ 1300 360 000) runs buses from Launceston to Conara Junction, then through Fingal ($13.20) and St Marys ($15.50) to St Helens ($19.20). It also runs a bus to Scottsdale ($9.30) and Derby ($13), where you can catch Broadby's bus to St Helens.

TRC fares from Hobart are: Fingal ($26.40), St Marys ($29.40) and St Helens ($31.70).

Broadby's (☎ 6376 3488) runs a weekday return service from St Helens to St Marys. It departs from the BP service station in St Helens at 7.45 am and leaves the post office in St Marys at 9 am; the fare is $3 one way. The same company also runs a bus from St Helens through Derby and Winnaleah and back to St Helens. This service connects with TRC's north-east service at Derby and Winnaleah. It departs from the post office in St Helens on weekdays at 10.45 am, leaves Derby at 12.45 pm and leaves Winnaleah at 1 pm. The fare is $5 one way to/from either Derby or Winnaleah.

TWT (☎ 1300 300 520) has a service from Hobart to St Helens via the east coast on Wednesday, Friday and Sunday, and also on Monday from early December to early April. The fare is $29.40.

Bicycle The Tasman Hwy (A3) is a winding narrow road that crosses two major passes as it heads west through Weldborough and Scottsdale. Cyclists need to be vigilant on this road. One alternative is to follow the rough unsealed roads around the coast. There is little traffic and you have fewer hills to climb. However, you'll need to carry a tent as there is no accommodation around

the coast between St Helens and Bridport; camping areas exist at both ends of Mt William National Park and at Tomahawk on the route from St Helens to Bridport.

SCAMANDER
• postcode 7215   • pop 420
Scamander township is stretched along some lovely white sand beaches.

The *Kookaburra Caravan & Camping Ground* (☎ 6372 5121) has sites ($10) and on-site vans ($25). The *Scamander Beach Resort Hotel* (☎ 6372 5255) is a three storey building with good views. It charges $50 to $75 a double. *Benson's* (☎ 6372 5587) has elegant B&B for $120 to $140 a double.

Surfside Motor Inn (☎ 6372 5177) charges $50/60 a single/double and has a family restaurant serving lunch and dinner.

ST HELENS
• postcode 7216   • pop 1500
St Helens, on Georges Bay, is the largest town on the east coast. First settled in 1830, this old whaling town has an interesting and varied history, which is recorded in the **history room**, at 59 Cecilia St, adjacent to the town's library. It's open weekdays from 9 am to 4 pm ($4).

St Helens is Tasmania's largest fishing port, with a big fleet based in the bay. Visitors can charter boats for game fishing or take a lazy cruise.

While the beaches in town are not particularly good for swimming, there are excellent scenic beaches at **Binalong Bay** (10km from St Helens), **Sloop Rock** (12km), **Stieglitz** (7km) and St Helens and Humbug points.

The information centre (☎ 6376 1329) is in the RACT office on Cecilia St. There are three banks in town and EFTPOS facilities are available at the service stations and supermarkets.

Places to Stay & Eat
The *St Helens Caravan Park* (☎ 6376 1290) is just out of town, south of the bridge on Penelope St. For two people, camp sites are $12, on-site vans $30 and cabins cost from $40.

The *St Helens Youth Hostel (☎ 6376 1661, 5 Cameron St)* is in a lovely, quiet spot by the beach and charges $13 a night. *Artnor Lodge (☎ 6376 1234)*, in Cecilia St, is a comfortable guesthouse with B&B from $35/45 for singles/doubles. Just south of the bridge and off the highway is the Edwardian *Wybalenna Guest House (☎ 6376 1611)*. Set in peaceful gardens among tall trees alive with birds, it has water views from the dining room, the verandah and the best of the bedrooms. Singles range from $85 to $110, while doubles range from $95 to $130. Wybalenna does not cater for children under 14.

For self-catering accommodation, try *Kellraine Units (☎ 6376 1169)*, on the highway west of the centre. At $35 a double, it is great value if you don't mind being away from the water. Alternatively, *Queechy Cottages (☎ 6376 1321)*, on a hill overlooking the water just south of the centre, has units for $50 a double and $10 for each extra person.

In the main street, the *Deli* is open daily. *Trimboli's Pizza*, in Circassian St, has good pizza and pasta. For something special, try *Tidal Water*, the seafood restaurant at Queechy.

ST COLUMBA FALLS

These falls are 24km from St Helens (turn left off the A3 at the sign between St Helens and Weldborough). At around 90m high, they are believed to be the state's highest falls. Although you can see them from the road, you get an entirely different and more impressive view from the platform at their base, an easy 10 minute walk from the car park. These falls are as good as Russell Falls in Mt Field National Park.

Six kilometres back along the road from the A3 to the falls is *St Columba Falls Hotel (☎ 6373 6121)*, which is more generally known as the Pub in the Paddock, an apt description. It has good hotel rooms with new, clean shared facilities for $20/30 a single/double and generous counter meals.

WELDBOROUGH

The Weldborough Pass, with its mountain scenery and dense rainforests, is quite spectacular. During the tin-mining boom last century, hundreds of Chinese migrated to Tasmania and many made Weldborough their base. The joss house now in Launceston's Queen Victoria Museum & Art Gallery was built in Weldborough.

The *Weldborough Hotel* is an idiosyncratic place for a drink and runs a small *camping ground* next door.

BAY OF FIRES

From St Helens a minor road heads northeast to meet the coast at the start of the Bay of Fires and continues up as far as The Gardens. The northern end of the bay can be reached on the C843, the road to the settlement of Ansons Bay and Mt William National Park. Early explorers named the bay after seeing Aboriginal fires along the shore. It is a series of sweeping beaches, rocky headlands, heathlands and lagoons. As well as being popular with today's tourists it was also popular with the Aborigines, who left behind high piles of shells known as middens. The foreshore, lagoons and heathlands are all part of a coastal reserve. If you are after some extremely scenic camping spots, then this is the place for you.

The ocean beaches provide some good surfing. The lagoons provide safe swimming; it is not advisable to swim in the ocean, due to the many rips along the beaches.

There are many places along the bay where free *camping* is allowed, although there are no toilets or fresh water. Just before Ansons Bay is the turn-off to **Policemans Point**, a camping spot close to dazzling beaches. This must be one of the most beautiful free-range camping spots in the state.

MT WILLIAM NATIONAL PARK

This little known park consists of sweeping sandy beaches, low ridges and coastal heathlands. The highest point, Mt William (one hour return on foot), is only 216m high yet provides some breathtaking views. The area was declared a national park in 1973 for the prime purpose of protecting the Forester kangaroo. **Musselroe Point** has a very large midden.

The main activities here include bird-watching, animal-watching, surf and boat fishing, swimming, surfing and diving around Stumpys Bay and Cape Naturaliste. Horse riding is allowed only under permit, so contact the ranger first on ☎ 6357 2108. Spotlighting is also permitted, but, again, the ranger (who can supply lights) must be advised in advance.

At the time of writing, Cradle Huts (☎ 6331 2006) was planning to offer a four day fully catered coastal walk through Mt William National Park from December to May for $1050 per person.

The impressive **Eddystone lighthouse**, at Eddystone Point, was built of granite blocks in the 1890s. A small picnic spot here overlooks a beach of red granite outcrops, while a short drive away, beside a lovely tannin-stained creek and yet another magnificent arc of white sand and aqua water, is the idyllic free *camping ground* of Deep Creek.

Camping in the park is very basic, with only pit toilets, bore water for washing and fireplaces provided. There is no power, and no fresh water except at Deep Creek. Camping is also allowed at four areas in *Stumpys Bay*, and at *Musselroe Top Camp*. Fires are only allowed in fireplaces and it is advisable to bring your own wood or, preferably, a portable stove. On days of total fire ban only gas cookers are permitted.

Getting There & Around

You can enter the park, which is well off the main roads, from the north or the south. The northern end is 12km from Gladstone, the southern end 50km from St Helens. From Bridport, take the road towards Tomahawk and continue on to Gladstone. Try to avoid driving here at night as that's the time the animals are most active. National park entry fees apply; on the access road there is a ranger station from which you can obtain a park pass.

DERBY

• postcode 7264   • pop 200

In 1874, tin was discovered in Derby and this little township flourished throughout the late 19th century. Today Derby is a classified historic town and some of the old mine buildings are now part of the excellent **Tin Mine Centre**, which features a mine museum with old photographs and mining implements, and a re-creation of an old mining shanty town. The centre opens daily from 9 am to 5 pm ($4/1.50).

Vegetarians and animal liberationists beware: the Derby information officer is the butcher. Drop into his shop from Monday to Friday and he'll give you all the hints you need while continuing to wield his blade over the rack of ribs on the chopping block.

Derby comes alive in late October when several thousand people arrive for the annual **Derby River Derby**, a 5km course for all sorts of inflatable craft.

Places to Stay & Eat

The *Dorset Hotel* (☎ 6354 2360) has singles/doubles for $35/55 with breakfast, and it also serves counter meals. Six kilometres from Winnaleah, near Derby, is *Merlinkei Farm Hostel* (☎ 6354 2152), which charges $12 a night. You can ring from Winnaleah and the manager will pick you up. The views across the rural valley to the Blue Tiers Mountains are arresting, but you must be able to appreciate the sound and smell of dairy cows at close range.

The *Crib Shed Tea Rooms* (part of the mine museum) serves delicious scones, while *Derby Sweet Thoughts* has sweets, pancakes, good coffee, pizza, chocolates and ice cream.

SCOTTSDALE

• postcode 7260   • pop 2000

Scottsdale, the major town in the north-east, services some of Tasmania's richest agricultural and forestry country. A camp site at the *Scottsdale Camping Ground* (☎ 6352 2017), on the road to Derby, costs $7.50. *Bellow's Backpacker & Budget Accommodation* (☎ 6352 2263) is a spick and span hostel in King St charging $15 for a dorm bed and $35 for single or double rooms with good shared facilities.

Anabel's of Scottsdale (☎ 6352 3277, 46 King St) has B&B in modern rooms in a beautiful garden for $70/80 a single/double, while ***Beulah's B&B*** *(☎/fax 6352 3723, 9 King St)* is a cottage run by friendly hosts who charge $95 a single or double for rooms with en suite and a cooked breakfast.

AROUND SCOTTSDALE

At Nabowla, 21km west of Scottsdale, is the **Bridestowe Lavender Farm**, open daily during the spectacular flowering season from mid-December to late January ($3). At other times it's open weekdays only and entry is free. **Bridport**, 21km north of Scottsdale, is a popular beach resort where there's plenty of accommodation.

Travelling west from Bridport on the B82 brings you to the **Pipers Brook** and **Pipers River** wine producing regions, where there are several wineries with free tastings and cellar-door sales. Established in 1974, Pipers Brook (☎ 6382 7527) is the best known vineyard in Tasmania and features an architecturally arresting winery. It is open every day except Christmas Day from 10 am to 5 pm. The restaurant at ***Rochecombe & Heemskerk Wines*** serves Tasmanian produce indoors or in its outdoor vine-covered eating area.

Launceston

• postcode 7250   • pop 67,800´

Founded by Lieutenant-Colonel William Paterson in 1805, Launceston is Australia's third oldest city and the commercial centre of northern Tasmania.

The Tamar River estuary was explored in 1798 by Bass and Flinders, as they attempted to circumnavigate Van Diemen's Land.

Launceston was the third attempt by the British to establish a permanent settlement on the Tamar River and was originally called Patersonia, after its founder.

In 1907 the city was renamed in honour of Governor King, who was born in Launceston, England, a town settled 1000 years before on the Tamar River in the county of Cornwall.

Orientation

The city centre is a grid pattern around the Brisbane St Mall, between Charles and St John Sts. Two blocks north, in Cameron St, there's another pedestrian mall called Civic Square. To the east is Yorktown Square, a charming and lively area of restored buildings that have been turned into shops and restaurants.

Information

The TTIC (Gateway Tasmania, ☎ 6336 3133), on the corner of St John and Paterson Sts, is open weekdays from 9 am to 5 pm, Saturday to 3 pm and Sunday and public holidays to noon.

For road maps and motoring information go to the RACT office, on the corner of George and York Sts. For bushwalking maps and camping gear go to Paddy Pallin, at 110 George St, or Allgoods, on the corner of York and St John Sts.

The Wilderness Society's shop at 174 Charles St, has information relevant to conservation issues. The Design Centre of Tasmania, on the corner of Brisbane and Tamar Sts, is a retail outlet displaying work by Tasmania's top artists and craftspeople. There's a craft market in Yorktown Square every Sunday.

Cataract Gorge

Only a 10 minute walk from the city centre is the magnificent Cataract Gorge. Here, almost vertical cliffs line the banks of the South Esk River as it enters the Tamar. The area around the gorge has been made a wildlife reserve and is one of Launceston's most popular tourist attractions.

Two walking tracks, one on either side of the gorge, lead up to First Basin, filled with water from the South Esk River. The walk takes about 30 minutes; the northern trail is the easier. There is a concrete swimming pool that you can use free of charge, an a la carte restaurant, a cafe and peacocks. The gorge is worth visiting at night when it's lit up.

A chairlift crosses the basin to the reserve ($5). A good walking track leads further up the gorge to Second Basin and Duck Reach, 45 minutes each way.

Penny Royal World

The Penny Royal entertainment complex has exhibits including working 19th century

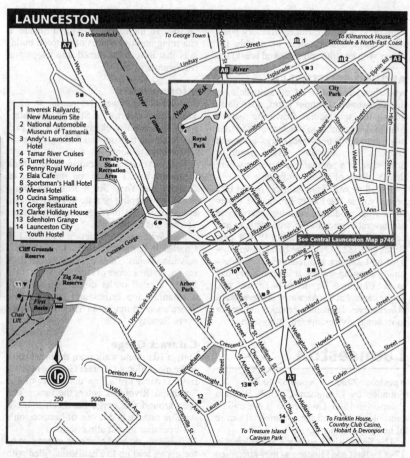

LAUNCESTON

1 Inveresk Railyards;
   New Museum Site
2 National Automobile
   Museum of Tasmania
3 Andy's Launceston
   Hotel
4 Tamar River Cruises
5 Turret House
6 Penny Royal World
7 Elaia Cafe
8 Sportsman's Hall Hotel
9 Mews Hotel
10 Cucina Simpatica
11 Gorge Restaurant
12 Clarke Holiday House
13 Edenholm Grange
14 Launceston City
   Youth Hostel

See Central Launceston Map p746

0 250 500m

water mills and windmills, gunpowder mills
and model boats. You can take a ride on a
barge or a restored city tram or take a 45
minute cruise part-way up the gorge on the
Lady Stelfox paddle-steamer. Some parts of
the complex are interesting, but overall it's
not worth the admission of $19.50/$9.50.
You can, however, just pay to see one of the
attractions.

Queen Victoria Museum & Art Gallery

The Queen Victoria Museum & Art Gallery,
built late last century, displays the splendour

of the period both inside and out. The splendid joss house was donated by descendants of
Chinese settlers. The centre is open Monday
to Saturday from 10 am to 5 pm and Sunday
from 2 to 5 pm. The gallery and museum are
free, while the planetarium costs $3.

The historic Johnstone & Wilmot warehouse, on the corner of Cimitiere and St
John Sts, dates from 1842. It houses the
community history branch of the museum
and operates a genealogical service. It is
open weekdays from 10 am to 4 pm.

At the time of writing, the Inveresk Railyards just across Victoria Bridge, to the

right of Invermay Rd, were being extensively redeveloped to house much of the museum's collection.

National Automobile Museum
This museum is a little out of the centre, on the corner of Cimitiere and Willis Sts. It's open from 9 am to 5 pm daily from September to May and from 10 am to 4 pm daily the rest of the year. Admission is $7.50/4 for adults/children.

Interesting Buildings
In Civic Square is **Macquarie House**, built in 1830 as a warehouse but later used as a military barracks and office building.

The **Old Umbrella Shop**, at 60 George St, was built in the 1860s and still houses a selection of umbrellas. Classified by the National Trust, it is the last genuine period shop in the state. The interior is lined with Tasmanian blackwood timber, and a good range of National Trust items are on sale.

On weekdays at 9.45 am there's a highly recommended one hour guided historic walk around the city centre and former waterfront. The tours leave from the Tasmanian Travel & Information Centre and cost $10.

On the Midland Hwy, 6km south of the city, is **Franklin House**, one of Launceston's most attractive Georgian homes. It was built in 1838 and has been beautifully restored and furnished by the National Trust. The house is open daily from 9 am to 5 pm (4 pm in winter; $6).

Parks & Gardens
Launceston is renowned for its beautiful public squares, parks and reserves.

The 13-hectare **City Park** is a fine example of a Victorian garden and features an elegant fountain, a bandstand, a monkey enclosure, a radio museum, a conservatory and a very old wisteria (behind the radio museum). **Prince's Square**, between Charles and St John Sts, features a bronze fountain bought at the 1855 Paris Exhibition, and a disconcerting statue of William Russ Pugh, credited with the first use of ether for surgical purposes in the southern hemisphere, descending stairs into the park.

Other public parks and gardens include **Royal Park**, near the junction of the North Esk and Tamar rivers; the **Punchbowl Reserve**, with its magnificent rhododendron garden; **Windmill Hill Reserve**; the **Trevallyn Recreation Area**; and the Cataract Gorge.

Organised Tours
The Coach Tram Tour Company has a comprehensive three hour tour of the city sights for $23. It leaves from TTIC (☎ 6336 3122). TRC (☎ 6331 3233), in George St, has half and full-day tours of city sights and the Tamar Valley ($34), the north-west coast ($38), the north-east ($42) and Cradle Mountain ($45). TWT (☎ 6334 4442) has tours to the Tamar Valley, Cradle Mountain and Freycinet Peninsula (all $59).

At Home Point in Royal Park, Tamar River Cruises (☎ 6334 9900) offers four-hour river cruises from $48 with lunch.

Places to Stay – Budget
Camping The *Treasure Island Caravan Park* (☎ 6344 2600, 94 Glen Dhu St) is 1km south of the city beside the expressway. It has camp sites ($14 a double), standard cabins ($54) and deluxe cabins ($60).

Hostels The friendly *Launceston City Backpackers* (☎ 6334 2327, 173 George St), in the centre of town, is an old, thoughtfully renovated house costing $14 per person in four-bed rooms.

Andy's Launceston Hotel (☎ 6331 4513, 1 Tamar St), above the Mallee Grill, has backpacker accommodation for $14 and rooms with shared facilities for $40 a double. *Irish Murphy's* (☎ 6331 4440, 211 Brisbane St) charges $14 for backpacker accommodation but can be noisy.

The independent *Launceston City Youth Hostel* (☎ 6344 9779, 36 Thistle St) is 2km from the centre of town. It has dorm beds and family rooms for $12 per person a night. The building dates from the 1940s and used to be the canteen for the Coats Patons woollen mill. The hostel has mountain bikes and bushwalking gear for hire.

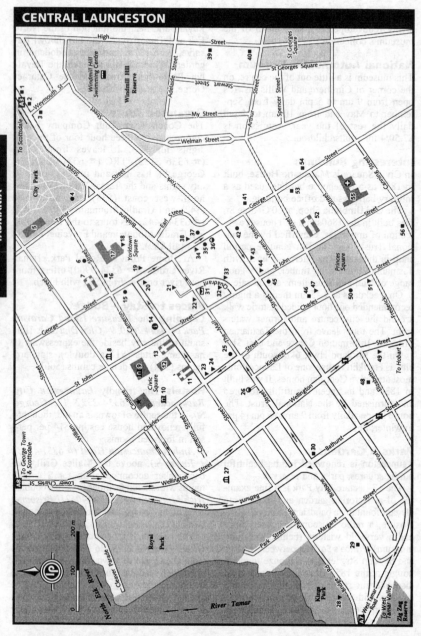

CENTRAL LAUNCESTON

CENTRAL LAUNCESTON

PLACES TO STAY
1 Sandors on the Park
2 North Lodge
3 Parklane Motel
16 Batman Fawkner Inn
17 Novotel Launceston
29 Rose Lodge
30 Irish Murphys
39 Windmill Hill Tourist Lodge
40 Ashton Gate Guest House
41 Fiona's B&B
46 Hotel Tasmania
48 YHA summer hostel
53 Colonial Motor Inn
54 Launceston City
   Backpackers
56 Canning Cottage

PLACES TO EAT
18 Tairyo Japanese Restaurant &
   Sushi Bar
19 La Cantina

20 Shrimps
21 Croplines Coffee
22 Banjo's
23 Arpar's Thai Restaurant
24 Star Bar
28 Ripples Restaurant
32 That Dear Little Coffee Shop
33 Pasta Resistance Too
34 Konditorei Café/Manfred
38 Pepperberry Cafe/Restaurant
43 Fu Wah
44 The Metz
47 Canton
49 Calabrisella Pizza
51 Fee & Me

OTHER
4 Design Centre of Tasmania
5 Albert Hall
6 Advance Car Rentals
7 Holy Trinity Anglican Church
8 Community History Museum

9 Town Hall
10 Macquarie House
11 Pilgrim Uniting Church
12 Library
13 St Andrews Church
14 Travel & Information Centre
15 Old Umbrella Shop
25 Qantas
26 Tamar Valley Coaches
27 Queen Victoria Museum &
   Art Gallery; Queen Vic Cafe
31 Post Office &
   Commonwealth Bank
35 Paddy Pallin
36 Tasmanian Redline Coaches
37 Tasmanian Wilderness
   Travel
42 RACT
45 Allgoods
50 The Wilderness Society Shop
52 St Johns Church
55 St Vincent's Hospital

TASMANIA

The YHA runs a *summer hostel (☎ 6334 4505, 132 Elizabeth St)*; advance bookings can be made through the Hobart YHA office.

Hotels Launceston has a good selection of hotels for a town of its size. One of the cheapest is the *Sportsman's Hall Hotel (☎ 6331 3968, 252 Charles St)*, where singles/doubles cost $35/50, including a cooked breakfast.

Apartments Although a little difficult to find, *Clarke Holiday House (☎ 6334 2237, 19 Neika Ave)*, about 1km out of town, is good value at $35 a double for an entire flat.

Places to Stay – Mid-Range

B&Bs *Fiona's B&B (☎ 6334 5965, 141 George St)* offers delightful singles/doubles for $60/80. *Rose Lodge (☎ 6334 0120, 270 Brisbane St)* provides friendly service and small but comfortable rooms with a cooked breakfast for $55/68. *Mews Motel (☎ 6331 2861, 89 Margaret St)* is closer to a guesthouse than a motel and is also reasonably priced at $55/68.

The *Windmill Hill Tourist Lodge (☎ 6331 9337, 22 High St)* charges $60/70. The lodge also has self-contained holiday flats at $75 a double.

The cosy *Turret House (☎ 6334 7033, 41 West Tamar Rd)* charges $70/100, including a cooked breakfast. It's north of Cataract Gorge, which makes for a delightful early morning walk.

Ashton Gate Guest House (☎ 6331 6180, 32 High St), on top of the hill, has rooms for $75/95 with a continental breakfast.

For something different, you could try renting your own fully furnished two bedroom colonial cottage. *Canning Cottage (☎ 6331 4876, 26-28 Canning St)* is actually two separate cottages. Both are very cosy and there are lots of steep steps and narrow doorways. The cost is a very reasonable $85 for a double with breakfast provisions.

Hotels & Motels The *Hotel Tasmania (☎ 6331 7355, 191 Charles St)*, better known as the Saloon, has singles/doubles for $45/58, including continental breakfast.

The rambling but mostly comfortable *Batman Fawkner Inn (☎ 6331 7222, 35 Cameron St)* has a range of single rooms from $25 to $42 and doubles for $65. The $25 rooms are small and dingy.

Most motels are east of the city centre, in either York or Brisbane St, and are about 1km from town. *North Lodge (☎ 6331 9966,*

7 Brisbane St) has rooms for $75 a double. Next door is *Parklane Motel (☎ 6331 4233, 9 Brisbane St)* where rooms are $85 a double and self-contained units are $95.

Sandors On The Park (☎ 6331 2055, 3 Brisbane St) provides good standard rooms for $70/80.

Places to Stay – Top End

B&Bs *Edenholme Grange (☎ 6334 6666, 14 St Andrews St)*, which is classified by the National Trust, is in a side street off Hillside Crescent before it meets Hill St, the road to First Basin, and charges $100 for singles and $130 to $160 for doubles, with a five-course cooked Tasmanian breakfast. Its theme rooms are so lavishly decorated that you may believe you've found your way into your very own bodice-ripper novel.

Kilmarnock House (☎ 6334 1514, 66 Elphin Rd) is 1.5km east of the city and charges $80/100 for lovely rooms with a continental breakfast.

Hotels At the *Novotel Launceston (☎ 6334 3434, 29 Cameron St)* rooms start at $145 a double, including a buffet breakfast.

If you really want to be pampered, try the *Country Club Casino (☎ 6335 5777)*, at Prospect Vale, 10 to 15 minutes drive from the city. Rooms are $245 a double.

Places to Eat

Croplines Coffee, in Brisbane Court, has the best coffee in town. *Banjo's* bakes all its own bread, pizza and cakes, and has two shops in town: one in Yorktown Square, and one at 98 Brisbane St. Both are open daily from 6 am to 6 pm.

The best bargain in the Quadrant has to be *Pasta Resistance Too*, with serves at $5 to $7. It's a tiny place packed full of customers. Just opposite is *That Dear Little Coffee Shop*, a matchbox-sized cafe with a great reputation for its home-made cakes and soups.

Ripples Restaurant, beside the Tamar in the Ritchies Mill Art Centre opposite Penny Royal, specialises in light meals.

Elaia (238-240 Charles St), which is a little south of the city centre near the Sportsman's Hall Hotel, is colourful, open

and sunny, and serves good coffee, lunches and dinners.

The *Queen Vic Cafe*, in the museum, has a pleasant outlook, seats on a balcony and good food.

Most of Launceston's many hotels have filling, reasonably priced counter meals. The *South Charles Cafe*, at the Sportsman's Hall Hotel, has restaurant-quality meals at reasonable prices. Central and extremely popular is the *Star Bar (113 Charles St)*, which is spacious and appealing, and has a wood-fired pizza oven. In a similar vein, *The Metz*, on the corner of York and St John Sts, is a bar, cafe and restaurant in what used to be the St George Hotel. Its 'On York's Meateaters Platter' features ostrich, quail and wallaby.

Calabrisella Pizza (☎ 6331 1958, 56 Wellington St) serves excellent, reasonably priced Italian food and is often packed.

Arpar's Thai Restaurant, on the corner of Charles and Paterson Sts, is well worth a visit. If you prefer Chinese, try the *Fu Wah (☎ 6331 6368, 63 York St)* or the upmarket *Canton (☎ 6331 9448, 201 Charles St)*, which has a separate menu for those who prefer authentic dishes. A great Japanese restaurant and sushi bar is the *Tairyo (☎ 6334 2620)*, at Yorktown Square.

Konditorei Cafe Manfred (☎ 6334 2490, 106 George St), well known for its delicious German rolls and pastries, now has a licensed restaurant upstairs offering Mediterranean and French fare. Across the road is the *Pepperberry Cafe/Restaurant (☎ 6334 4589, 91 George St)*, which has an emphasis on Tasmanian produce and uses pepperberries in dishes featuring game such as wallaby.

On the other side of town, just out of the centre, is *Cucina Simpatica (☎ 6334 3177)*, on the corner of Frederick and Margaret Sts. It's rather expensive but has a bright, relaxed atmosphere and great food.

La Cantina (☎ 6331 7835, 63 George St) and the upmarket *Shrimps (☎ 6334 0584, 72 George St)* have been recommended by readers.

The *Gorge Restaurant*, at Cataract Gorge, undoubtedly has the best setting in Launceston, while *Fee & Me (☎ 6331 3195, 190 Charles St)* offers elaborate fine dining.

Entertainment

There's quite a good range of evening entertainment in Launceston, most of which is advertised in the free *Launceston Week* newspaper or in *This Week in Tasmania*.

The *Pavilion Tavern*, in Yorktown Square, has music from Tuesday to Saturday nights and a cabaret-style nightclub. Despite its wild west setting, the *Hotel Tasmania (191 Charles St)* isn't a country and western venue but it does have bands on Wednesday, Friday and Saturday nights. *Irish Murphy's (211 Brisbane St)* has bands regularly and seems to attract half of Launceston. The *Star Bar (113 Charles St)* is a popular wine bar.

If you want to risk a few dollars, or just observe how the rich play, check out the *Launceston Federal Country Club Casino*, at Prospect Vale, 10 to 15 minutes drive from the city centre. You don't have to pay to get in and about the only article of clothing disapproved of these days is track shoes.

Getting There & Away

Air See the Getting There & Away section at the beginning of this chapter for details. Qantas is on the corner of Brisbane and Charles Sts.

Bus The main bus companies operating out of Launceston are: TRC (☎ 1300 360 000, 6331 3233), at 112 George St; TWT (☎ 1300 300 520, 6334 4442), at 101 George St; and Tamar Valley Coaches (☎ 6334 0828), at 4 Cuisine Lane.

TRC runs buses to Deloraine ($6.80), Devonport ($13.70), Hobart ($19.50), Burnie ($18.30), Wynyard ($20.90), Stanley ($29), Smithton ($29), George Town ($7.20), St Marys ($15.50), St Helens ($19.20), Bicheno ($21.60) and Swansea ($17.30). TWT services the west coast, including Cradle Mountain ($36.50, plus $7 to Dove Lake) and Queenstown ($43.10). TWT also has a Launceston to Bicheno service for $19.

Car There are plenty of car-rental firms in Launceston. Among the cheapest is Advance Car Rentals (☎ 6391 8000), at 32 Cameron St and the airport. Prices range from $30 to over $100 for one day, less for longer rentals.

Getting Around

To/From the Airport TRC operates an airport shuttle service that meets all incoming flights and picks up passengers an hour or so before all departures. The fare is $7. A taxi to the city costs about $20.

Bus The local bus service is run by Metro, and the main departure points are the two blocks in St John St between Paterson and York Sts. For $3.10 you can buy an unlimited travel Day Rover ticket that can be used all day at weekends and between 9 am and 4.30 pm and after 6 pm on weekdays. Most routes, however, do not operate in the evenings, and Sunday services are limited.

Bicycle Rent-a-Cycle, at the Launceston City Youth Hostel (☎ 6344 9779), has a good range of mountain bikes for $95 a week.

Around Launceston

HADSPEN

• postcode 7290   • pop 1500

The popular residential suburb of Hadspen, with some attractive 19th century buildings, including the **Red Feather Inn** and **Hadspen Gaol**, is 15km south-west of Launceston.

Just west of Hadspen is **Entally House**, one of Tasmania's best known historic homes. It was built in 1819 by Thomas Haydock Reibey and is now owned by the National Trust. Set in beautiful grounds, it creates a vivid picture of what life must have been like for the well-to-do on an early farming property. It's open daily from 10 am to 5 pm ($6/4).

Carrick Mill, 2km west of Hadspen, is an ivy-covered bluestone mill dating from 1810. On the side road near the mill, and beside the dramatic ruins of the burnt-out Archers Folly, is the **Tasmanian Copper Gallery**. The art is unusual, entry is free and all works are for sale.

AROUND LAUNCESTON

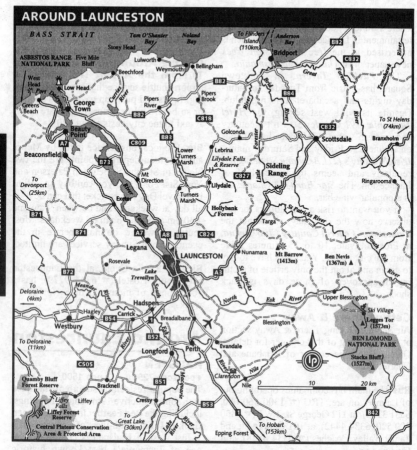

Places to Stay & Eat

On the corner of the Bass Hwy and Main Rd in Hadspen is the *Launceston Cabin & Tourist Park* (☎ 6393 6391). The park has good facilities and charges $10 for a camp site and $55 a double in pleasant, well equipped cabins.

The *Red Feather Inn* (☎ 6393 6331), built in 1844, has a restaurant upstairs and counter meals downstairs.

Thirteen kilometres from Carrick, at Whitemore and well signposted off the main roads, is the highly regarded *Gossips Restaurant* (☎ 6397 3148).

WESTBURY

● postcode 7303   ● pop 1285

The historic town of Westbury, 28km west of Launceston, is best known for its 1841 **White House**, featuring colonial furnishings, vintage cars and a collection of 19th century toys. It's open daily except Monday from 10 am to 4 pm ($6).

Pearn's Steam World, on the Bass Hwy, is open daily ($3). On the other side of the highway is the **Westbury Maze**, a hedge maze open daily from October to June ($3.50).

The *Westbury Hotel* has basic singles/doubles for $25/45, while *Fitzpatrick's Inn*

(☎ 6393 1153, Bass Hwy) has good value B&B for $40/70. A small range of quality goods baked in a wood-fired oven are available at the *White House*.

LIFFEY VALLEY

The Liffey Valley Forest Reserve protects the very beautiful rainforested valley at the foot of the Great Western Tiers and features the impressive **Liffey Falls**.

Liffey Valley Fernery, Tearooms and Gallery (☎ 6397 3213) is open most Saturdays, every Sunday and most public holidays from 11 am to 4 pm, but is closed from the June long weekend until the end of October. Liffey is 34km south of Carrick, via Bracknell, and is a good day trip from Launceston.

LONGFORD
* postcode 7301   * pop 2800

Longford, a National Trust classified town 27km from Launceston, is best known for its proximity to the historic estates of *Woolmers (☎ 6391 2230)* and *Brickendon (☎ 6391 1251)*, both of which are open to the public and offer accommodation.

The *Riverside Caravan Park (☎ 6391 1470)*, on the banks of the Macquarie River, has camp sites ($10) and on-site vans ($30). The *Country Club Hotel (☎ 6391 1155)* has recently renovated singles/doubles for $20/40 with a cooked breakfast. The *Old Rosary (☎ 6391 1662)*, off Malcombe St and hidden among magnificent gardens, is $130 a double. *Kingsley House (☎ 6391 2318)*, in Wellington St, has pleasant larger-than-average rooms for $80 a double.

EVANDALE
* postcode 7212   * pop 850

Evandale, 19km south of Launceston in the South Esk Valley, is another town classified by the National Trust. Many of its 19th century buildings are in excellent condition. In keeping with its old world atmosphere, Evandale hosts the **National Penny Farthing Championships** in February each year. A market is held here every Sunday morning.

The Tourism & History Centre (on your left as you enter town) is open daily from 10 am to 3 pm.

Eleven kilometres south of Evandale is the National Trust property of **Clarendon** (☎ 6398 6220), which was completed in 1838 and is one of the grandest Georgian mansions in Australia. It's open daily from 10 am to 5 pm (closing an hour earlier in winter); $6/4.

Places to Stay & Eat

The old *Clarendon Arms Hotel (☎ 6391 8181, 11 Russell St)* has singles/doubles from $25/35; breakfast is extra. Much more interesting, and great if you're travelling with kids, is *Greg & Gill's Place (☎ 6391 8248, 35 Collins St)*, in a lovely garden setting in a quiet corner of town ($50/75 with breakfast). *Solomon Cottage (☎ 6391 8331, 1 High St)* used to be a bakery, and the area that was once the oven is now the perfect alcove for a queen-size bed. B&B is $70/95.

Russells Restaurant, in Russell St, has meals for $10 to $16, while the pubs around town provide counter meals.

Getting There & Away

There is a TRC service from Launceston to Evandale ($2.40) on weekdays only.

LILYDALE

The small town of Lilydale, 27km from Launceston, stands at the foot of Mt Arthur. Three kilometres from the town is the **Lilydale Falls Reserve**, which has camping facilities and two easily accessible waterfalls. At the nearby town of Lalla, there's the century-old **rhododendron gardens**, which are spectacular in spring; entry is $2 per vehicle.

BEN LOMOND NATIONAL PARK

This 165 sq km park, 50km south-east of Launceston, includes the entire Ben Lomond Range and is best known for its skiing facilities. During the ski season, a kiosk, tavern and restaurant are open in the alpine village and there's accommodation at the *Creek Inn (☎ 6372 2444)*. High season backpacker accommodation costs $30 and units that sleep four adults are $180, including breakfast. Lift tickets and equipment-hire cost about half what they do on the mainland. The scenery at Ben Lomond is magnificent year round and the park is particularly noted for its wildflowers.

Getting There & Away

TWT (☎ 1300 300 520) has a daily return service ($29) between the ski fields and Launceston. (At the time of writing, this service was under review, so ring for details). TWT also runs a shuttle service from the bottom of Jacobs Ladder to the alpine village. The ladder is a very steep climb on an unsealed road with six hairpin bends and no safety barriers.

Tamar Valley & North Coast

Gently rolling hills and farmlands extend from the Tamar Valley north of Launceston and west to the Great Western Tiers. The best way to explore this area is to leave the highways and follow the quiet minor roads through the small towns. Most roads in this region are sealed.

The Tamar River separates the east and west Tamar districts and links Launceston with its ocean port of Bell Bay. Crossing the river near Deviot is Batman Bridge, the only bridge on the lower reaches of the Tamar. The river is tidal for the 64km to Launceston and wends its way through some lovely orchards, pastures, forests and vineyards.

The Tamar Valley and nearby Pipers River (see Around Scottsdale in the North-East section earlier in this chapter) are among Tasmania's main wine-producing areas and the dry, premium wines produced here have achieved wide recognition.

European history in the region dates from 1798, when Bass and Flinders discovered the estuary; settlement commenced in 1804. Slowly the valley developed, despite resistance from the Aboriginal people, first as a port of call for sailors and sealers from the Bass Strait islands and then as a sanctuary for some of the desperate characters who took to the bush during the convict days.

In the late 1870s, gold was discovered at Cabbage Tree Hill – now Beaconsfield –

and the fortunes of the valley took a new turn. The region boomed and for a time this was the third-largest town in Tasmania, before the mines closed in 1914.

Getting There & Around

On weekdays, Tamar Valley Coaches (☎ 6334 0828) has at least one bus a day running up and down the West Tamar Valley, but there are no weekend services. The fare from Launceston to Beaconsfield is $5.70.

TRC (☎ 1300 360 000) runs three buses every weekday and one bus on Sunday along the eastern side of the Tamar River from Launceston to Dilston, Hillwood and George Town ($7.20). On some services the bus will continue on to Low Head, but only if a booking has been made.

George Town is the point of arrival and departure for the summer-only *Devil Cat* service to Melbourne (see the Getting There & Away section at the start of this chapter). When the catamaran is running, a coach to and from Launceston meets the ferry each time it arrives and departs.

TRC has several services daily from Launceston to Devonport ($13.70), Ulverstone ($15.80) and Penguin ($16.20), some of which call at the ferry terminal in Devonport. It also runs weekday services from Launceston to Deloraine ($6.80).

Buses also run from both Launceston and Devonport to Cradle Mountain-Lake St Clair National Park. See The West later in this chapter for details.

ROSEVEARS

This is a tiny riverside settlement on a side road off the West Tamar Hwy. The main attraction is the **Waterbird Haven Trust**, a sanctuary for marine birds ($4). *B&B* is available beside the haven for $30/50 a single/double, but you'd have to be very fond of waterfowl to stay here. The *Rosevears Tavern* has pub meals but no accommodation.

The other feature here is the **Strathlynn Wine Centre** (☎ 6330 2388). This is an outlet for Pipers Brook and tastings are free. Meals featuring Tasmanian produce are also available at the centre.

BEACONSFIELD

- postcode 7270   • pop 1358

The once-thriving gold-mining town of Beaconsfield is still dominated by the ruins of its three original mine buildings. Two of these house the **Grubb Shaft Museum** complex, which is open daily from 10 am to 4 pm ($4/50c). It is a must-see if you're travelling with children as there are hands-on interactive exhibits including a noisy waterwheel-powered battery. A free display opposite the mine buildings has a reconstruction of a miner's cottage and old school. Beaconsfield Gold has opened up the old Hart shaft next to the museum and, using today's technology, mining for gold is again under way.

The *Club Hotel* serves counter meals daily, while *Garwoods Bakery* produces some tasty bread.

AROUND BEACONSFIELD

Further north is picturesque **Beauty Point**, the site of the Australian Maritime College. If you are cycling and wish to avoid using Batman Bridge, you may be able to cross to George Town with Tamar Boat Hire (☎ 6383 4744), at Beauty Point Marina, for $10 or $12.

At the mouth of the Tamar River are the quiet holiday and fishing resorts of **Greens Beach** and **Kelso**.

GEORGE TOWN

- postcode 7253   • pop 5000

George Town, on the eastern shore of the Tamar River close to the heads, is best known as the site where Lieutenant-Colonel Paterson landed in 1804, leading to the settlement of northern Tasmania.

In Cimitiere St, the **Grove** is a lovely Georgian stone residence built in the 1830s that has been classified by the National Trust. It's open daily from 10 am to 5 pm and admission is $4. Refreshments are available and lunch is served by staff in period costume.

The **old watch house**, in Macquarie St, dates from 1843 and has been turned into a community arts centre; it's open on weekdays and costs nothing to look around. Also of interest is the **St Mary Magdalen Anglican Church**, in Anne St.

Seal & Sea Adventure Tours (☎ 0419 357 028) has **seal spotting cruises**.

Places to Stay & Eat

The *Travellers Lodge* (☎ 6382 3261, 4 Elizabeth St) is a YHA hostel in a restored house that dates back to 1891. It has camp sites for $10, bunks for $14 and family rooms for $40.

The *Pier Hotel Motel* (☎ 6382 1300, 3 Elizabeth St) has singles/doubles for $40/50 and motel rooms from $99 a double. The hotel serves meals, including breakfast, daily. The *Grove* (☎ 6382 1336, Cimitiere St) has B&B for $60/75 and a licensed restaurant.

The *Buffalo Cafe*, in the main street, is open for lunch and dinner from Thursday to Sunday and has something of the atmosphere of a city wine bar. The *Cove Cafe* is another reasonable cafe.

LOW HEAD

- postcode 7253

Just north of George Town is Low Head, which provides the navigation aids for ships to enter the river. The **pilot station**, dating from 1835, is the oldest in Australia and houses an interesting **maritime museum** open daily ($3). There are several navigational lead lights (miniature lighthouses) around town that date from 1881. Penguins return to their burrows near the lighthouse daily at dusk. There is surf at **East Beach** on Bass Strait, and safe swimming in the river.

The *Beach Pines Holiday Village* (☎ 6382 2602, 192 Gunn Parade) has camp sites ($12 a double) and cabins ($60). Good, plain, waterfront accommodation is available in the *Pilot's House* (☎ 0417 503 292) at the Low Head pilot station for $60/70 a single/double.

DELORAINE

- postcode 7304   • pop 2100

Deloraine is Tasmania's largest inland town and, with its lovely riverside picnic area, superb setting at the foot of the Great Western Tiers, proximity to Cradle Mountain and good amenities, it makes a great base from which to explore the surrounding area. The visitor information centre (also the **folk museum**) is near the roundabout at the top of the main street.

Many of the town's Georgian and Victorian buildings have been restored. Places of interest include **St Mark's Church of England** and, 2km east of town, the **Bowerbank Mill** gallery. The **Tasmanian Craft Fair**, held in Deloraine over four days in late October and/or early November, is claimed to be Australia's largest working craft fair, and accommodation must be booked well in advance for this time of year.

Places to Stay & Eat

The *Apex Caravan Park* (☎ 6362 2345), in West Parade, is 500m from the town centre and has camp sites for $10. The park is in an attractive position but is subject to flooding.

The *Highview Lodge Youth Hostel* (☎ 6362 2996, 8 Blake St) is perched on a hillside and has magnificent views of the Great Western Tiers. It charges $12. Mountain bikes and touring bikes are available for rent.

The *Bush Inn* (☎ 6362 2365, 7 Bass Hwy) and *Deloraine Hotel* (☎ 6362 2022), in Emu Bay Rd, offer basic B&B pub accommodation for $20 and $25 per person respectively.

Next door to the Deloraine Hotel is the comfortable and friendly *Bonneys Inn* (☎ 6362 2974), which offers B&B in colonial accommodation for $60/75 for singles/doubles.

Excellent upmarket accommodation is available 2km east of town at *Bowerbank Mill* (☎ 6362 2628, 4455 Meander Valley Hwy) and, closer to town in East Barrack St, at the luxurious *Arcoona* (☎ 6362 3443).

The *Emu Bay Brasserie*, in the main street, is open daily from 8 am. The atmosphere is relaxed and the meals are reasonably priced. The *Delicatessen Coffee Shop* is also inviting. At the *Christmas Hills Raspberry Farm*, well signposted 8km from town on the road to Devonport, desserts are understandably heavy on the raspberries. A popular winter choice is hearty soup and damper followed by dessert ($9.50). Further out is *Villarett* (☎ 6368 1214), which has a

teahouse, a gallery and mid-range accommodation in established gardens.

MOLE CREEK
● postcode 7304   ● pop 250

About 25km west of Deloraine is Mole Creek, in the vicinity of which you'll find spectacular limestone caves, leatherwood honey and one of Tasmania's best wildlife parks. Today, many of the area's features have been protected as part of the **Mole Creek Karst National Park**.

Marakoopa Cave, a wet cave 15km from Mole Creek, features two underground streams and an incredible glow-worm display. **King Solomon Cave** is a dry cave with amazing calcite crystals that reflect light; it has very few steps in it, making it the better cave for the less energetic. In the high season, there are at least five tours in each cave daily. A visit to one cave costs $8/4, or you can visit both for $12/6. Current tour times are prominently displayed on access roads, or ring the ranger (☎ 6363 5182).

There are also some magnificent **wild caves** in the area, and Wild Cave Tours (☎ 6367 8142) provides caving gear and guides at $65 for half a day or $130 for a full day.

The leatherwood tree only grows in the damp western part of Tasmania, so honey made from its flower is unique to this state. From January to April, when the honey is being extracted, you can visit the **Stephens Leatherwood Honey Factory** and learn all about this fascinating industry. The factory is open weekdays.

Two kilometres from Chudleigh, east of Mole Creek, is the **Trowunna Wildlife Park**, which is worth a visit. It's open daily from 9 am to 5 pm ($8.50/4.50).

Places to Stay

Two kilometres west of town, at the turn-off to the caves and Cradle Mountain, is the *Mole Creek Camping Ground* (☎ 6363 1150). It has basic facilities and charges $8/10 a family for unpowered/powered sites.

The *Mole Creek Hotel* (☎ 6363 1102), in the main street, has singles/doubles for $30/55 and counter meals daily. The *Mole*

Creek Guest House (☎ *6363 1399*), also in the main street, has B&B from $70 a double. Out of town, *Mole Creek Holiday Village* (☎ *6363 6124, 1876 Mole Creek Rd)* has timber units for $68 a double, while the lovely *Blackwood Park* (☎ *6363 1208*), in Mersey Hill Rd, has upmarket self-contained accommodation for just $96 a double.

SHEFFIELD
● postcode 7306   ● pop 1000

Sheffield is often referred to as 'the town of murals'. Since 1986, 20 murals depicting the history of the area have been painted in and around this little town, with a further 10 in the surrounding district, and these have become a major tourist attraction.

The Visitor Information Centre is in Pioneer Crescent behind Flo's Country Kitchen. The free **Diversity Murals Theatrette**, at the western end of the main street, screens an interesting documentary about the paintings. It's open all day Monday to Saturday, and Sunday afternoons. Pick up a map of mural locations here.

The scenery around Sheffield is also impressive, with **Mt Roland** (1231m) dominating the peaceful farmlands, thick forests and rivers brimming with fish. Nearby is beautiful **Lake Barrington**, a major rowing venue. There is a **deer farm** with *camping* (☎ *6491 1628)* in the tiny township of Paradise, and a large **maze, lavender farm and pancake parlour** at Promised Land, near Lake Barrington.

Places to Stay & Eat
The bland and basic *Sheffield Caravan Park* (☎ *6491 1366)* is behind the town hall. Sites are $8. The *Roland Rock Motel & Hostel* (☎ *6491 1821, 47 Main St)* has backpacker accommodation for $15 and motel rooms for $45 a double.

The *Sheffield Hotel* (☎ *6491 1130)*, in Main St, has singles/doubles for $30/45 with a light breakfast. The new *Kentish Hills Retreat* (☎ *6491 2484, 2 West Nook Rd)* has attractive modern units from $75/80, while *Tanglewood* (☎ *6491 1854, 25 High St)* has B&B for $72/100. The visitors centre has listings of host farms and cottages in the surrounding hills.

Sixteen kilometres from town is Gowrie Park, at the base of Mt Roland, where very basic hostel accommodation at *Mt Roland Budget Backpackers* (☎ *6491 1385)* costs $10 a night. Behind the backpackers is the rustic *Weindorfers* restaurant, which serves hearty meals at reasonable prices. This is an excellent base for walks up Mt Roland.

Flo's Country Kitchen, in Main Street, was established by a former Federal politician who is as famous for her pumpkin scones as she is for being the wife of former Queensland premier Joh Bjelke-Petersen. The scones really are pretty good, and the decor is the stuff of legend – a couple of 80kg Atlantic giants in the middle of the floor and wall to wall Joh memorabilia.

The *Sheffield Hotel* serves counter meals, while the Irish-style licensed *Red Rose Cafe* is open for lunch and dinner.

DEVONPORT
● postcode 7310   ● pop 25,400

Nestled behind the lighthouse-topped Mersey Bluff, Devonport is the terminal for the *Spirit of Tasmania*, the vehicular ferry that runs between Victoria and Tasmania.

The Bluff Lighthouse was built in 1889 to direct the colony's rapidly growing sea traffic, and its light can be seen from up to 27km out to sea. Today, the port is still important and handles much of the export produce from the rich agricultural areas of northern Tasmania.

Devonport tries hard to attract tourists but its visitors are usually arriving or departing rather than actually staying.

Information
For information about Devonport and Tasmania in general, head for the Backpacker's Barn (☎ 6424 3628), at 12 Edward St, open daily from 9 am to 6 pm. It has a cafe, an excellent bushwalking shop, a fax service and showers that travellers can use for a small fee.

The Devonport Showcase (☎ 6424 8176), at 5 Best St, also has tourist information and demonstrations of arts and crafts. The centre is the official information centre (☎ 6424 4466) and is open daily from 9 am to 5 pm.

TASMANIA

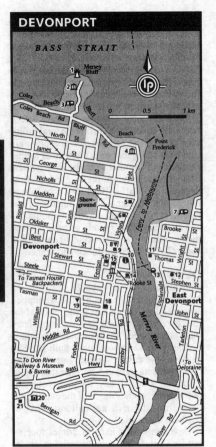

DEVONPORT

BASS STRAIT

Mersey Bluff

Coles Beach

Coles Beach Rd

Bluff Rd

North St

James St

George St

Nicholls St

Madden St

Oldaker St

Best St

Devonport

Stewart St

Steele St

Tasman St

To Tasman House Backpackers

William St

Middle Rd

Forbes St

To Don River Railway & Museum & Burnie

Bass Hwy

Berrigan Rd

Showground

Gunn St

Fenton St

Ferry to Melbourne

Point Frederick

Beach

Brooke St

Thomas St

Wright St

Rooke St

Stephen St

East Devonport

John St

Esplanade

Mersey River

Tarleton St

Formby Rd

River Rd

To Deloraine

0   0.5   1 km

DEVONPORT

PLACES TO STAY
3   Mersey Bluff Caravan Park
5   River View Lodge
6   Elimatta Motor Inn
7   Abel Tasman Caravan Park
9   Inner City Backpackers; Molly Molones
11 Edgewater Hotel & Motor Inn
14 Alexander & Formby Hotels
18 Mac Fie Manor
21 MacWright House (YHA)

PLACES TO EAT
8   Renusha's & Rialto Restaurants
19 Dangerous Liaisons

OTHER
1   Bluff Lighthouse
2   Tiagarra
4   Maritime & Folk Museum
10 Information Centre; Devonport Showcase; Old Devonport Town Coffee Shop
12 Rent-a-Bug
13 Spirit of Tasmania Ferry Terminal
15 Backpacker's Barn; Billabong Cafe
16 TRC Depot
17 Devonport Gallery
20 Home Hill

Tiagarra

The **Tasmanian Aboriginal Culture & Art Centre** is at Mersey Bluff, on the road to the lighthouse. It's known as Tiagarra, which is the Tasmanian Aboriginal word for 'keep', and was set up to preserve the art and culture of the Tasmanian Aborigines. The centre has a rare collection of more than 250 rock engravings, and is open daily from 9 am to 5 pm ($3).

Museums

The **Tasmanian Maritime & Folk Museum**, near the foreshore, has a display of model ships, old and new. It's recently been expanded and is open Tuesday to Sunday from 1 to 4.30 pm ($3).

The **Don River Railway & Museum**, 4km out of town on the Bass Hwy towards Ulverstone, features steam locomotives and passenger carriages, and you can take a ride on a vintage train along the banks of the Don River. It's open most days from 10 am to 4 pm; admission to the site costs $4, which is refunded if you pay for a steam train ride ($7/4).

Other Attractions

The **Devonport Gallery**, at 45-47 Stewart St, is open Monday to Friday from 10 am to 5 pm, and Sunday afternoons (free).

At 77 Middle Rd, not far from the YHA hostel, is **Home Hill**, which used to be the residence of Joseph and Dame Enid Lyons and is now administered by the National Trust. Joseph Lyons is the only Australian to have been both the premier of his state and prime minister of Australia, and Dame Enid Lyons was the first woman to become a member of the House of Representatives. Home Hill is open Tuesday to Thursday and weekends from 2 to 4 pm ($6).

Forest Glen Tea Gardens & Bird Sanctuary, 9km from town on the road to Sheffield, is a little sanctuary ringing with bird calls where you can view the endangered green swift parrot feeding among the tall trees.

Organised Tours

Tarkine Tours (☎ 6423 4690, 0418 143 057) runs tours to places like Cradle Mountain ($55), Pieman River ($70), Gordon River ($85), Arthur River ($65) and Leven Canyon ($50). Tasman Bush Tours (☎ 6492 1431), operating out of Tasman House Backpackers, also offers tours.

Places to Stay – Budget

The *Mersey Bluff Caravan Park* (☎ 6424 8655) is close to town, near Tiagarra. It's a pleasant place with some good beaches nearby. It has powered sites ($15), vans ($40) and cabins ($50). *Abel Tasman Caravan Park* (☎ 6427 8794, 6 Wright St) in East Devonport has camp sites ($10), on-site vans ($35 without linen) and cabins ($56).

Inner City Backpackers (☎ 6424 1898), above Molly Malones, provides backpacker accommodation for $13 per person. In *Tasman House Backpackers* (☎ 6423 2335, 169 Steele St) a dorm bed in former nurses' quarters costs $10 per person, a twin $12 per person, and an en suite double $28. It's a 15 minute walk from town and transport can be arranged when booking.

MacWright House (☎ 6424 5696, 115 Middle Rd), 400m past Home Hill, is Devonport's YHA hostel; it charges $10 a night and is a 40 minute walk from the town centre.

Two good hotels close to the centre of town are the *Alexander Hotel* (☎ 6424 2252, 78 Formby Rd), which charges $30/40 for comfortable singles/doubles and a continental breakfast; and the *Formby Hotel* (☎ 6424 1601, 82 Formby Rd), where rooms cost $35/45 with a cooked breakfast; en suite rooms are $15/20 dearer.

The *Edgewater Hotel & Motor Inn* (☎ 6427 8441, 2 Thomas St, East Devonport)

is not very attractive from the outside, but is close to the ferry terminal and charges from $45/50.

Places to Stay – Mid-Range

The friendly *River View Lodge* (☎ 6424 7357, 18 Victoria Parade), on the foreshore, has singles/doubles for $45/55 with shared facilities and $55/70 with en suite. The price includes breakfast. The lodge has a wheelchair friendly room and is deservedly popular.

Nearby, the *Elimatta Motor Inn* (☎ 6424 6555, 15 Victoria Parade) charges from $55/60.

Mac Fie Manor (☎ 6424 1719, 44 Macfie St) is a beautiful two storey Federation building charging $65/85 for B&B. Another great option is *Ochill Manor* (☎ 6428 2660), in the pretty town of Forth, 10km west of Devonport, where B&B is $85/120.

Places to Eat

The *Billabong Cafe* (12 Edward St), at the front of the Backpacker's Barn, has a largely vegetarian menu. The *Old Devonport Town Coffee Shop* in the Devonport Showcase is open daily and is good for a drink or a snack.

Most hotels have good counter meals for around $8 to $15; try *Molly Malones* (34 Best St).

Dangerous Liaisons (28 Forbes St), a short distance from the city centre, is open Tuesday to Friday for good value lunch and dinner (dinner only on Saturday). At the pleasant *Rialto Restaurant* (159 Rooke St), the pasta isn't fancy but service is swift. It's open Monday to Friday for lunch and every evening for dinner until late. Next door is *Renusha's* Indian restaurant.

Getting There & Away

Air See the Getting There & Away and Getting Around sections at the start of this chapter.

Bus TRC (☎ 1300 360 000) buses depart from and arrive at 9 Edward St, across the road from the Backpackers Barn. Buses also stop at the ferry terminal when the

TASMANIA

ferry is in town. TRC runs at least three services every day from Hobart to Launceston, on to Devonport and Burnie, and return. On weekdays most services continue to Smithton. At weekends, only one Saturday service operates to Smithton and there are no services on Sunday. The fare from Launceston to Devonport is $13.70.

TWT (☎ 1300 300 520) runs services to Sheffield, Gowrie Park, Cradle Mountain and the west coast. Similar services are provided by Maxwells (☎ 6492 1431), which runs buses on demand to Cradle Mountain, Lake St Clair, Walls of Jerusalem, Frenchmans Cap and other walking destinations. See The West section later in this chapter for details.

Outside the summer period, or if none of the scheduled services suit your particular needs, you can charter a minibus from Maxwells or the Backpackers Barn.

Car There are plenty of cheap car-rental firms such as Range/Rent-a-Bug (☎ 6427 9034), with VW Beetles for $25 to $40 a day. Major companies like Avis, Thrifty and Budget deliver to the ferry terminal.

Boat See the Getting There & Away section at the beginning of this chapter for details on the *Spirit of Tasmania* ferry service between Melbourne and Devonport. The TT Line terminal (☎ 1800 030 344) is on the Esplanade, East Devonport. You can't miss seeing the ferry, as it dominates the town when it's in port.

Getting Around

An airport bus meets every flight. A shuttle bus runs between accommodation options and the ferry. Local buses, operated by Mersey Coaches, run from Monday to Friday – pick up a timetable at the Devonport Showcase. A small ferry departs from just opposite the post office. On the eastern side of the river it docks next to the *Spirit of Tasmania*. It runs on demand weekdays and Saturday ($1.50 one way).

AROUND DEVONPORT

Formerly a farm, the **Asbestos Range National Park**, 25km from Devonport, was named after the highest peak in the park, Mt Asbestos, asbestos being one of many minerals discovered in the area. Asbestos hasn't been mined here for over 80 years, but the negative connotations are such that a new name is to be announced.

Animals and birds are prolific, and there are signposted walking tracks throughout the park. The **Springlawn Nature Walk** takes about an hour from the car park and includes a boardwalk over a wetland to a bird hide.

There are four *camp sites* in the park with pit toilets, bore water and firewood provided. For more information, contact the park ranger on ☎ 6428 6277.

ULVERSTONE
● postcode 7315　　　● pop 9800

With a number of excellent B&Bs and a seafood restaurant in a picture-perfect waterfront position, Ulverstone, at the mouth of the Leven River, has the potential to become a rather classy holiday retreat.

The **local history museum**, at 50 Main St, focuses on European pioneers and their activities in the region ($3/1).

If you're driving from Ulverstone to **Penguin**, consider taking the old Bass Hwy: as you approach Penguin the countryside takes on a 'Thomas the Tank Engine' feel as cottage gardens, a narrow-gauge railway track and the seaside somehow all fit into the scene. If you then travel from Penguin towards Gunns Plains, you'll pass the turn-off to **Pindari Deer Farm** (☎ 6437 6171), an animal park on a hilltop with sweeping views encompassing Mt Roland and Table Cape; admission is $7.50/5 for adults/children, and meals and upmarket accommodation are also available.

Gunns Plains can be reached directly from Ulverstone, about 30km north; daily guided tours of the spectacular **Gunns Plains wet cave** leave hourly from 10 am to 4 pm ($8/4). Also in Gunns Plains is the low key **Wings Farm Park** (☎ 6429 1335), where you can see cattle, rabbits, chickens, emus and reptiles, or fish for trout in the river, which we're told is also home to platypuses. Admission is $2. The park is really more of a budget accommodation option than anything else – a good place to stay with kids.

Further south (41km from Ulverstone) is **Leven Canyon**, a magnificent gorge with a number of walking tracks.

Places to Stay & Eat

The *Ulverstone Caravan Park (☎ 6425 2624)*, in Water St, is close to town and has camp sites ($12 a double), on-site vans ($35), en suite cabins ($45, or $52 with linen) and units with linen ($57).

Furner's Hotel (☎ 6425 1488, 42 Reibey St) has simple singles/doubles for $40/65, including a cooked breakfast. There is a bistro downstairs. More stylish is the *Lighthouse Hotel (☎ 6425 1197)*, on the corner of Victoria and Reibey Sts, which has rooms for $85/95. Meals, including children's meals, are available, and there is a good indoor play area.

There are four very good B&Bs in or around town: the *Ocean View Guest House (☎ 6425 5401, 1 Victoria St)*, which is in a great location 100m from the beach ($65/85); the circa 1800 *Winterbrook B&B (☎ 6425 6324, 28 Eastland Drive)*, which is in a large suburban garden ($75/90); *Westella House (☎ 6425 6222, Westella Drive)*, which is on the highway a little out of town but is spacious, warm and inviting ($110 to $128 a double); and, further out still, *Ochill Manor*, in the idyllic little town of Forth, east of Ulverstone. B&B is $85/120.

Pedro the Fisherman, down by the wharf, has cheap but filling takeaway fish and chips. Next door is *Pedro's the Restaurant*, an appealing upmarket seafood restaurant overlooking the water.

Mrs Simpson's, on Reibey St, is a combined deli, cafe and restaurant with an interesting menu and lots of home-made goodies.

Getting There & Away

See Getting There & Around at the start of this section. During the week, Metro Burnie (☎ 6431 3822) has regular local buses to Ulverstone for $2.80.

North-West

Tasmania's magnificent north-west coast is a land as rich in history as it is diverse in scenery. Its story goes back 40,000 years to a time when giant kangaroos and wombats roamed the area. Aboriginal tribes once took shelter in the caves along the coast, leaving a legacy of rock engravings and middens.

Europeans quickly realised the potential of the region and settlers moved further and further west, building towns along the coast and inland on the many rivers. The area was soon transformed into a vital part of the young colony's developing economy.

Getting There & Around

Air The airport for the region is in Wynyard, and is known as both Wynyard and Burnie airport. See the Getting There & Away and Getting Around sections at the start of this chapter for further information.

Bus TRC (☎ 1300 360 000) runs several buses daily from Hobart to Launceston ($19.50), then along the north coast to Devonport ($13.70) and Burnie ($18.30), from where you can catch another TRC service on weekdays and Saturday to Wynyard ($20.90), Stanley ($29) and Smithton ($29).

Car The main route from the north to the west coast is the Murchison Hwy from Somerset (near Burnie) to Queenstown. The Western Explorer is the name given to an alternative route from Smithton to the west coast that incorporates a difficult section between Arthur River and Corinna. Although this road can be negotiated by vehicles without 4WD and is promoted as a tourist route, it is remote, mostly unsealed and can get potholes, so should probably not be attempted in bad weather or at night. At Corinna, there is a vehicular ferry across the Pieman River, from where you can continue on to Zeehan and the rest of the west coast.

The other important road in the area is the road from the Murchison Hwy (A10) through to Cradle Mountain Lodge. This is the link road (C132) that enables cars and buses to travel directly from Devonport to

TASMANIA

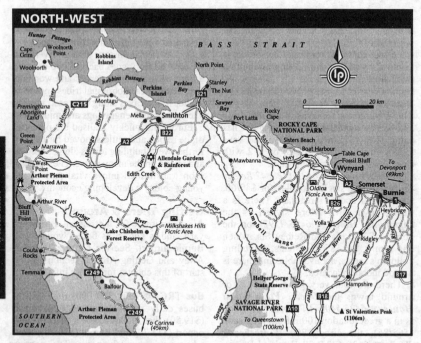

NORTH-WEST

Queenstown, thereby avoiding the north-west coast altogether.

BURNIE

- postcode 7320   • pop 21,000

Although Burnie sits on the shores of Emu Bay and is backed by rich farming land, it is factory smoke, not the views, that usually welcomes the visitor to Tasmania's fourth largest city. One of Burnie's main assets is its deep-water port, which makes cargo shipping an important industry.

The town started growing mainly potatoes, until the discovery of tin at Mt Bischoff in Waratah.

In 1878, the Van Diemen's Land Company opened a wooden tramway between the mine at Waratah and the port of Burnie. This was the humble beginning of the important Emu Bay Railway which, in the 1900s, linked the port of Burnie to the rich silver fields of Zeehan and Rosebery. The Emu Bay Railway, which travels through some

wild and impressive country, still operates today but it does not carry passengers.

The Tasmanian Travel & Information Centre (☎ 6434 6111), in Little Alexander St, attached to the Pioneer Village Museum, is a good source of information on Tasmania's north-west.

Things to See & Do

The **Pioneer Village Museum**, on Little Alexander St next to the Civic Plaza, has an authentic blacksmith's shop, printer and boot shop. This impressive museum is open Monday to Friday from 9 am to 5 pm, and weekends from 1.30 to 4.30 pm ($4.50/1.50).

Burnie Park is quite pleasant and features an animal sanctuary and the oldest building in town, the Burnie Inn.

The **Lactos cheese factory**, on Old Surrey Rd, is open daily and you can taste and purchase the products. The **Burnie Regional Art Gallery**, in Wilmot St, is open daily and is also worth a look.

There are a number of **waterfalls** and **viewpoints** in the Burnie area, including Roundhill Lookout and Fern Glade, just 3km from the city centre, and the impressive Guide Falls at Ridgley, 16km away. The impressive **Emu Valley Rhododendron Gardens**, 8km south of Burnie, is open daily between September and February ($3).

Places to Stay

It's unlikely that you'll want to spend a night in Burnie.

At Cooee, 4km west of Burnie on the Bass Hwy, the *Treasure Island Caravan Park* (☎ 6431 1925) has powered camp sites ($14 a double), on-site vans ($30/36 a single/double) and cabins ($45/55). It also has hostel accommodation for $12 per person. The associated *Ocean View Motel* has neat rooms for $55/65.

Among the cheapest of the hotels is the *Regent* (☎ 6431 1933, 26 North Terrace), which has rooms for $30/40. *Glen Osborne House* (☎ 6431 9866, 9 Aileen Crescent), about 1km from the town centre, is a beautiful period house with large en suite rooms for $80/100, including breakfast.

Apartments Down Town (☎ 6432 3219, 52 Alexander St) has self-contained Art Deco rooms from $80/95 with a continental breakfast.

Places to Eat

If you are staying in Burnie or just looking for somewhere to pick up a meal on your way further west, drop into the wonderful *Kinesis Health Eatery* (☎ 6431 5963, 53 Mount St). Its old club lounge chairs and country kitchen atmosphere are a welcome change from the more spartan decor of most of the town's cafes and takeaways. It opens at 8.30 am from Tuesday to Saturday and closes at 6 pm Tuesday to Thursday, late on Friday and at around 4 pm on Saturday.

The *Beach Hotel* (1 Wilson St), on the waterfront, usually has a good spread, while the *Mallee Grill* (26 North Terrace), in the Regent Hotel, serves reliable grilled steaks, gourmet sausages and kebabs.

The *Kasbah Pizza Hut* (25 Ladbrooke St) is open until late, and opposite is *Li Yin*

Chinese restaurant. The *Rialto Gallery Restaurant* (☎ 6431 7718, 46 Wilmot St) has good cheap pasta from $10.

Flannery's Restaurant (☎ 6431 9393, 104 Wilmot St) and the *Burnleigh Restaurant* (☎ 6431 3947, 8 Alexander St) offer a la carte meals. Out of the centre, at the West Park Nursery on Park Grove just past the Burnie Park, is the *Grove Country Kitchen*, a pleasant place for lunch.

Getting There & Away

See Getting There & Around at the start of the North-West section for details. During the week, Metro Burnie (☎ 6431 3822), at 30 Strahan St, has regular buses to Ulverstone, Penguin and Wynyard that depart from the bus stops in Cattley St.

HELLYER GORGE

Seven kilometres from Burnie is the small town of Somerset, at the junction of the Murchison and Bass highways. Hellyer Gorge is about 40km south of Somerset on the banks of the Hellyer River. The highway winds its way through the impressive gorge, where there is a picnic area.

WYNYARD

• postcode 7325   • pop 4500

Sheltered by the impressive Table Cape and Fossil Bluff, Wynyard sits on the seafront and the banks of the Inglis River.

Although there's not much to see in the town, Wynyard is a good base from which to explore the many attractions in the area. There is a Visitor Information Centre in Goldie St, not far from the wharves.

Places to Stay & Eat

Close to town, on the Esplanade, *Wynyard Caravan Park* (☎ 6442 1998) has hostel beds ($14), camp sites ($10), on-site vans ($34 a double) and cabins ($54 a double).

The *Wynyard Youth Hostel* (☎ 6442 2013, 36 Dodgin St) is one block south of the main street and has beds for $13. If you've arrived by air, it's only a five minute walk from the airport.

The *Federal Hotel* (☎ 6442 2056, 82 Goldie St), in the middle of town, has singles/

doubles for $35/55, including breakfast; the dining room is open from 7 am to 8 pm every day except Sunday, when it shuts at 2 pm.

Alexandria (☎ *6442 4411)*, at the start of the road to Table Cape, has good quality B&B for $65/85.

AROUND WYNYARD

Three kilometres from Wynyard is **Fossil Bluff**, where the oldest marsupial fossil ever found in Australia was unearthed. The soft sandstone here features numerous shell fossils deposited when the level of Bass Strait was much higher.

Other attractions in the area include **Table Cape**, which has unforgettable views, some of the best of which can be had from the stunning, modern *Skyescape* (☎ *6442 1876, 282 Tollymore Rd)*, where B&B is $130 to $180 a double. There is also a tulip farm and a lighthouse on the cape. **Boat Harbour Beach**, 14km from Wynyard, is a beautiful bay with white sand and crystal-blue water. If you want to stay the night, the *Boat Harbour Beach Backpackers* (☎ *6445 1273)*, in Strawberry Lane not far from the beach, charges $14 per person. Pick-up from the highway is available. The town also has a *caravan park*, a *motel* and *cottage* accommodation.

Nearby, in the **Rocky Cape National Park**, is Sisters Beach, an 8km expanse of glistening white sand with safe swimming and good fishing. Also in the park is the 10 hectare **Birdland Native Gardens**, which has information on many native bird species. You can also visit a number of waterfalls, including Detention Falls, which is 3km south of Myalla, and Dip Falls, near Mawbanna.

Unless you have your own transport, you will have to hitch to get to most of these places. Redline Coaches will drop you at the turn-off to Boat Harbour (3km) and Sisters Beach (8km).

STANLEY

• postcode 7331   • pop 600

Nestled at the foot of the extraordinary Circular Head (better known as The Nut), Stanley has changed little since its early days. In 1826 it became the headquarters of the London-based Van Diemen's Land Company, which was granted a charter to settle and cultivate Circular Head and the north-western tip of Tasmania.

The area prospered when it began shipping large quantities of mutton, beef and potatoes to Victoria's goldfields, and continued to prosper when settlers discovered rich dairying land behind Sisters Hills and tin reserves at Mt Bischoff.

Today, Stanley is a charming fishing village with many historic buildings. Information is available at the Nut chairlift. Pick up a copy of *Welcome to Stanley*, which has a map and details of historic buildings.

The Nut

This striking 152m-high volcanic rock formation, thought to be 12.5 million years old, can be seen for many kilometres around Stanley. It's a steep, 20 minute climb to the top, but the view is definitely worth it. A chairlift operates, weather permitting, from 9 am to 5.30 pm in the high season and 10 am to 4 pm in low season; rides cost $6/4/15 for adults/children/families. At the top you can take a leisurely stroll from one lookout to the next or catch the Nut Buggy ($5/free for adults/children).

Other Attractions

The old bluestone building on the seafront is the **Van Diemen's Land Company Store**, designed by colonial architect John Lee Archer and dating from 1844. The company's headquarters were at **Highfield**, 2km north of Stanley. This historic site is open Tuesday to Thursday and weekends ($2 entry to outbuildings and grounds, $5 entry to full site).

Near the wharf in Stanley is a particularly fine old bluestone building that used to be a grain store (now a restaurant). It was built in the mid-19th century from stones brought to Stanley as ship's ballast.

The little folk museum called the **Discovery Centre**, in Church St, is open daily for most of the year from 10 am to 4.30 pm ($3).

Other buildings of historical interest include **Lyons Cottage**, in Church St, which was the birthplace of former prime minister

Joseph Lyons (open from 10 am to 4 pm, admission by donation), and the **Presbyterian church**, which was probably Australia's first prefabricated building, bought in England and transported to Stanley in 1885.

Places to Stay
The *Stanley Youth Hostel (☎ 6458 1266)*, in Wharf Rd, is part of the *Stanley Caravan Park* and charges $12 a night. The caravan park has powered sites ($13), on-site vans ($30) and cabins ($40 to $50).

Pol & Pen (☎ 6458 1186, 8 Pearce St) is a pair of two-bedroom self-contained cottages, which are good value at $65 a double. The *Union Hotel (☎ 6458 1161)*, in Church St, has basic singles/doubles for $25/40; breakfast is extra. There are many B&Bs dotted around Stanley; prices range from $90 to $130 a double in the holiday season – bargain hard at other times, though some will be closed in winter. A list is available from the cafe at the Nut chairlift (☎ 6458 1286).

Places to Eat
The best of fresh fish and crayfish are available at a takeaway, cafe and *seafood restaurant (2 Alexander Terrace)*. The cafe and shop close at 6 pm when the restaurant opens.

Sullivans (25 Church St), a licensed restaurant, is open daily and serves light lunches, teas and dinner.

AROUND STANLEY
Twenty-two kilometres from Stanley, **Smithton** serves one of Tasmania's largest forestry areas and is also the administrative centre for Circular Head.

Allendale Gardens, on the B22 road to Edith Creek, is a good place to walk around or relax; the two-hectare property includes impressive botanical gardens, a rainforest walk, a wildflower section and a cafe serving Devonshire teas. The centre is open daily from 10 am to 6 pm, from October to April ($6.50/3).

Temperate rainforest and button-grass moorland can be found at **Milkshake Hills Forest Reserve**, 45km south of Smithton. A further 26km south-west of the reserve, set in lovely rainforest, is tranquil **Lake Chisholm**.

MARRAWAH
Marrawah, the most westerly town in Tasmania, is where the wild Indian Ocean occasionally throws up the remains of ships wrecked on the dangerous and rugged west coast. There is no regular public transport to Marrawah – a fact one can't help thinking is probably a blessing as well as a curse.

The area has seen little disturbance from European development and was once popular with the Tasmanian Aborigines. Many signs of these people remain, and particular areas have been proclaimed reserves to protect the remaining rock carvings, middens and hut depressions. The main **Aboriginal sites** are at Preminghana, near Green Point and West Point.

The township of Marrawah consists of a hotel serving daily counter meals, and a general store selling petrol and supplies. The hotel has no accommodation, but there is a basic *camp site* at beautiful Green Point, 2km from Marrawah, and at the time of research the general store was doing up a bus as backpacker accommodation. The pleasant *Glendonald Cottage (☎ 6457 1191)* is $70 a double. This region is good for fishing, canoeing, camping and bushwalking, or just for getting away from it all. Marrawah's main attraction, however, is its enormous **surf** – rounds of the state's surfing and windsurfing championships are held here each year.

ARTHUR RIVER
The sleepy town of Arthur River, 14km south of Marrawah, is mainly a collection of holiday houses belonging to people who come here to fish. There is no public transport.

Apart from the fishing, visitors come here to explore the **Arthur Pieman Protected Area** and to take a **cruise** on the Arthur River. Arthur River Cruises (☎ 6457 1158) departs at 10 am and returns around 3 pm. You cruise up the river to the confluence of the Arthur and Frankland rivers, where you enjoy a barbecue and guided walk. The cruise ($40 an adult) runs most days provided a minimum of eight people have booked.

West Coast Scenic River Cruises (☎ 6457 1288) also cruises the river. A barbecue lunch at the kiosk is included in the price of $35.

TASMANIA

Places to Stay & Eat

There is a *kiosk* with basic supplies and a *camp site* with basic facilities. Alternatively, you can stay at *Arthur River Holiday Units* (☎ *6457 1288*) for $60/70 a single/double, *Ocean View Holiday Cottage* (☎ *6452 1278*) for $85 a double or *Sunset Holiday Villas* (☎ *6457 1197*) for $80 a double.

The West

Nature at its most awe-inspiring is the attraction of Tasmania's rugged and magnificent west coast. Formidable mountains, button grass plains, ancient rivers, tranquil lakes, dense rainforests and a treacherous coast are all features of this compelling and beautiful region, some of which is now World Heritage Area.

Many centuries before the arrival of Europeans, this part of Tasmania was home to many of the state's Aboriginal people, and plenty of archaeological evidence, some of it more than 20,000 years old, has been found of these original inhabitants.

Prior to 1932, when the road from Hobart to Queenstown was built, the only way into the area was by sea, through the dangerously narrow Hells Gates into Macquarie Harbour. Despite such inaccessibility, early European settlement brought explorers, convicts, soldiers, loggers, prospectors, railway gangs and fishermen, while the 20th century has brought outdoor adventurers, naturalists and environmental crusaders.

It was over the wild rivers, beautiful lakes and tranquil valleys of Tasmania's south-west that battles between environmentalists and governments raged. The proposed damming of the Franklin and Lower Gordon rivers caused the greatest and longest-running environmental debate in Australia's history in the 1980s and has subsequently seen the boom of ecotourism in Strahan.

Getting There & Around

TWT (☎ 1300 300 520) runs one bus a day on Tuesday, Thursday, Friday and Sunday from Hobart to Bronte Junction ($20.60), Lake St Clair ($28.70), Derwent Bridge ($24.70) and Queenstown ($36.20). Buses return on the same day. Buses run on Tuesday, Thursday and Saturday from Queenstown to Zeehan ($5.60), Rosebery ($11), Tullah ($12.40), Cradle Mountain Lodge ($17.60), Gowrie Park ($24.70), Sheffield ($27.50), Devonport ($30.10) and Launceston ($43.10); there are return services on the same days. Buses for Strahan depart from Queenstown ($5.60) on Tuesday, Thursday, Saturday and Sunday, and for Queenstown from Strahan on Tuesday, Thursday and Sunday.

For information about alternative services for those walking the Overland Track, see Cradle Mountain-Lake St Clair later in this section.

CORINNA
• postcode 7321

Corinna, 28km south-west of Savage River, was once a thriving gold-mining settlement but is now little more than a ghost town. These days it's the scenery and the Pieman River Cruises (☎ 6446 1170) that attract visitors. The cruise passes an impressive gorge and forests of eucalypts, ferns and Huon pines on the way to Pieman Heads, strewn with massive logs. Costing $30 (children $15), the tours depart daily at 10.30 am and return at 2.30 pm.

The only accommodation is at the *Pieman Retreat Cabins* (☎ *6446 1170*). Cabins can sleep up to six people and cost $60 a double and $10 for each extra person. The cabins are self-contained and linen is available at extra cost.

The Pieman River Barge operates daily from 9 am to 5 pm ($10).

ROSEBERY
• postcode 7470   • pop 1900

Gold was discovered in Rosebery in the late 1800s and mining began early in the next century with the completion of the Emu Bay Railway between Burnie and Zeehan. However, when the Zeehan lead smelters closed in 1913 operations also closed in Rosebery. The Electrolytic Zinc Company

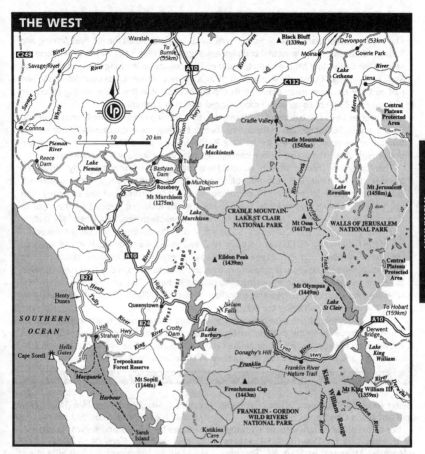

THE WEST

then bought and reopened the mine in 1936 and it has operated ever since.

Eight kilometres south of town, at the abandoned mining town of Williamsford, is the start of an excellent walk to the impressive **Montezuma Falls**.

ZEEHAN

● postcode 7469   ● pop 1100

In 1882 rich deposits of silver and lead were discovered in the quiet little town of Zeehan, and by the turn of that century it had become a booming mining centre known as Silver City, with a population that peaked at nearly 10,000. In its heyday Zeehan had 26 hotels, and its Gaiety Theatre seated 1000 people. In 1908, however, the mines began to fail and the town declined.

With the reopening and expansion of the Renison Tin Mine at Renison Bell, Zeehan experienced a revival in the late 1960s, becoming the housing base for Renison Ltd.

Things to See

Buildings that remain from the early boom days include the once-famous Grand Hotel, encompassing the Gaiety Theatre, which is

Abt Railway

This is why the company that mined Mt Lyell for so long was called the Mt Lyell Mining *and* Railway Company. If the industrial complex envisaged by its founders was to be a success, a railway line connecting Mt Lyell with the port of Teepookana on the King River, and later with Strahan, was vital. Construction began in 1894 and, by the time it was completed, the line had cost the company more than half its capital investment in the entire mining enterprise and covered 35km of some of the most rugged terrain in Australia.

Opened in 1896 and extended to Strahan in 1899, the line ran along the Queen River and up the one-in-16 Abt section to Rinadeena, before heading down the one-in-20 Abt section through magnificent rainforest to the King River. Here it crossed a stunning, curved 400m bridge high above the water, before continuing on to Teepookana and Regatta Point.

The Abt system (named after its inventor) was used to cover terrain originally considered too steep for the haulage of huge quantities of ore. In this arrangement, a third toothed rack rail is positioned between the two conventional rails, and locomotives are equipped with geared pinion wheels that lock into the rack rail, thereby making it possible for the trains to climb and descend gradients they would otherwise be unable to negotiate when fully loaded.

The railway, which was Queenstown's only link with the outside world before the opening of the Lyell Hwy in 1932, was closed in 1963 and soon fell into disrepair, but throughout the 1990s members of the Mt Lyell Abt Railway Society spent incalculable hours clearing vegetation, fixing drainage and mending bridges in the hope that one day they might be able to secure enough funding to reconstruct the railway. In July 1998 their dreams were realised when federal Cabinet approved the allocation of $20.45 million of Federation Funding to cover the full cost of restoring the line.

Today, the whole of the west coast, but particularly Queenstown, is pinning many of its hopes for prosperity on the drawing potential of this scenic and historic railway. All attempts will be made to have the first train running on the reconstructed line by the first week in January 2001, and it is expected that the journey will take between 1½ and 1¾ hours.

being renovated, the post office, the bank and St Luke's Church.

For an excellent insight into the workings of a mine, visit the **West Coast Pioneers' Memorial Museum**, in Main St. The museum also features an interesting mineral collection and an exhibit of early west-coast railways. It's open daily from 8.30 am to 5 pm ($5/3).

Trial Harbour, the original port for Zeehan, is a beautiful place for bush camping, while the **Henty Dunes** has expansive white sand dunes that should not be missed on the drive from Zeehan to Strahan.

Places to Stay & Eat

At the *Treasure Island West Coast Caravan Park* (☎ *6471 6633*), in Hurst St, there are camp sites ($12), on-site vans ($35) and

cabins ($60). The *Heemskirk Motor Hotel* (☎ *6471 6107*), in Main St, has singles/doubles for $73/79 and serves meals.

The old *Hotel Cecil* (☎ *6471 6221*), also in Main St, has rooms for $40/60 and self-contained holiday units that sleep four for $80 a double. Counter meals are available daily. The *Museum Coffee Lounge* (in the Pioneers' Museum) is a good place for a light lunch.

QUEENSTOWN
• postcode 7467   • pop 2500

The final, winding descent into Queenstown from the Lyell Hwy is unforgettable. With deep, eroded gullies and naked, multicoloured hills, there is no escaping that the destruction of the surrounding area is a direct result of mining.

The discovery of alluvial gold in the Queen River valley in 1881 brought prospectors to the area. Two years later, mining began on the rich Mt Lyell deposits and for nearly a decade miners extracted a few ounces of gold a day ignoring the mountain's rich copper reserves. In 1891, however, the Mt Lyell Mining Company began to concentrate on copper, which soon became the most profitable mineral on the west coast.

After 20 years of mining, the rainforested hills around Queenstown had been stripped bare – three million tonnes of timber had been felled to feed the furnaces. By 1900, uncontrolled pollution from the copper smelters was killing any vegetation that had not already been cut down, and bushfires – fuelled by the sulphur-impregnated soils and dead stumps – raged through the hills every summer. The west's high rainfall then washed away all the topsoil, preventing revegetation for many years. The smelters closed in 1969 and in recent years patches of green have begun to appear on the slopes.

Today the town is trying hard to promote itself as a tourist destination and has much to offer those interested in social and industrial history. The restoration of the Abt railway between Queenstown and Strahan is a major tourism project that it is hoped will revitalise the entire west coast. The station was originally on a site in Driffield St until recently occupied by the information centre, Lyell Tours (☎ 6471 2388). Following a fire, Lyell Tours moved across the road, and it is expected that a station will be established in its place to service the restored railway.

Queenstown has character and even, at times, a stark attractiveness, but it is not pretty. However, meals and accommodation are generally cheaper here than they are in Strahan, and if you are travelling on a budget and intend exploring more of the west than Strahan and the Gordon River, you might consider making it your base.

Things to See & Do

The **Galley Museum** started life as the Imperial Hotel (1898) and was the first brick hotel in Queenstown. The museum features an intriguing collection of old photographs with wonderfully idiosyncratic captions written by the photographer, Eric Thomas. From October to May it's open Monday to Friday from 10 am to 6 pm, and Saturday from 1 to 6 pm ($3). The rest of the year hours are 10 am to 4.30 pm and 1 to 4.30 pm respectively.

There are good views from **Spion Kop Lookout**, in the centre of town (follow Bowes St). If you look at the football oval you will notice that it is cream instead of green: Queenstown's footy team is tough – it plays on gravel, not grass.

There is a **chairlift** that rises 369m, giving good views of the multicoloured hills ($4/2).

The mine can be viewed on above or below-ground **mine tours** run by Lyell Tours (☎ 6471 2388). The impressive **Iron Blow**, the original open cut mine that is now abandoned, can be seen from a lookout off the Lyell Hwy.

Places to Stay

The *Queenstown Cabin & Tourist Park* (☎ 6471 1332, 17 Grafton St) is about 500m from the town centre and has bunkhouse accommodation ($15) and camp sites ($13). Infinitely prettier is the camping ground at *Lake Burbury*, just east of Bradshaw Bridge on the way to Hobart.

The *Mountain View Holiday Lodge* (☎ 6471 1163, 1 Penghana Rd) has very basic hostel accommodation for $10 a night and small motel units for $55 a double.

The *Empire Hotel* (☎ 6471 1699, 2 Orr St) is a lovely old hotel with pleasant singles/doubles from $20/35.

The *Mount Lyell Motor Inn* (☎ 6471 1888, 1 Orr St) has standard motel units from $35/45, while the *Gold Rush Motor Inn* (☎ 6471 1005) has attractive self-contained units for $80 a single or double.

Penghana Guesthouse (☎ 6471 2560), the former residence of the general manager of the Mt Lyell Mining Company, stands grandly above the town amid a surprising number of trees (surprising, given that this is Queenstown); upmarket B&B is $90 to $150 a double or twin.

Places to Eat

In Orr St, *Axel's* has good burgers and light snacks. Around the corner, in the BP service station, is the *Asian Eating House*. The *Empire Hotel* serves counter meals in a pleasant dining room with an open fire. *Smelters Restaurant* (☎ 6471 1511), at the Silver Hills Motor Inn on Penghana Rd, has an a la carte menu with mains around $17.

STRAHAN

• postcode 7468   • pop 800

Strahan, 37km from Queenstown on Macquarie Harbour, is the only town on this rugged and dangerous coast.

Treacherous seas, the lack of natural harbours and high rainfall discouraged early settlement of the region until Macquarie Harbour was discovered by sailors searching for the source of the Huon pine that frequently washed up on the southern beaches.

In those days, the area was totally inaccessible by land and very difficult to reach by sea, and in 1821 these dubious assets prompted the establishment of a penal settlement on **Sarah Island**, in the middle of the harbour. Its main function was to isolate the worst of the colony's convicts and to use their muscle to harvest the huge stands of Huon pine. The convicts worked upriver 12 hours a day, often in leg irons, felling the pines and rafting them back to the island's saw-pits where they were used to build ships and furniture.

Sarah Island appeared in Marcus Clarke's graphic novel about convict life *For the Term of His Natural Life*. In 1834, however, after the establishment of the 'escape-proof' penal settlement at Port Arthur, Sarah Island was abandoned.

As the port for Queenstown, Strahan reached its peak of prosperity with the west-coast mining boom and the completion of the Mt Lyell Mining Company's railway line in the late 1890s. Steamers operated regularly between Strahan and Hobart, and Launceston and Melbourne carrying copper, gold, silver, lead, timber and passengers. The closure of some of the mines and the opening of the Emu Bay Railway from Zeehan to Burnie led to the decline of Strahan as a port.

Convict Cannibalism

No story highlights more the desperation of the few convicts who dared to escape from Macquarie Harbour than that of Alexander Pearce. Managing to escape twice, Pearce took to the grisly habit of eating his fellow escapees. Upon his capture after a second attempt, he confessed to his crime and, to prove it, produced a bloody morsel of his mate from his pocket!

Strahan's harbourside main street is undeniably gorgeous, but the town itself is in danger of becoming a garishly folksy tourist trap. It draws droves of visitors longing for a wilderness-in-Reeboks experience aboard the Gordon River cruises and is believed to be the second most popular tourist destination in the state after Port Arthur.

Information

The architecturally innovative Strahan visitors centre (☎ 6471 7622), on The Esplanade, is a tourist attraction in its own right.

There is an office of the Department of Parks, Wildlife & Heritage in the old customs house building close to the town centre. This building also houses the post office. For banking, the post office is a Commonwealth Bank agent and the newsagent handles ANZ accounts.

Things to See

Beyond the Huon pine reception desk at the Strahan visitors centre is **West Coast Reflections**, an informative display about the history of the south-west. The centre is open daily from 10 am to 6 pm (8 pm in summer). Admission is $4.50 (children free), and from outside you can see a good deal of the display through the windows.

The **Union Steamship Building** (1894) and the **Customs House** are two imposing solid reminders of Strahan's former glory. The walk to **Hogarth Falls** starts east of the town centre at Peoples Park; allow one hour return.

Six kilometres from the town is the impressive 33km **Ocean Beach**, where the sunsets have to be seen to be believed. In October, when the birds return from their winter migration, the beach is also a mutton-bird rookery. About 14km along the road from Strahan to Zeehan are the spectacular **Henty Dunes**, which are sand dunes, many of them more than 30m high.

Organised Tours

Gordon River Cruise The traditional way of experiencing the beauty of the Gordon River is on one of the cruises that operate out of Strahan.

Gordon River Cruises (☎ 6471 7187) has trips from 9 am to 2 pm (and also 2 to 7 pm in January) for $45/25 for adults/children, including morning tea; and also, from October to May, from 9 am to 3.30 pm for $62/30, including a smorgasbord lunch.

World Heritage Tours (☎ 6471 7174) charges $44/20 for a trip from 9 am to 3.30 pm; its catamaran is purpose built and a smorgasbord lunch is available on board ($8).

All cruises include a visit to Sarah Island, a Heritage Rainforest Walk and views of Hells Gates (the narrow entrance to Macquarie Harbour).

West Coast Yacht Charters (☎ 6471 7422) offers various fishing and sightseeing cruises including a two day/two night cruise which costs $320/160; everything is included in the price.

Seaplane Tour A highly recommended way to see the river and surrounding World Heritage Area is on a seaplane tour with Wilderness Air (☎ 6471 7280). The planes take off from Strahan's wharf about every 1½ hours from 9 am onwards and fly up the river to Sir John Falls, where they land so that you can take a walk in the rainforest before flying back via Sarah Island and Ocean Beach. The 80 minute flight is well worth the $105. Demand for flights is heavy, so book ahead.

Jet-Boat Ride Wild Rivers Jet (☎ 6471 7174; book at Strahan wharf) offers 50-minute jet-boat rides up the King River for $39/25 for adults/children; the rides operate daily from 9 am to 5 pm.

Places to Stay

Although Strahan has a range of accommodation, places are often full in summer and closed in winter, so it's best to book. Outside the high season you should be able to negotiate very reasonable stand-by discounts if you make inquiries late in the day. Much of the accommodation in the central part of town is run by Strahan Village (☎ 6471 7191, fax 6471 7389) and can be booked through its new reservation office on the corner of The Esplanade and Esk St. Still more of the town's accommodation, including the hostel, is handled by Strahan Central (☎ 6471 7612), on the corner of The Esplanade and Harold St.

The **Strahan Caravan Park** (☎ 6471 7239), in Innes St, charges $10 for a camp site for two. There's also a **camping ground** with basic facilities 15km away at Macquarie Heads.

At $13, the **Strahan Youth Hostel** (☎ 6471 7255, 6471 7612), in Harvey St, has the cheapest accommodation in town. It also has serviced cabins at $43 a double. It is about a 10 minute walk from the town centre.

You can get B&B for $30 a person on a sailing boat moored at the wharf. Book through **West Coast Yacht Charters** (☎ 6471 7422); you have to disembark before 8 am, when cruises start.

Ring ☎ 6471 7191 to book the following: **Hamer's Hotel**, opposite the wharf, which has basic singles/doubles for $48/65; **Strahan Village**, a group of self-contained cottages on the waterfront built in various colonial styles ($99 to $155 a double); and **Strahan Inn**, the motel on the hill behind the Strahan Village reservations office ($85 to $115).

Upstairs at **Strahan Central** (☎ 6471 7612) are a number of attractive split level suites for $120 to $130 a double. Further around the harbour, **Gordon Gateway Chalet** (☎ 6471 7165) has attractive, modern units with views across the harbour for $110 to $150 a double.

Luxurious B&B is offered by **Franklin Manor** (☎ 6471 7311) for $110 to $208 a double and by **Ormiston House** (☎ 6471 7077) for $180 to $210 a double. Both are on the Esplanade.

For something different, hire an ocean kayak (inquire at the visitor centre) and head up to the *Boom Camp*, at Pine Landing on the Gordon River (the cruise companies should transport you and your craft, for a fee). Here you can spend a couple of days exploring the river. There's a seven bunk cabin with mattresses and basic facilities, but no cooking facilities or bedding, and we gather it's 'first in, first served'.

Places to Eat
Strahan Central has a pleasant cafe serving interesting meals. *Hamer's Hotel* and the *Regatta Point Tavern*, on the Esplanade, have counter meals; Hamer's Hotel is in the heart of Strahan, but the Regatta Point Tavern is the cheaper of the two. The *Strahan Inn*, in Jolly St, has a good restaurant.

You can get excellent meals at both *Franklin Manor (☎ 6471 7311)* and *Ormiston House (☎ 6471 7077)*, but it's best to book.

FRANKLIN-GORDON WILD RIVERS NATIONAL PARK
This World Heritage listed park includes the catchment areas of the Franklin and Olga rivers and part of the Gordon River, as well as the excellent bushwalking region known as Frenchmans Cap. It has a number of unique plant species and a major Aboriginal archaeological site at **Kutikina Cave**.

Much of the park is impenetrable rainforest, but the Lyell Hwy traverses its northern end and there are a few short walks that start from the road. These include hikes to **Donaghys Hill** (40 minutes return), from which you can see the Franklin River and the magnificent white quartzite dome of Frenchmans Cap, and a walk to **Nelson Falls** (20 minutes return).

Rafting the Franklin
The Franklin is a very wild river and rafting it can be hazardous. Whether you go with an independent group or a tour operator, you should contact the Queenstown PWS office (☎ 6471 2511) for the latest information on permits and regulations. You should also check out the excellent Franklin

River page on the PWS Web site at www.parks.tas.gov.au.

All expeditions should register at the booth at the junction between the Lyell Hwy and the Collingwood River, 49km west of Derwent Bridge. The trip, starting at Collingwood River and ending at Heritage Landing on the Franklin, takes about 14 days (you can do a shorter eight day one). From the exit point (the same for both trips), you can be picked up by a Wilderness Air seaplane, or 22km further down the river by a Gordon River cruise boat.

Tour companies with complete rafting packages include Rafting Tasmania (☎ 6239 1080), Tasmanian Wild River Adventures (☎ 0409 977 506) and Tasmanian Expeditions (☎ 1800 030 230). An all-inclusive rafting package costs around $180 a day. Tours run mainly from December to March.

CRADLE MOUNTAIN-LAKE ST CLAIR NATIONAL PARK
Tasmania's best known national park is the superb 1262 sq km World Heritage Area of Cradle Mountain-Lake St Clair. The spectacular mountain peaks, deep gorges, lakes and wild moorlands extend from the Great Western Tiers in Tasmania's north to Derwent Bridge on the Lyell Hwy in the south. It is one of the most glaciated areas in Australia and includes Mt Ossa (1617m), Tasmania's highest mountain, and Lake St Clair, Australia's deepest natural freshwater lake.

The preservation of this region as a national park is due, in part, to Gustav Weindorfer, an Austrian who fell in love with the area. In 1912 he built a chalet out of King Billy pine, called it *Waldheim* (German for Forest Home) and, from 1916, lived there permanently. Today, bushwalkers' huts have been constructed near his original chalet at the northern end of the park, and the area is named Waldheim, after his chalet.

There are plenty of day walks in both the Cradle Valley and Cynthia Bay (Lake St Clair) regions, but it is the spectacular 80km walk between the two that has turned this park into a bushwalkers' mecca. The Overland Track is one of the finest bushwalks in Australia and, in summer, up to 100 people a day can set off on it. The track can be walked in either direction, but most people walk from Cradle Valley to Cynthia Bay.

Cradle Valley

At the northern park boundary is the visitor centre and rangers' station (☎ 6492 1133), open from 8 am to 7 pm in summer and until 5 pm the rest of the year. The centre is staffed by rangers who can advise you about weather conditions, walking gear, maximum and minimum walking groups, bush safety, and bush etiquette.

For visitors in wheelchairs or with youngsters in prams, the centre also features an easy, but quite spectacular, 500m circular boardwalk through the adjacent rainforest.

Seair (☎ 6492 1132), which operates from the Cradle View Restaurant, offers flights over the park and surrounding areas.

Whatever time of the year you visit, be prepared for cold, wet weather in the Cradle Valley area – on average it rains on seven days out of 10, is cloudy eight days in 10, the sun shines all day only one day in 10, and it snows on 54 days each year!

Lake St Clair

Cynthia Bay, near the southern park boundary, also has an informative rangers' station (☎ 6289 1115) where you register to walk the Overland Track in the opposite direction. At the nearby kiosk (☎ 6289 1137) you can book a seat on the small *Idaclair!* ferry (see Getting Around later in this section), which is also available for charter, or hire dinghies.

The Overland Track

The best time to walk the Overland Track is during summer, when the flowering plants are most prolific, although spring and autumn also have their attractions. You can walk the track in winter, but only if you're very experienced.

The trail is well marked for its entire length and, at an easy pace, takes around five or six days to walk. There are many secondary paths leading up to mountains such as Mt Ossa or other natural features, so the length of time you actually take is only limited by the amount of supplies you can

carry. There are unattended huts along the track you can use for overnight accommodation, but in summer they can be full so make sure you carry a tent. Camp fires are banned so you must carry a fuel stove.

The most dangerous part of the walk is the exposed high plateau between Waldheim and Pelion Creek, near Mt Pelion West. The south-west wind that blows across here can be bitterly cold and sometimes strong enough to knock you off your feet.

If you are walking from Cradle Valley to Cynthia Bay, you have the option of radioing from Narcissus Hut for the *Idaclair!* ferry to come and pick you up, saving a 5½ hour walk.

More detailed descriptions of the walk are given in Lonely Planet's *Tasmania* guide and in its *Bushwalking in Australia*.

Places to Stay & Eat

Cradle Valley The cheapest place in this area is *Cosy Cabins Cradle Mountain* (☎ 492 1395), 2.5km outside the national park. It costs $16 a double to camp here in summer or $20 per person to stay in the bunkhouse. En suite cabins are $80 a double. Linen is $4 extra.

At *Waldheim*, 5km into the national park, there are basic huts containing gas stoves, cooking utensils and wood heaters, but no bedding. The minimum fees for these cabins are $55 to $75. Check in and bookings for the huts are handled by the Cradle Mountain Visitor Centre. The four-bunk cabins have recently been refurbished.

Just on the national park boundary is *Cradle Mountain Lodge* (☎ 6492 1303), where pleasant, self-contained cabins are $166 to $216 a double. The lodge has good facilities, an excellent restaurant (make sure you book first), the Tavern Bar and a general store. Petrol can be bought at the central lodge building. Expect prices to be higher than in other parts of the state.

Highlanders Cabins (☎ 6492 1116) has timber cottages with rustic appeal for $88 to $130 a double, including full breakfast provisions.

The *Cradle View Restaurant*, near the Cosy Cabins, serves reasonably priced home-style meals; you can also buy petrol and diesel from outside the restaurant.

On the way to Cradle Mountain from Devonport, near the crossroads at Moina, there is a turn-off to a luxurious mountain retreat, *Lemonthyme Lodge* (☎ 6492 1112). Accommodation ranges from $95 a double in the lodge to $220 a double in a spa cabin. It's a long drive in on a dirt road so make sure you book first.

Cynthia Bay, Derwent Bridge & Bronte Park

If you've got any sense, the moment you step off the Overland Track or the MV *Idaclair!*, you'll step straight into a Maxwells or TWT coach and head for the *Derwent Bridge Wilderness Hotel* (☎ 6289 1144) for a beer, a steak and some big talk about your big walk. The accommodation here is nothing special but the lounge bar is much more impressive than it looks from the outside. Hearty meals are available at standard prices, and its massive open fire, high ceilings and exposed wood also make it the perfect place to break the long drive from Queenstown to Hobart, even if all you want is a coffee. Bunks cost $20 per person, while rooms in the hotel are $75 to $85 a double, including a continental breakfast.

Derwent Bridge Chalets (☎ 6289 1000) is also at Derwent Bridge and charges $128 a double in summer.

Back at Cynthia Bay, at the southern end of Lake St Clair, *Lakeside St Clair Wilderness Holidays* (☎ 6289 1137) has a kiosk, tent sites for $5 a person (you must pay extra to use the campers' kitchen), backpacker accommodation for $20 a person and cabins for $165 a double. You can camp free at *Fergy's Paddock*, 10 minutes back along the Overland Track.

Just off the Lyell Hwy at Bronte Park, 26km east of Derwent Bridge, is the *Bronte Park Highland Village* (☎ 6289 1126), which is favoured by fishers trying their luck in Bronte Lagoon. It has a wide variety of budget and mid-range accommodation and the inviting chalet serves meals. You can arrange transport from Lake St Clair with Maxwells (☎ 6492 1431).

Getting There & Away

See Getting There & Around at the start of The West section. In summer TWT (☎ 1300 300 520) runs additional services to Cradle Mountain (Dove Lake) and Lake St Clair from Launceston and Hobart.

TWT can drop you off at one end of the Overland Track and pick you up at the other for $69 or $75. While you don't have to pay to have your luggage transported, you do have to pay $5 per bag for it to be stored until you are ready to collect it.

Maxwells (☎ 6492 1431) has services from Devonport to Cradle Mountain ($30), Launceston to Cradle Mountain ($40), Devonport and Launceston to Lake St Clair ($50), Lake St Clair to Bronte Park and Frenchmans Cap ($10) and Cradle Valley to Lake St Clair ($75).

It is possible that you might be able to find a more convenient or cheaper transport option by talking to staff at bushwalking shops or hostels.

Getting Around

TWT buses can be used to get from Cradle Mountain Lodge to Dove Lake for $7. Additionally, Maxwells (☎ 6492 1431) runs a shuttle bus on demand for $5 per person. Maxwells also runs an informal taxi to and from Cynthia Bay and Derwent Bridge for $5 (minimum two people), and this operates daily on demand. The TWT bus will also transport you between Derwent Bridge and Cynthia Bay for $5.

The MV *Idaclair!* does a one way ($15) or return ($20) trip to Narcissus Hut at the northern end of Lake St Clair ($25 if you break the trip for a couple of hours, $30 if you return on a different day) departing a number of times a day. Expect to pay more if there are fewer than four people on board. If using this at the end of your walk, you *must* radio the kiosk on arrival at Narcissus Hut.

South-West

SOUTHWEST NATIONAL PARK

There are few places left in the world as isolated and untouched as Tasmania's south-west wilderness, the state's largest national park. It is the home of some of the world's last tracts of virgin temperate rainforest, and these contribute much to the grandeur and extraordinary diversity of this ancient area.

The south-west is the habitat of the endemic Huon pine, which lives for more than 3000 years, and of the swamp gum, the world's tallest hardwood and flowering plant. About 300 species of lichen, moss and fern, some rare and endangered, dapple the rainforest in as many shades of green; glacial tarns with mirror reflections are drops of silver on the jagged mountains; and in summer, the alpine meadows are picture-perfect with wildflowers and flowering shrubs. Through it all run the wild rivers, with rapids tearing through deep gorges and waterfalls plunging over cliffs.

Each year more and more people venture into the heart of this incredible part of Tasmania's World Heritage Area, seeking the peace, isolation and challenge of a region as old as the last ice age.

The best-known walk in the park is the **South Coast Track**, between Port Davey and Cockle Creek, near Recherche Bay. This takes about 10 days and should only be tackled by experienced hikers, well prepared for the often vicious weather conditions. Light planes are used to airlift bushwalkers into the south-west and there is vehicle access to Cockle Creek. Detailed notes to some of the walks in this region are available in Lonely Planet's *Bushwalking in Australia*.

A whole range of escorted wilderness adventures are possible, involving flying, hiking, rafting, canoeing, mountaineering, caving and camping. More information on these can be obtained from the PWS (☎ 6233 6191). Entry fees apply even if you're just driving on the road through the park.

Getting There & Away
TWT (☎ 1300 300 520) runs services to Scotts Peak and the end of the South Coast Track at Cockle Creek.

Horizontal Can Be Vertical

Anodopetalum biglandulosum is a real mouthful. Otherwise known as 'horizontal', it's a form of scrub familiar to those who venture off the beaten track. Found only in Tasmania, it sends up thin, vigorous growth when an opening in the forest canopy occurs. This continual process creates the dense, tangled thickets so typical of Tasmania's native forest.

LAKE PEDDER & STRATHGORDON
At the northern edge of the south-west wilderness lies Lake Pedder, once a spectacularly beautiful natural lake considered the crown jewel of the region. In 1972, however, it was flooded to become part of the Gordon River power development. Together with nearby Lake Gordon, Pedder now holds 27 times the volume of water in Sydney Harbour and is the largest inland freshwater catchment in Australia.

Built to service HEC employees, the township of Strathgordon is the base from which to visit lakes Pedder and Gordon, the Gordon Dam and the power station. Strathgordon is also becoming a popular bushwalking, trout fishing, boating and waterskiing resort. The underground Gordon power station is the largest in Tasmania and on most days tours are available for $5. The visitors centre at the dam site has plenty of information about the scheme.

MARTIN HARRIS

Trout fishing is very popular in the lakes area.

TASMANIA

Places to Stay & Eat
On the southern side of Lake Pedder, fishers like to camp at *Lake Edgar Camping Ground*, which has water views, while bushwalkers tend to prefer the *Huon River Camping Ground*, which is hidden in tall forest near Scotts Peak Dam.

At Strathgordon, there's a camping ground and the *Lake Pedder Chalet (☎ 6280 1166)*, where singles/doubles cost from $55/65 to $80/90. Meals are also available from the restaurant at standard hotel prices.

Getting There & Away
TWT (☎ 1300 300 520) runs services to Scotts Peak.

Bass Strait Islands

Tasmania has two groups of islands, the Hunter and Furneaux groups, at the western and eastern entrances to Bass Strait respectively. Once the transient homes of sealers, sailors and prospectors, today these islands are inhabited by rural communities and are rich in wildlife and natural beauty.

KING ISLAND
• postcode 7256   • pop 1750

At the western end of Bass Strait in the Hunter Group, this small island has beautiful beaches and quiet lagoons. Discovered in 1798, King Island was soon known as a breeding ground for seals and sea elephants. Just as quickly, they were hunted close to extinction by brutal sealers and sailors known as the Straitsmen.

Over the years, the stormy seas of Bass Strait have claimed many ships and there are several wrecks around the island. The worst occurred in 1845 when the *Cataraqui*, an immigrant ship, went down with 399 people aboard.

King Island is best known for its dairy produce, although kelp and large crayfish are other valuable exports.

Things to See & Do
King Island's four **lighthouses** guard against its treacherous seas. The Cape Wickham lighthouse is the tallest in the southern hemisphere and is worth visiting for the view of the surrounding coastal scenery. The others are at Currie, Stokes Point and south of Naracoopa.

Currie Museum, originally the lighthouse keeper's cottage, is open from 2 to 4 pm daily except from July to mid-September. It features many maritime and local history displays and entry is $2. Kelp Industries Pty Ltd is the only kelp processing plant in Australia. From the roadside you can see kelp drying on racks.

The **King Island Dairy** is a must for visitors. It is open all day on weekdays and on Sunday from 12.30 to 4 pm, although times are liable to change.

Swimming at deserted **beaches** or in freshwater lakes, scuba diving among exotic marine life and shipwrecks, surfing and fishing are all popular.

If you're interested in a drier pastime, try **bushwalking**; there is abundant wildlife, including a small colony of fairy penguins at Grassy.

Organised Tours
King Island Coach Tours (☎ 6462 1138) and Top Tours (☎ 6462 1245) offer half-day trips from $25 or full-day trips from $55.

King Island Dive Charters (☎ 6461 1133, 1800 030 330) has single dives for $72 or day trips for $129, including equipment hire and lunch. King Island Bushwalks (☎ 6461 1276) runs short guided walks for $20, while Driftwood 4WD Tours (☎ 6462 1180) also offers trips around the island.

Places to Stay
Near Currie, the *Bass Caravan Park (☎ 6462 1260)* has on-site vans for $35/45 for singles/doubles. *Boomerang by the Sea (☎ 6462 1288)* has rooms with superb ocean views for $80/100.

In Naracoopa, *Boudins (☎ 6461 1110)* has self-contained units for up to $124 a double, while at Grassy (which is slowly being redeveloped as a holiday resort), *King Island Holiday Village (☎ 6461 1177)* has houses with water views for $150 and self-contained units for $110.

Places to Eat
Currie has many fine eating places within walking distance of most of the accommodation. The *Coffee Shop*, open daily, serves light meals, while the *Bakery* has home-made pies.

The restaurant at *Boomerang by the Sea* (☎ 6462 1288) features local produce and has spectacular ocean views; bookings are essential. The *Cataraqui Restaurant*, at Parers Hotel, offers a similar menu and the hotel also has a bistro.

On the other side of the island in Naracoopa, *Boudins* (☎ 6461 1110) serves lunch and dinner in its a la carte restaurant overlooking the bay.

Getting There & Away
Kendell Airlines (☎ 1800 338 894), King Island Airlines (☎ 9580 3777) and Tasair (☎ 1800 062 900) fly to the island. Regular flights are available from Melbourne ($121 one way), Launceston ($149) and Burnie/Wynyard ($105). Package deals are often the best value, with airfares, two nights accommodation plus a hire car for around $400 per person from Melbourne. Similar deals are available from Launceston.

Getting Around
There is no public transport on the island and most roads are gravel. Kendell Airlines can arrange airport transfers to Currie for $7 per person each way and to Naracoopa for $29 per person each way. Hire-car companies will meet you at the airport and should be booked.

Howell's Auto Rent (☎ 6462 1282) has cars from around $67 a day with insurance.

FLINDERS ISLAND
• postcode 7255   • pop 1130

Flinders Island is the largest of the 52 islands that comprise the Furneaux Group. First charted in 1798 by the British explorer Matthew Flinders, the Furneaux Group became a base for the Straitsmen, who not only slaughtered seals in their tens of thousands but also indulged in piracy.

The most tragic part of Flinders Island's history, however, was its role in the virtual annihilation of Tasmania's Aboriginal people between 1829 and 1834. Of the 135 survivors who were transported to Wybalenna (an Aboriginal word meaning Black Man's House) to be 'civilised', only 47 survived to make their final journey to Oyster Cove near Hobart in 1847.

Flinders Island has many attractions, including beautiful beaches, good fishing and scuba diving.

The island's main industries are farming, fishing and seasonal mutton-birding. Its administrative centre is Whitemark, and Lady Barron in the south is the main fishing area and deep-water port. Petrol is available in Whitemark and Lady Barron only.

Things to See & Do
Today all that remains of the unfortunate settlement at **Wybalenna** is the cemetery and the chapel, restored by the National Trust and open to visitors. In 1999 the site was returned to the descendants of those who had lived there.

Nearby, the **Emita Museum** displays a variety of Aboriginal artefacts as well as old sealing and sailing relics. It's open weekends from 2 to 5 pm and, during summer, on weekdays from 2 to 5 pm.

Bushwalking is popular, and many visitors climb **Mt Strzelecki**. The walk starts about 10km south of Whitemark, is well signposted and takes three to five hours return. The island supports a wide variety of **wildlife**, including many bird species, the most well known being the Cape Barren goose (now protected) and the mutton bird. Mutton birds are readily seen at dusk, and Flinders Island Adventures (☎ 6359 4507) runs evening tours from December to March from Lady Barron.

Mountain bicycles are available for hire from Flinders Island Bike Hire (☎ 6359 2000). Bikes cost $10 per day and can be collected at the airport on arrival if sufficient notice is given.

Scuba divers can visit several locations on the northern and western coasts. In many places you can enter from the beach or shelving rocks. There are **shipwrecks** around the island, some clearly visible from shore.

Rock and beach **fishing** are popular all year. Fishing tackle and bait can be purchased from many stores, however you need to bring your own rod. A more unusual pastime is **fossicking** for 'diamonds' (which are actually fragments of topaz) on the beach and creek at Killiecrankie Bay.

Jimmy's Island Tours (☎ 6359 2112) runs day-long coach tours for around $70 per person, while Leafmoor Four Wheeler Tours (☎ 6359 3517) takes tours through the hills on the eastern side of Mt Strzelecki down to a beach for $30 an hour.

Places to Stay

Flinders Park Units (☎ 6359 2188) is 5km north of Whitemark, next to the airport. It has self-contained cabins for $55 a double. The *Interstate Hotel* (☎ 6359 2114), in the centre of Whitemark, has singles/doubles with en suite for $48/75.

There are also a variety of holiday homes around the island, including *Echo Hills Holiday Units* (☎ 6359 6509) for $75 a double and *Seaview Cottage* (☎ 6359 2011) for $65 a double.

The *Flinders Island Lodge* (☎ 6359 3521), at Lady Barron overlooking the picturesque Franklin Sound, has doubles from $90 to $148. Rooms are spacious and the service is friendly.

Places to Eat

The *Bakery*, at Whitemark, sells pies, bread and cold drinks on weekdays, while *Sweet Surprises Coffee Shop* is a popular cafe open daily except Sunday.

The *Interstate Hotel*, in Whitemark, serves a range of reasonably priced counter meals from Monday to Saturday. The

Whitemark Sports Club has a cosy restaurant with a quality menu. Meals are also available in the bistro throughout the week in summer. Bookings for the restaurant are necessary.

Patterson's Store, in Lady Barron, is open daily and also acts as a post office and a Commonwealth Bank agency. The restaurant at the *Flinders Island Lodge*, in Lady Barron, has a fine selection of bistro meals every day. *Killiecrankie Enterprises* at Killiecrankie, provides snacks and drinks.

Getting There & Away

Air Island Airlines (☎ 1800 818 455) and Par Avion (☎ 1800 646 411) fly to the island. There are flights most days from Melbourne ($170) and Launceston ($114). Cheaper flights are available by booking three to 21 days in advance, but the cheapest way to see the island is by using one of the many package deals. These provide return airfares, accommodation for two or more nights and car hire with unlimited mileage. Costs vary according to season, but high season packages are around $450 from Melbourne.

Boat The southern Shipping Company (☎ 6356 1753) runs a ferry from Bridport on the north-east coast of mainland Tasmania to Flinders Island once a week. Once a month it continues on to Port Welshpool in Victoria.

Getting Around

In Whitemark, a number of companies offer cars for hire, including Bowman-Lees (☎ 6359 2388), charging around $50 or $60 a day.

Victoria

In 1803, a party of convicts, soldiers and settlers arrived at Sorrento (on Port Phillip Bay) but abandoned the settlement soon after. The arrival at Portland of the Henty family from Van Diemen's Land (Tasmania) in 1834 marked the first permanent European settlement in Victoria, and Melbourne was founded the following year by other enterprising Tasmanians.

In 1851 Victoria won separation from New South Wales (NSW). The same year, the rich Victorian goldfields were discovered and drew immigrants from around the world.

Victoria is the smallest mainland state, and its area of 227,420 sq km makes it roughly equivalent in size to Great Britain.

The variety of landscape in a relatively small area is perhaps Victoria's main attraction. The Western District is a huge volcanic plain; the Murray/Darling Basin, the beds of long-dry seas and lakes, takes in the Wimmera and Mallee districts; the Great Dividing Range running east-west across Victoria is the tail end of Australia's massive coastal range; heavily forested Gippsland is relatively untouched; and the Coastal Region has shorelines ranging from the 90-Mile Beach in Gippsland to the rock formations of Port Campbell National Park.

ABORIGINAL PEOPLE

As many as 100,000 people lived in Victoria before Europeans arrived; by 1860 there were as few as 2000 Aborigines left alive. Today there are around 20,000 Koories (Aborigines from south-eastern Australia), more than half living in Melbourne.

The Victorian people lived in 38 dialect groups who spoke 10 languages, with each group divided into clans and sub-clans. Each clan owned a distinct area of land, and the complex culture was largely based on a spiritual bond with that land.

Many cultures have been lost and no Victorian people live a purely traditional lifestyle. Some groups are attempting to revive their cultures and there are cultural

HIGHLIGHTS

Telephone code: ☎ 03
Population: 4.6 million
Area: 227,420 sq km

• Driving the spectacular Great Ocean Road from Anglesea to the Port Campbell National Park

• Enjoying adventure activities including skiing, bushwalking, hang-gliding and fly-fishing in the High Country

• Taking a leisurely cycling tour around the wineries of the Rutherglen area

• Visiting the re-created 1860s gold-mining town of Sovereign Hill, Ballarat

• Soaking up the history of the port of Echuca on the Murray River, with its evocative reminders of the paddle-steamer era

• Bushwalking among the wildflowers, wildlife and mystical beauty of the Grampians National Park

• Visiting Melbourne in spring – for the gardens, the Melbourne Cup, the Aussie Rules Grand Final and the Melbourne International Festival

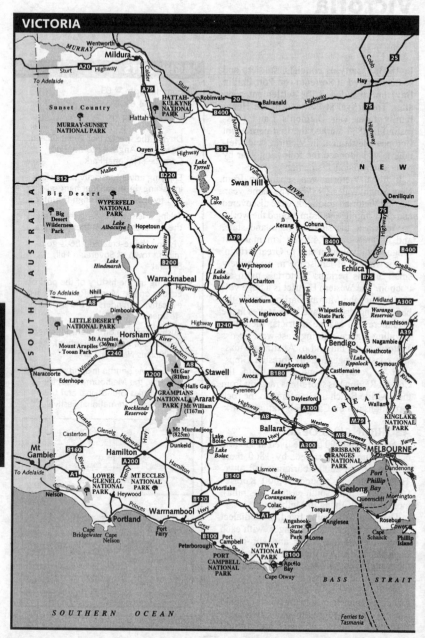

VICTORIA

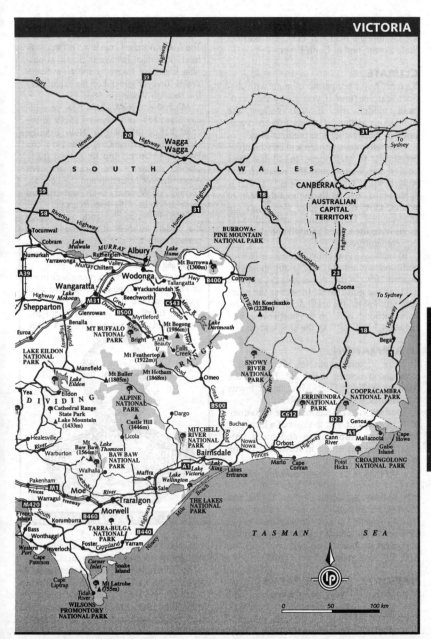

VICTORIA

centres around the state, including those in the Grampians National Park, the Barmah State Forest, and at Cann River.

CLIMATE

Victoria has a temperate climate with distinct seasons (four if you go by the European model, six if you follow the indigenous system). Locals take perverse pride in the weather's unpredictability.

Generally, the southern and coastal areas are similar to Melbourne, the alpine areas colder and wetter, and the northern and western areas warmer and drier. Rainfall is spread fairly evenly throughout the year. In winter, most of the higher mountains are snowcapped. The Wimmera and Mallee regions have the lowest rainfall and the highest temperatures.

In summer the average highest daily temperatures are around 25°C along the coast, around 20°C in the alpine areas, and up to 35°C in the north-west. In winter the average maximums are around 13°C along the coast, around 17°C in the north-west, and between 3 and 10°C in the alpine areas.

INFORMATION

Tourism Victoria promotes Victoria interstate and overseas; it has an office in the Melbourne Town Hall. Most larger towns have tourist information centres.

Tourism Victoria has an office in Sydney at 403 George St. For the cost of a local call you can get information and order brochures from anywhere in Australia: phone ☎ 1300 655 452.

The RACV's *Accommodation Guide* ($12, or $6 for members) lists hotels, motels, holiday flats, guesthouses, B&Bs and even some hostels. The RACV also publishes a *Tourist Park Accommodation* guide ($10, or $5 for members), that lists camping and caravan parks. You can buy both for $18; $9 for members.

NATIONAL & STATE PARKS

Victoria has 74 very diverse national and state parks. They are managed by Parks Victoria (☎ 13 1963 for 24 hour information). Parks Victoria does not have a shop

The Major Mitchell Trail

The Major Mitchell Trail is a 1700km 'cultural trail' which follows as closely as possible the route taken by the New South Wales surveyor general on his exploratory trip through Victoria in 1836.

Mitchell entered Victoria near present-day Swan Hill, and travelled south to the coast before returning to NSW through Hamilton, Castlemaine, Benalla and Wodonga. On his trip he named many places, including the Grampians, Mt Alexander, Mt Macedon and the Loddon, Glenelg and Wimmera rivers, and explored some previously little-known areas.

Mitchell was so pleasantly surprised by the verdant lushness of the land, in comparison with the dry expanses of NSW, that he named the area *Australia Felix* (Australia Fair).

The route today covers many back roads and is well signposted with distinctive small brown and blue signs. An excellent descriptive handbook is available from Parks Victoria and local tourist offices for $12.95.

TAMSIN WILSON

front, but it will mail brochures and it has a Web site, www.parks.vic.gov.au.

The Department of Natural Resources & Environment (NRE) has an Information Centre (☎ 9637 8080) at 8 Nicholson St, East Melbourne, which carries books and other information on parks and outdoor activities.

ACTIVITIES
Bushwalking
The High Country is popular, particularly with experienced walkers. Other popular areas include Wilsons Promontory, the Grampians and Croajingolong National Park.

Long-distance walks include The Great South-West Walk, a 250km loop beginning near Portland; the Australian Alps Walking Track, a 760km walk from near Walhalla in Victoria to Canberra in the Australian Capital Territory (ACT); and the Victorian section of the Bicentennial National Trail through the High Country.

There are more than 30 bushwalking clubs. Contact the Federation of Victorian Walking Clubs (☎ 9455 1876) at 332 Banyule Rd, Viewbank 3084 (its Web site is www.avoca.vicnet.net.au/~vicwalk), or have a look in the *Yellow Pages* under 'Clubs – Bushwalking'.

The NRE Information Centre in Melbourne sells walking guides, including *120 Walks in Victoria* by Tyrone T Thomas ($19.95) and *Melbourne's Mountains – Exploring the Great Divide* by John Siseman ($19.95). Lonely Planet's *Bushwalking in Australia* ($24.95) details some Victorian walks.

Cycling
Helmets are compulsory, as are front and rear lights at night.

Wine regions such as Rutherglen and the Pyrenees Ranges are popular for cycling tours, and the High Country is favoured by mountain bikers.

Bicycle Victoria (☎ 9328 3000, bicyclevic @bv.com.au), 19 O'Connell St, North Melbourne, is a mine of information and holds events such as the Great Victorian Bike Ride (November) and Easter Bike (April). It's Web site is www.bv.com.au. Cycle tourists can drop into Melbourne Bicycle Touring Club meetings (8 pm Thursday) at the same address. The club's Web site is at www.vicn et.net.au/~mbtc.

Bicycling Around Victoria (by Ray Peace, $19.95) is an excellent reference.

Many Melbourne bike shops rent bikes. A hybrid bike with panniers from touring specialists Christie Cycles (☎ 9818 4011) at 80 Burwood Rd, Hawthorn, costs $20 a day or $75 a week (including both weekends). Mountain bikes from St Kilda Cycles (☎ 9534 3074) at 11 Carlisle St, St Kilda, cost $20 a day, with panniers.

Skiing
Skiing in Victoria began in the 1860s when Norwegian goldminers introduced the sport in Harrietville. The season officially commences on the first weekend of June. Skiable snow usually arrives later in the month, and often stays until the end of September.

The Alpine Resorts Commission (ARC; ☎ 9895 6900) manages the main ski resorts. Parks Victoria manages Mt St Gwinear and Lake Mountain.

Surfing
With its exposure to the Southern Ocean swell, Victoria's coastline provides quality surf.

On the west coast you can take lessons with Go Ride a Wave (☎ 5263 2111), which holds lessons in Torquay, Anglesea and Lorne, or Westcoast Surf School (☎ 5261 2241) in Torquay. On Phillip Island try Island Surf School (☎ 5952 3443).

Telephone surf reports (☎ 1900 931 996 or 1900 983 268 for the Mornington Peninsula) are updated daily. A useful guide is *Surfinder Vic* ($20), available from surf and sports shops.

The three most popular areas are Phillip Island, the Mornington Peninsula and the west coast – all are less than two hours' drive from Melbourne.

Diving
Some of Victoria's diving is world class. Of course, it can get a little chilly and 7mm wetsuits or even drysuits are needed.

Port Phillip Bay has some excellent sites. The Bellarine Peninsula is also popular and Queenscliff is a good base. Other areas include Torquay, Anglesea, Lorne, Apollo Bay, Port Campbell and Portland (all on the Great Ocean Rd); Flinders, Sorrento and Portsea (on the Mornington Peninsula); and Kilcunda, Wilsons Promontory and Mallacoota (on the east coast).

VICTORIA

Sailing

There are yacht clubs around Port Phillip Bay – see Sailing in the Melbourne section, later. Other areas include the Gippsland Lakes and Lake Eildon. At some places you can hire yachts, which work out to be quite economical when shared between a few people. There are also schools where you can learn to sail.

Canoeing & Kayaking

Trips can be as short as a couple of hours, or extended adventures. The Glenelg River in the south-west has riverside camp sites for canoeists.

Rivers are graded according to their degree of difficulty. Grade one (such as parts of the Yarra River) are easy-flowing rivers; grade five (such as the Indi River and parts of the Murray) are long stretches of rapids, only suitable for very experienced canoeists.

Sea kayaking offers opportunities to see wildlife such as sea lions, gannets, penguins and dolphins.

For more information contact the Victorian Board of Canoe Education (☎ 9459 4251), 332 Banyule Rd, Viewbank 3084.

White-Water Rafting

Guided white-water rafting trips are run on various High Country rivers. The best times are during the snow melts from around August to December.

Costs range from around $130 per day, with everything from day trips to five-day expeditions. Operators include Peregrine Adventures (☎ 9662 2800) and Snowy River Expeditions (☎ 5155 0220). Paddle Sports (☎ 9478 3310), based in Preston in Melbourne, is another company offering guided rafting trips.

Horse Riding & Trekking

There are dozens of horse-riding ranches with rides from one hour (usually $20 or less) to a full day (around $80).

Treks – anything from overnight rides to week-long expeditions – are also available, usually costing between $100 and $130 per day. Operators include Bogong Horseback Adventures (☎ 5754 4849) at Mt Beauty,

Bright-Freeburgh Trail Rides (☎ 5755 1370) at Bright, Giltrap's Mt Bogong Packhorse Adventures (☎ 02-6072 3535) at Mitta Mitta and Mountain Saddle Safaris (☎ 5165 3365) at Erica. Stoney's Bluff & Beyond Trail Rides (☎ 5775 2212), near Mansfield, offers a three or four day ride in the mountains (around $450) and an 18 day marathon down to the coast.

Hang Gliding & Paragliding

Hang gliding and paragliding schools include the Eagle School of Hang Gliding (☎ 5750 1174) near Bright, and Wingsports Hang Gliding & Paragliding (☎ 0419-378 616) in Apollo Bay.

A two day course that has you in the air on the second day costs around $310; a seven to nine day HGFA (Hang Gliding Federation of Australia) licence course costs around $150 per day. A 20 hour powered hang gliding course costs about $120 per hour.

Most operators also offer tandem flights in powered hang gliders (from $70 for a 15 minute flight), as well as tandem paragliding or hang gliding (from around $100).

Rock Climbing

Mt Arapiles, in the Western District, is famous for its huge variety of climbs. Not far from here, in the Grampians National Park, rock climbing is increasingly popular. At Mt Buffalo there are good granite climbs.

There are plenty of other sites. The outdoor and adventure shops in Hardware St in Melbourne's city centre are good sources of information. The Victorian Climbing Club, which meets at 8 pm on the last Thursday of most months at the Australian Gemmological Association, 380-82 Spencer St, Melbourne, publishes *Rockclimbers Handbooks*. Write to The Secretary, GPO Box 1725P, Melbourne 3001.

Several operators in the Grampians and Natimuk (near Mt Arapiles) offer lessons and tours.

GETTING AROUND
Air

Kendall Airlines (book through Ansett, ☎ 13 1300) flies daily between Melbourne and

Mildura ($183), Portland ($137) and Albury ($133). Southern Australia Airlines (book through Qantas, ☎ 13 1313) also flies between Melbourne and Mildura ($183). Kendall and Southern Australia offer advance purchase discounts on one-way fares as well as return fares.

Several other small airlines fly to other destinations.

Train & Bus

Train and bus services within country Victoria are operated by V/Line, which has been leased to the UK company National Express. There's a chance that the name will change. As in all privatisations, the public has been assured that services will improve – Brits might be a little cynical about that.

Book tickets by phone (☎ 13 2232) daily between 7 am and 9 pm. In Melbourne you can buy tickets at Spencer St and Flinders St train stations, major suburban stations, and most travel agents.

One-way economy fares are quoted in this chapter. There are various special deals on return fares, most giving a discount of about 30%.

Most services do not require a reservation, although you do need one to travel on an interstate train (the *Overland*, the *Ghan* or the XPT) to a destination within Victoria.

Major Routes From Melbourne, the principal V/Line routes are:

South-west to Geelong ($8.60) then on the inland route to Warrnambool ($34.20); a daily bus service runs along the Great Ocean Rd from Geelong through Lorne ($21.90) and Apollo Bay ($26.90), continuing through to Warrnambool on Friday (also on Monday during summer).

North-west to Ballarat ($13.80), Stawell ($31.60), Horsham ($41.30) and on to Adelaide in South Australia; buses run from Stawell to Halls Gap in the Grampians.

North through Bendigo ($20.80) to Swan Hill ($43.40); buses continue from Bendigo to Echuca ($26.90).

North to Shepparton ($23.30) and Cobram ($31.60).

North to Albury-Wodonga ($38.90), continuing to Sydney; buses run from Wangaratta ($29.30) to Beechworth ($34.20) and Bright ($38.90).

VICTORIAN AIR FARES

Mildura · NEW SOUTH WALES · CANBERRA ACT · Albury · Merimbula · 183 · 133 · 197 · 137 · MELBOURNE · Portland · 199 · To Devonport · *All fares in Australian dollars One-way economy air fares*

East through Moe ($15.20) to Sale ($26.90); buses connect from Sale to Bairnsdale ($34.20), Lakes Entrance ($41.30), Orbost ($46.90), Cann River ($49) and Merimbula ($50).

Other Bus Services The major companies, Greyhound Pioneer (☎ 13 2030) and McCafferty's (☎ 13 1499), run between Melbourne and Adelaide (via Ballarat and Horsham) and between Melbourne and Sydney (via the Hume Hwy). Greyhound Pioneer also runs along the coastal Princes Hwy between Melbourne and Sydney. Stopovers can be made, for a fee.

For discounts and deals on buses check hostel noticeboards or contact a backpacker-oriented travel agency. A couple are listed in the Melbourne section.

Alternative Buses If you fast-track down the highways between Melbourne and either Sydney or Adelaide, you'll miss seeing some great places.

Wild-Life Tours (☎ 9747 1882) has tours of the Great Ocean Rd and the Grampians ($49 to $120) and a one-way trip between Melbourne and Adelaide via the Grampians (from $75) or via the Great Ocean Rd and the Grampians (from $119). You can stop over anywhere along the way.

The Wayward Bus touring company (☎ 1800 882 823) runs through southeastern Australia, mostly connecting Melbourne with Adelaide or Sydney. Try it's Web site at www.waywardbus.com.au. You can stop over along the way or stay on the bus (and get off for sights and activities) as

VICTORIA

it runs to Adelaide in three days via the Great Ocean Rd ($170), to Sydney via the High Country (and Canberra) in five days ($190) or to Sydney via East Gippsland in five days ($170). There's also a route between Sydney and Adelaide running through Mildura. Fares don't include accommodation, but the bus stops overnight where there's a hostel or other cheap accommodation.

ORGANISED TOURS

Various companies operate bus tours to destinations such as Sovereign Hill, Healesville Sanctuary, the Great Ocean Rd and Phillip Island.

Several operators run tours for backpackers. Well known outfits include Mac's Backpacker Bus (☎ 5241 3180) and Autopia Tours (☎ 9326 5536).

There's a wide range of activity-based tours. See the various sections in this chapter and check hostel notice boards. Echidna Walkabout (☎ 9646 8249) runs day trips with bushwalking and an introduction to Aboriginal culture ($95 or less), and trips to the Grampians, the Great Ocean Rd and East Gippsland. We have had good feedback about Eco Adventure Tours (☎ 5962 5115). Great Ocean Road Adventure Tours (☎ 5289 6841) offers walking, canoeing and other trips around the Great Ocean Rd, starting at $30.

Bogong Jack Adventures (☎ 08-8383 7198) has cycling, bushwalking and skiing tours through the High Country and wine regions.

Melbourne

• postcode 3000   • pop 3,321,700

Melbourne is a city of Victorian-era buildings, parks and gardens, and leafy boulevards. It's Australia's second-largest city and a vibrant, multicultural place characterised by its people rather than any geographical feature. Food, sports and the arts (high and low) are the main preoccupations.

In May 1835, John Batman bought about 240,000 hectares of land from the Aborigines of the Dutigalla clan, on behalf of the Tasmanian-based Port Phillip Association. The concept of buying or selling land was unknown to the Aborigines, but in exchange for their land they received tools, flour and clothing.

John Pascoe Fawkner arrived soon after and was a driving force behind the new settlement. By the time he died in 1869, Melbourne was flourishing and he was known as the 'Grand Old Man of Victoria', unlike Batman, who died soon after his 'deal' with the Aborigines, a victim of his own excesses.

By 1840 there were over 10,000 Europeans in the area. The wealth from the goldfields built a city that was known as 'Marvellous Melbourne' and this period of prosperity lasted until the great depression at the end of the 1880s. Recovering from this, Melbourne became Australia's financial and manufacturing centre.

In the years since WWII, Melbourne has been enriched by an influx of people and cultures from around the world.

ORIENTATION

Melbourne's suburbs sprawl around Port Phillip Bay, with the city centre (also known as the CBD – central business district) on the north bank of the Yarra River, about 5km inland from the bay.

The Yarra winds through Melbourne and divides the city in half, both geographically and socio-economically. The northern and western suburbs have always been working-class areas, the southern and eastern suburbs the more affluent areas.

Most places of interest to travellers are either within the inner-suburban area or beyond the urban fringe (see the Around Melbourne section, later).

Tourist information offices have free maps that cover the city and inner suburbs. Street directories are produced by Melway, UBD and Gregory's and Lonely Planet's Melbourne City Map ($7.95) gives good coverage of the city and environs.

If you're arriving from the airport, the freeway whisks you past the impressive but controversial Gateway, dominated by a huge, leaning, yellow beam. It hasn't yet attracted a nickname, but 'the cheese-stick' is a popular nomination.

City Centre

The CBD is bordered by the Yarra to the south, the Fitzroy Gardens to the east, Victoria St to the north and Spencer St to the west. However, the huge Docklands project is considerably extending the western border, Federation Square is changing the eastern border and Southgate has finally helped the city across the river.

The CBD is laid out in a grid one mile (1.61km) long and half a mile (805m) wide, once known as the Golden Mile. The main streets running east-west are Collins and Bourke Sts, crossed by Swanston and Elizabeth Sts. The heart of the CBD is the Bourke St Mall, between Swanston and Elizabeth Sts.

Long-distance buses and the airport bus arrive at either the Spencer St coach terminal (V/Line, Skybus, Firefly and McCafferty's) or the Melbourne Transit Centre on Franklin St (Greyhound Pioneer Australia and Skybus).

On the corner of Swanston and Flinders Sts, Flinders St train station is the main station for suburban trains. 'Under the clocks' at the station is a popular meeting place. The other major station, for country and interstate trains, is Spencer St train station. (Note that Melbourne Central is just a station on the underground rail loop – it takes its name from the shopping centre above it.)

The revitalised inner suburbs circling the city centre are East Melbourne, North Melbourne, Carlton, Fitzroy, Collingwood, Richmond, South Yarra and South Melbourne. Suburbs on the bay include St Kilda, which has long been Melbourne's most diverse and permissive area, and Williamstown, south-west of the city at the mouth of the Yarra, with a maritime flavour.

INFORMATION
Tourist Offices

Information booths in the Bourke St Mall and at Flinders St train station are open on weekdays from 9 am to 5 pm (Friday till 7 pm), Saturday from 10 am to 4 pm and Sunday from 11 am to 4 pm; the booth at the Queen Victoria Market is open on weekdays from 11 am to 5 pm and on weekends from 10 am to 4 pm. There's also a tourist booth in the international terminal at Melbourne airport.

Tourism Victoria (☎ 13 2842) is in the town hall on Swanston St. It's open daily from 9 am to 6 pm (5 pm on weekends). The City Experience Centre, also in the town hall, has multi-lingual touch-screen information.

Information Victoria (☎ 1300 366 356), 356 Collins St, stocks publications about Melbourne and Victoria. The NRE Information Centre (☎ 9637 8080), 8 Nicholson St, East Melbourne, carries information on parks and outdoor activities.

Backpacker-oriented travel agencies include Backpackers Travel Centre (☎ 9654 8477), Shop 19 Centre Place, 258 Flinders Lane; Backpackers World (☎ 9329 1990), 167 Franklin St; Travellers Contact Point (☎ 9642 2911), 29 Somerset Place (off Little Bourke St); and YHA Travel (☎ 6970 7991), 205 King St.

If you'd like to explore Melbourne in greater depth, Lonely Planet's *Melbourne* is a useful guide.

Post

The GPO, on the corner of Bourke and Elizabeth Sts, is open from 8 am to 6 pm on weekdays, and Saturday from 10 am to 1 pm. There's an efficient poste restante section.

Telephone

There are telephone booths all over the city, including at the GPO and just behind the GPO on Little Bourke St. There's also a Telstra Centre with phones and phonecard machines for international calls at 94 Elizabeth St; it's open daily from 6 am to midnight.

The telephone area code for Melbourne, Victoria (except some border regions) and Tasmania is 03. Omit the 0 if dialling from overseas.

There are a few call centres offering discount long-distance and international calls, including Global Gossip (☎ 9663 0511), 440 Elizabeth St, open daily between 8 am and midnight.

Email & Internet Access

Internet cafes come and go rapidly. Current places include: Cosmos Internet Services,

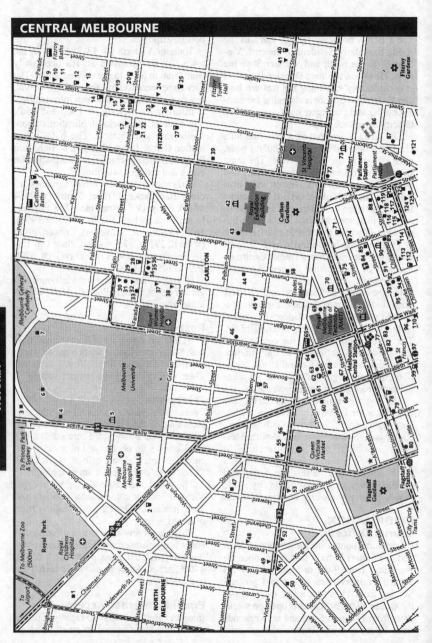

CENTRAL MELBOURNE

VICTORIA

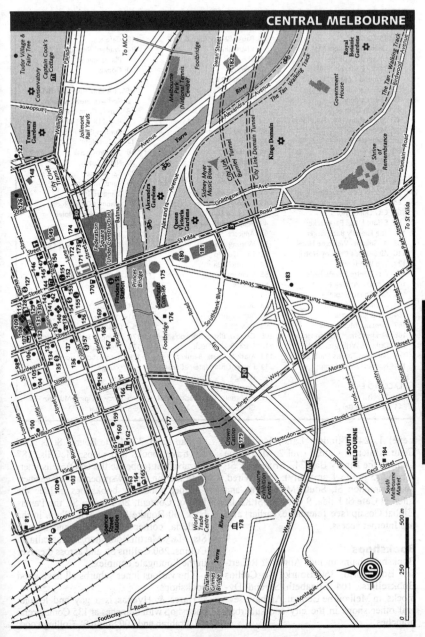

CENTRAL MELBOURNE

CENTRAL MELBOURNE

PLACES TO STAY
1 Chapman Gardens YHA Hostel
3 University College
4 Trinity College
6 Ormond College
7 Queen's College
39 The Nunnery
44 Carlton College
47 Queensbury Hill YHA Hostel
50 Miami Motel
58 Medley Hall
60 Hotel Y
61 Stork Hotel
66 Toad Hall
68 Hotel Bakpak
81 Astoria City Travel Inn
85 Rockman's Regency Hotel
88 City Limits Motel
94 Exford Hotel Backpackers
103 The Friendly Backpacker
109 All Seasons Welcome Hotel
116 All Seasons Crossley Hotel
123 The Windsor
125 City Centre Private Hotel
146 Victoria Vista Hotel
153 City Square Motel
163 Batman's Hill Hotel
164 Hotel Enterprize
167 Heritage Melbourne
168 Flinders Street Station Hostel
174 Duke of Wellington Hotel
176 Sheraton Towers Southgate
184 Nomads Market Inn

PLACES TO EAT
10 Bakers
11 The Vegie Bar

13 Babka Bakery Cafe &
   Charmaine's
15 The Fitz
16 Mario's
17 The Bull Ring
19 Rhumbarella's
22 Carmen Bar
23 Thai Thani
24 Black Cat Cafe
30 Jimmy Watson's
32 Tiamo
34 Shakahari
36 Brunetti's
37 University Cafe
38 Papa Gino's
41 Arcadia; Macedonia
45 Toto's Pizza House
48 Eldorado Hotel
49 Peppermint Lounge Cafe
51 Amiconi
52 Warung Agus
53 Don Camillo
54 La Porchetta
55 Vietnam House
56 Dalat's
91 Yamato
93 Stalactites
95 Supper Inn
96 Lounge
105 Campari Bistro; Schwob's
110 Dahu Peking Duck
113 Mask of China; Bernie's
114 Flower Drum; International
    Lounge
115 Florentino; Nudel Bar
117 Pellegrini's; Paperback; Hill of
    Content

118 Cafe K
124 Waiters' Restaurant; Meyer's
    Place; Spleen
130 Gopals

PUBS, BARS & NIGHTCLUBS
2 Redback Brewery Hotel
8 Dan O'Connell Hotel
9 Royal Derby Hotel
12 Punters Club Hotel
14 Evelyn Hotel
18 The Provincial
20 Night Cat
21 Bar Salona
25 Rainbow Hotel
27 Standard Hotel
28 Johnny's Green Room
40 Builders Arms Hotel
57 Dream
71 44
75 Bennett's Lane Jazz Club
78 Hardware
82 Rue Bebelons
99 Club 383
112 Billboard
120 Metro
134 Bass Station
161 Inflation
162 Grainstore Tavern
170 Young & Jackson's Hotel
173 The Forum
179 Automatic; Mercury
    Lounge

OTHER
5 Percy Grainger Museum
26 Binary Bar

Level 1, 247 Flinders Lane; Melbourne Central Internet Cafe, Level 2, Melbourne Central; the Binary Bar, 243 Brunswick St, Fitzroy (5 pm to 1 am daily); Cafe Wired, 363 Clarendon St, South Melbourne; and Internet Cafe St Kilda, 9 Grey St, St Kilda. Global Gossip (see Telephone, earlier) also has Internet access.

Bookshops

Bookshop chains include Angus & Robertson Bookworld, 360 Bourke St; Collins Booksellers, 104 Elizabeth St and Dymocks, in Melbourne Central. All have several other shops in the city and suburban branches.

Map Land, 372 Little Bourke St, is good for travel books and maps. McGills, 187 Elizabeth St (opposite the GPO), sells interstate and foreign newspapers and magazines.

Other good city bookshops include the Hill of Content, 86 Bourke St; the Paperback, 60 Bourke St; the ABC Shop, in the Galleria, corner of Elizabeth and Bourke Sts; Mary Martin Bookshop, in Australia on Collins, 260 Collins St, and across the river in the Southgate complex.

The various inner suburbs all have good bookshops.

Hares & Hyenas is a gay and lesbian bookshop with branches at 135 Commercial Rd, Prahran and 100 Smith St, Collingwood.

29 Lygon Court: Cinema Nova; Comedy Club
31 Readings
33 STA Travel
35 La Mama Theatre
42 Melbourne Museum
43 IMAX Cinema
46 Melbourne Sexual Health Centre
59 St James Old Cathedral
62 Melbourne Transit Centre
63 Qantas
64 Ansett
65 Melbourne City Baths
67 Global Gossip
69 Old Melbourne Gaol
70 Victoria Police Museum
72 NRE Information Centre
73 Eastern Hill Fire Station & Museum
74 Comedy Theatre
76 State Library
77 Melbourne Central & Daimaru
79 John Smith's House
80 Old Royal Mint
83 Technical Book Shop
84 Lumiere Cinema
86 St Patricks Cathedral
87 Tasma Terrace & National Trust
89 Po Hong Trading Company
90 Museum of Chinese Australian History
92 King of Kings; Sam Bear
97 Information Victoria
98 Map Land

100 Law Courts
101 Spencer St Coach Terminal
102 YHA Travel & Membership Office
104 Travellers' Medical & Vaccination Centre
106 McGills; Angus & Robertson Bookworld
107 GPO (Main Post Office)
108 Myer
111 David Jones
119 Princess Theatre
121 State Film Centre
122 Old Treasury Building
126 Kino
127 Thomas Cook Foreign Exchange
128 Tourist Information Booth
129 Travellers' Aid Society
131 Royal Arcade; Gog & Magog; Novatel on Collins
132 Half-Tix
133 ABC Shop
135 Bank of Australasia
136 Gothic Bank
137 Met Shop
138 Telstra Centre
139 Collins Booksellers
140 Sportsgirl Centre
141 Mary Martin Bookshop; Block Arcade
142 RACV Office
143 Capitol Theatre
144 Melbourne Town Hall; Tourism Victoria Information Centre
145 Athenaeum Theatre

147 Kay Craddock Antiquarian Bookseller
148 Collins Place
149 Hyatt Hotel
150 Regent Theatre
151 Tourist Information Booth
152 City Square
154 American Express
155 Backpackers Travel Cente; Cosmos Internet Services; Hell's Kitchen
156 Women's Information & Referral Exchange
157 Commonwealth Bank of Australia
158 National Mutual Building
159 Olderfleet Buildings
160 Rialto Towers & Observation Deck; Tourist Information Booth
165 Bus Booking Centre
166 Old Customs House: Immigration Museum & Hellenic Antiquities Museum
169 Coles Express
171 St Paul's Cathedral
172 Russell St Theatre
175 Melbourne Concert Hall
177 Melbourne Aquarium
178 Polly Woodside Maritime Museum
180 Theatres Building; Performing Arts Museum
181 National Gallery of Victoria
182 Sports & Entertainment Centre
183 Malthouse Theatre

VICTORIA

Medical Services

Travellers' Medical and Vaccination Centre (TMVC; ☎ 9602 5788), Level 2, 393 Little Bourke St in the city, is open weekdays from 9 am to 5 pm (Monday, Tuesday and Thursday till 8.30 pm) and Saturday from 9 am to 1 pm. Appointments are necessary.

The Melbourne Sexual Health Centre (☎ 9347 0244), 580 Swanston St, Carlton, provides free checkups and other medical services. Appointments are preferred.

The Victorian AIDS Council & Gay Men's Health Centre (☎ 9865 6700), 6 Claremont St, South Yarra, provides information and support for AIDS sufferers and operates a health centre.

Major public hospitals close to the city centre are:

Alfred Hospital
(☎ 9276 2000) Commercial Rd, Prahran
Royal Children's Hospital
(☎ 9345 5522) Flemington Rd, Parkville
Royal Melbourne Hospital
(☎ 9342 7000) Grattan St, Parkville
Royal Women's Hospital
(☎ 9344 2000) 132 Grattan St, Carlton
St Vincent's Hospital
(☎ 9288 2211) 41 Victoria Parade, Fitzroy

Emergency

Phone ☎ 000 for the police, ambulance or fire brigade. In the city centre, there's a 24 hour police station at 637 Flinders St (near Spencer St).

The Travellers' Aid Society (☎ 9654 2600), on the 2nd floor of 169 Swanston St, offers assistance for stranded travellers, advice, showers and toilets. It's open on weekdays from 8 am to 5 pm and Saturday from 10 am to 4 pm.

Address and numbers of other useful services include:

Automotive Breakdown
    Accident Towing Service (☎ 13 1176)
    RACV Emergency Roadside Service
    (☎ 13 1111)
Chemist
    Leonard Long Pharmacy, 8 am to midnight
    (☎ 9510 3977), corner of Williams Rd and
    High St, Prahran
    Tambassis Pharmacy, 24 hours (☎ 9387 8830),
    corner of Sydney and Brunswick Rds,
    Brunswick
Dentist
    Dental Emergency Service (☎ 9341 0222)
Interpreter Service
    Translating and Interpreting Service, 24 hours
    (☎ 13 1450)
Personal Crisis
    Crisis Line, 24 hour telephone counselling
    (☎ 9329 0300)
    Gay & Lesbian Switchboard, nightly between
    6 and 10 pm (Wednesday from 2 to 10 pm)
    (☎ 9510 5488)
    Lifeline Counselling, 24 hours, six languages
    (☎ 13 1114)
    Women's Refuge Referral, 24 hours (☎ 1800
    015 188)
Poisons
    Poisons Information Centre (☎ 13 1126)
Women's Health
    Women's Health Information Centre (☎ 9344
    2007), 132 Grattan St, Carlton
    Women's Health Information Service, 9 am to
    1 pm weekdays (☎ 9662 3755, information
    line ☎ 9662 3742), Level 2, 210 Lonsdale St

TRAM TOURS

For the price of a Zone 1 daily Met ticket ($4.40), you can spend the day travelling around the city and inner suburbs by tram – a great way to get a feel for Melbourne. The same ticket lets you use trains and buses too.

Try tram No 8. It starts along Swanston St in the city, rolls down St Kilda Rd beside the Kings Domain and continues up Toorak Rd through South Yarra and Toorak. Another good ride is on No 16, which cruises all the way down St Kilda Rd to St Kilda.

CITY CENTRE
Swanston St

The ugly duckling of the CBD, Swanston St was a pedestrian mall (with trams) for a few years, but is due to reopen to traffic, at night.

There are free tours of **Melbourne Town Hall**, corner of Collins St, at 10.30 am and 2.30 pm from Tuesday to Thursday but you must book (☎ 9658 9464). Opposite the town hall is the **Capitol Theatre** (1927). The ceiling is a kaleidoscopic creation.

On the corner of Swanston and Victoria Sts, the **Melbourne City Baths** was built in 1903; it's still a busy sports centre.

State Library The State Library was built in stages from 1854. The impressive domed Reading Room is worth seeing, but it might be closed for renovation when you arrive.

The library is open daily from 10 am to 6 pm (9 pm on Monday and Wednesday), with reduced hours in summer. There are free tours at 2 pm on weekdays and on the first and third Saturday of the month.

Collins St

The top end of Collins St was once known as the 'Paris End' but many of the finer buildings have gone. Facing each other on the north-west and north-east corners of Russell and Collins Sts are two historic churches, **Scots Church** (1873), No 140, and **St Michael's Church** (1866). **Kay Craddock's Antiquarian Bookseller**, No 156, is the place for bibliophiles. The **Athenaeum Theatre**, No 188, dates back to 1886, and you can use the library on the 1st floor. Across the road is the magnificent **Regent Theatre**.

The **Block Arcade**, running between Collins and Elizabeth Sts, is an intact 19th century shopping arcade. Taking tea in the old-fashioned **Hopetoun Tearooms** here is an elegant step back in time.

Melbourne's financial sector begins west of Elizabeth St. The interior of the **Commonwealth Bank of Australia (CBA)** building,

Melbourne Walking Tour

Start at the intersection of Flinders and Swanston Sts, with three landmarks. The grand old **Flinders St train station** is the main station for suburban trains. Across the road is one of Melbourne's best-known pubs, **Young & Jackson's**, which has the once scandalous painting *Chloe* in the upstairs bar. **St Paul's Cathedral** is a masterpiece of Gothic Revivalist architecture.

Also on this corner the big new **Federation Square**, with more attractions, was still under construction at the time of writing.

Up Swanston St, in the block between Flinders Lane and Collins St, is the **City Square**, yet again being redeveloped. Across Collins St is **Melbourne Town Hall**. Continue up Swanston to Bourke St and take a left into the **Bourke St Mall**. It's difficult for a pedestrian mall to work with 30-tonne trams barrelling through; nevertheless the mall is a focus for city shoppers.

Collect your mail from the GPO at the Elizabeth St end of the mall, then return to Swanston St and head north again. Across Little Lonsdale St you'll pass the **State Library** on your right, and in the next block is the **Royal Melbourne Institute of Technology**, with its bizarre architectural facades. Take a right into Franklin St and then another right into Russell St, and head down past the **Old Melbourne Gaol**.

At Little Bourke St, turn left and you've entered **Chinatown**. This narrow lane was a Chinese quarter even back in the gold-rush days and it's now a crowded couple of blocks of excellent restaurants, Asian supermarkets and shops.

At the top end of Little Bourke St, turn right into Spring St, which has some impressive old buildings, including the **Princess Theatre**, the **Windsor** hotel and the state **Parliament House**. Further down is the **Old Treasury Building**.

Cross Spring St into Collins St, and on your left are the towers of Collins Place, which house the five star **Sofitel Hotel**. The hotel's toilets on the 35th floor offer spectacular views. Back on ground level, head around to Flinders Lane (south of Collins Place). The **'top end' of Flinders Lane**, between Spring and Swanston Sts, was once the centre of the rag trade.

Continue down Flinders Lane as far as Swanston St and take a left. Pass Flinders St station, then turn right down the steps just before the river and stroll along the riverside. A footbridge takes you across the river to the **Southgate** complex, with its restaurants, bars and cafes. South of Southgate is Melbourne's **Arts Precinct**, and across St Kilda Rd are the parklands of the **Kings Domain**.

A shorter walk concentrating on the redevelopment along the Yarra begins at the Arts Precinct and follows the river down past the **casino** to Spencer St. Cross Spencer St to visit the **Polly Woodside** then cross the river and walk back by the river.

VICTORIA

333 Collins St, is worth a look, as are the interiors of the **Gothic Bank**, at 376, the former **National Mutual Life** building, No 395, and the former **Bank of Australasia**, at No 396.

The Gothic facade of the three **Olderfleet** buildings, No 471-477, has been preserved, and **Le Meridien at Rialto**, No 495, is an imaginative five-star hotel behind the facades of two Venetian Gothic buildings.

Rialto Towers Observation Deck This lookout (☎ 9629 8222) is on the 55th floor of Melbourne's tallest building, the Rialto Towers on Collins St. It offers spectacular 360° views. It's open daily from 10 am to 10 pm (until 11 pm on Friday and Saturday); entry costs $7.50 and includes a short film on Melbourne's history.

Bourke St

The area in and around the centre of Bourke St is the shopping heart of the city.

The north side of the mall is dominated by the Myer and David Jones department stores, and the GPO. On the south side, **Royal Arcade** houses **Gog and Magog**. These mythological giants, modelled on figures in London's Guildhall, have been striking the hour since 1892. The east end of Bourke St has some great cafes and restaurants, interesting book and record shops, mainstream cinemas and more fashion boutiques.

Spring St

At the top end of Collins St, the **Old Treasury Building** was built in 1858 with basement vaults to store much of the £200 million worth of gold from the Victorian goldfields. It now houses an exhibition on Melbourne's past and future, open daily (free).

Between Bourke and Little Collins Sts, the **Windsor Hotel** is a marvellous reminder of the 19th century. Opposite, the **State Houses of Parliament** are open on weekdays, with free tours when parliament isn't sitting. When Parliament is sitting you can watch from the public galleries.

Chinatown

Since the days of the gold rush, Little Bourke St has been a centre for Chinese people in Melbourne. The **Po Hong Trading Company**, on the corner of Cohen Place, has a huge assortment of Chinese knick-knacks.

The **Museum of Chinese Australian History**, 22 Cohen Place, documents the long history of Chinese people in Australia. The entrance is guarded by Dai Loong, the dragon who comes out to party on Chinese New Year. It's open daily from 10 am to 4.30 pm (Saturday from noon); admission is $5/3 for adults/children. It also conducts walking tours around Chinatown every morning, charging $15 (two hours) or $28 (three hours, including lunch). Book on ☎ 9662 2888.

There are many old buildings and warehouses in Little Bourke St and in the lanes that run off it.

Queen Victoria Market

This market, on the corner of Victoria and Peel Sts, has been running for more than 100 years. It's historic but also a great place to buy just about anything, or to just wander around.

Queen Victoria Market Walking Tours (☎ 9320 5822) runs two-hour tours around the market from Tuesday to Saturday. You get to visit all sorts of different stalls, meet a fascinating bunch of characters, and taste a variety of interesting goodies. The 'Foodies Dream' tour costs $18 and there's also a Heritage Tour ($12). Bookings are necessary.

Old Melbourne Gaol

This gruesome old gaol and museum (☎ 9663 7228) is a dark, dank, spooky place. Over 100 people were hanged here, including Aussie icon Ned Kelly. It is open from 9.30 am to 4.30 pm daily ($8 for adults, $5 for children, $6 for students or $23 for a family). There are also tours on Wednesday and Sunday nights at 7.45 pm (8.45 pm during daylight saving) for $17/9 for adults/children. Book through Ticketmaster (☎ 13 6100).

Melbourne Museum

Billed as 'the southern hemisphere's largest and most innovative museum', the new Melbourne Museum will open in late July 2000, in the Carlton Gardens by the Exhibition Building. The museum replaces the former Museum of Victoria in Swanston St. Its features include Bunjilaka, the Aboriginal Centre; a living forest gallery; a 3D interactive theatre and major exhibition galleries. Admission costs $5/12/30 for a child/adult/family.

Immigration Museum & Hellenic Antiquities Museum

In the old Customs House (1858-70) on Flinders St between William and Market Sts, the Immigration Museum (☎ 9927 2732) tells the story of Melbourne's immigrants. On the 2nd floor is the Hellenic Antiquities Museum, with changing exhibitions from Greece.

Both museums are open daily from 10 am to 5 pm. Admission to either is $7; to both it's $12.

Other Historic Buildings

The city's other historic buildings are too numerous to mention here. Some of the more notable ones are the simple Georgian **John Smith's House** (1848), 300 Queen St;

the massive **Law Courts** buildings (1874-84) in William St between Little Bourke and Lonsdale Sts; the **Old Royal Mint** (1872) in William St, adjacent to the Flagstaff Gardens; and **St James Old Cathedral** (1842), on the corner of King and Batman Sts, which is Melbourne's oldest surviving building.

Victoriana enthusiasts may also find some very small Melbourne buildings of interest – scattered around the city are some fine cast-iron men's urinals (like French *pissoirs*).

SOUTHBANK

Across the river from the city centre, the **Southgate** development has riverside walks and three levels of restaurants, cafes and bars, all of which enjoy a view of the city skyline and river.

Arts Precinct

This area to the east of Southbank, on St Kilda Rd, is the heart of Melbourne's high culture.

The fortress-like facade of the **National Gallery of Victoria** is enlivened by Deborah Halpern's quirky *Angel*, standing in the moat. Unfortunately, the gallery is closed until 2002 for a major make-over. Its Australian collection goes to a new home in Federation Square, and a small sample of the rest is on display in the State Library building. Regional galleries around the state also house some of the collection.

The **Victorian Arts Centre** is made up of two buildings – the Melbourne Concert Hall and the Theatres Building. The interiors of both buildings are stunning. The **Melbourne Concert Hall**, the circular building closest to the Yarra, is the main venue for major artists and companies, and the home of the Melbourne Symphony Orchestra. Most of the hall is below ground. The **Theatres Building** is topped by a spire, which is lit up at night. Underneath it are the State Theatre, the Playhouse and the George Fairfax Studio.

There are weekday tours of the concert and theatre complex at noon and 2.30 pm and on Saturday at 10.30 am and noon ($8). On Sunday you can visit the backstage areas at 12.15 pm ($12). Phone ☎ 9281 8198 for details, as backstage tours are not always available; children under 12 are not allowed backstage.

The **Performing Arts Museum** in the Theatres Building has changing exhibitions on all aspects of the performing arts. Admission is free and the museum is open whenever the building is.

Crown Casino

The operators refer to this megalith as Crown Entertainment Complex. It was fleetingly the world's largest casino and it's still the biggest in the southern hemisphere. The complex never closes and is worth a look if you're a fan of kitsch.

It's incredibly garish, noisy and crass, but what else would you expect from a casino? As well as gambling there are bars, cafes and restaurants, some of them cheapish, a cinema and the Planet Hollywood nightclub.

Across Clarendon St from the casino is the architecturally interesting **Melbourne Exhibition Centre**. It's known as Jeff's Shed, as it was built under the auspices of the former premier Jeff Kennett, and, well, it does somewhat resemble a shed.

Polly Woodside Maritime Museum

This museum (☎ 9699 9760) is on the riverfront, close to the Spencer St bridge. The *Polly Woodside* is an old sailing ship and is now the centrepiece of this maritime museum, open daily from 10 am to 5 pm. Admission is $8 for adults and $4 for children.

OTHER MUSEUMS

Scienceworks Museum, Booker St in Spotswood, under the shadow of the West Gate Bridge, is an interesting hands-on science museum. It's open daily from 10 am to 4.30 pm ($8/4). The museum is a 15 minute walk from Spotswood train station down Hudsons Rd.

The **Jewish Holocaust Centre** (☎ 9528 1985), 13 Selwyn St, Elsternwick (close to Elsternwick train station), tells a grim story and the guides are Holocaust survivors. It's open Monday to Thursday from 10 am to 2 pm

VICTORIA

and Sunday from 11 am to 3 pm (entry by donation).

Still under construction at the time of writing, **Melbourne Aquarium** will be an exciting place, with a huge tank extending into the Yarra. It's east of Kings Way, on the north side of the river.

PARKS & GARDENS

Victoria has dubbed itself the 'Garden State' and Melbourne has a wonderful array of public parks and gardens.

Kings Domain

The Royal Botanic Gardens form a corner of the huge Kings Domain.

Beside St Kilda Rd stands the massive **Shrine of Remembrance**, built as a memorial to Victorians killed in WWI. It's worth climbing to the top for fine views. The shrine is open daily from 10 am to 5 pm.

On Birdwood Ave near the shrine is Governor **La Trobe's Cottage**, the original Victorian government house, sent out from 'the mother country' in prefabricated form in 1840. It's open daily except Tuesday and Thursday ($2).

Imposing **Government House** (1872) is a copy of Queen Victoria's palace on England's Isle of Wight. There are guided tours on Monday, Wednesday and Saturday ($8). You need to book (☎ 9654 5528 – no tours from mid-December to the end of January).

On the other side of Birdwood Ave from La Trobe's cottage are the **Old Melbourne Observatory** and the **National Herbarium** at the main entrance to the Royal Botanic Gardens.

At the city end of the park is the **Sidney Myer Music Bowl**, an outdoor performance area.

Royal Botanic Gardens

The finest botanic gardens in Australia and among the finest in the world, a visit is a must. Pick up guide-yourself leaflets at the entrances. There are several entrance gates but the visitor centre is in the National Herbarium inside Gate F on Birdwood Ave. Free guided tours depart from here most

days at 10 and 11 am. The gardens are open daily from sunrise to sunset (free). The observatory cafe, opposite the Shrine, is open daily from 7 am to 5 pm and the cafe and kiosk beside the lake are open daily from 9 am to 5 pm (4.30 pm in winter).

There's a surprising amount of wildlife and if you peer over one of the small bridges you'll probably see some eels. A large colony of fruit bats lives in the trees of the fern gully.

The gardens are encircled by a former horse-exercising track known as the **Tan**, now a 4km running track that is Melbourne's favourite venue for joggers.

Fitzroy & Treasury Gardens

The Fitzroy Gardens divide the city centre from East Melbourne. By the kiosk in the centre of the gardens is a miniature **Tudor village** and the **Fairy Tree**, carved in 1932.

Captain Cook's Cottage is actually the former Yorkshire home of Cook's parents and is furnished as it would have been around 1750. There is an interesting exhibit on Cook's life and achievements. It is open daily ($3/1.50).

Nearby, the **Conservatory** has floral displays ($1).

In the early evening in the **Treasury Gardens**, you'll probably meet **possums**. If you must feed them (and they are cute), give them fruit, not bread or crisps, which can cause serious health problems.

Other Parks & Gardens

The **Flagstaff Gardens**, near the Queen Victoria Market, once provided good views of the bay, so a signalling station was set up here. Free lunchtime concerts are held in the gardens, particularly in warmer weather.

The **Carlton Gardens** surround the historic **Royal Exhibition Building**, built for the Great Exhibition of 1880.

ALONG THE YARRA RIVER

The Yarra is a surprisingly pleasant river. Despite being known as 'the river that flows upside down', it's just muddy, not particularly dirty.

Boat cruises along the river depart from Princes Walk (below Princes Bridge) and from Southgate. Bike paths (see the Bicycle entry in the Getting Around section later) start from the city and follow the river, and bikes can be hired from various places.

Yarra Bend Park

North-east of the city centre, the Yarra is bordered by the Yarra Bend parklands. To get there, follow Johnston St through Collingwood and turn into the scenic Yarra Blvd or hire a bike and ride around the riverside paths. By public transport, take tram No 42 from Collins St east along Victoria St to stop No 28, then walk up Walmer St and over the footbridge; or take bus No 201 or 203 from Flinders St train station, both of which go up Studley Park Rd.

The park has large areas of bushland and it's hard to believe the city's all around you. **Studley Park Boathouse** (☎ 9853 1972), open daily from 9.30 am to sunset, has a cafe and boats and canoes for hire. Kanes footbridge takes you across to the other side of the river, and it's about a 20 minute walk to **Dights Falls** at the confluence of the Yarra River and Merri Creek. You can also walk to the falls along the southern bank.

Further up river, Fairfield Park is the site of the **Fairfield Amphitheatre**, an open-air venue for plays, concerts and films. The **Fairfield Park Boathouse & Tea Gardens** (☎ 9486 1501) on Fairfield Park Drive, Fairfield, is a restored boathouse with a garden restaurant. It's open daily from October to March and on weekends the rest of the year.

YARRA PARK

Yarra Park is the large expanse of parkland to the south-east of the city centre, containing the Melbourne Cricket Ground, the Melbourne Park National Tennis Centre, Olympic Park and several other sports ovals.

Melbourne Cricket Ground

The Melbourne Cricket Ground (MCG or just 'the G') is one of the world's great sporting venues. The first game of Australian Rules Football was played near here in 1858, and in 1877 the first Test cricket match between Australia and England was played here. The MCG was the central stadium for the 1956 Melbourne Olympics, and will be used in the 2006 Commonwealth Games, hosted by Melbourne. The stadium will host some soccer matches during the 2000 Olympics and a semi-artificial surface will be laid – heresy!

The Melbourne Cricket Club (MCC) **Members' Pavilion** is the oldest stand. The pavilion houses the **MCC Cricket Library and Museum**. These are open weekdays from 10 am to 4 pm (except on match days) and admission is free.

Australian Gallery of Sport & Olympic Museum

In front of the members' entrance to the MCG (near the corner of Jolimont St and Jolimont Terrace), this museum is dedicated to Australia's sporting passions. It's open daily from 9.30 am to 4.30 pm, and admission ($9.50/6, or $25 for families) includes a tour of the MCG and the museum. Tours run hourly between 10 am and 3 pm, although they may be curtailed on match days.

Melbourne Park National Tennis Centre

A footbridge links the Melbourne Park National Tennis Centre with the MCG. The centre hosts the Australian Open (a Grand Slam event) in January and is also a concert venue. The centre's indoor and outdoor courts are available to the public (see the Activities section later).

CARLTON & PARKVILLE

This is a cosmopolitan old area that blends the intellectual with the gastronomic, the sporting with the cultural.

Royal Park

Royal Park, a large expanse of parklands, contains sports ovals and open spaces, netball and hockey stadiums, a public golf course and the Melbourne Zoo. In the corner closest to the University of Melbourne is a garden of Australian plants.

Melbourne Zoo

Melbourne's zoo is Australia's oldest (1861) and is the third oldest in the world.

It's a great place to visit and you should allow at least half a day.

The zoo is open daily from 9 am to 5 pm. Admission costs $14.50/7.20 or $39.30 for families. From the city, take tram No 55 or 56 from William St, or an Upfield-line train to Royal Park train station (no trains on Sunday!). A 1920s tourist tram runs from the city to the zoo on Sunday. Phone the Met (☎ 13 1638) for times.

University of Melbourne

This university, also known as Melbourne University, was established in 1853 and has some nice buildings, especially the colleges at the north end.

There are often bands in North Court (behind Union House), or you could sit in on a lecture, browse the Baillieu Library or visit the free galleries and museums. The most interesting is the Percy Grainger Museum, open weekdays, dedicated to the life and times of this eccentric composer.

Lygon St

Carlton is Melbourne's Italian quarter and Lygon St its stylish backbone. Lygon St was also Melbourne's first bohemian street. It no longer has much offbeat appeal, but not all of the hangouts have gone. Restaurants like Tiamo, Papa Gino's and Jimmy Watson's have resisted change; you can still play pool at Johnny's Green Room, and La Mama, a tiny experimental theatre, is still going strong in Faraday St.

Every November, the Lygon St Festa is a four day food-and-fun street party.

FITZROY & COLLINGWOOD

Fitzroy is where Melbourne's bohemians moved when the lights got too bright in Carlton.

Brunswick St, especially around Johnston St, is where you'll find some of the best food, the weirdest shops and the most interesting people. Johnston St is the centre of Melbourne's small Spanish-speaking community. It hosts the Hispanic Festival in November.

Smith St forms the border between Fitzroy and Collingwood, and is in turn becoming an exciting strip.

Carlton & United Breweries, maker of beers such as Fosters and Victoria Bitter, has a visitor centre at the Carlton Brewhouse with some interesting displays. It's actually in Abbotsford, a small suburb between Collingwood and Richmond, on the corner of Nelson and Thompson Sts, and is open from Monday to Saturday. Admission is $5 (including a tasting). On weekdays there are tours of the brewery at 10 and 11.30 am and 2 pm ($7.50). Book on ☎ 9420 6800.

EAST MELBOURNE

East Melbourne is a small residential pocket of elegant Victorian houses. Tasma Terrace, in Parliament Place behind Parliament House, is a magnificent row of terraces. It houses the National Trust, which has information on National Trust properties. Impressive St Patricks Cathedral is behind Parliament House.

Diagonally across Gisborne St from the cathedral is Eastern Hill Fire Station, which houses the Fire Services Museum of Victoria (☎ 9662 2907), open on Friday from 9 am to 3 pm and Sunday from 10 am to 4 pm ($5/2).

RICHMOND

As Carlton is to Italy so Richmond is to Vietnam, although there are still many Greek Australians living here, from a previous wave of immigrants. You might even find an Irish Australian from an earlier wave.

The Bridge Rd and Swan St areas are fashion centres, where designers sell their seconds and rejects alongside the outlets of good young designers. Dimmey's, 140 Swan St, is an old-fashioned department store that's one of the cheapest and most bizarre places to buy just about anything.

SOUTH YARRA & TOORAK

South Yarra and Toorak are on the 'right' side of the river – the high-society side of town. South Yarra is bustling, trendy and style-conscious. Further east, Toorak is the poshest suburb in Melbourne.

At the St Kilda Rd end of Toorak Rd stands the copper-domed Hebrew Synagogue (1930). On the south side of Toorak

Rd between Punt Rd and St Kilda Rd is **Fawkner Park**. **Como House**, 16 Como Ave, is one of Australia's finest colonial mansions, and it's open daily ($9).

At the Toorak end of Toorak Rd is the smaller and more exclusive group of shops known as **Toorak Village**, between Wallace Ave and Grange Rd.

The South Yarra end of Chapel St, between Toorak Rd and Commercial Rd, is Melbourne's most stylish centre for retail fashion. The **Jam Factory**, No 500, is a large shopping and entertainment complex.

PRAHRAN

Prahran is populated by people from a broad range of ethnic backgrounds and is enlivened by a variety of cultural influences.

Prahran's sector of **Chapel St** stretches from Malvern Rd down to Dandenong Rd, and is more diverse than the South Yarra sector. The delightful Prahran Market is just around the corner from Chapel St on

SOUTH YARRA & PRAHRAN

PLACES TO STAY		23	Cafe 151;
1	Albany Motor Inn		Alternative;
2	West End Private		Sandgropers
	Hotel	25	Sweet Basil
3	St James Motel	26	Blue Elephant;
8	Claremont		The Outlook
	Accommodation	27	Feedwell Cafe
21	Hotel Saville	28	Continental Cafe
		29	Globe Cafe
PLACES TO EAT		30	Saigon Rose
4	France Soir		
6	La Porchetta	**OTHER**	
11	Tamani Bistro	5	Longford
12	Chinois	7	Readings
13	Tanah Ria	9	Victorian AIDS
14	Corridor		Council & Gay
15	Caffe e Cucina		Men's Health
16	Chapelli's; That		Centre
	Little Noodle	10	Como Centre;
	Place		Hotel Como;
17	La Lucciola; STA		Como Cinemas
	Travel	20	Chasers
18	Frostbites	22	Exchange Hotel
19	Kush	24	Prahran Market

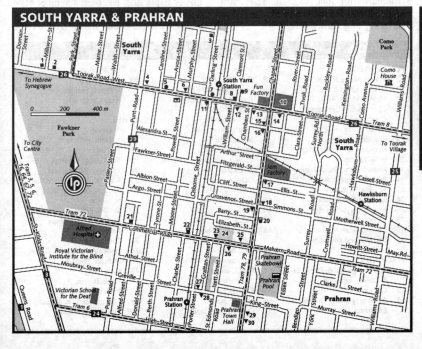

SOUTH YARRA & PRAHRAN

VICTORIA

Commercial Rd. **Commercial Rd** is a centre for the gay and lesbian community.

Running off Chapel St beside the Prahran Town Hall, **Greville St** has a quirky collection of offbeat clothing shops, galleries, bookshops, junk shops and some good bars and cafes.

ST KILDA

St Kilda is one of Melbourne's liveliest and most cosmopolitan areas.

In Melbourne's early days, St Kilda was a fashionable seaside resort but it gradually declined. By the 1960s it was pretty seedy and its decadent image of faded glories (and cheap rents) attracted immigrants and refugees, bohemians and down-and-outers.

St Kilda has undergone an image upgrade, although it's still a place of extremes – backpacker hostels and fine-dine restaurants, sports cars and junkies. It can still be perilous to wander the streets late at night, particularly for lone women. The main streets, **Fitzroy St** and **Acland St**, are full of interesting shops and eateries.

If you follow **Carlisle St** across St Kilda Rd and into East St Kilda, you'll find some great Jewish food shops and European delis. The **Jewish Museum of Australia** (☎ 9534 0083), 26 Alma Rd, houses displays relating to Jewish history and culture, as well as regular exhibitions. It's open Tuesday to Thursday from 10 am to 4 pm, and Sunday from 11 am to 5 pm ($5/3).

The **St Kilda Festival** in February is a showcase for local artists, musicians and writers, and features street parties, parades, concerts and *lots* more.

Seaside St Kilda

St Kilda Pier and breakwater is a favourite spot for strollers. Bicycles can be hired by the pier in summer. You can take a boat cruise with **Penguin Waters Cruises** (☎ 0412 187 202) to see a fairy penguin colony. Sunset cruises, including a barbecue and drinks, cost $30 from St Kilda Pier; $40 from Southbank.

The laughing face of **Luna Park**, on the Lower Esplanade, has been a symbol of St Kilda since 1912. It's an old-fashioned amusement park but that's part of the

ST KILDA

PLACES TO STAY
2   Robinson's by the Sea
3   Cabana Court Motel
4   Victoria House B&B
6   Charnwood Motor Inn
7   Crest international Hotel/Motel
11 St Kilda Coffee Palace
14 Kookaburra Backpackers
15 Enfield House
17 Hotel Tolarno; Bar & Bistro
21 Warwick Beachside
32 St Kilda Quest Inn
34 Olembia Guesthouse
36 Novotel Bayside Hotel
38 Carlisle Motor Lodge
39 Cosmopolitan Motor Inn
55 Barkly Quest Lodgings

PLACES TO EAT
10 The George Hotel, Public Bar & Gallery; Snakepit
12 Chichio's
13 Bar Ninety Seven; Chronicles Bookshop

16 Topolino's
18 Thai Panic Cafe
19 Leo's Spaghetti Bar
20 Cafe Menis; Bortoletto's
22 Hard Wok Cafe
23 Café Di Stasio
25 Chiata Ria – Blues
26 Street Cafe
28 Madame Joe Joe
37 Spuntino; Harley Court; Dog's Bar
41 Galleon
42 Vineyard Restaurant
.45 The Stokehouse
46 Pavilion
47 Bala's
48 Chinta Ria–Soul; Cafe Goa
49 Cafe Manna
50 Red Rock Noodle Bar
51 Blue Danube; Scheherezade
54 Cicciolina
56 Noodle Box
57 Orienta on Acland

58 Big Mouth
59 Wild Rice; Claypots Seafood Bar
61 Rasa's Vegie Bar

OTHER
1   Mansion
5   Corroboree Tree
8   The Ritz
9   The George Cinemas
24 Prince of Wales Hotel
27 Rock 'n' Roll 'n' Skate Hire
29 Royal Melbourne Yacht Squadron
30 St Kilda Baths
31 Esplanade Hotel; Espy Kitchen
33 Theatreworks
35 Linden Art Centre & Gallery
40 National Theatre
43 Luna Park
44 Palais Theatre
52 Internet Kennel Cafe
53 Cosmos Books & Music
60 Village Belle Hotel

VICTORIA

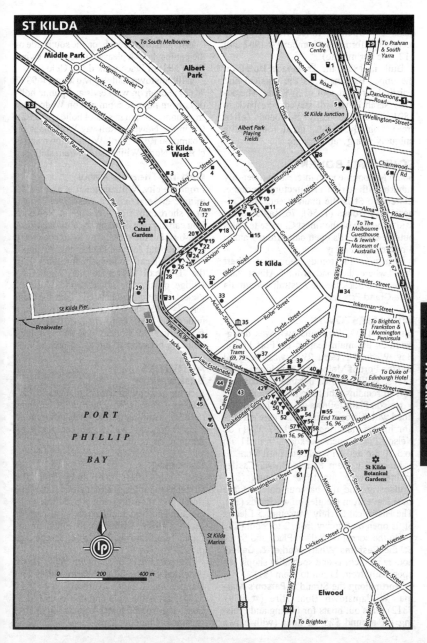

charm. Admission is free and each ride costs $3. Opening times vary; ring the recorded information number (☎ 1902 240 112, 30c per minute).

Built in 1880, the **Esplanade Hotel**, on the upper Esplanade, is the musical and artistic heart and soul of St Kilda. The actress Sarah Bernhardt stayed here back in 1891. Today the 'Espy' has bands (often free), comedy nights, great food and a uniquely grungy atmosphere.

SOUTH MELBOURNE

South Melbourne is an interesting inner-city suburb with a rich architectural heritage. **Clarendon St** is the main street. The **Chinese Joss House** (1856), 76 Raglan St, is said to be one of the finest Chinese temples outside China. It's open daily from 9 am to 4 pm, except Friday.

Nearby is the trendy suburb of **Albert Park**, where the road around Albert Park Lake is the track for the **Australian Formula One Grand Prix** race.

WILLIAMSTOWN

Back in 1837, Williamstown was designated as the main seaport on Port Phillip Bay. When the Yarra River was deepened and the Port of Melbourne developed in the 1880s, Williamstown became a secondary port. It remains a historic backwater.

Nelson Place follows the foreshore and is lined with historic buildings. There's a Visitor Information Booth (☎ 9397 3791) on Nelson Place, open weekdays from 11 am to 3.30 pm and on weekends until 5 pm.

Moored at Gem Pier is **HMAS Castlemaine**, now a maritime museum ($5). **Cruises** around the harbour on the *Little Gem* leave from the pier on weekends ($5). The **Historical Society Museum**, 5 Electra St, is open on Sunday from 2 to 5 pm ($3).

On the corner of Nelson Place and Syme St, the **Customs Wharf Market & Gallery** houses arts, crafts and speciality shops. It's open daily from 11 am to 6 pm ($1).

North along the Strand at **Parson's Marina**, Williamstown Boat Hire (☎ 9397 7312) rents out boats for fishing and cruising for around $25 an hour (with a two

hour minimum). It also hires tackle and sells bait.

Williamstown Beach, on the south side of the peninsula, is a pleasant place for a swim. From Nelson Place walk down Cole St.

Williamstown Railway Museum (☎ 9397 7412) is open on weekends and public holidays from noon to 5 pm and on Wednesday from noon to 4 pm in school holidays ($5/2). It's in the Newport Railway Workshops on Champion Rd in North Williamstown and is close to North Williamstown train station.

Getting There & Away

From the city, Williamstown is about a 10 minute drive across the West Gate Bridge, or a short train ride – change at Newport. You can also get there on the City Wanderer tour bus, but the nicest way to go is by ferry – see Getting Around later in this section.

A bicycle path follows the foreshore from the Timeball Tower to the West Gate Bridge, passing the Scienceworks Museum. Pedestrians and cyclists can take the Punt ferry (☎ 015 304 470) across the river from under the West Gate Bridge. It operates from Friday to Monday and during school holidays between 10 am and 5 pm ($3).

ACTIVITIES
Bushwalking

Pick up a copy of *Walking Around Melbourne – Bushwalking by Public Transport* ($12.95, available at the NRE information centre) for day walks you can reach by jumping on a train or bus.

Canoeing

The Yarra offers everything from flat stretches to rapids of about grade three (difficult and requiring some paddling technique). The best sections are in the upper reaches from Warburton to Fitzsimmons Lane, Templestowe. The lower reaches are mostly flat water.

The pamphlet *Canoeing the Upper Yarra*, provided by the Upper Yarra Valley and Dandenong Ranges Authority (☎ 5967 5222), gives the do's and don'ts and locations. The Youth Hostel Association (YHA) organises canoeing trips.

Studley Park Boat House, Melbourne, Vic

Victorian Arts Centre spire, Melbourne, Vic

Brighton beach bathing boxes and the city of Melbourne in the distance, Vic

Chalet at Dinner Plain Alpine Resort, Vic

Grade 21 'Kachoong', Mt Arapiles, Vic

Surf lifesavers, Great Ocean Road, Vic

Domain Chandon vineyard, Yarra Valley, Vic

For more sedate canoeing in the city, see the earlier Yarra Bend Park entry.

Windsurfing/Sailboarding

Elwood and Middle Park beaches are designated sailboarding areas. Repeat Performance Sailboards (☎ 9525 6475), 87 Ormond Rd, Elwood, hires out beginners' boards for $15 an hour or $35 for half a day, and specialised equipment for between $45 and $75 a half day. It offers packages for longer hires.

Fishing & Boating

Port Melbourne, Albert Park and St Kilda piers are popular places. Tackle shops like the Compleat Angler, 19 McKillop St in the city, are good places for advice.

Boats can be hired for fishing on the bay. Try Williamstown Boat Hire (☎ 9397 7312), Parson's Marina, Williamstown – the same people have Southgate Boat Hire, Berth 1 Southgate, with boats for cruising along the Yarra. Weather conditions can change quickly on the bay and it's shallow, so a vicious chop can spring up – be prepared.

Canoes and boats can also be hired along the Yarra – see the earlier Yarra Bend Park entry.

Sailing

There are about 20 yacht clubs around the bay and races are held most weekends (some clubs race on Wednesday as well). Some clubs welcome visitors as crew on racing boats. Phone the race secretary at one of the major clubs. (You might learn some new words, as we did after dropping a small but vital shackle-pin into the briny deep.)

The big clubs are: Royal Melbourne Yacht Squadron (☎ 9534 0227) in St Kilda; Royal Brighton Yacht Club (☎ 9592 3089); Sandringham Yacht Club (☎ 9598 7444) and Hobson's Bay Yacht Club (☎ 9397 6393) in Williamstown.

For more leisurely sailing, dinghies can be hired from the Jolly Roger School of Sailing (☎ 9690 5862) at Albert Park Lake.

You can learn to sail in Melbourne, in dinghies at the Jolly Roger School, or, to gain your Competent Crew certificate on yachts (handy if you plan to hitch a ride on

one), with a school such as Geoff Steadman's Melbourne Sailing School (☎ 9589 1433).

Melbourne's main ocean races are the Melbourne to Devonport and Melbourne to Hobart, held between Christmas and New Year.

Swimming

Swimming Pools The Melbourne City Baths, on the corner of Swanston and Victoria Sts, has a 25m indoor pool plus a gym, spas, saunas and squash courts. It's open weekdays from 6 am to 10 pm and weekends from 8 am to 6 pm. A swim, spa and sauna costs $6.50.

In the Albert Park Lake's parklands is the Melbourne Sports and Aquatic Centre. It's a great place for a swim, with a 75m pool and several other pools, plus a water-slide. It's open weekdays from 6 am to 10 pm and weekends from 7 am to 8 pm. Entry costs $4/3).

Other pools near the city include the outdoor Carlton Baths in Rathdowne St, Fitzroy Baths in Alexandra Parade, Prahran Pool in Essex St; the indoor Richmond Recreation Centre in Gleadell St and St Kilda Public Swimming Centre in Alma Rd. The outdoor pools are generally open from late October until April. One exception is the Harold Holt Swimming Centre in High St, Glen Iris (which must be the only pool in the world named after a prime minister who drowned). It's open year round and has indoor and outdoor pools, spas, saunas and aerobics.

In-Line Skating

The best tracks are around Port Phillip Bay from Port Melbourne to Brighton. You can hire from places like Rock 'n' Roll 'n' Skate Hire (☎ 9525 3434), 11 Fitzroy St in St Kilda. It charges $8 for the first hour (less for subsequent hours) and $25 for 24 hours.

Tennis & Squash

Tennis court hire is generally between $10 and $20 an hour. On weekends rates are often higher, and for floodlit or indoor courts you'll pay between $17 and $24 an hour.

Except in January during the Australian Open, you can hire an indoor or outdoor court at the Melbourne Park National Tennis Centre (☎ 9286 1244) on Batman Ave. For other public courts see the *Yellow Pages* phone book.

There are squash courts in the city at the Melbourne City Baths ($9 for half an hour in peak times, $6 in off-peak).

ORGANISED TOURS
City Bus Tours
Companies like AAT Kings (☎ 9663 3377), Australian Pacific (☎ 9663 1611) and Gray Line (☎ 9663 4455) run city tours and day trips to tourist destinations.

The City Explorer (☎ 9650 7000) does a continuous circuit around the city and inner suburbs, with stops at major attractions. Passes are sold on board and one/two-day passes cost $22/35. There's an information kiosk outside the town hall, which is the first stop. The first circuit begins here daily at 10 am and the last bus leaves at 4 pm.

The City Wanderer (☎ 9563 9788) does a similar circuit, as well as heading over the West Gate Bridge to the Scienceworks Museum and Williamstown. One-day passes cost $20. The first bus leaves the Town Hall at 10.30 am.

Tickets for both buses get you discounts at various attractions, and you can get on and off all day.

River Cruises
Melbourne River Cruises (☎ 9614 1215) departs half-hourly from Princes Walk (on the north bank of the river, east of Princes Bridge) and from Southgate. You can take a one hour cruise either upstream or downstream ($13) or combine the two for a 2½ hour cruise ($25). Southgate River Tours (☎ 9682 5711) offers an hour-long cruise upstream to Herring Island in the steampowered *Elizabeth Anne*, departing from Berth 4 at Southgate.

Maribyrnong River Cruises (☎ 9689 6431) has 2½-hour cruises up the Maribyrnong River, with a stopover at the interesting Living Museum of the West ($14), and one-hour cruises down to the West Gate Bridge and docklands ($7). Departures are from the end of Wingfield St in Footscray.

You can also cruise to the penguin colony at St Kilda pier – see the earlier St Kilda section for details.

Bicycle
City Cycle Tours (☎ 9585 5343) offers guided tours of the city by bike. Bicycles are supplied or you can 'bring your own' (BYO).

SPECIAL EVENTS
Melbourne has festivals year round. 'What's on' lists are available from tourist information offices. Tickets to most events can be booked through Ticketmaster (see Entertainment later in this chapter for phone details).

January
A public *New Year's Eve* party is often held at Southgate.
The *Australian Open*, a Grand Slam tennis championship, is held at the Melbourne Park Tennis Centre every January.
Australia Day (26 January) is celebrated in all sorts of ways, including fireworks at Albert Park Lake.
The eclectic *Montsalvat Jazz Festival* is held over three days at the artists' colony in Eltham and various other venues.

February
The *St Kilda Festival* is a week-long celebration of local arts, culture and food.
Chinatown comes to life with the celebration of *Chinese New Year* and the *Asian Food Festival*.
The gay and lesbian *Midsumma Festival* is held in early February.

March
The 10 day *Moomba* festival, in early March, is one of Melbourne's favourite and liveliest family events.
The *Formula 1 Grand Prix* is held at the Albert Park circuit in early March.
The *Melbourne Food and Wine Festival* is held over two weeks in late March.
Oh, and the *football season* kicks off in March too!

April
The brilliant *International Comedy Festival* takes over the town and the locals are joined by a swag of international acts.
Anzac Day, commemorating those who fell in war, is on 25 April. The day begins with a

dawn service at the Shrine of Remembrance, followed by a march along St Kilda Rd to the city.

July

The *International Film Festival* opens.

September

The *Australian Football League (AFL) Finals* series climax with the *Grand Final*, played on the last Saturday in September (but not in 2000 – due to Olympic commitments at the MCG the Grand Final will be held earlier in September).

Also in September is the *Royal Melbourne Show*, at the Royal Melbourne Showgrounds in Flemington.

October

The *Melbourne International Festival* combines the best of the performing arts, visual arts and music, and incorporates the *Melbourne Writers Festival* and the *Melbourne Fringe Arts Festival* – don't miss the weird and wild street party in Brunswick St.

On Phillip Island, the *Australian Motorcycle Grand Prix* is held.

November

The *Melbourne Cup* horse race is on the first Tuesday in November.

For the Italian *Lygon St Festa* in November, the street is filled with food stalls, bands and dancers; the entertainment also includes the manic waiters' race.

December

There are outdoor evening performances of plays such as *A Midsummer Night's Dream* and *Romeo and Juliet* in the Royal Botanic Gardens.

Since 1937 *Carols by Candlelight* have been held at the Myer Music Bowl. You'll need to book for all of these.

Head for the MCG on Boxing Day, when tens of thousands turn up for the first day of the international *Test Match*.

PLACES TO STAY

The city centre is convenient, although it can be a little lifeless at night. The alternative is to stay in one of the inner suburbs.

If you decide to stay longer, look in *The Age* classifieds on Wednesday and Saturday under 'Share Accommodation'. Also try the notice boards in hostels, and places like the

universities, Readings bookshop in Carlton, Cosmos Books & Music and the Galleon restaurant in St Kilda, and the Black Cat cafe in Fitzroy.

Camping & Caravan Parks

There are a few caravan/camping parks in the metropolitan area but none are close to the centre and most are in unattractive areas. *Hobsons Bay Caravan Park (☎ 9397 2395, 158 Kororoit Creek Rd, Williamstown)* is a long way from the city centre (about 15km) but Williamstown is a pleasant place. Sites cost $15 and cabins are $40/45 a single/double. The caravan park is about 2km west of Williamstown's shopping centre and 2.5km west of the bayfront.

The closest place to the city centre is *Melbourne Holiday Park (☎ 9354 3533, 265 Elizabeth St, Coburg East)*, 10km north of the city. For two people camping costs from $18 and cabins from $47.

Hostels

The following is a selection of hostels in popular areas, all good for your first night or two. After that you might want to look around for something that more closely matches your own style – there are lots to choose from. The prices listed are indicative only. The YHA hostels have the same prices all year, but at the others you can expect to pay a little less in winter and a little more in summer. Most offer cheaper weekly rates.

City Centre *Toad Hall (☎ 9600 9010, 441 Elizabeth St)* is within walking distance of the bus terminals. It's quiet and well equipped, and has off-street parking for $5. Dorm beds cost from $16; single/double/triple rooms cost about $30/48/52.

Exford Hotel Backpackers (☎ 9663 2697, 199 Russell St) is cheerful and well set up, in the upper section of a pub. Rates are marginally less than those at Toad Hall. The same people run the big, well equipped *Flinders Station Hostel (☎ 9620 5100)* on the corner of Elizabeth St and Flinders Lane. *Hotel Bakpak (☎ 9329 7525, 167 Franklin St)* gets good reports.

The *City Centre Private Hotel (☎ 9654 5401, 22 Little Collins St)* is clean and quiet, if somewhat prim. All rooms have shared bathrooms. Backpackers pay $18 in a three or four-bed room and doubles are $37; serviced singles/doubles are $37/50.

North Melbourne Both of Melbourne's YHA hostels are in North Melbourne, north-west of the city centre. From the airport you can ask the Skybus to drop you at the North Melbourne hostels.

The YHA showpiece is the huge *Queensberry Hill Hostel (☎ 9329 8599, 78 Howard St)*. It can feel a little soulless but it has excellent facilities. Dorms cost $18; rooms are $45/55, or $55/65 with bathroom, and there's an apartment for $95. Office hours are 7 am to 11 pm (there's 24 hour access after you check in). Catch tram No 55 from William St to stop No 11 (Queensberry St), or any tram north up Elizabeth St to stop No 8 (Queensberry St). Walk west on Queensberry St and turn right into Howard St.

Chapman Gardens YHA Hostel (☎ 9328 3595, 76 Chapman St) is smaller and older but can be a bit more intimate than Queensberry Hill. Beds in a dorm cost $15, singles $33, twin rooms $36 and doubles $44. From Elizabeth St in the city, take tram No 50 or 57 along Flemington Rd and get off at stop No 19, then walk down Abbotsford St. Chapman St is the first on the left.

Carlton *Carlton College (☎ 1800 066 551, 101 Drummond St, Carlton)* is a student residence in a fine triple storey terrace row – it becomes a hostel over summer. Dorm beds are $15 and rooms are just $25/40. This place has more of a hostel atmosphere than the colleges listed in the later Colleges section.

Fitzroy Well located on the fringe of the city and opposite the Exhibition Gardens, *The Nunnery (☎ 1800 032 635, 116 Nicholson St)* is one of the better hostels. Rates range from $18 in a twelve bed dorm to $21 in a three bed dorm; singles are around $40 and twins/doubles are around $55. Take tram No 96 heading east along Bourke St from the city centre and get off at stop No 13.

Richmond *Richmond Hill Hotel (☎ 9428 6501, 353 Church St)* is a big Victorian-era building with spacious living areas and clean rooms. Dorm beds cost about $18, singles/twins are $40/50, and it has a B&B section with good single/double rooms from around $60/80.

South Yarra *Lord's Lodge Backpackers (☎ 9510 5658, 204 Punt Rd)* is on a fairly hectic main road. This is a large, rambling old two storey mansion with a range of accommodation and prices a little lower than places in the city.

Windsor Nomad's new *Chapel St Backpackers (☎ 9533 6855, 22 Chapel St, Windsor)* is within walking distance of both South Yarra and St Kilda. It has dorms for $18, doubles for $50 and a double with bathroom for $60. Breakfast is free.

St Kilda From Swanston St in the city, tram No 16 takes you down St Kilda Rd to Fitzroy St, or there's the faster light-rail service (No 96 from Spencer St and Bourke St) to the old St Kilda train station and along Fitzroy and Acland Sts.

Enfield House (☎ 9534 8159, 2 Enfield St) is the original and probably the most popular of St Kilda's hostels. It's a huge Victorian-era building with over 100 beds that somehow manages to have a good atmosphere. There's a variety of dorms, singles and twins. The hostel's courtesy bus picks up travellers from the bus terminals, and from Station Pier in Port Melbourne where the Tasmanian ferries dock.

The excellent *Olembia Guesthouse (☎ 9537 1412, 96 Barkly St)* is more like a boutique hotel than a hostel. The rooms are quite small but clean and comfortable, and all have hand-basins and central heating. Dorm beds cost $18, singles are $40, and twins and doubles are $56. Book ahead.

St Kilda Coffee Palace (☎ 1800 654 098, 24 Grey St) is a big, spacious place with its own cafe and a modern kitchen. Dorms range from $16 to $18 ($20 in a four bed dorm) and doubles are $50. Around the corner, *Kookaburra Backpackers (☎ 9534 5457,*

56 Jackson St) is different from most St Kilda places in that it's small. Dorms are $16 and double rooms $45.

Middle Park Well located between Albert Park Lake and the bay, the *Middle Park Hotel (☎ 9690 1958)*, on the corner of Canterbury Rd and Armstrong St, is a pub in a trendy little shopping centre. The upstairs rooms have been renovated and to stay costs $15 in dorms, $25 for singles ($35 in larger rooms) and $50 for doubles, all with shared bathrooms.

South Melbourne Right by the South Melbourne Market, within walking distance of Southgate and close to both light-rail and tram lines, *Nomad's Market Inn (☎ 1800 241 445, 115 Cecil St)* is not really in the centre of things but it's still well located. And it's a pleasant hostel in a converted pub, charging about $15 to $18 in dorms and $45 for doubles. Breakfast is free.

Colleges

The following colleges at (or near) the University of Melbourne have accommodation in the vacation period from late November to mid-February and some also offer rooms during the semester breaks (July and the second half of September). You'll pay around $40 per single for B&B and about $10 extra for all meals.

Ormond, Queen's and Trinity are impressive 19th century piles – ask for a room in their old buildings.

International House (☎ 9347 6655, 241 Royal Parade, Parkville)
Medley Hall (☎ 9663 5847, 48 Drummond St, Carlton)
Ormond College (☎ 9348 1688, College Crescent, in University grounds)
Queen's College (☎ 9349 0500, College Crescent, in University grounds)
Ridley College (☎ 9387 7555, 160 The Avenue, Parkville)
Trinity College (☎ 9347 1044, Royal Parade, in University grounds)
University College (☎ 9347 3533, College Crescent, opposite the University)

Whitley College (☎ 9347 8388, 271 Royal Parade, Parkville)

Hotels, Guesthouses, Apartments & B&Bs

City Centre The *Duke of Wellington Hotel (☎ 9650 4984)*, on the corner of Flinders and Russell Sts, has comfortable rooms with shared bathrooms at $50/90 for singles/ doubles, including breakfast. The basic *Stork Hotel (☎ 9663 6237)*, on the corner of Elizabeth and Therry Sts, is close to the Franklin St bus terminal and Queen Victoria Market, charges from $39/49, and has a small guest kitchen. *Hotel Y (☎ 9329 5188, 489 Elizabeth St)*, run by the YWCA, is an award-winning budget hotel close to the Franklin St bus terminal. It has simple four-bed bunk-rooms for $25, singles/doubles/triples for $79/87/99 and deluxe rooms from $99/110/ 120. The 'Y' has good facilities including a budget cafe, communal kitchen and laundry.

Hotel Enterprize (☎ 9629 6991, 44 Spencer St) has rooms from $50/60, or from $95/100 with en suites. *Batman's Hill Hotel (☎ 9614 6344, 66-70 Spencer St)* has rooms from $140, and *Pacific International Terrace Inn (☎ 9621 3333, 16 Spencer St)* is reasonable and charges from $109. *Astoria City Travel Inn (☎ 9670 6801, 288 Spencer St)* has rooms from $84.

The big *Victoria Vista Hotel (☎ 9653 0441, 215 Little Collins St)* is a notch up from the cheapest hotels. Rooms with shared facilities cost $45/60, rooms with en suite and TV cost from $85/124. *City Square Motel (☎ 9654 7011, 67 Swanston St)* is fairly simple, but it's well located and charges from $70/90/100.

All Seasons Welcome Hotel (☎ 9639 0555, 265 Little Bourke St) is good value for $95 a room. *All Seasons Crossley Hotel (☎ 9639 1639, 51 Little Bourke St)* is a small four star hotel in Chinatown with rooms from $140. *City Limits Motel (☎ 9662 2544, 20-22 Little Bourke St)* has rooms with kitchenettes from $99.

Miami Motel (☎ 9329 8499, 13 Hawke St), north-west of the city centre in West Melbourne, is a cross between a motel and a backpacker hostel. It's clean and simple,

VICTORIA

with rooms with shared bathrooms for $40/60 or $68/84 with en suites.

Top-end hotels in the city centre include *Novotel Melbourne on Collins* (☎ 9650 5800, 270 Collins St) from $220 per room; *Heritage Hotel Melbourne* (☎ 9670 4101, 328 Flinders St) from $200 per room; *Rockmans Regency Hotel* (☎ 9662 3900), on the corner of Exhibition and Lonsdale Sts, from $210 per room; *The Windsor* (☎ 9633 6000, 103 Spring St) from $450 per room and *Sheraton Towers Southgate* (☎ 9696 3100, 1 Southgate Ave) from $405/465 a single/double.

East Melbourne Two convenient but uninspiring motels are *George Powlett Lodge* (☎ 9419 9488), on the corner of George and Powlett Sts, with older motel-style rooms with kitchenettes from $85/90, and *Treasury Motor Lodge* (☎ 9417 5281, 179 Powlett St) from $100/105.

Georgian Court Guesthouse (☎ 9419 6353, 21 George St) is an elegant B&B with rooms for $59/69, or $89/99 with bathroom; prices include a buffet breakfast.

Carlton & Parkville *Lygon Quest Lodging* (☎ 9345 3888, 700 Lygon St), opposite the Melbourne General Cemetery, has one and two-bedroom apartments from $110 to $165.

Park Avenue Motor Inn (☎ 9380 9222, 441 Royal Parade) has units and apartments from $76/87. One tram stop north is *Ramada Inn* (☎ 9380 8131, 539 Royal Parade) charging from $84/89.

South Yarra Tram No 8 from Swanston St in the city takes you along Toorak Rd.

The *West End Private Hotel* (☎ 9866 5375, 76 Toorak Rd West) has B&B with rooms for $40/55 – it's old-fashioned, but has a shabby charm.

Further east, the vast *Claremont Accommodation* (☎ 9826 8000, 189 Toorak Rd) has bright rooms with modern communal facilities. Rooms with shared bathrooms start at $46/58.

Hotel Saville (☎ 9867 2755, 5 Commercial Rd) has motel-style rooms from $84/88. *St James Motel* (☎ 9866 4455, 35 Darling St) is an older motel with rooms from $75. The *Albany Motor Inn* (☎ 9866 4485), corner Toorak Rd and Millswyn St, is opposite Fawkner Park and close to the Royal Botanic Gardens, with rooms from $75/80.

St Kilda & Albert Park Opposite St Kilda beach, *Warwick Beachside* (☎ 9525 4800, 363 Beaconsfield Parade) is a large complex of 1950s-style holiday flats. They're not glamorous, but they're quite well equipped. Costs range from $55 to $85 for a studio and from $90 to $110 for two bedrooms. Weekly rates are cheaper.

Stylish *Hotel Tolarno* (☎ 9537 0200, 42 Fitzroy St) is in the renovated flats above the Tolarno Restaurant and charges from $100 a double.

St Kilda has plenty of motels, but some are fairly dodgy. A couple of more respectable places are *Cabana Court Motel* (☎ 9534 0771, 46 Park St), which charges $99 a double, and the *Cosmopolitan Motor Inn* (☎ 9534 0781, 6 Carlisle St) charging from $95 a double. *Charnwood Motor Inn* (☎ 9525 4199, 3 Charnwood Rd) is on the inland side of St Kilda Rd and is a good motel in a quiet suburban street with rooms at just $55/65.

Opposite the beach, *Robinson's by the Sea* (☎ 9534 2683, 335 Beaconsfield Parade) is an elegant and impressive Victorian-era terrace house with B&B from around $130. The old *Hotel Victoria* (☎ 9690 3666, 123 Beaconsfield Parade, Albert Park) overlooks the bay. Doubles cost $60, from $90 with bathroom. *The Avoca* (☎ 9696 9090, 98 Victoria Ave, Albert Park) is a terrace house with good facilities, charging from $100/125 for B&B.

PLACES TO EAT
Melbourne is a marvellous place to have an appetite. Everywhere you go, there are restaurants, cafes, delicatessens, markets, bistros, brasseries and takeaways. If you're going to explore Melbourne's food options, Lonely Planet's *Out to Eat – Melbourne* is the best value guide for any budget. *The Age Good Food Guide* and its *Cheap Eats* are also useful.

For a reliable and inexpensive Italian restaurant, find the nearest member of the *La Porchetta* chain. There are La Porchettas in many areas, including North Carlton, South Yarra and Williamstown.

City Centre

Chinatown Area The area in and around Chinatown, which follows Little Bourke St from Spring St to Swanston Sts, is the CBD's most diverse food precinct.

Yamato (28 Corrs Lane) turns out excellent, inexpensive Japanese dishes. *King of Kings (209 Russell St)* is a cheap Chinese place (most dishes are $5 to $10) that stays open until 2.30 am. Another late closer is *Supper Inn*, hidden away at 15-17 Celestial Ave. It is worth searching out for its excellent and reasonably priced Chinese food.

Cafe K (☎ 9639 0414, 35 Little Bourke St) is a bistro with good dishes in the $15 to $20 range – you may need to book.

Just off Little Bourke St is the *Flower Drum (☎ 9662 3655, 17 Market Lane)*, one of Melbourne's finest (and most expensive – you might spend around $100 per person) restaurants, serving up the best Cantonese food this side of Hong Kong. For southern Chinese chiu chow food, try the *Mask of China (☎ 9662 2116, 117 Little Bourke St)*, another outstanding and expensive restaurant. *Dahu Peking Duck (☎ 9639 1381, 1st floor, 171 Little Bourke St)* isn't in the same league as these heavyweights, but it's worth trying.

Bourke St Area Off the top (east) end of Bourke St, the *Waiters' Restaurant (20 Meyer's Place)*, upstairs, serves good, cheap Italian food. Back on Bourke St, at No 66, is another Melbourne institution – *Pellegrini's*. The coffee is good and while the food is not outstanding, the atmosphere keeps people coming back.

Grossi Florentino (☎ 9662 1811, 80 Bourke St) has been an institution for 50 years. The upstairs restaurant is expensive, but *Florentino Grill* on street level is reasonable, and the downstairs *Florentino Cellar Bar* is a bargain, with pasta under $10 and a range of snacks.

Nearby at No 76, busy *Nudel Bar* is dedicated to noodles from European and Asian cuisines. The food is good and the prices reasonable – from $8.

Other City Centre Areas On Collins St, the *Hyatt Food Court* has a good range of reasonably priced food stalls.

Stalactites, on the corner of Lonsdale and Russell Sts, is a Greek restaurant best known for its bizarre decor and the fact that it's open 24 hours a day.

Lounge (1st floor, 243 Swanston St) is a groovy cafe/club with snags, stir-fries and salads from $8 to $10. *Gopal's (139 Swanston St)* is an extremely inexpensive vegetarian cafe run by Hare Krishnas.

As well as being the home of outdoor adventure shops, Hardware St is lined with cafes. At No 25 *Campari Bistro* has pastas for around $12 and other mains under $20. Nearby, *Schwob's* is a great place for a sandwich or roll; eat in or takeaway.

The three major department stores – Myer, David Jones and Daimaru – each have food emporiums. Particularly worth searching out is the *Daimaru Sushi Bar*, at level one in Melbourne Central.

Southgate, Arts Precinct & Casino

Southgate has a broad range of bars, cafes and restaurants, most of which have outdoor terraces and balconies.

On the ground level, *Blakes (☎ 9699 4100)* serves innovative food with mains in the $18 to $25 range. The centre of the ground floor is taken up by the *Wharf Food Market*, with a selection of stalls. One flight up, the casual *Blue Train Cafe* serves breakfasts, pastas and risottos, wood-fired pizzas and salads. Main courses are under $20 and there are lots of cheaper snacks. On the upper level is classy *Walter's Wine Bar (☎ 9690 9211)*. The food is simple modern Australian cuisine with main meals starting around $20. There are less expensive snacks, or you can just have a glass of wine.

In the Victorian Arts Centre, *Treble Clef* is in the Concert Hall overlooking the river, and opens from 11 am until around midnight,

VICTORIA

serving snacks, light meals or more substantial main courses. The casual *Cafe Vic* in the Theatres Building has pre-performance meals and post-performance coffee and cake.

There's a range of eateries in the casino, including some fairly cheap places.

North Melbourne

Amiconi (☎ 9328 3710, 359 Victoria St) is a traditional Italian bistro that has been a local favourite for decades, and you'll probably have to book. Across the road at No 488, the *Peppermint Lounge Cafe* is a top spot for breakfast or lunch, with specials around $7.

Warung Agus, No 305, is a simple restaurant that serves great Balinese food, with mains from $10 to $16. For Vietnamese food, head down towards the Queen Victoria Market. Across the road, *Vietnam House (284 Victoria St)* and *Dalat's*, No 270, both have good cheap food, especially at lunch time. *Don Camillo*, No 215, is another little Italian place that's been here for yonks, and it serves the basics in large portions. You'll pay about $15 for main courses.

The *Eldorado Hotel (46 Leveson St)* is an old pub that has been revitalised into a fun 'cafe saloon'.

Carlton

Tram Nos 1 and 21, running along Swanston St, get you there from the city centre, or stroll up Russell St.

In Lygon St, *Toto's Pizza House*, No 101, claims to be the first pizzeria in Australia. It's licensed, the pizzas are cheap and good and it stays open till after midnight. *Papa Gino's*, No 221, is a straightforward pizza-and-pasta joint. A block further north at No 305, *Tiamo* is another old Lygon St campaigner. *Jimmy Watson's*, No 333, is one of Melbourne's institutions. Wine and talk are the order of the day at this wine bar/restaurant – the annual Jimmy Watson trophy is Australia's best known red wine award, so you can count on the wines being drinkable.

Shakahari (☎ 9347 3848, 201 Faraday Street) is a long-running and innovative vegetarian restaurant.

Fitzroy & Collingwood

Brunswick St & Nearby There are many, many places to choose from – promenade along the street and consider your options. A few are listed here.

The *Black Cat Cafe*, No 252, was into retro before the term was invented. The 'Cat' has a good snack menu with most dishes under $8. *Thai Thani*, No 293, is a good option for Thai food. *The Provincial (☎ 9417 2228)*, on the corner of Brunswick and Johnston Sts, is stylish, with a bar, a great Italian bistro, and a burger/Asian bar next door. *Mario's (303 Brunswick St)* has a devout clientele and Italian-based food.

Around the corner on Johnston St, *Carmen Bar (☎ 9417 4794, 74 Johnston St)* is a hectic restaurant with Spanish food and flamenco from Wednesday to Saturday night. At No 95, the huge *Bull Ring* combines a Spanish restaurant, tapas bar and nightclub.

Rhumbarella's (342 Brunswick St) is a barn-sized cafe/restaurant with an art gallery upstairs. *Babka Bakery Cafe*, No 358, is famous for its breads and pastries. *Charmaine's* at No 370 has sensational ice creams and cakes.

On the corner of Rose St, *The Vegie Bar* has a great range of vegetarian meals for under $10 and snacks for around $2.

Across Alexandra Parade, where Brunswick St joins St Georges Rd, is another pocket of interesting places. *Tin Pot (284 St Georges Rd)* has good food at reasonable prices. Diagonally opposite, *The Toucan Club* serves inexpensive food and has cabaret in the evening.

On Gertrude St between Smith and Nicholson Sts, *Arcadia*, No 193, is a friendly cafe, and the nearby *Macedonia* does Balkan specialties at low prices. The *Builders Arms Hotel* on the corner of Gertrude and Gore Sts is a top spot for an ale and a bite.

Smith St The *Smith St Bar & Bistro (14 Smith St)* is a pleasant bar/restaurant. Further north at No 117, *Vegetarian Orgasm* is a vegie cafe. *Cafe Birko*, No 123, is a rustic bar/restaurant with salads, stir-fries, risottos and pastas. The *Soul Food Vegetarian Cafe*,

No 275, is a vegan cafe with salads and hot food for well under $10, and an organic grocer next door.

Closer to Johnston St, **Sinbad's Corner** sells good felafel – the owner is from Alexandria – and $7 gets you one with the lot.

Richmond

Victoria St Victoria St between Hoddle and Church Sts is lined with Asian supermarkets and groceries and dozens of inexpensive Vietnamese restaurants. Tram Nos 42 and 109 from Collins St get you there.

The food is fresh and authentic, and you can have a huge bowl of soup that's a meal in itself for around $4; main courses generally cost between $5 and $9.

Thy Thy 1 *(142 Victoria St)*, upstairs, is a dirt-cheap no-frills place, but the food is excellent. **Vao Doi**, No 120, is also good, as is **Victoria** across the road at No 311. **Tran Tran**, No 76, is also popular. **Tho Tho**, No 66, is a stylish bar/restaurant, but still inexpensive, with mains mostly from $7 to $10.

Swan St Richmond's Swan St, in the block east of Church St, is an enclave for Greek cuisine. From the city, take tram No 70 from Batman Ave to the corner of Swan and Church Sts.

Elatos Greek Tavern *(☎ 9428 5683, 213 Swan St)* is one of the best places, and the seafood is particularly good. Main courses cost about $12 and seafood about $16. Across the road **Salona** is also good, and a little cheaper. At No 256, **Kaliva** is fairly plain, although there's live bouzouki music Thursday to Sunday nights.

Bridge Rd Bridge Rd also has some great possibilities. Take tram No 48 or 75 from Flinders St.

Moose's Downtown Bar & Bistro *(14-16 Bridge Rd)* is a reasonably priced place serving Italian tucker. Next door is **Chilli Padi** *(☎ 9428 6432)*, with excellent Malaysian food. **Richmond Hill Cafe & Larder** *(48 Bridge Rd)* is a casual place with many dishes under $15. It's open from breakfast to past dinner daily except Sunday, when it closes at 5 pm.

Vlado's *(☎ 9428 5833)*, No 61, serves the best steaks in town. If you're into red meat you'll be happy to pay around $70 a head for the compulsory set menu.

Up at No 396, **The Curry Club Cafe** has inexpensive but unusually good Indian food.

South Yarra

Most of South Yarra's eateries are along Toorak Rd and Chapel St. Tram No 8 from the city gets you there.

There are many places on Toorak Rd in the blocks west of Chapel St, not all of them super expensive. For instance at No 11, **France Soir** *(☎ 9866 8569)*, one of the best brasseries in town, has mains in the $18 to $23 range. **Tamani Bistro**, No 156, is good for a hearty, inexpensive Italian meal. **Chinois** *(☎ 9826 3388)*, one of Melbourne's most acclaimed restaurants, has east-meets-west cuisine. The 'business lunch' menu is good value at $22.50 for two courses and a glass of wine. At No 210, **Tanah Ria** serves noodles for around $8 and curries and stir-fries for around $12. Across Chapel St at No 278, funky **Corridor** serves pasta and risotto from $13, plus other dishes.

Chapel St **Caffe e Cucina** *(9827 4139)*, No 581, is one of the coolest cafe/restaurants in town, with great Italian meals in the $14 to $22 range. Down at No 571 **Chapellis** is a bar/restaurant with good food and it never closes. At No 565, **That Little Noodle Place** is a hip cafe with noodle and rice dishes from around $10.

Further down, the Jam Factory complex has a few eateries.

La Lucciola, No 478, and **La Camera**, No 446, are good Italian restaurants with reasonable prices. **Kush**, No 427, is a hip cafe with light meals for around $10. Across at No 426 is **Frostbites**, a converted pub with meals around $7 to $15 plus frozen fruit cocktails.

Prahran

Commercial Rd is the border between South Yarra and Prahran. **Prahran Market** is a terrific place to shop, and within the market

VICTORIA

let's eat is an impressive 'food and wine emporium'. Before the market, at No 209, *Sweet Basil (☎ 9827 3390)* is a Thai place with noodle or curry dishes for around $13.

Opposite the market, *Blue Elephant (194 Commercial Rd)* is a funky cafe with meals from around $10 and breakfasts from around $5. Next door at No 196, *The Outlook, (☎ 9521 4227, theoutlook@hotmail .com)* combines cafe, gift and card shop, Internet access and a hair salon! Light meals are around $7, Internet access $7 an hour and haircuts from $15.

This stretch of Commercial Rd is a centre for Melbourne's gay and lesbian community, and past the market there's a string of cafes and restaurants, including *Cafe 151*, No 151, *Alternative* at No 149, and *Sandgropers*, No 133.

Heading south on Chapel St, the *Globe Cafe*, No 218, is open for breakfast, and lunch and dinner mains cost $12 to $15. *Saigon Rose*, No 206, serves inexpensive Vietnamese food. At No 135 *Patee Thai* is the best Thai restaurant in the area, with meals around $10 to $15.

The Windsor end of Chapel St has cafes like the cheap *Orange*, at No 126, and the more sophisticated *Ibiza* at No 116.

Greville St, running off Chapel St beside Prahran Town Hall, has the *Feedwell Cafe*, No 95, a vegetarian cafe serving wholesome food in the $5 to $10 range, and the *Continental Cafe*, No 132, with fabulous food at affordable prices and a sophisticated atmosphere.

St Kilda

Acland St Up at the north-west end of Acland St there's a cluster of places to eat and drink, including the hip *Dog's Bar*, No 54.

Heading south-east down Acland St, turn left up Carlisle St to the *Galleon*, No 9, a hold-out against the slickness of modern St Kilda. It has everything from toasted sandwiches to chicken and leek pie, at reasonable prices.

The unassuming *Vineyard Restaurant (71 Acland St)* has huge grills from $13 to over $30. Around the corner on Shakespeare Grove, *Bala's* has an inexpensive Indian-influenced menu to eat in or takeaway. Back on Acland St *Cafe Manna* is a simple Indian place where most mains are around $7.

Across the road, *Chinta Ria-Soul (☎ 9525 4664, 94 Acland St)* combines terrific Malaysian food with soul music. Main meals are $8 to $15, and you'll need to book. Next door, the quirky *Cafe Goa* serves Portuguese, Indian and vegetarian dishes, most at $9.50.

The low-key *Blue Danube (107 Acland St)* and *Scheherezade*, at No 99, serve central-European food in generous portions. Blue Danube is more Hungarian and Scheherezade is more Jewish. Further down at No 153, *Orienta on Acland* doesn't offer great food but it is cheap, with Asian-style dishes at $5 for as much as you can put on your plate.

Big Mouth, on the corner of Acland and Barkly Sts, has a downstairs cafe (most main courses are under $10) and an upstairs restaurant (most main courses well under $20). Across the street and round the corner, *Wild Rice (211 Barkly St)* is a good organic/ vegan cafe. Next door, *Claypots Seafood Bar* sells an intriguing breakfast of fresh sardines, eggs and potatoes ($6), as well as lunch and dinner. Around the next corner is *Rasa's Vegie Bar (5 Blessington St)*, with tofu or lentil burgers at $6.50 and other dishes from $8. It's closed Monday and Tuesday.

Fitzroy St Up at the beach end, the chic *Madame Joe Joe (☎ 9534 0000)* serves Mediterranean-style food with mains for around $18 to $25. Further along at No 23, the *Street Cafe* is a big cafe, bar and restaurant with something for everyone.

The tiny *Hard Wok Cafe*, No 49, has stir-fries, laksas and curries from $6 to $12. *Leo's Spaghetti Bar (55 Fitzroy St)* is an institution, with a coffee bar, bistro and restaurant, while further along at No 73 *Thai Panic Cafe* is a tiny Thai cafe with reasonable food from $7 to $9.

Across the road further up at No 42, the wonderful *Tolarno Bar & Bistro (☎ 9525 5477)* features the murals of artist Mirka Mora. The restaurant specialises in Mediterranean-style cuisine, with mains from $12.50 to $20. Next door, the small bar/eatery offers snacks and meals in the $7 to $18 range, including the best burgers in Melbourne ($9 with fries).

Back on the busy side of the street, **Topolino's**, No 87, is the place to go for a pizza or big bowl of pasta (try the spaghetti marinara for $12.50), especially late at night.

On the corner of Fitzroy and Grey Sts **The George Melbourne Wine Room** in the George Hotel features fine food and Victorian wines.

Seaside *The Stokehouse* (☎ 9525 5555, 30 Jacka Blvd), on the foreshore, has a fairly pricey restaurant upstairs and a downstairs bar/bistro with tasty tucker from $8 to $15.

The remarkable **Espy Kitchen** in the Esplanade Hotel is always busy and the food is great (mains from $10). After you've eaten you can play pool or check out a band.

Albert Park

There's a good range of places, most along Victoria Ave, but the only reason for a special trip is **Misuzu's** (7 Victoria Ave), a 'village-style' Japanese cafe. The food is quite different from the standard fare in formal Japanese restaurants; the prices are reasonable. It's open daily except Monday, for breakfast, lunch and dinner.

South Melbourne

The **Limerick Arms Hotel**, on the corner of Clarendon and Park Sts, is a revamped pub with a pleasant courtyard restaurant, and bar meals cost under $10.

If you transplanted a 1920s Aussie pub to provincial Italy, you'd end up with something like the **Locanda Veneta** (273 Cecil St). Pastas start at around $10 and main meals at around $15.

The **O'Connell Centenary Hotel**, on the corner of Montague and Coventry Sts, is known for its excellent food and inspiring menu. The restaurant is expensive but the bar isn't, and there are plenty of choices for vegetarians.

Williamstown

Hobson's Choice Foods (213 Nelson Place) is a popular cafe with great food. **Kohinoor**,

further up at No 223, looks pretty basic but serves good-value Indian food with main meals from $7 to $12.

On the Syme St corner is the Customs House Market & Gallery and next door is **Sam's Boatshed**, a bar/eatery built around an old clinker boat.

Elegant **Sails** (☎ 9397 2377, 231 Nelson Place), upstairs, has seafood mains for $20 to $25. Downstairs, the cafe is cheaper. The **Strand** (☎ 9397 7474), on the corner of The Strand and Ferguson St, also has good seafood for $15 to $28, and there's an upmarket takeaway fish and chip joint next door.

ENTERTAINMENT

The best source of 'what's on' information is the *Entertainment Guide (EG)*, which comes with the Friday *Age* newspaper. *Beat*, *Inpress* and *Storm* are free music and entertainment magazines available from pubs, cafes and venues.

Ticketmaster is the main booking agency. For inquiries ring ☎ 9645 7970, or ☎ 1800 338 998 from outside Melbourne. For credit card bookings for sport ring 13 6122, for theatre and the arts ☎ 13 6166 and for other events ☎ 13 6100. The telephone services operate Monday to Saturday from 9 am to 9 pm and Sunday to 5 pm. Ticketmaster has outlets in places such as Myer stores, major theatres and shopping centres.

The Half-Tix (☎ 9650 9420) booth in the Bourke St Mall sells half-price tickets on the day of the performance. Make sure you know where you'll be sitting – they don't sell the best seats at half price. Half-Tix opens Monday and Saturday from 10 am to 2 pm, and Tuesday to Thursday from 11 am to 6 pm and to 6.30 pm on Friday. Credit cards are not accepted.

Gay & Lesbian Switchboard Information Service (☎ 0055 12504) is a recorded service covering the entertainment scene as well as social and support groups.

Bars

If you're looking for activity without style, try an old-fashioned pub, if you can still find one – try the **Standard Hotel** (293 Fitzroy St, Fitzroy).

Melbourne has a great collection of fashionable bars. In the city try *Meyer's Place*, in tiny Meyer's Place, off the top end of Bourke St, *Lounge (1st floor, 243 Swanston St)*, *Bernie's (1 Coverlid Place)*, off Little Bourke St near Russell St, *International Lounge (18-24 Market Lane)*, *Rue Bebelons (267 Little Lonsdale St)* and *Spleen (41 Bourke St)*. *Hell's Kitchen (20 Centre Place)* is another worth trying.

There are plenty of bars over the river in the casino, including the cafe *Automatic* (☎ 9690 8500).

Brunswick St in Fitzroy, north of Johnston St, is a long string of funky bars. Chapel St in South Yarra, south of Toorak Rd, is where the wealthier hang out.

In St Kilda, the *Dog's Bar (54 Acland St)* is a hangout for social barflies. The front bar at *The George Hotel*, on the corner of Fitzroy and Grey Sts, is another popular local, and the *Snakepit* is a super-groovy bar in the same complex. Further along Fitzroy St, the main bar in the *Prince of Wales Hotel* has long been a hangout for gays, transvestites, showgirls, drunks and other St Kilda types. There's also the friendly *Tolarno Bar (42 Fitzroy St)*. Hardcore St Kilda residents drink at the *Village Belle Hotel (202 Barkly St)* or the *Greyhound (1 Brighton Rd)*.

Pubs & Music Venues

Melbourne's main music venues are the National Tennis Centre, the Concert Hall at the Victorian Arts Centre, the Sports and Entertainment Centre, and even the MCG for the occasional massive concert.

The sweaty grind around Melbourne's pubs has been the proving ground for many of Australia's best outfits. Acts like AC/DC, INXS, Crowded House and Nick Cave all had their roots in Melbourne's pub scene.

To find out who's playing where, look in the *EG*, *Beat* or *Inpress* or listen to the gig guides on FM radio stations like 3RRR (102.7) and 3PBS (106.7). Cover charges at pubs vary widely – some gigs are free, but generally you'll pay $5 to $10.

In the city, *Lounge (1st floor, 243 Swanston St)* is hip and semi-alternative. Down on Flinders St, on the corner of Russell St, *The Forum* is a fabulous old cinema that's been renovated into a music venue.

In Fitzroy, the *Rainbow Hotel*, a back-street pub at 27 St James St, has (free) bands nightly, from jazz, Cajun and blues to funk and soul. On the corner of Brunswick and Kerr Sts, the *Evelyn Hotel* is one of Fitzroy's major venues, while across the road the grungy *Punters Club Hotel (376 Brunswick St)* has bands most nights for $5 or less. The *Royal Derby Hotel*, on the corner of Brunswick St and Alexandra Ave, is another venue. The *Builders Arms Hotel (211 Gertrude St)* is another good Fitzroy watering hole.

In Collingwood, *The Club (132 Smith St)* attracts good bands and stays open until dawn-ish, while the *Prince Patrick Hotel (135 Victoria Parade)* alternates between bands and comedy. *The Tote (71 Johnston St)* is another fine pub with bands.

Richmond is something of an enclave for grungy rock pubs; they include the famous *Corner Hotel (57 Swan St)* and the *Central Club Hotel (293 Swan St)*.

At the *Continental* (☎ 9510 2788), 134 Greville St, Prahran, you can see a wide range of local and international acts close up. You have a choice of dinner-and-show deals ($35 to $65) or standing-room ($15 to $30). Not far away in Windsor, *Empire (174 Peel St)* is much larger but plays a similar range of acts, with clubbing nights as well.

In St Kilda, the famed *Esplanade Hotel*, on the Esplanade, has bands nightly and Sunday afternoons, often free. Around the corner and up Fitzroy St, *The Prince of Wales Hotel* at No 29 is a great, grungy venue.

Folk & Acoustic Music One of the main venues is the *Dan O'Connell Hotel*, *(225 Canning St, Carlton)*. Another popular Irish pub is *Molly Bloom's Hotel*, on the corner of Bay and Rouse Sts, Port Melbourne, with Irish music nightly. The *Great Britain Hotel (447 Church St, Richmond)* sometimes has folk music (and even when it doesn't, it's a nice place for a drink).

Jazz & Blues Down a lane off Little Lonsdale St (between Exhibition and Russell

Sts), *Bennett's Lane Jazz Club* is a dim, smoke-filled jazz venue, open nightly except Tuesday.

Quite a few pubs have jazz and blues sessions on certain nights – check the gig guide in the *EG*.

During January and February, the Melbourne Zoo has 'Zoo Twilights'; open-air sessions with jazz or big bands. Call the information line (☎ 9285 9333) for details.

Clubs

Melbourne has a huge (and constantly changing) collection of dance clubs, from the 'members only' variety to huge discos. Cover charges range from $5 to $15, although some places don't charge at all.

Most places have dress (or coolness) standards, generally at the discretion of the people on the door.

Mainstream Clubs The huge *Metro (20 Bourke St)* sometimes hosts quite big international acts, such as Grace Jones, Fat Boy Slim and Ben Harper.

King St in the city is a busy but somewhat seedy nightclub strip, with a cluster of places that include *Inflation*, No 60 and the *Grainstore Tavern* next door.

Billboard (170 Russell St), *Mercury Lounge* at the casino, *Silvers (445 Toorak Rd, Toorak)* and *Chasers (386 Chapel St, South Yarra)* are large, mainstream places with a variety of music on different nights.

Alternative Clubs Most venues host different club nights on different nights and names change as quickly as Melbourne's weather. The only way to keep up is to check the entertainment papers.

Dream Nightclub (229 Queensberry St, Carlton) has various themes – 'Revelations' on Thursday from 10 pm, 'Supermarket' from 10 pm on Saturday and from 10 am on Sunday it has '2000AD', an all day dance party. Other good venues, all in the city, include *Lounge (1st floor, 243 Swanston St)*, *Bass Station (12 McKillop St)*, *44 (44 Lonsdale St)* and *Club 383 (383 Lonsdale St)*.

In Fitzroy, the hip *Night Cat (141 Johnston St)* has jazz, soul and other bands from

Thursday to Sunday. Further down Johnston St at No 48, *Bar Salona* is a Latin-style dance club open nightly.

Gay & Lesbian Venues

Melbourne's gay scene is not confined to one strip, but is spread out over the city's inner suburbs, concentrating in Collingwood, Prahran and St Kilda. One of the only gay venues in the city centre is 'Jet Lounge', Friday nights at *Salon Rouge*, in the basement at 313 Flinders Lane.

Down in Prahran on Commercial Rd, known locally as the 'Gay Metre', you'll find a number of gay-run cafes and popular bars like the *Exchange Hotel (119 Commercial Rd)* and *The Market* at No 143.

The 'Front Bar' at *The Prince of Wales (29 Fitzroy St, St Kilda)* is the oldest gay bar in Melbourne. Also here, upstairs on Sunday nights, is 'Sunday Prince' (aka 'Homosexuelle') with the 'Pouffé Lounge' from 8 pm and 'Discothèque' until dawn.

North of the river, Collingwood has some good venues. *The Peel Dance Bar*, on the corner of Peel and Wellington Sts, is a late-night dance bar and *The Laird (149 Gipps St)* is a men-only pub, catering to a leather crowd and with a good beer garden. *Trade Bar (9 Peel St)* is a small bar with entertainment and there's also the *Star Hotel (176 Hoddle St)*.

The *Glasshouse Hotel*, on the corner of Gipps and Rokeby Sts, is a mixed pub with entertainment (anything from bingo to bands) nightly except Monday.

Cinema

The main chains are Village, Hoyts and Greater Union, and the main group of city cinemas is around the intersection of Bourke and Russell Sts. Tickets cost around $9 during the day and up to $12 at night.

There are many independent and art house cinemas, including the Art Deco nostalgia of the big *Astor (☎ 9510 1414)*, on the corner of Chapel St and Dandenong Rd, St Kilda, with double features for $10 nightly; the *Kino (☎ 9650 2100, Collins Place, 45 Collins St)* and the *Lumiere (☎ 9639 1055, 108 Lonsdale St)* in the CBD; *Cinema Nova (☎ 9347 5331,*

VICTORIA

380 Lygon St) in Carlton; the *Longford (☎ 9867 2700, 59 Toorak Rd, South Yarra)*; the *George Cinemas (☎ 9534 6922, 133 Fitzroy St, St Kilda)* and the *Westgarth Theatre (☎ 9482 2001, 89 High St, Northcote)*.

Melbourne's *IMAX Theatre (☎ 9663 5454)* is near the Exhibition Building in Carlton (enter on Rathdowne St). To experience one of the world's last drive-ins, head out to the *Village Drive-in*, Newlands Rd, Coburg.

Theatre

The *Victorian Arts Centre (☎ 9281 8000, St Kilda Rd)* is Melbourne's major venue for the performing arts.

In summer watch out for open-air productions in the Royal Botanic Gardens.

Comedy

During the International Comedy Festival, in April, local comedians join international acts to perform in pubs, clubs, theatres and streets.

The *Comedy Club (9348 1622, 380 Lygon St, Carlton)* is the main venue for comedy. The *Prince Patrick Hotel (135 Victoria Parade, Collingwood)* is an old stager in the comedy scene. Other stand-up venues include the *Waiting Room*, held each Sunday at 4 pm in the Esplanade Hotel's *Gershwin Room (11 The Esplanade, St Kilda)*, *Geebung Polo Club (85 Auburn Rd, Auburn)* and the *Nicholson Hotel (551 Nicholson St, North Carlton)*.

SPECTATOR SPORTS
Melbourne Cup

Horse races are held at Flemington, Caulfield, Moonee Valley and Sandown.

The Melbourne Cup, one of the world's great horse races, is the feature event of Melbourne's Spring Racing Carnival, which runs through October and finishes with the Melbourne Cup Carnival early in November. The cup brings the whole country to a standstill. Entry costs around $25 or book a seat in the Lawn Stand through Ticketmaster for around $75.

The Footy

Australian Rules football – otherwise known as 'the Footy' – is incredibly popular, with

---

The Melbourne Cup

If you happen to be in Melbourne on the first Tuesday in November, you can catch the greatest horse race in Australia – the prestigious Melbourne Cup, highlight of the city's Spring Racing Carnival. Although its status as the bearer of the largest prize for an Australian horse race is constantly under challenge, no other race can bring the country to a standstill.

For about an hour during the lead-up to the race each year, people all over the country get touched by Melbourne's spring racing fever. Serious punters and fashion-conscious racegoers pack the grandstand and lawns of the Victorian Racing Club's beautiful Flemington Racecourse; those who only bet once a year make their choice or organise Cup syndicates with friends; and the race is watched or listened to on TVs and radios in pubs, clubs and houses across the land. Australia virtually comes to a halt for three or so minutes while the race is run.

The two mile (3.2km) flat race attracts horses and owners from Europe, Asia and the Middle East, although often it's the New Zealand horses and trainers who leave with the coveted gold cup.

Some say that to be in Melbourne in November and not go to the Cup is like going to Paris and skipping the Louvre, or going to Pamplona and turning your back on the bulls.

---

games at the MCG regularly pulling crowds of 50,000 to 80,000; the grand final fills the ground with 100,000 fans. The sheer energy of the barracking at a big game is exhilarating and, despite the fervour, crowd violence is almost unknown.

Being the shrine of Aussie Rules, the MCG is the best place to see a match. Tickets can be bought at the ground for most games ($13.50 for adults, $7.50 concession and $2 for children under 14). Seats can be booked (this might be necessary at big games) through Ticketmaster for $23.50. Note that you aren't allowed to use umbrellas at the Melbourne Cricket Ground.

Motor Sports
Fans of blokes (and the odd 'sheila') driving in circles very fast will be pleased to know that the Australian Formula One Grand Prix is held at Albert Park in March, and the Australian round of the World 500cc Motorcycle Grand Prix runs at Phillip Island in October.

Cricket
In summer, an international Test match, one-day Internationals, the national cricket competition and local district matches are played at the MCG. General admission to international one-day matches is around $25; reserved seats start around $32. Finals cost more.

Tennis
For two weeks in January the National Tennis Centre (officially called Melbourne Park) on Batman Ave hosts the Australian Open, with top players from around the world competing in the year's first Grand Slam tournament. Tickets for the early rounds cost about $15 for general admission (which allows you to wander around the outside courts) or $25 for centre court. A ticket to the final rounds costs $80 to $90.

Other Spectator Sports
Basketball enjoyed phenomenal growth in the 90s and is still popular. The main venue is Melbourne Park. The season runs from October to March and tickets start at $12.50. The Melbourne Storm team is part of the national rugby league competition and plays at Olympic Park.

SHOPPING
Melbourne claims to be the shopping capital of Australia.

For late-night staples, head to Coles Express, 6-22 Elizabeth St, open 24 hours. Coles and Safeway supermarkets in the suburbs are open 24 hours at least some days of the week.

The major department stores are in the city centre: Myer (the main entrance is in the Bourke St Mall), David Jones (with shops on both sides of the Mall) and Daimaru (in the huge Melbourne Central shopping complex).

Most of Melbourne's more interesting shopping areas are in the inner suburbs.

Aboriginal Art
Although Melbourne is a long way from the Outback, there are galleries selling Aboriginal art. In the city centre, try the Aboriginal Gallery of Dreamings (73-77 Bourke St), the Aboriginal Art Galleries of Australia (31 Flinders Lane), Aboriginal Handcrafts, mezzanine level (130 Little Collins St), Alcaston Gallery (2 Collins St) and Emerald Hill Gallery (Level 8, 37 Swanston St).

Aussie Clothing
Sam Bear, 225 Russell St, a Melbourne institution since the 1950s, is a great place to go for durable hats, clothing and footwear. Other good shops include RM Williams at Melbourne Central and the Thomas Cook Boot & Clothing Co, 60 Hoddle St, Abbotsford.

A couple of places in the city for surfing equipment and clothing are the Melbourne Surf Shop in the Tivoli Arcade at 249 Bourke St and Surf Dive 'N' Ski at 213 Bourke St and in Melbourne Central.

Akubra hats are sold everywhere. Try City Hatters, beside the main entrance to Flinders St station or Melbourne's Top Hatters, shop 19, 259 Collins St.

Outdoor Gear
The best area for outdoor shops is around the intersection of Hardware St and Little Bourke St. Snowgum is around the corner at 366 Lonsdale St.

Fashion & Clothing
For female fashions try the Sportsgirl Centre, in Collins St between Swanston and Elizabeth Sts, and the Australia on Collins complex nearby. You'll find plenty of fashion houses along Bourke St, while Collins St is the home of expensive designer boutiques.

Bridge Rd and Swan St in Richmond are full of fashion warehouses, factory outlets and seconds shops. Brunswick St in Fitzroy has lots of offbeat clothing shops. Greville St in Prahran is the place for retro shops.

Chapel St in South Yarra is the most fashionable fashion zone. Toorak Rd in South Yarra is the ultimate in style and Lygon St in Carlton has upmarket and imported Italian clothes and shoes.

Duty-Free

Duty-free shops abound in the city centre. Remember that a duty-free item may not have had much duty on it anyway and could be available cheaper in an ordinary shop.

Film & Photography

There's a cluster of camera shops along Elizabeth St between Bourke and Lonsdale Sts. Little Bourke St (west of Elizabeth St) is another good area. Some sell second-hand gear, usually with a guarantee.

For camera repairs try the Camera Clinic (☎ 9419 5247), 19 Peel St, Collingwood.

Markets

Queen Victoria Market, on the corner of Victoria and Elizabeth Sts, has over 1000 stalls that sell just about everything, including fruit, vegetables, meat, fish, jeans and budgies. It opens Tuesday and Thursday from 6 am to 2 pm, Friday from 6 am to 6 pm, Saturday from 6 am to 3 pm and Sunday from 9 am to 4 pm (no fresh produce on Sunday). Over summer, part of the market is open on Wednesday until 10.30 pm.

Other major markets are South Melbourne Market, Cecil St, open on Wednesday, Friday, Saturday and Sunday; Prahran Market, Commercial Rd, open on Tuesday, Thursday, Friday and Saturday; and Footscray Market, on the corner of Hopkins and Leeds Sts, open on Thursday, Friday and Saturday.

In St Kilda, the Esplanade Art and Craft Market operates every Sunday on the upper Esplanade. One of the most popular 'trash and treasure' markets is the Camberwell Sunday Market (from dawn to mid-afternoon) in Station St, Camberwell.

Music

Independent shops selling recorded music include Gaslight, 85 Bourke St (great alternative music, open nightly till late, and the annual nude shopping day is world famous), Missing Link, 262 Flinders Lane and Au Go Go, 349 Little Bourke St. Discurio, 285 Little Collins St, has lots of classical, jazz, blues and world music.

Greville Records, 152 Greville St, Prahran, Polyester Records, 387 Brunswick St, Fitzroy, and Readings, 366 Lygon St, Carlton and 153 Toorak Rd, South Yarra, are other good shops.

JB Hi-Fi sells discounted tapes and CDs, and its shops include one in the city at 289 Elizabeth St.

GETTING THERE & AWAY

International and interstate flights operate out of Melbourne airport, long-distance trains run from Spencer St station, and there are two long-distance bus terminals – the Spencer St coach terminal (V/Line, McCafferty's and Firefly) and the Melbourne Transit Centre in Franklin St (Greyhound Pioneer).

GETTING AROUND
To/From the Airport

Melbourne airport is at Tullamarine, 22km north-west of the city centre. A taxi between the airport and city centre costs about $30.

The Skybus (☎ 9662 9275) shuttles between the airport and the city centre ($10), departing about half-hourly from Bay 30 at the Spencer St coach terminal and from the Melbourne Transit Centre in Franklin St. Buy tickets from the driver; bookings are not usually necessary. If there's room you can take your bicycle, with the front wheel removed.

Public transport between the city and the airport is limited. You could take tram No 59 from Elizabeth St to Moonee Ponds Junction – from there, Tullamarine Bus Lines (☎ 9338 3817) runs bus Nos 478 and 479 to the airport several times a day; bus No 500 runs to the airport from Broadmeadows train station. You can do either trip on a Zone 1 and 2 Met ticket. If you make the connections you could do it on a two-hour ticket ($3.90). If not you'll need an all-day ticket, which doesn't cost much less than the Skybus fare.

VICTORIA

Public Transport

The public transport system of buses, trains and trams has been privatised, but the following information is still pertinent.

For information, phone the Met Information Centre (☎ 13 1638), open daily from 7 am to 9 pm. The Met Shop, 103 Elizabeth St (open weekdays from 8.30 am to 5 pm and Saturday from 9 am to 3 pm), has information and sells souvenirs and tickets. Staffed train stations also have some information.

After the trams, buses and trains stop running (around midnight) night buses depart from the City Square in Swanston St for many suburban destinations. The fare is a flat $5.

Tickets & Zones There's an array of tickets and an unpopular automatic ticketing system. Once you've bought the ticket you have to validate it in another machine. Roving 'customer service officers' fine you $100 if you haven't managed to buy and validate a ticket.

The metropolitan area is divided into three zones. Zone 1 covers the city and inner area (including St Kilda), and most travellers won't venture beyond that unless they're going right out of town.

Zone 1 tickets cost $2.30 for two hours, $4.40 for all day and $19.10 for a week (longer periods are available). You can break your journey and change between trams, buses and trains with these tickets.

Short Trip tickets ($1.50) allow you to travel two sections on buses or trams in Zone 1, or you can buy a Short Trip 10 Card ($12.50), which gives you 10 short trips. You can't break your journey on a short trip ticket.

Buying a Ticket Small businesses, such as newspaper kiosks and milk bars, sell most tickets but not Short Trip tickets. Machines on trams sell *only* Short Trip and two-hour tickets, and only take coins. Machines at train stations sell many types of tickets but not Short Trip tickets. Large machines at train stations take coins, some notes and some bank cash cards; small machines at stations take coins only. Some stations have booking offices that sell most tickets. On

buses you can buy Short Trip, two-hour and all day tickets from the driver.

Disabled Travellers The *Mobility Map* is available from tourist information booths in the Bourke St Mall and Rialto Towers, and from the Melbourne City Council's information desk (☎ 9658 9763) on the corner of Swanston Walk and Little Collins St (ring and they will post one to you).

Tram Tram routes cover the city and inner suburbs. Tram stops are numbered out from the city centre. There are also 'light-rail' services to some suburbs. These are express trams running along disused rail lines.

In theory, trams run along most routes every six to eight minutes during peak hour and every 12 minutes at other times. Services are less frequent on weekends and late at night.

Be extremely careful getting on and off a tram: by law, cars are supposed to stop when a tram stops to pick up and drop off passengers, but that doesn't always happen.

Every 10 minutes or so between 10 am and 6 pm, free City Circle trams (painted burgundy and gold) travel along Flinders, Spring and Nicholson Sts to Victoria Parade, and then back along Latrobe and Spencer Sts.

Train Suburban trains are faster than trams or buses, but they don't go to many inner suburbs. Flinders St train station is the main terminal.

During the week, most trains start at 5 am and finish at midnight and should run every three to eight minutes during peak hour, every 15 to 20 minutes at other times and every 40 minutes after 7 pm. On Saturday they run every half-hour from 5 am to midnight, while on Sunday it's every 40 minutes from 7 am to 11.30 pm.

The city service includes an underground City Loop, which is a quick way to get from one side of town to the other.

Bicycles can be carried free on trains during off-peak times and at weekends.

Bus Generally, buses continue from where the trains finish, or go to places, such as hospitals, universities, suburban shopping centres and the outer suburbs, not reached by other services.

Car

Cars & Trams Treat trams with caution. You can only overtake a tram on the left and must *always* stop behind a tram when it halts to drop or collect passengers (except where there are central 'islands' for passengers).

Melbourne has a notoriously confusing road rule, known as the 'hook turn'. To turn right at many major intersections in the city centre, you have to pull to the left, wait until the light of the street you're turning into changes from red to green, then complete the turn. Look for the black-and-white hook sign hanging from overhead cables.

Parking If you're lucky enough to find a parking space in the city centre you'll pay about $2 an hour. Watch out for clearway zones that operate during peak hours. Parking in a clearway means big fines and maybe having your car towed away. Inner residential areas often have 'resident only' parking zones, or parking restrictions that run until midnight, rather than 5 or 6 pm as elsewhere. This makes parking near nightlife areas in Fitzroy or St Kilda nearly impossible – take a tram or a taxi.

Note that a sign telling you you're allowed to park for, say, two hours, reads 2P.

There are over 70 car parks in the city. Rates vary but you'll pay around $4 to $6 an hour or $14 to $25 a day during the week – less on weekends. There are often cheaper flat rates for parking after about 6 pm.

Car Rental Avis (☎ 1800 225 533), Budget (☎ 13 2727), Hertz (☎ 13 3039) and Thrifty (☎ 1300 367 227) have desks at the airport, and you can find plenty of others in the city.

For disabled travellers, Avis rents hand controlled vehicles and Norden Transport Equipment (☎ 9793 1066) has vans equipped with lifts.

The *Yellow Pages* lists lots of other car hire firms, including local operators who rent newer cars but don't have the nationwide

network (and overheads) of the big operators. Try Delta (☎ 13 1390) or National (☎ 13 1045).

Rent-a-wreck-style operators rent older vehicles at lower rates. Their costs and conditions vary widely and some companies only allow you to travel within a certain distance of the city, typically 100km. Try Rent-a-Bomb (☎ 9428 0088) in Richmond and Ugly Duckling (☎ 9525 4010) in St Kilda.

City Link A huge new road network called City Link should be operating by the time you read this – see the Melbourne map. City Link is a tollway system.

For visitors, the annoying thing about City Link isn't the cost but the inconvenience. Tolls are 'collected' electronically from a transponder in the car (an e-TAG). You don't have the option of paying cash. You have to either go to a post office (anywhere in Australia) or another Melbourne outlet and buy a day pass ($7.30), or open a City Link account, which gets you an e-Tag ($50 minimum, non-refundable). If you use City Link without an e-TAG or a day pass, you have until noon the next day to contact City Link (☎ 13 2629) and pay $8.50, or pay a fine of about $100.

Taxi

The main taxi ranks in the city are outside the big hotels, outside Flinders and Spencer St train stations, on the corner of William and Bourke Sts, on the corner of Elizabeth and Bourke Sts, in Lonsdale St outside Myer and outside Ansett in Franklin St. Finding an empty taxi in the city on Friday or Saturday night is difficult.

There are several taxi companies but all taxis are painted yellow. Major companies include Arrow (☎ 13 2211), Black Cabs (☎ 13 2227), Embassy (☎ 13 1755) and Silver Top (☎ 13 1008). All charge the same fares.

Accessible taxis for disabled travellers are plentiful. Try Black Cabs or Silver Top.

Bicycle

Melbourne's a great city for cycling. Bike paths run around Port Phillip Bay from Port

VICTORIA

Melbourne to Brighton, and up the Yarra for more than 20km – there are plenty of others. *Discovering Melbourne's Bike Paths* ($14.95) has maps and information. The *Melway* street directory is also useful.

Bicycles can be taken on suburban trains (free) during off-peak times.

Tram tracks are a major hazard: your wheel can get stuck in them and they're slippery, so take care cornering over them.

Quite a few places hire out bikes. A good mountain bike, helmet and lock costs about $20 a day. Try: St Kilda Cycles (☎ 9534 3074), 11 Carlisle St, St Kilda; Cycle Science (☎ 9826 8877), 320 Toorak Rd, South Yarra; City Cycle Tours (☎ 9585 5343), Treasury Gardens; and Fitzroy Cycles (☎ 9639 3511), 224 Swanston St.

Ferry

Two companies operate ferries between the city and Gem Pier in Williamstown, with hourly departures from Southgate between 10 am and 5 pm. The one-way/return fare is $10/18. You can ask to be dropped at Scienceworks and the *Polly Woodside*. On weekends there's a ferry between St Kilda Pier and Williamstown, departing St Kilda hourly between 11.30 am and 4.30 pm, and departing Williamstown hourly from 11 am to 4 pm. The fare is $6/10.

On Sunday between October and June the restored 1933 steam tug *Wattle* (☎ 9328 2739) runs between Station Pier in Port Melbourne and Gem Pier in Williamstown. It leaves Station Pier at 10.30 am, noon and 1.30 and 3 pm; the return fare costs $10.

Around Melbourne

There are some good excursions within an hour or so of the city. To the east are the Dandenong Ranges, north-east there's the Kinglake National Park, and to the north-west, the Macedon Ranges and Hanging Rock.

Then there's the Yarra Valley, known for its wineries and the Healesville Sanctuary; the rugged ocean beaches of the Mornington and Bellarine Peninsulas; and Phillip Island with its penguin parade and surf beaches.

MELBOURNE TO GEELONG

It's a one hour drive south-west down the Princes Freeway (M1) to Geelong. Leaving Melbourne over the soaring West Gate Bridge gives fine views of the city.

The **RAAF National Aviation Museum**, at the Point Cook RAAF base, has a collection of 20 aircraft and is open Tuesday to Friday from 10 am to 3 pm and until 5 pm on weekends; admission is by donation.

Werribee Park Mansion & Zoo is signposted off the freeway, about 30 minutes from Melbourne. The huge Italianate mansion (☎ 9741 2444) is surrounded by formal gardens. Entry to the gardens is free, but admission to the mansion costs $10/5. It's open from 10 am to 4.45 pm. The adjacent zoo (☎ 9731 9600) is a free-range park with African herbivores. Bus tours cost $14/7. Met trains run to Werribee train station and an infrequent bus service (none on Sunday) runs the 5km between the station and the park.

The **You Yangs** are a little range of volcanic hills just off the freeway. Ecologically, the park is quite degraded, but climbing up **Flinders Peak** gives fine views. In **Brisbane Ranges National Park** scenic Anakie Gorge is worth a visit and you might see koalas.

GEELONG

- postcode 3220 • pop 125,400

Geelong is a historic bayside city, with fine parks, good museums and galleries, and a lively nightlife. For most Victorians, the word 'Geelong' conjures up AFL football and Ford: the city is the home of the Cats and a major car factory.

Geelong boomed during the gold rush, as it was a major gateway to the goldfields. After the gold rush Geelong became the major port for the dispatch of wool and wheat from the Western District and the Wimmera.

Orientation & Information

Geelong is on the western shores of Corio Bay and the Barwon River winds through the city.

VICTORIA

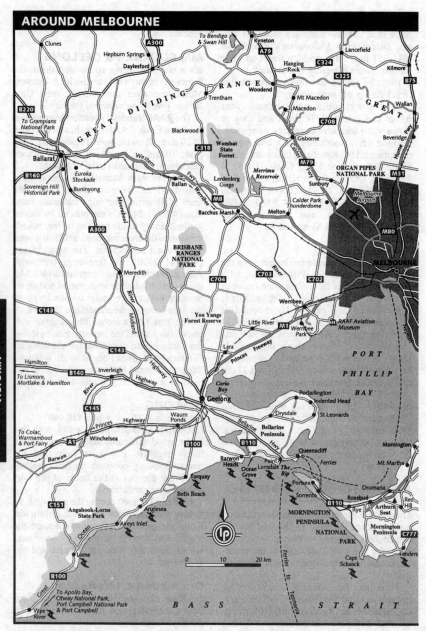

AROUND MELBOURNE

Clunes

To Bendigo & Swan Hill

Kyneton

Lancefield

A300

Hepburn Springs

Daylesford

A79

Hanging Rock

C324

Kilmore

B75

GREAT   DIVIDING   RANGE

Trentham

Woodend

Mt Macedon

Macedon

C708

GREAT

Wallan

Beveridge

Hume Fwy

B220

To Grampians National Park

Blackwood

C318

Wombat State Forest

Merrimu Reservoir

Gisborne

C79

Calder Fwy

ORGAN PIPES NATIONAL PARK

M31

Ballarat

B160

Eureka Stockade

Sovereign Hill Historical Park

Buninyong

Western   Fwy

Ballan

Lerderderg Gorge

Werribee Fwy

M8

Bacchus Marsh

Sunbury

Calder Park Thunderdome

Melton

Calder Fwy

Melbourne Airport

M80

MELBOURNE

A300

Meredith

BRISBANE RANGES NATIONAL PARK

C704

C703

C702

Werribee

M31

Moorabool   River

Werribee   River

C143

You Yangs Forest Reserve

Little River

M1

Werribee Park

RAAF Aviation Museum

Hamilton

B140

Inverleigh

To Lismore, Mortlake & Hamilton

C143

Lara

Princes   Freeway

PORT

River   Midland   Highway

Highway

PHILLIP

Geelong

Corio Bay

BAY

C145

Waurn Ponds

To Colac, Warrnambool & Port Fairy

A1

Winchelsea

Princes   Highway

Barwon   River

Portarlington

Indented Head

Drysdale

St Leonards

Bellarine   Hwy

Bellarine Peninsula

Mornington

Barwon Heads

B110

Queenscliff

Mt Martha

B100

Ocean Grove

Point Lonsdale

Ferries

Torquay

The Rip

Portsea

Dromana

Red Hill

Bells Beach

Sorrento

Rosebud

Rye

Arthurs Seat

C151

Angahook-Lorne State Park

Anglesea

Ocean   Road

MORNINGTON PENINSULA

B110

Mornington Peninsula

C777

Areys Inlet

NATIONAL

Lorne

PARK

Cape Schanck

Flinders

B100

Great   Ocean   Road

To Apollo Bay, Otway National Park, Port Campbell National Park & Port Campbell

Wye River

0   10   20 km

BASS   STRAIT

Ferries   to   Tasmania

VICTORIA

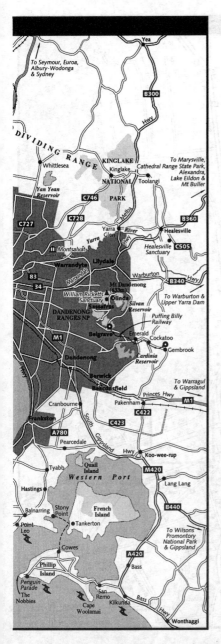

If you're driving in from the north, take the scenic foreshore route instead of the highway – even if you're just passing through. Turn left into Bell Parade (about 2km after the Ford factory) and follow the Esplanade along the foreshore.

Geelong Otway Tourism Centre (☎ 5275 5797 or 1800 620 888) is on the corner of the Princes Hwy and St Georges Rd, about 7km north of the centre. It's on the left as you come in from Melbourne. There are also tourist offices in the National Wool Museum and in the Market Square shopping centre.

Things to See & Do
Housed in a bluestone wool store (1872) on the corner of Moorabool and Brougham Sts, the impressive **Geelong National Wool Museum** (☎ 5227 0701) is open daily from 10 am to 5 pm ($7, students $5.80).

The **Naval & Maritime Museum** has an extensive collection of maritime bits and pieces, in the stables of **Osborne House**, a grand old homestead in Swinburne St, North Geelong. It's open daily, except Tuesday and Thursday, from 10 am to 4 pm ($2).

In Little Malop St, **Geelong Art Gallery** has mainly Australian art. Frederick McCubbin's *A Bush Burial* is the most famous painting. It's open on weekdays from 10 am to 5 pm and weekends from 1 to 5 pm ($3; free on Monday).

More than 100 buildings are classified by the National Trust, and several are open to the public, including the prefabricated **The Heights** (1855), 140 Aphrasia St, Newtown (open Wednesday to Sunday from 1 to 5 pm; $5) and neo-Gothic **Barwon Grange** (1856), Fernleigh St, Newtown (open Wednesday and weekends from 2 to 5pm; $4).

Eastern Beach, with its restored bathing pavilions and promenade, is a pleasant beach with good facilities. Various watercraft are rented on weekends and during the holiday seasons. Walk east along the foreshore towards Cunningham Pier to see some amusingly **painted bollards**.

The **Botanic Gardens**, in the centre of Eastern Park, is a great place for a stroll or picnic. Within the gardens, the **Old Customs**

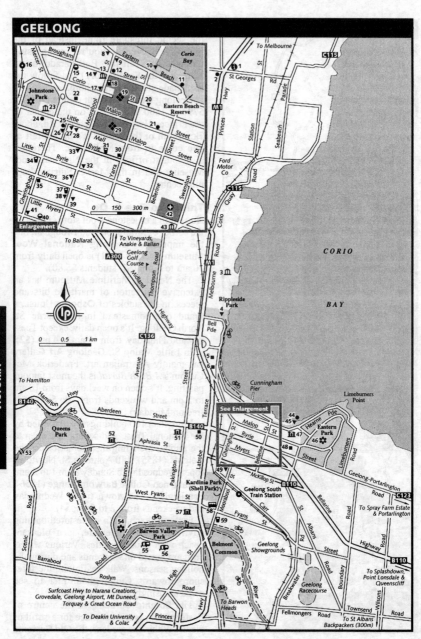

GEELONG

Enlargement

To Ballarat
To Vineyards, Anakie & Ballan
Geelong Golf Course
To Hamilton

CORIO BAY

Queens Park
Barwon Park

See Enlargement

Kardinia Park (Shell Park)
Geelong South Train Station
Belmont Common
Geelong Showgrounds
Geelong Racecourse

Limeburners Point
Eastern Park

To Spray Farm Estate & Portarlington

To Splashdown, Point Lonsdale & Queenscliff

Surfcoast Hwy to Narana Creations, Grovedale, Geelong Airport, Mt Duneed, Torquay & Great Ocean Road
To Deakin University & Colac
To Barwon Heads
To St Albans Backpackers (300m)

GEELONG

House is a tiny cottage said to be the oldest timber building in Victoria (1838).

Narana Creations (☎ 5241 5700) is an Aboriginal arts and crafts gallery and cultural centre, with an indigenous plant garden. It's near the airport at 410 Torquay Rd (the Surfcoast Hwy (B100)) in Grovedale, and is open on Wednesday.

Places to Stay
Camping & Caravan Parks Closest to the centre are the parks along Barrabool Rd on the south side of the Barwon River, which include **Billabong Caravan Park** (☎ 5243 6225) and **City Southside Caravan Park** (☎ 5243 3788). Camp sites range from $12 to $14 and cabins cost $45 a double.

St Albans Backpackers (☎ 5248 1229) is on a historic horse-stud property on Homestead Drive, Whittington. The old coach house has been converted into a hostel, with bunks for $17 and a double for $34. Ring for a pick-up.

The **colleges** at Deakin University (☎ 5227 1100), on the outskirts towards Colac, offer accommodation in the summer holidays.

Carlton Central Hotel (☎ 5229 1954, 21 Malop St) is an old-fashioned pub with reasonable singles/doubles/triples for $30/40/60, including a light breakfast. **Jokers on Ryrie** (☎ 5229 1104), on the corner of Ryrie and Yarra Sts, charges $25/45.

One of the cheapest motels is the **Kangaroo Motel** (☎ 5221 4022, 16 The Esplanade South) with units from $45/55. **Lucas Innkeepers Motor Inn** (☎ 5221 2177, 9 Aberdeen St) has doubles from $59 to $90.

Places to Eat
There are plenty of choices along Moorabool St and in Little Malop St west of the mall, and pubs all over the city have cheap counter lunches – some for $3.50. For a more upmarket pub meal, try the **Scottish Chief's Tavern & Brewery** (99 Corio St).

A couple of places with good lunch deals are **Pancake Kitchen** (48 Moorabool St) and **Spaghetti Deli** (188 Moorabool St). **Fujisan**, on Ryrie St near the corner of Moorabool, sells takeaway sushi.

There's a cluster of budget eateries and late-nighters on the Moorabool St hill. **Hill**

VICTORIA

Grill, No 228, has pastas, grills and seafood dishes mostly under $12. Across the road is *Joe's Cafe*, a souvlaki-and-burger joint that's open until 4 am.

Wholefoods Cafe (10 James St) has healthy tucker and is open on weekdays and Friday nights. At 90 Little Malop St, *Cat's* is a stylish cafe with curries, pastas and vegetarian dishes from $12 to $17.

Places by the bay include the *Fish Pier Restaurant* with fish dishes for around $20 and cheaper options, and *The Beach House* at Eastern Beach, with a restaurant, cafe and kiosk and a great location. For cheaper bayside eats, try *Gilligan's Fish & Chips*, across the road from Cunningham Pier.

Up at 51 McKillop St, Geelong Wintergarden is a restored church housing craft, souvenir and antique shops, and the good *Wintergarden Cafe*.

Entertainment

A surprising number of city pubs have bands, especially on weekends.

Lamby's at the National Wool Museum sometimes hosts quite big acts, and the *Wool Exchange Hotel* across Moorabool St is another venue. The barn-sized *Geelong Hotel (214 Moorabool St)* usually has something happening. In South Geelong, the big *Barwon Club Hotel (509 Moorabool St)* has bands from Thursday to Sunday.

The Max on Gheringhap St near the corner of Brougham has three floors with several bars and places to eat, and live music four nights a week. The *Lyric Nightclub*, on the corner of Gheringhap and Little Ryrie Sts, is probably the top nightspot. *Rebar Lounge (177 Ryrie St)* attracts a lot of students.

On winter Saturdays check to see if the mighty Cats are playing a home game at Kardinia Park (renamed Shell Stadium), just south of the city centre on Moorabool St.

Getting There & Away

Geelong train station is in Railway Terrace, beyond the west end of Corio St – V/Line trains and buses arrive here. Other long-distance buses use the Trans Otway Terminal, on the corner of Ryrie and Fenwick Sts.

Geelong Region Wineries

This area is known for its Pinot Noir and Cabernet Sauvignon. **Idyll Vineyard & Winery**, 265 Ballan Rd, Moorabool (open daily except Monday from 10 am to 5 pm) and tiny **Asher Vineyard**, 360 Goldsworthy Rd, Lovely Banks (open weekends from noon to 5 pm) are both about 8km north of Geelong.

The rustic **Mt Anakie Estate** (open daily, except Monday, from 10.30 am to 5 pm; on Sunday from 11 am to 6 pm) and **Staughton Vale Vineyard** (open Friday to Monday from 10 am to 5 pm) are both in Staughton Vale Rd, Anakie, about 40km north of Geelong on the Ballan road. **Mt Duneed Winery**, Feehans Rd, Mt Duneed, off the Surfcoast Hwy about 10km south, is open on weekends from 11 am to 5 pm.

There are also several wineries on the Bellarine Peninsula. **Kilgour Estate** is open on Saturday from 1 to 6 pm and Sunday from 11 am to 6 pm (open daily from Christmas to Easter). On weekends you can visit the historic **Spray Farm Estate** near Portarlington. The old homestead and stables are being restored – ring ☎ 5251 3176 to check opening hours.

Frequent trains make the one hour trip between Melbourne and Geelong ($8.60). Several trains a day run to Warrnambool ($24.50) and trains from North Shore station (two stations north of Geelong station) run to Ballarat ($24.50) twice on weekdays and once on Saturday.

At least twice daily V/Line buses run along the Great Ocean Rd to Apollo Bay ($18) via Torquay ($4.50) and Lorne ($11.20). On Friday (and Monday in summer), a bus goes on to Port Campbell and Warrnambool. V/Line buses run to Ballarat ($9.80) several times a day, then on to Castlemaine and Bendigo.

McHarry's Bus Lines (☎ 5223 2111) has frequent buses to the Bellarine Peninsula.

Gull Airport Service (☎ 5222 4966), 45 McKillop St, runs 13 buses a day between Geelong and Melbourne airport ($20).

Getting Around

The main city terminus is the Bus Port, on the corner of Gheringhap and Brougham Sts; drivers sell tickets.

Taxi companies include Bay City Cabs (☎ 1800 636 636).

There are bike paths throughout Geelong, and De Grandi Cycle & Sport (☎ 5222 2771), 72 Mercer St, rents bikes from around $25 a day.

BELLARINE PENINSULA

The Bellarine Peninsula forms the western side of the entrance to Port Phillip and there are some low-key resorts, such as Portarlington and St Leonards (which don't have surf) plus fashionable Queenscliff.

Accommodation prices soar between Christmas and the end of January and many caravan parks have a minimum stay requirement at this time.

McHarry's Bus Lines (☎ 5223 2111) operates the Bellarine Transit service with frequent buses from the Bus Port transit centre in Geelong and most places on the peninsula, including Barwon Heads and Ocean Grove (both $3.60) and Queenscliff and Point Lonsdale (both $5.55).

Car and passenger ferries sail daily between Queenscliff, Portsea and Sorrento – see the Mornington Peninsula Getting There & Away section later.

Geelong & Bellarine Mopeds (☎ 5258 4796) rents mopeds for $45 a day. You don't need a licence.

Queenscliff

• postcode 3225   • pop 3850

Queenscliff was established as a base for the pilots who steer ships through the treacherous Port Phillip Heads. This is one of the most dangerous seaways in the world and is known as 'the Rip'. The pilots weren't always successful – the coast is littered with shipwrecks.

In the 19th century, wealthy Melburnians and the squattocracy of the Western District flocked to the town on holiday, and some extravagant hotels and guesthouses were built. Queenscliff has been 'rediscovered' and is again a fashionable getaway town.

Things to See & Do The best way to get an overview of the (small) town centre is on the horse-drawn double-decker bus ($5) that leaves from the Vue Grand Hotel.

The most impressive old buildings are along Gellibrand St, including the **Ozone Hotel, Mietta's Queenscliff Hotel, Lathamstowe** and a row of old **pilots' cottages. Fort Queenscliff** was built in the 19th century to protect Melbourne from a feared Russian invasion. There are guided tours on weekends at 1 and 3 pm ($4/2) and weekdays at 1.30 pm ($5/2). Unfortunately, the government has decided to sell the fort – see it while you can.

The **Bellarine Tourist Railway** (☎ 1900 931 452 for recorded information) runs steam trains every Sunday, plus Tuesday and Thursday during school holidays, and daily from late December to late January.

The peninsula is popular for **diving and snorkelling**. Tanks can be filled at the general store in King St. The Queenscliff Dive Centre (☎ 5258 1188), 37 Learmonth St, and Dive Experience (☎ 5258 4058), 8 Wharf St, both run trips and courses and rent out equipment.

Bikes can be hired near the pier. Take the steam train to Drysdale and cycle back – it's downhill all the way.

The **Queenscliff Historical Centre**, Hesse St, displays various old relics and opens daily from 2 to 4 pm.

The **Marine Discovery Centre** (☎ 5258 3344), Weeroona Parade, holds programs and excursions in summer that are a fascinating way to discover Port Phillip. They also run a range of trips, including 'snorkelling with the seals' (about $40) and two-hour canoe trips ($12).

Several other operators run 'snorkelling with the seals' (and dolphins) trips. We've heard good reports about Sea-All Charters (☎ 5258 3889), which charges $50; $35 for non-snorkelling sightseers.

The small **Queenscliff Maritime Museum** is beside the Marine Studies Centre. It's open on weekends and daily during school holidays ($4/1.50).

Places to Stay The closest caravan park to the centre is at *Queenscliff Recreation*

VICTORIA

Reserve (Mercer St), with sites from $16.50 to $25. On the Bellarine Hwy 3.5km west of the centre, the modern *Beacon Resort Caravan Park* (☎ 5258 1133) has sites from $18.50 to $28 and units from $40 to $63.

The friendly Queenscliff Inn guesthouse always kept a few rooms for travellers, and is now the *Queenscliff Inn YHA* (☎ 5258 4600, 55 Hesse St). It has dorms for $15 and singles/doubles for $25/40. It's a nice place.

When it isn't full of divers, *Queenscliff Dive Centre* (☎ 5258 1188, 27 Learmonth St) offers dorm beds for $30, including breakfast.

Riptide Motel & Holiday Flats (☎ 5258 1675, 31 Flinders St) isn't glamorous, but the motel rooms and self-contained two-bedroom flats are good value, from $80 for four people. In the centre of town the pleasant *Queenscliff Inn* (☎ 5258 4600, 55 Hesse St) has rooms with shared bathrooms for $50 a single and doubles from $75 to $90, including breakfast.

Most of Queenscliff's old pubs have been renovated. The cheapest is the *Esplanade Hotel* (☎ 5258 1919), on the corner of Gellibrand and Symonds Sts, with rooms from $35. The *Royal Hotel* (☎ 5258 1669, 34 King St) charges from $70/80.

The *Ozone Hotel* (☎ 1800 804 753, 42 Gellibrand St), *Mietta's Queenscliff Hotel* (☎ 5258 1066, 16 Gellibrand St) and the *Vue Grand Hotel* (☎ 5258 1544, 46 Hesse St) are all expensive but worth considering for a splurge.

Places to Eat Hesse St has a collection of takeaways – try *Queenscliff Fish & Chips* at No 77. *Provender Deli*, at No 67 and, across the road, *Beaches Deli*, are good. *Thwaites Bakery*, near the corner of Hobson St, sells good takeaways, including seafood rolls for $3.35.

Harry's, in the foreshore park in Gellibrand St opposite the pier, is a quirky place with good food, especially the seafood. Mains are mostly under $20. Harry's closes in winter.

The *Ozone Hotel* has bar meals and a bistro serving upmarket pub food with mains around $18.

If you want to indulge yourself, head for *Mietta's Queenscliff Hotel* (☎ 5258 1066). It's a magnificently restored hotel, with consistently superb food. There's a formal dining room with a set menu at $62 a head, and a courtyard bistro with main courses around $20. Behind the hotel, with an entrance at the north end of Hesse St, *Mietta's Shop & Bar* is part bar, part gift shop and part eatery.

Point Lonsdale

Five kilometres west of Queenscliff (it's a pleasant walk along the beach between the two towns), Point Lonsdale is a laid-back little town centred around its **lighthouse** (1902).

Bring your mask or goggles to explore the rockpools around the headland at low tide.

Below the lighthouse is **Buckley's Cave**, where the 'wild white man', escaped convict William Buckley, who lived with Aborigines for 32 years, spent some time. This area is dotted with 'Buckley caves'!

The council-run *Royal Park Caravan Park* (☎ 5258 1765) is open between December and Easter and has camp sites for $16.50.

Ocean Grove

Ocean Grove is a sprawling and unattractive town, but the beach at the surf lifesaving club has good surf. There is good scuba diving on the rocky ledges of the bluff, and further out there are wrecks.

On the west side of town, *Riverview Family Caravan Park* (☎ 5256 1600) has camp sites from $15 to $25 – you'll need to book in summer. *Ocean Grove Motor Inn* (☎ 5256 2555, Wallington Rd), 1km north of the centre, has doubles from $60 to $114.

Barwon Heads

Barwon Heads is a smaller and prettier resort 4km west of Ocean Grove. (It is the location for the TV series *Sea Change*.) It has sheltered river beaches and, around the headland, **Thirteenth Beach** has excellent surf.

Barwon Heads Park (☎ 5254 1115) has sites from $15 to $23 and there are cabins and cottages for $50 to $170 a double. You'll need to book during school holidays.

Barwon Heads Hotel *(☎ 5254 2201, Ewing Blyth Rd)* has motel units from $70 to $110 a double. ***Early Settlers Motel*** *(☎ 5254 2369, 67 Hitchcock Ave)* has good units from $64 to $89 a double.

THE CALDER HIGHWAY

The Calder Hwy (large sections are freeway) runs north-west from Melbourne towards Bendigo.

Sunbury was the site for Woodstock-style rock festivals in the early 1970s. It is also where **the Ashes**, the Holy Grail of English and Australian cricket, originated. On Sunbury Rd are two historic wineries. **Goona Warra** and **Craiglee** were first planted in the 1860s – both are open daily.

Just north of Gisborne you can turn off the Calder Hwy and head past the small town of Macedon to **Mt Macedon** (1013m). The route up Mt Macedon Rd takes you over the mountain, past mansions with beautiful gardens. Beyond the summit turnoff, the road leads to Woodend, or take the first sealed road on the right to Hanging Rock. The nearby **Camel's Hump** is popular with rock climbers.

Hanging Rock was made famous by Joan Lindsay's novel and the subsequent film *Picnic at Hanging Rock* about the disappearance of some schoolgirls. It's a sacred site of the Wurrenjerrie Aborigines, and was a refuge for bushrangers. The reserve is popular for picnics, and there are walking tracks. You may see koalas. **Hanging Rock Picnic Race Meetings**, on New Year's Day and Australia Day, draw large crowds.

Hanging Rock Reserve (☎ 5427 0295) is 6km north-east of Woodend; admission costs $5 per car. There are daily trains from Melbourne to Woodend ($8.60) – from there, a taxi (☎ 5427 2641) to the rock costs about $12, or it's a fairly easy bicycle ride.

THE YARRA VALLEY & BEYOND

The Yarra Valley, not far beyond the northeastern outskirts of Melbourne, is a good area for cycling and bushwalking. There are

dozens of wineries, and there's also the famous Healesville Wildlife Sanctuary.

The Yarra Valley Visitor Information Centre (☎ 5962 2600) is off the highway in Healesville. There's also a Visitor Centre in the Upper Yarra Valley, on the highway at Warburton. Both are open daily.

In Toolangi, the NRE's impressive **Forest Discovery Centre** (☎ 5962 9314) has displays on various aspects of forest use. It's open daily ($2). There's a Parks Victoria/NRE office (☎ 5964 7088) at Woori Yallock.

There are quite a few state and national parks, most with walking trails and some with camping, including **Warrandyte State Park**, **Yarra Ranges National Park** and **Kinglake National Park**. The various information centres and Parks Victoria offices have information. Alternatively, drop into the NRE's shop in Melbourne before you leave.

The **Centenary Trail** follows a railway line between Warburton and Lilydale. At 38km it's a good bike ride.

There are some great scenic drives. The Warburton, Healesville and Marysville triangle takes you through some great countryside. Both the Acheron Way and Woods Point Rd are excellent drives along good gravel roads. It's a short drive from Warburton up to **Mt Donna Buang**, with the closest (but unskiable) snow to Melbourne in winter.

Getting There & Away

Suburban trains go as far as Lilydale. McKenzie's Bus Lines (☎ 5962 5088) has daily services from Lilydale to Healesville (Zone 3 Met ticket) and Yarra Glen, and direct services from the Spencer St coach terminal in Melbourne to Healesville (Zone 1, 2 & 3 Met ticket), and to Marysville ($11.20).

Martyrs Bus Service (☎ 5966 2035) runs from Lilydale train station to Yarra Junction and Warburton – fares are cheaper if you show your Met ticket.

Organised Tours

Yarra Valley Winery Tours (☎ 5962 3870) runs bus tours of the wineries from Melbourne. Eco Adventure Tours (☎ 5962 5115)

VICTORIA

has tours, including nocturnal walks, of the area's natural attractions. Adventure Canoeing (☎ 9844 3323), and other operators, hire canoes and organise canoeing trips.

Go Wild Ballooning (☎ 9890 0339) and Balloon Aloft (☎ 1800 028 568) offer dawn balloon flights over the valley.

Healesville Wildlife Sanctuary

Healesville Wildlife Sanctuary (☎ 5962 4022), Badger Creek Rd, Healesville, is one of the best places to see Australian fauna in the country. The Platypus House is likely to be the only place you'll see these amazing creatures, and certainly the only place you'll see their underwater activities.

The staff give regular demonstrations, such as snake shows. The best is the amazing Birds of Prey presentation, where raptors swoop above your head. It's held at noon and 3 pm (weather permitting), but get there early for a good seat. In summer the sanctuary has open-air music concerts.

The sanctuary is open daily from 9 am to 5 pm and admission is $14; $10.50 for students and $7 for children.

Galeena Beek Living Cultural Centre

Near the entrance to Healesville Wildlife Sanctuary, Galeena Beek (which means 'cleanse the earth'; ☎ 5962 1119, 22 Glen Eadie Ave) has an exhibition on Aboriginal history and offers a short interpretive bushwalk. You can usually try boomerang and spear throwing and, if you're here at the same time as a school group, you might be able to sit in on story-telling and didgeridoo playing. It is open on weekdays ($6.50).

Gulf Station

A couple of kilometres north of Yarra Glen, Gulf Station is a National Trust-classified farm dating back to the 1850s. It's open Wednesday to Sunday and on public holidays from 10 am to 4 pm ($7/4).

Marysville

• postcode 3779   • pop 625

In the 1920s this pretty little town was known as Melbourne's honeymoon capital.

Today, it's a getaway town, with its mountain setting, old-fashioned guesthouses, waterfalls and bushwalks.

Steavenson's Falls, the state's highest, are floodlit at night. **Cumberland Scenic Reserve**, with numerous walks and more waterfalls, is 16km east of Marysville. **Lady Talbot Drive** makes a 48km loop past some of the area's prettiest and most spectacular features.

Places to Stay *Marysville Caravan Park (☎ 5963 3443)* has sites from $12, on-site vans from $40 and bunkrooms where a bed costs $10 to $14, depending on the season.

Cheapest of the motels is the *Crossways Motel (☎ 5963 3290, Woods Point Rd)*, with units from $50/55 for singles/doubles.

Guesthouses include the enormous *Marylands Country House (☎ 5963 3204, 22 Falls Rd)*, with B&B from $190 a double; and *Mountain Lodge (☎ 5963 3270, 32 Kings Rd)*, with rooms from $80 per person, including meals.

THE DANDENONGS

On a clear day, the Dandenong Ranges can be seen from the centre of Melbourne – Mt Dandenong is the highest point (633m). The hills are about 35km east of the city.

By the end of the 19th century most of the forests had been cleared and the settlers planted deciduous trees. The landscape is now a blend of exotic and regrown native trees with a lush understorey of tree ferns.

Despite the encroaching urban sprawl, the Dandenongs retain much of their charm, although things can get a little hectic on the narrow roads on weekends.

Dandenong Ranges & Knox Visitor Information Centre (☎ 9758 7522) is at 1211 Burwood Hwy in Upper Ferntree Gully. The Parks Victoria office (☎ 9758 1342) is in the Lower Picnic Ground in Upper Ferntree Gully, at the start of the Mt Dandenong Tourist Rd. Rangers can provide maps of the parks and walking tracks.

Ferntree Gully National Park has walking trails that take around two hours. **Sherbrooke Forest** has a towering cover of mountain ash trees. The forest was famous for its lyrebirds, but feral cats have killed many of them.

Sherbrooke Forest was a haven for lyrebirds

Doongalla Forest, on the western slopes of Mt Dandenong, is not as accessible as the other areas, and is less crowded.

William Ricketts Sanctuary (☎ 13 1963), on Mt Dandenong Tourist Rd, features sculptures by William Ricketts. His work was inspired by the years he spent living with Aboriginal people and his philosophies permeate the sanctuary, which is in damp fern gardens. It's open daily from 10 am to 5 pm (last entry 4.30 pm) and admission costs $5. There are concerts here in summer.

There are some superb gardens, such as the **National Rhododendron Gardens** and the **Alfred Nicholas Memorial Gardens**, on Sherbrooke Rd in Sherbrooke.

Puffing Billy

Puffing Billy (☎ 9754 6800 for bookings and recorded information) is a steam train that puffs its way through the hills and fern gullies. Visit its Web site at www.pbr.org.au.

The train operates four times a day on weekdays outside school holidays, departing from the Belgrave Puffing Billy station, near Belgrave train station. One trip runs to Gembrook (return fare $25 for adults, $14 for children and $71 for families); the others run to Emerald Lakeside Park (return fare $18 for adults, $10 for children and $51 for families).

Places to Stay

The Dandenongs has numerous motels, guesthouses, B&Bs and cottages, and a few options for budget travellers. *Emerald Backpackers* (☎ 5968 4086) is on the edge of the Lakeside Reserve in Emerald. It's a comfortable hostel in an attractive setting, and the owners can often find work for travellers in nurseries and gardens. Dorm beds cost $13. There's also *Dougie's Place* (☎ 5958 3297, 22 Kings Rd, Emerald), run by an experienced traveller (from $15). In Belgrave, *Jaynes Retreat* (☎ 9752 6181, 27 Terrys Ave) is a B&B aimed at budget travellers, with good meals (from just $6.50 for dinner) and Sherbrooke Forest nearby. Prices start at around $20.

MORNINGTON PENINSULA

The Mornington Peninsula, separating Port Phillip and Western Port, is a little over an hour's drive from the city centre. It has been a summer resort since the 1870s.

Peninsula Tourism's main Visitor Information office (☎ 5987 3078 or 1800 804 009) is on the Nepean Hwy in Dromana. It's open daily from 9 am to 5 pm.

Getting There & Away

Bus & Train The Met's suburban trains from the city to Frankston take about an hour. Trains also run from Frankston to the Western Port side of the peninsula.

From Frankston train station, Portsea Passenger Buses (☎ 5986 5666) runs along the Nepean Hwy to Portsea ($6.90).

Ferry Peninsula Searoad Transport (☎ 5258 3244) runs a car and passenger ferry between Sorrento and Queenscliff on the Bellarine Peninsula. It runs daily and the crossing takes about half an hour, departing from Queenscliff at 7, 9 and 11 am, 1, 3 and 5 pm and returning from Sorrento at 8 and 10 am, noon and 2, 4 and 6 pm. During peak seasons (Friday and Sunday from mid-September to mid-December and then daily until Easter Tuesday), there are additional departures from Queenscliff at 7 pm and from Sorrento at 8 pm. Cars cost $32 to $36 plus $3 per adult and $2 per child; a motorcycle and

VICTORIA

rider costs $17; and pedestrians cost $7. Pedestrian tickets are valid for 12 months.

Mornington to Sorrento

Mornington and **Mt Martha** are attractive residential suburbs, but apart from their excellent bay beaches they hold little interest for travellers. Turn off the Nepean Hwy at Mornington and take the slower but much more scenic route around the coast, which rejoins the highway at **Dromana**. Just inland is the **Arthurs Seat** lookout, with a chairlift to the top ($7.50/5 return) on weekends and daily from September to April.

Sorrento

In summer Sorrento is a fashionable resort, with some fine 19th century buildings and good beaches. Dolphin-watching cruises in the bay are popular.

The **Nepean Historical Society Museum**, in the old Mechanic's Institute building on Melbourne Rd, is open on Sunday and during school holidays from 1.30 to 4.30 pm ($3). There's also a rather damp little **Marine Oceanarium**, open daily.

Places to Stay *Bell's Environmental YHA Hostel (☎ 5984 4323, 3 Miranda St, Sorrento)* is purpose-built and the facilities are very good. Horse trail rides and snorkelling trips can be organised. Beds cost $12 for YHA members ($14 in peak season). To get here from Melbourne take a train to Frankston, then take bus No 788 from the bus stop near to the station to stop 18.

Down near the back beach, the *Oceanic Motel (☎ 5984 4166, 234 Ocean Beach Rd)* has units from $45/90 to $55/100 a single/ double.

Portsea

Portsea, at the eastern tip of the peninsula, is where many of Melbourne's wealthiest families have seaside mansions. That little blue bathing box on the beach? It was snapped up for $185,000 in 1999.

Portsea has some great beaches. The back (ie, ocean) beach has good surf but can be dangerous, so head for the life-saving club and swim between the flags. The front (ie,

bay) beaches are safer for swimming, and if things get too hot you can wander up to the pub for a drink in the beer garden that overlooks the pier.

Dive Victoria (☎ 5984 3155) offers one-day beginner's dives (from $120, including gear and two dives) and snorkelling trips ($30 plus $15 for gear hire).

Accommodation is limited and generally expensive. The cheapest option is the *Portsea Hotel (☎ 5984 2213)*, with rooms with shared facilities from $60 plus a few en suite rooms from $110.

Mornington Peninsula National Park

Point Nepean National Park, on the tip of the peninsula, has expanded (and been renamed) to include the ocean beaches up to Cape Schanck and another large chunk called Green Bush.

There's a Visitors Centre (☎ 5984 4276) near the entrance. Admission costs $8.50 for adults, $4.50 for children and $19 for families if you want to take the two to four hour bus tour, less if you walk. You need to book if you're taking the bus tour and even if you aren't, booking is a good idea because visitor numbers are restricted.

There are several good walks, some quite long, and you can find yourself alone on wild surf beaches. Swimming is dangerous. On the fourth weekend of the month, the park holds 'bike & hike' days where, for a reduced entry fee of $5.50, cyclists and walkers can explore the park at their leisure.

Ocean Beaches – Portsea to Flinders

The south-western coast of the peninsula faces Bass Strait. Along here are the beautiful and rugged ocean beaches of Blairgowrie, Rye, St Andrews, Gunnamatta and Cape Schanck.

Surf life-saving clubs operate at Gunnamatta and Portsea during summer. There have been quite a few drownings along this stretch of coast, so only swim in patrolled areas.

At Cape Schanck is the **Cape Schanck Lighthouse Station** (☎ 5988 6154), an operational lighthouse built in 1859 with a kiosk, museum and information centre. It's open daily from 10 am to around 4 pm ($2). Guided tours are held half-hourly in summer, less often at other times, and cost $6.

Ace-Hi Ranch (☎ 5988 6262) in Cape Schanck is a horse-riding ranch with self-contained cabins costing $50 a double, plus $15 per extra adult. A short horse ride costs $15, a two hour ride is $25 and a 2¾ hour bush and beach ride is $35.

French Island
Off the coast in Western Port, French Island was once a prison farm and is virtually undeveloped. The prison has closed and two-thirds of the island is now a national park. The main attractions are bushwalks, bike rides, mutton-bird rookeries and koalas.

For information call ☎ 5980 1241; there's a ranger station by the ferry pier.

The *old prison farm (☎ 5678 0155)*, 2km from the ferry, has accommodation. Pick-ups from the ferry cost $10. Cells cost $15/25, and family dorms are $55 – if you prefer your windows without bars, try the *guesthouse* for $65 per person. Alternatively you can camp in the national park. There are toilets and drinking water (the only water in the park) at the *Fairhaven camping ground* on the western shore. You aren't allowed to light fires, so bring a fuel stove. Tankerton General Store sells limited supplies.

Inter Island Ferries (☎ 9585 5730) runs between Stony Point on the Mornington Peninsula and Phillip Island via French Island ($8 one way). There's at least one trip each day all year. A train runs between Melbourne and Stony Point.

PHILLIP ISLAND
At the entrance to Western Port, and 125km south-east of Melbourne by road, Phillip Island is a popular holiday resort. The island's main claim to fame is its excellent beaches, from world-renowned surf on the south coast to sheltered bay beaches on the north side. There's also the much hyped Penguin Parade.

The island was used by Aborigines as a pantry until they were hunted off by 19th century sealers.

Orientation & Information
The island is about 100 sq km in area. It is connected to the mainland by a bridge at San Remo.

Cowes, on the north coast, is the main town and has sheltered beaches.

The information centre (☎ 5956 7447) is on the main road, just after you cross the bridge. It is open daily from 9 am to 5 pm.

Penguin Parade
Every evening at Summerland Beach the little penguins that nest there emerge from the sea and waddle up the beach. Up to 4000 people also turn up, especially on weekends and holidays, so book ($9.50/5 and $24.50 for families) at the island's information centre, or at Phillip Island Nature Park (☎ 5956 8300 for recorded information) – the name of the penguin reserve. There's a visitors centre, open daily from 10 am.

Seal Rocks & The Nobbies
Off Point Grant, the extreme south-west tip of the island, a group of rocks called the Nobbies rises from the sea. Beyond these are Seal Rocks, home to Australia's largest colony of fur seals. The rocks are most crowded from October to December.

The new **Sea Life Centre** (☎ 1300 367 325) has some interesting displays, including live close-up video of the seals, but the really exciting project is a planned submarine tunnel out to the rocks. That's some way off yet. Admission is a hefty $15/7.50.

Beaches
The ocean beaches are on the south side and there's a life-saving club at Woolamai – this beach is notorious for its rips and currents, so swim only between the flags. Other surf beaches include Berry's Beach and Summerland. If you're not a good swimmer, head for the bay beaches around Cowes, or the quieter ocean beaches such as Smith's.

There are quite a few surf shops that rent equipment, and plenty of excellent breaks from Cat Bay to Woolamai. Island Surfboards (☎ 5952 3443) at Smith's Beach has surfing lessons for $25.

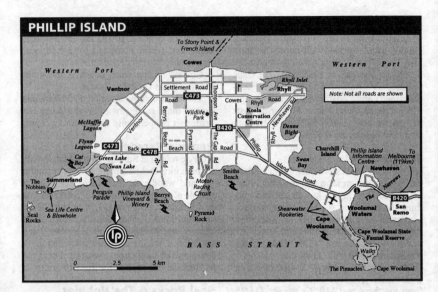

PHILLIP ISLAND

Dive Phillip Island (☎ 5674 2382) rents diving equipment and runs courses.

Koalas & Other Wildlife

The **Koala Conservation Centre** at Fiveways on the Phillip Island Rd has elevated boardwalks. It's open from 10 am to 6 pm ($5/2).

Phillip Island Wildlife Park, on Thompson Ave about 1km south of Cowes, has a good range of animals and is open daily ($9/4.50 and $25 for families). Off the island, on the highway about 10km from San Remo, **Wildlife Wonderland** also has animals, plus giant Gippsland earthworms ($6/11/31).

There are **mutton bird** (shearwater) colonies, particularly in the sand dunes around Cape Woolamai. These birds arrive on the same day each year – 24 September – and stay on the island until April. Your best chance of seeing them is at the penguin parade, as they fly in at dusk in spring and summer, or at the Forest Caves Reserve at Woolamai Beach.

Other Attractions

The old **Motor Racing Circuit** is now home to Australian Motorcycle Grand Prix. There's a visitors centre open daily from 10 am.

There are some walking tracks and a few cycling tracks. At rugged **Cape Woolamai**, access to the walking trail is from the Woolamai surf beach near the life-saving club. The information centre in Cowes and Amaroo Park Backpackers have information on other walks.

Small **Churchill Island** has a historic homestead and beautiful gardens. The island is connected to Phillip Island by a bridge and the turn-off is signposted about 1km out of Newhaven. The island is open daily from 10 am to 4 pm ($5).

There's a **museum** in the Heritage Centre on Thompson Ave in Cowes. It's open on Saturday morning and Sunday afternoon all year, plus some weekday afternoons during school holidays ($1).

Organised Tours, Flights & Cruises

Island Scenic Tours (☎ 5952 1042) runs trips most nights from Cowes to the penguin parade ($18, including entry) and also a three hour scenic tour ($18). Amaroo Park Backpackers also takes people to the penguin parade. Phillip Island airport (☎ 5956 7316) operates scenic flights, from a 15

Point Addis, Great Ocean Road, Vic

Ballarat Botanic Garden, Vic

The Nobbies, Phillip Island, Vic

Gibson Steps, Port Campbell, Vic

GARETH MCCORMACK

Mt Buffalo National Park, Vic

GREG ELMS

Post Office, Beechworth, Vic

BETHUNE CARMICHAEL

Croajingolong National Park, Vic

PAUL SINCLAIR

Snow laden tree in Mt Baw Baw National Park

minute zip around Cape Woolamai ($32) to a 45 minute loop around Western Port ($80).

Bay Connections Cruises (☎ 5678 5642) runs cruises, including trips to Seal Rocks ($35), and to French Island ($40; includes a bus tour of the island) from Cowes jetty, and evening 'shearwater cruises' ($27) from San Remo.

Places to Stay
Vacancies can be scarce at Christmas, Easter and during school holidays, and prices rise. The information centre has an accommodation booking service.

The places mentioned below are all in Cowes.

Camping, Caravan Parks & Hostels
Note that you aren't allowed to camp or even sleep in your car in any public area on the island.

There are a dozen or so caravan parks, about half of them in Cowes. Generally, sites range seasonally from $15 to $27, and on-site vans and cabins cost from $35 to $85.

Friendly *Amaroo Park YHA (☎ 5952 2548)*, on the corner of Church and Osborne Sts, close to the centre of Cowes, is a good hostel attached to a caravan park. It charges $14/17 in dorms for members/nonmembers, $17/20 per person in doubles and has tent sites for $7/10 per person. V/Line bus drivers will usually drop you off at the door and the hostel also runs Duck Truck packages, with three nights accommodation, two meals, entry to the penguin parade, an island tour, bike hire and transport to and from Melbourne – all for $75.

The caravan park has sites from $14 to $16, on-site tents for $16 and vans and cabins from $35 to $77 a double.

Other Accommodation The *Isle of Wight Hotel (☎ 5952 2301)* is on the Esplanade, and has motel rooms from $37/47 a single/double (expect to pay more in summer).

Also on the Esplanade is *The Anchor at Cowes (☎ 5952 1351)*, with motel units and suites ($62 to $72) and self-contained townhouses (from $92). There are several motels along Thompson Ave, the main road into

Cowes. They include the *Hollydene Motel (☎ 5952 2311)* at No 114, with rooms from $48, and *Banfield's (☎ 5952 2486)* at No 192, a large family-style motel with a bistro, cinema, swimming pool and rooms from $68/75.

Bayside Holiday Units (☎ 5952 2058, Beach St) has units sleeping from four people, from $60 to $100 per unit.

Places to Eat
Most eateries in Cowes are along the Esplanade or Thompson Ave. The *Isle of Wight Hotel* has pub meals in the bar and the upstairs bistro. Specials can cost as little as $5.

Isola de Capri on the main corner is a bustling Italian bistro, with pizzas and pastas from $12 to $15 and chicken, steak and seafood dishes from around $14. Across the road, *The Jetty (☎ 5952 2060)* has an upstairs cocktail bar and a cheaper cafe, *TVR*, next door. At 81 Thompson Ave, *Wing Ho* serves up Chinese tucker at reasonable prices.

Charmandene Cottage (☎ 5952 1386, 27-31 Osbourne Ave), the westward continuation of the Esplanade, specialises in old-fashioned roast dinners and great desserts for $20 a head. It's open on weekends and daily during holiday seasons.

Getting There & Away
V/Line's daily bus service between Melbourne and Cowes costs $13.50 and takes 2¼ hours. See the earlier Camping, Caravan Parks & Hostels entry for information on Duck Truck packages.

Inter Island Ferries (☎ 9585 5730) runs between Stony Point on Mornington Peninsula and Phillip Island via French Island, charging $8. There's at least one trip each day all year. A train runs between Melbourne and Stony Point.

Bay Connections (☎ 5678 642) also runs a ferry between Stony Point and Cowes ($15), via French Island but not daily and not at all in winter.

Getting Around
There is no public transport on the island. You can hire bikes from Phillip Island Bike

Hire (☎ 5952 2381), 11 Findlay St in Cowes, and from Amaroo Park Backpackers.

Great Ocean Road

The Great Ocean Rd (B100) is one of the world's most spectacular drives, especially between Anglesea and Apollo Bay. As well as great beaches, the beautiful Otway Ranges stretch from Aireys Inlet to Cape Otway and offer great bushwalking. One of the most popular trails is along the old railway line between Beech Forest and Colac. Most of the coastal section of the Otways is part of the Angahook-Lorne State Park.

Information centres in Lorne, Apollo Bay, Warrnambool, Port Fairy and Portland are open daily. There are smaller tourist offices in Torquay and Port Campbell. There's also a Web site: www.greatoceanrd.org.au.

Accommodation is scarce during the summer school holidays and Easter, and prices rise. Unless otherwise specified, where two prices are quoted in this section they refer to off peak/peak season.

Organised Tours

The larger companies such as V/Line (☎ 13 6196) run bus tours along the Great Ocean Rd from Melbourne. Smaller companies such as Autopia Tours (☎ 9326 5536) and Let's Go Bush Tours (☎ 9662 3969) run tours catering for backpackers.

Another good way to see the region is on the Wayward Bus (☎ 1800 882 823), which follows the coast on its three day run (well, amble) between Melbourne and Adelaide.

Great Ocean Road Adventure Tours (☎ 5289 6841) offers mountain-bike tours through the Angahook-Lorne State Park and the Otway Ranges, from $30. It also arranges bushwalking and other tours, which include discounts and accommodation for backpackers.

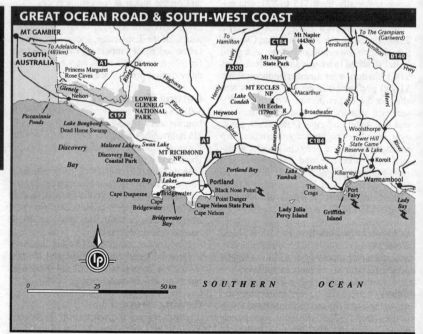

GREAT OCEAN ROAD & SOUTH-WEST COAST

Getting There & Away

V/Line buses operate from Geelong as far as Apollo Bay ($18) via Torquay ($4.50) and Lorne ($11.20) at least twice daily. On Friday, a V/Line bus continues on from Apollo Bay to Port Campbell and Warrnambool.

McHarry's Bus Lines (☎ 5223 2111) runs between Geelong and Torquay ($4.35).

TORQUAY

● postcode 3228   ● pop 6000

Torquay is a popular holiday town and the capital of Australia's surfing industry. There are loads of surf shops, with the big names like Rip Curl and Quicksilver at Surfcity Plaza on the Surfcoast Hwy.

The tourist information centre (☎ 5261 4219), at Surfcity Plaza, is open daily.

Things to See & Do

At Surfcity Plaza, the excellent **Surfworld Australia Surfing Museum** (☎ 5261 4606) is a must for visitors with any interest in waves. It's open daily and entry costs $6/4 and $16 for families.

Sheltered **Fisherman's Beach** is popular with families and the **Back Beach** is patrolled by life-savers during summer. About 3km south-west of Torquay, **Jan Juc** has good surf.

Surfing gear can be hired at several shops on the highway opposite Surfcity Plaza, or buy your own at the second-hand surf shops nearby in Baines Court. Go Ride a Wave (☎ 5263 2111) and Westcoast Surf School (☎ 5261 2241) have **surfing lessons**.

The **Surf Coast Walk** follows the coastline from Jan Juc to Moggs Creek, south of Aireys Inlet. The full distance takes about 11 hours.

About 7km from Torquay is the turn-off to the **Bells Beach Recreation Reserve.** The powerful point break at Bells is the site of a world-championship surfing contest every Easter.

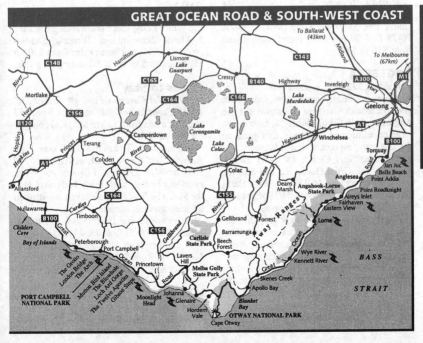

GREAT OCEAN ROAD & SOUTH-WEST COAST

VICTORIA

Places to Stay

Just behind the Back Beach, *Torquay Public Reserve* (☎ 5261 2496) has sites from $17 to $27 and cabins from $60 to $87. *Zeally Bay Caravan Park* (☎ 5261 2400), on the corner of Darian Rd and The Esplanade), is behind Fisherman's Beach and has sites from $15/17 and on-site vans and cabins for $38 to $75.

You can bunk down at *Bells Beach Backpackers* (☎ 5261 7070, 51-53 Surfcoast Hwy) for $17 ($20 in peak season).

Potter's Inn B&B (☎ 5261 4131, 40 Bristol Rd) has rooms from $60/85.

Places to Eat

Gilbert St, running at a right angle to the Esplanade, has a supermarket, an organic fruit and vegie shop, a bakery and several delis and takeaways. At the beach end of Gilbert St, *Yummy Yoghurt* provides healthy fare. At the other end, *The Lapin Agile Cafe* is a relaxed spot for a bite or cuppa. Across the road, *Sandbah Cafe* is another goody.

Micha's Mexican (☎ 5261 2460, 23 The Esplanade) caters well for vegetarians. The smoke-free *Surfrider Cafe* (☎ 5261 6477, 26-28 Bell St) has a big menu, with dishes from $16 to $19.

ANGLESEA

• postcode 3230　　• pop 2000

Anglesea is a family resort town. Other than good beaches, Anglesea is known for the **Anglesea Golf Club**, Noble St, home to a large population of kangaroos that graze on the fairways, especially towards dusk.

Anglesea Surf Centre (☎ 5263 1530), corner of the Great Ocean Rd and McMillan St, rents out boards. The **Anglesea Hang Gliding School** (☎ 015 841 107) offers tandem flights and certificate courses.

Angahook-Lorne State Park (22,000 hectares) extends between Fairhaven and Kennett River. There are basic camping areas, and some great walks, many beginning near Lorne and there's plenty of wildlife – contact the Parks Victoria office in Lorne for details.

Places to Stay

Anglesea Family Caravan Park (☎ 5263 1583, Cameron Rd) has sites from $17 to $24 and cabins and cottages from $47 (from $511 per week during summer and Easter). *Narambi Caravan Park* (☎ 5263 1362, 11 Camp Rd) has sites from $15 and cabins from $40.

Anglesea Backpackers (☎ 5263 2664, 40 Noble St) is a spotless place run by a local surfie. Dorm beds cost from $15 to $17 and doubles with bathroom cost from $20 per person. It's a couple of blocks along Noble St, which runs off the main road at the bridge.

The 1920s-style *Debonair Guesthouse & Motel* (☎ 5263 1440, fax 5263 3239) on the main road offers guesthouse rooms (some with shared bathrooms) for $75 to $95 a double, including breakfast, and motel units for $65 to $75. At the time of writing, it was due to be renovated, so these prices may change.

AIREYS INLET

• postcode 3231　　• pop 760

Aireys Inlet is less commercial than some other towns, and has good beaches and a good vibe.

Near **Split Point Lighthouse**, nicknamed the White Lady, there are walking tracks.

About 2km inland, Blazing Saddles (☎ 5289 7322) has **horse rides** from $20 for 1¼ hours to $35 for a 2¼ hour beach ride.

Places to Stay

Aireys Inlet Caravan Park (☎ 5289 6230, 19-25 Great Ocean Rd) has sites from $15 to $20, cabins from $45 to $65, and cottages for $80 to $95.

In Fairhaven, 1.5km towards Lorne from Aireys, *Surf Coast Backpackers* (☎ 5289 6886 or 0419 351 149, 5 Cowen Ave) is an excellent hostel, with bunk beds available for $17. The beach at Fairhaven is patrolled by life-savers in summer.

There are several B&Bs, such as *Bush to Beach B&B* (☎ 5289 6538, 43 Anderson St), with doubles from $90. *The Lightkeeper's Inn* (☎ 5289 6666, 64 Great Ocean Rd) is a motel charging from $70 to $100 a double.

LORNE

• postcode 3232　　• pop 1100

Lorne is the most popular and fashionable town on the west coast.

The visitor information centre (☎ 5289 1152), 144 Mountjoy Parade, is open daily from 9 am to 5 pm. Parks Victoria (☎ 5289 1732) is at 86 Polwarth Rd.

Lorne has some excellent beaches and life-savers patrol the main beach.

If you don't want to bushwalk, at least take a scenic drive through the hills behind town. Drive up to **Teddy Lookout**, follow the Deans Marsh-Lorne road into the Otways or take **Erskine Falls Rd** inland to the falls.

The **Lorne Historical Society**, on the corner of Otway St and the Great Ocean Rd, is open on weekends from 1 to 4 pm.

Paddle with the Platypus (☎ 5236 2119) offers half-day canoeing trips ($65 including transport) to the mysterious and lovely Lake Elizabeth in the Otways, where you have a good chance of seeing platypuses. Dawn is the best time to go. The trips require a minimum of two people and a maximum of six.

Special Events

New Year's Eve is a fairly wild time in Lorne and there's usually a big concert out at Erskine Falls. During the first week of January, the Pier to Pub Swim sees several thousand swimmers splash their way across Loutit Bay to the Lorne Hotel.

Places to Stay

There's a tremendous range of accommodation. For more than we can fit here, contact the visitor information centre or an agency such as the Great Ocean Rd Accommodation Centre (☎ 5289 1800) at 136 Mountjoy Parade.

Camping & Caravan Parks The Lorne Foreshore Committee (☎ 5289 1382) manages five good caravan parks. The main office is at *Erskine River Caravan Park*, beside the river. *Kia Ora Caravan Park* is nearby on the southern side of the river. *Ocean Road Park*, *Queens Park* and *Top Bank* only open at busier times of the year. You'll need to book well in advance for a site at Christmas or Easter.

Costs vary seasonally, with camp sites from $12 to $20 and cabins from $45 to $60

for two people. Over Christmas (19 December to 23 January) and Easter, cabins can only be booked weekly and cost $500 to $850.

Hostels *Erskine River Backpackers (☎ 5289 1496, 6 Mountjoy Parade)* is a top spot to hang out. Dorm beds cost $17 and doubles $50.

Great Ocean Road Cottages & Backpackers (☎ 5289 1070, Erskine Ave) is on a bushy hillside. Bunk beds cost $16 for YHA members, $18 for nonmembers. If you ask nicely, the V/Line bus can stop 200m from the front gate.

Pubs, Motels & Guesthouses Both of the town's pubs have rooms, although they also have bands, so nights can be noisy. *Lorne Hotel (☎ 5289 1409)*, on the corner of Mountjoy Parade and Bay St, has motel-style doubles from $80 to $110, and self-contained units from $120 to $160. *Grand Pacific Hotel/Motel (☎ 5289 1609, 268 Mountjoy Parade)* isn't as grand as it once was, although there are renovation plans. Rooms in the main building are a bit tired but they're large and have balconies. Doubles cost from $70 to $110, as do the motel-style units out the back.

There are half a dozen motels. *Ocean Lodge Motel (☎ 5289 1330, 6 Armytage St)* has singles/doubles (most with views) from $60/70 to $95/105. Right in the thick of things, *Sandridge Motel (☎ 5289 2180, 128 Mountjoy Parade)* has pleasant rooms from $60 to $100.

Erskine House (☎ 5289 1209, fax 5289 1185) is a splendid 19th century guesthouse with several hectares of gardens. The bedrooms are nothing special but the facilities are excellent. Tariffs range from $95 to $140 a double (from $120 to $165 with bathroom), including breakfast.

Self-Contained Cottages & Holiday Apartments The pick of the bunch is *Allenvale Cottages (☎/fax 5289 1450)*, 2km north-west of Lorne along Allenvale Rd. Prices for two range from $95 to $125, with deals for longer stays.

Back in town, **Great Ocean Road Cottages & Backpackers** (☎ 5289 1070, Erskine Ave) has cottages sleeping up to six, from $95 to $175.

Stylish **Phoenix Apartments** (☎ 5289 2000, 60 Mountjoy Parade) has studio apartments for $110 a double midweek and $260 for a two night stay on weekends.

Places to Eat

Kafe Kaos (☎ 5289 2639, 50a Mountjoy Parade) is a good place for a healthy lunch. Nearby **Lorne Ovenhouse** specialises in pizzas, pastas and focaccias.

The Arab (☎ 5289 1435, 94 Mountjoy Parade) has been a landmark since 1956. It's a bustling eatery open all day every day, and has breakfasts, pasta dishes from $10 to $15 and other main evening meals for around $18. For a good vibe, head to **Reif's** (☎ 5289 2366, 84 Mountjoy Parade), a bar and cafe with pasta dishes from $12 to $15 and a dinner menu that includes plenty of seafood; mains range from $14 to $20.

Kosta's Tavern (☎ 5289 1883, 48 Mountjoy Parade) has a Greek-influenced menu with main courses costing between $18 and $22. **Lorne Pier Seafood Restaurant**

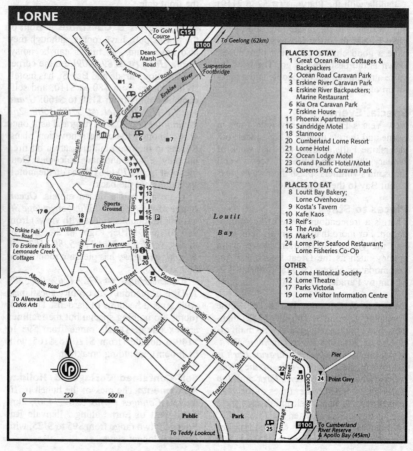

LORNE

PLACES TO STAY
1 Great Ocean Road Cottages & Backpackers
2 Ocean Road Caravan Park
3 Erskine River Caravan Park
4 Erskine River Backpackers; Marine Restaurant
6 Kia Ora Caravan Park
7 Erskine House
11 Phoenix Apartments
16 Sandridge Motel
18 Stanmoor
20 Cumberland Lorne Resort
21 Lorne Hotel
22 Ocean Lodge Motel
23 Grand Pacific Hotel/Motel
25 Queens Park Caravan Park

PLACES TO EAT
8 Loutit Bay Bakery; Lorne Ovenhouse
9 Kosta's Tavern
10 Kafe Kaos
13 Reif's
14 The Arab
15 Mark's
24 Lorne Pier Seafood Restaurant; Lorne Fisheries Co-Op

OTHER
5 Lorne Historical Society
12 Lorne Theatre
17 Parks Victoria
19 Lorne Visitor Information Centre

(☎ 5289 1119, Pier Head) is a low-key seaside cafe. Brunch and snacks are available from 11.30 am, and the dinner menu features mostly seafood with mains from $19 to $25. Next door, **Lorne Fisheries Co-op** sells fresh seafood.

APOLLO BAY
• postcode 3233 • pop 1000

The pretty port of Apollo Bay is a fishing town and another popular beach resort. It's a lot less trendy than Lorne.

The visitors centre (☎ 5237 6529), on the left as you arrive from Lorne, is open daily from 9 am to 5 pm. In the same building there's an impressive 'eco-centre'.

Things to See & Do

The **Old Cable Station Museum**, on the Great Ocean Rd 2km north of the centre, has local artefacts and a photographic display. It's open on weekends and during school holidays from 2 to 5 pm ($2). There's also a **shell museum**, 12 Noel St, open daily.

It's a 1km drive from town up to **Marriner's Lookout**, where a 500m walking trail climbs the hilltops, with great views. There's a good picnic area at **Paradise Valley**, 8km west of town, off the Beech Forest-Apollo Bay road.

Wild Dog Trails (☎ 5237 6441), based at a farm on Wild Dog Rd (signposted off the Great Ocean Rd 2.5km north-east of Apollo Bay), offers **horse rides** along the beaches ($25 for two hours or $70 all day). With 12 Apostles Great Ocean Road Air Tours (☎ 5237 7370), you can take a **flight** over Port Campbell National Park for $210 (the flight seats three).

Apollo Bay Boat Charters (☎ 5237 6214) offers 50-minute **scenic cruises** ($15) and half-day **fishing trips** ($55). Apollo Bay is also popular for **hang-gliding**, and the Wingsports Flight Academy (☎ 0419-378 616) is based here.

Places to Stay

Caravan parks include **Pisces Caravan Resort** (☎ 5237 6749) on the Great Ocean Rd 1.5km north of town, with sites from $17 to $30 for two, and cabins from $40 to $70;

and **Waratah Caravan Park** (☎ 5237 6562, Noel St), with sites for $16 to $28 and vans/cabins from $35/48.

Surfside Backpackers (☎ 5237 7263), on the corner of the Great Ocean Rd and Gambier St, is the closest hostel to the ocean and has bunks for $13/16 (YHA members/nonmembers), and doubles for $45. The larger **Apollo Bay Backpackers** (☎ 0419 340 362, 47 Montrose Ave) gets good reports from travellers and charges from $12 to $15.

Lighthouse Keepers Inn (☎ 5237 6278, 175 Great Ocean Rd) is good value with motel units from $70 to $110. Also good value, **Great Ocean View Motel** (☎ 5237 6527, 1 Great Ocean Rd) has doubles for $55 to $88.

Bayside Gardens (☎ 5237 6248, 219 Great Ocean Rd) has self-contained units from $65.

Places to Eat

An excellent place for breakfast and lunch, **The Bay Leaf Gourmet Deli** in the centre of town has an innovative menu. **The Wholefood Shop**, nearby, is another vegetarian option.

An offshoot of the renowned clifftop **Chris's Restaurant** in nearby Skenes Creek, **Sea-Grape Wine Bar & Grill** (☎ 5237 6610, 141 Great Ocean Rd) is a top spot for a meal or beverage. Evening mains cost around $20.

Apollo Bay Fishermen's Co-operative at the entrance to the harbour has crayfish and other seafood. Or try **Wayne's Craypot Bistro** (☎ 5237 6240, 29 Great Ocean Rd) at the 'top pub'.

The **Apollo Bay Hotel** (the 'bottom pub') has bistro meals for $12 to $17 and cheaper bar meals.

CAPE OTWAY & OTWAY NATIONAL PARK

From Apollo Bay the road temporarily leaves the coast to climb over Cape Otway. The main road winds through the Otway National Park with its relatively untouched rainforests, fern gullies and forests of mountain ash.

A couple of unsealed roads lead off the highway and run through the park down to the coast. The first turn-off, about 6km south-west of Apollo Bay, leads to the **Elliot River picnic area** and **Shelly Beach**. Seventeen kilometres past Apollo Bay is **Maits Rest Rainforest Boardwalk**, a 20 minute walk through a rainforest gully.

About 2km further on is the Otway Lighthouse Rd, which leads 12km down to Cape Otway. The lighthouse is open daily ($6).

Signposted off Otway Lighthouse Rd about 3km before the lighthouse, *Bimbi Park (☎ 5237 9246)* is a camping ground and horse riding ranch with walking tracks to remote beaches. Trail rides cost $18 an hour or $32 for a half-day trip. This place is also a hostel, with backpacker beds in on-site vans from $12 or in tents from $10. There are also camp sites from $11 and on-site vans from $25.

Blanket Bay Rd leads off the Otway Lighthouse Rd across to **Blanket Bay**, where there are walking tracks and a few bush camp sites that you'll need to book during summer – phone Parks Victoria in Apollo Bay (☎ 5237 6889).

PORT CAMPBELL NATIONAL PARK

Dramatic limestone cliffs tower above the ocean, and rock stacks, gorges, arches and blowholes are plentiful in this scenic area. **Gibson Steps** lead down to Gibson Beach. This beach, and others along this stretch of coast, is dangerous for swimming. You can walk along the beach, but beware of being stranded by high tides or stormy seas.

The **Twelve Apostles**, rock stacks in the ocean, are constantly pounded by waves; today only seven apostles can be seen. Port Campbell Boat Charters (☎ 5598 6463), in the township of Port Campbell, runs cruises to the Twelve Apostles and Bay of Islands ($30), and diving trips ($35 for one dive, $60 for two).

Loch Ard Gorge has a sad tale to tell:

In 1878 the iron-hulled clipper *Loch Ard* was driven onto the rocks around Mutton Bird Island on the final night of its voyage from England. Of the 55 people on board there were only two survivors. Eva Carmichael clung to wreckage and was washed into the gorge, where she was rescued

by apprentice officer, Tom Pearce. Eva and Tom were both 18, and the romantic aspects of the rescue led the press to speculate on a romance between the two, but Eva soon returned to Ireland and they never saw each other again.

West of Port Campbell township, the next features are **The Arch**, and **London Bridge**, which was once a rock platform linking a stack to the mainland. In 1990 it collapsed, stranding two surprised tourists – they were rescued by helicopter. On moonlit evenings this is a good spot to see penguins.

There's a Parks Victoria Information Centre (☎ 5598 6382) in Port Campbell township.

Places to Stay & Eat

Port Campbell township has several places to stay. *Port Campbell Caravan Park (☎ 5598 6492, Tregea St)* has camp sites from $12 to $15 and cabins from $55 to $80. Across the road is *Port Campbell YHA Hostel (☎/fax 5598 6305, 18 Tregea St)*. Dorm beds are $13, $16 for non-YHA members.

Port O'Call (☎ 5598 6206), opposite the pub, is more homey than the average motel and is good value for $55 to $70 a double.

Port Campbell Hotel (☎ 5598 6320) has inexpensive bar lunches, and the *Cray Pot Bistro*, out the back, has mains from $12 to $15. *Napiers Restaurant*, in the Southern Ocean Motor Inn, specialises in local seafood.

South-West

The Great Ocean Rd ends 12km east of Warrnambool where it meets the Princes Hwy, which continues westwards into South Australia (SA).

WARRNAMBOOL
• postcode 3280 • pop 26,000

Warrnambool was settled as a whaling and sealing station. Nowadays it is a major industrial and commercial centre, but it maintains a relaxed seaside feel.

The May Racing Carnival features the Grand Annual Steeplechase. This hellish

5.5km jumps race is held on the first Thursday in May. The carnival draws large crowds and you'll need to book accommodation.

The visitor information centre (☎ 5564 7837), 600 Raglan Parade, is open daily. Parks Victoria (☎ 5561 9900) is at 78 Henna St, and the RACV (☎ 5562 1555) is at 165 Koroit St.

Things to See & Do

The main swimming beach is sheltered **Lady Bay**. **Logans Beach** has the best surf, and there are good breaks at Levy's Beach and Second Bay.

Flagstaff Hill Maritime Village (☎ 5564 7841) is modelled on an early port, and on the lake are two restored ships. A small theatre continually screens old maritime films and documentaries. It's open daily from 9 am to 5 pm. Admission costs $9.50/4.50 and $26 for a family.

Warrnambool Art Gallery, 165 Timor St, has a good Australian collection and is open afternoons ($3).

The **Mahogany Walking Trail**, starting at the Thunder Point coastal reserve on the western edge of town, is a 22km coastal walk to Port Fairy.

Places to Stay

Surfside Holiday Park (☎ 5561 2611), Pertobe Rd, is by the beach. Sites cost from $15 to $23, and cabins from $45 to $75. Also on Pertobe Rd, *Ocean Beach Holiday Village* (☎ 5561 4222) has sites from $18 to $23 and cabin-vans from $38 to $64.

Closest to the sea, the friendly *Warrnambool Beach Backpackers* (☎/fax 5562 4874, 17 Stanley St) has good facilities and free pick-ups. Dorm beds cost $15; doubles $35. In the town centre, *Backpackers Barn* (☎ 5562 2073), on the corner of Liebig and Lava Sts, at the Victoria Hotel, has beds for $14 ($13 for YHA members). The *Western Hotel Motel* (☎ 5562 2011, 45 Kepler St) has backpacker singles/doubles for $18/30.

Hotel Warrnambool (☎ 5562 2377), on the corner of Koroit and Kepler Sts, has good pub rooms for $30/60, including breakfast (shared bathrooms). On Pertobe Rd near

Breakwater Rock, *Lady Bay Hotel* (☎ 5562 1544) has motel rooms from $35/45.

One of the best of the 23 motels is the *Olde Maritime Motor Inn* (☎ 5561 1415), on Merri St, not far from Flagstaff Hill Maritime Village. Standard units are $75.

O'Brien's B&B (☎ 5562 6241, 8 Mickle Crescent) charges $75/85 a room. The central *Pertobe B&B* (☎ 5561 7078, 10 Banyan St) is excellent value for $40/60. The whole house is available for $150 (sleeps seven).

Places to Eat

Many of the eateries are along Liebig St. The excellent *Fishtales Café* at No 63 is open all day for burgers ($5 to $7), gourmet fish and chips, vegetarian specials ($7 to $10), seafood and Asian dishes ($10 to $15) and huge breakfasts.

Next door, *Bojangles* has pastas and pizzas for $10 to $14, and other dishes for $15 to $20. *Malaysia* at No 69 serves fairly

The Shipwreck Coast

The Victorian coastline between Cape Otway and Port Fairy was a notoriously dangerous stretch of water in the days when sailing ships were the major form of transport. Navigation of Bass Strait was exceptionally difficult due to numerous barely hidden reefs and frequent heavy fog. More than 80 vessels came to grief on this 120km stretch in only 40 years.

The most famous wreck was that of the *Loch Ard* (see Port Campbell National Park in this chapter). Another was the *Falls of Halladale*, a Glasgow barque that ran aground in 1908 en route from New York to Melbourne. There were no casualties, but it lay on the reef, fully rigged and with sails set, for a couple of months.

Other vessels that came to grief included the *Newfield* in 1892 and *La Bella* in 1905.

All these wrecks have been investigated by divers, and relics are on display in the Flagstaff Hill Maritime Village in Warrnambool.

VICTORIA

WARRNAMBOOL

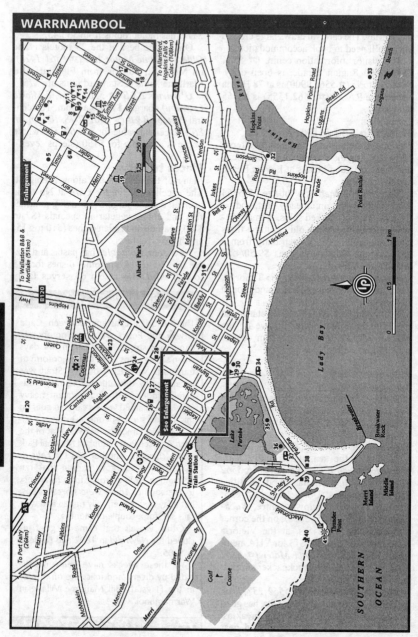

WARRNAMBOOL

PLACES TO STAY

3	Hotel Warrnambool
6	Western Hotel Motel
17	Pertobe B&B
18	Olde Maritime Motor Inn
20	Merton Manor
23	O'Brien's B&B
28	Backpackers Barn
34	Surfside Holiday Park
37	Ocean Beach Holiday Village
38	Lady Bay Hotel
39	Warrnambool Beach Backpackers

PLACES TO EAT

1	China City Chinese Restaurant
4	Sea Change Cafe; Capitol Cinema
8	Balenàs
10	Fishtales Cafe; Bojangles
11	Malaysia
12	Freshwater Cafe
13	Beach Babylon
14	Images; Seanchai
29	Mahogany Ship Bar & Restaurant

OTHER

2	RACV
5	Laundrette
7	Gallery Nightclub
9	Whaler's Inn Hotel
15	Warrnambool Performing Arts Centre
16	Warrnambool Art Gallery
19	History House
21	Warrnambool Botanic Gardens
22	Olympic Swimming Pool
24	Visitor Information Centre
25	Hospital
26	Caledonian Hotel (The Cally)
27	Criterion Hotel
30	Flagstaff Hill Maritime Village
31	Fletcher Jones Factory & Gardens
32	Proudfoot's Boathouse
33	Logans Beach Whale-Watching Platform
35	Lake Pertobe Adventure Playground
36	City of Warrnambool Lawn Tennis Club
40	Start of Mahogany Walking Trail
41	Thunder Point Lookout

good Malaysian and Chinese tucker plus a few Aussie specials, with mains in the $12 to $16 range.

Across the road, *Beach Babylon (☎ 5562 3714, 72 Liebig St)* is a pizza/steak/pasta joint. Steaks cost from $17 to $19; pasta dishes are around $13.

Entertainment
The *Criterion Hotel (151 Kepler St)* is a grungy rock pub with bands on Saturday night. The *Caledonian Hotel* (The Cally), in Fairy St, has a big entertainment lounge with pool tables, and the like. *Whalers' Inn Hotel*, on the corner of Liebig and Timor Sts, has bands on Wednesday, Friday and Saturday.

A great spot for some Guinness is *Seanchai (62 Liebig St)*, where there's live music every weekend.

Getting There & Away
The train station is on Merri St at the south end of Fairy St. There are daily services between Melbourne and Warrnambool, taking about three hours ($34.20).

Connecting V/Line buses continue to Port Fairy ($4.30), Portland ($12.20) and Mt Gambier ($26.90). There are also weekday buses to Ballarat ($18) and Hamilton ($6.10).

On Friday, a bus runs along the Great Ocean Rd to Apollo Bay ($20.80) and Geelong ($38.90).

PORT FAIRY
● postcode 3284   ● pop 2600

This seaside township was settled in 1835. The first arrivals were whalers and sealers, and Port Fairy still has a large fishing fleet.

The **Port Fairy Folk Festival**, one of Australia's foremost music festivals, is held on the Labour Day long weekend in early March. Accommodation is booked out well in advance.

The visitor information centre (☎ 5568 2682), on Bank St between Sackville and Barclay Sts, is open daily. A new centre is planned for the old railway site on Bank St near the river.

Things to See & Do
Brochures for the **Shipwreck Walk**, comprising three short walks, and the **History Walk** around town are available from the visitor information centre.

The **Port Fairy History Centre**, Gipps St, has shipping relics, old photos and costumes. It's open on Wednesday, weekends and daily during school holidays, from 2 to 5 pm ($3/50c).

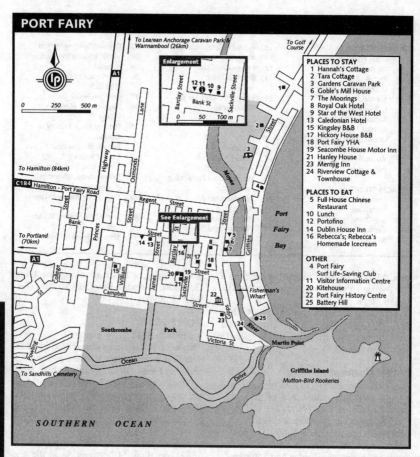

PORT FAIRY

To Learean Anchorage Caravan Park & Warrnambool (26km)

To Golf Course

Enlargement

PLACES TO STAY
1 Hannah's Cottage
2 Tara Cottage
3 Gardens Caravan Park
6 Goble's Mill House
7 The Moorings
8 Royal Oak Hotel
9 Star of the West Hotel
13 Caledonian Hotel
15 Kingsley B&B
17 Hickory House B&B
18 Port Fairy YHA
19 Seacombe House Motor Inn
21 Hanley House
23 Merrijig Inn
24 Riverview Cottage & Townhouse

PLACES TO EAT
5 Full House Chinese Restaurant
10 Lunch
12 Portofino
14 Dublin House Inn
16 Rebecca's; Rebecca's Homemade Icecream

OTHER
4 Port Fairy Surf Life-Saving Club
11 Visitor Information Centre
20 Kitehouse
22 Port Fairy History Centre
25 Battery Hill

To Hamilton (84km)

C184 Hamilton – Port Fairy Road

To Portland (70km)

See Enlargement

Port Fairy Bay

Fisherman's Wharf

Griffiths Island
Mutton-Bird Rookeries

Martin Point

SOUTHERN OCEAN

Griffiths Island, which is joined to the mainland by a narrow strip of land, is home to a colony of mutton birds (short-tailed shearwaters).

Mary S Tours (☎ 5568 1480) and Mulloka Cruises (☎ 5568 1790) offer half-hour cruises ($10) and fishing trips, departing from Fisherman's Wharf.

Places to Stay
Port Fairy has many B&Bs, guesthouses and cottages. It's impossible to list them all here so check with the visitor information centre.

Camping & Caravan Parks The closest place to town is *Gardens Caravan Park* (☎ 5568 1060, 111 Griffiths St), which has camp sites for $12 to $15 and two-bedroom cabins for $50 to $70. On the Princes Hwy 2km north of the centre, *Learean Anchorage Caravan Park* (☎ 5568 1145) has sites for $17 to $22 and vans and cabins for $30 to $72.

Hostels & Pubs *Port Fairy YHA Hostel* (☎ 5568 2468, 8 Cox St) is in a historic building and charges $13 ($16 for non-members).

Star of the West Hotel (☎ 5568 1715), on the corner of Bank and Sackville Sts, has pub rooms for $20 per person, with breakfast. Further down Bank St, the *Royal Oak Hotel* (☎ 5568 1018) has B&B for $30 per person (shared bathroom).

Seventeen kilometres north-west of Port Fairy in the tiny town of **Yambuk**, *Eumeralla Backpackers* (☎ 5568 4204) is an excellent new hostel run by a local Aboriginal trust. Bunks cost $10. Canoes can be hired for $5 a day to paddle down the Eumeralla River to Lake Yambuk.

Other Accommodation *Seacombe House Motor Inn* (☎ 5568 1082), on the corner of Cox and Sackville Sts, has units from $95 and B&B in the 1847 inn for $30 per person. The *Caledonian Hotel* (☎ 5568 1044), on the corner of Bank and James Sts, has motel units from $60 to $75.

Hanley House (☎ 5568 2709, 14 Sackville St) is a peaceful place dating from the 1850s with singles/doubles from $65/85. Also good are the *Hickory House B&B* (☎ 5568 2530, 4 Princes St), charging from $85/100, and the *Kingsley B&B* (☎ 5568 1269, 71 Cox St), which charges $55/85.

Hannah's Cottage (☎ 5568 1583, 177 Griffiths St) is a simple, three bedroom place sleeping up to seven people, costing $80 to $100 a double, plus $15 per extra person.

Places to Eat

A top spot for a daytime bite is *Rebecca's* (☎ 5568 2533, 72 Sackville St).

Lunch (☎ 5568 2642, 20 Bank St), in the old town hall, has modern Australian cuisine and a good vegetarian selection. Mains cost between $9 and $18.50. It's open Wednesday to Sunday from 8.30 am to 5 pm and for dinner on Friday, Saturday and Sunday.

Portofino (☎ 5568 1047, 28 Bank St) has pasta dishes for $14 to $16 and other mains for around $18.

The corner bar of the 1844 *Caledonian Hotel* (41 Bank St) serves dishes like mixed grills for around $7. The pub's dining room has mains in the $12 to $15 range. The restaurant at *Dublin House Inn* (57 Bank St) specialises in local produce and seafood.

Getting There & Around

Daily buses link Port Fairy and Warrnambool ($4.30), connecting with trains to/from Melbourne ($36.50). Daily buses run to Portland ($8.60) and Mt Gambier ($20.80).

Kitehouse (☎ 5568 2782), 27 Cox St, hires bikes from $20 a day.

PORTLAND

● postcode 3305   ● pop 9500

Portland is Victoria's oldest town. From early in the 19th century, it was a base for whaling and sealing. The first permanent settlers were the Henty family, who arrived from Van Diemen's Land (Tasmania) in 1834.

The Portland Aluminium Smelter produces something like 300,000 tonnes of aluminium a year.

The visitor information centre (☎ 5523 2671), at the Maritime Discovery Centre, is open daily from 9 am to 5 pm. The Parks Victoria office (☎ 5523 1180) is at 8-12 Julia St.

Things to See & Do

The **Maritime Discovery Centre**, Lee Breakwater Rd, has displays on exploration, whaling, wildlife and the Portland Lifeboat, Australia's oldest intact vessel. It's open daily and admission is $7/3 and $20 for families.

Burswood Homestead, 15 Cape Nelson Rd, was built for Edward Henty in 1850. The impressive gardens are open daily (closed during winter); admission is $3. Kingsley Homestead (1893), Bancroft St, the home of **Kingsley Wines**, is open afternoons. **History House** (☎ 5522 2266), Charles St, is full of interesting old stuff. It's open daily from 10 am to noon and 1 to 4 pm ($1).

Mary MacKillop worked in Portland from 1862 to 1866. MacKillop worked two miracles and has been beatified; the Vatican is investigating a third, which, if confirmed, may result in sainthood. A brochure *Walk in the footsteps of Mary MacKillop* is available from the information centre.

There are some good **surfing** spots, with sand breaks out at Bridgewater Bay (patrolled over summer). Around Point Danger, south of Portland, there are good point breaks at Black Nose Point and nearby

VICTORIA

Crumpets. A surf shop, Portland Surf-In, is at 98 Percy St.

Free two-hour tours of the **aluminium smelter** are held on Monday, Wednesday and Friday at 10 am (and several times daily during holiday periods). Bookings (☎ 5523 2671) are essential.

Places to Stay

Centenary Caravan Park (☎ 5523 1487, 184 Bentinck St) is on the waterfront. It has camp sites from $13, cabins from $40 and backpacker beds for $17 (BYO linen), although they are often booked out by visiting students.

The *Gordon Hotel (☎ 5523 1121, 63 Bentinck St)* has singles/doubles for $20/30, including breakfast. *Mac's Hotel Bentinck (☎ 5523 2188)*, on the corner of Gawler and Bentinck Sts, has motel units for $40/46, and suites from $120.

At Cape Bridgewater, 19 km from Portland, *Sea View Lodge B&B (☎ 5526 7276)* is a friendly guesthouse with doubles from $75 to $90, and there are backpacker B&B deals for $25.

Places to Eat

Julia's Treat (5 Julia St) – nice pun – looks like just another takeaway joint, but most nights Katrina turns the place into a fun and casual restaurant. It's BYO alcohol and meals cost up to $10.

A couple of doors up, *Canton Palace* has cheap Chinese smorgasbords at lunch and dinner. For a cheap feed, head to *Phoenix Diner* in Gore Place, where roasts and massive entree bowls of pasta cost $5. *Port of Call (85 Bentinck St)*, on the waterfront, is good value for breakfast or lunch. *Sunstream Wholefoods (49 Julia St)* has healthy tucker.

Edward's Waterfront Cafe-Restaurant (☎ 5523 1032, 101 Bentinck St), Portland's best eatery, is open for breakfast, lunch and dinner. Mains cost $15 to $18.

Getting There & Away

Daily V/Line buses run to Port Fairy ($8.60), Warrnambool ($12.20) and Mt Gambier ($11.20). Buses depart from Henty St, near the corner of Percy St.

PORTLAND TO SOUTH AUSTRALIA

From Portland, you can either head north to Heywood and rejoin the Princes Hwy, or north-west along the slower but more interesting Portland-Nelson road. There are turn-offs to beaches and some great national parks, including **Discovery Bay Coastal Park**, **Mt Richmond National Park** and **Lower Glenelg National Park**.

Great South-West Walk

This 250km walk between Portland and the South Australian border follows the coast to Nelson, then heads inland along the Glenelg River to the border before looping back to Portland. It takes at least 10 days but shorter sections are possible – see *Short Walks on and around the Great South-West Walk*, available at the Portland Parks Victoria office for $3.

There are camping sites with fireplaces, toilets and fresh water. A fuel stove is a good idea as firewood can be scarce, and you should carry water.

For more information, see Lonely Planet's *Bushwalking in Australia* or contact the Portland Visitor Information Centre.

Nelson

Nelson is a small village on the coast at the mouth of the mighty Glenelg River. It's the main access point for the **Lower Glenelg National Park**, popular with canoeists. The Parks Victoria office (☎ 08-8738 4051) issues permits for camp sites and is open on weekdays, except Tuesday, from 9 am to 4.30 pm.

Nelson Boat Hire (☎ 08-8738 4048) and South West Canoe Service (☎ 08-8738 4141) hire canoes for around $25 a day. Both will drop you upriver (for a fee) so you can paddle back to Nelson. For the less energetic there are also cruises.

River-Vu Caravan Park (☎ 08-8738 4123) has sites for $15 and cabins from $38 a double.

The *Nelson Hotel (☎ 08-8738 4011)* has basic singles/doubles from $20/30, including breakfast, and *Motel Black Wattle (☎ 08-8738 4008)* has doubles from $65.

On Black Swan Rd on the west side of the river, *Anchorage B&B* (☎ *08-8738 4220)* is a friendly place charging $35/50, including breakfast. The owner used to run a restaurant in Bali and can cook Indonesian dinners.

Princess Margaret Rose Cave
It's a pretty 12km drive from Nelson to Princess Margaret Rose Cave. Half-hour tours of the cave run approximately hourly from 10 am to 4.30 pm ($5.50). Interesting displays at the entrance explain the geology and history of the cave.

There are good camping facilities and cabins – to book, phone ☎ 08-8738 4171.

THE WESTERN DISTRICT
This region contains some of the best sheep and cattle country in Australia. It's also the third largest volcanic plain in the world.

Before Europeans arrived, much of this area belonged to the Dhauwurd wurrung people.

Hamilton
• postcode 3300   • pop 9250
Known as the 'Wool Capital of the World', Hamilton is the major town of the Western District. The area was settled in 1837.

The visitor information centre (☎ 5572 3746), Lonsdale St, opens daily from 9 am to 5 pm.

Things to See & Do Hamilton Art Gallery, Brown St, is an excellent gallery with a varied collection. It's open daily (afternoon only on Sunday). On Coleraine Rd 2km west of the centre, **The Big Woolbales** has wool-related displays. It's open daily (free).

Sir Reginald Ansett (founder of Ansett, the airline) began his empire in Hamilton in 1931. The **Sir Reginald Ansett Transport Museum** on Ballarat Rd is open daily from 10 am to 4 pm and costs $2/1.

The **Hamilton History Centre**, 43 Gray St, is open afternoons except Saturday. Next door there's a small **Aboriginal Keeping Place Museum**, although it's seldom open to the public – check with the information centre.

The eastern barred bandicoot colony on the banks of the Grange Burn Creek is the last in mainland Australia, and the **Hamilton Institute of Rural Learning**, 333 North Boundary Rd, is trying to establish new colonies. There's a nature trail in the institute's parklands.

Places to Stay *Lake Hamilton Caravan Park* (☎ *5572 3855, 8 Ballarat Rd)* has camp sites for $10, on-site vans from $28 and cabins from $38 to $50. Next door, *Peppercorn Lodge* (☎ *5571 9046)* has rooms for $12/20 a single/double.

The *Grand Central Hotel* (☎ *5572 2899, 141 Gray St)* has quite good rooms for $25/35.

Lenwin on the Lake Motor Inn (☎ *5571 2733, 2 Riley St)* has singles/doubles from $45/58. Riley St is off the Glenelg Hwy – coming from Melbourne, turn right after the Ansett Transport Museum.

Mt Eccles National Park
Mt Eccles National Park is about 9km west of the small town of Macarthur, which is 36km south of Hamilton. Mt Eccles erupted around 19,000 years ago. The main features are Mt Eccles itself, the scenic lake, lava caves and a huge koala population.

There are camp sites and a Parks Victoria ranger's station (☎ 5576 1338).

The Wimmera

The Wimmera is a major wheat and wool district. Much of the land has been cleared for farming and there are endless expanses of wheat fields and sheep properties.

The major attractions are the Grampians National Park, Mt Arapiles State Park, and the Little Desert National Park.

The main road through the Wimmera is the Western Hwy (A8), the main route between Melbourne and Adelaide.

Getting There & Away
The daily *Overland* train between Melbourne and Adelaide runs through the Wimmera, stopping at Ararat, Stawell, Horsham

and Dimboola. V/Line has train/bus services between Melbourne and the major towns in the Wimmera.

From Horsham, you can take a bus north to Mildura, west to Naracoorte or south to Hamilton.

ARARAT
• postcode 3377   • pop 7000

Chinese miners who were travelling overland from Adelaide to the Ballarat goldfields found gold in Ararat in 1857. They stayed and mined here until the early 1860s when the gold ran out, but the town continued to grow.

The Tourist Information Centre (☎ 1800 657 158) is on Town Hall Square on Barkly St and is open daily from 9 am to 5 pm.

Behind the pretty **Alexandra Gardens**, Vincent St, stands an old bluestone jail that was a prison for the criminally insane. Tours of **J Ward** are on weekdays at 11 am and on Sunday from 11 am to 3 pm ($6/3).

There's a *caravan park* (☎ 5352 2994) and several pubs and motels.

GREAT WESTERN
Great Western is a tiny town between Ararat and Stawell. There are three wineries in the area, and 'Great Western' is synonymous with Australian 'champagne' (now called 'sparkling wine' after protests from French champagne makers).

At *Allanvale* (☎ 5356 2201), a sheep property 3km east of Great Western, you can stay in shearers' quarters for $15 per person.

STAWELL
• postcode 3380   • pop 6250

Stawell is bypassed by the Western Hwy, although there's a string of motels and petrol stations along the highway about 5km south of the town centre.

Gold was found near here in 1853. The alluvial gold in the area soon ran out, but the discovery of rich quartz reefs in the Big Hill area led to the development of large-scale mining operations that lasted until the 1920s. Locals are resisting the opening of a mine in the centre of town.

The Stawell & Grampians Tourist Information Centre (☎ 1800 246 880) is on the Western Hwy, before the turn-off to Halls Gap. It has an accommodation booking service and is open weekdays from 9 am to 5pm and on weekends from 10 am to 4 pm.

Things to See
The **Stawell Gift** foot race has been run here on Easter Monday since 1878, and attracts up to 20,000 visitors. The **Stawell Gift Hall of Fame**, in Main St, opposite the Railway Hotel, is open weekday mornings and by appointment (☎ 5358 1326); admission costs $2.50.

Bunjil's Shelter, 11km south of Stawell and signposted off the road to Pomonal, is one of the most significant Aboriginal rock art sites in the state. Bunjil is the creator spirit of the Kooris of this region.

Places to Stay
Stawell Park Caravan Park (☎ 5358 2709), on the Western Hwy, has camp sites from $10 and cabins from $35 to $45.

In the town, the *Town Hall Hotel* (☎ 5358 1059), Main St, has basic rooms from $25/35 a single/double.

There's a string of motels along the Western Hwy. *Coorrabin Motor Inn* (☎ 5358 3933) is one of the cheapest with good units from $30/50 to $40/60. In town, *Diamond House Motor Inn* (☎ 5358 3366, 24 Seaby St) charges from $45/55 to $60/80.

Stawell Holiday Cottages (☎ 5358 2868), signposted off the Western Hwy, are in Errington Rd about 2km from Stawell. They sleep six people and cost from $60 to $70 a double, plus $10 for each extra person.

Places to Eat
Cafe Rasuli (139 Gold Reef Mall) serves snacks during the day and modern Australian meals for dinner, with mains from $11 to $16. The *Railway Hotel* (13 Main St) has bistro meals and has lunch specials on weekdays.

Getting There & Away
Stawell is on the Melbourne to Adelaide train line; the train station is about 1km

south of the centre in Napier St. In addition to the daily Adelaide train there are three to four services to/from Melbourne – a train to Ballarat with connecting bus to Stawell taking over 3½ hours ($31.60).

A bus connects Stawell with the Grampians.

GRAMPIANS NATIONAL PARK

Attractions here include an incredibly rich diversity of flora and fauna, rock formations, Aboriginal rock art, fine bushwalking and climbing and plenty of activities.

Orientation

The Grampians lie west of Ararat and stretch some 90km from Dunkeld in the south, almost to Horsham in the north.

Halls Gap is the only town in the Grampians. It has a supermarket, restaurants and cafes, and a range of accommodation. There are no banks, but the Mobil Service Station (☎ 5356 4206) has a Commonwealth Bank ATM; Halls Gap Newsagency (☎ 5356 4247) has EFTPOS and an ANZ agency open on Monday from 1.30 to 3.00 pm; the post office is a Commonwealth Bank agency for passbook holders only.

Information

The main tourist office for the region is on the Western Hwy at Stawell.

The excellent Grampians National Park Visitor Centre (☎ 5356 4381) is 2.5km south of Halls Gap and is open daily.

Brambuk Living Cultural Centre

This Aboriginal cultural centre (☎ 5356 4452), behind the visitor centre, is run by five Koori communities. There are interesting displays, a bush-tucker cafe and during the peak holiday periods there is Koori music and dance. Tours of rock art sites are run from here. See the following Organised Tours entry for more information. The Gariwerd Dreaming Theatre has a multi-media narration of traditional stories ($4).

Aboriginal Rock Art

There is a lot of rock art in the park, but not all is publicised or accessible. In the northern Grampians near Mt Stapylton, the main sites are Gulgurn Manja Shelter and Ngamadjidj Shelter. In the western Grampians, near the Buandik camping ground, the main sites are Billimina Shelter and Manja Shelter.

Wonderland Range

The Wonderland Range is close to Halls Gap and has some of the most spectacular and accessible scenery. There are scenic drives and walks –from an easy half-hour stroll to Venus Baths, to a four hour walk to Boroka Lookout. Walking tracks start from both Halls Gap and the Wonderland picnic ground.

Halls Gap Wildlife Park & Zoo

This small wildlife park, on Pomonal Rd behind Halls Gap, houses native and exotic animals. It's open Wednesday to Monday from 10 am to 5 pm ($7/5).

Zumstein

This is a reserve in the western Grampians where kangaroos congregate. They shoul not be fed or touched. A walking track follows the river to the base of the spectacular McKenzie Falls.

Activities

Adventure Activities Base Camp & Beyond (☎ 5356 4300) runs two to five-day rock-climbing and abseiling courses most weekends and during holiday periods, from $60 per day.

Action Adventures (☎ 5356 4654) runs introductory abseiling courses ($25), one-day rock-climbing and abseiling courses ($65), and canoeing and bicycle tours.

Grampians Adventure Services (☎ 5356 4556) offers rock climbing, abseiling, canoeing, bike tours, bushwalking and caving. They also combine two or three of these activities into a day for $40 to $60.

Bushwalking There are more than 150km of tracks, from half-hour strolls to overnight treks through difficult terrain. The rangers at the visitor centre have good advice on choosing a walk.

Wear appropriate footwear, take a hat and sunscreen in summer, and for longer walks

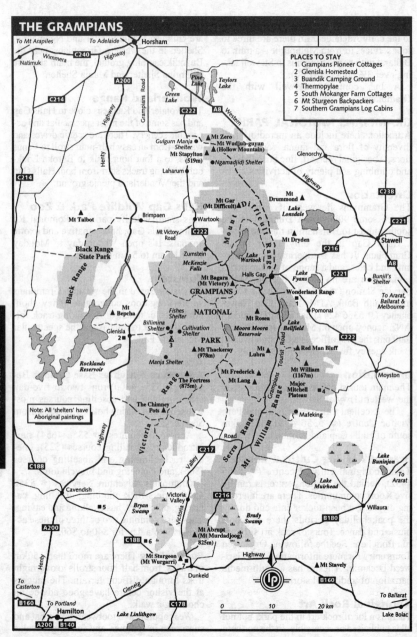

THE GRAMPIANS

PLACES TO STAY
1 Grampians Pioneer Cottages
2 Glenisla Homestead
3 Buandik Camping Ground
4 Thermopylae
5 South Mokanger Farm Cottages
6 Mt Sturgeon Backpackers
7 Southern Grampians Log Cabins

To Mt Arapiles
To Adelaide
Horsham
Natimuk
Wimmera
C240
Highway
A200
Grampians Road
C214
Pine Lake
Taylors Lake
Green Lake
A8
Western
C222
Highway
Mt Zero
Mt Wudjub-guyun (Hollow Mountain)
Gulgurn Manja Shelter
Mt Stapylton (519m)
Ngamadjidj Shelter
Glenorchy
Laharum
C214
Mt Talbot
Brimpaen
Mt Gar (Mt Difficult)
Wartook
Mt Drummond
Lake Lonsdale
C238
Black Range State Park
Mt Victory Road
Mt Dryden
C221
Stawell
A8
Zumstein
Lake Wartook
C216
McKenzie Falls
Mt Bagara (Mt Victory)
Halls Gap
Lake Fyans
C221
Bunjil's Shelter
Black Range
GRAMPIANS
Wonderland Range
To Ararat, Ballarat & Melbourne
Mt Bepcha
Fishes Shelter
NATIONAL
Mt Rosea
Pomonal
Glenisla
Billimina Shelter
Cultivation Shelter
PARK
Moora Moora Reservoir
Lake Bellfield
C222
Rocklands Reservoir
Manja Shelter
Mt Thackeray (978m)
Mt Lubra
Red Man Bluff
Moyston
The Fortress (875m)
Mt Frederick
Mt Lang
Mt William (1167m)
Major Mitchell Plateau
Note: All 'shelters' have Aboriginal paintings
The Chimney Pots
Grampians Tourist Road
Mafeking
Road
C217
Serra Range
C188
Lake Buninjon
Cavendish
Victoria Valley
C216
Lake Muirhead
Willaura
B180
Bryan Swamp
Brady Swamp
A200
C188
Mt Sturgeon (Mt Wurgarri)
Mt Abrupt (Mt Murdadjoog) 825m
Dunkeld
Mt Stavely
Highway
B160
To Casterton
To Portland
Hamilton
B160
B140
Lake Linlithgow
C178
Lake Bolac
To Ballarat
0   10   20 km

VICTORIA

carry water and let someone know where you're going (preferably the rangers).

Bike Hire Halls Gap Fun Park and Bike Hire (☎ 5356 4348), behind the main shopping centre, has mountain bikes from $15 a day; they also have a drop-off service if you want to ride to/from a particular area.

Joy Flights & Balloon Rides Grampians Balloon Flights (☎ 5358 5222), in Stawell, offers morning flights for $175 and Stawell Aviation Services (☎ 5357 3234) offers joy flights from $40.

Organised Tours

The Grampians Central Booking Office (☎ 5356 4654) in the Halls Gap Newsagency books many activities and tours. You can book Grampians Bushwalking Company tours here. Its walks and tours range from a two hour King Koala Hunt ($5), to a four hour sunrise or sunset tour ($48 with breakfast or dinner).

The Brambuk Living Cultural Centre (☎ 5356 4452) runs tours to rock art sites, departing from the centre most days at 9 am. Tours cost $12 and you need to book 24 hours in advance.

Grampians National Park Tours (☎ 5356 6221) runs daily, all-day 4WD tours of the park ($75). Bicycle Outback (☎ 9484 0284) has three-day bike tours through the national park for $235. Transport to and from Melbourne and all meals are provided. BYO bicycle and tent, although hire is available.

Places to Stay

During the busy seasons accommodation in Halls Gap fills up. Grampians Accommodation Booking Service (☎ 1800 246 880), at the Stawell & Grampians Tourist Information Centre, makes bookings.

Camping in the Park Be aware of fire restrictions – apart from the damage you could do to yourself and the bush, you stand a good chance of being arrested if you disobey them. Remember that you can be jailed for lighting *any* fire, including fuel stoves, on days of total fire ban.

Parks Victoria has about 10 camp sites in the park, all with toilets and fireplaces, and most with at least limited water. Permits cost $8.60, which covers one car and up to six people. You can self-register or pay at the visitor centre. Bush camping is permitted except in the Wonderland Range area, around Lake Wartook and in parts of the Serra and Victoria Ranges.

High Spirit Outdoor Adventures (☎ 019 403 620 or 0145 116 907) has a camp site beside the Moora Moora Reservoir in the Victoria Valley, where accommodation, meals, transport to bushwalks, use of canoes, a bush sauna, Aboriginal cultural talks and more costs $25 a day. This place is popular with travellers and gets very good reports.

Caravan Parks There are many caravan parks in and around the Grampians. In the centre of Halls Gap, *Halls Gap Caravan Park* (☎ 5356 4251) has camp sites from $12, on-site vans from $36 and cabins from $45 to $95. *Halls Gap Lakeside Caravan Park* (☎ 5356 4281), 5km south on the scenic shores of Lake Bellfield, has sites from $13 and on-site cabins and holiday flats from $38 to $94.

Other Accommodation *Brambuk Backpackers* (☎ 5356 4250), opposite the visitor centre, has dorm beds from $15 to $20, depending on the season. *Halls Gap YHA Hostel* (☎ 5356 6221) is 1km from the centre on the corner of Grampians Tourist Rd and Buckler St. Dorm beds are $13 ($16 for nonmembers), and family rooms cost $16 per person. At the time of writing, a new YHA hostel was planned.

See the earlier Camping in the Park section for High Spirit Outdoor Adventures, a sort of hostel in tents.

Five minutes from Dunkeld on the Cavendish Rd, *Mt Sturgeon Backpackers* (☎ 5577 2241) has beds for $20 in a house on a sheep property. BYO bedding and towel.

Cheaper motels in Halls Gap include *Halls Gap Motel* (☎ 5356 4209), with doubles from $59 to $85, and *Grand Canyon Motel* (☎ 5356 4280), from $55 to $93; both are on the Grampians Tourist Rd.

Close to the centre, *Halls Gap Kookaburra Lodge* (☎ 5356 4395, *14 Heath St*) has good double units from $70 to $90.

There are quite a few self-contained units and cottages. *Kingsway Holiday Flats* (☎ 5356 4202, *Grampians Tourist Rd*) is one of the cheapest places, with flats from $45 to $55 a double. *Grampians Wonderland Cabins* (☎ 5356 4264, *Ellis St*) has two-bedroom units from $85 to $135 a double.

For a farm stay that includes farm activities, *Thermopylae* (☎ 5354 6245), near Moyston, has self-contained or catered accommodation from $150 for a weekend.

Places to Eat

In Halls Gap there's a general store with a cafe and a takeaway section and a supermarket. The *Flying Emu Cafe* serves a good range of gourmet snacks and foods.

The excellent *Kookaburra Restaurant* (☎ 5356 4222), on Grampians Tourist Rd, makes use of fresh local produce. Main meals range from $15 to $22. It opens nightly for dinner and you'll need to book.

At the Mountain Grand Guesthouse, *The Balconies Restaurant* serves fine country cuisine, and has jazz on weekends; there's also a downstairs. *Suzy's Halls Gap Tavern* offers three-course set meals for $10; you can also order a la carte.

The *Bush Tucker Cafe* at the Brambuk Living Cultural Centre has bush snacks; a 'roo burger or kebab costs $6.

Getting There & Away

V/Line has a daily train/bus service from Melbourne to Halls Gap. The trip takes about four hours ($38.90).

A daily bus runs between Halls Gap and Stawell ($7.30).

The road from Stawell to Halls Gap is flat so it's an easy cycle of about 25km. It's a longer and hillier ride between Ararat and Halls Gap (via Moyston) but still fairly easy.

HORSHAM

• postcode 3402   • pop 12,600

The area around Horsham was first settled in 1841 and the town is the main commercial centre of the Wimmera. There's not a great deal of interest in the town, but it's a good base for the nearby Little Desert National and Mt Arapiles State parks and, for something kitsch, a visit to the Giant Koala at Dadswells Bridge.

The Tourist Information Centre (☎ 5382 1832), 20 O'Callaghan's Parade, is open daily from 9 am to 5 pm.

Things to See

Horsham Art Gallery, 80 Wilson St, is worth a visit. The main feature is the Mack Jost Bequest, a private collection of significant Australian artists. It opens Tuesday to Friday from 10 am to 5 pm, and on Sunday from 1 to 4.30 pm ($1).

The **Wool Factory**, in Golf Course Rd, is a community project providing employment and skills for handicapped people. It produces ultra-fine wool, and there's a walk-through sheep shed, a cafe and shop. Tours are held daily at 10.15 am, 11 am, 1.30 pm and 2.30 pm ($4).

Places to Stay & Eat

Horsham City Caravan Park (☎ 5382 3476), at the end of Firebrace St, has camp sites from $10 and on-site vans and cabins from $40.

A few pubs have rooms. Try the historic *Royal Hotel* (☎ 5382 1255, *132 Firebrace St*), which charges $20/35 a single/double.

There are more than 15 motels. One of the cheapest is *Glynlea Motel* (☎ 5382 0145, *26 Stawell Rd*), charging from $48 a double. See the tourist centre for B&Bs in the area.

Quirky *Cafe Bagdad*, on Wilson St near the corner of Firebrace St, is open Monday to Saturday and has good meals from $5 to $10. Bistro and counter meals at the pubs are popular, particularly at *The Commercial* in Wilson St.

MT ARAPILES STATE PARK

Mt Arapiles, 37km west of Horsham and 12km west of Natimuk, is probably Australia's best venue for rock climbing, with more than 2000 routes, from basic to advanced climbs. The park is also popular for walks. There are two short and steep walking

tracks from Centenary Park to the top of Arapiles – or you can drive up.

Climbing Instruction
Several operators, including the Climbing
Company (☎ 5387 1329) and Arapiles
Climbing Guides (☎ 5387 1284), offer
climbing and abseiling instruction. Group
instruction costs around $30 for a half-day;
private tuition is around $180 a day for in-
dividuals or $250 a day for small groups.

Places to Stay & Eat
There's a camp site known as '*the Pines*' in
Centenary Park at the base of the mountain.
Natimuk Lake Caravan Park (☎ 5387 1462)
is about 4km north of Natimuk and has camp
sites from $8 and on-site vans from $30.

In Natimuk, the *National Hotel (☎ 5387
1300, 65 Main St)* has comfortable pub
rooms for $17.50 per person. The pub serves
counter meals from Wednesday to Saturday
nights for around $10. They also have cabins
with a double bed and four bunks for $50 a
double and $10 for each extra adult. Friendly
Quamby Lodge (☎ 5387 1569, 71 Main St)
charges $15 per person with breakfast. Even
if you're not sleeping there you can have a
shower for $3 and do your laundry for $3.50.

Seven kilometres east of Natimuk, the
popular *Tim's Place YHA (☎ 5384 0236)*
has dorm beds for $15 and doubles for $35,
all including breakfast. The hostel arranges
climbing and abseiling instruction. You can
hire mountain bikes for $5 a day, go fishing,
yabbying, horse riding, swim in the dam or
enjoy an emu steak on the barbie. The hostel also runs a Koori cultural issues evening
three times a week for $15.

Natimuk Gallery and Cafe is open weekends from November to May and has excellent coffee and cakes. Vegetarian meals
are delicious and cost around $10.

Getting There & Away
The weekday bus service between Horsham
and Naracoorte drops people at Mt Arapiles
($4.50).

If you're planning to stay at Tim's Place
ring to find out about transport/accommo-
dation packages.

DIMBOOLA
• postcode 3414   • pop 1550
Dimboola, just off the Western Hwy, is a
country town with some fine old buildings.
It was made famous by Jack Hibberd's play,
Dimboola, about a country wedding, and
the subsequent film.

The Little Desert National Park starts
4km south of town. **Pink Lake** is a colourful
salt lake beside the Western Hwy about 9km
north-west of Dimboola. **Ebenezer Aboriginal Mission Station** was established in
Antwerp, 18km north of Dimboola, in
1859. It's signposted off the Dimboola-to-
Jeparit road. Walkabout Tours (☎ 5381
1691) run **Koori tours** in this area that include a visit to the mission ($15).

Places to Stay
Riverside Caravan Park (☎ 5389 1416) has
camp sites/on-site vans from $9/30.

The good *Victoria Hotel (☎ 5389 1630,
Wimmera St)* has singles/doubles for
$30/45. *Motel Dimboola (☎ 5389 1177)*, on
the Western Hwy at the edge of town, has
rooms from $42/50.

*Little Desert Log Cabins & Cottage
(☎ 5389 1122)* is 4km south of town and on
the edge of the Little Desert. Two-bedroom
cottages cost from $65 to $75 a double, plus
$10 per extra adult.

LITTLE DESERT NATIONAL PARK
The name of this park (132,000 hectares) is
misleading; the soil is mainly sandy but
there's a rich diversity of plants and the park
is famous for its springtime wildflowers.

Two sealed roads between the Western
and Wimmera highways pass through the
park: the Edenhope-to-Kaniva road and the
Harrow-to-Nhill road. There's also a good
gravel road from Dimboola into the park.
The tracks within the park are mostly suitable only for 4WD vehicles or walking, and
some are closed to 4WDs in the wet season
(from July to the end of September).

The best known resident here is the
mallee fowl, which can be seen in an aviary
at the Little Desert Lodge.

There are several short walks in the eastern block. Longer walks leave from the

camping ground south of Kiata including a 12km trek south to the Salt Lake – carry water and notify rangers before you set out.

Oasis Desert Adventures (☎ 5389 1957), 6km south of Dimboola, runs tours in and around the Little Desert. Little Desert Lodge (see Places to Stay) also has tours.

Places to Stay

Little Desert Lodge (☎ 5391 5232) is about 16km south of Nhill. It caters mainly for groups, but takes individuals when there are vacancies. B&B costs $45/60 for singles/doubles in en suite rooms and $25 in bunkrooms. Camp sites cost $9. There's an environmental study centre and a mallee fowl aviary ($5 entry). 4WD tours of the park cost $25/38 for a half/full day.

Parks Victoria has *camping grounds* at Horseshoe Bend and Ackle Bend, both on the Wimmera River south of Dimboola, and another about 10km south of Kiata. Sites have drinking water and toilets and cost $7.90.

You can bush camp on overnight walks in the central and western blocks, but speak to the rangers first at the Parks Victoria office, Wail Nursery Rd, south of Dimboola (☎ 5389 1204).

The Mallee

This dry area includes the one genuinely empty part of the state – the semi-arid wilderness known as 'Sunset Country'. You don't have to visit central Australia to get a taste of the Outback.

The Mallee takes its name from the mallee scrub that once covered the area. A mallee is a hardy eucalypt with chunky roots and multiple slender trunks. Mallee gums are canny desert survivors – root systems over 1000 years old are not uncommon. 'Mallee scrub' might look desolate but it's actually a rich biosystem.

Organised Tours

Sunset 4WD Tours (☎ 5023 1047), in Ouyen, runs 4WD tours of the Murray-Sunset, Wyperfeld and Hattah-Kulkyne national

parks and Big Desert Wilderness Park. Tours range from day trips to longer expeditions. Tours depart from Ouyen or Mildura.

Mallee Outback Experiences (☎ 5021 1621) runs tours to Hattah-Kulkyne National Park from Mildura.

Getting There & Away

V/Line runs buses from Melbourne nightly except Saturday through the Mallee to Mildura ($53.60) via Donald ($36.50) and Ouyen ($49.20). Alternatively, take a train to Bendigo and catch a bus from there.

The Henty Highway Coach (☎ 5382 4260 or 5023 5658) runs between Horsham and Mildura three times a week.

BIG DESERT WILDERNESS PARK

This 113,500 hectare park is a desert wilderness. There are no roads, tracks, facilities or water. Walking and camping are permitted but you should only do so if you are experienced and totally self sufficient. In summer, temperatures are usually way too high for walking. Notify the rangers in Wyperfeld National Park (☎ 5395 7221) before going.

The area is mostly sand dunes, red sandstone ridges and mallee, but there's an abundance of flora and fauna.

There are no roads into the Big Desert. A dry-weather road from Murrayville on the Mallee Hwy (B12) to Nhill separates this park from the Wyperfeld National Park. The road is buffered from the park by a 5km-wide strip of state forest. Parts of the road are very rough and may be impassable after rain.

There are basic camping sites in buffer zones at Big Billy Bore, the Springs, Moonlight Tank and Broken Bucket Reserve, all on the eastern side, and even more remote sites on the southern border.

MURRAY-SUNSET NATIONAL PARK

The park (663,000 hectares) includes the older **Pink Lakes State Park**. These lakes get their pink colour from microscopic organisms that concentrate an orange pigment in their bodies.

The park is arid and mainly inaccessible. An unsealed road leads from **Linga** on the

Mallee Hwy up to the Pink Lakes at the southern edge of the park, where there's a basic camping ground, but beyond here you need a 4WD. Don't go exploring in a two-wheel drive.

For more information contact the rangers in Underbool (☎ 5094 6267), on the Mallee Hwy, or Werrimull (☎ 5028 1218), north of the park.

Murray River

The Murray River is Australia's most important inland waterway, flowing from the mountains of the Great Dividing Range in north-eastern Victoria to Encounter Bay in SA, more than 2700km away. This makes it the third-longest navigable river in the world.

The river forms the border between Victoria and NSW. Most places of interest are on the Victorian side, although there's usually a 'twin' town on the NSW side.

Before roads and railways crossed the land, the Murray was an antipodean Mississippi, with paddle-steamers carrying supplies to and carting wool from remote sheep stations and homesteads.

In the 1880s Canadian irrigation experts, the Chaffey brothers, established an irrigation settlement at Mildura and installed irrigation systems, attracting thousands of new settlers.

Getting There & Away
Train Daily trains run between Melbourne and Swan Hill and there's a daily train/bus service between Melbourne and Echuca.

Bus Greyhound Pioneer and McCafferty's both go through Mildura daily on the Sydney to Adelaide run.

V/Line's Murraylink service connects towns along the Murray River between Mildura and Albury five days a week. You need a reservation on the Mildura-Kerang sector. V/Line's daily Speedlink service between Adelaide and Albury runs between Echuca and Albury, taking a fairly roundabout route. You need a reservation.

Car & Motorcycle The main route along the Murray is the Murray Valley Hwy, which starts near Mildura and follows the river all the way to Corryong.

While the highway links the towns, it rarely runs right beside the river. If you want a taste of less tamed river country, get some good maps and follow the web of back roads on the northern bank. This will add hours to your travel time, though.

MILDURA
• postcode 3500 • pop 24,000
After driving for hours through a dry and desolate landscape, you reach this thriving regional centre – a true oasis town, watered by the mighty Murray River.

The name 'Mildura' means 'red soil'.

As well as being one of the richest agricultural areas in Australia, Mildura is a tourist town – it promotes itself as a place of endless blue skies and sunshine.

Orientation
Once you penetrate the tacky development that extends kilometres from the city centre, downtown Mildura is reasonably compact. Deakin Ave is the main street and runs down to the Murray River. Langtree Ave, parallel to Deakin (and a block north) between Eleventh and Seventh Sts, is the main shopping street.

Mildura's urban sprawl extends south as far as Red Cliffs, a little town with a big tractor – Big Lizzie.

Information
The tourist information centre (☎ 5021 4424 or 1800 039 043 for bookings), on the corner of Deakin Ave and Twelfth St, is open daily from 9.30 am to 5.30 am (closes Sunday at 5 pm).

The Coles supermarket on the corner of Lime Ave and Eighth St never closes. The post office is on the corner of Eighth St and Orange Ave.

The NRE office (☎ 5022 3000) is at 253 Eleventh St. The RACV office (☎ 5021 3272) is on the corner of Ninth St and Lime Ave.

Fruit-Picking Work Contact the employment agency, Madec (☎ 5021 3359), on

Deakin Ave just west of Tenth St. The main harvest season runs from about January to March (call Madec's Harvest Office, ☎ 5022 1797, from November), but some casual work is available year-round.

After a few days, you'll get used to the back-breaking 10-hours-a-day labour. The official hourly rate for casual labour is $11.34. Some farmers provide a place to pitch a tent, but often you'll need to stay in town, so transport might be necessary. At least one of the backpacker hostels shuttles people to work.

Mildura Arts Centre & Rio Vista

This complex combines an art gallery, a theatre and a historical museum at Rio Vista, the former home of WB Chaffey. The grand homestead has been beautifully preserved. The gallery and museum are open weekdays from 9 am to 5 pm and weekends from 1 to 5 pm ($2.50).

Other Attractions

The tourist information centre has a brochure, *The Chaffey Trail*, which guides you around sights including the paddle-steamer wharf, the Mildura weir and lock, Old Mildura Homestead, the Mildara Blass Winery and the Old Psyche Bend Pump Station.

The **Old Mildura Homestead**, a cottage where WB Chaffey lived while Rio Vista was being built, is in a heritage park on the banks of the Murray in Pioneer Way. It is open daily from 9 am to dusk.

Wineries

All these wineries are open daily and have barbecue facilities.

Lindeman's Karadoc Winery (☎ 5051 3285), 20km south of Mildura, is a huge complex. There's a cafe (open noon to 3 pm). The winery is signposted off the Calder Hwy, south of Red Cliffs. It's open daily.

Mildara Blass specialises in fortified wines. It's on the Murray River at Merbein, 9km west of Mildura. On weekdays there are guided tours at 11 am and 2.30 pm.

In NSW, 12km from Mildura, the small **Trentham Estate Winery** has a restaurant open for lunch daily except Monday.

Paddle-steamer Cruises

PS *Melbourne* (☎ 5023 2200) is the only boat still driven by steam. Two-hour cruises depart daily at 10.50 am and 1.50 pm ($16).

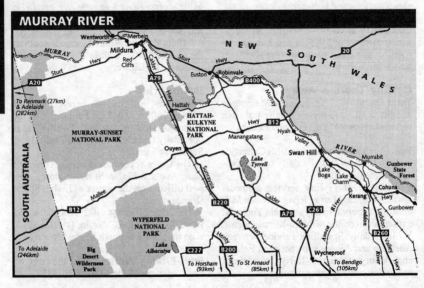

The PV *Rothbury* (☎ 5023 2200) has cruises to the Golden River Zoo and to Trentham Estate Winery; both cost $35, including lunch.

Showboat Avoca (☎ 5021 1166) has daily two-hour cruises ($16), and night cruises with dining and entertainment on Thursday and Saturday nights.

Paddle-steamer *Coonawarra* (☎ 1800 034 424) has three and five-day cruises from around $400.

Cruises depart from the Mildura Wharf at the end of Deakin Ave. Cruises operate more often during school holidays.

Boat Hire
The Buronga Boatman Boat Hire, on the NSW side of the Murray River opposite Mildura Wharf, hires out kayaks, canoes and power boats.

Organised Tours
Several Aboriginal operators run tours of the area, concentrating on culture, history (which covers 45,000 years if you go to Lake Mungo, north-east of Mildura, in NSW) and wildlife. The best known is Harry Nanya (☎ 5027 2076), with a wide range of tours, including a day trip to Mungo National Park

($43). Also good is Ponde Tours (book at the tourist information centre).

Mallee Outback Experiences (☎ 5021 1621) offers a range of tours, for a minimum of two people, in and around Mildura. It includes day trips to the Mungo or Hattah-Kulkyne national parks ($45).

On Monday, Wednesday and Friday, the Broken Hill Express Coach has day trips from Mildura to Broken Hill via Wentworth ($69 or $45 one way). Book at the tourist information centre.

Places to Stay
Camping & Caravan Parks There are nearly 30 caravan and camping grounds. Prices are relatively high, especially in school holidays.

Not the flashest but one of the best located is the *River Bend Tourist Park* (☎ 5023 6879), at Apex Park, Cureton Ave, about 4km west of the town centre. It's across the road from the river and has sites from $11, on-site vans from $26 to $36 and cabins from $40 to $65 (all prices for two people). *Buronga Riverside Caravan Park* (☎ 5023 3040), just across the river from the centre of town but a kilometre or two by

VICTORIA

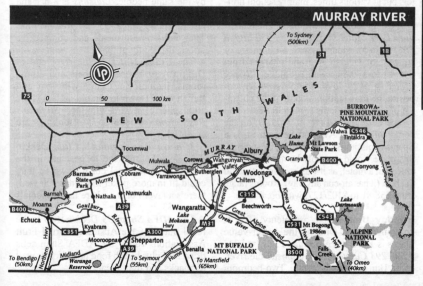

road, has tent sites from $11 and cabins from $35 a double.

Guesthouses & Hostels Friendly *Rosemont Guest House (☎ 5023 1535, 154 Madden Ave)* has simple doubles with bathroom from $45 and singles with shared bathroom for $22. This place is also a *YHA Hostel* and members are charged $15. All rooms have air-con, there's a pool, and rates include breakfast.

Mildura International Backpackers (☎ 5021 0133, 5 Cedar Ave) is good and the rooms have two beds (not bunks) for $14 a bed. The hostel has a van so you might be able to arrange a lift to work if you don't have a car.

The newcomer is *Riverboat Bungalow (☎ 5021 5315, 27 Chaffey Ave)* in a nice old house and fairly close to most things. It's well equipped and dorm beds cost around $15.

There's another hostel in Red Cliffs – *Red Cliffs Backpackers (☎ 5024 2905, 63 Indi Ave)*. It's over 15km from central Mildura, but might come in handy if you're here for work. Beds cost $13.

Motels & Hotels There are dozens of motels but at various times, mainly school holidays, vacancies are scarce and prices rise.

A good choice for a quiet night is *Mildura Park Motel (☎ 5023 0479, 250 Eighth St)*. It's in a residential area a kilometre or so west of Deakin Ave and charges from $45/49 to $79/84 a single/double. *Riviera Motel (☎ 5023 3696, 157 Seventh St)*, opposite the train station, is one of the cheapest places, with rooms from $38/42.

The *Grand Hotel (☎ 5023 0511)*, on the corner of Deakin Ave and Seventh St, is a Spanish mission-style building. In summer, this place would probably be more comfortable than a motel, as it was built to withstand the heat (it has air-con anyway). Rooms range from $58/81 to $102/127, with breakfast.

Holiday Units There are plenty of self-contained flats. One of the better-value places is *Yerre Yerre Holiday Flats (☎ 5022 1526, 293 Cureton Ave)*, opposite the river, about 1km north of the centre. Two-bedroom flats, each with a kitchen, laundry, TV and air-con, cost $46 to $68 for two people and sleep up to six. Weekly rates are a little lower.

Houseboats Staying on a houseboat is a great way to see the river. Houseboats range from two to 12-berth, from modest to luxurious, and are priced accordingly.

There are over 20 different companies and most have a minimum hire of three days with prices starting from around $100 a night or $600 a week, dramatically more in summer and school holidays. Contact the tourist information centre or the RACV for more details.

Places to Eat

The main restaurant precinct is along Langtree Ave, between the mall and the river.

Sandbar, on the corner of Langtree Ave and Eighth St, is a lively bar with a courtyard and entertainment from Wednesday to Saturday nights. It has snacks and meals in the $9 to $15 range. Across the street, *Restaurant Rendezvous (34 Langtree Ave)* is a classy place with entrees around $12 and mains around $20. Next door and run by the same people, *Liaisons* is a bar and bistro with a pleasant courtyard – and lower prices. *Siam Palace (35 Langtree Ave)* has Thai and Chinese meals and competitive prices, especially at lunch.

The *Grand Hotel*, at the river end of Deakin Ave, has several bars and dining rooms, including a casual wine bar and Italian cafe. Down in the old cellars is the atmospheric, award-winning, *Stefano's Restaurant (☎ 5023 0511)*. Bookings are essential.

Mildura Workingman's Club, Deakin Ave, once boasted the longest bar in the world, but some fool cut it down so they could fit in more poker machines. Oh well, there's a tavern bistro where lunch specials start at $3.

The *ADFA Shop (33 Deakin Ave)* is the retail outlet of the Australian Dried Fruit Association. Today the ADFA Shop sells dried fruit plus health food products, as well as snacks and light meals.

Getting There & Away

Air Mildura airport is about 10km west of the town centre, off the Sturt Hwy (A20). Kendall Airlines (book through Ansett ☎ 13 1300) flies daily between Melbourne and Mildura ($183), as does Southern Australia Airlines (book through Qantas ☎ 13 1313). Smaller operators fly to other destinations including Adelaide and Broken Hill.

Bus Between Melbourne and Mildura, V/Line has a bus nightly except Saturday, as well as several daily train/bus services via Bendigo or Swan Hill. The trip takes around eight hours ($52). V/Line also has a service connecting towns along the Murray River, including Swan Hill ($29.30), Echuca ($34.20) and Albury ($55).

Greyhound and McCafferty's have daily services between Mildura and Adelaide ($35) or Sydney ($74); Greyhound and Sunraysia Bus Lines have twice-weekly services to Broken Hill ($37).

Long-distance buses operate from near the train station on Seventh Ave.

Getting Around

There are bus services around town and as far out as Red Cliffs and Merbein, mostly during the week. The tourist information centre has timetables. The free coaches to the NSW gambling clubs leave from various points, including in front of Ron's Tours & Charters at 41 Deakin Ave.

Mildura Taxis (☎ 5023 0033) operates 24 hours a day.

HATTAH-KULKYNE NATIONAL PARK

Hattah-Kulkyne is a beautiful and diverse park. The vegetation ranges from sandy mallee country to the fertile riverside areas closer to the Murray.

The **Hattah Lakes** system fills when the Murray floods and supports many species of water bird.

The main access road is from the small town of **Hattah**, 70km south of Mildura on the Calder Hwy. About 5km into the park is an information centre. There are tracks through the park, but many are impassable after rain. The old camel tracks are great for cycling, but tell the rangers (in Hattah, ☎ 5029 3253) where you're going and carry water, a compass and a map.

There are camp sites at Lake Hattah and Lake Mournpall, but there is limited water. Camping is also possible anywhere along the Murray River frontage ($8.60).

SWAN HILL

• postcode 3585   • pop 9400

Swan Hill, the low hill on which the town of the same name sits, was named by Major Mitchell in 1836 after he was kept awake by swans in the nearby lagoon. The area was settled by sheep graziers soon after. Today, Swan Hill is a major regional centre surrounded by irrigated farms that produce grapes and other fruit.

Swan Hill's visitor information centre (☎ 5032 3033 or 1800 625 373), 306 Campbell St, is open daily.

Swan Hill Pioneer Settlement, in Monash Drive, re-creates a riverside port town and is worth visiting. The paddle-steamer PS *Pyap* makes short cruises along the Murray ($8.50 for adults; $4.50 for children). The settlement is open daily from 8.30 am to 5 pm ($13/6.50). Every night at dusk a 45 minute **sound & light show** is held ($8.50/4.50).

MV *Kookaburra* (☎ 5032 0003) has **lunch cruises**. The information centre sells tickets.

Tyntynder Homestead, 16km north of the town, has a small museum of pioneering and Aboriginal relics ($7.50); it's open daily. Built in 1886, **Murray Downs Homestead**, a couple of kilometres east of Swan Hill in NSW, is open daily except Monday ($7.50).

Buller's Caliope Winery is 14km north of town on the Murray Valley Hwy, and is open most days. **Best's St Andrews Vineyard** is 2km south-east of the town of Lake Boga, which is 17km south of Swan Hill. It specialises in fortified wines and brandies, and is open daily.

Places to Stay & Eat

Riverside Caravan Park (☎ *5032 1494*), on Monash Drive by the river, has camp sites from $13 and on-site vans and cabins from $30 to $75.

Camping Under Trees

Although you can camp in state forest right along the river, do not put up your tent beneath a river red gum – these mighty trees are notorious for dropping their huge branches without warning, whether it's windy or still.

The *White Swan Hotel* (☎ 5032 2761, 182 Campbell St) charges $25/35 a single/double; $45 for doubles with bathroom.

One of the cheapest motels is *Mallee Rest Motel* (☎ 5032 4541, 369 Campbell St), with doubles from $44 to $54.

Kookaburra Houseboats (☎ 5032 0003), just across the bridge in NSW, has houseboats from around $500 for two weekend nights from May to October and $800 for a week during the same months.

Whistling Kettle (392 Campbell St) serves light lunches during the day. *Tellers Cafe, Bar & Restaurant* (223 Campbell St) is a friendly place in a converted bank. The menu has a wide range of snacks and meals from around $7. Ask about backpacker specials.

The *White Swan Hotel* has good counter meals, from $6 at lunch time.

Getting There & Away
Trains and train/bus services run between Melbourne and Swan Hill ($43.40) via Bendigo. There are also buses four times weekly between Swan Hill and Mildura ($29.30), Echuca ($18) and Albury-Wodonga ($39.70).

GUNBOWER STATE FOREST
Gunbower State Forest is on Gunbower Island, which is almost 50km long, stretching from Koondrook in the north to near Torrumbarry in the south.

River red gum forest and swamps provide diverse habitats for the abundant bird and animal life.

Cohuna is the main access point, although there are tracks in from the highway. The tracks on the island are impassable after rain. There are plenty of walks and many riverside camp sites.

Gannawarra Wetlands Cruises (☎ 5453 3000), based at a mooring 16km north of Cohuna, runs the *Wetlander* into the wetland areas. Two-hour cruises operate daily except Thursday from mid-August to mid-May ($17/9).

ECHUCA
• postcode 3564   • pop 10,000
Echuca is located at the spot where the Goulburn and Campaspe rivers join the Murray. Appropriately, 'echuca' (pronounced 'e-choo-ka') means 'the meeting of the waters'.

The town was founded in 1853 by ex-convict Harry Hopwood, who established punt and ferry crossings over the Murray and Campaspe rivers. He built the Bridge Hotel in 1858 and watched his town grow into the busiest inland port in Australia. The wharf was once over a kilometre long and lined with shops and hotels.

Information
The tourist information centre (☎ 5480 7555) is off Heygarth St and is open daily from 9 am to 5 pm. It provides an accommodation booking service (☎ 1800 804 446).

There's a combined RACV and NRMA office (☎ 5482 1711) at 555 High St. The Coles supermarket on High St (corner of Darling St) never closes. There's a laundrette on Darling St near the corner of Hare St.

Historic Port of Echuca
The best feature of the old port area is that everything is original. You buy a 'passport' that admits you to the three main sections, the Star Hotel, the wharf and the Bridge Hotel.

The ticket box is at the entrance to the **wharf** via the old train station building. Across the road at the **Star Hotel** (1867) you can escape through the underground tunnel that was built to help drinkers avoid the police during the years when the pub was a 'sly grog shop'. At the **Bridge Hotel,** your ticket admits you to a historic upstairs gallery.

The Port of Echuca is open daily from 9 am to 5 pm, and tickets cost $7/5; admission plus a paddle-steamer cruise costs $16/9.

Other Port Area Attractions

The **Red Gum Works** has woodturners and blacksmiths at work using traditional equipment.

Sharp's Magic Movie House & Penny Arcade on Murray Esplanade has a collection of penny-arcade machines and showings of old movies (with authentic equipment). It is open daily from 9 am to 5 pm. Admission costs $10/6 for adults/children and the ticket is valid all day. The **Murray River Aquarium** shows denizens of the river deep such as a huge Murray cod ($5/2.50).

The World in Wax, 630 High St, features a cast of some 60 famous and gruesome people ($6/3).

You can take a tour in a horse-drawn coach ($4/2) with Cobb & Co (buy tickets at the PS *Canberra* office) and Flynn (PS *Pride of the Murray* office).

There are wine tastings at **Murray Esplanade Cellars** at the Port of Echuca in the old Customs House, on the corner of Leslie St. You can also sample some wine at the **William Angliss Wine Tasting Centre**, on the corner of Radcliffe St and Murray Esplanade.

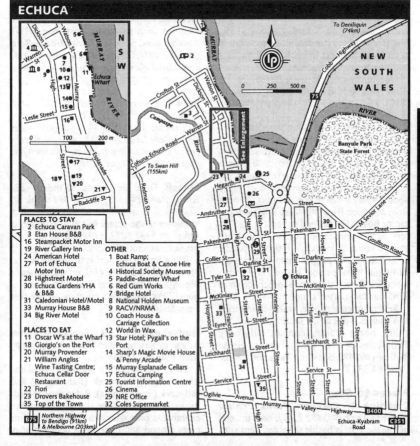

ECHUCA

NEW SOUTH WALES

To Deniliquin (74km)

Banyule Park State Forest

VICTORIA

PLACES TO STAY
2 Echuca Caravan Park
3 Etan House B&B
16 Steampacket Motor Inn
19 River Gallery Inn
24 American Hotel
27 Port of Echuca Motor Inn
28 Highstreet Motel
30 Echuca Gardens YHA & B&B
31 Caledonian Hotel/Motel
33 Murray House B&B
34 Big River Motel

PLACES TO EAT
11 Oscar W's at the Wharf
18 Giorgio's on the Port
20 Murray Provender
21 William Angliss Wine Tasting Centre; Echuca Cellar Door Restaurant
22 Fiori
23 Drovers Bakehouse
35 Top of the Town

OTHER
1 Boat Ramp; Echuca Boat & Canoe Hire
4 Historical Society Museum
5 Paddle-steamer Wharf
6 Red Gum Works
7 Bridge Hotel
8 National Holden Museum
9 RACV/NRMA
10 Coach House & Carriage Collection
12 World in Wax
13 Star Hotel; Pygall's on the Port
14 Sharp's Magic Movie House & Penny Arcade
15 Murray Esplanade Cellars
17 Echuca Camping
25 Tourist Information Centre
26 Cinema
29 NRE Office
32 Coles Supermarket

To Swan Hill (155km)

Northern Highway to Bendigo (91km) & Melbourne (203km)

Echuca-Kyabram Road

Other Attractions

Echuca's **Historical Society Museum** is at 1 Dickson St, in the old police station. It's open afternoons on Monday, Wednesday and weekends ($2).

At 7 Warren St, the **National Holden Museum** houses more than 40 restored Holdens and associated memorabilia ($5).

Activities

A **paddle-steamer cruise** along the Murray is almost obligatory. PS *Emmylou* (☎ 5480 2237) is driven by an original engine, offering one and 1½-hour cruises ($12 and $15). *Emmylou* also offers two-day and two-night cruises departing Wednesday evening (from $365), and an overnight cruise, usually on Saturday (from $135). She sleeps 18, so it wouldn't be too hard to get a group together to book the whole boat and thus receive a discount.

One-hour cruises are offered by PS *Alexandra Arbuthnot* ($12), PS *Canberra* ($10), PS *Pevensey* ($12) and PS *Pride of the Murray* ($9).

PS *Adelaide* is the oldest wooden hulled paddle-steamer still operating anywhere in the world; it occasionally has cruises. There's also MV *Mary Ann* (☎ 5480 2200); not a paddle-steamer but a cruising restaurant.

Based at the Victoria Park boat ramp about 700m north of the old port, Echuca Boat & Canoe Hire (☎ 5480 6208) hires out **motor boats**, **kayaks** and **canoes**. It also offers canoe cruises – they drive you upstream, you paddle back. A four hour paddle costs $50 for two people, three-day trips are $140 per two person canoe. A 10 day marathon from Yarrawonga to Echuca costs $285 per two person canoe.

Several operators offer **water-skiing** trips and classes – ask at the tourist office.

For **horse riding**, contact Billabong Trail Rides (☎ 5480 1222), Firedust Horse Riding (☎ 5482 5314) or Tarragon Lodge (☎ 5884 3387).

Places to Stay

Camping & Caravan Parks *Echuca Caravan Park* (☎ 5482 2157), near the end of Dickson St, is beside the river. Tent sites cost from $13, on-site vans from $35 and cabins from $48 a double. *Moama Riverside Caravan Park* (☎ 5482 3241), across the bridge in Moama (NSW) and close to the town centre, has similar prices.

Hostels & B&Bs *Echuca Gardens YHA* (☎ 5480 6522, 103 Mitchell St) has dorm beds for $16 ($19 nonmembers); everyone pays a small surcharge on long weekends and some major holidays). This place is also the pleasant *Echuca Gardens B&B*, with en suite doubles for $100 ($120 between Friday and Sunday).

Etan House B&B (☎ 5480 7477, 11 Connelly St) is a restored homestead with good facilities, including a tennis court and pool. Doubles with bathroom cost from $120. Another good place is *Murray House B&B* (☎ 5482 4944, 55 Francis St), with en suite singles/doubles from $95/165 and a two bedroom cottage for around $100.

Pubs The *American Hotel* (☎ 5482 5044), on the corner of Hare and Heygarth Sts, has pub rooms from $25/40 a single/double. The *Palace Hotel* (☎ 5482 1461), on the opposite corner, is slightly more upmarket and charges from $20 per person.

Motels There are around 20 motels. *Big River Motel* (☎ 5482 2522, 371 High St) has rooms from $40/50 to $48/58, while a bit closer to the centre of town, *Highstreet Motel* (☎ 5482 1013, 439 High St) has budget units at similar prices.

Right by the old port is the *Steampacket Motor Inn* (☎ 5482 3411), on the corner of Murray Esplanade and Leslie St, in a National Trust-classified building. Units cost from $64/87.

Houseboats Hiring a houseboat is a great way to experience river life. The boats sleep from four to 12 people.

There are three hire periods – weekend (three nights), midweek (four nights) and full week (seven nights). Rates vary according to the season and the size of the boat. For example, a boat with two double bedrooms costs around $800 per week between May and late December (except during school holidays). The tourist information centre has details and makes bookings.

Places to Eat

High and Hare Sts are full of eateries. *Murray Provender (568 High St)* is a good gourmet deli. *Drovers Bakehouse (513 High St)* is open during the day for light meals and has a deck overlooking the Campaspe River. In the Star Hotel on Murray Esplanade, *Pygall's on the Port* sells snacks and light meals during the day.

For a pub feed, try the *American Hotel*, with bar meals from $7 and a bistro. The *Caledonian Hotel Motel* is a renovated pub with an upmarket dining area.

Oscar W's at the Wharf is right on the wharf and overlooks the river. At lunch time snacks cost from $7.50 and main courses from $10. The *Echuca Cellar Door Restaurant (☎ 5480 6720, 2 Radcliffe St)*, at the William Angliss Wine Tasting Centre, has lunches for around $13.50 and a three course dinner for $19.50. Bookings are preferred.

Fiori, on the corner of Radcliffe and High Sts, is a smart Italian place, with entrees around $10 and mains around $20.

Top of the Town on the corner High and Service Sts has a good range of the piscine, including river fish – it isn't often that non-anglers get to sample these.

Across the river in Moama, the big *Rich River Golf Club* complex and the opulent *Moama Bowling Club* have a range of eateries; some are good value.

Getting There & Away

V/Line runs daily between Melbourne and Echuca ($26.90), changing from train to bus at Bendigo ($6.10 from Echuca). Four times a week V/Line buses connect Echuca with Albury-Wodonga ($34.20), Swan Hill ($18) and Mildura ($34.20). There's also a daily bus to Albury-Wodonga, which takes you to destinations in southern NSW.

BARMAH STATE PARK

This park is a wetland area created by the flood plains of the Murray River. The plains are forested with old river red gums, and the swampy understorey usually floods in winter, creating a breeding area for many bird species. It's the largest remaining redgum forest in Australia (and thus the world).

The **Dharnya Centre** (☎ 5869. 3302) is both the visitor information centre and a good little museum ($2) with displays on Aboriginal heritage and the park. It's open daily from 10.30 am to 4 pm. The centre is run by the Yorta Yorta people.

Although evidence in the area dates Aboriginal occupation at 'only' a thousand years or so, this is probably because the river has destroyed older evidence. It isn't far away, on drier land, that there is evidence of more than 40,000 years of continuous occupation. The Yorta Yorta people's Native Title claim for the area was rejected by the Federal Court in 1998.

The park starts 9km north of the small town of **Barmah**, which is 36km north-east of Echuca via Moama.

Gondwana Canoe Hire (☎ 5869 3347), midway between Barmah and the Dharnya Centre, hires canoes for $45 a day (less for longer rentals) and can advise on canoe trails. They can pick you up from as far afield as Echuca (for a fee).

The cruise boat *Kingfisher* (☎ 5869 3399) runs two-hour cruises on Monday, Wednesday, Thursday and Sunday (more often during holiday periods) for $16.

Places to Stay

You can camp anywhere in the park or at the Barmah Lakes camping area. The *Dharnya Centre (☎ 5869 3302)* has dorm accommodation ($15), but it's designed for groups and the minimum charge is $150. BYO bedding and food.

There are also *caravan parks* and a *hotel/motel* in the town of Barmah.

YARRAWONGA
● postcode 3730   ● pop 3400

On the western edge of the large Lake Mulwala, Yarrawonga is known for its aquatic activities on Lake Mulwala, and as a retirement centre.

The tourist information centre (☎ 5744 1989) is on Irvine Parade on the shores of

Lake Mulwala, beside the bridge. It's open daily from 9 am to 5 pm.

Two paddle-steamers, the *Lady Murray* and the *Paradise Queen*, operate cruises along the lake and the Murray River. Phil and Val Smith's Ski Rides (☎ 0419 211 122) rents a huge array of watercraft and offers water-skiing ($40 per half hour), para-sailing ($50 per flight) and other boat-towed thrills. You'll find them on the fore-shore in Mulwala, Yarrawonga's 'twin town' across the border in NSW.

There are about 10 caravan parks, 20 motels and many time-share resorts. The information centre makes bookings.

RUTHERGLEN

☎ 02   • postcode 3685   • pop 1900

Rutherglen is at the centre of one of Victoria's major wine-growing districts. It's a quaint little town dating from gold-rush days.

The **Rutherglen Historical Society Museum** is in an old school in Murray St behind the Victoria Hotel. It's open on Sunday from 10 am to 1 pm (free).

The visitor information centre (☎ 6032 9166), inside the historic Jolimont Wines complex, on the corner of Main and Drummond Sts, opens daily from 9 am to 5 pm. Note that this Victorian town is in the NSW telephone area, so you need to dial 02 if calling from a state other than NSW.

Special Events

The Winery Walkabout Weekend is held on the Queen's Birthday weekend in June. There's a wide range of events, as well as eating and drinking.

Other festivals include the Tastes of Rutherglen, held on the Labour Day week-end in March, and the Winemakers' Legends Weekend in mid-November. The Tour de Muscat, a bike ride around the wineries, is held in early November.

Accommodation in the area is likely to be tight during these festivals.

Places to Stay

Rutherglen Caravan Park (☎ 6032 8577, 72 Murray St) has sites from $15 and on-site vans from $30.

Victorian Wineries

Some of Australia's best wines are made in Victoria. Grape growing and wine production began with the gold rush of the 1850s and, before the turn of the century, the fine reputation of Victorian fortified wines was established in Europe. Then phylloxera, a disease of grapevines, devastated the Victorian vineyards. Changing tastes in alcohol completed the destruction.

In the 1960s the Victorian wine industry started to recapture its former glory and produce fine table wines, as well as fortified wines.

Victoria's oldest established wine-producing region is in the north-east, particularly around Rutherglen, but extending to Milawa, Glenrowan and beyond. Other fine wine-growing areas include the Yarra Valley and the Mornington Peninsula near Melbourne; the Geelong region; central Victoria around Bendigo and Heathcote; the Goulburn Valley; the Great Western and Pyrenees ranges (between Stawell, Ararat and Avoca); the Macedon ranges north of Melbourne; and the Murray River valley.

The *Victoria Hotel* (☎ 6032 8610, 90 Main St) has rooms for around $30/40 for singles/doubles and en suite rooms from $58 a double. Rates might be lower mid-week. Nearby, the *Star Hotel* (☎ 6032 9625) has basic rooms from $15 per person and motel units for $39 a double ($49 on weekends).

Motels include *Motel Woongarra* (☎ 6032 9588), on the corner of Main and Drummond Sts, with doubles from $48 to $62, and *Wine Village Motor Inn* (☎ 6032 9900), across the road, with doubles from $60 to $85.

Out in the countryside there are some excellent places to stay, including *Mt Ophir* (☎ 6032 8920), charging from $130 a double, *Lake Moodemere Homestead* (☎ 6032 8650), with doubles from $110 and *The House at Mt Prior* (☎ 6026 5256), charging from $210 a double.

Places to Eat
There are several good eateries along Main St. For light lunches and teas try *Shanty* or *Rutherglen Tearooms*. Both pubs serve bistro meals, and the Victoria has a pleasant beer garden.

The *Shamrock (152 Main St)* has reasonably priced, hearty dishes. *Rendezvous Courtyard (68 Main St)* is open for dinner nightly and has a Mediterranean-influenced menu.

Several wineries have cafes and restaurants, including *All Saints* (lunch and snacks daily), *St Leonards* (weekend lunches), *Cofield* (pre-order a picnic pack, daily), *Gehrig's* (lunch Thursday to Sunday), *Lake Moodemere* (pre-order a barbecue pack, daily) and *Pfeiffer* (pre-order a picnic hamper, daily).

The *House at Mt Prior (☎ 6026 5256)*, at the Mt Prior winery 14km north-east of Rutherglen, is probably the best restaurant in this area. There's also the less expensive *Terrace* restaurant here, open for lunch on weekends.

Getting There & Away
A V/Line bus runs to Wangaratta ($4.30) and connects with the Melbourne train on Wednesday, Friday and Saturday.

CHILTERN
☎ 03   • postcode 3683   • pop 1100
Just off the Hume Freeway, tiny Chiltern is one of Victoria's most historic townships. Gold was discovered here in 1859 and mining continued until the early 1900s – not much has changed since then.

There are a few places to see, such as the **Athenaeum Library & Museum**, now the historical society museum, and the **Star Hotel/Theatre**, but just wandering around is interesting.

Lake Anderson Caravan Park (☎ 5726 1298), Alliance St, has camp sites from $8 and on-site vans from $40. There's also a motel and a B&B or two.

In **Springhurst**, just off the Hume Freeway south of Chiltern, *Springhurst Tour-Tel Accommodation Centre (☎ 5726 5343)* offers B&B for $23. It's designed for groups but there's usually room for individuals. Trains between Melbourne and Albury (but not the XPT) stop at Springhurst.

WODONGA
☎ 02   • postcode 3690   • pop 25,800
The twin towns of Albury and Wodonga are separated by the Murray River and its flood plain.

The Gateway Tourist Information Centre (☎ 1800 800 743), on Lincoln Causeway between Wodonga and the Murray River, has information on both Victoria and NSW, and is open daily from 9 am to 5 pm.

The closest caravan park to the town centre is *Wodonga Caravan & Cabin Park (☎ 6024 2598, 186 Melbourne Rd)*, about 2km west. Sites cost $13 a double, on-site vans are $30 and cabins cost from $35.

There are two hostels across the river in Albury – see the South-West & the Murray section in the NSW chapter.

The *Provincial Motel (☎ 6024 1200, 10 High St)* has rooms from $50 to $60, and the *Terminus Hotel (☎ 6041 3544, 417 Dean St)* charges $30/40 for singles/doubles.

Getting There & Away
There are daily trains to/from Melbourne ($39.90).

WODONGA TO CORRYONG – THE UPPER MURRAY
The Murray Valley Hwy continues east of Wodonga through **Tallangatta**. Seven kilometres east of the town, there's a lookout point from which you can see the streetscape of Old Tallangatta, beneath the waters of the Hume Weir.

There's a turn off to the town of **Granya** 15km east of Tallangatta. About 6km north of Granya is *Herb & Horse (☎ 02-6072 9553)* – run by a friendly family, it's a great place to stay for a while and is popular with travellers. It's an 1890s homestead on a lakeside farm and riding ranch, with home-cooked meals, horse riding and canoe trips. You can stay in the homestead, in the barn or stables, or in a cottage overlooking the river. Shared rooms cost from $25, doubles from $75 and cottages with B&B from $70 per person. They can usually arrange free transport from Albury-Wodonga if you ring in advance.

The small town of **Corryong** is the Victorian gateway to the NSW Snowy Mountains and Mt Kosciuszko National Park. **Jack Riley's Grave**, found in the cemetery at the top of Pioneer Ave, is engraved with the words: 'In memory of the Man from Snowy River, Jack Riley, buried here 16th July 1914'. The **Man from Snowy River Folk Museum**, 55 Hansen St, isn't actually dedicated to the legend, but is more of a local history museum. Still, it houses a fascinating collection of items. It's open from 10 am to noon and 2 to 4 pm (closed between June and August). Admission costs $4.

Goldfields

The Goldfields region of central Victoria is a great area to explore, with quaint townships, impressive regional centres and pretty countryside. Take to the back roads and just go exploring. If you have a few days you could even hire a gypsy caravan. The *Colonial Way* (☎ *5437 3054*) rents caravans pulled by Clydesdale horses. The caravans sleep up to five and cost between $620 and $820 a week.

There's still gold in them thar hills. Metal detectors and other prospecting gear can be bought or hired in many towns.

Central Victoria is a major wine-producing area. The main regions are the Pyrenees Ranges near Avoca, the Heathcote region and around Bendigo.

The Goldfields Tourist Route takes in all the major gold-rush centres. A route map is available from most of the tourist information centres along the way.

BALLARAT
• postcode 3353   • pop 65,000
The area around present-day Ballarat was known to the local Kooris as 'Ballaarat' (resting place). European pastoralists arrived in 1837.

When gold was discovered at nearby Buninyong in 1851, thousands of diggers flooded into the area. After the alluvial goldfields were played out, deep shaft mines were

sunk, striking incredibly rich quartz reefs. The mines were worked until the end of WWI.

Ballarat grew into a major provincial town and there is a wealth of Victorian architecture here.

Information
The visitor information centre (☎ 5332 2694), on the corner of Sturt and Albert Sts, is open daily from 9 am to 5 pm.

The RACV (☎ 5332 1946), 20 Doveton St North, has an accommodation-booking service. Parks Victoria (☎ 5333 6782) is on the corner of Doveton and Mair Sts.

The Gold Shop, 8A Lydiard St North, in the old Mining Exchange building, sells miner's rights and rents out metal detectors.

Sovereign Hill Historical Park
This large re-creation of a gold-mining township of the 1860s is the best of its type in Australia. It's a living history museum with people performing their chores dressed in costumes of the time. You can pan for gold, and may find a speck or two.

Sovereign Hill is open daily from 10 am to 5 pm and admission is $18.50 for adults, $13.50 for students, $9 for children and $48 for families.

Sovereign Hill opens at night for the sound-and-light show 'Blood on the Southern Cross'; a simulation of the Eureka Stockade battle. It runs twice nightly from Monday to Saturday – commencement times depend on the time of sunset. Show-only tickets are $22.50; dinner-and-show costs $41. Bookings are essential – phone ☎ 5333 5777.

Gold Museum
Over the road from Sovereign Hill, this excellent museum has imaginative displays and gold nuggets and coins. It's open daily from 9.30 am to 5.20 pm. Admission is included in the Sovereign Hill ticket, or separate admission costs $5.

Ballarat Fine Art Gallery
This is the oldest and one of the best provincial galleries in the country. It's at 40 Lydiard St North and opens daily from 10.30 am to 5 pm ($4).

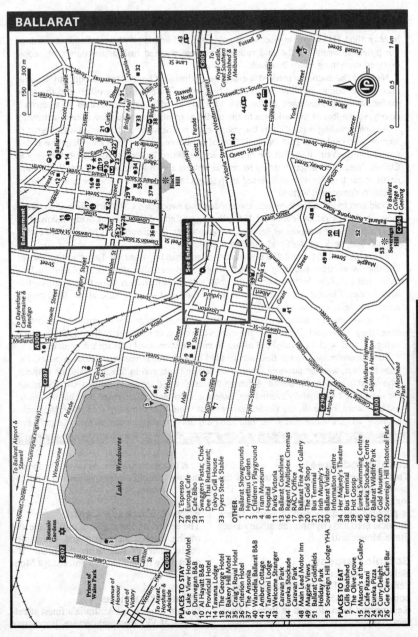

BALLARAT

Enlargement

See Enlargement

0 150 300 m

0 0.5 1 km

VICTORIA

To Daylesford;
Castlemaine & Bendigo

To Ballarat Airport &
Stawell

To Ararat;
Horsham &
Adelaide

To Kryal Castle,
Great Southern
Woolshed &
Melbourne

To Midland Highway,
Skipton & Hamilton

To Morshead
Park

To Ballarat
College &
Geelong

PLACES TO STAY
6   Lake View Hotel/Motel
9   Sunvegas B&B
10 Ai Hyatt B&B
12 Provincial Hotel
14 Tawana Lodge
18 The George Hotel
32 Bakery Hill Motel
35 Craig's Royal Hotel
36 Criterion Hotel
37 The Ansonia
40 Wandella Ballarat B&B
41 Amber Cottage
42 Tarwinni Lodge
43 Welcome Stranger
44 Eureka Stockade
     Caravan Park
48 Main Lead Motor Inn
49 Magpie Views
51 Ballarat Goldfields
     Holiday Park
53 Sovereign Hill Lodge YHA

PLACES TO EAT
5   Gills Boatshed
7   The Olive Grove
15 Mason's at the Gallery
23 Café Pazani
24 Eureka Pizza
25 Curry Delight
26 Gee Cees Cafe Bar

27 L'Espresso
28 Europa Cafe
29 Sweet Bito
31 Sweigers Pasta; Chok
     Dee Thai Restaurant;
     Tokyo Grill House
33 Dyers Steak Stable

OTHER
1   Ballarat Showgrounds
2   Hymettus Garden
3   Children's Playground
4   Tram Museum
8   Hospital
11 Parks Victoria
13 Ballarat Coachlines
16 Regent Multiplex Cinemas
17 RACV Office
19 Ballarat Fine Art Gallery
20 The Gold Shop
21 Fish Murphy's
22 Train Terminal
30 Ballarat Visitor
     Information Centre
34 Her Majesty's Theatre
38 Bus Terminal
39 Hot Gossip
45 Eureka Swimming Centre
46 Eureka Stockade Centre
47 Ballarat Wildlife Park
50 Gold Museum
52 Sovereign Hill Historical Park

Gold Fever

In May 1851 EH Hargraves discovered gold near Bathurst in NSW. Sensational accounts of the potential wealth of the find caused an unprecedented rush as thousands of people dropped everything to try their luck.

News of the discovery reached Melbourne at the same time as the accounts of its influence on the people of NSW. Sydney had been virtually denuded of workers and the same misfortune soon threatened Melbourne. Victoria was still being established as a separate colony, so the loss of its workforce to the northern goldfields would have been disastrous.

A public meeting was called by the young city's businessmen and a reward was offered to anyone who could find gold within 300km of Melbourne. In less than a week gold was discovered in the Yarra River but the find was soon eclipsed by a more significant discovery at Clunes. Prospectors began heading to central Victoria and over the next few months the rush north across the Murray was reversed as fresh gold finds and new rushes became an almost weekly occurrence in Victoria.

Gold was found in the Pyrenees, the Loddon and Avoca rivers, at Warrandyte and at Bunninyong. At Ballarat, in September 1851, the biggest gold discovery was made, followed by other significant discoveries at Bendigo, Mt Alexander, Beechworth, Walhalla, Omeo and in the hills and creeks of the Great Dividing Range.

By the end of 1851 about 250,000 ounces of gold had been claimed. Farms and businesses lost their workforces and in many cases were abandoned altogether as employers had no choice but to follow their workers to the goldfields. Hopeful miners came from England, Ireland, Europe, China and the failing goldfields of California – during 1852 about 1800 people arrived in Melbourne each week.

The government introduced a licence fee of 30 shillings a month for all prospectors, whether or not they found gold. This entitled the miners to a claim, limited to eight feet square, in which to dig for gold, and it provided the means to enforce improvised laws for the goldfields.

The administration of each field was headed by a chief commissioner whose deputies, the state troopers, were empowered to organise licence hunts and to fine or imprison any miner who failed to produce the permit. Although this later caused serious unrest on the diggings, for the most part it successfully averted the lawlessness that had characterised the California rush.

There were, however, the classic features that seem to accompany gold fever: the backbreaking work, the unwholesome food and hard drinking and the primitive dwellings. There

Lake Wendouree

This large artificial lake was used as the rowing course in the 1956 Olympics. The jogging and walking track around the lake is popular, and a favourite training venue for local hero and Olympic marathon runner Steve Moneghetti.

Botanic Gardens

Ballarat's excellent 40 hectare botanic gardens are beside Lake Wendouree. You can come face to face with the likes of Paul Keating and John Howard in Prime Ministers' Avenue, a collection of bronze busts.

A tourist tramway runs on weekends and during school holidays, departing from the tram museum.

Eureka Stockade Centre

The centre, on Eureka St, stands on the site of the Eureka Rebellion and has multimedia galleries simulating the battle. It's open daily from 9 am to 5 pm, except Monday ($8/4).

Other Attractions

Lydiard St is one of Australia's finest streetscapes of Victorian architecture. Impressive

Gold Fever

was the amazing wealth that was to be the luck of some, but the elusive dream of others; and for every story of success there were hundreds more of hardship, despair and death.

In *Australia Illustrated*, published in 1873, Edwin Carton Booth wrote of the 1850s goldfields:

> ... it may be fairly questioned whether in any community in the world there ever existed more of intense suffering, unbridled wickedness and positive want, than in Victoria at **that** time ... To look at the thousands of people who in those years crowded Melbourne, and that most miserable adjunct of Melbourne, Canvas Town, induced the belief that sheer and absolute unfitness for a useful life in the colonies ... had been deemed the only qualification requisite to make a fortunate digger.

The gold rush had its share of rogues, including the notorious bushrangers who attacked gold shipments being escorted to Melbourne, but it also had its heroes who eventually forced a change in the political fabric of the colony (see The Eureka Rebellion in the Ballarat section).

Above all, the gold rush ushered in a fantastic era of growth and material prosperity for Victoria and opened up vast areas of country previously unexplored by white people.

In the first 12 years of the rush, Australia's population increased from 400,000 to well over a million, and in Victoria alone it rose from 77,000 to 540,000. To cope with the moving population and the tonnes of gold and supplies, the development of roads and railways was accelerated.

The mining companies that followed the independent diggers invested heavily in the region over the next couple of decades. The huge shantytowns of tents, bark huts, raucous bars and police camps were eventually replaced by the timber and stone buildings that were the foundation of many of Victoria's provincial cities, most notably Ballarat, Bendigo, Maldon and Castlemaine.

The gold towns reached the height of splendour in the 1880s. Gold production gradually lost its importance after that time, but by then the towns of the region had stable populations, and agriculture and other activities steadily supplanted gold as the economic mainstay.

Gold also made Melbourne Australia's largest city and financial centre, a position it held for nearly half a century.

VICTORIA

buildings include Her Majesty's Theatre, the art gallery and Craig's Royal Hotel. A brochure is available from the information centre.

Ballarat Wildlife Park, on the corner of York and Fussel Sts, East Ballarat, has native animals and reptiles, and a few exotics. Guided tours are held daily at 11 am; on weekends there is a koala show at 2 pm, a wombat show at 2.30 pm and crocodile-feeding at 3 pm. The park is open daily from 9 am to 5.30 am ($10.50/5).

The Great Southern Woolshed, on the Western Hwy on the eastern outskirts of town, has shearing demos, trained dogs and woolly displays ($9/4). **Kryal Castle** is a kitsch but popular attraction, no doubt helped along by the hangings and whippings. The castle is 8km from Ballarat, towards Melbourne, and is open daily from 9.30 am to 5.30 pm ($12.50/7, less on weekdays outside school holidays).

Special Events

Ballarat's 100-year-old Begonia Festival (early March) attracts thousands of visitors. The Eureka Jazz Festival is held in April. In September/October the Royal South St

Eisteddfod is held – during this time accommodation can be hard to find.

Places to Stay

Camping & Caravan Parks *Ballarat Goldfields Holiday Park* (☎ 5332 7888, 108 Clayton St) is the closest to Sovereign Hill and has sites from $14, on-site vans from $37 and cabins from $45. Also convenient is the *Eureka Stockade Caravan Park* (☎ 5331 2281), Stawell St South, with sites for $11 and on-site vans from $25.

Welcome Stranger Caravan Park (☎ 5332 7722), 3km east of the city centre on the corner of Water St and Scott Parade, has excellent facilities. Sites are $14.50 and on-site vans and cabins range from $37 to $55.

Hostel & Pubs Adjacent to Sovereign Hill and off Magpie St, *Sovereign Hill Lodge YHA* (☎ 5333 3409) has dorm beds for $16 ($19 for nonmembers), singles/doubles from $27/46 (with bathroom from $86/95). It's excellent and often full.

The *Provincial Hotel* (☎ 5332 1845, 121 Lydiard St North), opposite Ballarat train station, has rooms for $20/40. The *Criterion Hotel* (☎ 5331 1451, 18 Doveton St South) charges $26/42.

Some of Ballarat's grand old pubs have been restored. The best is *Craig's Royal Hotel* (☎ 5331 1377, 10 Lydiard St South). There are old-fashioned rooms for $40, en suite rooms from $70 to $90 and suites from $120 to $160. The *George Hotel* (☎ 5333 4866, 27 Lydiard St North) has rooms (including breakfast) from $35/50, or $50/65 with bathroom.

Motels One of the cheapest central options is the *Lake View Hotel/Motel* (☎ 5331 4592, 22 Wendouree Parade), which charges from $50/60. Beside the train station, *Tawana Lodge* (☎ 5331 3461) is a ramshackle old private hotel/motel with rooms from $25/40 with shared bathrooms and motel-style rooms for $49/58.

One of the best and most central motels is the *Bakery Hill Motel* (☎ 5333 1363, 1 Humffray St), charging from $76/88.

B&Bs Sprawling *Wandella Ballarat Bed & Breakfast* (☎ 5333 7046, 202 Dawson St South) has rooms from $28.50/44.50. Quite a few old homes have been converted into B&Bs. Two goodies are *Dunvegan B&B* (☎ 5332 2505, 806 Mair St), from $75/100, and *Al Hayatt B&B* (☎ 5332 1396, 800 Mair St), from $70/90.

Places to Eat

L'Espresso (☎ 5333 1789, 417 Sturt St) has good food and coffee. Nearby, *Europa Cafe* serves all-day breakfasts, lunches such as Turkish *pide* or Spanish omelettes, and Mediterranean-style evening mains from $15 to $18. Also good for a meal is *Gee Cees Cafe Bar* (427 Sturt St).

Further east is the hip *Cafe Bibo* (205 Sturt St). Across the road, *Cafe Pazani* (102 Sturt St) is a bar/restaurant with in-vogue food.

There's a cluster of eateries in Bridge Mall. *Chok Dee Thai Restaurant* (☎ 5331 7361, 113 Bridge Mall) has Thai mains between $12 and $16. Next door is *Tokyo Grill House* (☎ 5333 3945), with dishes in the $15 to $19 range, or banquet menus between $22 and $37.

The best place for a steak is *Dyers Steak Stable* (☎ 5331 2850, 28 Little Bridge St), where you'll pay between $17 and $40.

There are plenty of cheap pub meals. The bistro at the *Lake View Hotel/Motel*, by the lake on Wendouree Parade, is popular. *Gills Boatshed*, nearby, serves snacks and drinks.

Entertainment

Hot Gossip (102 Dana St) plays funky dance music and has occasional bands. Also popular is *21 Arms* (21 Armstrong St). The *George Hotel* (☎ 5333 4866, 27 Lydiard St North) is one of the better venues for bands, as is *Irish Murphy's* (36 Sturt St).

Her Majesty's Theatre (☎ 5333 5800, 17 Lydiard St South) is Ballarat's main venue for the performing arts, and the main cinema complex is the *Regent Multiplex Cinemas* (☎ 5331 1399, 49 Lydiard St North).

Getting There & Away

Ballarat train station is off Lydiard St North. Trains run frequently between Melbourne

The Eureka Rebellion

Life on the goldfields was a great leveller, erasing all pre-existing social classes as doctors, merchants, ex-convicts and labourers toiled side by side in the mud. But as the easily won gold began to run out, the diggers began to recognise the inequalities between themselves and the privileged few who held land and government.

The limited size of claims, the inconvenience of licence hunts (see the 'Gold Fever' boxed text earlier in this chapter), coupled with the police brutality that often accompanied searches, the very fact that while they were in effect paying taxes they were allowed no political representation, and the realisation that they could not get good farming land, fired unrest among the miners and led to the Eureka Rebellion at Ballarat.

In September 1854 Governor Hotham ordered that the hated licence hunts be carried out twice a week. A month later a miner was murdered near a Ballarat hotel after an argument with the owner, James Bentley.

When Bentley was found not guilty, by a magistrate who just happened to be his business associate, a group of miners rioted over the injustice and burned his hotel. Bentley was re-tried and found guilty, but the rioting miners were also jailed, which fuelled their mounting distrust of the authorities.

Creating the Ballarat Reform League, the diggers called for the abolition of licence fees, the introduction of the miner's right to vote and increased opportunities to purchase land.

On 29 November about 800 miners tossed their licences into a bonfire during a mass meeting, and then set about building a stockade at Eureka where, led by the Irishman, Peter Lalor, they prepared to fight for their rights.

On 3 December, having already organised brutal licence hunts, the government ordered troopers to attack the stockade. There were only 150 diggers within the makeshift barricades at the time, and the fight lasted only 20 minutes, leaving 30 miners and five troopers dead.

Although the rebellion was short-lived, the miners were ultimately successful in their protest. They had won the sympathy of most Victorians, and had the full support of the goldfields' population behind them. The government deemed it wise to acquit the leaders of the charge of high treason.

The licence fee was abolished and replaced by a miner's right, which cost one pound a year. This gave the right to search for gold; the right to fence in, cultivate and build a dwelling on a moderate-sized piece of land; and the right to vote for members of the Legislative Assembly. The rebel miner Peter Lalor actually became a member of parliament himself some years later.

Norman Lindsay's *Peter Lalor* in watercolour and chalk

COURTESY BALLARAT FINE ART GALLERY; COPYRIGHT: HELEN, CATHERINE & ANDREW GLAD

VICTORIA

and Ballarat, taking about 1¾ hours ($13.80). Buses run to Ararat ($11.20) and Stawell ($15.20).

V/Line has daily buses to Geelong ($9.80) and Mildura ($46.90) via St Arnaud ($16.50), and weekday services to Warrnambool ($18), Hamilton ($24.50), Maryborough ($7.50) and Bendigo ($18) via Daylesford ($8.60) and Castlemaine ($13.80).

Passing through on the Melbourne-Adelaide run, McCafferty's and Greyhound buses stop at the train station.

Getting Around

Ballarat Transit (☎ 5331 7777) has two main terminals on either side of Bridge Mall; one in Curtis St and one in Little Bridge St. The information centre and the train station have timetables. Bus No 2 goes to the train station, No 15 goes to the botanic gardens and Lake Wendouree, and Nos 9 and 10 go to Sovereign Hill.

For a cab, call Ballarat Taxis (☎ 131 008).

CLUNES
● postcode 3370   ● pop 850
Clunes, a charming little town 32km north of Ballarat, was the site of Victoria's first significant gold discovery in June 1851. There is a small museum, the **William Barkell Arts & Historic Centre**, at 36 Fraser St.

Nearby **Mt Beckworth** is noted for its orchids and birdlife, and you can visit the old gold diggings of **Jerusalem** and **Ullina**.

Clunes Caravan Park (☎ 5345 3278), Purcell St, has sites from $8 and on-site vans and cabins from $30 to $40 a double.

DAYLESFORD & HEPBURN SPRINGS
● postcode 3460   ● pop 6000
The twin towns of Daylesford and Hepburn Springs are enjoying a revival as the 'spa centre of Victoria', a claim that was first made as long ago as the 1870s.

As well as attracting visitors from Melbourne, this area attracts escapees from the city rat race, and the population is an interesting blend of old-timers and alternative-lifestylers. There's a thriving gay and lesbian scene.

Daylesford is the larger of the towns; Hepburn Springs is a residential settlement just north of Daylesford. The visitor information centre (☎ 5348 1339) is next to the post office on Vincent St; it's open daily from 9 am to 5 pm.

Things to See & Do

Hepburn Spa Resort (☎ 5348 2034) is an impressive centre with services including heated spas, plunge pools, floatation tanks, beauty treatments, massages and saunas. A splash around in the indoor pool and spa costs $9, aero spas with oils cost $21/30 for singles/doubles, massages start at $36 and floatation tanks are $50 an hour. It gets pretty packed on weekends; prices are lower during the week.

The complex is open on weekdays from 10 am to 8 pm and weekends from 9 am to 8 pm.

In the reserve around the spa are a number of **mineral springs**, most pretty strong in flavour.

There are some good **walking trails**. The information centre has maps and guides.

The **Convent Gallery**, Daly St, is a massive 19th century convent converted into a craft and art gallery ($3). Lovely **Wombat Hill Botanic Gardens** is on top of the hill in Central Springs Rd and you can climb a tower for fine views.

At **Lake Daylesford** boats and kayaks can be hired. Even prettier is **Jubilee Lake**, about 3km south-east of town.

The **Historical Society Museum**, 100 Vincent St, is open on weekend afternoons and during school holidays ($2.50).

The **Central Highlands Tourist Railway** (☎ 5348 3503) has rides on old trains on Sunday between 10 am and 2.45 pm ($5). Also on Sunday morning at the train station, the **Daylesford Sunday Market** is held.

Places to Stay

There's a lot of accommodation, mostly pricey. It's impossible to list every place so check with the information centre or one of the agencies in town.

On weekends and during holidays, many places stipulate a minimum two-night stay.

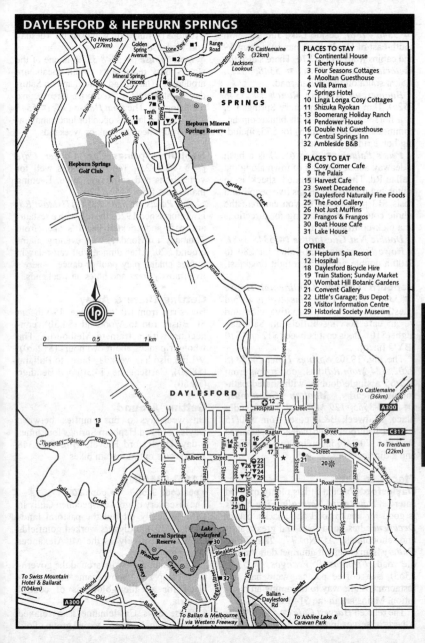

DAYLESFORD & HEPBURN SPRINGS

PLACES TO STAY
1 Continental House
2 Liberty House
3 Four Seasons Cottages
4 Mooltan Guesthouse
6 Villa Parma
7 Springs Hotel
10 Linga Longa Cosy Cottages
11 Shizuka Ryokan
13 Boomerang Holiday Ranch
14 Pendower House
16 Double Nut Guesthouse
17 Central Springs Inn
32 Ambleside B&B

PLACES TO EAT
8 Cosy Corner Cafe
9 The Palais
15 Harvest Cafe
23 Sweet Decadence
24 Daylesford Naturally Fine Foods
25 The Food Gallery
26 Not Just Muffins
27 Frangos & Frangos
30 Boat House Cafe
31 Lake House

OTHER
5 Hepburn Spa Resort
12 Hospital
18 Daylesford Bicycle Hire
19 Train Station; Sunday Market
20 Wombat Hill Botanic Gardens
21 Convent Gallery
22 Little's Garage; Bus Depot
28 Visitor Information Centre
29 Historical Society Museum

HEPBURN SPRINGS

Hepburn Mineral Springs Reserve

Hepburn Springs Golf Club

DAYLESFORD

To Newstead (27km)

To Castlemaine (32km)

Jacksons Lookout

To Castlemaine (36km)

To Trentham (22km)

To Swiss Mountain Hotel & Ballarat (104km)

To Ballan & Melbourne via Western Freeway

To Jubilee Lake & Caravan Park

Ballan - Daylesford Rd

Lake Daylesford

Central Springs Reserve

0   0.5   1 km

VICTORIA

Daylesford *Jubilee Lake Caravan Park* (☎ *5348 2186*), beside Lake Jubilee, 3km south-east of Daylesford, has sites from $9 and cabins from $35 to $70. There's also the *Victoria Caravan Park* (☎ *5348 3821*), 1.5km south on the Ballan road.

Boomerang Holiday Ranch (☎ *5348 2525*), 1km west on Tipperary Springs Rd, is a horse-riding farm with bunkroom accommodation (BYO linen) for $75, including horse riding and meals.

Pete's Palace (☎ *5348 6531*) is a bush hideaway about 5km out of town along the Ballan Rd. The self-contained 'shack' is no Hilton but it's cosy. It sleeps five people and costs $13 per person, or you can rent the whole cottage for $50. Ring for directions or a pick-up from town.

Double Nut Guesthouse (☎ *5348 3981, 5 Howe St)* is excellent value for $80 to $100 a double, including a light breakfast.

Hepburn Springs *Continental House* (☎ *5348 2005, 9 Lone Pine Ave)* is an old guesthouse with an alternative vibe and vegan cafe serving buffets on Saturday night ($10). Beds cost between $12 and $20 (BYO linen).

The big, 1930s *Springs Hotel* (☎ *5348 2202, 124 Main Rd)* has good rooms from $55/65 a single/double, with shared bathrooms. Nearby, *Mooltan Guesthouse* (☎ *5348 3555, 129 Main Rd)* is a friendly place. Midweek B&B costs from $50/75 (shared bathroom) and weekend packages start at $170/240, including two breakfasts and a dinner.

Places to Eat

Daylesford Vincent St has plenty of good eateries. *Daylesford Naturally Fine Foods* is good for health food and snacks. *Sweet Decadence* has good food and great cakes and chocolates. At No 77, *The Food Gallery* is an excellent gourmet deli. Across the road, *Frangos & Frangos* (☎ *5348 2363)* is a coffee palace, wine bar and restaurant, on its way to becoming an institution. Mains are in the $14 to $25 range.

The relaxed *Harvest Cafe* (☎ *5348 3994)*, Albert St, serves innovative vegetarian and 'aquatic' cuisine. Evening mains are in the $10 to $14 range. It is closed on Tuesday and Wednesday.

Lake House (☎ *5348 3329)* is one of the state's best restaurants. Main meals are around $25 (lunch and dinner) and on Saturday night there's a fixed price three course menu for $58. The *Boat House Cafe* (☎ *5348 1387)*, by the lake, is open for lunch and dinner – you'll need to book on weekends.

Hepburn Springs *Cosy Corner Cafe* (☎ *5348 3825)*, Tenth St, caters well for vegetarians and carnivores alike. Evening mains cost from $15 to $20.

The Palais (☎ *5348 1254, 111 Main Rd)* is a refurbished 1920s theatre with a restaurant, cafe and cocktail bar. It's open from Thursday to Monday, with evening mains around $20. After dinner, you can relax in lounge chairs, play pool or dance – there's live (mostly) jazz and blues on weekends.

Getting There & Away

Buses run from Little's garage, 45 Vincent St. Buses run to Woodend ($4.30), connecting with a train to Melbourne. The whole trip takes about two hours ($12.20). V/Line also has weekday buses to Ballarat ($8.60), Castlemaine ($4.30) and Bendigo ($8.60).

Getting Around

On weekdays a bus shuttles between Daylesford and Hepburn Springs four times a day. Daylesford Bicycle Hire (☎ 5348 1518) rents out mountain bikes.

CASTLEMAINE

● postcode 3450   ● pop 6700

The discovery of gold at Specimen Gully in 1851 radically altered the pastoral landscape as 30,000 diggers worked goldfields known collectively as the Mt Alexander Diggings.

Castlemaine grew up around the government camp and soon became the marketplace for all the goldfields of central Victoria.

These days Castlemaine is a relaxed country town, home to a varied group of old and new citizens. In April in odd-numbered years Castlemaine hosts the **State Festival**, one of Victoria's leading arts events.

The visitor information centre (☎ 5470 6200), in the Castlemaine Market building on Mostyn St, is open daily from 9 am to 5 pm.

Things to See

Dating from 1861, **Buda**, on the corner of Hunter and Urquhart Sts, was home to a Hungarian silversmith and then his descendants for 120 years. The family's art and craft collections and personal belongings are on display. It's open daily and admission is (a rather steep) $7 for adults and $3 for children.

The impressive **Castlemaine Art Gallery & Historical Museum**, Lyttleton St, has a collection of colonial and contemporary art. It's open weekdays and weekend afternoons ($3).

The imposing **Old Castlemaine Gaol** provides excellent views of the town from a hilltop on Bowden St. Guided tours are available on weekends at 11 am and 1 and 3 pm ($4).

Places to Stay

There's a lot of accommodation and we can't list everything, so check with the tourist centre for other options. There's also a booking service (☎ 5470 5866).

Botanic Gardens Caravan Park (☎ 5472 1125, Walker St), next to the gardens and swimming pool, has sites from $10 and onsite vans from $31.

The **Commercial Hotel** (☎ 5472 1173), on the corner of Forest and Hargreaves Sts, has basic rooms for $30/45 a single/double. The **Northern Hotel** (☎ 5472 1102, 359 Barker St) charges $20/30.

Campbell St Motor Lodge (☎ 5472 3477, 33 Campbell St) is in a building dating from 1886. The interior is relatively bland, but it's pleasant, with doubles from $65 to $85 and family units for $115. **Castlemaine Colonial Motel** (☎ 5472 4000, 252 Barker St) charges from $66/76.

The **Midland Private Hotel** (☎ 5472 1085, 2-4 Templeton St) has been sheltering travellers since 1879, and has good value rooms for $60/90 (shared bathrooms), with breakfast. **The Old Castlemaine Gaol**

(☎ 5470 5311), on the corner of Bowden and Charles Sts, has B&B in converted cells for $45 per person, or $65 with dinner. **Broadoaks** (☎ 5470 5827, 31 Gingell St) was the last home of Robert O'Hara Burke (of Burke and Wills), who was superintendent of police in Castlemaine before setting out on his ill-fated journey. Doubles cost $85, including breakfast.

Self-contained **Kraus Cottage** (☎ 5472 1936, Wills St) charges $70 a double, plus $10 for each extra person (sleeps four).

Places to Eat

Saffs Cafe (64 Mostyn St) serves breakfast, snacks and good coffee. **Tog's Place** (58 Lyttleton St) has light, healthy meals for around $9. **The Screaming Carrot Cafe & Sourdough Bakery** (☎ 5470 6555, 16 Lyttleton St) is a collectively-run vegetarian cafe, open from 10 am to 5.30 pm Wednesday and Thursday, and from 10 am until late on Friday and Saturday.

At the Theatre Royal, **The Mad Cow** is a good place for a meal before, or a nightcap after, the movies.

Pub grub is plentiful. The **Criterion Hotel**, on the corner of Mostyn and Barker Sts, and the **Bridge Hotel** (21 Walker St) have bar meals for $5.

Entertainment

At **Theatre Royal** (☎ 5472 1196, 30-34 Hargreaves St), patrons can dine while the movie's showing and dance afterwards. It's open Wednesday to Saturday.

Bands play at the **Criterion Hotel** on weekends.

Getting There & Away

Daily trains run between Melbourne and Castlemaine ($15.20) and continue on to Bendigo ($4.30) and Swan Hill ($26.90).

Weekday buses run to Daylesford ($4.30), Ballarat ($13.80) and Geelong ($24.50).

MALDON

● postcode 3463   ● pop 1250

The population of Maldon is a tiny proportion of the 20,000 who once worked the goldfields. The town is a well preserved relic of the era, and the National Trust has declared it a 'notable town'.

The visitor information centre (☎ 5475 2569), at the shire offices in High St, is open daily from 9 am to 5 pm. Pick up the *Information Guide* and *Historic Town Walk* brochures.

The **historical museum**, in the old marketplace in High St, has an interesting collection and is open in the afternoon. **Carmen's Tunnel Goldmine**, 2km south of town off Parkin's Reef Rd, was excavated in the 1880s, and tours run on weekends and during school holidays between 1.30 and 4 pm ($3.50/1.50).

Steam-train trips run on Sunday and Wednesday ($10 for adults, $6 for children and $29 for families). **Porcupine Township**, 2.5km out on the Bendigo road, is a re-created gold-mining village, open daily from 10 am to 5 pm. Admission is $7/5 and $20 for families.

The excellent **Maldon Folk Festival** is held in early November.

Places to Stay

Maldon Caravan Park (☎ 5475 2344), Hospital St, has sites from $10 and on-site vans and cabins from $29 to $48. *Derby Hill Accommodation Centre* (☎ 5475 2033), Phoenix St, is mostly used for youth camps but motel-style rooms are available on weekends and in school holidays for $30 per adult.

Even the motels in this town have appeal. *Maldon's Eaglehawk* (☎ 5475 2750, 35 Reff St) has comfortable units in pleasant grounds, with doubles from $84.

Other accommodation is mainly up-market B&Bs. Listed here is a small selection; check with the information centre for others. *The Barn & Loft* (☎ 5475 2015, 64 Main St) is a two-storey barn with two guest units. Doubles range from $85 to $95, including breakfast.

Other B&Bs include the grand *Calder House* (☎ 5475 2912, 44 High St), charging from $70/95 to $95/120 a single/double; and *McArthur's B&B* (☎ 5475 2519, 43 Main St), behind the restaurant of the same name, with doubles from $75.

There are plenty of self-contained cottages, many managed by Heritage Cottages of Maldon (☎ 5475 1094).

Places to Eat

There are several cafes and tearooms along the main street. The *Kangaroo Hotel*, High St, has a cosy bar and excellent bistro, with mains from $9 to $16.

McArthur's (☎ 5475 2519, 43 Main St) is an old-fashioned restaurant with everything from toasted sandwiches to whole trout; evening mains cost from $13 to $16. *Ruby's at Calder House* (☎ 5475 2912, 44 High St) is one of the state's best restaurants. Vegetarians are catered for and mains range from $15 to $20.

Getting There & Away

Castlemaine Bus Lines (☎ 5472 1455) runs two buses on weekdays between Maldon and Castlemaine ($2.80), which connect with the trains to and from Melbourne. The total journey takes about two hours.

MARYBOROUGH

● postcode 3465   ● pop 7400

Gold was discovered at White Hills and Four Mile Flat in 1854. A police camp at the diggings was named Maryborough, and at the height of the gold rush the population was over 40,000.

Built in 1892, **Maryborough Railway Station** was described by Mark Twain as 'a train station with a town attached'. It now houses the tourist information centre (☎ 5460 4511), open from 9 am to 5 pm, a mammoth antique emporium, gallery and cafe. **Worsley Cottage**, Palmerston St, is the historical society museum, open on Sunday afternoon.

Maryborough has held a **Highland Gathering** on New Year's Day since 1857.

Places to Stay & Eat

Maryborough Caravan Park (☎ 5460 4848, 7 Holyrood St), by a lake, has sites for $10 and cabins from $40 to $60.

The historic *Bull & Mouth Hotel* (☎ 5461 1002, 119 High St) has decent pub rooms for $30 a double; $40 with bathroom.

Cheapest of the motels is **Wattle Grove Motel** (☎ *5461 1877*), on the Ballarat road, with rooms from $42/48. Four kilometres south of town on Majorca Rd, **Davoren** (☎ *5461 2934*) is a mud-brick and stone cottage – good value for $70 a double.

In the station complex, **The Station Cafe** is a good daytime cafe. **Moonlight Inn** (☎ *5461 4598*), 5km west of town off the Avoca road, is an excellent French restaurant (BYO alcohol). Entrees are $10 and main meals around $18. It's signposted but hard to find, so phone for directions, and you'll need to book.

AVOCA & PYRENEES RANGES

Avoca is a small town and the centre of a rapidly expanding wine-growing region. The information centre (☎ 5465 3767), by the post office, is open most days from 10 am to 4 pm. Pick up the *Pyrenees & Grampians Wine Trail* brochure.

Mt Avoca, the highest peak in the nearby Pyrenees Ranges, reaches 760m. There are walking tracks, including the 18km **Pyrenees Trail**, which starts from the Waterfall Picnic Area 7km west of Avoca.

BENDIGO
● postcode 3550   ● pop 60,000

When gold was discovered at Ravenswood in 1851, thousands upon thousands of diggers converged on the fantastically rich Bendigo Diggings. The arrival of thousands of Chinese miners in 1854 had a lasting effect on the town and Bendigo still has a rich Chinese heritage.

During the boom years between the 1860s and 1880s mining companies poured money into the town; many examples of their fine Victorian architecture can still be seen. By the 1860s the surface gold was running out and deep mining began. Today Bendigo is a prosperous provincial city.

Information

The visitor information centre (☎ 5444 4445) and interpretive centre in the former post office on Pall Mall, opens daily from 9 am to 5 pm. The RACV (☎ 5443 9622) office is at 112 Mitchell St, and the Parks Victoria office (☎ 5444 6620) is at 57 View St.

Open-crown pediment on old National Bank of Australasia building in Bendigo

Chinese Joss House

The Chinese Joss House, on Finn St in North Bendigo, is one of the few remaining practising joss houses in Victoria. It is open daily from 10 am to 5 pm (4 pm in winter); admission costs $3.

Central Deborah Gold Mine

This 500m deep mine opened in the 1940s, and was connected to the two other Deborah shafts that date back to the early goldfield days. About 1000kg of gold was removed before it closed in 1954. The mine is being reworked and is also a tourist attraction. It's in Violet St, open daily from 9 am to 5 pm. You can take a self-guided surface tour ($6) or a 70 minute underground tour ($15.50/8). A combined ticket for the mine tour plus a ride on the 'talking tram' costs $21/11.

Talking Tram

A vintage tram makes a regular run from the Central Deborah mine, through the centre of the city and out to the tramways museum (free entry if you have a tram ticket) and the Chinese Joss House, with a commentary along the way ($8/4.50). It departs weekdays at 9.30 and 11.30 am and 1.30 and 3 pm from the Central Deborah mine, five minutes later from the Alexandra Fountain. On weekends, the tram departs every hour between 9.30 am and 3.30 pm (except 12.30 pm).

There's also **Bendigo Double-Decker Bus Tours** (☎ 5441 6969), which shuttles around the major sights. Tickets cost $8/4 and you can get on and off anywhere along the route.

BENDIGO

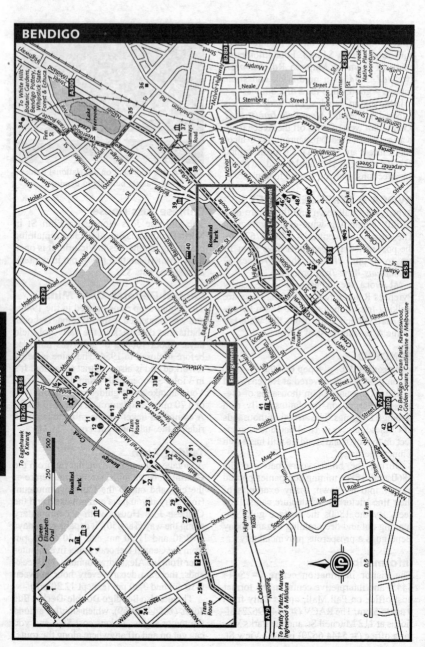

BENDIGO

PLACES TO STAY		15	Darby O'Gills	8	Sundance Saloon
1	Bendigo Central Motor	16	Cafe La Vache	11	Law Courts
	Lodge	17	The House of Khong	12	Visitor Information Centre;
13	Shamrock Hotel	20	Gillies' Pies		Old Post Office
18	Old Crown Hotel	22	Whirrakee Restaurant &	19	Eclipse
23	City Centre Motel		Wine Bar	21	Alexandra Fountain
24	Marlborough House	27	Rasoyee	26	Sacred Heart Cathedral
25	Cathedral Terrace B&B	28	Mexican Kitchen	33	Studio 54
35	Julie-Anna Inn Motel	29	Jo Joe's	34	Chinese Joss House
36	Fleece Inn Hotel	30	Bath Lane Cafe	37	Tramways Museum
38	Jubilee Villa	31	Green Olive Deli	39	Golden Dragon Museum &
42	Central City Caravan Park	32	Cafe au lait		Gardens
46	Hopetoun Hotel	49	Queens Arms Hotel	40	Aquatic Centre
				41	Fortuna Villa
PLACES TO EAT		OTHER		43	Central Deborah Gold Mine
4	Rifle Brigade Pub Brewery	2	Dudley House	44	The Vine
6	Bazzani	3	Bendigo Regional Arts Centre	45	Bendigo Cinemas
9	Clogs		(Capital Theatre)	47	RACV
10	Cafe Kryptonite	5	Bendigo Art Gallery	48	Discovery Science &
14	The Match Bar & Bakehouse	7	Conservatory Gardens		Technology Centre

Bendigo Art Gallery

The Bendigo Art Gallery, 42 View St, has an outstanding collection of Australian art and a surprising collection of 19th century European art. It is open daily from 10 am to 5 pm ($2) and there are guided tours at 2 pm.

Shamrock Hotel

Built in 1897 on the corner of Pall Mall and Williamson St, this is a fine example of Italianate late-Victorian architecture. The story goes that the floors were regularly washed down to collect gold dust brought in on the miners' boots. There are tours on weekends at 2.30 pm ($7.50).

Golden Dragon Museum & Gardens

The excellent Golden Dragon Museum in Bridge St houses the two Chinese processional dragons, Old Loong and Sun Loong (the world's longest dragon), which are the centrepieces of the annual Easter Fair parade. It opens daily from 9.30 am to 5 pm ($6/3 and $18 for a family). There are also Chinese gardens nearby ($2/50c; free with a museum ticket).

Bendigo Pottery

Bendigo Pottery, the oldest pottery works in Australia (1857), is on the Midland Hwy at Epsom, 6km north of Bendigo. There's a cafe, a sales gallery and historic kilns, and you can watch potters at work. It's open daily from 9 am to 5 pm (free entry).

Camel Rides

Sedgwick's Camel Farm (☎ 5439 6367), about 20km south of Bendigo near Sedgwick, offers a range of rides, from 10-minute rides ($7) to overnight treks into the bush ($145). The farm opens on weekends and school holidays between September and May (10 am to 5 pm) and weekdays by appointment. Entry costs $2.

Special Events

The Easter Fair attracts thousands of visitors with its carnival atmosphere and procession of Chinese dragons.

The November 'Swap Meet' attracts tens of thousands of people in search of that elusive vintage car part, and accommodation fills up.

Places to Stay

Camping, Caravan Parks & Hostels
There are about ten caravan parks in the area. *Central City Caravan Park (☎ 5443 6937, 362 High St, Kangaroo Flat)* has a basic hostel section in cabins. Beds cost $12. There are also tent sites for $12 and on-site

VICTORIA

vans and cabins from $32 to $55. It's about 2km south of the centre – you can get there on a Kangaroo Flat bus from Hargreaves St.

Hotels & Motels A good option is the central *Old Crown Hotel (☎ 5441 6888, 238 Hargreaves St)* with pub rooms with shared bathrooms for $30/48 a single/double. The *Fleece Inn Hotel (☎ 5443 3086, 139 Charlston Rd)*, opposite the cattle saleyards, has B&B for $20/40.

The splendid *Shamrock Hotel (☎ 5443 0333)* in Pall Mall has old-fashioned rooms with shared bathroom for $65 a double; motel-style rooms for $95 and suites from $125 to $150.

Two of the cheaper and more central motels are the *City Centre Motel (☎ 5443 2077, 26 Forest St)* and *Bendigo Central Motor Lodge (☎ 5443 9388, 181 View St)*, which have doubles from $55.

Places to Eat

In the Hargreaves St Mall, *Gillies'* pies are a Bendigo institution. You queue at the little window, then sit in the mall to eat your pie.

Good daytime cafes include *Cafe La Vache (47 Bull St)*, *Cafe au lait (20 Mitchell St)*, and *Bath Lane Cafe* and *Green Olive Deli*, both in Bath Lane. Several excellent cafe/restaurants that also open for dinner include *Cafe Kryptonite*, on Pall Mall, sophisticated *Bazzani*, Howard Place, with Italian and Asian influences and *Clogs*, 106 Pall Mall, a stylish pizza restaurant/bar.

There's plenty of pub food. *Darby O'Gills*, on the corner of Bull and Hargreaves Sts, has a good selection from focaccias ($8) to steak and seafood (around $14). They also have live music Thursday to Saturday nights. The *Rifle Brigade Pub Brewery (137 View St)*, has inexpensive bar meals as well as a bistro. Also popular is the corner bistro at the *Shamrock Hotel*.

For good Chinese food, try *The House of Khong (200 Hargreaves St)*, with an $8.50 smorgasbord lunch on weekdays.

Whirrakee Restaurant & Wine Bar (☎ 5441 5557, 17 View St) has a small wine bar and restaurant serving excellent 'modern Australian' cuisine in the $14 to $19 range.

Entertainment

Eclipse, on the corner of Williamson and Hargreaves Sts, has a contemporary hits dance floor on one level and a yesteryear hits disco upstairs. On the corner of Williamson and Queen Sts is *Studio 54*, a huge warehouse-style high-tech place.

One of the best live music venues is *The Vine (135 King St)*. *Sundance Saloon*, on the corner of Pall Mall and Mundy St, has bands on weekends.

Bendigo Regional Arts Centre (☎ 5441 5344, 50 View St), in the restored Capital Theatre, is the main venue for performing arts. *Bendigo Cinemas (☎ 5442 1666)* is at 107 Queen St.

Getting There & Away

Bendigo's train station is in Railway Place off Mitchell St. At least four trains run to Melbourne daily, taking about two hours ($20.80). Stops along the way include Castlemaine ($4.30) and Woodend ($9.80). Trains continue on to Swan Hill ($23.30).

Buses include daily services to Castlemaine ($4); weekday services to Ballarat ($18) and Geelong ($29.30); and Monday to Saturday services to Echuca ($6.10). There are also daily buses to Mildura ($46.90) via Swan Hill ($23.30).

Getting Around

Walkers Buslines (☎ 5443 9333) and Christian's Buslines (☎ 5447 2222) service the area. Timetables are available from the information centre. Tickets cost $1.30 and are valid for two hours.

For a taxi call Bendigo Associated Taxis (☎ 5443 0777).

The High Country

The High Country isn't particularly high in world terms – the highest point, Mt Bogong, reaches 1986m – but it contains some wild and diverse country.

This area offers a huge range of outdoor and adventure activities, including bushwalking, canoeing and white-water rafting, fishing, rock climbing, hang-gliding, para-gliding, horse trekking and skiing in winter.

This is an alpine environment, and weather conditions can change dramatically at any time of year. Bushwalkers should be self-sufficient, with a tent, a fuel stove, a sleeping bag, warm clothes and plenty of water. In summer you can walk all day in the heat without finding water, and then face temperatures below freezing at night.

Orientation & Information

The High Country's major tourist information centres are at Mansfield, Beechworth, Mt Beauty and Bright. The major ski resorts have Alpine Resort Commission (ARC) information offices, most open year-round. There are no banks in any of the ski resorts.

For snow conditions phone ☎ 1902 240 523, or go to the Web site at www.snowreport .vic.gov.au.

Getting There & Away

There are direct V/Line buses from Melbourne and connecting services from the train stations at Benalla and Wangaratta. Services vary seasonally.

Many roads can be impassable during winter. Check road conditions with a recorded information service (☎ 1902 240 523). In winter roads into the ski resorts can only be travelled if chains are carried.

ALPINE NATIONAL PARK

The Alpine National Park (646,000 hectares), joins the high country areas of NSW and the ACT. It is divided into the Bogong, Wonnangatta-Moroka, Cobberas-Tingaringy and Dartmouth areas.

During winter, skiing is the main activity. Most ski resorts are in or near the park, and otherwise the area is largely undeveloped. There are plenty of access roads, although in winter some are closed. Once the snow melts, the area is ideal for a great variety of outdoor activities.

There are a several camping areas and bush camping is allowed in most of the park. The region's many walking tracks include the Australian Alps Walking Track, which extends 655km from Walhalla to the outskirts of Canberra.

Parks Victoria has several offices in the region.

SKI RESORTS

As well as the main ski resorts there are five snowfields offering cross-country skiing or sightseeing, but without accommodation.

The closest snowfield to Melbourne is **Mt Donna Buang**, 95km east via Warburton. It's mainly for sightseeing.

Lake Mountain (☎ 5963 3288), 120km north-east from Melbourne via Marysville, has 40km of groomed cross-country trails.

Mt Stirling is another excellent cross-country area, a few kilometres north-east of Mt Buller Alpine Village, with over 60km of mostly groomed trails. The Mt Buller Rd from Mansfield is the main access route.

Mt St Gwinear (☎ 5165 3204) is 171km from Melbourne via Moe and has cross-country trails connecting with Mt Baw Baw. Around the summit of **Mt Bogong** there are some tough downhill skiing routes for the experienced.

Mt Baw Baw

- **elevation 1564m**

Mt Baw Baw Alpine Village (1480m) is in the Baw Baw National Park. It's good for novice skiers and is more relaxed than the big resorts. It's a three hour drive from Melbourne via Noojee.

The skiable downhill area is 25 hectares and the runs are 25% beginners, 64% intermediate and 11% advanced, with a vertical drop of 140m. It's also a base for cross-country trails, including one connecting to the Mt St Gwinear trails.

There's a small alpine village operating all year, and during the snow season there are places to eat and ski-hire is available.

The ARC information office (☎ 5165 1136, mtbawbaw@bawbawar.com.au) helps with accommodation bookings.

Snow season entry fees are $17 per car for the day car park. The lifts only operate if there is snow and cost $44 a day; lift-and-lesson packages cost $58. The cross-country daily trail fee is $3.

THE HIGH COUNTRY

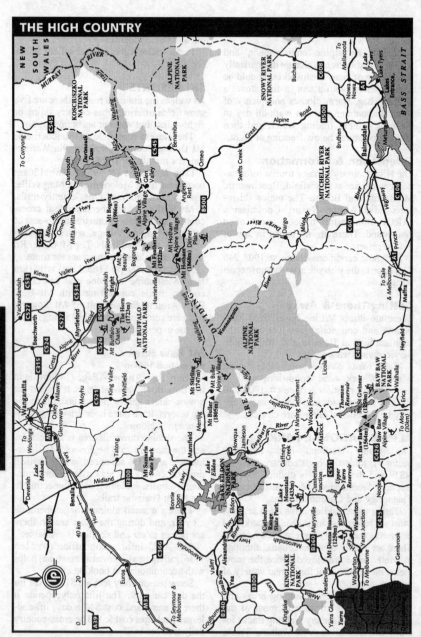

Mt Buller
- **elevation 1805m**

Mt Buller Alpine village (1600m) is Victoria's largest ski resort, 47km west of Mansfield and 237km (less than three hours drive) north-east of Melbourne.

The skiable downhill area is 162 hectares and runs are divided into 25% beginner, 45% intermediate and 30% advanced, with a vertical drop of 400m. Cross-country trails link Mt Buller with Mt Stirling.

Only a few restaurants, bars and places to stay are open outside the ski season. Horsehill Chairlift also runs during January and most weekends in February and March.

Raw NRG Mt Buller (☎ 5777 6887), in 'The Tunnel' Village Centre, rents out mountain bikes from $16 per hour and has one to four-day bike tours outside the ski season.

Information The Mt Buller Resort Management Board (☎ 5777 6077, mbresort@ mansfield.net.au) is located on Summit Rd, opposite the Village Centre Building and is open daily from 8.30 am to 5 pm in winter.

In summer, the information office shares with the post office on Summit Rd. It's open weekdays from 8.30 am to 5 pm and on weekends from 10 am to 4 pm. Check out the Buller Ski Lifts Ltd Web site at: www .skibuller.com.au.

Snow season entry fees are $18 per car for the day car park. Lift tickets for a full day cost $62. (Half day tickets are available in the afternoon.) Lift-and-lesson packages cost $95.

Places to Stay There are over 7000 beds on the mountain. Rates vary widely – for high and low seasons; mid-week and weekends; summer and the number of people sharing a room. Mt Buller Central Reservations (☎ 1800 039 049) books accommodation in commercial lodges from around $75 per person.

Club lodges generally have bunk accommodation and kitchen facilities; prices start from around $45. Most commercial lodges don't have kitchen facilities for the guests, but tariffs usually include breakfast and sometimes dinner.

Mt Buller Youth Hostel (☎ 5777 6181) is only open during the ski season and charges $45 for members, $49 for nonmembers. Book well in advance (☎ 9670 3802). *Preston Alpine Lodge* (☎ 5777 6336), at the end of Stirling Rd, has beds in summer from $15 and in winter from $50.

The *Kooroora Hotel* (☎ 5777 6050) is another winter-only place with basic, three or four-bed rooms with bathroom for around $70 per person on the weekends and $60 mid-week, with breakfast. *Avalanche Lodge* (☎ 9663 0811) has doubles from around $55 in summer and $75 per person in winter, including breakfast.

Places to Eat There's a supermarket in the Moloney's building in the village centre, but in summer it's not well stocked. In winter there are various kiosks and takeaway places.

Koflers is a ski-in bistro at the base of the Summit Run. Another winter-only place is the *Kooroora Hotel* in the village, which serves breakfast, lunch and dinner.

The restaurants, bars and cafes at the *Mt Buller Chalet Hotel* and the *Arlberg Hotel* are open all year.

Getting There & Around V/Line has buses twice-daily from Melbourne to Mansfield, $26.90 each way; Mansfield-Mt Buller Buslines (☎ 5775 2606) runs winter-only connecting buses up to Mt Buller, $19/31.20 one way/return. Mt Buller Snowcaper Day Tours (☎ 1800 033 023) has winter-only day trips ($110 weekends, $100 midweek), which include return transport from Melbourne, lift tickets and a lesson; gear hire is another $20.

Car parking during the ski season at Mt Buller is below the village. There is a 4WD taxi service; fares are $4 within the village and $8.50 between the car parks and the village.

If you're coming for the day you can take the quad chairlift from the Horsehill day car park into the skiing area and bypass the village – ski hire and lift tickets are available at the base of the chairlift. However, there

VICTORIA

is also a free bus service between the day car park and the village. Outside the ski season you can park in the village.

Mt Hotham
• elevation 1868m

Mt Hotham is 373km from Melbourne. The skiing is good – the skiable downhill area is 245 hectares (with about four beginners, 34 intermediate and 37 advanced runs), with a vertical drop of 428m. There is night skiing at the Big D and the Village Chairlift runs during January.

Mt Hotham is a skiers' mountain, with more emphasis on skiing than nightlife. Off-piste skiing in steep and narrow valleys is good. Cross-country skiing is also good and ski touring on the Bogong High Plains, which you can cross to Falls Creek, is excellent. This is also the starting point for trips across the Razorback to beautiful Mt Feathertop. Below the village, on the eastern side, there are trails running as far as Dinner Plain.

All these and other trails can be hiked during summer when Mt Hotham becomes an excellent base for hikes in the High Country.

Information Mt Hotham Alpine Resort Management (☎ 5759 3550) is in the village administration centre, open daily from 8 am to 5 pm during the snow season and weekdays the rest of the year. See its Web site at: www.hotham.net.au.

The snow season entry fee is $17 per car. Lift tickets for a full day cost $64/33 for adults/children and lift-and-lesson packages cost $87/59.

Places to Stay Mt Hotham Accommodation Service (☎ 1800 032 061, hotham@ netc.net.au), based in Lawlers Apartments, books accommodation – mainly club lodges from around $45. Mt Hotham-Falls Creek Reservation Centre (☎ 1800 354 555) in the Hotham Central building can book accommodation on the mountain. Skicom (☎ 1800 657 547), based in the Last Run Bar, deals mainly with apartments. Most accommodation is closed in summer, but these services can help you find something.

Some of the cheapest apartments are in *Jack Frost Lodge* (☎ 5759 3586). Studio-style apartments sleeping two people are up to $1218 per week and two-bedroom apartments sleeping up to six are up to $2800 per week. *Zirky's* (☎ 5759 3518) has double rooms for $110 per person.

The *Arlberg* (☎ 9809 2699) apartments have a bar, restaurant, disco, and supermarket. Two-bed apartments cost $216 to $480 in the high season; eight-bed apartments costs $495 to $1100 for two nights in the high season. During summer a double is $70 per night with a minimum two night stay.

In summer, *Snowbird Inn* (☎ 5759 3503) has beds in dorm-style rooms for $15 and rooms with bathroom for $30/50 a single/double; in winter, however, this place is not a bargain.

Places to Eat There's a small supermarket, and there are several restaurants, a few kiosks and takeaways. *Bedrock*, in the village administration centre, is good and stays open all year, as does the eatery in the General Store serving pizzas and pastas.

In winter only, *Zirky's* in the centre of the village is a good option for a bite. Two more expensive but good restaurants are *Frawley's* (☎ 5759 3586) at Jack Frost and *Herbies Bar & Grill* (☎ 5759 3626) below the White Crystal.

Getting There & Around By car, Mt Hotham can be reached from Melbourne via the Hume Freeway (M31) and Harrietville (4½ hours) or via the Princes Hwy and Omeo (5½ hours). Ring Mt Hotham Alpine Resort Management (☎ 5759 3550) for road conditions before deciding on a route.

In winter, Trekset Snow Services (☎ 9370 9055) has daily buses from Melbourne to Mt Hotham (twice on Friday), costing $75/105 one way/return. It also has daily services between Hotham and Myrtleford, Bright ($30/40) and Harrietville ($25/35).

If you want to ski Falls Creek for the day, jump on the 'Helicopter Lift Link' for $49 return if you have a lift ticket; they are transferable between the resorts. The flight costs more if you don't have a lift ticket. The six-minute flights are only possible on clear days.

The village is spread out, and free shuttle mini-buses frequently run along the ridge from 7 am to 3 am the next morning. Another shuttle service operates to Dinner Plain.

Dinner Plain

Dinner Plain is a stylish village 11km east of the Mt Hotham ski resort. In winter it's a base for skiers.

A shuttle bus runs to Mt Hotham and there are some excellent cross-country trails around the village, some of which lead to Mt Hotham. There is one lift for skiers. In summer it's an ideal base for enjoying the High Country, and there's accommodation year-round.

Apart from some of the best hiking in the country, you can also enjoy horse riding with Dinner Plain Trail Rides (☎ 5159 6445), who offers anything from one hour to seven-day rides.

All the accommodation is expensive in winter. Dinner Plain Central Reservations makes bookings (☎ 5159 6451 or 1800 670 019, dinnerplain@b150.aone.net.au). In summer, *Currawong Lodge* (☎ 9827 3996) charges from $25 per person, but in winter peak season expect to pay up to $140.

Mt Buffalo National Park

This area (31,000 hectares) was declared a national park in 1898. It is about a four hour drive (333km) from Melbourne. The main access road leads off the Great Alpine Rd at Porepunkah. A road leads to just below the summit of the 1723m Horn, the highest point on the massif.

Apart from Mt Buffalo itself (1500m), the park is noted for its scenery of granite outcrops, streams and waterfalls, and an abundance of birdlife and walks.

Winter Mt Buffalo becomes a fabulous ski resort in winter, with downhill and cross-country skiing.

There are two skiing areas: Cresta Valley and Dingo Dell. Cresta has five lifts – the skiable downhill area is 27 hectares, and runs are 45% beginner, 40% intermediate

and 15% advanced, with a vertical drop of 157m. Cresta Valley is the starting point for many of the cross-country trails. The chair-lift also operates on weekends in January.

There's a day visitors centre with a cafe, kiosk, ski hire and Mt Buffalo Lodge attached. Dingo Dell has a day visitor shelter with a kiosk.

Parks Victoria has an office (☎ 5755 1466) at the resort.

The entry fee to Mt Buffalo National Park is $8 per car ($11 in winter, but only if ski lifts are operating). Lift tickets for a full day cost $35/27. Lift-and-lesson packages cost $3721 for children.

Summer Mt Buffalo is a hang-glider's paradise (definitely not for beginners) and the walls of the Gorge provide some of the most challenging rock climbs in Australia. **Lake Catani** is good for swimming and canoeing.

Adventure Guides Australia (☎ 5728 1804) has abseiling, rock climbing, caving, ski touring/snow camping and other activities. Horse rides suitable for children can be arranged at the Chalet or phone ☎ 1800 037 038.

Places to Stay & Eat *Mt Buffalo Chalet* (☎ 5755 1500, buffalo@netc.net.au) is a huge guesthouse built in 1909. It retains a wonderfully old-fashioned feel, with simple bedrooms, large lounges and games rooms with open fires. Basic rooms with shared bathrooms cost around $115 per person; spacious rooms with bathroom cost around $145 per person – tariffs include all meals. The chalet is open all year.

The chalet's cafe is open to the public, as is the dining room when it's not booked out by house guests. Three course, buffet-style lunches cost $30 a head, and dinners are $35 a head.

Mt Buffalo Lodge (☎ 5755 1988) is a large inn with motel-style units and four-bunk rooms with shared bathrooms. Units cost from $75 per person with breakfast and dinner; bunks cost about $24 ($27 to $32 in winter). The lodge has a restaurant and ski hire.

During summer there are camp sites at *Lake Catani camping ground* for $14. Camping is also allowed at Rocky Creek but conditions apply – get a permit from the Parks Victoria ranger at the Mt Buffalo entrance station.

Getting There & Around There is no public transport to the plateau. From Bright, a taxi to Mt Buffalo costs about $40. Transport from Wangaratta train station can be arranged for chalet and lodge guests.

Falls Creek
• elevation 1780m

Falls Creek, on the edge of the Bogong High Plains, is a 4½ hour drive from Melbourne.

The skiing is spread over two main areas, the Village Bowl and Sun Valley. There are 19 lifts and the skiable downhill area is 451 hectares, with runs divided into 17% beginners, 60% intermediate and 23% advanced. The vertical drop is 267m. On Wednesday and Saturday there is night skiing in the Village Bowl. The Halley's Comet Chairlift also runs in January.

Some of the best cross-country skiing in Australia is here. A trail leads around Rocky Valley Pondage to some old cattlemen's huts, and the more adventurous can tour to the summits of Nelse, Cope and Spion Kopje. Australia's major cross-country skiing event, the Kangaroo Hoppet, is held on the last Saturday in August. It's part of the Worldloppet series of long-distance races.

Falls Creek is the most fashion-conscious of the resorts, and combines good skiing with plenty of nightlife. The village is large, with ski and equipment hire, ski schools, restaurants and cafes, pubs, discos and bars.

Falls Creek is also more of an all-seasons resort than the others, with a good range of accommodation year-round.

Information The Falls Creek Tourist Information Centre (☎ 5758 3490 or 1800 453 525), at the bottom of International Poma ski lift, is open daily from 9 am to 6 pm during the season, but closes at 5 pm in summer. Visit its Web site at www.skifallscreek .com.au.

The snow season entry fee is $17 per car. Lift tickets for a full day cost $64/33 and lift-and-lesson packages cost $87/59.

Summer Activities Some great hiking trails start at Falls Creek but there are many other activities, such as horse rides with Daily Trail Rides (☎ 5758 3655), and mountain biking; bikes can be hired from Viking Lodge.

Places to Stay There is little cheap accommodation in winter. Falls Creek Central Reservations (☎ 1800 033 079) makes bookings all year.

The cheapest places are club lodges such as *Alpha Lodge* (☎ 5758 3488), which in summer has bunk beds from $17, increasing to $40 in winter.

Viking Lodge (☎ 5758 3247, viking@ falls creek.albury.net.au) has two to six-bed rooms and kitchen facilities. A bed costs around $28 in summer to around $84 in the winter high season. *Silver Ski Lodge* (☎ 5758 3375 or 9886 8587) has double rooms with bathroom from $70 per person in the low season to around $105 per person in the high season, including breakfast and dinner.

Places to Eat There's a supermarket (open all year) in the Snowland Centre at the bottom of Halleys Comet Chairlift, and in winter the usual kiosks and snack bars are open.

Cafe Max, in the village bowl, is a lively bar/bistro that serves breakfast, lunch and dinner at reasonable prices. *Charcoal Grill Steakhouse* at Silver Ski Lodge is the place for fine steaks and wines. Both are open only during the ski season. If it's pizza you're after try *The Man*, all year.

Winterhaven (☎ 5758 3243), in the Winterhaven apartment building, is one of the best restaurants on the mountain and has dinner nightly in winter and on most weekends in summer.

Getting There & Around During the ski season, Pyle's Coaches (☎ 5754 4024) runs to/from Melbourne daily for $60/100 one way/return; it also has daily services to/from Albury ($30/52) and Mt Beauty ($17/29).

If you want to ski Mt Hotham for the day, jump on the 'Helicopter Lift Link' (see Getting There & Around, Mt Hotham, earlier in this section).

On the mountain, an over-snow transport service operates between the car parks and the lodges from 8 am until midnight – until 2 am on Friday night ($19 return).

EILDON
• postcode 3713   • pop 700

Eildon was built in the 1950s to house people constructing the Eildon Dam. It's a small town, with one pub and a few shops and is a recreation and holiday base for both Lake Eildon and the surrounding **Lake Eildon National Park**.

The tourist information centre (☎ 5774 2909), Main St, is open daily from 10 am to 2 pm.

Lake Eildon has a shoreline of over 500km and is a water-sports playground. **Horse rides**, from short trots to overnight rides, are offered by Great Divide Adventure Rides (☎ 5774 2122).

Snobs Creek Visitor Centre is a trout farm where you can watch short films on the fish hatchery and visit aquarium tanks. The centre is on the Goulburn Valley Hwy (B340), 6km south-west of Eildon, and opens daily during the school holidays from 10 am to 4 pm and the rest of the year from Saturday to Wednesday from 11 am ($5 for adults and $2.50 for children/concession).

Places to Stay

There are many caravan parks, as well as camp sites, in Lake Eildon National Park – you'll need to book camp sites during the holiday seasons by phoning Lake Eildon Camping & Cabins (☎ 5772 1293).

Eildon Caravan Park (☎ 5774 2105), Eildon Rd, has sites from $15 and on-site vans and cabins from $42 to $62. *Golden Trout Hotel/Motel (☎ 5774 2508)*, Eildon Rd, has units from $45/50 to $65/70 for singles/doubles.

Lake Eildon Holiday Boats (☎ 5774 2107) hires houseboats that sleep between six and 10 people. You'll pay between $750 and $4950 for a week.

Getting There & Away

McKenzie's Bus Lines (☎ 9853 6264) runs from Melbourne to Eildon daily ($18).

MT BEAUTY
• postcode 3699   • pop 1650

Mt Beauty and its twin town of Tawonga South are the gateway to the Falls Creek ski resort and the Bogong High Plains. There's a good choice of accommodation year-round, and winter facilities such as ski hire and transport to the mountain are available.

The tourist information centre (☎ 5754 4531) on the Kiewa Valley Hwy (C531) is open daily from 9 am to 5 pm. Parks Victoria (☎ 5754 4693) is on the Kiewa Valley Hwy in Tawonga South.

Next to the information centre is the small **Kiewa Valley Heritage Museum**.

Activities

Bogong Horseback Adventures (☎ 5754 4849) runs overnight treks from a farm 4km along Mountain Creek Rd (turn off the Kiewa Valley Hwy at the Bogong Hotel in Tawonga) to the Bogong High Plains.

Other activities include bike tours (book with Mountain Logistix; ☎ 5754 1676); Powered Hang Gliding (☎ 0417 496 264); fishing with Angling Expeditions (☎ 5754 1466); hiking, canoeing, ski touring and cross-country skiing with Ecotrek and Bogong Jack Adventures (☎ 5727 3382).

Places to Stay

The tourist information centre has an accommodation booking line (☎ 1800 808 277).

Tawonga Caravan Park (☎ 5754 4428) on Mountain Creek Rd (turn off the Kiewa Valley Hwy at the Bogong Hotel in Tawonga) has camp sites from $12, on-site vans from $35 and cabins from $40.

Baenschs (☎ 5754 4041, 16 St Bernaud Drive), in Tawonga South, has accommodation from $30 per person in doubles. *Carver's Log Cabins (☎ 5754 4863)*, Buckland St, Tawonga South, has cabins sleeping up to six people from $75 to $110.

The *Bogong Hotel (☎ 5754 4482)*, on the Kiewa Valley Hwy in Tawonga, has rooms with shared bathrooms for $30 per person. Cheapest of the motels is the *Meriki Motel (☎ 5754 4145)*, Tawonga Crescent, in Tawonga South, with rooms from $55 to $80 a double, including breakfast.

VICTORIA

Getting There & Away

V-Line operates a train/bus service via Wangaratta on weekdays. Pyle's Coaches (☎ 5754 4024), in Tawonga South, runs to Albury once a day all year and to Falls Creek in winter. They also have 4WD tours to Mt Feathertop outside the snow season for $65 a day.

MANSFIELD

• postcode 3722   • pop 2550

Mansfield is a good base town for the High Country, and is close to Mt Buller.

The graves of three police officers killed by Ned Kelly in 1878 are in **Mansfield cemetery** (at the end of Highett St), and there's a monument to them in the roundabout on the corner of High and Highett Sts.

The information centre (☎ 5775 1464), in the old train station on High St, opens daily from 9 am to 5 pm and has an accommodation booking service (☎ 1800 060 686). The NRE office (☎ 5733 0120) is at 33 Highett St.

Activities

Several companies offer horse-trail rides through the High Country, such as Stoney's Bluff and Beyond (☎ 5775 2212), Watson's Mountain Country Rides (☎ 5777 3552) and Merrijig Lodge (☎ 5777 5590).

Mountain Adventure Safaris (☎ 5777 3759, mas@mansfield.net.au) offers a wide range of activities, including mountain-biking, white-water rafting, trekking and abseiling. High Country Camel Treks (☎ 5775 1591), 7km south, offers one-hour rides ($18) as well as one, two and five-day treks.

Places to Stay

James Holiday Park Caravan Park (☎ 5775 2705), Ultimo St, has sites from $14 and on-site vans from $35.

Mansfield Backpackers' Inn (☎ 5775 1800, 112 High St) is part of the *Travellers Lodge*. It's well set up with doubles, four and six-bunk rooms from $15 per person ($20 in winter). Motel-type rooms cost from $60 a double.

The two pubs on the main roundabout, the *Mansfield Hotel* (☎ 5775 2101) and the *Delatite Hotel* (☎ 5775 2004), have B&B from $20 and $25 per person. The *Mansfield*

Motel (☎ 5775 2377, 3 Higheti St) has doubles from $61 to $73.

Alzburg Resort (☎ 5775 2367, 39 Malcolm St) is a large complex built around a century-old convent. The rooms sleep up to six people, some have kitchenettes, and prices start at $55 in summer and $75 in winter per double. *Highton Manor* (☎ 5775 2700), Highton Lane, is a historic homestead with beds for roughly $35 per person, and other more expensive options.

About half way between Mansfield and Mt Buller, **Merrijig** is a small settlement with off-mountain accommodation. *Arlberg Merrijig Resort* (☎ 5777 5633) has lodges, a restaurant, pool, tennis courts and motel-style rooms from $55 to $80 a double.

Places to Eat

Bon Apetit (39 High St) is an excellent deli and cafe. For a pub meal, try the bistros at either the *Mansfield Hotel* or the *Delatite Hotel* – both have mains from $9 to $16.

Come 'n' Get Stuffed, High St, has an inventive menu for breakfast, lunch and dinner from $4 to $17. The stylish *Sirens Restaurant* (☎ 5779 1600, 28 Highett St) specialises in pasta, steak and seafood. Mains cost around $13 to $18.

Getting There & Away

V-Line buses run twice daily (once on Sunday) from Melbourne ($26.90). In the ski season, Mansfield-Mt Buller Bus Lines (☎ 5775 2606) run daily from Mansfield to Mt Buller ($19).

HARRIETVILLE

Harrietville, 24km south of Bright, is a pretty little town at the foot of Mt Feathertop. It's the gateway to Mt Hotham, although the road sometimes closes in winter. During the ski season a bus shuttles between the town and Mt Hotham.

The town is also the starting and finishing point for various alpine walking tracks.

Places to Stay

Harrietville Caravan & Camping Park (☎ 5759 2523) is beside the river and has sites from $5 and on-site vans from $30.

The **Snowline Hotel** (☎ 5759 2524) has motel-style units starting from $35/50 for singles/doubles and standard pub meals. **Alpine Lodge Inn** (☎ 5759 2525) is a motel-style lodge with units from $30/60. **Cas Bak Holiday Flats** (☎ 5759 2531) offers self-contained one and two-bedroom cabins, from $60 a double.

BRIGHT

• postcode 3741   • pop 1900

Bright is a pretty holiday town in the Ovens Valley in the foothills of the High Country, and is a good base for year-round activities. It's about an hour's drive from Bright to the snowfields of Mt Hotham and Falls Creek, and Mt Buffalo National Park is about half an hour's drive away.

The tourist information centre (☎ 5755 2275), 119 Gavan St, is open daily from 9 am to 5 pm. Parks Victoria (☎ 5755 1577) is at 46 Bakers Gully Rd.

Things to See & Do

The **Bright & District Historical Society Museum** is in the old train station; it's open on Sunday from 2 to 4 pm (and Tuesday and Thursday afternoon in school holidays). **Centenary Park**, beside the Ovens River, has some good picnic areas and swimming spots.

Boynton's of Bright, about 8km northwest on the Great Alpine Rd, is an excellent winery, open daily.

There are plenty of walking trails and climbs to lookout points. The information centre has a *Short Walks around Bright* brochure. Bright Sports Centre (☎ 5755 1339) hires out mountain bikes, and Getaway Trailbike Tours (☎ 5752 2336) runs bike tours. Freeburgh Horse Trails (☎ 5755 1370) offers horse riding, from short trots to overnight treks.

Alpine Paragliding (☎ 5755 1753) and the Eagle School of Hang-Gliding (☎ 5750 1174) offer introductory flights and full certificate courses. There are also powered hang glider flights. Rapid Descents (☎ 02-6076 9111, rafting@rapiddescents.com.au) offers rafting tours, while River Mountain Guides (☎ 1800 818 466) has hiking, skiing, canoeing and canyoning trips.

Places to Stay

The tourist information office has an accommodation booking service (☎ 1800 500 117).

Camping, Caravan Parks & Hostels
Bright Caravan Park (☎ 5755 1141, yhalodge@bright.albury.net.au), Cherry Lane, has an excellent **YHA hostel**. Dorm beds cost $16 for YHA members, $19 non-members. Camp sites in the park cost from $17, and cabins from $48 to $82.

The well equipped **Bright Hikers Backpackers' Hostel** (☎ 5750 1244, 4 Ireland St, gwhite@netc.net.au) has dorm beds for $15 and twins/doubles for $32 – the owners can arrange numerous activities.

Other Accommodation The **Alpine Hotel** (☎ 5755 1366), on Anderson St, has single/double rooms for $30/45 and motel-style rooms for $35/50. One of the best motels for value and location is the **Elm Lodge Motel** (☎ 5755 1144, 2 Wood St) with rooms from $38/47 and backpacker discounts.

Bright Alps Guesthouse (☎ 5755 1197, 83-85 Delany Ave) has good rooms with shared bathrooms for $60 a double, with breakfast. There is also a self-contained apartment sleeping up to five people from $80 a double. **Rosedale Guesthouse** (☎ 5755 1059, 117 Gavan St) has rooms ranging from a single to a six bed family room. It's old fashioned and relaxed, and charges $40/65 for B&B, around $60 per person, including dinner.

Places to Eat

Liquid Am-Bar (8 Anderson St) has an interesting menu and a 10% discount for backpackers. Another trendy place is **Caffe Bacco** (2D Anderson St). **Tin Dog Cafe & Pizzeria**, corner of Gavan and Barnard Sts, has pizza and pasta from $7 and a Mexican menu with mains from $7.50 to $12.50.

Poplars (☎ 5755 1655), Star Rd, specialises in local produce such as beef, veal and trout from $16 to $20.

Getting There & Away

A train from Melbourne to Wangaratta and a connecting bus to Bright costs $39.80.

VICTORIA

MYRTLEFORD

• postcode 3737   • pop 2700

Myrtleford, the self-proclaimed 'gateway to the Alps', is at the foot of Mt Buffalo. It's mainly of interest as an overnight stop en route to the High Country.

Places to Stay

One of the best places is the *Happy Valley Hotel* (☎ *5751 1628*) in Ovens, 5km south-east of Myrtleford. This old country pub (1870) is excellent value with rooms for $35/55, including a light breakfast.

Back in Myrtleford, *Myrtleford Caravan Park* (☎ *5752 1598*), Lewis Ave, is close to the town centre and has sites from $12 and on-site vans from $25. *Myrtleford Hotel/Motel* (☎ *5752 1078*), on the corner of Standish and Smith Sts, has pub rooms from $20/30 or with bathroom from $30/45, and the *Railway Hotel/Standish Street Motel* (☎ *5752 1583*), Standish St, is restored and has good pub rooms from $35 and motel rooms from $38/58.

The *Golden Leaf Motor Inn* (☎ *5752 1566*), on the Great Alpine Rd, has rooms from $62/67.

BEECHWORTH

• postcode 3747   • pop 2950

Beechworth, a picturesque and historic town in the northern foothills of the High Country, is rated by the National Trust as one of Victoria's two 'notable' towns. From 1852, the town developed into the main centre for the Ovens Valley goldfields.

The tourist information centre (☎ 5728 3233), Ford St, is open daily from 9 am to 5 pm. Its Web site is www.beechworth-index.com.au. In the mornings during school holidays (not Sunday), a historian presents sessions on Ned Kelly and his association with Beechworth.

For information about walking tracks around the town, visit the NRE office (☎ 5728 1501), at La Trobe University's Beechworth Campus on Albert Rd, open in summer on weekdays from 9 am to 4.30 pm and the rest of the year until 1 pm Tuesday to Thursday, to 4.30 pm on Friday (closed Monday).

Things to See & Do

The **Burke Museum**, Loch St, has relics from the gold-rush era and an arcade with 16 shopfronts as they were over 100 years ago. It's open daily during school holidays from 9 am to 4.30 pm and the rest of the year to 3.30 pm. Entry is $5/3 and $14 for a family.

The **Gorge Scenic Drive**, a 5km tour around the outskirts of Beechworth, passes historic sites including the 1859 **Powder Magazine**, open daily from 10 am to noon and 1 to 4 pm, but only in the afternoon from February to August ($1.30).

In the cellar of **MB Historic Cellars**, on the corner of Last and William Sts, is an interesting collection relating to the old brewery (free), and upstairs you can buy its syrups and cordials. The **Historic Courthouse**, Ford St, was where Ned Kelly made his first court appearance and was committed to trial for the murders of constables Scanlon and Lonigan in August 1880. It's open daily from 10 am to 4 pm ($2).

The **Carriage Museum**, Railway Ave, has a collection of old horse-drawn carriages. It's open daily from 10 am to noon and 1 to 4 pm, but on weekends and in February it's only open in the afternoon ($1.50).

The **Beechworth Stagecoach** offers rides around town ($5). Two-hour 'Historic Town Tours' with Beechworth Bus Lines can be booked through the information centre ($12.50). Horse rides are offered by Woorage Trail Rides (☎ 5728 7282).

Places to Stay

Lake Sambell Caravan Park (☎ *5728 1421*), on McConville Ave and near the lake, has sites from $11, on-site vans from $28 and cabins from $40.

Tanswell's Commercial Hotel (☎ *5728 1480, 30 Ford St*) is a restored pub with good rooms and shared bathrooms from $25/40 ($35/55 on weekends), including a continental breakfast.

The *Armour Motor Inn* (☎ *5728 1466, 1 Camp St*) is central and charges from $70/75; the *Carriage Motor Inn* (☎ *5728 1830, 44 Camp St*) has comfortable rooms from $70/80.

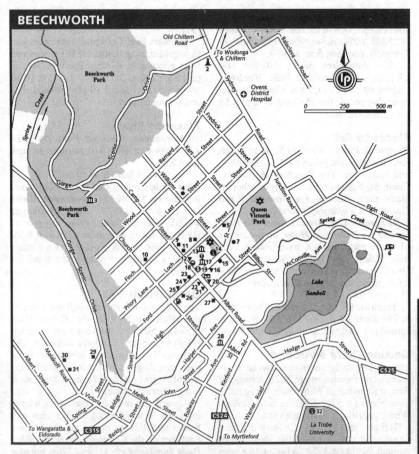

BEECHWORTH

BEECHWORTH

PLACES TO STAY
5   Kinross Guesthouse
6   Lake Sambell Caravan Park
8   Foxgloves B&B
9   Carriage Motor Inn
10 Finches of Beechworth
11 Rose Cottage
26 Tanswell's Commercial Hotel
27 Armour Motor Inn
29 Burnbrae B&B
30 Alba Country Rose
31 Country Charm Swiss
    Cottages

PLACES TO EAT
12 Hibernian Hotel
16 The Bank
20 Beechworth Provender
21 Chinese Village
22 Beechworth Bakery
24 The Parlour & Pantry;
    Commonwealth Bank (ATM)
25 Beechworth Pizza; Goldfields
    Greengrocer

OTHER
1   Beechworth Cemetery
2   Golden Horseshoes Monument

3   Powder Magazine
4   MB Historic Cellars
7   Beechworth Prison
13 Burke Museum
14 Shire Hall & Tourist
    Information Centre
15 Historic Courthouse
17 Left Bank Artists Co-operative
18 Beechworth Animal World
19 Bank of Melbourne (ATM)
23 Foodtown Supermarket
28 Carriage Museum
32 NRE Office

VICTORIA

Beechworth has a great selection of B&Bs and cottages. One of the best is *Rose Cottage* (☎ *5728 1069, ros-cot@hotkey.net.au, 42 Camp St)*, charging from $65/90.

Five kilometres north, off the Old Chiltern Rd, at Woolshed Falls, *Woolshed Cabins (☎ 5728 1035)* has cabins sleeping up to five people from $67 a double plus $8 for each extra adult.

Places to Eat
Parlour & Pantry (69 Ford St) is an excellent (if somewhat pricey) deli, coffee shop and restaurant. The *Beechworth Bakery*, Camp St, has hot bread, cakes and homemade pies. *Beechworth Provender (18 Camp St)* is a gourmet's paradise.

Tanswell's Commercial Hotel (30 Ford St) and the *Hibernian Hotel*, on the corner of Camp and Loch Sts, have bistros. *Chinese Village (11-15 Camp St)* has reasonable Chinese food at affordable prices. Very good pizzas are sold at *Beechworth Pizza (57 Ford St)*.

Beechworth's most upmarket restaurant is *The Bank (☎ 5728 2223, 86 Ford St)*, a formal licensed restaurant in a former bank.

Getting There & Around
V/Line has daily services between Melbourne and Beechworth ($34.20), changing from train to bus at Wangaratta. Wangaratta Coachlines (☎ 5722 1843) runs to Albury-Wodonga, Bright, Rutherglen etc.

Tickets for V/Line, Countrylink and Greyhound can be booked at Beechworth Animal World (☎ 5728 1374), at 36 Camp St, near the bus stop. Mountain bikes can also be hired here.

YACKANDANDAH
☎ 02   • postcode 3749   • pop 600
Yackandandah is another well preserved old gold-mining town and has been classified by the National Trust.

The tourist information centre (☎ 6027 1988) is in the Athenaeum on High St and has irregular opening hours.

The town has many fine buildings, including the 1850 **Bank of Victoria**, 21 High St, which is now a museum open on Sunday

afternoons and daily during school holidays ($2).

The **Kars Reef Goldmine Tour** takes you to a gold-mining tunnel (1888) where you learn about gold mining. Tours ($7/4) depart from 2 Kars St (☎ 6027 1757) at 10.30 am, noon, 1.30 and 3.30 pm on weekends and school holidays.

Places to Stay
Yackandandah Caravan Park (☎ 6027 1380) has sites from $10 and on-site vans from $30.

The tiny old *Star Hotel (☎ 6027 1493, 30 High St)* has rooms that it rents out occasionally for $25/40. *Yackandandah Motor Inn (☎ 6027 1155, 18 High St)* charges $45/65, with breakfast. There are several B&Bs, including *Serendipity B&B (☎ 6027 1881, 9 Windham St)*, which has a cottage for $80 a double or a room in the house for $50/90.

OMEO HIGHWAY
The only major route through the heart of the High Country is the Omeo Hwy (C543), which runs from the Murray Valley Hwy (A16) near Tallangatta to Omeo. The highway is unsealed in several sections (between Anglers Rest and Mitta Mitta) and often snow-bound during winter, but it is a memorable drive.

About 70km south of Mitta Mitta, a turn-off leads to the Bogong High Plains and Falls Creek (closed in winter). At **Anglers Rest**, beside the Cobungra River, the *Blue Duck Inn Hotel (☎ 5159 7220)* is popular with anglers, canoeists and bushwalkers. The tariff starts at $45 for a double room to $65 for a six bunk unit. You need to bring sheets, but pillows and doonas (duvets) are provided.

OMEO
☎ 03   • postcode 3898   • pop 300
This small town is on the southern access route to Mt Hotham, although the road is sometimes snow-bound.

Interesting old buildings include the **log gaol** (1858), the **courthouse** (1892), the **state school** (1860) and several churches.

The **historical society museum**, on the bend of Day Ave, is open on weekends.

There's an unofficial information centre in the **German Cuckoo Clock Shop** on Day Ave. The Bank of Melbourne is also on Day Ave.

Information and bookings for accommodation, horse riding, fishing, rafting, bike riding and hire, gold panning and ski hire are available from Omeo & High Country Booking Service (☎ 5159 1600 or bookings ☎ 1800 888 633). Overnight droving, mustering and trail rides (all on horseback) offered by High Plains Droving (☎ 5145 6055, treasure@tpgi.com.au) are highly recommended. The rides start at $240 for two days.

Places to Stay
Holston Tourist Park (☎ 5159 1351) has sites from $11 and on-site vans from $28. The *Omeo Alpine Camp (☎ 5159 1228)*, in the former convent on Day Ave next to the Catholic Church, has dorm beds for $15.

Colonial Bank House (☎ 5159 1388), Day Ave, has small self-contained units from $45/60 a single/double. The *Omeo Motel (☎ 5159 1297)* has units from $40/50. The *Golden Age Private Hotel (☎ 5159 1344)*, Day Ave, has gone upmarket and charges from $85 a double.

Getting There & Away
Omeo Bus Lines (☎ 5159 4231) runs daily between Omeo and Bairnsdale taking about two hours. During the ski season there is a bus most days to Dinner Plain and Mt Hotham.

Goulburn Valley & Hume Freeway

The Hume Freeway (M31) is Victoria's busiest freeway and isn't particularly scenic, although there are a few attractions off it.

West of the Hume is the Goulburn Valley, Victoria's fruit bowl. The valley's other main crop is wine, and several wineries are worth a visit, notably the impressive Chateau Tahbilk and Mitchelton wineries, both near Nagambie.

East of the freeway are the foothills of the High Country.

GLENROWAN
Ned Kelly's bushranging exploits came to a bloody end here in 1880. The story of Ned and his gang has become something of an industry in this small town.

Kellyland, an animated theatre, is the main attraction, with surprisingly lifelike characters telling the Kelly story. Be sure to read the promotional rhetoric out the front, with statements like '…most visitors to Glenrowan wouldn't know if the country shithouse fell on them!' The show starts half-hourly between 10 am and 4 pm, with extended hours during school holidays ($15/8 and $42 for families).

Places to Stay & Eat
Glenrowan Caravan Park (☎ 5766 2288) is 2km north of town and has sites from $11 and on-site vans and cabins from $26 a double.

Glenrowan Kelly Country Motel (☎ 5766 2202), Main St, has rooms from $40/45 a single/double. The *Glenrowan Hotel*, Main St, is refreshingly free of Kelly paraphernalia and serves bar and bistro meals.

WANGARATTA
• postcode 3677   • pop 15,500

Wangaratta (commonly called 'Wang') is at the junction of the Ovens and King rivers. Its name comes from two local Aboriginal words meaning 'resting place of the cormorants'. Wangaratta is the turn-off point for the Great Alpine Rd, which leads to Mt Buffalo, Myrtleford, Bright and the northern ski resorts of the High Country.

The visitor information centre (☎ 5721 5711) is just south of the town centre on the corner of the old highway and Handley St. It's open daily from 10 am to 4 pm. The RACV (☎ 5722 1292) has an agency at 10 Templeton St. The Coles supermarket on Greta Rd, just off the old highway, never closes. The NRE office (☎ 5721 5022) is in Tara Court on Ford St.

Wangaratta's main attraction is **Airworld**, an aviation museum at the airport, signposted 4km east of the freeway. It's open

Kelly Country

In the north-east of Victoria is 'Kelly Country', where Australia's most famous outlaw, Ned Kelly, had some of his more exciting brushes with the law. Kelly and his gang of bushrangers shot dead three police officers at Stringybark Creek in 1878, and robbed banks at Euroa and Jerilderie before their lives of crime ended in a siege at Glenrowan. Ned and members of his family were held and tried in Beechworth and Kelly was hanged at the Old Melbourne Gaol.

Not far to the east of the Hume Freeway are the Victorian Alps. In winter you'll catch glimpses of their snow-capped peaks from the highway near Glenrowan.

NED KELLY AT BAY.
FROM A SKETCH DRAWN ON THE SPOT BY MR. T. CARRINGTON.

VICTORIA

daily from 9 am to 5 pm ($6/4 and $12.50 for families). The **Wangaratta Jazz Festival** is one of Australia's premier music festivals. It's held on the weekend before the Melbourne Cup horse race, which is held on the first Tuesday in November.

Places to Stay
Painters Island Caravan Park (☎ 5721 3380), Pinkerton Crescent, on the banks of the Ovens River, is the most central caravan park. It has sites from $12 and on-site vans and cabins from $25 to $45 a double.

The *Pinsent Hotel (☎ 5721 2183, 20 Reid St)* is a renovated pub with reasonable motel-style rooms for $45/65. More traditional pubs include the *Royal Victoria Hotel (☎ 5721 5455, 25 Faithful St)* with rooms for $20/30 and the *Billabong Hotel (☎ 5721 2353, 12 Chisholm St)* charging from $24/40.

There are about a dozen motels. Coming from Melbourne, *Crana Motel (☎ 5721 4469)* is the first you come to on the old Hume Hwy, and it has good rooms from $37/42. On the northern side of town on the highway, *Millers Cottage (☎ 5721 5755)* is another good budget motel with rooms for $36/43.

Places to Eat
There are plenty of cafes and takeaways, mainly along Murphy St (the main street) and Reid St, which crosses Murphy St in the centre of town.

Scribbler's Coffee Lounge (66 Reid St) is a daytime cafe with good food at reasonable prices. Down Reid St, on the corner of Bickerton St, *Vespas* is another modern cafe. *Zippis (6 Roy St)* has a Tex-Mex menu plus other dishes. There are nightly specials, including all-you-can-eat deals on Friday and Saturday.

In the Bull's Head hotel on Murphy St, *Martini's* is a big restaurant with pizzas and other dishes, mainly Italian. The food is surprisingly good and reasonably priced.

The *Vine Hotel (☎ 5721 2605)* is an old pub with innovative food. It's about 4km north of town, on the road to Eldorado, and opens Monday to Saturday for dinner and Sunday for lunch. You might need to book.

Getting There & Away
Wangaratta train station is just west of the town centre in Norton St. Daily trains between Melbourne and Wangaratta cost $29. These trains continue on to Albury ($11).

V/Line buses run daily to Bright ($9.80) via Beechworth ($4.90) and Myrtleford ($6.10), and there's a daily (except Saturday) service to Rutherglen ($4.30) and Corowa ($4.90).

A bicycle and walking trail is being developed on disused railway lines, which will eventually connect Wangaratta with Wahgunyah (near Rutherglen) to the north, Beechworth to the east, Whitfield to the south and Bright to the south-east. The Beechworth and Bright sections will be finished first.

SHEPPARTON
● postcode 3632   ● pop 31,900
Shepparton is the regional centre of the Goulburn Valley. There's not a great deal for visitors, but you might come here to find fruit picking work.

The visitor information centre (☎ 5831 4400 or 1800 808 839) is in Wyndham St at the southern end of the Victoria Park Lake and opens daily from 9 am to 5 pm.

Tours of the **SPC cannery** (the largest in the southern hemisphere) are held during the canning season (from January to early April) on weekdays between 8.30 and 11 am and between noon and 3.30 pm – book at the information centre.

There are several wineries in the area around Shepparton and more are opening all the time. The closest is **Broken River Wines**, 8km east of town, open Thursday to Sunday.

Fruit Picking
From January to April it's fruit-picking season – a good time for casual work. Start looking in December as demand for jobs is high when the apricots, then peaches and pears ripen. The Harvest Office (☎ 1300 720 126), 361 Wyndham St, arranges employment. Some orchards offer basic accommodation or camp sites, but for others you'll need to stay in town and use your own transport.

VICTORIA

Places to Stay

There are half a dozen caravan parks. The most central is *Victoria Lake Caravan Park* (☎ *5821 5431*), right beside the lake and the information centre in Wyndham St, about a kilometre south of the town centre. It has sites from $9 and on-site vans and cabins from $30 to $48 a double.

Backpackers International (☎ *5831 8880, 129 Benalla Rd*) offers help in finding work and transport to get you there. Weekly rates are around $105, but phone before arriving to check the current situation.

Hotel Australia (☎ *5821 4011*), on the corner of Maude and Fryers Sts, has old pub rooms for $25/40 a single/double. The *Victoria Hotel* (☎ *5821 9955*), on the corner of Wyndham and Fryers Sts, has pub rooms from $29/39 and motel-style units for $45/55.

There are almost 20 motels, all fairly pricey. *Tudor House Motor Inn* (☎ *5821 8411, 64 Wyndham St*) is central and charges from $50/60.

Places to Eat

There are several snack bars on the Maude St Mall. On Maude St, west of the mall, is *La Porchetta*, with reasonably priced Italian dishes. For a pub meal, try *Hotel Australia*, or the *Victoria Hotel*.

The *Shepparton Family Restaurant* (*Shop 10, City Walk, 302 Wyndham St*) is a big place offering a cheap Chinese smorgasbord. It's open for lunch from 11.30 am to 2.30 pm, and for dinner from 5.30 to 9.30 pm.

Bosco's (☎ *5831 5858*), on the corner of Wyndham and High Sts, is a stylish Italian cafe and restaurant with main courses around $18. Another good Italian place is *Cellar 47 on High* (*170 High St*).

Getting There & Away

Shepparton train station is south of the town centre in Purcell St. There are daily trains and buses to Melbourne ($23.30) and connecting buses run to Cobram ($7.50).

V/Line buses also connect with Albury ($24.50) and Benalla ($7.50) daily, and with Mildura ($39.70) and Bendigo ($9.80) three times a week.

TATURA
● postcode 3616   ● pop 2800

Tatura is a small town 20km west of Shepparton. During WWII prisoner-of-war and internment camps were set up in the area between Tatura, Rushworth and Murchison, and there's a small **museum** here that records that period. It's open on weekend afternoons. There's a **German Military Cemetery** 2km west of Tatura.

NAGAMBIE
● postcode 3608   ● pop 1300

Nagambie is on the shores of **Lake Nagambie**, which was created by the construction of the Goulburn Weir back in 1887.

The visitor information centre (☎ 5794 2647), 145 High St, is open daily from 9 am to 5 pm.

Two of the best known **wineries** in Victoria, Chateau Tahbilk and Mitchelton, are south of town. A great way to visit these wineries is to take a **cruise** with Goulburn River Cruises (☎ 5794 2877). They run from October to the end of April on weekends and Wednesdays, with one cruise on Friday. The rest of the year there are cruises on Sunday.

There's a caravan park and motels.

Gippsland

Gippsland forms the south-eastern corner of Australia and has some of the most diverse and attractive scenery on the continent. The western part of Gippsland is divided into the Latrobe Valley, a coal mining and electricity generating centre, and South Gippsland, which includes the wonderful Wilsons Promontory National Park. East Gippsland, backed by the wild forests of the Great Dividing Range, includes the Lakes District and the Wilderness Coast.

For a holiday with a difference, try a horse-drawn gypsy-wagon tour through the Strzelecki Ranges. Two operators, Promway Horse Drawn Gypsy Wagons (☎ 5184 1258), based at Yarram, and Tarwin Valley Horse Drawn Wagons (☎ 5681 2244), based near Foster, have fully equipped gypsy-style

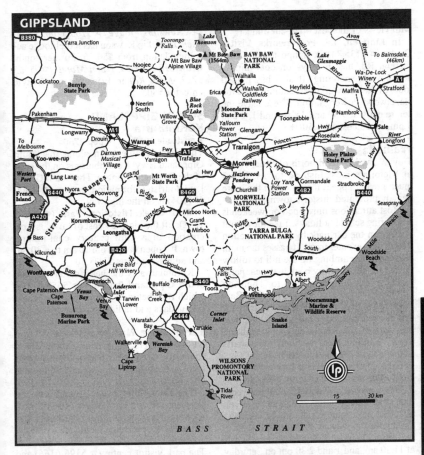

caravans (drawn by Clydesdale horses), which sleep five or six people and cost around $90 to $120 a day.

Ramrod Raft Tours (☎ 5157 5548), based 6km north of Bruthen, offers gentle raft trips down the Tambo River Gorge ($40).

Getting There & Away

Train Daily trains run between Melbourne and Sale.

Bus Daily V/Line buses from Melbourne run along the South Gippsland Hwy to Leongatha, Fish Creek, Foster and Yarram.

WEST GIPPSLAND & THE LATROBE VALLEY

From Melbourne, the Princes Hwy follows the powerlines back to their source in the Latrobe Valley. The region between Moe and Traralgon contains one of the world's largest deposits of brown coal, which is consumed by power stations at Yallourn, Morwell and Loy Yang.

Gippsland Heritage Park, off the Princes Hwy near Moe, is a re-creation of a 19th century community, open daily from 9 am to 5 pm. Entry costs $4/2/12 for adults/children/families. Also near Moe is the

Yallourn Power Station – there's a lookout with views of the vast open-cut mine.

In **Morwell**, the **Powerworks Visitor Centre** (☎ 5135 3415), signposted off Commercial Rd, has displays on coal-mining and power-generating. It also has guided tours of the Morwell open-cut mine and the Hazelwood Power Station. These leave the centre daily at 9.30 and 11 am and 1, 2 and 3 pm. Tours cost $8/3.50/18.

Walhalla

Tiny Walhalla, 46km north of Moe, is one of Victoria's most historic towns. It has much greater appeal than most of the more heavily promoted 'historic townships'.

Most attractions only open on weekends and during school holidays. Take the circuit walk from the car park by the information shelter as you enter town. It passes the main sights before climbing up the hill to follow the old timber tramway back to the car park.

There are longer walks to Thomson Bridge, Poverty Point or on to the Baw Baw Plateau. South of Walhalla there is a car park and marked trail to the summit of Mt Erica, the start of the Australian Alps Walking Track. Warning: there are many mine shafts in the area so keep to the marked tracks.

Guided tours of the **Long Tunnel Extended Gold Mine** are held Friday to Wednesday at 1.30 pm, and at 2.30 and 3.30 pm on weekends and school holidays ($4/2). You can also take a 40 minute ride on the **Walhalla Goldfields Railway** (☎ 0055 11788). It operates from Thomson Bridge and trains depart at 11.30 am, and 1 and 2.30 pm on Saturday and 11 am, and 12.30, 2 and 3.30 pm on Sunday and holidays. Return fares cost $7/5/20 for adults/children/families.

Most Sundays, Mountain Saddle Safaris (☎ 5165 3365) has horse rides from Erica up to Walhalla ($80 including lunch at the Walhalla pub). It also has horse treks through the High Country.

Places to Stay

There are good bush *camping* areas along Stringer's Creek. Simple, self-contained *Mill House* (☎ 5165 6227) sleeps up to six people and starts at $75.

There are more options in the area. To the east *Rawsons Village* (☎ 5165 3200, 1 Pinnacle Drive) in Rawson has motel/lodge accommodation from $50/36. Further south, *Crawford's Erica Hotel/Motel* (☎ 5165 3252, Main Rd) in Erica has motel-style units for $50.

SOUTH GIPPSLAND
Korumburra

• postcode 3950   • pop 2750

The first sizeable town along the South Gippsland Hwy, Korumburra is on the edge of the Strzelecki Ranges. The South Gippsland tourist information centre (☎ 1800 630704) is on the highway.

Coal Creek Historical Park (☎ 5655 1811), off the highway east of town, is a recreation of a 19th century coal-mining town. It's open daily from 10 am to 4.30 pm and admission costs $11/5.50.

Korumburra is the headquarters for the **South Gippsland Railway** (☎ 5658 1111), which runs between Nyora and Leongatha on Sundays and holidays.

Tarra-Bulga National Park

Tarra-Bulga (1230 hectares), about 30km south of Traralgon, is one of the last remnants of the forests that once covered southern Gippsland.

The Tarra Valley picnic ground is on the western side, off Tarra Valley Rd. A 2.2km walking track leaves from here to the **Cyathea Falls**. The Bulga picnic area is in the northern section, just off Grand Ridge Rd. The park visitor centre (☎ 5196 6166) and the 2km **Fern Gully Nature Walk** are here. Camping isn't allowed in the park.

Tarra-Bulga Guest House (☎ 5196 6141) is on Grand Ridge Rd near the park entrance. It's an old-fashioned guesthouse with rooms with shared bathrooms from $45/75 for single/double B&B, while packages including dinner start at $55 per person.

WILSONS PROMONTORY
NATIONAL PARK

The 'Prom' is one of the most popular national parks in Australia. It protects the peninsula that forms the southernmost part

WILSONS PROMONTORY NATIONAL PARK

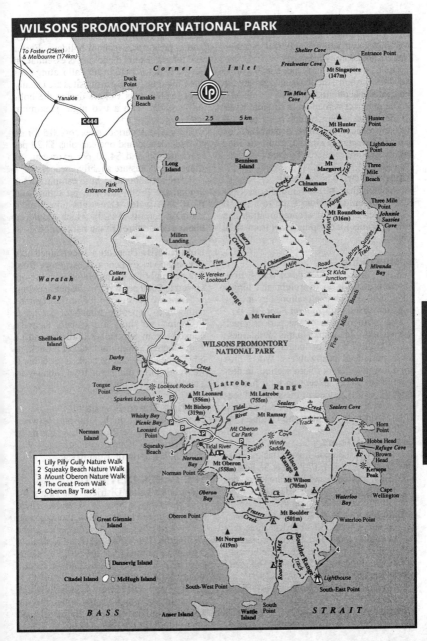

To Foster (25km)
& Melbourne (174km)

Corner Inlet

Shelter Cove
Freshwater Cove
Entrance Point
Mt Singapore (147m)

Duck Point
Yanakie
Yanakie Beach

Tin Mine Cove

Mt Hunter (347m)
Hunter Point

C444

0   2.5   5 km

Long Island
Bennison Island

Lighthouse Point
Three Mile Beach
Mt Margaret

Park Entrance Booth

Chinamans Knob

Three Mile Point
Johnnie Sussies Cove

Millers Landing

Mt Roundback (316m)

Vereker Range
Barn Creek
Five Mile Road
Chinaman
Margaret
Mount

St Kilda Junction
Miranda Bay

Cotters Lake
Vereker Lookout

Waratah Bay

Mt Vereker
Five Mile Beach

Shellback Island

WILSONS PROMONTORY
NATIONAL PARK

Darby Bay
Darby Creek

Tongue Point
Lookout Rocks
Latrobe   Range
The Cathedral

Sparkes Lookout
Mt Leonard (556m)
Mt Latrobe (755m)
Sealers Creek
Sealers Cove

Whisky Bay
Picnic Bay
Leonard Point
Mt Bishop (319m)
Tidal River
Mt Ramsay
Track
Horn Point

Norman Island
Cove
Windy Saddle
Hobbs Head
Refuge Cove
Brown Head

Squeaky Beach
Mt Oberon Car Park
Tidal River
Sealers
Wilson's Range
Kersops Peak

1 Lilly Pilly Gully Nature Walk
2 Squeaky Beach Nature Walk
3 Mount Oberon Nature Walk
4 The Great Prom Walk
5 Oberon Bay Track

Norman Bay
Mt Oberon (558m)
Norman Point
Growler
Mt Wilson (705m)
Cape Wellington

Great Glennie Island

Oberon Bay
Lighthouse Ck
Waterloo Bay

Oberon Point
Frasers Creek
Mt Boulder (501m)
Waterloo Point

Dannevig Island
Mt Norgate (419m)
Roaring Meg Ck
Boulder Range Track

Citadel Island   McHugh Island

Lighthouse
South-East Point

South-West Point

BASS
Anser Island
Wattle Island
South Point
STRAIT

VICTORIA

of the mainland. The Prom offers superb variety including more than 80km of walking tracks and some wonderful beaches. There's abundant wildlife.

The day visit fee is $8 per car. If you're staying overnight, the fee is incorporated in the cost of accommodation.

The one access road leads to Tidal River on the western coast, which has a park office and education centre, a petrol station and general store, a cinema, camp sites and cabins and lodges, all run by Parks Victoria.

Information

The park office (☎ 1800 350552) at Tidal River is open daily from 8 am to 6 pm. It takes reservations for accommodation and issues permits for camping away from Tidal River.

Bushwalking

The park office has details of walks, from 15-minute strolls to overnight and longer hikes. For serious exploration, buy a copy of *Discovering the Prom on Foot* ($6.95).

The northern area of the park is much less visited. Most walks in this 'Wilderness Zone' are overnight or longer, and mainly for experienced bushwalkers. Wood fires are allowed in the northern section, in designated fireplaces, except on total fire ban days. Fires are banned in the southern section (except in designated fireplaces in Tidal River between May and October).

Organised Tours

The owner of the good Foster Backpackers Hostel (☎ 5682 2614, 17 Pioneer St, Foster) runs a bus service to and from the Prom, departing Foster at 9 am most days ($10 each way) and rents out camping gear.

High Spirit Outdoor Adventures (☎ 0415 116 907 or 041 22 33 888) has three-day bushwalking trips for $165 per person which include transport from Melbourne, camping equipment and entrance fees, surf boards and all meals.

From Phillip Island, Amaroo Park Backpackers (☎ 5952 2548) runs day trips to the Prom for $45; you can stay a few nights at the Prom before returning to Phillip Island.

Places to Stay

Camping Tidal River has 500 camp sites, and at peak times (school holidays, Easter and long weekends) booking is essential. In fact, a ballot is held in July allocating sites for Christmas. A few camp sites are usually kept for overseas visitors during the holiday season, with a two night maximum stay.

During peak periods sites cost $15 for up to three people and one car, plus $3.20 per extra person and $4.60 per extra car. At other times rates are slightly cheaper.

There are another 11 bush camping areas around the Prom, all with pit toilets and most with water. Overnight hikers need camping permits ($4.20), which should be booked ahead through the park office.

Huts & Units There are self-contained huts sleeping up to six people. Costs range from $49 per night for a single/double in the off season to $660 per week in the peak season.

There are also group lodges, accommodating up to 30 people, from $486 per night.

Cabins and huts are usually heavily booked. From September until the end of April, there's a minimum stay of a week; at other times, they can be booked for either a weekend (three nights) or from Monday to Thursday (four nights).

Getting There & Away

There's no direct public transport between Melbourne and the Prom. V/Line has daily buses from Melbourne to Foster ($21.90), about 60km north of Tidal River.

THE LAKES DISTRICT

Gippsland's Lakes District is the largest inland waterway system in Australia. There are three main lakes, which interconnect: Lake King, Lake Victoria and Lake Wellington. The 'lakes' are actually shallow lagoons, separated from the ocean by a narrow strip of sand dunes known as the Ninety Mile Beach.

Lakes and Wilderness Tourism, which books accommodation and tours for the whole region, has offices in Bairnsdale and Lakes Entrance (☎ 1800 637 060).

Getting There & Away Daily trains run between Melbourne and Sale, where connecting buses run to Bairnsdale ($33.20 total fare), continuing on to Lakes Entrance ($40.10). V/Line and Greyhound Pioneer have daily buses continuing along the Princes Hwy into NSW.

From Bairnsdale V/Line buses run daily to Orbost ($17.50). Omeo Buslines (☎ 5159 4231) runs weekdays between Bairnsdale and Omeo ($23.60).

Sale

• postcode 3853   • pop 13,500

At the junction of the Princes and South Gippsland Hwys, Sale is a supply and residential centre for the Bass Strait oil fields. The town is connected by river to the Gippsland Lakes, and during the paddle-steamer era it was a busy port town.

The Sale Information Centre (☎ 5144 1108) on the Princes Hwy is open daily from 9 am to 5 pm.

Sale is the centre of the **Gippsland Wetlands**: lakes, waterways and billabongs that harbour more than 130 species of water bird. The **Wetlands Centre of Victoria**, on York St near Lake Guthridge, has information on the local wetlands and runs ecology tours of the district.

Ninety Mile Beach

This is a long, narrow strip of dunes backed by swamplands and lagoons, stretching from Seaspray to Lakes Entrance. The whole area is included in the Gippsland Lakes Coastal Park. There are many kangaroos in this area, so drive slowly, especially at night.

The beach is great for surf-fishing and walking, but can be dangerous for swimming.

The main access roads are from Sale to Seaspray or Golden Beach. There are shops and basic accommodation at **Seaspray** and **Loch Sport**.

In the centre of Ninety Mile Beach, **The Lakes National Park** is 2400 hectares of coastal bushland. The park is in Lake Victoria, and can be reached by road from Sale via Loch Sport or by boat from Paynesville.

The Parks Victoria office (☎ 5146 0278), at the park entrance near Loch Sport, opens for an hour in the morning and in the afternoon. The only camping is at *Emu Bight*, which has basic facilities. Book sites ($9.50 for up to six people) through the park office.

Rotamah Island is only accessible by boat. *Rotamah Island Bird Observatory* (☎ 5156 6398) has accommodation in an old homestead. There are bird hides and observation points, and wardens supervise study courses. The lodge sleeps up to 20 people in dorms and doubles, and the tariff of $65 per person includes meals and transport from the mainland.

Bairnsdale

• postcode 3875   • pop 11,000

Bairnsdale is the major town of this district.

The Visitor Information Centre (☎ 5152 3444) is at 240 Main St (between McDonald's and St Mary's Church). It's open daily from 9 am to 5 pm. **St Mary's Catholic Church**, beside the information centre, is notable for its extensive (but mediocre) murals.

At 37-53 Dalmahoy St the **Krowathunkoolong Keeping Place** (☎ 5152 1891) is a cultural centre with good displays on the local Aboriginal people. It opens weekdays from 9 am to 5 pm ($3.30/2.50).

Howitt Park is a good kids' playground, just off the Princes Hwy on the east side of town. The park is the starting point for the **East Gippsland Rail Trail** leading to **Bruthen**, 30km away.

The **historical museum** in MacArthur St, near the city oval, is open Wednesday, Thursday and Sunday afternoon ($3). Beyond the museum, **MacLeod Morass** is a swampy wetland reserve.

Places to Stay *Mitchell Gardens Caravan Park* (☎ 5152 4654), east of the centre and by the Mitchell River, has sites from $11 to $14 and vans and cabins from $35.

About 50m west of the train station, the small *Bairnsdale Backpackers' Hostel* (☎ 5152 5097, 119 McLeod St) has basic singles, doubles and dorms for $15 per person, including breakfast.

The *Commercial Hotel* (☎ 5152 3031), on the corner of Main and Bailey Sts, has pub rooms for $35 a double. There are plenty of motels along the highway.

Places to Eat *Oz Mex* (☎ 5152 4549), on the corner of Main and Service Sts, has a good range of 'Mexican-ish' eat-in and takeaway food. The *Commercial Hotel* has an excellent bistro with mains from $12 to $16. *Larrikins Cafe Deli* (☎ 5153 1421, 2 Wood St) has good snacks, salads and cakes.

The dining room at the *Riversleigh Country Hotel* (☎ 5152 6966, 1 Nicholson St) is one of country Victoria's better restaurants. Mains range from $14 to $19.

Mitchell River National Park

This park (12,000 hectares), about 40 km north-west of Bairnsdale, has three *camping* areas, and walking tracks including the two day, 18km Mitchell River Walking Track. The **Den of Nargun** is a small cave, which, according to Aboriginal legend, is haunted by a half-stone creature known as the Nargun.

Metung

- postcode 3904   • pop 500

Metung is smaller, more attractive and more fashionable than its big cousin, Lakes Entrance.

Riviera Nautic (☎ 1800 815 127) hires boats for cruising and sailing. A small motor boat takes up to six people and typically costs $80 a day. For overnight cruises there's a minimum hire of three days. Prices vary enormously, depending on the season and the size of boat. As a guide, a four berth yacht costs from $835 to $1050 per week.

Bull's Cruisers (☎ 5156 2208) also hires out motor boats.

If you don't want to skipper a boat yourself, there are a couple of cruises.

Places to Stay *Metung Tourist Park* (☎ 5156 2306), Stirling Rd, has sites from $14 and on-site vans and cabins from $45 to $55.

Metung Hotel (☎ 5156 2206) has good rooms with shared bathrooms from $30/40. *Maeburn Cottages* (☎ 5156 2736,

33 Mairburn Rd) has cottages from $60 to $75 a night, with a two-night minimum.

The enormous *Moorings at Metung* (☎ 5156 2750) has motel units from $89 and one, two and three-bedroom units from $115.

Lakes Entrance

- postcode 3909   • pop 5250

Lakes Entrance is a popular, if somewhat tacky, tourist town and the largest fishing port in Victoria.

The Tourist Information Centre (☎ 5155 1966) is on the corner of the Princes Hwy and Marine Parade, on the western edge of town. It's open daily from 9 am to 5 pm.

Things to See & Do A footbridge crosses the Cunninghame Arm inlet from the centre of town to the ocean and the **Ninety Mile Beach**. From there, a 2.3km track leads to the ocean 'entrance' to the lakes. From December until Easter, paddle-boats, canoes and sailboats can be hired by the footbridge.

Signposted off the Princes Hwy on the western side of town, **Jemmy's Point Lookout** has great views of the ocean, the lakes and the entrance.

The *Corque* (☎ 5155 1508) does two-hour **cruises** ($18/5), and trips to Wyanga Park Winery including a four hour lunch cruise ($30; daily). Peels Tourist & Ferry Services (☎ 5155 1246) runs cruises from the post office jetty, including lakes cruises ($15 to $24) and four-hour lunch cruises to Metung ($25). Mulloway Fishing Charters (☎ 014 943 154) has half-day fishing cruises ($25) and charters.

At Lake Tyers, the MB *Rubeena* (☎ 5155 1283) runs two-hour cruises on Tuesday, Thursday and Saturday (daily during holiday seasons) for $15. On Mondays, the *Rubeena* joins up with the East Gippsland Carriage Co wagonette for a 'Lake and Bush' tour ($65/40).

Victor Hireboats (☎ 5155 1888) and Portside Boat Hire (☎ 5155 3822), at jetties in Marine Parade, just down from the tourist information centre, rent out small motor boats from around $20 an hour, $60 for 4 hours and $80 for a day.

Places to Stay *Riviera Backpackers YHA* (☎ *5155 2444, 5 Clarkes Rd*) is just off the Esplanade. It has dorms, twins and doubles, all for $13 per person.

There are more than 20 caravan parks in the area. *Silver Sands Caravan Park* (☎ *5155 2343, 33 Myer St*) has $13 rates for backpackers. *Lakes Main Caravan Park* (☎ *5155 2365, 7 Willis St*) also has more basic beds for $10 and camp sites/on-site vans from $12/25.

There are dozens of motels and holiday units. One of the cheapest and most central is the *Glenara Motel* (☎ *5155 1555, 221 the Esplanade*) charging from $40 a double.

Places to Eat There are plenty of eateries along the Esplanade and most motels have restaurants. The health conscious will be cheered by the *Lakes Health Bar* on the corner of the Esplanade.

Tres Amigos (☎ *5155 2215*) is a cantina with main meals around $13 to $16, a cheaper takeaway menu and discounts for YHA members. For pizza, try *Egidios Wood Oven* (☎ *5155 1411, 357 the Esplanade*).

The *Fisherman's Co-op*, on Bullock Island at the western end of the Esplanade, sells fish fresh off the boats. For views, you can't beat the *Kalimna Hotel*, off the highway on the western side of Lakes Entrance. It has mains from $12 to $16.

Skippers Wine Bar & Restaurant (☎ *5155 3551, 481 the Esplanade*) specialises in seafood, but also serves game dishes, and is open for lunch and dinner daily. *Nautilus* (☎ *5155 1400*) is a licensed restaurant in a barge moored in the inlet, where you can tuck into seafood.

THE WILDERNESS COAST

This section of East Gippsland contains some of the most remote and spectacular national parks in the state. Much of the region was never cleared for agriculture, although logging of ancient forests is a hot issue here.

Orbost, which is the only sizeable town and the 'gateway' to the Wilderness Coast, has a tourist office incorporating a Parks Victoria office and rainforest centre. There

are other park offices at Cann River and Mallacoota.

Parks Victoria publishes several maps/brochures to the area, including *East Gippsland: A Guide for Visitors*. The Australian Conservation Foundation publishes *Car Touring & Bushwalking in East Gippsland*, although it's somewhat outdated.

Getting There & Away Daily buses run along the Princes Hwy from Bairnsdale into NSW. From Melbourne, take the train to Sale and connect with the bus there.

The Princes Hwy runs through the region, and good sealed roads lead off it to Mallacoota, Marlo, Cape Conran and Bemm River. The only other major route is the Monaro Hwy (B23), which runs north from Cann River into NSW.

Most other roads are unsealed, and some are closed during the wetter winter months. Check road conditions with park offices and you should keep an eye out for logging trucks.

Buchan

Buchan, a tiny and beautiful town in the foothills of the Snowy Mountains, is known for its limestone caves.

The scenic **Caves Reserve** is just north of town. The Parks Victoria office sells tickets for caves tours ($10). Between April and September tours run at 11 am and 1 and 3 pm; at other times tours of **Royal Cave** start at 10 am and 1 and 3.30 pm while those of **Fairy Cave** start at 11.15 am and 2.15 pm. The more adventurous can explore the Moon Hill caves – bring a torch (flashlight). The rangers also offer guided tours of more remote and undeveloped caves.

Activities Buchan is also the gateway to the Snowy River National Park. Snowy River Expeditions (☎ 5155 9353), based at Karoondah Park, runs activities including one, two and four-day rafting trips on the Snowy costing $75/150/380 respectively; half or full-day abseiling or caving trips ($25/55); and two-day 4WD, hiking and camping trips ($140). Most trips require a minimum of six people.

Detours Eco Adventures (☎ 5155 9464) offers adventures including half-day wild caving and abseiling from $45. It also has a half-day mystery trip for $25. The company is based in Nagaul Tipi Village just outside town.

Places to Stay *Buchan Caves Caravan Park (☎ 5155 9264)*, in the caves reserve, is very pretty and has good facilities. Camp sites cost from $10, and self-contained units cost from $45 to $55 a double – BYO linen.

Nagaul Tipi Village (☎ 5155 9464) has accommodation in tipis just outside Buchan for $20 per person. Just out of town, on Saleyard Rd, the excellent *Buchan Lodge Backpackers (☎ 5155 9421)* is a step above most hostels, and the owners can organise a wide range of activities. A dorm bed costs $15 – book ahead for peak periods.

Buchan Motel (☎ 5155 9201), on top of a hill behind the general store, has singles/doubles with great views from $45/55. *Buchan Valley Log Cabins (☎ 5155 9494)* is about 200m north of town and charges from $60 a double plus $15 per extra adult.

Places to Eat The *Caves Hotel* has a bistro with inexpensive meals and *The Willows*, opposite the pub, is a restaurant with great meals for $5 and $10.

Snowy River National Park

This is one of Victoria's most isolated and spectacular parks (95,000 hectares), dominated by gorges carved by the Snowy River.

The main access roads are Gelantipy Rd from Buchan and Bonang Rd from Orbost. These roads are joined by MacKillop's Rd (also known as Deddick River Rd), which runs across the northern border of the park from Bonang to just south of Wulgulmerang.

Along MacKillop's Rd you'll find **MacKillop's Bridge**. Near the bridge are the main camp sites, toilets and fireplaces, and sandy river beaches. There are several short walks, and the 15km Silver Mine walking track. The views from the lookouts over **Little River Falls** and **Little River Gorge**, the deepest in Victoria, are spectacular. The

lookouts are signposted and are about 20km to the west of MacKillop's Bridge.

There are other bush camping areas and picnic grounds. Bushwalking and canoeing are popular, but you need to be well prepared as conditions can change suddenly. The classic canoe or raft trip down the Snowy River from MacKillop's Bridge to a pull-out point near Buchan takes at least four days.

For information contact the park offices at Deddick (☎ 02-6458 0290), Orbost, Bairnsdale or Buchan.

Places to Stay Forty kilometres north of Buchan at Gelantipy, *Karoonda Park (☎ 5155 0220)* is a horse-riding ranch with YHA accommodation. Dorms, singles and doubles cost $14 per person and catered packages cost from $24 to $30 per person. The owners may have work available and lifts from Buchan can be arranged.

Delegate River Tavern (☎ 02-6458 8009) has bistro meals and accommodation in the adjacent *Tranquil Valley Resort*. Camp sites are $4 per person. One-bedroom cabins with shared bathroom cost $45 a double; two-bedroom cabins with bathroom cost $65 a double plus $10 per extra adult.

Orbost

• postcode 3888   • pop 2150

Orbost, by the Snowy River, is a service centre for the surrounding farms and logging areas. The Princes Hwy passes just south of the town, the Bonang Rd heads north towards the Snowy River and Errinundra national parks, and Marlo Rd follows the Snowy River south to Marlo, where the river meets the ocean, and continues along the coast to Cape Conran.

Parks Victoria's excellent **Rainforest & Information Centre** (☎ 1800 637 060), Lochiel St, is open daily from 9 am to 5 pm, and on weekends during school holidays from 10 am to 4 pm.

The scenic 113km **Murrungower Forest Drive** starts at Orbost and takes about three hours (without stops). One section can be closed in wet weather, so check with the parks office. The 262km **Baldwin Spencer Trail** also begins in Orbost and runs a circular route taking in both coast and high country. There are camping areas along the route. Many sections of the trail are unsealed, narrow, winding and steep, and often impassable in winter.

Places to Stay *Orbost Camp Park* (☎ 5154 1097), on the corner of Nicholson and Lochiel Sts, has sites from $12 and on-site vans from $30.

The *Commonwealth Hotel* (☎ 5154 1077, 159 Nicholson St) has double B&B from $35 and *Orbost Motel Lodge* (☎ 5154 1122), on the Princes Hwy, charges $40.

Errinundra National Park

The Errinundra Plateau contains Victoria's largest cool-temperate rainforest. The national park covers 25,100 hectares, but should be much larger – unfortunately the areas around the park are still being logged.

The Bonang Rd from Orbost passes the western side of the park, while the Errinundra Rd from Club Terrace runs through the centre. Both roads are unsealed, steep and winding, and are often closed in winter – check with the park office (☎ 02-6458 1456) at Bendoc, open weekdays from 8 am to 4.30 pm, or the park offices at Cann River or Orbost.

The only *camping* area is at Frosty Hollow on the western side, and there are a few basic picnic and camping areas on the park's edges – at Ada River, The Gap and Goongerah. There's a petrol station and general store at Bonang, a public phone at Goongerah, a pub at Bendoc (closed Sunday) and another pub and cabins at Delegate River.

Marlo

Marlo is a sleepy settlement at the mouth of the Snowy River, 15km south of Orbost.

Snowy River Entrance Retreat (☎ 5154 8504, 14 Stirling St) offers backpacker accommodation for $15, which includes an Orbost pick-up and drop-off. *Marlo Caravan Park* (☎ 5154 8226) has on-site vans from $25, self-contained cabins from $35 and motel units from $55. The *Municipal Park* (☎ 5154 8268) has sites from $10 to $14.

The nicest place is *Tabbara Lodge* (☎ 5154 8231, 1 Marlo Rd). Self-contained units that sleep up to five people cost from $45 a double, plus $5 for each extra person.

Cape Conran Marine Park

The 19km coastal route from Marlo to Cape Conran is especially pretty and there are some great beaches. A rough track leads from the cape to the mouth of the Yeerung River, which is 4km east and another good spot for swimming, canoeing and fishing. There are no shops at Cape Conran.

Places to Stay Parks Victoria (☎ 5154 8438) manages the accommodation, which you'll need to book at peak times. *Banksia Bluff Camping Area* has toilets, cold showers and fireplaces, but bring drinking water. Sites cost $11 to $15 seasonally.

Nearby, *Cape Conran Cabins & Lodge* has self-contained cabins. Cabins sleeping up to eight people range seasonally from $65 to $92 for up to four people, plus $12 to $14 per extra adult.

Gipsy Point

Gipsy Point is a tiny and idyllic settlement at the head of the Mallacoota Inlet.

Gipsy Point Lodge (☎ 1800 063 556) has a guesthouse and cottages sleeping three to five people, from $50. The lodge runs packages for birdwatchers and naturalists – ring for dates and details.

Mallacoota

- postcode 3892 • pop 980

Mallacoota is surrounded by the Croajingolong National Park. It's a sleepy place that becomes a crowded family holiday spot at Christmas and Easter.

The Parks Victoria (☎ 5158 0219) information centre opposite the main wharf is open weekdays from 9.30 am to noon and 1 to 3.30 pm.

Mallacoota Information & Booking Service (☎ 5158 0788), 57 Maurice Ave (a real estate agency), has a few brochures and maps.

Cruises & Boat Hire Mallacoota Inlet's 300km of shoreline is surrounded by national park. The brochure *Discovering Mallacoota Inlet* is a good guide.

Wallagaraugh River Wilderness Cruises (☎ 5158 0555) has a five hour cruise departing the main wharf at 10 am ($40, including lunch), and two and 2½-hour cruises for $15 and $20.

MV *Loch Ard* (☎ 5158 0144), a restored timber ferry, runs different cruises on different days: the two hour twilight cruise costs $15. It also has a five hour Gipsy Point cruise ($25) and a 3½ hour combined cruise and gold-mine walk ($18).

Rankin's Cruiser Hire (☎ 5158 0555), near the main wharf, hires fishing boats, as does Buckland's Boat Hire (☎ 5158 0660), which is about 4km north of the centre around Lakeside Drive – Bucklands also hires canoes.

Places to Stay Prices vary significantly with the seasons, and at Christmas or Easter you'll need to book ahead.

Mallacoota Camping Park (☎ 5158 0300), on the foreshore, charges from $11 to $14. *Beachcomber Caravan Park* (☎ 5158 0233, 85 Betka Rd) has on-site vans from $25 and cabins from $35; it may offer discounts to backpackers.

Mallacoota Lodge YHA (☎ 5158 0455), attached to the pub on Maurice Ave, has singles, doubles and dorm beds from $15 per person.

The *Silver Bream Motel* (☎ 5158 0305, 32 Maurice Ave) has doubles from $60. *Brew's Motor Inn* (☎ 5158 0544, 15 Maurice Ave) has units with kitchenettes from $50. The *Mallacoota Hotel/Motel* (☎ 5158 0455), Maurice Ave, has units from $45.

The best self-contained option is *Adobe Mudbrick Flats* (☎ 5158 0329, 17 Karbeethong Ave). The flats cost $45 for up to four people plus $10 per extra person; between December and May and during school holidays the base rate is $75. There are many other units, including *Harbour Lights Holiday Flats* (☎ 5158 0246, 88 Betka Rd) with simple units from $34.

Karbeethong Lodge (☎ 5158 0411), on Schnapper Point Drive, is a classic old-fashioned guesthouse. Doubles with shared bathrooms range from $50 to $70, family

rooms (sleeping up to five) from $75 to $105, and rooms with bathroom cost another $20.

Mallacoota Houseboats (☎ 5158 0775) has a houseboat with three double beds and a single bunk. Weekly rates are $1300 between December and March and $900 the rest of the year; there's a three night minimum hire.

Places to Eat At the Mallacoota Hotel, *Barnacles Seafood Bistro* has main courses from $10 to $16. *Watt's Cooking at the Tide* (☎ 5158 0100), on the corner of Maurice Ave and Allan Drive, specialises in seafood and opens daily for dinner, and for lunch on weekends. *Naomi's Deli* (☎ 5158 0064, 14 Allan Drive) opens daily for breakfast and lunch.

Getting There & Away Mallacoota is 23km off the Princes Hwy. Buses stop at Genoa and hitching from there is reasonably easy. Some accommodation places and tour operators will pick you up from Genoa if you ring in advance.

Croajingolong National Park

Croajingolong (87,500 hectares) is one of Australia's finest national parks. It stretches for about 100km from Bemm River to the NSW border and includes unspoiled beaches, inlets and forests. Mallacoota Inlet is the largest and most accessible area, and is covered in the previous section on Mallacoota.

There is a lot of wildlife and the reptile population includes huge goannas.

Access roads lead in from the Princes Hwy. All except Mallacoota Rd are unsealed and can be very rough. You can check road conditions with park offices in Cann River (☎ 5158 6351) and Mallacoota (☎ 5158 0219).

The main camping areas are at Wingan Inlet, Shipwreck Creek, Thurra River and Mueller Inlet. The Tamboon Inlet camping area can only be reached by boat from Furnell Landing. Secluded Wingan Inlet has the best facilities, with pit toilets, fireplaces and fresh water. Other bush camping areas (permits required) are along the Wilderness Coast Walk but you may need to bring drinking water. You'll need to book during the main holiday seasons; camping fees range from $6.90 to $11.50.

Point Hicks was the first part of Australia to be spotted by Captain Cook in 1888. The remote but comfortable *Assistant Light-keepers Residence (☎ 5158 4268)* can sleep up to eight and costs from $160 per night. This truly is a wilderness area.

Coopracambra National Park

Coopracambra (35,000 hectares) is remote and undeveloped. The landscape is rugged and spectacular, with deep gorges. The only access is a 4WD track from the Monaro Hwy to Genoa.

Coopracambra Cottage (☎ 5158 8277) is on a farm about 5km south of the park and costs $50 for up to four people, $60 for up to six. The cottage is 16km north-west of Genoa.

Western Australia

Western Australia (more commonly known as WA, or 'double-u-ay') is Australia's largest state. It's isolated from the country's eastern population and power centres, and many of its vast natural treasures are still being 'discovered' – although a push for tourism in recent years (millions were spent on an ad campaign starring Elle MacPherson) is attracting more visitors to the beauty and diversity of the west.

The region's position near the Indian Ocean trading routes led to very early European contact. The first known Europeans to land near the Western Australian coast were Dutch – including Dirk Hartog in 1616. Abel Tasman was the first to chart parts of the WA coastline in 1644.

William Dampier was the first Englishman to comprehensively chart the coast. He visited the area in 1688 on board the *Cygnet*, and his 1697 publication, *New Voyage around the World*, prompted funds for a subsequent trip in 1699 to what was then known as New Holland. On board the HMS *Roebuck*, he charted from the Houtman Abrolhos Islands as far north as Roebuck Bay, Broome.

Dampier's reports of a dry, barren land discouraged attempts at settlement. It was not until 1829, three years after Britain had formally claimed the land, that the first British settlers arrived in the Swan Valley (later Perth). Their presence was intended to forestall settlement by other European nations, particularly France.

Because of its isolation, the region was seen as a natural prison, and in June 1850 the first group of convicts was transported to the new colony. For the next 18 years, convicts were used in the construction of public buildings and roads. When settlers spread out into the south-west, many convicts went as their labour force.

WA's development as a British colony was painfully slow – hardly surprising, given its distance from the main Australian settlements in the east. It was not until the

HIGHLIGHTS

Telephone code: ☎ 08
Population: 1.8 million
Area: 2,525,500 sq km

- Clambering through the stunning gorges of Karijini National Park and admiring the view from Oxer's Lookout
- Diving in the clear waters of the Ningaloo Reef Marine Park
- Experiencing the remoteness and harsh beauty of the Kimberley along Gibb River Rd
- Canoeing down the Ord River near Kununurra
- Exploring the south-west's great beaches, historic towns, wineries and giant karri and tingle forests
- Enjoying vibrant Perth: sipping coffee in Fremantle, dining out in Northbridge, swimming at Cottesloe Beach or wandering around King's Park
- Seeing the spring wildflowers on the Midlands' Wildflower Way – perhaps the world's largest natural garden
- Seeing dolphins, whales and turtles all along the coast

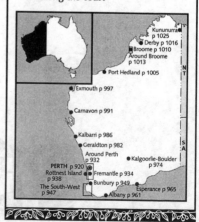

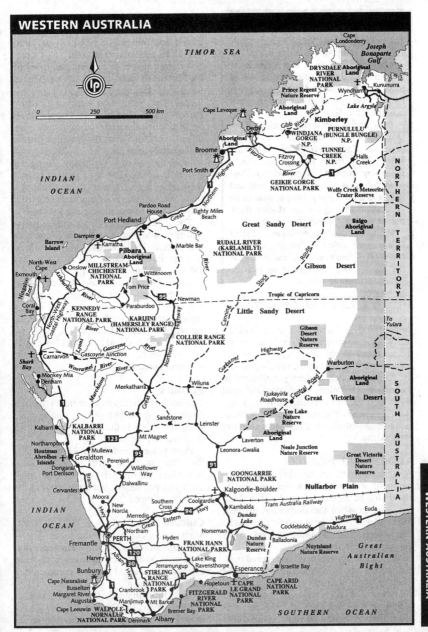

WESTERN AUSTRALIA

Sandgropers

You will often hear Western Australians colloquially referred to as sandgropers. The sandgroper is actually a subterranean insect known as a *cylindrachetid*, believed to be a descendant of the grasshopper family. Five species of sandgroper have been found in Australia.

Their bodies are perfectly adapted for 'groping' or burrowing in the sandy soils of the Swan Coastal Plain where they are found. They move through sand in a swimming motion, propelled by their powerful forelegs and with their mid and hind legs tucked away. They appear to be vegetarian, although some studies show that at least one species is omnivorous.

Humanoid sandgropers have a diet of Swan Lager, enjoy sunbathing and the footy, eat in Freo's cafe strip and holiday at the beach. They have yet to perfect the sand-swimming technique.

---

gold rushes of the 1890s that the colony really began to progress. Today, a larger and far more technologically advanced mineral boom forms the basis of the state's prosperity. As a result, WA is deeply embroiled in the native-title debate on Aboriginal land rights because of conflicting mining interests (see the Facts about the Country chapter for more information on land rights and native title).

ABORIGINAL PEOPLE

Western Australia has an Aboriginal population of over 47,250, which represents about 16% of the nation's total and is about the same as when the Europeans arrived. About a quarter of these people live in the state's north-west and along its border with the Northern Territory (NT).

Much evidence has been uncovered indicating that Aboriginal people lived as far south as present-day Perth at least 40,000 years ago. The state's archaeological record is rich, with a camp site (39,500 years old) unearthed at Swan Bridge, stone tools (30,000 years old) gathered from the Devil's Lair near Cape Leeuwin and ochre mined from Wilga Mia (30,000 years ago) in the Murchison as examples.

As elsewhere in Australia, the arrival of the Europeans had disastrous consequences for the Aborigines. Pushed off their traditional lands, many who were not killed by the colonisers died of European diseases, against which they had no immunity. Particularly hard hit were the Noongar people in the south-west.

From the end of WWII many Aboriginal people banded together in protest against their appalling treatment on the cattle stations. These protests were some of the first displays of a re-emerging consciousness.

The 1992 High Court Mabo ruling on native title prompted the WA government to pre-empt further legal restriction by rushing through its own Land Bill in December 1993. It also unsuccessfully challenged the validity of the Commonwealth Native Title Act in the High Court. Aboriginal people in WA have laid claims all across the state – mainly on Crown land – and the full implication of the High Court's Wik decision, which established that a pastoral lease does not necessarily extinguish native title, are still being realised.

Permits

You need a permit to enter or travel through Aboriginal land, but getting one is only really a problem in the remote communities in the east of the state.

Permits are issued by the Aboriginal Affairs Department in Perth (☎ 9235 8000); individual Aboriginal people apparently can't give permission, but access is often informally allowed.

Culture

Many tourists come wishing to see Aboriginal culture first-hand and many leave disappointed. Visitors are encouraged to make contact with the Aboriginal communities they pass through.

The only major Aboriginal cultural event in WA is the Stompem Festival held in Broome in October. National Aboriginal

Islander Day Observance Committee (NAIDOC) Week, in early July, brings together many groups, with displays of indigenous art and cultural performances.

One of the finest collections of traditional and contemporary Aboriginal art and artefacts can be found in the Berndt Museum of Anthropology, in the Social Sciences Building at the University of WA, Crawley. Magabala Books is a fine Aboriginal publishing house in Broome.

Tours on Aboriginal Land

Tours that incorporate aspects of Aboriginal life and culture provide the best opportunity for travellers to make meaningful contact with Aboriginal people. In the Kimberley, there are a number of options run by local Aboriginal people. Operators include Lombadina Tours, Kooljaman Resort and Bungoolee Tours (see the Kimberley section in this chapter).

The Purnululu Aboriginal Corporation and the Department of Conservation and Land Management (CALM) jointly manage the Purnululu (Bungle Bungle) National Park, one of the first attempts in Australia to balance the needs of local people with the demands of tourism. At Turkey Creek, near Purnululu, the Daiwul Gidja Cultural Centre (☎ 9168 7580) has half and full-day tours led by local Aboriginal people.

In the Pilbara, Aborigines have worked closely with CALM in establishing a cultural centre in the Karijini National Park and an information centre about the Yinjibarndi people's culture in Millstream-Chichester National Park.

GEOGRAPHY

Western Australia comprises a third of the Australian land mass. It has a small fertile coastal strip in its south-west corner. Hills rise behind the coast, but are much smaller than those of the Great Dividing Range in the east. Further north it's dry and relatively barren. Fringing the central-west coast is the Great Sandy Desert, an inhospitable region running right to the sea.

There are a couple of interesting variations, such as the Kimberley in the extreme north of the state – a wild and rugged area with a convoluted coastline and stunning inland gorges.

The Pilbara, in the north-west, is magnificent ancient rock and gorge country from which the state derives vast mineral wealth. Away from the coast most of WA is simply a huge empty stretch of outback: the Nullarbor Plain in the south, the Great Sandy Desert in the north, and the Gibson and Great Victoria deserts between.

CLIMATE

The main climate zones in WA are tropical (in the north), semi-arid (in the interior) and mild 'Mediterranean' (in the south-west). In general, rainfall decreases the further you get from the coast.

In the north the climate is characterised by the Dry and the Wet, rather than winter and summer. As the monsoon develops there is thunderstorm activity, high humidity (the 'build-up'), followed by the occasional tropical cyclone. Although it makes many roads impassable, the rain is generally welcomed. Port Hedland receives a cyclone at least every two years; Exmouth was devastated by Cyclone Vance in 1999 (see the boxed text 'The Day Vance came to Town' in the Exmouth section later in this chapter).

Further south, there is little rainfall during summer and the winds are generally hot, dry easterlies, though in the afternoon coastal areas receive sea breezes such as the famed 'Fremantle Doctor'.

NATIONAL PARKS

A visit to some of WA's national parks is a must. From the old growth karri forests in the south to the gorges of the Kimberley and Pilbara, most of WA's best natural attractions are protected in these areas. Most of the parks are managed by CALM, which has offices throughout the state. Its head office (☎ 9334 0333, 1800 199 287) is at 50 Hayman Rd, Como, Perth.

Camping is allowed in designated areas of some parks – it generally costs $8 per night for two people and $4 for each additional person. CALM produces informative brochures on the major national parks

National Parks Passes

Of the state's 63 national parks, 24 require a fee for vehicles (which is often the only way to get into the parks) – $8 per vehicle, per day ($3 for motorcycles or bus passengers). This can really add up. The answer is to buy a CALM park pass, which gives unlimited access to the state's national parks. There are a number of different passes: a good one is the Holiday Pass ($20), which gives unlimited entry for four weeks. If you need more time, the All Parks Annual Pass ($45) gives access for a year. Another option is the Annual Local Park Pass ($15), which gives 12 months entry to one park (or a group of local parks such as Karijini and Millstream-Chichester). Passes are available from CALM offices around the state.

and nature reserves in the state, as well as reams of other literature and maps. Call ☎ 9334 0333, or visit its Web site: www.calm.wa .gov.au.

ACTIVITIES
Bushwalking
There are a number of bushwalking clubs in Perth. The umbrella organisation is the Federation of WA Bushwalking Clubs (☎ 9362 1614). Its Web site is www.bushwalking .org.au/wapage.html.

Popular areas for walking include the Stirling Range and Porongurup national parks, both north-east of Albany. There are also good walking tracks in many coastal parks in the south and south-west, such as Fitzgerald River, Cape Le Grand, Walpole-Nornalup and Cape Arid. To the north, the Kalbarri, Karijini (Hamersley Range) and Purnululu national parks also provide a great hiking environment.

There are interesting and varied walks in the hills around Perth, and for real enthusiasts there's the 964km Bibbulmun Track (see the boxed text 'The Bibb Track' in this section for details). Information on this and many other tracks is available from CALM.

Bird-Watching
This can be an integral part of bushwalking, and WA is a fascinating destination for avifauna addicts. It is the only state with two Birds Australia observatories – at Eyre and Broome.

Cycling
This is a popular activity, with Rottnest Island, Perth and the south-west offering excellent conditions. For information contact the Cycle Touring Association through Bike West (☎ 9320 9301), 441 Murray St, Perth.

Rock Climbing & Caving
In the south, the sea cliffs of Wilyabrup, West Cape Howe and the Gap, and the huge cliffs of the Stirling and Porongurup ranges attract climbers. There are abseiling operations in the Murchison River gorges near Kalbarri and at Karijini National Park. The noncommercial caves of the Margaret River region and the lesser known 'holes' of Cape Range National Park offer plenty of opportunities for speleologists.

Water Sports
Swimming & Surfing People in Perth often claim to have the best surf and swimming beaches of any Australian city. Popular surfing areas around WA include Denmark, near Albany; the coast from Cape Naturaliste to Margaret River in the south-west; and Geraldton. There are fine swimming beaches all along the coast.

Diving Good diving areas include the large stretch of coast from Esperance to Geraldton, and between Carnarvon and Exmouth, particularly the Ningaloo Reef.

Fishing The coastal regions of WA offer excellent fishing. Some of the more popular areas include Rottnest Island, Albany, Geraldton and the Houtman Abrolhos Islands, Mackerel Islands, Shark Bay, Carnarvon, North-West Cape, Broome and Kununurra.

Fishing licences are required if you intend catching marron and rock lobsters, if you use a fishing net and for freshwater angling. They range from $15 to $25, or an annual licence

The 'Bibb' Track

The Bibbulmun Track is a classic walking trail that winds its way south from Kalamunda, near Perth, to Walpole and along the coast to Albany – a total of 964km.

The first stages of the track were officially opened and first traversed by walkers in 1979 as part of the celebrations of 150 years of European settlement. Completed in 1998, the track passes through a variety of forest areas and runs close to Dwellingup, Balingup, Pemberton, Northcliffe and Denmark along the way. Camp sites are spaced at regular intervals (there are 47), most with a three-sided shelter sleeping eight to 12 people, a water tank and pit toilets.

About 5000 walkers use the Bibbulmun each year, though most are only on the track for two or three days. For more information contact CALM on ☎ 9334 0265 or at bibtrack@calm.wa.gov.au. There are excellent guide books and maps available, and leaflets divided into convenient short sections, or look up the Web site, www.bibbulmuntrack.org.au. If you like bush walking, the Bibb Track has to rate as the best way to see WA's southern forests.

covering everything costs $60. They're available from the Fisheries Department (☎ 9482 7333), SGIO Building, 168-170 St George's Terrace, Perth, or its country offices.

Other Water Sports WA was once, briefly, the home of sailing's greatest prize, the America's Cup, and sailing is popular, especially on the sheltered Swan River.

The Amateur Canoe Association of WA (☎ 9387 5756) will provide information on the many good canoeing and kayaking rivers in the state. White-water rafting is not as widespread as on the eastern seaboard, but after heavy rains rivers such as the Murray, Avon and Ord are challenging.

Windsurfing is very popular, especially along Perth's city beaches and up in windy Geraldton. Lancelin and Ledge Point are the true sailboarders' meccas.

GETTING THERE & AWAY

WA is the largest, most lightly populated and isolated state in the country. You can drive across the Nullarbor from the eastern states to Perth, up the Indian Ocean coast and through the Kimberley to Darwin without leaving bitumen – but there's no way of covering all those kilometres cheaply. Sydney to Perth is around 4400km by road; a discounted air ticket costs about $600 return, a one-way economy rail ticket on the route is $424, while a full-fare seat on a Greyhound Pioneer bus costs around $295.

Hitching across the Nullarbor is not advisable; waits of several days are common. Driving yourself is probably the cheapest way of getting to WA from the eastern states if you have companions. Count on spending around $500 on fuel travelling coast to coast.

Train

The *Indian Pacific* (see Train in the Getting Around chapter) travels twice weekly between Sydney and Perth. One-way fares from Adelaide to Perth are $262 in an economy seat, $554 for an economy sleeper or $870 for a 1st class sleeper (includes meals). From Sydney, fares are $424/888/1350 for a seat/economy sleeper/1st class sleeper. Sleeper fares increase significantly during September and October.

You can make rail connections in Adelaide for the Melbourne *Overlander* to Melbourne and *The Ghan* to Alice Springs. You can also connect to *The Ghan* in Port Augusta.

Reservations for all these services are made with Great Southern Railways (☎ 13 2147, fax 08-8213 4491, enquiries@gsr.com.au) or look up www.gsr.com.au.

GETTING AROUND
Air

Ansett Australia (☎ 13 1300) and Skywest (☎ 9334 2288) connect Perth to most regional centres. Qantas Airways (☎ 13 1313) has flights to Broome, Port Hedland, Kalgoorlie and Darwin. As always, tickets are cheaper if booked ahead – Skywest offers reductions for two and seven-day advance purchases.

See the WA Airfares chart for the main domestic routes and flight costs.

Christmas & Cocos (Keeling) Islands

Christmas Island

☎ 08   • pop 1500   • 135 sq km

Christmas Island is a rugged mountain 360km south of Java and 2300km northwest of Perth. Part of Australia's Indian Ocean Territories, it was originally settled in 1888 to mine phosphate, which continues today. The island has an exotic blend of Chinese, Malay and Caucasian inhabitants. You will hear Bahasa Malaysian and Mandarin spoken, but English is widely understood.

The port area has excellent snorkelling in the dry season (April to October), and surfing during the wet or 'swell' season (November to March). Steep dropoffs 50m to 200m offshore and huge whale sharks from October to April attract divers worldwide.

Temperatures hover around 28°C. Frigate birds and boobies soar on gentle sea breezes, while endemic golden bosun birds with long streamer tail feathers swoop under the wharf where phosphate is loaded.

Christmas Island National Park covers 62% of the island, with tall tropical forests on the plateau (elevation 320m), rare nesting seabirds and soil riddled with crab burrows. Each November/December there is a spectacular breeding migration of red crabs to the sea: they cover roads, the golf course and anything else in their way. Robber crabs (known elsewhere as coconut crabs for breaking open coconuts) are common and will check out picnics at Martin Point cliff lookout. There are blowholes along the south coast and small beaches with coral rubble, rockpools and sand are dotted around the island, reached by forest walks or by boat.

Most of the island's shops and services are situated between Flying Fish Cove and the nearby clifftop area of Settlement. The Christmas Island Visitor Information Centre (☎ 9164 8382, fax 9164 8080, cita@christmas.net.au) coordinates accommodation, tours, diving, game fishing charters and car hire bookings, and has an excellent Web site (www.christmas.net.au) linking local businesses. Staff can also advise on the several weekly flights to Jakarta ($450 return). Visa requirements are as for Australia, and Australians should bring their passports.

Accommodation varies from backpackers ($18 dorms, $45 single rooms) to self-contained apartments and hotel-style suites. A casino-resort was built in 1993, but was in liquidation at the time of writing and should be open soon after this book's publication. Until it's in full swing, you can stay in the rooms, use the pool and have a continental breakfast for $140 a night.

There are several Malay and Chinese eating houses, mainland-style cafes and a wonderful colonial-style club house on the hill behind the Malay Kampong. Try roti ($1) for breakfast at the *Malay restaurants*, noodles ($3) for lunch at the *Chinese Literary Association* and dine in style at the *Rumah Tinggi* a la carte (mains for around $16).

A return Apex fare from Perth with National Jet (book through Qantas ☎ 13 1313) costs $998 and travels every Saturday (some Wednesdays) on a circle route with the Cocos Islands. In Perth, Island Bound Holidays (☎ 1800 804 420 or 9381 3644) and Christmas

Christmas & Cocos (Keeling) Islands

Island Travel (☎ 9481 1200, fax 9481 2005, info@citravel.com.au) both offer packages. To reach some of the remote parts of the island you need a 4WD. They can be hired from Kiat (☎/fax 9164 8276), which also runs tours – but there is plenty to see walking around Settlement.

Cocos (Keeling) Islands

'Altitude 10 feet', says the sign at the tiny airport. A chain of 27 islands around a clear azure lagoon, the Cocos Islands and Pulu Keeling, 24 km to the north, are the islands that inspired Charles Darwin's theory of atoll formation. Surf hums on the outer reef, echoing the mellow lifestyle, and a constant sea breeze keeps temperatures around 23°C to 29°C year-round. White sandy beaches and lots of reef without the resorts ... paradise!

First sighted in 1609 by Captain William Keeling (the history is written conveniently on the street signs), Cocos was settled by John Clunies Ross in 1826. Importing Malay workers, he established a coconut plantation, a shipbuilding business and a dynasty that survives today. The islands were sold to the Australian government in 1978 and now form, with Christmas Island 900km to the east, part of Australia's Indian Ocean Territories. The Cocos Islands are overgrown coconut plantations returning to natural vegetation, with crabs and feral chooks but few birds. In contrast, the uninhabited lone island atoll of Pulu Keeling National Park, which is accessible during good weather in 'the doldrums' from October to March, has retained its native vegetation and is an important seabird nesting site for huge numbers of frigatebirds, boobies, terns and rails.

Direction Island, also uninhabited and the mooring site for passing yachties during the 'trades' from April to September, is the classic desert island with a perfect protected beach. 'The Rip' is a channel, rich in marine life, between the lagoon and ocean with excellent snorkelling on the turn of the tide. Boat charter to reach 'DI' costs around $20 and charters can also take you deep-sea fishing or to various wild surfing locations. There are annual windsurfing clinics on the lagoon and the diving is truly special, with mantas, turtles, wild dolphins and astounding visibility commonplace.

West Island hosts the airport, administration and service workers (population 100). Accommodation on the island ranges from utilitarian rooms for $95 per night with canteen meals at *The Lodge*, to Bali-style self-catering bungalows at *Cocos Cottages* for $150 per night per double. Social life in this remote community revolves around *'the Club'* in the cyclone shelter. Sunday breakfast at *Saltwaters* is a must, and if you donate a mainland newspaper, locals will love you (the same applies on Christmas Island).

West Island is linked by a free ferry with Home Island, where the huge Clunies-Ross home sits abandoned and the Cocos Malay community lives (population 500). The cemetery and museum are also on Home Island, as well as *Bunga Melati*, a Malay restaurant open for dinner on Thursday ($14). The Home Island Malay community is more fundamentalist than on Christmas Island, so dress modestly to respect Islamic tradition.

Flights with National Jet on Saturday and sometimes Wednesday are $998 return Apex (ring Qantas ☎ 13 1313, or agents for Christmas Island). If you come through Jakarta (see Christmas Island earlier), a return Apex fare is $350 from Christmas Island. Cocos Islands Tourism Association (☎ 9162 6790, jenny.freshwater@cocos-tourism.cc) coordinates other bookings or visit its Web site at www.cocos-tourism.cc.

Jane Bennett

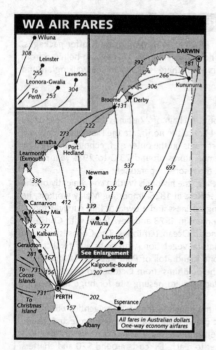

WA AIR FARES

Wiluna 308
Leinster 255
Laverton
Leonora-Gwalia 304
To Perth 253

DARWIN
392
181
266
306
Kununurra

Broome
131
Derby

273
222

Karratha
Port Hedland

Learmonth (Exmouth)
336

Newman
537
697

423 537 651

Carnarvon 412
Monkey Mia 339
86 277
Kalbarri
Geraldton
281 167
To Cocos Islands 731 156
To Christmas Island 731

PERTH 202
157

Albany

Wiluna
Laverton
See Enlargement

Kalgoorlie-Boulder
207

Esperance

*All fares in Australian dollars
One-way economy airfares*

Bus
Greyhound Pioneer (☎ 13 2030) buses run from Perth along the coast to Darwin ($436), and from Perth to Adelaide ($199) via Kalgoorlie. Most travellers buy a kilometre pass or one of the set route passes. With kilometre passes, bear in mind that Greyhound deducts double the kilometres for side trips off the main highway, such as to the Pinnacles, Kalbarri and Monkey Mia.

Perth Goldfields Express (☎ 1800 620 440) goes from Perth via Kalgoorlie to Leonora and Laverton. Integrity Coach Lines (☎ 9226 1339) is a new bus service that runs from Perth to Carnarvon ($90) on Tuesday, Thursday and Sunday, continuing to Exmouth ($160) on Thursday and Sunday. There's a 10% discount for YHA/VIP card holders.

South-West Coachlines (☎ 9324 2333) in the city bus port in Perth runs services from Perth to towns in the south-west such as Bunbury, Busselton, Nannup, Dunsborough, Augusta, Manjimup, Donnybrook and Collie.

Westrail (☎ 13 1053) goes to Augusta, York, Kalgoorlie, Hyden, Pemberton, Albany and Esperance, and north to Geraldton, Kalbarri and Meekatharra. There's a 50% discount for concession card holders, including YHA/VIP members. Its Web site is www.westrail.wa.gov.au.

Backpacker Transport An excellent alternative for travel in the south-west and the coast as far north as Exmouth is the jump-on jump-off bus run by Easyrider Backpackers (☎ 9226 0307, fax 9226 0309, tours@easyriderbp.com.au). The southern circuit (September to May) costs $149 and is valid for three months. It departs from Perth on Monday, Wednesday, Friday and Saturday stopping at Rockingham, Mandurah, Bunbury, Busselton, Margaret River, Dunsborough, Augusta, Nannup, Pemberton, Walpole, Denmark, Albany and Mt Barker.

The northern circuit pass is valid for six months, costs $299 and runs from Perth to Exmouth (one way), departing every Thursday. If you want to return to Perth, there's an express return for an extra $99. The route includes Lancelin, Cervantes, Dongara, Geraldton, Kalbarri, Denham and Monkey Mia, Carnarvon, Coral Bay and Exmouth.

It's a fun and relaxed way to travel and the bus drops you at the door of the hostel of your choice. Both trips can also be done as set tours – see Organised Tours in the Perth section.

Train
WA's domestic rail network, operated by Westrail, is limited to services between Perth and Kalgoorlie (the *Prospector*), the Midlands *(Avonlink)* and Bunbury (the *Australind)*; see Getting There & Away in the Perth section.

Car
See Getting Around in the Perth section for information on car rental.

Perth

• postcode 6000   • pop 1,097,000

Perth is a vibrant, cosmopolitan and modern city, pleasantly sited on the Swan River, with the port of Fremantle a mere 20km downstream. It's claimed to be the sunniest state capital in Australia and the most isolated capital city in the world. Around 80% of WA's 1.8 million people live in and around Perth.

Perth was founded in 1829 as the Swan River Settlement. It grew very slowly until 1850, when convicts were brought in to alleviate the labour shortage. Many of Perth's fine buildings, such as Government House and the Perth Town Hall, were built with convict labour.

Perth's development lagged behind that of the eastern cities, until the discovery of gold in the 1890s increased the population fourfold in a decade and initiated a building boom.

Orientation

The city centre is fairly compact, situated on a sweeping bend of the Swan River that borders the city centre to the south and east. The main shopping precinct is along the Hay St and Murray St malls and the arcades that run between them. St George's Terrace is the centre of the city's business district.

The railway line bounds the city centre on the northern side. Immediately north of it is Northbridge, a popular restaurant, entertainment and budget accommodation area. The western end of Perth slopes up to the pleasant Kings Park, which overlooks the city and Swan River.

Further north-west, suburbs extend as far as the Indian Ocean beaches, such as Scarborough and Cottesloe.

Information

Tourist Offices The Western Australia Tourist Commission's (WATC) efficient tourist centre (☎ 9483 1111, 1800 812 808, fax 9481 0190) is in Albert Facey House on Forrest Place opposite the Perth train station. It's open Monday to Thursday from 8.30 am to 5 pm, Friday until 6 pm, Saturday until 4.30 pm and Sunday from 10 am to 3 pm. You can get a wide range of maps and brochures on Perth and WA, and there's an accommodation and tours booking service. It's Web site is www.westernaustralia.net.

The Perth Tourist Lounge (☎ 9481 8303, fax 9321 1207), on Level 2 of the Carillon Arcade, has a relaxed, friendly environment with travel advice on all parts of WA. It's open Monday to Friday from 10 am to 5 pm and weekends from noon to 4 pm. For backpacker information and tours, the Travellers Club (☎ 9226 0660, 1800 016 969, fax 9226 0661), 499 Wellington St, is the best source of information. Look out for the numerous free guides to Perth, including *Your Guide to Perth & Fremantle* available from tourist centres, hostels and hotels.

Money All the major banks are well represented in and around Perth. American Express (☎ 9221 0777) has a foreign exchange office at 645 Hay St, and Thomas Cook (☎ 9321 2896) is at 704 Hay St.

Post & Communications Perth's main post office (☎ 9326 5211) is on Forrest Place, between Wellington St and the Murray St Mall. It's open Monday to Friday from 8 am to 5.30 pm, Saturday from 9 am to 12.30 pm and Sunday from noon to 4 pm. There are phones for international calls in the foyer.

Email & Internet Access There are plenty of places to access the Internet and send and receive email – most of the hostels have at least one terminal (usually coin-operated). The Travellers Club is the best place to surf, with some 60 terminals. The cost is $4 an hour and there's free tea and coffee.

Net.chat, 196A William St in Northbridge, offers access at 15c per minute. The Alexander Library has free Internet access, but you need to book in advance and it's wise to backpackers – no email allowed!

Bookshops City bookshops include Angus & Robertson, 199 Murray St and 625 Hay St; Dymocks, Hay St Mall; and Boffins Bookshop, 806 Hay St. For a more select

Perth Walking Tour

The civic mothers and fathers haven't been kind to central Perth – charming old buildings have been bulldozed and replaced with giant concrete and glass towers. This tour, which commences at the WATC tourist centre in Forrest Place, traces some remnants of the old Perth.

Pass the main post office, and proceed through one of the arcades to the Hay St Mall. Turn left and look out for **London Court** on your right. Between Hay St and St George's Terrace, the narrow, touristy London Court looks very Tudor English but only dates from 1937. At one end of this shopping court St George and the dragon pop out to do battle above the clock each quarter of an hour, while at the other end knights joust on horseback.

Turn left at the end of the court and follow St George's Terrace to Barrack St. The **Central Government Buildings** on the corner of Barrack St and St George's Terrace, recognisable by their patterned brick, were built between 1874 and 1902 (at one stage they housed the GPO). Uphill on Barrack St, on the corner of Hay St, is the **Perth Town Hall** (1867-70).

Head back to St George's Terrace and turn left, passing **St George's Cathedral**, constructed from local stone and jarrah in 1888. On the corner of Pier St is the **Deanery**, built in 1859 and restored after a public appeal in 1980. It's one of the few cottage-style houses that have survived from colonial days, but it's not open to the public. Across St George's Terrace are the Stirling Gardens. The old **courthouse**, next to the Supreme Court, is also here. One of the oldest buildings in Perth, it was built in Georgian style in 1836. A little further along St George's Terrace is **Government House**, a Gothic-looking fantasy built between 1859 and 1864.

Follow St George's Terrace to Hill St (at Victoria Ave, St George's Terrace becomes Adelaide Terrace). Turn left and head up to Hay St. On the right (entrance on Hay St) is the **Perth Mint** (see the Perth Mint entry in the main text). Continuing up to Goderich St and left to Victoria Square you'll find **St Mary's Cathedral** (1863), and a grassed area that's popular with office workers at lunch time. Follow Murray St, on the far side of the square, west to William St. Turn left into William St and head to St George's Terrace. On the corner of St George's Terrace is the grand and once extravagant **Palace Hotel** (1895), now a banking chamber. Turn right into St George's Terrace and head down to King St – on your left, at No 139, is the **Old Perth Boys' School** (1854), now a National Trust gift shop.

At King St turn right and follow it to Hay St. On the other side is the restored **His Majesty's Theatre** (1904); there are free daily foyer tours of the 'Maj' between 10 am and 4 pm, and back stage tours every Thursday morning at 10.30 am ($10). Return to St George's Terrace and turn right. Walk a short distance and, on the right, are the **Cloisters** (1858), noted for their beautiful brickwork. Originally a school, they are now part of a modern office development.

The distinctive **Barracks Archway**, at the western end of St George's Terrace, is all that remains of a barracks built in 1863 to house the pensioner guards of the British army – discharged soldiers who guarded convicts.

On the far side of the Mitchell Freeway is **Parliament House**. Tours of the Parliament buildings can be arranged on weekdays through the parliamentary information officer (☎ 9222 7222) – you will of course get a more extensive tour when parliament is not in session. Take the Red CAT from Harvest Terrace to return to the city centre. Fit walkers may wish to proceed to **Kings Park**.

range of reading matter the Arcane Bookshop, 212 William St, has an interesting collection, and the All Foreign Languages Bookshop, 101 William St, stocks a wide variety of travel books and language guides. The Perth Map Centre is at 884 Hay St.

Useful Organisations The Royal Automobile Club of Western Australia (RACWA; ☎ 9421 4444) is at 228 Adelaide Terrace. Membership is worth the reduced rate for its *WA Touring & Accommodation Guide*.

Disabled visitors can use the services of ACROD (☎ 9221 9055), 189 Royal St, East Perth.

The YHA (☎ 9227 5122, 1800 811 420) has its office and travel shop at 236 William St in Northbridge.

Medical Services The Traveller's Vaccination & Medical Clinic (☎ 9321 1977, fax 9321 1984, wa@tmvc.com.au) is at 5 Mill St, off St George's Terrace. The Royal Perth Hospital (☎ 9224 2244), on Victoria Square, is close to the city centre.

Emergency For general emergencies call ☎ 000, or contact the main police station on ☎ 9222 1111.

Kings Park

There are superb views across Perth and the river from this 4 sq km park. It includes a 17 hectare **Botanic Garden** with over 2500 WA plant species, and a section of natural bushland. In spring, there's a display of WA's famed wildflowers.

Free guided walks of Kings Park and the Botanic Garden start opposite the war memorial daily at 10 am throughout the year. The park also has a number of bike tracks; bikes can be rented ($4 per hour) from Koala Bicycle Hire on the western side of the main car park. An information centre (☎ 9480 3659), next to the car park, is open daily from 9.30 am to 4 pm.

Take the Red Central Area Transit (CAT) service to Kings Park entrance or walk up Mount St from the city, then cross the freeway overpass. The Perth Tram also runs up here (see its entry later in this section).

Perth Cultural Centre

Bounded by Roe, Francis, Beaufort and William Sts, just north of the Perth train station, the Perth Cultural Centre includes the state museum, gallery, library and the Perth Institute of Contemporary Arts (PICA).

The large Western Australian Museum (☎ 9427 2700) includes a recently updated gallery of Aboriginal culture, a marine gallery, vintage cars, a 25m blue whale skeleton and a large collection of meteorites, the biggest of which weighs 11 tonnes. A second building contains exhibitions of stuffed wildlife and the educational 'hands-on' Discovery Centre. The complex also includes Perth's original prison, built in 1856 and used until 1888. Out in the courtyard, set in its own preservative bath, is megamouth, a large species of shark with a huge mouth – only five specimens of this benign creature have ever been recorded. The museum is open Sunday to Friday from 10.30 am to 5 pm, and on Saturday from 1 to 5 pm (free).

The Art Gallery of Western Australia is housed in a modern building accessed from the footbridge directly behind the Perth train station. It has a fine permanent exhibition of European, Australian and Asia-Pacific art, including a rich display of Aboriginal art, and regular temporary exhibitions. It's open daily from 10 am to 5 pm, and admission is free.

The Perth Institute of Contemporary Arts (PICA; ☎ 9227 9339), 51 James St, promotes the creation and presentation of new and experimental art. Performances are regularly held in the Blue Room. It's open Tuesday to Sunday from 11 am to 8 pm.

Other Museums

The It's a Small World Museum, 12 Parliament Place, has the largest collection of miniatures in the country (open Monday to Friday from 10 am to 5 pm and Saturday from 2 pm to 5 pm; $5/4 for adults/children). The WA Fire Brigade Museum, on the corner of Irwin and Murray Sts, has displays of fire-fighting equipment and is open weekdays from 10 am to 3 pm (free).

Perth Mint

The Perth Mint (☎ 9421 7425), on the corner of Hill and Hay Sts, was originally opened in 1899 and still handles a tonne of gold every day – so security is tight! Interesting tours are held in conjunction with a

WESTERN AUSTRALIA

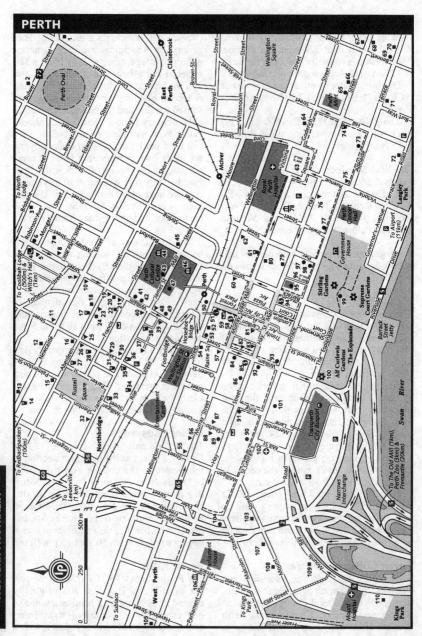

PERTH

WESTERN AUSTRALIA

PERTH

PLACES TO STAY
1 Rainbow Lodge
2 Cheviot Lodge
3 The Shiralee
7 Backpack City & Surf
12 Ozi Inn
13 Spinner's Backpackers
15 Lone Star City Perth Backpackers
16 Backpackers International
18 Field Touring Hostel
20 Britannia YHA
22 Northbridge YHA
24 Aberdeen Lodge
45 Court Hotel
52 Globe Backpackers; Traveller's Club
54 Royal Hotel
64 YMCA Jewell House
66 Hay Street Backpackers
67 Perth City Hotel
68 12.01 Backpackers
70 Exclusive Backpackers
71 Terrace Hotel
72 City Waters Lodge
79 Criterion Hotel
80 Murray Street Hostel
103 Emerald Hotel
105 CWA House
107 Mountway Holiday Units
108 Riverview on Mount Street
109 Adelphi Apartments Motel
110 Sullivan's Hotel

PLACES TO EAT
5 City Fresh Food Co
8 Asian Food Court
9 White Elephant Thai
10 Sri Melaka
11 Planet Cafe
19 Villa Italia
21 Chef Han's Cafe
23 Good, Bad & Ugly
25 The Street Cafe
26 Mamma Maria's
29 Glassby's Trains, Planes & Automobiles; Vinous; Redheads
30 James St Pavilion Food Hall
32 Lotus Vegetarian
37 Old Shanghai Markets
39 Sylvana Pastry
40 Brass Monkey Bar & Brasserie; Universal Bar
48 Tonic Cafe; Hare Krishna Food for Life
55 Fast Eddy's
56 Katong Singapore Restaurant; Taj Tandoor
57 Wentworth Plaza; Bobby Dazzler's; Moon & Sixpence
60 Ann's Malaysian Food
62 Hayashi
75 Cafe Cilento
76 Magic Apple Wholefoods
81 Carillon Food Hall
82 Fast Food Strip
83 Down Under Foos Hall
87 Durty Nelly's
88 Phoenician's Restaurant

PUBS & ENTERTAINMENT
14 The Bog
17 Aberdeen Hotel
27 The Post Office
28 Elephant & Wheelbarrow; The Church
31 Cinema Paradiso
33 Rosie O'Grady's
34 Metropolis City Nightclub
35 Paramount
36 Novak's Inn; O2
38 Connections
61 New Loft Nighclub
74 Grosvenor Hotel

OTHER
4 Mosque
6 Apex Car Rentals
41 YHA Travel Centre
42 Arcane Bookshop
43 Alexander Library
44 Western Australian Museum
46 Art Gallery of WA
47 PICA & The Blue Room
49 Net.chat
50 Westrail Booking Office
51 Western Australian Tourist Centre
53 Easyrider Backpackers
58 Commonwealth Bank
59 Main Post Office
63 St Mary's Cathedral
65 Cycle Centre
69 Bayswater Car Rental
73 RACWA
77 Ansett Australia
78 WA Fire Brigade Museum
84 All Foreign Languages Bookshop
85 Thomas Cook
86 Boffin's Bookshop
89 Perth Map Centre
90 Cloisters
91 His Majesty's Theatre
92 Qantas Airways
93 Palace Hotel
94 American Express
95 Perth Town Hall
96 St George's Cathedral
97 Playhouse Theatre
98 Deanery
99 Supreme Court
100 Allan Green Plant Conservatory
101 Old Perth Boy's School
102 Traveller's Vaccination & Medical Clinic
104 Barracks Archway
106 It's a Small World Museum

gold pour on the hour from 10 am to 3 pm weekdays and until noon on weekends. Visitors can also mint their own coins and handle a solid gold bar. The mint is open on weekdays from 9 am to 4 pm and weekends until 1 pm ($5/3).

Perth Zoo

Perth's popular zoo (☎ 9367 7988) is set in attractive gardens across the Swan River at 20 Labouchere Rd, South Perth. It has a number of interesting collections, including a nocturnal house (open daily from noon to 3 pm), an Australian wildlife park, numbat display and conservation discovery centre.

It's open daily from 9 am to 5 pm ($10/5/27.50 adult/child/family). You can reach the zoo on bus No 110 (No 108 on weekends) from the city bus port, or by the more pleasant option of taking the South

Perth ferry across the river from the Barrack St jetty ($2 return).

Perth Tram

The Perth Tram (☎ 9322 2006) is a replica of Perth's early trams (not unlike a San Francisco rattler) but it runs on wheels, taking in some of the city's main attractions (including commentary) between the Burswood Casino and Kings Park. It costs $12/6 and leaves from 565 Hay St at least six times daily, or pick it up at Kings Park or the casino.

Other Innercity Attractions

The **Allan Green Plant Conservatory**, on the Esplanade, houses a tropical and semitropical controlled-environment display (free). On Melville Place, south of the river, is one of Perth's landmarks: the finely restored, National Trust classified **Old Mill**, built in 1835. The former flour mill is open daily from 10 am to 4 pm ($2/1). Get there on bus No 108 or 109 from St George's Terrace.

The **Scitech Discovery Centre** on Railway Parade, West Perth, has over 160 hands-on and large-scale exhibits. It's open daily from 10 am to 5 pm ($11/7).

Beaches

There are calm bay beaches on the Swan River at **Crawley**, **Peppermint Grove** and **Como**. Better are the string of patrolled surf beaches on the Indian Ocean coast. These include the popular nude beach at **Swanbourne**; **Cottesloe**, a popular and safe swimming beach; **Port**; **City**; **Scarborough**, a wide, golden surf beach – great for sunbathing but recommended only for experienced swimmers; **Leighton**; **Floreat**; and **Trigg Island**, another surf beach that is dangerous when rough.

You can take any Fremantle-bound train for Cottesloe and Swanbourne – in each case there's a bit of a walk to get to the beach itself. Alternatively, bus No 70, 71 or 72 from the city busport will get you to Cottesloe. Bus No 36 goes to Swanbourne from St Georges Terrace. For Scarborough, take bus No 400 from the Wellington St bus station.

Markets

There are many lively markets in Perth. The **Subiaco Pavilion** on the corner of Roberts and Rokeby Rds is open Thursday to Sunday. The weekend **Galleria Market** on the causeway between the art gallery and the museum has a good range of local arts and crafts.

The **Wanneroo Markets**, north of Perth at 33 Prindiville Drive, Wangara, feature a large food hall and a variety of stalls; they're open weekends from 9 am to 6 pm.

Other markets include the historic **Fremantle Market** (see the Fremantle section later in the chapter); the weekend **Stock Rd Markets** at Bibra Lake, south of Perth; and the **Gosnells Railway Markets** from Thursday to Sunday.

Perth Suburbs

Lake Monger in Wembley, north-west of the city centre, is a hang-out for local feathered friends, particularly the famous black swans.

Near Armadale (a suburb 27km south-east of the city), **Tumbulgum Farm** has a number of Australian products for sale, and puts on farm shows ($12/6) and displays of Aboriginal culture ($9/ 4.50). It's open Wednesday to Sunday from 9.30 am to 5 pm.

In West Swan the **Caversham Wildlife Park** has a large collection of Australian animals and birds; it's open daily from 9 am to 5 pm ($8/3).

Swan Valley **vineyards** are dotted along the river from Guildford to the Upper Swan. Many are open for tastings and cellar sales. Houghton Wines on Dale Rd, Middle Swan, was established in 1842 and produced its first vintage in 1859.

In Subiaco, the **Museum of Childhood**, 160 Hamersley Rd, houses an interesting, nostalgic collection; it's open daily except Saturday. Across the Canning River, towards Jandakot airport on Bull Creek Drive, is the excellent **Aviation Heritage Museum**, with a collection of aviation memorabilia including a Spitfire and a Lancaster bomber. It's open daily from 10 am to 4 pm ($8/3).

Underwater World, north of the city at Hillarys Boat Harbour on West Coast Drive, is certainly not your run-of-the-mill aquarium. There's a fascinating 98m-long acrylic tunnel aquarium displaying 2500 examples of 200 marine species, including sharks and stingrays – it's about the closest most people will get to 'swimming' with sharks. Also in the complex are interactive displays such as a Touch Pool, Microworld, dolphin feeding and an audiovisual theatre. It is open daily from 9 am to 5 pm ($16.50/9). To get there from Perth station, take the Joondalup train to Warwick station then bus No 423 to Hillarys.

On Progress Drive, Bibra Lake, 15km south of Perth, are **Adventure World**, a large amusement park ($20/18), and **Bungee West**, both open daily. At the latter you can bungee jump from a 40m tower; the less adventurous can abseil. At **Cables Water Park**, Troode St, Spearwood (off Rockingham Rd), cables haul water-skiers along at 20 to 50km/h.

Organised Tours

Half-day city tours of Perth and Fremantle cost from about $35; for $59 you can get tours to the Swan Valley wineries, Cohunu Wildlife Park or Underwater World and the northern beaches.

The tour of the Swan Brewery (☎ 9350 0222), 25 Baile Rd, Canning Vale, is no longer free and it's a hassle to get there without your own transport. The cost is $7 (including drinks and snacks), and it's on Tuesday only at 10 am and 6.30 pm.

Planet Perth (☎ 9276 5295) is a small outfit that has been recommended by travellers for its day and evening tours. The popular afternoon wine-tasting tour (Friday) costs $29 and visits four wineries. There's an after dark trip into Caversham Wildlife Park on Monday ($29), and a horse-riding trip on Tuesday and Thursday ($65). It offers a 5% discount for YHA/VIP members.

Eco Bush Tours (☎ 9336 3050) includes national parks and lakes around Perth in its full-day tour ($120), and there's a two-day forest and farmland tour going as far as Walpole ($325, departs Saturday).

There are numerous companies offering day trips to the Pinnacles, two-day trips to Wave Rock and extended trips (from three days) to the south-west. Western Travel Bug (☎ 9561 5236, 1800 627 488) covers all the bases as far as Kalbarri and Esperance and

gets good reports. A Pinnacles day tour costs $65, a four day south-west tour is $325. Planet Perth's two day Wave Rock trip (departs Saturday) costs $160. Easyrider Backpackers (☎ 9226 0307) has three-day tours of the south-west for $159 and five-day tours north to Exmouth for $299.

Cruises A number of cruise companies operate tours from the Barrack St jetty, including Captain Cook Cruises (☎ 9325 3341), Boat Torque (☎ 9221 5844) and Oceanic Cruises (☎ 9325 1191). These include cruises on the Swan River, winery visits, trips to Fremantle, and lunch and dinner cruises.

From September to May, the Transperth ferry departs daily at 2 pm from the Barrack St jetty on a cruise of the Upper Swan ($10).

Boat Torque has a full-day Swan Valley wine cruise ($75) or a half-day lunch cruise ($29), and Captain Cook Cruises has a three hour river cruise around Perth and Fremantle ($24/12). Oceanic Cruises has a two hour city river tour as far as Tranby House daily at 2 pm ($12/5).

Whale-Watching & Dolphins Mills Charters (☎ 9246 5334) runs an informative whale-watching trip from Hillarys Boat Harbour. The three hour tour searches for humpback whales on their return to Antarctic waters after wintering off north-western Australia. Tours run from September to December, and cost $25/15 for adults/children on weekends and $20/10 on weekdays. To get to Hillarys take the train to Warwick and then bus No 423 from there.

Other whale-watching operators are Boat Torque (☎ 9246 1039) leaving from Hillarys, or Rottnest Express (☎ 9335 6406) and Oceanic Cruises (☎ 9430 5127) from Fremantle.

Rockingham Dolphins (☎ 0418-958 678) offers the rare chance to swim with wild dolphins from a boat. Tours depart from Wellington St in Perth daily from September to May ($130).

Special Events

Every year around February the Festival of Perth offers music, drama, dance and films.

WESTERN AUSTRALIA

The 'alternative' Northbridge Festival is also held around that time. The Perth Royal Show takes place every September/October, and the Artrage Festival is held in October. In early June, West Week is held to celebrate WA's foundation – there are historical recreations, art and craft events, concerts and sporting fixtures. Perth's Gay Pride march is held on the last weekend in October.

Places to Stay – Budget

Camping Perth is not well endowed with camping grounds convenient to the city centre, but there are many caravan parks in the suburbs. Rates at the following are for two people.

Armadale Tourist Village (☎ 9399 6376, South-West Hwy, Armadale) is 27km southeast of Perth and has powered sites for $14 and cabins at $40. *Kenlorn Tourist Park (☎ 9356 2380, 229 Welshpool Rd, Queens Park)*, 9km south-east, has tent/powered sites for $12/16 and park cabins for $60 (weekly rates available). On-site vans cost from $80 per week.

Perth Central Caravan Park (☎ 9277 1704, 34 Central Ave, Redcliffe), 8km east, has tent/powered sites for $12/20, cabins for $40 and self-contained units for $65.

Starhaven Caravan Park (☎ 9341 1770, 18-20 Pearl Parade, Scarborough), 14km north-west, has tent/powered sites for $8/16, on-site vans for $40 and holiday units for $65. *Swan Valley Tourist Village (☎ 9274 2828, 6851 West Swan Rd, Guildford)*, 19km north-west, has tent/powered sites for $14/15 and cabins from $35.

Hostels The budget traveller is well catered for in Perth – there are probably more backpacker hostels than the city needs. Competition is fierce; all provide similar facilities, and the choice often comes down to management, atmosphere and location. Most offer pick-ups from the bus and train stations, but few do airport pick-ups in summer when it's busy. Most of the backpackers give a $1 discount for VIP/YHA cards.

Northbridge Coolibah Lodge (☎ 9328 9958, rorysbak@ozemail.com.au, 194 Brisbane St) is in two clean, renovated colonial houses with pleasant gardens and a barbecue area. The atmosphere is friendly and there's a range of comfortable accommodation. Dorm beds are $16, singles $25 and twins/doubles $40 or $42.

Ozi Inn (☎ 9328 1222, 282 Newcastle St) is also good and closer to the Northbridge action. The large, renovated house has all the necessary facilities and friendly staff. Dorm beds are $15 and doubles/twins with air-con are $36. Over the road at 101-103 Lake St, a cheaper 'overflow' place used mainly by longer-term patrons charges $11 for a basic dorm.

The *Witch's Hat (☎ 9228 4228, 1800 818 358, 148 Palmerston St)* is a spotless and well-run new place. Again it has all the facilities and, perhaps because it's new, is a little quieter than the others and definitely has an air of class. The name comes from the Edwardian turret at the front – it's lit up like a beacon at night to guide you home from the pub! Dorms are $16 and twins/doubles are $40.

Northbridge YHA (☎ 9328 7794, 42-46 Francis St) is a relaxed place and popular with travellers. This former guesthouse has all the facilities; dorm beds are $15 ($18 for nonmembers) and doubles are $45. *Britannia YHA (☎ 9328 6121, 253 William St)*, just around the corner, is a huge place with endless rooms – great if you're after a single or double room, but not so good for atmosphere. It's an efficiently run place with dorm beds for $16, singles for $22 and doubles for $45 ($19/25/48 for nonmembers).

The Shiralee (☎ 9227 7448, 107 Brisbane St) is recommended. It's clean, air-conditioned, has pleasant recreation areas and the managers work hard to ensure an enjoyable stay; dorm beds are $16, twins and doubles are $40 and more upmarket doubles with en suite are $50.

Redbackpackers (☎ 9227 9969, 496 Newcastle St) is a classic 'party' hostel with young, enthusiastic staff. Dorm beds are $15, twins/doubles $36. The small *Backpack City & Surf (☎ 9227 1234, 41 Money St)* is tucked away in a leafy part of town; it's well run but the limited office hours are annoying. Dorm beds are $16, twins/doubles are $38. There's a twice-daily shuttle to Scarborough Beach, where its sister hostel is located.

Cheviot Lodge (☎ 9227 6817, 30 Bulwer St) is one of a couple of good hostels slightly removed from the Northbridge action. It has plenty of facilities, cheap dorm beds for $11 (with YHA/VIP), partitioned singles for $16 and twins for $32. *Rainbow Lodge (☎ 9227 1818, 133 Summers St)*, nearby, is a compact, busy place popular with Japanese travellers; dorm beds are $13 ($80 per week), singles $20 and twins/doubles $32. There's free coffee and toast for breakfast.

North Lodge (☎ 9227 7588, 225 Beaufort St) is another good alternative; the large, renovated old house has all the usual facilities and comfortable rooms. Dorms cost from $13, singles/doubles $30/34.

Other places to try include *Spinner's Backpackers (☎ 9328 9468, 342 Newcastle St)*, with a comfortable lounge and good kitchen facilities – it gets good reports (dorm beds from $14 per night, twins $36); the *Lone Star Perth City Backpackers (☎ 9328 6667, 156-158 Aberdeen St)*, made up of two renovated houses (dorm beds $14, doubles $40); *Field Touring Hostel (☎ 9328 4692, 74 Aberdeen St)*, a small and friendly place with dorm beds for $11 with VIP/YHA, singles for $18 and twins/doubles for $36; *Aberdeen Lodge (☎ 9227 6137, 79 Aberdeen St)*, centrally located but a bit run down (dorm beds $13, twins/doubles $32); and *Backpackers International (☎ 9227 9977, 110 Aberdeen St)*, a basic place with dorm beds for $11, singles for $13 and twins/doubles for $28/35.

Inner City Hay Street Backpackers (☎/fax 9221 9880, 266-268 Hay St, East Perth) has excellent facilities (including a pool), but is removed from the action of Northbridge and Leederville. Dorm beds for $15 and doubles for $36 ($45 with en suite) are good value.

12.01 East (☎ 9221 1666, 195 Hay St) has dorm beds for $11, smaller dorms for $14 and twins/doubles for $34/40. The rooms are air-conditioned, generally clean and some have fridges. *Exclusive Backpackers (☎ 9221 9991, 156 Adelaide Terrace)*, just around the corner, is in a beautifully restored building. It's a class above most of the others and is fairly quiet. Dorm beds are $15, singles $30 and doubles $40.

Globe Backpackers (☎ 9321 4080, 497 Wellington St) is a big, bustling former hotel and is well located near the Perth train station. Dorm beds are $14, singles $27 and doubles $40. The *Murray Street Hostel (☎ 9325 7627, 119 Murray St)* has little character; dorm beds are $15 and singles/doubles $30/35. A spanking new hostel had just opened at the time of writing: *Grand Central Backpackers (☎ 9421 1123, fax 9421 1650, 379 Wellington St)* is in a refurbished old building close to the Perth train station. Dorm beds are $15, and singles/doubles $30/40.

The *YMCA Jewell House (☎ 9325 8488, 180 Goderich St)* has over 200 comfortable, clean rooms; basic singles/doubles with shared facilities are $32/40. It's open 24 hours and has off-street parking.

Scarborough Close to the surf, Scarborough is a good alternative to Northbridge.

Western Beach Lodge (☎ 9245 1624, 6 Westborough St) is clean, airy and social; rates are $14 ($13 with VIP) in dorms and $30 in doubles ($34 with en suite). *Indigo Net Cafe & Lodge (☎ 9341 6655, 256 West Coast Hwy)* has a variety of good rooms (some with balconies) and, unsurprisingly, an Internet cafe. Dorm beds are $14, singles $25 and twins/doubles $38/40.

Sunset Coast Backpackers (☎ 9245 1161, 119 Scarborough Beach Rd) is about 1km back from the beach and has a shuttle bus from its sister hostel in Northbridge. Dorms are $15 and twins/doubles $36.

Mandarin Gardens (☎ 9341 5431, 20-28 Wheatcroft St), only 500m from the beach, is more of a budget holiday resort than a backpackers, with sizeable recreational areas and a pool. Dorm beds cost from $14, singles $26 and twins/doubles $30.

Places to Stay – Mid-Range

Guesthouses *CWA House (☎ 9321 6081, 1174 Hay St)* in West Perth (the entrance is at the rear) has comfortable rooms at a reasonable price. Singles with shared bathroom are $35, and singles/doubles with en suite are $50/61.50. A light breakfast is included.

Swanbourne Guesthouse (☎ 9383 1981, 5 Myera St) out at Swanbourne is gay-friendly and has good self-contained rooms from $55/85.

Motels & Holiday Flats Perth and the surrounding suburbs have an abundance of motels and holiday flats (see the Western Australia Accommodation & Tours Listing available from the tourist centre for more information). Most of these places have cheaper weekly rates.

City Waters Lodge (☎ 9325 1566, 118 Terrace Rd) is conveniently located by the river and good value. Rooms have cooking facilities, bathroom, TV and laundry, and cost $73/78 for singles/doubles.

The **Adelphi Apartments Motel** (☎ 9322 4666, 130a Mounts Bay Rd) has well-equipped self-contained units from $60/70, rising to $80/100 for rooms with a view.

A couple of places on Mount St (across the overpass) enjoy good views of the river and the city. **Mountway Holiday Units** (☎ 9321 8307, 36 Mount St) has economical rooms for $45/53. **Riverview on Mount Street** (☎ 9321 8963, 42 Mount St) is more upmarket with studio apartments for $75 and riverview apartments for $85.

Hotels There are a number of classic old-fashioned hotels around the city centre. The **Royal Hotel** (☎ 9324 1510, 300 Wellington St) has comfortable singles/doubles from $50/60, or $65/80 with en suite. The **Court Hotel** (☎ 9328 5292, 50 Beaufort St) is a gay-friendly place that was about to undergo renovations at the time of writing. Rooms are $30/40, or $70 for en suite doubles.

Sullivan's Hotel (☎ 9321 8022, 166 Mounts Bay Rd), about 2km from the city centre and next to Kings Park, is a popular family-run place with comfortable rooms from $89. It has a pool, restaurant and off-street parking.

Perth City Hotel (☎ 9220 7000, 200 Hay St) is a recommended new mid-range place. Twins/doubles with en suite and fridge are $69 and family units are $89.

Places to Stay – Top End

If you want something upmarket, you won't be disappointed in the city centre, where the top hotel chains are well represented.

The **Criterion Hotel** (☎ 9325 5155, 1800 245155, 560 Hay St), a refurbished Art Deco building, has friendly staff and excellent singles/doubles for $80/120 with breakfast.

The **Terrace Hotel** (☎ 9492 7777, 1800 098863, 195 Adelaide Terrace) has been recommended by readers. Studio rooms with en suite and kitchenette cost from $148 (ask about discounts).

The **Emerald Hotel** (☎ 9481 0866, 24 Mount St) is between the city and Kings Park, with excellent views over the city and river. Standard doubles cost from $103.

Places to Eat

City Centre There are two good and very popular food halls where you can fill up on a variety of international cuisines from as little as $6. They're usually open till about 9 pm. The **Down Under Food Hall**, downstairs from the Hay St Mall and near the corner of William St, has stalls offering Chinese, Mexican, Thai, Indian and many other types of food. The **Carillon Arcade Food Hall** in the Carillon Arcade off the Hay St Mall is slightly more upmarket. It also has sandwich shops, a seafood stall and fast-food outlets.

Magic Apple Wholefoods (445 Hay St) does delicious pitta sandwiches, cakes and fresh juices, but it's closed on weekends. **Cafe Cilento** (254 Adelaide Terrace) does cheap breakfasts, tasty lunches and has an outdoor seating area.

ANN JEFFREE

Marron is a local delicacy

WESTERN AUSTRALIA

Ann's Malaysian Food (137 Barrack St) is a good place for a quick, economical lunch or takeaway. *Hayashi (107 Pier St)* is a Japanese restaurant with excellent-value lunches, while *Bobby Dazzler's* at the Wentworth Plaza has an Australian menu and is a good place for a bite and a drink.

The *Moon & Sixpence (300 Murray St)*, is an English-style pub popular with the lunch-time office crowd (and backpackers) – it's hard to find a spare outdoor table on a sunny afternoon.

There's a cluster of restaurants west of the city centre near the corner of Murray and Milligan Sts. These include the popular 24 hour burger joint *Fast Eddy's*, and the cheap, highly recommended *Katong Singapore (446 Murray St)* for nyonya delights; lunch specials are $10. *Taj Tandoor*, next door at No 442, is a creditable Indian restaurant.

Shafto Lane, between Murray and Hay Sts, has undergone several transformations but remains a trendy spot. *Durty Nelly's* is a stylish new Irish pub with counter meals and outdoor tables, and opposite is the upmarket *Phoenician's Restaurant*.

Northbridge The area bounded by William, Lake, Roe and Newcastle Sts is full of ethnic restaurants to suit all tastes and budgets.

The *James St Pavilion Food Hall* on the corner of Lake and James Sts is good value. It's open from Wednesday to Sunday, and has some outdoor seating and a couple of bars. On James St, at the back of the small Roe St Chinatown, are the *Old Shanghai Markets*. The much smaller *Asian Food Court* is on the corner of William and Little Parry Sts.

William St boasts a real cornucopia of ethnic tastes. Near the Roe St corner, *Sylvana Pastry* is a Lebanese coffee bar with an amazing selection of sticky Middle Eastern pastries. *Hare Krishna Food for Life* at No 200 is the first stop for budget vegetarians. There's a $5 all-you-can-eat lunch from Monday to Friday and $2 takeaway meals between 5 and 6 pm.

Tonic Cafe, on the corner of William and James Sts, is an excellent spot for breakfast. On the left-hand side – in the next four blocks of William St heading north – you'll find the *Brass Monkey Bar & Brasserie (☎ 9227 9596)* at No 209, with a great selection of beers, a balcony with a view and good-sized counter meals; *Chef Han's Café (☎ 9328 8122)* on the corner of William and Francis St, a popular and cheap Vietnamese restaurant with most mains under $8; the busy *Villa Italia (☎ 9227 9030)*, at No 279, which serves fine coffee and light meals including good pasta; and a string of Asian restaurants, including *Sri Melaka* (Malaysian) at No 313 and *White Elephant Thai* at No 323.

Beyond Forbes St is the *City Fresh Fruit Co*, the place to buy healthy groceries and gourmet rolls. *Planet Cafe (264 Newcastle St)* is OK for a cheap breakfast in rustic surroundings and it has an Internet cafe. *Good, Bad & Ugly (69 Aberdeen St)* is a throbbing Mexican saloon bar with cheap meals, cheap drinks and various entertainment nights.

The Lake St strip is another restaurant enclave with several Italian eateries giving it a 'little Italy' feel. *Vinous (☎ 9228 2888)*, at No 44, is an upmarket wine bar and restaurant with some interesting Aussie cuisine. The *Street Cafe*, on the corner of Lake and Aberdeen Sts, serves good breakfasts including pancakes, and across the road is *Mamma Maria's (105 Aberdeen St)* with a pleasant ambience and a deserved reputation as one of Perth's best Italian eateries. *Glassby's Trains, Planes & Automobiles (48 Lake St)* is an institution; Wednesday is backpackers night.

Lotus Vegetarian (220 James St) has an all-you-can-eat buffet for under $10.

Leederville The area of Oxford St between Vincent and Melrose Sts, and Newcastle St has earned popularity with the 'cappuccino set'. Many cafes and eateries, as well as the art-house *Luna Cinema*, are here.

Cafes include *Villa*, *Oxford 130*, *Mazzini's*, *Giardini* and *Cino to Go*. The cuisines of the world are represented in an eclectic collection of eateries: *Cosmos Kebabs*, *Banzai Sushi & Noodle Bar*, *Halal Bros Egyptian*, *Anna Vietnamese*, *Shalimar* (Indian) and *Hawkers Hut* (Asian).

Subiaco This enclave, known as 'Subi', has a number of eateries, most of which are on (or just off) Rokeby Rd, with the best spots at the northern end.

Across from Forrest Way Mall on Churchill Ave is the small *Maggie's Kitchen*, a pleasant spot for a hearty breakfast ($7). *Mezza Villa* on the corner of Railway and Rokeby Rds has good atmosphere, staff and food. *Mackey's Seafood (118-120 Rokeby Rd)* has a reasonably priced menu and pleasant dining area. The *Witch's Cauldron*, with its renowned garlic prawns, is at No 89, and the popular *Bridie O'Reilly's* pub is just around the corner on Barker St.

Entertainment

Perth has plenty of pubs, clubs and live shows, which includes the Fremantle scene (see the Around Perth section). *Xpress*, the free weekly entertainment mag has a gig guide and is available at music shops and other outlets. Check the *West Australian* for listings of theatre, cinema and nightclub events.

Northbridge, Leederville and Subiaco (and Freo) are the main places to go after dark. There's revelry on weekend nights, particularly around Lake and James Sts in Northbridge, while the city centre remains relatively dead.

Pubs & Live Music Popular pubs (most with live music on weekends) in Northbridge include the *Brass Monkey Bar & Brasserie (209 William St)*; *Novak's Inn (147 James St)*; the *Elephant & Wheelbarrow (53 Lake St)*, a heaving new English-style pub with a beer garden facing the street; *Rosie O'Grady's (205 James St)*, which has Irish bands most nights of the week; the *Bog (361 Newcastle St)*, Perth's most happening Irish pub (open till 6 am); and the *Aberdeen Hotel*, the 'Deen', *(84 Aberdeen St)*, which has bands most nights and 'backpackers night' on Monday. The *Universal Bar*, next to the Brass Monkey on William St, is a trendy, open fronted bar with regular jazz sessions.

On Oxford St in Leederville, the *Leederville Hotel* has a legendary Sunday after-noon session. On Tuesday and Thursday many backpackers will be found at the *hip-e-club* behind the Leederville Village, enjoying free entry, a complimentary drink and lining up for hours for a sausage – the club provides a free bus back to local hostels.

The Sunday blast at the *Cottesloe Beach Hotel (104 Marine Parade)* goes off in the large beer garden, but the sunset view from the bar of the *Ocean Beach Hotel* (the 'OBH'), near North Cottesloe Beach, is much better.

Perth has the usual pub-rock circuit, with cover charges depending on the gig. Popular venues include the *Indi Bar & Bistro (23 Hastings St)*, Scarborough; the *Swanbourne Hotel (141 Claremont Crescent)*, Swanbourne; the *Junction (309 Great Eastern Hwy)*, Midland; and the *Grosvenor Hotel (339 Hay St)*, East Perth, where music's belted out Wednesday to Sunday.

Nightclubs Perth has plenty of places where you can dance into the wee small hours. In the city centre, the *New Loft Nightclub (104 Murray St)* has a variety of styles including retro on Sunday nights.

The majority of late-night venues are in Northbridge. Hard-core dance clubs include the *Church (69 Lake St)*, *Redheads (44 Lake St)* just across the road, and *O2 (Oxygen) (139 James St)*. The *Post Office*, on the corner of Parker and Aberdeen Sts, handles a slightly older crowd with aplomb (especially on Thursday at the over-30s session). Some of the best new venues are the smaller, more intimate clubs. *Paramount (163 Lake St)* is hugely popular – dancers on podiums at the front signal that you've found the place. *Metropolis City*, is the original big city nightclub and concert venue, but its popularity is waning.

Perth's glitzy *Burswood Casino*, over the Causeway from the city centre, is open all day every day; it hosts a cavalcade of prominent local and foreign entertainers.

Gay & Lesbian Venues The *Court Hotel* on the corner of Beaufort and James Sts has live music, drag shows and gay-friendly accommodation. *Connections* ('Connies';

The city from Kings Park, Perth, Western Australia, (WA)

Rottnest Island, WA

Cassidy headframe at sunrise, Kalgoorlie, WA

Oxer Lookout, Karijini National Park, WA

Lake Cave, Leeuwin-Naturalist National Park, WA

Mitchell Falls, Mitchell Plateau, WA

Wildflowers and Rossiter Bay, Cape Le Grand, WA

Thistle Cove, Cape Le Grand, WA

Mushroom Rock Gorge, Kalbarri National Park, WA

RICHARD I'ANSON

Boxed Text

Bold indicates maps.

81 James St) is popular for dance music and floorshows. *O2* has Trade on Thursday nights, and the *Rainbow Connection Cafe (615 Beaufort St, Mt Lawley)* is a happening venue with drag cabarets on Friday and Saturday.

Check the *Westside Observer (WSO)*, available from the above-mentioned places, for more venues and activities.

Concerts & Recitals The *Perth Concert Hall (☎ 9231 9900, 5 St George's Terrace)* and the *Entertainment Centre (☎ 9322 4766, 640 Wellington St)* are venues for concerts and recitals by local and international acts. For bookings, call BOCS ticketing (☎ 1800 193 300) for the Concert Hall and Red Tickets (☎ 1800 199 991) for the Entertainment Centre.

Cinemas & Theatres For quality arthouse films try *Cinema Paradiso* in the Galleria complex at 164 James St, Northbridge; *Luna* on Oxford St, Leederville; and the *Astor* on the corner of Beaufort and Walcott Sts in Mt Lawley. Mainstream films screen at Hoyts, Greater Union and Village city and suburban cinemas; budget night is Tuesday. The open air *Sunset Cinema (☎ 1902 290 087)* in Kings Park operates from February to April and is a great way to spend an evening with a bottle of wine and some munchies.

Popular theatres include *His Majesty's Theatre (☎ 9265 0900, 825 Hay St)*, the *Playhouse Theatre (☎ 9325 3344, 3 Pier St)* and the *Subiaco Theatre Centre (☎ 9382 3385, 180 Hamersley Rd)*. Session times and programs appear daily in the *West Australian* and tickets for all three can be booked through BOCS (☎ 1800 193 300).

Comedy The rear bar of the *Brass Monkey Bar & Brasserie* in Northbridge is a regular comedy venue (Wednesday night; $8).

Spectator Sports

The people of Perth, like most other Australians, are parochial in their support of local sporting teams. The West Coast Eagles and the Fremantle Dockers, Perth's two representatives in the Australian Football League (AFL), and the Perth Wildcats, in the National Basketball League (NBL), regularly play interstate teams in Perth. In the National Soccer League, Perth Glory is building a big base of fans. Check the *West Australian* for game details.

International one-day cricket and test matches are played in Perth at the Western Australian Cricket Association ground (WACA; ☎ 9265 7222).

Shopping

Perth has a number of excellent outlets for Aboriginal arts and crafts, including the Creative Native Gallery, 32 King St; Ganada, 71 Barrack St; and Artists in Residence Gallery at the Lookout, Fraser Ave, Kings Park. Other crafts can be found at the various markets – see the Markets section earlier in this section.

Getting There & Away

Air Qantas Airways (☎ 13 1313) and Ansett Australia (☎ 13 1300) have direct, one-way economy flights to/from Sydney ($725), Melbourne ($651), Adelaide ($582), Darwin ($697), Yulara for Uluru ($529) and Alice Springs ($555). In most cases, flights to Queensland (Brisbane and Cairns) involve stops in Melbourne or Sydney, although there are more direct flights via Alice Springs ($752 to Brisbane). Ansett's city office is at 26 St George's Terrace, and Qantas is at 55 William St.

Of course, major discounts on these fares are available: with the 21 day advance purchase fare you can get return tickets between Perth and Adelaide for $499, Melbourne $589, Sydney $599 and Brisbane $739 – possibly less if you shop around at travel agents.

Skywest (☎ 9334 2288, 13 1300), out on the Great Eastern Hwy, flies to many regional centres in WA, including Albany, Esperance, Exmouth, Carnarvon and Kalgoorlie.

Bus Greyhound Pioneer (☎ 13 2030) operates daily bus services out of Perth from its new terminal (☎ 9277 9962) at 250 Great Eastern Hwy, Belmont. The airport shuttle bus (see Getting Around in this section) stops here.

The daily coastal run to Darwin takes about 56 hours and costs $436. Greyhound also operates a twice weekly service to Port Hedland via the more direct, inland route through Newman. This trip is three hours shorter and the same price as via the coastal road. Integrity (☎ 9226 1339) operates from the Wellington St bus station and goes as far north as Exmouth.

Westrail (☎ 13 1053) has bus services from the East Perth terminal to numerous destinations – as far as Esperance, Kalgoorlie and Kalbarri. South West Coachlines (☎ 9324 2333) travels from the city bus port to Bunbury, Margaret River and the capes. See Getting Around earlier in this chapter for more information.

Readers recommend the Nullarbor Traveller (☎ 1800 816 858), of Adelaide, which does minibus trips along the coast from Adelaide to Perth. See the Bus section of the Getting Around chapter.

Train Perth train station is the terminal for the 65 hour *Indian-Pacific* trip to Sydney (see the Getting There & Away section earlier in this chapter).

The limited *AvonLink* from Perth to Northam (via Midland and Toodyay), and the *Prospector* to Kalgoorlie, depart from the East Perth terminal on West Parade. The *Prospector* has at least one service in each direction daily; the trip to Kalgoorlie takes about 7½ hours. From Monday to Saturday it leaves Perth around 8.45 am (check this in advance); on Sunday it departs at 2.50 pm.

The *Australind* to Bunbury departs from Perth train station to Bunbury (2¼ hours) at 9.30 am and 5.45 pm daily. Reservations can be made on ☎ 13 1053.

Hitching We *don't* advise hitching (see Hitching in the Getting Around chapter). If you must hitch, hostel notice boards are worth checking for lifts to points around the country. If you're hitching out of Perth to the north or east, take a train to Midland. For travel south, take a train to Armadale.

Getting Around

Perth's public transport organisation, Transperth (☎ 13 6213) operates buses, trains and ferries. Its Web site is www.transperth .wa.gov.au. There are Transperth information offices in the Plaza Arcade (off the Hay St Mall), the Perth train station, the city bus port on Mounts Bay Rd and at the Wellington St bus station. These offices are open Monday to Friday from 7.30 am to 5.30 pm, and the Plaza Arcade office is also open from 8 am to 5.30 pm on Saturday and noon to 6 pm on Sunday. The free *See Perth on Transperth* is useful.

There's a free transit zone in the city involving all Transperth buses and trains. You can travel free of charge within the area bounded by Northbridge (Newcastle St) in the north, the river in the south, Kings Park in the west and the Causeway in the east. For more information see the Bus entry in this section.

To/From the Airport The domestic and international terminals are about 11km and 15km from the city centre. A taxi (Swan Taxis; ☎ 13 1388) to the city costs around $18 and $24 respectively.

The privately run airport shuttle bus (☎ 9479 4131) meets all incoming domestic and international flights, and provides transport to the city centre, hotels and hostels. It costs $7 from the domestic terminal and $9 from the international terminal; a trip between the terminals costs $5. Travelling to the terminals, there are scheduled runs every two hours from 4.45 am to 10.30 pm. Call for more information on hotel and hostel pick-ups and timetables. The Fremantle Airport Shuttle (☎ 9838 4115) costs $12/15 from domestic/international terminals.

Alternatively, you can get into the city (William St) for $2.50 on Transperth bus No 200, 201, 202, 208 or 209. The buses depart from the domestic terminal every hour or so from 5.30 am to 10 pm (less frequently on weekends). Buses leave from bus stand No 32 on St George's Terrace for the domestic terminal.

Bus There are two free excellent Central Area Transit (CAT) services in the city centre. The buses are state of the art and there are computer read-outs (and audio services) at the stops telling you when the next bus is due. Using the two, you can get to most sights in the inner city.

The Red CAT operates east-west from Outram St, West Perth, to the WACA in East Perth; the service runs every five minutes on weekdays from 7 am to 6 pm. The Blue CAT operates north-south from the river to Northbridge, roughly in the centre of the Red CAT route; services run every 7½ minutes on weekdays from 7 am to 6 pm. A modified version of the Blue CAT runs every 10 minutes on weekends. Get a copy of the CAT User Guide from Transperth offices for more information.

On regular buses, a short ride of one zone is $1.70, two zones $2.50 and three zones $3.30. Zone 1 covers the inner suburbs (including Subiaco and Claremont) and Zone 2 extends all the way to Fremantle. A Multi-rider ticket gives 10 journeys for the price of nine, and day tickets (available after 9 am on weekdays) cost $6.50.

Train Transperth (☎ 13 6213) operates the Fastrak suburban train lines to Armadale, Fremantle, Midland and the northern suburb of Joondalup from around 5.20 am to midnight on weekdays, with reduced services on weekends. Free train travel (free transit zone) is between the Claisebrook and City West stations .

All trains leave from the Perth train station on Wellington St. Your rail ticket can also be used on Transperth buses and ferries within its zone.

Car & Motorcycle You'll have no trouble getting fuel between 7 am and 9 pm Monday to Saturday, but on Sunday you need to find out which fuel outlets are rostered to be open (usually from 7 am to 10 pm). For rostering details call ☎ 11 573.

Avis (☎ 13 6333), Budget (☎ 13 2727), Hertz (☎ 13 3039) and Thrifty (☎ 13 1286) are all represented in Perth (including at the airport), but better deals are available from the smaller operators. Apex (☎ 9227 9091), 400 William St, Northbridge, offers some of

the best rates in town; Bayswater Car Rental (☎ 9325 1000), 160 Adelaide Terrace, is also worth trying.

Bicycle Cycling is a great way to explore Perth. There are many bicycle routes along the river that continue all the way to Fremantle and along the Indian Ocean coast.

The Cycle Centre (☎ 9325 1176), 282 Hay St, hires bikes for $15 a day or, if you're in town for a while, it offers a useful guaranteed buy-back plan.

Boat Transperth ferries cross daily from the Barrack St jetty to the Mends St jetty in South Perth every half-hour (more frequently at peak times) between 6.50 am and 7.15 pm ($1/2 one way/return). Take this ferry to get to the zoo.

Around Perth

FREMANTLE
• postcode 6160   • pop 25,000

Despite recent development, Fremantle ('Freo' to the locals) has a far more laid-back feeling than gleaming, skyscrapered Perth. It's a place with a real sense of history and a pleasant atmosphere. Although considered virtually a suburb of Perth these days (many locals catch the train down for the afternoon or a night out), Fremantle has very much a separate identity.

Fremantle was founded in 1829, when HMS *Challenger*, captained by Charles Fremantle, first dropped anchor here. Like Perth, the settlement made little progress until it decided to take in convicts. This cheap and hard-worked labour force constructed most of the town's earliest buildings, some of them among the oldest and most treasured in WA. As a port, Fremantle was abysmal until the brilliant Irish engineer CY O'Connor built an artificial harbour in the 1890s and blasted away the limestone bar that was blocking passage to the Swan River.

In 1987 the city was the site of the unsuccessful defence of what was, for a brief period, one of Australia's most prized possessions – the America's Cup yachting trophy.

AROUND PERTH

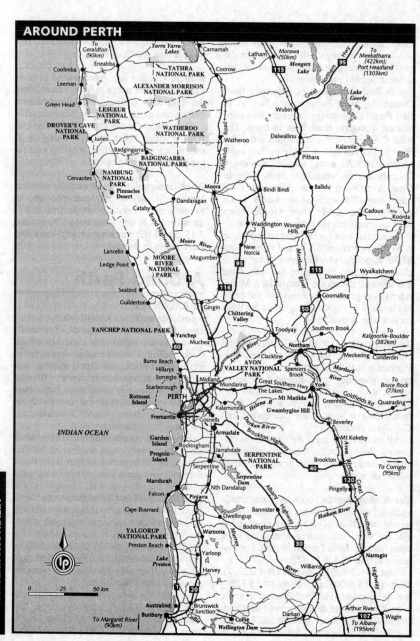

WESTERN AUSTRALIA

Preparations for the influx of tourists associated with the competition transformed Fremantle into a more modern, colourful and expensive city, though at the time many residents protested that their lifestyle and the character of their community were being damaged by development.

The town has numerous interesting old buildings, some excellent museums and galleries, lively produce and craft markets, and a diverse range of pubs, cafes and restaurants. Allow enough time to explore, sip coffee in an outdoor cafe and soak in the atmosphere.

Information

The busy tourist bureau (☎ 9431 7878, fax 9431 7755) is in the Fremantle Town Hall shop on King's Square. It's open Monday to Saturday from 9 am to 5 pm and Sunday from 10.30 am to 4.30 pm. Tramswest (☎ 9339 8719) also runs an information office on the Esplanade reserve (opposite the Esplanade Hotel) or try the WA Cafe on Margaret St. You can get information on national parks at CALM's WA Naturally shop (☎ 9430 8600) at 47 Henry St.

All the hostels have Internet access; Net.chat in the Wesley Arcade on Market St charges 15c a minute ($4 an hour from 8 am to 11 am and 8 pm to 11 pm).

Fremantle History Museum

The history museum, 1 Finnerty St, is housed in a building constructed as a lunatic asylum in the 1860s by convicts. It has a fine collection, including exhibits on Fremantle's Aboriginal history, the colonisation of WA and the early whaling industry. It also tells the intriguing story of the Dutch East India Company ships that first 'discovered' the western coast of Australia and in several instances were wrecked on its inhospitable shores. The museum is open daily from 10.30 am to 4 pm (1 to 5 pm on Saturday). Admission by donation.

WA Maritime Museum

On Cliff St, near the waterfront, this museum (www.mm.wa.gov.au) occupies a building constructed in 1852 as a commissariat store. The museum has a display on WA's maritime history, with emphasis on the famous wreck of the *Batavia*. One gallery features a preserved section of its timber hull and a huge stone portico facade intended as an entrance to Batavia Castle in what is now Jakarta, Indonesia. It was being carried by the *Batavia* as ballast when the vessel sank. A visit to this intriguing museum is a must. It's open daily from 10.30 am to 5 pm, and there are free tours at 11.30 am and 2 pm (admission by $2 donation).

Discover Duyfken

Bobbing in the harbour opposite the Esplanade Reserve is an exact replica of the *Duyfken* (Little Dove), a Dutch *jacht* (scout ship) for the Moluccan Fleet, which made the first recorded voyage to Australia in 1606. It was built in Fremantle, which has become something of a centre for replica boat building – the replica of James Cook's *Endeavour* was also built here.

The *Duyfken*, known to have reached Cape York Peninsula with about 20 crew, is very small for a sailing ship but it's worth a poke around if you're interested in maritime history. It's open from 9.30 am to 4.30 pm (adults/children $5/3).

The boat will be away from Fremantle for at least six months from April 2000 re-enacting its voyage around the northern coast of Australia.

Fremantle Market

A prime attraction is the colourful covered Fremantle Market on the corner of South Terrace and Henderson St. Originally opened in 1892, the market was reopened in 1975 and draws crowds looking for everything from craft items to vegetables, jewellery and antiques; there is also a great tavern where buskers often perform. The market is open on Friday from 9 am to 9 pm, Saturday until 5 pm and Sunday from 10 am to 5 pm. Late Sunday afternoon is the time to buy fruit and vegetables, which are sold at reduced prices before closing time.

Round House

On Arthur Head, at the western end of High St, is the Round House. Built in 1831, it's

FREMANTLE

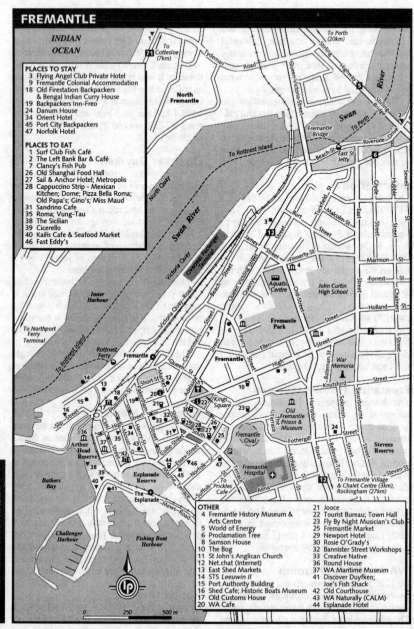

PLACES TO STAY
3 Flying Angel Club Private Hotel
9 Fremantle Colonial Accommodation
18 Old Firestation Backpackers
   & Bengal Indian Curry House
19 Backpackers Inn-Freo
24 Danum House
34 Orient Hotel
45 Port City Backpackers
47 Norfolk Hotel

PLACES TO EAT
1 Surf Club Fish Café
2 The Left Bank Bar & Café
7 Clancy's Fish Pub
26 Old Shanghai Food Hall
27 Sail & Anchor Hotel; Metropolis
28 Cappuccino Strip - Mexican
   Kitchen; Dome; Pizza Bella Roma;
   Old Papa's; Gino's; Miss Maud
31 Sandrino Cafe
35 Roma; Vung-Tau
38 The Sicilian
39 Cicerello
40 Kailis Cafe & Seafood Market
46 Fast Eddy's

OTHER
4 Fremantle History Museum &
   Arts Centre
5 World of Energy
6 Proclamation Tree
8 Samson House
10 The Bog
11 St John's Anglican Church
12 Net.chat (Internet)
13 East Shed Markets
14 STS *Leeuwin II*
15 Port Authority Building
16 Shed Cafe; Historic Boats Museum
17 Old Customs House
20 WA Cafe
21 Jooce
22 Tourist Bureau; Town Hall
23 Fly By Night Musician's Club
25 Fremantle Market
29 Newport Hotel
30 Rosie O'Grady's
32 Bannister Street Workshops
33 Creative Native
36 Round House
37 WA Maritime Museum
41 Discover Duyfken;
   Joe's Fish Shack
42 Old Courthouse
43 WA Naturally (CALM)
44 Esplanade Hotel

WESTERN AUSTRALIA

the oldest public building in WA. It actually has 12 sides and was originally the prison (in the days before convicts were brought into WA). It was also the site of the colony's first hanging.

Later, the building was used to hold Aboriginal prisoners before they were taken to prison on Rottnest Island. The site of the Round House is considered sacred by the Noongar people. It's open daily from 9 am to 5 pm and you can see the Jardine time gun fired daily at 1 pm (admission by $2 donation).

Old Fremantle Prison
This was one of the first building tasks of the convicts and a maximum security prison until 1991. The prison is open daily from 10 am to 6 pm ($10/4). Tours are held every half-hour, or you can take yourself on an audio handset tour of the prison grounds. These prices apply also for the eerie candle-light tours, held on Wednesday and Friday at 7.30 pm.

Gold Rush Landmarks
Fremantle boomed during the Western Australian gold rush of the 1890s and many buildings were constructed shortly before or during this period. They include **Samson House**, a well-preserved 1888 colonial home on Ellen St; open Thursday and Sunday from 1 to 5 pm. **St John's Anglican Church** (1882) on the corner of Adelaide and Queen Sts features a large stained-glass window.

Other buildings of the era are the **Fremantle Town Hall** (1887) on King's Square, and the Georgian-style **Old Customs House** on Cliff St. The **water trough** in the park in front of the Fremantle train station has a memorial to two men who died of thirst on an outback expedition. The **Proclamation Tree**, near the corner of Adelaide and Parry Sts, is a Moreton Bay fig that was planted in 1890.

Other Attractions
From the observation tower on top of the **Port Authority Building**, at the end of Cliff St, you can enjoy a panoramic view of the

harbour. You must take an escorted tour from the foyer (weekdays at 1.30 pm only). Nearby are the **East Shed Markets**, open from 10 am to 9 pm on Friday, and from 9 am to 5 pm on weekends.

For boat freaks only, the **Historic Boats Museum** displays boats from the last 100 years in the B-Shed at Victoria Quay. It's open weekdays from 10 am to 3 pm, and weekends from 11 am to 4 pm (admission by donation).

The **World of Energy**, 12 Parry St, has some entertaining and educational displays tracing the development of gas and electricity. It's open on weekdays from 9 am to 5 pm, and weekends from 1 to 5 pm ($2/1).

Fremantle is a popular centre for artisans and one of the best places to find them is at the imaginative **Bannister Street Workshops**. **Creative Native** is a gallery and shop of Aboriginal art at 65 High St. There's a large collection of hand-painted didgeridoos (from $150 to $300) and everything from boomerangs to painted T-shirts.

Organised Tours
The Fremantle Tram (☎ 9339 8719), very much like the Perth Tram, does a 45 minute historical tour of Fremantle with commentary for $8/3. There are two alternating tours – the Historical Trail and the Four Harbours tour – departing from the town hall daily on the hour from 10 am to 4 pm; there's also the 1½ hour Top of the Port tour at 1.15 pm ($10/5) and the immensely popular Fish & Chips dinner tour on Thursday at 6 pm ($20; book ahead).

You can combine a tour with a return cruise to Perth, and a tour on the Perth Tram for $35.

Special Events
The 10 day Festival of Fremantle in November is the city's biggest annual event. It features street parades, concerts, exhibitions and free performances. The Sardine Festival, held on the Esplanade in January, is devoted to gourmet food – yabbies, crocodile, seafood and Freo's sardines – but there's free entertainment too. There's also the Busker's Festival in April.

Places to Stay – Budget

The *Fremantle Village & Chalet Centre* (☎ 9430 4866, Lot 1 Cockburn Rd), about 3.5km from the city centre, has noisy en suite tent/powered sites at $15/18 and chalets at $70 for two.

Backpackers Inn Freo (☎ 9431 7065, fax 9336 7106, 11 Pakenham St) is a superb YHA hostel. It has been completely renovated and extended to include the warehouse next door; there are plenty of well designed communal areas and all the usual facilities, including a good cafe. Dorm beds are $14/16 for members/nonmembers, singles are $20/23 and twins or doubles are $34/39.

The *Old Firestation Backpackers* (☎ 9430 5454, 18 Phillimore St) is also pretty impressive – there are more free facilities here than you can point a hose at. Formerly the town's fire station (the new one is next door), it's a little basic but it's well managed and very secure (surveillance cameras, the works). It has free Internet access between 8 am and 6 pm, free use of washing machines, backpacker meals for $2.50 from 6 to 7 pm and, considerately, a female-only area with a separate lounge, kitchen, rooms and showers. The managers will also help you find work and arrange transport. Dorm beds are $14, singles $20 and doubles $36, and there are significantly cheaper weekly rates.

Port City Backpackers (☎ 9335 6635, 5 Essex St) is well located between the Esplanade and South Terrace, and is the smallest of Freo's hostels. Dorm beds cost from $12, twin/doubles are $35. If you stay here there's an opportunity to work with nearby Wyjalla Didjeridus and learn how to craft and play the instruments (and perhaps keep one).

Places to Stay – Mid-Range

The *Norfolk Hotel* (☎ 9335 5405, 47 South Terrace), with arguably the best beer garden in Perth, has small singles/doubles for $35/60 or $75/85 with en suite. The *Orient Hotel* (☎ 9336 2455, 39 High St) has good rooms with shared facilities for a reasonable $30/50. The *Flying Angel Club Private Hotel* (☎ 9335 5000, fax 9335 5321, 76 Queen Victoria St) in the International Seafarers' Centre has Bed & Breakfast rooms with en suite for $50/85.

B&B places are popular and historic Fremantle has some good ones – ask the tourist office for a list. *Fremantle Colonial Accommodation* (☎ 9430 6568, fax 9340 6568, 215 High St) is a charming place with elegant rooms from $75. The proprietors also have a licence to let the three former wardens' cottages adjoining the prison on the hill overlooking Fremantle. A two-bedroom, self-contained cottage with laundry facilities and generous breakfast supplies costs $130 a night. *Danum House* (☎ 9336 3735, 6 Fothergill St) charges from $80/90.

Places to Eat

Many a traveller's afternoon in Freo has been whiled away sipping beer or coffee and watching life go by from pavement tables on the South Terrace 'cappuccino strip'. Cafes and restaurants along here include the popular *Old Papa's* at No 17, which has great coffee and gelati; the trendy *Gino's* (the place to be seen) at No 1; *Dome*, which has a multicultural arts centre upstairs; and the large *Miss Maud*, with a pleasant terrace area, at No 33.

The historic *Sail & Anchor Hotel* (64 South Terrace), formerly the Freemason's Hotel, built in 1854, has been impressively restored to much of its former glory. It specialises in locally brewed Matilda Bay beers, and on the 1st floor is a brasserie serving snacks and full meals.

The *Mexican Kitchen*, next to Old Papa's, has mains from $10 to $15 (half-price nachos on Tuesday). On the other side of the road, *Pizza Bella Roma* is probably the most popular pizza and pasta joint in town.

The *Old Shanghai Food Hall* (4 Henderson St), opposite the market, is a small Asian food hall. You can get delicious and cheap Thai, Vietnamese, Japanese, Chinese and Italian food in large portions here till 9 pm most nights and it's busy on market days.

Fast Eddy's (13 Essex St), not far from South Terrace, is an American-theme diner with good breakfasts and a 24 hour licence. For something more upmarket, *Sandrino Cafe*, (☎ 9335 4487, 93 Market

St) has excellent Italian cuisine and seafood at moderate prices.

West End & Harbour *Roma (☎ 9335 3664, 13 High St)* is a reliable Freo institution, which serves home-made Italian fare. Even the rich and famous have to queue to eat here. For Vietnamese food, try the *Vung-Tau (19 High St)*. The *Bengal Indian Curry House*, in the old fire station on Phillimore St, has great cheap lunch specials.

Dining on fish and chips down by the fishing boat harbour is a Freo tradition. *Cicerello (44 Mews Rd)* and *Kailis's Fish Market Café (46 Mews Rd)* both serve deep-fried seafood for around $6. Kailis's also has a fresh seafood market.

For something a bit fancier, the *Sicilian (☎ 9430 7024, 47 Mews Rd)*, beneath Sails Restaurant on the harbour, is where you might end the evening – it's not cheap but enjoys a good reputation and also does a buffet breakfast. *Joe's Fish Shack (42 Mews Rd)*, alongside the Duyfken reconstruction, has a great waterfront location and reasonably priced seafood.

Other Areas Fashionable places include the *Left Bank Bar & Café (☎ 9319 1315, 15n Riverside Rd)*, down from the East St jetty, and the beachy, trendy *Surf Club Fish Café (☎ 9430 6866, Port Beach Rd)*, out at North Fremantle Beach, has both cheap and expensive sections).

Clancy's Fish Pub (Cantonment St) is a lively pub and nightspot specialising in good value seafood dishes.

Prickles Cafe (408 South Terrace) specialises in modern bush tucker – Aussie nouvelle cuisine (kangaroo, emu and crocodile – even witchetty grubs!) and a host of vegetarian dishes with a twist.

Entertainment

Freo buzzes like a fridge at night. There are many venues in town with music and/or dancing.

Home of the 'big gig' is still the *Metropolis (52 South Terrace)*. It's also a nightclub but is really only a good venue when the big bands are on. The *Orient Hotel (39 High St)* and the *Newport Hotel (2 South Terrace)* also have bands pumping out on the weekends.

Fly by Night Musician's Club on Parry St (in what looks like an aircraft hangar) is frequented by talented musicians specialising in world music, and occasionally has big name performers.

Jooce (80 High St), is the latest dance club with house and techno music and the Cigar Lounge upstairs. *Rosie O'Grady's* is an ever-popular Irish pub on William St, with live music three or four nights a week, but the latest Irish hot spot is the *Bog (189 High St)*, which is already emulating the success of its Perth counterpart.

Mojo's (237 Queen Victoria St) in North Fremantle (near the station) is the most popular indie music venue around.

Getting There & Around

The Fremantle Airport Shuttle (☎ 9383 4115) departs from Fremantle for the airport six times daily from 6.30 am to 9.30 pm, and picks up at your accommodation ($12/15 domestic/international terminal).

The train between Perth and Fremantle runs every 15 minutes or so throughout the day ($2.50). Bus Nos 106 and 111 from the city busport go along St George's Terrace to Fremantle via the Canning Hwy. Bus Nos 102, 103 and 104 depart from St George's Terrace (south side) but go to Fremantle via the north side of the river.

Oceanic Cruises has daily ferries from Perth's Barrack St jetty to Freo for $9/16 one way/return at 8.45, 10 and 11.45 am.

Fleet Cycles (☎ 9430 5414), 66 Adelaide St, hires bikes for $20 a day (closed Sunday).

ROTTNEST ISLAND
• postcode 6161　　• pop 400

'Rotto', as it's known to the locals, is a sandy island only 11km long and 4.5km wide about 19km off the coast from Fremantle. It was discovered by the Dutch explorer Willem de Vlamingh in 1696. He named it Rats' Nest because of the numerous king-size 'rats' he saw there (in fact, they were small wallabies called quokkas). The Rottnest settlement was established in 1838 as a prison for Aborigines from the

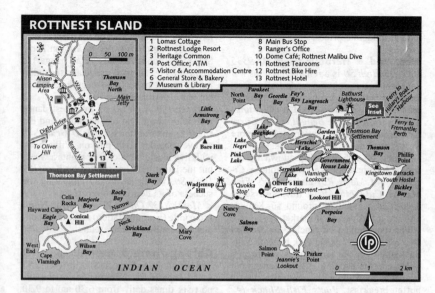

ROTTNEST ISLAND

1 Lomas Cottage
2 Rottnest Lodge Resort
3 Heritage Common
4 Post Office; ATM
5 Visitor & Accommodation Centre
6 General Store & Bakery
7 Museum & Library
8 Main Bus Stop
9 Ranger's Office
10 Dome Café; Rottnest Malibu Dive
11 Rottnest Tearooms
12 Rottnest Bike Hire
13 Rottnest Hotel

mainland – the early colonists had lots of trouble imposing their ideas of private ownership on the nomadic Aborigines. The prison was abandoned in 1903 and the island soon became an escape for Perth society.

During WWII Rottnest Island became an important military stronghold, primarily to protect the coast and Fremantle Harbour. Some 2500 personnel were based on the fortfied island by 1942, and the legacy of this period can be seen in the Kingstown barracks and the gun placement on Oliver Hill.

In the last 30 years, the island has developed as a popular day trip, and with numerous high-speed ferries making the trip over from Perth and Fremantle, a visit is a must.

So what do you do on Rotto? Well, you cycle around the island, laze in the sun on the many superb beaches, climb the low hills, go fishing, boating or surfing, ride in a glass-bottomed boat (the waters have some of the world's most southerly coral), swim in the crystal-clear water or go quokka spotting.

Information

The visitors centre (☎ 9372 9752) at the harbour in Thomson Bay (the island's largest settlement) is open weekdays from 8.30 am to 5 pm, Saturday from 9 am to 4 pm, and Sunday from 10 am to noon and 2.30 to 4 pm. The island's accommodation booking service (☎ 9432 9111) is also here. You can pick up useful publications detailing a walking tour of the old settlement buildings, heritage trails, various shipwrecks around the island and a cycling guide.

There's a post office and an ATM in Thomson Bay. Rottnest is very popular in summer, when ferries and accommodation are heavily booked – plan ahead.

Things to See & Do

The excellent little **museum** has exhibits about the island, its history, wildlife and shipwrecks. It's open daily in summer from 11 am to 4 pm ($2/50c). You can wander around the old convict-built buildings, including the octagonal 1864 'Quad' and Lomas Cottage. Rottnest Voluntary Guides (☎ 9372 9777) conducts free walking tours from the ranger's office daily at 11.30 am and 2.30 pm.

Vlamingh Lookout on View Hill, near Thomson Bay, offers panoramic views of the island. The main lighthouse, built on Wadjemup Hill in 1895, is visible from 60km out to sea. The island has a number of low-lying salt lakes and it's around these that you are most likely to spot **quokkas**. Bus tours have regular quokka-feeding points where the voracious marsupials appear on demand.

The restored **Oliver Hill Gun Emplacement**, west of Thomson Bay, is linked by the Oliver Hill railway line; trains leave Thomson Bay four times daily. The cost of $9/6 includes entry to see the guns and tunnels.

Some of Rotto's shipwrecks are accessible to snorkellers but getting to most of them requires a boat. There are marker plaques around the island telling the grim tales of how and when the ships sank. Snorkelling equipment, fishing gear and boats can be hired from Malibu Dive (☎ 9292 5111) in Thomson Bay.

KATE NOLAN
A local on Rottnest – a quokka

Organised Tours

There are two-hour bus tours around the island, departing from the visitors centre daily at 11 am and 1.30 pm ($12/6).

The *Underwater Explorer* is a boat with windows below the waterline for viewing shipwrecks and marine life; an interesting 45 minute trip costs $16/9. There are also snorkelling tours in summer ($18/15) and a twilight cruise ($17/15). Scenic flights over the island are available with Rottnest Air Taxi (☎ 1800 500 006); a 10 minute flight costs $18.

Places to Stay

Most visitors to Rotto come only for the day but it's worth staying overnight. You can camp at the *Allison camping ground* in Thomson Bay for $5 per person. There are also safari cabins from $28 for two people in the high season. Book cabins well in advance through the Rottnest Island Authority (☎ 9432 9111) or directly at the visitors centre. The authority has over 250 houses and cottages for rent in Thomson Bay and around Geordie, Fays and Longreach bays. There are bungalows (four bed) for $201/234 a week in winter/summer, and ocean-front villas from $447/560 per week.

The *Kingstown Barracks YHA* (☎ 9372 9780), 1.3km south-east of the ferry terminal, is in an old army barracks built in 1936;

dorm beds are $16 ($14 for nonmembers) and doubles are $38, linen included. *Rottnest Lodge Resort* (☎ 9292 5161, fax 9292 5158), in the former Quad (prison), is more inviting these days and has double rooms with en suite and TV from $130.

Places to Eat

Rottnest has a well-stocked *general store* and a *bakery* that's famed for its fresh bread and pies.

The new licensed *Rottnest Tearooms* has a pleasant balcony overlooking the bay, and serves a range of light meals, sandwiches and takeaways. There's a branch of the popular *Dome Cafe* nearby.

Brolley's in the Rottnest Hotel serves snacks and meals, and there's the licensed *Garden Lake* in the Lodge Resort.

Getting There & Away

Rottnest Air Taxi (☎ 1800 500 006) has a same day return flight to Rotto from Perth's Jandakot airport (from $50). It offers transfer to the airport from city locations, including Fremantle.

There are frequent ferries to Rottnest from Fremantle (30 minutes) and a few services from Perth (1½ hours) daily.

Boat Torque (☎ 9430 5844) has ferries every two hours from 7.30 am to 3.30 pm (and at 6.30 pm on Friday) departing from

Emma Place in North Fremantle. The cost for a same-day return is $35/12 for adults/children ($5 more for an extended stay); backpackers with YHA/VIP card pay $30 for the day return. From Perth's Barrack St jetty there are services at 8.45, 9.45 and 10.30 am and 2 pm (and 7.15 pm on Friday) for $52/47/15 adults/backpackers/children.

From Hillarys Boat Harbour (north of Perth), Boat Torque's *Sea Flyte* takes 45 minutes to get to Rottnest Island, departing daily at 8.30 and 10.30 am (and 4.30 pm in peak season); the cost is $45/35/13 for adults/backpackers/children.

Oceanic Cruises (☎ 9430 5127) departs from the East St jetty in Fremantle at 7, 8.30, 9.45 and 11.45 am and 4 pm; adult/child fares are $32/10 for same-day return, $37/14 for an extended stay ($5 discount for YHA/VIP card holders). From Pier 2A at the Barrack St jetty in Perth ferries depart at 8.45 and 10 am ($45/40/14 for same-day return).

Rottnest Express (☎ 9335 6406) conveniently departs from C Shed at Victoria Quay in Fremantle daily at 7.30, 9.30 and 11.15 am and 3.30 pm (and 6.45 pm on Friday). Same-day return is $34/29/10 adults/backpackers/children; extended return is $39/34/14.

Getting Around

Bicycles are the time-honoured way of getting around the island. The number of motor vehicles is strictly limited, which makes cycling a real pleasure, and the island is just big enough to make a day's ride fine exercise. Rottnest Bike Hire (☎ 9292 5105) in Thomson Bay hires adult bikes from $13 a day; a deposit of $20 is required and locks and helmets (both necessary) are provided.

A free bus departs regularly from the main jetty in Thomson Bay between 8.15 am and 5.45 pm. It goes to Geordie Bay, Kingstown and the airport.

The Bayseeker ($5/2) departs from Thomson Bay every half-hour from 8 am to 5.30 pm and does a circuit of the island, stopping at all the main bays and beaches.

SOUTH OF PERTH

The coast south of Perth has a softer appearance than the often harsh landscape to the north. This is a popular beach-resort area for Perth residents, many of whom have holiday homes along the coast.

Rockingham

- postcode 6168   • pop 49,900

Rockingham, 47km south of Perth, was founded in 1872 as a port, but that function was taken over by Fremantle. Today, Rockingham is a dormitory city (WA's second largest in terms of population) and a popular seaside resort with both sheltered and ocean beaches.

The tourist centre (☎ 9592 3464), 43 Kent St, is open on weekdays from 9 am to 5 pm and weekends until 4 pm.

Penguin Island, home to a colony of blue fairy penguins from late October to May, and **Seal Island** are part of the Shoalwater Islands Marine Park. Rockingham Sea Tours (☎ 9528 2004) operates a variety of trips daily from Mersey Point jetty, Shoalwater Bay. The boat to Penguin Island ($7.50/4.50) includes entry to the Penguin Experience Island Discovery Centre. There's also a 45 minute cruise of both islands ($18.50/9.50) and a snorkel cruise ($25/17).

Rockingham Dolphins (☎ 0418-958 678) has unique trips swimming with dolphins daily from September to May ($130) departing from the jetty on Palm Beach (there's also a free bus from Perth).

Places to Stay & Eat The *Palm Beach Caravan Park* (☎ 9527 1515, 37 Fisher St) has powered sites for $14 and on-site vans for $40. *Rockingham Beach Backpackers* (☎ 9592 1828, 26 Kent) is in a great location facing the beach but it's really just a charmless shell with a lot of potential. Still, a bed in a large dorm (no bunks) costs $15, singles are $35 and doubles $45.

The cosy *Anchorage Guest House* (☎ 9527 4214, 2 Smythe St) has B&B singles/doubles from $55/75.

The *Leisure Inn* (☎ 9527 7777), on the corner of Read St and Simpson Ave near the bus terminal, has motel units for $70/80.

There's a string of pleasant cafes with alfresco dining along Rockingham Rd on the beachfront. *Sinbad's Cafe*, at No 41, is open early for breakfast; the *Country Spot* at No 43 and *Oliver's Restaurant* at No 45 are also good. Otherwise, try the local hotels for a counter meal.

Getting There & Away Get to Rockingham on bus No 120 from Fremantle, or any South-West Coachlines Bunbury-bound bus from the city busport in Perth. The local bus depot is at the city shopping centre on Clifton St.

Mandurah
• postcode 6210   • pop 35,950

Situated on the calm Mandurah Estuary and 74km south of Perth, this is another popular beach resort. Dolphins are often seen in the estuary, and the waterways in the area are noted for good fishing, prawning and crabbing.

The Tourist Bureau (☎ 9550 3999), near the boat harbour on Mandurah Terrace, has transport schedules, maps and other information. Attached is the **Peel Discovery Centre** ($2/1), a walk-through exhibition covering the region's history and attractions.

Parrots of Bellawood Park, on Furnissdale Rd, is a fauna park where you can see and feed several species of parrot; there's also a breeding program for endangered species and a walk-in aviary. It's open Thursday to Monday from 10 am to 4 pm ($6.50/3.50).

The **Mandurah City Tram** is similar to those in Perth and Fremantle and does a city tour from the tourist bureau daily at 10 am and 11 am ($6/4).

Various **cruises** up the estuary leave from the jetty near the tourist bureau several times a day. One-hour cruises are $8/5, luncheon cruises cost $30/16. Prolific bird life can be seen on the Peel Inlet and the narrow coastal salt lakes, Clifton and Preston, to the south. Avocet Wildlife Cruises concentrates on this aspect of the waterways with eco-cruises from $10. All cruises can be booked at the tourist bureau.

Places to Stay & Eat There's plenty of accommodation, including a string of caravan parks with tent sites and on-site vans on

the way into town. *Timbertop Caravan Park* (☎ 9535 1292), on the corner of Peel and Rockford Sts, has powered sites for $14 and on-site vans for $35.

Albatross House (☎ 9581 5597, 26 Hall St) has good value B&B for $45/90 for singles/doubles. The *Blue Bay Motel* (☎ 9535 2743, 11 Oversby St), about 200m from the beach, is also reasonable at $55/70.

A 15 minute drive south of town, across the Dawesville Channel on Melrose Beach, is *Yalgorup Eco Park* (☎ 9582 1320, 8 Henry Rd), a pleasant retreat with provision for backpackers (being built at the time of writing). It has tent/powered sites at $14/15, four-bed cabins with kitchenette at $38 for two ($5 for each extra person) and more luxurious accommodation.

The *Hog's Breath Cafe (115 Mandurah Terrace)* is good for lunch and dinner, and there's a branch of the *Dome Cafe* on the waterfront next to the jetty.

Jetty Fish & Chips (Mandurah Terrace) serves big and tasty portions. Next door is *Yo Yo's* for ice creams.

Getting There & Away Bus No 116 from the Perth city busport, or No 117 from Fremantle, will get you to the Dower St depot in Mandurah. South-west Coachlines and Westrail have daily buses from Perth, dropping off in Sutton St.

Pinjarra & Dwellingup
Pinjarra (population 1900), 86km south of Perth, was the scene of a bloody battle between white settlers and Aborigines in 1834. Only five years after first settling the area, colonists massacred members of the Bindjareb Nyoongar tribe in reprisal for a series of raids and the killing of a soldier. It has a number of old buildings picturesquely sited on the banks of the Murray River.

The Pinjarra tourist centre (☎ 9531 1438) is in historic **Edenvale**, on the corner of George and Henry Sts.

About 4km south of town is **Old Blythewood**, an 1859 colonial farm and National Trust property.

The new **Forest Heritage Centre** (☎ 9538 1395) in Acacia St, Dwellingup, 24km south-east of Pinjarra, has wood-working displays and a tree-top walk through the jarrah forest ($5/2). Dwellingup is also the terminus for the **Hotham Valley Railway** (☎ 9221 4444), which runs a variety of steam train trips between May and October. The Etmilyn Forest Tramway does a 1½ hour diesel-hauled journey from Dwellingup on Tuesday, Thursday and weekends ($8/3.50), passing through blooming wildflowers and virgin jarrah forests. On weekends between May and October the service is steam-hauled ($9/4.50). There are also steam train journeys from Pinjarra station on Wednesday from April to November ($15/9.50).

Places to Stay & Eat The *Pinjarra Motel* (☎ 9531 1811) offers singles/doubles for $45/65. *Fairbridge* (☎ 9531 1177), about 5km north of Pinjarra, is a peaceful 'mini-village' with accommodation from $15 per person and numerous recreation facilities. It's big with school groups – you'll need your own transport to get here.

The *Heritage Tearooms* in Pinjarra has light meals, such as sandwiches and quiche. *Ravenswood Sanctuary* on Sutton St, Pinjarra, has a pleasant cafe and restaurant open on weekends only, and a program of folk and classical music in summer.

THE DARLING RANGE

The hills that surround Perth are popular for picnics and bushwalks. The **Araluen Botanic Garden** with its waterfalls and terraced gardens, the **Mt Dale** fire lookout and **Churchman's Brook** are all off the Brookton Hwy. Other places of interest include the hairpin bends of the former **Zig Zag** railway at Gooseberry Hill and the walking trails of **Lake Leschenaultia**. CALM provides a good free pamphlet *The Hills Forest*.

Mundaring

- postcode 6073   • pop 1900

Mundaring, 35km east of Perth, is the site of the Mundaring Weir, completed in 1900 to supply water to the goldfields over 500km to the east. The reservoir has an attractive setting and there are a number of walking tracks. The **CY O'Connor Museum** has ex-

hibits about the water pipeline to the goldfields – in its time it was one of the country's most audacious engineering feats. It's open weekdays (except Tuesday) from 10.30 am to 3 pm and Sunday from noon to 5 pm.

The **John Forrest National Park** near Mundaring has protected areas of jarrah and marri trees, native fauna, waterfalls, a swimming pool and an old railway tunnel.

Places to Stay The *Mundaring Caravan Park* (☎ 9295 1125, Great Eastern Hwy), 2km west of town, has powered sites for $10 for two.

Djaril Mari YHA (☎ 9295 1809, Mundaring Weir Rd), 8km south of town in a rustic location near the reservoir, has dorm beds from $14. Staff can arrange pick up from Mundaring and meals if booked in advance.

The *Mundaring Weir Hotel* (☎ 9295 1106, Mundaring Weir Rd) is popular with Perth residents for weekend breaks. Its quality rammed-earth units cost from $70 for two ($100 on weekends).

AVON VALLEY

The lush Avon Valley, about 100km north-east of Perth, looks very English and was a delight to homesick early settlers. In the spring, this area is particularly rich in wildflowers. The valley was first settled in 1830, only a year after Perth was founded, so there are many historic buildings. The picturesque Avon River is very popular with canoeing enthusiasts.

Getting There & Away

The Avon Valley towns all have bus connections to Perth with Westrail (☎ 13 1053), and you can also get to Toodyay and Northam by train on either *Avonlink* or the *Prospector*. The bus fare to York is $9.70; the bus/train fare to Northam is $11.40 and to Toodyay it's $9.70. The best way to see the valley, however, is in your own car.

Toodyay

- postcode 6566   • pop 670

There are numerous old buildings in this charming and historic town, many built by convicts. The tourist centre (☎ 9574 2435)

Connor's Mill – grinding on

is on Stirling Terrace in the 1870s **Connor's Mill**, which still houses a working flour mill. It's open daily from 9 am to 5 pm.

The **Old Newcastle Gaol Museum** on Clinton St is open daily from 11 am to 3 pm ($3/2); the Moondyne Gallery within tells the story of bushranger Joseph Bolitho Johns (Moondyne Joe). Close to town is **Coorinja** winery, which dates from the 1870s (open daily except Sunday).

Places to Stay & Eat *Avon Banks Caravan Park (☎ 9574 2612, Railway Rd)* has tent/powered sites for $10/14, on-site vans for $30 and self-contained cabins for $50.

Victoria Hotel/Motel (☎ 9574 2206, Stirling Terrace) has singles/doubles with shared facilities from $20/40 and motel rooms for $30/55; meals are available.

Cafes along Stirling Terrace include the *Stirling House Cafe*, with pleasant outdoor seating and a BYO restaurant for evening meals, the *Lavender Cafe* and the *Toodyay Bakery. Connor's Cottage Restaurant (☎ 9574 2613, 5 Piesse St)* is the best place in town.

Avon Valley National Park

This national park, down river from Toodyay, is an area of granite outcrops, diverse fauna and transitional forests. It is the northern limit of the jarrah forests, where jarrah and marri mix with wandoo woodlands. There are camp sites with basic facilities for $8 (two people); contact the ranger (☎ 9574 2540). National park fees apply for vehicles. The park is 30km from Toodyay and the entrance is 5km off the main road.

Northam

• postcode 640   • pop 6300

Northam, the major town of the Avon Valley, is a farming centre on the railway line to Kalgoorlie. At one time, the line from Perth ended here and miners had to trek hundreds of kilometres to the goldfields. Every year Northam is packed on the first weekend in August for the start of the gruelling 133km Avon Descent race for power boats and canoeists.

The friendly and modern Avon Valley Tourist Bureau (☎ 9622 2100), 2 Grey St, overlooks the Avon River and includes a cafe and a free exhibition explaining the role of two post-war refugee camps that were set up in Northam to house European immigrants. It's open daily from 9 am to 5 pm.

The 1836 **Morby Cottage** served as Northam's first church and school, and now houses a museum, open on Sunday from 10.30 am to 4 pm ($2/1). The **old railway station**, listed by the National Trust, has been restored and turned into a museum; it's open on Sunday from 10 am to 4 pm ($2/50c). Also of interest in town is the colony of **white swans** on the Avon River, the descendants of birds introduced from England in the early 1900s.

If you have the funds, try **ballooning** over the Avon Valley (weekends from March to November; $190 per person).

Places to Stay & Eat The *Northam Guesthouse (☎ 9622 2301, 51 Wellington St)* is a bit shambolic in the communal areas but most of the rooms are OK and it's cheap at $15 per person. There are no dorms so you may get a decent double room for that price.

CHRIS MELLOR

The *Colonial Tavern* (☎ 9622 1074, 197 Duke St) has excellent value singles/doubles for $25/40 in large rooms. It's in a peaceful part of town and also serves good food.

The *Shamrock Hotel* (☎ 9622 1092, 112 Fitzgerald St) is one of the nicest places in town, with elegant en suite bedrooms; a double costs from $99. This is also the place for an upmarket evening meal as it has a good cafe/bistro.

Egoline Reflections (☎ 9622 5811, Toodyay Rd), 7km out of town, is an excellent farmstay with B&B from $85/120.

Bruno's Pizza Bar (Fitzgerald St) does tasty pizza to eat in or take away. *Central Cafe*, a few doors along, is open early for a cheap breakfast.

York

- postcode 6302   - pop 1900

The oldest inland town in WA, York was settled in 1831. It is one of the highlights of the Avon Valley, even though its efforts to preserve and promote its Englishness (complete with old red phoneboxes) are a bit over the top. A stroll down the main street, with its many restored old buildings, is a step back in time and the whole town is classified by the National Trust.

The tourist centre (☎ 9641 1301) is in one of the finest buildings, the old **town hall** on the corner of Avon Terrace and Joaquina St. It's open Monday to Friday from 10 am to 4 pm, Saturday from 9.30 am to 4.30 pm and Sunday from 9 am to 4 pm.

The excellent 1850s **Residency Museum**, Brook St, is open Tuesday to Thursday from 1 to 3 pm and weekends until 5 pm ($2/1). The **Castle Hotel**, at 97 Avon Terrace (which dates from coaching days and claims to be WA's oldest inland hotel), is photogenic, as are the police station, gaol, courthouse and Settlers House.

The classy **Motor Museum**, 116 Avon Terrace, houses Australia's best collection of vintage, classic and racing cars, including the Saudi Williams driven by former world champion Alan Jones. It's open daily from 9.30 to 4 pm ($7).

York loves a good festival, with no fewer than a dozen major annual events.

The better patronised ones are the Jazz Festival in October, the Flying 50s Vintage & Veteran car race in August and Rally Australia in November.

Places to Stay & Eat The *Mt Bakewell Caravan Park* (☎ 9641 1421, Eighth Rd) has tent/powered sites at $13/15 and on-site vans for $34 for two.

The *Castle Hotel* (☎ 9641 1007, 97 Avon Terrace) has good value rooms in its historic hotel section for $35 per person, and motel rooms for $65/90 a single/double. The *Settlers House* (☎ 9641 1096, 125 Avon Terrace) has stylish B&B for $69/118.

There are a number of quality B&Bs and farmstays in the region from about $70 to $200 for two people; inquire at the tourist bureau.

From the wide selection of eateries along Avon Terrace, try the *Settlers House* for breakfast, *Cafe Bugatti* for cappuccino and Italian food, *York Village Bakehouse* for freshly baked bread and cakes, and *Jule's Shoppe* for delicious home-made pasties. The *York Imperial Inn*, opposite the town hall, has a cafe with a pleasant outdoor dining area and a gallery, and the *Castle Hotel* serves decent counter meals.

Beverley

- postcode 6304   - pop 790

South of York, also on the Avon River, Beverley was founded in 1838 and is noted for its fine **aeronautical museum**, open daily from 9 am to 4 pm. Exhibits include a locally built biplane, *Silver Centenary*, constructed between 1928 and 1930. The tourist bureau (☎ 9646 1555) is housed in this building on Vincent St, easily recognised by the Vampire jet mounted on the front lawn!

The 7 sq km **Avondale Discovery Farm**, 6km west of Beverley, has a large collection of agricultural machinery, a homestead, workshop and stables.

The *Beverley Caravan Park* (☎ 9646 1200, 136 Vincent St), at the shire offices, has tent/powered sites for $5/10 for two people. The ordinary *Beverley Hotel* (☎ 9646 1190, 137 Vincent St) has singles/doubles for $22/45.

NORTH OF PERTH

The coast north of Perth is scenic, but quickly becomes the inhospitable terrain that deterred early explorers. The **Yanchep National Park**, 51km north of Perth, is natural bushland with a colony of 'imported' koalas, some fine caves (including the limestone Crystal and Yondemp caves), Loch McNess and the Yaberoo Budjara Aboriginal Heritage Trail. The town of Yanchep has an atmospheric pub and nearby is the Two Rocks fishing marina with attached shopping complex.

On weekdays, one bus goes to Yanchep from Perth's Wellington St bus station.

Some 43km north of Yanchep is **Guilderton**, a popular holiday resort beside the mouth of the Moore River. The *Vergulde Draeck* (Gilt Dragon), a Dutch East India Company ship, ran aground near here in 1656. See the boxed text 'Dutch Shipwrecks' later in this chapter.

Lancelin
• postcode 6044   • pop 600

The sealed coast road ends at Lancelin, a small crayfishing port and up-and-coming resort 130km north of Perth.

An off-shore reef provides good surfing and windsurfing conditions, and the town is backed by expansive dunes that are great for **sand boarding**. This is the home of the amazing 'Bigfoot' – supposedly the world's largest 4WD tour coach and a sight to behold. It does trips into the dunes daily ($25/15); contact Sandgroper Safaris (☎ 9405 3074).

Windswept Lancelin is the end of the annual Ledge Point Windsurfing Race. There are many opportunities in Lancelin to learn **windsurfing** – Werner's Hot Spot, usually set up on the beach, hires out equipment and has beginners' lessons for $10 an hour.

Places to Stay & Eat *Lancelin Lodge YHA (☎ 9655 2020, fax 9655 2021, Hopkins St)* is a friendly, well-equipped, purpose-built backpacker place. It's run by Trish and Trev, who are knowledgeable and passionate about the local area. A comfortable dorm bed is $15 ($14 for YHA members) and neat doubles are $40 ($50 in the high season).

Windsurfer Beach Units (☎/fax 9655 1454, 1 Hopkins St) occupies a prime spot by the entrance to the beach. Fully self-contained units sleeping six are $75 a night for two people.

The *Endeavour Tavern (Gin Gin St)*, near the jetty, is a classic pub with a beer garden right on the beach and excellent counter meals (including local crayfish). The *Offshore Café (Hopkins St)* is good for coffee, snacks and light meals, and it's licensed.

Getting There & Away Catch-a-bus (☎ 019-378 987) is a shuttle service that picks up in Perth on Monday, Wednesday and Friday at 9.30 am and returns the same days at around 1 pm ($20 one way). If you're coming down from the north by Greyhound, Lancelin Lodge may be able to arrange a pick-up from Regan's Ford (you'll have to tell the bus driver you want to get off there).

A 4WD-only coast road continues up to Cervantes.

Pinnacles Desert

The small seaport of **Cervantes** (population 480), 257km north of Perth, is the entry point for the bizarre and haunting Pinnacles Desert. Here, in coastal **Nambung National Park**, the flat sandy desert is punctured with peculiar limestone pillars, some only a few centimetres high, others towering up to 5m. The park is also the scene of an impressive wildflower display from August to October. Entry costs $8 per car or $3 for bus passengers.

Try to visit the Pinnacles Desert early in the morning. Not only is the light better for photography but you will avoid the crowds, especially in peak holiday times. Sunset is also a great time for photography, when the pillars cast long shadows and the late afternoon sun produces orange and purple hues.

The park is 13km from Cervantes and part of the drive is along a bumpy unsealed road. Conventional vehicles are usually OK on the park roads – as long as you stick to them – but check in Cervantes if conditions are wet. A coastal gravel road runs north to **Jurien**, a crayfishing centre, and south to Lancelin.

Organised Tours Cervantes Pinnacles Adventure Tours (☎ 9652 7236) offers a range of tours, including 4WD trips into the dunes. The standard Pinnacles tour is $20, and sunrise, sunset or full moon trips are $25. It also runs an informative cruise, covering aspects of the local rock lobster (crayfish) industry for $80.

Happyday Tours (☎ 9652 7244) runs a tour of the Pinnacles from Cervantes daily at 8.30 am, connecting with the Greyhound bus at the Brand Hwy turn-off. The tour costs $12 (plus $3 entry), or it can be included on your Greyhound pass if you have one.

Places to Stay There is accommodation in Cervantes but not in the national park. The *Pinnacles Caravan Park (☎ 9652 7060, 35 Aragon St)* on the beachfront has tent/powered sites for $11/15 and on-site vans/cabins from $25/35.

Pinnacles Beach Backpackers (☎ 9652 7377, 91 Seville St) is a friendly purpose-built place close to the beach with a well-equipped kitchen, plenty of recreation space and cramped but tidy rooms; dorm beds are $15, doubles $40 and the family room with en suite $50. Internet access is available.

The *Pinnacles Motel (☎ 9652 7145, 227 Aragon St)* has doubles for $90.

The South-West

South-west WA's coastline is magnificent with two prominent capes and many national parks, including the region of 'tall trees'. It's a green, fertile area that contrasts with the dry and barren country found in much of the state. There are also whale-watching opportunities, famous surfing beaches, prosperous farms, the Margaret River wineries and, in season, beautiful wildflowers.

Getting There & Away

Westrail (☎ 13 1053) buses go daily from Perth to Bunbury ($16.30), Busselton ($21.30), Yallingup ($24.50), Margaret River ($24.50) and Augusta ($29.10).

South-West Coachlines (☎ 9324 2333) also services the region daily from Perth to Bunbury ($16), Busselton ($20), Dunsborough ($22), Margaret River ($23) and Augusta ($28). From Monday to Friday it has services to Collie ($20), Donnybrook ($20), Balingup ($23), Bridgetown ($23), Nannup ($24) and Manjimup ($27).

SOUTH-WEST HINTERLAND

Inland from the south-west coast, the town of **Harvey** (population 2570) is in a popular bushwalking area of rolling green hills. The **Yalgorup National Park**, with its peculiar thrombalites on the shores of Lake Clifton, is north-west of the town. The tourist bureau (☎ 9729 1122) on the South-Western Hwy is open daily.

Donnybrook (population 1650), 37km south of Bunbury, is the centre of an apple-growing area and a popular (and fruitful) base for backpackers seeking casual work. Vineyards are also appearing here, which should further boost work opportunities. The apple-picking season is roughly from November to June. The Donnybrook-Balingup tourist bureau (☎ 9731 1720), next to the old train station, can help with finding work, as can Brook Lodge (see the following Places to Stay entry).

Collie (population 7200) is WA's only coal town and the home of the state's new $575 million power station. It has an interesting replica of a coal mine, mining and steam-locomotion museums, and there are tours of the old Muja power station. Pleasant bushwalking country surrounds the town. The tourist bureau (☎ 9734 2051), 156 Throssell St, is open on weekdays from 9 am to 5 pm and weekends from 10 am to 4 pm.

Places to Stay

The *Rainbow Caravan Park (☎ 9729 2239, 199 King St)* in Harvey has unpowered/powered camp sites for $6/7 and single/double on-site vans for $30. In Collie, *Mr Marron Holiday Village (☎ 9734 5088, Porter St)* has camping and basic backpacker dorms for $15 per person.

In Donnybrook, *Brook Lodge (☎ 9731 1520, 3 Bridge St)* is a well-run, friendly backpackers place with kitchen and laundry

THE SOUTH-WEST

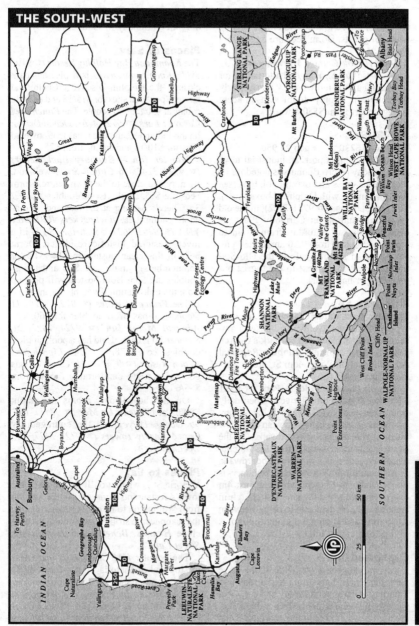

facilities. It's gradually being renovated and the owners have a good system of finding work for guests. Dorm beds are $12 ($75 a week).

Donnybrook Cottage Workstay (☎ 9731 0384, 11 Collins St) is a good alternative for something a little more homey (particularly for couples). Roomy doubles in adjacent cottages start from $150 a week.

BUNBURY

- postcode 6230   • pop 24,950

As well as being a port, an industrial town and a holiday resort, Bunbury is noted for its blue manna crabs and playful dolphins (see the 'Swimming with Dolphins' boxed text). The tourist bureau (☎ 9721 7922), in the old 1904 train station on Carmody Place, is open Monday to Saturday from 9 am to 5 pm and Sunday from 9.30 am to 4.30 pm.

There's an Internet cafe in the Old Station Coffee Lounge next to the tourist bureau ($5 per half-hour).

Things to See

The town's **old buildings** include King Cottage at 77 Forrest Ave, which houses a museum, the Rose Hotel and St Mark's Church (1842). The interesting **Bunbury Regional Art Galleries**, on Wittenoom St, are in a restored convent.

The **Big Swamp Wildlife Park** (☎ 9721 8380) on Prince Philip Drive is open daily from 10 am to 5 pm ($3/2) and includes many examples of native fauna. You can also view birdlife from a nearby boardwalk. On the Leschenault Inlet, across from the dolphin discovery centre, is a **mangrove boardwalk**.

At Australind, 7km north of Bunbury, is the **St Nicholas Church**, which, at just 4m by 7m, is said to be the smallest church in Australia. There is a scenic drive between Australind and Binningup along the shores of the **Leschenault Inlet**.

Organised Tours

Town walking tours (☎ 9795 9261) leave from the tourist bureau on Wednesday and Saturday at 10 am and Friday at 1 pm ($6). Cheese and wine cruises on Koombana Bay are a great way to spend the afternoon – the MV *Paddlewheeler* (☎ 9721 2933) operates at 2 pm on Sunday in summer ($10/5).

Places to Stay

The *Koombana Bay Holiday Resort (☎ 9791 3900, Koombana Drive)* is a pleasant park close to the Dolphin Discovery Centre and has tent/powered sites for $15/18 and en suite cabins at $50 for two people. The *Punchbowl Caravan Park (☎ 9721 4761, Ocean Drive)*, on the Indian Ocean beach, has tent/powered sites for $10/13 and cabins from $25.

Wander Inn – Bunbury Backpackers (☎ 9721 3242, 16 Clifton St) is well run, friendly and close to the town centre. Dorm beds are $15, singles/twins/doubles $20/32/36. There's parking at the rear and an outdoor seating area. *Backpackers Residency YHA (☎ 9791 2621, 55 Stirling St)* is in a lovely restored historic residence. Dorm beds in this clean hostel are $14 ($17 for nonmembers), singles are $18 and twins/doubles are $35. Both hostels will pick up from the train station if you phone ahead.

The *Prince of Wales (☎ 9721 2016, 41 Stephen St)* has B&B doubles for $60. The *Admiral Motor Inn (☎ 9721 7322, 56 Spencer St)* is central and has a pool; singles/doubles cost $78/95. The *Lighthouse Beach Resort (☎ 9721 1311, Carey St)* has good views and comfortable rooms from $55/65.

On the beachfront, rooms are about $50/65 at *Chateau La Mer (☎ 9721 3166, 99 Ocean Drive)* and the courageously named *Fawlty Towers (☎ 9721 2427, 205 Ocean Drive)*.

Places to Eat

Victoria St is where you'll find most of the town's restaurants and cafes – the section from Wellington to Eliot Sts is aptly named the 'cappuccino strip'. Places along here include *Henry's*, *Benessé* and *Jumpin' J's Street Cafe*.

The popular *HM Customs House*, near the top end of Victoria St, has four outlets including a brasserie.

L'Amour de la Femme (18 Wittenoom St) is an intimate, trendy place for lunch or dinner, and the *Ex-Tension Cafe (Ocean*

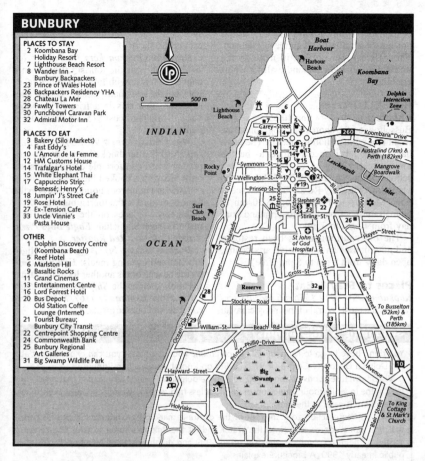

BUNBURY

PLACES TO STAY
2 Koombana Bay
   Holiday Resort
7 Lighthouse Beach Resort
8 Wander Inn -
   Bunbury Backpackers
23 Prince of Wales Hotel
26 Backpackers Residency YHA
28 Chateau La Mer
29 Fawlty Towers
30 Punchbowl Caravan Park
32 Admiral Motor Inn

PLACES TO EAT
3 Bakery (Silo Markets)
4 Fast Eddy's
10 L'Amour de la Femme
12 HM Customs House
14 Trafalgar's Hotel
15 White Elephant Thai
17 Cappuccino Strip:
   Benessé; Henry's
18 Jumpin' J's Street Cafe
19 Rose Hotel
27 Ex-Tension Cafe
33 Uncle Vinnie's
   Pasta House

OTHER
1 Dolphin Discovery Centre
   (Koombana Beach)
5 Reef Hotel
6 Marlston Hill
9 Basaltic Rocks
11 Grand Cinemas
13 Entertainment Centre
16 Lord Forrest Hotel
20 Bus Depot;
   Old Station Coffee
   Lounge (Internet)
21 Tourist Bureau;
   Bunbury City Transit
22 Centrepoint Shopping Centre
24 Commonwealth Bank
25 Bunbury Regional
   Art Galleries
31 Big Swamp Wildlife Park

Drive), overlooking the sea, is open daily from 7 am.

The *Rose Hotel* on the corner of Wellington and Victoria Sts does good counter meals and has a variety of beers on tap, and bistro meals in the lounge of *Trafalgar's Hotel (36 Victoria St)* are recommended.

White Elephant Thai (38 Victoria St) has a $7.50 lunch special and mains from $12. *Fast Eddy's (31 Victoria St),* open 24 hours, is always good for a burger or hot breakfast.

Uncle Vinnie's Pasta House (113 Spencer St), south of the city centre, is a good Italian place where you can fill up on pasta for $15.

Popular night spots are the *Lord Forrest (20 Symmons St)*, *Rose* and *Trafalgar's* hotels. The *Reef Hotel (8 Victoria St)*, an unmistakable bright orange and purple, is still the top pub with the young crowd.

Getting There & Around

Westrail (☎ 13 10 53) and Southwest Coachlines (☎ 9791 1955) have regular buses between Bunbury and Perth, and to points south and east. The *Australind* train also runs to Perth twice daily (except Friday). It departs from Bunbury at 6.15 am and 2.40 pm ($18).

Bunbury City Transit (☎ 9791 1955) covers the region around the city as far north as Australind and south to Gelorup. The office (open daily) is next to the tourist bureau and can handle all transport bookings.

BUSSELTON

• postcode 6280   • pop 10,650

Busselton, on the shores of Geographe Bay, is another popular holiday resort. The town has a 2km **jetty** once reputed to be the longest timber jetty in Australia. The Busselton tourist bureau (☎ 9752 1288) on the corner of Causeway Rd and Peel Terrace is open Monday to Friday from 8.30 am to 5 pm, Saturday from 9 am to 4 pm and Sunday from 10 am to 3 pm.

The old **courthouse** has been restored and now houses an impressive arts centre, open daily from 9 am to 5 pm (free).

Places to Stay & Eat

Kookaburra (☎ 9752 1516, 66 Marine Terrace) is the most central of the many caravan parks and has a camper's kitchen. Powered sites cost $15.50, on-site vans are $30 and cabins $35 for two.

Busselton Backpackers (☎ 9754 2763, 14 Peel St), near the tourist office, is in a converted house with limited kitchen facilities, but the new management is doing a lot to ensure that this is a friendly, reliable place. Dorm beds cost $15, singles $20 and doubles $35.

Motel Busselton (☎ 9752 1908, 90 Bussell Hwy) is often booked out – hardly surprising when comfortable double units are only $35 with a cooked breakfast.

There are numerous holiday resorts in the region; inquire at the tourist bureau.

Takeaway places on the Bussell Hwy, just off Queen St, include *Eagle Boys Pizza*, *Aussie Cafe* and *Red Rooster*.

Darbies (Kent St) is good for light lunches and evening meals. *Equinox Cafe* on the beachfront is another local favourite.

Hotels such as the *Ship Resort* (2 Albert St) and the *Esplanade* (167 Marine Terrace) serve counter meals.

Swimming with Dolphins

You don't have to go to Monkey Mia to commune with dolphins – you can experience it at the Dolphin Discovery Centre (☎ 9791 3088) on Koombana Beach in Bunbury.

Visits from three pods of about 100 bottlenose dolphins (Tursiops truncatus) that regularly feed in the Inner Harbour usually occur daily but less frequently in winter; the most likely time to see them is early in the morning.

A dolphin interaction zone in front of the centre is marked by white floats, and it's here that you can wade or swim into the water and let the dolphins come to you. The centre, staffed by helpful volunteers, was set up in 1989 and dolphins started to interact with the public in early 1990. A brochure explains the simple rules of contact with dolphins; if in doubt, ask a volunteer. The centre's museum and interpretive theatre is a must ($5/2 for adults/children).

Boat trips aboard the *Dolphin Dancer* or *Naturaliste Lady* (☎ 9755 2276) depart from outside the Dolphin Discovery Centre daily at 11 am and 2 pm, weather permitting ($15/10). You'll probably see the dolphins 'surfing' along in front of the boat on these excellent cruises.

MARTIN HARRIS

DUNSBOROUGH

• postcode 6281   • pop 1150

Dunsborough, west of Busselton, is a pleasant little coastal town that makes a good base for visiting nearby beaches and wineries. The tourist bureau (☎ 9755 3299) is in the shopping centre.

North-west of Dunsborough, the Cape Naturaliste Rd leads to excellent beaches such as **Meelup**, **Eagle Bay** and **Bunker Bay**, some fine coastal lookouts and the tip of **Cape Naturaliste**, which has a lighthouse and a network of walking trails. The lighthouse is open daily (except Monday) from 9.30 am to 4.30 pm ($4/2).

In season you can see humpback and southern right whales from the lookouts over Geographe Bay. At scenic **Sugarloaf Rock** is the southernmost nesting colony of the rare red-tailed tropicbird.

Organised Tours

Bay Dive & Adventures (☎ 9756 8846) and Cape Dive (☎ 9756 8778) organise snorkelling trips ($22) and diving ($44) out at the wreck of the Australian naval frigate HMAS *Swan*, sunk in Geographe Bay in 1997 specifically for diving.

For a winery tour with a difference, take a Clydesdale-drawn wagon tour from the Bootleg Brewery about 20km south of Dunsborough. Tours (minimum of four) depart weekdays at 11 am ($65). Book at the tourist bureau.

Places to Stay & Eat

Green Acres Beachfront Caravan Park (☎ 9755 3087, 77 Gifford Rd) has tent/powered sites for a pricey $20/21 for two people in the high season, and park homes from $75; prices drop by 25% out of season.

The *Three Pines Resort YHA (☎ 9755 3107, 285 Geographe Bay Rd)* in Quindalup, 2km south-east of Dunsborough, has a great beachfront location. The office is closed during the afternoon. Dorm beds are $15, twins are $18 per person. Bikes and canoes are available for hire.

Dunsborough Inn (☎ 9756 7277, Dunn Bay Rd), close to the shopping centre, is a spotless new purpose-built backpackers

with a large kitchen and modern facilities, including provision for disabled travellers. Dorm beds are $16, twins/doubles are $40 and there are some self-contained units available for groups or families. The friendly owners run a shuttle bus to nearby beaches for surfing and snorkelling. Another new place is *Dunsborough Lodge (☎ 9756 8866, 13 Dunn Bay Rd)*, which combines a backpackers section with motel-style accommodation in a fairly flash set-up. Dorm beds are $16, doubles $49 and en suite doubles $69. There's a coffee shop at the front.

Dunsborough Rail Carriages (☎ 9755 3865, Commonage Rd) are quaint, fully equipped recycled dwellings that cost $110 for two people ($90 in winter).

The *Naturaliste Forum Food Centre* has a variety of eating places, including a fine bakery. *Enjoia*, next to the Dunsborough Inn, is a good place for wood-fired pizzas, coffee or a few drinks. *Simmo's Ice Creamery (Commonage Rd)* serves 26 home-made flavours.

YALLINGUP

• postcode 6282   • pop 500

Yallingup, a mecca for surfers, is surrounded by spectacular coastline and some fine beaches.

Nearby is the stunning **Ngilgi Cave**, which was discovered, or rather stumbled upon, in 1899. The cave is open daily from 9.30 am to 4.30 pm (last entry 3.30 pm) and self-guided tours go every half-hour ($10/4).

The *Yallingup Beach Caravan Park (☎ 9755 2164, Valley Rd)* has a good location but exorbitant high season rates. *Caves House Hotel (☎ 9755 2131, Caves Rd)* is a classic old-world lodge with ocean views and an English garden; doubles start at $90 ($80 with shared facilities).

MARGARET RIVER

• postcode 6285   • pop 2850

Margaret River is a popular holiday spot due to its proximity to fine surf (Margaret River Mouth, Gnarabup, Suicides and Redgate) and swimming beaches (Prevelly and Gracetown), some of Australia's best wineries and spectacular scenery.

The Margaret River-Augusta tourist office (☎ 9757 2911) is on the corner of the Bussell Hwy and Tunbridge Rd. It has a wad of information on the area, including an extensive vineyard guide ($5.95) and details on the many art and craft places in town.

Eagles Heritage, 5km south of Margaret River on Boodjidup Rd, has a fascinating collection of raptors (birds of prey) in a natural bush setting; it's open daily from 10 am to 5 pm ($7/3), and there are flight displays at 11 am and 1.30 pm.

Everybody in Margaret's wants to surf (or so it seems) – if you don't know how to, the Surf Academy (☎ 9757 3850) offers lessons for $25.

Organised Tours

Margaret River's wineries are a major attraction and a good way to see a few is on a wine tour. Milesaway Tours (☎ 1800 818 102) has a popular half-day minibus tour visiting four or five wineries for $40. It departs from the tourist office on Monday, Wednesday and Friday at 12.30 pm. Margaret River Tour Company (☎ 041-9917166) takes groups by 4WD ($40) or a full day tour for $65, or it will custom-make tours by request.

An interesting three hour tour, conducted by Helen of **Cave Canoe Bushtucker Tours** (☎ 9757 9084) at Prevelly Park, takes you on a search for forest secrets. The tour combines walking and canoeing up the Margaret River, entering deep inside a wilderness cave and learning Aboriginal culture, bushcraft, flora and fauna; it costs $30/15 and is well worthwhile.

Leeuwin-Naturaliste Caves

There are several limestone caves dotted throughout the Leeuwin-Naturaliste Ridge between the capes (around 350), but most of those open to the public are along Caves Rd between Margaret River and Augusta.

In **Mammoth Cave**, 21km south of Margaret River, a fossilised jawbone of *Zygomaturus trilobus*, a giant wombat-like creature, can be seen. Limestone formations are reflected in the still waters of an underground stream in **Lake Cave**, 25km from Margaret River. The vegetated entrance to this cave is spectacular and includes a karri tree with a girth of 7m. Fossilised remains of a Tasmanian tiger *(thylacine)* have been discovered in **Jewel Cave**, 8km north of Augusta. **Moondyne Cave**, also 8km north of Augusta, is unlit and a guide takes visitors on a two hour caving adventure daily at 2 pm ($25).

CaveWorks (☎ 9757 7411) is an interpretive centre based at Lake Cave with state-of-the-art computerised displays, a theatrette, audiovisuals and a boardwalk. Guided cave tours, the only way to see these caves, operate daily for $12/5, or you can buy a pass for Jewell, Lake and Mammoth caves for $30. Both Jewel and Lake are open on the half-hour from 9.30 am until

Surfing WA

The beaches between Capes Leeuwin and Naturaliste offer powerful beach and reef breaks, both right and left-handers. The wave at Margaret River ('Margaret's') has been described by surfing supremo Nat Young as 'epic', and by world surfing champ Mark Richards as 'one of the world's finest'.

The better locations include Rocky Point (short left-hander), The Farm and Bone Yards (right-hander), Three Bears (Papa, Mama and Baby, of course), Yallingup ('Yal's'; breaks left and right), Injidup Car Park and Injidup Point (right-hand tube on a heavy swell; left-hander), Guillotine/Gallows (right-hander), South Point (popular break), Left-Handers and Margaret River (with Southside or 'Suicides').

Get a free copy of the *Down South Surfing Guide*, which indicates wave size, wind direction and swell size, from the Dunsborough and Busselton tourist bureaus. The Margaret River Surf Classic in March attracts some of the world's best surfers and is well worth being around for.

4 pm, Mammoth is open on the hour from 9 am to 4 pm and Moondyne at 2 pm only (these times vary depending on the season, so contact CaveWorks).

Places to Stay
Margaret River Caravan Park (☎ 9757 2180, Station Rd) is central and has tent sites for $7 per person plus $2 for power, and on-site vans for $33 for two. *Riverview Caravan Park* (☎ 9757 2270, Willmott Ave) is another possibility with tent/powered sites at $15/16 for two, and cabins from $55 ($45 in winter).

Margaret River Lodge (☎ 9757 2532, 220 Railway Terrace) is a good backpacker hostel, about 1.5km south-west of the town centre. The rammed earth buildings have every facility, and the manager runs a courtesy bus to pick up guests and take them to surf beaches. Dorm beds cost from $15, singles are $32 and doubles are $42, but prices vary depending on the type of room.

Margaret River Inne Town Backpackers (☎ 9757 3698, 93 Bussell Hwy) is almost opposite the tourist office. It's in a converted (but slightly run down) house with a nice patio and is popular with long-termers working in the area. Dorm beds are $15, twins and doubles $40.

Surf Point Lodge (☎ 9757 1777, Riedle Drive), at Gnarabup Beach, is one of the nicest budget places you could hope to stay in. In addition to the beachside location, it has a large, fully equipped kitchen and recreation areas. There is also a courtesy bus to/from Margaret River. Dorm beds are $20, twins/doubles are $57 and en suite rooms $67.

There are many other cottages, B&Bs and farmstays; inquire at the tourist office.

Places to Eat
Most of Margaret River's cafes and restaurants are strung out along the Bussell Hwy between the tourist office and Wallcliffe Rd.

The *Settler's Tavern* (114 Bussell Hwy) has good counter meals from $12 – there's also live music on weekends. The Margaret River Motel Hotel has meals in its *Rivers Bistro*.

At the southern end of town is the *Margaret River Tuckshop*, a bit of an institution, with friendly owners. Nearby, the *Arc of Iris* (☎ 9757 3112, 1/151 Bussell Hwy) is a cool BYO place with an interesting menu ranging from a Thai salad ($12) to crispy duck ($20). *Cafe Forte* (☎ 9757 3101, 101 Bussell Hwy) serves great Aussie cuisine.

AUGUSTA
• postcode 6290   • pop 2000
A popular holiday resort, Augusta is 5km north of Cape Leeuwin. The cape, the most southwesterly point in Australia, has a rugged coastline and a **lighthouse**, built in 1895 (open daily from 9 am to 4 pm; $3.50/1.50). Views from the 40m high tower extend over two oceans – the Indian and the Southern. Not far away is a salt-encrusted **water wheel**.

Cape Leeuwin took its name from a Dutch ship that passed here in 1622. The **Matthew Flinders memorial** on Leeuwin Rd commemorates Flinders' mapping of the Australian coastline, which commenced at the cape on 6 December 1801. There's a small historical museum on Blackwood Ave ($2/1).

The tourist bureau (☎ 9758 0166), 75 Blackwood Ave, is open daily from 9 am to 5 pm. The telecentre at 65 Allnutt Terrace has email and Internet access.

Organised Tours
Whale-watching is good from Cape Leeuwin between late May and September. Naturaliste Charters (☎ 9755 2276) has three-hour trips to see southern right and humpback whales, bottlenose dolphins and a colony of NZ fur seals on Flinders Island (June to September) for $38/22. The *Leeuwin Lady* (☎ 9758 1770) also has three-hour tours for $35/15, as well as fishing charters and leisurely cruises of the Blackwood River ($20/10). *Miss Flinders* (☎ 9758 1944) also sails up the Blackwood River, leaving from the Ellis St jetty. From September to June it leaves at 2 pm on Tuesday, Thursday and Saturday ($14/7).

Places to Stay & Eat
There are a number of basic *camping grounds* in the Leeuwin-Naturaliste National

Park, including at Boranup Drive, Alexandra Bridge and Conto's Field, near Lake Cave ($5 per person).

The *Doonbanks Caravan Park* (*☎ 9758 1517, Blackwood Ave*) is central and has tent/powered sites for $11/14, on-site vans for $25 and park cabins from $35 ($45 with en suite).

Baywatch Manor Resort (*☎ 9758 1290, fax 97581291, 88 Blackwood Avenue*), a purpose-built, Federation-style place, has been named Australia's No 1 YHA for two years running, so it's doing something right! It's modern and well equipped with comfortable rooms, and is well managed – definitely not a party place. Dorm beds (for YHA members) cost $15, double and twin rooms $40 and en suite doubles are $55.

The *Augusta Bakery*, at the north end of Blackwood Ave, is known for its pizzas, buns and home-baked pies; there's a Dome cafe attached. The *Cosy Corner* has $7 breakfasts and tasty focaccias. *Squirrels* serves delicious burgers and various health foods.

SOUTHERN FORESTS

A visit to the forests of the south-west is a must for any traveller to WA. Here, magnificent towering jarrah, marri and karri trees protect the natural, vibrant garden beneath. Unfortunately, parts of these forests are still threatened by logging, the major industry in this region.

The area of 'tall trees' (not 'tall timber', as that predetermines their fate) lies between the Vasse and South-Western Hwys, and includes the timber towns of Nannup, Bridgetown, Manjimup, Pemberton and Northcliffe. A trip will be more rewarding with CALM's brochure *Karri Country* ($1).

Getting There & Away

Westrail (*☎ 13 1053*) has daily services from Perth to Pemberton; some go via Bunbury, Donnybrook and Manjimup ($30.60), or the longer cape route via Margaret River and Augusta ($40.30). From Albany to Pemberton ($27) the daily service takes about three hours. South-West Coachlines has weekday buses as far as Manjimup ($27) and Bridgetown ($23).

Trees Versus Timber

One of the most divisive and emotive issues in WA is the logging of old-growth forest in the state's south-west.

Conservationists have been chaining themselves to bulldozers for years in protest at the felling of ancient karri, marri and jarrah trees, while the multi-million dollar timber industry employs some 20,000 people and is the economic mainstay of many south-west towns.

In April 1999 the WA government announced the Regional Forest Agreement (RFA), which identifies the areas of forest that will be preserved in the long-term and what concessions will be made to the timber industry. It's a complex document (aren't they all?), but the RFA promises to protect 67% of all old-growth forest (100% if it is rare or depleted) and increase protected reserves by 12%, cut the annual level of jarrah and karri sawlog cut, and offer the timber industry $41.5 million to help with retrenchments and more efficient technology.

The RFA will also create 12 new national parks and sink $17.5 million into tourism-related projects, such as new accommodation and scenic drives.

Nannup

- postcode 6275   • pop 520

Nannup is a peaceful, historical and picturesque town in the heart of forest and farmland. The tourist centre (*☎ 9756 1211*) in the old (1922) police station on Brockman St is open daily from 9 am to 5 pm.

In town there are some fine old buildings, several craft shops, a jarrah sawmill and an arboretum. One of Australia's great canoe trips is the descent of the **Blackwood River** from the forest to the sea. Blackwood Forest Canoeing (*☎ 9756 1252*) has more sedate half-day trips for $17.50.

Black Cockatoo (*☎ 9756 1035, 27 Grange Rd*) is an excellent permaculture-conscious backpackers lodge. Its cool owners contribute to the mellow nature of the place. As well as rustic rooms at $15 per person, there's a teepee and a caravan set up in the extensive back yard. You can pitch your own tent for half price.

There are several good eateries along Warren Rd, the main street through town. *Hamish's Cafe* serves tasty light meals and coffee. For local cuisine, the *Mulberry Tree (62 Warren Rd)* is the town's top restaurant.

Bridgetown
• postcode 6255   • pop 2100

This quiet country town on the Blackwood River is in an area of karri and jarrah forests and farmland. Bridgetown has some old buildings, including the mud-and-clay **Bridgedale House**, built by the area's first settler in 1862. There is a local history display in the tourist bureau (☎ 9761 1740) on Hampton St.

Interesting features of the Blackwood River valley are the burrawangs (grass trees) and large granite boulders. In **Boyup Brook**, 31km north-east of Bridgetown, there is a flora reserve, a country and western music collection (some 2000 titles), and a large butterfly and beetle display. Nearby is **Norlup Pool** with glacial rock formations.

One of Bridgetown's major attractions is the **Blues at Bridgetown** festival, held in the second week in November each year. Phone ☎ 9761 1280 for a program of events.

Places to Stay *Bridgetown Caravan Park (☎ 9761 1053, South-Western Hwy)* has a camper's kitchen; tent/powered sites cost $13/15, and on-site vans/cabins from $28/40.

The *Old Well (☎ 9761 2032, 16 Gifford St)* has B&B singles/doubles for $40/75. *Nelson's of Bridgetown (☎ 9761 1641, 38 Hampton St)* has motel rooms from $53/65 to $80/125 for luxury spa units.

Manjimup
• postcode 6258   • pop 4500

Manjimup, the agricultural centre of the south-west, is noted (and sometimes vilified) for its woodchipping industry. The **Timber Park Complex**, on the corner of Rose and Edwards Sts, includes museums, old buildings and the tourist bureau (☎ 9771

1831). You can get a feel for the town and its timber industry on one of the free mill tours that depart from the tourist office on Monday, Wednesday and Friday.

One Tree Bridge, or what's left of it after the 1966 floods, is 22km down Graphite Rd, west of Manjimup. It was constructed from a single karri log. The **Four Aces**, 1.5km from One Tree Bridge, are four superb karri trees believed to be over 300 years old. About 9km south of town is the 51m-high karri **Diamond Tree**. You can climb most of the way up to a platform from where there are great views over forest and farmland.

Perup, 50km east of Manjimup, is in the centre of a forest that boasts six rare mammals – the numbat, chuditch, woylie, tammar wallaby, ringtail possum and southern brown bandicoot. You can stay at the *Perup Forest Ecology Centre* for $25 a night, including guided bushwalks and spotlighting; contact the CALM office in Manjimup (☎ 9771 7988) for bookings.

Places to Stay & Eat The *Manjimup Caravan Park (☎ 9771 2093, South-West Hwy)* has a backpackers lodge with lounge and cooking facilities for $12/75 per night/week. The owners help travellers find work in the apple-picking season (March to June). There are also tent/powered sites for $12/15 and on-site vans from $30. The *Barracks (☎ 9771 1154, 8 Muir St)* is mainly for casual workers. Beds are $17/90 a night/week.

The *Manjimup Hotel (☎ 9771 1322, Giblett St)* can be noisy. The staff are friendly and the singles/doubles, most with bathrooms, are worth the $38/50.

The food in Manjimup is nothing to get excited about, but there are a couple of places on Giblett St, including *Tuk Tuk Thai* and *Déjà vu Cafe*, which is also an Internet cafe.

Pemberton
• postcode 6260   • pop 1000

Deep in the karri forests is the delightful township of Pemberton. The well-organised Karri visitors centre (☎ 9776 1133, 1800 671133) on Brockman St incorporates the tourist centre, pioneer museum and karri forest discovery centre ($2/1). It's open daily from 9 am to 5 pm. Internet access ($8 per half-hour) is available at the telecentre next door.

National park passes or day passes ($8 per car) are available from the visitors centre or the CALM office on Kennedy St.

Pemberton has some interesting **craft shops**, the pretty **Pemberton Pool** surrounded by karri trees and a **trout hatchery** that supplies fish for the state's dams and rivers.

The nerve-wracking 60m climb to the top of the **Gloucester Tree**, one of the highest fire lookout trees in the world, is not for the faint-hearted – apparently only one visitor in four ascends (more like three out of four backpackers though), but the view makes it well worthwhile. It's in the Gloucester National Park, 3km from town.

Also of interest in the area are the **Cascades** (when the water level is high) and **Beedelup National Park**, the 100-year-old forest (it was logged over 100 years ago and has since regrown), which stands as a defence against the supposed low impact of careful logging. There are forest drives through the **Warren National Park**; the **Dave Evans Bicentennial Tree**, pegged specially for tourists in 1988 and, at 68m, the tallest of the local 'climbing trees', is in this park.

Organised Tours The scenic **Pemberton Tramway**, through lush marri and karri forests, is one of the area's main attractions. Trams leave Pemberton train station for Warren River (adults/children $13/6.50) daily at 10.45 am and 2 pm, and for Northcliffe ($26/13) at 10.15 am on Tuesday, Thursday and Saturday. In the steam season (Easter to November), steam trains run to the Eastbrook ($19.50/9.50) and Lyall ($26/13) sidings at 10.30 am and 2.15 on Saturday, and 10.30 am on Sunday.

The Pemberton Hiking Company (☎ 9776 1559) has half/full-day eco walks ($25/50) through beautiful stands of karri (overnight trips are available). Forest Discovery Tours (☎ 9776 1825) has free tours covering the timber industry from the Forest Industries Centre on Brockman St (Monday to Saturday at 10.30 am). For a third perspective, Bwooka Boodja Dreaming Tours visits the forests with an Aboriginal guide, looking at Dreamtime sites and learning about bush tucker ($90/45 full/half day); book through the tourist bureau.

Places to Stay Camping is permitted at three sites in Warren National Park; contact CALM (☎ 9776 1207) for details. *Pemberton Caravan Park (☎ 9776 1300, 1 Pump Hill Rd)* has powered sites for $18 and cabins from $65 for two people (high season rates).

Pimelea Chalets YHA (☎ 9776 1153, Stirling Rd) is in a beautiful forest location 10km north-west of Pemberton. Its manager runs trips into town twice a day, although readers have reported some problems getting transport to this hostel in the past – phone for a pick up before arriving in Pemberton. Dorm beds are $14 in a variety of rustic timber houses with log fires; twins are $30 and doubles $35 (nonmembers pay $3 extra per person). Bikes can be hired for $10 a day.

Warren Lodge (☎ 9776 1105, 7 Brockman St) is central but lacks any sort of charm for the traveller; it's popular with people working in the area. Dorm beds cost from $14 and doubles from $38.

Kookaburra Cottage (☎ 9776 1246, 2 Kennedy St) is a recommended, friendly B&B with singles/doubles for $55/65 or $75 for an en suite double. *Gloucester Motel (☎ 9776 1266, Ellis St)* is reasonably good value with rooms from $45/60.

The lovely *Marima Cottages (☎/fax 9776 1211, Old Vasse Rd)* in Warren National Park is a good option for groups or families in the summer; two-bedroom, self-contained chalets with barbecue facilities and a good view (look for kangaroos in the morning) cost from $100.

Places to Eat For a town of its size, Pemberton has many places to eat; most have local trout and marron on their menus. The *Pemberton Bakehouse (4 Brockman St)* has tasty pies and cakes, while the *10K Cafe (Brockman St)* has basic, cheap snacks.

Rug 'n' Jo's (17 Brockman St), opposite the Forest Industries Centre, is a BYO cafe/restaurant with a broad, reasonably priced menu, including marron. For a Devonshire tea or a light lunch, the *Lavender and Berry Farm*, 5km east of town, makes a worthwhile excursion.

Shannon National Park

This 535 sq km national park on the South-Western Hwy, 50km south of Manjimup, is well worth a visit. The 48km **Great Forest Trees Drive** takes you through the old-growth karri forest with the bonus of on-board commentary if you tune your radio into 100FM when you see the signs (there are eight). The free *Shannon National Park and the Great Forest Trees Drive* brochure is informative, and *The Great Forest Trees Drive* ($12.95), is a detailed guidebook; both are available from CALM.

There is a fine *camping ground* in the spot where the original timber milling village used to be (it was closed in 1968). Camping fees are $8 for two adults, and there are huts equipped with pot belly stoves (also $8) – all fees are on a self-registration basis.

Northcliffe

• postcode 6262   • pop 240

Northcliffe, 32km south of Pemberton, has a **pioneer museum** and a nearby **forest park**, with good walks through stands of grand karri, marri and jarrah trees. The tourist centre (☎ 9776 7203) is by the pioneer museum on Wheatley Coast Rd.

Windy Harbour, on the coast 29km south of Northcliffe, has prefabricated shacks and a sheltered beach; true to its name, it is windy. The *camping ground (☎ 9776 8398)* has basic tent sites for $6 for two. The cliffs of the fine **D'Entrecasteaux National Park** are accessible from here. Experienced riders can go on three or four-day horse riding treks ($150 per day) through the park with South West Timber Trekking Co (☎ 9776 7199). There are also short trail rides ($25) for the less experienced.

The *Pinetree Caravan Park (☎ 9776 7193, Zamia Rd)* has tent/powered sites for $8/10. *Northcliffe Travellers Rest (☎ 9776 6060, 14 Wheatley Coast Rd)* has clean en suite singles/doubles for $40/79, including breakfast.

The South Coast

To the east of the capes and the karri forests is the vast area of the South Coast, sometimes called the Great Southern, stretching from Walpole-Nornalup in the west to Cape Arid, east of Esperance.

This area has some of the state's best coastal parks and inland, north of Albany, are two of the best mountain parks in Australia – the 'ecological islands' of the Stirling Range, which rise abruptly 1000m above the surrounding plains, and the ancient granite spires of the Porongurups.

Getting There & Away

Skywest (☎ 9334 2288) flies daily from Perth to Albany ($157) and Esperance ($202).

Westrail (☎ 13 1053) has a daily service from Perth to Albany (via Bunbury) using a combination of the *Australind* and road coach ($44.70), which passes through Denmark ($41.50) and Walpole ($36.70), and takes about eight hours. Another daily bus service from Perth to Albany ($35.10) goes inland via Williams and stops in Mt Barker ($30.60).

Westrail also has daily buses from Perth to Esperance ($52.60; 10 hours) and four buses a week from Albany to Esperance ($45.90).

WALPOLE-NORNALUP AREA

The heavily forested **Walpole-Nornalup National Park** covers 180 sq km around the Nornalup Inlet and Walpole; it contains beaches, rugged coastline, inlets and the famous Valley of the Giants.

Scenic drives include Knoll Drive, Hilltop Road, which leads to the **Giant Tingle Tree**, and the Valley of the Giants Road.

The Walpole tourist bureau (☎ 9840 1111) and CALM (☎ 9840 1027), both on the South Coast Hwy in Walpole, can provide more information. WOW Wilderness Cruises (☎ 9840 1036) runs 2½ hour trips through the inlets and river systems daily at 10 am ($18/10).

Valley of the Giants

Four species of rare eucalypts grow within 4km of each other in this region and nowhere else in the world: red, yellow and Rates tingle *(Eucalyptus jacksonii, E. guilfoylei, E. cornuta)*, in inland areas, and the red flowering gum *(E. ficifolia)*, closer to the coast.

The Valley of the Giants is the best place to see the giant tingle trees. The impressive **Tree Top Walk**, a 600m-long wheelchair-accessible ramp structure, allows visitors to get high up into the canopy of the giant trees. At its highest point it is 40m above the ground; the views below and above are stunning. Also from the Tingle shelter at the start of the tree-top walk is the **Ancient Empire**, a 600m ground level boardwalk through the giant trees.

The Tingle shelter (☎ 9840 8263) is open from 9 am to 4.15 pm, March to November, and from 8 am to 5.15 pm, December to February; entry to the Tree Top Walk costs $5/2/12 for adults/children/families. The Ancient Empire walk is free.

Places to Stay & Eat

There are a number of camping grounds in the Walpole-Nornalup National Park, including *tent sites* at Crystal Springs and *caravan parks* at Peaceful Bay and Coalmine Beach. There are CALM *huts* at Fernhook Falls and Mt Frankland.

Dingo Flat (☎ 9840 8073, Dingo Flat Rd) is the only backpackers and it's quite good if you have your own transport. It's on a quiet farm about 22km east of Walpole off the Valley of the Giants Rd. It may be possible to arrange a pick up from Bow Bridge or Walpole if you phone in advance. Rustic dorm beds are $12.

Tingle All Over (☎ 9840 1041, Nockolds St) in Walpole has budget rooms but, as the owners will gladly tell you, it's no backpackers. Singles cost $25 and twins/doubles are $34/38. The *Rest Point Tourist Centre (☎ 9840 1032, Rest Point Rd)*, perfectly sited on the Walpole Inlet, has self-contained cottages for around $20 per person.

You can get counter meals at the *Walpole Motel/Hotel*, and everything from a burger to a Thai curry at the smart (and licensed) *Top Deck Cafe (☎ 9840 1344, 25 Nockolds St)*.

DENMARK
* postcode 6333   • pop 2000

Denmark, or Koorabup ('Place of the Black Swan'), has some rare evidence of Aboriginal settlement in its Wilson Inlet – 3000-year-old fish traps.

The town is about 54km west of Albany and was first established to supply timber for goldfield development. It has some fine **beaches** (especially Ocean Beach for surfing), several notable wineries and is a good base for trips into the tingle forests.

The tourist office (☎ 9848 2055) on Strickland St has heritage trail brochures. They include the **Mokare Trail** (a 3km trail along the Denmark River) and the **Wilson Inlet Trail** (a 6km trail that starts from the river mouth).

The **William Bay National Park**, 15km west of Denmark, has fine coastal scenery of rocks and reefs. **Green's Pool** and **Elephants Rocks** are both calm and safe for swimming.

Organised Tours

There are 2½ hour cruises up the Denmark River on the *Sandpiper II* daily from October to May ($13/7), departing from the wharf opposite the Denmark Hotel. Denmark Southern Wonders (☎ 9848 1055) has a range of tours, including a full day to the tingle trees ($90), canoe trips on the Frankland River ($90) and half-day winery tours ($45).

Places to Stay

The idyllic *Rivermouth Caravan Park (☎ 9848 1262, Inlet Drive)* is the closest of several caravan parks to town (1km south); tent/powered sites are $11/14, on-site vans from $30 and cabins $36 for two.

The *Denmark Waterfront (☎ 9848 1147, 63 Inlet Drive)* was building a backpackers section with a common room and self-catering kitchen at the time of writing – a much-needed addition in Denmark. It's beautifully located on the water's edge and the management seems well in tune with what travellers want. Dorm beds will cost $17 ($15 after the first night). There are also motel units from $50/60 for singles/doubles. Phone ahead for a pick up from town.

Edinburgh House (☎ 9848 1477, 1800 671 477, 31 South Coast Hwy) in the centre of town is a friendly B&B with clean en suite rooms for $50/70.

There are many types of farmstays, B&Bs, chalets and cottages in the Denmark area; the tourist office keeps a current list.

Places to Eat

Bill's and *Day's Lunch Bar* are a couple of bakeries on the highway, and the *Walker St Pizzeria* is near the corner of Walker and Strickland Sts.

The *Riverview Coffee Shop (18 Holling Rd)* is excellent value – most meals are around $6. *Bellini's (12 Holling Rd)* has a great balcony with views of the river. The food is Greek and it's open daily (except Tuesday) for lunch and dinner.

The *Mary Rose (11 North St)* is a quaint place with a balcony; it serves tasty light meals including vegetarian dishes.

MT BARKER

• postcode 6324   • pop 1650

This pleasant town is 50km north of Albany and about 64km south of the Stirling Range. The tourist bureau (☎ 9851 1163) is in the restored 1923 train station building on the Albany Hwy, and is open on weekdays from 9 am to 5 pm, Saturday until 3 pm and Sunday from 10 am to 3 pm.

There are panoramic views of the area from the **Mt Barker Lookout**, 5km south of town. South-west of town is the picturesque 1873 **St Werburgh's Chapel**.

The **Old Police Station Museum** on the Albany Hwy is worth a visit – as well as the restored 1868 police station and lock-up, there's an amazing collection of local historical memorabilia. It's open on weekends from 10 am to 4 pm and the $3/1 admission may include an impromptu tour.

The **Banksia Farm** (☎ 9851 1770) on Pearce Rd has supposedly the world's only complete collection of all 76 banksia species. There's a museum and a one hour guided tour ($5).

The region has a reputation for wine production and there are numerous **wineries** with cellar sales near town – the tourist bureau has locations and opening times. The Mt Barker wine festival is held in February.

Places to Stay & Eat

The *Mount Barker Caravan Park* (☎ 9851 1691, Albany Hwy) has tent/powered sites for $11/14, cabins from $35 for two ($40 with en suite) and single budget cabins for $15.

The *Plantagenet Motel Hotel* (☎ 9851 1008, 9 Lowood Rd) has singles/doubles with shared facilities (in the older section) for $25/40 and motel units for $35/50. It's also a good spot for a counter meal. *Tippett's Diner (43 Lowood St)* is recommended for lunch.

PORONGURUP & STIRLING RANGES

Porongurup National Park (24 sq km) has beautiful panoramic views and scenery, large karri trees, 1100-million-year-old granite outcrops and some excellent bushwalking. Trails include the short Tree in the Rock stroll, the intermediate Castle Rock walk (two hours), the harder Haywards and Nancy Peaks (four hours) and the excellent Devil's Slide and Marmabup Rock (three hours) walks. A scenic 6km drive along the park's northern edge starts at the ranger's residence.

In the 1156 sq km **Stirling Range National Park**, Toolbrunup Peak (for views and a good climb), Bluff Knoll (at 1073m, the highest peak in the range) and Toll Peak (prolific wildflowers) are popular half-day

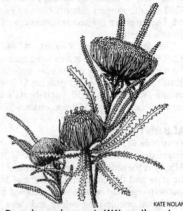

KATE NOLAN

Dryandra can be seen in WA's south-west, especially in the Stirling Ranges

walks. The 96km range is noted for its spectacular colour changes through blues, reds and purples. The mountains rise abruptly from the surrounding flat and sandy plains, and the area is known for its fine flora and fauna – the Stirling Bells are especially magnificent in bloom.

National park fees apply to vehicles entering both of these parks. For further information contact the CALM offices on Bolganup Rd, Mt Barker; Chester Pass Rd, Stirling Range; or Albany Highway, Albany.

Places to Stay & Eat

There's no camping in the Porongurups but there's a *tourist park* (☎ 9853 1057) in Porongurup township, with tent/powered sites for $14/16 and cabins at $40 for two people.

Porongurup Shop & Tearooms (☎ 9853 1110, Porongurup Rd) has a friendly and well-run YHA hostel behind the shop. Beds are $13 per person in dorms or double rooms ($14 for nonmembers). The owners will arrange pick up from Albany or Mt Barker if you book in advance, and they're a good source of information on walking or working in the area.

Karribank Country Retreat (☎ 9853 1022, Porongurup Rd) has comfortable doubles from $70.

You can camp in the Stirling Range National Park at *Moingup Springs* (☎ 9827 9230 for the ranger) just off Chester Pass Rd. Facilities are limited and sites cost $8 for two people.

The *Stirling Range Retreat (☎ 9827 9229, Chester Pass Rd)* is a caravan park on the northern boundary of the park opposite Bluff Knoll. Tent/powered sites are $12/16, on-site vans from $30, self-contained rammed-earth cabins $59 and chalets $79.

ALBANY

• postcode 6330   • pop 20,500

Established shortly before Perth in 1826, Albany is the oldest European settlement in the state and the commercial centre of the southern region. The area was occupied by Aboriginal people long before and there is much evidence, especially around Oyster Harbour, of their earlier presence.

With its excellent harbour on King George Sound, Albany was a thriving whaling port until the late 1970s. When steamships started travelling between the UK and Australia, Albany was also a coaling station for ships bound for the east coast. During WWI, it was the gathering point for troopships of the 1st Australian Imperial Force (AIF) before they sailed for Egypt.

The coast near Albany has some of the country's most rugged and spectacular scenery, and Middleton Beach, 3km east of town, is good for swimming.

Information

The tourist bureau (☎ 9841 1088, 1800 644 088), in the old train station on Proudlove Parade, is open on weekdays from 8.30 am to 5.30 pm and weekends from 9 am to 5 pm. The CALM and RACWA offices are on the Albany Hwy.

Internet access is available at the Yak Bar, 28 Stirling Terrace, for $5 per half-hour – you can have a curry while surfing. The town's two hostels also have Internet access. You can buy, sell or swap books at the Gemini Book Exchange on York St.

Historic Buildings

Albany has some fine colonial buildings – Stirling Terrace is noted for its Victorian shopfronts. The 1852 Old Gaol on Lower Stirling Terrace is now a folk museum, open daily from 10 am to 4.15 pm. The $3.50 admission includes entry to the 1832 wattle-and-daub Patrick Taylor Cottage on Duke St, the oldest dwelling in WA.

The Albany Residency Museum, opposite the Old Gaol, was built in the 1850s as the home of the resident magistrate; it's open daily from 10 am to 5 pm (free). Displays include seafaring subjects, flora and fauna, and Aboriginal artefacts. The excellent Eclipse building across the car park features a lighthouse optic among the displays rescued from Eclipse Island.

Alongside the museum is a full-scale replica of the brig, *Amity*, that brought Albany's founders to the area in 1826 ($2/50c).

The restored post office (1870) on Lower Stirling Terrace houses a classy restaurant

Cockburn Range, Kimberley, WA

Desert wildflowers, Kalbarri National Park, WA

Pinnacles Desert, Nambung National Park, WA

Gantheaume Point, Broome, WA

Geikie Gorge National Park, WA

Lake Argyle Diamond Mine, WA

Bungle Bungle (Purnululu) National Park, WA

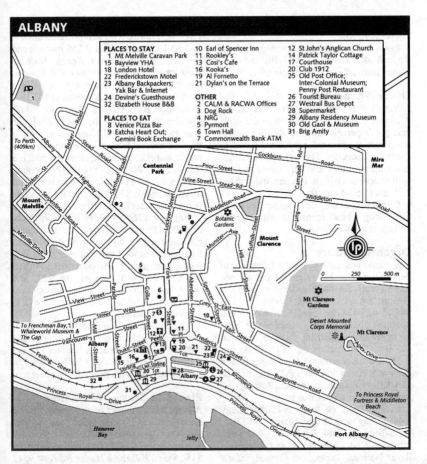

ALBANY

PLACES TO STAY
1 Mt Melville Caravan Park
15 Bayview YHA
18 London Hotel
22 Frederickstown Motel
23 Albany Backpackers;
   Yak Bar & Internet
24 Devine's Guesthouse
32 Elizabeth House B&B

PLACES TO EAT
8 Venice Pizza Bar
9 Eatcha Heart Out;
   Gemini Book Exchange

10 Earl of Spencer Inn
11 Rookley's
13 Cosi's Cafe
16 Kooka's
19 Al Fornetto
21 Dylan's on the Terrace

OTHER
2 CALM & RACWA Offices
3 Dog Rock
4 NRG
5 Pyrmont
6 Town Hall
7 Commonwealth Bank ATM

12 St John's Anglican Church
14 Patrick Taylor Cottage
17 Courthouse
20 Club 1912
25 Old Post Office;
   Inter-Colonial Museum;
   Penny Post Restaurant
26 Tourist Bureau
27 Westrail Bus Depot
28 Supermarket
29 Albany Residency Museum
30 Old Gaol & Museum
31 Brig Amity

and the Inter-Colonial Museum, with its collection of communications equipment; it's open daily from 10 am to 4 pm (free).

Other historic buildings include **St John's Anglican Church**, the elegant home **Pyrmont**, the **courthouse** and the **Town Hall**. A free brochure detailing a walking tour of Albany's colonial buildings is available from the tourist bureau.

Viewpoints

There are fine views over the coast and inland from the twin peaks, **Mt Clarence** and **Mt Melville**, which overlook the town. On top of Mt Clarence is the Desert Mounted Corps Memorial, originally erected in Port Said as a memorial to the events of Gallipoli. It was moved here when the Suez Crisis (1956) made colonial reminders less than popular in Egypt.

Mt Clarence can be climbed along a track accessible from the end of Grey St East; turn left, take the first street on the right and follow the path by the water tanks. The walk is tough but the views make it worthwhile. The easier way is to drive to the car park at the end of Apex Drive. There's a whale-watch walk from Marine Drive on

Mt Adelaide to the harbour entrance (45 minutes return).

Panoramic views are also enjoyed from the lookout tower on Mt Melville; the signposted turn-off is off Serpentine Rd.

Other Attractions

Albany's **Princess Royal Fortress** on Mt Adelaide was built in 1893 when the strategic port's perceived vulnerability to naval attack was considered a potential threat to Australia's security. The restored buildings, gun emplacements and fine views make it well worth a visit. It is open daily from 7.30 am to 5.30 pm (free).

Dog Rock, a deformed boulder that looks like a dog's head (complete with painted collar), is on Middleton Rd.

Organised Tours

The whale-watching season is from July to September – southern right whales are observed near the bays and coves of King George Sound. Southern Ocean Charters (☎ 015-423 434) has trips ($25/16) and also operates diving, fishing, underwater photography and snorkelling tours on demand.

Silver Star Cruises (☎ 9841 3333) has 2½ hour cruises around King George Sound daily at 9.30 am and 1 pm ($25/16), as well as whale-watching in season. Both operators depart from the town jetty.

Escape Tours (☎ 9844 1945) has many half/full-day tours around Albany for $33/65. Do-a-Tour (☎ 9844 3509) has 4WD tours into the West Cape Howe and Fitzgerald River National Parks, and Coastal Safaris (☎ 9841 7652) has good value half/full-day trips for about $35/70 with discounts for backpackers. Design a Tour (☎ 9841 7778) has a day tour of the region ($85) and a five day tour from Perth to Albany ($540); the tourist bureau has details on all these tours.

Albany Wine Tours (☎ 1800 644 088) visits Denmark and Mt Barker wineries ($40), and has a full day tour taking in the whole region ($75).

Places to Stay – Budget

There are caravan parks aplenty in Albany: try the *Mt Melville Caravan Park* (☎ 9841 4616, 22 Wellington St), just off the Albany Hwy 1km north, with tent/powered sites at $12.50/16.50 and cabins at $50 for two; and the spotless *Middleton Beach Holiday Park* (☎ 9841 3593, 1800 644 674, Middleton Rd), 3km east, with tent/powered sites for $15/17 and tidy park cabins at $45.

Albany Backpackers (☎ 9841 8848, Spencer St) is possibly the best hostel in the state for atmosphere. The people who run it make everyone feel at home, and the free coffee and cake gathering every evening is a real winner. With the YHA/VIP discount, dorm beds cost $14, a single room is $27 and a twin/double is $36. You can hire mountain bikes ($12 a day) and surfboards ($15) here.

Bayview YHA (☎ 9842 3388, 49 Duke St), 400m from the town centre, is also well run and friendly. Not to be outdone, it has free pancakes for breakfast every morning – take your pick! Dorm beds cost $14 ($15 for nonmembers), singles are $20, and twins and doubles are $34. You can rent bikes, surfboards and even a car here ($35 a day for the latter).

The historic *London Hotel* (☎ 9841 1048, 106 Stirling Terrace) is an interesting budget alternative with backpacker beds for $15 and singles/doubles for $25/35 ($35/45 with en suite). There's a kitchen and lounge here too.

Places to Stay – Mid-Range

Albany has a number of reasonably priced guesthouses and B&Bs. Good ones include: *Devines Guesthouse* (☎/fax 9841 8050, 20 Stirling Terrace), with singles/doubles from $45/65; and *Elizabeth House B&B* (☎ 9842 2734, 9 Festing St), with rooms at $40/65. The *Discovery Inn* (☎ 9842 5535, 9 Middleton Rd) out near Middleton Beach has rooms for $35/55.

The *Frederickstown Motel* (☎ 9841 1600, 1800 808 544, Spencer St) is central, with standard rooms from $72/79.

Places to Eat

Stirling Terrace, York St and Frederick St are the main areas for eating out.

Dylan's on the Terrace (82 Stirling Terrace) has an excellent range of light meals, including hamburgers and pancakes; it's open late most nights and early for breakfast. *Eatcha Heart Out (154 York St)* and *Cosi's Cafe (Peels Place)* are also recommended.

Al Fornetto (132 York St) has a popular open-air dining area and pasta dishes from $11, and the *Venice Pizza Bar*, further north on York St, has good value pizzas. *Rookley's (36 Peels Place)* has an alfresco courtyard and specialises in lunches, deli meals and fine takeaways. It's closed in the evenings.

The *Earl of Spencer Inn*, a British-style pub on Spencer St, serves good counter meals and is a convivial place for an evening out.

For more upmarket dining, *Kooka's (☎ 9841 5889, 204 Stirling Terrace)* is in a restored old house where you can enjoy an excellent country-style three-course meal for $35, and the *Penny Post Restaurant*, in the old post office on Stirling Terrace, has mains from $17.

Entertainment
NRG (38 Middleton Rd) and *Club 1912 (120 York St)* are the town's late-night venues – Club 1912 often has live music on the weekends. The *Earl of Spencer Inn* has a range of international beers on tap, and the *Esplanade Hotel* at Middleton Beach usually has a band at its lively Sunday session.

Getting Around
Love's runs bus services around town on weekdays and Saturday morning. Buses go along the Albany Hwy from Peel Place to the main roundabout, and to Spencer Park, Middleton Beach, Emu Point and Bayonet Head (once a week). A short trip costs 80c.

AROUND ALBANY
South of Albany, off Frenchman Bay Rd, is a stunning stretch of coastline. It includes the **Gap** and **Natural Bridge** rock formations; the **Blowholes**, which are especially interesting in heavy seas when air is blown with great force through the rock face; the **rock-climbing** areas of Peak Head and West Cape Howe; steep, rocky coves such as **Jimmy Newhill's Harbour** and **Salmon Holes** (popular with surfers, although these coves are considered quite dangerous); and **Frenchman Bay**, which has a caravan park,

a fine swimming beach and a grassed barbecue area. This coastline is dangerous; beware of king-sized waves.

Whaleworld Museum
The Whaleworld Museum at Frenchman Bay, 21km from Albany, is based at the Cheynes Beach Whaling Station (which only ceased operations in November 1978). There's the rusting *Cheynes IV* whalechaser and station equipment to inspect outside. The museum screens a gore-spattered film on whaling and has displays, including harpoons, whaleboat models and scrimshaw (etching on whale bone and teeth).

Whaleworld is open daily from 9 am to 5 pm ($8/3). There are guided tours on the hour from 10 am to 4 pm.

National Parks & Reserves
There are a number of excellent natural areas along the coast both west and east of Albany where you can explore many different habitats.

West Cape Howe National Park is a playground for naturalists, bushwalkers, rock climbers and anglers. **Torndirrup National Park** includes the region's two popular attractions, the Natural Bridge and the Gap, as well as the Blowholes. Southern right whales can be seen from the cliffs during the season.

East of Albany is **Two People's Bay**, a nature reserve with a good swimming beach, scenic coastline and a small colony of noisy scrub-birds, a species once thought extinct.

Probably the best of the national parks, but the least visited, is **Waychinicup**, which includes Mt Manypeaks and other granite formations, also east of Albany. Walking in the area is restricted because of dieback, a fungal disease that attacks the roots of plants and causes them to rot. Its spread can be prevented by observing 'no go' road signs and by cleaning soil from your boots where you're instructed to do so.

ALBANY TO ESPERANCE
From Albany, the South Coast Hwy runs north-east along the coast before turning inland to skirt the Fitzgerald River National Park and ending in Esperance.

WESTERN AUSTRALIA

Ongerup, a small Wheatbelt town 153km north-east of Albany, has an annual wildflower show in September/October with hundreds of local species on display. **Jerramungup**, north-east of Albany on the South Coast Hwy, has an eclectic military museum.

Bremer Bay
• postcode 6338   • pop 220

This fishing and holiday town, at the western end of the Great Australian Bight, is 61km east of the South Coast Hwy. It's a good spot to observe southern right whales. Information is available from the BP Roadhouse (☎ 9837 4093).

The *Bremer Bay Caravan Park* (☎ *9837 4018*) has tent/powered sites for $14/16 and cabins from $30 for two. *Quaalup Homestead* (☎ *9837 4124*), 18km east of Bremer Bay, is a nice place to stay in the Fitzgerald River National Park. Camping costs $5 per person, single/double units are $40/45, chalets $55 and cottages $100.

Ravensthorpe & Hopetoun
Ravensthorpe (population 350) was once the centre of the Phillips River goldfield. Copper mining followed but now the area depends on farming. The ruins of a disused smelter and the Cattlin Creek copper mine are near town, and there's a wildflower show in the first two weeks of September. The Ravensthorpe information centre (☎ 9838 1277), Morgans St, is open daily from 8.30 am to 5 pm.

Hopetoun (population 320), 50km south of Ravensthorpe, has fine beaches and bays, and is the eastern gateway to the Fitzgerald River National Park. The information centre (☎ 9838 3228) is in Gerry's Ocean Obsessions on Veal St.

About 150km north of Ravensthorpe, the **Frank Hann National Park** has a range of typical sand-plain flora.

Places to Stay & Eat
The *Ravensthorpe Caravan Park* (☎ *9838 1050, South Coast Hwy*) has tent/powered sites for $10/14, on-site vans for $25 and cabins for $30. The *Palace Motor Hotel* (☎ *9838 1005, Morgans St*) has a few backpacker beds for $20; single/double motel units are $45/60.

The *Hopetoun Caravan Park* (☎ *9838 3096, Spence St*) has tent/powered sites for $11/13 and on-site vans for $30 for two. The *Port Hotel* (☎ *9838 3053, 1 Veal St*), in Hopetoun, has singles/doubles for $30/40, or $15 for backpacker beds.

At Munglirup, 90km east of Ravensthorpe, the *Singing Winds* (☎ *9075 1018, Fuss Rd*) provides B&B at $35 for long-distance cyclists.

There is a sumptuous cake selection at the *Country Kitchen* in Ravensthorpe. In Hopetoun, *Cafe Barnacles*, run by a Swiss chef and specialising in seafood, is the place to dine out.

Fitzgerald River National Park
This 3300 sq km park contains beautiful coastline, sand plains, the rugged Barren mountain range and deep, wide river valleys. The wilderness bushwalking route from Fitzgerald Beach to Whalebone Beach is recommended, though there is no trail and no water. Clean your shoes at each end of the walk to discourage the spread of dieback.

The park contains half of the orchid species in WA (over 80 species, 70 of which occur nowhere else), 22 mammal species, 200 species of birds and 1700 species of plants. It is also the home of those floral marvels the royal hakea and Quaalup bell.

Access is from Bremer Bay (west), Hopetoun (east) or from the South Coast Hwy along Devils Creek, Quiss and Hamersley Rds. *Camping* is allowed at numerous sites within the park.

ESPERANCE
• postcode 6450   • pop 8650

Esperance, or the Bay of Isles, has become a popular resort due to its temperate climate, magnificent coastal scenery, clear blue waters, squeaky white beaches and good fishing. It's 721km south-east of Perth and 200km south of Norseman.

Although the first settlers came to the area in 1863, it was during the 1890s gold rush that the town really became established as a port. When the gold fever subsided, Esperance went into a state of suspended animation until after WWII. In the 1950s, it was discovered that adding missing trace elements to the soil around Esperance restored it to fertility – since then the town has rapidly grown into an agricultural centre.

Information

The helpful tourist bureau (☎ 9071 2330) on Dempster St is open daily from 9 am to 5 pm, and can book tours to the islands and the surrounding national parks, as well as onward transport.

Internet facilities can be found at the hostels, the Village Cafe (near the tourist bureau) or at Top End Takeaways on Dempster St.

Things to See & Do

The **Museum Village**, between the Esplanade and Dempster St, contains the tourist bureau and various old buildings, including a gallery, smithy's forge, cafe and craft shop. The municipal museum itself is open daily from 1.30 to 4.30 pm ($3/1). It features a display on Skylab – the US space station that was launched in May 1973 and crashed to earth in 1979, passing right over Esperance.

The 36km **Great Ocean Drive** heads south from town and includes vistas from the Rotary Lookout and Observatory Point, the **Pink Lake**, stained by the salt-tolerant algae *Dunalella salina*, and the popular swimming spots of Twilight Bay and Picnic Cove.

There are about 100 small islands in the **Recherche Archipelago**, home to colonies of fur seals, penguins and a wide variety of water birds. There are regular trips to Woody Island, a wildlife sanctuary where you can stay overnight; see the Organised Tours and Places to Stay entries in this section.

Esperance has excellent **fishing** – many a traveller has caught dinner using a handline from the town jetty. There is good **diving** around the many islands and, for experienced scuba divers, the wrecks of the *Sanko Harvest* and the *Lapwing* are worth exploring. Esperance Diving and Fishing (☎ 9071 5111), 72 the Esplanade, organises trips and hires equipment.

Organised Tours

Vacation Country Tours (☎ 9071 2227) runs trips around Esperance, including a

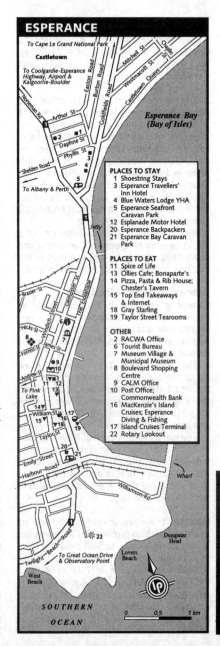

ESPERANCE

To Cape Le Grand National Park
Castletown
To Coolgardie-Esperance Highway, Airport & Kalgoorlie-Boulder

Esperance Bay (Bay of Isles)

To Albany & Perth

PLACES TO STAY
1 Shoestring Stays
3 Esperance Travellers' Inn Hotel
4 Blue Waters Lodge YHA
5 Esperance Seafront Caravan Park
12 Esplanade Motor Hotel
20 Esperance Backpackers
21 Esperance Bay Caravan Park

PLACES TO EAT
11 Spice of Life
13 Ollies Cafe; Bonaparte's
14 Pizza, Pasta & Rib House; Chester's Tavern
15 Top End Takeaways & Internet
18 Gray Starling
19 Taylor Street Tearooms

OTHER
2 RACWA Office
6 Tourist Bureau
7 Museum Village & Municipal Museum
8 Boulevard Shopping Centre
9 CALM Office
10 Post Office; Commonwealth Bank
16 MacKenzie's Island Cruises; Esperance Diving & Fishing
17 Island Cruises Terminal
22 Rotary Lookout

To Pink Lake
To Great Ocean Drive & Observatory Point
Lovers Beach
West Beach

SOUTHERN OCEAN

0   0.5   1 km

Wharf
Dempster Head

WESTERN AUSTRALIA

town-and-coast tour for $28 and a Cape Le Grand tour for $45. More adventurous is Aussie Bight Expeditions (☎ 9071 7778), with 4WD safaris to secluded beaches and bays and to national parks from around $48 for a half day.

Tours on the waters of the Bay of Isles are a must. MacKenzie's Island Cruises (☎ 9071 5757) regularly tours the bay ($42/16), including a stop on Woody Island. Expect to see NZ fur seals, Australian sea lions, sea eagles, Cape Barren geese, common dolphins and a host of other wildlife on these cruises. Full-day tours, including lunch, cost $65/27. Book tours at its Esplanade office, but if you're staying at the local hostels it's cheaper to book through them.

Esperance 4WD & Dive Tours (☎ 9071 3357) takes small groups out on diving and snorkelling trips as far as Cape Arid in the east and Stokes National Park in the west.

Places to Stay – Budget

Camping There are half a dozen caravan parks around Esperance with camp sites, on-site vans and cabins; the usual rates for tent/powered sites are $14/16 and cabins are around $40 for two.

The *Esperance Bay Caravan Park* (☎/fax 9071 2237, 162 Dempster St) is near the wharf at the southern end of town, and the *Esperance Seafront Caravan Park* (☎ 9071 1251, fax 9071 7003, Goldfields Rd) is at the other end of town.

You can camp on peaceful *Woody Island* (☎ 9071 5757) for $7 per night in your own tent or from $25 to $48 per person in safari tents. MacKenzie's Island Cruises goes there daily, and there's an additional direct ferry ($27) in January.

Hostels There are three good hostels in town, all of which provide a pick-up service if you arrive by bus, and all have Internet, laundry and cooking facilities.

Shoestring Stays (☎ 9071 3396, 040 892 9461, fax 9072 0298, 23 Daphne St) is a new backpacker place under the Nomads group. It's spacious with a big back yard, modern facilities, free bike hire, lockers in all rooms and even a spa. There are 4WD

trips and other activities on offer. Dorm beds cost $15 ($14 with YHA/VIP) and doubles are $40 ($38). There's also a self-contained family unit, which is a bargain at $60.

Esperance Backpackers (☎ 9071 4724, 018 93 4541, 14 Emily St) is the most centrally located, and is tidy and homey. Dorm beds are $14, and twins/doubles are $35 (with YHA/VIP). Staff run tours for the guests: trips to the national parks are $40, while Jurg's excellent fishing trips are $30.

Blue Waters Lodge YHA (☎/fax 9071 1040, 299 Goldfields Rd) is a large, popular place with dorm beds for $14 ($17 for non-members), singles for $20 ($25) and doubles for $35 ($41). It has a nice breakfast area with views over the water.

Places to Stay – Mid-Range

The tourist bureau has a list of the many motels and B&Bs in Esperance.

Esperance Travellers' Inn Hotel (☎ 9071 1677, fax 9071 1190, Goldfields Rd), near the YHA, is a clean place with budget motel rooms for $45/55 for singles/ doubles, family units for $70 and backpacker accommodation (private rooms with shared facilities) for only $15.

The *Esperance Motor Hotel* (☎ 9071 1555, fax 9071 1495, 14 Andrew St) is in the middle of town and good value at $20/35 for rooms in the hotel section (shared facilities) and $50/60 for standard motel rooms.

Places to Eat

Esperance has a good number of cafes. *Taylor Street Tearooms* is popular, being right on the waterfront. Other options are *Ollie's Cafe* on the Esplanade, and the *Village Cafe* in the Museum Village complex.

Pizza, Pasta & Rib House, on the corner of William and Dempster Sts, is the best known of the takeaways but there are also a number of fish and chip places, including *Top End Takeaways* on Dempster St.

Spice of Life (22a Andrew St) has a varied health-food menu. *Esperance Motor Hotel* is hard to beat for value with its $5 counter meals, and the *Traveller's Inn* does $6.50 set meals four nights a week.

For more upmarket dining, *Bonaparte Seafood Restaurant (☎ 9071 7727)*, above Ollie's Cafe on the Esplanade, is the place for seafood, and the *Gray Starling Restaurant (☎ 9071 5880, 126 Dempster St)* has a select menu with mains from $16.

AROUND ESPERANCE

There are four national parks in the Esperance region. The closest and most popular is **Cape Le Grand**, extending from about 20km to 60km east of Esperance. The park has spectacular coastal scenery, some good beaches and excellent walking tracks. There are fine views from **Frenchman's Peak** at the western end of the park, and good fishing, camping and swimming at Lucky Bay and Le Grand Beach.

Further east is the coastal **Cape Arid National Park** at the start of the Great Australian Bight. It is a rugged and isolated park with abundant flora and fauna, good bushwalking, beaches and camp sites. Much of the park is only accessible by 4WD.

Other national parks include **Stokes**, 92km west of Esperance, with an inlet, long beaches and rocky headlands; and **Peak Charles**, 130km north. For more information on all these parks, contact CALM (☎ 9071 3733), Dempster St, Esperance.

If you are going into the national parks, take plenty of water as there is little or no fresh water in most of these areas. Also, be wary of spreading dieback. Entry fees apply to vehicles ($8).

Places to Stay & Eat

Limited-facility tent sites are $10 (for two people) at *Cape Le Grand (☎ 9075 9022)* and free at *Cape Arid (☎ 9075 0055)*; apply for permits at the park entrances. There are basic camp sites at *Stokes (☎ 9076 8541)* for $8 and *Peak Charles (☎ 9071 3733)*, which offers free camping.

Between Cape Le Grand and Cape Arid, the friendly *Orleans Bay Caravan Park (☎ 9075 0033)* has sandy tent sites for $12, powered sites for $14 and park homes from $30.

Merivale Farm, just off Merivale Rd on the way to Cape Le Grand, is famous for its tasty cakes and tortes.

The Midlands

This huge area stretches from the base of the Pilbara down to the Wheatbelt towns some 300km or so south of the Great Eastern Hwy. Much of it is commonly referred to as the Wheatbelt. The area is noted for its unusual rock formations, many Aboriginal sites and *gnamma* (water holes), and magnificent displays of wildflowers in spring.

WILDFLOWER WAY

The best place to see the famous carpet of wildflowers, mainly everlastings, is in the Midlands, north of Perth. Follow the Great Northern Hwy (SH95) via New Norcia to Dalwallinu. From here, travel north-west on the Wildflower Way to Mullewa. You can return to Perth on the Midland Road (SH116) via Mingenew or on the Brand Hwy (Hwy 1) via flora-rich sand-plain parks.

New Norcia

● postcode 6509   ● pop 80

The small, meditative community of New Norcia is an incongruity, Australia's very own setting for Umberto Eco's *The Name of the Rose*. Established as a Spanish Benedictine mission in 1846, it has changed little since and boasts a fine collection of buildings with classic Spanish architecture.

The museum and art gallery building also contains the tourist office (☎ 9654 8056). Daily tours of the monastery (adults/children $10/5) take in the interior of chapels and other cloistered and secret places (11 am and 1.30 pm).

Just past the museum is the *New Norcia Hotel (☎ 9654 8034, Great Northern Hwy)* with its interesting decor, including a grand staircase. Singles/doubles cost from $40/60.

Benedictine monks still live and work in New Norcia. You can experience monastery life by staying in their *guesthouse*; $40 per person for bed and all meals.

Midlands Scenic Roads

To the north of New Norcia is **Moora**, a farming community in an area known for its colourful spring wildflowers. The area was devastated by floods in 1999.

WESTERN AUSTRALIA

Blooming Wildflowers

WA is famed for its 8000 species of wild-flower, which bloom in greatest number from August to October. Even some of the driest regions put on a colourful display after a little rainfall, and at any time of the year.

The south-west has over 3000 species, many of which are unique to this region. They're commonly known as everlastings because the petals stay attached after the flowers have died. You can find flowers almost everywhere in the state, but the jarrah forests in the south-west are particularly rich. The coastal national parks, such as Fitzgerald River and Kalbarri, also have brilliant displays. Near Perth, the Badgingarra, Alexander Morrison, Yanchep and John Forrest national parks are excellent choices. There's also a wildflower display in Kings Park, Perth. As you go further north, they tend to flower earlier in the season. Common flowering plants include various species of banksia, wattles, mountain bells, Sturt's desert pea, kangaroo paw and many orchids.

Pick up a copy of *Wildflower Discovery – a Guide for the Motorist* free from the WATC in Perth.

RACHEL BLACK

WA's floral emblem, the kangaroo paw

Towns such as **Dalwallinu**, **Perenjori**, **Morawa** and **Mullewa** are part of the Wildflower Way – famous for its brilliant spring display of wildflowers, including wreath leschenaultia, foxgloves, everlastings and wattles. This area is the gateway to the Murchison goldfields; there are gold-mining centres and ghost towns near Perenjori.

The return option is SH116 further west, known locally as the Midlands Scenic Way. It's an interesting alternative route for travel between Perth and Geraldton. At **Watheroo**, the old *Watheroo Station Tavern* (☎ 9651 7007, George St) offers accommodation, meals and activities, such as bushwalking, wildflower walks, tennis and horse-riding. It's worth the detour.

Coorow is 262km north of Perth and nearby is the **Alexander Morrison National Park**. **Carnamah**, near the Yarra Yarra Lakes, is noted for its bird life.

Mingenew has an historical museum in an old primary school. The tourist centre (☎ 9928 1081) is on Midlands Rd.

GREAT NORTHERN HIGHWAY

Although most people heading for the Pilbara and the Kimberley travel up the coast, the Great Northern Hwy is more direct. The bitumen highway extends from Perth to Newman and then skirts the eastern edge of the Pilbara on its way to Port Hedland – a distance of 1638km.

The highway is not the most interesting in Australia, mainly passing through flat and featureless country. The Murchison goldfields and towns of Mt Magnet, Cue, Meekatharra and Newman punctuate the monotony. (For information on Newman, see the Company Towns section later in this chapter.)

Greyhound Pioneer (☎ 13 2030) goes from Perth to Port Hedland on Friday and Sunday ($163). Westrail (☎ 13 1053) has a twice weekly service from Perth to Meekatharra ($67.30), via Geraldton, stopping at Mt Magnet ($56) and Cue ($60.50).

Mt Magnet Area

Gold was found at Mt Magnet in the late 19th century and mining is still the town's lifeblood. Some 11km north of town are the ruins of **Lennonville**, once a busy town. There are some interesting old solid stone buildings in **Cue**, 80km north of Mt Magnet, and **Walga Rock**, 48km to the west, is a large monolith with a gallery of Aboriginal art (*walga* means 'ochre painting' in the local Warragi language). **Wilgie Mia**, 64km northwest of Cue via Glen Station, is the site of a 30,000-year-old Aboriginal red ochre quarry.

The *Mt Magnet Caravan Park* (☎ 9963 4198, Hepburn St) has tent/powered sites and neglected on-site vans. *Cue Caravan Park* (☎ 9963 1107, Austin St) also has sites.

Meekatharra
● postcode 6642   ● pop 1270

Meekatharra is also a mining centre. At one time it was a railhead for cattle brought down from the NT and the east Kimberley along the Canning Stock Route. There are ruins of various old gold towns and operations in the area. From Meekatharra you can travel southeast via Wiluna and Leonora to the Kalgoorlie goldfields, mostly on unsealed road.

The *Meekatharra Caravan Park* (☎ 9981 1253, Main St) has tent/powered sites at $12/13.50 and cabins at $40 for two. The *Royal Mail Hotel* (☎ 9981 1148, Main St) charges $65/80 a single/double.

GREAT EASTERN HIGHWAY
This highway runs east from Perth to the gold mining centre of Kalgoorlie-Boulder. An earthquake in 1968 badly damaged **Meckering**, 40km east of Northam. The museum on Forrest St in **Cunderdin**, 24km east, has exhibits relating to that event, as well as an interesting collection of farm machinery and equipment.

Merredin (population 2900), the largest centre in the Wheatbelt, is the proud home of the 'world's longest road train'. On Easter Saturday, 1999, a Kenworth truck pulled a whopping 45 trailers weighing 603 tonnes and measuring 610m for 8km along the highway here to set the world record.

The tourist centre (☎ 9041 1666) is on Barrack St. The 1920s train station is now a museum with a vintage 1897 locomotive and an old signal box ($2/1). Merredin was the site of numerous WWII defence installations

and its Military Museum now houses a diverse collection of war memorabilia.

Although the gold quickly gave out, **Southern Cross**, further east, was the first gold-rush town on the WA goldfields. The Yilgarn History Museum in the courthouse has local displays.

Places to Stay & Eat
The *Cunderdin Motor Hotel* (☎ 9635 1104, Olympic Ave) has singles/doubles for $45/60.

The *Merredin Caravan Park* (☎/fax 9041 1535, 2 Oats St), just off the highway, has tent/powered sites from $8/12 and on-site vans for $30. The *Commercial Hotel* (☎ 9041 1052, Barrack St) in Merredin has singles/doubles for $25/45 and good counter meals.

In Southern Cross, there's a *caravan park* (☎ 9049 1212, Coolgardie Rd) and a couple of hotels. The *Palace Hotel* (☎ 9049 1555, Antares St) is a restored country pub with real charm, a large bar and a restaurant; there are single backpacker rooms for $30 and standard hotel rooms are $49/75 for a single/en suite double.

WAVE ROCK & HYDEN
● postcode 6359   ● pop 190

Famous Wave Rock is 4km from the tiny town of Hyden. The perfect wave just about to break, it's 15m high and frozen in solid rock streaked with different coloured bands. It's impressive but hardly justifies the 700km return trip from Perth, which many people make in a day!

Other interesting rock formations in the area bear names like the **Breakers, Hippo's Yawn** and the **Humps. Mulka's Cave** has Aboriginal rock paintings. The information centre (☎ 9880 5182) is in the Wave Rock Wildflower Shop opposite the site, and there's a small museum in the kiosk at the caravan park ($2). There's a parking fee of $5 per car ($2 for motorcycles) within the Wave Rock reserve.

The *Wave Rock Caravan Park* (☎ 9880 5022) is literally right next to the rock. Tent/powered sites cost $12/15, on-site vans $35 and en suite cabins $55 for two.

WESTERN AUSTRALIA

There's backpacker accommodation in four-bed cabins at $15 per person.

The *Wave Rock Hotel-Motel (☎ 9880 5052, fax 9880 5041, 2 Lynch St)*, back in Hyden, is a reasonably luxurious place with well-appointed singles/doubles for $55/85.

Wave-a-Way Backpackers (☎ 9880 5129, Worland Rd), a peaceful farmhouse about 22km north-west of the rock, is a pleasure to stay in. The enthusiastic owners, Joy and Marino, will take you on an interesting tour of the farm, including their wildflower craft centre – the area is ablaze with wildflowers in spring. Beds are $15, and there is separate B&B accommodation in the main house for $35 per person. If you arrive in Hyden by bus, phone ahead for a pick up.

A Westrail (☎ 13 1053) bus to Hyden leaves Perth on Tuesday and returns on Thursday ($30.60; five hours).

OTHER WHEATBELT TOWNS

Most sizeable Wheatbelt towns have a caravan park, a pub that serves counter meals, a motel, a takeaway, a trio of wheat silos, a pervading ennui and little else.

There is a fine rock formation, known as **Kokerbin** (Aboriginal for 'High Place'), 45km west of Bruce Rock. **Corrigin** has a folk museum, a craft cottage and a miniature railway. About 5km west of town is a 'Buried Bone' canine cemetery with some elaborate headstones, crosses and epitaphs in memory of Lassie, Shep, Dusty, Trigger and many more (can you believe it?).

Narrogin (population 4500), 189km south-east of Perth, is an agricultural centre with a courthouse museum, a railway heritage park and the **Albert Facey Homestead**, 39km to the east and close to Wickepin; it's well worth a visit, especially if you have read Facey's popular book *A Fortunate Life*. The Narrogin tourist centre (☎ 9881 2064) is on Egerton St.

Some 26km north of Narrogin is the magnificent **Dryandra Woodland**, a remnant of the open eucalypt woodlands that once covered most of the Wheatbelt. It supports many animal species, including numbats, and is good for bird-watching, walking and, in season, wildflowers.

Wagin (population 1350), 229km south-east of Perth, has a kitsch 15m-high fibreglass ram (a tribute both to the surrounding merino industry and civic bad taste). It is the biggest in the southern hemisphere – are there actually more? The Wagin tourist centre (☎ 9861 1177) on Arthur Rd will reveal more regional delights.

Near **Dumbleyung**, 40km east of Wagin, is the lake upon which Donald Campbell broke the world water-speed record (444.66km/h) in 1964; today it hosts a variety of bird life.

Katanning, south of Wagin, has a large Muslim community (Christmas Islanders), and a mosque built in 1980. The old flour mill on Clive St houses the tourist centre (☎ 9821 2634), open on weekdays from 10 am to 4 pm and Saturday until noon.

Southern Outback

The Southern Outback is a vast area stretching from the goldfields city of Kalgoorlie-Boulder across to South Australia (SA) and the NT.

Fifty years after its establishment in 1829, the Western Australian colony was still going nowhere, so the government in Perth was delighted when gold was discovered at Southern Cross in 1887. That first strike petered out quickly, but more discoveries followed and WA profited from the gold boom for the rest of the century. Gold finally gave WA the population to make it viable in its own right, rather than being just a distant offshoot of the east-coast colonies.

The major strikes were made in 1892 at Coolgardie and, a year later, at Kalgoorlie, but in the goldfields area today Kalgoorlie is the only large town remaining.

Coolgardie's period of prosperity lasted until just 1905 and many other gold towns went from nothing to populations of 10,000 then back to nothing in just 10 years. Nevertheless, the towns capitalised on their prosperity while it lasted, as the many magnificent public buildings attest.

Life on the early goldfields was terribly hard. This area of WA is extremely dry – rainfall is erratic and usually low – and the little rain that does fall quickly disappears into the porous soil. Many early gold-seekers, driven more by enthusiasm than common sense, died of thirst while seeking the elusive mineral. Others succumbed to disease in the unhygienic shanty towns. The supply of water to the goldfields by pipeline in 1903 was a major breakthrough and ensured the continuation of mining.

Today, Kalgoorlie is the main goldfields centre. Elsewhere, a string of fascinating ghost and near-ghost towns and modern nickel mines make a visit to WA's gold country a must.

COOLGARDIE

● postcode 6429   ● pop 1260

A popular pause in the long journey across the Nullarbor, and also the turn-off for Kalgoorlie, Coolgardie really is a ghost of its former self. You only have to glance at the huge town hall and post office building along the broad Bayley St to appreciate the size that Coolgardie once was.

Gold was discovered here in 1892, and by the turn of the century the population had boomed to 15,000. When the precious metal petered out the town withered away just as quickly.

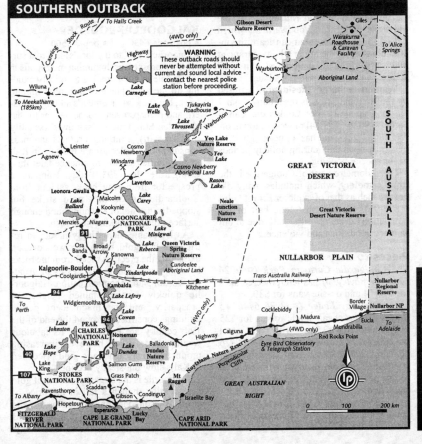

The tourist office (☎ 9026 6090) in the Warden's Court on Bayley St is open daily from 9 am to 5 pm.

Things to See & Do

The many historical markers scattered in and around Coolgardie describe the history of its buildings and sites. The **Goldfields Exhibition**, in the same building as the tourist bureau, has a fascinating display of goldfield memorabilia – you can even find out about former US president Herbert Hoover's days on the WA goldfields. It's open daily from 9 am to 5 pm and is worth the $3/1 entry, which includes a film.

The **Railway Station Museum** is in the old train station on Woodward St, which closed in 1971. Here you can learn the incredible story of the miner who was trapped 300m underground by floodwater in 1907 and rescued by divers 10 days later.

Warden Finnerty's Residence, restored by the National Trust, is open daily from 9 am to 4 pm ($2). The **Coolgardie Camel Farm** (☎ 9026 6159), 4km west of town, offers camel treks and has a museum but it's generally open only during holiday periods or for special bookings.

One kilometre west of Coolgardie is the **town cemetery**, which includes many old graves such as that of explorer Ernest Giles (1835-97). It's said that 'one half of the population buried the other half' due to unsanitary conditions and violence.

Places to Stay & Eat

The *Coolgardie Caravan Park (☎ 9026 6238, 99 Bayley St)* has tent/powered sites for $10/14 and on-site vans for $30.

The *Railway Lodge (☎ 9026 6446, 75 Bayley St)* has cheap single rooms for $25 and doubles for $35, all with continental breakfast. The *Coolgardie Motel (☎ 9026 6080, fax 9026 6300, Bayley St)* is the most comfortable option in town with en suite rooms for $50/65, and it has a licensed restaurant.

The *Denver City Hotel (Bayley St)* does counter meals, and the *Coolgardie Pizza Bar* is next door.

Getting There & Away

Greyhound Pioneer (☎ 13 2030) passes through Coolgardie on the Perth to Adelaide run; the one-way fare from Perth to Coolgardie is $91, and from there to Adelaide it's $199. Perth Goldfields Express (☎ 1800 620 440) has a similar service to Perth but is much cheaper at $65. Golden Lines runs on weekdays from Kalgoorlie to Coolgardie ($4.60).

The *Prospector* from Perth to Kalgoorlie stops at Bonnie Vale train station, 14km away, daily (only westbound on Saturday); the one-way fare from Perth is $47. For bookings call the tourist bureau or Westrail (☎ 13 1053). There's no public transport from the train station into Coolgardie.

KALGOORLIE-BOULDER
● postcode 6430   ● pop 30,500

Kalgoorlie ('Kal' to the locals) is a real surprise – a prosperous, humming metropolis in the middle of nowhere. It's a raw city exuding all the atmosphere of a frontier mining town, but at the same time it's adding a modern and perhaps even urbane veneer to that character. Still, tattoos, 'skimpies' (scantily clad bar staff), gambling, brothels and mass consumption of alcohol are the rule in Kal.

Kalgoorlie rose to prominence later than Coolgardie. In 1893 Paddy Hannan, a prospector from way back, set out from Coolgardie for another gold strike but stopped at the site of Kal and found enough surface gold to spark another rush.

As it became increasingly harder to retrieve surface gold, the miners went deeper, extracting the precious metal from the rocks by costly and complex processes of grinding, roasting and chemical action. Kalgoorlie quickly reached fabled heights of prosperity, and the magnificent public buildings constructed around the end of the 19th century are evidence of its fabulous wealth. After WWI, however, increasing production costs and static gold prices led to Kal's slow but steady decline.

Kalgoorlie is the largest producer of gold in Australia, though a fall in the price of gold has resulted in some mine closures and job losses – certainly, casual mining work is not as easy to find as it once was. Large mining conglomerates have been at the forefront of new open-cut mining operations in the Golden Mile – gone are the old headframes and corrugated iron homes. These days a busy tourist trade combines with mining and pastoral development to ensure Kal's continuing importance as an outback centre.

Overall the cool winter months are the best time to visit. From late August to the end of September the town is packed because of wildflower tours and the local horse races, making accommodation of any type hard to find.

Orientation

Although Kalgoorlie sprang up close to Paddy Hannan's original find, mining soon shifted a few kilometres away to the Golden Mile, a square mile that was one of the richest gold-mining areas for its size in the world; the satellite town of Boulder, 5km south, developed to service it. The two towns amalgamated in 1989 into Kalgoorlie-Boulder city.

Kalgoorlie itself is a grid of broad, tree-lined streets. The main street, Hannan St, is flanked by imposing buildings and is wide enough to turn a camel train – a necessity in early goldfield towns. You'll find most of the hotels, restaurants and offices on or close to Hannan St.

Information

The helpful tourist centre (☎ 9021 1966), 250 Hannan St, has a free map of Kal and loads of information on the area. It's open on weekdays from 8.30 am to 5 pm and weekends from 9 am to 5 pm.

Goldfields Net Zone, 109 Maritana St, has Internet access for $10 per hour.

The RACWA office (☎ 9021 1511) is on the corner of Porter and Hannan Sts, and CALM (☎ 9021 2677) is in the post office building on Hannan St. If you need some new reading matter, Goldfields Book Exchange is on Hannan St.

Hannans North Tourist Mine

This former mine (☎ 9091 4074), about 5km north of town on Broad Arrow Rd, is one of Kalgoorlie's biggest attractions. You can take the lift-cage down into the bowels of the earth and take a guided tour, given by an ex-miner, around the drives and cross-cuts of the mine .

The entry ($7.50/15/38 children/adults/family) covers the underground tour, an audiovisual display, a tour of the surface workings and a 'gold pour'. You can also try your hand at gold panning. The complex is open daily from 9 am to 5 pm, and the underground tours are usually at 12.30 pm. Fully enclosed shoes must be worn when you go underground.

Golden Mile Loopline Railway

The 'Rattler', a ramshackle tourist train, makes an interesting one hour loop around the Golden Mile daily at 10 am (adults/children $9/5). On Sunday it also runs at 11.45 am. It departs from the Boulder train station (☎ 9021 7077).

Museum of the Goldfields

The impressive Ivanhoe mine headframe at the north-eastern end of Hannan St marks the entrance to this excellent museum. It's open daily from 10 am to 4.30 pm (entry by donation) and has a wide range of exhibits, including an underground gold vault full of nuggets, a restored miner's cottage and historic photographs. The tiny British Arms Hotel (the narrowest hotel in Australia) is part of the museum, though the interior is not an example of a goldrush hotel. You can take a lift to the top of the 31m-high headframe for a good view over town.

Other Attractions

Kalgoorlie has a legal Bush Two-Up school in a corrugated-iron amphitheatre 6km out along the Menzies road – follow the signs from Hannan St. Two coins are tossed into the ring and bets are placed on whether heads or tails result. A lot of money changes hands in this frenetic Australian gambling game, but you're welcome just to watch. The action starts at 4.30 pm.

A block north-west of Hannan St is Hay St, one of Kal's more famous 'attractions'. Quietly ignored in tourist brochures, this is

WESTERN AUSTRALIA

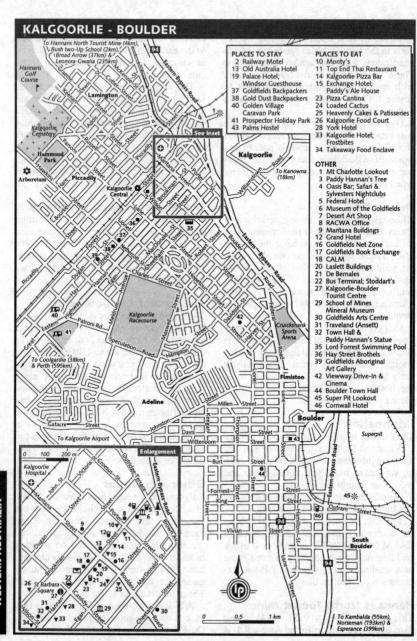

KALGOORLIE - BOULDER

PLACES TO STAY
2 Railway Motel
13 Old Australia Hotel
19 Palace Hotel;
    Windsor Guesthouse
37 Goldfields Backpackers
38 Gold Dust Backpackers
40 Golden Village
    Caravan Park
41 Prospector Holiday Park
43 Palms Hostel

PLACES TO EAT
10 Monty's
11 Top End Thai Restaurant
14 Kalgoorlie Pizza Bar
15 Exchange Hotel;
    Paddy's Ale House
23 Pizza Cantina
24 Loaded Cactus
25 Heavenly Cakes & Patisseries
26 Kalgoorlie Food Court
28 York Hotel
33 Kalgoorlie Hotel;
    Frostbites
34 Takeaway Food Enclave

OTHER
1 Mt Charlotte Lookout
3 Paddy Hannan's Tree
4 Oasis Bar; Safari &
    Sylvesters Nightclubs
5 Federal Hotel
6 Museum of the Goldfields
7 Desert Art Shop
8 RACWA Office
9 Maritana Buildings
12 Grand Hotel
16 Goldfields Net Zone
17 Goldfields Book Exchange
18 CALM
20 Laslett Buildings
21 De Bernales
22 Bus Terminal; Stoddart's
27 Kalgoorlie-Boulder
    Tourist Centre
29 School of Mines
    Mineral Museum
30 Goldfields Arts Centre
31 Traveland (Ansett)
32 Town Hall &
    Paddy Hannan's Statue
35 Lord Forrest Swimming Pool
36 Hay Street Brothels
39 Goldfields Aboriginal
    Art Gallery
42 Viewway Drive-In &
    Cinema
44 Boulder Town Hall
45 Super Pit Lookout
46 Cornwall Hotel

WESTERN AUSTRALIA

a strip of brothels where working women beckon passing men to their galvanised-iron doorways. A blind eye has been turned to this activity for so long that it has become an accepted, historical part of the town.

The **Mt Charlotte Lookout**, only 200m from the north-eastern end of Hannan St, offers a good view over town. The **Super Pit** lookout, just off the Eastern Bypass Road near Boulder, gives a good insight into modern mining practices and the immensity of the operations; it's open daily from 7 am to 6 pm but it's worth trying to be there for the blasting, usually at around 4.45 pm (the lookout is closed if blasting is within 400m).

The **Royal Flying Doctor Service** (☎ 9093 1500) has a base at Kalgoorlie-Boulder airport. There's a visitor centre here, open from 11 am to 3 pm.

There's an art gallery upstairs in the decorative Kalgoorlie **town hall**, while outside is a replica of a statue of Paddy Hannan holding a water bag. The original is inside – safe from nocturnal spray-painters.

Organised Tours

Goldrush Tours (☎ 1800 620 440) is the main local operator with tours of Kal ($40), Coolgardie and nearby ghost towns. Book through the tourist centre.

Aboriginal Bush Tours (☎ 9093 3745), run by Geoff Stokes, has recommended, informative trips covering bush tucker, tracking and Dreamtime stories. Day trips cost $70, twilight tours cost $30 and camping trips are available. There are 4WD tours (☎ 0419-915 670) to ghost towns and for outback gold detecting. For a trip around town with a difference, Red Desert Trike Tours (☎ 0408-955 300) has three-wheel motorbike tours from $30.

You can see the Golden Mile mining operations from above with Goldfields Air Services (☎ 9093 2116) and AAA Charters (☎ 9093 4115); flights cost from $25 per person (minimum of two).

Special Events

The Kalgoorlie-Boulder Race Around is the biggest outback horse racing carnival in WA, drawing thousands of punters. It's held around the first week in September, culminating with the 2300m Kalgoorlie Cup. The event coincides with the popular wildflower season, so getting a bed in town can be difficult.

Places to Stay – Budget

Caravan Parks There are a number of caravan parks in Kal. *Golden Village Caravan Park* (☎ 9021 4162, 406 Hay St), 2km south-west of the train station, has tent/powered sites for $13/16.50, and park homes for $50 ($70 in the high season). *Prospector Holiday Park* (☎ 9021 2524, Great Eastern Hwy) has tent/powered sites $17/18 and standard/en suite cabins for $56/66; it has a pool, a grassed area for campers and a campers' kitchen.

Hostels There are two good hostels on Hay St; both have pools and pick up travellers from the bus or train on request. *Goldfields Backpackers* (☎ 9091 1482, 0412-110 001, 166 Hay St) is well managed and definitely the pick; dorm beds are $16 ($14 for YHA members); doubles/twins are $34 to $36 for members. A separate homestay, next door at No 164, is in a former brothel and caters for long-termers. *Gold Dust Backpackers* (☎ 9091 3737, 192 Hay St) has similar facilities including a large kitchen, and staff can help in finding work; with a discount, dorm beds are $14, twins/doubles $30/35.

Windsor Guesthouse (☎ 9021 5483, 147 Hannan St) is a new place for backpackers with beds in comfortable twin rooms for $15 per person. It's next door to, and run by, the Palace Hotel. Although the guesthouse wasn't complete at the time of writing, it looked like a reasonable option.

The *Palms* (☎/fax 9093 1620, 35 Wittenoom St), another new place, is a little out of the action at Boulder, but it's a notch above the other places for comfort. In a renovated old corner hotel, it has dorm beds for $14 and furnished singles/doubles with character for $20/36. Some rooms open out onto the balcony, and you get free bikes, free laundry and free use of the spa! Phone for a pick up from the bus or train station.

Places to Stay – Mid-Range

There are several pleasantly old-fashioned hotels right in the centre of Kal, including the *Palace Hotel (☎ 9021 2788)* on the corner of Maritana and Hannan Sts, which has singles/doubles with en suite and air-con for $50/70.

The *Old Australia Hotel (☎ 9021 1320, Maritana St)*, diagonally opposite the Palace, is a private hotel (not a pub) with rooms for $55/75 or $85 for en suite doubles.

The *Railway Motel (☎ 9088 0000, 51 Forrest St)*, opposite the train station, is one of many good motels. Standard doubles are $115/95 weekdays/weekends.

Places to Eat

Kalgoorlie has plenty of reliable pubs for counter meals (where they skimp on clothing, not the servings), and a growing number of trendy cafes and restaurants.

The *Kalgoorlie Food Court (90 Brookman St)* has a selection of about six types of food from around $6. *Heavenly Cakes & Patisseries*, on the corner of Boulder Rd and Egan St, lives up to its name with mouthwatering cakes, rolls and smoothies. For pizza, try *Pizza Cantina (211 Hannan St)* or the *Kalgoorlie Pizza Bar* at No 123.

If you don't mind being in a pub with scantily clad barmaids first thing in the morning, the $5 'big breakfast' in the front bar (the 'Wild West Saloon') of the *Exchange Hotel* is unbeatable. For counter meals, try the *York Hotel (259 Hannan St)*, or *Tommy Pepper's* in the Palace Hotel, which has lunchtime roasts for $4.90.

Top End Thai Restaurant (☎ 9021 4286, 71 Hannan St) is good for a splurge – it has a wide range of prawn, curry and noodle dishes from $15. *Monty's (80 Hannan St)* is a 24 hour Italian-style place with wicker chairs, alfresco dining and half-price pasta on Tuesday.

The *Loaded Cactus (☎ 9022 8028, 90 Egan St)* adds to the multicultural picture. It's a BYO Mexican restaurant with moderately priced standards.

Entertainment

Pubs feature heavily in the night scene, but the days of the rough and ready, frontier-type men-only bar rooms are waning in modern Kal. For a taste of the original Kalgoorlie pub – skimpies and all – the *Federal Hotel* and *Grand Hotel* on Hannan St are good places to start.

One of the most popular pubs in town is *Paddy's Ale House* in the Exchange Hotel. It has a convivial atmosphere, live music nightly and a range of international beers. *De Bernales (193 Hannan St)* is a great place for a relaxed drink and also has occasional live music. The *Kalgoorlie Hotel (319 Hannan St)*, with its Frostbites bar (the one with cocktails spinning in washing machines), is popular with a younger crowd.

Nightclubs include *Safari* and *Sylvesters*, in the same building at the top end of Hannan St. Like any late night venue, it can get rough here at times.

Shopping

The Goldfields Aboriginal Art Gallery on Dugan St and the Desert Art shop, next to the Museum of the Goldfields, have crafts for sale. Kal is a good place to buy gold nuggets fashioned into relatively inexpensive jewellery – shop along Hannan St.

Getting There & Away

Air A surprising number of flights go from Kalgoorlie to many parts of Australia. Ansett (☎ 13 1300) and Qantas Airlink (☎ 13 1313) fly between Perth and Kal at least twice a day ($217). Skywest (☎ 13 1300) also has a direct flight daily and is marginally cheaper.

Traveland, 314 Hannan St, is the local Ansett agent. Stoddart's (☎ 9021 2796), 248 Hannan St, is the Qantas agent.

Bus Greyhound Pioneer (☎ 13 2030) buses stop in Kalgoorlie daily between Perth and Adelaide. Perth Goldfields Express (☎ 1800 620 440) has a service from Perth to Kal, continuing north to Leonora ($35 from Kal) and Laverton ($50) on Sunday, Wednesday and Friday. A fourth service on Thursday runs between Perth and Kal only ($65).

Westrail (☎ 13 1053) runs a bus three times a week to Esperance – twice via Kambalda and once via Coolgardie; the trip takes 5½ hours and costs $18 to Norseman, $33.50 to Esperance. Westrail also has a bus between Perth and Kal on Monday, Wednesday and Friday. Buses stop outside the tourist office on Hannan St.

Train The daily *Prospector* service from Perth takes around 7½ hours ($49.30). The *Indian-Pacific* train also goes through Kal on Wednesday and Saturday.

Getting Around

There's a regular bus service between Kal and Boulder, operated by Goldenlines (☎ 9021 2655) between 8 am and 6 pm. There are also daily buses to Kambalda and Coolgardie (during school terms only).

Kalgoorlie Adventure Bus (☎ 9091 1958) is a new 'backpacker' bus that runs twice daily to Hannan's North Tourist Mine ($3) and the Super Pit at Boulder ($3). Return trips to either are $5 and a round-trip covering the lot is $9. Trips leave from Goldfields Backpackers, or you can be picked up. The service may expand, depending on demand, and trips to other places of interest can be organised.

NORTH OF KALGOORLIE-BOULDER

The road north is surfaced from Kal all the way to the three 'Ls' – Leonora-Gwalia (237km), Laverton (368km) and Leinster (361km). Off the main road, however, traffic is virtually nonexistent and rain can quickly close dirt roads.

Places of interest include the ghost town **Kanowna**, 22km north-east of Kalgoorlie-Boulder along a dirt road. In 1905 this town had a population of 12,000, 16 hotels, many churches and an hourly train service to Kal. Today, apart from the train station and the odd piles of rubble, not much remains. **Broad Arrow**, further north, has a population of 20, compared with 2400 at the beginning of the 20th century. One of the town's original eight hotels operates in a virtually unchanged condition. **Menzies**, 132km north of Kal, has about 110 people today, compared with 5000 in 1900. Many early buildings remain, including the train station with its 120m-long platform and the town hall with its clockless clock tower – the ship (SS *Orizaba*) bringing the clock from England sank en route.

Leonora (population 1150) serves as the railhead for the nickel from Windarra and Leinster. In adjoining **Gwalia** (once a ghost town) is the Sons of Gwalia gold mine, the largest in WA outside Kalgoorlie. At one time the mine was managed by Herbert Hoover, later to become president of the USA. The Gwalia Historical Society is housed in the 1898 mine office – this fascinating local museum is open daily from 10 am to 4 pm ($2).

South of Leonora-Gwalia, 25km off the main road, is **Kookynie**, another interesting once-flourishing mining town with just a handful of inhabitants. The 1901 *Grand Hotel* (☎ 9031 3010) has single/doubles for $40/45 with continental breakfast. Nearby **Niagara** is also a ghost town; the Niagara Dam was built with cement carried in by a 400-strong camel train.

From Leonora-Gwalia, you can turn north-east to **Laverton** (population 670), where the surfaced road ends. The population here declined from 1000 in 1910 to 200 in 1970, when the Poseidon nickel discovery revived mining operations in nearby Windarra. There are many abandoned mines in the area. From here, it's just 1710km to Alice Springs via the Warburton road.

North of Leonora-Gwalia, the road is surfaced to **Leinster** (population 1450), another modern nickel town. Nearby, **Agnew** is another old gold town that has all but disappeared. From here, it's 170km north to **Wiluna** (population 260) and then another 185km west to Meekatharra and the surfaced Great Northern Hwy. Throughout the 1930s, due to the mining of arsenic, Wiluna was a modern, prosperous town with a population of 9000. The ore ran out in 1948 and the town quickly declined. There is a *caravan park* (☎ 9981 70 21), and the *Club Hotel/Motel* (☎ 9981 7012) has double units for $100.

Warburton Road

For those interested in an outback experience, the unsealed road from Laverton to Yulara

WESTERN AUSTRALIA

(near Uluru), via Warburton, provides a rich scenery of red sand, spinifex, mulga and desert oaks. The road is well maintained and suitable for conventional vehicles, although a 4WD would give a much smoother ride. There are plans to seal this stretch of highway to create the Great Central Desert Road.

You should take precautions relevant to travel in such an isolated area – tell someone reliable of your travel plans and take adequate supplies of water, food, petrol and spare parts. Don't even consider doing it from November to March when the heat is extreme. Conditions should not be taken lightly – in 1994 a Japanese motorcyclist, equipped with just four leaky 1L milk bottles, nearly met his end here. See the Getting Around chapter for more details on outback travel.

Petrol and supplies are available at Laverton, Warburton, Docker River and Yulara. Between Warburton and Laverton (about 315km from Laverton), *Tjukayirla Roadhouse* (☎ *9037 1108*) also has fuel, limited meals and accommodation for $25 per person. At **Giles**, about 105km west of the NT border, is a weather station with a friendly 'Visitors Welcome' sign and a bar.

As this road passes through Aboriginal land, transit permits are required from the Central Land Council in Alice Springs (☎ 8951 6211) for the NT end and from Aboriginal Affairs in Perth (☎ 9235 8000) for the WA end. These permits take up to two weeks to issue.

SOUTH OF KALGOORLIE-BOULDER
Kambalda
• postcode 6442   • pop 1200

Today this is a major mining centre 79km south of Kalgoorlie-Boulder. Nickel was discovered here in 1966, the town having died as a gold-mining town in 1906. There are two town centres, Kambalda East and Kambalda West, about 4km apart. Nearby is **Lake Lefroy**, a large saltpan and a popular spot for land yachting.

The tourist bureau (☎ 9027 1446) is on Emu Rocks Rd in Kambalda West. There's a *caravan park* and *motel* in Kambalda West.

Norseman
• postcode 6443   • pop 1500

Norseman is a major crossroads town from where you start or finish the Eyre Hwy (Nullarbor) journey. From here you can also head south to Esperance or north to Kalgoorlie.

The tourist bureau (☎ 9039 0171), 68 Robert St, is open daily from 9 am to 5 pm. Behind it is a rest park with showers and barbecue facilities, open from 7 am to 6 pm. There's a telecentre nearby on Robert St with Internet and email facilities.

The **Historical & Geological Collection** in the old School of Mines has items from the gold-rush days; it's open daily except Thursday and Sunday from 10 am to 1 pm ($2/1). You can fossick for gemstones (agate) on a property about 12km north of town. Get a permit ($5) from the tourist bureau.

There are excellent views of the town and the surrounding salt lakes from the **Beacon Hill Mararoa Lookout**, down past the mountainous tailings dumps. One of these contains 4.2 million tonnes of rock, the result of 40 years of mining.

Also worth a look are the views at sunrise and sunset of the dry, expansive **Lake Cowan**, north of the town. South of Norseman, just under halfway along the road to Esperance, is the small township of **Salmon Gums**, named after the prevalent local gum trees that acquire a rich, pink bark in late summer and autumn.

Places to Stay & Eat The *Gateway Caravan Park* (☎ *9039 1500, Prinsep St*) is a tidy place with tent/powered sites for $14/16 and on-site vans/cabins for $35/45 for two. There are a couple of backpackers rooms for $15/20 a single/double.

Lodge 101 (☎ *9039 1541, 101 Prinsep St*) is a very welcoming place to stay. The comfortable dorm beds for $15 will be a godsend to weary cross-Nullarbor cyclists, and there are singles/doubles for $25/40. It's run by a lovely couple and there's a pleasant outdoor sitting area.

The *Norseman Hotel* (☎ *9039 1023, 90 Roberts St)* has rooms for $30/45 including continental breakfast, and the *Norseman*

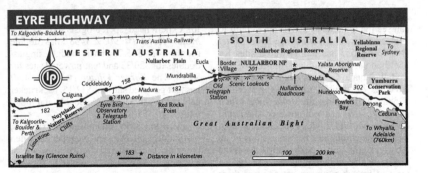

EYRE HIGHWAY

Eyre Motel (☎ 9039 1130, Roberts St) charges $62/69 for its rooms. The motel has a bar and restaurant.

The *Rainbow Drive Cafe* (93 Roberts St) does hot breakfasts, burgers and light meals.

EYRE HIGHWAY

It's a little over 2700km between Perth and Adelaide – not much less than the distance from London to Moscow. The long and sometimes lonely Eyre Hwy crosses the southern edge of the vast **Nullarbor Plain** – Nullarbor is bad Latin for 'no trees' and indeed there is a small stretch where you see none at all.

The road across the Nullarbor takes its name from John Eyre, the explorer who, in 1841, was the first European to make the east-west crossing. It was a superhuman effort that involved five months of hardship and resulted in the death of Eyre's companion, John Baxter. In 1877 a telegraph line was laid across the Nullarbor, roughly delineating the route the first road would take. Later in the 19th century, miners en route to the goldfields followed this telegraph-line route across the empty plain. In 1896 the first bicycle crossing was made and in 1912 the first car was driven across.

In 1941 WWII inspired the building of a transcontinental highway, just as it had the Alice Springs to Darwin route. It was a rough-and-ready track and in the 50s only a few vehicles a day made the crossing. In the 60s the traffic flow increased to more than 30 vehicles a day, and in 1969 the WA government surfaced the road as far as the South

Australian border. Finally, in 1976, the last stretch was surfaced and now the Nullarbor crossing is an easy, but still long, drive.

The surfaced road runs close to the coast on the South Australian side. Along this coastline, the Nullarbor region ends dramatically at the cliffs of the Great Australian Bight. The Trans Australia Railway runs across the true Nullarbor Plain, while the highway is mainly to the south of the treeless area.

From Norseman it's 725km to the WA-SA border, near Eucla, and a further 480km to Ceduna (meaning 'a place to sit down and rest' in the local Aboriginal language) in SA. From Ceduna, it's still another 793km to Adelaide via Port Augusta. It's a long way!

Crossing the Nullarbor

Although the Nullarbor is no longer the torture trail of old, it's wise to prepare adequately to avoid difficulties.

The longest distance between fuel stops is about 200km, so if you're foolish enough to run low on petrol midway, it can be a long trip to get more. Getting help for a mechanical breakdown can be very expensive and equally time-consuming, so make sure you have good tyres and at least a basic kit of simple spare parts. Carry some drinking water (at least 4L per person) just in case you do have to sit it out by the roadside on a hot summer day.

Norseman to Eucla

From Norseman, the first settlement you reach is **Balladonia**, 193km to the east.

WESTERN AUSTRALIA

After Balladonia, near the old station, you can see the remains of stone fences built to enclose stock. The *Balladonia Hotel Motel* (☎ *9039 3453)* has tent/powered sites for $8/12 and singles/doubles from $58/68.

Balladonia to **Caiguna** is one of the longest stretches of straight road in the world – 145km. At Caiguna, the *John Eyre Motel* (☎ *9039 3459)* has tent/powered sites from $8/15 for two and singles/doubles for $50/65.

At **Cocklebiddy** are the stone ruins of an Aboriginal mission. Cocklebiddy Cave is the largest of the Nullarbor caves – in 1983 a team of French explorers set a record there for the deepest cave dive in the world. With a 4WD, you can travel south to Twilight Cove, with its 75m-high limestone cliffs. At Cocklebiddy, the *Wedgetail Inn Motel Hotel* (☎ *9039 3462)* has expensive fuel, tent/powered sites for $9/15, basic singles/doubles for $40/48 and motel rooms for $60/70.

Birds Australia's *Eyre Bird Observatory* (☎ *9039 3450)*, housed in the former **Eyre Telegraph Station**, 50km south of Cocklebiddy on the bight, is a haven for twitchers. Full board is $70 per person per day (with reductions after the first night). Return transport from Cocklebiddy is available for overnight guests, otherwise you'll need a 4WD with good clearance.

Madura, 90km east of Cocklebiddy, is close to the Hampton Tablelands. At one time, horses were bred here for the Indian Army. The *Madura Pass Oasis Inn* (☎ *9039 3464)* has tent/powered sites for $12/15, budget rooms for $52, and single/double motel rooms for $69/86.

Mundrabilla, 116km to the east, has a *caravan park*, and the *Mundrabilla Motel Hotel* (☎ *9039 3465)* has rooms from $55.

Just before the South Australian border is **Eucla**. South of the town, on the Great Australian Bight, are picturesque ruins of an old **telegraph repeater/weather station**, first opened in 1877. The telegraph line now runs along the railway line to the north. The station, 5km from the roadhouse, is gradually being engulfed by sand dunes (just the chimneys protrude).

The Eucla area has many caves, such as the famous **Koonalda Cave** with its 45m-high chamber. Like most Nullarbor caves, it's only for experienced speleologists. The *Eucla Motor Hotel* (☎ *9039 3468)* has double rooms from $65/75, basic budget singles/doubles for $20/35 and tent/powered sites for $4/10. The *Border Village* (☎ *9039 3474)* has tent/powered sites for $12/15, backpacker cabins for $20/35 a single/double and motel units from $55/65.

There are strict quarantine restrictions, particularly on fruit and vegetables, when crossing the border; checkpoints are at Eucla and Ceduna.

Eucla to Ceduna
See the South Australia chapter for the section of highway between the border and Ceduna.

Central West Coast

After leaving Perth's north coastal region, the North-West Coastal Hwy (Hwy 1) passes through three interesting regions – the Batavia Coast (evoking memories of the area's many shipwrecks, and including Geraldton and Kalbarri); the Shark Bay World Heritage region; and the Gascoyne, with Carnarvon and Mt Augustus.

DONGARA-DENISON
* postcode 6525   * pop 1900

The Brand Hwy hits the coast at Dongara. This is a pleasant little port with fine beaches, lots of crayfish and a tourist centre (☎ 9927 1404), housed in the old police station at 5 Waldeck St. There's a small historical display in the adjacent old gaol. **Russ Cottage**, built in 1870, is open on Sunday from 10 am to noon ($2).

Just over the Irwin River is **Port Denison**. The mouth of the Irwin is a great place for bird-watching – you'll see pelicans and cormorants in particular.

Places to Stay & Eat
Caravan parks include the *Dongara Denison Tourist Park* (☎ *9927 1210, 8 George St)*, with powered sites from $14 and on-site vans from $25, and the friendly *Seaspray*

(☎ 9927 1165, 81 Church St), with powered sites/cabins for $15/60.

Dongara Backpackers YHA (☎ 9927 1581, 32 Waldeck St) is a simple place with rooms in an old house or in a nearby train carriage – it gets good reports for the laid back atmosphere. Dorm beds cost $14, singles $20 and twins/doubles $28/32 (YHA members pay $1 less).

The *Priory Lodge Historic Inn (☎/fax 9927 1090, 6 St Dominics Rd)* is a bit of gem. The priory was built in 1881, and the accommodation section (1920) was originally a ladies college. Now fully restored, it has modern bathroom facilities, a self-catering kitchen, a cosy lounge and a pool. Singles/doubles cost $35/50.

Toko's Restaurant (☎ 9927 1497, 38 Moreton Terrace) is open for lunch and dinner with an a la carte menu. In Port Denison, the *Port Store* has a bakery, coffee shop and takeaway food section, and the *Octopus's Garden Restaurant (☎ 9927 2207, 60 Point Leander Drive)*, open from 6 pm, is a good place for an evening meal (it's BYO and licensed).

GREENOUGH
• postcode 6530   • pop 100

Further north, only about 20km south of Geraldton, is Greenough, once a busy little mining town but now a quiet farming centre. There's quite a bit to see in the area – local information is available at the Midwest Centre (☎ 9926 1660), just off the highway.

The **Greenough Historical Hamlet** contains 11 buildings constructed in the 19th century and now restored by the National Trust. There are guided tours on weekends – at other times you can take a self-guided tour. Either way it's well worth a visit. The hamlet is open daily from 9 am to 4 pm (adults/children $4.50/2.50). The **Pioneer Museum**, open daily from 10 am to 4 pm ($2/50c), has some fine historical displays. In the local paddocks, look out for the bizarre 'leaning trees', river red gums *(Eucalyptus camaldulensis)* bent over by salt winds off the ocean.

The *Greenough Rivermouth Caravan Park (☎ 9921 5845)* is well situated and has

tent/powered sites for $15 and on-site vans/cabins for $26/45. The *Hampton Arms Inn (☎ 9926 1057, Company Rd)* is a classic historic inn (1863) and a great place for a quiet beer or a bed. The old fashioned rooms have many original fittings and are good value at $48/65 for singles/doubles with a light breakfast.

GERALDTON
• postcode 6530   • pop 25,250

Geraldton, the major town in the mid-west, is on a rugged stretch of coast, with the mystical Houtman Abrolhos Islands offshore. The area has a fine climate, particularly in winter. If you are tempted by fresh lobster or are a windsurfing enthusiast, this is the place to visit – in summer it is extremely windy here.

Information
The tourist bureau (☎ 9921 3999) is in the Bill Sewell complex on Chapman Rd. It's open on weekdays from 8.30 am to 5 pm, Saturday from 9 am to 4.30 pm and Sunday from 9.30 am to 4.30 pm. The main post office is on Durlacher St and most of the banks are in the Mall on Marine Terrace.

Phoenix, on the corner of Augustus and Gregory Sts, has email and Internet access for $5 per hour.

Geraldton Museum
The town's captivating museum on Marine Terrace tells the story of early wrecks and has assorted relics from the doomed Dutch ships, including the *Batavia* and the *Zeewijk* – see the boxed text 'Dutch Shipwrecks'. A feature is the carved wooden sternpiece from the *Zuytdorp*, found in 1927 on top of cliffs near where the ship had grounded. An experimental yellow submarine, built locally in 1969, sits out the front.

The museum is open daily from 10 am to 4 pm (admission by donation).

St Francis Xavier Cathedral
The cathedral is one of a number of buildings in Geraldton and the mid-west designed by Monsignor John Hawes, an unusual priest-cum-architect who left WA

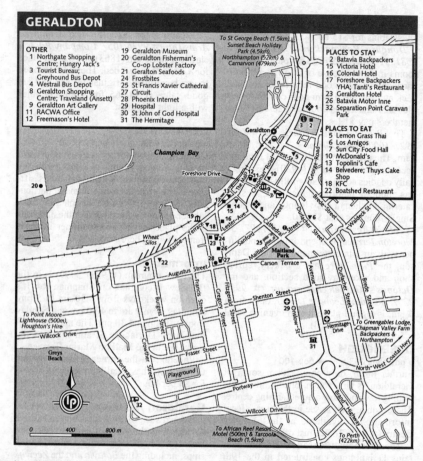

GERALDTON

OTHER
1 Northgate Shopping Centre; Hungry Jack's
3 Tourist Bureau; Greyhound Bus Depot
4 Westrail Bus Depot
8 Geraldton Shopping Centre; Traveland (Ansett)
9 Geraldton Art Gallery
11 RACWA Office
12 Freemason's Hotel
19 Geraldton Museum
20 Geraldton Fisherman's Co-op Lobster Factory
21 Geralton Seafoods
24 Frostbites
25 St Francis Xavier Cathedral
27 Circuit
28 Phoenix Internet
29 Hospital
30 St John of God Hospital
31 The Hermitage

PLACES TO STAY
2 Batavia Backpackers
15 Victoria Hotel
16 Colonial Hotel
17 Foreshore Backpackers YHA; Tanti's Restaurant
23 Geraldton Hotel
26 Batavia Motor Inne
32 Separation Point Caravan Park

PLACES TO EAT
5 Lemon Grass Thai
6 Los Amigos
7 Sun City Food Hall
10 McDonald's
13 Topolini's Cafe
14 Belvedere; Thuys Cake Shop
18 KFC
22 Boatshed Restaurant

To St George Beach (1.5km); Sunset Beach Holiday Park (4.5km); Northampton (52km) & Carnarvon (479km)

Champion Bay

Foreshore Drive

To Point Moore Lighthouse (500m), Houghton's Hire

Greys Beach

To African Reef Resort Motel (500m) & Tarcoola Beach (1.5km)

To Greengables Lodge, Chapman Valley Farm Backpackers & Northampton

To Perth (422km)

0   400   800 m

---

in 1939 and spent the rest of his life as a hermit on a Caribbean island. Construction of the Byzantine-style cathedral commenced in 1916, a year after Hawes' arrival, but his plans were too grandiose and the building was not completed until 1938.

The architecture is a blend of styles. External features include the twin towers of the west front with their arched openings, a large central dome similar to Brunellesci's famous cupola in Florence and a cone roofed tower that would not be out of place in the Loire Valley. The interior is just as striking, with Romanesque columns, huge arches beneath an octagonal dome and zebra-striped walls. Hawes felt that he had 'caught the rhythm of a poem in stone'.

Other Attractions

The **Geraldton Art Gallery**, Chapman Rd, is open daily (free). The Geraldton Fisherman's Co-op free **lobster factory tour** is worth doing. It gives a good insight into this multi-million dollar industry – learn how a live rock lobster gets from the ocean floor to a Hong Kong restaurant table. Guided tours are held Monday to Friday at 9.30 am and 2 pm (November to June).

Organised Tours

Touch the Wild Safaris (☎ 9921 8435) does trips ($65/80 half/full day) into the hinterland surrounding Geraldton, where you get the chance to see a wide range of flora and fauna. Shine Aviation (☎ 9923 3600) and Geraldton Air Charters (☎ 9923 3434) have scenic flights over the mid-west, including the Houtman Abrolhous Islands.

Places to Stay – Budget

Camping & Hostels *Separation Point (☎ 9921 2763, Willcock Drive)* is the closest caravan park to the town centre. It has tent/powered sites for $12/14 and cabins for $36 for two.

Sunset Beach Holiday Park (☎ 9938 1655, Bosley St, Sunset Beach) is an excellent caravan park a little way north of town but well worth it for its beach location; tent/powered sites are $13/16, on-site vans $30 and tidy cabins are from $30/40 for two.

Foreshore Backpackers YHA (☎ 9921 3275, 172 Marine Terrace) is in the former Grantown Guesthouse. It's a friendly place with plenty of old-style private rooms. Dorm beds are $14 ($13 for members), singles are $20 ($18) and doubles $36 ($33).

Batavia Backpackers (☎ 9964 3001, Chapman Rd) is in the Bill Sewell complex, right behind the tourist office. It's a big place with good facilities (it caters for groups as well as travellers). Dorm beds in partitioned rooms are $14 ($13 with VIP), singles are $18 ($17) and doubles $40 ($38).

Chapman Valley Farm Backpackers (☎ 9920 5160, Murphy Norris Rd), 25km out of town, is in an historic homestead. It offers pick up from Geraldton if you book ahead; beds are $10.

Hotels Cheap rooms are available at some of the older-style hotels, such as the *Colonial* on Fitzgerald St, the *Victoria* on Marine Terrace and the *Geraldton* ('the Gero') on Gregory St; count on about $20 per person.

Places to Stay – Mid-Range

Greengables Lodge (☎ 9938 2332, 7 Hackett Rd), about 5km from town off Chapman Valley Rd, is a classy B&B that comes highly recommended. Standard singles/doubles cost $65/75 and evening meals are available.

The *Batavia Motor Inne (☎ 1800 014 628, 54 Fitzgerald St)* is central and has rooms for $75. The *African Reef Resort Motel Hotel (☎ 9964 5566, 5 Broadhead Ave)* has all sorts of facilities and varied accommodation from caravan sites to ocean view motel units for $80/95. Self-contained apartments start at $70.

Places to Eat

The *Sun City Food Hall (56 Durlacher St)* has Indian, Chinese and Italian food, roasts and fish and chips. The food is excellent and you can get a good feed for $8.

There are a number of small snack bars and cafes along Marine Terrace including *Thuys Cake Shop* at No 202 and *Belvedere* at No 149, with standard cafe food at down-to-earth prices. *Topolini's Cafe (☎ 9964 5866, 158 Marine Terrace)* is a trendy licensed restaurant with pasta dishes from $8.50 and main meals around $15.

Lemon Grass Restaurant (☎ 9964 1172, 18 Snowdon St) and *Tanti's (☎ 9964 2311, 174 Marine Terrace)* are both popular Thai restaurants; the latter is particularly good value. *Los Amigos (105 Durlacher St)* is a deservedly popular, licensed Mexican place. The *Boatshed (☎ 9921 5500, 357 Marine Terrace)* is Geraldton's top seafood restaurant. A little further along Marine Terrace is *Geraldton Seafoods* where you can buy it fresh; a small cooked lobster costs around $11 and makes for a great gourmet picnic.

Entertainment

The *Gero* occasionally has live bands and its Beachcomber beer garden is pleasant in summer. The *Freemason's* ('the Freo') in the Mall is a popular pub, and the city's nightclubs are *Frostbites* (next to the Geraldton Hotel) and *Circuit* on Fitzgerald St.

Getting There & Around

Skywest (☎ 13 1300) has flights from Perth to Geraldton daily. There are also flights from Geraldton to Carnarvon and Exmouth twice a week.

WESTERN AUSTRALIA

Westrail (☎ 13 1053) and Greyhound Pioneer (☎ 13 2030) have regular bus services from Perth to Geraldton for around $40 one way. Integrity (☎ 9226 1339) goes from Perth to Geraldton three times a week ($35). Westrail services continue north-east to Meekatharra (twice weekly) or north to Kalbarri (three weekly). Westrail stops at the old train station, while Greyhound Pioneer and Integrity stop at the Bill Sewell complex.

A city bus service (☎ 9923 1100) provides access to all nearby suburbs. Houghtons Hire (☎ 9964 1722) has the cheapest car hire rates. Bikes can be hired from the Geraldton tourist bureau for $10 a day.

HOUTMAN ABROLHOS ISLANDS

There are more than 100 islands in this group, located about 60km off the Geraldton coast, and they are a bird-watcher's paradise. The beautiful but treacherous reefs surrounding the islands have claimed many ships over the years, including early Dutch vessels – see the boxed text 'Dutch Shipwrecks'.

Much of the beauty of the Abrolhos lies beneath the water, where the *Acropora* family of corals abounds. Air and diving tours to these protected, spectacular islands can be taken from Geraldton, but you can't camp overnight.

Sea-Jay Abrolhos Island Tours (☎ 9921 3771) has trips out to the islands for $150 per person per day. For an extra fee you can avoid the boat trip and get there on a float plane.

NORTHAMPTON

• postcode 6535   • pop 850

This town, 50km north of Geraldton, has a number of historic buildings and access to good beaches at **Horrocks** (22km west) and

---

Dutch Shipwrecks

During the 17th century, ships of the Dutch East India Company sailing from Europe to Batavia in Java headed due east from the Cape of Good Hope and then beat up the WA coast to Indonesia. It took only a small miscalculation for a ship to run aground on this unknown and uncharted coast and a few did just that, with disastrous results.

Four wrecks of Dutch East Indiamen have been located, including the *Batavia*, the earliest and, in many ways, the most interesting wreck.

In 1629 the *Batavia* went aground on the Houtman Abrolhos Islands, off the coast of Geraldton. The survivors set up camp, sent off a rescue party to Batavia (now Jakarta) in the ship's boat and waited. It took three months for a rescue party to arrive, and in that time a mutiny had taken place and more than 120 of the survivors had been murdered. The ringleaders were hanged and two mutineers were unceremoniously dumped on the coast just south of modern-day Kalbarri.

In 1656 the *Vergulde Draeck* (Gilt Dragon) struck a reef about 100km north of Perth and, although a party of seven survivors made it to Batavia, no trace of those who stayed behind was found, other than a few scattered coins.

The *Zuytdorp* ran aground beneath the towering cliffs north of Kalbarri in 1712. Wine bottles, other relics and the remains of fires have been found on the cliff top. The discovery of the extremely rare Ellis van Creveld syndrome (rife in Holland at the time the ship ran aground) in children of Aboriginal descent suggests that *Zuytdorp* survivors might have passed the gene to Aboriginal people.

In 1727 the *Zeewijk* followed the *Batavia* to destruction on the Houtman Abrolhos Islands. Again a small party of survivors made its way to Batavia, but many of the remaining sailors died before they could be rescued. Many relics from these shipwrecks, particularly the *Batavia*, can be seen in the maritime museums in Fremantle and Geraldton. A good account of the wrecks is *Islands of Angry Ghosts* by Hugh Edwards, leader of the expedition that discovered the wreck of the *Batavia*.

Port Gregory (47km north-west). The town was founded to exploit the lead and copper deposits discovered in 1848. Today it's an agricultural centre.

The tourist bureau (☎ 9934 1488) is in the old library on the main road and is open weekdays from 9 am to 4 pm and until 2 pm on Saturday.

Chiverton House, an early mining home, is a fine municipal museum open daily except Tuesday and Wednesday from 10 am to noon and 2 to 4 pm ($2).

Places to Stay

There are *caravan parks* near Northampton *(☎ 9934 1202)*, Port Gregory *(☎ 9935 1052)* and Horrocks *(☎ 9934 3039)*; all have tent sites, and the Horrocks and Port Gregory caravan parks have on-site vans.

The *Nagle Centre (☎ 9934 1692, 61 North West Coastal Hwy)*, formerly the Sacred Heart Convent, has budget beds for $12 per person, or $15 with linen; it has all the usual facilities. The pubs in town offer rooms.

Lynton Homestead (☎ 9935 1040, Port Gregory Rd), next to the ruined convict settlement about 40km west of Northampton, has backpacker beds in two bunkhouses (with shared facilities and kitchen) for $15 and one fully self-contained cottage at $30 per person ($60 for four).

KALBARRI
• postcode 6536   • pop 1800

A deservedly popular spot with backpackers, Kalbarri is on the coast at the mouth of the Murchison River, 66km west of the main highway. The area has an alluring coastline, stunning gorges and haunting Dutch shipwreck stories. The *Zuytdorp* was wrecked about 65km north-west of Kalbarri in 1712; earlier, in 1629, two *Batavia* mutineers were marooned at Wittecarra Gully, an inlet just south of the town.

The tourist bureau (☎ 9937 1104, 1800 63 9568), Grey St, is open daily from 9 am to 5 pm; it has plenty of information and handles bookings for various tours and activities. Internet access is available at the library next door, or at the Kalbarri Explorer dive shop in the arcade ($5 per half-hour).

Things to See & Do

Rainbow Jungle is an interesting bird park and parrot breeding centre 4km south of town on Red Bluff Rd ($7/2). Kalbarri Boat Hire (☎ 9937 1245) has canoes, rowboats, motorboats and surfboards for hire, and tours can be taken on the river aboard the *Kalbarri River Queen* ($20/15); book at the tourist bureau.

Riverside Recollections, on Grey St, is an unusual museum crammed with local history memorabilia, a large collection of dolls from around the world and a replica underground mine ($4). Across the road, pelicans arrive on cue each morning at around 8.45 am for a feed.

South of town is a string of rugged cliff faces, including Red Bluff, Rainbow Valley, Pot Alley, Eagle Gorge and Natural Bridge. A walking/cycling path goes almost as far as Red Bluff.

There are some excellent surfing breaks along the coast – Jakes Corner, 3.5km south of town, is among the state's best.

Kalbarri National Park

This park boasts over 1000 sq km of bushland and scenic gorges on the Murchison River. From Kalbarri, it's about 40km to the Loop and Z-Bend, two impressive gorges. Short walking trails lead down into the gorges from road access points and there are also longer walks, such as the two day walk between the Z-Bend and the Loop.

Further east along the Ajana-Kalbarri road are two lookouts: Hawk's Head (a must) and Ross Graham. The park has a particularly fine display of wildflowers in spring, including everlastings, banksias, grevilleas and kangaroo paws.

Organised Tours

All sorts of tours covering adventure and wildlife activities are on offer. For views over the Murchison River gorges, take a flight with Kalbarri Air Charter (☎ 9937 1130); a 20 minute coastal flight is $29, the 'grand tour' is $125.

Kalbarri Safari Tours (☎ 9937 1011), led by livewire local Frank Seidler, is the most popular local outfit. Tours include a

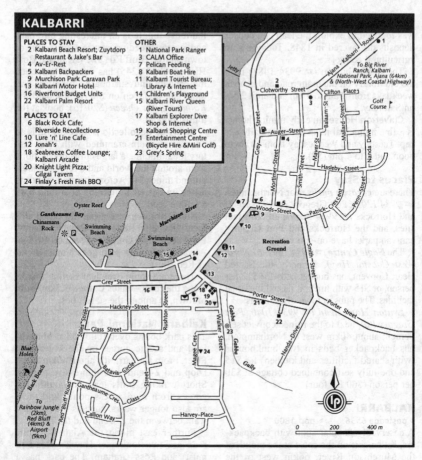

KALBARRI

PLACES TO STAY
2 Kalbarri Beach Resort; Zuytdorp
  Restaurant & Jake's Bar
4 Av-Er-Rest
5 Kalbarri Backpackers
9 Murchison Park Caravan Park
13 Kalbarri Motor Hotel
16 Riverfront Budget Units
22 Kalbarri Palm Resort

PLACES TO EAT
6 Black Rock Cafe;
  Riverside Recollections
10 Lure 'n' Line Cafe
12 Jonah's
18 Seabreeze Coffee Lounge;
   Kalbarri Arcade
20 Knight Light Pizza;
   Gilgai Tavern
24 Finlay's Fresh Fish BBQ

OTHER
1 National Park Ranger
3 CALM Office
7 Pelican Feeding
8 Kalbarri Boat Hire
11 Kalbarri Tourist Bureau;
   Library & Internet
14 Children's Playground
15 Kalbarri River Queen
   (River Tours)
17 Kalbarri Explorer Dive
   Shop & Internet
19 Kalbarri Shopping Centre
21 Entertainment Centre
   (Bicycle Hire & Mini Golf)
23 Grey's Spring

sandboarding trip out to the 'Superbowl', which they claim is the highest razorback dune in Australia (who are we to argue?), and the enthralling Z-Bend wilderness trip to Kalbarri National Park (both $50). Two-day bush camping tours to the Shark Bay area are also available.

Kalbarri Coach Tours (☎ 9937 1161) visits the Murchison River gorges and ocean gorges ($38). You can also abseil into the Z-Bend gorge ($50); book at the tourist bureau or Kalbarri Backpackers. If that's not enough, there are diving and fishing charters, camel safaris, horse riding and stargazing tours.

Places to Stay

Kalbarri is a popular resort and accommodation can be tight during school holidays, when prices generally increase.

Of the town's caravan parks, **Murchison Park** (☎ 9937 1005), on the corner of Woods and Grey Sts, is the most central. Tent/powered sites are $14/15, on-site vans are $35.

Kalbarri Backpackers (☎ 9937 1430, 52 Mortimer St) is a modern, lively YHA place with a pool and covered barbecue area. The arrival of the Greyhound shuttle is handled with army-camp efficiency. Dorm beds cost from \$15 (\$14 for YHA), singles/doubles are \$25/38 (\$22/34), and there are family and disabled units from \$45. It's a great place to relax, or you can book tours and activities here.

Av-Er-Rest (☎ 9937 1101, Mortimer St) is a quieter budget alternative. It has fully self-contained units with dorm beds at \$13, and units sleeping six at \$45 for two plus \$6 per extra person. *Riverfront Budget Units (☎ 9937 1144, Grey St)* enjoys a good location. The units are nothing special, but they're cheap at \$45 for two plus \$5 per extra person (they sleep six).

There are plenty of holiday units and resorts. The *Kalbarri Beach Resort (☎ 1800 096002, Clotworthy St)* has comfortable two-bedroom units from \$65. The *Kalbarri Palm Resort (☎ 9937 2333, 8 Porter St)* has units with kitchenette from \$55 (\$75 during school holidays). For family villas, ring the Kalbarri Accommodation Service (☎ 9937 1700).

Places to Eat
Finlay's Fresh Fish BBQ, in an old ice works on Magee Crescent, is a legendary place for a meal (from \$10). The decor is no frills, but the meals and self-serve salads (50c extra) are filling, it's BYO and the atmosphere is great. A sing-song around the camp fire is on the cards here.

The *Black Rock Cafe (62 Grey St)* is not particularly cheap, but it's across from the pelican feeding area and opens early for breakfast. It also does fondue, and an all-you-can-eat barbecue grill for \$15. *Lure 'n' Line Cafe*, also on Grey St, is BYO and has an open eating area, but serves up fairly forgettable Chinese food. The *Sea Breeze Coffee Lounge*, in the arcade, is popular and has a range of burgers, sandwiches and light meals.

For fish and chips try *Jonah's* on Grey St and for pizza go to *Knight Light Pizza* in the shopping centre.

The *Kalbarri Palm Resort* has a \$15 dinner including a film in its restaurant cinema, which shows current reel films (as opposed to videos). It's a great way to spend an evening.

Behind the Zuytdorp Restaurant in the Kalbarri Beach Resort is *Jake's*, a 1970s-style bar, with good bistro meals.

Getting There & Around
Western Airlines (☎ 1800 998 097) has return flights from Perth to Denham via Kalbarri on Monday, Wednesday and Friday; the one-way/return fare to Perth is \$167/334. The fare is \$86 from Kalbarri to Denham.

Westrail (☎ 13 1053) buses from Perth come into Kalbarri on Monday, Wednesday and Friday (\$59.40), returning Tuesday, Thursday and Saturday at 6 am. A daily return shuttle run by Kalbarri Backpackers connects with Greyhound Pioneer (☎ 13 2030) at Ajana on the North-West Coastal Hwy.

Bicycles can be rented from the Kalbarri Entertainment Centre on Porter St for \$10 a day.

SHARK BAY AREA
The **Shark Bay World Heritage & Marine Park** has spectacular beaches, important sea-grass beds, the stromatolites at Hamelin Pool and the famously predictable dolphins of Monkey Mia.

The first recorded landing on Australian soil by a European took place at Shark Bay in 1616 when Dutch explorer Dirk Hartog landed on the island that now bears his name. He nailed an inscribed plate to a post on the beach but a later visitor collected it; there's a copy in the Geraldton Museum.

Denham, the main centre of Shark Bay, is 132km off the North-West Coastal Hwy from the Overlander Roadhouse.

Getting There & Around
Western Airlines (☎ 1800 998 097) has return flights from Perth to Denham on Monday, Wednesday and Friday; the one-way/return fare is \$249/498.

The Overlander Roadhouse, 290km north of Geraldton, is the turn-off to Shark Bay. A shuttle bus connects daily with the north and south-bound Greyhound Pioneer (☎ 13 2030) bus at the Overlander, dropping off at Denham and Monkey Mia. The full fare from Perth to Denham or Monkey Mia is \$127.

In addition to the Greyhound shuttle, Majestic Tours (☎ 9948 1640) has a shuttle bus from the Denham tourist bureau to Monkey Mia at 8 am (\$8).

WESTERN AUSTRALIA

Overlander Roadhouse to Denham

The first turn-off (27km from the highway) is the 5km road to **Hamelin Pool**, a marine reserve that contains the world's best known colony of **stromatolites** (see the 'Stromatolites' boxed text in this section). There's a boardwalk for viewing them, but it's best to visit at low tide when they're not completely submerged. Information on these unique living rock formations can be found in the 1884 **Telegraph Station** (☎ 9942 5905) which served as a telephone exchange until 1977. Camping, caravan sites and food are also available here.

The stunning 110km-long Shell Beach consists of solid shells up to 10m deep. In places in Shark Bay, the shells (mainly cardiid cockles Fragum erugatum) are so tightly packed that they can be cut into blocks and used for building construction, as can be seen at Hamelin Pool. This is also a fine swimming beach – the crystal waters are no more than knee deep for at least 100m out.

Nanga Station has a pioneer museum and is the only station in Australia licensed to serve alcohol, and at **Eagle Bluff**, halfway between Nanga and Denham, there are superb cliff-top views. The *Nanga Bay Holiday Resort (☎ 9948 3992)* on the station has tent and powered sites, backpacker beds for $12 and cabins for $45 per night.

Denham

• postcode 6537   • pop 1140

The most westerly town in Australia, this was once a pearling port. Today, prawns and tourism are the local moneymakers. There's little to do in Denham itself, but this is a good base for visiting Monkey Mia, 26km away.

The Shark Bay tourist bureau (☎ 9948 1253) at 71 Knight Terrace is open daily from 7.30 am to 6.30 pm. The CALM office (☎ 9948 1208), also on Knight Terrace, has plenty of information on the World Heritage area. There are some buildings in town made of shell blocks – the most notable is the Old Pearler restaurant on Knight Terrace.

Organised Tours If you want to see Shark Bay from the air, Kalbarri Air Charter

Stromatolites

The dolphins at Monkey Mia aren't the only reason Shark Bay is listed as a World Heritage region. The most significant feature was the stromatolites at Hamelin Pool. These lumpy masses, consisting of layers of calcareous material formed by the prolific growth of microbes, are thousands of years old. What's more, their evolutionary history spans an amazing 3.5 billion years, right back to the dawn of life on earth.

Hamelin Pool is suited to the growth of stromatolites because of the clarity and hypersalinity of the water. Each stromatolite is covered in a form of cyanobacterial microbe shaped like algae which, during daily photosynthesis, wave around. At night the microbes fold over, trapping calcium and carbonate ions dissolved in the water. The sticky chemicals they exude constantly add new layers to the surface of the stromatolite.

These are the most accessible stromatolites in the world, spectacularly set amid the turquoise waters of Hamelin Pool.

RICHARD I'ANSON

(☎ 9948 1445) has a Zuytdorp Cliffs tour from $65 per person, and an 'around the bay' tour for $85.

Majestic Tours (☎ 9948 1640) has full-day 4WD tours into François Péron National

WESTERN AUSTRALIA

Park ($79), trips to Hamelin Pool and Shell Beach ($69), or just Shell Beach ($33). Design-A-Tour (☎ 9948 1880) has similar tours from Denham and Monkey Mia for $80.

Shark Bay Under Sail (☎ 9948 1616) has a good-value full-day eco-cruise, including lunch ($60). It leaves from the Denham jetty at 8.30 am. Tours can all be booked through the tourist bureau.

Places to Stay & Eat The *Seaside Caravan Park (☎ 9948 1242, Knight Terrace)* is a friendly, tidy place on the foreshore with tent/powered sites for $11/15 and park homes for $50.

Bay Lodge (☎ 9948 1278, 1800 812780, 95 Knight Terrace) is YHA affiliated and the best budget place in town – if nothing else it offers a free courtesy bus (run by Majestic Tours) into Monkey Mia and back daily. Beds cost $16 per person ($14 for YHA/VIP members) and are in modern, self-contained units, so that a kitchen, lounge and bathroom is shared by no more than six people. Singles cost $34, doubles $38 and family units $85 ($65 in the low season).

Shark Bay Holiday Cottages (☎ 9948 1206, Knight Terrace) has bedsits from $40 and one-bedroom cottages for $55. Shark Bay Accommodation Services (☎ 9948 1323) can help with finding villas and self-contained units from $50 a night.

The *Old Pearler Restaurant (☎ 9948 1373, Knight Terrace)* is full of character. Evening meals cost $18 to $28, good value three-course lunch specials are $12 and local seafood is a speciality. There are two *pubs* serving counter meals on Knight Terrace, and a couple of standard *cafes*.

François Péron National Park

About 4km from Denham on the Monkey Mia Rd is the turn-off·to the fascinating, wild François Péron National Park. The park is known for its arid scenery, wilderness feel and landlocked salt lakes. National park entry fees apply ($8 per vehicle per day). There's a visitor centre at the Péron Homestead, 6km from the main road, where there are two **artesian bore tanks**, one with

water at 35°C and the other at a hot 43°C – you can soak in the former (sunset is a great time). *Camp sites* with limited facilities are located at Big Lagoon, Gregories, Bottle Bay, South Gregories and Herald Bight ($8 per night for two people).

The road to the homestead is usually suitable for 2WD vehicles (check conditions with CALM as it gets very sandy) but a 4WD is necessary to go any further into the park. Stick to the roads and *don't* try to cross a *birrida* (salt pan) – you will get bogged. Majestic Tours and Design-A-Tour both run 4WD tours into the park (see Organised Tours in the previous Denham entry).

Just before the turn-off to the park is the shallow but eye-catching **Little Lagoon**.

Monkey Mia

This pleasant spot is 26km north-east of Denham on the other side of the Péron Peninsula. The Dolphin Information Centre (☎ 9948 1366), near the beach viewing area, has lots of information on dolphins and also screens a 45 minute video on Shark Bay. A new $800,000 visitor centre, complete with interpretive display, was due to open early in 2000.

It's believed that bottlenose dolphins have been visiting Monkey Mia since the early 1960s, although it's only in the last 15 years that their visits have become famous. Monkey Mia's dolphins swim into knee-deep water in the 'dolphin interaction zone' several times a day, nudge up against the circus of awestruck tourists, and follow the ranger up and down the shore until it's time for the fish to be handed out. The rangers select a few people at random from the crowd to hand-feed the dolphins. They generally come in daily year-round, although less frequently in early to mid-summer, and more often in the early morning. It's worth waiting around for the mid-morning appearance as there should be fewer people around. The dolphins may arrive alone or in groups of five or more.

Always observe the rules of behaviour outlined in your entry brochure, and do as the ranger says when you're with the dolphins.

Entry to the reserve is $5 (children $2, family $10). You can buy a term pass ($8), which is valid for the length of your stay. CALM national park passes seem to allow a whole vehicle-load of people in, but since Monkey Mia is a self-funding reserve rather than a national park, this may change in the future.

Cruises The most popular activity in Monkey Mia other than dolphin ogling is taking a cruise to see other marine wildlife, including sea turtles and the enigmatic dugongs. Two catamarans operate from the jetty. The *Aristocat II*, a luxury catamaran with viewing areas and access for the disabled, has morning and afternoon cruises ($35) and a sunset cruise ($25). Full day Cape Peron cruises can also be arranged. The *Shotover* is a former ocean racer, which is good for all round viewing and sunbathing. The morning cruise is $34, afternoon cruise $39 and a supremely relaxing sunset cruise is $29. If you take the afternoon cruise on either vessel, the sunset cruise is free.

Places to Stay & Eat Monkey Mia is not a town, but simply the resort and beachfront.
Monkey Mia Dolphin Resort (☎ 9948 1320, 1800 653611, sales@monkeymia.com.au) dominates the scene and has a wide range of accommodation. Tent/powered sites cost from $14/18 for two (a beachfront site is a whopping $22), backpacker beds in stylish two-tented condos (with kitchen and en suite) are $14, on-site vans from $35, park homes for $80 and motel-style villas from $140; discounts are available in the low season.

At the *Bough Shed* join the elite and watch the dolphins feed while you do; there's also a bar here. There's a *takeaway cafe* and a small *grocery shop*, but the cheaper option is to buy supplies in Denham – takeaway alcohol cannot be purchased anywhere in Monkey Mia.

CARNARVON
• postcode 6701   • pop 6900
Situated at the mouth of the Gascoyne River, Carnarvon is a nondescript place noted for its tropical fruit (particularly bananas) and

fine climate – although it can become very hot in the middle of summer and is periodically subjected to floods and cyclones. Quite a few travellers break their journey in Carnarvon to seek fruit picking work.

The main street, Robinson St, is 40m wide and a reminder of the days when camel trains used to pass through, and the palm-lined Fascine esplanade is a pleasant place for a stroll.

Carnarvon's tourist bureau (☎ 9941 1146), in the civic centre on the corner of Robinson and Stuart Sts, is open Monday to Friday from 8.30 am to 5 pm and Saturday from 9 am to 2 pm. As well as plenty of information, it has a nifty control console rescued from the NASA tracking station that was set up in Carnarvon in 1964 but has since been demolished.

Internet access is available at Gascoyne Photographics on Robinson St.

Things to See
The **Historic Precinct** on Babbage Island includes the 'one mile' jetty and the Lighthouse Keeper's Cottage Museum ($3). The jetty is a popular fishing spot – it costs $2 to walk on, or $4 if you take the 'ocean tram'. A train line linking the historic precinct with the town has been restored to resurrect the *Kimberley* steam train.

If you're interested in how outback kids get an education, the **Carnarvon School of the Air** (☎ 9941 1015), on Carnarvon Rd, has tours on Monday and Thursday mornings ($2) that include sitting in on a lesson.

There are tours of **banana plantations**, ending with the almost obligatory eating of a chocolate-coated frozen banana; Munro's, on South River Rd, about 12km from Carnarvon, has a tour daily (except Saturday) at 11 am ($3), and Westoby, 5km from town on Robinson St, has very informal tours daily (except Tuesday) at 11 am and 2 pm ($4).

Organised Tours
Tropical Tripper Tours (☎ 9941 1146) has half-day tours around town for $15 and an all-day tour that includes Lake Macleod, Cape Cuvier, the *Korean Star* wreck and

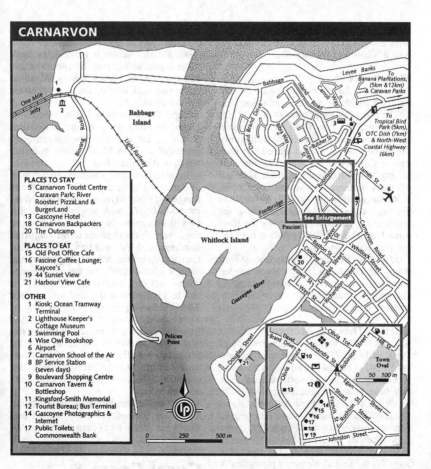

CARNARVON

PLACES TO STAY
5 Carnarvon Tourist Centre
Caravan Park; River
Rooster; PizzaLand &
BurgerLand
13 Gascoyne Hotel
18 Carnarvon Backpackers
20 The Outcamp

PLACES TO EAT
15 Old Post Office Building
16 Fascine Coffee Lounge;
Kaycee's
19 44 Sunset View
21 Harbour View Cafe

OTHER
1 Kiosk; Ocean Tramway
Terminal
2 Lighthouse Keeper's
Cottage Museum
3 Swimming Pool
4 Wise Owl Bookshop
6 Airport
7 Carnarvon School of the Air
8 BP Service Station
(seven days)
9 Boulevard Shopping Centre
10 Carnarvon Tavern &
Bottleshop
11 Kingsford-Smith Memorial
12 Tourist Bureau; Bus Terminal
14 Gascoyne Photographics &
Internet
17 Public Toilets;
Commonwealth Bank

blowholes for $40. West Coast Safaris (☎ 1800 621625) has 4WD tours into Mt Augustus (Burringurrah) National Park and the Kennedy Ranges.

Places to Stay

There are seven caravan parks in Carnarvon; the closest to the town centre is the *Carnarvon Tourist Centre Caravan Park* (☎ 9941 1438, 90 Robinson St), with powered sites/on-site vans at $13.50/29 for two. *Wintersun Caravan Park* (☎/fax 9941 8150, Robinson St) is a very tidy park with a pool and mini-golf course; tent/powered sites cost $13.50/15, on-site vans are $40 and self-contained cabins are $60.

Carnarvon Backpackers (☎ 9941 1095, 46 Olivia Terrace) is a reasonably friendly place that looks after travellers wanting to find work locally, but it's one of those places where the office never seems to be attended. Dorm beds cost from $14, twins are $36 ($1 less per person with YHA/VIP).

The *Gascoyne Hotel* (☎ 9941 1412, 88 Olivia Terrace) has motel rooms for $45/55 for singles/doubles, or rooms in the hotel for $35/45. *The Outcamp* (☎ 9941 2421, 16 Olivia Terrace), on the Fascine, is a luxurious

WESTERN AUSTRALIA

B&B in the town's best location. You can relax in comfort here in its rooms for $60/90, with a 'silver service' breakfast.

Places to Eat

Fascine and *Kaycee's*, almost side by side on Robinson St, are standard coffee lounges.

The BYO *Old Post Office (☎ 9941 4231, Robinson St)* is one of the best places in town to eat out. Its verandah, with sturdy timber benches, is a good place to be on a balmy Carnarvon evening. The menu is mainly Italian (pasta dishes from $10) and it's open Wednesday to Sunday from 5 pm.

44 Sunset View (☎ 9941 1116, 44 Olivia Terrace) makes great homemade food for lunch and dinner. For seafood, try the *Harbour View Cafe (☎ 9941 2288)* at the fishing port on Douglas St.

Munro's Banana Plantation (South River Rd) is set in a shady tropical garden and serves an array of scones, pancakes, smoothies and light meals – most featuring bananas or mangoes.

Getting There & Around

Skywest (☎ 13 1300) flies to Carnarvon from Perth daily ($277). A Greyhound Pioneer (☎ 13 2030) bus passes through Carnarvon late at night on its way north or south. The fare from Perth is $120. Integrity (☎ 9226 1339) has a bus from Perth to Carnarvon on Tuesday, Thursday and Sunday, returning on Monday, Wednesday and Friday ($90).

A local bus service makes daily trips to places of interest including the One Mile Jetty, OTC dish and Westoby's plantation. A single trip costs $1; buses depart from the tourist bureau. Bicycles are available for hire from Carnarvon Backpackers for $5 a day.

GASCOYNE AREA

Good beaches near Carnarvon are **Bush Bay** to the south off the North-West Coastal Hwy (turn-off 20km) and **New Beach** (37km).

The frenzied **blowholes**, 70km north of Carnarvon, are well worth the trip – though several people have drowned here after being swept off the rocks by king waves, so be careful. There's a fine beach about 1km south of the blowholes with a primitive *camping ground* (no fresh water available). You can camp at *Quobba Station (☎ 9941 2036)* for $6 – power is limited, but fresh water is available. About 1km south of this homestead is the **HMAS Sydney Memorial** to the ship sunk here by the German raider *Kormoran* in 1941.

Cape Cuvier, where salt is loaded for Japan, is 30km north of the blowholes. Nearby is the wreck of the *Korean Star*, grounded in 1988 (don't climb over the wreck as it's dangerous).

Remote Gascoyne Junction, 164km east of Carnarvon in the gemstone-rich **Kennedy Range**, has the welcome *Junction Hotel (☎ 9943 0504)*, with singles/doubles for $40/50. From here, the adventurous can continue through the Outback to **Mt Augustus (Burringurrah) National Park**, 450km from Carnarvon, to see **Mount Augustus**, the biggest – but certainly not the most memorable – rock (or monadnock) in the world. It can be climbed in a day and you can see Aboriginal rock paintings along the way.

At *Cobra Station (☎ 9943 0565)*, 50km from Mt Augustus, there are single/twin station rooms for $45/60 and motel units for $60/80. At the *Mt Augustus Outback Tourist Resort (☎ 9943 0527)* tent/powered sites are $16/20 for two and single/double units are $40/60.

For more information on accommodation at outback stations, get a copy of the free *Gascoyne Station Stays* from the Carnarvon tourist bureau.

Coral Coast & Pilbara

The Coral Coast extends from Coral Bay to Onslow and is, without doubt, one of the richest eco-tourism destinations in the world. The North-West Cape boasts the scintillating Ningaloo Reef and the rugged Cape Range National Park. Here you can snorkel over the world's largest west-coast reef and swim with the famous benign whale shark, dugongs, manta rays and a host of tropical fish.

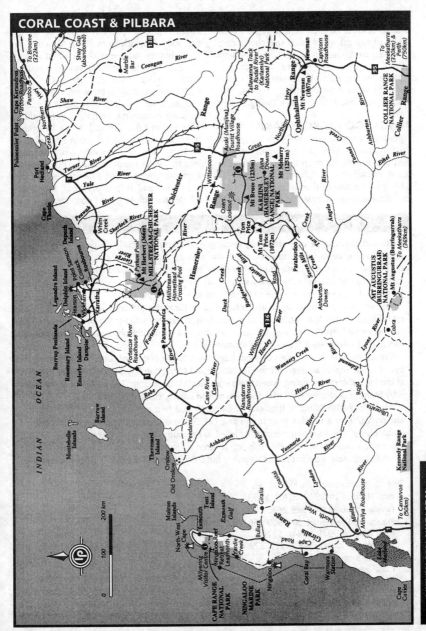

CORAL COAST & PILBARA

The Pilbara, composed of the world's oldest rocks, is an ancient, arid region with a glut of natural wonders. It stretches along the coast from Onslow to Port Hedland and inland beyond the superb Millstream-Chichester and Karijini national parks, and includes several hoary mining towns. The Pilbara is outback WA at its alluring best.

NINGALOO MARINE PARK

Running alongside the North-West Cape for 260km, from Bundegi Reef in the northeast to Amherst Point in the south-west, is the stunning Ningaloo (Point of Land) Reef. This mini version of the Great Barrier Reef is actually more accessible than its east-coast counterpart – in places it is less than 100m offshore. The bays enclosed by the reef vary in width from 200m to 6km.

Within the marine park are eight sanctuary zones where fishing is banned – you can only observe. Over 220 species of coral have been recorded in the waters of the park, ranging from the slow-growing bommies to delicate branching varieties. For eight to nine nights after the full moon in March, there is a synchronised mass spawning of coral, with eggs and sperm being released into the water simultaneously. For more information, see CALM's *Coral Reefs of WA*.

In June and July every year, humpback whales pass close by the coast on their way

Whale Sharks & Other Marine Life

Visitors to Australia are often morbidly fascinated by sharks, especially the deadly great white shark that frequents the Southern Ocean. The whale shark *(Rhiniodon typus)* is the largest of the sharks, but it is a gentle giant. One of the few places in the world where you can come face to face underwater with this leviathan is off Ningaloo Reef, near Exmouth. To swim with these sharks is to experience one of the natural wonders of the world.

The whale shark weighs up to 40,000kg, is up to 18m long and drifts slowly on ocean currents filtering water through its 300 or more bands of minute teeth for the plankton and small fish on which it feeds. These sharks also eat an awful lot of rubbish: a wallet, boot, bucket and part of an oar were found in the stomach of one.

Whale-shark observing goes on from late March to the middle of June. The largest number of whale sharks are seen off the Tantabiddi and Mangrove Bay areas. The season begins at the time of coral spawning, when there is also a plankton bloom. The best way to see them is by licensed charter vessel (after they have been initially spotted by aircraft).

About eight boats make trips out of Exmouth and two out of Coral Bay. They charge around $220 for a full day with snorkelling ($199 if you have your own gear) or $240 for scuba diving. The following companies listed in Exmouth have a 'no sighting policy' where you can go out on the next available trip for free if whale sharks are not encountered. The Coral Bay operators do not have this policy but they generally report a high encounter rate.

Operators in Exmouth include:
  Blue Horizon (☎ 9949 1620), $199
  Diving Ventures (☎ 9949 2635), $220
  Exmouth Dive Centre (☎ 1800 655 156, whaleshark@exmouthdiving.com.au), $220
  King Dive (☎ 9949 1094), $220
  Ningaloo Blue (☎ 9949 1119), $220
Operators from Coral Bay are:
  Coral Bay Adventures (☎ 9942 5955), $250
  Ningaloo Reef Dive (☎ 9942 5824), $250

Costs indicated are for snorkelling with gear provided.

north to their calving grounds, probably near the Montebello Islands. In October and November they pass by again, on their return journey to Antarctica. Huge whale sharks also gather to feed along the reef each year – see the 'Whale Sharks & Other Marine Life' boxed text.

Between November and January, near the top of North-West Cape, turtles come up the beaches at night to lay their eggs. Mauritius, Janz and Jacobz beaches are the best places to observe this fascinating event.

Contact the CALM office in Exmouth for more specific information and get a copy of the excellent *Parks of the Coral Coast* pamphlet (it has a reasonable map of the cape).

Coral Bay
● pop 950

At the southern end of the Ningaloo Marine Park, 150km south of Exmouth, Coral Bay is a great place for snorkelling, swimming and sunbathing. It's a tiny resort settlement on the edge of a picturesque bay with some stunning beaches to the north and south. The supermarket (☎ 9942 5988) in the Coral Bay Arcade offers information and brochures. Internet access is available at Ningaloo Reef Dive in the arcade.

Ningaloo Reef Dive (☎ 9942 5824) and Coral Dive (☎ 9942 5830) arrange scuba adventures and PADI dive courses, fill tanks and rent equipment. A good time to dive is

---

Whale Sharks & Other Marine Life

Manta rays are seen from July to November, and to 'fly' with one is an awesome experience. However, it is not guaranteed that you will see them every day. Ningaloo Experience (☎ 9942 5877) in Coral Bay specialises in manta ray trips ($80).

Five-day PADI open water dive courses at Exmouth or Coral Bay cost around $260. Recommended operators in Exmouth include Exmouth Dive Centre (☎ 1800 655 156), Village Dive (☎ 9949 1101) and WAGS (☎ 9949 2661), a small owner-operator outfit that gets good reports.

Dive trips are available to the Muiron Islands, 10km north-east of the cape. These islands are a breeding sanctuary for three species of turtle: green, loggerhead and hawksbill. During dives you can hand feed the 1.5m-long potato cod *(Epinephalus tukula)* at the 'cod house'.

Other marine life you might see include humpback whales, dugongs and a few species of turtles, as well as a host of fish species. If you're interested in identifying fish consider getting *The Marine Fishes of North-West Australia* by G Allen & R Swainston.

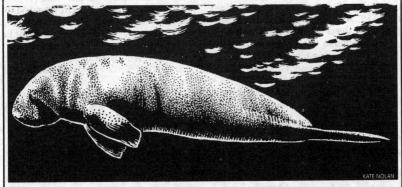

KATE NOLAN

One of the many wonders of the marine world, the dugong.

WESTERN AUSTRALIA

during the coral spawning in March and April. You can rent snorkelling equipment for $7.50/12 per half/full day or go 'snuba' diving (using an air hose) for $40 per person.

Glass Bottom Boats (☎ 9942 5885) and Sub-Sea Explorer (☎ 9942 5955) trips allow you to see beneath the waves without getting wet; they cost $20 for an hour and both have ticket booths near the dunes. You can also inquire here about the variety of scenic flights over Coral Bay and Ningaloo Reef (from $50 for half an hour).

The latest Coral Bay craze is a spin around the dunes on four-wheeled motorbikes. Quad-Treks (book through Ningaloo Experience ☎ 9942 5877) and ATV Eco Tours (☎ 9942 5873) offer similar outings, including a sunset tour ($40) and snorkelling tour ($55).

See the following Exmouth section for information on transport to Coral Bay.

Places to Stay & Eat *Bayview Holiday Village* (☎ 9942 5932) has a range of accommodation including tent/powered sites from $14/16, cabins with shared facilities from $40 and chalets from $70.

Coral Bay Backpackers (☎ 9942 5934) is behind the Ningaloo Reef Resort; as well as a basic bed for $15, you get access to the resort's pool and bar.

Bayview Backpackers (☎ 9942 5932) is a similar set-up behind the Bayview Holiday Village. Beds in cramped twin units cost $18. A planned purpose-built backpackers in Coral Bay will really help here.

The *Ningaloo Reef Resort* (☎ 9942 5934) has tidy, well-appointed motel rooms from $95/110 for singles/doubles or self-contained apartments for $105/115.

There's not a great deal of choice for eating out in Coral Bay. *Fin's Cafe*, just past Bayview Holiday Village, opens early and has a pleasant alfresco dining area. The *Reef Cafe*, next to the Bayview Holiday Village, does pizzas and a few expensive meals.

EXMOUTH

• postcode 6707   • pop 3050

Exmouth was established in 1967 largely as a service centre for the huge US navy communications base. These days tourism is the town's mainstay and Exmouth provides a focus for the many great eco-activities in the area. On no account should it be allowed to become a supply and administrative centre for multi-national companies drilling in and around Ningaloo Marine Park!

The helpful Exmouth tourist bureau (☎ 9949 1176), in a new building on Murat Rd, is open daily from 8.30 am to 5 pm. CALM (☎ 9949 1676) is on Maidstone Crescent. The telecentre in Learmonth St (open daily except Sunday) has email and Internet facilities.

About 13km south of town is **Pebbly Beach**, a safe swimming beach covered in colourful pebbles. The wreck of the SS *Mildura*, beached in 1907, pokes out of the water near the tip of the cape, and the **Vlaming Head Lighthouse**, further round the cape, offers sensational views from its hilltop location.

Part of North-West Cape is dominated by the 13 low-frequency transmitter stations of the Harold Holt Communications Station. Twelve are higher than the Eiffel Tower (321m) and serve to support the 13th, which is 396m high.

Organised Tours

Tours in the area range from gulf and gorge safaris to reef and fishing trips. Neil McLeod's Ningaloo Safari Tours (☎ 9949 1550) has a full-day trip (10 hours; $110) recommended by many travellers; it takes in Cape Range, Ningaloo Reef and Yardie Creek, as well as snorkelling at Turquoise Bay and Vlaming Head lighthouse – and you get to try Neil's mum's legendary boiled fruit cake.

Other operators with similar itineraries are West Coast Safaris (☎ 1800 621 625), charging $90 and $75 for backpackers, and Exmouth Eco Tours (☎ 9949 2809), who charges $100.

Ningaloo Ecology Cruises (☎ 9949 2255) operates two-hour glass bottom boat tours from Tantabiddi on the west coast where you can expect to see reef sharks, turtles and manta rays. The cost is $30/25/10 adults/backpackers/children.

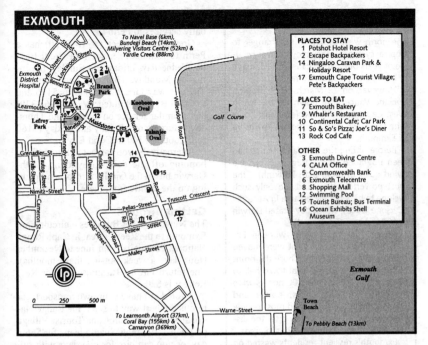

EXMOUTH

To Navel Base (6km),
Bundegi Beach (14km),
Milyering Visitors Centre (52km) &
Yardie Creek (88km)

Exmouth
District
Hospital

Brand
Park

Learmonth-St

Lefroy
Park

Kooboorroo
Oval

Golf Course

Talanjee
Oval

Willersdorf Road

Grenadier—St

Nimitz—Street

Cameron-Street

Pelias—Street

Truscott Crescent

Maley—Street

Exmouth
Gulf

Town
Beach

0   250   500 m

To Learmonth Airport (37km),
Coral Bay (155km) &
Carnarvon (369km)

Warne—Street

To Pebbly Beach (13km)

PLACES TO STAY
1 Potshot Hotel Resort
2 Excape Backpackers
14 Ningaloo Caravan Park &
    Holiday Resort
17 Exmouth Cape Tourist Village;
    Pete's Backpackers

PLACES TO EAT
7 Exmouth Bakery
9 Whaler's Restaurant
10 Continental Cafe; Car Park
11 So & So's Pizza; Joe's Diner
13 Rock Cod Cafe

OTHER
3 Exmouth Diving Centre
4 CALM Office
5 Commonwealth Bank
6 Exmouth Telecentre
8 Shopping Mall
12 Swimming Pool
15 Tourist Bureau; Bus Terminal
16 Ocean Exhibits Shell
    Museum

Places to Stay

Exmouth Cape Tourist Village (☎ 9949 1101, 1800 621 101, Murat Rd) still looked well kept and in good shape when we visited, despite the cyclone damage! Tent/powered sites cost $16/19, and cabins with cooking facilities are $60. It incorporates ***Pete's Backpackers*** in converted four-bed units (with cooking facilities) at $15 per person ($14 for YHA/VIP members); a new purpose-built backpackers section is planned.

Base Lodge (☎ 9949 1474, 1800 241 474) is a relatively new backpackers. Housed in one of the sturdy accommodation blocks at the naval base 6km north of town, its austere appearance is part of the appeal. Beds in spotless twin rooms are good value at $15 ($14 for YHA/VIP). There's a kitchen and common room on each of the two floors, and you get to use the base facilities. A shuttle bus runs into town twice a day.

The swanky ***Potshot Hotel Resort*** (☎ 9949 1200, Murat Rd) has all types of accommodation from 'homestead' singles/doubles with en suite for $70/85 to three-bedroom apartments for $165. ***Excape Backpackers*** (☎ 1800 655 156) is incorporated in the resort but is run by the Exmouth Dive Centre (it's behind the dive shop). Beds costs $15 ($14 for YHA/VIP) or $18 ($17) in twin rooms. There's a new kitchen, common room and free barbecues, and you're tantalisingly close to the town's main pub.

The ***Ningaloo Caravan Park & Holiday Resort*** (☎ 9949 2377, Murat Rd) was in a complete rebuilding phase – even before the cyclone hit. As well as tent and caravan sites, the complex will include a 64-bed backpackers section with kitchen facilities, upmarket cabins, a restaurant and a pool with built-in aquarium.

Places to Eat

There are a number of takeaways and cafes in the main shopping area, including ***So and***

The Day Vance Came to Town

The north-west of WA is no stranger to tropical cyclones – they blow in every couple of years but usually cause little damage in this sparsely populated region.

However, on 22 March 1999, Tropical Cyclone Vance bore down on the North West Cape, and within a few short hours it had wreaked havoc in the tiny township of Exmouth.

Before hitting the mainland, Vance had been upgraded to a Category 5 cyclone (wind gusts of more than 280kmh) – the most powerful rating and the only such cyclone to hit a populated area in Australia (Cyclone Tracey, which devastated Darwin in 1974, was a Category 4).

About 120 backpackers were in Exmouth at the time and most were moved from caravan parks (which bore the brunt of the damage) to the local town hall to ride out the storm. Over 100 homes were flattened like matchsticks, power and water supplies were lost, and most people were evacuated immediately after the disaster (miraculously, no-one was injured).

Exmouth's resilient residents wasted no time in recovering and rebuilding their town. Just five weeks after the cyclone, it was open for business – the marine-based eco-tourism it has become famous for. By the time you read this, the only real evidence of the cyclone will be the new buildings – and a lot of tales about the day Vance came to town.

So's Pizza, *Joe's Diner* and the *Continental Cafe* for good coffee. *Whaler's Restaurant* (☎ 9949 2416, 5 Kennedy St) has a nice verandah and has some good dinner specials, particularly in the seafood department. It's licensed and BYO. The *Rock Cod Cafe (Maidstone Crescent)* has takeaways and light meals from $7, and a great buffet for $15.

Getting There & Away

There are Skywest (☎ 13 1300) flights between Learmonth (37km from Exmouth)

and Geraldton ($271) on weekdays, and daily services to Perth ($336).

Greyhound Pioneer (☎ 13 2030) has a Perth to Exmouth service (via Coral Bay) on Wednesday, Friday and Sunday, returning on Monday, Thursday and Saturday. The one-way fare to Exmouth is $176 and to Coral Bay $159. Integrity (☎ 9226 1339) has a similar service on Sunday and Thursday, returning on Monday and Friday ($160 to Exmouth, $140 to Coral Bay).

Alternatively, you can get to Exmouth by hopping off the daily Greyhound Perth-Darwin bus at the Giralia turn-off and picking up the shuttle from there.

Getting Around

The Ningaloo Reef Bus does a circuit from Exmouth to the Reef Retreat in Cape Range National Park daily from June to December (four days a week outside these months). The return fare to Turquoise Bay or Reef Retreat is $20.

If you don't have your own transport, car hire is the best way to see Cape Range National Park. Exmouth Cape Tourist Village (☎ 9949 1101) rents Suzuki jeeps for $66 a day, or you can hire for two days with full camping kit (swags etc) for $90.

CAPE RANGE NATIONAL PARK

This 510 sq km park, which runs down the west coast of the cape, includes a variety of flora and fauna, good swimming and snorkelling beaches, rugged scenery, several gorges (the Shothole, Charles Knife and Yardie Creek), Owl's Roost Cave and opportunities for camping.

The modern and informative Milyering visitor centre (☎ 9949 2808) has a comprehensive display of the area's natural and cultural history, and there's a coffee shop next door. It's usually open daily from 10 am to 4 pm during the high season.

A park fee of $8 per vehicle applies; there's an honesty box near the park entrance or you can pay at the visitor centre. Equipped (4WD) vehicles can continue south to Coral Bay via the coast (check first at the visitor centre to see if Yardie Creek is passable).

Montebello Islands

The Montebellos are a group of more than 100 flat limestone islands off the north-west coast of WA between Onslow and Karratha. In 1992 they were gazetted as a conservation park.

In 1622 the survivors of the shipwrecked *Tryal* camped here before setting off to the East Indies. The islands were named by the French explorer Baudin, in 1801 after the battle of Monte Bello. The pearlers who came next introduced the black rat and the cat, which ensured the extinction of the golden bandicoot and the spectacled hare-wallaby on the island.

In 1952 the British detonated an atomic weapon mounted on HMS *Plym*, anchored in Main Bay off Trimouille Island. Two further atomic tests were carried out in 1956, on Alpha and Trimouille islands. Some 40 years later you can now step ashore and get close to the point of detonation. It will be interesting to see how long the radiation warning signs last before being souvenired by collectors of the macabre.

Nature is resilient and the islands have thriving populations of both land and marine fauna and more than 100 plant species, including a stand of mangroves. The legless lizard *Aprasia rostrata* is found on Hermite Island and two species of marine turtle are known to nest on the islands, as are a number of seabirds.

Hour-long boat tours (☎ 9949 2659) are conducted up scenic **Yardie Gorge** on Monday, Wednesday and Saturday (daily during school holidays) for $20/10 for adults/children.

There are several *camping grounds* along the coast within the park; facilities and shade are usually minimal, but several have toilets. Bigger sites include Ned's Camp and Mesa, while Lakeside and Osprey Bay are good options. The cost is $8 per night for two people; no camp fires or dogs are allowed in the park.

Ningaloo Reef Retreat (☎ 9949 1776), in the dunes near the entrance to Mandu Mandu Gorge Rd, is a wilderness experience where you camp out in swags under the stars (April to November). The camp includes a kitchen and toilet facilities, and you cook your own meals with food provided. There are guided nature walks and snorkelling. It's not cheap at $95/155/195 for one/two/three nights but this includes all food, transport to and from Exmouth and activities.

ONSLOW
- postcode 6710   • pop 600

Onslow has the dubious distinctions of being the southernmost WA town to be bombed in WWII and later of being used as a base by the British for nuclear testing in the Montebello Islands.

The tourist centre (☎ 9184 6644) is on Second Ave. The **Old Onslow ruins**, 48km south-west of the town, were abandoned in 1925. They include a gaol and post office, and are worth a look. There's also good swimming and fishing in the area.

The *Ocean View Caravan Park (☎ 9184 6053, Second Ave)* has tent/powered sites for $13/15 and units with kitchen for $50. There are expensive *resorts* on Thevenard and Direction islands (part of the Mackerel Islands group), 11km and 22km offshore respectively. The islands are very popular with sporting fishermen; for more information call ☎ 9388 2020.

KARRATHA
- postcode 6714   • pop 10,050

Karratha (Good Country) is the commercial centre of the Pilbara. The town developed due to the rapid expansion of the Hamersley Iron and Woodside LNG projects. Karratha is an access point for Karijini and Millstream-Chichester national parks, and a good place to break the long coastal drive between Carnarvon and Port Hedland.

The area around Karratha is replete with evidence of Aboriginal occupation, such as middens, carvings, grindstones and etchings, and can be found on the 3.5km **Jaburara Heritage Trail**, which starts by the tourist bureau. Pick up a copy of the heritage trail leaflet ($1.50) and walk the trail in the morning or early evening.

The Karratha Tourist Bureau (☎ 9144 4600) on Karratha Rd has heaps of information on what to see and do in the Pilbara, and is the place to book tours of the major industrial plants. The CALM office (☎ 9143 1488) is on Anderson Rd in the light industrial estate 4km south of town.

The Fe-NaCl-NG Festival (pronounced 'fenarkling') is held in August each year. The title combines the chemical abbreviations of the region's main natural resources – iron, salt and natural gas.

Places to Stay & Eat

Fleetwood's Rosemary Rd Caravan Park (☎ 9185 1855, fax 9144 1243, *Rosemary Rd*) has tent/powered sites at $14/18, on-site vans at $45 and en suite chalets at $75.

Karratha Backpackers (☎ 9144 4904, *110 Wellard Way*) is in much better shape these days thanks to a change of management. It caters for a mixture of travellers and semi-permanents, but the atmosphere is good, it has all the necessary facilities (including email and a good kitchen) and there's a pleasant courtyard. Dorm beds are $15 and singles/doubles $30/40.

Banksia House B&B (☎ 9144 4143, *1 Gregory Way*) is central and costs $55 for a double.

Pearlers Rest (☎ 9144 1741), behind the Video Ezy store on Balmoral Rd, is a good licensed restaurant with a pleasant outdoor dining area. It serves a roast lunch on Sunday. For snacks, there are *cafes* and *takeaways* (and *McDonald's*) in the Karratha shopping centre. *Al's Burgers* on Balmoral Rd has an interesting array of fast food.

Getting There & Around

Qantas/Airlink (☎ 13 1313) and Ansett (☎ 13 1300) have direct daily flights from Perth.

Greyhound Pioneer (☎ 13 2030) has daily services from Perth ($139) and Darwin; the Shell Roadhouse on Searipple Rd

is the depot. The bus goes on to Dampier and returns to pick up in Karratha for the north and southbound journeys.

Free Car Hire (☎ 9185 1003) rents older cars (in reasonable condition) for $30 a day with unlimited kilometres (but limited to within a 50km radius of Karratha), which is perfect for exploring the Dampier and Roebourne areas. Karratha Cycle Hire (☎ 9144 2984) rents bikes for $12 a day.

DAMPIER
• postcode 6713 • pop 1400

Dampier is on King Bay, across from the 41 islands of the Dampier Archipelago (named after William Dampier, who visited the area in 1699). It's a Hamersley Iron town, the port for Tom Price and the Paraburdoo iron-ore operations. Gas from the natural-gas fields of the North-West Shelf is piped ashore nearby on the Burrup Peninsula. From there, it is piped to other parts of the Pilbara and Perth, or liquefied as part of the Woodside Petroleum project and exported to Japan and South Korea.

Tours of the port facilities ($5/3) leave from the Hamersley training centre at 9 am on weekdays from April to November (Monday and Thursday only from November to April). Dampier Salt also runs half-day tours for a whopping $16/8. The free Northwest Gas Shelf visitor centre (☎ 9183 8100), overlooking the plant, is open weekdays from 10 am to 4 pm during the tourist season.

The **Burrup Peninsula** has some 10,000 Aboriginal rock engravings depicting fish, turtles, kangaroos and a Tasmanian tiger. The **Dampier Archipelago** is renowned as a game-fishing mecca and each year in August it hosts the Dampier Classic fishing competition.

Places to Stay & Eat

The *Transit Caravan Park* (☎ 9183 1109, *the Esplanade*) has tent/powered sites for $7/14.

Peninsula Palms Resort (☎ 9183 1888, *the Esplanade*) has 'singles men's quarters' – tidy single rooms for $35 with shared ablutions. Standard motel rooms cost $95 a night.

Barnacle Bob's, on the Esplanade and overlooking Hampton Harbour, has good fish and chips, and is a licensed seafood restaurant.

ROEBOURNE AREA

The Roebourne area is a busy little enclave of historic towns and modern port facilities. Information is available from the Roebourne tourist bureau (☎ 9182 1060) in the Old Gaol on Queen St.

Roebourne

• postcode 6718   • pop 950

Roebourne is the oldest existing town in the Pilbara, with a history of grazing, and gold and copper mining. There are still some fine old buildings, including the **Old Gaol** (now a museum), an 1894 church and the Victoria Hotel, which is the last of five original pubs. The town was once connected to Cossack, 13km away, by a horse-drawn tram.

From May to October, Robe River Iron conducts a free three hour tour from the Roebourne tourist bureau, taking in Cossack, Wickham and the Cape Lambert port facilities.

The *Harding River Caravan Park* (☎ 9182 1063) has tent/powered sites at $8/15 and on-site vans from $34 for two.

Cossack

Originally known as Tien Tsin Harbour, Cossack, at the mouth of the Harding River, was a bustling town and the main port for the district in the mid to late 19th century. Its boom was short-lived and Point Samson soon supplanted it as the chief port for the region.

This fascinating collection of ghost town buildings, dating from 1870 to 1898, includes an **art gallery**, **museum** and a hostel. Beyond town, there's a **pioneer cemetery** with a small Japanese section dating from the old pearl-diving days. WA's first major pearl-fishing industry was started at Cossack in the 1870s – it later moved to Broome when oysters were discovered in Roebuck Bay in the 1890s. There are good lookouts and excellent beaches in the area; get a copy of the *Cossack Historic Walk* brochure from Roebourne tourist bureau or in Cossack.

Cossack Backpackers (☎ 9182 1190) is one of those gems of the road if you like to be transported back in time. It's housed in the old police barracks, built in 1897. Dorm rooms are $15 and family rooms are $35, and there's a kitchen. There's a small cafe open during the day, but there are no shops so you'll need to bring your own food. If you ring in advance the proprietors will pick you up from Roebourne (where the Greyhound stops).

Wickham & Point Samson

Wickham (population 1650) is the Robe River Iron company town. The company handles its ore-exporting facilities 10km away at Cape Lambert, where the jetty is 3km long. Ore is railed to the coast from the mining operations inland at Pannawonica. The Robe River Visitor Centre (open from May to October) has a massive yellow haul truck parked out the front.

Point Samson (population 250), beyond Wickham, took the place of Cossack when the old port silted up. In turn, it has been replaced by the modern port facilities of Dampier and Cape Lambert. There are **beaches** at Point Samson and at nearby Honeymoon Cove.

The *Solveig Caravan Park* (☎ 9187 1414, Samson Rd), next to the tavern in Point Samson, has tent/powered sites for $15/20. *Delilah's B&B* (☎ 9187 1471), also in Point Samson, has just one comfortable double room for $85.

It's worth making the trip to Point Samson for lunch if you're in the area. At *Moby's Kitchen* you can get excellent fish and chips with salad ($8), and the *Trawler's Tavern* upstairs has a pleasant balcony for relaxing with a beer.

Whim Creek

The first significant Pilbara mineral find was at Whim Creek, 80km east of Roebourne. It once had a copper mine but today all that's left is the *Whim Creek Hotel* (☎ 9176 4914), which has accommodation and a restaurant; tent sites are $8 for two, backpacker beds are $15 and units are from $50/70 for singles/doubles.

MILLSTREAM-CHICHESTER NATIONAL PARK

This impressive 2000 sq km national park, in the middle of a semi-arid environment, includes a number of freshwater pools. **Python Pool** was once an oasis for Afghani camel drivers and is still a good place to pause for a swim.

The **Millstream Homestead** is 150km south of Roebourne and 21km from the Wittenoom road. It has been converted into an information centre, with much detail on the Millstream ecosystems and the lifestyle of the Yinjibarndi people.

The **Chinderwarriner Pool**, near the information centre, is a pleasant oasis with pools, palms (including the unique Millstream palm) and lilies. The park also has a number of walking/driving trails, including Cliff Lookout Drive, the Murlunmunyjurna Trail (6.8km) and the 8km Chichester Range Camel Track.

There are basic but pleasant *camp sites* (☎ 9184 5144) at Snake Creek, Crossing Pool and Deep Reach Pool (where you can swim) which have gas barbecues, fire places and pit toilets ($8 for two).

KARIJINI NATIONAL PARK

Like other gorges in central Australia, those of Karijini (Hamersley Range) National Park are spectacular in their sheer rocky faces, varied colours and great size. In early spring, the park is often carpeted with colourful wildflowers.

There is an interpretive centre (☎ 014-511 1285) at the junction of Juna Downs, Joffre Falls and Yampire Gorge roads, in the south-east corner of the park. It's run by Aboriginal people, the traditional dwellers of Karijini, and they are enthusiastic and informative. Get a copy of CALM's free *Karijini: Visitor Information/Walk Trail Guide* to assist in planning your visit.

The 10km road into **Dales Gorge** starts just south of the interpretive centre. About 200m along the Dales Gorge track is a turn-off to a giant termite mound. Continuing on you come first to the **Fortescue Falls** walk. The descent offers excellent views of the only permanent falls in Karijini.

Further along is **Circular Pool** and a nearby lookout. The walk from Circular Pool along the floor of Dales Gorge to the falls is recommended.

The Joffre Falls road leads to **Knox Gorge**. Nearby is a 1.5km return walk to Red Gorge lookout.

From the Joffre Falls turn-off it is 16km to the truly spectacular **Oxers Lookout**, at the junction of the Red, Weano, Joffre and Hancock gorges – one of Australia's great sights. To get down into the gorges proper, take the steps down to Handrail Pool (turn to the right at the bottom) in Weano Gorge, or the more difficult but dramatic walk down into stunning Hancock Gorge, which starts by descending a ladder.

In the north-west of the park on the Nanutarra-Munjina road, you pass through the small **Rio Tinto Gorge**. Just beyond this, 4km from the main road, is the relatively small but spectacular **Hamersley Gorge** with it's unique folded rock formations.

The 'ghost' town of Wittenoom (population 25) is at the northern end of the park and **Wittenoom Gorge**, infamous because of many asbestos-related deaths in the region, is immediately south of the town. A road runs the 13km into the gorge, passing old asbestos mines, small gorges and pretty pools.

Some 18km from the Great Northern Hwy is the turn-off to **Yampire Gorge**, where blue veins of asbestos can be seen in the rock. This road is no longer maintained and can only be negotiated by 4WD (check conditions beforehand).

The best access to the park is via the sealed road from the Great Northern Hwy, some 35km south of the Auski (Munjina) Roadhouse, or via Tom Price to the west.

Warning

Even after 25 years, there is a potential health risk from airborne asbestos fibres in Wittenoom township, and in the Wittenoom and Yampire gorges. Avoid disturbing asbestos tailings in the area and keep your car windows closed on windy days. If you are concerned, seek medical advice before going to Wittenoom.

WESTERN AUSTRALIA

Places to Stay

There are three basic *camping grounds* within Karijini, with pit toilets and gas barbecues: the Fortescue camping ground near Dales Gorge; Weano Gorge; and at the turn-off to Joffre Falls ($8 for two people) – call ☎ 9189 8157 for information.

Wittenoom is still a good accommodation base if you're prepared to brave the possible asbestos risk (as many are). *Bungarra Bivouac (☎ 9189 7026)*, run by Dave of the gorge trips fame, has beds for $8. It's a rickety old place, but that goes with the town. *Wittenoom Guest House (☎ 9189 7060)*, in a former convent, is a surprisingly pleasant place with clean, comfortable rooms. Dorm beds are $10 and singles/doubles $20/35, including linen and towels.

Auski Tourist Village (☎ 9176 6988, Great Northern Hwy) is asbestos-free but overpriced: tent/powered sites are $10/20 for two, austere budget cabins $30/45 for singles/doubles and motel rooms $110.

Mt Florance Station (☎ 9189 8151), halfway between Millstream-Chichester and Karijini, has camp sites for $5 per person and beds in the shearers' quarters for $15.

Organised Tours

The best way to tackle the 'Miracle Mile', a challenging route through some of the best parts of Karijini, is on a tour. Dave's Gorge Tours (☎ 9189 7026) are legendary and receive rave reviews from our readers. They cost $70/150 for one/two days. Design-a-Tour (☎ 9144 1460) also has good one-day tours of the gorges from Auski or Tom Price, including lunch ($80). Snappy Gum Safaris (☎ 9185 1278) runs two-day camping trips from Karratha to Karijini and Millstream-Chichester ($190) and Lestok Tours (☎ 9189 2032), based in Tom Price, has day trips to Karijini for $80.

Scenic helicopter flights (☎ 9176 6979) over the gorges depart from the Auski Roadhouse; a 30 minute flight is $150 per person (minimum two). Red Rock Abseiling Adventures (☎ 9189 2206) will lower you into the gorges for $95. The starting point for a half-day adventure is the Weano Gorge parking area.

COMPANY TOWNS

There are two large, company-run, iron-ore towns near Karijini – Tom Price (population 3900) to the west, and Paraburdoo (population 1980) to the south-west. Another, Newman (population 4800), is 450km south of Port Hedland. Pannawonica, very much a 'closed' town, is 46km east of the North-West Coastal Hwy.

Company towns usually have sports facilities, which are second in popularity to the pub or workers' club. In **Tom Price** you can tour the Hamersley Iron mine site – if nothing else, the scale of it will impress you; the 1½ hour tours cost $12/6 and should be booked through the tourist bureau on ☎ 9188 1112. Mt Nameless, 4km west of Tom Price, offers excellent views of the area, especially at sunset. It's a three hour return walk, or you can drive to the top if you have a 4WD vehicle. Tom Price is about 80km from the entry to Karijini via a sealed road.

At **Newman**, a BHP town which only came into existence in the 1970s, the iron-ore mountain Whaleback is being systematically taken apart and railed north to the coast at Port Hedland. Guided 1½-hour tours of these engrossing operations leave across from the tourist centre weekdays at 8.30 am and 1 pm and Saturday at 8.30 am ($7). Like Tom Price, Newman is a modern company town built to service the mine; the friendly tourist bureau (☎ 9175 2888) is on the corner of Fortescue Ave and Newman Drive.

The scenic drive through the **Ophthalmia Range** is spectacular in wildflower season.

Places to Stay & Eat

Tom Price The *Tom Price Tourist Park (☎ 9189 1515)* has tent/powered sites for $14/18 for two, en suite cabins for $75 and self-contained A-frame units for $90. *Hillview Lodge (☎ 9189 1110, Stadium Rd)* has budget twin rooms for $55 and motel rooms for $95. It also has counter meals and an excellent buffet ($18).

The *Red Emperor* in the shopping mall does reasonable food.

Newman *Dearlove's Caravan Park (☎ 9175 2802, Cowra Drive)* has tent and powered sites for $14 and $18 and motel-style units at $50 for two.

The *All Seasons Newman Hotel* has good counter meals, and there are several roadhouses and takeaways in town.

MARBLE BAR

• postcode 6760   • pop 320

Reputed to be the hottest place in Australia, Marble Bar had a period in the 1920s when the temperature exceeded 37°C for 160 consecutive days. On one day in 1905 the mercury soared to 49.1°C. From October to March, days over 40°C are common. But in late winter, as the spring wildflowers begin to bloom, Marble Bar is actually quite an attractive place.

The town, 203km south-east of Port Hedland, is the centre of a 377,000 sq km shire (larger than New Zealand). It takes its name from the red jasper bar across the Coongan River, 5km to the west. The tourist centre (☎ 9176 1041) is across from the Ironclad Hotel.

The 1895 government buildings in town, made of local stone, are still in use. The **Comet Gold Mine**, 10km south of Marble Bar, still operates and has a mining museum.

The *Ironclad Hotel (☎ 9176 1066, 15 Francis St)*, one of the area's colourful drinking spots, has a range of rooms; backpacker beds cost from $15. Meals are also available.

PORT HEDLAND

• postcode 6721   • pop 12,850

This port handles a massive tonnage, as it's from here that much of the Pilbara's iron ore is shipped overseas. The main highway into Port Hedland enters along a 3km causeway. About 15km south of the port is South Hedland, the modern residential centre.

Even before the Marble Bar gold rush of the 1880s, the town had been important. It became a grazing centre in 1864 and during the 1870s a fleet of 150 pearling luggers was based here. By 1946, however, the population had dwindled to a mere 150.

Information

The helpful tourist bureau (☎ 9173 1711) is at 13 Wedge St (reputedly the shortest main street in Australia). It has showers ($2), Internet access and loads of information, including a good map and guide. It's open weekdays from 8.30 am to 5 pm and weekends until 4.30 pm (closed Sunday from November to May).

Things to See & Do

You can survey the town from the 26m **observation tower** behind the tourist office (you have to sign a waiver to climb it and you'll need closed-in shoes; $2/1). Below are huge ore carriers, stockpiles and a town encrusted in red Pilbara dust (even the local pigeons are red). The iron-ore trains are up to 2.6km in length. The informative 1½-hour BHP Iron Ore & Port Tour leaves from the tourist office on weekdays at 9.30 am ($10/2). There's also a town tour on Monday, Wednesday and Friday at 1.30 pm ($10/2). BHP's new Hot Briquetted Iron (HBI) plant on Finucane Island lights up like a fairy castle at night – it's best seen at dusk from Richardson St.

Pretty Pool, 7km east of the town centre on the waterfront, is a tidal pool where shell-collectors have fun. The tidal flats just north of here are the best viewing area for Port Hedland's own 'Stairway to the Moon' on full moon nights.

There are **Aboriginal petroglyphs** (rock engravings), including turtles and a whale, near the BHP gate at Two-Mile Ridge; you need to get the key from the Department of Aboriginal Affairs office in the Boulevard shopping centre on Wilson St.

Between October and March **flatback turtles** nest on some of the nearby beaches, including Munda, Cooke Point, Cemetery and Pretty Pool. At Munda, up to 20 turtles may nest in a night. The tourist office keeps track of the turtles' location during the nesting season.

Four-hour **whale-watching** trips are operated by Big Blue Dive (☎ 9173 3202) in season ($70); trips are dependent on tides and numbers. Majestic humpbacks are often seen in pods of five to six.

Places to Stay

Cooke Point Caravan Park (☎ 9173 1271, Athol St) is well situated close to Pretty

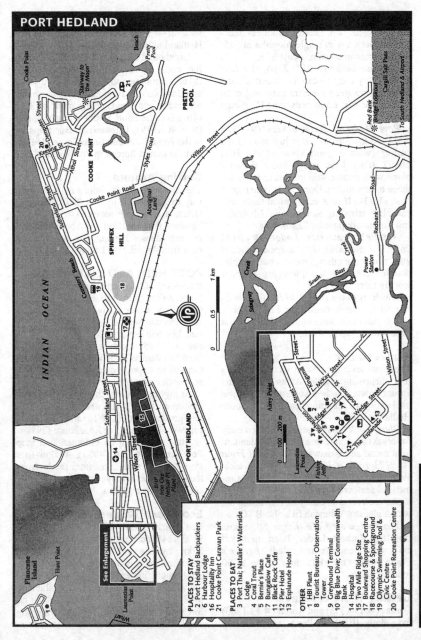

PORT HEDLAND

PLACES TO STAY
2 Port Hedland Backpackers
6 Harbour Lodge
16 Hospitality Inn
21 Cooke Point Caravan Park

PLACES TO EAT
3 Port Thai; Natalie's Waterside Lodge
4 Coral Trout
5 Bernie's Place
7 Bungalow Cafe
11 Black Rock Cafe
12 Pier Hotel
13 Esplanade Hotel

OTHER
1 HBI Plant
8 Tourist Bureau; Observation Tower
9 Greyhound Terminal
10 Big Blue Dive; Commonwealth Bank
14 Hospital
15 Two Mile Ridge Site
17 Boulevard Shopping Centre
18 Racecourse & Sportground
19 Olympic Swimming Pool & Civic Centre
20 Cooke Point Recreation Centre

Pool; tent/powered sites in this tidy park are $14/19 for two. There's a spotless backpacker section with singles/doubles at $25/45; self-contained cabins cost $75.

Harbour Lodge (☎ 9173 2996, *11 Edgar St*) is a very cosy place with rooms around a central lounge, a pleasant patio and even a 10-seater spa; dorm beds are $15, rooms $30/40.

Port Hedland Backpackers (☎ 9173 3282, *20 Richardson St*) is just around the corner (with a good view of the HBI plant). It's a little rough but a friendly place with good outdoor seating areas for those balmy nights. Dorm beds/twin rooms cost $15/34. It runs economical three-day camping trips to Karijini on Mondays (minimum six people; $220).

Natalie's Waterside Lodge (☎ 9173 2635, *7 Richardson St*) is a good choice if you want something more comfortable; doubles are $60 and there are cheaper weekly rates.

The *Hospitality Inn* (☎ 9173 1044, *Webster St*) has motel rooms from $142. There's also accommodation in South Hedland, but little reason to stay there.

Places to Eat
There are several cafes on Wedge St and a few surprisingly good Asian restaurants around town. The best supermarkets are in the Boulevard shopping centre and at South Hedland.

Black Rock Cafe (*Wedge St*) is open early for breakfast, and serves a range of standard light meals and takeaways. The *Coral Trout* (☎ 9173 1003, *4 Richardson St*) is a takeaway and BYO restaurant with recommended seafood. *Port Thai* (☎ 9173 4585, *7 Richardson St*) is an excellent Thai restaurant with a pleasant verandah (it's also BYO).

The *Bungalow Cafe* (*Edgar St*), across from the Harbour Lodge, is an upmarket cafe with focaccias and salads. *Bernie's Place* in the Port Plaza does filling $7.50 lunch specials.

Getting There & Away
Qantas (☎ 13 1313) and Ansett (☎ 13 1300) have daily flights to Perth, and there are

services to Broome, Derby and Kununurra. Merpati (☎ 9172 2700) flies direct from Port Hedland to Bali every Friday ($740 return).

Greyhound Pioneer (☎ 13 2030) goes up the coast from Perth to Port Hedland ($163), Broome and Darwin. There's also an inland service from Perth (via Newman) on Friday and Sunday. The main booking office is at the South Hedland tourist bureau (☎ 9140 1919), Throssell St. Bus stops are at the Ampol Roadhouse in South Hedland and the tourist bureau in Port Hedland.

Getting Around
The airport is 13km from town; the only way to get there is by taxi ($20). There's a Hedland Bus Lines service (☎ 9172 1394) between Port Hedland and South Hedland; the trip takes 40 minutes to an hour and runs from Monday to Friday ($2.80).

PORT HEDLAND TO BROOME
It's 604km of fairly dull highway to Broome. Some 84km from Port Hedland is the **De Grey River**, where many bird species can be seen. *Pardoo Station* (☎ 9176 4930), 133km out, has tent/powered sites for $12/14 for two and singles/doubles for $25/40. Not far from the Pardoo Roadhouse (154km) is the turn-off to **Cape Keraudren**, a great fishing spot with *camp sites* ($5 per vehicle).

At **Eighty Mile Beach**, 245km from Port Hedland, there's a *caravan park* with tent/powered sites ($12/16) and cabins ($55 for two). The Sandfire Roadhouse (295km) is little more than an enforced fuel stop. **Port Smith** (☎ 9192 4983), 477km from Port Hedland and 23km from the highway turn-off, comes highly recommended; *camp sites* are $6 per person.

Eco Beach Wilderness Retreat
Eco Beach Yardoogarra (☎ 9192 4844, fax 9192 4845, ecobeach@tpgi.com.au) is only 27km by sea and 130km by road from Broome. There is a 15km stretch of white-sand beach, timber huts on stilts with superb views of the Indian Ocean, and abundant marine and bird life. Activities include nature walks, horse-riding, fishing, swimming, snorkelling or just relaxing. There are no

TVs, telephones or room service but the back-to-nature theme compensates.

A two day package cost $250 per person with all meals and transfers included. Otherwise, singles/twins cost from $155 and 4WD transfers are $50 return. Call for directions if you're driving a 4WD.

COLLIER RANGE & RUDALL RIVER NATIONAL PARKS

Two of the state's most isolated national parks are found in the Pilbara.

The **Collier Range National Park** is the more accessible, as the Great Northern Hwy bisects it near the Kumarina Roadhouse, 256km north of Meekatharra. Here, at the upper reaches of the Ashburton and Gascoyne rivers, the ranges vary from low hills to high ridges bounded by cliffs.

Even more remote is the **Rudall River (Karlamilyi) National Park**, a breathtakingly beautiful desert region of 15,000 sq km, 300km east of Newman. Visit in July and August when daytime temperatures are tolerable – although the nights can be exceptionally cold. The Martu Aboriginal people still live in the park. At least two vehicles, equipped with HF radios, are needed for off-road trips into these parks and visitors must be self-sufficient. There are no facilities.

The Kimberley

The rugged Kimberley, in the north of WA, is one of Australia's last great frontiers. Despite enormous advances in the past decade this is still a little-travelled and remote area of great rivers and magnificent scenery.

The Kimberley suffers from climatic extremes – heavy rains in the Wet followed by searing heat in the Dry – but the irrigation projects in its north-east have made great changes to the region. Rivers and creeks can rise rapidly following heavy rain and become impassable torrents within 15 minutes. Unless it's a brief storm, it's quite likely that watercourses will remain impassable for some days. After two or three days of rain the Fitzroy River can swell from its normal 100m width to over 10km.

The best time to visit is between April and September. By October it's already getting hot as the build-up begins (with daily temperatures of 35°C), and later in the year temperatures of more than 40°C are common until it starts to rain. On the other hand, the Wet is a spectacular time to visit – ethereal electrical storms, waterfalls close to the towns and magic carpet of green rejuvenated landscape.

Get a copy of the free annual *Kimberley Holiday Planner* from the Broome or Kununurra tourist bureau.

BROOME

- postcode 6725   • pop 11,350

Broome is often seen as Australia's true getaway – an isolated oasis with wide, sandy beaches and a relaxed cosmopolitan atmosphere. Although it is isolated, Broome has certainly been discovered and today it's a popular travellers' centre, with the attendant good and bad characteristics.

Broome's busy season is May to September (peaking in July and August); if you visit during the Wet you'll find a lot of tours and businesses not operating, but accommodation will be cheaper.

This small, dusty old port is noted for its Chinatown (or what's left of it) and the influences of early Japanese pearlers. Pearling in the waters off Broome started in the 1880s and peaked in the early 1900s, when the town's 400 pearling luggers, worked by 3000 men, supplied 80% of the world's mother-of-pearl (used mainly for buttons). The introduction of plastic buttons in the early 1950s brought about the demise of the thriving mother-of-pearl industry, and today only a handful of boats operate. The development of cultured pearls in the late 1950s went some way to reviving the industry, but pearl farms have largely replaced open sea diving. The divers were from various Asian countries and rivalry between the nationalities was always intense and sometimes ugly. The *Broome Heritage Trail* pamphlet merges the past with the present.

Broome became a target during WWII when, in 1942, 10 Japanese fighter planes bombed the harbour. Up to 100 people,

WESTERN AUSTRALIA

THE KIMBERLEY

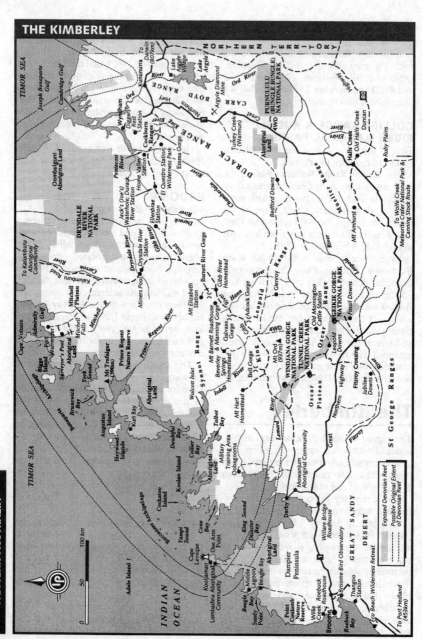

WESTERN AUSTRALIA

Bird-Watching at Roebuck Bay

Roebuck Bay is the most significant site in Australia for observing migratory waders – some 800,000 birds migrate here annually. The wide variety of habitats encourages a vast range of species: over 300 species have been recorded, more than one-third of Australia's species. Of these, the 49 species of waders represent nearly a quarter of all wader species in the world, and 22 of the 24 raptor (birds of prey) species found in Australia can be observed here.

The Broome Bird Observatory (☎ 9193 5600), administered by Birds Australia, is on Crab Creek Rd, not far from the shores of Roebuck Bay and about 25km from Broome. You can stay here and take part in economical tours with the observatory staff. The Shorebird, Crab Creek Bird Walk and Bushbird tours cost $25 from the observatory, or $45 if taken from Broome. It's worth checking tide times and heights for the most favourable viewing times before heading out. Tent/powered sites are $12/16 for two people, single/double (bunk) rooms are $25/32, and a six-bed, self-contained chalet is $80 a double and $10 per extra person.

George Swann of Kimberley Birdwatching (☎ 9192 1246) has a number of excellent bird-watching tours. Happy twitching!

ANN JEFFREE

Osprey

---

mainly Dutch refugees, were killed and 16 Australian flying boats were hit.

Information

The efficient tourist bureau (☎ 9192 2222, fax 9192 2063, tourism@broome.wt.com.au) is on the corner of Broome Rd and Bagot St. It's open daily from 8 am to 5 pm from April to November, and from 9 am to 5 pm on weekdays and until 1 pm on weekends during the rest of the year.

The post office is in the Paspaley shopping centre in Chinatown. The busy Broome Telecentre is at the southern end of Dampier Terrace. Internet access costs $10 per hour and it's open Monday to Friday from 9 am to 5 pm and Saturday until 1 pm; there are plenty of terminals but you may still have to queue.

Chinatown

The term 'Chinatown' refers to the old part of town, although there is really only one block or so that is truly multicultural and historic. Some of the plain and simple wooden buildings that line Carnarvon St still house Chinese merchants, but most are now restaurants and tourist shops. The bars on the shop windows aren't there to deter outlaws but to minimise cyclone damage.

You can take a morning or evening stroll through Chinatown and learn some history from local Aboriginal guide Stephen 'Baamba' Albert for $25/30. Phone ☎ 0417 988 328 for bookings.

Pearl Fishing

Pearl Luggers (☎ 9192 2059), on Dampier Terrace, takes an informal and informative look at Broome's pearling past – two of the original pearl boats have been restored and are on display along with a store house of old pearling equipment and photographs. Historical 'tours' are given by former pearl divers at 9.30 and 11 am, and 1.30 and 3 pm ($15/8). There's also an extended evening tour that includes a tasting of pearl meat from the Pinctada Maxima oyster – it costs a hefty $60, but then, pearl meat sells for up to $100 a kilo!

The **Broome Historical Society Museum** on Saville St has exhibits both on Broome and its pearling industry. It's in the old

BROOME

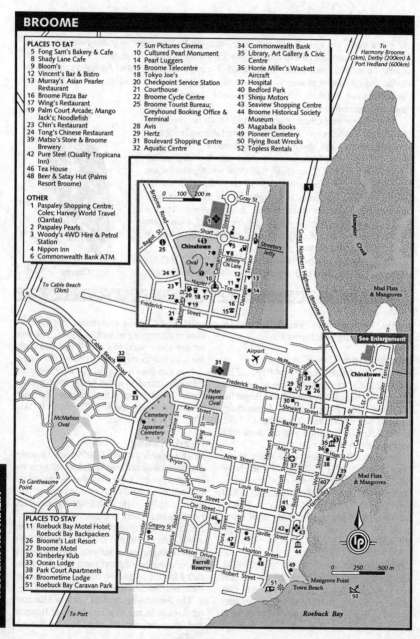

PLACES TO EAT
5 Fong Sam's Bakery & Cafe
8 Shady Lane Cafe
9 Bloom's
12 Vincent's Bar & Bistro
13 Murray's Asian Pearler Restaurant
16 Broome Pizza Bar
17 Wing's Restaurant
19 Palm Court Arcade; Mango Jack's; Noodlefish
23 Chin's Restaurant
24 Tong's Chinese Restaurant
39 Matso's Store & Broome Brewery
42 Pure Steel (Quality Tropicana Inn)
46 Tea House
48 Beer & Satay Hut (Palms Resort Broome)

OTHER
1 Paspaley Shopping Centre; Coles; Harvey World Travel (Qantas)
2 Paspaley Pearls
3 Woody's 4WD Hire & Petrol Station
4 Nippon Inn
6 Commonwealth Bank ATM

7 Sun Pictures Cinema
10 Cultured Pearl Monument
14 Pearl Luggers
15 Broome Telecentre
18 Tokyo Joe's
20 Checkpoint Service Station
21 Courthouse
22 Broome Cycle Centre
25 Broome Tourist Bureau; Greyhound Booking Office & Terminal
28 Avis
29 Hertz
31 Boulevard Shopping Centre
32 Aquatic Centre

34 Commonwealth Bank
35 Library, Art Gallery & Civic Centre
36 Horrie Miller's Wackett Aircraft
37 Hospital
40 Bedford Park
41 Shinju Motors
43 Seaview Shopping Centre
44 Broome Historical Society Museum
45 Magabala Books
49 Pioneer Cemetery
50 Flying Boat Wrecks
52 Topless Rentals

PLACES TO STAY
11 Roebuck Bay Motel Hotel; Roebuck Bay Backpackers
26 Broome's Last Resort
27 Broome Motel
30 Kimberley Klub
33 Ocean Lodge
38 Park Court Apartments
47 Broometime Lodge
51 Roebuck Bay Caravan Park

WESTERN AUSTRALIA

customs house opposite the Seaview shopping centre and is open daily from 10 am to 1 pm ($3/50c).

Mother-of-pearl and, more recently, cultured pearls have long been a Broome speciality. There are **pearl shops** along Dampier Terrace, and Short and Carnarvon Sts in Chinatown.

The **cemetery**, near Cable Beach Rd, testifies to the dangers that accompanied pearl diving when equipment was primitive and the knowledge of diving techniques limited. In 1914 alone, 33 divers died of the bends, while in 1908 a cyclone killed 150 seamen caught at sea. The Japanese section is one of the largest and most interesting.

Other Attractions

The 1888 **courthouse** was once used to house the transmitting equipment for the old cable station. The cable ran to Banyuwangi on Java.

Housed in an odd building on Weld St is a **Wackett aircraft** that used to belong to Horrie Miller, founder of MacRobertson Miller Airlines (now part of Ansett). There's a **pioneer cemetery** near Town Beach at the end of Robinson St.

If you're lucky enough to be in Broome on a cloudless night when a full moon rises you can witness the **Staircase to the Moon**. The reflections of the moon from the rippling mud flats create a wonderful golden stairway effect, best seen from Town Beach. The effect is most dramatic about two days after the full moon, as the moon doesn't rise until after the sky has had a chance to darken. A lively evening market is held and the town takes on a carnival air. Check with the tourist bureau for dates and times.

Cable Beach

The most popular swimming beach in Broome, Cable Beach is about 4km from town. It's azure waters and classic white sand as far as the eye can see, and watching the sun go down here is almost obligatory. You can hire surfboards, wave skis and other beach equipment – parasailing is popular. The northern side beyond the rocks is a popular nude-bathing area. You can also

Japanese cemetery, Broome

take vehicles (other than motorbikes) onto this part of the beach, although at high tide access is limited because of the rocks – don't get stranded.

Red Sun and Ships of the Desert operate popular sunset camel rides on the beach ($25 per hour). Broome Camel Safaris has half-hour morning rides for $15; book these at the tourist bureau. Cable Stables (☎ 0417 979 957) has two-hour horse riding trips for $40.

Broome Crocodile Park (☎ 9192 1489) on Cable Beach Rd is open from April to October on weekdays from 10 am to 5 pm and weekends from 2 to 5 pm ($12/5). There are guided tours at 3 pm.

The long sweep of Cable Beach eventually ends at **Gantheaume Point**, 7km south of Broome. The cliffs here have been eroded into curious shapes. At extremely low tides 120 million-year-old **dinosaur tracks** are exposed, though not easy to find. You can inspect casts of the footprints on the cliff top. **Anastasia's Pool** is an artificial rock pool, on the northern side of the point, built by the lighthouse keeper for his crippled wife.

Organised Tours

There are loads of tours available in and around Broome. Broome Day Tours (☎ 1800 801068) has a half-day tour of the Broome

WESTERN AUSTRALIA

RICHARD I'ANSON

Broome Festivities

The people of Broome love nothing more than a good party and there are plenty of festivals, mainly between May and November, to look out for. Exact dates of these festivals vary from year to year, so contact the Broome tourist bureau for more information.

The **Broome Fringe Arts Festival**, where the alternative performers and artists have their day, is held in early June. There are markets, Aboriginal art exhibitions and impromptu jamming sessions. The **Broome Race Round** in June/July is a major outback horse-racing meeting and one of Broome's big social events.

The biggest annual event is the **Shinju Matsuri** (Festival of the Pearl), which commemorates the early pearling years and the town's multicultural heritage. The week-long festival is usually held between mid-August and early September, and features street parades, the Shinju Ball and dragon boat races. It's well worth being in Broome for this festival, but it's also the busiest time of year and accommodation is hard to find, so book well in advance. Many traditional Japanese ceremonies are featured, including the **O Bon Festival** (Festival of the Dead). It concludes with a beach concert and a huge fireworks display.

The **Stompem Festival**, held in early October, is a celebration of Aboriginal arts and music from the Kimberley.

The **Mango Festival** is held in late November and celebrates the harvest of this sweet tropical fruit. The three day event features a Mango Cocktail Party, the Great Chefs of Broome Mango Cook-off and open-air concerts.

Other events include the **Chinatown Street Party** in March, the **Dragon Boat Classic** in early April, the **Broome Sailfish Tournament** (a tag and release event) in July and evening markets on the many nights of the Staircase to the Moon.

peninsula ($39). You can take twilight cruises in the replica pearl lugger *Willie* for $60.

Other options include jet boat tours (☎ 9193 6415) up Dampier Creek (weekends only; $30/20), and examinations of the star-studded Kimberley night sky with Astro Tours (☎ 9193 5362); $45 includes pick up and supper. Windrider Safaris (☎ 015-010 772) is a new outfit catering to adventurous young travellers. The one day tour involves sailing your own trimaran from Cable Beach to Willie Creek and back ($115), or there's a two day camping tour ($195). The tourist bureau can direct you to more tours and make bookings.

Several companies offer adventure 4WD trips from Broome to Darwin – expect to pay at least $110 a day.

Places to Stay – Budget

During the high season, accommodation in Broome, even tent sites, can be hard to find. If you can, book ahead.

Camping The *Roebuck Bay Caravan Park* (☎ 9192 1366, Walcott St) has a great location right on town beach and is the closest park to town; tent/powered sites are $14/19 for two and on-site vans cost from $45. There's a good camper's kitchen in the Mango Camping Ground section. *Broome Vacation Village* (☎ 9192 1057, Port Drive) is halfway between town and the jetty. It has powered/en suite sites for $20/25 and park homes for $90.

Cable Beach Caravan Park (☎ 9192 2066, Millington Rd) has tent/powered sites for $15/18 and cottages for $600 a week.

Hostels Broome has embraced backpackers in recent years, creating some competition for budget beds. The flashy *Kimberley Klub* (☎ 9192 3233, fax 9192 3530, Frederick St) sets a high standard in purpose-built backpacker accommodation – it's more like a holiday resort than a hostel. As a result it lacks personality but makes up for that in facilities. There's a bar and barbecue overlooking the swimming pool, sand volleyball court, a big TV/games room, tour booking service and large, noisy rooms. A bed in 10/four-bed rooms costs $15/17 and twins/doubles are $55.

Broome's Last Resort (☎ 9193 5000, 1800 801 918, 2 Bagot St) is the original party hostel and is close to the tourist bureau and airport. It's smaller and less sterile than the Kimberley Klub – there's a small, convivial bar and a good pool. Dorm beds are $14/15/16 in eight/six/four-bed rooms and doubles (some with air-con) are $45 ($1 less for YHA members).

The *Roebuck Bay Backpackers (☎ 9192 1183, Dampier Terrace)*, part of the Roebuck Bay Motel Hotel, is very central and the cheapest of the lot, but it's also the least well maintained. A dorm bed is $13 ($11 for YHA/VIP members) and musty air-con doubles with bathroom are $43 ($39).

Cable Beach Backpackers (☎ 9193 5511, 1800 655 011, 33-37 Lullfitz Drive) not only has the ideal beach location but it's probably the most laid back and pleasant of Broome's backpacker hostels. It's an open-plan design with a well-equipped kitchen, pool and volleyball court. Dorm beds cost $16 ($15 for YHA/VIP), doubles cost $42. There's a free shuttle bus into town five times a day, and it rents bikes ($10 a day) and mopeds ($25).

Places to Stay – Mid-Range
Ocean Lodge (☎ 9193 7700, fax 9193 7496, Cable Beach Rd), near the junction of Port Drive, has self-contained units from $75 to $95 in the high season. There's a pool and shady courtyard.

The *Broometime Lodge (☎ 9193 5067, 1800 804 322, 59 Forrest St)* is clean and comfortable with air-con singles for $50 and en suite twins/doubles for $70. It's not in a great location but has a homey atmosphere with a pool, barbecue area, lounge and kitchen.

The *Broome Motel (☎ 9192 7775, 1800 683 867, 51-57 Frederick St)* is a brand new place in a good location. Spotless rooms have en suite, kitchenette, and a small verandah. High season doubles cost $95 with a small reduction for stays of more than one night.

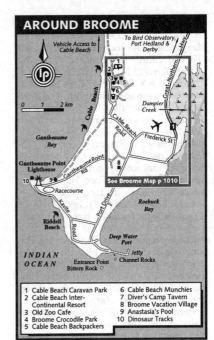

AROUND BROOME

1 Cable Beach Caravan Park
2 Cable Beach Inter-Continental Resort
3 Old Zoo Cafe
4 Broome Crocodile Park
5 Cable Beach Backpackers
6 Cable Beach Munchies
7 Diver's Camp Tavern
8 Broome Vacation Village
9 Anastasia's Pool
10 Dinosaur Tracks

The *Roebuck Bay Hotel Motel (☎ 9192 1221, 1800 098 824, Carnarvon St)* has noisy motel units for $80, or better singles/doubles for $90/100.

Park Court Apartments (☎ 9193 5887, 1800 801 225, Haas St) has units with all facilities from $80 to $160 (and cheaper weekly rates).

Harmony Broome (☎ 9193 7439, Broome Highway), 5km north of town, has cosy B&B rooms for $50/80.

Places to Stay – Top End
The *Cable Beach Inter-Continental Resort (☎ 9192 0400, 1800 095 508, Cable Beach Rd)* is a beautifully designed, upmarket place covering a large area; a studio room costs from $300 (high season).

Places to Eat
Cafes & Fast Food *Bloom's (Carnarvon St)* serves a generous cappuccino and has excellent croissants. The Palm Court Arcade

on the corner of Hamersley and Frederick Sts has a few takeaway places, including *Mango Jack's* for hamburgers, kebabs and fish and chips. The *Broome Pizza Bar (Napier Terrace)* is a good place for pizzas.

Fong Sam's Bakery & Cafe in China-town is average and pricey, but it's always busy around lunch time. The Seaview shopping centre also has a *bakery*, as well as a *Coles supermarket* (there's a 24 hour Coles in Chinatown's Paspaley centre). The *Shady Lane Cafe (Johnny Chi Lane)* has a range of focaccias, coffees and light lunches. (Ignore the 'Food Hall' signs in Johnny Chi Lane – it's long gone.)

Cable Beach Munchies (Cable Beach Rd) is open daily for breakfast, lunch and dinner.

Pubs & Restaurants The Roebuck Bay Hotel Motel (the 'Roey') has the airy *Vincent's Bar & Bistro*, with an alfresco dining area, while the Palms Resort Broome, Hopton St, has the eternally popular (and very good) *Beer & Satay Hut*.

Pure Steel is another good restaurant upstairs in the Quality Tropicana Inn on Robinson St. *Matso's Store & Broome Brewery (☎ 9193 5811, 60 Hamersley St)* comes recommended for intimate dining, good food and its boutique beers.

Asian restaurants are naturally plentiful and usually good value in Broome. *Noodlefish (☎ 9192 5529, Hamersley St)* is a great little BYO Thai place with alfresco seating and lightning service. *Chin's Restaurant (☎ 9192 1466, 7 Hamersley St)* has a variety of dishes from all over Asia, and *Wing's (Napier Terrace)* and *Tong's (Broome Rd)*, around the corner, are Chinese specialists.

Murray's Pearler Restaurant (☎ 9192 2049), in the thick of the pearl shops on Dampier Terrace, is another very popular place for an evening meal.

The *Tea House (☎ 9193 6025, Dora St)*, in a mud-brick building with an outdoor dining area, has a great range of Thai and seafood dishes, and BYO is permitted.

The *Old Zoo Cafe (☎ 9193 6200, Challenor Drive)*, near Cable Beach, is a good spot for breakfast and lunch – evening meals are pricier and you'll probably have to book.

Entertainment
Sun Pictures (Carnarvon St) is an open-air cinema dating from 1916. It screens recent releases ($10) and settling back on a deck chair to watch the 'flicks' here is a must. The *Roey* still rocks along with various 'special' nights (cheap drinks, competitions etc) to attract punters. The Sports Bar has a big screen showing international events.

Broome's nightclubs are the *Nippon Inn (Dampier Terrace)* and *Tokyo Joe's (Napier Terrace)* – entry to either is usually $5.

Getting There & Away
Ansett (☎ 13 1300) and Qantas (☎ 13 1313) have daily flights to Perth, Darwin and other regional centres. Ansett also has a weekly flight to Denpasar, Bali, departing on Wednesday. Qantas' Broome agent is Harvey World Travel (☎ 9193 5599) in the Paspaley centre.

Greyhound Pioneer stops in Broome on its daily Perth-Darwin service; the terminal and booking office (☎ 9192 1561) is at the tourist bureau.

Getting Around
The Town Bus (☎ 9193 6585) plies hourly between the town and Cable Beach, with one service a day to Gantheaume Point. A sector fare is $2.50/1 and a day pass is $8/4. The bus stops close to most places to stay and discounted tickets are available from the hostels.

The Broome Cycle Centre, on the corner of Hamersley and Frederick Sts, hires bikes for around $12 a day.

There are several local car hire operators. Topless Rentals (☎ 9193 5017) on Hunter St is one of the cheapest with sedans from $30 and 4WDs from $50.

DAMPIER PENINSULA
The **Willie Creek Pearl Farm** (☎ 9193 6000) is 38km north of Broome, off the Cape Leveque Rd. It offers a rare chance to see a working pearl farm and learn something about the science of culturing pearls. Guided tours are held daily at 9 am and 2.30 pm ($17.50/9); the farm is only open at guided tour times and you should book in advance. During the Wet the road is open

WESTERN AUSTRALIA

only to 4WD vehicles. Broome Coachlines (☎ 1800 801 068) runs tours to Willie Creek for $45, including admission.

It's about 200km from the turn-off, 9km out of Broome, to the Cape Leveque Lighthouse at the tip of the Dampier Peninsula. This flora and fauna paradise is a great spot for humpback whale-watching. On the west coast of the peninsula is **Coulomb Point Nature Reserve**, established to protect the unique pindan vegetation and the rare bilby. It's accessed by the coastal Manari Rd.

About halfway to the lighthouse is a diversion to the **Beagle Bay Aboriginal community** (☎ 9192 4913), which has a beautiful church in the middle of a green. Inside is an altar stunningly decorated with mother-of-pearl. A fee of $5 is charged for entry to the community. There's no camping here; fuel is available from 8 am to around 3 pm on weekdays only.

About 20km before Cape Leveque is the **Lombadina Aboriginal community** (☎ 9192 4936), which has a lovely church built from mangrove wood. Day and overnight mud-crabbing and traditional fishing tours are available with the Bardi people. Petrol and diesel are available on weekdays. A $5 car permit is required from the office.

Cape Leveque, has a lighthouse and wonderful beaches beneath stunning red cliffs. Sunset here is truly memorable and a great photo opportunity. There is accommodation at *Kooljaman* (☎ 9192 4970). In the high season, tent/powered sites are $10/15, exotic beach shelters are $30 for two and family units are $50; all prices, except for camping, drop in the low season. Bushtucker and mud-crabbing tours are available, as is unleaded and diesel fuel.

Take note that the communities won't want you to stay on their land, but if you want to see their churches or buy something from their shops they will be helpful. Permission to visit other areas must be obtained in advance; check with the Broome tourist bureau about road conditions and permits.

Organised Tours
Over the Top Adventure Tours (☎ 9192 3977, overtop@broome.wt.com.au) and Flak Track (☎ 9192 1487) in Broome have one-day 4WD tours of the peninsula for $175 and $170 respectively. Over the Top also has a two day camping tour for $275.

DERBY
● postcode 6728   ● pop 3200

This major administrative centre for the west Kimberley, 220km from Broome, is a good point from which to travel to the spectacular gorges in the region. The Great Northern Hwy beyond Derby continues inland to Fitzroy Crossing (256km) and Halls Creek (288km further on). Alternatively, there's the much wilder Gibb River Rd.

Derby is on a point of land jutting into King Sound, north of the mouth of the mighty Fitzroy River. The whole town is surrounded by huge expanses of tidal mud flats, baked hard in the Dry and occasionally flooded by king tides.

The tourist bureau (☎ 9191 1426, 1800 621 426), 1 Clarendon St, is open on weekdays from 8.30 am to 4.30 pm, and weekends from 9 am to 1 pm (until noon on weekends from November to April). Staff here are enthusiastic and helpful.

The Derby Telecentre on Ashley St has Internet and email. It's open daily from 9 am to 5 pm ($5 per half-hour).

Things to See
The **Prison Tree**, 7km south of town, is probably Derby's most famous attraction. This huge boab has a girth of 14m, a hollow trunk and is said to be over 1000 years old. Prisoners were supposedly locked up here years ago before being taken to Derby gaol. Nearby is **Myall's Bore** with its 120m-long cattle trough.

There's a small, shady botanic garden just behind the library off Clarendon St. **Wharfinger's House**, at the end of Loch St, contains some local historical information – you can get the key from the tourist bureau.

Derby's lofty **wharf** was brought back into action for shipping by Western Metals in late 1997. Zinc and lead are now brought to the port from the Cadjeput mines east of Fitzroy Crossing and shipped to Asia.

WESTERN AUSTRALIA

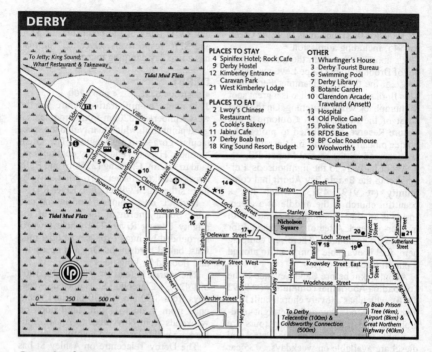

DERBY

PLACES TO STAY
4 Spinifex Hotel; Rock Cafe
9 Derby Hostel
12 Kimberley Entrance
    Caravan Park
21 West Kimberley Lodge

PLACES TO EAT
2 Lwoy's Chinese
   Restaurant
5 Cookie's Bakery
11 Jabiru Cafe
17 Derby Boab Inn
18 King Sound Resort; Budget

OTHER
1 Wharfinger's House
3 Derby Tourist Bureau
6 Swimming Pool
7 Derby Library
8 Botanic Garden
10 Clarendon Arcade;
    Traveland (Ansett)
13 Hospital
14 Old Police Gaol
15 Police Station
16 RFDS Base
19 BP Colac Roadhouse
20 Woolworth's

Organised Tours

The Kimberley Entrance Caravan Park (see Places to Stay) runs 1½ hour town tours of Derby, including the wharf and the prison tree ($6).

From Derby there are flights over King Sound to Cockatoo Island, which is partly owned by BHP and has recently opened to visitors; *Cockatoo Island Resort (☎ 9191 7477)* has an excellent value three night package including air transfer from Derby for $195. Scenic flights over the Buccaneer Archipelago and the west Kimberley coast are available with Aerial Enterprises (☎ 1800 066 132) and Derby Air Services (☎ 1800 180 075) from $160 (minimum of two).

Hot Land Safaris (☎ 9193 1312) has two to 14-day camping tours into remote areas of the Kimberley for $165 per day, including meals, fishing and camping gear. Bush Track Safaris (☎ 9191 1547) goes into the remote Walcott Inlet and Mitchell Plateau for around $195 per day.

West Kimberley Tours (☎ 9193 1442) goes to the Devonian Reef gorges on Tuesday, Thursday and Saturday ($80), and Gibb River Rd gorges ($300 for two days). For something different, One Tide Charters (☎ 9191 1426) has mud-crabbing trips on King Sound for $75.

Special Events

The Boab Festival, held over the first two weeks of July, is Derby's big annual event. Among the events are concerts, sports (including the unique mud footy) and street parades. If, for some reason, you're in Derby over Christmas, the Boxing Day Sports is another biggie – featuring the famous watermelon seed spitting contest.

Places to Stay

The *Kimberley Entrance Caravan Park (☎ 9193 1055, Rowan St)* has sites for $7 per person plus $3 for power, and on-site vans for $40 for up to four people. It's a friendly place with a great barbecue area at the front.

The **Spinifex Hotel** (☎ 9191 1233, Clarendon St), known as 'the Spinny' to all, has backpacker beds in very basic twin-share rooms for $15 per person, budget singles/doubles at $40/50 and 'deluxe' (en suite) rooms at $50/65. It's conveniently close to the tourist bureau and Greyhound drop-off.

Goldsworthy Connection (☎ 9193 1246, Lot 4 Guildford St) has several good value self-contained units plonked out in a quiet bush setting just off the main road into town. It costs $50 for a twin room in air-conditioned three-bedroom units, or $150 to rent the whole unit. The comfortable backpackers cottage has beds for $20 (discounts for stays of more than one night).

Derby Hostel (☎ 9191 1867, 233-235 Villiers St), run by Aboriginal Hostels Ltd, is often full with semi-permanents and transient indigenous people, but it welcomes backpackers. If available, a bed in a reasonably clean twin-share room is $16 per person including continental breakfast; dinner costs $8, and there's also a self-catering kitchen.

West Kimberley Lodge (☎ 9191 1031, Sutherland St), on the eastern edge of town, has small but clean rooms for $45/50, and en suite units with TV for $65. There's a kitchen, pleasant tropical garden and a pool.

Places to Eat

Cookie's Bakery (Clarendon St) is good for lunch and has a fine selection of sandwiches. The air-conditioned **Jabiru Cafe** has a nice garden setting and is open early for breakfast.

The **Spinny**, **Derby Boab Inn Hotel** and the **King Sound Resort Hotel** all do counter meals, roughly in ascending order of price. Attached to the Spinny is the relatively stylish **Rock Café**, which has a great buffet dinner every Thursday.

At the end of Loch St there's **Lwoy's Chinese Restaurant** (☎ 9191 1554), and at the jetty is the BYO **Wharf Restaurant & Takeaway** (☎ 9191 1195) with local seafood specialities.

Tidal Waterfalls

One of the most remarkable features of the Kimberley's rugged coastline are the spectacular tidal 'waterfalls', which are not actual waterfalls but immense tidal currents that hurtle through the narrow coastal gorges. The speed they attain, from 20 to 30 knots in places, gives the impression of a waterfall flowing horizontally.

The waterfalls are spectacular at **Talbot Bay**, north of King Sound. At the south end of the bay, two narrow hard sandstone gorges, both about 30m high, protect the inner and outer bays (flooded valleys). The high tide fills both bays with water and, as the tide goes out, the water in the bays is released. The narrow gorges restrict the outflow, resulting in a vertical difference of 1m between the first bay and the open sea of Talbot Bay, and of 2m between the first and second bays. Water then thunders through both the outer 70m-long gorge and the impressive 100m-long inner gorge.

The Aborigines of the now-extinct Meda tribe and the Worora people knew the waterfalls as 'Wolbunum' and once had a system of *bidi* (tracks) running to these valleys as food was abundant there. Nowadays, most people see the waterfalls from the air (see Organised Tours in the Derby section).

Getting There & Away

Ansett (☎ 13 1300) flies daily (except Sunday) to Perth via Broome. The Ansett office is at Traveland (☎ 9193 1488) in Shop 6 in the Clarendon Arcade on Clarendon St.

Greyhound Pioneer's daily Perth-Darwin service stops in Derby at the tourist bureau at 10 pm on its way north and 4.35 am southbound.

GIBB RIVER ROAD

This is the 'back road' from Derby to Wyndham or Kununurra. At 667km it's more direct by several hundred kilometres than the Fitzroy Crossing to Halls Creek route. It's almost all dirt, although it does not require a 4WD if it happens to have been recently graded. However, in the Wet the road is impassable. Tackling the Gibb River Rd in its entirety is not recommended for conventional 2WD vehicles, but some of the main gorges can be reached from Derby or Kununurra (for example, you can drive to Windjana Gorge from Derby, then continue on to the Great Northern Hwy).

Get a copy of *The Gibb River and Kalumburu Roads Travellers Guide* ($2) from information centres in Broome, Derby or Kununurra. There's little traffic of any sort along the Gibb River Rd, so don't bother trying to hitch (see Organised Tours under Kalumburu Road further in this chapter for operators covering this route).

Derby to Mt Barnett Station

The road is bitumen for the first 62km from Derby. It's 119km to the Windjana Gorge (21km) and Tunnel Creek (51km) turn-off, and you can continue down that road to the Great Northern Hwy near Fitzroy Crossing (see the Devonian Reef National Parks section later in this chapter).

The Lennard River bridge is crossed at 120km and at 145km you pass through the Yamarra Gap in the King Leopold Range. At 184km you can turn off to the beautiful *Mt Hart Homestead (☎ 9191 4645)*, which is 50km down a rough 4WD-only dirt road. You need to book if you want to stay here; dinner and B&B is $105/50 for adults/children (no camping). The 5km-long **Lennard River Gorge**, 8km off the Gibb River Rd, has a waterfall just north of the entrance and a refreshing pool.

About 26km on from the Mt Hart turn-off is the turn-off to **Bell Gorge**, 29km off the road along a 4WD-only track. This gorge is one of the west Kimberley's finest and has a picturesque waterfall. You can *camp* here for $7.

At 246km the adventurous can head to the *Old Mornington Cattle Station (☎ 9191 7035)* on the Fitzroy River, 100km south (no access to Mt House Station); camping is $8 and tent accommodation (with hot showers) is $40. Meals are also available.

At the 251km mark is the road into *Beverley Springs Homestead (☎ 9191 4646)*. This is a working station, 43km off the Gibb River Rd, with a variety of accommodation; camping costs $8 per person, chalets with dinner and B&B are $95, homestay with dinner and B&B is $89, and self-contained two-bedroom cabins are $85 a night.

The turn-off to **Adcock Gorge** is at 267km. This gorge is 5km off the road and is good for swimming. You can *camp* here, although the site is rocky and there's little shade.

Horseshoe-shaped **Galvans Gorge** is less than 1km off the road, at the 286km mark. The gorge has a swimming hole, but no camping. It's then another 20km to Mt Barnett Roadhouse.

Mt Barnett & Manning Gorge

The Mt Barnett Roadhouse (☎ 9191 7007) is at the 306km point and is owned and run by the Kupingarri Aboriginal community. The *roadhouse* and small *general store* (ice is available) are open daily from 7 am to 6 pm, from May to October. It's also the access point for **Manning Gorge**, 7km off the road along an easy dirt track. The $7 entry fee covers camping.

The *camping ground* is by a lovely waterhole, but the best part of the gorge is about a 1¼-hour walk along the far bank – walk around the right of the waterhole to pick up the track, which is marked with empty drink cans strung up in trees. It's a strenuous walk; carry some drinking water.

Mt Barnett to Wyndham-Kununurra Road

The **Barnett River Gorge** turn-off is at 328km. This is another good swimming spot, 3km down a side road. *Mt Elizabeth Station (☎ 9191 4644)* lies 30km off the road at the 338km mark. Homestead accommodation is available but must be arranged in advance ($105/60 per adult/child for dinner and B&B). Camping is $7 per person.

At 406km you come to the turn-off to the spectacular **Mitchell Plateau** (172km) and the **Kalumburu Aboriginal community** (267km). This is remote, 4WD-only territory and should not be undertaken without adequate preparation; an entry permit is required for Kalumburu (see the following Kalumburu Rd section).

There's magnificent scenery between the Kalumburu turn-off and Jack's (Joe's) Waterhole on **Durack River Station** (☎ 9161 4324) at 524km. There is no camping at Campbell Creek (451km) or the Durack River (496km). At 476km there is a turn-off to *Ellenbrae Station* (☎ 9161 4325), 6km further down a side road; camping costs $7, and dinner and B&B is $95 per person.

Jack's Waterhole is 8km down a side road at 524km and, apart from fuel, there's homestead accommodation ($20 per person; $55 with meals) and camping here ($6).

At 579km you get some excellent views of the Cockburn Ranges to the north, as well as the Cambridge Gulf and the twin rivers (the Pentecost and the Durack). Shortly after (2km or so) is the turn-off to *Home Valley Station* (☎ 9161 4322), which has camping ($6/3 for adults/children) and bunkhouse accommodation for $25 per person ($75 with meals).

The large **Pentecost River** is forded at 590km and this crossing can be dodgy if there's water in the river.

El Questro Station & Wilderness Park (☎ 9169 1777) is the best known station in the east Kimberley – it's close enough to Kununurra to visit on a day trip and it's usually accessible by conventional vehicle. Attractions include **El Questro Gorge**, **Zebedee Springs** and boat rides up the **Chamberlain Gorge**. There are excellent riverside camp sites for $10 per person, comfortable bungalows for $105/140 and expensive homestead accommodation for a whopping $640 per person, as well as a bar, restaurant and shop. Also part of El Questro Wilderness Park is **Emma Gorge**, back on the Gibb River Rd at 623km. It's about a 40 minute walk along this spectacular gorge to a pool with a high droplet waterfall. Wilderness *cabin accommodation* costs $70/103 ($120 with en suite), and there's a good licensed restaurant, bar and pool. The $5 fee to walk Emma Gorge is waived if you stay or eat here.

At 630km you cross King River and at 647km you finally hit the bitumen road;

Wyndham lies 48km to the north-west, Kununurra 52km east.

KALUMBURU ROAD

This dirt road traverses extremely rocky terrain in an isolated area. Distances in the following description are given from the junction of the Gibb River and Kalumburu roads. The junction is 419km from the Derby Hwy and 248km from the Great Northern Hwy (Wyndham to Kununurra).

It's recommended that you get a permit before entering Kalumburu Reserve. Phone the community on ☎ 9161 4300 (or fax 9161 4331) weekdays between 7 am and noon.

Gibb River Road to Mitchell Plateau

The Gibb River is crossed at 3km and Plain Creek at 16km. The first fuel stop is at *Drysdale River Station* (☎ 9161 4326) at 59km; the homestead is 1km down a side road. You can also buy supplies and camp here ($2.50) or stay in B&B units for $25.

At 62km you can turn off to the **Miners Pool** picnic and *camping area*. It is 3.5km to the river and the last 200m is slow going; entry is $2/1.

The road reaches the Mitchell Plateau turn-off at 172km. From this junction it is 70km along the Mitchell Plateau Rd to the turn-off to the spectacular, multi-tiered **Mitchell Falls**. The falls are 16km downhill from this turn-off; from the last car park (13km) it's a 3km walk (allow a full day for the excursion). You usually can't get into the falls until late May.

As this is a remote area, be sure to bring plenty of basic necessities. In the Dry the falls are like any other, with water falling from the centre of the terraces. In the Wet they are vastly different – the muddied water stretches from escarpment to escarpment and thunders down submerged terraces.

You can *camp* at the King Edward River (don't use soap in the watercourse) and at Mitchell Falls car park.

Mitchell Plateau to Kalumburu

From the Mitchell Plateau turn-off, the road heads north-east towards Kalumburu, passing *Theda Station* (☎ 9161 4329) where there is camping ($9) or homestead accommodation ($85). There are also Aboriginal Bradshaw painting tours here. You cross the Carson River at 247km.

The **Kalumburu Aboriginal community** (☎ 9161 4300) is at 267km, about 5km from the mouth of the King Edward River and King Edward Gorge. The picturesque mission is set among giant mango trees and coconut palms. There is *accommodation* (entry is $25 per vehicle) and a *store*; food and all types of fuel are available from Monday to Friday from 7 to 11 am and 1.30 to 4 pm, and on Saturday until 11 am.

Drysdale River National Park

Very few people get into 4000 sq km Drysdale River, WA's most northern national park, 150km west of Wyndham. It's one of the most remote parks in Australia – it has no road access – and is the home of the mysterious, ancient Bradshaw art figures and the more recent Wandjina art figures. (See the 'Aboriginal Art' special section for details.)

Rainforest, which until 1965 was thought not to exist in WA, is found in pockets along the Carson Escarpment and in some gorges. At the mouth of the King George River are the spectacular, split **King George Falls**, best seen from the air.

A permit is necessary to enter this national park; get one from the CALM offices in Derby or Kununurra.

Organised Tours

An increasing number of 4WD outfits cross the Gibb River Rd from both directions.

Wandjina rock art

Kununurra's Desert Inn (☎ 1800 805 010) runs five-day camping trips along the Gibb River Rd (from Kununurra or Broome) for $650. Kimberley Wilderness Adventures (☎ 1800 804 005) has a four day tent safari from Broome for $695, or a seven day trip with station accommodation from Kununurra for $1695. Its five day Mitchell Plateau Explorer is $895.

DEVONIAN REEF NATIONAL PARKS

The west Kimberley boasts three national parks, based on gorges which were once part of a western coral 'great barrier reef' in the Devonian era, 350 million years ago.

The magnificent **Geikie Gorge** is 18km north-east of Fitzroy Crossing. Part of the gorge, on the Fitzroy River, is in a small national park. During the Wet the river rises nearly 17m and in the Dry it stops flowing, leaving only a series of water holes.

The vegetation around this beautiful gorge is dense and there is also much wildlife, including freshwater crocodiles, wallaroos and the rare black-footed wallaby. Visitors must stick to the prescribed 1.5km west-bank walking track at all times.

During the Dry (April to November) CALM operates a one hour boat trip up the river daily at 8 and 11 am and 3 pm ($17.50/2).

You can visit the spectacular formations of Windjana Gorge and Tunnel Creek from the Gibb River Rd, or make a detour off the main highway between Fitzroy Crossing and Derby onto Leopold Station Rd.

The walls of **Windjana Gorge** soar 90m above the Lennard River, which rushes through in the Wet but becomes just a series of pools in the Dry. You'll almost certainly see freshwater crocodiles sunning themselves on the sand banks or gliding through the pools here. It gets very hot in the gorge during the afternoon so bring plenty of water, especially if you intend to make the 7km return walk from the camping ground to the end of the gorge. *Camping* costs $8 for two.

Three kilometres from the river are the ruins of **Lillimooloora**, an early homestead and, from 1893, a police outpost. It was here that Aboriginal tracker Jandamarra shot Constable Richardson (see the 'Jandamarra ('Pigeon')' boxed text).

Tunnel Creek is a 750m-long passage that the creek has cut through a spur of the Napier Range. The tunnel is generally from 3m to 15m wide and you can walk all the way along it. You'll need a torch and a change of shoes (preferably sandals); be prepared to wade through cold, knee deep water in places. Don't attempt it during the Wet, as the creek may flood suddenly. There are several Aboriginal paintings on the walls at either end of

Jandamarra ('Pigeon')

Windjana Gorge, Tunnel Creek and Lillimooloora were the setting for the legendary exploits of the outlaw Aboriginal tracker Jandamarra, nicknamed 'Pigeon'. As a teenager Jandamarra, a member of the Bunuba tribe, was a highly skilled stockman working on the Lennard River Station. His skills eventually led him to become an armed tracker working with the local police to capture Aborigines who were spearing sheep.

In October 1894, Pigeon's tribal loyalty got the better of him – he shot a police colleague at Lillimooloora, freed his captured tribesmen and escaped to lead a band of dissident Bunuba people who evaded search parties for almost three years. Despite being seriously wounded in a shootout at Windjana Gorge only a month after his escape, Pigeon survived and continued to taunt the settlers with raids and vanishing acts.

During this time Pigeon killed another four men. In 1897 he was finally trapped and killed near his hideout at Tunnel Creek. He and his small band had hidden in the seemingly inaccessible gullies of the adjoining Napier Range.

For the full story, get a copy of the *Pigeon Heritage Trail* from the Derby or Broome tourist bureaus ($1.50), or the more detailed *Jandamarra and the Bunuba Resistance* by Howard Pedersen & Banjo Woorunmurra.

the tunnel. Halfway through, a collapse has created a shaft to the top of the range.

Over the Top Adventure Tours (☎ 9193 7700) operates popular two-day trips from Broome, combining Windjana and Tunnel Creek with Geikie Gorge ($275). For details of day tours out of Derby and Fitzroy Crossing, see those sections in this chapter.

FITZROY CROSSING
- postcode 6765 • pop 1150

A tiny settlement where the Great Northern Hwy crosses the Fitzroy River, this is a convenient access point for Geikie and Windjana gorges. The old town site is on Russ St, north-east of the present town. The Crossing Inn, near Brooking Creek, is the oldest pub in the Kimberley.

The flash Fitzroy Crossing tourist bureau (☎ 9191 5355) is on the highway next to the service station and is also the depot for the Perth-Darwin Greyhound (which unfortunately arrives at 1.30 am going in either direction). It's open daily from 9 am to 6 pm from April to October (fewer hours during the Wet), and there's a gallery of Aboriginal art inside.

See the previous Devonian Reef National Parks section for information on nearby Geikie Gorge.

Organised Tours
Bungoolee Tours and Fitzroy Crossing Tours work in conjunction to offer excellent 4WD day trips to Windjana Gorge and Tunnel Creek on Tuesday, Thursday, Friday and Sunday (May to September). The cost is $85 and tours can be booked at the tourist bureau. Bungoolee Tours, run by Bunuba guide, Dylan, is also planning cultural camping trips onto traditional Aboriginal land – again ask at the tourist bureau.

You can also take an informative 1½ hour stroll along the Fitzroy River banks with Dylan, who explains bush tucker and the area's significance to the local Aboriginal people ($15).

Places to Stay & Eat
The *Fitzroy River Lodge Motel Hotel & Caravan Park* (☎ 9191 5141, 1800 355

WESTERN AUSTRALIA

266, Great Northern Hwy), 2km east of town beside the Fitzroy River, is overpriced but has an excellent camping area with tent/powered sites for $16/18 for two. Single/double self-contained air-con safari tents cost $90/110 and motel units cost $115/140.

The ***Darlngunaya Backpackers*** *(☎ 9191 5140, Russ Rd)* is in the Old Post Office, about 4km from town. It has beds from $15 and self-contained houses for $110 for two. There are bikes and canoes for hire. Pick-up from the Greyhound bus (which stops outside the tourist office) costs $5. Swollen waterways can make Darlngunaya inaccessible by car, so it closes in the wet.

The *Crossing Inn* (☎ 9191 5080, Sanford Rd) has standard en suite rooms for $70/85. It can get pretty noisy here as there is a boisterous (and at times unsavoury) bar next door, but the motel part is kept separated. There's also a reasonably priced a la carte restaurant here – call ahead if you just want to stop by for lunch or dinner.

There's not much incentive to dine out in Fitzroy Crossing. *Maxine's* in the Fitzroy River Lodge serves expensive but reasonable meals and there's a bar.

HALLS CREEK
• postcode 6770   • pop 1260

Halls Creek, in the centre of the Kimberley and on the edge of the Great Sandy Desert, was traditionally the land of the Jaru and Kija people. White pastoralists arrived in the 1870s and gold was found at Halls Creek, 14km from the present town, in 1885. This was WA's first gold rush, but it didn't last long and all that remains are a few abandoned mines and the crumbling ruins of the original settlement.

The Halls Creek tourist centre (☎ 9168 6262) on the Great Northern Hwy is open daily from 8 am to 4 pm from April to November; it handles bookings for tours.

Five kilometres east of Halls Creek and then about 1.5km off the road is the **China Wall**. This subvertical quartz vein is short, but picturesquely situated.

Halls Creek **Old Town** is a great place for fossicking. All that remains of the once bustling mining town are the ant-bed and

spinifex walls of the old post office, the cemetery and a huge bottle pile where a pub once stood. You can swim in Caroline Pool, Sawpit Gorge and Palm Springs.

Places to Stay & Eat
The *Halls Creek Caravan Park* (☎ 9168 6169, 1800 355 228, Roberta Ave) has tent/powered sites for $12/14 and on-site vans for $38 for two.

The *Kimberley Hotel* (☎ 9168 6101, Roberta Ave), opposite, has a variety of overpriced 'budget' singles/doubles (at the front) for $60/80, and a much nicer deluxe version for $115/140. The hotel has a pleasant bar with standard counter meals as well as a swish restaurant with smorgasbord meals.

The *Halls Creek Motel* (☎ 9168 6001, 194 Great Northern Hwy) has air-con units for $63/78.

Getting There & Away
Greyhound Pioneer buses pass through Halls Creek early in the morning (northbound) and late at night (southbound), stopping at the Poinciana Roadhouse.

WOLFE CREEK METEORITE CRATER
The 835m-wide and 50m-deep Wolfe Creek meteorite crater is the second-largest crater in the world where meteorite fragments have been found. To the local Jaru Aboriginal people, the crater, which they call 'Kandimalal', marks the spot where a huge snake emerged from the ground.

The turn-off to the Wolfe Creek Crater is 16km out of Halls Creek towards Fitzroy Crossing and from there it's 130km by unsealed road to the south. It's accessible without 4WD (with care), but you'll need to carry enough fuel, food and water for a return trip. If you can't handle one more outback road, you can fly over the crater from Halls Creek for $100 (per person): try Oasis Airlines (☎ 9168 6462).

BUNGLE BUNGLE (PURNULULU) NATIONAL PARK
The 3000 sq km Bungle Bungle (Purnululu) National Park should not be missed. It's an

amazing spectacle with its spectacular rounded rock towers, striped like tigers in alternate bands of orange (silica) and black (lichen). The only hitches are that the formations are hard to get to, and because the rock is fragile you are not allowed to climb them. The name purnululu means sandstone in the local Kija dialect and bungle bungle is thought to be a misspelling of bundle bundle, a common grass.

Echidna Chasm in the north or **Cathedral Gorge** in the south are only about a one hour walk from the car park. The soaring **Piccaninny Gorge** is an 18km round trip that takes eight to 10 hours to walk. Access to the park costs $8 per vehicle (CALM park passes are valid), plus $7 a night for two people camping. The restricted gorges in the northern part of the park can only be seen from the air, but they are a memorable sight.

From the main highway it's 55km to a track junction known as Three Ways. From here it's 20 minutes north to *Kurrajong Camping Area* and 45 minutes south to *Bellburn Camping Area*. Fire sites and firewood are supplied. Kurrajong, for casual visitors, has long-drop toilets, drinking water and fireplaces with firewood. Bellburn is mainly for tour groups and is similarly equipped.

Scenic Flights & Tours
As the range is so vast, flights and helicopter rides over the Bungles are popular – it's money well spent, although on the flights from Kununurra your time over the range itself is quite short. The chopper rides, operated by Heliwork WA (part of Slingair, ☎ 9168 7337), are more impressive as they fly right in, among and over the deep, narrow gorges, while light planes must remain above 700m. Helicopter rides cost $160 for a 45 minute flight from Purnululu airstrip, or $170 in a faster helicopter from Turkey Creek on the main highway. This latter flight is a popular alternative option for people without a 4WD.

Flights from Kununurra are $160 (see that section later). Out of Halls Creek, flights are $120 with Oasis Air (☎ 9168 6462).

If you don't have a 4WD the best option is a tour from Kununurra or Turkey Creek.

Desert Inn 4WD Adventure (☎ 1800 805 010) offer two/three-day tours for $260/390. East Kimberley Tours (☎ 9168 2213) charges $318/528 for a day/overnight combined flight-4WD trip.

Alternatively, you can hire a 4WD at the Poinciana Roadhouse (☎ 9168 6164) in Halls Creek for $100 a day.

WYNDHAM
● postcode 6740   ● pop 850
Wyndham is a sprawling town consisting of the present town centre and the historic port area 5km further on. It suffers from Kununurra's boom in popularity and from being well off the main Perth-Darwin route, but the **Five Rivers Lookout** on top of Mt Bastion is still a must. From there you can see the King, Pentecost, Durack, Forrest and Ord rivers enter the Cambridge Gulf. The view is particularly good at sunrise and sunset.

Local information is available from Kimberley Motors (☎ 9161 1281) on the Great Northern Hwy. This is real crocodile country (a hideous 20m concrete croc greets you as you arrive in town) and when the tide is right you can observe (from a distance) large saltwater crocs near the water. Safer, but no less awesome, is the **Wyndham Crocodile Farm** on Barytes Rd. There are some monster salties here, as well as a breeding program and Komodo dragons. It's open daily from 8.30 am to 4 pm, with guided tours at 11 am ($10).

Not far from Wyndham is the **Marlgu Billabong** on Parry Lagoons Reserve, a wetlands that hosts many bird species.

Kimberley Pursuits (☎ 9161 1029), at Digger's Rest Station, 35km from Wyndham, has **horse trekking** from two to seven days ($250 to $890 all inclusive).

Places to Stay & Eat
The *Three Mile Caravan Park (☎ 9161 1064, Baker St)* has tent sites for $7 per person ($3 extra for power) and a massive boab tree. *Gulf Breeze Guest House (☎/fax 9161 1401, 6 O'Donnell St)* in Wyndham Port is a laid back little place with a kitchen, garden and pool. Singles are $30, twins $50

and there's a large family room that groups can use for $50.

The **Wyndham Town Hotel** (☎ *9161 1202, O'Donnell St*) nearby has single/double motel units for $50/80. You can also get reasonable counter meals here and breakfast from 7.30 am.

KUNUNURRA
● postcode 6743   ● pop 4900

In the Miriwoong language, this region is known as 'gananoorrang' – Kununurra is the European version of this word. Founded in the 1960s, Kununurra is in the centre of the Ord River irrigation scheme, and is quite a modern and bustling little town. Tourism has developed quickly here and there are enough adventure and recreational activities, mostly water-based, to keep you busy for a week.

This is also a popular place to seek work. The main fruit picking season starts in May and ends in September. Ask at the Kununurra Backpackers, Desert Inn or the tourist bureau.

Information
The tourist bureau (☎ 9168 1177) on Coolibah Drive has lots of information on the town and the Kimberley, including some colourful publications on the Gibb River Rd and Ord River area. It's open daily from 8 am to 5.30 pm.

The telecentre on Banksia St (next to Slingair) has Internet access for $10 an hour (no minimum). For national park information and passes, the CALM office (☎ 9168 0200) is on Konkerberry Drive.

There's a 1½ hour time difference between Kununurra and Katherine in the NT. Strict quarantine restrictions apply when entering WA (don't bring fruit etc).

Lake Kununurra (Diversion Dam)
Lily Creek Lagoon is a mini-wetlands beside the town and has plenty of bird life. Lake Kununurra, also called the Diversion Dam, has picnic spots and is popular with water-skiers and boating enthusiasts. There's good fishing below the Lower Dam, and also on the Ord River at **Ivanhoe Crossing** (on the old road to Wyndham) – popular with locals for barra fishing. If you dare to swim there, be careful of the crocs.

Other Attractions
There are good views of the irrigated fields from **Kelly's Knob**, a favourite sunset viewpoint. During the Wet, distant thunderstorms are spectacular when viewed from the lookout, although the knob is frequently struck by lightning.

Hidden Valley, in **Mirima National Park** and only 2km from the town centre, is a wonderful area with a steep gorge, great views and short walking tracks. The banded formations in the park are reminiscent of the Bungle Bungles and are of great spiritual importance to the Miriwoong people.

The **Packsaddle Plains**, 6km south-east of town, has the touristy Zebra Rock Gallery. Further along this road you'll find farms (producing bananas and mangos) that are open to the public. It's worth a trip out to the **Kimberley Dairy**, a working dairy farm just off Ivanhoe Rd, to try a milkshake – 34 flavours of bliss!

Organised Tours & Flights
Self-guided canoe trips on the Ord River, between Lake Argyle and the Diversion Dam, are popular with travellers and a lot of fun. The best place to arrange them is at the backpacker hostels. Big Waters Kimberley Canoe Safaris (☎ 1800 641 998) has recommended three-day trips for $120. Kimberley Canoeing Experience (☎ 1800 805 010) also has three-day tours for $120 with camping at established river sites, as well as one/two day trips ($105/160) for the less adventurous.

Barramundi is the major fishing attraction, but other fish are also caught and there are several charter operators. Full-day boat trips with Macka's Barra Camp (☎ 9169 1759) cost $190. Triple J Tours (☎ 9168 2682) has high speed cruises along 55km of the Ord between Lake Argyle and Kununurra. A morning cruise in the high season costs $60/30 for adults/children.

Duncan's Ord River Tours (☎ 9168 1823) on Lake Kununurra visit banana plantations on Packsaddle Plains and areas of prolific

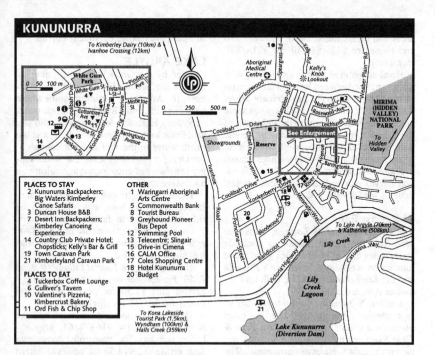

KUNUNURRA

To Kimberley Dairy (10km) &
Ivanhoe Crossing (12km)

PLACES TO STAY
2 Kununurra Backpackers;
   Big Waters Kimberley
   Canoe Safaris
3 Duncan House B&B
7 Desert Inn Backpackers;
   Kimberley Canoeing
   Experience
14 Country Club Private Hotel;
   Chopsticks; Kelly's Bar & Grill
19 Town Caravan Park
21 Kimberleyland Caravan Park

PLACES TO EAT
4 Tuckerbox Coffee Lounge
6 Gulliver's Tavern
10 Valentine's Pizzeria;
   Kimbercrust Bakery
11 Ord Fish & Chip Shop

OTHER
1 Waringarri Aboriginal
   Arts Centre
5 Commonwealth Bank
8 Tourist Bureau
9 Greyhound Pioneer
   Bus Depot
12 Swimming Pool
13 Telecentre; Slingair
15 Drive-in Cimena
16 CALM Office
17 Coles Shopping Centre
18 Hotel Kununurra
20 Budget

To Kona Lakeside
Tourist Park (1.5km),
Wyndham (100km) &
Halls Creek (359km)

bird life; the four hour tour is $50/30. Kununurra Cruises (☎ 9168 1718) has economical sunset cruises for $27/15.

Kimberley Ecotours (☎ 9168 2116) has two interesting and informative wildlife tours. The morning tour (from 6 to 8 am) focuses on wetland bird species ($30/20) and the evening tour (from 5 to 7 pm) on crocodile biology and nocturnal wildlife ($35/25).

Flights over Purnululu are popular and cost about $160 a person. They take about two hours, and also fly over Lake Argyle, the Argyle and Bow River diamond mines and the irrigation area north of the town. Contact Alligator Airways (☎ 1800 632 533) or Slingair (☎ 1800 095 500). Most of these tours can also be booked through the tourist bureau.

Places to Stay

The **Town Caravan Park** (☎ 9168 1763, Bloodwood Drive) is central and has tent/powered sites from $16/18, on-site vans for $60 ($50 in the low season) and cabins for $90. There's a camp kitchen with fridge. **Kimberleyland Caravan Park** (☎ 9168 1280, Victoria Hwy) charges $14/16 for tent/powered sites.

Kona Lakeside Tourist Park (☎ 9168 1031, Lakeview Drive), the pick of the parks, is about 1km from town and well situated on the lake. Tent/powered sites are $14/16, on-site vans are $50 and budget cabins are $65.

Kununurra Backpackers (☎ 9169 1998, 1800 641 998, 112 Nutwood Crescent) is a friendly, well-run place about five minutes walk from the town centre. One section is set aside for travellers working in the area, so long and short termers are well looked after. Dorm beds cost $16, triples $17 and twins/doubles $40 ($1 discount for YHA/VIP). There's a big back yard and shaded pool, and the owners run adventure tours.

The **Desert Inn Backpackers** (☎ 9168 2702, 257 Konkerberry Drive), opposite Gulliver's Tavern in the centre of town, is secure and again has a pool, plenty of sitting areas and offers tours. Dorm beds are $16 and twins are $42 ($15/40 for YHA/VIP members).

Hotel accommodation is expensive, with a big variation between low and high season tariffs. The *Country Club Private Hotel* (☎ 9168 1024, 76 Coolibah Drive) has some pokey budget twin rooms in the older part of the complex for $50/60 for one/two people with shared facilities – well overpriced. Motel rooms start at $140 in the high season.

Duncan House (☎ 9168 2436, 167 Coolibah Drive) is a stylish B&B with singles/doubles for $85/95.

Places to Eat

The *Tuckerbox Coffee Lounge*, across the road from the tourist bureau, is good for sandwiches and rolls, and does good value lunches on weekdays. *Valentine's Pizzeria* and the *Kimbercrust Bakery*, both on Cottontree Ave, are open daily.

Gulliver's Tavern (Konkerberry Drive) is a popular drinking spot and is a good place for a counter meal. The *Ord Fish & Chip Shop* nearby is the place to go if you haven't caught your own barramundi. The Country Club has the Chinese *Chopsticks* (main courses for $17.50) and its *Kelly's Bar & Grill* has excellent steaks served in a tropical setting.

Getting There & Away

Ansett (☎ 13 1300) has flights to Darwin and Perth daily. The Perth service stops in Broome.

Greyhound Pioneer (☎ 13 2030) passes through Kununurra on the Darwin-Perth route at 9.45 am southbound and 5 pm

northbound; the terminal is in the shire office car park next to the tourist bureau.

LAKE ARGYLE

Created by the Ord River Dam, Lake Argyle is the second-biggest storage reservoir in Australia, holding somewhere between nine and 18 times as much water as Sydney Harbour, depending on who you ask. Prior to its construction, there was too much water in the Wet and not enough in the Dry. By providing a regular water supply the dam has encouraged agriculture on a massive scale.

There's also some of the most spectacular scenery in WA here, with high, steep red ridges plunging into the lake's blue waters.

There's a **pioneer museum** in the old Argyle Homestead, moved here when its original site was flooded.

The *Lake Argyle Tourist Village* (☎ 9168 7360, Parker Rd) has tent sites for $6 per person plus $3.50 for power, and motel rooms for $65/75 for singles/doubles.

There are two boat trips operated by Lake Argyle Cruises (☎ 9168 7361, argyle@hobbit.com.au). The *Bowerbird* does a two hour cruise ($29/14.50 for adults/children) at 10 am, and the *Silver Cobbler* a six hour cruise ($95/60) at noon. There's also a sunset cruise at 3 pm ($35/17.50). These cruises are thoroughly recommended – the immensity of this inland sea is not fully appreciated until you are out in the middle of it all.

About 150km south of Kununurra is the huge **Argyle Diamond Mine**, which produces around 35% of the world's diamonds, although most are only of industrial quality. A six hour fly-in tour costs $220 per person – book through Belray's (☎ 1800 632 533).

Glossary

Australian English

Any visitor from abroad who thinks Australian (that's 'Strine') is simply a weird variant of English/American will soon have a few surprises. For a start many Australians don't even speak Australian – they speak Italian, Lebanese, Vietnamese, Turkish or Greek.

Those who do speak the native tongue are liable to lose you in a strange collection of Australian words. The meaning of some words in Australia is completely different from that in other English-speaking countries; some commonly used words have been shortened almost beyond recognition. Others are derived from Aboriginal languages, or from the slang used by early convict settlers.

There is a slight regional variation in the Australian accent, while the difference between city and country speech is mainly a matter of speed. Some of the most famed Aussie words are hardly heard at all – 'mates' are more common than 'cobbers'. If you want to pass for a native try speaking slightly nasally, shortening any word of more than two syllables and then adding a vowel to the end of it, making anything you can into a diminutive (even the Hell's Angels become mere 'bikies') and peppering your speech with as many expletives as possible. Lonely Planet publishes an *Australian phrasebook*, which is an introduction to both Australian English and Aboriginal languages, and the list that follows may also help:

arvo – afternoon

back o' Bourke – back of beyond, middle of nowhere
bail out – leave
banana bender – resident of Queensland
barbie – barbecue (BBQ)
barrack – cheer on team at sporting event, support (ie 'who do you barrack for?')
bastard – general form of address which can mean many things, from high praise or respect ('He's the bravest bastard I know') to dire insult ('You rotten bastard!'). Only use on males, and avoid if unsure!
bathers – swimming costume (Victoria)
battler – hard trier, struggler
beaut, beauty, bewdie – great, fantastic
bevan – *bogan* in Queensland
big mobs – a large amount, heaps
bikies – motorcyclists
billabong – water hole in dried up riverbed; more correctly an ox-bow bend cut off in the dry season by receding waters
billy – tin container used to boil water in the bush
bitumen – surfaced road
black stump – where the 'back o' Bourke' begins
block, do your – lose your temper
bloke – man
blokey – exhibiting characteristics considered typically male
blow-in – stranger
blowies, blow flies – large flies
bludger – lazy person, one who refuses to work
blue – to have an argument or fight (ie 'have a blue')
bogan – young, unsophisticated person
bonzer – great, ripper
boogie board – half-sized surf board
boomer – very big; a particularly large male kangaroo
boomerang – a curved flat wooden instrument used by Aboriginal people for hunting
booner – *bogan* in ACT
booze bus – police van used for random breath testing for alcohol
bot – to scrounge or obtain by begging or borrowing
bottle shop – liquor shop, off-licence
Buckley's – no chance at all, ie 'you've got Buckley's'
bug (Moreton Bay bug) – a small, edible crustacean
bull dust – fine and sometimes deep dust on outback roads; also bullshit
bunyip – mythical bush spirit

burl – have a try (ie 'give it a burl')

bush, the – country; anywhere away from the city

bushbash – to force your way through pathless bush

bushranger – Australia's equivalent of the outlaws of the American wild west (some goodies, some baddies)

bush tucker – native foods, found in the Outback

BYO restaurant – one that allows you to 'bring your own' alcohol

camp oven – large, cast-iron pot with lid, used for cooking on an open fire

cark it – to die

cask – wine box (another great Australian invention)

CDEP – Community Development Employment Program (work for the dole scheme)

chiga – *bogan* in Tasmania

Chiko roll – vile Australian junk food

chocka – completely full; from 'chock-a-block'

chook – chicken

chuck a U-ey – do a U-turn, turn a car around within a road

clobber – to hit; also clothes

clout – to hit

cobber – friend, mate (archaic)

cocky – small-scale farmer

come good – turn out all right

coolamon – Aboriginal wooden carrying dish

cool drink – soft drink in WA

counter meal, countery – pub meal

cow cocky – small-scale cattle farmer

cozzie – swimming costume (NSW)

crack the shits – lose your temper; also 'crack a mental'

crook – ill, badly made, substandard

crow eater – resident of SA

cut lunch – sandwiches

dag, daggy – dirty lump of wool at back end of a sheep; also an affectionate or mildly abusive term for a socially inept person

daks – trousers

damper – bush loaf made from flour and water and cooked in a camp oven

dead horse – rhyming slang for tomato sauce

dead set – true, dinkum

deli – *milk bar* in SA and WA, but a delicatessen elsewhere

didgeridoo – cylindrical wooden musical instrument traditionally played by Aboriginal men

Digger – mate (archaic; from Australian and New Zealand soldiers in WWI)

dill – idiot

dilly bag – Aboriginal carry bag

dinkum, fair dinkum – honest, genuine

dinky-di – the real thing

dip out – to miss out or fail

dob in – to tell on someone

donga – small, transportable building widely used in the Outback

drongo – worthless or stupid person

Dry, the – dry season in northern Australia (April to October)

duco – car paint

dunny – outdoor lavatory

earbash – talk nonstop

esky – large insulated box for keeping beer etc cold

fair dinkum – see *dinkum*

fair go! – give us a break

flake – shark meat, used in fish and chips

flat out – very busy or fast

floater – meat pie floating in pea soup – yum!

flog – sell, steal

fossick – hunt for gems or semiprecious stones

freshie – freshwater crocodile (the harmless, unless provoked, one); new *tinny* of beer

furphy – a rumour or false story

galah – noisy parrot, thus noisy idiot

game – brave (ie 'game as Ned Kelly')

gander – look (ie 'have a gander')

g'day – good day; traditional Australian greeting

gibber – Aboriginal word for a stone or rock, hence gibber plain or desert

give it away – give up

gnamma – Aboriginal water holes

good on ya – well done

grazier – large-scale sheep or cattle farmer
grog – general term for alcoholic drinks
grouse – very good

homestead – residence of a station owner or manager
hoon – idiot, hooligan, yahoo
how are ya? – standard greeting (expected answer: 'good, thanks, how are you?')

icy-pole – frozen lollipop, ice lolly
iffy – dodgy, questionable
indie – independent music bands

jackaroo – young male trainee on an outback station (farm)
jillaroo – young female trainee on an outback station
jocks – men's underpants
journo – journalist
jumped-up – a person who is full of self-importance, arrogant

kick the bucket – to die
Kiwi – New Zealander
knacker – testicle
knackered – broken; tired
knock – criticise, deride
knocker – one who knocks; woman's breast
Koori – Aboriginal person (mostly south of the Murray River)

lair – layabout, ruffian
lairising – acting like a lair
lamington – square of sponge cake covered in chocolate icing and coconut
larrikin – hooligan, mischievous youth
lay-by – put a deposit on an article so the shop will hold it for you
lemon – faulty product, a dud
lob in – drop in (to see someone)
lollies – sweets, candy
lurk – a scheme

mate – general term of familiarity, whether you know the person or not
milk bar – small shop selling milk and other basic provisions
Mod Oz – innovative adaptation of international cuisines
mozzies – mosquitoes

nature strip – strip of land between two carriageways where trees and bushes are grown
never-never – remote country in the Outback
no-hoper – hopeless case
no worries – no problems; that's OK

ocker – an uncultivated or boorish Australian; a knocker or derider
off-sider – assistant or partner
Outback – remote part of the bush, back o' Bourke

paddock – a fenced area of land, usually intended for livestock
pastoralist – large-scale grazier
pavlova – traditional Australian meringue and cream dessert, named after the Russian ballerina Anna Pavlova
perve – to gaze with lust
piker – someone who doesn't pull their weight, or chickens out
piss – beer
piss turn – boozy party, also piss-up
pissed – drunk
pissed off – annoyed
piss weak – no good, gutless
plonk – cheap wine
pokies – poker machines
Pom – English person
postie – mailman
pot – large beer glass (Victoria); beer gut; to sink a billiard ball

Queenslander – a high-set weatherboard house, noted for its wide verandah and sometimes ornate lattice-work

rapt – delighted, enraptured
ratbag – friendly term of abuse
ratshit (RS) – lousy
reckon! – you bet!, absolutely!
rego – car registration (ie 'car rego')
rellie – relative
ridgy-didge – original, genuine
ring-in – a substitute or outsider
ripper – good (also 'little ripper')
road train – a large truck; a semitrailer towing several trailers
root – have sexual intercourse
rooted – tired; broken

ropable – very bad-tempered or angry
RSL – Returned Serviceman's League
rubbish – deride, tease (ie 'to rubbish')

saltie – saltwater crocodile (the dangerous one)
Salvo – member of the Salvation Army
sandgroper – resident of WA
scallops – fried potato cakes (Queensland, NSW); shellfish
schooner – large beer glass (NSW, SA)
scrub – bush
sea wasp – deadly box jellyfish
sealed road – bitumen road
session – lengthy period of heavy alcohol drinking
shanks's pony – to travel on foot
shark biscuit – an inexperienced surfer
sheila – woman
shellacking – comprehensive defeat
she'll be right – no problems, no worries
shonky – unreliable
shoot through – leave in a hurry
shout – buy a round of drinks (ie 'it's your shout')
sickie – day off work ill (or malingering)
skimpy – scantily clad barmaid
slab – carton of beer bottles or cans
smoko – tea break
snag – sausage
spag bol – spaghetti bolognese
sparrow's fart – dawn
squatter – pioneer farmer who occupied land as a tenant of the government
station – large farm
sticky beak – nosy person
stinger – jellyfish
strides – trousers, *daks*
stroppy – bad-tempered
Stubbies – popular brand of men's work shorts
stubby – 375ml bottle of beer
sunbake – sunbathe (well, the sun's hot in Australia)
swag – canvas-covered bed roll used in the Outback; also a large amount

tall poppies – achievers (*knockers* like to cut them down)
tea – evening meal
thingo – thing, whatchamacallit, doovelacki, thingamajig
thongs – flip-flops; an ocker's idea of formal footwear
tinny – 375ml can of beer; also a small, aluminium fishing dinghy (NT)
togs – swimming costume (Queensland, Victoria)
too right! – absolutely!
Top End – northern part of the NT
trucky – truck driver
true blue – dinkum
tucker – food
two-pot screamer – person unable to hold their drink
two-up – traditional heads/tails gambling game

ute – utility, pick-up truck

wag – to skip school or work (ie 'to wag')
walkabout – lengthy walk away from it all (ie 'to go walkabout')
weatherboard – timber cladding on house
Wet, the – rainy season in the north (November to May)
whinge – complain, moan
wobbly – disturbing, unpredictable behaviour (ie 'throw a wobbly')
woomera – stick used by Aboriginal people for throwing spears
woop-woop – Outback; miles from anywhere
wowser – someone who doesn't believe in having fun; a spoilsport; teetotaller

yabbie – small freshwater crayfish
yakka – work (from an Aboriginal language)
yobbo – uncouth, aggressive person
yonks – ages, a long time
youse – plural of you; pronounced 'yooze'; only used by the grammatically challenged

Acknowledgments

THANKS

Many thanks to the travellers who used the last edition and wrote to us with helpful hints, useful advice and interesting anecdotes:

A E Vletter, A J Saddler, A Keller, Abby Harwood, Adam Stott, Aidan Kenny, Alan & Baryl Camp, Alan Blackshaw, Alan Boyle, Alan Hakim, Alan Kendall, Albert Baques, Alec Bamber, Alex Gardner, Alexandra Saidy, Alexandre Choueiri, Alicia McCoy, Alicia Reid, Alison & Simon Porges, Alison Cameron, Alison Moore, Alisson Ogle, Allison Horsfell, Amanda Beaman, Amir Alon, Amy Reiter, Ana Lamo, Andor Savelkouls, Andre Neumann, Andrea Intelligenza, Andreas Huber, Andrew Forbes, Andrew Geer, Andrew Holden, Andy Penney, Angela Caviglia, Angela Cole, Anice Paterson, Anja-Katharina Munster, Ann Sy, Anna Dowding, Anna Hargreaves, Anne Miek Eisenberger, Anne Miller, Anne Phillips, Anne Scott, Annegret Habel, Annemarie Schuitemaker, Anouk Rengelink, Antti Saarela, Anu Moulee, April Bryant, Arnold Bartels, Aroha Russell, Aron Wahl, Arthur Schultz, Astrid van Leeuwen, Avishai Weissberg, Aylish Frauklin, B J Haynes, Barbara Jehle Ulmer, Barnie Jones, Barry & Victoria Price, Barry Carter, Barry Kowal, Barry O'Callaghan, Becca & Lara, Becki Wood, Belinda Park, Ben Robinson, Benjamin Pecoud, Benjamin Pippenger, Benjamin R Day, Bernard Koch, Beth Russell, Bill Mitchell, Bill Spivey, Birgit & Jorn Lein-Mathisen, Birte Helmer, Bob Tanner, Brendan Finn, Brent Boyer, Brian Lea, Bridgid Seymour-East, Bruce Paterson, Bruce Webster, Bryn Taylor, Byron Gardiner, C P Hollis, Cameron Hallmark, Cara Walsh, Carl Schedlich, Carol Conway, Carol Lewis, Caroline Bilney, Caroline Cross, Caroline East, Caroline Hulsman, Caroline Kennedy, Caroline Liardet, Carolyn Evens, Carrie Marsh, Carrie Wood, Carsten Poulsen, Catherine McConachie, Catherine Pembrey, Cathy O'Callaghan, Celia Moslener, Cello Rueegg, Ceredwyn Bensley, Charles Massey, Charlotte Moss, Charlotte Williams, Cheryl & John Bredin, Cheryl Haisch, Cheryle Edwards, Chiara Fantoni, Chris Dunning, Chris Friesen, Chris King, Chris Lawler, Chris Peake, Christina Bamberg, Christine Van den Winckel, Christopher Wilkins, Claire Allen, Claire Gripton, Claire Harness, Claire Kidson, Claire King, Claire Laidlaw, Clare Goodman, Clare Huish, Clare Marston, Claudia Cleff, Claudia Paolicelli, Colin Cowell, Colin Kirley, Colleen Boyle, Connie Norheim, Corinne Toune, Cornelia Nauck, Craig Walsh, Cris Best, D E M Blackie, D Holloway, D W E Fuller, Dan Oleskevich, Dani Powell, Danny Byrne, Danny Saddler, Danny Southern, Darina Eades, Darren Flemming, Daryl & Kim Hughes, Dave & Barbara Lowe, Dave Bacon, David Brown, David Cole, David Coster, David Dawson, David Farkas, David Hugh Smith, David Mandel, David McClelland, David V Oheimb, Debbie Dear, Debbie Gibson, Deborah Berthold, Deborah O'Byrne, Deirdre & Patrick Ruttledge, Deirdre Keating, Denise & Dave Murray, Denise Bouvier, Dennis Fleurant, Dennis Fuller, Dennis Paradine, Desiree Cauchie, Dianne & Paul Morrison, Dianne MsGrath, Dimitri Zaphiris, Dimitrios Dimiropoulos, DI & DC Baker, Dominik Giel, Doris Eickmeyer, Dorothea Heimeier, Dorothy M Collins, Doug Durst, Dr John Thorne, Dr Mark Tronson, Dr Michael Alpers, Dr Rosana Pellizzari, Dudley McFadden, Duncan Millar, Duncan Priestley, Dunja & Heinrich Wiechers, E A Harris, E M Linnan, Edi Weinberger, Eileen Roberts, Elain Genser, Elaine Gavin, Elaine K Harding, Eleanor Swain, Ellen Visscher, Elsa Haugen, Emma Scragg, Emmie Thomas, Eric Clam, Eric Clark, Eric K Federing, Erika Petersons, Erin & Steve Freeman, Erin Marshall, Erwin Kanters, Esmee Verouden, Esther & Roland Birchmeier, Esther Lehmann, Eva George, Eyal Levin, Fernando & Annalisa, Fiona Hearn, Fiona Malcolmson, Francesco Peracchini, Frank Barbaro, Frank Verlegh, Franz Schmausser, Fred Burke, Frida Caroline Bjerkman, Gaetano & Cristina Pizzitola, Gareth Farbon, Gary Baptiste, Gary Cowper, Gary McDonnell, Gary Spinks, Gary Stephens, Gavin Reynolds, Geertje Korf, Gemma Hearn, Gemma Smith, Geoffrey Dyer, Gilles Gut, Gillian Ling, Giselle Sweet-Escott, Godfrey Guinan, Graham Eason, Graihagh Farrell, Greg & Kelli Carson, Greg James, Guido Kats, Guy & Janet Pinneo, Gwynn Jones, Hagay Shemesh, Hayden & Helen Robinson, Hayley Amanda, Heike Hora Adema, Helen Banks, Helen Cohen, Helen Leudar, Helen Vines, Helen Woodward, Helen Wraithmell, Helle Hansen, Henrietta Somers, Heule Harry, Hilde Kamminga, Iain A Chalmers, Iain Mackay, Ian Carson, Ian Duckworth, Ian Garman, Ian Loftus, Ian Newton, Ian Smart, Ilja Rijnen, Illan Peri, Ingrid & Wolfgang, Ingrid Rotter, Irene Esquivel, Iris Meban, Isabell Blomer, Itai Guberman, Ivan & Barbara Stander, Ivan Stander, Ivo Nijhuis, Izzy Perko, J A Coombs, J E Lilley, James Beringer-Pooley, James Downey, James S Grant, Jamie Hook, Jan Schut, Jane & Chris Meaden, Jane Curne, Jane Dunn, Jane Hamilton, Jane Matthews,

Jane Oldfield, Janet Jones, Janet Richards, Janine Pittaway, Jarlath Dunford, Jaron & Mary Beth Goldberg, Javier Estebaranz, Jean-Jacques Dupont, Jeff Major, Jen Campbell, Jennie Foster, Jenny Hein, Jenny Hill, Jenny Lock, Jens Hultman, Jenuna Prittie, Jeraen Beuckels, Jerry Fries, Jesper Poulsen, Jesse Holliday, Jessica Krakow, Jessica Oman, Jill Anderson, Jill Litwin, Jim Aylett, Jim Hill, Jim Houser, Jo Chick, Jo Hartley, Jo Perriss, Jo Pope, Jo Train, Jo Wise, Joanna Gidney, Joanna Higgs, Joanne Cochrane, Joanne Owen, Joanne Rich, Joanne Schaefer, Job Heimerikx, Jody McLean, Joel & Maria Teresa Prades, Joel Siegfried, John & Wenche Cumming, John Arwe, John Atwood, John Bielinski, John Gourley, John Heetan, John Lam-Po-Tang, John Medley, John Parkinson, John Petherick, John Taylor, John Van Schagen, Jolene Pestel, Jon Willis, Jorg Scheede, Jose Caballera, Josie Simmonds, Josien Dikkers, Joyanne Manning, Joyce Lomax, Julia Holten, Julia Holzemer, Julie Costello, Julie Firmstone, Julie Kenyon-Muir, June Martin, Jurgen Veys, Justin Perkins, K J Storer, Karen & Bryan Geon, Karen Kissinger, Karen Sthamer, Karen Widdowson, Karin Bauer, Karin Oberlin, Karinda Agnew, Karsten Mikkelsen, Karsten Moos, Kate Paxton, Kate Storer, Kate Stubbs, Kate Witners, Kathryn Saunders, Katie Graves, Keith Hughes, Keith Moir, Kelly Wasyluk, Kerrie Williams, Kevin Ruben, Kim Stadtler, Kirsty Matthewson, Kitty Gushee, Klaus & Ute Martini, Knut Magne Arneson, Konrad Fink, Kor Hoon Tan, Kris Mowren, Krista Dalby, Kristi & Jeff Layton, L Hertog, L Smith, Larissa Wilson, Laura Preston, Laura Teunissen, Laura Totti, Laura Zentveld, Laurie Hood, LB Lister, Leanne Tanner, Lee Snowden, Leesa Yeo, Lenora Ahlan, Leonado Pagliarin, Leonie Debnam, Leonie Lene, Lesley Bonney, Lianne de Zeeuw, Liesbeth Barnhoorn, Lina Morgera, Linda Bissinger, Linda Knight, Linda Meagher, Lindsay Edkins, Lindsey Martin, Lisa Appleyard, Lisa Prior, Liz Allen, Liz Reilly, Lloyd Griscom, Lori H Johnson, Lori Lockinger, Lorraine Farrell, Louise Harvey, Louise Pocock, Lucy Carter, Ludovic Smets, Luiz Alencar, Lynn & Al Reece, Lynn Tai, M & E Taylor, M Wheeler, Maarten Brouwer, Maarten Vankan, Madeleine Pitt, Mads eg Sorensen, Maeve Conroy, Magaret & Hugh Kennon, Maire O'Connor, Mairead Loftus, Malcolm & Pat Grainper, Malcolm Allan, Malcolm Walshe, Malinda Quartel, Manita Visser, Manon de Vries, Marc Beelen, Marc Wise, Marcelino & Charlotte Arconada, Marco Riolfo, Maresli Saiko, Margaret & Hans de Roo, Margaret Johnston, Margaret Scott, Margaret Sherley, Margrit Altstadt, Mari Fagin, Maria Mitelman, Maria Walsh, Marin Smith, Marina Zwittlinger, Mark Capellaro, Mark de Vries, Mark Foley, Mark Harford, Mark Hoskin, Mark Meares, Mark Parkes, Mark Richardson, Mark Surridge, Mark Taylor, Markus Vogel, Martein Beversluis, Martijn Nielen, Martin & Marie Lycett, Martin Borowski, Martin Emslie, Martin Haddrell, Martina Weigelt, Mary Carroll, Mary Steen, Mary Steer, Maryangel, Mat Carlsberg, Matt Murray, Matt Whiteway, Maureen Cutfield, Max & Joyce Taylor, Meg Ruffel, Megan Berkle, Meghan Pepper, Melanie Martin, Melchior Bussink, Melissa Quigley, Michael & Rosette Malone, Michael Caourville, Michael Cave, Michael Chambers, Michael Coggins, Michael Paterson, Michael S Anacker, Michel Goossens, Michele Bennett, Michelle vld Veen, Mike Krosin, Mike Landau, Mike McNamee, Mike Nixon, Mike Talbot, Mike Tate, Mirja Leinonen, Moira McBride, Monica Campion, Monique Ingwes, Moya Anchisi, Ms Wheeldon, Murray Sugden, Nadia Dimassi, Nancy Booth, Nancy Mazuryk, Nancy van Rooij-de Goede, Natasha Montgomery, Natasha Quadt, Nathan A Schwartz, Neil & Jean Webster, Nelly Ballistreri, Nelson Wirtz, Nick Coles, Nick Iles, Nicola Copland, Nicola Isendahl, Nicolas Burton, Nicole Fraser, Nicole Mirane, Nicole Partington, Nigel Brown, Nigel Leach, Nova Flitter, Orla Baxter, Par Lindstrom, Patric Endenberg, Patricia Navarro, Patricia Parker, Patrick Dodd, Paul Brookes, Paul Greenaway, Paul Hudson, Paul Logan, Paul Vinton, Penny van Leeuwen, Per Anderson, Per Hilmskou Hansen, Pete Smith, Peter & Mandy, Peter Bayliss, Peter Bleekrode, Peter Camps, Peter Dixon, Peter Driscoll, Peter Gillen, Peter Hiscock, Peter Mako, Peter Schmitz-Gortz, Petra Vondrasek, Phil Nepszy, Phil Scott, Philip Britton, Philip McKernan, Philip Row, Philip Teasdale, Pichaya Saisaengchan, Pieter Mostert, PJ Ellis, Quinten Foppe, Quirine Krull, R J Hateley, R Shoesmith, Rachael Large, Rachel Sant, Rafael Ford, Ralf Wahner, Ralph Schwer, Ray Mosher, Rebecca Flood, Regula Krattiger, Ren Berkerley, Renate Vink, Renee Clark, Richard A Smith, Richard Barton, Richard Bean, Richard Humble, Richard Koiak, Richard Mastenbroek, Richard Nutter, Richard Patterson, Richard Tomlinson, Rick Briggs, Rikke Gregers, Rita & Erik Ronning, Rita-Claire Edmonds, Rixta de Bode, Rob Dudley, Robert Hia, Robert Morgan, Robert Passey, Robert van Beemen, Robin Hounslow, Robina von Kolczynski, Rocco Chin, Rocio Da Riva, Rod Daldrey, Rod Myers, Rodney Croome, Rodney Wilkinson, Roel Mulder, Roga Bishta, Roisin Ryan, Roland Nebel, Roland Soper, Roland Stayt, Ron Eisele, Ronan O'Reilly, Rosa Heuvelmans, Ross Willaims, Russel Griffin, Russell Chan, Russell Hall, Rutger Bezema, Ruth Boreham, Ruth Kennard, Ryan Wainwright, Ryon Rosvold, S A A Boyen, S Hampton, S Steiner, S Vishalakshi, Sadi Batool, Sally Tong, Sam Bush, Samantha Newstead, Sandra de Souza, Sandra

Shaw, Sandra Wild, Sara Eeman, Saragh Kenny, Sarah Churchward, Sarah Coleman, Sarah Deakin, Sarah Hill, Sarah Schnapp, Sa'sdiah Johari, Saskia van Stockum, Scott Hackett, Sean Coxy, Shabnam Hussain, Shane O'Rourke, Shannon Boyer, Shannon Haintz, Sharon England, Sharyn Roberts, Sherry Vaughn, Shirley Hardy-Rix, Sian Mackenzie, Sian Williamson, Sibylla C Cressy, Sigrid van der Geest, Silvia Mertens, Simon Bowker, Simon Hagger, Simon Lesser, Simon Martin, Simon Walker, Simone de Wet, Sinead Fahy, Siobhan Robinson, Siok Han Tjoa, Sonja Haas, Stef de Bock, Stefan Mueller-Morungen, Steffen Pauls, Stephane Cosandey, Stephen Walsh, Stewart Atkinson, Stuart Anderson, Stuart Bowes, Sue Masters, Sue Straughair, Susan B Boyd, Susan Bucciero, Susan Gutierrez, Susanne & Manner, Susanne Heckeroth, Susanne Vogt, Susie Quinn, Susie Stephens, Suzanne Brown, Sven Bestmann, T Cobb,

Tang Huihong, Tania, Tania Buffin, Terry George, Teveli Gabor, Thomas J LeCompte, Tim & Rachel Broome, Tim Brown, Tim Quantrill, Timothy Easterday, Tina Johnson, Tine Skov Olsen, Tom Edmonds, Tom Sperlinger, Ton de Gouw, Ton Theelen, Tony Bradshaw, Tony Hansen, Tony Woodham, Torsten Poitzsch, Tove Hagman, Tracey Boyd, Tracy Platana, Tricia Bauman, Trish Ryding, Ulf Schlierenhlaemper, Ulrich Fischer, Valda Laidlaw, Vanessa Smith-Holburn, Verstrepen Goort, Vicky Calderwood, Vicky Page, Vicky Rodger, Victoria Graham, Vru Eigenheer, Wayng Spalding, Wendy A Macklin, Wendy Hughes, Wendy James, Wieke Myjer, Will Anderson, Will Carless, Will Gardner, William Carless, William K Howle, William Wentworth, Winnie Sorensen, Winston Jackson, Yaron Kaspi, Yeal Lahat, Yolanda Cruz, Yukiko Nishimura, Yuko Iloka, Yvonne Pickering, Zahid Ali.

LONELY PLANET

ON THE ROAD

Travel Guides explore cities, regions and countries, and supply information on transport, restaurants and accommodation, covering all budgets. They come with reliable, easy-to-use maps, practical advice, cultural and historical facts and a rundown on attractions both on and off the beaten track. There are over 200 titles in this classic series, covering nearly every country in the world.

 Lonely Planet Upgrades extend the shelf life of existing travel guides by detailing any changes that may affect travel in a region since a book has been published. Upgrades can be downloaded for free from **www.lonelyplanet.com/upgrades**

For travellers with more time than money, **Shoestring** guides offer dependable, first-hand information with hundreds of detailed maps, plus insider tips for stretching money as far as possible. Covering entire continents in most cases, the six-volume shoestring guides are known around the world as 'backpackers bibles'.

For the discerning short-term visitor, **Condensed** guides highlight the best a destination has to offer in a full-colour, pocket-sized format designed for quick access. They include everything from top sights and walking tours to opinionated reviews of where to eat, stay, shop and have fun.

CitySync lets travellers use their Palm™ or Visor™ hand-held computers to guide them through a city with handy tips on transport, history, cultural life, major sights, and shopping and entertainment options. It can also quickly search and sort hundreds of reviews of hotels, restaurants and attractions, and pinpoint their location on scrollable street maps. CitySync can be downloaded from **www.citysync.com**

MAPS & ATLASES

Lonely Planet's **City Maps** feature downtown and metropolitan maps, as well as transit routes and walking tours. The maps come complete with an index of streets, a listing of sights and a plastic coat for extra durability.

Road Atlases are an essential navigation tool for serious travellers. Cross-referenced with the guidebooks, they also feature distance and climate charts and a complete site index.

LONELY PLANET

ESSENTIALS

Read This First books help new travellers to hit the road with confidence. These invaluable predeparture guides give step-by-step advice on preparing for a trip, budgeting, arranging a visa, planning an itinerary and staying safe while still getting off the beaten track.

Healthy Travel pocket guides offer a regional rundown on disease hot spots and practical advice on predeparture health measures, staying well on the road and what to do in emergencies. The guides come with a user-friendly design and helpful diagrams and tables.

Lonely Planet's **Phrasebooks** cover the essential words and phrases travellers need when they're strangers in a strange land. They come in a pocket-sized format with colour tabs for quick reference, extensive vocabulary lists, easy-to-follow pronunciation keys and two-way dictionaries.

Miffed by blurry photos of the Taj Mahal? Tired of the classic 'top of the head cut off' shot? **Travel Photography: A Guide to Taking Better Pictures** will help you turn ordinary holiday snaps into striking images and give you the know-how to capture every scene, from frenetic festivals to peaceful beach sunrises.

Lonely Planet's **Travel Journal** is a lightweight but sturdy travel diary for jotting down all those on-the-road observations and significant travel moments. It comes with a handy time-zone wheel, a world map and useful travel information.

Lonely Planet's **eKno** is an all-in-one communication service developed especially for travellers. It offers low-cost international calls and free email and voicemail so that you can keep in touch while on the road. Check it out on **www.ekno.lonelyplanet.com**

FOOD & RESTAURANT GUIDES

Lonely Planet's **Out to Eat** guides recommend the brightest and best places to eat and drink in top international cities. These gourmet companions are arranged by neighbourhood, packed with dependable maps, garnished with scene-setting photos and served with quirky features.

For people who live to eat, drink and travel, **World Food** guides explore the culinary culture of each country. Entertaining and adventurous, each guide is packed with detail on staples and specialities, regional cuisine and local markets, as well as sumptuous recipes, comprehensive culinary dictionaries and lavish photos good enough to eat.

LONELY PLANET

OUTDOOR GUIDES

For those who believe the best way to see the world is on foot, Lonely Planet's **Walking Guides** detail everything from family strolls to difficult treks, with 'when to go and how to do it' advice supplemented by reliable maps and essential travel information.

Cycling Guides map a destination's best bike tours, long and short, in day-by-day detail. They contain all the information a cyclist needs, including advice on bike maintenance, places to eat and stay, innovative maps with detailed cues to the rides, and elevation charts.

The **Watching Wildlife** series is perfect for travellers who want authoritative information but don't want to tote a heavy field guide. Packed with advice on where, when and how to view a region's wildlife, each title features photos of over 300 species and contains engaging comments on the local flora and fauna.

With underwater colour photos throughout, **Pisces Books** explore the world's best diving and snorkelling areas. Each book contains listings of diving services and dive resorts, detailed information on depth, visibility and difficulty of dives, and a roundup of the marine life you're likely to see through your mask.

LONELY PLANET

OFF THE ROAD

Journeys, the travel literature series written by renowned travel authors, capture the spirit of a place or illuminate a culture with a journalist's attention to detail and a novelist's flair for words. These are tales to soak up while you're actually on the road or dip into as an at-home armchair indulgence.

The range of lavishly illustrated **Pictorial** books is just the ticket for both travellers and dreamers. Off-beat tales and vivid photographs bring the adventure of travel to your doorstep long before the journey begins and long after it is over.

Lonely Planet **Videos** encourage the same independent, tough-minded approach as the guidebooks. Currently airing throughout the world, this award-winning series features innovative footage and an original soundtrack.

Yes, we know, work is tough, so do a little bit of deskside dreaming with the spiral-bound Lonely Planet **Diary** or a Lonely Planet **Wall Calendar**, filled with great photos from around the world.

TRAVELLERS NETWORK

Lonely Planet Online. Lonely Planet's award-winning Web site has insider information on hundreds of destinations, from Amsterdam to Zimbabwe, complete with interactive maps and relevant links. The site also offers the latest travel news, recent reports from travellers on the road, guidebook upgrades, a travel links site, an online book-buying option and a lively travellers bulletin board. It can be viewed at **www.lonelyplanet.com** or AOL keyword: lp.

Planet Talk is a quarterly print newsletter, full of gossip, advice, anecdotes and author articles. It provides an antidote to the being-at-home blues and lets you plan and dream for the next trip. Contact the nearest Lonely Planet office for your free copy.

Comet, the free Lonely Planet newsletter, comes via email once a month. It's loaded with travel news, advice, dispatches from authors, travel competitions and letters from readers. To subscribe, click on the Comet subscription link on the front page of the Web site.

Lonely Planet Guides by Region

Lonely Planet is known worldwide for publishing practical, reliable and no-nonsense travel information in our guides and on our Web site. The Lonely Planet list covers just about every accessible part of the world. Currently there are 16 series: Travel guides, Shoestring guides, Condensed guides, Phrasebooks, Read This First, Healthy Travel, Walking guides, Cycling guides, Watching Wildlife guides, Pisces Diving & Snorkeling guides, City Maps, Road Atlases, Out to Eat, World Food, Journeys travel literature and Pictorials.

AFRICA Africa on a shoestring • Botswana • Cairo • Cairo City Map • Cape Town • Cape Town City Map • East Africa • Egypt • Egyptian Arabic phrasebook • Ethiopia, Eritrea & Djibouti • Ethiopian Amharic phrasebook • The Gambia & Senegal • Healthy Travel Africa • Kenya • Malawi • Morocco • Moroccan Arabic phrasebook • Mozambique • Namibia • Read This First: Africa • South Africa, Lesotho & Swaziland • Southern Africa • Southern Africa Road Atlas • Swahili phrasebook • Tanzania, Zanzibar & Pemba • Trekking in East Africa • Tunisia • Watching Wildlife East Africa • Watching Wildlife Southern Africa • West Africa • World Food Morocco • Zambia • Zimbabwe, Botswana & Namibia
Travel Literature: Mali Blues: Traveling to an African Beat • The Rainbird: A Central African Journey • Songs to an African Sunset: A Zimbabwean Story

AUSTRALIA & THE PACIFIC Aboriginal Australia & the Torres Strait Islands •Auckland • Australia • Australian phrasebook • Australia Road Atlas • Cycling Australia • Cycling New Zealand • Fiji • Fijian phrasebook • Healthy Travel Australia, NZ & the Pacific • Islands of Australia's Great Barrier Reef • Melbourne • Melbourne City Map • Micronesia • New Caledonia • New South Wales • New Zealand • Northern Territory • Outback Australia • Out to Eat – Melbourne • Out to Eat – Sydney • Papua New Guinea • Pidgin phrasebook • Queensland • Rarotonga & the Cook Islands • Samoa • Solomon Islands • South Australia • South Pacific • South Pacific phrasebook • Sydney • Sydney City Map • Sydney Condensed • Tahiti & French Polynesia • Tasmania • Tonga • Tramping in New Zealand • Vanuatu • Victoria • Walking in Australia • Watching Wildlife Australia • Western Australia
Travel Literature: Islands in the Clouds: Travels in the Highlands of New Guinea • Kiwi Tracks: A New Zealand Journey • Sean & David's Long Drive

CENTRAL AMERICA & THE CARIBBEAN Bahamas, Turks & Caicos • Baja California • Belize, Guatemala & Yucatán • Bermuda • Central America on a shoestring • Costa Rica • Costa Rica Spanish phrasebook • Cuba • Cycling Cuba • Dominican Republic & Haiti • Eastern Caribbean • Guatemala • Havana • Healthy Travel Central & South America • Jamaica • Mexico • Mexico City • Panama • Puerto Rico • Read This First: Central & South America • Virgin Islands • World Food Caribbean • World Food Mexico • Yucatán
Travel Literature: Green Dreams: Travels in Central America

EUROPE Amsterdam • Amsterdam City Map • Amsterdam Condensed • Andalucía • Athens • Austria • Baltic States phrasebook • Barcelona • Barcelona City Map • Belgium & Luxembourg • Berlin • Berlin City Map • Britain • British phrasebook • Brussels, Bruges & Antwerp • Brussels City Map • Budapest • Budapest City Map • Canary Islands • Catalunya & the Costa Brava • Central Europe • Central Europe phrasebook • Copenhagen • Corfu & the Ionians • Corsica • Crete • Crete Condensed • Croatia • Cycling Britain • Cycling France • Cyprus • Czech & Slovak Republics • Czech phrasebook • Denmark • Dublin • Dublin City Map • Dublin Condensed • Eastern Europe • Eastern Europe phrasebook • Edinburgh • Edinburgh City Map • England • Estonia, Latvia & Lithuania • Europe on a shoestring • Europe phrasebook • Finland • Florence • Florence City Map • France • Frankfurt City Map • Frankfurt Condensed • French phrasebook • Georgia, Armenia & Azerbaijan • Germany • German phrasebook • Greece • Greek Islands • Greek phrasebook • Hungary • Iceland, Greenland & the Faroe Islands • Ireland • Italian phrasebook • Italy • Kraków • Lisbon • The Loire • London • London City Map • London Condensed • Madrid • Madrid City Map • Malta • Mediterranean Europe • Milan, Turin & Genoa • Moscow • Munich • Netherlands • Normandy • Norway • Out to Eat – London • Out to Eat – Paris • Paris • Paris City Map • Paris Condensed • Poland • Polish phrasebook • Portugal • Portuguese phrasebook • Prague • Prague City Map • Provence & the Côte d'Azur • Read This First: Europe • Rhodes & the Dodecanese • Romania & Moldova • Rome • Rome City Map • Rome Condensed • Russia, Ukraine & Belarus • Russian phrasebook • Scandinavian & Baltic Europe • Scandinavian phrasebook • Scotland • Sicily • Slovenia • South-West France • Spain • Spanish phrasebook • Stockholm • St Petersburg • St Petersburg City Map • Sweden • Switzerland • Tuscany • Ukrainian phrasebook • Venice • Vienna • Wales • Walking in Britain • Walking in France • Walking in Ireland • Walking in Italy • Walking in Scotland • Walking in Spain • Walking in Switzerland • Western Europe • World Food France • World Food Greece • World Food Ireland • World Food Italy • World Food Spain **Travel Literature:** After Yugoslavia • Love and War in the Apennines • The Olive Grove: Travels in Greece • On the Shores of the Mediterranean • Round Ireland in Low Gear • A Small Place in Italy

Lonely Planet Mail Order

onely Planet products are distributed worldwide. They are also available by mail order from Lonely Planet, so if you have difficulty finding a title please write to us. North and South American residents should write to 150 Linden St, Oakland, CA 94607, USA; European and African residents should write to 10a Spring Place, London NW5 3BH, UK; and residents of other countries to Locked Bag 1, Footscray, Victoria 3011, Australia.

INDIAN SUBCONTINENT & THE INDIAN OCEAN Bangladesh • Bengali phrasebook • Bhutan • Delhi • Goa • Healthy Travel Asia & India • Hindi & Urdu phrasebook • India • India & Bangladesh City Map • Indian Himalaya • Karakoram Highway • Kathmandu City Map • Kerala • Madagascar • Maldives • Mauritius, Réunion & Seychelles • Mumbai (Bombay) • Nepal • Nepali phrasebook • North India • Pakistan • Rajasthan • Read This First: Asia & India • South India • Sri Lanka • Sri Lanka phrasebook • Tibet • Tibetan phrasebook • Trekking in the Indian Himalaya • Trekking in the Karakoram & Hindukush • Trekking in the Nepal Himalaya • World Food India **Travel Literature:** The Age of Kali: Indian Travels and Encounters • Hello Goodnight: A Life of Goa • In Rajasthan • Maverick in Madagascar • A Season in Heaven: True Tales from the Road to Kathmandu • Shopping for Buddhas • A Short Walk in the Hindu Kush • Slowly Down the Ganges

MIDDLE EAST & CENTRAL ASIA Bahrain, Kuwait & Qatar • Central Asia • Central Asia phrasebook • Dubai • Farsi (Persian) phrasebook • Hebrew phrasebook • Iran • Israel & the Palestinian Territories • Istanbul • Istanbul City Map • Istanbul to Cairo • Istanbul to Kathmandu • Jerusalem • Jerusalem City Map • Jordan • Lebanon • Middle East • Oman & the United Arab Emirates • Syria • Turkey • Turkish phrasebook • World Food Turkey • Yemen **Travel Literature:** Black on Black: Iran Revisited • Breaking Ranks: Turbulent Travels in the Promised Land • The Gates of Damascus • Kingdom of the Film Stars: Journey into Jordan

NORTH AMERICA Alaska • Boston • Boston City Map • Boston Condensed • British Columbia • California & Nevada • California Condensed • Canada • Chicago • Chicago City Map • Chicago Condensed • Florida • Georgia & the Carolinas • Great Lakes • Hawaii • Hiking in Alaska • Hiking in the USA • Honolulu & Oahu City Map • Las Vegas • Los Angeles • Los Angeles City Map • Louisiana & the Deep South • Miami • Miami City Map • Montreal • New England • New Orleans • New Orleans City Map • New York City • New York City City Map • New York City Condensed • New York, New Jersey & Pennsylvania • Oahu • Out to Eat – San Francisco • Pacific Northwest • Rocky Mountains • San Diego & Tijuana • San Francisco • San Francisco City Map • Seattle • Seattle City Map • Southwest • Texas • Toronto • USA • USA phrasebook • Vancouver • Vancouver City Map • Virginia & the Capital Region • Washington, DC • Washington, DC City Map • World Food New Orleans **Travel Literature:** Caught Inside: A Surfer's Year on the California Coast • Drive Thru America

NORTH-EAST ASIA Beijing • Beijing City Map • Cantonese phrasebook • China • Hiking in Japan • Hong Kong & Macau • Hong Kong City Map • Hong Kong Condensed • Japan • Japanese phrasebook • Korea • Korean phrasebook • Kyoto • Mandarin phrasebook • Mongolia • Mongolian phrasebook • Seoul • Shanghai • South-West China • Taiwan • Tokyo • Tokyo Condensed • World Food Hong Kong • World Food Japan **Travel Literature:** In Xanadu: A Quest • Lost Japan

SOUTH AMERICA Argentina, Uruguay & Paraguay • Bolivia • Brazil • Brazilian phrasebook • Buenos Aires • Buenos Aires City Map • Chile & Easter Island • Colombia • Ecuador & the Galapagos Islands • Healthy Travel Central & South America • Latin American Spanish phrasebook • Peru • Quechua phrasebook • Read This First: Central & South America • Rio de Janeiro • Rio de Janeiro City Map • Santiago de Chile • South America on a shoestring • Trekking in the Patagonian Andes • Venezuela **Travel Literature:** Full Circle: A South American Journey

SOUTH-EAST ASIA Bali & Lombok • Bangkok • Bangkok City Map • Burmese phrasebook • Cambodia • Cycling Vietnam, Laos & Cambodia • East Timor phrasebook • Hanoi • Healthy Travel Asia & India • Hill Tribes phrasebook • Ho Chi Minh City (Saigon) • Indonesia • Indonesian phrasebook • Indonesia's Eastern Islands • Java • Lao phrasebook • Laos • Malay phrasebook • Malaysia, Singapore & Brunei • Myanmar (Burma) • Philippines • Pilipino (Tagalog) phrasebook • Read This First: Asia & India • Singapore • Singapore City Map • South-East Asia on a shoestring • South-East Asia phrasebook • Thailand • Thailand's Islands & Beaches • Thailand, Vietnam, Laos & Cambodia Road Atlas • Thai phrasebook • Vietnam • Vietnamese phrasebook • World Food Indonesia • World Food Thailand • World Food Vietnam

ALSO AVAILABLE: Antarctica • The Arctic • The Blue Man: Tales of Travel, Love and Coffee • Brief Encounters: Stories of Love, Sex & Travel • Buddhist Stupas in Asia: The Shape of Perfection • Chasing Rickshaws • The Last Grain Race • Lonely Planet ... On the Edge: Adventurous Escapades from Around the World • Lonely Planet Unpacked • Lonely Planet Unpacked Again • Not the Only Planet: Science Fiction Travel Stories • Ports of Call: A Journey by Sea • Sacred India • Travel Photography: A Guide to Taking Better Pictures • Travel with Children • Tuvalu: Portrait of an Island Nation

Notes

Index

Bold indicates maps.

Bold indicates maps.

N

Bold indicates maps.